World Cancer Research Fund

American Institute for Cancer Research

D0520319

SUMMARY

Food, Nutrition, Physical Activity, and the Prevention of Cancer:

a Global Perspective

WORLD CANCER RESEARCH FUND GLOBAL NETWORK

OUR VISION

We help people make choices that reduce their chances of developing cancer

OUR HERITAGE

We were the first cancer charity

To create awareness of the relationship between diet and cancer risk

To focus funding on research into diet and cancer prevention

To consolidate and interpret global research to create
a practical message on cancer prevention

OUR MISSION

Today the World Cancer Research Fund global network continues

Funding research on the relationship of nutrition,
physical activity and weight management to cancer risk

Interpreting the accumulated scientific literature in the field

Educating people about choices they can make to reduce
their chances of developing cancer

The World Cancer Research Fund global network consists of the following charitable organisations:
The American Institute for Cancer Research (AICR); World Cancer Research Fund (WCRF UK);
Wereld Kanker Onderzoek Fonds (WCRF NL); World Cancer Research Fund Hong Kong (WCRF HK);
Fonds Mondial de Recherche contre le Cancer (FMRC FR) and the umbrella association, World Cancer
Research Fund International (WCRF International).

Please cite the Report as follows:
World Cancer Research Fund / American Institute for Cancer Research.
Food, Nutrition, Physical Activity, and the Prevention of Cancer: a Global
Perspective. Washington, DC: AICR, 2007

First published 2007 by the American Institute for Cancer Research
1759 R St. NW, Washington, DC 20009

Introduction

This summary provides an abbreviated version of the full Report. It highlights the wealth of information and data studied by the Panel and is designed to give readers an overview of the key issues contained within the Report, notably the process, the synthesis of the scientific evidence, and the resulting judgements and recommendations.

The first and second Reports

Food, Nutrition and the Prevention of Cancer: a global perspective, produced by the World Cancer Research Fund together with the American Institute for Cancer Research, has been the most authoritative source on food, nutrition, and cancer prevention for 10 years. On publication in 1997, it immediately became recognised as the most authoritative and influential report in its field and helped to highlight the importance of research in this crucial area. It became the standard text worldwide for policy-makers in government at all levels, for civil society and health professional organisations, and in teaching and research centres of academic excellence.

Since the mid-1990s the amount of scientific literature on this subject has dramatically increased. New methods of analysing and assessing evidence have been developed, facilitated by advances in electronic technology. There is more evidence, in particular on overweight and obesity; on physical activity; and on whole life course events. Also, cancer survivors is a new field. The need for a new report was obvious; and in 2001 WCRF International in collaboration with AICR began to put in place a global process in order to produce and publish the Report in November 2007.

How this Report has been achieved

The goal of this Report is to review all the relevant research, using the most meticulous methods, in order to generate a comprehensive series of recommendations on food, nutrition, and physical activity, designed to reduce the risk of cancer and suitable for all societies. This process is also the basis for a continuous review of the evidence.

Organised into overlapping stages, the process has been designed to maximise objectivity and transparency, separating the collection of evidence from its assessment and judgement. First, an expert task force developed a method for systematic review of the voluminous scientific literature. Second, research teams collected and reviewed the literature based upon this methodology. Third, an expert

Panel has assessed and judged this evidence and agreed recommendations. The results are published in the full Report and summarised here. A more detailed explanation of this process is given in Chapter 3 of the Report and the research teams and investigators involved are listed on pages viii–xi.

The Report is a guide to future scientific research, cancer prevention education programmes, and health policy around the world. It provides a solid evidence base for policy-makers, health professionals, and informed and interested people to draw on and work with.

The World Cancer Research Fund (WCRF) global network

Since its foundation in 1982, the World Cancer Research Fund global network has been dedicated to the prevention of cancer. All the members of the global network have the same goal: to prevent cancer worldwide.

The WCRF global network consists of WCRF International and its member organisations. These are national charities based in the USA, the UK, the Netherlands, France, and Hong Kong.

Each member organisation is supported by donations from the public and is independent of government. Each is a separate legal entity, responsible to its own board and accountable to the donors who support it. All member organisations determine their own programmes, which are designed to be most effective in national and local environments. Through national education and research programmes, a primary goal of the WCRF global network is to help promote changes that will decrease rates of cancer incidence. WCRF International provides each member with financial, operational and scientific services and support.

From its beginnings in the early 1980s, the WCRF global network has consistently been a pioneer and a leader of research and education on food, nutrition, physical activity and the prevention of cancer. The network has a special commitment to creation of the most reliable science-based recommendations, and their translation into messages that form the basis for action by professionals, communities, families and individuals. This work is being done for these organisations in the USA, the UK, the Netherlands, France, and Hong Kong, and on behalf of people in all countries. The global network will remain one of the leaders of the international cancer prevention movement, in the broader context of better personal and public health, worldwide.

The Expert Report Panel

The Report is the result of a five year process. This has included examination of the world's literature by a panel of the world's leading scientists, supported by observers from United Nations and other international organisations. Here they are.

Sir Michael Marmot MBBS MPH PhD FRCP FFPH (Chair)
University College London, UK
Epidemiology and public health

Tola Atinmo PhD
University of Ibadan, Nigeria
Nutrition and obesity

Tim Byers MD MPH
University of Colorado, Denver, CO, USA
Cancer prevention and epidemiology

Junshi Chen MD
Chinese Centre for Disease Control and Prevention, Beijing, China
Nutrition and food safety

Tomio Hirohata MD DrScHyg PhD
Kyushu University, Fukuoka City, Japan
Cancer and epidemiology

Alan Jackson CBE MD FRCP FRCPCH FRCPath
University of Southampton, UK
Public health nutrition and developmental origins of health and disease

W. Philip T. James CBE MD DrSc FRSE FRCP
International Obesity Task Force, London, UK
Obesity and nutrition

Laurence Kolonel MD PhD
University of Hawai'i, Honolulu, HI, USA
Epidemiology and cancer epidemiology

Shiriki Kumanyika PhD MPH
University of Pennsylvania School of Medicine, Philadelphia, PA, USA
Biostatistics, epidemiology and obesity

Claus Leitzmann PhD
Justus Liebig University, Giessen, Germany
Nutrition and food science

Jim Mann DM PhD FFPHM FRACP
University of Otago, Dunedin, New Zealand
Human nutrition

Hilary J. Powers PhD RNutr
University of Sheffield, UK
Human nutrition, micronutrients

K. Srinath Reddy MD DM MSc
Institute of Medical Sciences, New Delhi, India
Chronic disease

Elio Riboli MD ScM MPH
Imperial College London, UK
**Cancer epidemiology and
prevention**

Juan A. Rivera PhD
Instituto Nacional de Salud Publica,
Cuernavaca, Mexico
Nutrition and health

Arthur Schatzkin MD DrPH
National Cancer Institute,
Rockville, MD, USA
Cancer epidemiology and genetics

Jacob C. Seidell PhD
Free University Amsterdam,
the Netherlands
Obesity and epidemiology

David E.G. Shuker PhD FRSC
The Open University, Milton Keynes, UK
**Diet and cancer, chemistry and
biomolecules**

Ricardo Uauy MD PhD
Instituto de Nutricion y Technologia de los
Alimentos, Santiago, Chile
Public health nutrition and child health

Walter C. Willett MD DrPH
Harvard School of Public Health,
Boston, MA, USA
Epidemiology, nutrition and cancer

Steven H. Zeisel MD PhD
University of North Carolina, Chapel
Hill, NC, USA
Human nutrition and cancer

Robert Beaglehole ONZM FRSNZ DSc
Chair 2003
Was at: World Health Organization (WHO)
Geneva, Switzerland
Now at: University of Auckland
New Zealand

Panel observers

Mechanisms Working Group
John Milner PhD

Methodology Task Force
Jos Kleijnen MD PhD
Gillian Reeves PhD

**Food and Agriculture Organization of the
United Nations (FAO)**
Rome, Italy
Guy Nantel PhD
Prakash Shetty MD PhD

**International Food Policy Research Institute
(IFPRI)**
Washington, DC, USA
Lawrence Haddad PhD
Marie Ruel PhD

International Union of Nutritional Sciences (IUNS)
Mark Wahlqvist MD AO

Union Internationale Contre le Cancer (UICC)
Geneva, Switzerland
Annie Anderson PhD
Harald zur Hausen MD DSc
Curtis Mettlin PhD

United Nations Children's Fund (UNICEF)
New York, NY, USA
Ian Darnton-Hill MD MPH
Rainer Gross Dr Agr

World Health Organization (WHO)
Geneva, Switzerland
Ruth Bonita MD
Denise Coitinho PhD
Chizuru Nishida PhD MA
Pirjo Pietinen DSc

Additional members
for policy panel

Nick Cavill MPH
British Heart Foundation Health Promotion
Research Group
Oxford University, UK

Barry Popkin PhD MSc BSc
Carolina Population Center, University of North
Carolina, Chapel Hill, NC, USA

Jane Wardle PhD MPhil
University College London, UK

Overview of the second expert Report

The Report of which this is a summary has a number of inter-related general purposes. One is to explore the extent to which food, nutrition, physical activity, and body composition modify the risk of cancer, and to specify which factors are most important. To the extent that environmental factors such as food, nutrition, and physical activity influence the risk of cancer, it is a preventable disease. The Report specifies recommendations based on solid evidence which, when followed, will be expected to reduce the incidence of cancer.

Part 1 — Background

Chapter 1 shows that patterns of production and consumption of food and drink, of physical activity, and of body composition have changed greatly throughout human history. Remarkable changes have taken place as a result of urbanisation and industrialisation, at first in Europe, North America, and other economically advanced countries, and increasingly in most countries in the world. Notable variations have been identified in patterns of cancer throughout the world. Significantly, studies consistently show that patterns of cancer change as populations migrate from one part of the world to another and as countries become increasingly urbanised and industrialised. Projections indicate that rates of cancer in general are liable to increase.

Chapter 2 outlines current understanding of the biology of the cancer process, with special attention to the ways in which food and nutrition, physical activity, and body composition may modify the risk of cancer. Cancer is a disease of genes, which are vulnerable to mutation, especially over the long human lifespan. However, evidence shows that only a small proportion of cancers are inherited. Environmental factors are most important and can be modified. These include smoking and other use of tobacco; infectious agents; radiation; industrial chemicals and pollution; medication; and also many aspects of food, nutrition, physical activity, and body composition.

Chapter 3 summarises the types of evidence that the Panel has agreed are relevant to its work. No single study or study type can prove that any factor definitely is a cause of, or is protective against, any disease. In this chapter, building on the work of the first report, the Panel shows that reliable judgements on causation of disease are based on assessment of a variety of well-designed epidemiological and experimental studies.

The prevention of cancer worldwide is one of the most pressing challenges facing scientists and public health policy-makers, among others. These introductory chapters show that the challenge can be effectively addressed and suggest that food, nutrition, physical activity, and body composition play a central part in the prevention of cancer.

Part 2 — Evidence and Judgements

The judgements made by the Panel in Part 2 are based on independently conducted systematic reviews of the literature commissioned from academic institutions in the USA, UK, and continental Europe. The evidence has been meticulously assembled and, crucially, the display of the evidence was separated from assessments derived from that evidence. Seven chapters present the findings of these reviews. The Panel's judgements are displayed in the form of matrices that introduce five of these chapters, and in the summary matrix on the fold-out page inside the back cover.

Chapter 4, the first and longest chapter in Part 2, is concerned with types of food and drink. The judgements of the Panel are, whenever possible, food- and drink-based, reflecting the most impressive evidence. Findings on dietary constituents and micronutrients (for example foods containing dietary fibre) are identified where appropriate. Evidence on dietary supplements, and on patterns of diet, is included in the two final sections of this chapter.

Chapters 5 and 6 are concerned with physical activity and with body composition, growth, and development. Evidence in these areas is more impressive than was the case up to the mid-1990s; the evidence on growth and development indicates the importance of an approach to the prevention of cancer that includes the whole life course.

Chapter 7 summarises and judges the evidence as applied to 17 cancer sites, with additional briefer summaries based on narrative reviews of five further body systems and cancer sites. The judgements shown in the matrices in this chapter correspond with the judgements shown in the matrices in the previous chapters.

Obesity is or may be a cause of a number of cancers. Chapter 8 identifies what aspects of food, nutrition, and physical activity themselves affect the risk of obesity and associated factors. The judgements, which concern the biological and associated determinants of weight gain, overweight, and obesity, are based on a further systematic literature review, amplified by knowledge of physiological processes.

The relevance of food, nutrition, physical activity, and body composition to people living with cancer, and to the prevention of recurrent cancer, is summarised in Chapter 9.

Improved cancer screening, diagnosis, and medical services are, in many countries, improving survival rates. So the number of cancer survivors — people living after diagnosis of cancer — is increasing.

The Panel agreed that its recommendations should also take into account findings on the prevention of other chronic diseases, and of nutritional deficiencies and nutrition-related infectious diseases, especially of childhood. Chapter 10, also based on a systematic literature review, is a summary of the findings of expert reports in these areas.

The research issues identified in Chapter 11 are, in the view of the Panel, the most promising avenues to explore in order to refine understanding of the links between food, nutrition, physical activity, and cancer, and so improve the prevention of cancer, worldwide.

Part 3 — Recommendations

Chapter 12, the culmination of the five-year process, presents the Panel's public health goals and personal recommendations. These are preceded by a statement of the principles that have guided the Panel in its thinking.

The goals and recommendations are based on 'convincing' or 'probable' judgements made by the Panel in the chapters in Part 2. These are proposed as the basis for public policies and for personal choices that, if effectively implemented, will be expected to reduce the incidence of cancer for people, families, and communities.

Eight general and two special goals and recommendations are detailed. In each case a general recommendation is followed by public health goals and/or personal recommendations, together with further explanation or clarification as required. Chapter 12 also includes a summary of the evidence, justification of the goals and recommendations, and guidance on how to achieve them.

The process of moving from evidence to judgements and to recommendations has been one of the Panel's main responsibilities, and has involved discussion and debate until final agreement has been reached. The goals and recommendations in the Report have been unanimously agreed.

The goals and recommendations are followed by the Panel's conclusions on the dietary patterns most likely to protect against cancer. In order to discern the 'big picture' of healthy and protective diets, it is necessary to integrate a vast amount of detailed information. The Panel used a broad, integrative approach that, while largely derived from conventional 'reductionist' research, has sought to find patterns of food and drink consumption, of physical activity, and of body fatness, that enable recommendations designed to prevent cancer at personal and population levels.

The goals and recommendations are designed to be generally relevant worldwide and *the Panel recognises* that in national settings, the recommendations of the Report will be best used in combination with recommendations, issued by governments or on behalf of nations, designed to prevent

chronic and other diseases. In addition, the Panel cited three specific cases where the evidence is strong enough to be the basis for goals and recommendations, but which currently are relevant only in discrete geographical regions: maté in Latin America, Cantonese-style salted fish particularly in the Pearl River Delta in Southern China, and arsenic contaminating water supplies in several locations. Further details on nutritional patterns and regional and special circumstances can be found in section 12.3.

The main focus of the full Report is on nutritional and other biological and associated factors that modify the risk of cancer. *The Panel is aware* that as with other diseases, the risk of cancer is also modified by social, cultural, economic, and ecological factors. Thus the foods and drinks that people consume are not purely because of personal choice; likewise opportunities for physical activity can be constrained. Identifying the deeper factors that affect cancer risk enables a wider range of policy recommendations and options to be identified. This is the subject of a separate report to be published in late 2008.

The public health goals and personal recommendations of the Panel that follow are offered as a significant contribution towards the prevention and control of cancer throughout the world. On the following pages of this summary, the recommendations themselves are shown, together with key passages from the whole text in the full Report.

The Panel's recommendations

The Panel's goals and recommendations that follow are guided by several principles, the details of which can be found in Chapter 12. The public health goals are for populations, and therefore for health professionals; the recommendations are for people, as communities, families, and individuals.

The Panel also emphasises the importance of not smoking and avoiding exposure to tobacco smoke.

Format

The goals and recommendations begin with a general statement. This is followed by the population goal and the personal recommendation, together with any necessary footnotes. These footnotes are an integral part of the recommendations. The full recommendations, including further clarification and qualification, can be found in Chapter 12 of the full Report.

The Panel's judgements

This matrix displays the Panel's judgements of the strength of the evidence causally relating food, nutrition and physical activity with the risk of cancer of the sites reviewed, and with weight gain, overweight and obesity. It is a synthesis of all the matrices introducing the chapters in Parts 1 and 2 of the Report, and shows judgements of "convincing", "probable", "limited - suggestive", and "substantial effect on risk unlikely", but not "limited – no conclusion". Usually judgements of convincing and probable generate public health goals and personal recommendation. These are shown on the following pages.

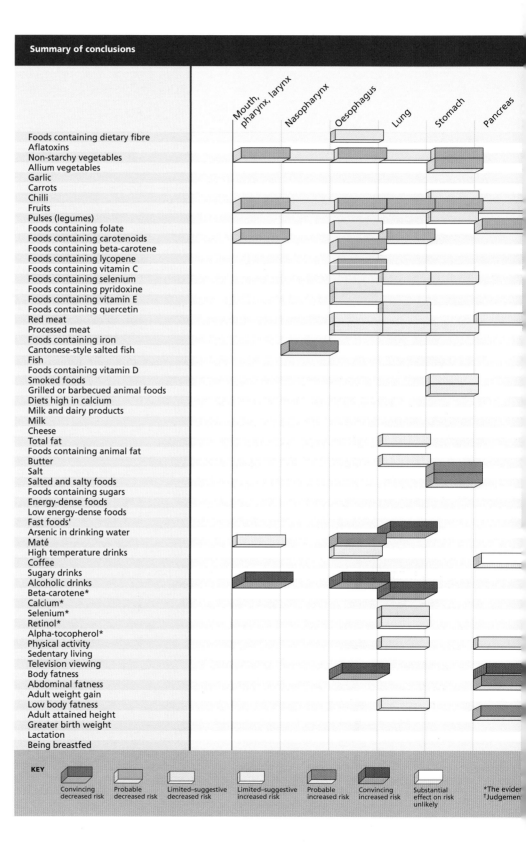

Summary of conclusions

Mouth, pharynx, larynx · Nasopharynx · Oesophagus · Lung · Stomach · Pancreas

Foods containing dietary fibre
Aflatoxins
Non-starchy vegetables
Allium vegetables
Garlic
Carrots
Chilli
Fruits
Pulses (legumes)
Foods containing folate
Foods containing carotenoids
Foods containing beta-carotene
Foods containing lycopene
Foods containing vitamin C
Foods containing selenium
Foods containing pyridoxine
Foods containing vitamin E
Foods containing quercetin
Red meat
Processed meat
Foods containing iron
Cantonese-style salted fish
Fish
Foods containing vitamin D
Smoked foods
Grilled or barbecued animal foods
Diets high in calcium
Milk and dairy products
Milk
Cheese
Total fat
Foods containing animal fat
Butter
Salt
Salted and salty foods
Foods containing sugars
Energy-dense foods
Low energy-dense foods
Fast foods'
Arsenic in drinking water
Maté
High temperature drinks
Coffee
Sugary drinks
Alcoholic drinks
Beta-carotene*
Calcium*
Selenium*
Retinol*
Alpha-tocopherol*
Physical activity
Sedentary living
Television viewing
Body fatness
Abdominal fatness
Adult weight gain
Low body fatness
Adult attained height
Greater birth weight
Lactation
Being breastfed

KEY

Convincing decreased risk · Probable decreased risk · Limited–suggestive decreased risk · Limited–suggestive increased risk · Probable increased risk · Convincing increased risk · Substantial effect on risk unlikely

*The evider
†Judgemen

RECOMMENDATION 1

BODY FATNESS

**Be as lean as possible within
the normal range[1] of body weight**

PUBLIC HEALTH GOALS

Median adult body mass index (BMI) to be
between 21 and 23, depending on the
normal range for different populations[2]

The proportion of the population that is overweight
or obese to be no more than the current level,
or preferably lower, in 10 years

PERSONAL RECOMMENDATIONS

Ensure that body weight through
childhood and adolescent growth projects[3] towards the
lower end of the normal BMI range at age 21

Maintain body weight within
the normal range from age 21

Avoid weight gain and increases in
waist circumference throughout adulthood

[1] 'Normal range' refers to appropriate ranges issued by national governments or
the World Health Organization
[2] To minimise the proportion of the population outside the normal range
[3] 'Projects' in this context means following a pattern of growth (weight and
height) throughout childhood that leads to adult BMI at the lower end of the
normal range. Such patterns of growth are specified in International Obesity
Task Force and WHO growth reference charts

Justification
**Maintenance of a healthy weight throughout life may be
one of the most important ways to protect against cancer.
This will also protect against a number of other common
chronic diseases.**

Weight gain, overweight, and obesity are now generally much
more common than in the 1980s and 1990s. Rates of overweight
and obesity doubled in many high-income countries
between 1990 and 2005. In most countries in Asia and Latin
America, and some in Africa, chronic diseases including obesity
are now more prevalent than nutritional deficiencies and
infectious diseases.

Being overweight or obese increases the risk of some cancers.
Overweight and obesity also increase the risk of conditions
including dyslipidaemia, hypertension and stroke, type
2 diabetes, and coronary heart disease. Overweight in childhood
and early life is liable to be followed by overweight and
obesity in adulthood. Further details of evidence and judgements
can be found in Chapters 6 and 8. Maintenance of a
healthy weight throughout life may be one of the most important
ways to protect against cancer.

RECOMMENDATION 2

PHYSICAL ACTIVITY

Be physically active as part of everyday life

PUBLIC HEALTH GOALS

The proportion of the population that is sedentary[1]
to be halved every 10 years

Average physical activity levels (PALs)[1] to be above 1.6

PERSONAL RECOMMENDATIONS

Be moderately physically active, equivalent
to brisk walking,[2] for at least 30 minutes every day

As fitness improves, aim for 60 minutes or more
of moderate, or for 30 minutes or more of
vigorous, physical activity every day[2][3]

Limit sedentary habits such as watching television

[1] The term 'sedentary' refers to a PAL of 1.4 or less. PAL is a way of representing
the average intensity of daily physical activity. PAL is calculated as total energy
expenditure as a multiple of basal metabolic rate
[2] Can be incorporated in occupational, transport, household, or leisure activities
[3] This is because physical activity of longer duration or greater intensity is more
beneficial

Justification
**Most populations, and people living in industrialised and
urban settings, have habitual levels of activity below levels
to which humans are adapted.**

With industrialisation, urbanisation, and mechanisation,
populations and people become more sedentary. As with
overweight and obesity, sedentary ways of life have been
usual in high-income countries since the second half of the
20th century. They are now common if not usual in most
countries.

All forms of physical activity protect against some cancers,
as well as against weight gain, overweight, and obesity; correspondingly,
sedentary ways of life are a cause of these cancers
and of weight gain, overweight, and obesity. Weight
gain, overweight, and obesity are also causes of some cancers
independently of the level of physical activity. Further
details of evidence and judgements can be found in
Chapters 5, 6, and 8.

The evidence summarised in Chapter 10 also shows that
physical activity protects against other diseases and that
sedentary ways of life are causes of these diseases.

| RECOMMENDATION 3 | RECOMMENDATION 4 |

FOODS AND DRINKS THAT PROMOTE WEIGHT GAIN

**Limit consumption of energy-dense foods[1]
Avoid sugary drinks[2]**

PUBLIC HEALTH GOALS

Average energy density of diets[3] to be lowered towards 125 kcal per 100 g

Population average consumption of sugary drinks[2] to be halved every 10 years

PERSONAL RECOMMENDATIONS

Consume energy-dense foods[1 4] sparingly

Avoid sugary drinks[2]

Consume 'fast foods'[5] sparingly, if at all

[1] Energy-dense foods are here defined as those with an energy content of more than about 225–275 kcal per 100 g
[2] This principally refers to drinks with added sugars. Fruit juices should also be limited
[3] This does not include drinks
[4] Limit processed energy-dense foods (also see recommendation 4). Relatively unprocessed energy-dense foods, such as nuts and seeds, have not been shown to contribute to weight gain when consumed as part of typical diets, and these and many vegetable oils are valuable sources of nutrients
[5] The term 'fast foods' refers to readily available convenience foods that tend to be energy-dense and consumed frequently and in large portions

Justification

Consumption of energy-dense foods and sugary drinks is increasing worldwide and is probably contributing to the global increase in obesity.

This overall recommendation is mainly designed to prevent and to control weight gain, overweight, and obesity. Further details of evidence and judgements can be found in Chapter 8.

'Energy density' measures the amount of energy (in kcal or kJ) per weight (usually 100 g) of food. Food supplies that are mainly made up of processed foods, which often contain substantial amounts of fat or sugar, tend to be more energy-dense than food supplies that include substantial amounts of fresh foods. Taken together, the evidence shows that it is not specific dietary constituents that are problematic, so much as the contribution these make to the energy density of diets.

Because of their water content, drinks are less energy-dense than foods. However, sugary drinks provide energy but do not seem to induce satiety or compensatory reduction in subsequent energy intake, and so promote overconsumption of energy and thus weight gain.

PLANT FOODS

Eat mostly foods of plant origin

PUBLIC HEALTH GOALS

Population average consumption of non-starchy[1] vegetables and of fruits to be at least 600 g (21 oz) daily[2]

Relatively unprocessed cereals (grains) and/or pulses (legumes), and other foods that are a natural source of dietary fibre, to contribute to a population average of at least 25 g non-starch polysaccharide daily

PERSONAL RECOMMENDATIONS

Eat at least five portions/servings (at least 400 g or 14 oz) of a variety[2] of non-starchy vegetables and of fruits every day

Eat relatively unprocessed cereals (grains) and/or pulses (legumes) with every meal[3]

Limit refined starchy foods

People who consume starchy roots or tubers[4] as staples also to ensure intake of sufficient non-starchy vegetables, fruits, and pulses (legumes)

[1] This is best made up from a range of various amounts of non-starchy vegetables and fruits of different colours including red, green, yellow, white, purple, and orange, including tomato-based products and allium vegetables such as garlic
[2] Relatively unprocessed cereals (grains) and/or pulses (legumes) to contribute to an average of at least 25 g non-starch polysaccharide daily
[3] These foods are low in energy density and so promote healthy weight
[4] For example, populations in Africa, Latin America, and the Asia-Pacific region

Justification

An integrated approach to the evidence shows that most diets that are protective against cancer are mainly made up from foods of plant origin.

Higher consumption of several plant foods probably protects against cancers of various sites. What is meant by 'plant-based' is diets that give more emphasis to those plant foods that are high in nutrients, high in dietary fibre (and so in non-starch polysaccharides), and low in energy density. Non-starchy vegetables, and fruits, probably protect against some cancers. Being typically low in energy density, they probably also protect against weight gain. Further details of evidence and judgements can be found in Chapters 4 and 8.

Non-starchy vegetables include green, leafy vegetables, broccoli, okra, aubergine (eggplant), and bok choy, but not, for instance, potato, yam, sweet potato, or cassava. Non-starchy roots and tubers include carrots, Jerusalem artichokes, celeriac (celery root), swede (rutabaga), and turnips.

Continued on next page

RECOMMENDATION 5

ANIMAL FOODS

Limit intake of red meat[1] and avoid processed meat[2]

PUBLIC HEALTH GOAL

Population average consumption of red meat to be no more than 300 g (11 oz) a week, very little if any of which to be processed

PERSONAL RECOMMENDATION

People who eat red meat[1] to consume less than 500 g (18 oz) a week, very little if any to be processed[2]

[1] 'Red meat' refers to beef, pork, lamb, and goat from domesticated animals including that contained in processed foods
[2] 'Processed meat' refers to meat preserved by smoking, curing or salting, or addition of chemical preservatives, including that contained in processed foods

Justification

An integrated approach to the evidence also shows that many foods of animal origin are nourishing and healthy if consumed in modest amounts.

People who eat various forms of vegetarian diets are at low risk of some diseases including some cancers, although it is not easy to separate out these benefits of the diets from other aspects of their ways of life, such as not smoking, drinking little if any alcohol, and so forth. In addition, meat can be a valuable source of nutrients, in particular protein, iron, zinc, and vitamin B12. *The Panel emphasises* that this overall recommendation is not for diets containing no meat — or diets containing no foods of animal origin. The amounts are for weight of meat as eaten. As a rough conversion, 300 g of cooked red meat is equivalent to about 400–450 g raw weight, and 500 g cooked red meat to about 700–750 g raw weight. The exact conversion will depend on the cut of meat, the proportions of lean and fat, and the method and degree of cooking, so more specific guidance is not possible. Red or processed meats are convincing or probable causes of some cancers. Diets with high levels of animal fats are often relatively high in energy, increasing the risk of weight gain. Further details of evidence and judgements can be found in Chapters 4 and 8.

RECOMMENDATION 6

ALCOHOLIC DRINKS

Limit alcoholic drinks[1]

PUBLIC HEALTH GOAL

Proportion of the population drinking more than the recommended limits to be reduced by one third every 10 years[1][2]

PERSONAL RECOMMENDATION

If alcoholic drinks are consumed, limit consumption to no more than two drinks a day for men and one drink a day for women[1][2][3]

[1] This recommendation takes into account that there is a likely protective effect for coronary heart disease
[2] Children and pregnant women not to consume alcoholic drinks
[3] One 'drink' contains about 10–15 grams of ethanol

Justification

The evidence on cancer justifies a recommendation not to drink alcoholic drinks. Other evidence shows that modest amounts of alcoholic drinks are likely to reduce the risk of coronary heart disease.

The evidence does not show a clear level of consumption of alcoholic drinks below which there is no increase in risk of the cancers it causes. This means that, based solely on the evidence on cancer, even small amounts of alcoholic drinks should be avoided. Further details of evidence and judgements can be found in Chapter 4. In framing the recommendation here, the Panel has also taken into account the evidence that modest amounts of alcoholic drinks are likely to protect against coronary heart disease, as described in Chapter 10.

The evidence shows that all alcoholic drinks have the same effect. Data do not suggest any significant difference depending on the type of drink. This recommendation therefore covers all alcoholic drinks, whether beers, wines, spirits (liquors), or other alcoholic drinks. The important factor is the amount of ethanol consumed.

The Panel emphasises that children and pregnant women should not consume alcoholic drinks.

Recommendation 4, continued from previous page
The goals and recommendations here are broadly similar to those that have been issued by other international and national authoritative organisations (see Chapter 10). They derive from the evidence on cancer and are supported by evidence on other diseases. They emphasise the importance of relatively unprocessed cereals (grains), non-starchy vegetables and fruits, and pulses (legumes), all of which contain substantial amounts of dietary fibre and a variety of micronutrients, and are low or relatively low in energy density. These, and not foods of animal origin, are the recommended centre for everyday meals.

RECOMMENDATION 7

PRESERVATION, PROCESSING, PREPARATION

**Limit consumption of salt[1]
Avoid mouldy cereals (grains) or pulses (legumes)**

PUBLIC HEALTH GOALS

Population average consumption of salt from all sources to be less than 5 g (2 g of sodium) a day

Proportion of the population consuming more than 6 g of salt (2.4 g of sodium) a day to be halved every 10 years

Minimise exposure to aflatoxins from mouldy cereals (grains) or pulses (legumes)

PERSONAL RECOMMENDATIONS

Avoid salt-preserved, salted, or salty foods; preserve foods without using salt[1]

Limit consumption of processed foods with added salt to ensure an intake of less than 6 g (2.4 g sodium) a day

Do not eat mouldy cereals (grains) or pulses (legumes)

[1] Methods of preservation that do not or need not use salt include refrigeration, freezing, drying, bottling, canning, and fermentation

Justification

The strongest evidence on methods of food preservation, processing, and preparation shows that salt and salt-preserved foods are probably a cause of stomach cancer, and that foods contaminated with aflatoxins are a cause of liver cancer.

Salt is necessary for human health and life itself, but at levels very much lower than those typically consumed in most parts of the world. At the levels found not only in high-income countries but also in those where traditional diets are high in salt, consumption of salty foods, salted foods, and salt itself is too high. The critical factor is the overall amount of salt. Microbial contamination of foods and drinks and of water supplies remains a major public health problem worldwide. Specifically, the contamination of cereals (grains) and pulses (legumes) with aflatoxins, produced by some moulds when such foods are stored for too long in warm temperatures, is an important public health problem, and not only in tropical countries.

Salt and salt-preserved foods are a probable cause of some cancers. Aflatoxins are a convincing cause of liver cancer. Further details of evidence and judgements can be found in Chapter 4.

RECOMMENDATION 8

DIETARY SUPPLEMENTS

Aim to meet nutritional needs through diet alone[1]

PUBLIC HEALTH GOAL

Maximise the proportion of the population achieving nutritional adequacy without dietary supplements

PERSONAL RECOMMENDATION

Dietary supplements are not recommended for cancer prevention

[1] This may not always be feasible. In some situations of illness or dietary inadequacy, supplements may be valuable

Justification

The evidence shows that high-dose nutrient supplements can be protective or can cause cancer. The studies that demonstrate such effects do not relate to widespread use among the general population, in whom the balance of risks and benefits cannot confidently be predicted. A general recommendation to consume supplements for cancer prevention might have unexpected adverse effects. Increasing the consumption of the relevant nutrients through the usual diet is preferred.

The recommendations of this Report, in common with its general approach, are food based. Vitamins, minerals, and other nutrients are assessed in the context of the foods and drinks that contain them. *The Panel judges* that the best source of nourishment is foods and drinks, not dietary supplements. There is evidence that high-dose dietary supplements can modify the risk of some cancers. Although some studies in specific, usually high-risk, groups have shown evidence of cancer prevention from some supplements, this finding may not apply to the general population. Their level of benefit may be different, and there may be unexpected and uncommon adverse effects. Therefore it is unwise to recommend widespread supplement use as a means of cancer prevention. Further details of evidence and judgements can be found in Chapter 4.

In general, for otherwise healthy people, inadequacy of intake of nutrients is best resolved by nutrient-dense diets and not by supplements, as these do not increase consumption of other potentially beneficial food constituents. *The Panel recognises* that there are situations when supplements are advisable. See box 12.4.

SPECIAL RECOMMENDATION 1

BREASTFEEDING

Mothers to breastfeed; children to be breastfed[1]

PUBLIC HEALTH GOAL

The majority of mothers to breastfeed
exclusively, for six months[2] [3]

PERSONAL RECOMMENDATION

Aim to breastfeed infants exclusively[2]
up to six months and continue
with complementary feeding thereafter[3]

[1] Breastfeeding protects both mother and child
[2] 'Exclusively' means human milk only, with no other food or drink, including
water
[3] In accordance with the UN Global Strategy on Infant and Young Child Feeding

Justification
The evidence on cancer as well as other diseases shows
that sustained, exclusive breastfeeding is protective for the
mother as well as the child.

This is the first major report concerned with the prevention
of cancer to make a recommendation specifically on breastfeeding, to prevent breast cancer in mothers and to prevent
overweight and obesity in children. Further details of evidence and judgements can be found in Chapters 6 and 8.
   Other benefits of breastfeeding for mothers and their children are well known. Breastfeeding protects against infections in infancy, protects the development of the immature
immune system, protects against other childhood diseases,
and is vital for the development of the bond between mother and child. It has many other benefits. Breastfeeding is
especially vital in parts of the world where water supplies
are not safe and where impoverished families do not readily have the money to buy infant formula and other infant
and young child foods. This recommendation has a special
significance. While derived from the evidence on being
breastfed, it also indicates that policies and actions designed
to prevent cancer need to be directed throughout the whole
life course, from the beginning of life.

SPECIAL RECOMMENDATION 2

CANCER SURVIVORS[1]

**Follow the recommendations
for cancer prevention[2]**

RECOMMENDATIONS

All cancer survivors[3] to receive nutritional care
from an appropriately trained professional

If able to do so, and unless otherwise advised,
aim to follow the recommendations for
diet, healthy weight, and physical activity[2]

[1] Cancer survivors are people who are living with a diagnosis of cancer, including
those who have recovered from the disease
[2] This recommendation does not apply to those who are undergoing active
treatment, subject to the qualifications in the text
[3] This includes all cancer survivors, before, during, and after active treatment

Justification
Subject to the qualifications made here, *the Panel has
agreed* that its recommendations apply also to cancer
survivors. There may be specific situations where this
advice may not apply, for instance, where treatment has
compromised gastrointestinal function.

If possible, when appropriate, and unless advised otherwise
by a qualified professional, the recommendations of this
Report also apply to cancer survivors. The Panel has made
this judgement based on its examination of the evidence,
including that specifically on cancer survivors, and also on
its collective knowledge of the pathology of cancer and its
interactions with food, nutrition, physical activity, and body
composition. In no case is the evidence specifically on cancer survivors clear enough to make any firm judgements or
recommendations to cancer survivors. Further details of evidence and judgements can be found in Chapter 9.
   Treatment for many cancers is increasingly successful, and
so cancer survivors increasingly are living long enough to
develop new primary cancers or other chronic diseases. The
recommendations in this Report would also be expected to
reduce the risk of those conditions, and so can also be recommended on that account.

SUMMARY

Food, Nutrition, Physical Activity, and the Prevention of Cancer:
a Global Perspective

The most definitive review of the science to date, and the most authoritative basis for action to prevent cancer worldwide.

- *Recommendations based on expert judgements of systematic reviews of the world literature.*

- *The result of a five-year examination by a panel of the world's leading scientists.*

- *Includes new findings on early life, body fatness, physical activity, and cancer survivors.*

- *Recommendations harmonised with prevention of other diseases and promotion of well-being.*

- *A vital guide for everybody, and the indispensable text for policy-makers and researchers.*

SECOND EXPERT REPORT

Printed in Mexico

World Cancer
Research Fund
International

American Institute
for Cancer Research

World Cancer
Research Fund

Wereld Kanker
Onderzoek Fonds

World Cancer
Research Fund
Hong Kong

Fonds Mondial
de Recherche
contre le Cancer

Food, Nutrition, Physical Activity, and the Prevention of Cancer:

a Global Perspective

World Cancer Research Fund

American Institute for Cancer Research

Please cite the Report as follows:
World Cancer Research Fund / American Institute for Cancer Research.
Food, Nutrition, Physical Activity, and the Prevention of Cancer: a Global Perspective.
Washington DC: AICR, 2007

First published 2007 by the American Institute for Cancer Research
1759 R St. NW, Washington, DC 20009

ISBN: 978-0-9722522-2-5

CIP data in process

Printed in the United States of America by RR Donnelley

Food, Nutrition, Physical Activity, and the Prevention of Cancer:

a Global Perspective

A project of
World Cancer Research Fund
International

World Cancer Research Fund

American Institute for Cancer Research

Preface

I am very grateful to the special group of distinguished scientists who made up the Panel and Secretariat for this major review of the evidence on food, nutrition, physical activity and cancer. The vision of WCRF International in convening this Panel and confidence in letting a strong-willed group of scientists have their way is to be highly commended.

In our view, the evidence reviewed here that led to our recommendations provides a wonderful opportunity to prevent cancer and improve global health. Individuals and populations have in their hands the means to lead fuller, healthier lives. Achieving that will take action, globally, nationally, and locally, by communities, families, and individuals.

It is worth pausing to put this Report in context. Public perception is often that experts disagree. Why should the public or policy-makers heed advice if experts differ in their views? Experts do disagree. That is the nature of science and a source of its strength. Should we throw up our hands and say one opinion is as good as another? Of course not. Evidence matters. But not evidence unguided by human thought. Hence the process that was set up for this review: use a systematic approach to examine all the relevant evidence using predetermined criteria, and assemble an international group of experts who, having brought their own knowledge to bear and having debated their disagreements, arrive at judgements as to what this evidence means. Both parts of the exercise were crucial: the systematic review and, dare I say it, the wisdom of the experts.

The elegance of the process was one of the many attractions to me of assuming the role of chair of the Panel. I could pretend that it was the major reason, and in a way it was, but the first reason was enjoyment. What a pleasure and a privilege to spend three years in the company of a remarkable group of scientists, including world leaders in research on the epidemiology of cancer, as well as leaders in nutrition and public health and the biology of cancer, to use a relatively new methodology (systematic literature reviews), supported by a vigorous and highly effective Secretariat, on an issue of profound importance to global public health: the prevention of cancer by means of healthy patterns of eating and physical activity. It was quite as enjoyable as anticipated.

Given this heady mix, the reasons why I might have wanted to take on the role of Panel chair were obvious. I did question the wisdom of WCRF International in inviting me to do it. Much of my research has been on cardiovascular disease, not cancer. What I described as my ignorance, WCRF International kindly labelled impartiality.

WCRF also appreciated the parallels between dietary causes of cardiovascular disease and cancer. There is a great deal of concordance. In general, recommendations in this Report to prevent cancer will also be of great relevance to cardiovascular disease. The only significant contradiction is with alcohol. From the point of view of cancer prevention, the best level of alcohol consumption is zero. This is not the case for cardiovascular disease, where the evidence suggests that one to two drinks a day are protective. The Panel therefore framed its recommendation to take this into account.

The fact that the conclusions and recommendations in this Report are the unanimous view of the Panel does not imply that, miraculously, experts have stopped disagreeing. The Panel debated the fine detail of every aspect of its conclusions and recommendations with remarkable vigour and astonishing stamina. In my view, this was deliberation at its best. If conclusions could simply fall out of systematic literature reviews, we would not have needed experts to deliberate. Human judgement was vital; and if human, it cannot be infallible. But I venture to suggest this process has led to as good an example of evidence-based public health recommendations as one can find.

Throughout the Panel's deliberations, it had in mind the global reach of this Report. Most of the research on diet and cancer comes from high-income countries. But noncommunicable diseases, including cancer, are now major public health burdens in every region of the world. An important part of our deliberations was to ensure the global applicability of our recommendations.

One last point about disagreement among experts: its relevance to the link between science and policy. A caricature would be to describe science as precise and policy-makers as indecisive. In a way, the opposite is the case. Science can say: could be, might be, some of us think this, and some think that. Policy-makers have either to do it or not do it — more often, not. Our effort here was to increase the precision of scientific judgements. As the Report makes clear, many of our conclusions are in the 'could be' category. None of our recommendations is based on these 'could be' conclusions. All are based on judgements that evidence was definite or probable. Our recommendations, we trust, will serve as guides to the population, to scientists, and to opinion-formers.

But what should policy-makers do with our judgements? A year after publication of this Report, we will publish a second report on policy for diet, nutrition, physical activity, and the prevention of cancer. As an exercise developing out of this one, we decided to apply, as far as possible, the same principles of synthesis of evidence to policy-making. We enhanced the scientific panel that was responsible for this Report with experts in nutrition and food policy. This policy panel will oversee systematic literature reviews on food policy, deliberate, and make recommendations.

The current Report and next year's Policy Report have one overriding aim: to reduce the global burden of cancer by means of healthier living.

Michael Marmot

Contents

CHAPTER BOXES

Acknowledgements

Panel

Sir Michael Marmot
MB BS MPH PhD FRCP FFPH
Chair
University College London
UK

Tola Atinmo PhD
University of Ibadan, Nigeria

Tim Byers MD MPH
University of Colorado Health
Sciences Center
Denver, CO, USA

Junshi Chen MD
Chinese Centre for Disease
Control and Prevention
Beijing, People's Republic of
China

Tomio Hirohata MD
DrScHyg PhD
Kyushu University
Fukuoka City, Japan

Alan Jackson CBE MD FRCP
FRCPCH FRCPath
University of Southampton
UK

W Philip T James CBE MD
DSc FRSE FRCP
International Obesity Task
Force
London, UK

Laurence N Kolonel MD PhD
University of Hawai'i
Honolulu, HI, USA

Shiriki Kumanyika PhD MPH
University of Pennsylvania
Philadelphia, PA, USA

Claus Leitzmann PhD
Justus Liebig University
Giessen, Germany

Jim Mann DM PhD FFPH
FRACP
University of Otago
Dunedin, New Zealand

Hilary J Powers PhD RNutr
University of Sheffield, UK

K Srinath Reddy MD DM MSc
Institute of Medical Sciences
New Delhi, India

Elio Riboli MD ScM MPH
Was at: International Agency
for Research on Cancer
(IARC), Lyon, France
Now at: Imperial College
London, UK

Juan A Rivera PhD
Instituto Nacional de Salud
Publica
Cuernavaca, Mexico

Arthur Schatzkin MD DrPH
National Cancer Institute
Rockville, MD, USA

Jacob C Seidell PhD
Free University Amsterdam
The Netherlands

David E G Shuker PhD FRSC
The Open University
Milton Keynes, UK

Ricardo Uauy MD PhD
Instituto de Nutricion y
Tecnologia de los Alimentos
Santiago, Chile

Walter C Willett MD DrPH
Harvard School of Public
Health
Boston, MA, USA

Steven H Zeisel MD PhD
University of North Carolina
Chapel Hill, NC, USA

Robert Beaglehole ONZM
FRSNZ DSc
Chair 2003
Was at: World Health
Organization (WHO)
Geneva, Switzerland
Now at: University of
Auckland, New Zealand

Panel observers

Food and Agriculture
Organization of the United
Nations (FAO)
Rome, Italy
Guy Nantel PhD
Prakash Shetty MD PhD

International Food Policy
Research Institute (IFPRI)
Washington DC, USA
Lawrence Haddad PhD
Marie Ruel PhD

International Union of
Nutritional Sciences (IUNS)
Mark Wahlqvist MD AO

Mechanisms Working Group
John Milner PhD

Methodology Task Force
Jos Kleijnen MD PhD
Gillian Reeves PhD

Union Internationale Contre
le Cancer (UICC)
Geneva, Switzerland
Annie Anderson PhD
Curtis Mettlin PhD
Harald zur Hausen MD DSc

United Nations Children's
Fund (UNICEF)
New York, NY, USA
Ian Darnton-Hill MD MPH
Rainer Gross Dr Agr

World Health Organization
(WHO)
Geneva, Switzerland
Denise Coitinho PhD
Ruth Bonita MD
Chizuru Nishida PhD MA
Pirjo Pietinen DSc

Additional members for policy panel

Barry Popkin PhD MSc BSc
Carolina Population Center,
University of North Carolina,
Chapel Hill, NC, USA

Jane Wardle PhD MPhil
University College London, UK

Nick Cavill MPH
British Heart Foundation
Health Promotion
Research Group
University of Oxford, UK

Systematic Literature Review Centres

University of Bristol, UK

George Davey Smith
FMedSci FRCP DSc
University of Bristol , UK

Jonathan Sterne PhD MSc MA
University of Bristol, UK

Chris Bain MB BS MS MPH
University of Queensland
Brisbane, Australia

Nahida Banu MB BS
University of Bristol, UK

Trudy Bekkering PhD
University of Bristol, UK

Rebecca Beynon MA BSc
University of Bristol, UK

Margaret Burke MSc
University of Bristol, UK

David de Berker MB BS MRCP
United Bristol Healthcare
Trust, UK

Anna A Davies MSc BSc
University of Bristol, UK

Roger Harbord MSc
University of Bristol, UK

Ross Harris MSc
University of Bristol, UK

Lee Hooper PhD SRD
University of East Anglia
Norwich, UK

Anne-Marie Mayer PhD MSc
University of Bristol, UK

Andy Ness PhD FFPHM MRCP
University of Bristol, UK

Rajendra Persad ChM FEBU
FRCS
United Bristol Healthcare
Trust & Bristol Urological
Institute, UK

Massimo Pignatelli MD PhD
FRCPath
University of Bristol, UK

Jelena Savovic PhD
University of Bristol, UK

Steve Thomas MB BS PhD
FRCS
University of Bristol, UK

Tim Whittlestone MA MD
FRCS
United Bristol Healthcare
Trust, UK

Luisa Zuccolo MSc
University of Bristol, UK

Istituto Nazionale Tumori Milan, Italy

Franco Berrino MD
Istituto Nazionale Tumori
Milan, Italy

Patrizia Pasanisi MD MSc
Istituto Nazionale Tumori
Milan, Italy

Claudia Agnoli ScD
Istituto Nazionale Tumori
Milan, Italy

Silvana Canevari ScD
Istituto Nazionale Tumori
Milan, Italy

Giovanni Casazza ScD
Istituto Nazionale Tumori
Milan, Italy

Elisabetta Fusconi ScD
Istituto Nazionale Tumori
Milan, Italy

Carlos A Gonzalez PhD MPH
MD
Catalan Institute of Oncology
Barcelona, Spain

Vittorio Krogh MD MSc
Istituto Nazionale Tumori
Milan, Italy

Sylvie Menard ScD
Istituto Nazionale Tumori
Milan, Italy

Eugenio Mugno ScD
Istituto Nazionale Tumori
Milan, Italy

Valeria Pala ScD
Istituto Nazionale Tumori
Milan, Italy

Sabina Sieri ScD
Istituto Nazionale Tumori
Milan, Italy

Johns Hopkins University, Baltimore, MD, USA

Anthony J Alberg PhD MPH
University of South Carolina
Columbia, SC, USA

Kristina Boyd MS
Johns Hopkins University
Baltimore, MD, USA

Laura Caulfield PhD
Johns Hopkins University
Baltimore, MD, USA

Eliseo Guallar MD DrPH
Johns Hopkins University
Baltimore, MD, USA

James Herman MD
Johns Hopkins University
Baltimore, MD, USA

Genevieve Matanoski MD
DrPH
Johns Hopkins University
Baltimore, MD, USA

Karen Robinson MSc
Johns Hopkins University
Baltimore, MD, USA

Xuguang (Grant) Tao MD
PhD
Johns Hopkins University
Baltimore, MD, USA

University of Leeds, UK

David Forman PhD FFPH
University of Leeds, UK

Victoria J Burley PhD MSc
RPHNutr
University of Leeds, UK

Janet E Cade PhD BSc
RPHNutr
University of Leeds, UK

Darren C Greenwood MSc
University of Leeds, UK

Doris S M Chan MSc
University of Leeds, UK

Jennifer A Moreton PhD MSc
University of Leeds, UK

James D Thomas
University of Leeds, UK

Yu-Kang Tu PhD MSc DDS
University of Leeds, UK

Iris Gordon MSc
University of Leeds, UK

Kenneth E L McColl FRSE
FMedSci FRCP
Western Infirmary
Glasgow, UK

Lisa Dyson MSc
University of Leeds, UK

London School of Hygiene & Tropical Medicine, UK

Alan D Dangour PhD MSc
London School of Hygiene & Tropical Medicine, UK

Shefalee Mehta MSc
London School of Hygiene & Tropical Medicine, UK

Abigail Perry MSc
London School of Hygiene & Tropical Medicine, UK

Sakhi Kiran Dodhia MSc
London School of Hygiene & Tropical Medicine, UK

Vicki Pyne MSc
London School of Hygiene & Tropical Medicine, UK

University of Teesside, UK

Carolyn Summerbell PhD SRD
University of Teesside
Middlesbrough, UK

Sarah Kelly PhD
University of Teesside
Middlesbrough, UK

Louisa Ells PhD
University of Teesside
Middlesbrough, UK

Frances Hillier MSc
University of Teesside
Middlesbrough, UK

Sarah Smith MSc
University of Teesside
Middlesbrough, UK

Alan Batterham PhD
University of Teesside
Middlesbrough, UK

Laurel Edmunds PhD
University of Teesside
Middlesbrough, UK

Vicki Whittaker MSc
University of Teesside
Middlesbrough, UK

Ian Macdonald PhD
University of Nottingham, UK

Penn State University, University Park, PA, USA

Terryl J Hartman PhD MPH RD
Penn State University, University Park, PA, USA

David Mauger PhD
Penn State College of Medicine,
University Park, PA, USA

Lindsay Camera MS
Penn State College of Medicine,
University Park, PA, USA

M Jenny Harris Ledikwe PhD
Penn State University, University Park, PA, USA

Linda Kronheim MS
Penn State University, University Park, PA, USA

Keith R Martin PhD MTox
Penn State University, University Park, PA, USA

Tara Murray
Penn State University, University Park, PA, USA

Michele L Shaffer PhD
Penn State College of Medicine,
University Park, PA, USA

Kim Spaccarotella PhD
Rutgers, The State University of New Jersey, New Brunswick, NJ, USA

Kaiser Permanente, Oakland, California, USA

Elisa V Bandera MD PhD
The Cancer Institute of New Jersey
New Brunswick, NJ, USA

Lawrence H Kushi ScD
Kaiser Permanente
Oakland, California, USA

Dirk F Moore PhD
The Cancer Institute of New Jersey
New Brunswick, NJ, USA

Dina M Gifkins MPH
The Cancer Institute of New Jersey
New Brunswick, NJ, USA

Marjorie L McCullough RD ScD
American Cancer Society
New York, NY, USA

Wageningen University, The Netherlands

Pieter van 't Veer PhD
Wageningen University
The Netherlands

Ellen Kampman PhD
Wageningen University
The Netherlands

Marije Schouten PhD
Wageningen University
The Netherlands

Bianca Stam MSc
Wageningen University
The Netherlands

Claudia Kamphuis MSc
Wageningen University
The Netherlands

Maureen van den Donk PhD
Wageningen University
The Netherlands

Marian Bos MSc
Wageningen University
The Netherlands

Akke Botma MSc
Wageningen University
The Netherlands

Simone Croezen MSc
Wageningen University
The Netherlands

Mirjam Meltzer MSc
Wageningen University
The Netherlands

Fleur Schouten MSc
Wageningen University
The Netherlands

Janneke Ploemacher MSc
Wageningen University
The Netherlands

Khahn Le MSc
Wageningen University
The Netherlands

Anouk Geelen PhD
Wageningen University
The Netherlands

Evelien Smit MSc
Wageningen University
The Netherlands

Salome Scholtens MSc
Wageningen University
The Netherlands

Evert-Jan Bakker PhD
Wageningen University
The Netherlands

Jan Burema MSc
Wageningen University
The Netherlands

Marianne Renkema PhD
Wageningen University
The Netherlands

Henk van Kranen PhD
National Institute for Health and the Environment (RIVM)
Bilthoven, the Netherlands

Narrative review authors

Liju Fan PhD
Ontology Workshop
Columbia, MD, USA

Luigino Dal Maso ScD
Aviano Cancer Center
Italy

Michael Garner MSc
University of Ottawa
Ontario, Canada

Frank M Torti MD MPH
Wake Forest University,
Comprehensive Cancer Unit
Winston-Salem, NC, USA

Christine F Skibola PhD
University of California,
Berkeley, CA, USA

Methodology Task Force

Martin Wiseman FRCP
FRCPath
Chair
Project Director
WCRF International

Sheila A Bingham PhD
FMedSci
MRC Dunn Human Nutrition
Unit
Cambridge, UK

Heiner Boeing PhD
German Institution of Human
Nutrition
Berlin, Germany

Eric Brunner PhD FFPH
University College London,
UK

H Bas Bueno de Mesquita MD
MPH PhD
National Institute of Public
Health and the Environment
(RIVM)
Bilthoven, the Netherlands

David Forman PhD FFPH
University of Leeds, UK

Ian Frayling PhD MRCPath
Addenbrookes Hospital
Cambridge, UK

Andreas J Gescher DSc
University of Leicester, UK

Tim Key PhD
Cancer Research UK
Epidemiology Unit,
University of Oxford
Oxford, UK

Jos Kleijnen MD PhD
Was at: University of York, UK
Now at: Kleijnen Systematic
Reviews, York, UK

Barrie Margetts MSc PhD
MFPH
University of Southampton,
UK

Robert Owen PhD
German Cancer Research
Centre
Heidelberg, Germany

Gillian Reeves PhD
Cancer Research UK
Epidemiology Unit,
University of Oxford
Oxford, UK

Elio Riboli MD ScM MPH
Was at: International Agency
for Research on Cancer
(IARC), Lyon, France
Now at: Imperial College
London, UK

Arthur Schatzkin MD DrPH
National Cancer Institute
Rockville, MD, USA

David E G Shuker PhD
The Open University
Milton Keynes, UK

Michael Sjöström MD PhD
Karolinska Institute
Stockholm, Sweden

Pieter van 't Veer PhD
Wageningen University
The Netherlands

Chris Williams MD
Cochrane Cancer Network
Oxford, UK

Mechanisms Working Group

John Milner PhD
Chair
National Cancer Institute
Rockville, MD, USA

Nahida Banu MBBS
University of Bristol, UK

Xavier Castellsagué Pique
PhD MD MPH
Catalan Institute of Oncology
Barcelona, Spain

Sanford M Dawsey MD
National Cancer Institute
Rockville, MD, USA

Carlos A Gonzalez PhD MPH
MD
Catalan Institute of Oncology
Barcelona, Spain

James Herman MD
Johns Hopkins University
Baltimore, MD, USA

Stephen Hursting PhD
University of North Carolina
Chapel Hill, NC, USA

Henry Kitchener MD
University of Manchester, UK

Keith R Martin PhD MTox
Penn State University
University Park, PA, USA

Kenneth E L McColl FRSE
FMedSci FRCP
Western Infirmary
Glasgow, UK

Sylvie Menard ScD
Istituto Nazionale Tumori
Milan, Italy

Massimo Pignatelli MD PhD
MRCPath
University of Bristol, UK

Henk van Kranen PhD
National Institute of Public
Health and the Environment
(RIVM)
Bilthoven, the Netherlands

Peer reviewers and other contributors

David S Alberts MD
Arizona Cancer Center
Tucson, AZ, USA

Chris Bain MBBS MPH
University of Queensland
Brisbane, Australia

Amy Berrington de Gonzalez
DPhil MSc
Johns Hopkins University
Baltimore, MD, USA

Sheila A Bingham PhD
FMedSci
MRC Dunn Human Nutrition
Unit
Cambridge, UK

Diane Birt PhD
Iowa State University
Ames, IA, USA

Steven Blair PED
University of South Carolina
Columbia, SC, USA

Judith Bliss MSc
The Institute of Cancer
Research
Sutton, UK

Cristina Bosetti ScD
Istituto di Recherche
Farmacologiche "Mario
Negri"
Milan, Italy

Paul Brennan PhD MSc
International Agency for
Research on Cancer (IARC)
Lyon, France

Johannes Brug PhD FFPH
Institute for Research in
Extramural Medicine
(EMGO),
VU University Medical Centre
Amsterdam, the Netherlands

Eric Brunner PhD FFPH
University College London,
UK

H Bas Bueno de Mesquita MD
MPH PhD
National Institute of Public
Health and the Environment
(RIVM)
Bilthoven, the Netherlands

Noel Cameron BEd MSc
Loughborough University, UK

Moira Chan-Yeung MBBS
FRCP FACP
University of Hong Kong
China

Robert Clarke DSc PhD
Lombardi Comprehensive
Cancer Center, Georgetown
University
Washington DC, USA

Steven K Clinton MD PhD
The Ohio State University
Columbus, OH, USA

Karen Collins MS RD
Nutrition Advisor
AICR

Brian Cox MBChB PhD
FAFPHM
University of Otago
Dunedin, New Zealand

Cindy Davis PhD
National Cancer Institute
Rockville, MD, USA

Diana Dyer MS RD
Ann Arbor, MI, USA

Jonathan Earle MB BCh FCAP
Memorial Sloan Kettering
Cancer Center
New York, NY, USA

Alison Eastwood MSc
University of York, UK

Ibrahim Elmadfa PhD
University of Vienna
Austria

Dallas English PhD MSc
University of Melbourne
Victoria, Australia

Michael Fenech PhD MSc BSc
Commonwealth Scientific and
Industrial Research
Organization (CSIRO)
Adelaide, Australia

Justin Fenty MSc
University of Nottingham, UK

Lynn Ferguson DSc DPhil MSc
Univerity of Auckland
New Zealand

Elizabeth TH Fontham DrPH
Louisiana State University of
Public Health
New Orleans, LA, USA

Terrence Forrester MB BS DM
FRCP
University of the West Indies
Kingston, Jamaica

Teresa Fung ScD RD MSc
Simmons College and
Harvard School of Public
Health
Boston, MA, USA

John Garrow MD PhD FRCP
University of London, UK

Glenn Gibson PhD
University of Reading, UK

Ian Gilmore MD PRCP
Royal College of Physicians
London, UK

Vay Liang W Go MD
University of California
Los Angeles, CA, USA

Per Hall MD PhD
Karolinska Institutet
Stockholm, Sweden

Laura Hardie PhD
University of Leeds, UK

Peter Herbison MSc
University of Otago
Dunedin, New Zealand

Melvyn Hillsdon PhD
University of Bristol, UK

Edward Hurwitz DC PhD
University of Hawai'i
Honolulu, HI, USA

Susan Jebb PhD
MRC Human Nutrition
Research
Cambridge, UK

Stanley B Kaye MD FRCP
FMedSci
The Institute of Cancer
Research
Sutton, UK

Tim Key PhD
Cancer Research UK
Epidemiology Unit,
University of Oxford
Oxford, UK

Victor Kipnis PhD
National Cancer Institute
Rockville, MD, USA

Paul Knekt PhD
National Public Health
Institute
Helsinki, Finland

Thilo Kober PhD
Cochrane Haematological
Malignancies Group
Cologne, Germany

Suminori Kono PhD MD MSc
Kyushu University
Fukuoka, Japan

Nancy Kreiger PhD MPH
Cancer Care Ontario and
University of Toronto
Canada

Petra Lahmann PhD
University of Queensland
Brisbane, Australia

Fabio Levi MD MSc
Institut Universitaire de
Médecine Sociale et
Préventive
Lausanne, Switzerland

Ruth Lewis MSc
Cardiff University, UK

Albert B Lowenfels MD
New York Medical College
New York, NY, USA

Graham A MacGregor FRCP
St George's University of
London, UK

Geoffrey Marks PhD MS
University of Queensland
Brisbane, Australia

John Mathers PhD DipNutr
University of Newcastle, UK

Sam McClinton MD FRCS
NHS Grampian
Aberdeen, UK

Fiona Mensah
University of York, UK

Margaret McCredie PhD
University of Otago
Dunedin, New Zealand

Tony McMichael MB BS PhD
FAFPHM
The Australian National
University
Canberra, Australia

Dominique Michaud ScD
Harvard School of Public
Health
Boston, MA, USA

Anthony B Miller MD FRCP
FACE
University of Toronto
Canada

Sidney Mirvish PhD
University of Nebraska
Omaha, NE, USA

Max Parkin MD
International Agency for
Research on Cancer (IARC)
Lyon, France

Charlotte Paul MB ChB PhD
University of Otago
Dunedin, New Zealand

John Reilly PhD
University of Glasgow, UK

Richard Rivlin MD
Strang Cancer Research
Laboratory
New York, NY, USA

Andrew Roddam DPhil
Cancer Research UK
Epidemiology Unit
University of Oxford
Oxford, UK

Leo Schouten MD PhD
Nutrition and Toxicology
Research Institute Maastricht
The Netherlands

Jackilen Shannon PhD MPH
RD
Oregon Health and Science
University
Portland, OR, USA

Keith Singletary PhD
University of Illinois
Urbana, IL, USA

Rashmi Sinha PhD
National Cancer Institute
Rockville, MD, USA

ACKNOWLEDGEMENTS

Rachael Stolzenberg-Solomon
PhD MPH RD
National Cancer Institute
Baltimore, MD, USA

Boyd Swinburn MB ChB MD
Deakin University
Melbourne, Australia

Peter Szlosarek MRCP PhD
St Bartholomew's Hospital
London, UK

Paul Talalay MD
Johns Hopkins University
Baltimore, MD, USA

Margaret Thorogood PhD
University of Warwick, UK

Stewart Truswell MD DSc
FRCP
University of Sydney
Australia

Paolo Vineis MD MPH
Imperial College
London, UK

Steven Waggoner MD
Case Comprehensive Cancer
Center
Cleveland, OH, USA

Christopher P Wild PhD
University of Leeds, UK

Anthony Williams DPhil FRCP
FRCPCH
St George's University of
London, UK

Frederic M Wolf PhD MEd
University of Washington
Seattle, WA, USA

Jian-Min Yuan MD PhD
University of Minnesota,
Minneappolis, MN, USA

Maurice Zeegers PhD MSc
University of Birmingham, UK

**WCRF/AICR Report
Executive Team**

Marilyn Gentry
President
WCRF Global Network

Kelly Browning
Chief Financial Officer
WCRF Global Network

Kate Allen PhD
Director
WCRF International

Kathryn L Ward
Senior Vice-President
AICR

Deirdre McGinley-Gieser
WCRF International

Jeffrey R Prince PhD
Vice-President for Education
and Communications
AICR

Secretariat

Martin Wiseman FRCP
FRCPath
Project Director
WCRF International

Geoffrey Cannon
Chief Editor
WCRF International

Ritva R Butrum PhD
Senior Science Advisor
AICR

Greg Martin MB BCh MPH
Project Manager
WCRF International

Susan Higginbotham PhD
Director for Research
AICR

Steven Heggie PhD
Project Manager
WCRF International
From 2002 to 2006

Alison Bailey
Science Writer
Redhill, UK

Poling Chow BSc
Research Administration
Assistant
WCRF International

Kate Coughlin BSc
Science Programme Manager
WCRF International

Cara James
Associate Director for
Research
AICR
From 2003 to 2005

Jennifer Kirkwood
Research Administration
Assistant
WCRF International
From 2003 to 2004

Anja Kroke MD PhD MPH
Consultant
University of Applied Sciences
Fulda, Germany
2002

Kayte Lawton
Research Administration
Assistant
WCRF International
From 2006 to 2007

Lisa Miles MSc
Science Programme Manager
WCRF International
From 2002 to 2006

Sarah Nalty MSc
Science Programme Manager
WCRF International

Edmund Peston
Research Administration
Assistant
WCRF International
From 2004 to 2006

Serena Prince
Research Administration
Assistant
WCRF International
From 2004 to 2005

Melissa Samaroo
Research Administration
Assistant
WCRF International
From 2006 to 2007

Elaine Stone PhD
Science Programme Manager
WCRF International
From 2001 to 2006

Rachel Thompson PhD
RPHNutr
Review Coordinator

Ivana Vucenik PhD
Associate Director for
Research
AICR

Joan Ward
Research Administration
Assistant
WCRF International
From 2001 to 2003

Julia Wilson PhD
Science Programme Manager
WCRF International

Art & production

Chris Jones
Design and Art Director
Design4Science Ltd
London, UK

Emma Copeland PhD
Text Editor
Brighton, UK

Rosalind Holmes
Production Manager
London, UK

Mark Fletcher
Graphics
Fletcher Ward Design
London, UK

Ann O'Malley
Print Manager
AICR

Geoff Simmons
Design & Production Manager
WCRF UK

Summary

Introduction

This summary provides an abbreviated version of the full Report. It highlights the wealth of information and data studied by the Panel and is designed to give readers an overview of the key issues contained within the Report, notably the process, the synthesis of the scientific evidence, and the resulting judgements and recommendations.

The first and second Reports

Food, Nutrition and the Prevention of Cancer: a global perspective, produced by the World Cancer Research Fund together with the American Institute for Cancer Research, has been the most authoritative source on food, nutrition, and cancer prevention for 10 years. On publication in 1997, it immediately became recognised as the most authoritative and influential report in its field and helped to highlight the importance of research in this crucial area. It became the standard text worldwide for policy-makers in government at all levels, for civil society and health professional organisations, and in teaching and research centres of academic excellence.

Since the mid-1990s the amount of scientific literature on this subject has dramatically increased. New methods of analysing and assessing evidence have been developed, facilitated by advances in electronic technology. There is more evidence, in particular on overweight and obesity and on physical activity; food, nutrition, physical activity, and cancer survivors is a new field. The need for a new report was obvious; and in 2001 WCRF International in collaboration with AICR began to put in place a global process in order to produce and publish the Report in November 2007.

How this Report has been achieved

The goal of this Report is to review all the relevant research, using the most meticulous methods, in order to generate a comprehensive series of recommendations on food, nutrition, and physical activity, designed to reduce the risk of cancer and suitable for all societies. This process is also the basis for a continuous review of the evidence.

Organised into overlapping stages, the process has been designed to maximise objectivity and transparency, separating the collection of evidence from its assessment and judgement. First, an expert task force developed a method for systematic review of the voluminous scientific literature. Second, research teams collected and reviewed the literature based upon this methodology. Third, an expert Panel has assessed and judged this evidence and agreed recommendations. The results are published in this Report and summarised here. A more detailed explanation of this process is given in Chapter 3 and the research teams and investigators involved are listed on pages viii–xi.

This Report is a guide to future scientific research, cancer prevention education programmes, and health policy around the world. It provides a solid evidence base for policy-makers, health professionals, and informed and interested people to draw on and work with.

Overview of the second expert Report

This Report has a number of inter-related general purposes. One is to explore the extent to which food, nutrition, physical activity, and body composition modify the risk of cancer, and to specify which factors are most important. To the extent that environmental factors such as food, nutrition, and physical activity influence the risk of cancer, it is a preventable disease. The Report specifies recommendations based on solid evidence which, when followed, will be expected to reduce the incidence of cancer.

Part 1 — Background

Chapter 1 shows that patterns of production and consumption of food and drink, of physical activity, and of body composition have changed greatly throughout human history. Remarkable changes have taken place as a result of urbanisation and industrialisation, at first in Europe, North America, and other economically advanced countries, and increasingly in most countries in the world. Notable variations have been identified in patterns of cancer throughout the world. Significantly, studies consistently show that patterns of cancer change as populations migrate from one part of the world to another and as countries become increasingly urbanised and industrialised. Projections indicate that rates of cancer in general are liable to increase.

Chapter 2 outlines current understanding of the biology of the cancer process, with special attention to the ways in which food and nutrition, physical activity, and body composition may modify the risk of cancer. Cancer is a disease of genes, which are vulnerable to mutation, especially over the long human lifespan. However, evidence shows that only a small proportion of cancers are inherited. Environmental factors are most important and can be modified. These include smoking and other use of tobacco; infectious agents; radiation; industrial chemicals and pollution; medication; and also many aspects of food, nutrition, physical activity, and body composition.

Chapter 3 summarises the types of evidence that the Panel has agreed are relevant to its work. No single study or study type can prove that any factor definitely is a cause of, or is protective against, any disease. In this chapter, building on the work of the first report, the Panel shows that reliable judgements on causation of disease are based on assessment of a variety of well-designed epidemiological and experimental studies.

The prevention of cancer worldwide is one of the most pressing challenges facing scientists and public health policy-makers, among others. These introductory chapters show that the challenge can be effectively addressed and suggest that food, nutrition, physical activity, and body composition play a central part in the prevention of cancer.

Part 2 — Evidence and Judgements

The judgements made by the Panel in Part 2 are based on independently conducted systematic reviews of the literature commissioned from academic institutions in the USA, UK, and continental Europe. The evidence has been meticulously assembled and, crucially, the display of the evidence was separated from assessments derived from that evidence. Seven chapters present the findings of these reviews. The Panel's judgements are displayed in the form of matrices that introduce five of these chapters, and in the summary matrix on the fold-out page inside the back cover.

Chapter 4, the first and longest chapter in Part 2, is concerned with types of food and drink. The judgements of the Panel are, whenever possible, food- and drink-based, reflecting the most impressive evidence. Findings on dietary constituents and micronutrients (for example foods containing dietary fibre) are identified where appropriate. Evidence on dietary supplements, and on patterns of diet, is included in the two final sections of this chapter.

Chapters 5 and 6 are concerned with physical activity and with body composition, growth, and development. Evidence in these areas is more impressive than was the case up to the mid-1990s; the evidence on growth and development indicates the importance of an approach to the prevention of cancer that includes the whole life course.

Chapter 7 summarises and judges the evidence as applied to 17 cancer sites, with additional briefer summaries based on narrative reviews of five further body systems and cancer sites. The judgements shown in the matrices in this chapter correspond with the judgements shown in the matrices in the previous chapters.

Obesity is or may be a cause of a number of cancers. Chapter 8 identifies what aspects of food, nutrition, and physical activity themselves affect the risk of obesity and associated factors. The judgements, which concern the biological and associated determinants of weight gain, overweight, and obesity, are based on a further systematic literature review, amplified by knowledge of physiological processes.

The relevance of food, nutrition, physical activity, and body composition to people living with cancer, and to the prevention of recurrent cancer, is summarised in Chapter 9. Improved cancer screening, diagnosis, and medical services are, in many countries, improving survival rates. So the number of cancer survivors — people living after diagnosis of cancer — is increasing.

The Panel agreed that its recommendations should also take into account findings on the prevention of other chronic diseases, and of nutritional deficiencies and nutrition-related infectious diseases, especially of childhood. Chapter 10, also based on a systematic literature review, is a summary of the findings of expert reports in these areas.

The research issues identified in Chapter 11 are, in the view of the Panel, the most promising avenues to explore in order to refine understanding of the links between food, nutrition, physical activity, and cancer, and so improve the prevention of cancer, worldwide.

Part 3 — Recommendations

Chapter 12, the culmination of the five-year process, presents the Panel's public health goals and personal recommendations. These are preceded by a statement of the principles that have guided the Panel in its thinking.

The goals and recommendations are based on 'convincing' or 'probable' judgements made by the Panel in the chapters in Part 2. These are proposed as the basis for public policies and for personal choices that, if effectively implemented, will be expected to reduce the incidence of cancer for people, families, and communities.

Eight general and two special goals and recommendations are detailed. In each case a general recommendation is followed by public health goals and/or personal recommendations, together with further explanation or clarification as required. Chapter 12 also includes a summary of the evidence, justification of the goals and recommendations, and guidance on how to achieve them.

The process of moving from evidence to judgements and to recommendations has been one of the Panel's main responsibilities, and has involved discussion and debate until final agreement has been reached. The goals and recommendations here have been unanimously agreed.

The goals and recommendations are followed by the

Panel's conclusions on the dietary patterns most likely to protect against cancer. In order to discern the 'big picture' of healthy and protective diets, it is necessary to integrate a vast amount of detailed information. The Panel used a broad, integrative approach that, while largely derived from conventional 'reductionist' research, has sought to find patterns of food and drink consumption, of physical activity, and of body fatness, that enable recommendations designed to prevent cancer at personal and population levels.

The goals and recommendations are designed to be generally relevant worldwide and *the Panel recognises* that in national settings, the recommendations of this Report will be best used in combination with recommendations, issued by governments or on behalf of nations, designed to prevent chronic and other diseases. In addition, the Panel cited three specific cases where the evidence is strong enough to be the basis for goals and recommendations, but which currently are relevant only in discrete geographical regions: maté in Latin America, Cantonese-style salted fish in the Pearl River Delta in Southern China, and arsenic contaminating water supplies in several locations. Further details on nutritional patterns and regional and special circumstances can be found in section 12.3.

The main focus of this Report is on nutritional and other biological and associated factors that modify the risk of cancer. *The Panel is aware* that as with other diseases, the risk of cancer is also modified by social, cultural, economic, and ecological factors. Thus the foods and drinks that people consume are not purely because of personal choice; likewise opportunities for physical activity can be constrained. Identifying the deeper factors that affect cancer risk enables a wider range of policy recommendations and options to be identified. This is the subject of a separate report to be published in late 2008.

The public health goals and personal recommendations of the Panel that follow are offered as a significant contribution towards the prevention and control of cancer throughout the world.

The Panel's recommendations

The Panel's goals and recommendations that follow are guided by several principles, the details of which can be found in Chapter 12. The public health goals are for populations, and therefore for health professionals; the recommendations are for people, as communities, families, and individuals.

The Panel also emphasises the importance of not smoking and avoiding exposure to tobacco smoke.

Format
The goals and recommendations begin with a general statement. This is followed by the population goal and the personal recommendation, together with any necessary footnotes. These footnotes are an integral part of the recommendations. The full recommendations, including further clarification and qualification, can be found in Chapter 12.

RECOMMENDATION 1

BODY FATNESS

Be as lean as possible within the normal range[1] of body weight

PUBLIC HEALTH GOALS

Median adult body mass index (BMI) to be between 21 and 23, depending on the normal range for different populations[2]

The proportion of the population that is overweight or obese to be no more than the current level, or preferably lower, in 10 years

PERSONAL RECOMMENDATIONS

Ensure that body weight through childhood and adolescent growth projects[3] towards the lower end of the normal BMI range at age 21

Maintain body weight within the normal range from age 21

Avoid weight gain and increases in waist circumference throughout adulthood

[1] 'Normal range' refers to appropriate ranges issued by national governments or the World Health Organization

[2] To minimise the proportion of the population outside the normal range

[3] 'Projects' in this context means following a pattern of growth (weight and height) throughout childhood that leads to adult BMI at the lower end of the normal range. Such patterns of growth are specified in International Obesity Task Force and WHO growth reference charts

Justification

Maintenance of a healthy weight throughout life may be one of the most important ways to protect against cancer. This will also protect against a number of other common chronic diseases.

Weight gain, overweight, and obesity are now generally much more common than in the 1980s and 1990s. Rates of overweight and obesity doubled in many high-income countries between 1990 and 2005. In most countries in Asia and Latin America, and some in Africa, chronic diseases including obesity are now more prevalent than nutritional deficiencies and infectious diseases.

Being overweight or obese increases the risk of some cancers. Overweight and obesity also increase the risk of conditions including dyslipidaemia, hypertension and stroke, type 2 diabetes, and coronary heart disease. Overweight in childhood and early life is liable to be followed by overweight and obesity in adulthood. Further details of evidence and judgements can be found in Chapters 6 and 8. Maintenance of a healthy weight throughout life may be one of the most important ways to protect against cancer.

RECOMMENDATION 2

PHYSICAL ACTIVITY

Be physically active as part of everyday life

PUBLIC HEALTH GOALS

The proportion of the population that is sedentary[1] to be halved every 10 years

Average physical activity levels (PALs)[1] to be above 1.6

PERSONAL RECOMMENDATIONS

Be moderately physically active, equivalent to brisk walking,[2] for at least 30 minutes every day

As fitness improves, aim for 60 minutes or more of moderate, or for 30 minutes or more of vigorous, physical activity every day[2,3]

Limit sedentary habits such as watching television

[1] The term 'sedentary' refers to a PAL of 1.4 or less. PAL is a way of representing the average intensity of daily physical activity. PAL is calculated as total energy expenditure as a multiple of basal metabolic rate

[2] Can be incorporated in occupational, transport, household, or leisure activities

[3] This is because physical activity of longer duration or greater intensity is more beneficial

Justification

Most populations, and people living in industrialised and urban settings, have habitual levels of activity below levels to which humans are adapted.

With industrialisation, urbanisation, and mechanisation, populations and people become more sedentary. As with overweight and obesity, sedentary ways of life have been usual in high-income countries since the second half of the 20th century. They are now common if not usual in most countries.

All forms of physical activity protect against some cancers, as well as against weight gain, overweight, and obesity; correspondingly, sedentary ways of life are a cause of these cancers and of weight gain, overweight, and obesity. Weight gain, overweight, and obesity are also causes of some cancers independently of the level of physical activity. Further details of evidence and judgements can be found in Chapters 5, 6, and 8.

The evidence summarised in Chapter 10 also shows that physical activity protects against other diseases and that sedentary ways of life are causes of these diseases.

RECOMMENDATION 3

FOODS AND DRINKS THAT PROMOTE WEIGHT GAIN

**Limit consumption of energy-dense foods[1]
Avoid sugary drinks[2]**

PUBLIC HEALTH GOALS

Average energy density of diets[3] to be lowered
towards 125 kcal per 100 g

Population average consumption of sugary drinks[2]
to be halved every 10 years

PERSONAL RECOMMENDATIONS

Consume energy-dense foods[1][4] sparingly

Avoid sugary drinks[2]

Consume 'fast foods'[5] sparingly, if at all

---

[1] Energy-dense foods are here defined as those with an energy content of more than about 225–275 kcal per 100 g

[2] This principally refers to drinks with added sugars. Fruit juices should also be limited

[3] This does not include drinks

[4] Limit processed energy-dense foods (also see recommendation 4). Relatively unprocessed energy-dense foods, such as nuts and seeds, have not been shown to contribute to weight gain when consumed as part of typical diets, and these and many vegetable oils are valuable sources of nutrients

[5] The term 'fast foods' refers to readily available convenience foods that tend to be energy-dense and consumed frequently and in large portions

Justification

Consumption of energy-dense foods and sugary drinks is increasing worldwide and is probably contributing to the global increase in obesity.

This overall recommendation is mainly designed to prevent and to control weight gain, overweight, and obesity. Further details of evidence and judgements can be found in Chapter 8.

'Energy density' measures the amount of energy (in kcal or kJ) per weight (usually 100 g) of food. Food supplies that are mainly made up of processed foods, which often contain substantial amounts of fat or sugar, tend to be more energy-dense than food supplies that include substantial amounts of fresh foods. Taken together, the evidence shows that it is not specific dietary constituents that are problematic, so much as the contribution these make to the energy density of diets.

Because of their water content, drinks are less energy-dense than foods. However, sugary drinks provide energy but do not seem to induce satiety or compensatory reduction in subsequent energy intake, and so promote overconsumption of energy and thus weight gain.

RECOMMENDATION 4

PLANT FOODS

Eat mostly foods of plant origin

PUBLIC HEALTH GOALS

Population average consumption of non-starchy[1]
vegetables and of fruits to be at least 600 g (21 oz) daily[2]

Relatively unprocessed cereals (grains) and/or pulses
(legumes), and other foods that are a natural source of
dietary fibre, to contribute to a population average
of at least 25 g non-starch polysaccharide daily

PERSONAL RECOMMENDATIONS

Eat at least five portions/servings
(at least 400 g or 14 oz) of a variety[2] of
non-starchy vegetables and of fruits every day

Eat relatively unprocessed cereals (grains)
and/or pulses (legumes) with every meal[3]

Limit refined starchy foods

People who consume starchy roots or tubers[4]
as staples also to ensure intake of sufficient
non-starchy vegetables, fruits, and pulses (legumes)

---

[1] This is best made up from a range of various amounts of non-starchy vegetables and fruits of different colours including red, green, yellow, white, purple, and orange, including tomato-based products and allium vegetables such as garlic

[2] Relatively unprocessed cereals (grains) and/or pulses (legumes) to contribute to an average of at least 25 g non-starch polysaccharide daily

[3] These foods are low in energy density and so promote healthy weight

[4] For example, populations in Africa, Latin America, and the Asia-Pacific region

Justification

An integrated approach to the evidence shows that most diets that are protective against cancer are mainly made up from foods of plant origin.

Higher consumption of several plant foods probably protects against cancers of various sites. What is meant by 'plant-based' is diets that give more emphasis to those plant foods that are high in nutrients, high in dietary fibre (and so in non-starch polysaccharides), and low in energy density. Non-starchy vegetables, and fruits, probably protect against some cancers. Being typically low in energy density, they probably also protect against weight gain. Further details of evidence and judgements can be found in Chapters 4 and 8.

Non-starchy vegetables include green, leafy vegetables, broccoli, okra, aubergine (eggplant), and bok choy, but not, for instance, potato, yam, sweet potato, or cassava. Non-starchy roots and tubers include carrots, Jerusalem artichokes, celeriac (celery root), swede (rutabaga), and turnips.

Continued on next page

RECOMMENDATION 5

ANIMAL FOODS

**Limit intake of red meat[1] and
avoid processed meat[2]**

PUBLIC HEALTH GOAL

Population average consumption of red meat
to be no more than 300 g (11 oz) a week,
very little if any of which to be processed

PERSONAL RECOMMENDATION

People who eat red meat[1]
to consume less than 500 g (18 oz) a week,
very little if any to be processed[2]

---

[1] 'Red meat' refers to beef, pork, lamb, and goat from domesticated animals including that contained in processed foods
[2] 'Processed meat' refers to meat preserved by smoking, curing or salting, or addition of chemical preservatives, including that contained in processed foods

RECOMMENDATION 6

ALCOHOLIC DRINKS

Limit alcoholic drinks[1]

PUBLIC HEALTH GOAL

Proportion of the population drinking
more than the recommended limits to be
reduced by one third every 10 years[1][2]

PERSONAL RECOMMENDATION

If alcoholic drinks are consumed,
limit consumption to no more than two drinks a day
for men and one drink a day for women[1][2][3]

---

[1] This recommendation takes into account that there is a likely protective effect for coronary heart disease
[2] Children and pregnant women not to consume alcoholic drinks
[3] One 'drink' contains about 10–15 grams of ethanol

Justification

An integrated approach to the evidence also shows that many foods of animal origin are nourishing and healthy if consumed in modest amounts.

People who eat various forms of vegetarian diets are at low risk of some diseases including some cancers, although it is not easy to separate out these benefits of the diets from other aspects of their ways of life, such as not smoking, drinking little if any alcohol, and so forth. In addition, meat can be a valuable source of nutrients, in particular protein, iron, zinc, and vitamin B12. *The Panel emphasises* that this overall recommendation is not for diets containing no meat — or diets containing no foods of animal origin. The amounts are for weight of meat as eaten. As a rough conversion, 300 g of cooked red meat is equivalent to about 400–450 g raw weight, and 500 g cooked red meat to about 700–750 g raw weight. The exact conversion will depend on the cut of meat, the proportions of lean and fat, and the method and degree of cooking, so more specific guidance is not possible. Red or processed meats are convincing or probable causes of some cancers. Diets with high levels of animal fats are often relatively high in energy, increasing the risk of weight gain. Further details of evidence and judgements can be found in Chapters 4 and 8.

Justification

The evidence on cancer justifies a recommendation not to drink alcoholic drinks. Other evidence shows that modest amounts of alcoholic drinks are likely to reduce the risk of coronary heart disease.

The evidence does not show a clear level of consumption of alcoholic drinks below which there is no increase in risk of the cancers it causes. This means that, based solely on the evidence on cancer, even small amounts of alcoholic drinks should be avoided. Further details of evidence and judgements can be found in Chapter 4. In framing the recommendation here, the Panel has also taken into account the evidence that modest amounts of alcoholic drinks are likely to protect against coronary heart disease, as described in Chapter 10.

The evidence shows that all alcoholic drinks have the same effect. Data do not suggest any significant difference depending on the type of drink. This recommendation therefore covers all alcoholic drinks, whether beers, wines, spirits (liquors), or other alcoholic drinks. The important factor is the amount of ethanol consumed.

The Panel emphasises that children and pregnant women should not consume alcoholic drinks.

Recommendation 4, continued from page xviii

The goals and recommendations here are broadly similar to those that have been issued by other international and national authoritative organisations (see Chapter 10). They derive from the evidence on cancer and are supported by evidence on other diseases. They emphasise the importance of relatively unprocessed cereals (grains), non-starchy vegetables and fruits, and pulses (legumes), all of which contain substantial amounts of dietary fibre and a variety of micronutrients, and are low or relatively low in energy density. These, and not foods of animal origin, are the recommended centre for everyday meals.

RECOMMENDATION 7

PRESERVATION, PROCESSING, PREPARATION

Limit consumption of salt[1]
Avoid mouldy cereals (grains) or pulses (legumes)

PUBLIC HEALTH GOALS

Population average consumption of salt from all sources to be less than 5 g (2 g of sodium) a day

Proportion of the population consuming more than 6 g of salt (2.4 g of sodium) a day to be halved every 10 years

Minimise exposure to aflatoxins from mouldy cereals (grains) or pulses (legumes)

PERSONAL RECOMMENDATIONS

Avoid salt-preserved, salted, or salty foods; preserve foods without using salt[1]

Limit consumption of processed foods with added salt to ensure an intake of less than 6 g (2.4 g sodium) a day

Do not eat mouldy cereals (grains) or pulses (legumes)

[1] Methods of preservation that do not or need not use salt include refrigeration, freezing, drying, bottling, canning, and fermentation

Justification

The strongest evidence on methods of food preservation, processing, and preparation shows that salt and salt-preserved foods are probably a cause of stomach cancer, and that foods contaminated with aflatoxins are a cause of liver cancer.

Salt is necessary for human health and life itself, but at levels very much lower than those typically consumed in most parts of the world. At the levels found not only in high-income countries but also in those where traditional diets are high in salt, consumption of salty foods, salted foods, and salt itself is too high. The critical factor is the overall amount of salt. Microbial contamination of foods and drinks and of water supplies remains a major public health problem worldwide. Specifically, the contamination of cereals (grains) and pulses (legumes) with aflatoxins, produced by some moulds when such foods are stored for too long in warm temperatures, is an important public health problem, and not only in tropical countries.

Salt and salt-preserved foods are a probable cause of some cancers. Aflatoxins are a convincing cause of liver cancer. Further details of evidence and judgements can be found in Chapter 4.

RECOMMENDATION 8

DIETARY SUPPLEMENTS

Aim to meet nutritional needs through diet alone[1]

PUBLIC HEALTH GOAL

Maximise the proportion of the population achieving nutritional adequacy without dietary supplements

PERSONAL RECOMMENDATION

Dietary supplements are not recommended for cancer prevention

[1] This may not always be feasible. In some situations of illness or dietary inadequacy, supplements may be valuable

Justification

The evidence shows that high-dose nutrient supplements can be protective or can cause cancer. The studies that demonstrate such effects do not relate to widespread use among the general population, in whom the balance of risks and benefits cannot confidently be predicted. A general recommendation to consume supplements for cancer prevention might have unexpected adverse effects. Increasing the consumption of the relevant nutrients through the usual diet is preferred.

The recommendations of this Report, in common with its general approach, are food based. Vitamins, minerals, and other nutrients are assessed in the context of the foods and drinks that contain them. *The Panel judges* that the best source of nourishment is foods and drinks, not dietary supplements. There is evidence that high-dose dietary supplements can modify the risk of some cancers. Although some studies in specific, usually high-risk, groups have shown evidence of cancer prevention from some supplements, this finding may not apply to the general population. Their level of benefit may be different, and there may be unexpected and uncommon adverse effects. Therefore it is unwise to recommend widespread supplement use as a means of cancer prevention. Further details of evidence and judgements can be found in Chapter 4.

In general, for otherwise healthy people, inadequacy of intake of nutrients is best resolved by nutrient-dense diets and not by supplements, as these do not increase consumption of other potentially beneficial food constituents. *The Panel recognises* that there are situations when supplements are advisable. See box 12.4.

SPECIAL RECOMMENDATION 1	SPECIAL RECOMMENDATION 2

BREASTFEEDING

Mothers to breastfeed; children to be breastfed[1]

PUBLIC HEALTH GOAL

The majority of mothers to breastfeed
exclusively, for six months[2] [3]

PERSONAL RECOMMENDATION

Aim to breastfeed infants exclusively[2]
up to six months and continue
with complementary feeding thereafter[3]

[1] Breastfeeding protects both mother and child
[2] 'Exclusively' means human milk only, with no other food or drink, including water
[3] In accordance with the UN Global Strategy on Infant and Young Child Feeding

CANCER SURVIVORS[1]

**Follow the recommendations
for cancer prevention[2]**

RECOMMENDATIONS

All cancer survivors[3] to receive nutritional care
from an appropriately trained professional

If able to do so, and unless otherwise advised,
aim to follow the recommendations for
diet, healthy weight, and physical activity[2]

[1] Cancer survivors are people who are living with a diagnosis of cancer, including those who have recovered from the disease
[2] This recommendation does not apply to those who are undergoing active treatment, subject to the qualifications in the text
[3] This includes all cancer survivors, before, during, and after active treatment

Justification

The evidence on cancer as well as other diseases shows that sustained, exclusive breastfeeding is protective for the mother as well as the child.

This is the first major report concerned with the prevention of cancer to make a recommendation specifically on breastfeeding, to prevent breast cancer in mothers and to prevent overweight and obesity in children. Further details of evidence and judgements can be found in Chapters 6 and 8.

Other benefits of breastfeeding for mothers and their children are well known. Breastfeeding protects against infections in infancy, protects the development of the immature immune system, protects against other childhood diseases, and is vital for the development of the bond between mother and child. It has many other benefits. Breastfeeding is especially vital in parts of the world where water supplies are not safe and where impoverished families do not readily have the money to buy infant formula and other infant and young child foods. This recommendation has a special significance. While derived from the evidence on being breastfed, it also indicates that policies and actions designed to prevent cancer need to be directed throughout the whole life course, from the beginning of life.

Justification

Subject to the qualifications made here, *the Panel has agreed* that its recommendations apply also to cancer survivors. There may be specific situations where this advice may not apply, for instance, where treatment has compromised gastrointestinal function.

If possible, when appropriate, and unless advised otherwise by a qualified professional, the recommendations of this Report also apply to cancer survivors. The Panel has made this judgement based on its examination of the evidence, including that specifically on cancer survivors, and also on its collective knowledge of the pathology of cancer and its interactions with food, nutrition, physical activity, and body composition. In no case is the evidence specifically on cancer survivors clear enough to make any firm judgements or recommendations to cancer survivors. Further details of evidence and judgements can be found in Chapter 9.

Treatment for many cancers is increasingly successful, and so cancer survivors increasingly are living long enough to develop new primary cancers or other chronic diseases. The recommendations in this Report would also be expected to reduce the risk of those conditions, and so can also be recommended on that account.

Introduction

The proposals that cancer might be preventable, and that food, nutrition, physical activity, and body composition might affect the risk of cancer, were first made before science emerged in its modern form in the 19th and 20th centuries. Throughout recorded history, wise choices of food and drink, and of habitual behaviour, have been recommended to protect against cancer, as well as other diseases, and to improve well-being.

Reports such as this, which incorporate systematic examination of all relevant types of research, differ from ancient, historical, and even relatively recent accounts, and descriptive studies of the type detailed in Chapter 1, not only in the quantity and quality of evidence, but also in the reliability of the judgements and recommendations that derive from it.

The purpose of this Report

This Report has been commissioned and resourced by the World Cancer Research Fund (WCRF) International and its sister organisation the American Institute for Cancer Research (AICR), who provided the Secretariat that has supported the Panel responsible for the Report. Panel members, observers, review centres, and other contributors are listed on the preceding pages. The five-year project that has resulted in this Report follows a previous five-year project that resulted in the first WCRF/AICR report published in 1997, which was the responsibility of the former distinguished international multidisciplinary panel chaired by Professor John Potter.

This Report has two overall general purposes. The first is to summarise, assess, and judge the most comprehensive body of evidence yet collected and displayed on the subject of food, nutrition, physical activity, body composition, and the risk of cancer, throughout the life-course. The second purpose is to transform the evidence-derived judgements into goals and personal recommendations that are a reliable basis for sound policies and effective actions at population, community, family, and individual level, in order to prevent cancer, worldwide.

What is already known

The Panel is aware of the general consensus shared by scientists, health professionals, and policy-makers on the relationships between food, nutrition, physical activity, body composition, and the risk of cancer.

This consensus, based on the findings of a rapidly growing mass of increasingly well-designed epidemiological and experimental studies and other relevant evidence, emerged in the early 1980s. Thus: 'It is

abundantly clear that the incidence of all the common cancers in humans is determined by various potentially controllable external factors. This is surely the most comforting fact to come out of cancer research, for it means that cancer is, in large part, a preventable disease'.[1] This is the conclusion of a report on diet and the prevention of cancer published a quarter of a century before this Report.

Since the early 1980s, relevant United Nations agencies, national governments, authoritative non-governmental organisations, and researchers and other experts in the field have agreed that food and nutrition, physical activity, and body composition are individually and collectively important modifiers of the risk of cancer, and taken together may be at least as important as tobacco.

By the mid-1990s the general consensus became more solidly based on methodical assessment of the totality of the relevant literature. Thus: 'It is now established that cancer is principally caused by environmental factors, of which the most important are tobacco; diet and factors related to diet, including body mass and physical activity; and exposures in the workplace and elsewhere.' This statement introduces the recommendations made in the first WCRF/AICR report.

Expert reports may be accompanied by guidebooks written for general readers. Thus: 'A healthy eating strategy… is an important part of protecting yourself against a long list of diseases. These include heart disease, stroke, several common cancers, cataract formation, other age-related diseases, and even some types of birth defects. When combined with not smoking and regular exercise, this kind of healthy diet can reduce heart disease by 80 per cent, and stroke and some cancers by 70 percent, compared with average rates'.[2] This is a conclusion of a book written by a member of the Panel responsible for this Report.

Some general judgements are now well known and not a matter for serious debate. Cancer in general, and cancers of different types and sites, are agreed to have various causes, among which are inherited genetic predisposition and the increasing likelihood that cells will accumulate genetic defects as people age. This is discussed in more detail in Chapter 2. Also, people die less frequently from nutritional deficiencies, infectious diseases, predation, and accidents, whereas chronic diseases including cancer — which are more common in older people — become more common.

However, cancer is not an inevitable consequence of ageing, and people's susceptibility to it varies. There is abundant evidence that the main causes of patterns of cancer around the world are environmental. This does indeed mean that at least in principle, most cancer is preventable, though there is still discussion about the relative importance of various environmental factors.

But what are these environmental factors, what is their relative importance, and how may they vary in different times in the life-course and in different parts of the world, and how might they interact with each other? Many thousand epidemiological and experimental studies have looked for answers. Some answers are now agreed to be unequivocal. Thus, smoking is the chief cause of lung cancer. Alcohol is also an established carcinogen in humans, as are types of radiation such as those used in medical treatments and as released by nuclear weapons and accidents. Certain infectious agents are undoubtedly a cause of some cancers.

The need for a new initiative

Many questions, particularly in the field of food, nutrition, and associated factors, remain. Some are fundamental. Do statements such as those quoted above remain valid? Do they apply worldwide? Have the reviews and reports so far published overlooked key findings? How do the large prospective studies, meta-analyses, pooling projects, and randomised controlled trials undertaken and published since the mid-1990s impact on earlier conclusions and recommendations? Are there areas in this field that have been neglected? Is entirely new evidence coming to light?

Questions such as these led to the commissioning of this Report by WCRF/AICR in 2001. The Panel responsible for the Report first convened in 2003, and has met twice a year until 2007. The terms of reference accepted by the Panel at its first meeting were to:

- Judge the reviews of the scientific and other literature prepared for the Panel by the assigned review teams

- Devise a series of dietary, associated, and other recommendations suitable for all societies, designed to reduce the risk of cancer

- Evaluate the consistency between such recommendations and those designed to prevent other food-related diseases.

The Panel believes that these terms of reference have been fulfilled. The public policy implications of the recommendations made in this Report are the subject of a further report, to be published in late 2008.

Special features of this Report

This Report in part adapts and builds on the work of the previous WCRF/AICR report. It also has central features that are new. It is not simply an 'update' of the previous report. Since the mid-1990s a substantial body of relevant literature has been published in peer-reviewed journals. Further, the executive officers of WCRF/AICR, its Secretariat, and the Panel responsible, decided at the outset that developments in scientific method since the mid-1990s, notably in systematic approaches to synthesising evidence, and as enabled by the electronic revolution, have been so remarkable that a whole new process was justified.

Systematic literature reviews

This process (described in Appendix A) has involved systematic literature reviews (SLRs), which have been used as the main basis for the Panel's judgements in this Report. These are described in more detail in Chapter 3. They were undertaken by independent centres of research and review excellence in North America and Europe, to a common agreed protocol, itself the product of an expert Methodology Task Force. As a result, the judgements of the Panel now are as firmly based as the evidence and the state of the science allow. Some are new. Some are different from those previously published. Findings that may at first reading seem to repeat those of the first report are in fact the result of an entirely new process.

Rigorous criteria to assess evidence

The criteria used in this Report to assess the evidence presented in the SLRs and from other sources are more precise and explicit than, and in some respects different from and more stringent than, those used in the previous report. During its initial meetings, the Panel reviewed and agreed these criteria before embarking on the formal evidence review. More details are given in Chapter 3.

Nevertheless, readers and users of this Report should be able to see how and why the development of scientific method and research since the mid-1990s has resulted in conclusions and recommendations here that sometimes vary from, sometimes are much the same as, and sometimes reinforce those of the previous Report.

Graphic display of Panel judgements

The Panel has retained the matrix technique of displaying its judgements, which introduce the chapters and chapter sections throughout Part 2 of this Report. This technique, pioneered in the first report, has been adapted by the

World Health Organization in its 2003 report on diet, nutrition, and the prevention of chronic diseases. Some members of the expert consultation responsible for the WHO report, including its chair and vice-chair, have served as members of the Panel responsible for this Report.

In further adapting the format of the matrices used in the first report, the Panel was careful to distinguish between evidence strong enough to justify judgements of convincing or probable causal relationships, on which recommendations designed to prevent cancer can be based, and evidence that is too limited in amount, consistency, or quality to be a basis for public and personal health recommendations, but which may nevertheless in some cases be suggestive of causal relationships.

Food-based approach

Since the 1990s a broad food- and drink-based approach to interpreting the evidence on food, nutrition, and the risk of cancer has increasingly been used, in contrast to the overwhelming research emphasis on individual food constituents. The previous report included three chapters showing the findings on dietary constituents (including 'energy and related factors', notably physical activity), foods and drinks, and food processing (meaning production, preservation, processing, and preparation), in that order.

This Report has taken a food-based approach, as shown throughout Chapter 4, more closely reflecting the nature of the evidence. Thus many findings on dietary constituents and micronutrients, when their dietary sources are from foods rather than supplements, are here identified as, for example, findings on 'foods containing dietary fibre' or 'foods containing folate'. Findings on methods of food processing are, wherever possible, shown as part of the evidence on the associated foods, so that, for example, meat processing is integrated with the evidence on meat. The evidence and judgements focused on cancer are summarised and displayed in Chapter 7.

Physical activity

The scope of the work of this Panel is wider than that of the previous panel. The previous report judged that the evidence that physical activity protects against cancer of the colon was convincing. Since then evidence on physical activity (and physical inactivity, especially when this amounts to generally sedentary ways of life) has become more impressive. Correspondingly, the review centres were requested specifically to examine the literature on physical activity (and inactivity) as well as on foods and drinks. The results of this work, and the Panel's judgements, are shown in Chapter 5.

Body fatness

As with physical inactivity, the evidence that body fatness — including degrees of fatness throughout the range of body weight, from underweight and normal to overweight and obesity, as well as any specific effect of weight gain — directly influences risk of some cancers has also become more impressive. The previous report judged that the evidence that greater body fatness (there termed 'high body mass') is a convincing or probable cause of cancers of the endometrium, breast (postmenopausal), and kidney. For this Report, the commissioned SLRs not only included the evidence linking body fatness directly with cancer, but a separate review was also commissioned specifically on the biological and associated determinants of body fatness itself. The evidence and the Panel's judgements, which include assessment of the physiology of energy metabolism, are summarised in Chapters 6 and 8.

The Panel is aware that weight gain, overweight, and obesity, and their antecedent behaviours, are critically determined by social, cultural, and other environmental factors. This is one topic for the separate report on policy implications to be published in late 2008.

Cancer survivors

There are increasing numbers of cancer survivors — people who have at some time been diagnosed with cancer. What should those people living with cancer do? Particularly since the 1990s, this question is being asked increasingly, as more and more people are diagnosed with and treated for cancer, and are seeking ways in which they can add to their medical or surgical management to help themselves to remain healthy. Are the circumstances of people who have recovered from cancer any different from those of people who are free from cancer? Questions such as these are addressed in Chapter 9.

Life-course approach

Unlike this Report, the reviews conducted for the first report did not consider the literature on food and nutrition in the first two years of life. Increasingly, evidence is accumulating on the importance of early life-events on later health. Evidence and judgements on the impact of birth weight and adult attained height on cancer risk are presented in Chapter 6, though the detailed processes underpinning these associations with cancer risk are not yet clear. Findings on the relationship between not being breastfed and later overweight and obesity in children are reported in Chapter 8, and on lactation and lower breast cancer risk in the mother are reported in Chapter 7. These findings form part of a general 'life-course' approach summarised in Chapter 2, reflecting an appreciation of the importance of the accumulation of nutritional and other experiences throughout life, as well as genetic endowment, in influencing susceptibility to disease.

Goals and recommendations

The Panel's recommendations are set out in Chapter 12 and in abbreviated form in the Summary, on the preceding pages.

The previous report agreed 14 recommendations. This Report makes eight general and two special recommendations for specific target groups. These are set out in more detail than in the previous report. As before, principles that guide the goals and recommendations are set out. The recommendations themselves are displayed in boxes and are accompanied by text that justifies them, and by practical guidance. The recommendations are addressed to people, as members of communities and families and also as individuals.

Recommendations and options addressed to UN and other international organisations, national governments, industry, health professional and civil society organisations, and the media are set out in the separate report on policy implications, to be published in late 2008.

A note of caution

The Panel is confident that its findings are soundly based, and that its recommendations, when translated into effective public policy programmes and personal choices, will reduce the risk of cancer. That said, the available evident is imperfect. The Panel's conclusions derive from the best evidence now available, which reflects past and recent research priorities mostly in high-income countries, though synthesised and judged in as meticulous and rigorous way as possible. What is here is therefore an incomplete picture.

The tendency of reports such as this is to consider diseases in isolation. In the case of this Report, the relationship of weight gain, overweight, and obesity on the risk of some cancers is so clear that determinants of these factors have also been considered. But *the Panel agrees*, as evident in Chapters 10 and 12, that many chronic diseases, including type 2 diabetes and its precursors, cardiovascular diseases and their precursors, and also perhaps other diseases of the digestive, musculoskeletal, and nervous systems, are to a large extent caused by environmental factors, including inappropriate food and nutrition, physical inactivity, overweight and obesity, and associated factors. Following from this, future reports should consider the promotion of health and the prevention of disease as a whole.

How much cancer is preventable?

As shown in its title, the purpose of this Report is to prevent cancer. The term 'prevention' needs definition. It does not mean the elimination of cancer. It means reduction in its occurrence, such that at any age fewer people have cancer than otherwise would be the case.

If all factors are taken into account, cancer is mostly a preventable disease. The authors of a landmark study published in the early 1980s concluded: 'It is highly likely that the United States will eventually have the option of adopting a diet that reduces its incidence of cancer by approximately one third, and it is absolutely certain that another one third could be prevented by abolishing smoking.'[3] Cancers of some sites, notably of the colon, are generally agreed to be greatly or mostly affected by food and nutrition.

Since then, authoritative estimates of the preventability of cancer by means of food and nutrition and associated factors have been in broad agreement with the 'around one third' figure. The estimate of the previous WCRF/AICR Report was that cancer is 30 to 40 per cent preventable over time, by appropriate food and nutrition, regular physical activity, and avoidance of obesity. On a global scale this represents over 3 to 4 million cases of cancer that can be prevented in these ways, every year.

In many of its forms, cancer is a disease that can cause great suffering and claims many lives. The overall commitment of scientists and other professionals committed to disease prevention, as exemplified by this Report, is to reduce the rates not just of cancer, but of all diseases, so that more people enjoy good health until they eventually die in old age.

References

[1] National Research Council. *Diet, Nutrition and Cancer.* Washington DC: National Academy of Sciences, 1982

[2] Willett W. Summary. In: *Eat, Drink, and Be Healthy. The Harvard Medical School Guide to Healthy Eating.* New York: Free Press, 2003

[3] Doll R, Peto R. The causes of cancer: quantitative estimates of avoidable risks of cancer in the United States today. *J Natl Cancer Inst* 1981;66:1191-308.

Part 1

Background

Introduction to Part 1

This Report has a number of inter-related general purposes. One is to explore the extent to which food, nutrition, physical activity, and body composition modify the risk of cancer, and to specify as far as possible the importance of specific factors. To the extent that environmental factors such as food, nutrition, and physical activity influence risk of cancer, it is a preventable disease. The Report specifies recommendations based on solid evidence which, when followed, will be expected to reduce the incidence of cancer.

Part 1 of the Report begins with two chapters summarising the first lines of evidence from observations of human populations, and from experimental and basic science, pointing to the conclusion that cancer is preventable. The third chapter summarises the types of evidence that are relevant in identifying the causes of cancer, and explains the process used by the Panel to assess the strength of this evidence and to come to judgement.

Chapter 1 shows that patterns of production and consumption of food and drink, of physical activity, and of body composition have changed greatly throughout different periods of human history. Remarkable changes have taken place as a result of urbanisation and industrialisation, at first in Europe, North America, and other economically advanced countries, and increasingly in most countries in the world.

With the establishment of reliable records in the second half of the 20th century, notable variations have been identified in patterns of cancer throughout the world. Some cancers, such as those of the upper aerodigestive tract, stomach, liver, and cervix, are more common in lower income countries; others, such as those of the colorectum, breast, ovary, endometrium, prostate, and lung, are more common in higher income countries.

More significant, as shown in Chapter 1, are studies consistently showing that patterns of cancer change as populations migrate from one part of the world to another and as countries become increasingly urbanised and industrialised. Projections indicate that rates of cancer in general are liable to increase.

Chapter 2 outlines current understanding of the biology of the cancer process, with special attention given to the ways in which food and nutrition, physical activity, and body composition may modify it.

Cancer is a disease of genes, which are vulnerable to beneficial or harmful mutation, especially over the long human lifespan. Nutritional factors are important in determining the likelihood of some mutations, as well as in changing the functions of genes even without mutation. However, both epidemiological and experimental evidence shows that only a small proportion of cancers are inherited. Environmental factors are most important and can be modified. These include smoking and other use of tobacco; infectious agents; radiation; industrial chemicals and pollution; medication — and also many aspects of food, nutrition, physical activity, and body composition. Essentially this is good news. It means that healthy environments can stop cancer before it starts. The evidence also indicates that such environments, including the factors that are the subject of this Report, may be able to check the cancer process after it has started.

The third chapter summarises the types of evidence that the Panel has agreed are relevant to its work. No one study can prove that any factor definitely is a cause of or is protective against any disease. Also while some study designs are more reliable than others, they often cannot be used to answer many types of question; so no one kind of study, however careful its methods, can ever produce definitive results. In this chapter, building on the work of the first report, the Panel shows that all study designs have strengths and weaknesses, and that reliable judgements on causation of disease are based on assessment of a variety of well designed epidemiological and experimental studies.

The judgements made by the Panel in Part 2 of this Report are based on independently commissioned and conducted systematic reviews of the literature. This has ensured that the evidence has been assembled using methods that are as meticulous as possible, and that the display of the evidence is separated from assessments derived from this evidence, which are made in Part 2.

The prevention of cancer worldwide is one of the most pressing challenges facing scientists and public health policy-makers, among others. These introductory chapters show that the challenge can be effectively addressed. They also suggest that food and nutrition, physical activity, and body composition all play a central part in the prevention of cancer.

CHAPTER 1

International variations and trends

The first lines of evidence suggesting that cancer is a largely preventable disease have come from studies noting variations in cancer incidence across time and place. The most impressive initial evidence showing that patterns of cancer are altered by environmental factors, and are not mainly genetically determined, comes from studies describing changes in the rates of different cancers in genetically identical populations that migrate from their native countries to other countries. Such studies consistently show that changes in the rates of some of the most common cancers, including those of the stomach, colorectum, breast, and prostate, can be remarkable, even over one or two generations.

This first introductory chapter summarises current knowledge of the variations in food, nutrition, physical activity, body composition, and cancer in different parts of the world. This assessment provides strong circumstantial evidence that continues to prompt systematic studies including interventions of various types, and also reports such as this, which collect and judge the available evidence. Such systematic work has already led the United Nations and other international bodies, national governments, and authoritative independent organisations to be confident that most cancers are largely preventable.

Patterns of food and drink, of physical activity, and of body composition have changed remarkably throughout human history. With industrialisation and urbanisation, food supplies usually become more secure, and more food is available for consumption. In general, diets become more energy dense, containing fewer starchy foods, more fats and oils, sugars, and additives, and often more alcoholic drinks. At the same time, patterns of physical activity change: populations become increasingly sedentary, their need for energy from food drops, and rates of overweight and obesity increase.

These changes correlate with changes in the patterns of cancer throughout the world. Middle- and low-income regions and countries within Africa, Asia, and Latin America have generally experienced comparatively high rates of cancers of the upper aerodigestive tract (of the mouth, pharynx, larynx, nasopharynx, and oesophagus), and of the stomach, liver (primary), and cervix. Rates of some cancers, especially stomach cancer, are now generally decreasing.

In contrast, high-income countries, and urbanised and industrialised areas of middle- and low-income regions and countries, have higher rates of colorectal cancer and of hormone-related cancers (of the breast, ovary, endometrium, and prostate). Lung cancer is now the most common type in the world because of the increase in tobacco smoking and exposure to environmental tobacco smoke. Rates of these cancers, some of which may have been historically rare, are increasing.

Globally, the number of people with cancer is projected to double by the year 2030, with most of this increase likely to occur in middle- and low-income countries. Such an increase would only partly be accounted for by the projected rise in the size and average age of the global population. This makes the task of cancer prevention all the more urgent and important.

This chapter outlines the historic, recent, and current variations and trends in food, nutrition, physical activity, overweight and obesity, and in patterns of cancer.

People's diets reflect the times and situations in which they live. It is only relatively recently in history that urban–industrial ways of life have evolved, with many or most people living in towns and cities rather than in the countryside. In much of Africa and Asia, most people still live in rural communities, and peasant–agricultural and urban–industrial ways of life still coexist in most countries. Such patterns change very rapidly as countries become increasingly urbanised and industrialised.

The different food systems and diets that are part of these diverse ways of life affect people's levels of physical activity, their body composition and stature, their life expectancy, and patterns of disease, including cancer. With the move to urban–industrial ways of life, populations have become taller and heavier, their life expectancy has increased, and they are usually adequately nourished (although poverty, and even destitution, remains a major problem in most big cities). On the other hand, urban populations are at increased risk of chronic diseases such as obesity, type 2 diabetes, coronary heart disease, and also some cancers.

This chapter also summarises some available information on eight common cancers, irrespective of any recognised links to food, nutrition, and physical activity; these factors are dealt with later in the Report. Four are endemic in middle- and low-income countries: cancers of the oesophagus, stomach, liver, and cervix. Four are endemic in high-income countries, and are in general increasing in middle- and low-income countries: cancers of the lung, colon and rectum, breast, and prostate. Information on the trends and projections of levels of physical activity, and overweight and obesity, is summarised.

Descriptive epidemiology, including studies of changing disease patterns in migrant populations, is covered. These studies can generate hypotheses about relationships between food, nutrition, physical activity, and the risk of cancer. However, they serve mainly as a foundation for studies that provide stronger evidence.

The 12 national examples provided throughout this chapter summarise some of the trends in foods and drinks, obesity, physical activity, and cancer in countries around the world. These are Egypt and South Africa (Africa); China, India, and Japan (Asia); the UK, Poland, and Spain (Europe); the USA, Brazil, and Mexico (the Americas); and Australia (Asia-Pacific).[1-47]

1.1 Food systems and diets: historical and current

Throughout history, food systems, and thus human diets, have been and are shaped by climate, terrain, seasons, location, culture, and technology. They can be grouped into three broad types: gatherer–hunter, peasant–agricultural, and urban–industrial. These and other food systems (for example, pastoralist, the semi-mobile farming of herds of large animals such as sheep and cattle) have their roots in history. All have coexisted in recent millennia with the exception of industrial food systems, which are the consequence of the industrial revolution that began in Europe in the late 18th century. These systems still exist in the world today.

1.1.1 Gatherer–hunter

Since the emergence of *Homo sapiens* around 250 000 years ago, gatherer–hunter food systems have taken different forms, depending on the environments in which people lived. These systems still exist in parts of the world that are remote from cities and roads. They supply diets that usually include moderate amounts of starchy foods, and which are high in dietary fibre and low in sugar, mostly from fruits and honey.[48] Methods of food preparation include pulverising, drying, and roasting. These diets are usually high in foods of animal origin (ranging from large animals to insects, and also fish and other seafood, depending on location), and thus in animal protein. It is sometimes thought that gatherer–hunter diets are high in fat, which is not the case because wild animals are lean. Recent analyses suggest that gathered food generally provides rather more dietary bulk and energy than hunted food.[49]

People in gatherer–hunter societies are necessarily physically active, and are often tall and usually lean (only chiefs, or old or incapacitated people might be overweight or obese). The diets of food-secure gatherer–hunter societies may be diverse and high in micronutrients.[50] [51] Diets are liable to become monotonous and deficient in various nutrients, as well as in energy, when food supplies are chronically insecure, or at times of acute food shortage. It is sometimes claimed that gatherer–hunter food systems generate diets to which the human species is best adapted.[48] However, life expectancy in gatherer–hunter societies is and has been usually relatively low.

Evidence of cancer has occasionally been found in human and other fossil and ancient remains.[52] Historically, cancer

Egypt

In 2004 Egypt had a population of just over 74 million. Nearly the whole population lives within the Nile Valley and the Nile Delta, less than 4 per cent of the country's total area. Egypt has a lower-middle-income economy, with a gross domestic product of 4274 international dollars per person (figure 1.3). Life expectancy at birth is 66 years for men and 70 for women (figure 1.1).[46]

Chronic diseases account for 83.6 per cent of deaths, while infectious diseases, maternal, perinatal, and nutritional condi-

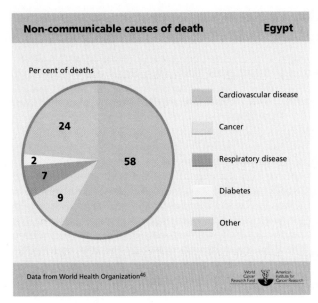

Non-communicable causes of death   **Egypt**

Per cent of deaths

- 58
- 24
- 2
- 7
- 9

Cardiovascular disease

Cancer

Respiratory disease

Diabetes

Other

Data from World Health Organization[46]

World Cancer Research Fund / American Institute for Cancer Research

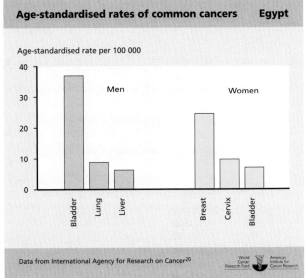

Age-standardised rates of common cancers   **Egypt**

Age-standardised rate per 100 000

Men: Bladder, Lung, Liver

Women: Breast, Cervix, Bladder

Data from International Agency for Research on Cancer[20]

World Cancer Research Fund / American Institute for Cancer Research

of any type seems to have been uncommon among gatherer–hunter peoples, if only because their average life expectancy was low. In modern gatherer–hunter societies, the incidence of cancer rises after contact with industrialised and urbanised ways of life, which usually involve shifts in patterns of diet and physical activity.[53] These points generally also apply to pastoralist societies.

1.1.2 Peasant–agricultural

In recent millennia, and until very recently in history, almost all human populations have been rural and mostly peasant–agricultural, and the majority still are in most regions of Asia, many regions of Africa, and some parts of Latin America. Peasant–agricultural food systems involving the cultivation of wheat may have first developed around 9000 years ago in the 'Fertile Crescent' of the Middle East, including the region between the Tigris and Euphrates rivers (within modern Iraq). These systems also developed independently in Asia, with rice as the staple food, and in the Americas, with corn (maize) as the staple.[54] The key factor in these systems is land settlement, itself determined by the cultivation and breeding of crops and also animals, birds, and fish for human consumption and use.[55] In and around Egypt, people began to make bread from wheat about 6000 years ago.[56]

Typically, diets derived from these systems are plant-based: they are high or very high in cereals (grains), complemented with animal sources of protein. These diets are therefore high in starchy foods and usually in dietary fibre (unless the cereals are refined). They include varying amounts of foods of animal origin, and of vegetables and fruits, depending on relative food security. Surplus food is stored for consumption in winter and during hard times, and methods of food preparation also include fermentation, used for foods as well as for the production of alcoholic drinks (see chapters 4.8 and 4.9).

The dominant indigenous cereal crop varies in different parts of the world: wheat is grown in the Middle East; barley, rye, and oats in colder, northern climates; millet and rice in Asia; maize (corn) in the Americas; and sorghum and teff in Africa. Indigenous staple crops also include roots and tubers such as cassava (manioc), yams, potatoes, and also plantains. Pulses (legumes) are also farmed to ensure agricultural and nutritional balance; and other crops such as vegetables and fruits are also cultivated. Birds and animals are domesticated and bred for food, and fish and seafood contribute to the diets of communities living beside water.[57]

As with gatherer–hunters, the diets of peasant–agricultural societies may be diverse and high in micronutrients. Again, when food supplies are chronically insecure, or at times of acute food shortage (including times of war), diets are liable to become monotonous and deficient in various nutrients, as well as in energy.

Peasant–agricultural societies are necessarily physically active, although not constantly so: the main times of intensive physical work include building field systems, sowing, harvesting, and storing. The level of energy balance and of physical activity varies greatly, depending in part on how dif-

tions account for 12.2 per cent; 4.2 per cent of deaths are due to injuries. The first figure gives a breakdown of deaths caused by chronic diseases.[46]

Bladder cancer is the most common type of cancer in men, followed by cancers of the lung and liver.[20] In women, the dominant cancers include those of the breast, cervix, and bladder (for age-standardised rates of these cancers, see the second figure).[20] The high incidence of bladder cancer is likely to be related to bilharzia, a parasitic infection of the bladder.[20] There is also a high incidence of hepatitis C virus, a cause of liver cancer.[20] Also see box 7.8.1 It is predicted that there will be a 3.5-fold increase in liver cancer by 2030.[12]

For the period 1991–1994, 46 per cent of men and 48 per cent of women between the ages of 20 and 44 were classified as sedentary.[46] In 2003, women aged 15–49 had a mean body mass index (BMI) of 28.6. In teenagers (13–19 year olds), average BMI was 23.9; women in their 30s had a mean BMI of 29.0, while those over 45 had a BMI of 31.3. In total, 77.3 per cent of women aged 15–49 had a BMI of over 25. In 1992,

23.5 per cent of all women had a BMI of over 30. By 2000, this figure had risen to 41 per cent.[46] Fewer data are available for men, but in 1994, the mean BMI for men aged 20–44 was 26.6, rising to 28.4 for men over 45. In 2002, among all men, 45 per cent had a BMI of between 25 and 29.99 and 20 per cent had a BMI of over 30.[15] See figure 1.4 for projections of the proportions of men and women predicted to have a BMI of 30 or more in 2015.[46]

The average amount of available food energy rose between 1964 and 2004, from around 2240 to 3290 kcal/person per day (9400 to 13 800 kJ/person per day).[1] Early dietary studies in Egypt demonstrated that corn bread was the staple food and that protein intake was about 100 g/day.[15] People from higher-income households consumed more dairy products and those from urban households consumed a wider variety of foods. Between 1950 and 1990, there was a shift towards a dependence on wheat rather than other cereals (grains), and a sustained rise in the consumption of meat, fish, and dairy products.[15]

Consumption of sugars and oils increased substantially and pulses (legumes) decreased in importance.[15] Since the 1970s, consumption of all major food groups has increased. However, between 1990 and 1994 there was a 20 per cent decrease in total household food consumption, because subsidies were removed and food prices rose sharply.[15] A national study in 1981 found that only 24 per cent of urban and 15 per cent of rural households ate ready-made foods, and meat was eaten more frequently in urban households compared with rural households.[15] A repeat survey in 1998 found that poultry had become the main source of animal protein and that wheat bread was the most popular type, although homemade wheat-maize bread was common in rural areas. Another study highlighted differences in dietary fat intake: in urban women, 27.5 per cent of dietary energy came from fat (mainly as vegetable oil) compared with 22.5 per cent in rural women.[15] Between 1981 and 1998, people increasingly ate meals away from home (20.4 per cent of all meals in 1981 compared with 45.8 per cent in 1998).[15]

ficult it is to cultivate the land. The degree of physical activity and so of body mass in peasant–agricultural communities depends mostly on relative food security.[58]

People in these societies who are prosperous, especially those who own land farmed by others, may quite often become overweight or obese. But in general, and largely because of the nature of their dietary staples, peasant–agriculturalists are usually short and lean. This is still evident in rural peasant communities whose food systems remain traditional: for instance, in Africa, Latin America, and in Asia, notably India and China.[58]

Agriculture enabled the development of towns and then cities: throughout the world, walled, urban settlements became surrounded by fields cultivated by peasants. These people subsisted on the food they produced, and the surplus fed the community living within the walls. In times of war, the fortified settlement became a refuge for the farmers. This crowding of populations into towns and cities caused a sharp rise in the rates of infectious diseases, mostly notably among infants and young children, pregnant and lactating women, and infirm and old people.[59]

The average life expectancy of peasant–agriculturists in general is probably a little longer than that of gatherer–hunters, with a greater percentage of people surviving into what would be regarded as late-middle and old age.

The prevalence and incidence of various cancers in traditional rural societies is often uncertain, even following the establishment of cancer registers in many countries: records

are less reliable than those kept in urbanised societies. But there is reasonable evidence that relatively common cancers in peasant–agricultural societies include those causally associated with chronic infections, such as cancers of the stomach, liver, and cervix.[60]

1.1.3 Urban–industrial

Indigenous or traditional peasant–agricultural systems have coexisted with urban–industrial food systems in most countries since the creation and growth of cities, and the beginning of the 'industrial revolution'. This movement started in Europe in the 18th century, and then spread to North America and elsewhere. Britain is one exception to this coexistence: it was the first country to become mostly urban, with hired workers replacing peasants on increasingly large and relatively mechanised farms. The Americas are another exception: settlers, mostly from Europe, displaced native populations and developed mechanised agricultural systems.[61] In continental Europe, some balance between rural and urban ways of life has been preserved. Throughout the Mediterranean coastal regions, and in the Middle East, modern food systems have deep, historical roots.[62] In most of Africa and Asia, including countries with large cities, the basic economies and cultures have remained predominantly rural, but this is changing.[63]

Urban–industrial food systems have characteristics distinct from peasant–agricultural and gatherer–hunter systems. Their original purpose was to ensure reliable and adequate supplies of food of an agreed minimum nutritional quality

South Africa

In 2001 South Africa had a population of nearly 47.5 million.[3] The country has a middle-income economy, with a gross domestic product of 8506 international dollars per person (figure 1.3), which masks extreme socioeconomic inequalities.[46] Life expectancy at birth is 47 years for men and 49 for women (figure 1.1).[46]

Chronic diseases account for 53.9 per cent of deaths, while infectious diseases, maternal, perinatal, and nutritional conditions account for 40.2 per cent; 5.9 per cent of deaths are due to injuries. The figure below gives a breakdown of deaths caused by chronic diseases.[46]

The most common cancers in men are those of the prostate, lung, oesophagus, colorectum, and bladder.[20] Since HIV and AIDS became epidemic, Kaposi's sarcoma has become more common in both men and women. For women, the most common cancers are those of the cervix, breast,

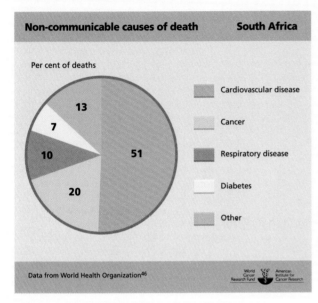

Non-communicable causes of death — **South Africa**

Per cent of deaths

- Cardiovascular disease
- Cancer
- Respiratory disease
- Diabetes
- Other

Data from World Health Organization[46]

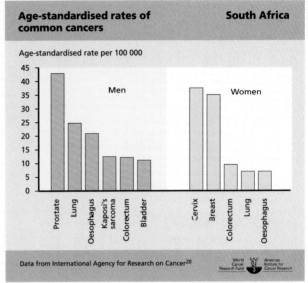

Age-standardised rates of common cancers — **South Africa**

Age-standardised rate per 100 000

Data from International Agency for Research on Cancer[20]

to entire populations. Technology has been the main driving force behind these systems. For instance, various food-preservation techniques were developed as part of the industrial revolution, and there has been further innovation since that time. These include bottling, canning, refrigeration, and packaging; the extensive use of sugar and salt; and technologies that suppress, convert, or eliminate perishable qualities in fresh foods (see chapters 4.6 and 4.9). The clearing of land to rear cattle and sheep, and the development of railways, refrigeration, and other technologies, have made meat, milk, and their products cheap and plentiful all year round. Sugar derived from cane is the most profitable edible cash crop, and sugars and syrups made from cane, beet, and now also corn are used to sweeten and preserve breakfast foods, baked foods, desserts, soft drinks, and a vast array of other manufactured products.[64][65] Steel roller mills, invented in the 1870s, separate the components of wheat and enable production of uniform quality white bread, which has become a staple food.[66] Hydrogenation, which converts oils to hard fats (see chapter 4.5), has made margarine a basic item of food, and provides ingredients used in the manufacturing of many processed foods.[67] Perhaps the most remarkable change following the industrialisation of food systems has been the precipitate drop in breastfeeding.[68] At various times, urban–industrial food systems have been adjusted in response to the then current knowledge of nutrition and pub-

lic health recommendations, notably when food security has been threatened by wars.[69]

Urban–industrial food systems generate relatively energy-dense diets. These are fairly high in meat, and milk and their products, and in total fats, hardened fats, processed starches and sugars, salt, baked goods, soft drinks, and often also alcoholic drinks. These diets are relatively low in both dietary fibre and starchy staple foods, other than products made from wheat, which has become the dominant cereal in most countries outside Asia and Africa. Recent advances in food technology have further altered patterns of food production and consumption, particularly in high-income countries. Patterns of production and consumption of vegetables and fruits and fish vary between different urban–industrial food systems, depending on factors such as climate and geographical location.[70]

Efficient urban–industrial food systems can ensure the constant supply of food to all sections of the population, even to the lowest-income and marginalised groups. In higher-income countries and regions, this, together with basic public health initiatives, has helped to greatly reduce rates of nutritional deficiencies and other diseases, which people are more vulnerable to if they have inadequate food supplies. As a result of these food systems, people have become generally taller and heavier.

Since the industrial revolution, as populations have moved

colorectum, lung, and oesophagus (for age-standardised rates of these cancers, see the second figure).[20] Diseases of poverty and chronic diseases coexist, but it is predicted that by 2010, deaths from AIDS will account for twice as many deaths as those from all other causes combined.[5 41]

For the period 2002–2003, 44 per cent of men and 49 per cent of women aged 18–69 were classified as sedentary (figure 1.6).[46] Some regional studies suggest that young women who did not finish school have low levels of physical activity.[24] There is a lack of physical education in schools, and poor environment and high crime rates prevent leisure activity outside school.[24]

In 1998 men aged 15–24 had an average body mass index (BMI) of 21.1; for those aged 35–65, average BMI remained constant at around 25. Just 7.8 per cent of men aged 25–34 had a BMI of over 30 compared with 17.3 per cent of men aged 45–54. In the same year, women aged 15–24 had an average BMI of 23.7; for those aged 35–64, average BMI remained constant at around 29. In women aged 25–34, 27 per cent had a BMI of over 30 compared with 45 per cent of women aged 45–64.[46] Although under-nutrition remains a problem among rural children, obesity and associated diseases are

also prevalent. There has been a misconception of 'benign obesity': being thin is associated with HIV and AIDS, and moderately overweight women are thought of as attractive and affluent.[24] Overall, in 1998, 21.1 per cent of men and 25.9 per cent of women had a BMI of at least 25; 10.1 per cent of men and 27.9 per cent of women had a BMI of at least 30. See figure 1.4 for projections of the proportions of men and women who will have a BMI of 30 or more in 2015.

The average amount of available food energy rose between 1964 and 2004, from around 2700 to 3000 kcal/person per day (11 400 to 12 600 kJ/person per day). In the same period, sugar consumption dropped from 420 to 370 kcal/person per day (1800 to 1500 kJ/person per day).[1] The National Food Consumption survey of 1999 found that stunting was the most common nutritional disorder, affecting almost one fifth of children aged 1–9, with the lowest levels in urban areas. There was a similar pattern for underweight, where 10 per cent of children aged 1–3 consumed less than half of their suggested daily dietary needs, and 26 per cent consumed less than two thirds.[25] In rural areas, adults from lower-income households were shorter and had a lower

BMI, and commonly consumed foods were maize, sugar, tea, milk, and brown bread. Urban households ate less maize porridge but more vegetables and fruits, animal-based products, and fats and oils. It was only in urban areas that fruits and milk appeared in the top 10 list of foods and drinks consumed by more than 85 per cent of people. In men, alcoholic drinks made a significant contribution to dietary energy (10–14 per cent). People living in rural areas obtained a higher proportion of total dietary energy from carbohydrates, whereas the most urbanised populations derived one third of their energy from animal foods high in protein.

Urbanisation is generally accompanied by an improvement in micronutrient intakes, but this way of life is also associated with increases in overweight and obesity.[44] Other studies have suggested shifts towards a Western dietary pattern in people living in both urban and rural areas, typified by a decrease in starchy foods and dietary fibre consumption, and an increase in fat. They have also shown that half of the population does not eat the locally recommended four portions of fruits and vegetables each day, while a quarter eats none.[10]

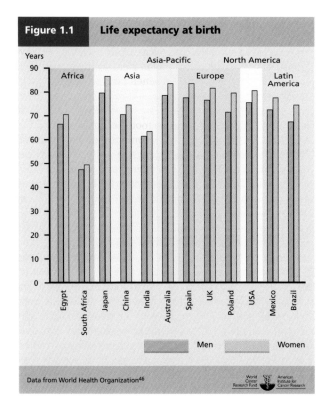

Figure 1.1   Life expectancy at birth

Years

Africa — Egypt, South Africa

Asia-Pacific — Asia: Japan, China, India, Australia

Europe: Spain, UK, Poland

North America — USA

Latin America — Mexico, Brazil

Men   Women

Data from World Health Organization[46]

from rural to urban areas, there have been rapid and profound changes in both the nature and quality of their foods and drinks, and the patterns of diseases they suffer.[71] Urban–industrial food systems have evidently improved people's strength and health in early life. They are also a factor in the doubling of average life expectancy since 1800, and the increase in global population from around 1 billion in 1800 to 6.5 billion in 2006.[72] The range of current life expectancy in selected countries is illustrated in figure 1.1.

In the second half of the 20th century, attention focused on the apparent ill-effects of these food systems on people, mostly in later life. By the 1980s, it was generally agreed that these industrialised diets increase the risk of some chronic diseases, usually of later life, which had become common or epidemic in higher-income industrialised countries. These included obesity, type 2 diabetes, and coronary heart disease. At the same time, in examining patterns of both diet and cancer across the world, and among migrants, it was increasingly thought that these diets were partly responsible for some cancers, notably those of the colon and rectum, breast, ovary, endometrium, and prostate.[73-75]

In the last decades of the 20th century, the demographic, nutritional, and epidemiological transitions that had, until then, largely been apparent only in higher-income countries became global. Since the 1990s, and outside Europe, North America, and other high-income countries, economic glob-

China

In 2004 China had a population of over 1.3 billion. The one-child policy introduced in 1979 has reduced annual population growth to 1.07 per cent. The United Nations estimates that the population will have increased to nearly 1.5 billion by 2025.[46] The country has a lower-middle-income economy, with a gross domestic product of 5581 international dollars per person (figure 1.3). Life expectancy at birth is 70 years for men and 74 for women (figure 1.1).[46]

Chronic diseases account for 78.9 per cent of deaths, while infectious diseases, maternal, perinatal, and nutritional conditions account for 11.7 per cent; 9.3 per cent of deaths are due to injuries.[46] The figure below gives a breakdown of deaths caused by chronic diseases.[46] A study published in 2004 found that there has been a shift towards nutrition-related chronic diseases such as type 2 diabetes, cancer, and cardiovascular disease.[14]

Stomach cancer is the most common type of cancer in men, although it has declined slightly since 1980.[20] Lung cancer has risen steadily over the same period.[20] Liver cancer has risen since 1990, although levels are now

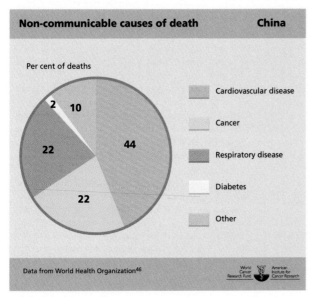

Non-communicable causes of death China

Per cent of deaths

- Cardiovascular disease
- Cancer
- Respiratory disease
- Diabetes
- Other

Data from World Health Organization[46]

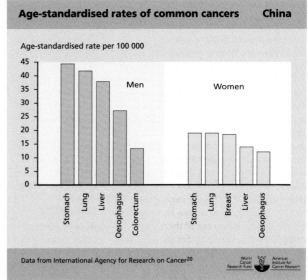

Age-standardised rates of common cancers China

Age-standardised rate per 100 000

Men — Stomach, Lung, Liver, Oesophagus, Colorectum

Women — Stomach, Lung, Breast, Liver, Oesophagus

Data from International Agency for Research on Cancer[20]

alisation is thought to be the single main force shifting populations from the countryside into cities, changing the dominant food systems from peasant–agricultural to urban–industrial, and transforming patterns of disease. This phenomenon includes the unprecedented and accelerating movement of money, goods, and ideas. All this has been made possible by new international, political, and economic policies, by the creation of supranational regulatory bodies such as the World Trade Organization, and by the electronic revolution.[76-78]

People's levels of physical activity have also changed dramatically as a result of the move from peasant–agricultural to urban–industrial ways of life. In 1950, the UN 'reference man' weighing 65 kg (143 lbs) was estimated to be in energy balance at an average of 3200 kilocalories (kcal)/day (13 398 kilojoules [kJ]/day); the 'reference woman' weighing 55 kg (121 lbs) was estimated to be in energy balance at 2300 kcal/day (9630 kJ/day). Today in the USA, average weights are much higher, yet the figure for the 'reference person' (men and women combined) is taken to be 2000 kcal/day (8374 kJ/day) for the purposes of nutrition food labelling. The reason for this drop in human energy requirements is because three of the four settings for physical activity — occupational, household, and transport — (see Chapter 5) have become increasingly mechanised. Energy-dense food systems, essen-

tial to sustain young populations that walk or cycle to work that is physically demanding, are unsuitable for ageing populations who sit for most of the day, even if they engage in some recreational physical activity.

There is some evidence that these very recently introduced urban–industrial food systems have lowered the rates of nutritional deficiencies and infectious diseases of early life in middle- to low-income countries and regions. But the apparent impact on the rates of chronic diseases in these areas is of increasing public health concern. In most of these regions, with the exception of sub-Saharan Africa, childhood overweight, obesity, and type 2 diabetes have become common and, in some countries, epidemic.[70]

The Panel emphasises that there is no reason to think that urban–industrial food systems are intrinsically harmful. They were first developed using relatively crude technologies, and at a time when something was known of their positive impact on growth and strength, but little of their long-term impact on health. Since then, many new technologies have been developed, and there is a clearer understanding that some methods of preserving and processing food are beneficial, whereas others are a factor in increasing the risk of disease. Future developments can ensure universal food security, avoid earlier mistakes, and reduce the risk of chronic diseases, including cancer.

stabilising.[20] The incidence of cancer of the oesophagus has remained stable since the 1980s and cancers of the colorectum are also relatively common.[20] For women, the most common cancers are those of the lung, stomach, and breast, which have risen steadily since the 1980s; of the liver, which has risen since 1990; and of the oesophagus. For age-standardised rates of these cancers, see the second figure.[20]

For the period 2002–2003, 10 per cent of men and 12 per cent of women aged 18–69 were classified as sedentary (figure 1.6).[46] These figures are likely to increase, with further urbanisation and greater use of vehicles for transport. Between 1980 and 2003, the number of cars produced in China quadrupled to more than 2 million.[84]

In 1997 men aged 24–64 had an average body mass index (BMI) of around 25; just 2.1 per cent of men aged 20–74 had a BMI of over 30. In the same year, women aged 25–29 had an average BMI of 22.2, and those aged 35–64 had a BMI of around 25. Just 3.7 per cent of women had a BMI of over 30.[46] In 2002, 18.9 per cent of men and women aged 18 and above had a BMI of over 25, and 2.9 per cent of them had a BMI of over 30. See figure 1.4 for projections of the proportions of men and women who will have a BMI of 30 or more in 2015.

The average amount of available food energy rose between 1964 and 2004, from around 1850 to 2940 kcal/person per day (7760 to 12 290 kJ/person per day). This is largely due to an increase in the availability of fats and oils, meat, and sugar.[1] The 1957–1962 famine was followed by a liberalisation of food production. Economic growth has reduced poverty and Chinese diets now are influenced by the Western pattern: cereals (grains) and lower-fat mixed dishes are being replaced with animal foods and edible fats.[14] Recent national nutritional surveys show that energy intake from animal sources increased from 8 per cent in 1982 to 25 per cent in 2002, and that energy from fat, particularly among people living in urban areas, increased from 25 to 35 per cent over the same period.[84] Intake of cereals (grains) has also decreased substantially since the mid-1980s among urban and rural populations, with a larger decrease in the consumption of coarse grains compared with refined varieties. The biggest drop in cereal intake has been among people in the lowest-income groups. Vegetable and fruit intakes have decreased since 1989, although they are highest in urban populations. Fat intake is also increasing and many adults obtain 30 per cent or more of their overall energy intake from fat.[14] Regional variations also exist: for example, the dietary pattern around the city of Hangzhou is very varied, resulting in a diet low in saturated fatty acids and high in n-3 polyunsaturated fatty acids; people there eat green, leafy vegetables with almost every meal.[26] The incidence of nutrition-related diseases and deaths from these diseases are lower in this region than in other parts of China.

Snacking contributes minimal energy intake to Chinese diets (0.9 per cent). However, snacking and eating food away from home are increasing among children from middle- and high-income groups. Foods commonly eaten away from home include cereals (grains), vegetables and fruits, meat, eggs, and fish. Between 1991 and 1997, the proportion of children from low-income households eating foods away from home did not change, but there was an increase among children from higher-income groups, with a 10 per cent increase in the consumption of foods from animal sources eaten away from home. Eating food prepared away from home accounted for 15 per cent of total energy intake for all Chinese children during this period.[27] Despite these statistics, only 10 per cent of Chinese children and young people consumed any snacks during the study period, and there was little evidence then that they consumed significant amounts of soft drinks, although this is now changing rapidly.

1.2 Foods and drinks, physical activity, body composition

1.2.1 Foods and drinks

Substantial changes have occurred in the patterns of foods and drinks supplied and consumed throughout the world, and these changes are becoming increasingly rapid. Also see Chapter 4.

Economic development is generally accompanied by quantitative and qualitative changes in food supplies and therefore in diets. This 'nutrition transition' may reduce the risk of some dietary deficiencies and improve overall nutrition. But it can also be accompanied by adverse shifts in the composition of diets, for instance, with a greater proportion of energy coming from fats and oils, and added sugars. Over recent years, such dietary changes have been rapid in the middle- and low-income countries of Asia, Africa, the Middle East, and Latin America.[63 79 80]

The Food and Agriculture Organization (FAO) of the UN records global differences in the availability of food crops and commodities (box 1.1). These data provide information on the average amounts of food available for consumption, rather than actual food consumption. Animal products have traditionally made up a small proportion of food availability in low-income countries; most dietary energy comes from plant sources such as roots and tubers, cereals (grains), and fruits.

However, this pattern is changing, with proportionally more dietary energy available for consumption now coming from animal sources. Since the 1960s, estimates for animal sources for low-income countries have risen from around 160 to 340 kcal/day (670 to 1400 kJ/day). During the same period, estimates of the energy available for consumption from plant sources have also risen, from 1900 to 2340 kcal/day (7900 to 9800 kJ/day) (figure 1.2). There have been similar changes in the availability of both animal and plant sources of energy in high-income countries. However, in these cases, the proportion of energy from animal sources is much greater: around one third or 940 kcal/day (3900 kJ/day).[81] The proportion of dietary energy available from cereals (grains) has remained constant at around 50 per cent, though dietary energy available from cereals (grains), in particular rice and wheat, have decreased slightly in low-income countries. This trend is likely to continue until the 2030s in middle- and low-income countries.[81]

Large variations exist across the world in the amounts of fat available for consumption. The highest availability is in Europe and North America; the lowest is in Africa. The quantity of available fat in diets has increased globally since the 1960s, with the exception of sub-Saharan Africa.[81] These

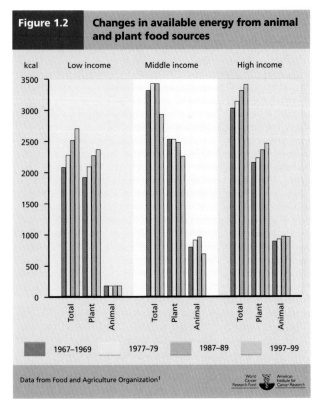

Figure 1.2 — Changes in available energy from animal and plant food sources

Food energy from animal and plant food sources in selected low-, middle-, and high-income countries, 1967–1999

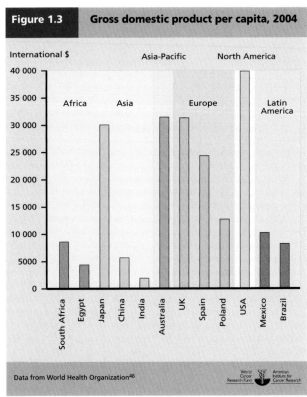

Figure 1.3 — Gross domestic product per capita, 2004

Current gross domestic product per capita for selected countries in international dollars

changes are accounted for by an increase in the availability and consumption of plant oils in lower-income countries.[82] Palm oil intake is increasing in South-East Asia, and olive oil is now consumed widely in Europe and not just in Mediterranean countries.

Analysis of food balance sheet data suggests that available energy for consumption has increased steadily on a world-wide basis. Since the 1960s, this has increased globally by approximately 450 kcal/person per day (1900 kJ/person per day), and by more than 600 kcal/person per day (2500 kJ/person per day) in low-income countries.[81] Regional differences exist. For example, there has been little change in sub-Saharan Africa, and in Asia the amount of available energy has risen dramatically: in China by almost 1000 kcal/person per day (4200 kJ/person per day). These data need to be interpreted with caution, as they do not relate directly to energy consumption (box 1.1). Global average available energy is predicted to rise from around 2800 kcal/person per day (11700 kJ/person per day) (1997–1999 average) to 2940 (12300 kJ) in 2015, and to 3050 (12800 kJ) in 2030. Again, see box 1.1.

With increasing socioeconomic status, the proportion of energy in diets from staples such as cereals (grains) and roots and tubers declines, whereas the proportion of energy from fats and oil, and animal protein (including from meat, milk, and eggs) increases. For example, in China, energy intake from foods of animal origin has increased significantly: the average Chinese adult now consumes more than 1300 kcal/day (5400 kJ/day) from these foods.[83] In low-income countries between the 1960s and 1990s, consumption of meat rose by 150 per cent, and of milk and dairy products by 60 per cent. By 2030, it is predicted that consumption of animal products could rise by a further 44 per cent, with the biggest contribution coming from poultry. If stocks of fish can be maintained, fish consumption is likely to rise by 19–20 kg/person in the same period. Owing to decreases in the cost of these foods in real terms, low-income countries have higher levels of meat and fat consumption at much lower levels of gross domestic product (GDP) than was the case in countries that underwent socioeconomic transition in the 1960s and 1970s. Figure 1.3 shows the GDP of selected countries.

According to food consumption surveys, only a minority of the world's adult population consumes the commonly recommended minimum daily amount of vegetables and fruits of 400 g/person. Low-income countries have the lowest intakes of vegetables and fruits, and vegetables are generally more readily available than fruits.[43] In India, for example, levels of vegetable and fruit intake have remained static at 120–140 g/day. Australia, Japan, and North America have high levels of intake, for example 300 g/day in Australia. In Europe, average consumption is between 250 and 350 g/day — often much higher in Mediterranean countries, for instance 550 g/day in Spain — and Scandinavian countries have particularly high fruit intakes.[43] Countries in Europe, Latin America, North America, and South-East Asia have seen an increase in the availability of vegetables and fruits for con-

Box 1.1	Measurement of food supply and consumption

The data here on energy, foods, and drinks are taken from food balance sheets compiled by the Food and Agriculture Organization of the United Nations. These are statistical data on the production, trade, and use of agricultural commodities for all countries. Food balance sheets are the most common and widely used data sets for food supply estimates. A food balance sheet provides estimates of the food available for human consumption, and an overall picture of a country's food supply during a specified period of time, which can be compared between countries.

It follows that these estimates of availability are not measures of consumption. They record information about the supply of food (production, imports, stock changes, and exports) and about how it is used (as feed and seed, in processing, and wastage, as well as food). The amounts of foods and drinks recorded on these balance sheets are expressed 'per person' (in kg/person per year or kcal/person per day).

The estimates in food balance sheets that need to be treated with most caution are those of energy. Balance sheets overestimate food consumption in high-income countries, where substantial amounts of food are wasted or fed to pets. They underestimate consumption in countries that are not dominated by urban–industrial food systems, and where many people grow their own food, raise animals, or gather wild food such as fungi and berries. It follows that balance sheet data showing increases in food energy over time tend to reflect economic development and greater use of money, rather than actual increases in availability.

The accuracy of a food balance sheet also depends on the reliability of the underlying statistics of supply, use, and population. Also, the data do not take into account regional differences, so the information may not be representative of the entire country. In countries where there is wide variation in income and food access, for example, the overall supply picture provided by the balance sheet is of limited use. In such cases, food balance sheets can be complemented with national nutrition surveys or household income/expenditure surveys.

Household income/expenditure surveys, such as the World Bank's Living Standards Measurement Study, look at multiple aspects of household welfare and behaviour, and collect data on the quantities of food purchased by a representative sample of households. These surveys provide detailed information about foods consumed in and away from the home over a limited time period, and can be used to document differences in regional, geographical, or household socioeconomic characteristics. While these surveys are generally more useful than food balance sheets for assessing household consumption, they are less readily available. Balance sheets are often available for a large number of countries and for most years.

Food balance sheets, household income/expenditure surveys, and methods of assessing individual dietary intakes (see Chapter 3) all provide information on food supply and consumption, and they have different purposes, uses, and limitations.

---

sumption since the 1960s. In contrast, in eastern and central Africa, availability has decreased since the mid-1980s.

Studies in children suggest that their eating patterns vary around the world. For instance, children living in the USA and the Philippines consume one third of their daily energy away from home, and snacks provide one fifth of their daily energy. In contrast, children living in Russia and China eat very little food away from the home. Snacks provide about 16 per cent of dietary energy for Russian children, but account for only 1 per cent in Chinese children.[2]

A US study showed that between 1977 and 2001, consumption of sweetened drinks increased by 135 per cent. During the same period, milk consumption decreased by 38 per cent, resulting in an overall daily increase of 278 kcal (1164 kJ) from drinks.[31]

1.2.2 Overweight and obesity

There have been rapid changes in rates of overweight and obesity throughout the world since the 1980s, at the same time as the urbanisation and industrialisation of middle- and low-income countries. Such countries often experience the dual burden of nutritional deficiencies and chronic diseases. Also see Chapters 6 and 8.

The most recent estimates suggest that in 2002 there were 1 billion overweight or obese people worldwide, with Chinese people accounting for approximately one fifth. The example of China is remarkable. Historically, China, which is classed as a lower-middle-income economy by the World Bank, had a lean population. But the prevalence of underweight adults has decreased and the numbers of people who are either overweight or obese have risen considerably. In 2002, there were 184 million overweight and 31 million obese people in China, out of a population of 1.3 billion.[14] The prevalence of overweight and obesity among 7–18 year olds increased substantially between 1985 and 2000.[84] Between 1989 and 1997, one study estimated that the proportion of overweight and obese men in China rose from 6.4 to 14.5 per cent, and in women from 11.5 to 16.2 per cent.[85] Another study, in nine Chinese provinces, found that between 1989 and 2000 there was a 13.7 per cent increase in the proportion of men, and a 7.9 per cent increase in the proportion of women, who were overweight or obese. During the same period, there was an average 2 per cent decrease in the number of men and women who were classified as underweight.[86]

The World Health Organization MONICA Project monitored 10 million adults in 21 countries over a 10-year period in the 1980s and 1990s. During this time, the mean body mass index (BMI) increased in most populations, with the largest increases in regions of Australia and the USA. Over the course of the project, the overall average BMI increased by 1.5.[87] However, average BMI decreased in Russia and Central Europe, and in certain regions of Italy and Switzerland. The UK has one of the highest rates of excess weight in Europe. This has increased threefold since 1980; in 2003, 65 per cent of men and 56 per cent of women were overweight, with 22 per cent of men and 23 per cent of women classified as obese.[88]

Historically, food insecurity, undernutrition, and underweight, and their likely contribution to infection, have been

India

In 2004 India had a population of over 1.1 billion, growing at a rate of about 1.2 per cent a year; it was the next country after China to reach the 1-billion mark.[46] India has a low-income economy, with a gross domestic product of 1830 international dollars per person (figure 1.3). Life expectancy at birth is 61 years for men and 63 for women (figure 1.1).[46]

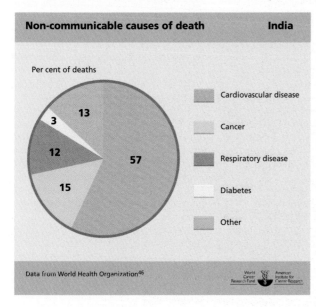

Non-communicable causes of death   **India**

Per cent of deaths

- Cardiovascular disease
- Cancer
- Respiratory disease
- Diabetes
- Other

Data from World Health Organization[46]

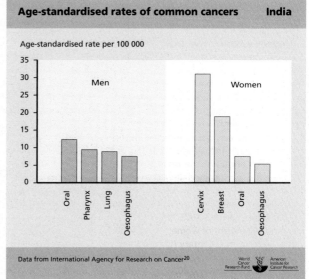

Age-standardised rates of common cancers   **India**

Age-standardised rate per 100 000

Data from International Agency for Research on Cancer[20]

the main nutrition-related public health issues in middle- and low-income countries. This is no longer the case. Thus, surveys of women between 1992 and 2000 found that overweight exceeds underweight in most middle- and low-income countries, including those in North Africa and the Middle East, Central Asia, China, and Latin America. Indeed, there has been a disproportionate increase in, and prevalence of, obesity among the lowest-income groups in most countries. It is more likely that people will be overweight if they live in urban areas compared with rural areas, and countries with a higher GDP have a greater ratio of overweight to underweight women.[89] North Africa and the Middle East are two areas of the world with middle- and low-income countries that are experiencing very high rates of overweight and obesity, often higher in women than in men.[82]

The rise of overweight and obesity since the mid-1970s has been much faster in lower-income countries.[63] In Europe and the USA, the prevalence has risen relatively slowly, by 0.3–0.5 per cent each year; but the figures are two- to four-fold higher in many low-income countries.[90] Projections from existing data suggest that by 2015, levels of obesity could be as high as 50 per cent in the USA, between 30 and 40 per cent in the UK and Australia, and more than 20 per cent in Brazil.[46] See figure 1.4. It is estimated that more than 12 million adults in England will be obese by 2010, while 25 per cent of children who live in households with obese parents will become obese themselves.[88]

1.2.3 Physical activity

Changes in degrees of physical activity throughout the world have also been rapid since the 1970s, as paid and household

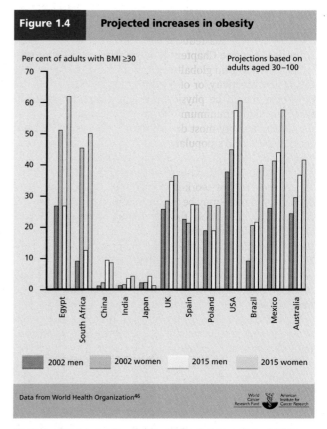

| Figure 1.4 | **Projected increases in obesity** |

Per cent of adults with BMI ≥30

Projections based on adults aged 30–100

- 2002 men
- 2002 women
- 2015 men
- 2015 women

Data from World Health Organization[46]

Projected increases in obesity (BMI of above 30 kg/m²) in selected countries, 2002–2015

Chronic diseases account for 58.1 per cent of all deaths, while infectious diseases, maternal, perinatal, and nutritional conditions account for 32.9 per cent; 9 per cent of deaths are due to injuries.[46] The first figure gives a breakdown of deaths caused by chronic disease.[46]

Common cancers in men include those of the oral cavity and pharynx.[20] Although these cancers have declined since the late 1970s, the incidence remains high.[20] Cancers of the oesophagus and lung have also decreased slightly in the same period.[20] In women, cancer of the cervix is the most common type, and has been since the 1970s; breast cancer has increased steadily during this time.[20] Cancers of the oral cavity and oesophagus have declined slightly since the late 1970s (for age-standardised rates of these cancers, see the second figure).[20]

For the period 2002–2003, 10 per cent of men and 16 per cent of women aged 18–69 were classified as sedentary (figure 1.6).[46]

In 2000 men aged 20–24 had an average body mass index (BMI) of 20.7, while those aged 40–54 had an average BMI of 23.6.[46] For men aged 20–70, 25.4 per cent had a BMI of over 25.[46] Women aged 20–24 had an average BMI of 20.9, rising to an average of 24 at age 30; and women aged 30–69 also had a BMI of around 24.[46] In total, 35.8 per cent of women aged 20–70 had a BMI of over 25.[46] A review from 2002 established that the prevalence of preschool obesity was about 1 per cent, but stunting remained a problem in over half of all children.[39] Obesity has been uncommon in India and varies with socioeconomic status, being more common in high-income households. In the 1970s, 2.1 per cent of men and 2.9 per cent of women had a BMI of 25 or more, while less than 0.5 per cent of men and women had a BMI of 30 or more.[46] By 1998 these figures had risen: 4.4 per cent of men and 4.3 per cent of women had a BMI of 25 or more.[46] See figure 1.4 for projections of the proportions of men and women who will have a BMI of 30 or more in 2015.[46]

The average amount of available food energy rose between 1964 and 2004, from around 2050 to 2470 kcal/person per day (8580 to 10 360 kJ/person per day).[1] Recently, though, there have been large increases in the consumption of animal products, fats, and sugars. The proportion of energy from fat has increased each year, although within India there are differences: for higher-income groups, 32 per cent of energy comes from fat, compared with 17 per cent in lower-income groups.[39]

Since 1975 there has been a reduction in cereal (grains) consumption, particularly coarse grains, although this has not affected overall energy consumption. This is probably due to large increases in intakes of fats and animal protein, and also of milk and milk products. In lower-income households, fat comes mainly from vegetable foods, with very little consumption of animal fats, whereas in the highest-income households, the majority of fat is from animal sources. India is a major producer of vegetables and fruits, much of which are exported.

work has become increasingly mechanised, and vehicles are used more often for transport. Occupational and household physical activity has reduced dramatically in high-income countries. Also see Chapters 5, 6 and 8.

There is as yet no globally accepted, quantified definition of physical inactivity, or of the extent to which populations or people should be physically active. In 2002, the WHO recommended a minimum of 30 minutes moderate-intensity physical activity most days; it found that at least 60 per cent of the world's population fails to achieve this level of physical activity.[91]

The proportion of people employed in agriculture can reflect the level of work-related activity undertaken in a country, and there may be a linear relationship between the two.[91] Thus, it is likely that, compared with high-income countries, transport-related and occupational and household physical activity is higher in low-income countries. Transport-related physical activity (cycling, walking) is higher in those countries with the lowest gross domestic product and low car ownership, and this differs little between men and women.

Data on physical activity in Africa are limited. Several studies are available for South Africa, but these cannot be used to predict or generalise about activity levels across the entire continent. Some small regional studies have been performed, in Ethiopia, for example, which provide useful local information, but they are not nationally representative.

Data from Europe, where recreational physical activity accounts for a greater proportion of total activity, suggest that approximately half of all walking and cycling trips are less than 3 km. Therefore, almost half of European adults do not do enough physical activity getting from one place to another.[91] In Europe, people living in more northerly regions such as Scandinavia have higher levels of activity than those living further south, for example, in Mediterranean countries. Women tend to exercise less than men and this difference is greatest in southern European countries.[42]

A study conducted in 1953 demonstrated that more than half of US school children failed a minimum standard of

Figure 1.5	Projected levels of inactivity in selected regions in 2020	
	Insufficient	**Inactive**
Africa	45–55	10–20
USA/Canada	35–50	17–30
Latin America	25–45	17–47
Middle East	30–42	15–30
Europe	30–60	15–40
India/Bangladesh	30–42	14–25
New Zealand/Australia/Japan	48–56	15–20
China	40	15–22

Data from Bull et al[93]

Percentage of adults projected to have insufficient levels of physical activity or to be inactive in 2020 in selected regions

Japan

In 2004 Japan's population was just over 128 million, with 79 per cent living in urban areas.[46] The country has a high-income economy, with a gross domestic product of 30 039 international dollars per person (figure 1.3). Life expectancy at birth is 79 years for men and 86 for women (figure 1.1).[46]

Chronic diseases account for 78.7 per cent of all deaths, while infectious diseases, maternal, perinatal, and nutritional conditions account for 10.5 per cent; 10.8 per cent of deaths are due to injuries. The first

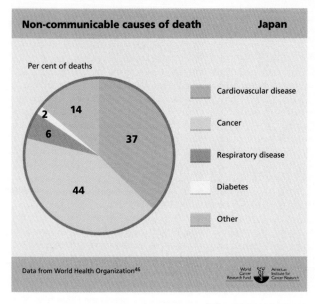

Non-communicable causes of death Japan

Per cent of deaths

- Cardiovascular disease
- Cancer
- Respiratory disease
- Diabetes
- Other

Data from World Health Organization[46]

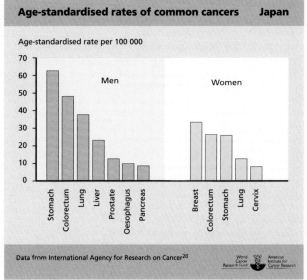

Age-standardised rates of common cancers Japan

Age-standardised rate per 100 000

Men / Women

Men: Stomach, Colorectum, Lung, Liver, Prostate, Oesophagus, Pancreas
Women: Breast, Colorectum, Stomach, Lung, Cervix

Data from International Agency for Research on Cancer[20]

---

fitness, compared with less than 10 per cent of European children.[92] Another study in 2001 found that only 0.2 per cent of US adults were physically active in both occupational and transport settings, compared with 29 per cent of Chinese adults.[91] In the USA, while socioeconomic status has a large impact on whether someone participates in recreational physical activity, there are only small differences between men and women, and activity levels decline with age. Similar trends exist for men and women and for socioeconomic status in Australia.[42]

A number of factors will affect levels of physical activity in future. Economic development has the effect of reducing levels of occupational, household, and transport physical activity. It reduces the amount of physical activity in the workplace, often because of a shift from agriculture to manufacturing and service industries. Improved public transport in middle- and low-income countries reduces transport-related activity. Similarly, as people gain more disposable income, they are more likely to own a car, which means that they will make fewer journeys by bicycle or foot. Recreational activity is the only area in which physical activity may increase as economies develop and countries become increasingly urbanised and mechanised, although people may not necessarily use their leisure time for active pursuits.[91]

Other factors constrain physical activity in cities, such as personal safety: crime rates are often high and it may be unsafe to walk, jog, or cycle in the streets. Furthermore, city and town planning may not encourage people to be active — for example, people can only walk, run, ride, and play if

| Figure 1.6 | Sedentary behaviour in adults in selected countries (age 18–69) |

Per cent of adults classified as sedentary

	Men	Women
Brazil	28	31
China	10	12
India	10	16
Mexico	17	18
South Africa	44	49
Spain	27	33

Data from World Health Organization[46]

Sedentary behaviour is defined as less than 30 minutes of moderate physical activity (equivalent to brisk walking) on fewer than 5 days/week, or less than 20 minutes of vigorous physical activity (equivalent to running) on fewer than 3 days/week. Also defined in terms of 'metabolic equivalents' (METs) as achieving less than 60 MET–hours/week of any combination of activity on fewer than 5 days/week (also see chapter 5.2)

there are sidewalks/pavements, parks, or other areas where they can move around freely and safely. Cultural and religious customs may also limit activity levels, particularly for women.

By 2020 it is predicted that more adults will be physically

figure gives a breakdown of deaths caused by chronic diseases.[46]

In men, cancer of the stomach is the most common type of cancer. This is followed by colorectal, lung, liver, and prostate cancers, which have increased since the 1960s. Cancer of the oesophagus has remained steady since the 1960s, although the incidence of cancer of the pancreas has increased since then.[20] In women, breast cancer is the most common type and its incidence has risen since the 1970s.[20] Colorectal cancer is the next most common type, and this has also increased. Stomach cancer incidence has decreased since the 1960s, but the rate remains high; lung cancer has risen steadily since the 1960s.[20] The incidence of cancer of the cervix increased during the 1960s and remained high in the 1970s, but has since declined (for age-standardised rates of these cancers, see the second figure). [20] However, the total numbers of new cancer cases and cancer deaths are set to rise because Japan has an ageing population. Cancer has been the leading cause of death in Japan since 1981 and projections indicate that in 2015 almost 900 000 people will develop cancer and 450 000 will die from cancer.[47]

Regional studies suggest that 68–70 per cent of men and 70–82 per cent of women, aged 20–70, are physically inactive.

In men there has been a steady increase in body mass index (BMI) since the mid-1970s. In 2002, 17.5 per cent of men aged 20–29 and around 30 per cent of those aged 30–60 had a BMI of over 25. Only 7 per cent of women aged 20–29, 19 per cent of those aged 40–49, and 25.6 per cent of those aged 50–59 had a BMI of over 25. See figure 1.4 for projections of the proportions of men and women who will have a BMI of 30 or more in 2015.

The average amount of available food energy rose between 1964 and 2004, from around 2570 to 2760 kcal/person per day (10 780 to 11 540 kJ/person per day). Meat consumption also increased during this time.[1] Steamed rice was the staple food until 1950, and accounted for 80 per cent of energy intake before 1935. Dietary intake of cereals (grains), almost all rice, has decreased, from 75 per cent of energy in the 1940s to 41.3 per cent in 2000. Energy from fat increased from 6.9 per cent in 1949 to 25 per cent in 1988, and to 26.5 per cent in 2002. Total fat intake has increased significantly following the country's economic growth, from 15 g/person per day in the 1940s to 59 g in 1983, remaining at around this level in 2002. The percentage of energy in diets from protein has risen from 12.4 per cent in the 1940s to 15.9 per cent in 2000. However, there has been a larger increase in the percentage of protein from animal sources: from 18.6 per cent in the 1940s to more than 50 per cent in 2000. In 2002, people were continuing to eat more green and yellow vegetables, with people over 50 tending to eat the most vegetables. Fruit intake peaked in 1975 and has since decreased and stabilised. In 2002, Japanese diets did not provide the recommended intake of calcium: although consumption of milk and dairy products had increased, consumption of fish and shellfish had declined slightly. Salt intake remained high, at over 12 g/person per day. [23]

inactive.[91] Clearly, levels of physical activity will vary in different areas and countries around the world. In Europe, for example, the former Soviet Union states and countries in eastern Europe are at the lower end of the estimates, with western European countries at the higher end. Indeed, these figures are expected to rise further in western Europe and it is estimated that 50–60 per cent of adults will not be sufficiently physically active by 2020. Also see figure 1.5. The percentage of adults currently classified as sedentary in selected national examples is shown in figure 1.6. Using different definitions, the amount of adults (aged over 16 years) classified as sedentary for the UK are 60 per cent of men and 66 per cent of women. For the USA 52 per cent of men and 65 per cent of women (aged over 18 years) are classified as sedentary.[46]

1.2.4 Cancer

Patterns of cancer and trends, incidence, and projections vary greatly in different parts of the world. Also see Chapter 7.

In 2002 there were more than 10 million new cases of cancer (excluding non-melanoma skin cancers) recorded worldwide, and nearly 7 million cancer deaths. By 2020 these figures are estimated to rise to over 16 million new cases, with 10 million deaths. There may be more than 20 million new cases of cancer in 2030.[93] Indications suggest that, at that time, 70 per cent of cancer deaths will be in low-income countries.

This projected increase is accounted for by a combination of factors: the projected increase in global population; an ageing world population; improved screening, detection, and treatment, which increases the number of people living with a diagnosis of cancer (see Chapter 9); the projected increases in tobacco smoking in many countries; and the increase in the number of people with HIV/AIDS in some countries. The global age-adjusted incidence of cancer is also likely to increase. Also see box 1.2.

Globally, the most commonly diagnosed cancers (excluding all types of skin cancer) are those of the lung, colon and rectum, and breast, with lung cancer being the leading cause of cancer death.[94 95] Geographical and socioeconomic differences exist for the most common cancers. In low-income countries, the most prevalent cancers include those of which infectious agents are a major cause, while in high-income countries, they include hormone-related cancers. In high-income countries, and among men, prostate cancer is the most common type, followed by cancers of the lung, stomach, and colon and rectum. In low-income countries, and among men, lung cancer is the most common type, followed by cancers of the oesophagus, stomach, and liver. Breast cancer is the most common type among women living in high-income countries, followed by cancers of the lung, colon and rectum, and endometrium. Breast cancer is also the most frequent type among women living in low-income countries, followed by cancers of the lung, stomach, and cervix.[94 96]

1.2.4.1 Oesophagus

Oesophageal cancer is the seventh most common type of cancer worldwide, with more than 460 000 new cases record-

UK

In 2001 the UK population was nearly 60 million.[30] The UK is a high-income economy, with a gross domestic product of 31 300 international dollars per person (figure 1.3). Life expectancy at birth is 76 years for men and 81 for women (figure 1.1).

Chronic diseases account for 84 per cent of all deaths, while infectious diseases, maternal, perinatal, and nutritional conditions account for 11 per cent; 4.9 per cent

of deaths are due to injuries. The first figure below gives a breakdown of deaths caused by chronic diseases.[46]

Prostate cancer is the most common cancer type in men and has increased steadily since the 1970s.[20] Lung cancer incidence peaked in the 1960s, remained high until the mid-1980s, and is now declining.[20] Colorectal cancer has risen steadily since 1960.[20] Bladder cancer, which had been ris-

ing steadily since the 1960s, is now decreasing, and stomach cancer incidence has declined since the 1960s.[20] In women, breast cancer is the most common type, and although rates were fairly constant during the 1960s and 1970s, they have risen steadily since then.[20] The incidence of colorectal cancer has remained steady since the 1960s.[20] Lung cancer rose from the 1960s to 1980s, and has remained steady since

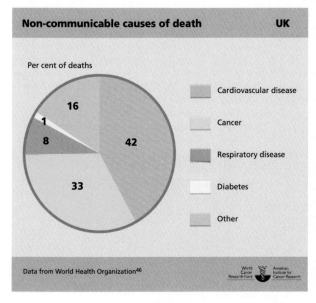

Non-communicable causes of death — **UK**

Per cent of deaths

- Cardiovascular disease — 42
- Cancer — 33
- Respiratory disease — 8
- Diabetes — 1
- Other — 16

Data from World Health Organization[46]

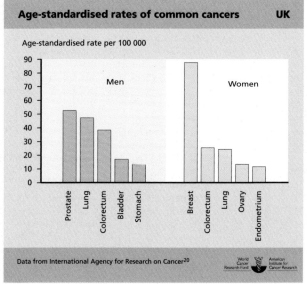

Age-standardised rates of common cancers — **UK**

Age-standardised rate per 100 000

Men: Prostate, Lung, Colorectum, Bladder, Stomach
Women: Breast, Colorectum, Lung, Ovary, Endometrium

Data from International Agency for Research on Cancer[20]

ed in 2002. Because it has a poor survival rate, it is the fifth most common cause of cancer death, responsible for nearly 390 000 deaths in 2002.

Incidence rates vary widely between countries. Studies suggest that cancer of the oesophagus is 100 times

more common in parts of China than in Europe and North America.[94] [97] Other areas of high risk include southern and eastern Africa, south-central Asia, and some countries in South America.

Geographical variability of exposure to established car-

Box 1.2 — Measurement of cancer incidence and mortality

After cancer registers were established in various countries in the second half of the 20th century, descriptive studies showed reliably for the first time that rates and trends of different cancers vary, sometimes substantially across different countries. This variation suggested that cancer is not just genetically inherited and that different cancers have different causes.

Many countries publish annual incidence and mortality rates for cancer. The incidence rate refers to the number of new cancer cases reported; the mortality rate refers to the number of deaths from can-

cer. These rates are usually expressed as the number of new cases (or deaths) each year for every 100 000 people.

Cancers are not usually diagnosed until they produce symptoms, so there is a period of time between the first stages of cancer development and its identification. This length of time can vary greatly, and there are also considerable differences in survival times and how types of cancer respond to treatment.

Many countries and international agencies track mortality statistics with causes of death, and national or regional cancer

registries prepare cancer-incidence statistics. With types of cancer where survival is high, cancer mortality statistics will not reflect occurrence rates. But globally, it is easier to obtain statistics for mortality than for incidence, so these are often used for comparisons between population groups.

It can also be difficult to compare cancer incidence globally: not all countries and regions are covered by cancer registries, and these organisations may use different definitions and collect different data, both geographically and over time.

then.[20] Cancer of the ovary has increased slightly since the 1960s, and rates of cancer of the endometrium have remained the same since the 1960s (for age-standardised rates of these cancers, see the second figure).[20] The incidence of childhood cancer has been rising at an average rate of 1.1 per cent each year and, between 1978 and 1997, the age-standardised incidence increased from 120 to 141 cases/million children.[22] Children in the British Isles have the highest rates of skin cancer in Europe.[11]

In 2003, 64 per cent of men and 76 per cent of women aged 16–69 were classified as sedentary.[46] A study to examine exercise patterns in adults in 1991 and again in 1999 found that only 4 in 10 adults had managed to meet and maintain the current recommended level of activity, or to increase their level. During the study period, the majority either reduced their activity level or maintained it below the recommended level, and 15 per cent of the sample was inactive, both in 1991 and 1999.[33]

In the UK, body mass index (BMI) has risen steadily since the mid-1970s. For the proportions of men and women in 1980 and in 2003 with a BMI of between 25 and 29.9, or of over 30, see the figure on this page. Also see figure 1.4 for projections of the proportions of men and women who will have a BMI of 30 or more in 2015.

The average amount of available food energy rose between 1964 and 2004,

from around 3280 to 3480 kcal/person per day (13730 to 14570 kJ/person per day).[1] Consumption of pasta, rice, cereals (grains), yogurt, soft drinks, savoury snacks, and nuts has increased since the mid-1980s. Over the same period, intakes of fish and fish dishes and eggs and egg dishes have decreased.[19] Large studies suggest that fat intake has decreased because people now consume less whole milk, butter, and red meat, and more vegetables and fruits.[35] Men surveyed between 2000 and 2001 were more likely to eat foods containing fats, oils, and sugars, as well as meat and meat products, and soft and alcoholic drinks.

In the same survey, and compared with older men and all women, young men were more likely to eat savoury snacks and soft drinks, and less likely to eat eggs, fish, and fruit.[19] Women ate more fruit, although only 13 per cent of men and 15 per cent of women ate the recommended five daily

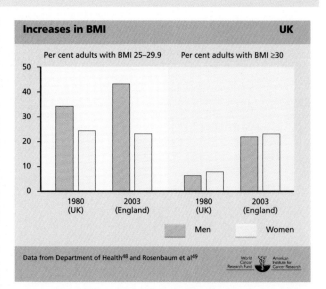

Increases in BMI — UK

Data from Department of Health[48] and Rosenbaum et al[49]

portions of vegetables and fruits. Instead, men ate an average of 2.7 portions while women had 2.9.[19] The survey also showed that vegetable and fruit consumption was particularly low in young adults, and that people from low-income households were less likely to eat fruit and yogurt.[19] It appears that more-educated adults put dietary guidelines into practice, reducing the amount of fat in their diets and increasing the amount of vegetables and fruits they eat.[3]

cinogens can explain some of these differences. In high-income countries, alcohol and smoking tobacco are the main carcinogenic agents, whereas chewing tobacco is more common in India. Pockets of high incidence occurring in parts of China and in the Caspian littoral of Iran may be due to general nutritional deficiencies. Incidence of adenocarcinoma of the lower third of the oesophagus is steadily increasing in the USA and Europe, which is likely to be linked to an increasing incidence of acid reflux from the stomach due to obesity.[94][95] Also see chapter 7.3.

1.2.4.2 Lung

Lung (pulmonary) cancer has been the most common type of cancer in the world since 1985, with around 1.35 million new cases recorded in 2002. It is also the most common cause of cancer death. In 2002, 1.2 million people died from lung cancer.

Between 1985 and 2002, the estimated number of lung cancer cases worldwide rose by 51 per cent, and the number of cases in middle- and low-income countries has increased steadily over recent years. Previous estimates indicated that the majority of lung cancer cases occurred in

high-income countries (almost 70 per cent in 1980); almost half were predicted to occur in middle- and low-income countries in 2005.[94][95] The USA and Europe have the highest numbers of lung cancer cases for both men and women, but the incidence appears to have peaked, and may now be declining in the USA and in parts of northern Europe. It is, however, still increasing in southern and eastern Europe.

Men are more likely to develop lung cancer than women, almost certainly because, on average, they smoke more than women. Worldwide, 1 billion men and 250 million women currently smoke tobacco. It is estimated that throughout the 20th century, 100 million people died from tobacco use.[93] Also see chapter 7.4.

1.2.4.3 Stomach

Stomach (gastric) cancer is now the fourth most common type of cancer worldwide, with around 925000 new cases recorded in 2002. It is the second most common cause of death from cancer, with around 700000 deaths annually.

Until about the mid-1980s, stomach cancer was the most common type in the world. Since then, rates have fallen substantially in all high-income countries, and overall rates are

Poland

In 2004 Poland had a population of around 38.5 million. The country has an upper-middle-income economy, with a gross domestic product of 12647 international dollars per person (figure 1.3).[46] Life expectancy at birth is 71 years for men and 79 for women (figure 1.1).[46]

Chronic diseases account for 88.2 per cent of all deaths, while infectious diseases, maternal, perinatal, and nutritional conditions account for 3.9 per cent; 7.9 per cent of deaths are due to injuries. The first figure gives a breakdown of deaths caused by chronic diseases.[46]

Lung cancer is the most common type of

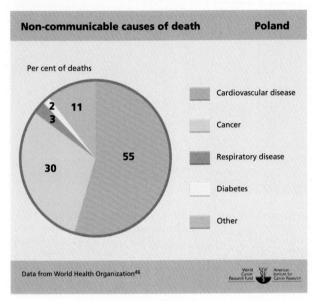

Non-communicable causes of death — **Poland**

Per cent of deaths

- Cardiovascular disease
- Cancer
- Respiratory disease
- Diabetes
- Other

Data from World Health Organization[46]

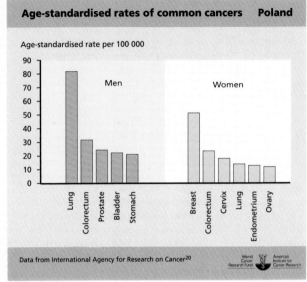

Age-standardised rates of common cancers — **Poland**

Age-standardised rate per 100 000

Data from International Agency for Research on Cancer[20]

now about 15 per cent lower than in 1985.[94-96]

Stomach cancer is now much more common in Asia than in the USA or Europe. Indeed, 42 per cent of cases occur in China alone.[94 97] High-risk areas are China, Japan, eastern Europe, and Central and South America. Low-risk areas are South-East Asia, northern and eastern Africa, the USA, and Australia and New Zealand. In most countries, incidence has dropped by about 15 per cent compared with 1985.

The bacterium *Helicobacter pylori* is an established cause of stomach cancer. Reduction in stomach cancer rates can be explained partly by reduced exposure to *H pylori* and partly by increased use of refrigeration to preserve foods.[94 97] Also see chapter 7.5.

1.2.4.4 Liver

Liver (hepatic) cancer is the sixth most common type of cancer worldwide, with around 625000 new cases recorded in 2002. The poor prognosis makes it the third most common cause of cancer death, with around 600000 deaths in 2002.

In most countries, the incidence of liver cancer is stable and there is little difference in survival rates between high- and low-income countries. More than 80 per cent of cases occur in middle- and low-income countries. Areas with a high incidence are China (55 per cent of all new cases), sub-Saharan Africa, and eastern and south-eastern Asia. Incidence is lower in high-income countries and in Latin America, although Japan and areas of southern Europe have intermediate incidence levels.[94 96]

Exposures to the hepatitis B and C viruses are known to increase the risk of developing liver cancer; 85 per cent of cases in low-income countries are attributed to exposures to these two viruses. Also see chapter 7.8.

1.2.4.5 Colon and rectum

Colorectal cancer (of the colon or rectum) is the third most common type of cancer worldwide, with just over 1 million new cases recorded in 2002. Mortality is approximately half that of the incidence, and nearly 530000 deaths were recorded in 2002, making it the fourth most common cause of death from cancer.

There is a large geographical difference in the global distribution of colorectal cancers. Incidence varies up to 25-fold between countries with the highest rates (the USA, Australia and New Zealand, and in parts of Europe) and those with the lowest rates (in Africa and Asia). Intermediate levels occur in South America.

Incidence of colorectal cancer may be stabilising in parts of northern and western Europe, and possibly declining gradually in the USA. Elsewhere, however, the incidence is increasing rapidly, particularly in Japan and in middle- and low-income countries.[94 96]

As shown in 1.3, the incidence of colorectal cancer increases quickly when people migrate from low- to high-risk areas of the world. Indeed, the incidence rate is higher in Japanese people born in the USA than in white people born in the USA. Also see chapter 7.9.

cancer in men and age-adjusted incidence has remained stable since the 1970s.[20] The incidence of colorectal cancer has increased since 1990, and both prostate and bladder cancers have increased slightly since the 1970s.[20] Stomach cancer incidence peaked in the late 1970s and has declined steadily since. Breast and colorectal cancers are the most common types in women and their rates have risen steadily since the 1970s.[20] Cancer of the cervix has remained steady since the mid-1970s, whereas cancers of the lung, ovary, and endometrium have increased in this period (for age-standardised rates of these cancers, see the second figure).[20]

In 1996, 31 per cent of men and 32 per cent of women aged 15–75 were classified as sedentary.[46]

In 1996 men aged 15–29 had an average body mass index (BMI) of 23.1.[46] This rose to 25.9 for men aged 30–44, while those aged 45–75 had a BMI of between 26 and 27.[46] Only 2.4 per cent of men aged 15–29 had a BMI of over 30, rising to 10.8 per cent of those aged 30–44, and 17.5 per cent of 45–59 year olds.[46] In the same year, women aged 15–29 had an average BMI of 21.2.[46] Women aged 30–44 had a BMI of 24.1, while those aged 45–59 had a BMI of 26.7.[46] Only 1.5 per cent of women aged 15–29 had a BMI of over 30, rising to 22.5 per cent of those aged 45–59, and 23.7 per cent of women aged 60–74.[46] In a study of adults in Warsaw, the average adult BMI remained stable between 1983 and 1993 at approximately 27.[46] Overall in 1996, 10.3 per cent of men and 12.4 per cent of women had a BMI of 30 or more.[46] See figure 1.4 for projections of the proportions of men and women who will have a BMI of 30 or more in 2015.[46]

The average amount of available food energy rose between 1964 and 2004, from around 3310 to 3520 kcal/person per day (13850 to 14730 kJ/person per day). The amount of energy available from sugars and meat increased during this period, while the energy available from animal fats fell substantially.[1] In 1989 Poland began the transition from a centrally planned to a market economy. This resulted in dramatic increases in food prices, and although the transition gave people a better choice of foods, there was a decline in food demand and alterations in dietary patterns.[37]

Tobacco smoking and alcoholic drink consumption are underlying factors in overall mortality trends in eastern Europe. An analysis of national household budget and individual dietary surveys carried out in the 1990s found that, each day, the average person ate around 300 g of dairy products and the same amount of cereals (grains) and roots and tubers, although consumption of pulses (legumes) was very low.[38] A study of students found that women ate meat and drank beer less frequently than men, and they ate more fruit and drank more milk.[8] Another local study, in Warsaw, reported decreases in intakes of total energy, dietary cholesterol, and dietary animal fats, and an increase in vegetable oil intake between 1984 and 2001.[45] Another study found that between 1990 and 2000, the proportion of men eating fruit each day increased from 36 to 42 per cent. Levels of intake were stable in women, with around 60 per cent eating fruit every day. In contrast, over the same decade, only 22–23 per cent of men limited their fat intake, although more women did during this period (an increase from 23 to 45 per cent).[40]

1.2.4.6 Breast

Breast cancer is the most common type of cancer in women, and the third most common cancer overall. Incidence rates are increasing in most countries, with an estimated 1.15 million new cases recorded in 2002. Breast cancer is the sixth most common cause of death from cancer overall. However, it is the second most common cause of cancer death in women, with just over 410000 deaths recorded in 2002.

The incidence of breast cancer is highest in high-income countries (although not in Japan) and more than half of all cases occur in these countries. Although breast cancer has been less common in women living in low-income countries, age-adjusted incidence is increasing, and the rates of increase are often greater in these countries.

Globally, estimates indicate that breast cancer incidence has increased by 0.5 per cent annually since 1990. However, certain cancer registries, such as those in China and other parts of Asia, are recording annual increases in incidence of up to 4 per cent. Rates are low in Africa, with the lowest incidence in central Africa.[94 96]

Migrant studies show that breast cancer rates change when women move to a new country. See 1.3. Also see chapter 7.10.

1.2.4.7 Cervix

Cancer of the cervix is the second most common type of cancer among women, and the eighth most common cancer overall, with around 500000 new cases recorded in 2002.

Cervical cancer is the seventh most common cause of death from cancer overall, and the third most common in women, and was responsible for nearly 275000 deaths in 2002.

Over 80 per cent of cases occur in low-income countries. Areas with the highest incidence rates are sub-Saharan Africa, the Caribbean, Central and South America, and south-central and South-East Asia. Incidence rates are lowest in Europe, the USA, Japan, China, and Australia and New Zealand.

The incidence has dropped substantially in high-income countries following the introduction of cervical screening programmes. The major established cause of cervical cancer is infection with certain subtypes of human papilloma viruses (HPV). Other cofactors (parity, contraception, HIV infection, and smoking) can also modify the risk of this cancer in women infected with HPV.[94 96 97] Also see chapter 7.13.

1.2.4.8 Prostate

Prostate cancer is the third most common type of cancer in men, and the sixth most common cancer overall, with nearly 680 000 new cases recorded in 2002. The majority of cases are diagnosed in men over the age of 65, and this cancer accounted for just over 220000 cancer deaths in 2002. This made it the eighth most common cause of death from cancer overall, and the sixth most common in men.

Prostate cancer is more common in high-income countries, but the incidence remains low in Japan. Incidence rates have been influenced by screening programmes, which increase

Spain

In 2004 Spain had a population of over 43 million. The country has a high-income economy, with a gross domestic product of 24 325 international dollars per person (figure 1.3).[46] Life expectancy at birth is 77 years for men and 83 for women (figure 1.1).[46]

Chronic diseases account for 87.4 per cent of all deaths, while infectious diseases, maternal, perinatal, and nutritional conditions account for 5.5 per cent; 6.9 per cent of deaths are due to injuries. The first figure below gives a breakdown of deaths due

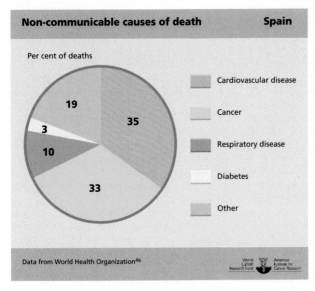

Non-communicable causes of death   **Spain**

Per cent of deaths

- Cardiovascular disease — 35
- Cancer — 33
- Respiratory disease — 10
- Diabetes — 3
- Other — 19

Data from World Health Organization[46]

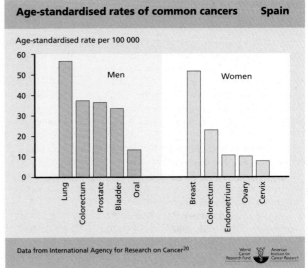

Age-standardised rates of common cancers   **Spain**

Age-standardised rate per 100 000

Men: Lung, Colorectum, Prostate, Bladder, Oral
Women: Breast, Colorectum, Endometrium, Ovary, Cervix

Data from International Agency for Research on Cancer[20]

---

diagnosis rates. This has resulted in a huge increase in the number of recorded cases in the USA in recent years, although the incidence in several high-income countries has declined since the 1990s. Prostate cancer incidence is increasing rapidly in low-income countries, particularly in Latin American countries (such as Costa Rica, Colombia, and Ecuador) and in China. Again, this may partly be due to increased awareness and screening.

Mortality from prostate cancer is lower (5.8 per cent of cancer deaths in men),[94] and may give a better indication of actual disease patterns.[97] Even so, mortality is approximately 10 times more common in the USA and Europe than in Asia. Also see chapter 7.14.

1.3 Migrant and other ecological studies

Ecological studies (also called correlation studies) examine the relationships between environmental factors and disease outcomes, often in different countries, at an aggregate level (see chapter 3.1.2). These provided the first systematically gathered evidence suggesting that the principal causes of cancer are environmental, and that food, nutrition, and physical activity are among these factors. Early studies showed strong correlations among countries between, for instance, dietary fat intake and breast cancer rates.[98]

While not providing strong evidence for causation, such studies generated hypotheses for possible links between

Figure 1.7	Mortality from stomach and colorectal cancer in European migrants to Australia

Length of residence (years) Country of origin	Stomach cancer		Colon cancer		Rectal cancer	
	<16	>16	<16	>16	<16	>16
Yugoslavia	2.22	1.23	0.47	0.66	0.46	1.34
England	1.47	1.24	0.99	1.04	1.23	1.04
Scotland	1.84	1.46	1.47	1.24	1.05	1.08
Ireland	1.77	1.21	0.62	1.06	1.17	1.18
Poland	1.69	1.71	1.02	1.14	0.43	1.34
Greece	1.35	1.15	0.36	0.69	0.34	0.7
Italy	1.43	1.49	0.37	0.7	0.48	0.8
Australia	1.0	1.0	1.0	1.0	1.0	1.0

Data from McMichael et al[102]

Relative risk of death from cancer of the stomach, colon, and rectum in European migrants to Australia (1962–1976) compared with people born in Australia

specific nutritional factors and cancers at particular sites, and for the general proposition that patterns of cancer might be altered as a result of changing patterns of eating and other ways of life. Part 2 of this Report explores the degree

to chronic diseases.[46]

Lung cancer is the most common cancer type in men and incidence rates have increased dramatically since the 1970s.[20] Rates of colorectal, prostate, bladder, and oral cancers have risen since records began in the 1970s.[20] Breast cancer is the most common type in women and the rate has doubled since the 1970s.[20] Colorectal cancer is the next most common type, which has seen a steady rise during this period.[20] Cancers of the endometrium and cervix have remained steady since the 1970s, but cancer of the ovary has risen (for age-standardised rates of these cancers, see the second figure).[20]

A survey in 1997 found that 76 per cent of adults aged 16 and over did no regular exercise during their leisure time[29]; 46 per cent of adults were classified as sedentary, with only 7 per cent of adults recording any physical activity each week.[29]

Between 1994 and 1997, men aged 25–34 had an average body mass index (BMI) of 25, while those aged 35–44 had a BMI of 26, and 45–75 year olds had a BMI of 27.[46] In total, 35 per cent of men aged 25–64 had a BMI of over 27, and 12.2 per cent had a BMI of over 30.[46] Women aged 25–34 had an average BMI of 23, while those aged 35–44 had a BMI of 25, and 45–74 year olds had a BMI of between 27 and 28.[46] Overall, 25.7 per cent of women aged 25–64 had a BMI of over 27, and 12.1 per cent had a BMI of over 30.[46]

Over the period 1977–1993, the proportion of people with energy-intensive jobs halved. In children aged 6–7, there has been a marked increase in obesity and overweight, higher even than in US children of the same age. Obesity in adolescents is also among the highest in the world.[29] Between 1990 and 2000, 45 per cent of men and 32.2 per cent of women had a BMI of 25 or more, and 13.4 per cent of men and 15.8 per cent of women had a BMI of 30 or more. See figure 1.4 for projections of the proportions of men and women who will have a BMI of 30 or more in 2015.[46]

The average amount of available food energy rose between 1964 and 2004, from around 2700 to 3480 kcal/person per day (11 330 to 14 590 kJ/person per day), due largely to an increase in the availability of sugars and meat.[1] The Mediterranean-style diet is often seen as the healthiest in Europe, but Spanish diets have recently shifted towards being high in fat and dairy products, with only moderate amounts of vegetables. Dairy and fruit intakes are the highest in Europe, but so is the proportion of energy in diets from fat.[29] Between 1964 and 1990, consumption of plant-based foods decreased from 1289 to 995 g/person per day. In the same period, intakes of cereals (grains), pulses (legumes), and potatoes all halved. While consumption of other vegetables remained stable, fruit intake doubled to 327 g/person per day. Consumption of animal products increased from 407 to 743 g/person per day due to a large increase in the amounts of meat, poultry, milk, and dairy products in people's diets, although intakes of animal fats decreased.[29]

Figure 1.8	Cancer among female Iranian migrants to British Columbia, Canada

Age-standardised incidence in women per 100 000

Cancer	Ardabil province (Iran)	Kerman province (Iran)	Iranian migrants to British Columbia	British Columbia general
Breast	7.6	16.9	68.5	81.4
Colorectal	Not done	5.9	11.6	26.6

Data from Yavari et al[104]

World Cancer Research Fund American Institute for Cancer Research

Age-standardised incidence of breast and colorectal cancer is increased in Asian migrants to Canada compared with source population

Figure 1.9	Incidence of colorectal cancer in Asian migrants to USA and their descendants

Ethnicity	Birth place	Incidence rate per 100 000 people	
		Men	Women
White	USA	89.9	64.3
Chinese	USA	66.9	40.9
	China	87.8	44.7
Japanese	USA	142.5	90.1
	Japan	69.3	63.5
Filipino	USA	57.2	14.2
	Philippines	44.4	25.7

Data from Flood et al[106]

World Cancer Research Fund American Institute for Cancer Research

Age-standardised incidence of colorectal cancer is increased in the descendants of Japanese migrants to the USA

to which such hypotheses are upheld or refuted by the totality of the relevant published literature, including more robust observational and also experimental types of study.

The most compelling evidence, suggesting that the main causes of cancers of most sites are environmental (due to factors that people are exposed to) rather than genetically inherited comes from studies of migrant populations.

There are many migrant populations. Examples include people who have migrated from eastern Asia to the Americas; from the Indian subcontinent to Africa and the UK; from Europe to Australia; and from Africa to the Caribbean, and then to the UK. All of these population movements are accompanied by marked changes in patterns of diet, physical activity, and disease.

Migrations from Japan to the USA, from the Caribbean to the UK, and from European countries to Australia have been

USA

In 2004 the USA had a population of almost 300 million. The country has a high-income economy, with a gross domestic product of 39 901 international dollars per person (figure 1.3), which masks socioeconomic inequalities.[46] Life expectancy at birth is 75 years for men and 80 for women (figure 1.1).[46]

Chronic diseases account for 84.7 per cent of all deaths, while infectious diseases, maternal, perinatal, and nutritional conditions account for 6.7 per cent; 8.6 per cent of deaths are due to injuries. The first figure below gives a breakdown of deaths caused by chronic diseases.[46]

Prostate cancer is the most common type of cancer in men and the incidence rate has more than doubled since the 1970s.[20] Lung cancer peaked in the early 1980s and has since declined slightly.[20] Rates of colorectal and bladder cancer have remained stable, although melanoma has increased steadily.[20] Breast cancer is the most common type in women, followed by lung cancer, and both have increased since the 1970s.[20] Over the same period, the incidence of cancers of the colon and rectum and of the ovary have remained stable, while cancer of the endometrium has decreased slightly (for age-standardised rates of these cancers, see

the second figure below).[20]

In 2003, 22 per cent of men and 27 per cent of women aged 20–65 were classified as sedentary; physical inactivity was more prevalent among people with a low income.[91]

In 2002 men aged 20–24 had an average body mass index (BMI) of 26.2, while those aged 25–29 had a BMI of 27, and men aged 30–65 had a BMI of between 27 and 29.[46] While 19.7 per cent of men aged 20–24 had a BMI of over 30, this rose to 23.6 per cent of those aged 30–34, and 30 per cent of 40–44 year olds.[46] Women aged 20–24 had an average BMI of 26.2, while those aged

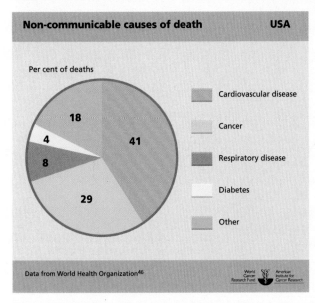

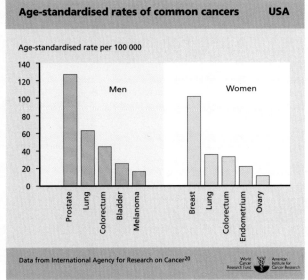

studied in some detail, as have movements of populations from rural to urban areas within countries. Both types of migration result in dietary changes, which are followed, within one or two generations, by changes in disease patterns. Patterns of cancer among migrant groups often change faster than they do among people who remain in their home country or among people native to the host country.

In the 1980s, one study demonstrated that breast cancer incidence increased almost threefold in first-generation Japanese women who migrated to Hawaii, and up to fivefold in the second generation. Colorectal cancer incidence increased almost fourfold in the first generation but did not increase further with subsequent generations.[99] In this same population, the incidence of stomach cancer dropped by almost half in the first generation, and dropped further in the second generation.[99]

Another study, published in 1980, of European migrants to Australia demonstrated a reduction in the death rate from

stomach cancer, which corresponded to the length of time the migrants stayed in Australia. However, their risk of colorectal cancer increased proportionally to the length of their stay.[100] See figure 1.7. A later study demonstrated that deaths from breast cancer among Italian migrants to Australia were half that of Australian-born women during the first five years after emigrating. However, after 17 years, Italian migrants had similar death rates (due to breast cancer) to women born in Australia.[101]

Following migration, the incidence of certain cancers may increase, whereas the incidence of other cancers may decrease. Thus among Iranian immigrants to Canada, in women, breast cancer incidence rate increased fourfold, and colorectal cancer incidence rate doubled; but there was a dramatic decrease in cancers of the stomach and oesophagus in both sexes.[102] See figure 1.8.

Another study showed that breast cancer incidence increased threefold within one generation in Polish migrants

25–29 had a BMI of 27.4, and 30–65 year olds had a BMI of between 28 and 30.[46] While 23.1 per cent of women aged 20–24 had a BMI of over 30, this rose to 30.9 per cent of women aged 25–29, and to more than 40 per cent of those aged 55–64.[46] The obesity epidemic began earlier in the USA than in other high-income countries. Between 1906 and 1962, 10.4 per cent of men and 15 per cent of women had a BMI of 30 or more.[46] By 1999/2000, these figures had increased to 27.7 per cent of men and 34 per cent of women (see figure).[46] In 2002 a US health survey found that almost 75 per cent of people were trying to prevent weight gain.[106] See figure 1.4 for projections of the proportions of men and women who will have a BMI of 30 or more in 2015.[46]

The average amount of available food energy rose between 1964 and 2004, from around 2930 to 3750 kcal/person per day (12 250 to 15 690 kJ/person per day).[1] Between 1977 and 1996, the average proportion of meals eaten in restaurants or fast-food outlets rose from 9.6 to 23.5 per cent, and fast food now accounts for 20 per cent of dietary energy.[2]

Vegetable and fruit intakes have increased since the 1980s across all income levels, and people now eat more fresh and frozen vegetables and fruits than canned. Potatoes are commonly eaten. Bananas are the most popular fruit.[34] More than 80 per cent of men and 70 per cent of women aged 20–64 fail to eat the recommended five daily portions of vegetables and fruits. Between 1970 and 2000, average population consumption of meat and poultry per person increased by 11 per cent: people ate less beef but more poultry.[16] Analysis of national food surveys demonstrated that between 1977 and 2001, people consumed more sweetened drinks and less milk. The portion sizes of sweetened drinks increased and they contributed more energy to diets: an increase from 50 to 140 kcal/person per day (210 to 600 kJ/person per day). During the same period, fruit drinks increased from 20 to 45 kcal/person per day (80 to 190 kJ/person per day); energy intake from milk dropped from 140 to 100 kcal/person per day (600 to 410 kJ/person per day), with the largest drop in milk consumption among those aged 2–18.[31] Another study revealed that 93 per cent of young people ate snack foods and they consumed one third of their total energy away from home.[2] Energy from soft drinks, fast foods, and salty snacks doubled between 1977 and 1996, and soft drinks now provide 8.5 per cent of total energy in young people's diets.[2]

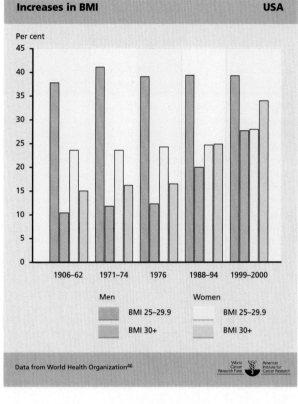

Increases in BMI — **USA**

Per cent

Men: BMI 25–29.9, BMI 30+
Women: BMI 25–29.9, BMI 30+

(1906–62, 1971–74, 1976, 1988–94, 1999–2000)

Data from World Health Organization[46]

to the USA.[103] Japanese, Chinese, and Filipino people who migrate to the USA have a higher risk of colorectal cancer than their counterparts who do not migrate. One study of US-born Japanese men demonstrated incidence rates of colorectal cancer twice as high as Japanese men born in countries other than the USA or Japan and 60 per cent higher than in white people born in the USA (figure 1.9).[104]

Data from more recent migrant studies show that cancer incidence rates generally become similar to those of the adopted country in second-generation immigrants.[17 105] This is illustrated in first-generation immigrants to Sweden, where the incidence of all cancers was 5 and 8 per cent lower for men and women, respectively, compared with native Swedes.[17] By the second generation, however, the incidence was only marginally below the figures for people native to Sweden.[105]

Correlation studies, and migrant studies in particular, prove that the main determinants of patterns of cancer are environmental and suggest that patterns of food, nutrition, and physical activity are important among these causes. Migrants share a common genetic background, as do their parents and children: the genetic pool of any population does not change within a generation or two. But as shown in Chapter 2, different patterns of environmental exposure can and do alter patterns of DNA damage and gene expression, and so cancer, in a relatively short time.

1.4 Conclusions

Between the early 2000s and 2030, the global absolute number of cancer cases is projected by UN agencies to double, most of all in the middle- and low-income countries of Africa and Asia. Some of this increase can be attributed to the

Continued on page 29

Mexico

In 2004 Mexico had a population of over 107 million. The country has an upper-middle-income economy, with a gross domestic product of 10 158 international dollars per person (figure 1.3). Life expectancy at birth is 72 years for men and 77 for women (figure 1.1).[46]

Chronic diseases account for 72.4 per cent of all deaths, while infectious diseases, maternal, perinatal, and nutritional conditions account for 16.5 per cent; 16.49 per cent of deaths are due to injuries. The first figure below gives a breakdown of the deaths caused by chronic diseases.[46]

Prostate cancer is the most common type of cancer in men, followed by lung, stomach, and colorectal cancers. Cancer of the cervix is the most common type in women, followed by cancers of the breast, stomach, and ovary (for age-standardised rates of these cancers, see the second figure below).[20] Women living in rural areas have a higher risk of cancer of the cervix compared with those living in urban areas.[32] Stomach cancer incidence has risen since 1980, and this increase is more evident in men.[20]

In 2002–2003, 17 per cent of men and 18 per cent of women aged 18–69 were classified as sedentary (figure 1.6).[46]

Between 1995 and 1999, the prevalence of overweight and obesity in children rose from 13.6 per cent to 19.5 per cent.[18] Geographically, the highest prevalence of overweight and obesity is in Mexico City and in the northern region. Across the country as a whole, girls are more likely to be overweight or obese.[18] One fifth of school-age children are overweight or obese, and the risk of body fatness rises if their mother has a school education and higher socioeconomic status.[18] Men aged 20–29 had an average body mass index (BMI) of 25.2, while those aged 30–39 had a BMI of 26.9, and men aged 40–59 had a BMI of 27.5. While 11.8 per cent of men aged 20–29 had a BMI of over 30,[46] this rose to 20.9 per cent of 30–39 year olds.[46] Around 25 per cent of men aged between 40 and 69 had a BMI of over 30. Women aged 20–29 had an average BMI of 25.6.[46] This rose to 27.9 for those aged 30–39, and to 29 for those aged 40–69. While 16.7 per cent of women aged 20–29 had a BMI of over 30, this rose to 29.6 per cent of those aged 30–39. Around 40 per cent of women aged 40–59 had a BMI of over 30.[46] See figure 1.4 for projections of the proportions of men and women who will have a BMI of 30 or more in 2015.[46]

The average amount of available food energy rose between 1964 and 2004, from around 2470 to 3150 kcal/person per day (10 350 to 131 780 kJ/person per day).[1] In 1999, micronutrient deficiencies remained a problem.[36] Undernutrition was more prevalent in the indigenous population, in people of lower socioeconomic status, and in rural areas and the south. One in five children under the age of 5 years was stunted, and 2 per cent were classified as suffering from wasting. Rates of stunting and wasting were three times higher in rural than urban areas, and were higher in the south of the country than north.

Folate intakes were lower in urban areas, in the north of the country, and in Mexico City, compared with the south and in rural areas.[7] This demonstrates regional differences in diets, particularly in the amounts of green, leafy vegetables people eat. Preschool children in the north and in Mexico City had the highest intakes of fat and the lowest intakes of dietary fibre. Children in the south, those indigenous to the country, and those of lower socioeconomic status had higher intakes of dietary fibre and starchy foods, the lowest fat intakes, and the highest risk of inadequate micronutrient intakes for vitamin A, vitamin C, folate, calcium, iron, and zinc.[7] In women, there was a risk of inadequate vitamin A, vitamin C, and folate intake. Consumption of starchy staple foods and intakes of folate, calcium, and iron were significantly higher in rural women compared with those living in urban areas. Saturated fatty acid consumption was lower in the south, reflecting the greater contribution of beans and cereals (grains) in diets.[6] Women in urban areas, and those of higher socioeconomic status, consumed more cholesterol, saturated fatty acids, and total fat.[6] Across the country as a whole, dietary fibre consumption was found to be inadequate, but intakes were higher in central and south Mexico, mainly because people's diets contained beans and cereals (grains), although their intake of vegetables and fruits was low.

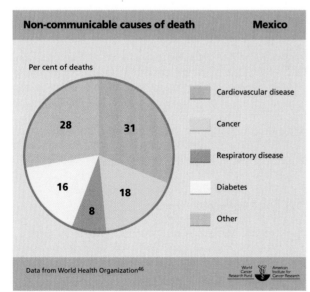

Non-communicable causes of death   **Mexico**

Per cent of deaths

- Cardiovascular disease
- Cancer
- Respiratory disease
- Diabetes
- Other

28, 31, 18, 8, 16

Data from World Health Organization[46]

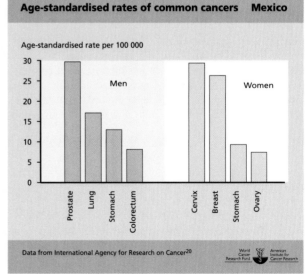

Age-standardised rates of common cancers   **Mexico**

Age-standardised rate per 100 000

Men: Prostate, Lung, Stomach, Colorectum
Women: Cervix, Breast, Stomach, Ovary

Data from International Agency for Research on Cancer[20]

Australia

In 2004 the population of Australia was over 20 million. The country has a high-income economy, with a GDP of 31 454 international dollars per person (figure 1.3).[46] Life expectancy at birth is 78 years for men and 83 for women (figure 1.1).[46]

Chronic diseases account for 86.9 per cent of all deaths, while infectious diseases, maternal, perinatal, and nutritional conditions account for 4.7 per cent; 8.4 per cent of deaths are due to injuries. The first figure below gives a breakdown of the deaths due to chronic diseases.[46]

In men, prostate cancer is the most common type and rates have doubled since the 1970s. Colorectal cancer has increased and lung cancer has declined slightly. There has been a large increase in the incidence of melanoma and a slight increase in bladder cancer. In women, breast cancer is the most common type and the rate has increased since the 1970s. Colorectal cancer is the next most common type, although this has remained stable. There has been a large increase in melanoma, and lung cancer has doubled since the late 1970s, although cancer of the endometrium has remained stable (for age-standardised rates of these cancers, see the second figure below).[20]

In 2001, 30 per cent of men and 32 per cent of women aged 15–75 were classified as sedentary.[46]

In the same year, men aged 18–24 had an average body mass index (BMI) of 24.3, while those aged 25–29 had a BMI of 25.3, and men aged 30–75 had a BMI of between 26 and 27.5.[46] Of men aged 18–24, 34.3 per cent had a BMI of over 25.[46]

This rose to 43.8 per cent of those aged 25–29, and to between 50 and 70 per cent of men aged 30–75.[46] Between 17 and 20 per cent of men aged 35–69 had a BMI of over 30.[46] The average BMI of women aged 18–24 was 22.8.[46] This rose to 24.9 for women aged 30–34, and those aged 40–75 had a BMI of between 25 and 27.1.[46] The proportion of women with a BMI of over 25 increased with age: 19.9 per cent of women aged 18–24, and 34–55 per cent of those aged 30–75. Overall, between 15 and 20 per cent of women aged 30–75 had a BMI of over 30.[46] There has been a steady increase in BMI since 1980, when 40.6 per cent of men and 20.2 per cent of women had a BMI of 25 or more, and 9.3 per cent of men and 8 per cent of women had a BMI of 30 or more.[46] In 2000, 48.2 per cent of men and 29.9 per cent of women had a BMI of 25 or more, and 19.3 per cent of men and 22.2 per cent of women had a BMI of 30 or more.[46] See figure 1.4 for projections of the proportions of men and women who will have a BMI of 30 or more in 2015.[46]

The average amount of available food energy remained stable between 1964 and 2004: around 3130 and 3120 kcal/person per day (13 100 and 13 070 kJ/person per day), respectively.[1] The most recent National Nutritional Survey in 1995 found that 90 per cent of the people surveyed ate cereals (grains) or cereal products, and milk or milk products, the day before the interview. However, half of the men and one third of the children had not eaten fruit, and 20 per cent of children had not eaten vegetables the day before the interview. Fruit con-

sumption was decreasing in adolescents, although the intake of milk products was declining only among girls. Fewer adolescents ate cereals (grains) compared with other age groups, although cereals and cereal products contributed 34–37 per cent of their total dietary energy. Cereal products contributed the greatest amount of food by weight to adults' diets, followed by milk and milk products, then pulses (legumes). Fruit consumption increased with age, whereas intakes of cereals (grains), milk, meat, and poultry decreased. Adults in the Northern Territory consumed more meat, poultry, game, and alcoholic drinks, and less vegetables and fruits, than people living in other areas. Men were slightly more likely to eat food away from home (64 per cent) compared with women (57 per cent). Almost one third of adults thought that they should be eating more fruit, and 25 per cent thought they should eat fewer high-fat foods.[4] Fruit and vegetable consumption was highest in 18–39 year-olds, with 40–50 per cent consuming a combination of at least one portion of fruit and three portions of vegetables each day, although this amount then declined steadily with age. Only 37.6 per cent of children (12–17 year olds) ate this quantity of vegetables and fruits and, in total, 37.2 per cent of people over the age of 12 failed to eat this amount. A study of people aged 20–75 living in Queensland found that 63 per cent of participants drank too much alcohol, 40 per cent were not sufficiently physically active, and less than half ate the recommended levels of fruits and vegetables.[13]

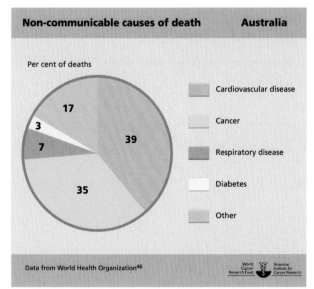

Non-communicable causes of death **Australia**

Per cent of deaths

- Cardiovascular disease
- Cancer
- Respiratory disease
- Diabetes
- Other

17, 3, 7, 39, 35

Data from World Health Organization[46]

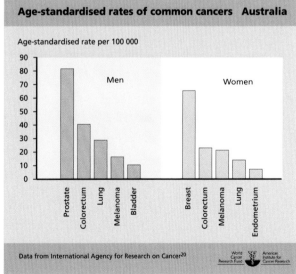

Age-standardised rates of common cancers **Australia**

Age-standardised rate per 100 000

Men: Prostate, Colorectum, Lung, Melanoma, Bladder

Women: Breast, Colorectum, Melanoma, Lung, Endometrium

Data from International Agency for Research on Cancer[20]

Brazil

In 2004 Brazil had a population of over 185 million. The country has a middle-income economy, with a gross domestic product of 8140 international dollars per person (figure 1.3), which masks extreme socioeconomic inequalities.[46] Life expectancy at birth is 67 years for men and 74 for women (figure 1.1).[46]

Chronic diseases account for 75.3 per cent of all deaths, with infectious diseases, maternal, perinatal, and nutritional conditions accounting for 16.2 per cent; 8.5 per cent of deaths are due to injuries. The first figure below gives a breakdown of deaths caused by chronic diseases.[46]

Prostate cancer is the most common type of cancer in men. This is followed by lung, stomach, colorectal, and bladder cancers. Breast cancer is the most common type in women, followed by cancers of the cervix, colorectum, stomach, and lung (for age-standardised rates of these cancers, see the second figure below).[20] Age-standardised mortality rates for childhood cancers have declined since 1980 and there has been a decrease in mortality from oral and pharyngeal cancers since the early 1980s.[9] These figures may represent

improved provision of healthcare rather than changes in incidence.

In 1997, 28 per cent of men and 31 per cent of women aged 18–69 were classified as sedentary (figure 1.6).[46]

In 1997 men aged 20–65 had an average body mass index (BMI) of between 23 and 25.[46] Just 2.1 per cent of men aged 20–24 had a BMI of over 30, rising to 9.1 per cent of 30–34 year olds, 11.4 per cent of 40–44 year olds, and 12.3 per cent of men aged 50–54.[46] Women aged 20–39 had an average BMI of between 22.5 and 24.9, while from age 40 onwards, average BMI remained between 25 and 27.[46] Just 5.2 per cent of women aged 20–24 had a BMI of over 25, rising to 17.4 per cent of those aged 40–44, and 25.5 per cent of women aged 60–64.[46] The proportion of men and women with a BMI of 30 or more has increased steadily since the mid-1970s.[46] In 1975, just 2.1 per cent of men and 6 per cent of women had a BMI of 30 or more; this rose to 6.4 per cent and 12.4 per cent in 1996/7.[46] See figure 1.4 for projections of the proportions of men and women who will have a BMI of 30 or more in

2015.[46] In 1975, for every obese woman, approximately another two were underweight. Between 1975 and 1989, the prevalence of underweight almost halved, while the prevalence of obesity doubled; so by 1997 there were two obese women for every underweight woman.[28]

The average amount of available food energy rose between 1964 and 2004, from 2313 to 3157 kcal/person per day (9684 to 13 218 kJ/person per day), largely due to an increase in the availability of meat and oils.[1] In one study, people living in urban areas ate more vegetables and fruits than those living in rural areas; intake increased with age, schooling, and income. However, only 41 per cent of adults reported eating fruit every day and 30 per cent reported daily vegetable intake.[21] Wasting and stunting in children due to undernutrition have decreased rapidly since 1975, although it remains a major problem in the north-eastern region of the country. Obesity among children is low, but those from higher income households in the economically developed south-eastern region are more likely to be overweight.[28]

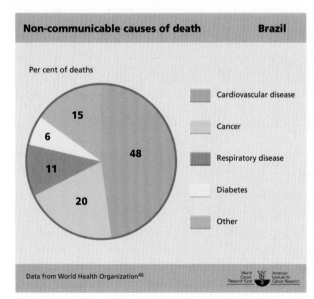

Non-communicable causes of death **Brazil**

Per cent of deaths

- Cardiovascular disease
- Cancer
- Respiratory disease
- Diabetes
- Other

Data from World Health Organization[46]

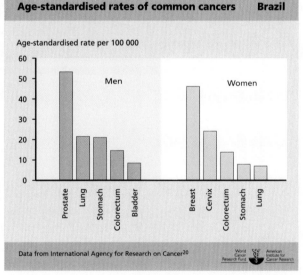

Age-standardised rates of common cancers **Brazil**

Age-standardised rate per 100 000

Men: Prostate, Lung, Stomach, Colorectum, Bladder

Women: Breast, Cervix, Colorectum, Stomach, Lung

Data from International Agency for Research on Cancer[20]

Continued from page 25

general projected increase in global population; to ageing populations; and to improved surveillance, detection and, in the case of prostate cancer, screening and diagnosis. Nevertheless, at the global level, a real, age-adjusted, population-adjusted increase in cancer rates is projected. These projections show that any global 'war on cancer' is not being won. It follows that soundly based policies and effective programmes to prevent cancer — which is to say, to decrease the risk of cancer — need not be accompanied by a decrease in the overall numbers of people suffering and dying from cancer.

This ominous prospect should be put in context. First, both actual numbers and also age-adjusted rates of some cancers are decreasing in high-income countries, and rates of stomach cancer are generally decreasing worldwide. Second, the remarkable differences in the numbers of different cancers, and in their incidence over time, show that most cancer is, at least in principle, preventable. Third, the theme of this Report, correlations between changes in patterns of diet, physical activity, body composition, and changes in patterns of cancer provide evidence that these factors are important modifiers of cancer risk.

Furthermore, as shown in Part 2 of this Report, overall the evidence is a reliable basis for recommendations designed to prevent cancer. The evidence shows that, together with exposure to tobacco smoke, key aspects of food and nutrition, physical activity, and body composition are or may be causes of important cancers of some sites. Unlike tobacco, the evidence also shows that other aspects protect against a number of common cancers. This indicates that many cancers are preventable not only in principle, but potentially also in practice.

CHAPTER 2

The cancer process

Food and nutrition modify the risk of cancers at a large number of sites. This means that some foods and drinks, dietary constituents (or their balance in diets), and methods of food production, processing, preservation, and preparation influence the development of some cancers. More recently, evidence has accumulated about the effects of physical activity and body composition on the risk of a number of cancers, suggesting that bioenergetics is another factor determining cancer risk and tumour behaviour.

Since the mid-1990s, great progress has been made in understanding the cancer process, and which internal and external factors modify cancer risk. Mapping of the human genome has enabled the establishment and development of new disciplines devoted to understanding biological processes at the most basic level, including those that prevent cancer, those that cause cancer, and those that modify its behaviour.

Evolution in living organisms depends on the accumulation of adaptations as a result of changes in the expression of the genetic information carried in DNA. Even with no changes in the DNA, alterations in how the message in the genetic code is translated can lead to functional changes. More importantly, the DNA itself is susceptible to mutation — changes in the genetic code itself — as a result of damage from external causes such as radiation or simply due to the process of metabolism. Such mutations are the essential basis for human evolution, by producing adaptations that are beneficial in particular environmental circumstances. At the same time, some mutations can contribute to the harmful changes in cells that eventually lead to cancer.

The integrity of the genetic information is protected by many systems that prevent DNA damage, or remove or repair damaged DNA if it occurs. Imperfections in these systems limit the ability to block all damage and allow both helpful and harmful mutations to occur. Cancers result when sufficient mutations have accumulated, most presenting at an age that was rarely reached in the evolutionary past of human beings. The development of cancer may be seen as a corollary of

the ability of humans to evolve and adapt.

Ultimately it is both the genetic information (genotype) and its expression that control the characteristics (or phenotype) of an individual. Any exposure during the life course that affects the genotype or its expression may also have an effect on the phenotype. At any point in time, the phenotype is related not only to the genotype but also to a host of environmental factors, including nutritional exposures. This accumulated metabolic experience may begin during maternal and early life, and proceed throughout a person's lifetime.

The purpose of this second introductory chapter is to summarise current knowledge and thinking on the biology of the cancer process, with special reference to food and nutrition, physical activity, and body composition. In Part 2 of this Report, epidemiological and mechanistic evidence is summarised, and the Panel's assessments and judgements are made, based on a balance of all relevant evidence.

This chapter summarises the wealth of biological evidence that documents the ability of food and nutrition, physical activity, and body composition to influence several stages of the process of the development of cancer.

Nutrients and food constituents have effects that can either inhibit several events that lead to cancer, or contribute to cancer development, by altering DNA itself, or by altering how the genetic message in DNA is translated. Physical activity and variations in body composition also appear to influence cancer risk. Indeed, overall dietary patterns can indirectly influence cell growth by way of changes in general metabolic, regulatory, and endocrine effects.

The normal functioning of all biological processes, including those of the human body, depends on the availability of substrate and nutrients. Good nutrition — defined as appropriate provision of food and nutrients from the level of the whole organism to the cellular and intracellular level — is needed for normal structure and function. When a person is not suitably nourished, either through under- or overnutrition, this impacts on the tissue microenvironment, compromising both structure and function.

Understanding the mechanisms underlying cancer development is central to improving its prevention and treatment. The main body of this Report comprises the Panel's judgements on a series of systematic literature reviews (SLRs) on evidence linking food, nutrition, and physical activity to cancer. All evidence on the mechanisms of the cancer process is also based on rigorous review criteria. However, the evidence presented in this chapter is a summary of this literature, and the references cited are illustrative examples only. Full details of the methods used for the reviews are contained in the SLR specification manual. The full SLRs and this manual are contained on the CD included with this Report.

2.1 Basic concepts and principles

2.1.1 Cancer

Cancer is a group of more than 100 diseases characterised by uncontrolled cellular growth as a result of changes in the genetic information of cells. Cells and tissues are complex systems with critical stages and checkpoints to ensure normal growth, development, and function. Normally the division, differentiation, and death of cells are carefully regulated. All cancers start as a single cell that has lost control of its normal growth and replication processes.

Human adults are made up of around 10^{13} (or 10 000 000 000 000) cells, which are renewed and replaced constantly. About 5–10 per cent of cancers result directly from inheriting genes associated with cancer, but the majority involve alterations or damage accumulated over time to the genetic material within cells. The causes of damage are both endogenous (internal) and exogenous (environmental). Food, nutrition, and physical activity are important environmental factors in the development of cancer.

Cancer can also be seen as a group of diseases that affects many different tissues and types of cell, and can be defined by their tissue of origin. Approximately 85 per cent of adult cancers develop from the epithelial cells of the inner and outer linings of the body and are called carcinomas. Cancers of glandular tissue such as the breast are called adenocarcinomas; cancers from bone and muscle derived from mesoderm cells (embryonic cells that grow to form muscle, blood, bone, and connective tissue), are called sarcomas.

Each type of cancer has different characteristics, but one feature of all these diseases is unregulated cell growth and/or cell death. Apart from haematological cancers such as leukaemias, this results in a tumour or mass, and cancerous cells often invade the surrounding tissue. Spread of cancer cells from the primary site to other parts of the body is called metastasis. Benign tumours do not invade or metastasise. Malignant tumours do not remain localised but can invade and/or metastasise.

2.1.2 Genetic material

The genetic material of mammalian cells is composed of double-stranded DNA made from four organic bases — cytosine, guanine, adenine, and thymine — within a helical spine comprising deoxyribose (a sugar) and phosphate. The combination of a base with phosphate and deoxyribose is called a nucleotide. Humans have 3 billion base pairs in the DNA code that encode approximately 30 000 different genes.

The nucleus of a cell contains DNA, and the information in the code is 'read' to generate proteins in the cytoplasm of the cell. This is achieved by transcribing the DNA into RNA, and then translating the information in RNA to synthesise protein. For transcription, the two DNA strands separate and an intermediary, complementary copy of the DNA is made from mRNA (which differs slightly in structure from DNA and is single stranded). For translation, the RNA leaves the nucleus and binds to an organelle in the cytoplasm called the ribosome. The RNA nucleotides encode for 21 different

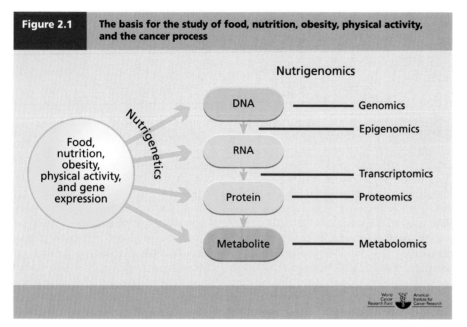

Figure 2.1 The basis for the study of food, nutrition, obesity, physical activity, and the cancer process

The genetic message in the DNA code is translated into RNA, and then into protein synthesis, and so determines metabolic processes. Research methods called '-omics' address these different stages.

amino acids, with the ribosome moving along the RNA molecule and translating the genetic code into a sequence of amino acids that build into a protein.

The normal metabolic processes in cells are controlled by proteins, each of which is a product of a single gene from the DNA in the nucleus. Although each cell in the body contains exactly the same genes, cells from different organs have different structures and functions because there is a process of regulation that determines which genes are expressed; that is, which genes are turned on and which are not (see 2.2.2). This differential gene expression varies not only from tissue to tissue but also from time to time over the course of a person's life, from embryonic and fetal stages onwards (box 2.1). Gene expression is regulated by promoter regions of genes in the DNA, as well as by epigenetic factors — those that alter gene expression without changing the nucleotide sequence (see 2.2.3). The availability of nutrients within the immediate environment influences these processes (figure 2.1).

2.1.3 Nutrigenomics and cancer

Unravelling links between diet and cancer is complex, as thousands of dietary components are consumed each day; a typical diet may provide more than 25000 bioactive food constituents.[1] Assessing intakes of some constituents is difficult due to wide variations in the amounts of bioactive components within a particular food.[2][3] Dietary constituents modify a multitude of processes in both normal and cancer cells.[4][5]

The response is further complicated since a single, bioactive food constituent can modify multiple steps in the cancer process. Likewise, many of these processes can be influenced by several food components. Normal and cancer cells also differ in their responses to bioactive food components in terms of the dose (quantity), timing, and duration of exposure required to bring about effects. To unravel the contribution of nutrition to cancer, the biological processes underpinning cancer development need to be understood. Extensive evidence exists for nutritional factors in several processes related to cancer development (figure 2.2). However, because of the complexity of the process, it is not possible to conclude that modifying any one, or more, of these processes influences cancer risk.

The recent expansion of knowledge in molecular biology has allowed new techniques to be developed to explain these mechanisms. Nutrigenomics is a new field with profound implications in cancer prevention and therapy, since it seeks to clarify the impact of nutrition in the maintenance of genome stability, and to dissect out the influence of genotype in determining our response to diet. Nutrigenomics is the study of nutritional influences on the phenotypic variability of individuals based on genomic diversity (figure 2.1). This determines the sequence and functions of genes, and studies single nucleotide polymorphisms (SNPs), and amplifications and deletions within the DNA sequence as modifiers of the response to foods and beverages and their constituents. Nutritional epigenomics is another key determinant of gene expression patterns. It includes non-coding modification of genes (such as methylation, changes in histone homeostasis, miRNA, and DNA stability) in response to nutrition. Nutritional transcriptomics is the study of gene expression patterns at the RNA level, and it can identify common nutritional response elements in gene promoters that can be modulated by diet. Proteomics studies the proteins that can be expressed by a cell, many of which can be influenced by nutrition. Metabolomics studies the range of metabolic processes in a cell and metabolic regulation in cells or tissues, which again are heavily influenced by food, nutrition, and physical activity.

2.2 Cellular processes

The role of nutrition in cancer depends on how it impacts on fundamental cellular processes including the cell cycle (figure 2.3; also see 2.5.1). To understand cancer biology, it is important first to understand normal cellular processes. The integrity of tissues and organs depends on a regulated balance between cell proliferation and death, and appropriate cell differentiation. This regulation is controlled by several types of genes including oncogenes and tumour suppressor genes (box 2.2), and factors in the cellular environment that influence their expression. Maintenance of the DNA sequence and structure as cells divide is essential: several cellular mechanisms exist to ensure this is achieved.

2.2.1 Cell signalling

Cells detect and respond to external stimuli and send messages to other cells through a molecular mechanism known as cell signalling.

Cells within a tissue normally communicate with each other through a network of locally produced chemicals called cytokines (including some growth factors). Cell proliferation is a tightly controlled and coordinated process, and is stimulated by growth factors. These soluble proteins can be produced locally, either from the same cell (autocrine), or from different cells (paracrine), or as hormones (endocrine) produced by a distant tissue and transported in the blood. Growth factors bind to specific receptors on the cell surface and transmit a signal into the cell, which is relayed to the nucleus. In the nucleus, genes are switched on to produce the proteins necessary for cell division.

Getting the growth signal from the outside of the cell to the nucleus requires a series of steps. The shape of the receptor changes when the growth factor binds to it, which causes part of the receptor to become activated, usually by a process called phosphorylation. A regulated process of phosphorylation and dephosphorylation is necessary for the appropriate initiation, transmission, and cessation of signals.

2.2.2 Gene expression

Gene expression is the process by which the information within a gene is 'turned on' or 'turned off'. The information is used to create the associated proteins and modify the amounts produced. Also see figure 2.1.

Transcription factors are proteins involved in the regulation of gene expression and carry the signal from the cytoplasm to the nucleus. They bind to the promoter regions of genes and have the effect of either switching gene expression on or off. There are also nuclear receptors, such as retinoic acid receptors, that function as transcription factors by binding directly to specific DNA sequences.

Some so-called 'housekeeping' genes are expressed by almost all cell types. These genes generally encode proteins that participate in basic cell functions such as metabolic pathways and synthesis, and processing of DNA, RNA, or proteins. Other genes have more restricted expression, and are expressed only in specific cell types, and/or stages of development.

Gene expression can also be influenced by changes outside the DNA of genes. DNA is closely organised and tightly packaged in the nucleus of cells. To achieve this, DNA is spooled around proteins called histones. Histone structure can be modified either, like DNA itself, by methylation, or more commonly by acetylation (addition of an acetyl group). Acetylation and deacetylation (removal) are mediated by the enzymes histone acetyl transferase (HAT) and histone deacetylase (HDAC), respectively. HATs relax the packaged DNA structure, which is associated with enhanced transcription, whereas HDACs stabilise the structure with higher levels of packaging, and so suppress transcription. Butyrate, produced in the colon by bacterial fermentation of non-starch polysaccharide (dietary fibre), diallyl disulphide from garlic and other allium vegetables, and sulphoraphane, a glucosinolate from cruciferous vegetables, can behave as histone deacetylase inhibitors,[16] and act to maintain DNA stability or enhance transcription.

Micro RNAs (miRNAs) are

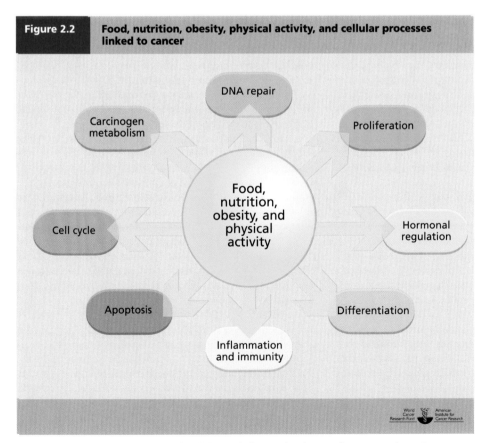

| Figure 2.2 | Food, nutrition, obesity, physical activity, and cellular processes linked to cancer |

DNA repair

Carcinogen metabolism

Proliferation

Cell cycle

Food, nutrition, obesity, and physical activity

Hormonal regulation

Apoptosis

Differentiation

Inflammation and immunity

Food, nutrition, obesity, and physical activity can influence fundamental processes shown here, which may promote or inhibit cancer development and progression.

Nutrition over the life course

The best understanding of the impact of endogenous and exogenous factors on the cancer process will come from studies of the whole life course, and particularly of critical periods within it.

Early nutritional exposure is an important determinant of phenotypic expression during later life and is likely to affect vulnerability to chronic diseases, including cancer.[6] During pregnancy, the nutrient demands of the fetus have to be satisfied. Although the mother's dietary intake is important in maintaining her own nutrient reserves, it is her nutrition status on entering pregnancy that determines her capacity to deliver appropriate nutrients to the fetus. Any stress that modifies her nutritional state, either by changing appetite or altering nutrient demand, can impact on the availability of nutrients to the fetus.[7] In experimental models, pregnant rats fed a low-protein diet resulted in overexposure of the fetus to maternal glucocorticoids. This led to a permanent alteration in hormonal status and metabolic responses in the offspring.[8][9] These effects were attributed to differential methylation of certain glucocorticoid genes and could be mitigated by maternal folic acid supplementation.[4]

Lower birth weight, followed by exposure to periods of rapid rates of growth, possibly due to energy-dense diets, is associated with development of metabolic syndrome during adult life.[6] This is the clustering of several cardiovascular risk factors including hypertension, abdominal obesity, insulin resistance, and type 2 diabetes. Type 2 diabetes has been associated with increased prevalence of some cancers, and risk of cancer shows a graded relationship with glycated haemoglobin (a measure of blood glucose control) throughout the normal range.[10] Metabolic syndrome may also increase cancer risk,[11] suggesting that the metabolic disturbances associated with this syndrome promote genetic instability.

Growth and development are dependent on the supply of adequate energy and nutrients to match a person's needs. Famine exposure in women affects breast dysplasia later in life: girls exposed to famine before the age of 10 years have less dysplasia in later life, whereas those exposed after 18 years of age have more dysplasia than non-exposed women. This illustrates the importance of timing of nutrition during key stages of development.[12]

Greater body fatness later in life is linked to development of metabolic syndrome and related health problems, including insulin resistance. The inflammatory state associated with obesity also promotes cancer.[13] In contrast, energy restriction (box 2.5) delays the onset of many age-related diseases, including cancer.

RNA molecules that do not encode proteins; instead they function as negative regulators of gene expression. Some mutations in miRNAs have been associated with human cancers, and they can function as oncogenes or tumour suppressor genes (box 2.2). miRNAs are short, single-stranded RNA molecules of approximately 22 nucleotides. For instance, to silence (turn off) genes, they may bind to complementary mRNA sequences and degrade them before they have been translated. Profiling miRNA signatures within cancer cells may aid the diagnosis, classification, and treatment of cancer. For example, a certain miRNA that is downregulated in lung cancer is associated with decreased survival.[17] Research on the interactions between nutrition and non-coding RNA molecules is at an early stage but is potentially relevant to cancer.

2.2.3 Epigenetic regulation

Gene expression can also be altered without changing the DNA sequence. This is called epigenetic modulation.

Methylation of DNA — the addition of a methyl group (CH_3) — plays a role in gene silencing. Methylation occurs only to cytosine residues located next to guanine bases in the DNA sequence. These CpG dinucleotide sequences are found throughout the genome; in about half of all genes, clusters of CpG sequences, so-called 'CpG islands', are located in the promoter region that normally functions to promote expression of the gene. Transcription factors cannot bind to these sites when methylated and so the gene is silenced. For active genes, the CpG islands in the promoter regions are generally not methylated.

Controlled DNA methylation also provides a mechanism for cell differentiation. In normal cells, genes may be permanently silenced so that they can no longer be expressed, in a way that is transmitted into daughter cells during cell division (see 2.5.1), so maintaining the particular structural and functional characteristics of the cells of specific tissues.

Dietary constituents contribute to epigenetic modulation of promoter regions in both normal and malignant cells. For example, dietary folate and other methyl-donors such as choline, methionine, and betaine are essential for DNA synthesis and epigenetic regulation of DNA. Appropriate gene expression is maintained by appropriate patterns of methylation; folate is an important determinant of normal methylation. In addition, dietary constituents such as genistein, which do not provide methyl groups, have also been reported to modify DNA methylation.

Imbalances or lack of specific dietary constituents may potentially increase the risk of cancer by inducing an imbalance in DNA precursors, leading to altered DNA synthesis and repair, and may impair appropriate patterns of DNA methylation, with consequences for gene expression. For example, inadequate folate availability means cells tend to incorporate uracil into DNA in place of thymine. Global hypomethylation of DNA is an early epigenetic event in cervical carcinogenesis, and the degree of hypomethylation increases with the grade of cervical cancer.[18][19] Global hypomethylation of DNA and site-specific hypermethylation may also be relevant in colorectal cancer.[20] A host of bioactive food constituents from alcohol to zinc has been reported to influence DNA methylation patterns. Nevertheless, it remains to be determined how important these changes are in the overall cancer process. The potential cancer-protective effects of green, leafy vegetables (see chapter 4.2) are often attributed to their folate content. Folates function as a coenzyme in the metabolism of single-carbon compounds for nucleic acid synthesis and amino acid metabolism.

2.2.4 Differentiation

Cells become specialised to perform their particular function through a process known as differentiation.

Although each cell within the body contains the entire genome with the same genes, only some genes are active in any one cell at any one time. Gene expression controls the subset of genes expressed and the timing of expression, and this distinguishes one cell type from another by determining their particular structure and function.

Hundreds of different cell types arise from one fertilised egg during development; this is achieved by proliferation and differentiation of stem cells. Stem cells are unspecialised but can give rise to different specialised cell types. A small population of cells within the tumour mass of several forms of human cancer, which have both the properties of stem cells and also the characteristics of transformed cells, may be important for the development of these tumours. As yet, our understanding of cancer stem cells is basic, although the concept was proposed as early as 1875.[22] Several groups have now isolated and identified cancer stem cells in both haematopoietic and epithelial cancers, including cancers of the breast,[23] brain,[24 25] ovary,[26] prostate,[27] colon,[28] and stomach.[29] It is clear that subtle changes in exposure to bioactive food constituents can have a profound effect on the differentiation of these cells.

In early embryos, proliferation of embryonic stem cells increases the total number of cells. As the organism develops, cells differentiate and become specialised to their particular function. Transcription factors specific to that cell type turn on genes for that particular lineage of cells, so determining its structure and function.

At various stages of differentiation, cells become sensitive to different growth factors. In the cancer process, one characteristic of cells that are accumulating DNA damage is that they become de-differentiated and undergo epithelial-mesenchymal transition (EMT), characterised by loss of cell adhesion and increased cell mobility. In addition, during differentiation, other genes can be silenced by chromatin modification, including DNA methylation and histone modifications such as methylation and acetylation (see 2.2.2).

Stem cells are found among differentiated cells in almost all adult tissues, where they maintain and regenerate tissues. Examples include haemopoietic stem cells for continuous generation of red and white blood cells, and stem cells in the basal layer of the epidermis and at the base of hair follicles in the skin, which can give rise to keratinocytes and hair follicles. Cellular differentiation also continues in solid tissues such as mammary tissue, which during pregnancy differentiates for later milk production. A systematic review has shown that long-chain n-3 polyunsaturated fatty acids (PUFAs) in fish oils promote differentiation of colonic epithelial cells.[30 31] Vitamin D and retinoic acid may also promote differentiation of cells.

2.2.5 DNA damage and repair

Each time a cell divides into two new daughter cells, there is potential for an error in replication of the DNA (see 2.5.1). These mutations result in non-functioning genes or in proteins with altered amino acid sequences that can change cell function.

DNA is continuously exposed to damage from products of normal intracellular metabolism, including reactive oxygen species, hydroxyl radicals, and hydrogen peroxide; and also to damage from external factors such as ultra-violet (UV)

Box 2.2   Oncogenes and tumour suppressor genes

Oncogenes and tumour suppressor genes are present in all cells, and in their normal, non-mutated form contribute to the regulation of cell division and death. In cancer, both types of gene are often mutated, and these alterations contribute to the cancer process. The combined effect of activation of oncogenes and inactivation of tumour suppressor genes is an important driver of cancer progression.

Oncogenes increase the rate of transformation from a normal to a cancerous cell. Oncogene function is changed by mutation so that the protein product is produced either in greater quantities or has increased activity. The normal, non-mutated form of an oncogene is called a proto-oncogene.

More than 100 oncogenes have been identified, including ERBB2 in breast and ovarian cancers, members of the Ras family in cancers of the lung, colorectum, and pancreas, and MYC in lymphomas. Amplification of the ERBB2 gene occurs in around 30 per cent of breast cancers, and RAS mutations occur in approximately 30 per cent of all human cancers (and in 75–90 per cent of pancreatic cancers).

Tumour suppressor genes prevent excessive growth of a cell, either by controlling cell proliferation or by controlling DNA repair and genomic stability. Mutation of a tumour suppressor gene results in the loss of function of the protein product.

Common tumour suppressor genes include p53 and the retinoblastoma (Rb) gene. The p53 gene was the first tumour suppressor gene to be identified, and is considered to be the guardian of the genome.[14] Under normal circumstances, p53 is involved in several processes such as cell proliferation, DNA repair, apoptosis, and angiogenesis. p53 is activated by cellular stresses that could facilitate tumour development such as hypoxia, lack of nucleotides, and in particular, DNA damage.

In response, p53 can either halt the cell cycle to allow DNA repair, or induce apoptosis. It can bind to the promoter regions of approximately 300 different genes, thereby having an important regulatory role in various molecular pathways. The p53 pathway is altered in most cancers, and the mutated protein product cannot protect the genome, allowing mutations to accumulate.

In the absence of a functional Rb gene, the retinoblastoma protein pRb is not made and its inhibitory role of inactivating cell cycle transcription factors is absent. This leads to increased, uncontrolled proliferation, and thereby increased risk of further mutations. More than 2000 inactivating mutations of p53 have been identified in human tumours. Both p53 and pRb can also be inactivated by the human papilloma virus. Development of lung cancer is associated with loss of function of both genes. Li-Fraumeni syndrome, a result of a germ line mutation in p53, leads to inherited susceptibility to a wide range of cancers. Patients with Li-Fraumeni syndrome have a 25-fold increased risk of developing cancer compared with the general population.[15]

light, as well as other environmental factors including food, nutrition, and physical activity (see 2.4). There are several mechanisms for DNA repair (box 2.3), a vital defence in maintaining cellular integrity and preventing a cell being transformed from normal to cancerous.

Various studies suggest that nutritional status and/or certain food constituents may influence DNA repair. Data from observational studies suggest that severe malnutrition can impair DNA repair.[34] Nucleotide excision repair has been found to be lower in adults with the lowest intakes of folate.[35] Studies of healthy adults consuming kiwi fruits,[36] cooked carrots,[37] or supplements of coenzyme Q$_{10}$ (an important cofactor in metabolism)[38] have demonstrated improved DNA repair in vitro. Selenium induces base-excision repair in vitro via p53 activation in cultured fibroblasts.[39]

Evidence exists that some dietary components can modify DNA damage and gene expression in exfoliated colonocytes. For example, the amount of single-strand breaks in exfoliated colorectal mucosal cells was significantly lower in healthy individuals consuming a vegetarian diet compared with a diet high in meat.[40] Similarly, DNA damage in exfoliated lung epithelial cells can be influenced by dietary components. Consumption of a lycopene-rich vegetable juice was associated with significantly decreased damage to the DNA of lung epithelial cells in healthy volunteers.[41]

Defects in any of the DNA repair mechanisms can predispose to cancer. Several inherited conditions link such defects to cancer incidence. For example, patients with hereditary non-polyposis colorectal cancer have defective mismatch repair (see chapter 7.9.2).

Although the processes of cell development, signalling, and DNA repair are tightly controlled, errors will occur during the trillions of cell divisions that occur over a lifetime. This may result in inappropriate proliferation or failure of damaged cells to die. These changes could provide the altered cell with a growth advantage over the normal cells in the tissue. If additional alterations occur, this can result in a cell with the potential to become cancerous.

2.3 Carcinogen metabolism

The chance of carcinogenesis occurring and then progressing is modified by many factors, including food and nutrition. Dietary constituents that modify carcinogenesis include selenium, allyl sulphur, sulphuraphane, and isoflavonoids.

Most dietary carcinogens require activation to produce reactive intermediates that bind to and damage DNA. Phase I and phase II metabolising enzymes in the liver and in other tissues are involved in this process. These are enzymes that catalyse the metabolic detoxification of xenobiotics, drugs, and carcinogens produced through aerobic metabolism, and thus protect cells against oxidative stress and reactive electrophilic carcinogen metabolites.

Metabolic activation of carcinogens is generally catalysed by the cytochrome P450 (CYP) family of phase I enzymes through oxidation, which usually makes the molecule more water soluble. Some of the intermediates formed during this process may be carcinogenic, and can bind to DNA, forming

DNA adducts. These adducts distort the structure of DNA and disrupt its replication, potentially causing mistranslation. They can also break the DNA strand, which can result in mutations or deletions of genetic material.

In addition to P450 enzymes, other systems such as peroxidases (including the cyclooxygenases) and certain transferases, such as N-acetyltransferase and sulphotransferase, can influence carcinogen bioactivation.[42-44]

Competing with this metabolic activation of carcinogens is the detoxification process catalysed by a second group of enzymes, known as phase II enzymes.[45] They catalyse conjugation reactions, producing molecules that can be excreted in bile or urine. Examples include acetyltransferases, glutathione-S-transferases (GSTs), UDP-glucuronyltransferases, NAD(P)H:quinone oxidoreductase, and sulphotransferases. The induction of phase II enzymes is mediated by the antioxidant response element, which is located in the promoter region of specific genes.[46]

Each of these enzymes represents a potential target for dietary components to influence carcinogen activation. Specificity in response is evident since isothiocyanates from cruciferous vegetables have been shown to induce expression of phase II detoxification enzymes without affecting expression of phase I enzymes.

The carcinogenic properties of polycyclic hydrocarbons, aromatic amines, N-nitroso compounds, and aflatoxins result from the metabolism of these compounds, which produces carcinogenic by-products. Metabolising enzyme activity can be modulated by dietary factors. The enzyme CYP3A4 participates in the metabolism of over half of all pharmaceutical agents, and is especially sensitive to dietary effects. For example, interactions have been reported between grapefruit juice, red wine, garlic, and various drugs.[47] Food–drug interactions involving CYP1A2, CYP2E1, glucuronysyltransferases, and GSTs have also been documented.[48]

The activity of phase I and II enzymes, and thus carcinogen metabolism and cancer development, varies between individuals. SNPs in several phase I and phase II enzymes have been shown to modulate cancer risk.[49 50] There is some difficulty in synthesising this evidence and some studies may give false positive results. Nevertheless, the literature shows tantalising evidence that relates genetic diversity to these enzymes in various processes linked to cancer development. Some specific examples of SNPs in cancer are listed below.

GSTs are involved in the metabolism of environmental carcinogens and reactive oxygen species. People who lack these enzymes may be at higher risk for cancer because of a reduced capacity to dispose of activated carcinogens.[51] As shown in chapter 4.1, aflatoxins — produced by moulds that contaminate certain types of foods such as cereals (grains) and peanuts — are carcinogens that are activated by phase I enzymes in the liver into reactive DNA metabolites that cause DNA adducts. However, the number of adducts and therefore the potency of aflatoxin B are influenced by other enzymes such as GSTs, which eliminate carcinogens before they can bind to DNA. Individuals with low expression of GSTs are also at higher risk for colorectal cancer; however, a diet high in isothiocyanates (derived from glucosinolates

| Box 2.3 | Mechanisms for DNA repair |

Mammals have five types of DNA repair system[32] [33]:

- Direct reversal corrects rather than removes damaged DNA bases.
- Base-excision repair corrects DNA damage caused by reactive oxygen species, deamination, and hydroxylation arising from cellular metabolism and spontaneous depurination.
- Nucleotide-excision repair removes lesions that distort the structure of the DNA helix, such as pyrimidine dimers and DNA adducts.
- Homologous recombination and non-homologous end-joining repair double-strand breaks. Homologous recombination is used when a second identical DNA copy is available, for example after replication; non-homologous end-joining re-links the 'broken' ends of a double-strand break.
- DNA mismatch repair detects and repairs copying errors made during replication.

in cruciferous vegetables) can ameliorate this.[52]

Epidemiological evidence supports the idea that individuals possessing these genotypes are predisposed to a number of cancers, including those of the breast, prostate, liver, and colon[53]; it also shows that nutrition influences cancer risk. Thus, an SNP in the methylenetetrahydrofolate reductase (MTHFR) gene appears to influence folate metabolism by reducing MTHFR activity, and is associated with a reduction in the risk of developing colorectal cancer.[54] Certain SNPs in the N-acetyltransferase gene alter the activity of the enzyme (involved in the metabolic activation of heterocyclic amines from meat cooked at high temperatures), and may also increase the risk of colon cancer.

Again, as described in chapter 4.3, people whose diets are high in red and processed meat and who also carry an insert variant in CYP2E1, a key activating enzyme of many nitrosamines, have a greater risk of rectal cancer.[55] Consumption of cruciferous vegetables protects against lung cancer in individuals lacking the GSTM1 gene.[56] In addition, genes that predispose to obesity may promote obesity-related cancers (box 2.4).

Dietary components can either be, or be activated into, potential carcinogens through metabolism, or act to prevent carcinogen damage. For instance, as summarised in chapter 4.3, high intake of red meat may result in more absorption of haem iron, greater oxidative stress, and potential for DNA damage.[57] [58] In addition, iron overload can also activate oxidative responsive transcription factors and inflammation in the colon.[59] Red meat consumption is also associated with the formation of N-nitroso compounds. This increases the level of nitrogenous residues in the colon and is associated with the formation of DNA adducts in colon cells.[60]

Cruciferous vegetables contain glucosinolates, which are transformed by food preparation into isothiocyanates (ITCs), which alter the metabolism of carcinogens. Indoles and ITCs, two major glucosinolate breakdown products, attenuate the effects of polycyclic aromatic hydrocarbons and nitrosamines via induction of GSTs and inhibition of cytochrome P450 isoenzymes, respectively.

Human intervention studies with cruciferous vegetables have demonstrated induction of GSTs by consumption of Brussels sprouts and red cabbage varieties, but not with white cabbage and broccoli. The particular isoform of the enzyme induced may protect against bladder cancer. Cruciferous vegetables also affect drug metabolism in humans, and red cabbage leads to specific changes in the patterns of meat-derived urinary mutagens. ITCs may also protect against mutations formed by tobacco carcinogens.[61]

In a variety of animal studies, certain dietary components have shown a reduction in experimentally induced cancers. Rats fed ITCs developed significantly fewer oesophageal cancers due, in part, to inhibition of cytochrome P450-mediated bioactivation of the carcinogen. Dietary indole-3-carbinol inhibited spontaneous occurrence of endometrial adenocarcinoma and preneoplastic lesions in rats.[62]

Flavonoids (polyphenolic compounds found in plant foods) may also alter carcinogen metabolism. Quercetin has been shown to inhibit the expression of cytochrome P450 and phase I enzymes, and may reduce tobacco carcinogen activation.[63]

Exposure of vulnerable populations to excess amounts of dietary constituents, irrespective of whether they are nutrients or not, may actually increase the risk of cancer. In one example, consumption of beta-carotene supplements in smokers was associated with increased incidence of lung cancer.[64] For most dietary components, there will be an upper threshold beyond which people may be exposed to adverse effects. There are also concerns regarding excessive supplementation with folic acid, iron, copper, iodide, and selenium.[65]

2.4 Causes of cancer

A number of different types of exogenous (environmental) factors are known causes of cancer. These include some aspects of food and nutrition that are established as carcinogenic by the International Agency for Research on Cancer, although it is difficult to estimate the proportion of cancers directly attributable to these.[74] Known causes of cancer include tobacco smoking and its use, infectious agents, medication, radiation, and industrial chemicals, and also some factors within the scope of this report — carcinogenic agents in food and drink.

Sometimes the extent to which cancer in general, or specific cancers, may be modified by any factor, are calculated, and some of these figures are given here. However, these estimates should be treated with some caution. First, they are estimates, and cannot be exact, and so are best given as ranges. Second, individual causes of cancer often interact with one another to increase or decrease risk, or are modifiers or precursors of others; and some act together to produce a multiplicative effect. This point is particularly important with food and nutrition, which may have a substantial effect on the risk of a cancer with environmental causes other than food, nutrition, and physical activity. Third, it is sometimes assumed that once all factors that decrease (or increase) risk are added together, with allowance for unknown factors, such estimates should add up to 100 per cent. This is not so. Reasonable estimates for a number of separate or interactive factors may add up to well over 100 per cent because of the interactions.

2.4.1 Endogenous causes
2.4.1.1 Inherited germ line mutations
As mentioned, only a minority (5–10 per cent) of cancers are linked to single inherited genes. Such inherited alterations are termed germ line mutations, and are passed on from egg or sperm DNA. Individuals with inherited germ line mutations will not definitely get cancer but have an increased risk of developing cancer compared with the general population.

Often mutations in tumour suppressor genes (box 2.2) increase the chance of developing cancer at a young age. These include retinoblastoma (a rare cancer of the eye), Li-Fraumeni syndrome, multiple endocrine neoplasia type 1, and kidney cancer in Von Hippel-Lindau disease. Mutations in the BRCA1 and BRCA2 (breast cancer susceptibility) genes cause 5–10 per cent of all breast cancer cases. These genes normally produce DNA repair proteins. Patients with the syndrome familial adenomatous polyposis coli have a predisposition to colorectal cancer due to mutations in the adenomatosis polyposis coli tumour suppressor gene.[75] Other common cancers, including those of the ovary, prostate, pancreas, and endometrium, may be related to inherited mutations, but only in a small percentage of cases.

The other type of genetic mutation — somatic gene changes — develops during the life course. Such somatic mutations are not passed on to offspring. This DNA damage is caused by exposure to external factors such as radiation or carcinogens, or harmful products of normal aerobic metabolism.

2.4.1.2 Oxidative stress
Reactive oxygen species generated through normal oxidative metabolism have the potential to cause extensive DNA damage. The body has several mechanisms, which can scavenge reactive oxygen species to prevent such damage occurring, or block the effects.

Reactive oxygen species cause oxidative damage to DNA. During repair (see 2.2.5), the damaged, oxidised bases are excreted in the urine. Levels of urinary 8-hydroxy-2'-deoxyguanosine, an oxidative DNA damage adduct, can be used as an indicator of oxidative DNA damage in humans and rodents. Antioxidants can scavenge reactive oxygen species. Vitamins C and E can donate electrons to free radicals and block their damaging activity. Dietary constituents such as ITCs and polyphenols can also activate the signalling pathways that lead to activation of the antioxidant response element (see 2.3), and upregulation of the expression of detoxifying enzymes.

2.4.1.3 Inflammation
Inflammation is a physiological response to infection, foreign bodies, trauma, or chemical or other irritation, and in the acute phase can be helpful. However, chronic inflammation can result in DNA damage and cancer promotion.

Chronically inflamed tissue is infiltrated with a variety of inflammatory cells that produce a wide variety of bioactive chemicals. These include cytokines, growth factors, reactive oxygen and nitrogen species, cyclooxygenase, and lipoxygenase products. A chronic inflammatory environment can increase proliferation and differentiation, inhibit apoptosis (programmed cell death), and induce angiogenesis (generation of new blood vessels). Chronic inflammatory conditions, such as Barrett's oesophagus and ulcerative colitis, predispose to cancer. In Barrett's oesophagus, reflux of acid can cause the cells lining the gullet to undergo EMT, and some areas can develop dysplasia and ultimately cancer. Around 1 per cent of people with Barrett's oesophagus will develop oesophageal cancer (this is between 30 and 125 times higher than the general population). Also see chapter 7.3.2. Approximately 5 per cent of patients with ulcerative colitis, a form of irritable bowel disease, will develop colon cancer. Also see chapter 7.9.2. Epidemiological and experimental evidence has demonstrated that long-term use of non-steroidal anti-inflammatory drugs can inhibit cancer development in a number of tissues including colon, oesophagus, and breast.[76]

Cancer induced by inflammation may be susceptible to nutritional influences. Thus, dietary constituents could be involved in generation of reactive oxygen species, could influence antioxidant defences, or could suppress the inflammatory process. For example, the glucocorticoid receptor pathway and the vitamin D receptor are capable of suppressing inflammation.

The immune system can be divided into innate and adaptive responses. Innate immunity provides initial defences. Adaptive immunity develops later and involves activation of lymphocytes and their differentiation into effector and memory cells. The 'immune surveillance' hypothesis proposes that both the innate and adaptive immune systems constantly survey for and eliminate newly formed cancer cells, and that onset and progression of cancer are kept under control by the immune system.[77] Immunosurveillance requires that the immune system recognises something different about cancer cells compared with normal cells within the same tissue – often different proteins (termed tumour antigens) that are expressed on the surface of a cancer cell.

This recognition of 'altered self' allows the immune system to generate a response to these tumour antigens. They can be proteins that are only expressed by cancer cells, and newly expressed during cancer development; or proteins that have become mutated during the cancer process and so are different from the non-mutated protein; or proteins expressed due to differentiation of cancer cells (termed differentiation antigens); or proteins that are normally expressed by cells but that are expressed at much higher levels by cancer cells. Evasion of immunosurveillance is sometimes referred to as a further hallmark of cancer[78] (see 2.5), although the evidence remains speculative.

Specialised mucosal cells form the interface between the inside and outside of the body.[79] These are normally an efficient barrier against pathogens. The gut barrier consists of gut-associated lymphoid cells that can sense pathogens, and participate in innate and adaptive responses.[80] The function of these cells is dependent on nutrition.[81][82] For example, n-3 PUFAs can enhance immunity, whereas high concentrations

Box 2.4	Body fatness and attained height

As shown in Chapter 6, the overall evidence that body fatness is a cause of a number of cancers is convincing. Some of the mechanisms by which body fatness increases the risk of cancer are well understood.

Obesity influences the levels of a number of hormones and growth factors.[66] Insulin-like growth factor 1 (IGF-1), insulin, and leptin are all elevated in obese people, and can promote the growth of cancer cells. In addition, insulin resistance is increased, in particular by abdominal fatness, and the pancreas compensates by increasing insulin production. This hyperinsulinaemia increases the risk of cancers of the colon and endometrium, and possibly of the pancreas and kidney.[13] Increased circulating leptin levels in obese individuals are associated with colorectal[67] and prostate cancers.[68]

Sex steroid hormones, including oestrogens, androgens, and progesterone, are likely to play a role in obesity and cancer. Adipose tissue is the main site of oestrogen synthesis in men and postmenopausal women.[13] The increased insulin and IGF-1 levels that accompany body fatness result in increased oestradiol in men and women,[13] and may also result in higher testosterone levels in women (extreme obesity can lead to polycystic ovary disease). Increased levels of sex steroids are strongly associated with risk of endometrial and postmenopausal breast cancers,[69] [70] and may impact on colon and other cancers. As shown in Chapter 6, body fatness probably protects against premenopausal breast cancer; this may be because obese women tend to have anovulatory menstrual cycles and thus reduced levels of oestrogen.

Obesity is characterised by a low-grade chronic inflammatory state, with up to 40 per cent of fat tissue comprising macrophages. The adipocyte (fat cell) produces pro-inflammatory factors, and obese individuals have elevated concentrations of circulating tumour necrosis factor (TNF)-alpha,[13] interleukin (IL)-6, and C-reactive protein, compared with lean people,[71] as well as of leptin, which also functions as an inflammatory cytokine.[72] Such chronic inflammation can promote cancer development.

Also as shown in Chapter 6, factors that lead to greater adult attained height, or its consequences, are a cause of a number of cancers. Adult height is related to the rate of growth during fetal life and childhood. The number of cell divisions in fetal life and childhood, health and nutrition status in childhood, and age of sexual maturity can alter the hormonal microenvironment, and affect circulating levels of growth factors, insulin, and oestrogens.

Taller people have undergone more cell divisions stimulated by IGF-1 and pituitary-derived growth hormone,[73] and there is therefore more potential for error during DNA replication, which may result in cancer development.

of n-6 unsaturated fatty acids can have a suppressive effect.[83] Various factors have been shown to modulate both inflammation and immunity, including vitamins A and E, copper, selenium, zinc, PUFAs, and epigallocatechin-3-gallate (EGCG) from green tea.[84] Zinc deficiency can lead to abnormalities in adaptive immune responses.[85]

Immune status and chronic inflammation may explain patterns of cancer in different parts of the world. Cancers caused by infectious agents, such as those of the liver and cervix (see chapter 7.8 and 7.13) are more common in low-income countries, where undernutrition may impair people's immune responses. Undernutrition, with deficiencies in specific micronutrients such as vitamin A, riboflavin, vitamin B12, folic acid, vitamin C, iron, selenium, and zinc, suppresses most immune functions and may fail to control chronic inflammation.[86] [87] By contrast, hormone-related cancers such as those of the breast and prostate are more common in developed countries.

The cytokine IL-6 can act as a pro- or anti-inflammatory cytokine. In cancer, IL-6 can either stimulate proliferation or exert anti-tumour effects by enhancing both innate and adaptive immunity.[88] Dietary phytoestrogens, such as soy isoflavones, downregulate IL-6 gene expression and thus potentially influence the development of hormone-related cancers.[89]

Circulating levels of IL-6 increase (up to 100-fold) following exercise; this reduces chronic inflammation by reducing pro-inflammatory mediators and elevating anti- inflammatory mediators.[90] Regular moderate and occasional vigorous physical activity has been associated with enhanced immunity,[91] but prolonged and intense physical activity can cause immune suppression that cannot be counteracted by nutritional supplements or antioxidants.[83] Physical activity does not increase pro-inflammatory cytokines, but instead increases anti-inflammatory mediators.

Chronic consumption of alcohol alters both innate and adaptive immunity. Heavy drinkers are more vulnerable to infections and, as shown in chapter 4.8, to liver cancer.[92] One possible mechanism is alteration in hepatic metabolism resulting in functional iron deficiency that impairs immune function.[93-95]

2.4.1.4 Hormones

Lifetime exposure to oestrogen — increased by early menarche, late menopause, not bearing children, and late (over 30) first pregnancy — raises the risk of, and may be seen as a cause of, breast, ovarian, and endometrial cancers in women. The reverse also applies: a reduction in lifetime exposure to oestrogen due to late menarche, early menopause, bearing children, and early pregnancy may reduce the risk of hormone-related cancers. Age at menarche and menopause are influenced by nutrition, with high-energy diets leading to early puberty and late menopause, and low-energy diets delaying puberty and advancing menopause.

The oral combined contraceptive pill (containing both oestrogen and progesterone) has been estimated to halve the risk of ovarian cancer, if taken for 5 years or more.[96] This protective effect can last for up to 15 years after women stop taking these oral contraceptives.[97] Using any type of oral contraceptive may also have a slight protective effect against bowel cancer.[98] In contrast, combined oral contraceptives can cause a slight and transient increase in breast cancer risk, but only for the duration of use.[99] There may also be an increase in the risk of cervical cancer, although this is partly related to sexual behaviour.[100]

Studies of women taking oestrogen-only hormone replacement therapy have suggested that the risk of endometrial cancer is doubled after 5 years of use,[101] and the risk of ovarian cancer rises by 25 per cent after the same length of use.[97 102] However, use of hormone replacement therapy that combines oestrogen and progesterone does not increase ovarian cancer risk and may even protect against endometrial cancer.[102 97 101]

2.4.2 Exogenous causes

2.4.2.1 Tobacco use

Tobacco causes an estimated 20 per cent of all cancer deaths, and an estimated total of 1.2 million in 2002.[75] Smokers have increased risk of a number of different cancers (see Chapter 7). Worldwide, around 80 per cent of lung cancer cases in men and 50 per cent in women are caused by tobacco smoking.[103 104] In 2002, out of all new cases of cancer in low-income countries, over 1 in 5 in men and almost 4 per cent in women were attributable to tobacco. In high-income countries, one third of all new cancer cases in men and just over 1 in 8 in women were attributed to tobacco smoking.

Cigarette smoke contains at least 80 known mutagenic carcinogens, including arsenic, cadmium, ammonia, formaldehyde, and benzopyrene. Each will have a separate mechanism for causing cancer. For example, following metabolic activation, the activated derivative of benzopyrene, benzo(a)pyrenediol epoxide, can form DNA adducts in lung epithelial cells.[105]

Cigarette smoke is a powerful carcinogen and also a source of oxidative stress. Compared with non-smokers, active smokers have lower circulating concentrations of several antioxidant micronutrients including alpha-carotene, beta-carotene, cryptoxanthin, and ascorbic acid.[106]

2.4.2.2 Infectious agents

Infectious agents, including viruses, bacteria, and parasites, can induce DNA damage and promote cancer development. Some infectious agents, including hepatitis viruses, the bacterium *Helicobacter pylori (H pylori)*, and parasites, also promote cancer by causing chronic inflammation (see 2.4.1.3).

Both DNA and RNA viruses can cause cancer, although the mechanisms differ.[75] DNA viruses encode viral proteins that block tumour suppressor genes, whereas RNA viruses or retroviruses encode oncogenes (box 2.2). Human papilloma virus is an established cause of cervical cancer, Epstein-Barr virus of nasopharyngeal cancer and lymphoma, and hepatitis B and C infection of liver cancer.

As summarised in Chapter 7, *H pylori* is associated with stomach cancer, liver flukes (from eating raw or undercooked freshwater fish) with liver cancer, and *Schistosoma haematobium* infection with bladder cancer.

In most cases, infection with these agents by itself does not lead to cancer but is a contributory or necessary factor in the cancer process. Multiple factors are thought to be important in determining why cancer is the result in only some cases.

Approximately 1 in 4 cancers in low-income countries are estimated to be attributable to infection. In 2002, this represented some 1.9 million cancers or close to 1 in 5 of all cancers worldwide[104]. Inadequate nutrition or dietary imbalances can lead to immunodeficiencies and increased susceptibility to infections.

Dietary factors may influence host susceptibility to the viral infection or persistence of the infection. For example, high folate intake is thought to reduce the susceptibility to and the persistence of human papilloma virus.[107]

2.4.2.3 Radiation

Both ionising radiation and UV radiation damage DNA and act as carcinogens. This includes radiation used in X-ray radiographs and in the treatment of cancer. In 1982, the various forms of radiation were calculated to account for 3 per cent of all cancer deaths.[74]

Ionising radiation can cause DNA damage, both directly by causing breaks in the DNA strands, and indirectly by interacting with water molecules and generating reactive oxygen species that damage DNA.

Although sunlight causes DNA damage, it also induces production of vitamin D. One of its metabolites, 1-25-hydroxy-vitamin D, has antiproliferative and pro-differentiation effects in some cells mediated through the vitamin D receptor.

Exposure to ionising radiation comes from cosmic radiation (air travel increases exposure), natural radioactivity present in rocks and soil, medical exposure through X-rays, or atomic radiation from weapons and nuclear accidents. Ionising radiation increases the risk of various cancers, in particular leukaemias, and breast and thyroid cancers.

UV light from sunlight or sunlamps is divided into three bands of wavelengths: UVA, UVB, and UVC. UVB is the most effective carcinogen and is absorbed by bases in the DNA, causing characteristic patterns of DNA damage. UVA damages DNA through generation of reactive oxygen species. UVC in sunlight is absorbed by ozone in the atmosphere and does not reach the surface of the earth. UV radiation causes both malignant melanoma and non-melanoma skin cancer.

It has been difficult to separate the effects of nutrients on DNA damage from those on repair, at least in animal or human studies. There is some evidence that vitamin C and carotenoids can protect DNA against oxidative damage in some experimental settings.[108]

2.4.2.4 Industrial chemicals

Certain industrial chemicals and pesticides persist in the environment and become concentrated in the food chain. Some of these are within the scope of this Report and are summarised in Part 2. In 1982, industrial chemicals were calculated to account for less than 1 per cent of cancer deaths.[74]

Polychlorinated biphenyls (PCBs), organic compounds previously used in plasticisers, adhesives, paints, and various oils, do not readily degrade. They are soluble in fat rather than water and thus accumulate in carnivorous fish such as salmon, and can be absorbed by people who eat these types of fish.[109] They also accumulate in human milk, and can be passed to the infant during breastfeeding. There is limited experimental evidence suggesting that PCBs have sex steroid activity and alter oestrogen levels, which may contribute to breast cancer risk.[109]

Arsenic is genotoxic, causes gene mutations, and is carcinogenic to humans; arsenic in drinking water is absorbed from the gastrointestinal tract.[75] The Panel's judgements on arsenic are summarised in chapter 4.7. Arsenic can modify the urinary excretion of porphyrins in animals and humans. It also interferes with the activities of several enzymes of the haem biosynthetic pathway. There is clear evidence that selenium binds heavy metals such as arsenic and thus modifies their absorption.[75]

2.4.2.5 Medication

A number of medical treatments modify the risk of some cancers. As indicated in 2.4.2.3, X-rays are carcinogenic, as is radiation used as cancer treatment.

The most notorious example has been diethylstilboestrol, once prescribed in pregnancy and now withdrawn, which caused cancers of the vagina and cervix of female children born to mothers who received this drug. Treatments that affect hormonal status have been studied extensively and are described in 2.4.1.4. Chemotherapy as cancer treatment during childhood is followed by an increased risk of lymphoma in adulthood.[110]

2.4.2.6 Carcinogenic agents in food

Food may be contaminated with natural or man-made carcinogenic toxicants. These are within the scope of this Report, and are assessed and judged in Part 2.

Moulds and the toxins produced by some moulds cause DNA adducts and are carcinogenic. Aflatoxin B, a product of the *Aspergillus* fungus and a common contaminant of cereals (grains) and peanuts, is an established cause of liver cancer (see chapter 4.1). Fumonisin B, a toxin produced by the fungus *Fusarium verticillioides*, may be found on maize and may be carcinogenic, although epidemiological studies are lacking.

Some carcinogenic compounds are formed during food preparation (see chapter 4.3 and 4.9). Heterocyclic amines are formed by cooking meat at high temperatures, and polycyclic aromatic hydrocarbons can be produced in meat and fish that has been grilled (broiled) or barbecued (charbroiled) over a direct flame. Also see box 4.3.4. High environmental concentrations of polycyclic aromatic hydrocarbons, which also come from pollution caused by traffic and industry, can contaminate other foods such as cereals, vegetables, and fruits.

Some *N*-nitroso compounds are carcinogens, and are formed in foods containing added nitrates or nitrites; examples include fish and meat preserved with salting or preservatives, and smoking or drying. These carcinogens can also be generated from ingested foods containing nitrate or nitrite. *N*-nitroso compounds are also produced endogenously in the stomach and colon of people who eat large amounts of red meat or take nitrite supplements. Also see box 4.3.2.

2.5 Nutrition and cancer

The majority of cancers are not inherited. Cancer is, however, a disease of altered gene expression that originates in changes to DNA, the carrier of genetic information. For a cell to be transformed from normal to cancerous, it has to acquire different phenotypic characteristics that result from alterations to the genotype. Most cancers develop to the stage of being clinically identifiable only years or decades after the initial DNA damage.

Cancer development, or carcinogenesis, requires a series of cellular changes. No single gene causes cancer. It is a multistep process caused by accumulated errors in the genes that control cellular processes. One genetic mutation may allow a single trait (such as increased survival) to be acquired by a lineage of cells, and descendants of these cells may then acquire additional genetic mutations. However, cancer only develops when several genes are altered that confer growth and survival advantages over neighbouring normal cells.

The capacity of a cell to achieve effective cancer prevention or repair is dependent on the extracellular microenvironment, including the availability of energy and the presence of appropriate macro- and micronutrients. Tumours are not simply masses of cancer cells. Rather, they are heterogeneous collections of cancer cells with many other cell types — so-called stromal cells; cancer cells communicate with stromal cells within the tumour. The tumour microenvironment comprises many cell types including infiltrating immune cells such as lymphocytes and macrophages, endothelial cells, nerve cells, and fibroblasts. All these cell types can produce growth factors, inflammatory mediators, and cytokines, which can support malignant transformation and tumour growth, and attenuate host responses. In addition, factors produced by the cancer cells themselves modulate the activity and behaviour of the tumour stroma.

Initiation is the exposure of a cell or tissue to an agent that results in the first genetic mutation. This can be an inherited mutation or an exogenous or endogenous (produced through oxidative metabolism) factor. Even without external oxidative stress, hundreds of sites within DNA are damaged each day but are normally repaired or eliminated.

Exposure to the carcinogen initiates DNA damage, usually via the formation of DNA adducts. If left uncorrected, these adducts can be transferred to daughter cells during division and confer the potential for neoplastic (new and abnormal) growth.

Initiation alone is insufficient for cancer to develop. An initiated cell must go through a process of clonal expansion during promotion to become neoplastic; the larger the number of initiated cells, the greater the risk of progressing to cancer. Promotion involves exposure of the initiated cell to a promoting agent. This may allow alterations in the rate of proliferation or additional DNA damage to occur, leading to further mutations within the same cell, which alter gene expression and cellular proliferation. Finally, these initiated and promoted cells grow and expand to form a tumour mass. DNA damage continues at this stage and cancer cells often contain multiple copies of chromosomes. This clear, sequential process is typical of experimentally induced cancers but may be less clear in sporadic cancers in humans.

At the end of the multistage process of carcinogenesis, the cell will bear some or all of the hallmarks of cancer[111] (figure 2.4). Several genes can contribute to each hallmark and one gene (for example p53) can contribute to several of the hallmarks. These hallmarks or traits are shared by most, if not all, cancer cells. The six hallmarks of cancer cells are self-sufficiency in growth signals; insensitivity to antigrowth signals; limitless replicative potential; evasion of apoptosis; sustained angiogenesis; and tissue evasion and metastasis.[111] Food, nutrition, and physical activity-related factors influence cellular processes and lead to cells accumulating these traits (figure 2.5).

2.5.1 Cell proliferation

Three hallmarks of cancer, namely growth signal autonomy, evasion of growth inhibitory signals, and unlimited replication, promote enhanced cell proliferation. Over a normal human lifetime, approximately 10^{16} (10 000 000 000 000 000) cell divisions will take place. The sequence of stages of a cell dividing into two daughter cells is called the cell cycle (figure 2.3). Normal cells require external signals from growth factors, which stimulate them to divide. Proliferation of normal cells depends, in part, on the presence in the cellular environment of signals that both promote and inhibit growth, and the balance between them.

Most cells in adults are not in the process of actively dividing, but are in an inactive or quiescent state termed G. To re-enter the cell cycle, cells must be stimulated with growth factors and have sufficient space and nutrients for division.

During the G_1 phase, the cell increases in size, and synthesises RNA and proteins. At the end of the G_1 phase, cells must pass through the G_1 checkpoint, which arrests the cycle if damaged DNA is detected, ensuring that it is not replicated. During the S phase, DNA is replicated. The S phase ends when the DNA content of the nucleus has doubled and the chromosomes have been replicated.

When DNA synthesis is complete, the cell enters the G_2 phase, during which the cell continues to increase in size and produce new proteins. The G_2 checkpoint leads to arrest of the cell cycle in response to damaged or unreplicated DNA; otherwise the cell divides into two daughter cells during the M (mitosis) phase, and the M checkpoint ensures each daughter cell receives the correct DNA. The cell cycle is controlled by a set of proteins called cyclins and their specific cyclin-dependent kinases (CDKs). These join to form cyclin–CDK complexes, which activate transcription factors. This in turn activates transcription of the genes required for the next stage of the cell cycle, including the cyclin genes.

In this section, examples are given to illustrate the known interactions between nutritional factors and these physiological processes.

Among the modulators of cell-cycle progression are specific nutrients, which can either function as energy sources or regulate the production and/or function of proteins needed to advance cells through the replicative cycle. Vitamin A, vitamin B12, folic acid, vitamin D, iron, zinc, and glucose all contribute to the control of cell cycle progression (figure 2.3).

2.5.1.1 Growth signal autonomy

Unlike normal cells, cancer cells are not dependent on external growth factors to stimulate their division. Instead, they can generate their own signals or respond to lower concentrations of external signals. This frees cancer cells from the growth constraints of normal cells.

2.5.1.2 Insensitivity to antigrowth signals

Normal cells also receive growth inhibitory signals. Indeed, most cells of the body are quiescent and not actively dividing. Cells respond to negative environmental signals such as contact with other cells. Cancer cells have acquired mutations that interfere with these pathways and so do not respond to growth inhibitory signals.

2.5.1.3 Limitless replicative potential

Normal cells can divide a finite number of times. Once they have replicated 60 or 70 times they stop — a process termed senescence, which is thought to constitute a protective mechanism against unlimited proliferation. This preordained number of cell doublings is controlled by telomeres. Telomeres are segments of DNA on the ends of chromosomes, which are shortened during each round of DNA replication. Eventually when the telomeres are too short, the cell can no longer divide and it undergoes apoptosis.

By contrast, cancer cells have acquired the ability to maintain the length of their telomeres, which means they can replicate endlessly. Recent work has suggested that senescence can be induced prematurely, particularly in premalignant cells, by activation of the normal, non-mutated forms of genes such as p53 and Rb.[111] This senescence is a normal active process involving genetic and phenotypic changes that may protect against cancer development; for example, it may be one mechanism preventing benign moles from progressing to malignant melanoma. However, in malignant melanoma, cell markers of senescence are lost.[112]

In experimental conditions, many constituents of food such as retinol, calcium, allyl sulphide, n-3 fatty acids, and genistein are known to influence progression of cells through the cell cycle. These studies, when conducted in cells in culture, need to be assessed cautiously because they may not always adequately reflect events in vivo. However, they can and do provide evidence additional to that gained from epidemiological studies. Also see chapter 3.1 and 3.2.

Specific dietary components have effects on cell cycle progression and proliferation in experimental settings. Some known or hypothesised benefits of some dietary constituents are summarised here.

Vitamin A (in the form of retinol) can lead to cell cycle arrest.[113] Retinoids and carotenoids inhibit proliferation by binding retinoid receptors on the cell surface. Reduced expression of retinoid receptors occurs during development of lung cancer[114]; retinoic acid receptor silencing is also common in other malignancies. Retinoic acid, a metabolite of vitamin A, has been used as a chemopreventive and therapeutic agent in cervical cancer.[115] Retinoids can inhibit proliferation of initiated cells by inducing apoptosis or inducing differentiation of abnormal cells back to normal.[116] Retinoids may also cause regression of precancerous lesions in the cervix.[117]

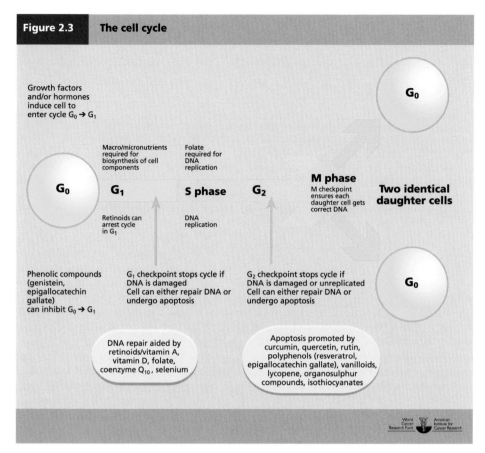

Figure 2.3   The cell cycle

Growth factors and/or hormones induce cell to enter cycle $G_0 \rightarrow G_1$

Macro/micronutrients required for biosynthesis of cell components

Folate required for DNA replication

G_0

G_0 G_1 S phase G_2

M phase
M checkpoint ensures each daughter cell gets correct DNA

Two identical daughter cells

Retinoids can arrest cycle in G_1

DNA replication

Phenolic compounds (genistein, epigallocatechin gallate) can inhibit $G_0 \rightarrow G_1$

G_1 checkpoint stops cycle if DNA is damaged Cell can either repair DNA or undergo apoptosis

G_2 checkpoint stops cycle if DNA is damaged or unreplicated Cell can either repair DNA or undergo apoptosis

G_0

DNA repair aided by retinoids/vitamin A, vitamin D, folate, coenzyme Q_{10}, selenium

Apoptosis promoted by curcumin, quercetin, rutin, polyphenols (resveratrol, epigallocatechin gallate), vanilloids, lycopene, organosulphur compounds, isothiocyanates

World Cancer Research Fund   American Institute for Cancer Research

Nutrition may influence the regulation of the normal cell cycle, which ensures correct DNA replication. G_0 represents resting phase, G_1 the growth and preparation of the chromosomes for replication, S phase the synthesis of DNA, G_2 the preparation of the cell for division, and M represents mitosis.

Butyrate and diallyl disulphide can act as histone deacetylase inhibitors[16] (see 2.2.2), and arrest the cell cycle. Folate is a necessary cofactor for DNA synthesis, and deficiency can reduce cell proliferation due to decreased DNA synthesis.

Phenolic compounds, including genistein and EGCG, can inhibit some cyclins and cyclin-dependent kinases.[118] Specifically, in people with oral leukoplakia, green tea (which contains EGCG) has been associated with significant decreases in the size of cancers and of micronuclei formation in exfoliated oral cells.[119]

Phytoestrogens are found in high concentrations in soya beans, and have been shown in vitro to exhibit a plethora of different anti-cancer effects, including inhibiting proliferation.[120][121] Glucosinolates from cruciferous vegetables are converted in the liver to ITCs, which can arrest cell cycle progression, as well as induce phase 2 enzymes, which can promote carcinogen excretion (see 2.3). Only about one third of people have the types of microbial flora in their gut that are capable of metabolising the dietary isoflavone daidzein to equol. Compared with Western populations, Asian populations are more likely to produce equol, and this affects the expression of genes involved in cell signalling and differentiation, and cell division. Equol can also modulate oestrogen-responsive genes.[122]

Calcium has a growth inhibiting action on normal and tumour gastrointestinal cells.[123] However, certain dietary compounds can also stimulate proliferation in experimental cell lines, for example, colonic cells can be induced to hyperproliferate by dietary haem iron.[124]

In a variety of animal studies, certain dietary components have shown reductions in experimentally induced cancers. Allyl sulphides in garlic inhibit experimentally induced colon tumour formation. Although this is not completely understood, experiments with diallyl disulphide suggest a block in the G_2/M phase in the progression of the cell cycle, and induction of apoptosis.[125]

Fish oil supplements decrease the number of tumours in experimental models of colorectal cancer.[126] Long-chain n-3 PUFAs in fish oils can limit tumour cell proliferation[30][31] by modifying signalling pathways,[127][128][129] for example, by decreasing signalling of activated oncogenes.[130] Animals that receive a diet supplemented with n-3 fatty acids have fewer colonic tumours than those fed a diet supplemented with corn oil,[131] due to dietary fibre-altering, fatty acid-binding, protein expression in colonocytes during tumour development.

Various growth factors and hormones involved in normal cell processes can be used or produced by cancer cells to maintain or augment uncontrolled cell proliferation. The receptor for IGF-1 is overexpressed on many cancer cells. IGF-1 can enhance the growth of a variety of cancer cell lines[132] by stimulating progression of the cell cycle from G_1 to S phase.[13]

Insulin itself can also act as a growth factor for tumour cell proliferation, both by binding to the insulin receptor on cancer cells and by stimulating increased IGF-1 production by the liver.[13][133] Insulin resistance increases with body fatness, in particular abdominal fatness, and the pancreas compensates by increasing insulin production. This hyperinsulinaemia is associated with a risk of cancers of the colon and endometrium, and possibly of the pancreas and kidney.[13] Leptin, a hormone produced by fat cells, can also stimulate proliferation of many premalignant and malignant cell types,[134] as can a number of sex steroid hormones (see Chapter 6, and box 2.4).

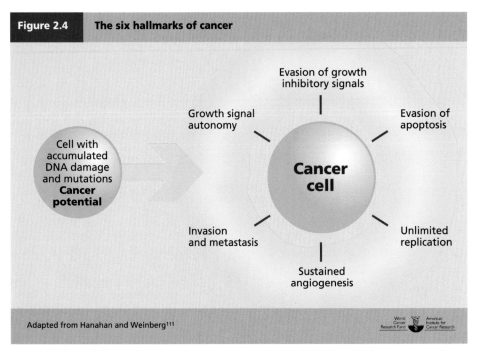

Figure 2.4   The six hallmarks of cancer

Cell with accumulated DNA damage and mutations **Cancer potential**

Growth signal autonomy

Evasion of growth inhibitory signals

Evasion of apoptosis

Cancer cell

Invasion and metastasis

Unlimited replication

Sustained angiogenesis

Adapted from Hanahan and Weinberg[111]

Cancer cells have different characteristics from normal cells. The six 'hallmarks' shown here are the phenotypic changes that need to be accumulated over time as a result of genetic changes (mutations and epigenetic factors) in order for a cell to become cancerous.

Physical activity improves insulin sensitivity and decreases levels of insulin.[135] However, exercise has little or no long-term effects on circulating IGF-1 levels.[136-138] IGF binding activity may increase with physical activity, and thus overall IGF-1 bioavailability and activity may decrease. Physical activity decreases serum oestrogen and androgens in postmenopausal women. In premenopausal women, it decreases circulating oestrogens, increases cycle length, and decreases ovulation, all of which provide a protective effect for breast and endometrial cancers. Also see Chapter 5.

In experimental animals, energy restriction leads to a reduction in cell proliferation[66] (box 2.5). At the molecular level, dietary energy restriction affects levels of cell cycle control proteins (decreased cyclins, increased levels of cyclin-dependent kinase inhibitors, and decreased cyclin-dependent kinases), leading to reduced Rb phosphorylation and inhibited cell cycle progression.[139] This, in turn, may directly inhibit tumour growth and/or indirectly reduce cancer development by reducing the number of cell divisions, thus reducing the chances for incorrect DNA replication or preventing damaged DNA from being replicated.

2.5.2 Evasion of apoptosis

Apoptosis is the tightly regulated process of cell death that controls cell numbers, removes damaged cells, and prevents damaged cells being replicated, thereby maintaining tissue integrity and protecting against cancer. Ultimately, cells break into small membrane-surrounded fragments (apoptotic bodies) that are phagocytosed without inducing inflammation.

Triggers for apoptosis in normal cells include DNA dam-

age, disruption of the cell cycle, hypoxia, reactive oxygen species, and physical or chemical insult. Two non-exclusive pathways, the intrinsic (mitochondrial) pathway or the extrinsic (death-receptor) pathway, can be activated. Both involve activation of caspases, a family of protease enzymes that cleave intracellular proteins.[143] In apoptosis, p53 functions as a transcriptional activator of genes encoding apoptosis effectors. p53 can also exert a direct apoptotic effect by damaging mitochondria.[144] Cancer cells have acquired mutations in genes regulating apoptosis and therefore can evade apoptotic signals. Defects in apoptosis are often observed in established cancers. In cancer cells, many signals that normally induce apoptosis, such as damaged DNA or expression of activated oncogenes, are present but apoptosis is not induced. This avoidance of apoptosis allows further opportunity for additional mutations to develop. In cancer cells with mutations in p53 or other members of this family, apoptosis may not occur. Additionally, mutations in genes that would normally activate p53 or regulate its activity, or in genes that should be switched on as a result of p53 activation, can have the same effect. Cancer cells with upregulated expression of IGF-1R and increased responses to IGF-1 have decreased apoptosis.[133]

In experimental settings, energy restriction creates a pro-apoptotic environment, adjacent to premalignant and malignant breast pathologies.[145] Long-chain n-3 PUFAs in fish oils limit tumour cell proliferation, increasing apoptotic potential along the crypt axis, promoting differentiation and limiting angiogenesis.[30 31 126]

Reactive oxygen species can induce apoptosis, but it is also possible that scavenging of reactive oxygen species by dietary antioxidants can delay or inhibit apoptosis, and thus favour survival of premalignant cells. Indeed, this could explain why dietary antioxidant intervention trials have produced mixed results.[146 147]

Many dietary components have been shown to induce apoptosis in cultured cancer cells and in experimental mod-

Maintenance of healthy cells depends on regulated processes, which can be influenced by factors related to food, nutrition, and physical activity, either to protect the cell from or to promote cancer. The evidence for what is shown here comes from a variety of experimental studies.

Figure 2.5 The influences of food, nutrition, obesity, and physical activity on the processes shown in figure 2.2

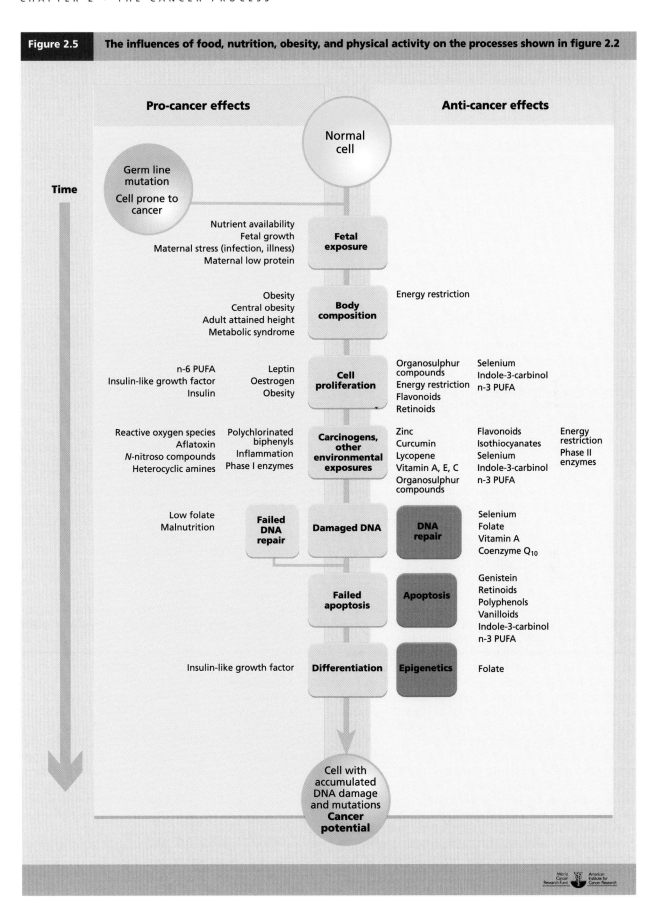

Box 2.5	**Energy restriction**

Restriction of energy intake from food is the most effective single intervention for preventing cancer in experimental animals. It increases the lifespan of rodents, and suppresses tumour development in mice. In addition, energy restriction can suppress the pro-cancer effects of many carcinogens in experimental animal models.[66]

Energy restriction leads to a reduction in cell proliferation.[66] This may directly inhibit tumour growth, and also indirectly reduce cancer development by reducing overall proliferation, thus reducing the chances for incorrect DNA replication, or by preventing damaged DNA from being replicated. Reduced metabolism results in reduced generation of reactive oxygen species, and therefore less exposure of DNA to damaging oxygen radicals.

Dietary energy restriction reduces levels of circulating IGF-1[66 140] and insulin, which are growth factors for many cells, including breast cancer.[141] IGF-1 stimulates progression through the cell cycle from G_1 to S phase, and high levels of insulin increase production of IGF-1.[13] Energy restriction also decreases expression of cyclins and cyclin-dependent kinases (CDKs), and increases levels of CDK inhibitors, leading to reduced Rb phosphorylation and inhibited cell cycle progression.[139] Energy restriction also decreases other inflammatory markers.[66] Conversely, increased glucose levels associated with increased energy intake are associated with increased DNA synthesis and levels of some cyclins and CDKs.[113] Energy restriction may also create a pro-apoptotic environment and reduce blood vessel density, as shown in pre-malignant and malignant breast pathologies.[139] It may also activate other protective pathways, such as the activation of protein deacetylases.[142]

The data on energy restriction must be interpreted with caution, as all studies have been performed in experimental animals and there is an absence of epidemiological and mechanistic data in humans. Therefore the relevance of these findings in experimental animals to the human condition is not yet clear.

---

els of cancer.[148] These include EGCG, curcumin, genistein, indole-3-carbinol, resveratrol, ITCs, lycopene, capsaicin, and organosulphur compounds.[149] In premalignant cells, retinoids, polyphenols, and vanilloids stimulate apoptosis.[150] Alpha-tocopherol (a form of vitamin E) has been shown both to induce[151] and to protect against apoptosis.[152]

2.5.3 Sustained angiogenesis

Angiogenesis, the formation of new blood vessels, is essential for the supply of nutrients and oxygen to any growing tissue, including tumours. Most cells within tissues reside within 100 mm of a capillary blood vessel. The generation of blood vessels in adults is fairly constant and tightly controlled by a balance of angiogenesis inducers and inhibitors. For a cancer to progress to a larger size, it must acquire the ability to induce angiogenesis. Currently about 35 proteins have been identified as angiogenesis activators or inhibitors.[153]

In experimental settings, one of the first dietary components for which a beneficial anti-angiogenic effect was clearly demonstrated was EGCG from green tea.[154] Now some 20 different compounds consisting mainly of flavonoids and isoflavones (including genistein) are documented as being able to modulate the angiogenic process. Diets high in n-6 fatty acids are associated with poor prognosis in breast cancer patients, whereas those high in n-3 fatty acids appear to suppress angiogenesis.[155] Long-chain n-3 PUFAs in fish oils limit angiogenesis in other experimental cancers.[30 31] Curcumin, quercetin, and resveratrol have all been shown to inhibit the angiogenic factor, vascular endothelial growth factor (VEGF), in cultured cancer cells. Garlic extract may inhibit experimentally induced angiogenesis, as it can suppress endothelial cell motility, proliferation, and tube formation.[156] Phytoestrogens found in high concentrations in soya beans have also been shown to inhibit angiogenesis.[120] Energy restriction reduces blood vessel density in pre-malignant and malignant breast pathologies.[145] Exercise increases the levels of a circulating endogenous VEGF-inhibitor in healthy people, which could decrease plasma levels of VEGF.[157]

2.5.4 Tissue invasion and metastasis

Normal cells in solid tissues maintain their position in the body and generally do not migrate. As a cancer increases, it eventually reaches the membrane encapsulating the organ. Tumour cells secrete enzymes such as matrix metalloproteases (MMPs), which digest the membrane and allow the cancer to invade adjacent tissue. Once through the membrane, cancer cells can access other sites via the blood and lymphatic systems. This migration of cancer cells, or metastasis, is a common characteristic of most cancer deaths.

There is limited evidence for dietary components to influence these late stages of cancer, although in vitro, EGCG, resveratrol, quercetin, curcumin, and genistein can inhibit one or more MMPs. Vitamin C can inhibit MMP production by a number of human cancer cell lines and prevent invasion of these lines in vitro.[158] Vitamin E can inhibit metastasis of pre-established tumours in mouse models of breast cancer.[159]

2.6 Conclusions

Great progress has been made since the mid-1990s in the understanding of the cancer process. Evidence is accumulating that shows or suggests that food and nutrition, and physical activity and associated factors, are important in modification of the cancer process. Moreover, there is increased evidence that specific dietary patterns, foods and drinks, and dietary constituents can and do protect against cancer, not only before the process starts, but also afterwards.

Understanding the mechanisms that control cell structure and function, and so influence the cancer process, will aid not only understanding of cancer as a whole, but also the development of preventive strategies.

CHAPTER 3

Judging the evidence

The task of expert committees responsible for reports such as this is to collect, discuss, and judge scientific evidence, as a basis for recommendations made in the public interest. The purpose of this third introductory chapter is to summarise the process the Panel has used in the five years of its work, in order to ensure that its assessments, judgements, and recommendations made in the chapters that follow are reliable.

As shown in the previous chapters, while cancer is a disease of cells and tissues, the main determinants of many cancers are environmental, which means that most cancers are, at least in theory, preventable. Environmental factors that modify the risk of cancer include food and nutrition, physical activity, and body composition. One purpose of scientific research in this field is to determine which aspects of these factors protect against, and which are causes of, cancers of various sites. Such research is also concerned with which aspects are most important — that is, which have the most powerful or general effects.

Some of the methods used by the Panel responsible for this Report are new. Others are developed from those used elsewhere, including in the previous report. The best evidence that aspects of food, nutrition, physical activity, and body fatness can modify the risk of cancer does not come from any one type of scientific investigation. It comes from a combination of different types of epidemiological and other studies, supported by evidence of plausible biological mechanisms. Such comprehensive evidence has been collected in the form of 20 systematic literature reviews specially commissioned as the basis for this Report, compiled by nine independent centres of scientific excellence, covering 20 cancer sites, the determinants of obesity, and recommendations made by other authoritative reports. These reviews amount to a comprehensive examination of the relevant types of epidemiological and experimental evidence, organised using a common methodology. Their findings, as summarised for and then assessed and judged by the Panel, are shown in Part 2 of this Report. The full systematic literature reviews are contained on the CD included with this Report.

Judgements of the Panel are shown in the form of matrices at the beginning of the chapters of Part 2 of this Report. Two key judgements in these matrices, and in the text, are those of 'convincing' and 'probable'. These denote the Panel's judgements that the evidence of causality — that a factor either decreases or increases the risk of cancer — is strong enough to justify population goals and personal recommendations, which are made in Part 3. The criteria agreed by the Panel for grading the evidence 'convincing', 'probable', or 'limited', or else showing that any substantial effect on the risk of cancer is unlikely, are also specified in this chapter.

Since the mid-1990s, the discipline of epidemiology has placed increasing emphasis on the use of meta-analyses and systematic reviews, both of which have informed the Panel responsible for this Report. Taken together with lines of evidence from other types of study, these provide a reliable basis for judgements and recommendations designed to improve public health.

The task of the Panel, with the supporting Secretariat, has been to commission, summarise, and display a comprehensive range of evidence; to assess and judge this evidence; and to draw conclusions and make recommendations based on this systematic and transparent process. Also see Appendix A.

This chapter details the nature of the science relevant to the work of the Panel. It also summarises the processes developed from initial work done by a Methodology Task Force. Its findings have been a foundation for the work of the Panel. The two most important parts of this process are the systematic literature reviews (SLRs), explained in box 3.4, and the criteria the Panel has agreed for grading the evidence, described in box 3.8. These and other methods have determined the Panel's approach to gathering, summarising, assessing, and judging evidence, and agreeing on population goals and personal recommendations as a basis for the prevention of cancer.

3.1 Epidemiological evidence

Epidemiological research describes and seeks to explain the distribution of health and disease within human populations. The methods used are based mainly on comparative observations made at the level of whole populations, special groups (such as migrants), or individuals within populations. This type of investigation is known as observational. By relating differences in circumstances and behaviour to differences in the incidence of disease, associations are identified that may be causal. In epidemiological studies, an 'exposure' is a factor or condition that may increase or decrease the risk of disease. In this Report, food, nutrition, physical activity, and body composition are the 'exposures' investigated. The methods summarised here and applied to cancer are also used to study and understand other diseases.

3.1.1 Descriptive studies
The most basic information about cancer comes from statistics on cancer incidence and mortality. See chapter 1.2.4,

the introductory passages of the sections of Chapter 7, and box 7.1.1.

The International Agency for Research on Cancer (IARC), a branch of the World Health Organization, compiles international cancer statistics using data from national and regional cancer registries around the world.[1] Cancer incidence rates are usually specified by gender and age. Cancer mortality rates, generally derived from data collected routinely on causes of death, are more widely available than cancer incidence rates.

Descriptive epidemiology informs cancer surveillance programmes, and is a basic tool for determining patterns of cancer, relative rates of cancer and other diseases, and changes in patterns and trends over time. Remarkable changes in the incidence of cancers (for example, the general drop in rates of stomach cancer or the increase in rates of lung cancer in many middle- and low-income countries) provide first lines of evidence pointing to causation due to corresponding changes in environmental circumstances.

Like all types of study, descriptive epidemiology has limitations. Apparent trends in cancer incidence and mortality may be due in part to changes and developments in screening, diagnosis, or treatment. For example, the rapid rise in the recorded incidence of prostate cancer in the USA, the UK, and other higher-income countries is largely due to widespread use of diagnostic techniques that identify early evidence of this cancer.

3.1.2 Ecological studies
Ecological studies are designed to explore relationships between environmental factors and disease amongst populations rather than individuals.

Within the scope of this Report, ecological studies compare relationships between estimated levels of consumption of foods and drinks, levels of physical activity, and degrees of body fatness with rates of cancer for populations. For example, as already mentioned, early observations found impressive correlations between national per capita intake of total dietary fat and rates of breast cancer mortality, mapped across many countries,[2] leading to the hypothesis that relatively high consumption of total fat was an important cause of breast cancer.

The findings of ecological studies, together with those from migrant and laboratory studies (see 3.1.3 and 3.2), were important factors leading to judgements and recom-

Box 3.1 Issues concerning interpretation of the evidence

Interpretation of epidemiological evidence on any and all aspects of foods and drinks, physical activity, body composition, and associated factors, with the risk of cancer, is never simple. General considerations include the following, which need to be taken into account when evidence is assembled and assessed. This emphasises that expert judgement is essential.

Patterns and ranges of intakes. Most studies are carried out in high-income countries. Their findings may have limited application in countries where dietary and physical activity patterns are different. They may also be unrevealing in their own countries if the ranges examined are relatively narrow. Some foods that are important dietary constituents outside high-income countries are often not examined.

Classification. Following from the above, studies usually classify foods and drinks, and physical activity in ways that correspond to the patterns of high-income countries. Their findings may over-emphasise the significance (or insignificance) of foods and drinks commonly consumed in high-income countries, and they may overlook other foods and drinks consumed in other parts of the world. The same points apply to types of physical activity. This may impede understanding, not only in

middle- and low-income countries, but also globally.

Measurement. Many study exposures are difficult to determine and are thus measured imprecisely. It is easier to measure food intakes than intakes of dietary constituents of foods. This can lead to an undue degree of importance being given to studies of aspects of food and nutrition that happen to be more easily measured.

Terminology. For some foods and drinks, and dietary constituents, there are no generally agreed definitions. Examples include 'dietary fibre' and 'processed meat'. Also, some common definitions may disguise real differences: different types of 'dietary fibre' have different biological effects.

Study design. The relative merits of different types of epidemiological study design, and the relative value of epidemiological evidence compared with experimental evidence, are likely to remain to some extent a matter of opinion. The special power of randomised controlled trials (see 3.1.6), most often used to test the effects of dietary constituents as opposed to whole diets, could lead to over-emphasis of the importance of isolated constituents which, within the context of food and diets, may have other effects.

Confounding. A confounder is a factor associated with both the outcome (in this case, cancer) and the exposure being studied, but is not an effect of the exposure. It is never possible from observational studies to eliminate completely the possibility that an evident effect of a constituent, or aspect of a food or drink, is at least in part caused by another factor.

Reporting bias. Studies reliant on self-reporting of dietary intake are prone to systematic bias. People tend to over-report consumption of foods and drinks they believe to be healthy, and under-report foods and drinks they believe to be unhealthy. Under-reporting of energy intake has been shown to be associated with factors such as age, overweight and obesity, perceived body size, and other personal characteristics.[7-14] Allowance for this is an inexact science. Also see 3.3.

Production, preservation, processing, preparation. Studies of foods and drinks, and of food groups, may neglect the effects of methods of production, preservation, processing, and preparation (including cooking). They are also inclined to underestimate the significance of foods and drinks combined in dishes or meals, and as components of whole dietary patterns.

---

mendations made in reports on diet and cancer published in the 1980s.[3-5]

While ecological studies, like other observational studies, may suggest a relationship between a specific environmental factor (such as an aspect of food and nutrition) and disease, the actual causal relationship may be with a different 'confounding' factor, which may or may not be associated with the environmental factor being investigated.[6] The example of total fat consumption and breast cancer is a case in point: total fat consumption, disposable income, and consumption of alcoholic drinks might all correlate with one another, and also with breast cancer. See box 3.1.

Ecological studies are often used to identify associations or trends that warrant further investigation. They have special strengths, particularly when conducted between populations, either internationally, or cross-culturally among different populations within a country. Thus, the contrast in dietary intake between countries is often much larger than the contrast within countries. In addition, average national diets are likely to be more stable over time than the diets of communities, families, or individual people. For most countries, the changes in overall national dietary intakes over a decade or two are relatively small.

3.1.3 Migrant studies
Migrant studies compare cancer rates for migrants, and for their offspring, in their current country of residence, with rates in their country of origin.[16] These studies show that populations migrating between areas with different cancer incidence rates acquire the rates characteristic of their new location for some cancers, often after only one or two generations. This shows that environmental, rather than inherited, factors are primarily responsible for the large differences in cancer rates in different regions and countries (see chapter 1.3).[17] Those diseases for which incidence shifts with migration, such as cancer, are diseases with evidently important environmental causes.

3.1.4 Case-control studies
In case-control studies, individuals diagnosed with a specific type of cancer ('cases') are compared with otherwise similar individuals who have not been diagnosed with cancer ('controls'). The control group is a sample of the population from which the cases arose, and provides an estimate of how the exposures being studied are distributed in that population. Identifying and enrolling appropriate controls is a major challenge in case-control studies.[18-20]

Case-control studies are subject to recall bias, which can occur when participants' reporting of various exposures (dietary intake, medication, physical activity, and so on) is differentially affected by whether they are cases or controls in the study. Selection bias is an increasing problem in high-income countries, where participation rates among both case and control groups may be substantially less than 100 per cent, and where participation may be related (in different ways) to various exposures. However, case-control studies are usually less expensive than cohort studies, and can be completed over shorter periods of time.

A 'nested' case-control study is carried out within an existing cohort study (see 3.1.5). In this type of study, all of the cases in the cohort are compared with a sample of the non-cases. A nested case-control study has the strengths of a cohort study — notably that diet is assessed among study participants prior to the diagnosis of cancer, so avoiding recall bias — but is less expensive to conduct, since only a sample of the non-cases are included in the analysis.

3.1.5 Cohort studies

In prospective cohort studies (usually simply called cohort studies), the diets, body compositions, and/or physical activity levels of a large group (cohort) of people who are assumed to be healthy are assessed, and the group is followed over a period of time. During the follow-up period, some members of the cohort will develop and be diagnosed with cancer, while others will not, and comparisons are then made between these two groups. Because measurements are made before any cancer diagnosis, cohort studies are not subject to recall bias. A single cohort study allows examination of the effects of diet and physical activity on multiple types of cancer and other diseases. Also, in cohort studies, blood and tissue samples are often collected and stored for future analysis. Finally, cohort studies provide the opportunity to obtain repeated assessments of participants' diets at regular intervals, which may improve the dietary assessment.

Cohort studies may need to be very large (up to tens or even hundreds of thousands of participants) to have sufficient statistical power to identify factors that may increase cancer risk by as little as 20 or 30 per cent. Also, meaningful comparisons between cases and non-cases can be made only for factors that vary sufficiently within the cohort.

Cohort studies are expensive, so they have been conducted mostly in high-income countries. The European Prospective Investigation into Cancer and Nutrition (EPIC), started in 1992, is a cohort of more than 520 000 men and women in 10 European countries.[21 22] In the US, large cohorts include the Nurses' Health Study, established in 1976, and the Nurses' Health Study II, established in 1989, each with a cohort of more than 100 000 women.[23-25] Increasing numbers of cohort studies are now being conducted in middle- and low-income countries.

3.1.6 Randomised controlled trials

A randomised controlled trial (RCT) is an experiment in which participants are randomly assigned to groups, often called intervention and control groups, to receive or not receive an experimental intervention. The main use of RCTs has generally been to test the efficacy of drugs and other medical treatments.

In a 'double blind' RCT, neither the participants nor the investigators know to which group (intervention or control) the participant has been assigned. Blinding is used because the knowledge of group assignment might influence study results, but it is usually impossible to achieve with trials involving physical activity, or those investigating foods and drinks in their usual form.

An effective use of RCTs is to test the effects of supplementation with specified doses of dietary micronutrients (as pills or by other means). However, pharmacological doses of supplements are often studied — doses much higher than can be derived from diets — and results may not be directly relevant to dietary intakes of that micronutrient.

Such trials may yield powerful evidence of the effect of a specific dietary constituent. However, they are often conducted as a result of promising epidemiological studies that have shown protective effects of a particular group of foods, and there is always a possibility that the actual active agent or combination of agents in the foods has not been used in the trial. Dietary constituents that are or may be protective when contained within foods may have unexpected effects in isolation, especially at doses higher than those found in normal diets. For example, in the Alpha-Tocopherol, Beta-Carotene Cancer Prevention Trial (ATBC Trial) of male smokers in Finland, high dose beta-carotene supplementation was associated with increased incidence of lung cancer.[26]

RCTs are also used to test interventions designed to change behaviour, including dietary intakes and physical activity. Such trials require a high level of commitment by participants, and learning how to conduct them well is a topic of active investigation.

A unique and important strength of sufficiently large RCTs is that confounding variables, both known and unknown, will on average be distributed equally between the treatment and control groups, and will therefore not bias the study results.

3.1.7 Meta-analysis

Meta-analysis is a method used to combine the results of several studies addressing similar questions. Unless an epidemiological study is sufficiently large, modest but potentially important associations can be missed, simply because of the inadequate statistical power of the individual study. Meta-analysis is used to provide summaries of selected collections of studies.

Study-level meta-analysis provides single estimates of effect using information from multiple studies of the same design. These summary estimates can provide evidence regarding the presence or absence of an association, as well as examining possible dose-response relationships (box 3.2). Meta-analysis, often displayed graphically on a forest plot (box 3.3), can also identify heterogeneity between studies. This heterogeneity can be quantified using a measure called I^2, which ranges from 0 to 100 per cent, and indicates the

Box 3.2 Dose response

'Dose response' is a term derived from pharmacology, where it denotes a change in the effect of a drug according to the dose used. This concept can be applied to any exposure, including food, nutrition, and physical activity. For example, different amounts of food and drink consumed, or of physical activity taken, may lead to a different likelihood of any particular outcome, such as cancer. Such a graded response, or biological gradient, may show that higher exposure leads to increased risk, or to reduced risk, and vice versa.

Dose responses take different forms. The effect may be linear, shown in graphic form as a straight line. There may be a 'threshold' below which there is no effect, but above which there is an effect. This is shown as a horizontal line that inclines once the threshold is reached. Or the effect may be to influence risk one way at both

low and high levels of exposure, but the other way at intermediate levels of exposure, shown as 'J'- or 'U'-shaped curves. In such cases, the exposure is evidently beneficial or harmful only within certain ranges.

Throughout Chapters 4–6, this Report uses two forms of dose-response graph as a means of displaying graded responses. These show the direction and shape of the association, and allow estimates to be made of levels of exposure that may influence risk. In order to combine and quantify study results, the dose-response curves are also presented with the exposure variable displayed per standard unit of increase. The demonstration of a biological gradient adds weight to evidence that an exposure may be causal. Diet and physical activity exposures are continuous variables, but are often reported in discrete

categories. Although this is done for statistical reasons and can make effects easier to detect, the number and location of category boundaries may obscure the true relationship between exposure and the outcome, and non-linear effects of exposure may be missed if insufficient categories are used.

Evidence of dose response is important when framing recommendations. For example, if the evidence for cancer showed no threshold of effect for alcoholic drinks, such that the risk of cancer increased from having any amount of alcoholic drink, however modest, then a recommendation based on the evidence for cancer would be to avoid alcoholic drinks. However, if there is clear evidence of no effect below a certain level of consumption, then the recommendation would differ accordingly. Also see chapter 4.8.

percentage of total variation across studies that is not due to chance. In general, an I^2 of 25 per cent or less indicates low heterogeneity; around 50 per cent indicates moderate heterogeneity; and 75 per cent or more indicates high heterogeneity.[27]

For this Report, RCTs and ecological, cohort, and case-control studies have been the subjects of systematic review, and, when possible (and separately) of study-level meta-analysis. Studies were included in a meta-analysis only when sufficient data were included in the publication. In addition to effect measures and their standard errors (or confidence intervals, see box 3.3), key elements of adequate reporting included the number of people with and without disease for each exposure category, and boundaries of exposure categories.

The SLRs on which the conclusions of this Report are based include original study-level meta-analyses undertaken by the independent centres of scientific excellence. The Panel considered all studies identified in the SLR, not just the results of the meta-analyses. Full details of the methods used for the meta-analyses are contained in the SLR specification manual. The full SLRs and the manual are contained on the CD included with this Report. Also see box 3.4.

Pooled analysis is a type of meta-analysis where original individual-level data from various published epidemiological studies of the same type — usually prospective cohort studies — are combined and reanalysed. The combination of data from multiple studies creates a larger data set and increased statistical power. Published studies from pooling projects, in addition to the SLR study-level results generated specifically for this Report, were taken into account by the Panel in making its assessments and judgements.

3.2 Experimental evidence

Epidemiological studies all have strengths and limitations. So do laboratory and mechanistic studies; their main strength is control. The environment of these research studies is defined by chosen experimental conditions: precise manipulations can be made and relatively exact measures taken. Occasionally the test participant is a human volunteer, but usually these studies are conducted in animals (in vivo) or using human or animal cells grown in the laboratory (in vitro).

Rodents (usually rats or mice) are the most commonly used animals in laboratory experiments. Their relatively short lifespan provides comparatively fast results in cancer studies, and they offer a 'whole body system' suited to a wide variety of tests. Rodent studies can show how nutrients and other compounds might affect the cancer process. But it is known that some interventions that affect rodents do not affect humans, or do not affect them in the same ways or to the same degrees, and vice versa. Also, experiments on animals may be highly artificial, using special breeds of rodents initially given massive doses of carcinogenic agents, and then fed nutrients or other substances at levels far higher than humans would normally consume, or could ethically be given.

Human or animal cells, sometimes derived from particular cancers, can be grown in vitro in the laboratory and used in experiments to help researchers understand mechanisms that may lead to the development of cancer. The Panel's decision on what types of experimental studies were admissible as evidence for this Report is summarised in box 3.5.

3.2.1 Human feeding studies

Human volunteers can be studied in a controlled environment, such as within a metabolic unit, where their diets and

Box 3.3	Forest plots

The graphic device known as a 'forest plot' is the usual method of presenting the results of meta-analysis of a number of studies. In the forest plot below, studies are presented that examine the relationship between alcoholic drinks and oesophageal cancer. This plot is also shown as figure 4.8.5.

This plot shows 1 cohort study and 23 estimates from 20 case-control studies. The horizontal axis of the plot shows the relative risk (RR) and is bisected by the vertical axis, which represents 'no difference in effect on risk' between the exposure categories that are compared (the RR is 1.00). Also see 3.4.3.

The squares represent the results of each individual study. Each square is centred on the point estimate of the RR for that study. The point estimate is the extent to which any exposure (in this case, alcoholic drinks) is associated with the risk of cancer (in this case, of the oesophagus). The line running through the squares represents the 95 per cent confidence interval (CI) of the estimate. Where no line is apparent, the CI falls within the square. The CI is an indication of how much random error underlies the point estimate; it does not take into account confounding and other forms of systematic bias.[15] A confidence level of 95 per cent indicates a 95 per cent probability that the true population value falls within the CI.[28]

When the CI does not cross the vertical axis representing 'no difference', the estimate is considered statistically significant. Looking at the example above, the value

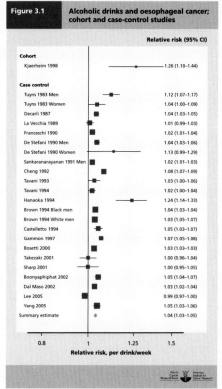

Figure 3.1 Alcoholic drinks and oesophageal cancer; cohort and case-control studies

Relative risk (95% CI)

Cohort	
Kjaerheim 1998	1.26 (1.10–1.44)
Case control	
Tuyns 1983 Men	1.12 (1.07–1.17)
Tuyns 1983 Women	1.04 (1.00–1.09)
Decarli 1987	1.04 (1.03–1.05)
La Vecchia 1989	1.01 (0.99–1.03)
Franceschi 1990	1.02 (1.01–1.04)
De Stefani 1990 Men	1.04 (1.03–1.06)
De Stefani 1990 Women	1.13 (0.99–1.29)
Sankaranarayanan 1991 Men	1.02 (1.01–1.03)
Cheng 1992	1.08 (1.07–1.09)
Tavani 1993	1.03 (1.00–1.06)
Tavani 1994	1.02 (1.00–1.04)
Hanaoka 1994	1.24 (1.14–1.33)
Brown 1994 Black men	1.04 (1.03–1.04)
Brown 1994 White men	1.03 (1.05–1.07)
Castelletto 1994	1.05 (1.03–1.07)
Gammon 1997	1.07 (1.05–1.08)
Bosetti 2000	1.03 (1.03–1.03)
Takezaki 2001	1.00 (0.96–1.04)
Sharp 2001	1.00 (0.95–1.05)
Boonyaphiphat 2002	1.05 (1.04–1.07)
Dal Maso 2002	1.03 (1.02–1.04)
Lee 2005	0.99 (0.97–1.00)
Yang 2005	1.05 (1.03–1.06)
Summary estimate	1.04 (1.03–1.05)

Relative risk, per drink/week

of meta-analysis is demonstrated: of the 20 case-control studies, 6 are non-significant or only marginally so, of which 1 suggests a protective effect (that is, it has an RR of less than 1.00). But taken together, as shown by the summary diamond, an overall significant effect, consistent with a judgement that alcoholic drinks are a cause of oesophageal cancer, is shown.

There is only one cohort study shown on the forest plot, and it has a wide CI, but the estimate is statistically significant and consistent with results from the case-control studies.

The size of each square on the plot represents each study's calculated weight (influence) on the combined (summary) estimate (the diamond). The size of the square is calculated taking a number of factors into account, such as the number of people in the study, and the event rate (here, the rate of oesophageal cancer occurrence). The diamond summarises the meta-analysis. The width of the diamond represents the 95 per cent CI of the overall estimate. Unless indicated otherwise, random effects models, which do not assume that the links between exposure and outcome are the same in different studies, were used to generate the forest plots presented in this Report. The Panel's judgement for this particular example is given in chapter 4.8.5. The forest plots presented in this Report do not contain all of the studies identified in the SLRs. Sometimes, more studies could be included in a comparison between those at the highest levels compared with the lowest levels of exposure in different studies. This can give an indication as to whether or not there is an association between exposure and outcome. However, because the actual levels of exposure vary between studies, this cannot give a quantified summary estimate of effect. The Panel discussed all studies identified, not just those included in a meta-analysis.

---

activity levels can be highly regulated and measured. In some studies, subjects live at the metabolic unit for short periods of time, eating only foods and meals provided as part of the study. Since the nutrient composition of such diets can be controlled and manipulated, investigators can study the effects of various changes in nutrient intakes on factors such as hormone levels or cell proliferation assays, which may be important predictors of cancer or other diseases. These are intermediate markers, however, and relating the results to cancer occurrence may be problematic.

3.2.2 Live animal models

Laboratory animals can be used to test the effects of food, nutrition, and physical activity on the development of cancer. Human genes can be added to animals' DNA (creating transgenic animal models) or key genes can be removed (creating 'knockout' animal models) to address specific research

questions. Often the animals have tumours produced by irradiation, viruses, chemicals, or other carcinogens, or they may be genetically prone to develop cancer. The effect of dietary or other interventions on the prevention or progression of such tumours is then investigated.

As indicated in 3.2, the strength of these studies is the tight control of experimental conditions. Their limitations are their artificiality and the fact that no effect on rodents, however unequivocal, can be assumed to apply to humans. Rather like the results of population ecological studies, results from animal studies provide first lines of evidence that may prompt more persuasive research; they can also corroborate such findings.

3.2.3 In vitro studies

In vitro studies are conducted using cells or other test systems. Human cells, animal cells, mechanistic test systems,

Box 3.4	Systematic literature reviews

The main basis for the Panel's work in coming to judgement on the causal relationships between food, nutrition, physical activity, and cancer is a series of 20 specially commissioned systematic literature reviews (SLRs). These have all been conducted according to a common, detailed specification, following recommendations made by the Methodology Task Force, which completed its work before the Panel's first meeting. The SLRs form the main evidence basis for the assessments and judgements made by the Panel in Part 2 of this Report, on which the Panel's population goals and personal recommendations in Part 3 are based.

This approach differs from that used to prepare most other expert reports. Previously, expert reports concerned with the prevention of disease, and other topics, have relied on less formal methods to collect and assess relevant literature. Until the 1980s, most such reports were assembled by members of panels of scientists who, assisted by secretariats, wrote drafts of chapters themselves using their own knowledge, either with or without additional research. The panel then reviewed the draft report until consensus was achieved. In some cases, report authors took total responsibility for assembling and judging the evidence. In the 1990s, more ambitious reports placed greater emphasis on secretariats, which tended to take more responsibility for drafting the report, and for some original research, as directed by the panel. More recently, panels have sometimes been informed by 'narrative reviews' commissioned from specialists and prepared independently from the panel process. Such reviews are usually written from the specialists' existing knowledge, and form background 'substrate' for the reports. Narrative reviews may be published separately.[29]

Current practice, when resources allow, is to separate the process of collecting and displaying evidence from that of discussing and judging evidence. Evidence is collected systematically, after agreeing criteria for inclusion or exclusion for review. As well as reducing possible bias, this is a more comprehensive and transparent approach. This process was used by the previous report, which at the time of its publication was the most comprehensive in its and allied fields. This current Report has made a step-change in this process, by commissioning independent SLRs, and making full use of electronic resources.

The Panel, in commissioning the SLRs and supplementary work, decided to require evidence from all relevant epidemiological and experimental studies, together with biological findings. The alternative approach would have been to agree a hierarchy of epidemiological evidence, perhaps with one study type given pre-eminent importance. Instead, while allowing for some types of epidemiological study being more or less prone to bias than others, the Panel has based its conclusions and judgements on evidence accumulated from different types of study. For the Panel to be convinced that a relationship between an exposure and cancer is causal, or that it is probably causal, consistent evidence from different types of study was required, with the exception of randomised controlled trials.

The teams responsible for producing the SLRs gathered relevant studies in a common, systematic fashion, using a protocol designed to limit the potential for bias in deciding which evidence should be included or excluded from analysis.

The first stage of the SLRs was a comprehensive search of the scientific literature and other sources catalogued on electronic databases, using all relevant keywords

and terms. The papers identified were assessed for relevance using reproducible criteria. Study characteristics and results were extracted and recorded. Data from different studies were combined and analysed, using meta-analysis when appropriate. Key features of selected studies are presented in graphic form in Chapters 4–6 and 8, to aid comparison and quality assessment. Existing SLRs were also identified to ensure, as far as possible, that all relevant papers were included.

An important aspect of an SLR is that all stages of searching, selection, assessment, and analysis are prespecified, objective, reproducible, openly documented, and subject to peer review at critical stages. As stated, full details of the approach taken can be found in the SLR specification manual contained on the CD included with this Report (together with the SLRs).

The SLRs included evidence published up to the end of 2005, and the Panel's conclusions are based on these SLRs. To ensure that the Panel's recommendations, which are derived from their conclusions and judgements, take into account developing evidence, a further review of studies published during 2006 was conducted. This review was more limited than the full SLRs: it was confined to exposures that had been judged 'convincing', 'probable', 'substantial effect on risk unlikely', and 'limited–suggestive', based on the SLRs. (See box 3.8 for an explanation of these terms.) At this second review stage, no further meta-analyses were performed and a review of study quality was not included. For these reasons, the results of this 2006 review have been noted but have not been used to alter the Panel's judgements based on the full SLRs. A further process has been established for a continuous review of evidence published since 2006, after publication of this Report.

and bacterial systems can be used.

Cell cultures can be primary, where tissue (such as a tumour biopsy) is taken directly from humans or animals and then cultured; or secondary, where the original cells are cultured a number of times. Such cell lines are commonly used in laboratory research, and can become immortal — cultured again and again. The cells or tissues are subjected to potential carcinogens, and then markers of damage are measured.

Conducting studies in vitro has two main advantages. First, specific, well defined interventions can be tested; and second, intracellular mechanisms can be examined. However, these studies do not allow the study of integrated systems, such as how organs or the whole body responds to the

interventions. Therefore extrapolation of results to humans is limited.

3.2.4 Biological pathways

Epidemiological and experimental evidence indicating a causal association between an aspect of diet and cancer is strengthened when there is evidence of a plausible biological pathway or mechanism by which the cancer process may be modified. *The Panel agreed* that simply identifying such plausible mechanisms is not sufficient evidence for a causal relationship; but it also agreed that the case for a causal relationship is strengthened when there is evidence of biological plausibility.

Narrative reviews of experimental studies and of evidence of plausible biological mechanisms were included in the SLRs that inform this Report. Summaries of these SLRs are presented in Part 2, Chapters 4–10. Also see box 3.4.

3.3 Methods of assessment

Some exposures are easier to measure than others. Thus, it is relatively easy to assess the impact of tobacco smoking and exposure to tobacco on cancer risk. Although tobacco smoke is a mixture of many chemicals, and its interactions with the body are complex, tobacco can be considered a single exposure.

By contrast, diets are multidimensional exposures and in free-living populations cannot be measured with complete accuracy. Moreover, the foods and drinks people consume every day contain thousands of constituents, some well known, others unknown and unmeasured. The relationships between food, nutrition, physical activity, and health and disease are complex and difficult to untangle. The presence or absence of effect modification (box 3.6) can create additional challenges.

3.3.1 Foods, drinks, and nutrients

People's dietary intake varies from day to day and over the course of their lives. There are interrelationships between food components, between foods in whole diets, and between diets and other behavioural characteristics such as physical activity or smoking. There are several methods for assessing food and drink consumption, all with their own weaknesses and strengths.

3.3.1.1 Dietary assessment methods

Food intakes can be measured for populations, groups, or individuals. The most commonly used techniques for assessing food and drink consumption are diet histories, 24-hour dietary recalls, food frequency questionnaires, and food diary or food record methods. Most of the studies included in this Report used dietary assessment data from individuals, recorded using food frequency questionnaires.

Diet histories take the form of unstructured enquiries, more useful in clinical settings than in research studies. Dietary recalls may use structured or unstructured methods, and are often administered many times over the course of a study. In a 24-hour dietary recall, a record is made of everything a person can recall eating or drinking over the previous 24 hours. Automated systems for collecting and analysing dietary recalls have been developed, which facilitate the use of this method of assessment in large studies.[32]

Food frequency questionnaires collect information on food consumption patterns, typically over the past year. A record is made of the frequency of consumption of perhaps 100 to 150 items, and often includes information on serving sizes. Food frequency questionnaires may be designed to gain detailed information about specific aspects of diets, such as intakes of fats or dietary fibre, leaving other components less well characterised. A questionnaire for whole diets cannot adequately capture the full variety and composition of individual diets without becoming unwieldy. Food frequency questionnaires are inexpensive, however, and are practical for use in large-scale epidemiological studies.

Food diary or food record methods rely on the participants in the study recording everything they eat and drink over the course of one or more days. Participants may be asked to estimate portion sizes, or weigh foods and drinks.

All dietary assessment methods that rely on self-reporting are subject to measurement error. Further errors are introduced by the conversion of food data to nutrient data, using tables of the chemical composition of foods, which give average nutrient contents for defined foods. This implicitly assumes that all participants eat foods that have the same standard composition and portion size. But in reality, food composition varies widely, depending on soil quality,

---

Box 3.5	**Experimental findings**

The Panel agreed a 'hierarchy of robustness' recommended by the Methodology Task Force, which completed its work before the Panel's first meeting. The 'hierarchy of robustness' was designed to determine which types of human and animal experimental study are likely to be most applicable to human cancer. This was done for practical and scientific reasons. The body of experimental literature is very much larger than the body of epidemiological literature, and an exhaustive systematic review of this literature would have been impractical. Also, most experimental work, such as that conducted as a guide to toxicological regulations, either has no evident relevance to the work of the Panel, or else would be unlikely to sig-nificantly influence judgements derived from consideration of the collective weight of evidence from all other types of study.

For these reasons, eight types of experimental evidence were identified and split into three classes:

Class 1
- In vivo data from studies in human volunteers (controlled human feeding studies).
- In vivo data from studies using genetically modified animal models related to human cancer (such as gene knockout or transgenic mouse models).
- In vivo data from studies using rodent cancer models designed to investigate modifiers of the cancer process.

Class 2
- In vitro data from studies using human cells validated with an in vivo model; for example, a transgenic model.
- In vitro data from studies using primary human cells.
- In vitro data from studies using human cell lines.

Class 3
- In vitro data from studies on animal cells.
- Data from mechanistic test systems; for example, isolated enzymes or genes.

For the systematic literature reviews in this Report, only class 1 evidence was reviewed. Illustrative evidence from in vitro studies is included only in Chapter 2.

| Box 3.6 | **Effect modification** |

Effect modification (or effect-measure modification) occurs when a measure of effect for an exposure changes over levels of another variable (the modifier).[30] Effect modifiers can sometimes even change the direction of an effect. For example, a pooled analysis of seven cohort studies found an association between body fatness and decreased risk of breast cancer in premenopausal women, but with increased risk in postmenopausal women.[31] In this case, menopausal status modifies the effect of body fatness on breast cancer risk.

harvesting conditions, animal feed, storage, and food processing, for example. Furthermore, food tables can be incomplete: for instance, they may not include information on phytochemical or fatty acid levels in foods. In many countries, there may be no records of the composition of traditional and indigenous foods.

Multiple-day food records or 24-hour dietary recalls have been used as reference instruments to check the validity of food frequency questionnaires.[33 34] However, studies using biomarkers (see 3.3.1.2) have shown that food record and recall methods are also liable to measurement error, and that these errors are correlated with errors from food frequency data. This means that the use of food record or recall methods to validate food frequency data results in an overestimation of the validity of the food frequency data.[35-38]

Often, estimated intakes of macro- and micronutrients are adjusted for energy intake (box 3.7).

3.3.1.2 Biomarkers

'Recovery' biomarkers, such as doubly labelled water or 24-hour urinary nitrogen excretion, can be used to assess the accuracy of various dietary assessment methods. The doubly labelled water test accurately measures a person's total energy expenditure, which equals energy intake when a person is in energy balance.[39] Urinary nitrogen excretion is used as a biomarker of protein consumption.[40] Studies using these recovery biomarkers suggest that measurement errors from all types of dietary assessment instruments are larger than previously appreciated.[35 38 41]

'Concentration' biomarkers, such as blood levels of fatty acids or vitamins, can be used to indirectly estimate dietary intake of these compounds. However, blood levels are determined not only by a person's intake of the compound, but also by factors such as the compound's bioavailability and excretion, intakes of other dietary components, personal characteristics such as smoking, and individual variation in metabolism. These determinants — and therefore the relations between true intakes and the biomarkers — vary among people, and this can bias observed diet–cancer associations.[9]

For some compounds, such as selenium, biomarkers are a more accurate indicator of dietary intakes than data from food frequency questionnaires.[42 43] Many studies examine concentration biomarkers as indirect proxies for intake, and there is growing interest in combining these data with results from self-report dietary assessment instruments.

3.3.2 Nutrition status

Nutrition status is not simply a function of dietary intake. It includes energy and nutrient intakes, and also body nutrient stores and body composition, all of which can be studied at various levels of complexity. Nutrition status cannot be completely measured by any one method, and judging which methods are most useful is an important aspect of the science in this field.

Some aspects of nutrition status can be assessed relatively accurately. These include body fatness and measurements of weight and height at birth, during growth, and in adulthood.

Nutrition status is affected by other biological and behavioural factors, and also by social and environmental factors. Social factors include economic and political drivers of food supplies, availability of food, and tradition and culture.

3.3.3 Physical activity

Study of the effects of physical activity on health requires reliable and valid measurements of physical activity in whatever setting it occurs — occupational, household, transport, and recreational — and also of frequency, duration, and intensity. Effects of physical activity are not just a function of total overall energy expenditure. A person may expend the same amount of energy during a short period of intense exercise or in a longer period of moderate activity, but the physiological effects may be different. Also see Chapter 5.

Assessments of physical activity may use objective biochemical, physiological, or other methods, but these are expensive and not commonly used in large studies. Epidemiological studies usually rely on self-completed questionnaires. These vary in the duration and type of physical activity, the length and detail of the questionnaire, and how the physical activity measures are calculated.

As with food questionnaires, physical activity questionnaires have limitations. Activities may be over-reported when participants overestimate their recreational activity, for example, or under-reported, such as when participants do not take account of everyday activities, such as walking around their home or office. Many questionnaires ask only about occupational activity or recreational activity, and therefore do not provide a comprehensive account of people's total physical activity.

Results from questionnaires are commonly reported in terms of energy expenditure. This is usually done by assigning an 'energy cost' (derived from published guides) to the energy value of various activities, and multiplying this by the duration and frequency of the activity. But there are large variations in the energy values of different activities depending on age, gender, body mass, skill, and level of fitness; these can lead to significant errors in estimates.

3.3.4 Cancer outcomes

In studies of food, nutrition, physical activity, and cancer, accurate identification of cancer occurrence is as important as making accurate measures of food and drink consumption, and of physical activity. In most epidemiological studies, data from cancer registries are used, or else participants report whether they have been diagnosed as having cancer.

Studies may also require participants to undergo clinical examination, or provide tissue biopsy samples.

The duration of a study can also affect whether the full effects of exposures are identified. Relatively short-term prospective studies may miss any late effects on cancers. This is one reason why results from studies with long-term follow-up periods are particularly valuable.

Population-based cancer registries collect cancer incidence and mortality data for the areas they serve, and produce cancer registers.

In the US, the Surveillance, Epidemiology, and End Results (SEER) programme collects population-based data on newly diagnosed cancers from registries that cover approximately 23 per cent of the US population.[49] The European Network of Cancer Registries represents population-based cancer registries in Europe.[50] Population-based registries are becoming increasingly available in middle- and low-income countries. In total, 57 countries and 186 cancer registries are represented in Volume VIII of the *Cancer Incidence in Five Continents* series published by IARC.[1] Also see box 1.2.

Cancer incidence data are coded in a standardised way, using International Classification of Disease (ICD) codes that have been established for oncology.[51] These 10-digit codes specify the site of origin of the tumour (topography), the tumour or cell type (morphology), the behaviour of the tumour (malignant, benign, or in situ), and the tumour grade or degree of differentiation.

In addition to providing cancer incidence and mortality statistics, cancer registries are used by researchers to identify people who are eligible to enrol in a case-control study, or to collect information on cancer diagnosis relating to people who are enrolled in a cohort study.

3.4 Causation and risk

One of the Panel's tasks has been to devise a transparent and objective method that enables evidence of relationships between diet, physical activity, body fatness, and associated factors, and cancer of one or more sites, to be judged as causal, with varying degrees of confidence.

3.4.1 Inferring causation

The Panel endorses the view of the panel responsible for the previous report, that causal relationships between food and nutrition, and physical activity can be confidently inferred when epidemiological evidence, and experimental and other biological findings, are consistent, unbiased, strong, graded, coherent, repeated, and plausible. Individually, none of these factors is likely to be sufficient to infer a causal relationship with confidence. Also, individual relationships may be deficient in various respects, but collectively can still be judged as causal because of their cumulative weight.

Many types of evidence can contribute to causal inference. However strong the evidence from any single study, it will rarely justify a conclusion of causality. Increasing 'survivability' of an observed relationship, when supported by further studies, or which produces corroborative evidence in other categories, as listed above, strengthens the evidence for a causal relationship.[52] [53]

With regard to food and nutrition, and physical activity, single exposures are unlikely to act alone to cause or prevent cancer. In general, many factors act together as contributory or component causes, forming a complete causal process. Component causes can interact biologically, even when exerting their effects at different times.[30]

| Box 3.7 | **Energy adjustment** |

One of the basic principles in controlled human and animal feeding experiments to evaluate the effect of a specific dietary factor is that the diets should be isocaloric (i.e., total energy intake is the same in both groups). This is because differences in energy intake between two groups would cause one group to gain or lose more weight than the other. The effects of the dietary factor being investigated could not then be distinguished from the effects of changes in weight. This is important, because differences in weight themselves may have different physiological effects.

In epidemiological studies, there are similar reasons to conduct isocaloric analyses. These use statistical methods to 'adjust' intakes of the dietary factor under study for total energy intake. The rationale for energy-adjusted intakes is that the absolute intake of a nutrient is a function of two factors: first, the total amount of food consumed, represented by total energy intake; and second, the composition of

diets. The total amount of food consumed is determined primarily by body size and physical activity.

Body size and physical activity are of interest in their own right, but their effects need to be disentangled from the effects of a specific nutrient. This can be done by using energy-adjusted nutrient intakes. Expressed another way, studies designed to change the intake of a specific nutrient usually should do so by changing the composition of diets rather than total energy intake. Epidemiological studies therefore should adjust for energy and not rely on absolute intakes, which reflect both dietary composition and variation in total energy intake due to differences in body size and physical activity.

The best method to adjust for total energy intake has been a matter of considerable discussion.[44-48] The two basic approaches are to use the nutrient density (for example, expressing intake per unit of energy or, for macronutrients, as a per-

centage of total energy) or regression analysis to calculate nutrient residuals. In an epidemiological analysis, the nutrient density does not adequately adjust for total energy intake if energy intake itself is associated with disease risk. In this case, total energy intake must be added as a separate term to the model. Another method, that of 'energy partition', has been used in some studies, but this is not an 'isocaloric' analysis and thus does not control for total energy intake.

An additional advantage of energy-adjusted nutrient intakes is that they are often measured with less error than absolute nutrient intakes. This is because over- or under-reporting of specific nutrients tends to be strongly correlated with over- or under-reporting of total energy intake, especially for macronutrients, being calculated from the same foods. These errors are highly correlated, so tend to cancel each other when calculating nutrient densities or energy-adjusted intakes.

3.4.2 The 'portfolio' approach

Many different types of study, all of which have strengths and weaknesses, investigate links between food, nutrition, physical activity, and cancer. Persuasive evidence comes from different types of epidemiological study, supported by experimental findings that indicate a relevant biological mechanism.

The Panel's judgements, presented in Part 2 of this Report, are based on its assessment of the evidence available in the scientific literature, with due consideration given to the advantages and disadvantages of each type of study design, and to the quality of individual studies. An inclusive or 'portfolio' approach has been taken, recognising the relative strengths and weaknesses of different types of study, but in which no single type of study design is given pre-eminence. In general, the strongest evidence comes from consistent findings from different types of studies, preferably also in diverse populations.

3.4.3 Quantification of risk

Quantification of the risk of any disease is an essential basis for public health policy planning. It also guides people in making their own decisions about how they lead their lives. It is not enough to know that the risk of cancer is affected by diet. It is also important to know by how much. For example, if consumption of alcohol increases the risk of breast cancer, and diets high in vegetables decrease the risk of various cancers, to what extent may the incidence of cancer on a population basis be affected by these factors? And on a personal level, how can people best judge how their current diets and ways of life, and any changes they might want to make, are likely to affect their own risk of cancer? Quantifying risk helps to answer such questions.

The strength of a relationship between any risk factor and the occurrence of disease is commonly expressed in terms of relative risk (RR). In cohort studies, this is the ratio of risk (or incidence) of a disease among people with a particular characteristic (say, high consumption of red meat) to that among people without that characteristic (in this example, low or no consumption of red meat). In case-control studies, the odds ratio is used, which is the ratio of the odds of exposure among cases to the odds of exposure among controls. Relative risks below 1.0 imply a protective effect: so a relative risk of 0.5 for high compared with low vegetable consumption implies a halving of risk. Relative risks above 1.0 indicate an increased risk.

Absolute risk is also important. Small RR values, when consistent, are important when the number of people affected is large. A large RR of a rare type of cancer amounts to only a small absolute risk, which may reasonably be considered not significant, either by public health planners or by individuals assessing their own choices. By contrast, a small RR may amount to a large number of cases for a common type of cancer. For example, an increased risk of 10 per cent implied by a RR of 1.10 amounts to many extra cases of colorectal and breast cancer in Europe and North America, where these cancers are common. Assessment of small RRs depends on the size and quality of the studies in which such risks are identified. Small RRs may

amount to strong evidence if consistently found in large, well designed studies.

3.5 Coming to judgement

A crucial part of the process that has informed this Report is the methods used by the Panel in judging whether the evidence that a relationship between aspects of food, nutrition, physical activity, and body fatness, and cancers of the sites specified, is or may be causal. The need for evidence from different types of study and the characteristics looked for in such studies have been outlined already. Here, the precise methods used by the Panel are explained.

The previous report broke new ground in a number of respects. One was to display panel judgements in the form of matrices within which panel judgements on causal relationships, of different degrees of confidence, were shown, and repeated in the text of the report. This method has been adapted in other reports.[29] Another was the specification of criteria guiding these judgements. The previous report also used explicit statements explaining why, on occasion, the panel had made judgements that did not obviously derive from the evidence as presented. One general principle was that of transparency. Readers and users of the previous report have been able to follow its reasoning, to challenge any judgements that might seem questionable, and to modify or reinforce judgements in the light of further and better evidence.

The Panel responsible for this Report decided to adapt those innovative approaches, and use them as the basis for its work. Some of the judgements made in this Report are different from those based on the evidence available a decade previously, while others confirm or strengthen previous judgements.

3.5.1 The matrix approach

An example of a matrix used in this Report is shown in figure 3.1. This particular matrix displays the Panel's judgements on the likelihood that physical activity modifies the risk of cancers of specified sites. This matrix is used here as an example, to explain the nature of the matrices displayed in all chapters in Part 2 of this Report. This matrix and its judgements are discussed fully in Chapter 5.

The title of the matrix is self-explanatory. In this and other cases, the introductory words are important: here, the footnote specifies that the physical activity referred to is of all types.

The matrices display the Panel's judgements on whether particular aspects of food and nutrition, physical activity, and body composition do or may modify (or not modify) the risk of cancers of specific sites. The matrices are of course shorthand, and the entries cannot convey all nuances. Necessary clarifications and qualifications are stated in footnotes to the matrices.

Matrix entries themselves need to be explained. For example, an entry 'fruits' or 'foods containing dietary fibre' in a matrix column headed 'decreases risk' means that the Panel has judged that these foods are or may be protective against

PHYSICAL ACTIVITY, AND THE RISK OF CANCER

In the judgement of the Panel, physical activity[1] modifies the risk of the following cancers. Judgements are graded according to the strength of the evidence.

	DECREASES RISK	INCREASES RISK
Convincing	**Colon[2]**	
Probable	**Breast (postmenopause) Endometrium**	
Limited — suggestive	Lung Pancreas Breast (premenopause)	
Substantial effect on risk unlikely	None identified	

1 Physical activity of all types: occupational, household, transport, and recreational.
2 Much of the evidence reviewed grouped colon cancer and rectal cancer together as 'colorectal' cancer. *The Panel judges* that the evidence is stronger for colon than for rectum.

For an explanation of the terms used in the matrix, please see chapter 3.5.1, the text of this chapter, and the glossary.

World Cancer Research Fund   American Institute for Cancer Research

Figure 3.1 Example of a matrix

the cancer specified. The judgements are derived from analysis of studies in which relatively high intakes of (in this example) fruits and foods containing dietary fibre are compared with relatively low intakes. The same point applies to matrix entries 'physical activity' and 'body fatness' in columns headed 'decreases risk' and 'increases risk', respectively, which are derived from analysis of studies of people whose physical activity levels or degree of body fatness is relatively high compared with people whose physical activity levels or degree of body fatness is relatively low.

In some cases, analysis may show that any effect begins or ends, or is less apparent, below or above evident 'thresholds'. For example, it has been thought that alcoholic drinks increase the risk of some cancers only above certain levels of consumption. Such amounts would be specified in a footnote to the relevant matrices, and could be reflected in Panel recommendations. When matrices include no such footnotes, this is because no lower or upper threshold of effect has been identified. In such cases, matrix entries showing or suggesting a causal association should be taken to mean that the effect is across the whole range of dietary intake, amounts of physical activity, or degrees of body fatness found in the studies analysed. The implications of the nature of the dose-response relationships for recommendations are further discussed in Chapter 12, in Part 3 of this Report.

3.5.2 Levels and types of judgement

The top half of the matrix in figure 3.1 shows that the evidence of causality, either of decreased risk or increased

risk, is judged to be convincing, or else probably causal. A judgement of 'convincing' in turn generally justifies a recommendation designed to inform policies and programmes designed to prevent cancer. A judgement of 'probable' also normally justifies a recommendation. So in the case of the matrix shown, it follows that the Panel would make a recommendation on physical activity designed to reduce the risk of cancer.

The top two rows of the matrix are separated from the row below, which shows judgements that the evidence is too limited, for a variety of reasons (see 3.5.5), to conclude that a relationship is causal, but that there are enough data to suggest that such a relationship might exist. Normally, a judgement of 'limited — suggestive' does not justify any recommendation. The matrices used in Chapter 7 also include a row showing judgements where the evidence is so limited (again for a variety of reasons) that no judgement can be made whether any association exists or not. For this reason, such judgements of 'limited — no conclusion' do not indicate whether the evidence is in the direction of decreasing or increasing risk. The final, bottom row of the matrix, 'substantial effect on risk unlikely', shows judgements for which the evidence, equivalent to a judgement of 'convincing' or 'probable', shows that no causal relationship is likely to exist.

Terms used in the text and matrices to refer to foods and drinks, physical activity, body fatness, and other factors are necessarily shorthand. Thus, in chapter 4.2, the matrix displays judgements that 'non-starchy vegetables' probably protect against a number of cancers. The matrix in chapter 4.8 displays judgements that the evidence that 'alcoholic drinks' cause a number of cancers is convincing. What is meant by 'non-starchy vegetables' and by 'alcoholic drinks' is defined in the text of these sections.

Further, when 'non-starchy vegetables' is used as a matrix entry and contained in Panel judgements, it means 'relatively high consumption of non-starchy vegetables and/or foods containing them'. The same point applies to many other matrix entries and also to the accompanying text.

Within all matrix cells, exposures are listed in the order of the contents of the Report. There are a number of cancer sites where a substantial number of related exposures meet the criteria for matrix entry. The Panel has judged that it is often appropriate to aggregate such exposures. For example, if both 'alcoholic drinks' and 'wine' are judged as exposures that probably increase the risk of a type of cancer, then only 'alcoholic drinks' will appear in the matrix for that cancer site.

The matrices used in this Report differ from those used in the previous report in a number of respects. The previous report used categories of 'possible' and 'insufficient' defined differently from the categories of 'limited — suggestive' and 'limited — no conclusion' used here. Also, the previous report allowed for different weights of evidence for no causal relationship, whereas this Report includes just the one judgement of 'substantial effect on risk unlikely'. The judgements of 'convincing' and 'probable', both agreed to be a sufficient basis for recommendations, are common to both reports, although the criteria allowing such judgements have been refined for this Report (see 3.5.5).

Box 3.8   Criteria for grading evidence

This box lists the criteria finally agreed by the Panel that were necessary to support the judgements shown in the matrices and text of the Part 2 chapters. The grades shown here are 'convincing', 'probable', 'limited — suggestive', 'limited — no conclusion', and 'substantial effect on risk unlikely'. In effect, the criteria define these terms.

Convincing

These criteria are for evidence strong enough to support a judgement of a convincing causal relationship, which justifies goals and recommendations designed to reduce the incidence of cancer.

A convincing relationship should be robust enough to be highly unlikely to be modified in the foreseeable future as new evidence accumulates. All of the following were generally required:

- Evidence from more than one study type.
- Evidence from at least two independent cohort studies.
- No substantial unexplained heterogeneity within or between study types or in different populations relating to the presence or absence of an association, or direction of effect.
- Good quality studies to exclude with confidence the possibility that the observed association results from random or systematic error, including confounding, measurement error, and selection bias.
- Presence of a plausible biological gradient ('dose response') in the association. Such a gradient need not be linear or even in the same direction across the different levels of exposure,

so long as this can be explained plausibly.
- Strong and plausible experimental evidence, either from human studies or relevant animal models, that typical human exposures can lead to relevant cancer outcomes.

Probable

These criteria are for evidence strong enough to support a judgement of a probable causal relationship, which would generally justify goals and recommendations designed to reduce the incidence of cancer.

All the following were generally required:

- Evidence from at least two independent cohort studies, or at least five case-control studies.
- No substantial unexplained heterogeneity between or within study types in the presence or absence of an association, or direction of effect.
- Good quality studies to exclude with confidence the possibility that the observed association results from random or systematic error, including confounding, measurement error, and selection bias.
- Evidence for biological plausibility.

Limited — suggestive

These criteria are for evidence that is too limited to permit a probable or convincing causal judgement, but where there is evidence suggestive of a direction of effect. The evidence may have methodological flaws, or be limited in amount, but shows a generally consistent direction of effect. This almost always does not justify recom-

mendations designed to reduce the incidence of cancer. Any exceptions to this require special explicit justification.

All the following were generally required:

- Evidence from at least two independent cohort studies or at least five case-control studies.
- The direction of effect is generally consistent though some unexplained heterogeneity may be present.
- Evidence for biological plausibility.

Limited — no conclusion

Evidence is so limited that no firm conclusion can be made.

This category represents an entry level, and is intended to allow any exposure for which there are sufficient data to warrant Panel consideration, but where insufficient evidence exists to permit a more definitive grading. This does not necessarily mean a limited quantity of evidence. A body of evidence for a particular exposure might be graded 'limited — no conclusion' for a number of reasons. The evidence might be limited by the amount of evidence in terms of the number of studies available, by inconsistency of direction of effect, by poor quality of studies (for example, lack of adjustment for known confounders), or by any combination of these factors. Exposures that are graded 'limited — no conclusion' do not appear in the matrices presented in Chapters 4–6, but do appear in Chapters 7 and 8.

When an exposure is graded 'limited — no conclusion', this does not necessarily indicate that the Panel has judged that there is evidence of no relationship. With

3.5.3 The food-based approach

Terms used in the text of this Report and in the matrices reflect the Panel's decision that the Report, and its judgements and recommendations, should whenever possible be based on foods and drinks rather than on nutrients. This food- (and drink-) based approach is also apparent in the overall structure of the Report. Chapter 4, the first chapter in Part 2, on foods and drinks, is the longest chapter. This is in part because dietary constituents associated with foods are grouped with these foods. Thus, matrix entries in chapter 4.1 identify 'foods containing dietary fibre' (rather than dietary fibre), and in 4.8 identify 'alcoholic drinks' (rather than alcohol or ethanol). Chapters 4, 5, and 6 also include material presented graphically, such as the forest plots described in box 3.3.

The food-based approach is also justified because of the uncertainty that any food constituent is a true causal factor,

rather than simply a marker for the particular foods in which it is found; or for other dietary constituents found in the same foods; or other associated health-related factors. In chapter 4.10, some micronutrients appear in matrices graded as 'convincing' or 'probable'. These judgements are derived from the findings of good quality, randomised, controlled trials, sometimes also supported by observational studies, clearly showing that supplements of these micronutrients, rather than the foods containing them, affect the risk of cancer.

Sometimes the studies that are the basis for the Panel's work have used markers of exposure. Thus, many epidemiological studies use body mass index as a marker of body fatness. When there is clear evidence of an underlying mechanism for body fatness, the Panel has agreed that the term 'body fatness' best represents the causal factor. Usually, anthropometric indices — other examples being waist to hip ratio and waist

further good quality research, any exposure graded in this way might in the future be shown to increase or decrease the risk of cancer. Where there is sufficient evidence to give confidence that an exposure is unlikely to have an effect on cancer risk, this exposure will be judged 'substantial effect on risk unlikely'.

There are also many exposures for which there is such limited evidence that no judgement is possible. In these cases, evidence is recorded in the full SLR reports contained on the CD included with this Report. However, such evidence is usually not included in the summaries and is not included in the matrices in this printed Report.

Substantial effect on risk unlikely

Evidence is strong enough to support a judgement that a particular food, nutrition, or physical activity exposure is unlikely to have a substantial causal relation to a cancer outcome. The evidence should be robust enough to be unlikely to be modified in the foreseeable future as new evidence accumulates.

All of the following were generally required:
- Evidence from more than one study type.
- Evidence from at least two independent cohort studies.
- Summary estimate of effect close to 1.0 for comparison of high versus low exposure categories.
- No substantial unexplained heterogeneity within or between study types or in different populations.
- Good quality studies to exclude, with

confidence, the possibility that the absence of an observed association results from random or systematic error, including inadequate power, imprecision or error in exposure measurement, inadequate range of exposure, confounding, and selection bias.
- Absence of a demonstrable biological gradient ('dose response').
- Absence of strong and plausible experimental evidence, either from human studies or relevant animal models, that typical human exposures lead to relevant cancer outcomes.

Factors that might misleadingly imply an absence of effect include imprecision of the exposure assessment, an insufficient range of exposure in the study population, and inadequate statistical power. Defects in these and other study design attributes might lead to a false conclusion of no effect.

The presence of a plausible, relevant biological mechanism does not necessarily rule out a judgement of 'substantial effect on risk unlikely'. But the presence of robust evidence from appropriate animal models or in humans that a specific mechanism exists, or that typical exposures can lead to cancer outcomes, argues against such a judgement.

Because of the uncertainty inherent in concluding that an exposure has no effect on risk, the criteria used to judge an exposure 'substantial effect on risk unlikely' are roughly equivalent to the criteria used with at least a 'probable' level of confidence. Conclusions of 'substantial effect

on risk unlikely' with a lower confidence than this would not be helpful, and could overlap with judgements of 'limited — suggestive' or 'limited — no conclusion'.

Special upgrading factors

These are factors that form part of the assessment of the evidence that, when present, can upgrade the judgement reached. So an exposure that might be deemed a 'limited — suggestive' causal factor in the absence, say, of a biological gradient, might be upgraded to 'probable' in its presence. The application of these factors (listed below) requires judgement, and the way in which these judgements affect the final conclusion in the matrix are stated.
- Presence of a plausible biological gradient ('dose response') in the association. Such a gradient need not be linear or even in the same direction across the different levels of exposure, so long as this can be explained plausibly.
- A particularly large summary effect size (an odds ratio or relative risk of 2.0 or more, depending on the unit of exposure) after appropriate control for confounders.
- Evidence from randomised trials in humans.
- Evidence from appropriately controlled experiments demonstrating one or more plausible and specific mechanisms actually operating in humans.
- Robust and reproducible evidence from experimental studies in appropriate animal models showing that typical human exposures can lead to relevant cancer outcomes.

circumference — do not appear in the matrices.

As exceptions to this approach, the Panel has made judgements on 'adult attained height' and 'greater birth weight', as shown in the matrices. Many epidemiological studies have reported on height and birth weight. It is thought that associations between height, birth weight, and cancer risk reflect some causal association with a combination of genetic, hormonal, nutritional, and other factors. Uncertainty as to the mechanisms underlying the observations with 'adult attained height' and 'birth weight' mean that the Panel was not able to determine the appropriate causal factors to be shown in the matrices. Instead, the anthropometric markers have been included, with appropriate footnotes.

3.5.4 The basis for robust judgements

The Panel has been particularly careful in deciding the criteria for judgement on causal relationships (or lack of such

relationships). Its decisions here have been enlightened by the rapid development since the mid-1990s of the technique of systematic review, using search techniques enabled by the electronic revolution.

Since the mid-1990s, about as many studies in the field of this Report have been published as were published in the previous 35 years. This development has not just been one of quantity but also of design and quality. In particular, many cohort studies have been published in the period analysed by the SLRs, and some of these have also been pooled. The Panel agreed that in general, cohort studies provide more impressive evidence than case-control and other epidemiological study designs, and this decision affected the criteria for judgement. For this reason, while the best evidence comes from a number of different study designs, the Panel agreed that reasonably strong and consistent evidence was needed from studies where biases could reasonably be excluded. Usually this evidence came from cohort studies with a prospective design or, where available and appropriate, from randomised controlled trials, to allow a judgement of 'convincing' or 'probable'. This was not a requirement specified for the previous report. See box 3.8.

A consequence is that the same amount of evidence for any particular association has sometimes led to a different judgement and level of matrix entry from the previous report. Sometimes, in cases where there is a greater quantity of evidence, this might not lead to a 'higher' classification, and could even possibly lead to a 'lower' one. These refinements are intended to give as robust an assessment as possible, given current understanding. In these respects, the criteria used by the Panel are more stringent than those pioneered by the previous panel.

The Panel agreed that the criteria for their judgements should be detailed and precise. But such criteria do not lead to automatic judgements. However meticulous, they cannot replace expert judgement. If a reviewer or a Panel member felt that important considerations had been overlooked by the overall agreed process, this was discussed, and the Panel's final judgement specified, with reasons provided.

3.5.5 The grading criteria

Specification of criteria for the grading of judgements enables a common, transparent approach. But as indicated, any such criteria cannot fully capture the sophistication and nuances of all the studies considered, or the nature and quality of different studies.

In using the criteria specified here, the Panel has taken into account additional factors including, but not confined to, the type, number, and size of studies; their design and execution; the nature of any intervention; the definition of cases and non-cases; the selection of any comparison group; methods of characterising exposure and outcome; length and completeness of follow-up; and the methods used to ascertain cases.

Other factors might lead to one or another grading. Failure to achieve a higher grade might result from several small deficits against a number of standards, or from a major shortfall in one particular aspect of evidence. Panel expertise was essential in judging whether criteria were met, or 'upgrading factors' (box 3.8) were applicable, as well as deciding what constituted substantial heterogeneity, high-quality study design, and so on. The criteria provide a consistent basis for judgement, not a 'set of boxes to be ticked'. As well as these 'upgrading factors', particular reasons why any specific judgement was reached are presented under the relevant exposure and cancer site in Chapters 4–7.

The following grading criteria specify the quantity, quality, and nature of evidence that can lead to associations being graded differently.

Convincing, probable
In considering the criteria allowing a judgement that the evidence of a causal relationship was convincing, or that the evidence showed a probable causal relationship, the Panel was conscious that both judgements were liable to generate public health goals and personal recommendations.

Limited and 'below'
For the two types of 'limited' judgement, the evidence falls short of a 'higher' judgement for a variety of reasons. There are also many exposures for which evidence was so limited that it did not warrant detailed consideration. In these cases, evidence is recorded in the full SLR reports contained on the CD included with this Report. However, this evidence is not included in the summaries or matrices in this printed Report.

Absence of a causal relation
The strength of this judgement corresponds to that for 'convincing' or 'probable' (and replaces the previous report's 'no relationship' category). This judgement does not reflect the absence of evidence, which in itself is not evidence of absence of effect. As with judgements of 'convincing' or 'probable', evidence from both observational studies and randomised trials contribute to such an inference.

3.6 Conclusions

Reports such as this address issues of public importance. They are informed by a process of collection, display, discussion, and judgement of evidence as the basis for recommendations made in the public interest.

We, the members of the Panel responsible for this Report, have had the responsibility to ensure that the judgements we have made in Part 2, and the public health goals and personal recommendations we have specified in Part 3, are clearly and reliably based on current evidence.

In the five years of our work, we have built on the work of the previous report, and have been supported by the findings of a preliminary Methodology Task Force; by the evidence gathered and presented by independent SLR centres; by observers from United Nations and other international organisations; and by the Report's Secretariat. As far as we know, the whole process, which has also included eight face-to-face Panel meetings, each lasting up to four days, is the most comprehensive and rigorous of its kind yet undertaken.

As this chapter shows, no method used to ascertain causal relationships between food, nutrition, physical activity, and cancer is perfect. But we believe that the integrated and sometimes innovative approaches we have taken, summarised here, have enabled us to make sound judgements and reliable recommendations. We have also done our best to make sure that the methods we have used are explained and displayed transparently, so they can be readily accessed and challenged as science develops, or from different points of view. We believe this best serves science, and also the cause of cancer prevention.

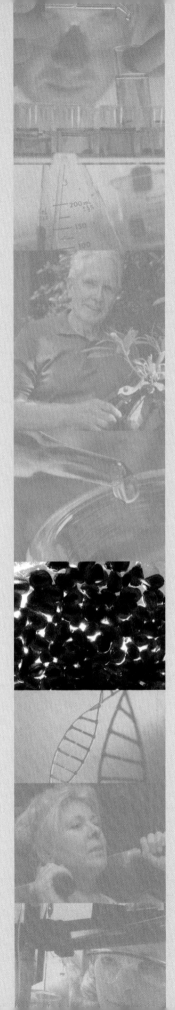

Part 2

Evidence and judgements

2

Introduction to Part 2

The brief of the Panel, and of the systematic literature review teams that provided the basis for the Panel's work, has included the task of presenting a clear, strong, and reliable foundation for the final recommendations. These in turn form the basis of sound policies and effective programmes to reduce the rates of cancer in populations, and the risk of cancer in people, whether as members of communities, or as families, or as individuals.

In this central part of the Report, seven chapters display the findings of the independently assembled systematic literature reviews, and the judgements of the Panel derived from these reviews and other evidence as needed. The Panel's judgements are displayed in the form of matrices that introduce five of these chapters. Judgements of 'convincing' and 'probable' causal relationships, shown in the top part of these matrices, are the basis for recommendations made in Part 3 of the Report.

Chapter 4, the first and longest chapter that follows, is concerned with types of food and drink. The judgements of the Panel are generally food- and drink-based, reflecting the evidence. Findings on dietary constituents and micronutrients are identified as, for example, on 'foods containing dietary fibre' or 'foods containing folate'. For consistency, findings on methods of food processing are, where possible, shown as part of the whole evidence on the associated foods so that, for example, the processing and preparation of meat is integrated with the evidence on meat. Evidence specifically on dietary supplements and on patterns of diet is included in the two final sections of this chapter.

Chapters 5 and 6 are concerned with physical activity, and with body composition, growth, and development. Evidence in these areas is more impressive than was the case up to the mid-1990s; the evidence on growth and development indicates the importance of a whole life-course approach to the prevention of cancer. As with the chapter on foods and drinks, these chapters include detailed summaries of the evidence collected in the systematic literature reviews together with graphic representations of the most significant evidence.

Chapter 7 summarises and judges the evidence as applied to 17 cancer sites, with briefer summaries based on narrative reviews on cancers of five other body systems and sites. The judgements as shown in the matrices in this chapter correspond with the judgements shown in the matrices in the previous chapters.

Chapter 8, in which judgements are also based on the evidence from the systematic literature reviews amplified by knowledge of physiological processes, concerns the biological and associated determinants of weight gain, overweight, and obesity. Before work on this chapter began, the Panel agreed that a comprehensive review of the evidence would be likely to show that obesity is or may be a cause of a number of cancers. It was therefore important to identify what aspects of food, nutrition, and physical activity themselves affect the risk of obesity and associated factors.

Improved screening, diagnosis, and medical services, including therapy and surgery, are in many countries improving the rates of survival for people with cancer. The number of cancer survivors — people living after diagnosis of cancer — is therefore increasing. The relevance of food, nutrition, physical activity, and body composition to people living with cancer, and to the prevention of recurrent cancer, is summarised in Chapter 9.

The Panel agreed that its final recommendations should be principally based on the evidence concerning cancer, and also should take into account findings on food, nutrition, physical activity, and the prevention of other chronic diseases, and of nutritional deficiencies and nutrition-related infectious diseases, especially of childhood. Chapter 10, which is also based on a systematic literature review, is a summary of the findings of expert reports in these areas.

The proposals for further research contained in Chapter 11 are, in the view of the Panel, the most promising avenues to explore in order to refine understanding of the links between food, nutrition, physical activity, and cancer, and so improve the prevention of cancer, worldwide.

As expected, a comprehensive assessment of all relevant types of evidence relating to food, nutrition, physical activity, body composition, and the risk of cancer has proved to be a massive task. The Panel was impressed not only by the quantity but also the quality of much of the evidence, and the degree to which a great deal of the evidence was consistent. As a result, recommendations designed to prevent cancer in general can be made with confidence. These are contained in Part 3.

CHAPTER 4

Foods and drinks

This chapter, with the following chapters in Part Two, forms the basis for the population goals and personal recommendations in Part Three.

The Panel decided that the evidence on food, nutrition, and cancer is generally most persuasive for foods rather than for specific nutrients or other food constituents; and that the evidence from epidemiological and experimental studies in this field, usually undertaken to address questions about cancers of specific or related sites, is most usefully synthesised in terms of foods and drinks.

The detailed evidence on foods and drinks is presented in this chapter, and that on physical activity and on body composition in the following two chapters. These three chapters include summaries of the evidence, including meta-analyses presented in graphic form, as well as the Panel's judgements. Chapter 7 presents the evidence on cancer sites in more summarised form.

In this chapter, whenever possible and appropriate, the evidence on dietary constituents, and on food production, preservation, processing, and preparation (including cooking), is integrated with the evidence on foods and drinks. So here, for example, the evidence on carotenoids is considered together with the evidence on vegetables and fruits; the evidence on methods of cooking meats is considered with the evidence on red meat and on processed meats; and the evidence on ethanol is considered with alcoholic drinks.

The result is not perfect. There is no single, ideal way of categorising the evidence on food and nutrition. But an approach emphasising foods and drinks is consistent with the generally accepted view that food-based dietary guidelines and recommendations are particularly valuable as a foundation for policies designed to improve public health.

The first two sections of this chapter summarise and judge the evidence on plant foods; the next two sections that on animal foods; and the following two sections that on fats and oils, and sugars and salt. The next two sections concern drinks, the second of which covers alcoholic drinks. These are followed by sections concerned with those aspects of dietary constituents, and with food

production, preservation, processing, and preparation (including cooking), that have not been incorporated in previous sections. The final section summarises evidence on dietary patterns, including being breastfed.

The pattern that emerges, though different in some important respects, is largely similar to that based on the evidence gathered in the mid-1990s, although the confidence with which various exposures are judged to cause or protect from cancer has sometimes changed.

4.1 Cereals (grains), roots, tubers, and plantains

CEREALS (GRAINS), STARCHY ROOTS AND TUBERS, PLANTAINS, AND THE RISK OF CANCER

In the judgement of the Panel, the factors listed below modify the risk of cancer. Judgements are graded according to the strength of the evidence.

	DECREASES RISK		INCREASES RISK	
	Exposure	**Cancer site**	**Exposure**	**Cancer site**
Convincing			**Aflatoxins[1]**	**Liver**
Probable	**Foods containing dietary fibre[2]**	**Colorectum**		
Limited — suggestive	Foods containing dietary fibre[2]	Oesophagus		
Substantial effect on risk unlikely		None identified		

1 Foods that may be contaminated with aflatoxins include cereals (grains), and also pulses (legumes), seeds, nuts, and some vegetables and fruits (see chapter 4.2).
2 Includes both foods naturally containing the constituent and foods which have the constituent added (see chapter 3.5.3). Dietary fibre is contained in plant foods (see chapter 4.2 and box 4.1.2).

For an explanation of all the terms used in the matrix, please see chapter 3.5.1, the text of this section, and the glossary.

These starchy plant foods have been the staple sources of dietary energy and bulk for humans since the development of settled communities and agriculture. They have to be prepared in some way to make them edible. In whole or relatively unprocessed forms, they are also sources of dietary fibre and various micronutrients. Cereals in whole form contain essential fats. When the outer layers of these foods are removed and they are refined, most of what remains is starch and protein.

In general, with industrialisation and urbanisation, consumption of these foods decreases, and more is consumed in the form of cereal products, which are typically more energy-dense and which may contain substantial amounts of fat, sugar, or salt. Pure starch from these foods is also used as an ingredient in many processed foods. Wheat, rice, maize (corn), and potatoes and their products are now the main cereals and roots/tubers produced and consumed globally.

Overall, *the Panel judges* that evidence indicating that cereals (grains), roots, tubers, or plantains affect the risk of any cancer, remains insubstantial.

The Panel judges as follows:
Foods containing dietary fibre probably protect against colorectal cancer; and there is limited evidence suggesting that such foods protect against oesophageal cancer. Dietary fibre is found in plant foods: vegetables, fruits, and pulses (legumes) (see chapter 4.2), as well as in cereals, roots, tubers, and plantains. All these foods are highest in dietary fibre when in whole or minimally processed form.

Foods high in dietary fibre may have a protective effect because of being bulky and relatively low in energy density. See chapters 6.1, 7.3, 7.9, and Chapter 8 for discussion of the role of energy density in weight gain, overweight, and obesity, and of weight gain, overweight, and obesity in the risk of some cancers, including those of the oesophagus and colorectum.

The Panel also judges that the evidence that foods contaminated with aflatoxins are a cause of liver cancer is convincing. Cereals (grains) and peanuts (see chapter 4.2) are the foods most commonly infested by these fungal toxins. Contamination is most widespread in countries with hot, damp climates and poor storage facilities.

Within the remit of this Report, the strongest evidence, corresponding to judgements of 'convincing' and 'probable', shows that foods containing dietary fibre probably protect against colorectal cancer; and that foods contaminated with aflatoxins are a convincing cause of liver cancer. Also see chapter 4.2 for judgements of probable protective effects of foods containing various micronutrients also found in cereals, roots, and tubers, particularly when relatively unprocessed.

Cereals (grains) are the staple foods in large parts of the world, supplying most of the energy and bulk in diets. In some regions, roots, tubers, or plantains are staple foods as well as or instead of cereals (grains). These generalisations apply to practically all settled rural and most urban populations. Monotonous 'poverty diets' containing very high levels of these foods, particularly if refined, are low and sometimes inadequate in protein and other nutrients. Gatherer–hunter and pastoral communities usually consume less of these starchy foods. Their nutrient content is variable, largely depending on the degree to which they are refined.

Consumption of cereals, roots, and tubers in general gradually drops with industrialisation and urbanisation, and an increasing amount of wheat in particular is grown for animal feed. These foods are increasingly used as a basis for or ingredients in processed products that are often energy-dense, high in fats or sugars, and sometimes salt. In lower-income countries, total population consumption of these foods may amount to 60–80 per cent of total energy, and in high-income countries, usually to less than 30 per cent. Also see Chapter 1.

Early reports concerned with nutritional deficiencies generally did not pay much attention to these foods and instead gave priority to energy- and nutrient-dense foods of animal origin, such as milk, eggs, and meat. Beginning in the 1970s, interest in dietary fibre increased, following informal epidemiological findings that diets high in dietary fibre were associated with a lower risk of a number of chronic diseases.[1] [2] By the 1990s, it was generally agreed that diets relatively high in cereals (grains) and other starchy staple foods, preferably relatively unrefined, protect against obesity, type 2 diabetes, coronary heart disease, and perhaps also digestive disorders.[3] [4] Evidence that such diets protect against cancer of any site has been less impressive, but epidemiological studies tend not to distinguish between degrees of refinement of cereals, roots, and tubers.

This section (4.1) includes cereal products and dietary fibre. It also includes contamination by aflatoxins, though this may also affect other plant foods (also see chapter 4.2). Non-starchy root vegetables such as carrots are included in chapter 4.2. Micronutrients found in plant foods are included in chapter 4.2, though most of these are also found in cereals (grains), roots, tubers, and plantains.

4.1.1 Definitions, sources

Cereals (grains)
Cereals (grains) are the seeds and energy stores of cultivated grasses. The main types are wheat, rice, maize (corn), millet, sorghum, barley, oats, and rye. In some countries, 'cereal' is also a term for dry foods made from grains and other ingredients, often eaten with milk for breakfast.

Roots, tubers, plantains
Roots and tubers are energy stores of plants. Names and definitions can vary around the world — potatoes are tubers, which are the tips of underground stems that swell with starch (a polysaccharide) and water. While potatoes are often classed as vegetables (in the USA, for instance), they are grouped separately from non-starchy vegetables in this Report. Sweet potatoes, sometimes called 'yams' in North America, are a type of storage root rather than a tuber, but true yams are starchy tubers. Cassava (manioc) and yucca are elongated roots, and sago is a starchy food made from the pith of some types of palm tree. Taro is cultivated for its edible leaves, as well as its starchy corm, which is similar to a tuber. Plantains are one of several fruits used as vegetables: they grow on trees and look like bananas, but only a small proportion of the starch is converted to sugar during the ripening process, which makes them similar to potatoes to cook with.

Box 4.1.1	Wholegrain and refined cereals and their products

Many of the cereals (grains) that we consume are refined. Grains are first broken into pieces and then refined, sifting away the bran, germ and, usually, the aleurone layer. This removes most of the fibre, oil, and B vitamins, as well as approximately 25 per cent of the protein. Polishing, as often performed on rice, removes additional nutrients. Many high-income countries therefore fortify refined cereals, including flour, with B vitamins and iron. Wholegrain products generally contain the constituents of the grain but, given the absence of an internationally accepted definition, intact grains are present to a variable extent. The extent to which the grain remains intact influences physiological processes in the bowel and hence health.

Cereal foods may be eaten in wholegrain form, although consumption in refined forms, such as white rice, bread, or pasta, is generally much more common, particularly in high-income countries. Refined grains are considered easier than wholegrains to cook and to chew; are light in colour — which is attractive to many consumers; and also have a longer shelf-life than wholegrain products, as the oil in bran goes rancid relatively quickly.

Breakfast cereals, particularly in the United States and parts of Europe, also account for a significant proportion of grain eaten. Many breakfast cereals, although based on grains (whole or refined), may contain substantial amounts of added sugars. Grains are further processed to provide ingredients such as corn syrup, starch, or alcohol. They also form the basis of many animal feeds.

Processed grains have a higher glycaemic index than unprocessed grains and, generally, the greater the degree of processing, the greater the glycaemic index (box 4.1.3).

Box 4.1.2 **Foods containing dietary fibre**

The concept of dietary fibre arose from observations of the low prevalence of colon cancer, diabetes, and coronary heart disease in parts of Africa amongst people whose diets were high in unrefined carbohydrates and whose stools were typically bulky, and often or sometimes semisolid. Considerable efforts have been dedicated to characterising the dietary components of what has come to be called dietary fibre that might confer health benefit. Naturally occurring dietary fibre is only derived from plant foods. Pulses (legumes) and minimally processed cereals are particularly concentrated sources, but vegetables and fruits also contain significant amounts. Dietary fibre isolated from plant cell walls and in synthetic forms are increasingly entering the food supply.

High intakes of dietary fibre, variously defined, have been associated with reduced risk of cardiovascular disease as well as of some cancers. Definitions of dietary fibre vary. Some are based on chemical analyses of the components of plant cell walls, such as non-starch polysaccharide, others on physiological effects — the carbohydrates that enter the large bowel having escaped digestion in the small intestine being defined as dietary fibre. The latter definition includes oligosaccharides and resistant starch. The World Health Organization and Food and Agriculture Organization have recently proposed that only polysaccharides which form part of plant cell walls should be regarded as dietary fibre and that the health benefits of resistant starch and oligosaccharides are more appropriately considered separately.

This section refers to starchy roots, tubers, and plantains. Carrots, beets, parsnips, turnips, and swedes are non-starchy roots, and are classified as non-starchy vegetables in this Report. Also see chapter 4.2.

4.1.2 Composition

Cereals (grains)
The relative amounts of dietary constituents in cereals and cereal foods depend largely on the degree of refinement and other forms of processing (box 4.1.1). Starch makes up about 70 per cent of the raw weight of the storage tissues (endosperm) of unprocessed cereal grains. The outer parts of the grain (the bran and the aleurone layer) contain non-starch polysaccharide, a type of carbohydrate that characterises dietary fibre (box 4.1.2).

Cereals also contain variable amounts of protein, oils, B vitamins, vitamin E and tocotrienols, iron, and various trace elements, as well as phytochemicals, some of which, such as the antioxidants, are bioactive (box 4.1.2). The germ is the embryonic part of cereal plants and contains oils, proteins, and fibre. Various cereals contain other specific components. Wheat contains gluten (a mixture of proteins). Rye has high levels of pentosans and oats contain beta-glucans, both of which are non-starch polysaccharides, a characterising feature of dietary fibre.

Cereals (grains) and pulses (legumes) may be contaminated with aflatoxins. See box 4.1.4.

Box 4.1.3 **Glycaemic index and load**

The degree to which different foods and meals raise blood glucose depends not only on the nature of the carbohydrate, but also on the characteristics of the foods consumed. Glycaemic index (GI) is a measure of the degree to which a food raises blood glucose compared with a standard food (usually glucose or white bread) under standard conditions. The test food must contain the same amount of available carbohydrate (usually 50 grams) as the standard. GI was originally used as an aid to food choice in diabetes and has more recently been applied to people without diabetes. The rise in blood glucose after consuming a food depends not only on the GI but also on the amount of food eaten. A related measure, glycaemic load (GL), takes into account both the GI of a food as well as the actual amount of carbohydrate consumed. The GL of a food may be measured directly or calculated by multiplying the GI of a food by the number of carbohydrate grams in a serving of the food.

Factors that influence the GI of a food include the type of carbohydrate, how the food is processed or cooked, and the other components present in the food (for example, fat, protein, fibre). There is some relationship (inverse) between GI and fibre content, although some foods high in fibre have a high GI and vice versa. Factors can affect GI by influencing speed of absorption, for instance higher fat foods tend to have a low GI. The calculated GI of a mixed meal or whole diet has been shown in some studies to correlate with the actual GI obtained by feeding a mixed meal. Although the concept of GI has been controversial, the GI and GL of diets have predicted risks of type 2 diabetes and coronary heart disease and related biomarkers, independent of dietary fibre, in prospective epidemiological studies, suggesting that GI and GL may be useful markers.

The relevance to cancer might lie in the fact that the rise in blood glucose after a meal is closely linked to that of insulin, which apart from its crucial role in carbohydrate and lipid metabolism, is also one of a family of important growth factors (also see Chapter 2).

Roots, tubers, and plantains
Roots and tubers are less concentrated stores of starch, although this accounts for almost all of their raw weight apart from water. Starch content varies from around 15–20 per cent in sweet potatoes to 25–30 per cent in cassava and yams, which translates into around 80–95 per cent of the dietary energy of these roots and tubers. Cooking sweet potatoes makes them taste sweet because an enzyme converts as much as 75 per cent of the starch into maltose (a disaccharide). Roots and tubers eaten with the skin on are high in dietary fibre. These foods are generally poor sources of protein, so although protein deficiency is uncommon, populations that subsist on these foods, and do not eat protein-rich pulses (legumes), are at risk of deficiency, especially children weaned on thin gruels made with these low-protein foods. They contain variable amounts of other nutrients. Potatoes contain vitamin C, for example, and the orange varieties of sweet potatoes contain carotenoids. Yams contain many bioactive compounds and taro corms are high in vitamin B6, fibre, and manganese.

Box 4.1.4   Aflatoxins

Mycotoxins are toxins produced by certain moulds or fungi. Although moulds that contaminate foods are usually destroyed by cooking temperatures, the toxins they produce may remain. Aflatoxins are one type of mycotoxin. All naturally occurring aflatoxins are classified as human carcinogens (group 1) by the International Agency for Research on Cancer; other mycotoxins, such as fumonisins, are suspected carcinogens.[5] It is common to find co-contamination by more than one species of mycotoxin-producing fungus. In Europe, the Joint FAO/WHO Expert Committee on Food Additives and Contaminants recommends that aflatoxin concentrations in foods be kept as low as possible.[6]

The main foods that may be contaminated by aflatoxins are all types of cereal (grain), including wheat, rice, maize (corn), barley, and oats; and pulses (legumes) — notably peanuts. Nuts and seeds may also be contaminated. Feedstuffs for farm animals may also be contaminated with aflatoxins, which can then be secreted in milk or accumulated in tissues.

Aflatoxins, which are produced by *Aspergillus flavus* and *A. parasiticus*, are most problematic in countries with hot, damp climates and poor storage facilities. Under these conditions, foods may become contaminated with fungi and then accumulate such toxins. Such foods are marketed and consumed in the countries in which they are produced; they are also exported to neighbouring countries and intercontinentally. Aflatoxin contamination is therefore a international issue.

Levels of aflatoxin contamination tend to be highest in countries where rates of liver cancer are high, such as some African countries and South-East Asia, including China. In general, rates are low in Europe, but relatively high rates of contamination have on occasion been found in the USA.

Aflatoxin exposure levels are low in Europe and Australia, higher in the USA, and high in many low-income countries. This is particularly the case in tropical and subtropical regions where grains and nuts are stored for long periods under non-ideal conditions.

Rates are reduced by inspection, use of fungicides, and screening of imported foods. However, monitoring of levels of aflatoxin contamination in low-income countries is generally lacking.

4.1.3 Consumption patterns

Cereals and grains

As societies moved to more settled, agricultural ways of life 10–15 000 years ago, cereals became the main staple foods; the types of cereal crops grown depended largely on climate and terrain. Wheat, barley, oats, and rye are traditionally staple foods for people living in the Middle East and Europe; and with rice in Asia; maize (corn) in the Americas; and sorghum and millet in Africa. But the market for cereals and their products is now global, although some, such as sorghum, remain largely regional.

The importance of starchy staples in food systems and diets is broadly connected to economic and industrial development. Both in higher-income countries and across the world, there has been a long-term decline in their consumption. With increasing urbanisation in lower-income countries, wheat and maize are replacing traditional staple foods. An important exception is Asia, where rice remains the staple grain. Cereal cultivation and consumption tends to be highest in most of Asia and lowest in Oceania, parts of Europe, and North America.

Globally, cereal foods provide more than 45 per cent of dietary energy; diets based on these foods tend to be bulky with a low energy density (see chapter 8.8.4). Cereals provide more than 50 per cent of dietary energy in low-income countries, but only around 30 per cent in high-income countries. While grains contribute roughly 20 per cent of dietary energy in Australia, North America, and central Europe, they can provide as much as 70 per cent in parts of Asia (mainly from rice). Although more wheat is grown than rice on a global basis, much of it is used for animal feed. Rice is the principal food for half of the world's population.

Cereals are very versatile once they have been processed from the raw grain. Wheat is mainly milled to make flour for bread, pastries, cakes, and pasta. Maize (corn) is a staple food in Latin America and parts of Asia and Africa, where it is used to make grits, cornmeal (used for polenta as well as corn breads), corn flour, tortillas, tamales, and corn chips. It is also the basis of corn starch (a thickener), corn syrup (a sweetner), and corn oils. Sweetcorn is also eaten as a vegetable, either on or off the cob. Rice is usually processed to remove the bran and aleurone layers, turning 'brown rice' into 'white'. It is also used to make flour (the basis for gluten-free breads), rice powder, noodles, rice paper, rice milk, Japanese mochi, and lao-chao (Chinese fermented rice). Barley is used primarily in Asia (tsampa and miso soya paste) and in North Africa (soups, porridges, and flat breads). Whole rye grains are milled and used to make bread in some north and east European countries. Whole oats are made into porridges and used in muesli and baked goods, such as biscuits. Fonio, millet, sorghum, teff, and triticale are traditional crops and staples in parts of Africa and Asia. Many grains are also fermented to make alcoholic drinks (see chapter 4.8.1).

Roots, tubers, and plantains

Roots, tubers, and plantains are staple foods in some parts of the world. For instance, populations in some regions of sub-Saharan Africa, Latin America, and Oceania base their diets on these foods. Globally, starchy roots provide around 5 per cent of dietary energy. Consumption is highest in the Pacific islands and parts of Africa, with cassava and yams providing more than 40 per cent of dietary energy in Ghana. Potatoes can provide as much as 10 per cent of dietary energy in North America and Europe. Globally, plantains provide less than 0.5 per cent of dietary energy, but they are locally important in some African, Latin American, and Caribbean countries, where they can provide more than 15 per cent of dietary energy. Some populations do not rely on any of these foods — for instance, pastoralist societies such as the Maasai hunters in East Africa, and the Inuit and other Arctic populations, maintain their traditional ways of life and diets.

Dietary fibre

Dietary fibre intake, measured as non-starch polysaccharides, varies from 10–13 grams (g)/day in Japan and the UK to 15–20 g/day or more in Africa and India. Intake among individuals in a population may vary between 7 and 25 g/day.[7]

4.1.4 Interpretation of the evidence

Interpretation of the evidence on any and all foods and drinks, their constituents, their methods of production, preservation, processing and preparation, and other factors, with the risk of cancer, is never simple, for general and specific reasons.

4.1.4.1 General

For general considerations that may affect interpretation of the evidence, see chapters 3.3 and 3.5, and boxes 3.1, 3.2, 3.6, and 3.7.

'Relative risk' (RR) is used in this Report to denote ratio measures of effect, including 'risk ratios', 'rate ratios', 'hazard ratios', and 'odds ratios'.

4.1.4.2 Specific

Some considerations specific to cereals (grains), roots, tubers, and plantains are as follows.

Classification. 'Cereals' is a broad classification. Different cereals have different nutritional composition and biological effects, as do different types of dietary fibre. Any effects of specific cereals or their constituents may not become apparent.

Patterns and ranges of intake. Little evidence relates to roots, or tubers other than potatoes, or plantains, some of which, such as cassava (manioc) or yams, are staple foods in some parts of the world.

Terminology. Potatoes are usually (as here) defined as tubers, but are sometimes (in the USA especially) included with vegetables. Bananas, a significant item in many diets, may be (as here) defined as a fruit, or else with plantains as a starchy food. There is no internationally agreed definition for dietary fibre (box 4.1.1).

Measurement. Non-starch polysaccharides are measured precisely by the Englyst method,[8] but there are fewer epidemiological data on non-starch polysaccharides specifically than for dietary fibre. The various analytical techniques used to assess the fibre content of foods give widely different results.

Confounding. In high-income countries, high intakes of wholegrain cereal products tend to go together with other health-conscious dietary and other habits. Also there is possible confounding between dietary fibre and other dietary constituents and in general with 'healthier' dietary patterns and ways of life. Data on dietary fibre come predominantly from dietary sources, that is, plant-based foods (also see box 4.1.1 and chapter 4.2); therefore, no effect can be attributed to different types and sources of dietary fibre.

Production, preservation, processing, preparation. Few studies distinguish between unrefined and refined cereals and their products. Many processed foods grouped as cereal products, such as ready-to-eat breakfast cereals, are high in added sugars and sometimes salt. The ways in which cereals are processed, prepared, and consumed varies greatly in different cultures.

4.1.5 Evidence and judgements

The full systematic literature review (SLR) is contained on the CD included with this Report.

4.1.5.1 Cereals (grains)

The evidence was too limited in amount, consistency, or quality to draw any conclusions.

4.1.5.2 Roots, tubers, and plantains

The evidence was too limited in amount, consistency, or quality to draw any conclusions.

4.1.5.3 Foods containing dietary fibre
Colorectum

Sixteen cohort studies[9-37] and 91 case-control studies investigated dietary fibre and colorectal cancer. The Harvard pooling project also analysed original data from 13 separate cohort studies.[38]

An association was apparent from many, though not all, cohort studies. Ten studies showed decreased risk when comparing high with low intake groups,[14 19 21 25-29 33 34] which was statistically significant in one (figure 4.1.1).[28] Two reported non-significant increased risk,[36 39] one showed no effect on risk,[30] and one reported no association.[18] One study reported non-significant decreased risk in women and non-significant increased risk in men[23]; one study reported non-significant increased risk in women and non-significant decreased risk in men.[37] Meta-analysis was possible on eight studies, giving a summary effect estimate of 0.90 (95% confidence interval (CI) 0.84–0.97) per 10 g/day increment, with moderate heterogeneity (figure 4.1.2). A dose-response relationship was apparent from cohort data.

Because of the abundant prospective data from cohort studies, case-control studies were not summarised.

The Harvard pooled analysis from 13 prospective cohort studies (725 628 participants, followed up for 6 to 20 years, 8081 colorectal cancer cases) gave a significant inverse association in the age-adjusted model (0.84, 95% CI 0.77–0.92).[38] However, the association was attenuated and no longer statistically significant after adjusting for other risk factors (0.94, 95% CI 0.86–1.03). One comparison group was statistically significant when maximally adjusted, others were not. Compared with dietary fibre intake of 10 to < 15 g/day, the pooled effect estimate was 1.18 (95% CI 1.05–1.31) for less than 10 g/day (low compared with moderate intake). All other measures were not associated with risk of colorectal cancer. The pooled analysis therefore found that, after accounting for other dietary risk factors, high dietary fibre intake was not associated

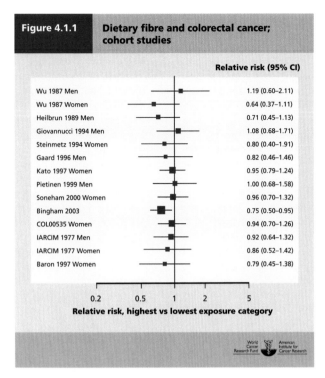

Figure 4.1.1 Dietary fibre and colorectal cancer; cohort studies

Relative risk (95% CI)

	Relative risk (95% CI)
Wu 1987 Men	1.19 (0.60–2.11)
Wu 1987 Women	0.64 (0.37–1.11)
Heilbrun 1989 Men	0.71 (0.45–1.13)
Giovannucci 1994 Men	1.08 (0.68–1.71)
Steinmetz 1994 Women	0.80 (0.40–1.91)
Gaard 1996 Men	0.82 (0.46–1.46)
Kato 1997 Women	0.95 (0.79–1.24)
Pietinen 1999 Men	1.00 (0.68–1.58)
Soneham 2000 Women	0.96 (0.70–1.32)
Bingham 2003	0.75 (0.50–0.95)
COL00535 Women	0.94 (0.70–1.26)
IARCIM 1977 Men	0.92 (0.64–1.32)
IARCIM 1977 Women	0.86 (0.52–1.42)
Baron 1997 Women	0.79 (0.45–1.38)

Relative risk, highest vs lowest exposure category

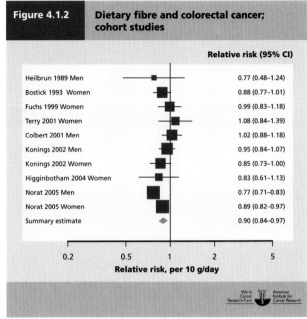

Figure 4.1.2 Dietary fibre and colorectal cancer; cohort studies

Relative risk (95% CI)

	Relative risk (95% CI)
Heilbrun 1989 Men	0.77 (0.48–1.24)
Bostick 1993 Women	0.88 (0.77–1.01)
Fuchs 1999 Women	0.99 (0.83–1.18)
Terry 2001 Women	1.08 (0.84–1.39)
Colbert 2001 Men	1.02 (0.88–1.18)
Konings 2002 Men	0.95 (0.84–1.07)
Konings 2002 Women	0.85 (0.73–1.00)
Higginbotham 2004 Women	0.83 (0.61–1.13)
Norat 2005 Men	0.77 (0.71–0.83)
Norat 2005 Women	0.89 (0.82–0.97)
Summary estimate	0.90 (0.84–0.97)

Relative risk, per 10 g/day

with a reduced risk of colorectal cancer.

Fibre exerts several effects in the gastrointestinal tract but the precise mechanisms for its probable protective role are not clearly understood. Fibre dilutes faecal contents, decreases transit time, and increases stool weight.[40] Fermentation products, especially short-chain fatty acids, are produced by the gut flora from a wide range of dietary carbohydrates that reach the colon. Short-chain fatty acids, particularly butyrate, can induce apoptosis and cell cycle arrest, and promote differentiation. Fibre intake is also strongly correlated with intake of folate.

> **A clear dose-response relationship is apparent from generally consistent cohort studies, supported by evidence for plausible mechanisms, but residual confounding could not be excluded. Foods containing dietary fibre probably protect against colorectal cancer.**

The Panel is aware that since the conclusion of the SLR, six cohort studies[41-46] and one case-control study[47] have been published. This new information does not change the Panel judgement (see box 3.8).

Oesophagus

One cohort study,[48] nine case-control studies,[49-58] and two ecological studies[59 60] investigated dietary fibre and cancer of the oesophagus.

There was some evidence of an association between dietary fibre and reduced oesophageal cancer risk. The single cohort study reported decreased risk when comparing high with low intakes, with an effect estimate of 0.50, though no assessment of statistical significance was included.[48]

The nine case-control studies produced 13 independent effect estimates. Of these, 11 estimates were of decreased risk,[50-53 55 56 58 61] which were statistically significant in eight. One estimate indicated no effect on risk[54] and one other gave non-significant increased risk.[62] The data were most consistent when stratified for adenocarcinomas; of six studies, five reported significant decreased risk; results were less consistent for squamous cell carcinoma. All studies were adjusted for alcohol and smoking except one, which was adjusted for alcohol but not smoking.[50]

The ecological studies were inconclusive. Neither was statistically significant, with one in the direction of increased and the other of decreased risk.

There is no evidence of a plausible biological mechanism through which dietary fibre reduces the risk of oesophageal cancer. It is not possible to conclude whether an as yet unknown mechanism is responsible for an apparent reduction in risk, or whether it is due to other components found in the vegetables and fruits that contain dietary fibre.

> **There is limited evidence from sparse and inconsistent case-control studies only, suggesting that foods containing dietary fibre protect against oesophageal cancer.**

4.1.5.4 Aflatoxins

(Also see box 4.1.4; chapter 4.9; and chapter 7.8). There are two approaches to measuring aflatoxin intake. The first uses local food tables to estimate exposure to aflatoxins from diet. The second approach uses biomarkers of exposure. These are derived from knowledge of aflatoxin metabolism. In humans, metabolised products of aflatoxins can be detected in blood, urine, or breastmilk. Biomarkers of exposure are more accurate and precise.

Liver

Five cohort studies[63-70] and seven case-control studies[71-79] assessed associations between biomarkers of exposure to aflatoxin and hepatocellular carcinoma.

The cohort studies used a variety of different biomarkers for exposure to aflatoxin, some in blood and some in urine. Despite this variety, all five studies reported increased risk for the highest levels when compared to the lowest, and all of these reported at least one measure that resulted in a statistically significant increased risk (figure 4.1.3). Studies that adjusted for hepatitis virus infection tended to show the greater effects.[65 66] There is some evidence of an interaction whereby the risk is increased by a multiplicative effect if aflatoxin exposure is combined with hepatitis infection. One study showed that people with hepatitis virus antibodies and biomarkers of aflatoxin exposure had a higher risk than those with hepatitis virus antibodies alone, with an effect estimate of 10.0 (95% CI 1.6–60.9).[65]

There is evidence from some of the cohort studies for interaction with glutathione-*S*-transferase (GST) genotype.[63 64] GST is an enzyme involved in the metabolic pathway that 'detoxifies' aflatoxins. Different genotypes show varying efficiencies at this task. Two genes (GSTT1 and GSTM1) were assessed separately. For each, it is possible to have a positive or negative genotype. In each case, a negative genotype increases risk of hepatocellular carcinoma when exposed to aflatoxins. There is clear, consistent evidence that GSTM1/GSTT1 positive genotypes protect against the increased risk of liver cancer from hepatitis infection combined with aflatoxin exposure, which supports a causal role for aflatoxins in hepatocellular carcinoma.

Four case-control studies showed statistically significant increased risk for the highest levels of biomarkers when compared to the lowest.[71 74 78 79] Two studies showed no effect on risk.[73 77] One study showed a non-significant decreased risk.[72] Heterogeneity may be explained by the diversity in methods of exposure assessment.

A dose-response relationship is apparent from most cohort

studies and some of the case-control studies.

The areas in the world where there is considerable aflatoxin contamination of foods coincide with the areas where primary liver cancer rates are high. The epoxide product of aflatoxin AFB_1 is known to be genotoxic and is formed in the liver.[80] It damages DNA, causing G:C base pairs to become T:A. GST enzymes can repair this damage with varying efficiency between genotypes. Recent studies have shown that aflatoxins can damage the p53 gene, which is an important regulator of normal growth.[67] Damage to p53 DNA can lead to increased proliferation of abnormal cells and formation of cancers.

The synergistic effect of hepatitis virus infection and aflatoxin exposure might be explained by hepatitis virus increasing the production of the enzyme (CYP1A2) that produces the genotoxic metabolite of aflatoxin.[81] It is also possible that the hepatitis virus increases the number of G:C to T:A transversions, or that it inhibits nucleotide repair, or that it acts as a tumour promoter.

The evidence is ample and consistent and is supported by strong evidence for mechanisms operating in humans. A dose response is apparent from both cohort and case-control studies. The evidence that aflatoxins and aflatoxin-contaminated foods are a cause of liver cancer is convincing.

4.1.6 Comparison with previous report

The previous report concluded that dietary fibre/non-starch polysaccharides possibly protect against cancers of the pancreas, colorectum, and breast. The previous report also concluded that wholegrain cereals possibly decrease the risk of stomach cancer and that refined cereals possibly increase the risk of oesophageal cancer.

Since the mid-1990s, evidence for a protective effect of dietary fibre against colorectal and oesophageal cancer risk has become somewhat stronger. The finding of the previous report, suggesting that the degree of refinement (other than relative amounts of dietary fibre) may be a factor in modification of the risk of some cancers, was not found.

The previous report classified bananas as plantains. Here they are classified as fruits. The previous report considered dietary fibre separately from cereals (grains) and other plant foods. Here, dietary fibre is considered in the context of cereals (grains) and other plant foods.

4.1.7 Conclusions

The Panel concludes:
The direct evidence that cereals (grains), roots, tubers, or plantains affect the risk of any cancer remains unimpressive.

However, foods containing dietary fibre probably protect against colorectal cancer; and there is limited evidence suggesting that such foods protect against oesophageal cancer. Dietary fibre is mostly found in cereals, roots and tubers, and also in vegetables, fruits, and pulses (legumes) (see chapter

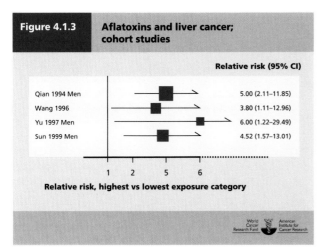

Figure 4.1.3 — **Aflatoxins and liver cancer; cohort studies**

Relative risk (95% CI)

	Relative risk (95% CI)
Qian 1994 Men	5.00 (2.11–11.85)
Wang 1996	3.80 (1.11–12.96)
Yu 1997 Men	6.00 (1.22–29.49)
Sun 1999 Men	4.52 (1.57–13.01)

Relative risk, highest vs lowest exposure category

4.2). All of these are highest in dietary fibre when in whole or minimally processed forms.

Foods high in dietary fibre may also have a protective effect indirectly because they are relatively low in energy density. See chapters 6.1, 7.3, 7.9, and 8 for discussion of the role of energy density in weight gain, overweight, and obesity, and of weight gain, overweight, and obesity in the risk of some cancers, including those of the oesophagus and colorectum.

The evidence that foods contaminated with aflatoxins are a cause of liver cancer is convincing. Cereals (grains) and peanuts (see chapter 4.2) are the foods most commonly infested by these fungal toxins. Contamination is most widespread in countries with hot, damp climates and poor storage facilities.

4.2 Vegetables, fruits, pulses (legumes), nuts, seeds, herbs, spices

Vegetables and fruits are generally low in energy density (with a few exceptions) and, when consumed in variety, are sources of many vitamins, minerals, and other bioactive compounds (phytochemicals). Many non-starchy vegetables, including salad vegetables and fruits, may be eaten raw and may also be cooked. Pulses (legumes) are high in protein. Traditional diets all over the world combine cereals (grains) with pulses (legumes) and, in this way, ensure sufficient protein of adequate quality, usually with small amounts of animal foods. Nuts and seeds are concentrated sources of numerous micronutrients and of essential fatty acids. All these foods are sources of dietary fibre. Many herbs and spices have potent pharmacological as well as culinary properties.

Consumption of vegetables and fruits is very variable: high around the Mediterranean littoral and some tropical countries; low in many low-income countries, including some in which fruits are abundant. Consumption of pulses (legumes) is also very variable: beans and chickpeas and their products are basic foods in a number of Latin American, Middle Eastern, and Asian countries, but pulses are insignificant in typical North American and most European diets. Consumption of nuts, seeds, herbs, and spices also varies. Traditional Middle Eastern and Indian cuisines use a great variety of herbs and spices; garlic, usually classified as a herb, is consumed in remarkable quantities in some countries.

In general, *the Panel judges* that findings from cohort studies conducted since the mid-1990s have made the overall evidence, that vegetables or fruits protect against cancers, somewhat less impressive. In no case now is the evidence of protection judged to be convincing. However, in a substantial number of cases, a judgement of probable is justified. Evidence on legumes (pulses), nuts, seeds, and (with two exceptions) herbs and spices remains insubstantial.

The Panel judges as follows:
Non-starchy vegetables probably protect against cancers of the mouth, pharynx, and larynx, and those of the oesophagus and stomach. There is limited evidence suggesting that they also protect against cancers of the nasopharynx, lung, colorectum, ovary, and endometrium. Allium vegetables probably protect against stomach cancer. Garlic (an allium vegetable, commonly classed as a herb) probably protects against colorectal cancer. There is limited evidence suggesting that carrots protect against cervical cancer; and that pulses (legumes), including soya and soya products, protect against stomach and prostate cancers. Fruits in general probably protect against cancers of the mouth, pharynx, and larynx, and those of the

oesophagus, lung, and stomach. There is limited evidence suggesting that fruits also protect against cancers of the nasopharynx, pancreas, liver, and colorectum. There is limited evidence suggesting that chilli is a cause of stomach cancer.

Fruits and non-starchy vegetables are generally low energy-dense foods. For a discussion of the effect of such foods and drinks on weight gain, overweight, and obesity, and the role of weight gain, overweight, and obesity in the risk of some cancers, see Chapters 6, 7, and 8.

Evidence that vegetables and fruits protect against some cancers is supported by evidence on foods containing various micronutrients, found especially in vegetables, fruits, and pulses (legumes), and nuts and seeds, as well as in cereals, roots, tubers, and other plant foods. Foods containing folate probably protect against pancreatic cancer, and there is limited evidence suggesting that these foods also protect against oesophageal and colorectal cancers. Foods containing carotenoids probably protect against cancers of the mouth, pharynx, and larynx, and also lung cancer. Foods containing the carotenoid beta-carotene probably protect against oesophageal cancer; and foods containing lycopene probably protect against prostate cancer. Foods containing vitamin C probably protect against oesophageal cancer. There is limited evidence suggesting that foods containing quercetin protect against lung cancer.

Evidence also relevant to chapter 4.1 is grouped here. Foods containing selenium (also found in animal foods) probably protect against prostate cancer; and there is limited evidence suggesting that they protect against stomach and colorectal cancers. There is limited evidence suggesting that foods containing pyridoxine protect against oesophageal and prostate cancers; and that foods containing vitamin E protect against oesophageal and prostate cancers.

The strongest evidence, here corresponding to judgements of 'probable', shows that non-starchy vegetables and also fruits probably protect against cancers of the mouth, larynx, pharynx, oesophagus, and stomach, and that fruits also probably protect against lung cancer; and that allium vegetables, and garlic specifically, probably protect against stomach cancer. The case that vegetables, fruits, and pulses (legumes) may be protective against cancers of some sites is supported by evidence on foods containing micronutrients found in these and other plant foods. Thus, foods containing carotenoids probably protect against cancers of the mouth, pharynx, larynx, and lung; foods containing beta-carotene and also vitamin C probably protect against oesophageal cancer; foods containing selenium and also lycopene probably protect

VEGETABLES,[1] FRUITS,[1] PULSES (LEGUMES), NUTS, SEEDS, HERBS, SPICES, AND THE RISK OF CANCER

In the judgement of the Panel, the factors listed below modify the risk of cancer. Judgements are graded according to the strength of the evidence.

	DECREASES RISK		INCREASES RISK	
	Exposure	Cancer site	Exposure	Cancer site
Convincing				
Probable	**Non-starchy vegetables[1]**	**Mouth, pharynx, larynx** **Oesophagus** **Stomach**		
	Allium vegetables[1]	**Stomach**		
	Garlic[1]	**Colorectum**		
	Fruits[1]	**Mouth, pharynx, larynx** **Oesophagus** **Lung** **Stomach**		
	Foods containing folate[2]	**Pancreas**		
	Foods containing carotenoids[2]	**Mouth, pharynx, larynx** **Lung**		
	Foods containing beta-carotene[2]	**Oesophagus**		
	Foods containing lycopene[2 3]	**Prostate**		
	Foods containing vitamin C[2 4]	**Oesophagus**		
	Foods containing selenium[2 5]	**Prostate**		
Limited — suggestive	Non-starchy vegetables[1]	Nasopharynx Lung Colorectum Ovary Endometrium	Chilli[1]	Stomach
	Carrots[1]	Cervix		
	Fruits[1]	Nasopharynx Pancreas Liver Colorectum		
	Pulses (legumes)[7]	Stomach Prostate		
	Foods containing folate[2]	Oesophagus Colorectum		
	Foods containing pyridoxine[2 8]	Oesophagus		
	Foods containing vitamin E[2 6]	Oesophagus Prostate		
	Foods containing selenium[2 5]	Lung Stomach Colorectum		
	Foods containing quercetin[2]	Lung		
Substantial effect on risk unlikely	Foods containing beta-carotene[9]: prostate; skin (non-melanoma)			

1 Judgements on vegetables and fruits do not include those preserved by salting and/or pickling.
2 Includes both foods naturally containing the constituent and foods which have the constituent added (see chapter 3.5.3).
3 Mostly contained in tomatoes and tomato products. Also fruits such as grapefruit, watermelon, guava, and apricot.
4 Also found in some roots and tubers — notably potatoes. See chapter 4.1.
5 Also found in cereals (grains) and in some animal foods. See chapters 4.1 and 4.3.
6 Also found in plant seed oils. See chapter 4.5.
7 Including soya and soya products.
8 Vitamin B6. Also found in cereals. See chapter 4.1.
9 The evidence is derived from studies using supplements and foods containing beta-carotene: see chapter 4.10.

For an explanation of all the terms used in the matrix, please see chapter 3.5.1, the text of this section, and the glossary.

against prostate cancer; and foods containing folate probably protect against pancreatic cancer. Also see chapter 4.1 for the evidence that foods containing dietary fibre, found in plant foods (particularly when in whole or relatively unprocessed forms), probably protect against colorectal cancer.

Vegetables and fruits (including berries), nuts and seeds, and herbs and spices, where they grow and can be cultivated, have always been part of human diets. Gatherer–hunters and pastoral peoples probably consumed more than relatively impoverished urban dwellers: for them, vegetables were the main sources of many vitamins, and fruits were a main source of energy, from sugar (also found in wild honey). They are consumed abundantly as part of many long-established traditional cuisines, around the Mediterranean littoral, the Middle East, in many Asian countries, and the Pacific islands, where substantial amounts of meat, dairy products, and other animal foods are traditionally consumed only occasionally. In contrast, monotonous 'poverty' diets include few of these foods.

Globally, consumption of these foods is lower than now generally recommended. Vegetables and fruits are sometimes seen as relatively expensive. Well stocked supermarkets usually now display a variety of local and imported fresh vegetables and fruits, although supplies in smaller stores are more variable. Consumption of fresh vegetables and fruits in many tropical countries in Africa and Latin America is low: on average people in Brazil, for example, consume roughly the same as people in Britain. The explanation may be that in Africa, many rural communities are obliged to grow cash crops that displace gardens, and that in Latin America knowledge of the value — and pleasure — of many indigenous vegetables and fruits has been lost. Many programmes in tropical countries are now dedicated to regaining this knowledge.[1]

Even before the discovery of vitamins as essential nutrients beginning in the early 20th century, vegetables and fruits have been recommended as 'protective foods'. Early reports concerned with nutritional deficiencies paid less attention to pulses (legumes), nuts, and seeds, even though these plant foods contain protein, and nuts and seeds are nutrient- and also energy-dense, perhaps because they are not much consumed in the countries where most such reports were compiled. Instead, as already mentioned, priority was given to energy- and nutrient-dense foods of animal origin. By the 1980s, most reports concerned with prevention of chronic diseases recommended relatively high intakes of vegetables and fruits and sometimes also pulses (legumes), either because these foods were seen as nourishing substitutes for energy-dense fatty or sugary foods, or else because they were identified as positively protective against cardiovascular disease.[2] Evidence that vegetables and fruits might be protective against some cancers emerged in the 1990s.[3] A common recommendation has been for at least five portions (or at least 400 g) of vegetables and fruits a day.[4]

Non-starchy root vegetables such as carrots are included

here. Chapter 4.1 includes dietary fibre, only found naturally in plant foods. Chapter 4.1 also includes aflatoxins, which also contaminate pulses (legumes), notably peanuts, nuts and seeds, and other plant foods. The micronutrients included here, as contained in vegetables, fruits, pulses (legumes), nuts and seeds, are also found in other plant foods, and some also in animal foods.

4.2.1 Definitions, sources

Vegetables and fruits are defined in this Report by their culinary use, and are grouped for discussion below as vegetables and fruits, pulses (legumes), nuts and seeds, and herbs, spices, and condiments.

Vegetables and fruits

Vegetables are the edible parts of plants, usually including fungi. Typical examples include cultivated or gathered leaves, roots, stalks, bulbs, and flowers. Some foods are culinary vegetables but are classified botanically as fruits; these include cucumbers, peppers, squash, and tomatoes. Non-starchy vegetables are included here, while starchy root vegetables are considered in chapter 4.1. Non-starchy vegetables can be further divided into green, leafy vegetables, such as spinach and lettuce; cruciferous vegetables (the cabbage family), for example, bok choy, broccoli, cabbage, and watercress; and allium vegetables, such as onions, garlic, and leeks.

A fruit is the seed-containing part of the plant; but only those that are eaten as fruits are included in the culinary definition, for example, apples, bananas, berries, figs, grapes, mangoes, and melons. This also includes citrus fruits such as oranges, grapefruits, lemons, and limes; and also dried fruits, such as apricots, figs, and raisins.

Pulses (legumes)

Leguminous plants produce their fruits as pods and are considered here separately. The dried, edible seeds of this family are often called pulses, although this term is used interchangeably with legumes. They include beans, lentils, peas, and peanuts (groundnuts). The dried forms, which have matured and dried on the plant, are eaten most widely. But some varieties are eaten as a green vegetable, such as peas; the pods are sometimes eaten like this too, for example, green beans and runner beans. Some legumes can also be sprouted (germinated) and eaten, such as beansprouts.

Nuts and seeds

Nuts are edible seeds surrounded by a tough, dry shell. This definition includes true nuts (such as hazelnuts and chestnuts), as well as seeds that most people think of as nuts (including Brazil nuts, macadamia nuts, and cashews). Other seeds commonly eaten include sunflower, sesame, pumpkin, and poppy seeds. Nuts and seeds are processed for their oil, ground into pastes, used as ingredients, or eaten raw or roasted as snack foods. Cereals (grains) are also the seeds of plants, but these are discussed separately in this Report (see chapter 4.1). Seeds, like nuts, have a relatively high oil

Box 4.2.1   Micronutrients and other bioactive compounds and cancer risk

Vegetables, fruits, pulses (legumes), nuts, and seeds are sources of a wide variety of micronutrients and other bioactive compounds. Foods containing several of these constituents have been identified in the systematic literature reviews, on which this chapter is based, as being associated with cancer risk. These are carotenoids (including beta-carotene and lycopene), folate, vitamin C, vitamin D, vitamin E, quercetin, pyridoxine, and selenium. Mechanisms by which they might affect cancer risk are discussed in chapter 4.2.5. However, it is not possible to ascribe the association between these foods and lower cancer risk to a causal effect of specific compounds with confidence, as each food contains a complex mixture of different constituents, all of which might also contribute to any effect.

Carotenoids are found in varying concentrations in all vegetables, particularly those that are red or orange. They are a family of more than 600 fat-soluble red/orange pigments that comprise xanthophylls (such as lutein) and carotenes (such as alpha- and beta-carotene, and lycopene). Some carotenoids, most importantly beta-carotene, can be converted by the body to retinol and are sometimes called pro-vitamin A carotenoids. These compounds tend to be the main dietary source of vitamin A in low-income countries.

Only about half of the 50 or so carotenoids in human diets can be absorbed. They have antioxidant and other bioactivities that are discussed in chapter 4.10. Sources of carotenoids include spinach, kale, butternut squash, pumpkin, red (bell) peppers, carrots, tomatoes, cantaloupe melon, and sweet potatoes.

Beta-carotene is found in yellow, orange, and green fruits and green, leafy vegetables including carrots, spinach, lettuce, tomatoes, sweet potatoes, broccoli, cantaloupe melon, oranges, and winter squash (pumpkin).

As a rule of thumb, the greater the intensity of the colour of the fruit or vegetable, the more beta-carotene it contains.

The most concentrated source of lycopene is tomatoes, but it is also present in watermelon, red (bell) peppers, pink or red grapefruit, pink-fleshed guava, and persimmons.

The B-vitamin folate is a family of compounds essential for human health. Folic acid, the synthetic form, is used to fortify manufactured cereal products, spreads, and, in some countries, flour or grains. Folates are involved in a number of metabolic pathways, especially in the synthesis of purines and pyrimidines, which are important for DNA synthesis and cell replication (also see chapter 4.2.5.4). Sources of dietary folate include liver, beans, spinach, broccoli, romaine lettuce, chicory, oranges, and papaya.

Vitamin C (ascorbic acid) is a water-soluble vitamin. Humans, like a small number of other animals, cannot synthesise vitamin C, so it is an essential part of diets. Vitamin C is essential for collagen synthesis and also has antioxidant activity. Severe deficiency causes scurvy. It is added to many foods, including bread and soft drinks, in small amounts as an antioxidant preservative. Natural dietary sources are vegetables, tubers, and fruits, including red/yellow (bell) peppers, kiwi fruits, broccoli, papaya, citrus fruits, strawberries, and potatoes, but it is destroyed by heat or contact with the air (for instance, when vegetables are chopped), or lost into cooking water.

Vitamin E is a fat-soluble vitamin and a potent antioxidant that occurs as eight different forms: alpha- and gamma-tocopherol are the most common. The most important dietary sources of vitamin E are vegetable oils such as palm, sunflower, corn, soya bean, and olive oils. Nuts, sunflower seeds, and wheatgerm are also sources. Wholegrains, fish, peanut butter, green, leafy vegetables, and fortified

breakfast cereals also contain this vitamin.

Pyridoxine is one of a group of water-soluble compounds collectively known as vitamin B6. This vitamin is involved in neurotransmitter synthesis, red blood cell formation and function, niacin (vitamin B3) formation, steroid hormone function, and nucleic acid synthesis (also see chapter 4.2.5.5).[15] Food sources include bananas, fish, poultry, liver, potatoes eaten with the skin, green, leafy vegetables, beans, pulses (legumes), nuts, wholegrains, and fortified breakfast cereals.

Selenium is a mineral element that occurs in different chemical forms. It is toxic in large amounts, but is essential in the diet at trace levels. It is present at varying concentrations in different soils; and since plants take up selenium from the soil, these levels determine the amount present in vegetables. Thus selenium deficiency is more prevalent in regions where the soil selenium content is low. Selenium is a component of the amino acids selenocysteine and selenomethionine, which are integrated into proteins to form selenoproteins. Selenoproteins include antioxidant enzymes such as glutathione peroxidases, thioredoxin reductase, which is important for DNA synthesis, and iodothyronine deiodinase, which is important for the synthesis of thyroid hormones.[16] Dietary sources of selenium include brazil nuts, fish, wholegrains, wheatgerm, and sunflower seeds.

Quercetin is a flavonoid, which is a type of polyphenol; it is not an essential dietary component. Many studies in cultured cells and animals suggest that quercetin has antioxidant activity, which could give rise to a range of biological activities, including reducing inflammation (also see chapter 4.2.5.9). Quercetin is found in apples, green and black tea, onions, raspberries, red wine, red grapes, citrus fruits, leafy, green vegetables, cherries, elderberries, broccoli, blueberries, cranberries, and bilberries.

---

content, and the oils produced from them are considered in chapter 4.4.

Herbs, spices, and condiments

Herbs and spices, which are generally used to flavour or preserve foods, are of plant origin, although a very small number of animal products are classed as spices (such as ambergris). Definitions of herbs and spices vary, but herbs are usually the fresh or dry leaves or whole plant, while spices are produced from other parts of the plant, such as the seeds, and are usually dried.[5] Many different parts of

plants are used as herbs or spices, such as the leaves (sage, bay, or basil), stems (ginger, lemongrass), bark (cinnamon), rhizomes (ginger), roots (horseradish), flower buds (cloves), stamens (saffron), seeds (mustard, cumin), kernels (nutmeg), and fruits (peppers).

A condiment is a substance that adds taste to other foods; the term is often used for sauces added at the table, which are usually of plant origin. Examples include vinegars, ketchups, chutneys, harissa, mustard, and soy sauce. Salt is neither a herb nor a spice, although it is used as a condiment (see chapter 4.5).

Phytochemicals

Plants contain a wide range of biologically active compounds, some of which are known as phytochemicals. There may be as many as 100 000 different compounds, which determine particular properties in plants, and in the fruits and vegetables they produce, such as flavour and colour. Phytochemicals are classified according to their chemical structure and functional characteristics, and include salicylates, phytosterols, saponins, glucosinolates, polyphenols, protease inhibitors, monoterpenes, phytoestrogens, sulphides, terpenes, and lectins.

It is widely believed that the health benefits of diets high in fruits and vegetables are likely to be due partly to the presence of phytochemicals. For instance, several act as antioxidants, preventing oxidative damage to cells, proteins, and DNA. It is likely that other bioactive phytochemicals have yet to be identified, and those that are known may have additional properties in the body that are not yet understood. But it is thought that nutrients, phytochemicals, and other, as yet unknown, bioactive components act together to influence physiological responses.

Although many phytochemicals are bioactive, they are not essential in the diet and there is no daily requirement, so they are not classed as nutrients. Humans have developed tastes for some phytochemicals, such as the hot flavours of mustard oil, bitter alkaloids, and irritating capsaicins. There is genetically inherited variation in sensitivity to some tastes, for example, the bitter taste of isothiocyanates in cruciferous vegetables such as cabbage.

4.2.2 Composition

Vegetables and fruits

The composition of fruits and vegetables depends both on species and on subtype, as well as on the environmental, farming, production, and storage conditions. These include factors such as sun exposure, soil quality, agricultural practices, harvesting time, ripeness, length of time between harvest and consumption, and preservation and preparation methods. For instance, the outer leaves of lettuces can have higher levels of some micronutrients than the inner leaves; and harvested, unripe fruit that ripens in transit may have lower levels of nutrients than fruits ripened on the plant (box 4.2.1).[6]

Vegetables and fruits contain vitamins, minerals, dietary fibre, and other bioactive compounds, such as phytochemicals (box 4.2.2). This is a collective term for a variety of plant components that often perform important functions in the plant, such as providing colour, flavour, or protection, but are not essential in the human diet. They include salicylates, flavonoids, glucosinolates, terpenes, lignans, and isoflavones. All of these groups of compounds have been shown either in humans or in laboratory experiments to have potentially beneficial health effects when they are included in diets. However, the bioavailability of these compounds is variable (box 4.2.3) and their ultimate heath effects uncertain.

Plant cell walls are the main source of dietary fibre, and all whole fruits and vegetables (but not their juices) contain varying amounts of fibre (box 4.2.4). Most vegetables and fruits are low energy-dense foods, although there are exceptions, for example, avocados, nuts, and seeds.

Some families of fruits and vegetables have characteristic components that may confer a particular health benefit (or risk) to the whole family. For instance, cruciferous vegetables are sources of glucosinolates and their products isothiocyanates and indoles. Allium vegetables and others, such as chicory and Jerusalem artichokes, store energy as inulin (chains of fructose sugars) rather than starch (chains of glucose sugars). The body cannot digest inulin, which is called a prebiotic — a substance that is claimed to have health benefits by promoting the growth of certain types of gut bacteria. Allyl sulphides and allicin in garlic are distinctive flavour molecules that give vegetables of the onion family their 'sting' (box 4.2.3). Green, leafy vegetables are sources of folate, and tomatoes have high levels of lycopene. All of these components, as well as other phytochemicals (box

Preparation of vegetables and nutrient bioavailability

While some vegetables, often termed 'salad vegetables', are commonly eaten raw, many are cooked before they are eaten. In most cases, whether a vegetable is eaten raw depends on personal choice. Most forms of cooking reduce the total nutrient content of vegetables, although the degree to which this happens varies between nutrients and with cooking methods. However, cooking also increases the bioavailability of some nutrients.[12] Therefore, although raw vegetables have higher amounts of nutrients overall, the body may absorb more of a nutrient from the cooked vegetable.

For instance, carotenoid absorption in the small intestine is relatively inefficient (5–50 per cent); the bioavailability of carotenes is increased by cooking and pureeing vegetables, particularly by adding oil, because these compounds are fat soluble.[13] Similarly, processing tomatoes increases the bioavailability of lycopene, another carotenoid: it is four times more bioavailable from tomato paste than from fresh tomatoes. Thus processed tomato products such as pasteurised tomato juice, soup, sauce, and ketchup provide the most bioavailable lycopene. Cooking and crushing tomatoes (as in the canning process) and including them in oil-rich dishes (such as pasta sauce or pizza) greatly increases lycopene absorption from the digestive tract.

The biological response to garlic can also be influenced by the way that it is processed. Peeling and chopping garlic releases an enzyme, alliinase, which is known to promote the formation of some sulphur compounds that are not only odoriferous but may provide some health benefits. Heating garlic without peeling inactivates this enzyme and has been found to substantially reduce or eliminate the active properties. If garlic is peeled or chopped and allowed to stand for 15–20 minutes, the active agents that are formed are not destroyed by normal cooking procedures.[14]

The ways in which vegetables and fruits are produced and stored may affect nutrient levels as much as cooking, or more. For example, nutrient levels tend to fall rapidly after harvest.

Box 4.2.4 Foods containing dietary fibre

The concept of dietary fibre arose from observations of the low prevalence of colon cancer, diabetes, and coronary heart disease in parts of Africa amongst people whose diets were high in unrefined carbohydrates and whose stools were typically bulky, and often or sometimes semisolid. Considerable efforts have been dedicated to characterising the dietary components of what has come to be called dietary fibre that might confer health benefit. Naturally occurring dietary fibre is only derived from plant foods. Pulses (legumes) and minimally processed cereals are particularly concentrated sources, but vegetables and fruits also contain significant amounts. Dietary fibre isolated from plant cell walls and synthetic forms are increasingly entering the food supply.

High intakes of dietary fibre, variously defined, have been associated with reduced risk of cardiovascular disease as well as of some cancers. Definitions of dietary fibre vary. Some are based on chemical analyses of the components of plant cell walls, such as non-starch polysaccharide, others on physiological effects — the carbohydrates that enter the large bowel having escaped digestion in the small intestine being defined as dietary fibre. The latter definition includes oligosaccharides and resistant starch. The World Health Organization and Food and Agriculture Organization have recently proposed that only polysaccharides which form part of plant cell walls should be regarded as dietary fibre and that the health benefits of resistant starch and oligosaccharides are more appropriately considered separately.

This box also appears as box 4.1.2 in the previous section

4.2.2), have been shown to have potentially beneficial effects in laboratory experiments, as detailed in the evidence in chapter 4.2.5 (also see Chapter 2).[7-9]

Pulses (legumes)

Dry pulses are seeds and are higher in protein than most other plant foods. Soya beans and peanuts contain 37 g per 100 g and 26 g per 100 g protein dry weight respectively, although, on average, pulses contain around 20 g per 100 g protein dry weight.[10] These foods are typically high in carbohydrates and non-starch polysaccharides (dietary fibre), and are generally low in fat. Soya beans and peanuts are exceptions, being relatively high in fat with 8 g per 100 g and 47 g per 100 g fat, respectively (mostly mono- and polyunsaturated fatty acids). They also contain oligosaccharides that are not digested in the gut but are fermented by bacteria in the colon. Soya beans are distinct from other legumes in that they have a high content of bioactive isoflavones, or phytoestrogens, which have hormone-like effects in the body. They are also good sources of saponins and phytosterols, which decrease cholesterol absorption. Many legumes contain deguelin, which has been shown to have anti-tumour effects in laboratory experiments.[11] Most pulses are virtually indigestible and inedible before cooking; immature legumes that are eaten green have higher levels of sugar and lower levels of non-digestible polysaccharides than dried pulses.

Nuts and seeds

Other seeds and nuts are also relatively high in protein and fat; some contain as much as 60 g fat per 100 g. They are therefore energy-dense foods (see Chapter 8), as well as being nutrient-dense. Weight-for-weight, nuts provide more calories than either meat or cereals (grains), although chestnuts are the exception as they are relatively low in fat. Most nuts contain mainly monounsaturated fatty acids, although the exceptions are coconuts, which contain a high proportion of saturated fatty acids, and walnuts and pecans, which contain mostly polyunsaturated fatty acids (see chapter 4.5.2). Nuts and seeds are high in dietary fibre (box 4.2.4), especially when they are eaten with their skins or hulls; the fibre content is typically 5–11 g per 100 g. Nuts and seeds are also high in vitamins and minerals, particularly the B vitamins, vitamin E, and folate; and the seed coats contain phenolic compounds.

Herbs and spices

Nearly all herbs and spices contain aromatic compounds, which are volatile molecules that are usually fat- rather than water-soluble. The flavour compounds may make up as much as 15 g per 100 g of a spice by weight, although herbs contain much lower levels — typically around 1 g per 100 g. Many plants have evolved to contain these compounds because they act as deterrents to herbivores. Some of these aromatic compounds may be bioactive, although possibly not at the levels found in most diets. Isothiocyanates are responsible for the spicy/hot flavour of mustard and horseradish, produced from glucosinolates in cruciferous plants. Chives and garlic (allium vegetables) contain the distinctive sulphides discussed above. Terpenoids are common components in herbs and spices, providing distinctive flavours. Examples include monoterpenes, such as geranial in lemon grass, and linalool in bergamot; sesquiterpenes, such as bisabolene in ginger; triterpenoids, such as the saponin glycrrhizic acid, found in liquorice root; and tetraterpenoids, such as the carotenoid, lycopene.

4.2.3 Consumption patterns

Fruits and vegetables

The global average for vegetable consumption (based on availability and not including vegetable oils) is 2.6 per cent of total daily energy intake.[17] It is generally highest in North Africa, the Middle East, parts of Asia, the USA and Cuba, and in southern Europe. Although consumption levels are similar in countries of high and low economic status, vegetables represent a greater proportion of daily energy intake in the low-income countries. Intakes range from 5.3 per cent in parts of Asia to as little as 0.2 per cent in sub-Saharan Africa. On average, the availability of vegetables is increasing globally.

The global average for fruit consumption (based on availability) is 2.7 per cent of total daily energy intake. Fruit consumption is generally higher than vegetable consumption, but it shows a greater degree of variability. Fruit consumption is higher in high-income countries, although it represents a similar percentage of total available dietary energy to that seen in low-income countries. Intakes are highest in some parts of Africa, the Middle East, southern Europe, and Oceania, and lowest in other parts of Africa and Asia. Fruit consumption also tends to be low in north-eastern Europe. Intakes range from as much as 20 per cent of daily energy in parts of Africa to as little as 0.5 per cent in parts of Asia. The availability of fruit has increased globally in recent decades, although there was a slight decrease in the 1990s.

Most countries have national recommendations for the daily amount of vegetables and fruits that need to be eaten to maintain optimal health (Chapter 10). These vary, but they tend to recommend three or more servings per day of vegetables and two or more servings per day of fruits; a serving is about 80 g (or half a US cup). In most high-income countries for which data were available, daily consumption of vegetables fell short of this target, although this is not due to lack of availability; indeed, availability is high due to the wide use of refrigeration. Fruit consumption tended to be closer to national targets. Seasonal availability influences overall availability, although less so in high-income countries where vegetables and fruits are more likely to be imported.

Pulses (legumes)
Globally, pulses supply 2 per cent of total energy intake (based on availability) and 3.5 per cent of daily protein intake.[17] The highest availability is in parts of Africa, South America, Asia, and the Middle East. In these areas, pulses are a dietary staple, and can account for as much as 20 per cent of daily energy intake and 50 per cent of protein intake. In societies with high intakes of meat and other foods of animal origin, pulses are less important in diets, and are usually consumed infrequently or in small amounts. Peanuts and soya beans account for most of the legume products eaten around the world.

Soya bean availability per person represents 0.5 per cent of daily energy intake globally, but it is notably high in parts of Asia, and higher than average in parts of Africa and Central America. In parts of Asia, soya beans account for up to 4.9 per cent of daily energy availability and 15 per cent of protein.

Pulses are eaten in a variety of ways around the world; for instance, Japanese and Chinese bean curd (tofu), Chinese mung bean sprouts, Mexican chilli and refried beans, Indian dahl, Middle Eastern falafel and hummus, Indonesian cultured soya bean cakes (tempeh), Cuban black beans and rice, Boston baked beans, French cassoulet, Brazilian feijoada, Swedish pea soup, and US peanut butter. Soya beans are particularly versatile and their products are a common feature in manufactured foods, although they are not commonly eaten whole. Soya foods include soya drinks and flour, tofu, tempeh, textured vegetable protein, and the many products that can be prepared from these foods. Fermented soya beans produce soy sauce and miso. Soya bean oil is also used widely (see chapter 4.5.3).

Nuts and seeds
Nuts and seeds were an important part of human diets before the advent of agriculture and they remain locally important in a few areas. Globally, tree nuts supply 0.4 per cent of daily energy availability. The highest availability is in the Middle East and parts of Europe, and the lowest is in South America and parts of Africa; intakes range from 3 per cent of total energy in parts of the Middle East to virtually zero in many low-income countries.

Coconuts represent 0.5 per cent of daily energy availability globally, although coconuts can be locally important in tropical islands, for instance in parts of Oceania, Asia (Sri Lanka and Indonesia), the Caribbean, and in the African islands. In parts of Oceania, for example, coconuts provide as much as 20 per cent of energy in the diet.

Sunflower, rape, mustard, and sesame seeds together supply 0.2 per cent of daily energy intake globally. There are fewer data available for seeds than for many other foods, although sesame seed intake is relatively high in parts of Africa and Asia, providing a maximum of 3.9 per cent of energy in parts of central Africa. Oils from seed crops are widely used (see chapter 4.5.3).

Herbs, spices, and condiments
Although spices are consumed in small amounts to flavour food, they are such a regular feature of some diets that they account for a measurable quantity of daily energy intake. Worldwide, spices provide 0.3 per cent of available dietary energy and in parts of Asia they constitute as much as 1.8 per cent. Herbs and spices tend to be part of the traditional diet in the areas from which they originate, and many traditional cuisines are characterised by the use of herbs, spices, and condiments. Most are now available worldwide, although their use still varies greatly in different parts of the world. Many herbs and spices are believed to have medicinal or tonic value and have been used in this way at least since the times of the earliest medical records. Many modern pharmaceuticals are derived from herbs and other plants.

Many herbs and some spices are biologically very potent: the modern pharmacopoeia lists drugs, many of which have been isolated from herbs, sometimes known as 'plants with healing powers'. There are some in vivo experimental data for potentially beneficial effects in the cases of turmeric, saffron, ginger, pepper, garam masala (a herb and spice mix), and also eugenol and myristin, constituents of a number of herbs and spices.

Conversely, it is at least theoretically possible that some condiments have adverse effects. Two examples are hot chilli juices and harissa, a fiery condiment; both are consumed in substantial quantities in Mexico and the Mahgreb countries of North Africa, respectively, and both irritate the mouth and throat.

4.2.4 Interpretation of the evidence

4.2.4.1 General
For general considerations that may affect interpretation of the evidence, see chapter 3.3 and 3.5, and boxes 3.1, 3.2, 3.6 and 3.7.

'Relative risk' (RR) is used in this Report to denote ratio measures of effect, including 'risk ratios', 'rate ratios', 'hazard ratios', and 'odds ratios'.

4.2.4.2 Specific

Considerations specific to vegetables, fruits, pulses (legumes), nuts, seeds, herbs, and spices include:

Patterns and ranges of intake. Most studies of consumption of vegetables, fruits, and pulses (legumes) have been conducted in populations that have relatively homogeneous diets. The limited data on nuts, seeds, herbs, spices, and condiments come mainly from a few human case-control studies and some experimental animal studies.

Classification. There is no general agreement on classification. Some studies have included cereals such as corn, and tubers such as potatoes, as vegetables, and plantains as fruit. Broccoli and green peppers are included as 'green vegetables' in some studies, while only leafy greens are included in this category in others; tomatoes are considered 'yellow-orange vegetables' in some but not in others. Some studies report results only for broad categories (for example, 'all vegetables' or 'all fruits'), whereas others have reported results for more narrowly defined categories (for example, 'raw vegetables', 'green vegetables', 'citrus fruits') or for individual food items (for example, 'spinach', 'carrots', 'tomatoes'). In some studies, vegetables and fruits have been categorised according to botanical classification; in others, categorisation has been according to culinary usage. In this report, the terms 'vegetables' and 'fruits' are used according to their culinary definition. Some studies have included pulses as vegetables whereas others have classified these as a separate entity or not at all. Many older studies have not differentiated between retinol and carotenoids. Vitamin E intakes are difficult to quantify since much comes from the vegetable oils used in food preparation, and intakes within populations are usually homogenous because of the widespread occurrence of vitamin E in commonly consumed foods.

Measurement. Assessment of selenium intake is problematic because the content of selenium in foods depends to a large extent on the soil selenium content of the area in which the foods were grown. Blood and toenail levels of selenium are thought to be fairly accurate indicators of intake and have been used in several studies.

Confounding. Smokers consume fewer vegetables and fruits than non-smokers.[18][19] Fat intake inversely correlates with vegetable and, particularly, fruit intake in the USA.[20] Recent studies of the effects of fruits and vegetables in cancers thought to be caused by smoking have controlled for the effect of smoking. Folate intake is correlated with intake of non-starchy polysaccharide (dietary fibre).

Reporting bias. Studies using self-reporting tend to over-report vegetable and fruit consumption. Where an effect exists, results from such studies are liable to underestimate the extent to which vegetables and fruits modify the risk of cancer.

4.2.5 Evidence and judgements

The full systematic literature review (SLR) is contained on the CD included with this Report.

4.2.5.1 Non-starchy vegetables
Mouth, pharynx, and larynx

Thirty-one case-control studies[21-50] and 3 ecological studies[51-53] investigated non-starchy vegetables and mouth, pharynx, or larynx cancers; 1 cohort study[54] and 6 case-control studies[33][39][45][55-57] investigated non-starchy vegetables and fruits; 23 case-control studies investigated raw vegetables[24][27][28][33][36-43][45][47][50][58-65]; 1 cohort study,[66] 14 case-control studies,[24][26-29][39][41][43][45-47][50][63][67] and 1 ecological study[68] investigated cruciferous vegetables; 1 cohort study[66] and 10 case-control studies[24][26-29][39][47][61][67][69] investigated green, leafy vegetables; 3 cohort studies[66][70][71] and 18 case-control studies[23][24][26-29][39][41-43][46][49][50][63][65][72-75] investigated carrots; and 1 cohort study[66] and 12 case-control studies[26-29][39-43][46][50][58][62][65] investigated tomatoes.

Non-starchy vegetables

Most studies showed decreased risk with increased intake of non-starchy vegetables. Twenty-two studies reported comparisons of high against low intake (figure 4.2.1).[22][23][25][26][29-31][33][35-46][49][50] Of these, 19 showed decreased risk for the highest intake group,[22][25][26][30][31][33][35-44][46][49][50] which was statistically significant in 13.[22][25][30][31][35][37][38][40][42][43][46][49][50] The other 3 studies showed non-significant increased risk.[23][29][45]

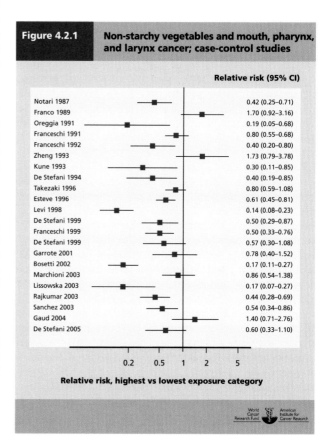

Figure 4.2.1	Non-starchy vegetables and mouth, pharynx, and larynx cancer; case-control studies

Relative risk (95% CI)

	Relative risk
Notari 1987	0.42 (0.25–0.71)
Franco 1989	1.70 (0.92–3.16)
Oreggia 1991	0.19 (0.05–0.68)
Franceschi 1991	0.80 (0.55–0.68)
Franceschi 1992	0.40 (0.20–0.80)
Zheng 1993	1.73 (0.79–3.78)
Kune 1993	0.30 (0.11–0.85)
De Stefani 1994	0.40 (0.19–0.85)
Takezaki 1996	0.80 (0.59–1.08)
Esteve 1996	0.61 (0.45–0.81)
Levi 1998	0.14 (0.08–0.23)
De Stefani 1999	0.50 (0.29–0.87)
Franceschi 1999	0.50 (0.33–0.76)
De Stefani 1999	0.57 (0.30–1.08)
Garrote 2001	0.78 (0.40–1.52)
Bosetti 2002	0.17 (0.11–0.27)
Marchioni 2003	0.86 (0.54–1.38)
Lissowska 2003	0.17 (0.07–0.27)
Rajkumar 2003	0.44 (0.28–0.69)
Sanchez 2003	0.54 (0.34–0.86)
Gaud 2004	1.40 (0.71–2.76)
De Stefani 2005	0.60 (0.33–1.10)

0.2   0.5   1   2   5

Relative risk, highest vs lowest exposure category

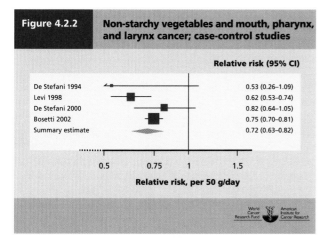

Figure 4.2.2 Non-starchy vegetables and mouth, pharynx, and larynx cancer; case-control studies

	Relative risk (95% CI)
De Stefani 1994	0.53 (0.26–1.09)
Levi 1998	0.62 (0.53–0.74)
De Stefani 2000	0.82 (0.64–1.05)
Bosetti 2002	0.75 (0.70–0.81)
Summary estimate	0.72 (0.63–0.82)

Relative risk, per 50 g/day

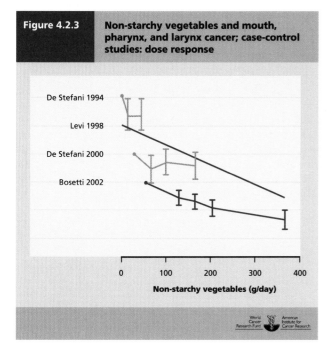

Figure 4.2.3 Non-starchy vegetables and mouth, pharynx, and larynx cancer; case-control studies: dose response

Non-starchy vegetables (g/day)

The remaining studies showed no consistent association, probably due to varying exposure definitions and study design.[21 24 27 28 32 34 47 48] Meta-analysis was possible on 4 case-control studies, giving a summary effect estimate of 0.72 (95% confidence interval (CI) 0.63–0.82) per 50 g/day, with moderate heterogeneity (figure 4.2.2). All studies adjusted for sex, smoking, and alcohol consumption.

A dose-response relationship is apparent from the four case-control studies that could be meta-analysed (figure 4.2.3). There is some suggestion that the greatest effect appears to be with the first increment. That is, any increase above the lowest levels of vegetable consumption confers a protective effect. However, it is not clear that the effect continues in a linear fashion with increased dose.

Of the three ecological studies, one (Hong Kong) study found a significant negative association between vegetable consumption and cancer incidence[51]; the other two

(international) found no significant association with cancer mortality.[52 53]

Non-starchy vegetables and fruits

A cohort study that reported results for non-starchy vegetables and fruits in combination reported a statistically significant protective effect in the highest consumers (0.55, 95% CI 0.32–0.95).[54] All six case-control studies looking at the same exposure group reported reduced risk estimates in similar comparisons,[33 39 45 55-57] which were statistically significant in four.[33 39 55 57] All of these studies adjusted for smoking and alcohol consumption.

Raw vegetables

Twenty-three case-control studies reported separate risk estimates for raw vegetable consumption.[24 27 28 33 36-43 45 47 50 58-65] All of these reported comparisons of risk between high and low intake groups, which produced reduced risk estimates in 22[24 27 28 33 36-43 45 47 50 58 60-65]; 16 of these were statistically significant.[24 33 36-40 42 43 47 50 60-63 65] No studies reported statistically significant increased risk estimates. Meta-analysis of 7 case-control studies gave an effect estimate of 0.71 (95% CI 0.59–0.86) per 50 g/day, with moderate heterogeneity.[37 39 42 45 59 62 65] These studies also provided evidence of a dose-response relationship. The heterogeneity could be partially explained by variable exposure definitions. These results are consistent with data for non-starchy vegetables.

Cruciferous vegetables

One cohort study,[66] 14 case-control studies,[24 26-29 39 41 43 45-47 50 63 67] and 1 ecological study[68] reported separate risk estimates for cruciferous vegetable consumption.

The single cohort study showed a non-significant increased risk for increased intake of cauliflower and a non-significant decreased risk for cabbage.[66] Four case-control studies showed statistically significant decreased risk with increased intake, either overall or in specific subgroups.[24 29 43 47] One study showed statistically significant increased risk associated with eating kimchi or pickled cabbage.[67] The other nine studies showed inconsistent and non-significant associations.[26-28 39 41 45 46 50 63] The ecological study showed a statistically significant decreased risk.[68]

Green, leafy vegetables

One cohort study[66] and 10 case-control studies[24 26-29 39 47 61 67 69] reported separate risk estimates for green, leafy vegetable consumption.

The single cohort study showed no effect for the highest intake group of lettuce when compared to the lowest.[66] Nine case-control studies showed decreased risk with increased intake,[24 26 27 29 39 47 61 67 69] which was statistically significant in four.[24 39 61 69] One study showed non-significant increased risk.[28]

Carrots

Three cohort studies[66 70 71] and 18 case-control studies[23 24 26-29 39 41-43 46 50 63 65 72-75] investigated non-starchy root vegetables and mouth, larynx, or pharynx cancers. There was variation in the exposure classification in studies. Most assessed carrots, but some looked at 'tubers and carrots' or 'non-starchy root vegetables' or 'yellow/orange vegetables'.

One cohort study, looking at 'tubers and carrots', reported a non-significant increased risk when comparing high against low intakes, with a wide confidence interval (1.9, 95% CI 0.6–6.0).[66] Another that reported on 'carotene-rich fruits and vegetables' found a non-significant reduced risk when comparing the highest intake group against the lowest (0.50, p value for linear trend 0.10).[70] The third, which evaluated yellow/orange vegetables in postmenopausal US women, reported a significant reduced risk for the same comparison (0.58, 95% CI 0.39–0.87).[71]

All of the 18 case-control studies reported comparisons of risk between high- and low-intake groups.[23 24 26-29 39 41-43 46 49 50 63 65 72-75] Sixteen reported reduced risk estimates,[23 26-29 39 41-43 50 63 65 72-75] 6 of which were statistically significant.[49 72 75] The other 2 were non-significant in the direction of increased risk.[24 27 28 39 43 46] The majority of studies were hospital-based and analysed carrots as a separate exposure.

Tomatoes

One cohort study[66] and 12 case-control studies[26-29 39-43 46 50 58 62 65] investigated tomatoes and mouth, larynx, or pharynx cancers.

The cohort study reported a non-significant increased risk when comparing the highest intake group against the lowest, with a wide confidence interval (1.7, 95% CI 0.8–3.7).[66]

Of the 12 case-control studies,[26-29 39-43 46 50 58 62 65] 10 reported reduced risk estimates,[26 29 39-43 46 50 58 62 65] 5 of which were statistically significant.[26 29 39 40 62] Only 2 reported an increased risk, which was non-significant.[27 28] These studies were also the only studies not to adjust for both smoking and alcohol intake.

The general mechanisms through which vegetables could plausibly protect against cancers of the mouth, larynx, and pharynx are outlined below.

Although all of the studies mentioned here adjust for smoking behaviour and nearly all adjust for alcohol, the relative risk of smoking is large (particularly when combined with alcoholic drinks). It is therefore difficult to eliminate confidently the possibility of residual confounding with ways of life associated with smoking: for instance, smokers consume fewer vegetables than non-smokers.

A substantial amount of consistent evidence on non-starchy vegetables, including specific subtypes, mostly from case-control studies, shows a dose-response relationship. There is evidence for plausible mechanisms. Non-starchy vegetables probably protect against mouth, pharynx, and larynx cancers.

The Panel is aware that since the conclusion of the SLR, two cohort[76 77] and two case-control studies[78 79] have been published. This new information does not change the Panel judgement (see box 3.8).

Oesophagus

Five cohort studies,[70 80-83] 37 case-control studies[22 40 60 84-115] and 6 ecological studies[51 52 116-119] investigated non-starchy

vegetables and oesophageal cancer. Eight case-control studies investigated vegetable and fruit consumption (combined)[95 104 107 114 120-123]; 16 case-control studies investigated raw vegetables[40 60 85 95-97 103 109 113 114 124-129]; 1 cohort study[66] and 5 case-control studies[86 93 107 124 125] investigated cruciferous vegetables; 1 cohort study[82] and 8 case-control studies[86 101 103 107 109 111 129 130] investigated allium vegetables; 1 cohort study[66] and 11 case-control studies[86 96 98 111 124 127 131-135] investigated green, leafy vegetables; 1 cohort study[66] and 9 case-control studies[58 62 109 111 113 129-132 136] investigated tomatoes.

Non-starchy vegetables

Data suggest an association with reduced risk. Of the five cohort studies, three reported decreased risk when comparing the highest intake group against the lowest, one of which was statistically significant (0.66, 95% CI 0.44–0.99, non-starchy vegetables[82]; 0.5, p value for linear trend 0.1, yel-

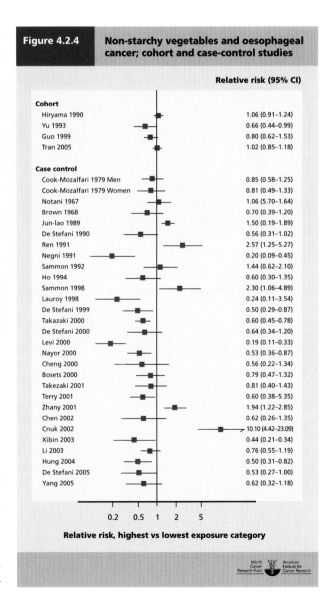

Figure 4.2.4 **Non-starchy vegetables and oesophageal cancer; cohort and case-control studies**

Relative risk (95% CI)

Cohort
	Relative risk (95% CI)
Hiryama 1990	1.06 (0.91–1.24)
Yu 1993	0.66 (0.44–0.99)
Guo 1999	0.80 (0.62–1.53)
Tran 2005	1.02 (0.85–1.18)

Case control
Cook-Mozalfari 1979 Men	0.85 (0.58–1.25)
Cook-Mozalfari 1979 Women	0.81 (0.49–1.33)
Notani 1967	1.06 (5.70–1.64)
Brown 1968	0.70 (0.39–1.20)
Jun-lao 1989	1.50 (0.19–1.89)
De Stefani 1990	0.56 (0.31–1.02)
Ren 1991	2.57 (1.25–5.27)
Negni 1991	0.20 (0.09–0.45)
Sammon 1992	1.44 (0.62–2.10)
Ho 1994	0.60 (0.30–1.35)
Sammon 1998	2.30 (1.06–4.89)
Lauroy 1998	0.24 (0.11–3.54)
De Stefani 1999	0.50 (0.29–0.87)
Takazaki 2000	0.60 (0.45–0.78)
De Stefani 2000	0.64 (0.34–1.20)
Levi 2000	0.19 (0.11–0.33)
Nayor 2000	0.53 (0.36–0.87)
Cheng 2000	0.56 (0.22–1.34)
Bosets 2000	0.79 (0.47–1.32)
Takezaki 2001	0.81 (0.40–1.43)
Terry 2001	0.60 (0.38–5.35)
Zhany 2001	1.94 (1.22–2.85)
Chen 2002	0.62 (0.26–1.35)
Cnuk 2002	10.10 (4.42–23.09)
Xibin 2003	0.44 (0.21–0.34)
Li 2003	0.76 (0.55–1.19)
Hung 2004	0.50 (0.31–0.82)
De Stefani 2005	0.53 (0.27–1.00)
Yang 2005	0.62 (0.32–1.18)

0.2 0.5 1 2 5

Relative risk, highest vs lowest exposure category

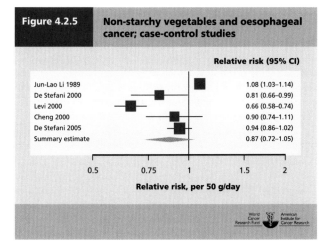

Figure 4.2.5 — Non-starchy vegetables and oesophageal cancer; case-control studies

Relative risk (95% CI)

Study	Relative risk (95% CI)
Jun-Lao Li 1989	1.08 (1.03–1.14)
De Stefani 2000	0.81 (0.66–0.99)
Levi 2000	0.66 (0.58–0.74)
Cheng 2000	0.90 (0.74–1.11)
De Stefani 2005	0.94 (0.86–1.02)
Summary estimate	0.87 (0.72–1.05)

Relative risk, per 50 g/day

low/orange vegetables[70]; and 0.8, 95% CI 0.60–1.0 and p value for trend 0.08, stated as not statistically significant, non-starchy vegetables[80]). The other two reported a non-significant increased risk (1.06, 95% CI 0.91–1.24, non-starchy vegetables[81]; and 1.02, 95% CI 0.88–1.19, fresh non-starchy vegetables[83]) (figure 4.2.4).

Most (29) of the case-control studies published decreased risk estimates when comparing the highest intake group against the lowest,[40 60 85-90 94-99 101-105 107-109 111-115] which were statistically significant in 14 (figure 4.2.4).[40 88 89 94 97-99 101 102 104 105 109] Five studies reported statistically significant increased risk.[84 91 93 100 106 110] Meta-analysis was possible on 5 of the case-control studies, giving a summary effect estimate of 0.87 (95% CI 0. 72–1.05) per 50 g/day increment, with high heterogeneity (figure 4.2.5). A potential cause of heterogeneity is the disparate nature of the exposure definition in different studies, some of which included pickled and cured vegetables, cooked or uncooked vegetables.

Two of the ecological studies reported a statistically significant, positive association between vegetable consumption and cancer incidence[116 117]; one reported a statistically significant, negative association between vegetable consumption and cancer incidence[51]; and the other three reported no significant association between vegetable consumption and cancer mortality.[52 118 119]

The Panel is aware that data from the European Prospective Investigation into Cancer and Nutrition (EPIC; 521 457 participants from 10 European countries; 65 cases of adenocarcinomas of the oesophagus), published after the conclusion of the SLR,[140] showed a non-significant reduced risk (0.72, 95% CI 0.32–1.64) per 100 g/day increase in vegetable consumption (adjusted for several variables including smoking and alcohol, red meat, and processed meat).

Non-starchy vegetables and fruits

Eight case-control studies investigated vegetable and fruit consumption (combined) and oesophageal cancer. All reported a decreased risk with increased consumption.[95 104 107 114 120-123] Six of these were statistically significant.[95 104 107 114 120 121]

Raw vegetables

Sixteen case-control studies investigated raw vegetables and oesophageal cancer.[40 60 85 95-97 103 109 113 114 124-129]

All of these studies reported associations with decreased risk, which were statistically significant in 10.[40 60 85 95 97 109 113 126 127 129] Dose-response meta-analysis was possible on five studies, giving a summary effect estimate of 0.69 (95% CI 0.58–0.83) per 50 g/day increment (figures 4.2.6 and 4.2.7).

This exposure category could be less disparate than other vegetable groupings, as it is clear that preserved vegetables are not included and variation in cooking methods is removed. This may account for the lack of heterogeneity in direction of effect in this subcategory of vegetables.

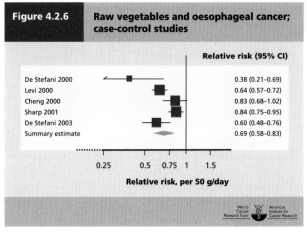

Figure 4.2.6 — Raw vegetables and oesophageal cancer; case-control studies

Relative risk (95% CI)

Study	Relative risk (95% CI)
De Stefani 2000	0.38 (0.21–0.69)
Levi 2000	0.64 (0.57–0.72)
Cheng 2000	0.83 (0.68–1.02)
Sharp 2001	0.84 (0.75–0.95)
De Stefani 2003	0.60 (0.48–0.76)
Summary estimate	0.69 (0.58–0.83)

Relative risk, per 50 g/day

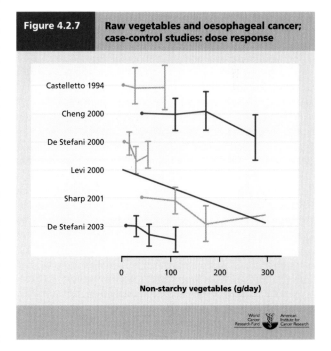

Figure 4.2.7 — Raw vegetables and oesophageal cancer; case-control studies: dose response

Castelletto 1994
Cheng 2000
De Stefani 2000
Levi 2000
Sharp 2001
De Stefani 2003

Non-starchy vegetables (g/day)

Non-starchy root vegetables and tubers

One cohort study[66] and six case-control studies[114 122 128 132 136 141 142] reported separate risk estimates for consumption of non-starchy root vegetables and tubers.

The single cohort study showed a non-significant increased risk for the highest intake group when compared to the lowest, after adjustment.[66] All six case-control studies showed non-significant decreased risk with increased intake.[114 122 128 132 136 141 142]

Cruciferous vegetables

One cohort study[66] and five case-control studies[86 93 107 124 125] reported separate risk estimates for consumption of cruciferous vegetables.

The single cohort study showed a non-significant decreased risk for increased intake of cauliflower or swede and a non-significant increased risk for cabbage, after adjustment.[66] Three case-control studies showed decreased risk with increased intake,[93 107 124] which was statistically significant in two.[93 124] One study showed a non-significant increased risk[125]; and one study showed a non-significant increased risk in women and a non-significant decreased risk in men.[86]

Allium vegetables

One cohort study[82] and eight case-control studies[86 101 103 107 109 111 129 130] reported separate risk estimates for allium vegetable consumption.

The single cohort study showed that garlic intake had no effect on risk.[82] Four case-control studies showed non-significant decreased risk with increased intake.[101 103 107 130] Two studies showed non-significant increased risk.[86 111] One study showed a statistically significant decreased risk for garlic and that onions/leeks had no effect on risk[109]; and one study showed a statistically significant reduced risk for onions and a non-significant increased risk for garlic.[129]

Green, leafy vegetables

One cohort study[66] and 11 case-control studies[86 96 98 111 124 127 131-135] reported separate risk estimates for green, leafy vegetable consumption.

The single cohort study showed no effect for the highest intake group of lettuce when compared to the lowest.[66] Ten case-control studies showed decreased risk with increased intake,[96 98 111 124 127 131-135] which was statistically significant in five.[96 127 132-134] One study showed a non-significant increased risk in women and a non-significant decreased risk in men.[86]

Tomatoes

One cohort study[66] and nine case-control studies[58 62 109 111 113 129-132 136] reported separate risk estimates for consumption of tomatoes.

The single cohort study showed a non-significant increased risk for the highest intake group of lettuce, when compared to the lowest, after adjustment.[66] Eight case-control studies showed decreased risk with increased intake,[58 62 109 111 113 129 131 132 136] which was statistically significant in two.[62 129] One study showed no effect on risk.[130]

The general mechanisms through which vegetables could plausibly protect against oesophageal cancer are outlined below.

There is more evidence, including on vegetable subtypes, from case-control studies than from cohort studies, but both are moderately consistent and there is some evidence for a dose-response relationship. There is evidence for plausible mechanisms. Non-starchy vegetables probably protect against oesophageal cancer.

The Panel is aware that since the conclusion of the SLR, one cohort[140] and two case-control studies[78 143] have been published. This new information does not change the Panel judgement (see box 3.8).

Stomach

Ten cohort studies,[71 80 140 144-150] 45 case-control studies,[109 151-195] and 19 ecological studies[51 52 116-119 196-209] investigated total vegetables. Eleven cohort studies,[71 144 150 210-218] 21 case-control studies,[89 165 169 178 179 188 191 219-232] and 8 ecological studies[233-240] investigated green-yellow vegetables; 6 cohort studies[70 140 144 146 150 241], 13 case-control studies,[162 174 175 179 180 187 223 227 229 230 232 242 243] and 2 ecological studies[202 240] investigated green, leafy vegetables; 3 cohort studies[70 146 241] and 19 case-control studies[58 109 129 152 156 164 171 172 174 232 243-251] investigated tomatoes; 2 cohort studies[150 214] and 6 case-control studies[157 165 169 226 228 243] investigated white or pale vegetables; 6 cohort studies,[146 148 214 252-254] 25 case-control studies,[109 129 161 162 167 172 174 183 184 191 219 225 226 243 247 248 250 255-264] and 3 ecological studies[202 208 238] investigated raw vegetables; 5 cohort studies[144 146 148 253 265] and 6 case-control studies[158 161 162 164 257 266 267] investigated non-starchy vegetables and fruits.

Non-starchy vegetables

Of 12 independent estimates from the 10 cohort studies that investigated non-starchy vegetable consumption, none was statistically significant.[71 80 140 144-150] Seven studies showed non-significant reduced risk[71 140 144-147 150] and 2 reported non-significant increased risk.[80 149] One study showed non-significant increased risk in women and non-significant decreased risk in men.[148] Most effect estimates were close to 1. Meta-analysis was possible on 9 independent estimates from 7 cohort studies, giving a summary effect estimate of 0.98 (95% CI 0.91–1.06) per 100 g/day, with moderate heterogeneity (figure 4.2.8).

Of 45 case-control studies that reported on non-starchy vegetable consumption, 28 reported statistically significant decreased risk.[109 151-153 156-160 163 164 168 169 171 173 176-179 181 182 184 185 187 190 192] The majority of the 17 remaining studies that reported no significant effect on risk were in the direction of decreased risk.[155 162 165-167 170 172 174 183 191 194 195] Four studies showed non-significant increased risk,[180 188 189 193] 1 study showed no effect on risk,[154] and 1 study stated that there was no significant association.[175] One study showed non-significant decreased risk in women and non-significant increased risk in men[186]; and 1 study showed statistically significant

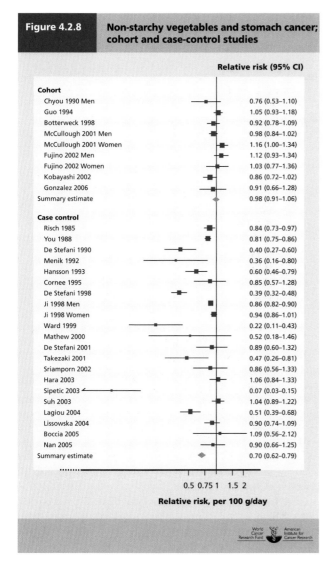

Figure 4.2.8 — Non-starchy vegetables and stomach cancer; cohort and case-control studies

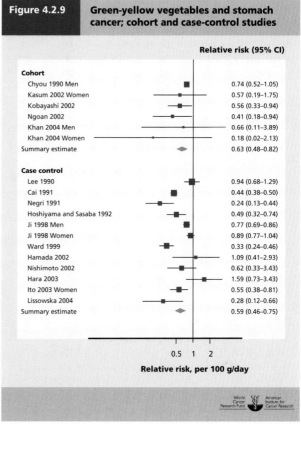

Figure 4.2.9 — Green-yellow vegetables and stomach cancer; cohort and case-control studies

decreased risk in men and non-significant increased risk in women.[161] No studies reported statistically significant increased risk. Meta-analysis was possible on 20 studies, giving a summary effect estimate of 0.70 (95% CI 0.62–0.79) per 100 g/day, with high heterogeneity (figure 4.2.8). This heterogeneity tended to reflect differences in size, rather than direction, of effect.

A dose-response relationship was apparent from case-control but not cohort data.

Results from ecological studies reporting on non-starchy vegetable consumption were mixed, with almost as many studies reporting increased risk as reported decreased risk.[51 52 116-119 196-209]

Green-yellow vegetables

Eight of the 11 cohort studies that reported on green-yellow vegetable consumption showed decreased risk,[71 144 150 210 211 214-217] statistically significant in 4.[150 210 215 216] Two other studies showed non-significant increased risk[212 213] and 1 other study reported no statistically significant association.[218]

Meta-analysis was possible on 6 independent estimates from 5 studies, giving a summary effect estimate of 0.63 (95% CI 0.48–0.82) per 100 g/day, with no heterogeneity (figure 4.2.9).

Of the 21 case-control studies that reported on green-yellow vegetable consumption, 16 showed decreased risk,[89 165 169 178 179 191 219 220 222-228 230-232] statistically significant in 12.[89 165 169 178 179 191 220 222 223 226 231 232] The remaining 5 studies reported increased risk,[111 188 221 229] 1 of which was statistically significant.[221] Meta-analysis was possible on 12 independent estimates from 11 studies, giving a summary effect estimate of 0.59 (95% CI 0.46–0.75) per 100 g/day, with high heterogeneity (figure 4.2.9).

All of the studies adjusted for age and sex; none was adjusted for infection with *Helicobacter pylori*. Nine studies were maximally adjusted, seven of which reported a significant negative association with higher consumption of green-yellow vegetables, and the other two reported no significant association.

A dose-response relationship was apparent from both

Figure 4.2.10	Green-yellow vegetables and stomach cancer; cohort and case-control studies: dose response

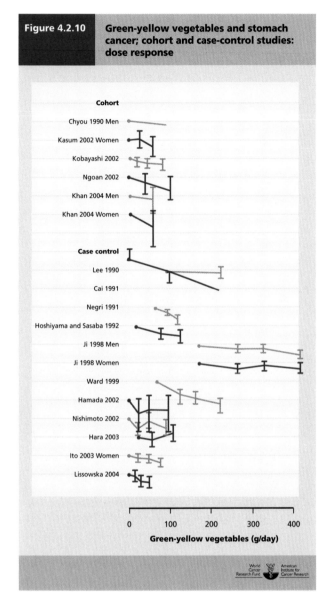

Figure 4.2.11	White or pale vegetables and stomach cancer: cohort and case-control studies

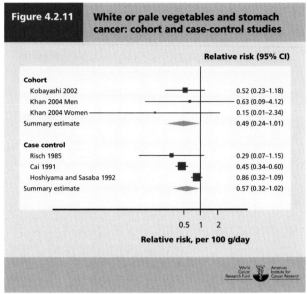

cohort and case-control data on green-yellow vegetable consumption (figure 4.2.10).

Five out of the eight ecological studies that reported on green-yellow vegetable consumption showed decreased risk with increased consumption,[236-240] two showed no association,[233 234] and one study showed increased risk.[235]

This exposure included green-yellow vegetables, green vegetables, yellow vegetables, yellow-orange vegetables, carrots and pumpkins, and high-carotenoid vegetables.

Green, leafy vegetables

Four cohort studies showed non-significant decreased risk with increased intake[70 144 146 150]; two studies showed non-significant increased risk.[140 241] Meta-analysis was possible on four cohort studies, giving a summary effect estimate of 0.85 (95% CI 0.58–1.25) per 100 g/day, with no heterogeneity.[140 144 146 150]

Nine case-control studies showed decreased risk with increased intake,[179 187 223 227 229 230 232 242 243] which was statistically significant in three,[223 232 243] and in men, but not women, in a fourth study.[227] Two further studies showed non-significant increased risk[174 180]; one study showed no effect on risk[162]; and one study stated that there was no significant association.[175] Meta-analysis was possible on six case-control studies, giving a summary effect estimate of 0.90 (95% CI 0.70–1.16) per 100 g/day, with no heterogeneity.[162 179 180 187 229 230]

One ecological study showed statistically significant decreased risk[240] with high intake, the other showed non-significant increased risk.[202]

One cohort study[146] and 15 case-control studies[152 156 164 167 172 231 243-246 261 268-271] also reported separately on lettuce and salad leaves. The single cohort study showed a non-significant decreased risk with increased intake. The effect estimate was 0.88 (95% CI 0.38–2.60) per 50 g/day.[146] Twelve case-control studies showed decreased risk with increased intake of lettuce or salad leaves,[152 156 164 167 231 243 246 261 268-271] which was statistically significant in 7.[156 243 246 261 268-270] Two studies showed non-significant increased risk.[172 245] One study showed no effect on risk.[244] Meta-analysis was possible on 5 case-control studies that investigated lettuce or salad leaves, giving a summary effect estimate of 0.43 (95% CI 0.24–0.77) per 50 g/day, with high heterogeneity.[152 231 268-270] Heterogeneity was related primarily to the size, and not the direction, of the effect.

Tomatoes

Two cohort studies showed a non-significant increased risk with increased intake.[146 241] One study stated that there was a non-significant decreased risk (unquantified).[70] The effect estimates were 1.81 (95% CI 0.85–3.85) per 100 g/day,[146] and 1.1 (95% CI 0.76–1.60) for women and 1.19 (95% CI 0.88–1.61) for men (both for the highest

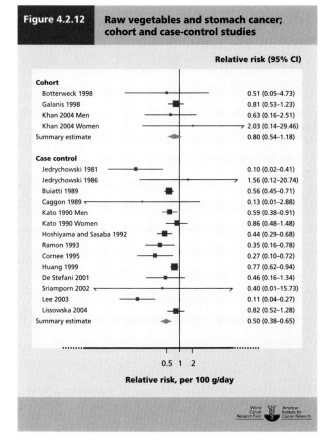

Figure 4.2.12 Raw vegetables and stomach cancer; cohort and case-control studies

Relative risk (95% CI)

Cohort
		Relative risk (95% CI)
Botterweck 1998		0.51 (0.05–4.73)
Galanis 1998		0.81 (0.53–1.23)
Khan 2004 Men		0.63 (0.16–2.51)
Khan 2004 Women		2.03 (0.14–29.46)
Summary estimate		0.80 (0.54–1.18)

Case control
Jedrychowski 1981		0.10 (0.02–0.41)
Jedrychowski 1986		1.56 (0.12–20.74)
Buiatti 1989		0.56 (0.45–0.71)
Caggon 1989		0.13 (0.01–2.88)
Kato 1990 Men		0.59 (0.38–0.91)
Kato 1990 Women		0.86 (0.48–1.48)
Hoshiyama and Sasaba 1992		0.44 (0.29–0.68)
Ramon 1993		0.35 (0.16–0.78)
Cornee 1995		0.27 (0.10–0.72)
Huang 1999		0.77 (0.62–0.94)
De Stefani 2001		0.46 (0.16–1.34)
Sriamporn 2002		0.40 (0.01–15.73)
Lee 2003		0.11 (0.04–0.27)
Lissowska 2004		0.82 (0.52–1.28)
Summary estimate		0.50 (0.38–0.65)

Relative risk, per 100 g/day

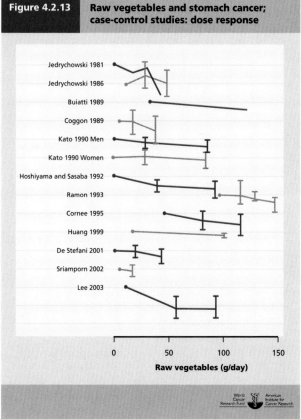

Figure 4.2.13 Raw vegetables and stomach cancer; case-control studies: dose response

Raw vegetables (g/day)

intake group when compared to the lowest).[241]

Most case-control studies showed decreased risk with increased intake, which was statistically significant in 10.[58] [109 152 156 164 171 232 246-248] No studies showed statistically significant increased risk. Meta-analysis was possible on 6 case-control studies, giving a summary effect estimate of 0.40 (95% CI 0.19–0.82) per 100 g/day, with high heterogeneity.[109 152 171 232 244 250]

White or pale vegetables

This incorporates a wide range of vegetables. For example, in Japan white vegetables such as daikon (radish) are commonly consumed. Descriptions used for this exposure were white vegetables, pale green or light green vegetables, and raw chicory.

Both cohort studies showed non-significant decreased risk with increased intake.[150 214] Meta-analysis was possible on both studies, giving a summary effect estimate of 0.49 (95% CI 0.24–1.01) per 100 g/day, with no heterogeneity (figure 4.2.11).

All six case-control studies showed decreased risk with increased intake,[157 165 169 226 228 243] which was statistically significant in three.[165 169 243] Meta-analysis was possible on three studies, giving a summary effect estimate of 0.57 (95% CI 0.32–1.02) per 100 g/day, with high heterogeneity, which was caused by varying size, not direction of the effect (figure 4.2.11).

Raw vegetables

Of seven independent estimates from six cohort studies that reported on raw vegetables, four reported non-significant reduced risk,[146 214 253 254] two reported non-significant increased risk,[214 252] and the other reported a significant increased risk.[148] Two of the increased risk estimates, including the one that reached statistical significance, were stratified for women only. Meta-analysis was possible on four estimates from three studies (not including the one that was statistically significant), giving a summary effect estimate of 0.80 (95% CI 0.54–1.18) per 100 g/day, with no heterogeneity (figure 4.2.12).

Of the 25 case-control studies that reported on raw vegetables, 21 reported decreased risk,[109 129 161 162 167 172 174 183 184 191 219 225 226 243 247 248 250 255 256 258 260 261 264] which was statistically significant in 13.[129 161 172 174 225 226 243 247 248 256 260 261 264] None of the remaining 4 studies that reported increased risk reached statistical significance.[257 259 262 263] Meta-analysis was possible on 14 independent estimates from 13 case-control studies, giving a summary effect estimate of 0.50 (95% CI 0.38–0.65) per 100 g/day, with moderate heterogeneity (figure 4.2.12).

A dose-response relationship was apparent from case-control but not cohort data (figure 4.2.13).

Of the three ecological studies, two reported statistically significant reduced risk[208 238] and one reported a non-significant increased risk with increased raw vegetable consumption.[202]

Non-starchy vegetables and fruits

All five cohort studies showed decreased risk for the highest intake group when compared to the lowest,[144 146 148 253 265] which was statistically significant in two,[253 265] and in men, but not women, in a third study.[148] Meta-analysis was possible on two cohort studies, giving a summary effect estimate of 0.81 (95% CI 0.58–1.14) per 100 g/day.[146 253] All six case-control studies showed decreased risk with increased intake,[158 161 162 164 257 266 267] which was statistically significant in four.[158 162 164 257] Meta-analysis was possible on two case-control studies, giving a summary effect estimate of 0.79 (95% CI 0.63–0.99) per 100 g/day.[162 267]

The stomach is a particularly unusual chemical environment and it is possible that, in addition to the general mechanisms described below, specific mechanisms apply, for instance, in relation to nitrosamine formation.

A substantial amount of evidence is available, including on specific subtypes, particularly green-yellow vegetables, with a dose-response relationship in case-control, but not cohort data. There is evidence for plausible mechanisms. Vegetables probably protect against stomach cancer.

Nasopharynx

Five case-control studies[272-276] and two ecological studies[51 277] investigated non-starchy vegetables and nasopharyngeal cancer; a further four case-control studies investigated green vegetables.[278-281] Preserved vegetables were excluded from all categories.

Eight of the case-control studies reported reduced risk when comparing high against low intake groups,[272 273 275 276 278-281] which was statistically significant in three of the non-starchy vegetable studies[272 275 276] and in two of the green vegetable studies.[279 280] One other study stated that there was no significant association.[274] All studies were based in China.

The ecological studies produced mixed results. One showed significant correlations between the consumption of fresh vegetables and reduced risk of nasopharyngeal carcinoma after adjusting for age (r^2 = -0.77, p = 0.009 among men and r^2 = -0.75, p = 0.013 among women).[51] The second study showed an increasing risk with increases in local consumption of non-starchy vegetables (r^2 = 2.36).[277] This study did not report any adjustments for potential confounding variables or whether the finding was significant.

The general mechanisms through which vegetables could plausibly protect against nasopharyngeal cancer are outlined below.

The evidence for non-starchy vegetables is sparse but generally consistent. There is limited evidence suggesting that non-starchy vegetables protect against nasopharyngeal cancer.

Lung

Seventeen cohort studies,[282-300] 27 case-control studies,[301-331] and 6 ecological studies[52 116 332-335] investigated total vegetables and lung cancer (some studies did not separate non-starchy vegetables from this grouping); in addition, there was 1 relevant pooling project publication.[336] Three cohort studies[337-339] and 1 case-control study[321] investigated non-starchy vegetables specifically; 5 cohort studies[285 292 299 340 341] and 17 case-control studies[65 301 307 312 320-322 326 330 342-350] investigated green, leafy vegetables (excluding cruciferous); 2 cohort studies investigated non-starchy root vegetables and tubers[289 291]; and 6 cohort studies,[285 289 293 299 339 341] 21 case-control studies,[65 261 304 307 313 320-322 325-327 342 344 346-348 351-358] and 1 ecological study[333] investigated carrots specifically.

Total vegetables

Out of 19 effect estimates from 17 cohort studies, 14 showed reduced risk with higher levels of vegetable consumption,[282 283 286-289 291-297 299 300] which was statistically significant in 3[286 297 299 300] and in women only in another[285]; 1 reported no effect on risk,[298] 2 showed increased risk,[284 290] none of which was statistically significant, and 2 showed non-significant increased risk in men but not women.[285 296] Meta-analysis was possible on 10 studies, all of which adjusted for smoking, giving a summary effect estimate of 0.95 (95% CI 0.92–0.98) per 80 g serving/day, with no heterogeneity.[282 283 285-287 292 296 297 300] Two studies did not adjust for smoking, 1 of which showed a non-significant lower vegetable intake in cases than in controls,[295] and the other reported no effect on risk.[298]

Pooled analysis from 8 cohort studies (over 430 000 participants, followed up for 6 to 16 years, more than 3200 lung cancer cases) showed a non-significant reduced risk when comparing high against low intake groups (0.88, 95% CI 0.78–1.00), with a p value for trend of 0.12.[336]

Out of 27 case-control studies, 17 showed reduced risk with higher levels of vegetable consumption,[301-304 306-312 314 316 317 319 322 325-331] which was statistically significant in 8[303 304 306 308-310 314 316 319 325-328]; 7 studies showed non-significant increased risk[305 313 315 318 320 323 324] and 1 study showed no effect on risk.[321] Meta-analysis was possible on 10 studies, all of which adjusted for smoking, giving a summary effect estimate of 0.67 (95% CI 0.53–0.86) per serving/day, with high heterogeneity.[303 308 309 313 316 317 323 325 326 328 329] Three studies did not adjust for smoking, all of which showed statistically significant decreased risk.[306 316 319]

A dose-response relationship was apparent from both cohort and case-control data.

Most of the ecological studies are suggestive of an association between increased vegetable consumption and decreased risk.

Non-starchy vegetables

All three cohort studies reported non-significant reduced risk when comparing highest and lowest vegetable intakes, with effect estimates of 0.9 (lung cancer mortality, 95% CI 0.61–1.33),[337] 0.75 (95% CI 0.41–1.37),[338] and 0.54 (p value for trend 0.2, squamous and small-cell carcinomas only) when comparing the highest with the lowest intake groups.[339] The single case-control study reported a non-significant increased risk when comparing high and low vegetable intakes.[321]

Green, leafy vegetables

All five cohort studies reported reduced risk when comparing high to low intake groups,[285 292 299 340 341] which was statistically significant in one.[299] Dose-response meta-analysis was possible on three cohort studies, giving a summary effect estimate of 0.91 (95% CI 0.89–0.93) per serving/day, with no heterogeneity.[285 340] The two non-included studies reported high-versus-low effect estimates of 0.89 (95% CI 0.66–1.19)[292] and 0.45 (95% CI 0.26–0.78).[299] All five cohort studies adjusted for smoking.

Of the 17 case-control studies, 12 reported decreased risk[65 301 307 320 321 326 330 342 343 345-348] (reaching statistical significance in 2[343 345 348] and 5 reported non-significant increased risk.[312 322 344 349 350] Dose-response meta-analysis was possible on 8 case-control studies, giving a summary effect estimate of 0.96 (95% CI 0.91–1.02) per serving/day, with moderate-to-high heterogeneity.[65 322 326 343 346-349] Some of this heterogeneity may be due to variation in exposure classification, with some studies listing 'green vegetables' being included in this category.

Total non-starchy root vegetables and tubers

Both cohort studies reported reduced risk with increased consumption,[289 291] with effect estimates of 0.56 (95% CI 0.36–0.88)[289] when comparing the highest with the lowest intake groups, and 0.70 (95% CI 0.53–0.93) when comparing the third highest quartile with the lowest (the highest intake group had a non-significant decreased risk).[291] Both studies adjusted for smoking.

Carrots

All six cohort studies reported reduced risk,[285 289 293 299 339 341] which was statistically significant in one (0.4, p value for trend 0.003).[341] The other, non-significant, risk estimates ranged from 0.61 to 0.82.[285 289 293 299 339]

Twenty of the 21 case-control studies showed decreased risk when comparing high against low intake groups,[65 261 304 307 313 321 322 325-327 342 344 346-348 351-358] which was statistically significant in 8.[261 304 321 325 327 346 347 351 353 356-358] One study reported no effect.[320] Meta-analysis on studies that adjusted for smoking was possible on 11 studies, giving a summary effect estimate of 0.81 (95% CI 0.73–0.89), per serving/day increment, with high heterogeneity.[65 307 313 322 325-327 347 348 351 352 354-357]

There was some evidence of publication bias for both cohort and case-control studies.

The single ecological study reported lower mean intake of carrots in an area of high lung cancer risk.[333]

The general mechanisms through which vegetables could plausibly protect against lung cancer are outlined below.

A substantial amount of evidence is available but some studies were not adjusted for smoking. A dose-response relationship is apparent from both cohort and case-control studies. There is limited evidence suggesting that non-starchy vegetables protect against lung cancer.

Colorectum

Seventeen cohort studies[81 359-379] and 71 case-control studies investigated non-starchy vegetables and colorectal cancer.

Of 20 effect estimates from 17 cohort studies that reported comparisons of the highest and lowest intake groups, 11 were in the direction of reduced risk,[81 362 364 366 371-374 376-378] 3 of which were statistically significant.[81 366 371 377] One study showed non-significant decreased risk in women and non-significant increased risk in men.[360] The other 8 reported non-significant increased risk.[359 361 363 365 367-370 375] One study stated that there was no significant association.[379] Meta-analysis was possible on 9 independent estimates from 6 studies, giving a summary effect estimate of 1.00 (95% CI 0.90–1.11) per 2 servings/day increment, with moderate to high heterogeneity.[360 362-364 366 370]

Because of the abundant prospective data from cohort studies, case-control studies were not summarised.

The general mechanisms through which vegetables could plausibly protect against colorectal cancer are outlined below.

A substantial amount of evidence is available but it is inconsistent. There is limited evidence suggesting that non-starchy vegetables protect against colorectal cancer.

The Panel is aware that since the conclusion of the SLR, three case-control studies[78 261 380] have been published. This new information does not change the Panel judgement (see box 3.8).

Ovary

Five cohort studies,[381-385] eight case-control studies,[89 386-392] and two ecological studies[393 394] investigated non-starchy vegetables, and three cohort studies[381-383] and two case-control studies[395 396] investigated green, leafy vegetables.

Non-starchy vegetables

All of the cohort studies reported decreased risk with increased vegetable consumption.[381-385] Meta-analysis was possible on four cohort studies, giving a summary effect estimate of 0.64 (95% CI 0.33–0.97) for an increase of one serving/day, with no heterogeneity.[381 383-385] The study that could not be included reported an effect estimate of 0.76 (95% CI 0.42–1.37) for the highest intake group when compared with the lowest.[382]

Pooled analysis from 12 cohort studies (over 560 000 participants, followed up for 7 to 22 years, more than 2100 lung cancer cases) showed a non-significant reduced risk when comparing high against low intake groups (0.90, 95% CI 0.78–1.04), with a p value for trend of 0.06.[397]

All of the case-control studies reported reduced risk,[89 386-392] which was statistically significant in five.[89 386 387 391 392]

One ecological study reported a non-significant positive regression/correlation between continents[393] and the other reported a negative regression/correlation between countries.[394]

Green, leafy vegetables

All three cohort studies reported decreased risk with increased green, leafy vegetable consumption.[381-383] Meta-analysis was possible on two cohort studies, giving a summary effect estimate of 0.96 (95% CI 0.88–1.03) per two servings/day, with no heterogeneity.[381 383] The third cohort study reported a statistically significant reduced risk (0.44, 95% CI 0.25–0.79) when comparing the highest and lowest intake groups.[382]

Both case-control studies reported reduced risk from increased consumption of green, leafy vegetables,[395 396] one of which was statistically significant.[396]

The general mechanisms through which vegetables could plausibly protect against ovarian cancer are outlined below.

Evidence from cohort and case-control studies is sparse. There is limited evidence suggesting that non-starchy vegetables protect against ovarian cancer.

The Panel is aware that since the conclusion of the SLR one case-control study[78] has been published. This new information does not change the Panel judgement (see box 3.8).

Endometrium

Ten case-control studies investigated non starchy vegetable consumption.[398-407] Seven case-control studies investigated cruciferous vegetables and endometrial cancer.[398-400 405 407-410]

Of the 10 studies that reported on non-starchy vegetables, 7 showed decreased risk when comparing the highest with the lowest intake groups,[400-405 407] which was statistically significant in 5.[400 402-404 407] Two reported a non-significant increased risk[398 406] and the other showed no effect on risk.[399] Meta-analysis was possible on 8 studies, giving a summary estimate of 0.90 (95% CI 0.86–0.95) per 100 g of vegetable intake/day, with low heterogeneity.[399 401-407] A dose-response relationship was apparent from these data.

Five out of the seven case-control studies that investigated cruciferous vegetables reported reduced risk when comparing high to low intake groups,[399 405 407-410] which was statistically significant in one.[405] The other two studies reported non-significant increased risk.[398 400] Meta-analysis was possible on five studies, giving a summary effect estimate of 0.79 (95% CI 0.69–0.90) per 100 g/day, with no heterogeneity.[399 405 407 409 410] The two studies that could not be included suggested increased risk, though not statistically significant.[398 400]

A dose-response relationship is apparent from case-control data.

The general mechanisms through which vegetables could plausibly protect against endometrial cancer are outlined below. Cruciferous vegetables contain glucosinolates. Certain hydrolysis products of glucosinolates, including indoles and isothiocyanates, have shown anti-carcinogenic properties in laboratory experiments and in diets in live experiments in animals.[411] The human genotype of glutathione *S*-transferase has been shown to have a significant role in the metabolism of these phytochemicals and may therefore influence potential anti-cancer properties.[412]

Evidence comes from case-control studies only. There is limited evidence suggesting that non-starchy vegetables protect against endometrial cancer.

General mechanisms — non-starchy vegetables

Also see Chapter 2. Non-starchy vegetables provide a plethora of potentially cancer-preventive substances, including several antioxidant nutrients (such as carotenoids and vitamin C), dietary fibre, as well as phytochemicals (such as glucosinolates, dithiolthiones, indoles, chlorophyll, flavonoids, allylsulphides, and phytoestrogens). Phytochemicals might influence cancer risk through their antioxidant activities, modulation of detoxification enzymes, stimulation of the immune system, antiproliferative activities, and/or modulation of steroid hormone concentration and hormone metabolism, to name a few possible mechanisms. Non-starchy vegetables are also a source of folate, which plays an important role in synthesis and methylation of DNA. Abnormal DNA methylation has been linked to aberrant gene expression and also to cancers at several sites, and may be particularly important in rapidly dividing tissues. It is difficult to unravel the relative importance of each constituent and likely that a protective effect may result from a combination of influences on several pathways involved in carcinogenesis.

Carrots are a source of carotenoids, particularly alpha-carotene and beta-carotene, as well as other vitamins and phytochemicals with potentially protective effects. Tomatoes are a source of vitamin C and carotenoids, particularly lycopene. Potential mechanisms of inhibition include the antioxidant properties of carotenoids and ligand-dependent signalling through retinoid receptors (see chapter 4.2.5.3).

There is a complex mixture of phytochemicals present in whole vegetables and these may have additive and synergistic effects responsible for anti-cancer activities.

4.2.5.1.1 Allium vegetables
Stomach

Two cohort studies,[413 414] 27 case-control studies,[109 129 152 162 164 171 178 182 185 187 191 194 195 232 243-245 247 248 251 266 270 415-419] and 2 ecological studies[202 208] investigated allium vegetables and stomach cancer; 1 cohort study,[413] 16 case-control studies,[109 129 182 184 195 232 246 247 251 262 418 420-422] and 2 ecological studies[203 208] investigated garlic and stomach cancer. There was also 1 relevant intervention study that combined allitridium and selenium supplements.[423 424]

Allium vegetables

Both cohort studies reported decreased risk,[413 414] which was statistically significant in one.[413] Meta-analysis was possible on both, giving a summary effect estimate of 0.55 (95% CI 0.35–0.87) per 100 g/day, with no heterogeneity (figure 4.2.14).[413 414]

Twenty of the case-control studies showed reduced risk when comparing high with low intake groups,[129 152 162 164 171 178 182 185 187 191 194 195 232 243 247 248 270 416 418 419] which was statistically significant in 12.[129 152 162 164 182 187 194 243 248 270 416 418] Four studies showed increased risk,[109 245 266 415] which was statistically significant in 2,[245] and the remaining 3 reported no significant effect on risk.[244 251 417] Meta-analysis was possible

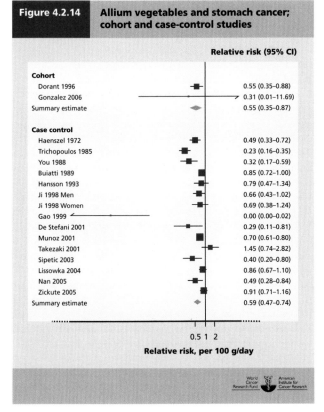

Figure 4.2.14 | **Allium vegetables and stomach cancer; cohort and case-control studies**

Relative risk (95% CI)

Cohort
Dorant 1996		0.55 (0.35–0.88)
Gonzalez 2006		0.31 (0.01–11.69)
Summary estimate		0.55 (0.35–0.87)

Case control
Haenszel 1972		0.49 (0.33–0.72)
Trichopoulos 1985		0.23 (0.16–0.35)
You 1988		0.32 (0.17–0.59)
Buiatti 1989		0.85 (0.72–1.00)
Hansson 1993		0.79 (0.47–1.34)
Ji 1998 Men		0.66 (0.43–1.02)
Ji 1998 Women		0.69 (0.38–1.24)
Gao 1999		0.00 (0.00–0.02)
De Stefani 2001		0.29 (0.11–0.81)
Munoz 2001		0.70 (0.61–0.80)
Takezaki 2001		1.45 (0.74–2.82)
Sipetic 2003		0.40 (0.20–0.80)
Lissowka 2004		0.86 (0.67–1.10)
Nan 2005		0.49 (0.28–0.84)
Zickute 2005		0.91 (0.71–1.16)
Summary estimate		0.59 (0.47–0.74)

0.5 1 2

Relative risk, per 100 g/day

World Cancer Research Fund / American Institute for Cancer Research

on 14 studies, giving a summary effect estimate of 0.59 (95% CI 0.47–0.74) per 100 g/day, with high heterogeneity (figure 4.2.14).[109 129 152 162 171 178 182 187 191 194 232 247 270 416]

Both ecological studies reported statistically significant decreased risk with increased consumption.[202 208]

A statistically significant dose-response relationship is apparent from cohort and case-control data.

Garlic
The single cohort study, which was specific to supplementary garlic, showed a non-significant increased risk when comparing garlic supplement use versus no supplement use (1.29, 95% CI 0.62–2.67).[413]

Fifteen of the case-control studies showed decreased risk when comparing highest to lowest intake groups,[109 129 182 184 195 232 246 247 251 418 420-422] which was statistically significant in seven.[129 182 232 246 247 418 420 422] One study showed a non-significant increased risk.[262] Meta-analysis was possible on five studies, giving a summary effect estimate of 0.41 (95% CI 0.23–0.73) per serving/day.[109 129 182 232 421]

One ecological study showed statistically significant decreased risk with increased intake[208]; the other showed no significant association.[203]

Intervention study
The double-blind, randomised trial had an intervention duration of 3 years, and a 5- and 10-year follow-up, and more than 5000 participants, all of whom had been identified as being at increased risk of stomach cancer. The intervention

was a combined selenium/allitridium supplement.[423 424] The 5-year follow-up suggested that the intervention was effective in reducing stomach cancer incidence in men (0.36, 95% CI 0.14–0.92) but not in women (1.14, 95% CI 0.22–5.76).[423] The statistically significant protective effect for men had dissipated at the 10-year follow-up.[424] (Also see chapter 4.2.5.8.)

Allium vegetables are high in flavonols and organosulphur compounds. They also, particularly garlic, have antibiotic properties. Although this may act directly against *H pylori* (a known cause of stomach cancers), a study in humans has not shown this effect.[425] It is also possible that antibacterial effects of garlic might inhibit the secondary colonisation of the stomach after *H pylori*-induced atrophy. At present, there is no evidence to support or refute this mechanism. An animal study provides evidence that dietary garlic can reduce the severity of *H pylori*-associated gastritis.[426]

The evidence, though not copious and mostly from case-control studies, is consistent, with a dose-response relationship. There is evidence for plausible mechanisms. Allium vegetables probably protect against stomach cancer.

Colorectum
Garlic
Two cohort studies[361 362] and six case-control studies[427-435] investigated garlic consumption.

Both cohort studies reported non-significant decreased risk when comparing the highest with the lowest intake groups, with effect estimates of 0.77 (95% CI 0.51–1.16)[361] and 0.68 (95% CI 0.46–1.01) (figure 4.2.15).[362]

All six case-control studies showed decreased risk for the highest consumers of garlic,[427-435] which was statistically significant in three (figure 4.2.16).[431 432]

There is considerable preclinical evidence with model carcinogens and transplantable tumours that supports an anti-cancer effect of garlic and some of its allyl sulphur components. Animal studies demonstrate that allyl sulphides effectively inhibit colon tumour formation and also can inhibit cell growth in the laboratory.[436-439]

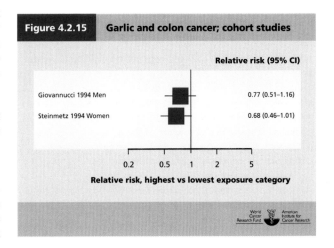

Figure 4.2.15 | **Garlic and colon cancer; cohort studies**

Relative risk (95% CI)

Giovannucci 1994 Men		0.77 (0.51–1.16)
Steinmetz 1994 Women		0.68 (0.46–1.01)

0.2 0.5 1 2 5

Relative risk, highest vs lowest exposure category

World Cancer Research Fund / American Institute for Cancer Research

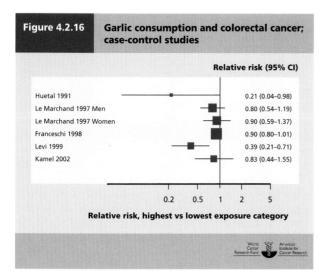

Figure 4.2.16 | **Garlic consumption and colorectal cancer; case-control studies**

The evidence, though not copious and mostly from case-control studies, is consistent, with a dose-response relationship. There is evidence for plausible mechanisms. Garlic probably protects against colorectal cancer.

The Panel is aware that since the conclusion of the SLR, one case-control study[78] has been published. This new information does not change the Panel judgement (see box 3.8).

In addition to this judgement, data on garlic have contributed to the evidence base for allium vegetables and stomach cancer (also see chapter 7.5).

4.2.5.1.2 Carrots
Cervix

Five case-control studies[440-444] and one ecological study[445] investigated carrots and cervical cancer.

Case-control studies were consistent in showing reduced risk for the highest levels of consumption, which was statistically significant in three.[440-442] All studies used hospital-based controls and none adjusted for human papilloma virus status. The single ecological study showed non-significant increased risk with high intake of carrots.[445]

Some carotenoids, including beta-carotene and alpha-carotene, which are found at high levels in carrots, are precursors of vitamin A. They also have properties independent of their pro-vitamin A activity. Carotenoids are recognised antioxidants and low blood levels of dietary antioxidants are associated with human papilloma virus persistence.[446]

The evidence, from case-control studies only, is sparse but consistent. There is limited evidence suggesting that carrots protect against cervical cancer.

Data on carrots have contributed to the evidence base for non-starchy vegetables and mouth, pharynx, and larynx cancers (chapter 7.1) and lung cancer (chapter 7.4). Also see chapter 4.2.5.1.

4.2.5.2 Fruits
Mouth, pharynx, and larynx

One cohort study,[447] 35 case-control studies[21 22 24-26 28 30-33 35 36 39-50 59-61 63 64 67 69 72 74 448-450] and 2 ecological studies[52 68] investigated fruits and mouth, pharynx, and larynx cancers; and 1 cohort study,[66] 23 case-control studies[23 26-29 31 33 34 37-39 41-43 45-47 50 63 65 75 451 452] and 1 ecological study[52] investigated citrus fruits. In addition, 1 cohort study[54] and 6 case-control studies[33 39 45 55-57] investigated non-starchy vegetables and fruits in combination (also see evidence on non-starchy vegetables, chapter 4.2.5.1).

General fruits

The single cohort study, which adjusted for smoking, showed a non-significant decreased risk for the highest when compared to the lowest intake groups, with an effect estimate of 0.82 (95% CI 0.64–1.04) (figure 4.2.17).[447]

Most (32) of the case-control studies reported decreased risk associated with higher intake of fruits,[24-26 28 30-33 35 36 39-48 50 59-61 63 64 69 72 74 448 450] which was statistically significant in 17.[26 31 32 35 39-43 46-48 50 63 64 69 72 448] No study reported statistically significant increased risk. Meta-analysis was possible on 7 studies (all of which adjusted for smoking), giving a summary effect estimate of 0.72 (95% CI 0.59–0.87) per 100 g/day, with high heterogeneity (figure 4.2.17).[30 39 42 44 45 69 72] Heterogeneity came from the varying size, not direction, of effect.

One ecological study showed a weak inverse correlation between fruits and oral cancer.[68] The other observed inverse correlations among women for fruit and both oral and laryngeal cancers and positive correlations among men for the same two sites.[52]

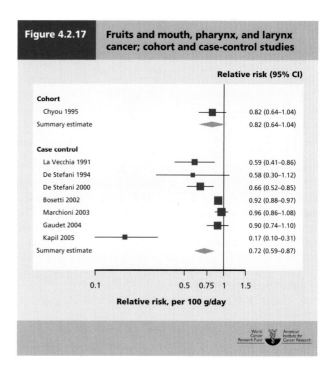

Figure 4.2.17 | **Fruits and mouth, pharynx, and larynx cancer; cohort and case-control studies**

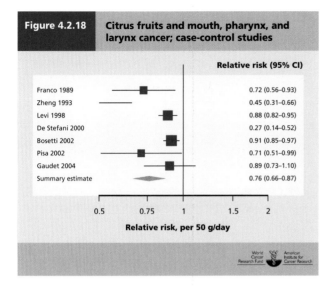

Figure 4.2.18 | Citrus fruits and mouth, pharynx, and larynx cancer; case-control studies

Relative risk (95% CI)

Franco 1989	0.72 (0.56–0.93)
Zheng 1993	0.45 (0.31–0.66)
Levi 1998	0.88 (0.82–0.95)
De Stefani 2000	0.27 (0.14–0.52)
Bosetti 2002	0.91 (0.85–0.97)
Pisa 2002	0.71 (0.51–0.99)
Gaudet 2004	0.89 (0.73–1.10)
Summary estimate	0.76 (0.66–0.87)

Relative risk, per 50 g/day

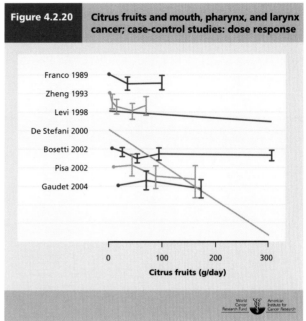

Figure 4.2.20 | Citrus fruits and mouth, pharynx, and larynx cancer; case-control studies: dose response

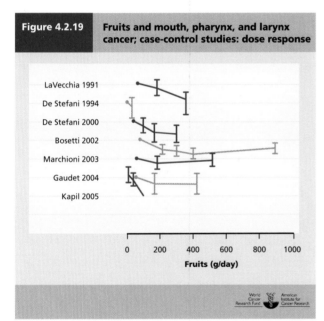

Figure 4.2.19 | Fruits and mouth, pharynx, and larynx cancer; case-control studies: dose response

Citrus fruits

The single cohort study, which was specific to oranges and was adjusted for smoking, showed a non-significant decreased risk for the highest when compared to the lowest intake groups, with an effect estimate of 0.50 (95% CI 0.30–1.00), with a p value for trend of 0.03.[66] This risk estimate was for cancers of the upper aerodigestive tract.

Twenty-two of the case-control studies showed decreased risk associated with higher intake of fruits,[23 27-29 31 33 34 37-39 41-43 45-47 50 63 65 75 451 452] which was statistically significant in 13.[23 27-29 31 33 37 39 42 43 47 50 75] The 23rd study showed no effect on risk.[26] Meta-analysis was possible on 7 studies (all of which adjusted for smoking), giving a summary effect estimate of 0.76 (95% CI 0.66–0.87) per 50 g/day, with high heterogeneity (figure 4.2.18).[23 29 37 39 42 45 65] Heterogeneity

came from the varying size, not direction, of effect.

A dose-response relationship was apparent from case-control but not cohort data for both general and citrus fruits (figures 4.2.19 and 4.2.20). There is some suggestion that the greatest effect appears to be with the first increment. That is, some fruit consumption confers a protective effect compared to none. However, it is not clear that the effect continues in a linear fashion with increased doses.

One ecological study found no significant association between citrus fruit consumption and cancer mortality in men or women.[52]

Studies that reported on combined intake of non-starchy vegetables and fruits showed evidence of an association with decreased risk (see chapter 4.2.5.1).

The general mechanisms through which fruits could plausibly protect against mouth, pharynx, and larynx cancer are outlined below.

The evidence, including on fruit subtypes, though mostly from case-control studies, is consistent, with a dose-response relationship. There is evidence for plausible mechanisms. Fruits probably protect against mouth, pharynx, and larynx cancers.

The Panel is aware that since the conclusion of the SLR, two cohort studies[76 77] and one case-control study[79] have been published. This new information does not change the Panel judgement (see box 3.8).

Oesophagus

Four cohort studies,[80 82 83 447] 36 case-control studies[22 40 60 84 86 87 89 94-96 98-100 102 104 108-110 112-115 125-129 134-136 138 453-456] and 7 ecological studies[52 68 116 118 119 234 457 458] investigated fruits and oesophageal cancer; 1 cohort study,[66] 16 case-control

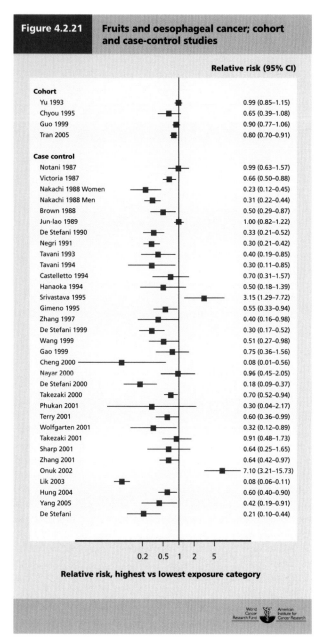

Figure 4.2.21 | Fruits and oesophageal cancer; cohort and case-control studies

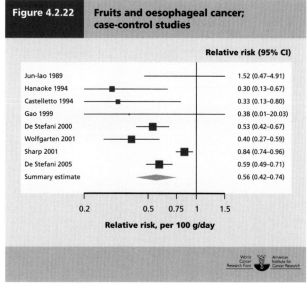

Figure 4.2.22 | Fruits and oesophageal cancer; case-control studies

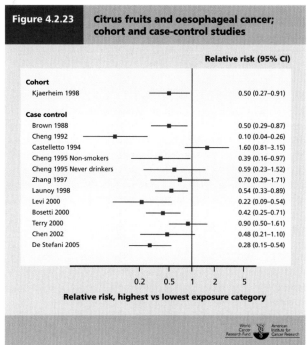

Figure 4.2.23 | Citrus fruits and oesophageal cancer; cohort and case-control studies

studies,[33 85 86 88 90 97 105 111 113 124 125 128 130 132 133 136 459] and 1 ecological study[52] investigated citrus fruits.

General fruits

All of the cohort studies reported reduced risk with higher intakes of fruit,[80 82 83 447] which was statistically significant in two.[83 447] One study reported a statistically significant dose-response relationship, with a risk estimate of 0.68 (95% CI 0.53–0.88) per 100 g/day after adjustment for smoking.[447] The other three reported risks for the highest intake groups relative to the lowest, with risk estimates of 0.8 (95% CI 0.7–0.9; not adjusted for smoking),[83] 0.9 (95%

CI 0.8–1.1; adjusted for smoking),[80] and 0.99 (95% CI 0.85–1.15; not adjusted for smoking).[82]

Thirty-two of the case-control studies reported reduced risk for the highest intake groups when compared to the lowest (figure 4.2.21),[22 40 60 84 86 87 89 95 96 98 99 102 104 108-110 113-115 125-129 134-136 138 453-456] which was statistically significant in 24.[40 60 84 86 87 89 95 96 102 104 110 113-115 127 134-136 138 454-456] One study reported statistically significant increased risk,[100] one reported no effect on risk,[112] and one reported no statistically significant association.[94] Meta-analysis was possible on eight studies, giving a summary effect estimate of 0.56 (95% CI 0.42–0.74) per 100 g/day, with high heterogeneity (figure

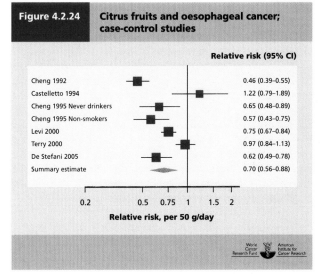

Figure 4.2.24 Citrus fruits and oesophageal cancer; case-control studies

Relative risk (95% CI)

Cheng 1992	0.46 (0.39–0.55)
Castelletto 1994	1.22 (0.79–1.89)
Cheng 1995 Never drinkers	0.65 (0.48–0.89)
Cheng 1995 Non-smokers	0.57 (0.43–0.75)
Levi 2000	0.75 (0.67–0.84)
Terry 2000	0.97 (0.84–1.13)
De Stefani 2005	0.62 (0.49–0.78)
Summary estimate	0.70 (0.56–0.88)

Relative risk, per 50 g/day

4.2.22). Heterogeneity may be partially explained by differential adjustment for confounders between studies.

All seven ecological studies reported reduced risk with increased intake,[52 68 116 118 119 234 457 458] which was statistically significant in one.[68 458]

Citrus fruits

The single cohort study, which was specific to oranges and was adjusted for smoking, showed a non-significant decreased risk for the highest when compared to the lowest intake groups, with an effect estimate of 0.50 (95% CI 0.30–1.00), with a p value for trend of 0.03.[66] This risk estimate was for cancers of the upper aerodigestive tract; 22 out of 71 cases were oesophageal cancers.

Fifteen of the case-control studies reported decreased risk for the highest intake groups when compared to the lowest,[33] [85 86 88 90 97 105 111 113 124 125 130 132 133 136 459] which was statistically significant in 10 (figure 4.2.23).[33 85 86 88 97 105 113 132 133 136 459] The other study reported a non-significant increased risk.[128] Meta-analysis was possible on six studies, giving a summary effect estimate of 0.70 (95% CI 0.56–0.88) per 50 g/day, with high heterogeneity (figure 4.2.24).[33 97 128 130 132 133] Four of these studies adjusted for smoking.[33 97 128 132 133] Heterogeneity may be partially explained by differential adjustment for confounders between studies.

The single ecological study reported a non-significant increased risk.[52]

The general mechanisms through which fruits could plausibly protect against cancer are outlined below.

The evidence, including on fruit subtypes, though mostly from case-control studies, is consistent, with a dose-response relationship. There is evidence for plausible mechanisms. Fruits probably protect against oesophageal cancer.

The Panel is aware that since the conclusion of the SLR, one cohort study[140] and two case-control studies[143 460] have been published. *This new information does not change the Panel judgement (see box 3.8).*

Lung

Twenty-five cohort studies,[214 216 282-300 337 339 360 461-467] 32 case-control studies,[261 303-306 308-318 320-322 324 326-328 330 331 343 346 349 350 352 355 357 358 468-472] and 7 ecological studies[52 116 332-334 473 474] investigated fruits and lung cancer.

Twenty of the cohort studies showed decreased risk for the highest intake groups when compared to the lowest,[214 216 282-289 291-294 296 297 299 300 337 461-467] which was statistically significant in four.[216 289 292 300 461 464] Four studies showed non-significant increased risk[290 295 339 360] and the other reported no statistically significant association.[298] Meta-analysis was possible on 14 cohort studies, giving a summary effect estimate of 0.94 (95% CI 0.90–0.97) per 80 g serving/day, with low heterogeneity (figure 4.2.25). All but one of these studies adjusted for smoking.[462]

Pooled analysis from 8 cohort studies (over 430 000 participants, followed up for 6 to 16 years, more than 3200 lung

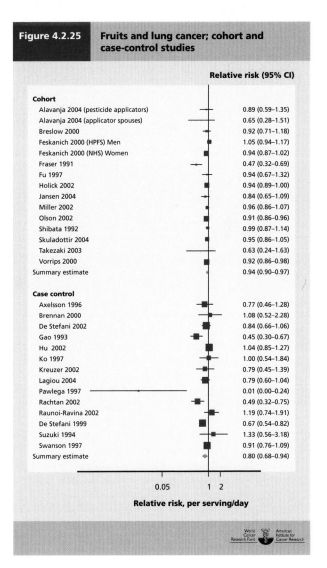

Figure 4.2.25 Fruits and lung cancer; cohort and case-control studies

Relative risk (95% CI)

Cohort

Alavanja 2004 (pesticide applicators)	0.89 (0.59–1.35)
Alavanja 2004 (applicator spouses)	0.65 (0.28–1.51)
Breslow 2000	0.92 (0.71–1.18)
Feskanich 2000 (HPFS) Men	1.05 (0.94–1.17)
Feskanich 2000 (NHS) Women	0.94 (0.87–1.02)
Fraser 1991	0.47 (0.32–0.69)
Fu 1997	0.94 (0.67–1.32)
Holick 2002	0.94 (0.89–1.00)
Jansen 2004	0.84 (0.65–1.09)
Miller 2002	0.96 (0.86–1.07)
Olson 2002	0.91 (0.86–0.96)
Shibata 1992	0.99 (0.87–1.14)
Skuladottir 2004	0.95 (0.86–1.05)
Takezaki 2003	0.63 (0.24–1.63)
Vorrips 2000	0.92 (0.86–0.98)
Summary estimate	0.94 (0.90–0.97)

Case control

Axelsson 1996	0.77 (0.46–1.28)
Brennan 2000	1.08 (0.52–2.28)
De Stefani 2002	0.84 (0.66–1.06)
Gao 1993	0.45 (0.30–0.67)
Hu 2002	1.04 (0.85–1.27)
Ko 1997	1.00 (0.54–1.84)
Kreuzer 2002	0.79 (0.45–1.39)
Lagiou 2004	0.79 (0.60–1.04)
Pawlega 1997	0.01 (0.00–0.24)
Rachtan 2002	0.49 (0.32–0.75)
Raunoi-Ravina 2002	1.19 (0.74–1.91)
De Stefani 1999	0.67 (0.54–0.82)
Suzuki 1994	1.33 (0.56–3.18)
Swanson 1997	0.91 (0.76–1.09)
Summary estimate	0.80 (0.68–0.94)

Relative risk, per serving/day

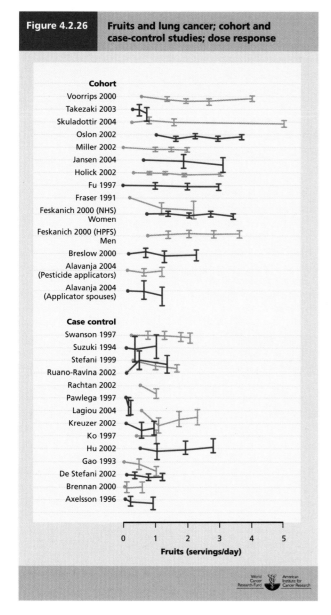

Figure 4.2.26 | **Fruits and lung cancer; cohort and case-control studies; dose response**

Of the seven ecological studies, four reported non-significant decreased risk in areas of higher fruit consumption,[52 332 473 474] one reported no consistent association,[334] and two reported non-significant increased risk.[116 333]

The general mechanisms through which fruits could plausibly protect against cancer are outlined below. In addition, flavonoids found in fruit directly inhibit expression of CYP1A1 (a cytochrome P450 enzyme that helps to metabolise toxins), resulting in decreased DNA damage.[475] Elevated CYP1A1 activity has been associated with increased risk of lung cancer, primarily in smokers.[476] The protective association of flavonoids is associated with specific CYP1A1 genotypes, which supports the importance of flavonoids and potentially explains heterogeneous results.[476 477]

> **The evidence is ample and consistent. A dose-response relationship is apparent from both cohort and case-control studies and there is evidence for plausible mechanisms operating in humans. The evidence that fruits protect against lung cancer is convincing.**

The Panel is aware that since the conclusion of the SLR, one case-control study[478] has been published. This new information does not change the Panel judgement (see box 3.8).

Stomach

Sixteen cohort studies,[71 80 144-147 149 150 213-217 252-254 414] 51 case-control studies,[89 109 129 151 154 156 158-163 167-169 174-176 178-180 182 184-187 189-191 193 195 219 221 222 224-227 229 230 246 255-258 260 261 264 270 479-482] and 23 ecological studies[52 116 118 119 197 198 200-202 204-209 234 236-240 483-485] investigated fruits.

Ten cohort studies reported decreased risk for the highest intake groups when compared to the lowest,[71 80 144 146 150 214-217 253 254] which was statistically significant in one,[253] and in women only in a second study.[216] Six studies showed increased risk,[145 147 149 213 214 252 414] which was statistically significant in one.[213] Meta-analysis was possible on eight studies, giving a summary effect estimate of 0.95 (95% CI 0.89–1.02) per 100 g/day, with low heterogeneity (figure 4.2.27).

One of the cohort studies considered in the meta-analysis above (EPIC, more than 521 000 participants in over 10 European countries) reported results stratified by *H pylori* status. The effect estimate for the *H pylori*-negative group was 0.72 (95% CI 0.39–1.33) and 0.98 (95% CI 0.81–1.2) for the positive group.[140]

Forty case-control studies showed decreased risk for the highest intake groups when compared to the lowest,[89 109 151 156 158-160 162 163 167-169 174 176 178-180 184 186 187 189-191 195 219 221 222 225 226 229 230 246 256-258 260 261 264 270 479-481] which was statistically significant in 25.[89 109 151 158-160 162 163 167-169 174 176 178 186 187 190 191 221 222 226 229 246 256 261 264 479 481] Seven showed increased risk,[129 161 182 185 193 224 482] which was statistically significant in two.[182 193] One study showed non-significant increased risk in men and non-significant decreased risk in women.[227] Two studies showed no effect on risk[154 255] and the remaining one reported that there was no significant association.[175] Meta-analysis was possible on 26 studies, giving a summary effect estimate of 0.67 (95% CI 0.59–0.76) per 100 g/day, with

cancer cases) showed a statistically significant reduced risk for the highest intake group when compared to the lowest (0.77, 95% CI 0.67–0.87), with a p value for trend of < 0.001.[336]

Twenty-one case-control studies showed decreased risk for the highest intake groups when compared to the lowest,[261 303 305 306 308 309 311 312 315 317 318 320-322 324 327 328 331 343 346 349 350 355 357 358 468 469 472] which was statistically significant in 7.[261 309 311 324 327 343 346 357 358 468 472] Three studies reported no effect on risk[310 316 330 352] and 8 showed increased risk,[304 313 314 326 470 471] which was statistically significant in 3.[304 326 470] Meta-analysis was possible on 14 case-control studies, giving a summary effect estimate of 0.80 (95% CI 0.68–0.94) per serving/day, with moderate heterogeneity (figures 4.2.25 and 4.2.26). All but 2 of these studies adjusted for smoking, and exclusion of these 2 studies did not significantly alter the meta-analysis.[316 352]

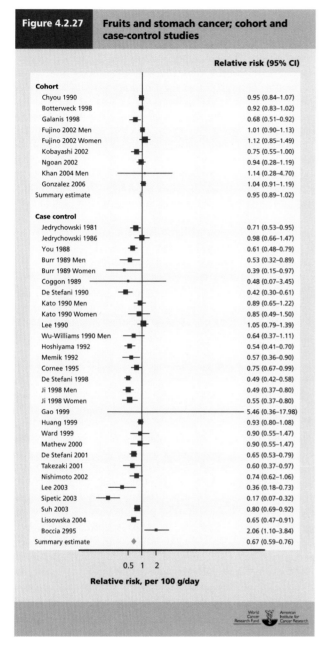

Figure 4.2.27 | **Fruits and stomach cancer; cohort and case-control studies**

Relative risk (95% CI)

Cohort
Chyou 1990	0.95 (0.84–1.07)
Botterweck 1998	0.92 (0.83–1.02)
Galanis 1998	0.68 (0.51–0.92)
Fujino 2002 Men	1.01 (0.90–1.13)
Fujino 2002 Women	1.12 (0.85–1.49)
Kobayashi 2002	0.75 (0.55–1.00)
Ngoan 2002	0.94 (0.28–1.19)
Khan 2004 Men	1.14 (0.28–4.70)
Gonzalez 2006	1.04 (0.91–1.19)
Summary estimate	0.95 (0.89–1.02)

Case control
Jedrychowski 1981	0.71 (0.53–0.95)
Jedrychowski 1986	0.98 (0.66–1.47)
You 1988	0.61 (0.48–0.79)
Burr 1989 Men	0.53 (0.32–0.89)
Burr 1989 Women	0.39 (0.15–0.97)
Coggon 1989	0.48 (0.07–3.45)
De Stefani 1990	0.42 (0.30–0.61)
Kato 1990 Men	0.89 (0.65–1.22)
Kato 1990 Women	0.85 (0.49–1.50)
Lee 1990	1.05 (0.79–1.39)
Wu-Williams 1990 Men	0.64 (0.37–1.11)
Hoshiyama 1992	0.54 (0.41–0.70)
Memik 1992	0.57 (0.36–0.90)
Cornee 1995	0.75 (0.67–0.99)
De Stefani 1998	0.49 (0.42–0.58)
Ji 1998 Men	0.49 (0.37–0.80)
Ji 1998 Women	0.55 (0.37–0.80)
Gao 1999	5.46 (0.36–17.98)
Huang 1999	0.93 (0.80–1.08)
Ward 1999	0.90 (0.55–1.47)
Mathew 2000	0.90 (0.55–1.47)
De Stefani 2001	0.65 (0.53–0.79)
Takezaki 2001	0.60 (0.37–0.97)
Nishimoto 2002	0.74 (0.62–1.06)
Lee 2003	0.36 (0.18–0.73)
Sipetic 2003	0.17 (0.07–0.32)
Suh 2003	0.80 (0.69–0.92)
Lissowska 2004	0.65 (0.47–0.91)
Boccia 2995	2.06 (1.10–3.84)
Summary estimate	0.67 (0.59–0.76)

0.5 1 2

Relative risk, per 100 g/day

World Cancer Research Fund   American Institute for Cancer Research

high heterogeneity (figure 4.2.27).

A dose-response relationship is apparent from case-control but not cohort data. There is statistically significant heterogeneity between study types.

Eighteen ecological studies showed decreased risk with increased intake of fruits,[116 118 197 200 201 204-208 234 237-239 484 485] which was statistically significant in eight.[204-208 237] Four studies showed increased risk with increased intake,[52 118 119 202 239 240] which was statistically significant in one.[240] Two studies showed non-significant decreased risk in women and non-significant increased risk in men[209 236]; one study showed non-significant decreased risk in men and non-significant increased risk in women[198]; and one study

showed non-significant increased risk in white men and Japanese men and women, and non-significant decreased risk in white women.[483]

The stomach is a particularly unusual chemical environment and it is possible that, in addition to the general mechanisms described below, specific mechanisms apply, for instance, in relation to nitrosamine formation.[486] It is also plausible that bioactive constituents in fruit would protect against *H pylori*-induced damage, particularly inflammation, which is implicated in the development of stomach cancers.

The evidence is ample and more consistent with a dose-response relationship for case-control studies than for cohorts. There is evidence for plausible mechanisms. Fruits probably protect against stomach cancer.

The Panel is aware that since the conclusion of the SLR, three case-control studies[487-489] have been published. This new information does not change the Panel judgement (see box 3.8).

Nasopharynx

Six case-control studies investigated general fruits and nasopharyngeal cancers[274 275 281 490-492]; a further five case-control studies investigated citrus fruits.[273 278-281] Preserved fruits were excluded from all categories.

Of the six case-control studies that investigated general fruits, four reported decreased risk for the highest intake groups when compared to the lowest,[275 281 491 492] which was statistically significant in two.[275 491] The other two studies reported that there was no significant effect on risk, without further detail.[274 490] All five of the case-control studies that investigated citrus fruits reported decreased risk for the highest intake groups when compared to the lowest,[273 278-281] four of which were statistically significant.[273 278-280]

Preserved fruits were excluded as they introduced substantial heterogeneity.

The general mechanisms through which fruits could plausibly protect against nasopharyngeal cancer are outlined below. In addition, it is possible that active constituents in fruit could act directly on Epstein-Barr virus infection.[493]

The evidence, from case-control studies only, is sparse. There is limited evidence suggesting that fruits protect against nasopharyngeal cancer.

Pancreas

Six cohort studies,[214 216 252 494-496] 16 case-control studies,[219 497-511] and 8 ecological studies[52 197 485 512-515] investigated fruits and pancreatic cancer.

All six cohort studies showed decreased risk for the highest intake groups when compared to the lowest,[214 216 252 494-496] which was statistically significant in one.[496] Meta-analysis was possible on three cohort studies, giving a summary effect estimate of 0.92 (95% CI 0.81–1.04) per 100 g/day, with no heterogeneity.[216 494 495]

Eleven case-control studies showed decreased risk for the highest intake groups when compared to the lowest,[219 497 498 500 501 503-509 511] which was statistically significant in four,[503]

[504 508 511] and in men but not women in a fifth study,[506] and in women but not men in a sixth.[501] One study reported a statistically significant increased risk for men and a statistically significant decreased risk for women.[510] No other study reported statistically significant increased risk. Meta-analysis was possible on eight case-control studies, giving a summary effect estimate of 0.89 (95% CI 0.82–0.98) per 100 g/day, with high heterogeneity.[497 498 502 503 505 506 508 510] Heterogeneity could be partly explained by proxy reporting, poor study quality, and varying adjustment for known confounders.

A dose-response relationship is apparent from case-control, but not cohort data.

Ecological studies show no consistent association.[52 197 485 512-515]

The general mechanisms through which fruits could plausibly protect against pancreatic cancer are outlined below.

The evidence is inconsistent. There is limited evidence suggesting that fruits protect against pancreatic cancer.

The Panel is aware that since the conclusion of the SLR, one cohort study[516] has been published. This new information does not change the Panel judgement (see box 3.8).

Liver cancer
One cohort study[216 517] and five case-control studies[89 518 521] investigated fruits and liver cancer.

The single cohort study showed non-significant decreased risk for the highest intake groups when compared to the lowest (0.98, 95% CI 0.75–1.21).[216 517]

Four case-control studies showed decreased risk for the highest intake groups when compared to the lowest,[89 518 520 521] which was statistically significant in two.[89 518] One study showed non-significant increased risk.[519] Heterogeneity could be partly explained by poor study quality and varying adjustment for known confounders.

The general mechanisms through which fruits could plausibly protect against liver cancer are outlined below. In addition, grape extracts and auraptene (from citrus fruit) have shown protective effects against the development of hepatocellular carcinoma in rats.[522-525]

The evidence is sparse and inconsistent. There is limited evidence suggesting that fruits protect against liver cancer.

The Panel is aware that since the conclusion of the SLR, one case-control study[526] has been published. This new information does not change the Panel judgement (see box 3.8).

Colorectum
Twenty cohort studies[214 216 359-372 374-376 378 379 527-529] and 57 case-control studies investigated fruits and colorectal cancer.

Thirteen cohort studies showed decreased risk with increased intake,[214 216 360-364 366 371 374-376 378] which was statistically significant in two.[360 364] No studies reported statistically significant increased risk. Meta-analysis was possible on eight cohort studies, giving a summary effect estimate of 0.97 (95% CI 0.92–1.03) per serving/day, with high heterogeneity.[360 362-364 366 370 529] When results were stratified by

sex, a statistically significant decreased risk was apparent in women (0.81, 95% CI 0.85–0.98 per serving/day based on five studies), with low heterogeneity.

Because of the abundant prospective data from cohort studies, case-control studies were not summarised.

The mechanism for this sex difference is unknown. There is speculation the mechanism could be related to the (partly understood) explanation for protective effects observed in postmenopausal women provided with hormone replacement therapy. Another possibility is that the result could be artifactual if men are poorer at reporting their diets than women.

The general mechanisms through which fruits could plausibly protect against colorectal cancer are outlined below.

There is a substantial amount of evidence but it is inconsistent. There is limited evidence suggesting that fruits protect against colorectal cancer.

The Panel is aware that since the conclusion of the SLR, one cohort[530] and five case-control studies [261 380 531-533] have been published. This new information does not change the Panel judgement (see box 3.8).

General mechanisms — fruits
Fruits, in particular citrus fruits, are sources of vitamin C and other antioxidants, such as phenols and flavonoids, as well as potentially bioactive phytochemicals. Vitamin C traps free radicals and reactive oxygen molecules, protecting against oxidation damage. It also regenerates other antioxidant vitamins such as vitamin E.[534] Vitamin C also inhibits the formation of carcinogens and protects DNA from mutagenic attack.[535]

Beta-carotene and other carotenoid antioxidants are also found in fruits. Some fruits contain high levels of flavonoids, including apples (quercetin) and grapefruit (naringin). Flavonoids have antioxidant effects and can also inhibit carcinogen-activating enzymes. Flavonoids can also alter the metabolism of other dietary agents. For instance, quercetin directly inhibits expression of CYP1A1 (a cytochrome P450 enzyme that helps to metabolise toxins), resulting in decreased DNA damage.[475] The phytochemical antioxidants contained in fruit could reduce free-radical damage generated by inflammation. A single study reported that apples given in physiological quantities inhibited carcinogen-induced mammary cancer in rodents in a dose-response manner.[536]

There is a complex mixture of phytochemicals present in whole vegetables and these may have additive and synergistic effects responsible for anti-cancer activities.

4.2.5.3 Foods containing carotenoids
Mouth, pharynx, and larynx
Two cohort studies[537 538] investigated total serum carotenoids and two case-control studies[539 540] investigated total dietary carotenoids and mouth, pharynx, and larynx cancers. Ten case-control studies investigated pro-vitamin A carotenoids.[26-29 47 48 450 451 541-544] Three cohort studies investigated serum alpha-carotene[537 538 545]; one cohort study

investigated dietary alpha-carotene[71]; three cohort studies[537] [538] [545] and two case-control studies[546] [547] investigated serum beta-carotene; one cohort study[71] and seven case-control studies[34] [35] [67] [74] [540] [548] [549] investigated dietary beta-carotene. One cohort study[71] and four case-control studies[62] [450] [540] [543] [548] investigated dietary lycopene; one cohort study[538] and one case-control study[547] investigated serum lycopene.

Total carotenoids

The two cohort studies both showed decreased risk,[537] [538] one was statistically significant for the highest serum levels of total carotenoids when compared to the lowest (0.33, p value for trend 0.05; not adjusted for smoking and alcohol); and 0.22 (95% CI 0.05–0.88; adjusted for smoking and alcohol).[537]

The two case-control studies showed decreased risk for the highest intake group when compared to the lowest,[539] [540] which was statistically significant in men but not women in one study[539] and statistically significant for all in the other.[540] Both case-control studies adjusted for smoking.

Pro-vitamin A carotenoids

Nine case-control studies reported decreased risk,[26-29] [47] [48] [450] [541-544] which was statistically significant for five studies.[29] [48] [541-543] One other study reported decreased risk for men and increased risk for women but neither was statistically significant.[451] All studies adjusted for smoking.

Alpha-carotene

All four cohort studies reported decreased risk for the highest intake group or serum level compared to the lowest,[71] [537] [538] [545] which was statistically significant in three,[71] [537] [545] although one of the latter reported a separate estimate specific to oral cancers, which suggested a non-significant increased risk.[545] Only one study adjusted for smoking.[537] The effect estimates were 0.62 (95% CI 0.41–0.94) for dietary alpha-carotene,[71] and 0.48 (laryngeal cancers, p value for trend 0.18), 1.26 (oral cancers, p value for trend 0.54),[545] 0.20 (95% CI 0.05–0.75; adjusted for smoking),[537] and 0.37 (p value for trend 0.06) for serum levels.[538] These tended to be based on a relatively small number of cases.

Beta-carotene

The single cohort study that investigated dietary beta-carotene intake reported that there was no significant association, but provided no further details.[71] All three cohort studies that investigated serum levels showed decreased risk for the highest group when compared to the lowest,[537] [538] [545] which was statistically significant in one.[537] The effect estimates were 0.10 (95% CI 0.02–0.46; adjusted for smoking),[537] 0.42 and 0.88 for oral/oropharyngeal and laryngeal cancers, respectively (not adjusted for smoking),[545] and 0.5 (p value for trend 0.17), which was attenuated after adjustment for smoking (0.69).[538]

Five case-control studies reported decreased risk,[34] [35] [74] [540] [549] which was significant in two.[35] [549] One study reported non-significant increased risk[548] and one study reported a significant increased risk.[67]

Lycopene

One cohort study[71] and four case-control studies[62] [450] [540] [543] [548] investigated dietary lycopene and mouth, larynx, and pharynx cancers; one cohort study[538] and one case-control study[547] investigated serum lycopene.

One cohort study reported a non-significant decreased risk for the highest serum lycopene levels when compared to the lowest (0.61; p value for trend 0.37).[538] The other stated that there was no relationship between dietary lycopene and risk.[71]

All four case-controls that investigated dietary lycopene reported decreased risk for the highest intake groups when compared to the lowest,[62] [450] [540] [543] [548] which was statistically significant in two.[62] [548] The single case-control that investigated serum lycopene reported contrary results, showing that levels were significantly higher in cases than controls.[547]

The general mechanisms through which foods containing carotenoids could plausibly protect against mouth, pharynx, and larynx cancer are outlined below.

There is a considerable amount of evidence, and though it is for different carotenoid types, it is generally consistent, with a dose-response relationship. There is evidence for plausible mechanisms. Foods containing carotenoids probably protect against mouth, pharynx, and larynx cancers.

The Panel is aware that since the conclusion of the SLR, one cohort study[76] has been published. This new information does not change the Panel judgement (see box 3.8).

Lung

Eleven cohort studies,[284] [286] [288] [289] [298] [299] [341] [550-555] 16 case-control studies,[306-308] [310] [311] [321] [322] [327] [330] [342] [344] [350] [352] [556-561] and 1 ecological study[333] investigated total dietary carotenoids and lung cancer; 4 cohort studies[298] [562-566] and 5 case-control studies[567-571] investigated total serum or plasma carotenoids; 7 cohort studies,[286] [289] [293] [341] [552] [566] [572] [573] 8 case-control studies,[306] [308] [320] [321] [327] [350] [560] [574] and 1 ecological study[333] investigated dietary beta-cryptoxanthin; 6 cohort studies[563-566] [575-577] and 1 case-control study[578] investigated serum or plasma beta-cryptoxanthin.

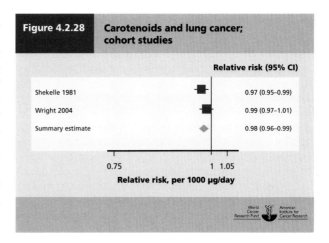

Figure 4.2.28 Carotenoids and lung cancer; cohort studies

Relative risk (95% CI)

	Relative risk (95% CI)
Shekelle 1981	0.97 (0.95–0.99)
Wright 2004	0.99 (0.97–1.01)
Summary estimate	0.98 (0.96–0.99)

0.75   1 1.05

Relative risk, per 1000 µg/day

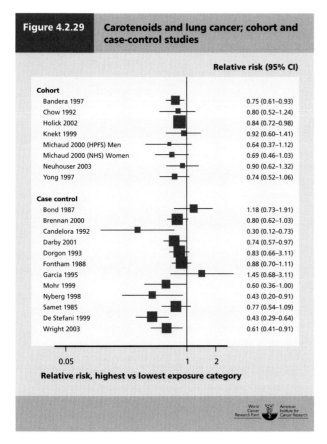

Figure 4.2.29 Carotenoids and lung cancer; cohort and case-control studies

Relative risk (95% CI)

Cohort
Bandera 1997	0.75 (0.61–0.93)
Chow 1992	0.80 (0.52–1.24)
Holick 2002	0.84 (0.72–0.98)
Knekt 1999	0.92 (0.60–1.41)
Michaud 2000 (HPFS) Men	0.64 (0.37–1.12)
Michaud 2000 (NHS) Women	0.69 (0.46–1.03)
Neuhouser 2003	0.90 (0.62–1.32)
Yong 1997	0.74 (0.52–1.06)

Case control
Bond 1987	1.18 (0.73–1.91)
Brennan 2000	0.80 (0.62–1.03)
Candelora 1992	0.30 (0.12–0.73)
Darby 2001	0.74 (0.57–0.97)
Dorgon 1993	0.83 (0.66–3.11)
Fontham 1988	0.88 (0.70–1.11)
Garcia 1995	1.45 (0.68–3.11)
Mohr 1999	0.60 (0.36–1.00)
Nyberg 1998	0.43 (0.20–0.91)
Samet 1985	0.77 (0.54–1.09)
De Stefani 1999	0.43 (0.29–0.64)
Wright 2003	0.61 (0.41–0.91)

0.05   1   2

Relative risk, highest vs lowest exposure category

World Cancer Research Fund / American Institute for Cancer Research

Dietary carotenoids

All 11 cohort studies showed decreased risk of lung cancer for the highest intake group when compared to the lowest,[284] [286 288 289 298 299 341 550-555] which was statistically significant in three.[286 550 553] Meta-analysis was possible on two cohort studies, giving a summary effect estimate of 0.98 (95% CI 0.96–0.99) per 1000 μg/day, with no heterogeneity (figure 4.2.28).[553 554] All cohort studies adjusted for smoking.

Twelve of the case-control studies showed decreased risk of lung cancer for the highest intake group when compared to the lowest,[306-308 310 311 321 322 327 330 344 350 352 556 559-561] which was statistically significant in seven (figure 4.2.29).[306-308 321 322 327 344 556 560] Three studies reported increased risk,[342 557 558] which was statistically significant in one,[557] and one reported no effect on risk.[350] Heterogeneity was high, which may be partially explained by varying adjustment for known confounders. Four case-control studies did not adjust for smoking.[306 352 556-558]

The single ecological study showed an association between increased carotenoid intake and decreased lung cancer risk.[333]

Serum or plasma or carotenoids

All four of the cohort studies showed decreased risk of lung cancer for the highest serum or plasma levels when compared to the lowest,[298 562-566] which was statistically significant in three.[298 562 563] Effect estimates were 0.27 (95% CI

0.1–0.7; adjusted for age, sex, smoking habits, alcohol drinking, and cholesterol),[563] 0.57 (95% CI 0.35–0.93; adjusted for age, smoking habits, and the intake of other nutrients, foods, and supplements),[298] 1.84 (low compared to high; p value for trend 0.033; adjusted for age and smoking),[562] and 0.84 (95% CI 0.48–1.47; adjusted for age and smoking).[566]

All five of the case-control studies showed decreased risk of lung cancer for the highest serum or plasma levels when compared to the lowest[567-571]; one was statistically significant.[568]

Dietary beta-cryptoxanthin

All seven cohort studies showed decreased risk with increased intake of beta-cryptoxanthin,[286 289 293 341 552 566 572 573] which was statistically significant in one.[293 566] Meta-analysis was possible on two studies, giving a summary effect estimate of 0.98 (95% CI 0.96–1.00) per 10 μg/day, with no heterogeneity.[286 572]

Pooled analysis from 7 cohort studies (almost 400 000 participants, followed up for 7 to 16 years, more than 3100 lung cancer cases) showed a statistically significant decreased risk when comparing high against low intake groups (0.76, 95% CI 0.67–0.89), p value for trend < 0.001.[579]

Six case-control studies showed increased risk for the highest intake groups when compared to the lowest,[306 308 321 327 560 574] which was statistically significant in four.[306 308 327 560] Two studies showed non-significant increased risk.[320 350]

The single ecological study showed an association between increased intake and increased risk.[333]

Serum or plasma beta-cryptoxanthin

Five cohort studies showed decreased risk with increased intake,[563-566 575 576] which was statistically significant in three.[563 566 575] One study showed statistically significant increased risk.[577] Meta-analysis was possible on two studies (including the latter described study), giving a summary effect estimate of 0.95 (95% CI 0.69–1.29) per 0.05 μmol/l, with high heterogeneity.[563 577]

The single case-control study showed a non-significant decreased risk with increased consumption.[578]

Data on beta-carotene supplements (see chapter 4.10.6.4.2) provide convincing evidence that high-dose supplements have a contrasting effect, at least in smokers, increasing the risk of lung cancer. Data on dietary beta-carotene (15 cohort studies, a pooled analysis, 32 case-control studies, 2 ecological studies) and serum or plasma beta-carotene (13 cohort studies, 16 case-control studies, 1 ecological study) showed no consistent evidence of an association. The full SLR is contained on the CD included with this Report.

The general mechanisms through which foods containing carotenoids could plausibly protect against lung cancer are outlined below.

There is a substantial amount of evidence available from both cohort and case-control studies. A clear dose-response relationship is apparent from cohort studies. Foods containing carotenoids probably protect against lung cancer.

Oesophagus

Three cohort studies[537 545 580] and one case-control study[581] investigated serum beta-carotene; 10 case-control studies investigated dietary beta-carotene and oesophageal cancer[95 107 125 141 548 582-587]; one cohort study[70] and three case-control studies[86 585 587] investigated dietary pro-vitamin A carotenoids.

Serum beta-carotene

One of the cohort studies showed decreased risk for the highest levels when compared to the lowest, which was statistically significant after adjusting for smoking (0.11, 95% CI 0.04–0.34).[537] Another cohort study showed no effect on risk (RR 1.0) and was specific for squamous cell carcinoma.[580] Another study reported a non-significant association but did not provide further details.[545]

The single case-control study showed that serum beta-carotene levels were non-significantly lower in cases than controls.[581]

Dietary beta-carotene

Nine of the case-control studies showed decreased risk for the highest intake group when compared to the lowest,[95 107 125 141 582-587] which was statistically significant in six.[95 141 582-585] One study reported a non-significant decreased risk (figure 4.2.30).[548]

Dietary pro-vitamin A carotenoids

The single cohort study showed a non-significant decreased risk for the highest intake group when compared to the lowest, with an effect estimate of 0.70 (95% CI 0.29–1.71) (figure 4.2.30).[70]

All case-control studies showed decreased risk for the highest intake group when compared to the lowest,[86 585 587] which was statistically significant in one[585] and in men, but not women, in another (figure 4.2.30).[86]

The general mechanisms through which foods containing carotenoids, including beta-carotene, could plausibly protect against oesophageal cancer are outlined below.

> **There is a substantial amount of consistent evidence available from both cohort and case-control studies. Foods containing beta-carotene probably protect against oesophageal cancer.**

Prostate

Five cohort studies,[588-594] 9 case-control studies,[595-608] and 3 ecological studies[609-611] investigated tomatoes; 3 cohort studies[590 591 612-615] and 14 case-control studies[595 596 598 599 601 602 606 616-625] investigated dietary lycopene; 6 cohort studies[576 594 626-630] and 2 case-control studies[596 608 619] investigated serum or plasma lycopene.

Tomatoes

Three of the cohort studies showed decreased risk for the highest intake groups when compared to the lowest,[588 591 592] which was statistically significant in two.[591 592] One study showed a non-significant increased risk[589] and one study reported that there was no statistically significant association.[594] Meta-analysis was possible on four of the cohort studies, giving a summary effect estimate of 0.69 (95% CI 0.43–1.08) per serving/day, with moderate heterogeneity.[588 589 591 592] One of these studies reported an effect estimate of 0.24 (95% CI 0.13–0.47) per 15 g/day for cumulative intake of tomato sauce.[591] Two of the cohort studies reported on advanced or aggressive prostate cancer.[590 591 594] One reported a risk estimate of 0.11 (95% CI 0.02–0.70) per increase in serving/day for tomato sauce[590] and the other found no statistically significant association.[594]

Seven of the case-control studies showed decreased risk for the highest intake groups when compared to the lowest,[595 598-600 602 603 608] which was statistically significant in one.[602] One study reported non-significant increased risk[597] and the other stated that there was no significant association without further details.[606] Meta-analysis was possible on five relatively high quality studies[595 597-600] and two relatively low quality ones.[602 603] The former gave a summary effect estimate of 0.97 (95% CI 0.91–1.03) per serving/day, with no heterogeneity; the latter gave a summary effect estimate of 0.33 (95% CI 0.04–2.74) per serving/day, with high heterogeneity.

The three ecological studies showed no consistent association.[609-611]

Dietary lycopene

Two cohort studies showed non-significant decreased risk for the highest intake groups when compared to the lowest,[590 614] the other study showed non-significant increased risk.[613] Meta-analysis was possible on all three cohort studies, giving a summary effect estimate of 0.97 (95% CI 0.64–1.45) per 5 mg/day, with low heterogeneity (figures 4.2.31 and

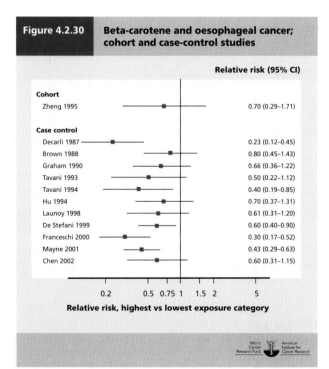

Figure 4.2.30	Beta-carotene and oesophageal cancer; cohort and case-control studies

Relative risk (95% CI)

Cohort
Zheng 1995 — 0.70 (0.29–1.71)

Case control
Decarli 1987 — 0.23 (0.12–0.45)
Brown 1988 — 0.80 (0.45–1.43)
Graham 1990 — 0.66 (0.36–1.22)
Tavani 1993 — 0.50 (0.22–1.12)
Tavani 1994 — 0.40 (0.19–0.85)
Hu 1994 — 0.70 (0.37–1.31)
Launoy 1998 — 0.61 (0.31–1.20)
De Stefani 1999 — 0.60 (0.40–0.90)
Franceschi 2000 — 0.30 (0.17–0.52)
Mayne 2001 — 0.43 (0.29–0.63)
Chen 2002 — 0.60 (0.31–1.15)

0.2   0.5   0.75 1   1.5   2   5

Relative risk, highest vs lowest exposure category

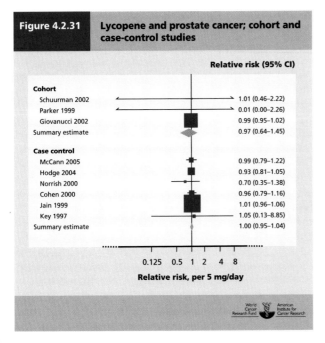

Figure 4.2.31 Lycopene and prostate cancer; cohort and case-control studies

Figure 4.2.32 Dietary lycopene and prostate cancer; cohort and case-control studies: dose response

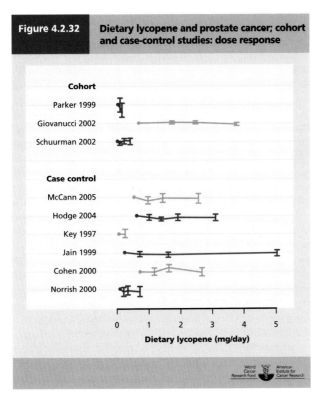

or aggressive cancer, giving estimates of 0.89 (95% CI 0.28–2.84) per 5 mg /day[613] and 0.57 (95% CI 0.37–0.87) for the highest intake groups when compared to the lowest.[591]

Nine case-control studies showed decreased risk for the highest intake groups when compared to the lowest,[595 598 602 606 616 617 619 621 624] which was statistically significant in one.[602] Five studies reported non-significant increased risk.[596 599 601 620 625] Meta-analysis was possible on six relatively high quality case-control studies[595 598 599 601 616 617] and three relatively low quality ones.[602 619 620] The former gave a summary effect estimate of 0.995 (95% CI 0.95–1.04) per 5 mg/day, with no heterogeneity and the latter gave a summary estimate of 0.56 (95% CI 0.23–1.36) per 5 mg/day, with high heterogeneity (figures 4.2.31 and 4.2.32).

Serum or plasma lycopene

Five cohort studies showed a non-significant reduced risk for the highest intake groups when compared to the lowest[576 626-628]; the other study showed a non-significant increased risk.[629] Meta-analysis was possible on four cohort studies, giving a summary estimate of 0.96 (95% CI 0.926–0.999) per 10 $\mu g/l$, with no heterogeneity.[576 626 627] All cohort studies were fully adjusted.

Both case-control studies of serum or plasma lycopene showed a statistically significant reduced risk for the highest intake groups when compared to the lowest.[596 619]

Lycopene is most bioavailable from cooked and pureed tomatoes. The best measures of systemic exposure are therefore studies on tomato sauce, particularly of cumulative consumption, or on serum or plasma lycopene. The Panel also gave emphasis to studies on advanced or aggressive cancers, which may be better linked to prognosis than studies that include early stage or latent disease, or screening-detected disease.

The general mechanisms through which foods containing carotenoids, including lycopene, could plausibly protect against prostate cancer are outlined below. In addition, amongst the common carotenoids, lycopene is thought to be the most efficient antioxidant in the body.[631]

> There is a substantial amount of consistent evidence, in particular on tomato products, from both cohort and case-control studies. There is evidence for plausible mechanisms. Foods containing lycopene probably protect against prostate cancer.

The Panel is aware that since the conclusion of the SLR, two cohort studies[632 633] and one case-control study[634] have been published. This new information does not change the Panel judgement (see box 3.8).

Prostate

Also see chapter 4.10.6.4.2 for evidence on beta-carotene supplements. Six cohort studies[147 360 591 594 613 635 636] and 21 case-control studies[595 598 599 602 616 617 619-621 624 625 637-648] investigated dietary beta-carotene and prostate cancer.

Ten cohort studies[576 594 626 628-630 635 649-652] and five case-control studies[584 596 608 619 653] investigated serum or plasma beta-carotene.

4.2.32). One of these studies also reported cumulative measures of lycopene consumption, which is a robust measure of long-term consumption.[590] The effect estimate was 0.95 (95% CI 0.92–0.99) per 5 mg/day. All studies were fully adjusted.

Two of the cohort studies reported separately on advanced

Dietary beta-carotene

Three cohort studies showed non-significant increased risk with increased intake.[594 635 636] Three studies showed no effect on risk.[360 591 613] Meta-analysis was possible on all six cohort studies, giving a summary effect estimate of 1.00 (95% CI 0.99–1.01) per 700 μg/day, with no heterogeneity.[360 591 594 613 635 636]

Two cohort studies reported results separately for advanced/aggressive prostate cancer.[594 613] Meta-analysis was possible on both studies, giving a summary effect estimate of 0.97 (95% CI 0.88–1.06) per 700 μg/day, with no heterogeneity.

Fourteen case-control studies showed decreased risk with increased intake,[595 599 602 616 617 619-621 625 637 638 642 646 648] which was statistically significant in two relatively low quality studies.[602 646 648] Four studies showed no effect on risk[624 639 644 645] and three studies showed non-significant increased risk.[598 640 641] Meta-analysis was possible on nine relatively high quality[595 598 599 616 617 637-640] and six relatively low quality case-control studies,[602 619 620 624 641 642] giving summary effect estimates of 0.99 (95% CI 0.98–1.00) and 0.98 (95% CI 0.94–1.01) per 700 μg/day, with no and moderate heterogeneity, respectively.

Serum or plasma beta-carotene

Five cohort studies showed decreased risk with increased intake,[576 626 628 649 651 652] which was statistically significant in one.[649] Four studies showed non-significant increased risk.[594 626 629 635] Meta-analysis was possible on seven cohort studies, giving a summary effect estimate of 1.00 (95% CI 0.91–1.09) per 10 μg beta-carotene/100 ml, with moderate heterogeneity.[576 626 629 635 649]

Four case-control studies showed decreased risk with increased intake,[584 608 619 653] which was statistically significant in one relatively low quality study.[653] One study showed non-significant increased risk.[596]

It is unlikely that foods containing beta-carotene have a substantial effect on the risk of prostate cancer.

The Panel is aware that since the conclusion of the SLR, two cohort studies[632 633] have been published. This new information does not change the Panel judgement (see box 3.8).

Skin

Also see chapter 4.10.5.1 for evidence on beta-carotene supplements. Two cohort studies[654 655] and seven case-control studies[656-663] investigated dietary beta-carotene and skin cancer. Three cohort studies[655 664-666] and one case-control study[657] investigated beta-carotene from food and supplements combined; eight cohort studies[545 630 651 655 667-672] and three case-control studies[584 673 674] investigated serum or plasma beta-carotene.

Dietary beta-carotene

Both cohort studies showed non-significant increased risk with increased intake, both for basal cell carcinoma.[654 655] One case-control study showed a non-significant decreased risk of basal cell carcinoma for the highest intake group when compared to the lowest[662]; one showed a non-significant

increased risk of squamous cell carcinoma.[658 659] Three case-control studies showed decreased risk of melanoma for the highest intake group when compared to the lowest,[657 661 663] which was statistically significant in two.[657 663] Two studies showed non-significant increased risk of melanoma.[656 660]

Beta-carotene from foods and supplements

Two cohort studies showed increased risk of basal cell carcinoma for the highest intake group when compared to the lowest.[655 665] One cohort study showed non-significant increased risk of squamous cell carcinoma.[666] One cohort study showed a non-significant increased risk of melanoma.[664] One case-control study showed a statistically significant decreased risk of melanoma for the highest intake group when compared to the lowest.[657]

Serum or plasma beta-carotene

Two studies showed decreased risk for skin cancer of unspecified type with increased serum or plasma beta-carotene,[669 671] which was statistically significant in one.[669] One cohort study showed non-significant decreased risk of non-melanoma skin cancer.[667] One cohort study (fully adjusted) showed a non-significant decreased risk for basal cell carcinoma[672]; two showed a non-significant increased risk[630 655]; and one a non-significant increased risk in women and a non-significant decreased risk in men.[651] Two studies showed non-significant decreased risk on squamous cell carcinoma.[668 672] Two studies showed decreased risk of melanoma, which was statistically significant in one[545 670]; and one study showed non-significant increased risk.[630] Meta-analysis was possible on both cohort studies that investigated squamous cell carcinoma, giving a summary effect estimate of 0.99 (95% CI 0.98–1.00) per μg beta-carotene/100 ml, with no heterogeneity.[668 672] Meta-analysis was possible on two cohort studies that investigated melanoma, giving a summary effect estimate of 0.90 (95% CI 0.78–1.03) per μg beta-carotene/100 ml, with moderate heterogeneity.[545 670]

One case-control study showed a statistically significant decreased risk of non-melanoma skin cancer, which, at 0.999 per μg/100 ml (95% CI 0.999–0.999), was close to no effect.[673] One case-control study showed non-significant increased risk of basal cell carcinoma for the highest intake group when compared to the lowest.[584] The same study showed non-significant increased risk of squamous cell carcinoma and non-significant increased risk of melanoma.[584] One additional study showed non-significant decreased risk of melanoma.[674]

It is unlikely that foods containing beta-carotene have any substantial effect on the risk of non-melanoma skin cancer.

General mechanisms — foods containing carotenoids

Carotenoids are antioxidants, which can prevent lipid oxidation and related oxidative stress. Oxidative stress induced by free radicals causes DNA damage. Base mutation, single- and double-strand breaks, DNA cross-linking, and chromosomal breakage and rearrangement can all occur if this initial damage is left unrepaired. This damage could plausibly be prevented or limited by dietary antioxidants found in fruits and vegetables.[675]

Many of the carotenoids, including beta-carotene, are also retinoid (vitamin A) precursors. The pro-vitamin A carotenoids may be converted to retinol where they function in cellular differentiation, immunoenhancement, and activation of carcinogen-metabolising enzymes.[580 676]

Lycopene is the most potent carotenoid antioxidant, has an antiproliferative effect, reduces plasma low-density lipoprotein cholesterol, improves immune function, and reduces inflammation.

4.2.5.4 Foods containing folate

Foods naturally containing folates are vegetables, fruits, and liver, but increasingly foods such as breakfast cereals are fortified with folic acid.

Pancreas

Three cohort studies,[677 678] two case-control studies,[509 679] and one ecological study[515] investigated folate from foods and/or supplements, and pancreatic cancer.

One cohort study reported a statistically significant reduced risk for the highest intake groups (without specifying the source of folate) when compared to the lowest[677]; one reported no effect on risk in men[678] and the other reported a non-significant increased risk in women.[678] Meta-analysis was possible on all three cohort studies, giving a summary effect estimate of 0.94 (95% CI 0.80–1.11) per 100 μg/day, with high heterogeneity.[677 678]

When these results were stratified according to dietary or supplemental folate, this heterogeneity was removed. Two cohort studies reported separately on dietary folate.[678] Both reported non-significant decreased risk; meta-analysis was possible on both, giving a summary effect estimate of 0.86 (95% CI 0.73–1.00) per 100 μg/day, with no heterogeneity (figure 4.2.33). All three cohort studies reported separately on supplemental folate, showing non-significant increased risk, with no heterogeneity.[677 678]

In addition, one of the cohort studies included a nested case-control study investigating blood folate levels. This reported a statistically significant decreased risk for the highest levels when compared to the lowest, with an effect estimate of 0.45 (95% CI 0.24–0.82).[680]

The Panel is aware of an additional cohort study, published after the conclusion of the literature review, which showed a statistically significant decreased risk for the highest intake groups when compared to the lowest.[681] The effect estimate was 0.25 (95% CI 0.11–0.59) for dietary folate and 0.33 (95% CI 0.15–0.72) for total folate (combining dietary and supplemental sources). No association was observed with folate supplements only.

One of the case-control studies reported a statistically significant reduced risk for the highest intake groups when compared to the lowest.[679] The other reported a non-significant decreased risk in women and no effect on risk in men.[509]

The ecological study showed a statistically significant decreased risk in areas of high folate intake.[515]

The possible differential effect between folate from foods and from supplements could be explained by folate serving as a marker for fruit and vegetable intake, by a different metabolic effect of the folic acid in supplements, or by confounders associated with supplement use.

The general mechanisms through which foods containing folate could plausibly protect against pancreatic cancer are outlined below.

> **The evidence available is sparse but a dose-response relationship was apparent from cohort studies. There is limited evidence suggesting that foods containing folate protect against pancreatic cancer.**

The Panel is aware that since the conclusion of the SLR, one cohort study[681] has been published. This new information does not change the Panel judgement (see box 3.8).

Oesophagus

Eight case-control studies investigated dietary folate[113 124 125 136 548 583 585 587] and two case-control studies investigated red cell and/or plasma folate.[682-684]

All eight case-control studies that investigated dietary folate reported decreased risk for the highest intake groups when compared to the lowest,[113 124 125 136 548 583 585 587] which was statistically significant in two.[583 587] Most studies adjusted for smoking and alcohol.

Both case-control studies that investigated red cell and/or plasma folate reported that levels were lower (statistically significant) in cases than controls.[682-684] One study was adjusted for smoking and alcohol.[684]

The general mechanisms through which foods containing folate could plausibly protect against oesophageal cancer are outlined below. In addition, folate may reduce human papilloma virus proliferation in cells.[685]

> **The evidence, from case-control studies only, is sparse. There is limited evidence suggesting that folate protects against oesophageal cancer.**

The Panel is aware that since the conclusion of the SLR, one case-control study[78] has been published. This new information does not change the Panel judgement (see box 3.8).

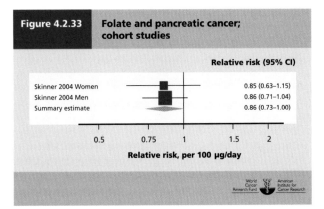

Figure 4.2.33 — Folate and pancreatic cancer; cohort studies

Relative risk (95% CI)

	Relative risk (95% CI)
Skinner 2004 Women	0.85 (0.63–1.15)
Skinner 2004 Men	0.86 (0.71–1.04)
Summary estimate	0.86 (0.73–1.00)

Relative risk, per 100 μg/day

Colorectum

Nine cohort studies investigated dietary folate and colorectal cancer.[686-694] Two cohorts investigated serum folate.[694 695]

Seven cohort studies that investigated dietary folate showed decreased risk for the highest intake groups when compared to the lowest, [686-690 692 693] which was statistically significant in one.[689] Two cohort studies reported non-significant increased risk.[691 694] Meta-analysis was possible on four studies, giving a summary effect estimate of 0.84 (95% CI 0.76–0.93) per 100 μg/day, with low heterogeneity (figure 4.2.34).[686 689 692 696]

One study of serum folate levels showed statistically significant decreased risk for the highest intake groups when compared to the lowest, with an effect estimate of 0.52 (95% CI 0.27–0.97).[695] The other showed a non-significant decreased risk for colon cancer (0.96, 95% CI 0.4–2.3) and a non-significant increased risk for rectal cancer incidence (2.94, 95% CI 0.84–10.33).[694]

Because of the abundant prospective data from cohort studies, case-control studies were not summarised.

A published meta-analysis of seven cohort studies and nine case-control studies reported a statistically significant decreased risk of colorectal cancer for the highest dietary folate intake when compared to the lowest (0.75, 95% CI 0.64–0.89).[697]

The general mechanisms through which foods containing folate could plausibly protect against colorectal cancer are outlined below. In addition, folate intake is also strongly correlated with intake of dietary fibre, which probably prevents colorectal cancer (also see chapter 7.1).

The evidence from cohort studies is plentiful, with a dose-response relationship, but there is unexplained inconsistency. Residual confounding from dietary fibre is possible. There is limited evidence suggesting that foods containing folate protect against colorectal cancer.

The Panel is aware that since the conclusion of the SLR, four cohort[698-701] and two case-control studies[380 702] have been published. This new information does not change the Panel judgement (see box 3.8).

General mechanisms — foods containing folate

Also see Chapter 2. Folate plays an important role in the synthesis and methylation of DNA.[703] Abnormal DNA methylation leading to aberrant gene expression has been demonstrated in several types of cancer. Folate deficiency may produce misincorporation of uracil instead of thymine into DNA. The effects of folate deficiency and supplementation on DNA methylation are gene- and site-specific, and appear to depend on cell type, target organ, stage of transformation, and degree and duration of folate depletion.

Animal studies have shown that dose and timing of folate intervention are critical in determining its effect: exceptionally high folate doses, and intervention after the formation of microscopic neoplastic foci, may promote rather than suppress colorectal carcinogenesis, at least in the animal models studied.[704]

There is a known interaction between folate and alcohol and the risk of some cancers.

4.2.5.5 Foods containing pyridoxine (vitamin B6)
Oesophagus

Six case-control studies investigated foods containing pyridoxine and oesophageal cancer.[88 125 548 583 585 587]

All six studies showed decreased risk for the highest intake groups when compared to the lowest,[88 125 548 583 585 587] which was statistically significant in four.[88 125 583 585] All studies adjusted for alcohol and five adjusted for smoking.

Together with folate and cobalamin (B12), vitamin B6 is involved in one-carbon metabolism and thus is important for DNA synthesis, repair, and methylation.

The evidence, from case-control studies only, was sparse. There is limited evidence suggesting that pyridoxine protects against oesophageal cancer.

The Panel is aware that since the conclusion of the SLR, one case-control study[78] has been published. This new information does not change the Panel judgement (see box 3.8).

4.2.5.6 Foods containing vitamin C
Oesophagus

One cohort study,[70] 19 case-control studies,[86 88 94 95 104 105 107 113 120 121 124 125 136 548 583 585-587 705-707] and 3 ecological studies[118 203 708] investigated vitamin C and oesophageal cancer.

The single cohort study reported a non-significant reduced risk for the highest intake groups when compared to the lowest after adjustment for smoking, with an effect estimate of 0.70 (95% CI 0.3–1.7).[70]

Eighteen of the case-control studies showed decreased risk for the highest intake groups when compared to the lowest,[86 88 94 95 104 105 107 113 120 121 124 136 548 583 585-587 705-707] which was statistically significant in 13 (figure 4.2.35).[86 88 95 104 105 113 120 121 136 548 583 585 705 707] Three studies showed a non-significant increased risk, all specific to adenocarcinoma.[124 125 706]

None of the ecological studies reported a statistically significant association.[118 203 708]

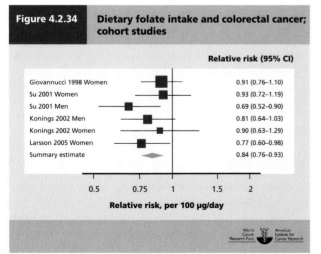

Figure 4.2.34 | **Dietary folate intake and colorectal cancer; cohort studies**

Relative risk (95% CI)

	Relative risk (95% CI)
Giovannucci 1998 Women	0.91 (0.76–1.10)
Su 2001 Women	0.93 (0.72–1.19)
Su 2001 Men	0.69 (0.52–0.90)
Konings 2002 Men	0.81 (0.64–1.03)
Konings 2002 Women	0.90 (0.63–1.29)
Larsson 2005 Women	0.77 (0.60–0.98)
Summary estimate	0.84 (0.76–0.93)

Relative risk, per 100 µg/day

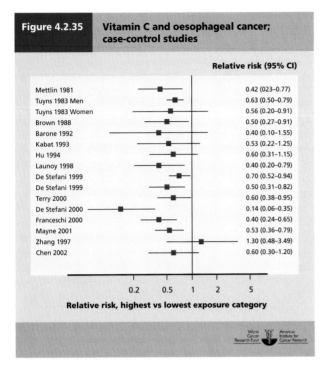

Figure 4.2.35 | **Vitamin C and oesophageal cancer; case-control studies**

Relative risk (95% CI)

	Relative risk (95% CI)
Mettlin 1981	0.42 (023–0.77)
Tuyns 1983 Men	0.63 (0.50–0.79)
Tuyns 1983 Women	0.56 (0.20–0.91)
Brown 1988	0.50 (0.27–0.91)
Barone 1992	0.40 (0.10–1.55)
Kabat 1993	0.53 (0.22–1.25)
Hu 1994	0.60 (0.31–1.15)
Launoy 1998	0.40 (0.20–0.79)
De Stefani 1999	0.70 (0.52–0.94)
De Stefani 1999	0.50 (0.31–0.82)
Terry 2000	0.60 (0.38–0.95)
De Stefani 2000	0.14 (0.06–0.35)
Franceschi 2000	0.40 (0.24–0.65)
Mayne 2001	0.53 (0.36–0.79)
Zhang 1997	1.30 (0.48–3.49)
Chen 2002	0.60 (0.30–1.20)

Relative risk, highest vs lowest exposure category

It is biologically plausible that vitamin C should protect against cancer. It traps free radicals and reactive oxygen molecules, protecting against lipid peroxidation, reducing nitrates, and stimulating the immune system.[586 709] Moreover, it can recycle other antioxidant vitamins such as vitamin E.[534] Vitamin C has also been shown to inhibit formation of carcinogens and protect DNA from mutagenic attack.[535] However, evidence supporting a specific mechanism in the oesophagus is limited.[586]

A substantial amount of consistent evidence is available, from both cohort and case-control studies. Foods containing vitamin C probably protect against oesophageal cancer.

The Panel is aware that since the conclusion of the SLR, one case-control study[710] has been published. This new information does not change the Panel judgement (see box 3.8).

4.2.5.7 Foods containing vitamin E
Oesophagus
One cohort study,[70] nine case-control studies,[86 88 95 105 125 548 583 585 587] and one ecological study[708] investigated dietary vitamin E and oesophageal cancer. Three cohort studies[537 545 711] and four case-control studies[581 682 683 712] investigated serum vitamin E.

Dietary vitamin E
The single cohort study showed decreased risk for the highest intake groups when compared to the lowest, with an effect estimate of 0.8 (95% CI 0.3–2.0; adjusted for smoking).[70]

Eight case-control studies reported decreased risk for the highest intake groups when compared to the lowest,[86 88 95 105 125 548 583 585] which was statistically significant in seven[86 88 95 105 548 583 585]; the other study reported no effect on risk.[587] All studies adjusted for alcohol and all but one also adjusted for smoking.

The single ecological study reported no association.[708]

Serum vitamin E
All three cohort studies showed decreased risk for the highest intake groups when compared to the lowest,[537 545 711] which was statistically significant in two. The effect estimates were 0.63 (95% CI 0.44–0.91) for alpha-tocopherol (the same study showed no significant association with serum gamma-tocopherol),[711] and 0.39 (95% CI 0.19–0.80) for gamma-tocopherol.[537] The third cohort study found lower mean values in cases than controls (8.52 vs 10.21 mg/l), which was not statistically significant.[545] The two former studies were maximally adjusted.[537 711]

Two case-control studies reported that cases had higher plasma vitamin E than controls,[682 683] statistically significant in one.[683] One study reported statistically significant lower levels in cases than those in controls[712]; and another reported no significant difference.[581] None of these studies was well adjusted.

The general mechanisms through which foods containing vitamin E could plausibly protect against oesophageal cancer are outlined below.

Much of the evidence on vitamin E, mostly from case-control studies, was of poor quality. There is limited evidence suggesting that foods containing vitamin E protect against oesophageal cancer.

Prostate
Two cohort studies,[147 613 650 713] 13 case-control studies,[595 599 601 604 607 616 619-621 625 637 714-717] and 1 ecological study[708] investigated dietary vitamin E and prostate cancer; 4 cohort studies[629 630 718-722] and 1 case-control study[716] investigated serum vitamin E; 8 cohort studies[576 626 627 629 635 650 652 713 718 723-725] and 2 case-control studies[619 653] investigated serum or plasma alpha-tocopherol; 6 cohort studies[576 626 627 629 650 718 724] and 1 case-control study[619] investigated serum gamma-tocopherol.

Dietary vitamin E
Most studies showed non-significant decreased risk, although there is heterogeneity in the direction of effect reported and effect estimates are usually very close to 1 (no effect). One cohort study reported an effect size of 0.96 (0.75–1.2) per 10 mg/day for advanced/aggressive prostate cancer.[613] Meta-analysis was possible on seven relatively good quality case-control studies, giving a summary effect estimate of 1.04 (95% CI 0.99–1.11) per 10 mg/day, with low heterogeneity.[595 599 601 616 637 714 715] Dietary studies produce no consistent effect.

Serum or plasma alpha-tocopherol
Seven cohort studies showed decreased risk for the highest

intake groups when compared to the lowest,[576] [626] [629] [635] [650] [652] [713] [718] [723-725] which was statistically significant in one.[576] One cohort study showed no effect on risk.[627] Meta-analysis was possible on seven cohort studies, giving a summary effect estimate of 0.99 (95% CI 0.97–1.00) per mg/l, with no heterogeneity.[576] [626] [713] [723-725]

Both case-control studies showed decreased risk for the highest intake groups when compared to the lowest,[619] [653] which was statistically significant in one.[653]

Serum gamma-tocopherol
All six cohort studies showed decreased risk for the highest intake groups when compared to the lowest,[576] [626] [627] [629] [650] [718] [724] which was statistically significant in two.[650] [724] Meta-analysis was possible on all six cohort studies, giving a summary effect estimate of 0.90 (95% CI 0.81–0.996) per mg/l, with moderate heterogeneity.

The single case-control study showed non-significant decreased risk for the highest intake groups when compared to the lowest.[619]

The general mechanisms through which foods containing vitamin E could plausibly protect against prostate cancer are outlined below. Vitamin E has also been shown to inhibit the growth of human prostate tumours induced in mice.[726]

The evidence, mostly from case-control studies, was inconsistent. There is limited evidence suggesting that foods containing vitamin E protect against prostate cancer.

The Panel is aware that since the conclusion of the SLR, two cohort studies[632] [633] have been published. This new information does not change the Panel judgement (see box 3.8).

General mechanisms — foods containing vitamin E
Vitamin E is an antioxidant that has been reported to prevent DNA damage, enhance DNA repair, prevent lipid peroxidation, and prevent activation of carcinogens such as nitrosamines. Vitamin E protects vitamin A and selenium in the body. In addition to acting as a free-radical scavenger, vitamin E enhances the body's immune response, which may play a role in cancer defences.[727]

4.2.5.8 Foods containing selenium
Data from selenium levels in serum or nails can be interpreted more robustly than dietary data because they are less prone to certain sources of error; serum data are a short-term reflection of intake; levels in nails are cumulative and reflect long-term intake.

It is not possible to rule out residual confounding between selenium levels and healthy lifestyles. Individuals with higher selenium levels may be more likely to be following several strategies to improve their health, including taking supplements.

It is plausible that an effect attributed to selenium could only be apparent in areas of selenium deficiency.

Lung
Two cohort studies,[288] [464] two case-control studies,[469] [557] and two ecological studies[728] [729] investigated dietary selenium and lung cancer.

Ten cohort studies,[463] [575] [577] [730-738] seven case-control studies,[570] [571] [739-743] and four ecological studies[729] [744-746] investigated plasma or serum selenium; three cohort studies[747-749] investigated selenium levels in nails.

Dietary selenium
One cohort study showed non-significant decreased risk for the highest intake group when compared to the lowest.[464] One cohort study showed non-significant increased risk in non-smokers and non-significant decreased risk in smokers.[288] Both case-control studies showed a non-significant increased risk for the highest intake group when compared to the lowest.[469] [557] One ecological study showed statistically significant decreased risk in high-intake areas,[728] the other showed no consistent association.[729]

Plasma or serum selenium
Seven cohort studies showed decreased risk for the highest selenium levels when compared to the lowest,[463] [575] [731-734] [736-738] which was statistically significant in two.[733] [737] Four studies showed increased risk,[577] [730] [735] [738] which was statistically significant in two.[735] [738] Meta-analysis was possible on four cohort studies, giving a summary effect estimate of 0.969 (95% CI 0.940–0.999) per 10 μg/l, with low heterogeneity.[577] [731] [733] [736]

Six case-control studies showed decreased risk for the highest levels when compared to the lowest,[570] [739-743] which was statistically significant in four.[739] [740] [742] [743] One study showed non-significant increased risk.[571]

One ecological study showed statistically significant decreased risk in areas of high plasma selenium[729]; the others showed no consistent effect.[729] [744-746]

Nails
Two cohort studies showed decreased risk for the highest selenium levels when compared to the lowest,[748] [749] which was statistically significant in one.[749] One study showed non-significant increased risk.[747]

The general mechanisms through which selenium could plausibly protect against lung cancer are outlined below.

The evidence available is sparse. There is limited evidence to suggest that foods containing selenium protect against lung cancer.

Prostate
One cohort,[713] [750] 7 case-control studies,[599] [601] [639] [715] [716] [751] [752] and 2 ecological studies[729] [753] [754] investigated dietary selenium; 12 cohort studies[652] [730] [732] [755-765] and 4 case-control studies[716] [741] [752] [754] [766] [767] investigated serum or plasma selenium; and 3 cohort studies,[615] [724] [768] 3 case-control studies,[717] [769] [770] and 1 ecological study[771] investigated levels in nails. Further to this, 1 randomised controlled trial[772] [773] and 2 cohorts[612] [628] [713] investigated selenium supplements (see chapter 4.10.6.4.5).

Dietary selenium

One cohort study showed a statistically significant decreased risk. The effect estimate was 0.66 (95% CI 0.44–0.98) per 50 µg/day.[713] This study did not adjust for confounders.

Two case-control studies showed non-significant decreased risk for the highest intake groups when compared to the lowest[751 752]; five showed increased risk,[599 601 639 715 716] one of which was statistically significant.[715] Meta-analysis was possible on three studies, giving a summary effect estimate of 1.07 (95% CI 0.92–1.25) per increase in 50 µg/day, with no heterogeneity.[599 601 639]

The two ecological studies reported that increasing selenium intake was associated with decreasing prostate cancer levels.[729 753 754]

Serum or plasma selenium

Eight cohort studies that investigated serum or plasma selenium showed decreased risk for the highest intake groups when compared to the lowest,[652 732 755-759 761 763 764] which was statistically significant in two. Four reported non-significant increased risk.[730 760 762 765] Meta-analysis was possible on nine of these studies, giving a summary effect estimate of 0.95 (95% CI 0.89–1.00) per 10 µg/l, with moderate heterogeneity (figure 4.2.36).[732 755 757 758 761 762 764 765]

Two of these 12 cohort studies reported separately on advanced/aggressive cancer.[730 755 758] Both showed decreased risk for the highest intake groups when compared to the lowest, which was statistically significant in one.[758] Meta-analysis was possible on both, giving a summary effect estimate of 0.87 (95% CI 0.79–0.97) per 10 µg/l, with no heterogeneity (figure 4.2.37).[755 758]

A dose-response relationship is apparent from the studies on advanced or aggressive disease (figure 4.2.38).

All four of the case-control studies showed decreased risk for the highest intake groups when compared to the lowest,[716 741 752 766 767] which was statistically significant in three.[741 752 767]

Nails

Two cohort studies investigated selenium levels in nails for all prostate cancer. Both showed non-significant decreased risk for the highest intake groups when compared to the lowest. Meta-analysis was possible on both studies, giving a summary effect estimate of 0.91 (95% 0.81–1.02) per 100 ng/g, with moderate heterogeneity.[724 768]

Two cohort studies investigated selenium levels in nails for advanced or aggressive prostate cancer. Both showed statistically significant decreased risk for the highest intake groups when compared to the lowest. Meta-analysis was possible on both studies, giving a summary effect estimate of 0.80 (95% 0.69–0.91) per 100 ng/g, with no heterogeneity.[615 768]

One case-control study showed non-significant decreased risk for the highest intake groups when compared to the lowest,[770] one showed no effect on risk[717] and the other showed a non-significant increased risk.[769]

The single ecological study reported a non-significant association.[771]

These data are supported by data on supplements, which have been shown to decrease prostate cancer risk (see chapter 4.10.6.4.5).

There is no significant heterogeneity within the meta-

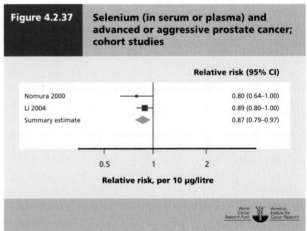

| Figure 4.2.37 | Selenium (in serum or plasma) and advanced or aggressive prostate cancer; cohort studies |

Relative risk (95% CI)

Nomura 2000 — 0.80 (0.64–1.00)
Li 2004 — 0.89 (0.80–1.00)
Summary estimate — 0.87 (0.79–0.97)

Relative risk, per 10 µg/litre

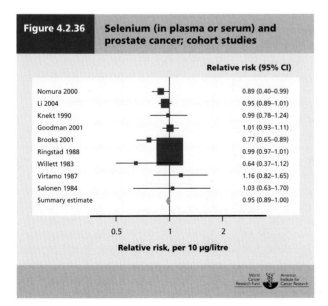

| Figure 4.2.36 | Selenium (in plasma or serum) and prostate cancer; cohort studies |

Relative risk (95% CI)

Nomura 2000 — 0.89 (0.40–0.99)
Li 2004 — 0.95 (0.89–1.01)
Knekt 1990 — 0.99 (0.78–1.24)
Goodman 2001 — 1.01 (0.93–1.11)
Brooks 2001 — 0.77 (0.65–0.89)
Ringstad 1988 — 0.99 (0.97–1.01)
Willett 1983 — 0.64 (0.37–1.12)
Virtamo 1987 — 1.16 (0.82–1.65)
Salonen 1984 — 1.03 (0.63–1.70)
Summary estimate — 0.95 (0.89–1.00)

Relative risk, per 10 µg/litre

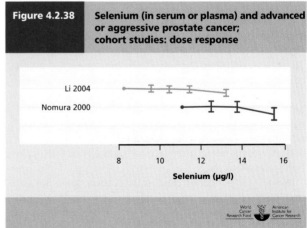

| Figure 4.2.38 | Selenium (in serum or plasma) and advanced or aggressive prostate cancer; cohort studies: dose response |

Li 2004
Nomura 2000

Selenium (µg/l)

analyses of advanced/aggressive cancer. The low to moderate heterogeneity observed for other outcomes and different study types may be explained by the variable inclusion of latent cancers in the outcome and by variations in study quality.

The general mechanisms through which foods containing selenium could plausibly protect against prostate cancer are outlined below. In addition, selenoproteins are involved in testosterone production, which is an important regulator of both normal and abnormal prostate growth.[774 775]

The evidence from cohort and case-control studies is consistent, with a dose-response relationship. There is evidence for plausible mechanisms. Foods containing selenium probably protect against prostate cancer.

Stomach

One case-control study[776] and five ecological studies[238 729 777-779] investigated dietary selenium and stomach cancer. Three cohort studies,[731 732 736] nine case-control studies,[738 741 754 780-785] and three ecological studies[236 729 786] investigated blood selenium. One cohort study[787] and one case-control study[788] investigated selenium in toenails or hair. In addition, one randomised controlled trial and one combined trial investigated selenium supplements.[423 424]

Dietary selenium
The single case-control study showed that dietary selenium was not significantly associated with risk of stomach cancer.[776]

Most ecological studies showed that low selenium levels were associated with increased stomach cancer risk,[238 777-779] one of which was statistically significant.[779]

Blood selenium
All three cohort studies that investigated blood selenium levels showed decreased risk for the highest levels when compared to the lowest,[731 732 736] which was statistically significant in men in one study.[732] Meta-analysis was possible on all three, giving a summary effect estimate of 0.89 (95% CI 0.78–1.00) per 0.1 μmol/l, with moderate heterogeneity.[731 732 736]

All nine case-control studies showed statistically significant decreased risk for the highest levels when compared to the lowest.[738 741 754 780-785] Meta-analysis was possible on six of these, giving a summary effect estimate of 0.44 (95% CI 0.35–0.55) per 0.1 μmol/l, with high heterogeneity.[741 754 782-785] This heterogeneity was caused by varying size, not direction, of effect.

All three ecological studies reported inverse associations between blood or plasma selenium and stomach cancer mortality,[236 729 786] which were statistically significant in two.[236 786]

A dose-response relationship is apparent from case-control but not cohort data.

Two additional cohort studies, both from China, stratified results according to tumour location.[789 790] The apparent protective effect was strengthened for cardia cancers, but disappeared for proximal.

Nails and hair
The single cohort study that investigated selenium in nails showed statistically significant decreased risk for the highest levels when compared to the lowest in men, but not women. The effect estimates were 0.4 in men (95% CI 0.17–0.96; 72 cases) and 1.68 in women (95% CI 0.43–6.54; 20 cases).[787]

The single case-control study found that mean hair selenium levels were significantly lower in the 15 stomach cancer cases than in controls.[788]

The general mechanisms through which foods containing selenium could plausibly protect against stomach cancer are outlined below. In addition, selenoproteins with powerful antioxidant activity may provide protection against the inflammatory effect of *H pylori*, which can lead to gastric cancer in infected individuals.[791]

A substantial amount of evidence was available on selenium, from dietary questionnaires, as well as blood, nails, and hair, mostly from case-control studies. There is limited evidence suggesting that foods containing selenium protect against stomach cancer.

Colorectum

Fifteen case-control studies investigated dietary selenium and colorectal cancer.[738 785 792-795]

Dietary, serum or plasma, toenail selenium
Meta-analysis was possible on six independent effect estimates from five case-control studies, giving a summary effect estimate of 0.86 (95% CI 0.78–0.95) per 10 μg/dl serum, with high heterogeneity.[785 792-795] All of these studies reported decreased risk, which was statistically significant in four of the five studies.[792-795] The heterogeneity is therefore derived from varying size, but not direction of effect. The remaining 10 studies reported non-significant decreased risk.[738] These data are supported by limited evidence suggesting that there is also a protective effect from selenium supplements (see chapter 4.10.6.4.5).

The general mechanisms through which foods containing selenium could plausibly protect against colorectal cancer are outlined below.

A substantial amount of data was available, from case-control studies only. There is limited evidence suggesting that foods containing selenium protect against colorectal cancer.

General mechanisms — foods containing selenium
Dietary selenium deficiency has been shown to cause a lack of selenoprotein expression. Twenty-five selenoproteins have been identified in animals and a number of these have important anti-inflammatory and antioxidant properties.[796] Four are glutathione peroxidises, which protect against oxidative damage to lipids, lipoproteins, and DNA. These enzymes are rapidly degraded during selenium deprivation. Three are thioredoxin reductases and, amongst other functions, these regenerate oxidised ascorbic acid to its active antioxidant form.

Selenoproteins appear to reach their maximal levels relatively easily at normal dietary selenium intake and not to increase with selenium supplementation. It is, however, plausible that supraphysiological amounts of selenium might affect programmed cell death, DNA repair, carcinogen metabolism, immune system, and anti-angiogenic effects.[797]

4.2.5.9 Foods containing quercetin

Lung

Two cohort studies[147 798] and three case-control studies[327 477 799] investigated foods containing quercetin and lung cancer.

Both cohort studies showed statistically significant decreased risk for the highest intake groups when compared to the lowest.[147 798] The effect estimates were 0.63 (95% CI 0.52–0.78)[147] and 0.42 (95% CI 0.25–0.72).[798] Both studies adjusted for smoking.

Two case-control studies showed decreased risk for the highest intake groups when compared to the lowest,[327 477] which was statistically significant in one.[327] One study reported non-significant increased risk.[799] The effect estimates were 0.58 (95% CI 0.39–0.85),[327] 0.7 (95% CI 0.4–1.1),[477] and 1.89 (95% CI 0.72–4.92).[799] The latter study may have been over-adjusted.

Quercetin is a flavonoid. It is an antioxidant and also directly inhibits expression of CYP1A1 (a cytochrome P450 enzyme that helps to metabolise toxins), resulting in decreased formation of DNA adducts.[475] Elevated CYP1A1 activity has been associated with increased risk of lung cancer, primarily in smokers.[476] The evidence for CYP1A1/flavonoid interactions is supported by the observation that protective associations of flavonoids are associated with specific CYP1A1 genotypes.[476 477]

> **The evidence available is sparse and inconsistent. There is limited evidence suggesting that foods containing quercetin protect against lung cancer.**

4.2.5.10 Pulses (legumes)

Studies conducted in Western countries, as most cohorts have been, are likely to have limited power to detect an association between pulses, and particularly soya intake, and cancer risk because consumption tends to be low.

Stomach

Three cohort studies,[144 146 241] 22 case-control studies,[109 157 161 162 165 175 179 180 185-187 190 219 224 243 244 247 249-251 270 271 482] 2 cross-sectional studies,[196 800] and 16 ecological studies[116-119 197 198 200-203 208 209 236 238 239 801] investigated pulses (legumes) and stomach cancer. Two cohort studies,[802 803] 9 case-control studies,[109 129 159 178 184 194 226 229 262] and 2 ecological studies[208 804] investigated soya and soya products.

Pulses (legumes)

All three cohort studies reported decreased risk with increased intake of pulses (legumes),[144 146 241] which was statistically significant in one.[146] Meta-analysis was possible on two studies, giving a summary effect estimate of 0.93 (95% CI 0.82–1.05) per 20 g/day, with moderate heterogeneity.[144 146]

Twelve case-control studies showed decreased risk for the highest intake groups when compared to the lowest,[109 157 161 165 179 185-187 190 219 247 249 250 271] which was statistically significant in six.[109 161 165 179 190 249] Six studies reported increased risk,[162 224 243 251 270 482] which was statistically significant in two.[224 243 270] The remaining four studies reported no effect on risk,[180 244] or stated that there was no significant effect on risk.[175] Meta-analysis was possible on eight studies, giving a summary effect estimate of 0.93 (95% CI 0.87–0.99) per 20 g/day, with moderate to high heterogeneity.[157 162 179 180 186 187 247 249]

A dose-response relationship is apparent from case-control but not cohort data.

One ecological study reported a statistically significant association, so that higher soya consumption was associated with lower stomach cancer risk.[208] The other 15 reported no significant association.[116-119 197 198 200-203 209 236 238 239 801]

Soya and soya products

Both cohort studies showed decreased risk for the highest intake groups when compared to the lowest,[802 803] which was statistically significant in one.[803] The effect estimates were 0.60 (44 cases, 95% CI 0.40–1.10)[802] and 0.86 (121 cases, 95% CI 0.77–0.96) per 20 g/day.[803] The smaller study was not adjusted for any confounders.

All nine case-control studies showed decreased risk for the highest intake groups when compared to the lowest,[109 129 159 178 184 194 226 229 262] which was statistically significant in five.[129 159 178 184 226] Meta-analysis was possible on seven studies, giving a summary effect estimate of 0.82 (95% CI 0.72–0.94) per 20 g/day, with high heterogeneity.[109 129 159 178 194 226 229] Heterogeneity is derived from the size, and not the direction, of the effect.

A dose-response relationship is apparent from case-control data, as well as from one of the two cohort studies.

Both ecological studies reported statistically significant inverse relationships, with stomach cancer risk decreasing in areas of increased soya consumption.[208 804]

The general mechanisms through which pulses (legumes), soya and soya products could plausibly protect against stomach cancer are outlined below. In addition, laboratory experiments have shown that genistein slows down the development of stomach cancers promoted by sodium chloride by increasing apoptosis, and lowering cell proliferation and blood vessel growth.[805] Additionally, in a rodent model, a diet containing miso inhibited *N*-nitrosamine-induced stomach tumours.[806]

> **The evidence, mostly from case-control studies, is inconsistent. There is limited evidence suggesting that pulses (legumes), including soya and soya products, protect against stomach cancer.**

Prostate

Three cohort studies,[589 592-594] 11 case-control studies,[595 597 599-601 604 608 617 620 624 715] and 6 ecological studies[116 118 609 807-809] investigated pulses (legumes) and prostate cancer. Four cohort studies,[597 810-813] 4 case-control studies,[603 715 814-816] and 2 ecological studies[804 808] investigated soya and soya products.

Pulses (legumes)

Two cohort studies reported statistically significant decreased risk with increased intake[589 592]; the third study reported that there was no significant association.[594] The reported effect estimates were 0.93 (95% CI 0.87–0.996)[589] and 0.817 (95% CI 0.714–0.934)[592] per serving/week. The latter was specific to beans and lentils.

Eight of the case-control studies showed decreased risk with increased intake,[595 597 599 608 617 620 624 715] which was statistically significant in two.[597 624] One study showed a non-significant increased risk[604] and the other reported no effect on risk.[600] One study showed a non-significant increased risk for dried beans and lentils and a non-significant decreased risk with fresh beans and lentils.[601] Meta analysis was possible on four relatively good quality case-control studies, giving a summary effect estimate of 0.97 (95% CI 0.95–0.98) per serving/week, with no heterogeneity.[595 597 599 601]

A dose-response relationship is apparent from two of the cohort studies, as well as case-control data.

The five ecological studies generally fail to show a clear relationship between consumption of pulses and prostate cancer risk; correlations range from -0.15 to -0.63.[116 118 609 807-809]

Soya and soya products

The cohort studies reported a wide range of results based on different specific exposures.[810-813] One study, which reported on soya and soya products, showed a non-significant decreased risk for the highest intake groups when compared to the lowest, with an effect estimate of 0.79 (95% CI 0.53–1.18).[810] One study reported a statistically significant decreased risk with increased intake of soya milk (0.93, 95% CI 0.87–0.99) per serving/week and a non-significant decreased risk with increased intake of vegetarian soya products (0.93, 95% CI 0.85–1.01) per serving/week.[813] One reported no association between soya bean paste soup intake and prostate cancer.[811] The final study reported non-significant harmful effects for miso soup and foods cooked in soy sauce, with effect estimates of 1.05 (95% CI 0.94–1.18) and 1.06 (0.474, 2.39) respectively per serving/day.[812]

All four case-control studies showed non-significant decreased risk with increased intake.[597 603 715 814-816] Meta analysis was possible on two case-control studies, giving a summary effect estimate of 0.98 (95% CI 0.95–1.00).[597 715]

The two ecological studies reported no clear relationship between soya consumption and prostate cancer.[804 808]

Heterogeneity is likely to be derived from the wide variety in specific foods being investigated.

The general mechanisms through which pulses (legumes), soya and soya products could plausibly protect against prostate cancer are outlined below. In addition, phytoestrogens in pulses and soya can have an androgenic effect, potentially inhibiting testosterone-induced growth of the prostate.

The evidence, mostly from case-control studies, is inconsistent. There is limited evidence suggesting that pulses (legumes), including soya and soya products, protect against prostate cancer.

General mechanisms — pulses (legumes)

Pulses (legumes), particularly soya foods, contain various compounds that may have anti-cancer effects, including protease inhibitors, saponins, and phytoestrogens, such as genistein and daidzein, which are found in high concentrations in soya.[817] These compounds could plausibly influence oestrogen metabolism. They have also been shown to have antioxidant effects, inhibit the growth of blood vessels to a tumour, and may influence apoptosis and cell growth.[818]

4.2.5.11 Nuts and seeds

The evidence was too limited in amount, consistency, or quality to draw any conclusions

4.2.5.12 Herbs and spices

Garlic can be classified as a herb or as an allium vegetable. Data on garlic have contributed to the evidence base for allium vegetables and stomach cancer (see chapter 4.2.5.1.1) and garlic also probably protects against colorectal cancer (see chapter 4.2.5.1.1).

4.2.5.12.1 Chilli

Stomach

Fourteen case-control studies investigated chilli use and stomach cancer.[171 175 176 180 182 187 189 219 246 247 259 415 819-821]

Nine studies showed increased risk for the highest intake groups when compared to the lowest,[175 176 180 187 189 219 259 415 820 821] which was statistically significant in four,[175 180 259 821] statistically significant in men but not women in a fifth study,[219] and statistically significant in non-drinkers of alcohol, but not alcohol drinkers, in a sixth.[176] Four studies showed decreased risk,[171 182 246 247] which was statistically significant in three.[182 246 247] One study reported no significant effect on risk.[819]

Chilli may be used to disguise 'off' flavours in foods, therefore these data may be confounded by socioeconomic status, the availability of refrigeration, and *H pylori* infection.

Some constituents of chilli are irritants which could therefore plausibly increase inflammation in the stomach.

The evidence, from case-control studies only, is inconsistent. There is limited evidence suggesting that chilli is associated with an increased risk of stomach cancer.

4.2.4 Comparison with previous report

The previous report concluded that the evidence that diets high in vegetables and fruits protect against cancers of the mouth, pharynx, oesophagus, lung, and stomach was convincing; and that the evidence that diets high in vegetables protect against colorectal cancer was also convincing. The previous report also judged that diets high in vegetables and fruits probably protected against cancers of the larynx, pancreas, breast, and bladder. The panel also noted a pattern whereby diets high in vegetables and fruits possibly protected against cancers of the cervix, ovary, endometrium, and thyroid; and that diets high in vegetables possibly protected against cancers of the liver, prostate, and kidney.

Since the mid-1990s, a number of cohort studies have somewhat weakened the overall evidence for the protective effects of vegetables and fruits. A number of judgements of probable protective effects are made for non-starchy vegetables and for fruits (mouth, pharynx, larynx, oesophagus, stomach, and (fruits only) lung). In general, the reason for this is that the more recent cohort studies failed to show the effect seen in case-control studies.

The previous report also made judgements on types of vegetables and fruits in a footnote, while choosing not to enter these into the matrix. The evidence that green vegetables protected against lung and stomach cancer was judged convincing; and probable for mouth and oesophageal cancer. The evidence that cruciferous vegetables protected against colorectal and thyroid cancer was judged probable. The evidence that allium vegetables protected against stomach cancer was judged probable. The evidence that raw vegetables and citrus fruits protected against stomach cancer was judged convincing. These classifications are somewhat different from those made in this Report, but mostly also generated more confident judgements than are made here.

Vitamins, minerals, and other bioactive constituents of foods and drinks were assessed as such in the previous report, whereas here they are assessed either as contained in foods and drinks or (see chapter 4.10) as supplements. The previous report judged that carotenoids (in food) probably protected against lung cancer; that vitamin C (in food) probably protected against stomach cancer; and that these vitamins and vitamin E possibly protected against cancers of a number of sites.

The previous panel regretted the lack of evidence on pulses (legumes), nuts, seeds, herbs, and spices, and made no significant judgements. Since then, evidence on soya and its products, and on garlic (as well as allium vegetables in general) and chilli, has increased and allowed some judgements.

The previous report judged that aflatoxin contamination was a probable cause of liver cancer. Since then, the overall evidence, particularly on the underlying mechanisms, has strengthened.

The previous report emphasised evidence on vegetables and on fruits as a whole, while noting evidence on categories of vegetables and fruits. This Report has not made any separate judgement on raw vegetables and fruits. The previous report classified bananas as plantains. Here they are classified as fruits. The previous report considered micronutrients and phytochemicals contained in foods of plant origin in separate chapters. Here, the evidence has been characterised in terms of foods containing specified micronutrients, and they are considered together with vegetables and fruits, pulses (legumes), nuts and seeds, and other plant foods. Similarly, the previous report considered dietary fibre separately from cereals (grains) and other plant foods. Here, dietary fibre is considered in the context of cereals (grains) and other plant foods, including those assessed in this section.

4.2.7 Conclusions

The Panel concludes:

Findings from cohort studies conducted since the mid-1990s have made the overall evidence that vegetables, or fruits, protect against cancers, somewhat less impressive. In no case now is evidence of protection judged to be convincing. However, there is evidence that some types of vegetables, and fruits in general, probably protect against a number of cancers. The few judgements on legumes (pulses), nuts, seeds, and (with two exceptions) herbs and spices, reflect the small amount of epidemiological evidence.

Non-starchy vegetables probably protect against cancers of the mouth, pharynx, and larynx, and those of the oesophagus and stomach. There is limited evidence suggesting that they also protect against cancers of the nasopharynx, lung, colorectum, ovary, and endometrium. Allium vegetables probably protect against stomach cancer. Garlic (an allium vegetable, commonly classed as a herb) probably protects against colorectal cancer.

Fruits in general probably protect against cancers of the mouth, pharynx, and larynx, and of the oesophagus, lung, and stomach. There is limited evidence suggesting that fruits also protect against cancers of the nasopharynx, pancreas, liver, and colorectum.

There is limited evidence suggesting that carrots protect against cervical cancer; and that pulses (legumes), including soya and soya products, protect against stomach and prostate cancers. There is limited evidence suggesting that chilli is a cause of stomach cancer.

Fruits and non-starchy vegetables are low energy-dense foods. For a discussion of the effect of such foods and drinks on weight gain, overweight, and obesity, and the role of weight gain, overweight, and obesity in the risk of some cancers, see Chapters 6, 7, and 8.

Evidence that vegetables, fruits, and pulses protect against some cancers is supported by evidence on various micronutrients, which act as markers for consumption of vegetables, fruits, and pulses (legumes), and other plant foods. Foods containing folate probably protect against pancreatic cancer, and there is limited evidence suggesting that these also protect against oesophageal and colorectal cancers. Foods containing carotenoids probably protect against cancers of the mouth, pharynx, and larynx, and also lung cancer. Foods containing the carotenoid beta-carotene probably protect against oesophageal cancer; and foods containing lycopene, found in tomatoes and also fruits such as watermelon, guavas, and apricots, probably protect against prostate cancer. Foods containing vitamin C, found in some vegetables, citrus and other fruits, and potatoes, probably protect against oesophageal cancer. There is limited evidence suggesting that foods containing quercetin, such as apples, tea, and onions, protect against lung cancer.

Evidence on foods containing other micronutrients is grouped here, for ease of reference. Foods containing selenium probably protect against prostate cancer; there is limited evidence suggesting that they protect against stomach and colorectal cancers. There is limited evidence suggesting that foods containing the B vitamin pyridoxine protect against oesophageal and prostate cancers; and that foods containing vitamin E protect against oesophageal and prostate cancers.

4.3 Meat, poultry, fish, and eggs

MEAT, POULTRY, FISH, EGGS, AND THE RISK OF CANCER

In the judgement of the Panel, the factors listed below modify the risk of cancer. Judgements are graded according to the strength of the evidence.

	DECREASES RISK		INCREASES RISK	
	Exposure	**Cancer site**	**Exposure**	**Cancer site**
Convincing			**Red meat[1]** **Processed meat[2]**	**Colorectum** **Colorectum**
Probable			**Cantonese-style salted fish[3]**	**Nasopharynx**
Limited — suggestive	Fish Foods containing vitamin D[4 7]	Colorectum Colorectum	Red meat[1] Processed meat[2] Foods containing iron[4 5] Smoked foods[6] Grilled (broiled) or barbecued (charbroiled) animal foods[6]	Oesophagus Lung Pancreas Endometrium Oesophagus Lung Stomach Prostate Colorectum Stomach Stomach
Substantial effect on risk unlikely		None identified		

1 The term 'red meat' refers to beef, pork, lamb, and goat from domesticated animals.
2 The term 'processed meat' refers to meats preserved by smoking, curing, or salting, or addition of chemical preservatives.
3 This style of preparation is characterised by treatment with less salt than typically used, and fermentation during the drying process due to relatively high outdoor temperature and moisture levels. This conclusion does not apply to fish prepared (or salted) by other means.
4 Includes both foods naturally containing the constituent and foods which have the constituent added (see chapter 3.5.3).
5 Although red and processed meats contain iron, the general category of 'foods containing iron' comprises many other foods, including those of plant origin.
6 The evidence is mostly from meats preserved or cooked in these ways.
7 Found mostly in fortified foods and animal foods.

For an explanation of all the terms used in the matrix, please see chapter 3.5.1, the text of this section, and the glossary.

These animal foods are sources of protein and micronutrients. The amount and nature of the fat content of meat, poultry, and fish depends on methods of rearing, processing, and preparation, as well as the type of animal.

Production and consumption of red meat and processed meat generally rise with increases in available income. Consumption of beef and products made with beef is still increasing, notably in China and other middle- and low-income countries. In many countries, poultry is now also intensively reared and consumption has increased greatly. Much fish is now farmed.

In general, *the Panel judges* that the evidence on red meat and processed meat is stronger than it was in the mid-1990s. Epidemiological evidence on other methods of preserving and preparing meats and other animal foods is sparse; the overall evidence remains suggestive, at most. The evidence on poultry, fish, and eggs is generally insubstantial.

The Panel judges as follows:
The evidence that red meats and processed meats are a cause of colorectal cancer is convincing. Cantonese-style salted fish is a probable cause of nasopharyngeal cancer. This finding does not apply to any other type of fish product. Cantonese-style salted fish is also subject to fermentation.

There is limited evidence suggesting that fish, and also foods containing vitamin D, protect against colorectal cancer. There is limited evidence suggesting that red meat is a cause of cancers of the oesophagus, lung, pancreas and endometrium; that processed meat is a cause of cancers of the oesophagus, lung, stomach and prostate; and that foods containing iron are a cause of colorectal cancer. There is also limited evidence that animal foods that are grilled (broiled), barbecued (charbroiled), or smoked, are a cause of stomach cancer.

Red meat can be relatively high in animal fats. For a discussion of the role of animal fats on cancer, see chapter 4.4 and Chapter 7. Meat can also be energy dense. For discussion on the role of energy-dense foods on weight gain, overweight, and obesity, and the role of weight gain, overweight, and obesity in the risk of some cancers, see Chapters 6 and 8.

The strongest evidence, corresponding to judgements of 'convincing' and 'probable', shows that red meat and processed meat are causes of colorectal cancer, and that Cantonese-style salted fish is probably a cause of nasopharyngeal cancer. *The Panel also notes* limited evidence suggesting that red meat and processed meat are causes of other cancers.

It is generally, though not universally, agreed that humans evolved as omnivores, and that healthy diets usually include foods of plant and of animal origin — including meat, poultry, fish, and eggs, as well as milk and other dairy products.

Most people who do not eat meat, flesh, or any food of animal origin do so for religious or ethical reasons. Impoverished communities eat little flesh and meat is reserved for feasts. Partly because meat-eating is a sign of prosperity and partly because many people enjoy eating meat, poultry, and fish, production and consumption generally rise as available income increases. Consumption of beef is, for example, now increasing very rapidly in China, and consumption of 'burgers' made from beef is increasing worldwide.

Early reports concerned with nutritional deficiencies identified meat, poultry, and fish as good sources of protein, iron, and other nutrients, and eggs as a 'complete food', especially for children. By contrast, in the second half of the 20th century, reports on meat, poultry, fish, and eggs tended to focus on red meat as a source of fat and saturated fatty acids and on eggs as a source of dietary cholesterol in the causation of coronary heart disease. These reports promoted poultry and fish as better choices than red meat, either because they contain less fat and saturated fatty acids or, in the case of oily fish, they contain unsaturated fats identified as protective. Little attention has been given to flesh from wild animals and birds, despite this being known to have a different nutritional profile — lower in total fat and higher in unsaturated fatty acids. On the other hand, since the mid-1990s more attention has been given in epidemiological studies to processed meat as a cause or possible cause of cancers of some sites.

For discussion of the role of red meat and processed meat in energy-dense foods and drinks, the effect of energy-dense foods and drinks on weight gain, overweight, and obesity, and the role of weight gain, overweight, and obesity in the risk of some cancers, see Chapters 6 and 8.

In this Report, methods of production, preservation, processing, and preparation (including cooking), that are solely or mainly to do with meat and other animal foods, are included here. Processed meat as a category is included here. The mineral iron is also covered here, although it is also found in plant foods.

4.3.1 Definitions and sources

Meat and poultry
In this Report, meat includes all animal flesh apart from fish and seafood. Meat can be further classed as either red meat, which generally refers to flesh from animals that have more red than white muscle fibres (in this Report, beef, goat, lamb, and pork), or poultry, which usually has more white than red muscle fibres (from birds such as chickens, guinea fowl, and turkeys). Meat can also be categorised by dividing it into meats from skeletal muscles or the internal organs (offal, such as the brain, liver, heart, intestines, and tongue). Meat can also be divided according to whether the animal was domesticated or wild. Most meats consumed around the world today are from domesticated animals. 'Wild' meats, that is from non-domesticated or free-ranging species, are a significant source of protein and energy among some populations. Some non-domesticated animals, such as deer or buffalo, are also farmed. However, the evidence presented in this chapter applies only to meat from domesticated animals. Some meats are processed in various ways (box 4.3.1).

Fish
This Report uses the culinary definition of fish, which includes shellfish. There are more than 27 000 species of salt and freshwater fish; many more crustaceans, bivalves, and cephalopods can also be eaten. Fish and shellfish are the only foods that, globally, are still obtained in significant quantities from the wild. But many species are on the verge of commercial extinction and aquaculture is increasing worldwide. For instance, more than a third of the salmon eaten worldwide is farmed. Like meat, fish is also processed, for instance by drying, salting, and smoking.

Eggs
Eggs are the ova of animals and in this Report mean only

Box 4.3.1   Processed meat

What is 'processed meat'? The question is important because, as shown here, the evidence that processed meat is a cause of colorectal cancer is convincing.

In the broad sense of the word, most meat is processed — cooking is a process. But as commonly used, the term 'processed meat' refers to meats (usually red meats) preserved by smoking, curing, or salting, or by the addition of preservatives. Meats preserved only by refrigeration, however they are cooked, are usually not classified as 'processed meat'.

There is no generally agreed definition of 'processed meat'. The term is used inconsistently in epidemiological studies. Judgements and recommendations are therefore less clear than they could be.

Ham, bacon, pastrami, and salami are processed meats. So are sausages, bratwursts, frankfurters, and 'hot dogs' to which nitrites or nitrates or other preservatives are added (box 4.3.2). Minced meats sometimes fall inside this definition, often if they are preserved chemically, but not always. The same point applies to 'hamburgers'. Given the importance of this issue, transnational burger caterers should specify the methods they use to process their products.

those of birds; because they are generally eaten before they have been fertilised, they do not contain an embryo. Eggs are eaten both on their own and as an ingredient in a variety of baked goods, sauces, and other composite foods. Chicken eggs are most commonly eaten, although people also eat duck, ostrich, and quail eggs. Fish eggs (roe) and turtle eggs are not included here.

4.3.2 Composition

Meat and poultry

Meat contains around 20–35 per cent protein by weight. The fat content by weight ranges from less than 4 per cent in lean poultry to 30–40 per cent in fatty meat from domesticated, farmed animals. About 50 per cent of the fatty acids in lean meat are monounsaturated fatty acids, while saturated fatty acids make up around 40–50 per cent (see chapter 4.4.2). Poultry contains a lower proportion of saturated fatty acids (30–35 per cent) and a higher proportion of polyunsaturated fatty acids (15–30 per cent compared with 4–10 per cent).[1] There are differences between meats from domesticated animals and wild meats. Wild animals are typically more mature, leaner, and contain a greater variety of aromatic compounds than farmed animals. They will have received no medication and their diets will have been uncontrolled. Wild animals are not only lower in fat, but also have a higher proportion of polyunsaturated fatty acids than farmed varieties and a lower proportion of saturated fatty acids.

Two iron-containing components of muscle tissue, myoglobin and cytochromes, give meat its red colour. It also contains relatively high levels of B vitamins, particularly B6 (pyridoxine) and B12, as well as vitamin D, and provides

---

Box 4.3.2 Nitrates, nitrites, and N-nitroso compounds

Nitrate occurs naturally in plants; levels vary between species and with different soil conditions and the amount of fertiliser used. In high-income countries, vegetables account for 70–97 per cent of dietary nitrate intake.[2] Between 5 and 20 per cent of the nitrate in diets is converted by the body into nitrite, a substance that is also found in some vegetables (notably potatoes). Nitrite is used to preserve processed meats (it is extremely toxic to bacteria) and gives cured meats their recognisable colour and flavours. The addition of nitrite and nitrate to food is regulated and monitored in most countries.

Nitrite can react with the degradation products of amino acids to form N-nitroso compounds (nitrosamines or nitrosamides). These may be formed in meat during the curing process or in the body (particularly in the stomach) from dietary nitrite (or nitrate).

Several N-nitroso compounds are known human or animal carcinogens.[3] There is concern that nitrite, from processed meats for example, nitrates in vegetables, and preformed nitrosamines may be involved in carcinogenesis, particularly in the stomach (see Chapter 2). Dietary nitrates and nitrites are probable human carcinogens because they are converted in the body to N-nitroso compounds.[3]

Box 4.3.3 Foods containing iron

Iron deficiency is the most common and widespread nutritional disorder in the world. It is most common among children and premenopausal women, and results in iron deficiency anaemia.

Haem iron is found only in foods of animal origin, such as meat and meat products, fish, and blood products. Non-haem iron is found in plant foods, such as lentils, beans, leafy vegetables, tofu, chickpeas, black-eyed peas, figs, and apricots. The amount of dietary iron needed to meet the body's requirements depends on its bioavailability from the diet. This varies with the diet, as well as factors related to the consumer such as their iron status. Iron from animal sources is better absorbed than iron from plant sources, but non-haem iron absorption is enhanced when the body's iron status is low, or when iron-rich foods are eaten together with vitamin-C rich foods or with meat.

Iron has a central role in metabolism. It is involved in oxidative metabolism within cells and is a component of a number of enzymes. Free iron can also catalyse the generation of free radicals, which cause oxidative damage to specific cell components including DNA, protein, and membrane lipids. Iron metabolism and transport are strictly regulated to reduce the likelihood of cells being exposed to free iron and so to oxidative damage; most iron in living tissues is bound to proteins, such as transferrin and ferritin, which prevent its involvement in free-radical generation. Also see chapter 4.10.

---

readily absorbable iron, zinc, and selenium. Eating red meat increases levels of N-nitroso compounds in the body (box 4.3.2), which may be partially due to its high haem content (box 4.3.3). If meat is cooked over an open flame, at high temperatures, and charred or 'well done', heterocyclic amines or polycyclic aromatic hydrocarbons can be formed (box 4.3.4).

Vitamin D is a fat-soluble vitamin that plays a critical role in calcium and bone metabolism and in controlling cell differentiation. Low levels may lead to osteomalacia or, in children, rickets and possibly osteoporosis, with increased fracture risk. Most vitamin D is derived from the action of sunlight on the skin. Foods such as milk or fat spreads (see chapter 4.9) may be fortified, and then become the major dietary source of vitamin D; natural sources include sardines and other oily fish, meat, and eggs.

Fish

Fish has similar levels of protein to meat. It has a fat by weight content of between 0.5 per cent in low-fat fish such as cod or skate to as much as 20 per cent in oily fish such as Atlantic salmon or eels. Fat from fish contains lower levels of saturated fatty acids (around 20–25 per cent) than meat.

Fish oils from saltwater fish contain long-chain n-3 fatty acids (see chapter 4.4.2). Wild fish have a lower fat content than farmed fish, with a higher proportion of n-3 fatty acids. Only marine algae and phytoplankton produce these fatty acids, so the fish that feed on them are the primary dietary sources. These fatty acids are essential to the development and function of the brain and retina; they also reduce inflammation, blood clotting, and cholesterol production. The body

Box 4.3.4 **Heterocyclic amines and poly-cyclic aromatic hydrocarbons**

Heterocyclic amines are formed when muscle meats such as beef, pork, fowl, and fish are cooked. High cooking temperatures cause amino acids and creatine (a chemical found in muscles) to react together to form these chemicals. So far, 17 different heterocyclic amines have been identified as being formed by cooking muscle meats and which may pose a cancer risk (also see Chapter 2).

Temperature is the most important factor in the formation of these chemicals. Frying, grilling (broiling), and barbecuing (charbroiling) produce the largest amounts because these cooking methods use very high temperatures. Oven roasting and baking involve lower temperatures, so meats cooked in this way are lower in heterocyclic amines, but gravy made from meat drippings contains substantial amounts. Meats that are partially cooked in a microwave oven before being cooked by other higher-temperature methods also have lower levels of these chemicals.[4]

Polycyclic aromatic hydrocarbons (PAHs) are a group of over 100 different chemicals formed when organic substances like tobacco or meat are burnt incompletely. Grilling (broiling) and barbecuing (charbroiling) meat, fish, or other foods with intense heat over a direct flame results in fat dropping on the hot fire; this produces PAHs that stick to the surface of food. The more intense the heat, the higher the level of contamination; using wood creates more PAHs than charcoal. Cereals contaminated with PAHs are also a common source of these chemicals in the diet. Levels in cereals are considerably lower than in grilled meats, but their overall contribution to diets is larger.[5] Taken together, cereals and meat and meat products account for more than 50 per cent of dietary levels of these chemicals. Intakes are thought to be relatively high in Europe, particularly in northern Europe, although measures are only available from a few, generally high-income, countries.[6]

can convert alpha-linolenic acid (found in plant foods and essential in the diet) to eicosapentaenoic acid and docosohexanoic acid, which are found in fish oils, but the rates of conversion are low.

Fish contain lower levels of B vitamins, iron, and zinc than meat and poultry, but oily fish are a source of retinol and vitamin D. Fish are also a source of calcium if the bones are eaten with the flesh, for example, when canned.

Fish and shellfish have the potential to accumulate pollutants that are washed into rivers and oceans, and these tend to accumulate in their fat. These pollutants can include heavy metals and organic compounds, some of which are known carcinogens. Farmed fish are exposed to veterinary medicines, and some environmental toxins may reach high concentrations in their food. But farmed fish are less likely than wild fish to become contaminated with environmental pollutants. The balance of risks and benefits of eating fish at various stages of the life course needs to be determined. Also see chapter 4.9.

Eggs

Eggs, like meat, poultry, and fish, contain all the essential amino acids needed by humans. A typical large hen's egg has roughly equal weights of protein and fat, with 60 per cent of the energy coming from fat. A typical large shelled egg contains 6 g protein; 1 g carbohydrate; 4.5 g fat (2.0 g monounsaturated, 0.5 g polyunsaturated, and 1.5 g saturated fatty acids); and about 200 mg cholesterol. It also contains retinol, folate, thiamin, riboflavin, vitamin B12, vitamin D, and iron. The yolk's colour comes from carotenoids, and contains all of the fat and cholesterol and most of the iron, thiamin, and retinol. The white is 90 per cent water and is virtually fat free, containing mainly protein, with some vitamins, and traces of glucose.

In Asia, eggs containing 2–3 week old chick fetuses may occasionally be included in diets. There is no nutritional difference between these and unfertilised eggs, except that fertilised eggs contain additional calcium absorbed from the shell.

4.3.3 Consumption patterns

Meat and poultry

Globally, meat accounts for about 8 per cent of total energy availability, 18 per cent of dietary protein, and 23 per cent of dietary fat. Meat consumption is considerably higher in high-income countries (10 per cent of total energy intake compared with 7 per cent in low-income countries), and is particularly high in the USA, parts of South America, some parts of Asia, northern Europe, and most of Oceania. Consumption is particularly low in most of Africa and other parts of Asia where vegetarian ways of life are commonplace. Bangladesh has the lowest level of intake (0.6 per cent) and Mongolia the highest (28 per cent).[7]

As a general rule, meat consumption increases with economic development. Worldwide, between 1961 and 2002, meat consumption per person doubled, with pork and poultry showing the greatest increases; in Japan it increased nearly six-fold. Globally, overall energy availability increased in the same period by just 12 per cent. Consumption of meat and other animal foods from wild and undomesticated animals is low on a global basis, but these foods are important parts of diets within many middle- and low-income countries, as well as being delicacies in high-income countries.

Fish

Worldwide, fish (including shellfish) account for 1 per cent of available dietary energy; these foods are particularly important in island and coastal communities. For instance, in the Maldives, marine fish account for 15 per cent of dietary energy, but in some landlocked, low-income countries, this figure is practically zero. In general, fish consumption is highest in Asia and Oceania. Freshwater fish provide a relatively small proportion of dietary energy (0.3 per cent), but they are a more important source of dietary energy in low-income countries, and are particularly important in regions with large lakes and rivers. Salting is a traditional method of preserving raw fish throughout much of the world (box 4.3.5).

Cantonese-style salted fish

Salting is a traditional method of preserving raw fish throughout much of the world. The freshness of the fish and the salting and drying conditions vary considerably between regions, although fish are usually dried outside, in direct sunlight. This results in varying levels of fermentation and/or insect infestation. Salted fish is a component of diets typical of Asia, Africa, and parts of the Mediterranean.

Depending on the precise conditions, salt-preserved fish may also undergo fermentation. The degree of fermentation that occurs depends on the freshness of the raw fish, the amount of salt used, the outdoor temperature, and the duration of the drying process. In general, excluding the factor of freshness, salted fish is less likely to be fermented in the northern part of China compared with the southern part of China (where nasopharyngeal cancer is more common). Cantonese-style salted fish is characterised by using less salt and a higher degree of fermentation during the drying process, because of the relatively high outdoor temperature and moisture levels.

Cantonese-style salted fish are a traditional part of the diet in southern China, Taiwan, Malaysia, and Singapore.

Eggs

Worldwide, eggs provide 1.2 per cent of available food energy. Egg consumption is highest in the Far East, North America, and Europe, ranging from nearly 3 per cent in these areas to virtually zero in many African countries; it is significantly higher in high-income countries. Preserved eggs (pickled, salted, or cured) are traditional in some cultures.

4.3.4 Interpretation of the evidence

4.3.4.1 General

For general considerations that may affect interpretation of the evidence, see chapters 3.3 and 3.5, and boxes 3.1, 3.2, 3.6 and 3.7.

'Relative risk' (RR) is used in this Report to denote ratio measures of effect, including 'risk ratios', 'rate ratios', 'hazard ratios', and 'odds ratios'.

4.3.4.2 Specific

Some considerations specific to meat, poultry, fish, and eggs include:

Classification. 'Fish' is a broad classification. Different fish have different nutritional profiles and biological effects, one obvious example being white fish and oily fish. These are often not distinguished in epidemiological studies.

Terminology. As yet, there is no agreed definition for 'processed meat'. Some studies count minced meat, or ham, bacon, and sausages as processed meats; others do not. See the footnote to the matrix and box 4.3.1.

Confounding. People who consume large amounts of meat and processed meats tend to consume less poultry, fish, and vegetables, and vice versa. So an apparent effect of meat and processed meat could possibly be due, at least in part, to low intakes of these other foods.

Production, processing, patterns. Practically all the evidence relates to these foods as preserved, processed, or prepared (cooked) in some way. Evidence on meat, poultry, and increasingly on fish, is practically all from these foods as produced industrially. There is very little evidence on wild animals and birds, despite the quantity and nature of their body fat, and other aspects of their nutritional profile, being different. Epidemiological evidence on specific methods of preservation, processing, and preparation/cooking of meat, poultry, and fish is mostly patchy, despite some of these being known to generate carcinogens established as such in experimental studies. Also see chapter 4.9.

4.3.5 Evidence and judgements

The full systematic literature review (SLR) is contained on the CD included with this Report.

4.3.5.1 Meat
4.3.5.1.1 Red meat

Some studies may have included processed meats in their classification of red meat intake.

Colorectum

Sixteen cohort studies[8-24] and 71 case-control studies investigated red meat and colorectal cancer.

All of the cohort studies that reported analyses of risk for the highest intake group when compared to the lowest showed increased risk (figure 4.3.1),[8-24] which was statistically significant in four (one of these was specific to rapid-acetylator genotypes).[9 10 12 18 23] Meta-analysis was possible

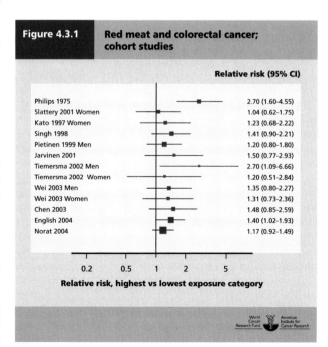

Figure 4.3.1 **Red meat and colorectal cancer; cohort studies**

Relative risk (95% CI)

	Relative risk (95% CI)
Philips 1975	2.70 (1.60–4.55)
Slattery 2001 Women	1.04 (0.62–1.75)
Kato 1997 Women	1.23 (0.68–2.22)
Singh 1998	1.41 (0.90–2.21)
Pietinen 1999 Men	1.20 (0.80–1.80)
Jarvinen 2001	1.50 (0.77–2.93)
Tiemersma 2002 Men	2.70 (1.09–6.66)
Tiemersma 2002 Women	1.20 (0.51–2.84)
Wei 2003 Men	1.35 (0.80–2.27)
Wei 2003 Women	1.31 (0.73–2.36)
Chen 2003	1.48 (0.85–2.59)
English 2004	1.40 (1.02–1.93)
Norat 2004	1.17 (0.92–1.49)

0.2 0.5 1 2 5

Relative risk, highest vs lowest exposure category

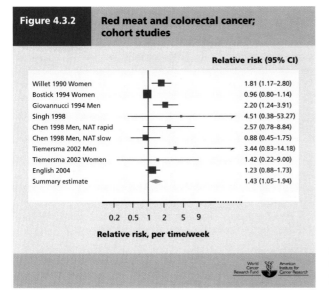

Figure 4.3.2   Red meat and colorectal cancer; cohort studies

Relative risk (95% CI)

	Relative risk (95% CI)
Willet 1990 Women	1.81 (1.17–2.80)
Bostick 1994 Women	0.96 (0.80–1.14)
Giovannucci 1994 Men	2.20 (1.24–3.91)
Singh 1998	4.51 (0.38–53.27)
Chen 1998 Men, NAT rapid	2.57 (0.78–8.84)
Chen 1998 Men, NAT slow	0.88 (0.45–1.75)
Tiemersma 2002 Men	3.44 (0.83–14.18)
Tiemersma 2002 Women	1.42 (0.22–9.00)
English 2004	1.23 (0.88–1.73)
Summary estimate	1.43 (1.05–1.94)

Relative risk, per time/week

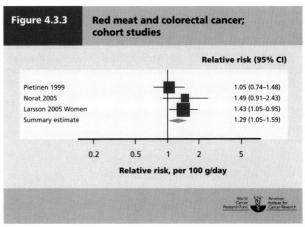

Figure 4.3.3   Red meat and colorectal cancer; cohort studies

Relative risk (95% CI)

	Relative risk (95% CI)
Pietinen 1999	1.05 (0.74–1.48)
Norat 2005	1.49 (0.91–2.43)
Larsson 2005 Women	1.43 (1.05–0.95)
Summary estimate	1.29 (1.05–1.59)

Relative risk, per 100 g/day

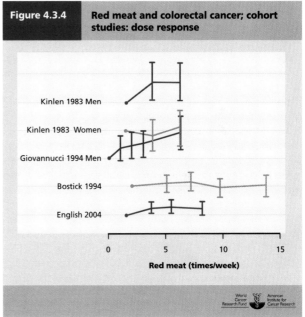

Figure 4.3.4   Red meat and colorectal cancer; cohort studies: dose response

Red meat (times/week)

on seven studies that measured red meat intake in 'times per week' and three studies that measured grams per day. The summary effect estimates were 1.43 (95% confidence interval (CI) 1.05–1.94) per times/week and 1.29 (95% CI 1.04–1.60) per 100 g/day, respectively (figures 4.3.2 and 4.3.3). There was moderate heterogeneity in the former analysis and low heterogeneity in the latter.

A dose-response relationship is apparent from cohort data (figure 4.3.4).

These data are supported by a recently published meta-analysis of 15 prospective studies, which reported a summary effect estimate of 1.28 (95% CI 1.18–1.39) per 120 g/day.[25]

Because of the abundant prospective data from cohort studies, case-control studies were not summarised.

The general mechanisms through which red meat could plausibly cause cancer are outlined below. In addition, dietary haem iron induces colonic cytotoxicity and hyper-proliferation.[26]

A substantial amount of data from cohort and case-control studies showed a dose-response relationship, supported by evidence for plausible mechanisms operating in humans. Red meat is a convincing cause of colorectal cancer.

The Panel is aware that since the conclusion of the SLR, six cohort[27-32] and four case control studies[33-36] have been published. This new information does not change the Panel judgement (see box 3.8).

Oesophagus

Twelve case-control studies[37-50] investigated red meat and oesophageal cancer.

Eight studies reported increased risk for the highest intake group when compared to the lowest,[37-39 41-45 49 50] which was statistically significant in five.[37 41 42 45] Three studies reported

non-significant decreased risk[38 40 46]; one study reported no significant effect on risk,[47 48] but did not provide further details. Most of these studies adjusted for smoking and alcohol.

The general mechanisms through which red meat could plausibly cause cancer are outlined below.

There is limited evidence, from case-control studies, some of which were poor quality, suggesting that red meat is a cause of oesophageal cancer.

The Panel is aware that since the conclusion of the SLR, one cohort study[51] has been published. This new information does not change the Panel judgement (see box 3.8).

Lung

One cohort study[52] and nine case-control studies[53-62] investigated red meat and lung cancer.

The single cohort study showed increased risk for the highest intake group when compared to the lowest, with an effect estimate of 1.6 (95% CI 1.0–2.6; p value for trend < 0.014), based on 158 cases.[52]

Seven case-control studies showed increased risk for the highest intake group when compared to the lowest,[53-58 60 61] which was statistically significant in four.[54 55 60 61] One study reported non-significant decreased risk[59] and one study showed no effect on risk.[62] All except the latter study adjusted for smoking.

The general mechanisms through which red meat could plausibly cause cancer are outlined below.

There is limited evidence, mostly from inconsistent case-control studies, suggesting that red meat is a cause of lung cancer.

Pancreas

Seven cohort studies[63-69] and four case-control studies[46 70-72] investigated red meat and pancreatic cancer.

Six cohort studies showed increased risk for the highest intake group when compared to the lowest,[63-65 67-69] which was statistically significant in one,[64] and two of the studies also had statistically significant tests for trend.[65 67] One study reported a non-significant increased risk that was very close to no effect.[66] Meta-analysis was possible on two studies, giving a summary effect estimate of 1.00 (95% CI 0.95–1.05) per 20 g/day, with no heterogeneity.[63 66] However, the two included studies were not typical. The effect estimates for the highest intake group when compared to the lowest in the other five cohort studies were 1.45 (95% CI 1.19–1.76),[64] 1.73 (95% CI 0.99–2.98; with a statistically significant test for trend),[65] 2.4 (95% CI 1–6.1; with a statistically significant test for trend),[67] 1.1 (95% CI 0.9–1.2),[68] and 1.4 (95% CI 0.4–4.8) for men and 2.7 (95% CI 0.8–8.9) for women.[69]

All of the case-control studies showed increased risk for the highest intake group when compared to the lowest,[46 70-72] which was statistically significant in three.[46 71 72] Meta-analysis was possible on three case-control studies, giving a summary effect estimate of 1.11 (95% CI 1.08–1.15) per 20 g/day, with no heterogeneity.[46 71 72]

The general mechanisms through which red meat could plausibly cause cancer are outlined below. In addition, both the secretory function of the pancreas and cell turnover within the pancreas are altered by the types of foods eaten.[73] Amino acids and fatty acids stimulate more pancreatic secretions than do carbohydrates.[74]

Evidence from cohort studies is less consistent than that from case-control studies. There is limited evidence suggesting that red meat is a cause of pancreatic cancer.

Endometrium

One cohort study[75] and seven case-control studies[46 76-81] investigated red meat and endometrial cancer.

The single cohort study showed a non-significant increased risk for the highest intake group when compared to the lowest, with an effect estimate of 1.10 (95% CI 0.70–1.73).[75]

Five case-control studies showed increased risk for the highest intake group when compared to the lowest,[46 76-79] which was statistically significant in two.[77 78] Two studies showed non-significant reduced risk.[80 81] Meta-analysis was possible on six studies, giving a summary effect estimate of 1.20 (95% CI 1.03–1.39) per 50 g red meat/day, with moderate heterogeneity.[46 76-80]

The general mechanisms through which red meat could plausibly cause cancer are outlined below.

The evidence, mostly from case-control studies, is sparse. There is limited evidence suggesting that red meat is a cause of endometrial cancer.

The Panel is aware that since the conclusion of the SLR, one case-control study[82] has been published. This new information does not change the Panel judgement (see box 3.8).

General mechanisms

There are several potential underlying mechanisms for an association between red meat consumption and cancer, including the generation by stomach and gut bacteria of potentially carcinogenic *N*-nitroso compounds. Some red meats are also cooked at high temperatures, resulting in the production of heterocyclic amines and polycyclic aromatic hydrocarbons (box 4.3.4). Haem promotes the formation of *N*-nitroso compounds and also contains iron. Free iron can lead to production of free radicals (box 4.3.3). Iron overload also activates oxidative responsive transcription factors, pro-inflammatory cytokines, and iron-induced hypoxia signalling.[83]

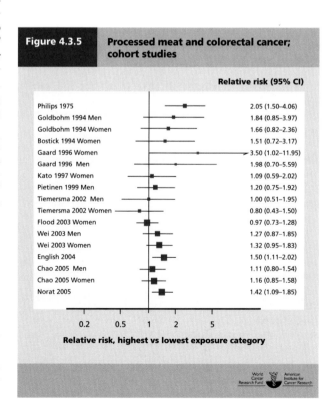

Figure 4.3.5	Processed meat and colorectal cancer; cohort studies

Relative risk (95% CI)

	Relative risk (95% CI)
Philips 1975	2.05 (1.50–4.06)
Goldbohm 1994 Men	1.84 (0.85–3.97)
Goldbohm 1994 Women	1.66 (0.82–2.36)
Bostick 1994 Women	1.51 (0.72–3.17)
Gaard 1996 Women	3.50 (1.02–11.95)
Gaard 1996 Men	1.98 (0.70–5.59)
Kato 1997 Women	1.09 (0.59–2.02)
Pietinen 1999 Men	1.20 (0.75–1.92)
Tiemersma 2002 Men	1.00 (0.51–1.95)
Tiemersma 2002 Women	0.80 (0.43–1.50)
Flood 2003 Women	0.97 (0.73–1.28)
Wei 2003 Men	1.27 (0.87–1.85)
Wei 2003 Women	1.32 (0.95–1.83)
English 2004	1.50 (1.11–2.02)
Chao 2005 Men	1.11 (0.80–1.54)
Chao 2005 Women	1.16 (0.85–1.58)
Norat 2005	1.42 (1.09–1.85)

0.2   0.5   1   2   5

Relative risk, highest vs lowest exposure category

4.3.5.1.2 Processed meat

The variation in definitions for processed meat used by different studies (see chapter 4.3.1) is likely to contribute to the observed heterogeneity.

Colorectum

Fourteen cohort studies[8-10 14-19 21 27 69 84 85] and 44 case-control studies investigated processed meat and colorectal cancer.

Twelve cohort studies showed increased risk for the highest intake group when compared to the lowest (figure 4.3.5),[8-10 14-19 21 27 69 85] which was statistically significant in three.[9 14 15 85] One study reported non-significant decreased risk and one study reported that there was no effect on risk.[84] Meta-analysis was possible on five studies, giving a summary effect estimate of 1.21 (95% CI 1.04–1.42) per 50 g/day, with low heterogeneity (figures 4.3.6 and 4.3.7). What heterogeneity there is could be explained by the disparity in category definitions between studies, as well as by improved adjustment for confounders in recent studies. A dose-response relationship was also apparent from cohort studies that measured in times/day (figure 4.3.8).

The majority of case-control studies showed increased risk with increasing intake of processed meat. Because of the abundant prospective data from cohort studies, case-control studies were not summarised.

These data are supported by a recently published meta-analysis of 14 cohort studies, which reported a summary effect estimate of 1.09 (95% CI 1.05–1.13) per 30 g/day.[25]

The general mechanisms through which processed meat could plausibly cause cancer are outlined below.

> **There is a substantial amount of evidence, with a dose-response relationship apparent from cohort studies. There is strong evidence for plausible mechanisms operating in humans. Processed meat is a convincing cause of colorectal cancer.**

The Panel is aware that since the conclusion of the SLR, five cohort[28 30 32 86 87] and two case-control studies[36 88] have been published. This new information does not change the Panel judgement (see box 3.8).

Oesophagus

Two cohort studies[89 90] and eight case-control studies[40 41 43 44 49 50 91-94] investigated processed meat and oesophageal cancer.

Both cohort studies showed non-significant increased risk for the highest intake groups when compared to the lowest.[89 90] The effect estimates were 1.24 (95% CI 0.73–2.1)[90] and 1.6 (95% CI 0.4–6.9).[89] Both analyses adjusted for age, smoking, and alcohol.

Six case-control studies showed increased risk for the highest intake groups when compared to the lowest,[43 44 49 50 91-93] which was statistically significant in one.[93] Two studies showed non-significant reduced risk.[40 41 94]

The general mechanisms through which processed meat could plausibly cause cancer are outlined below.

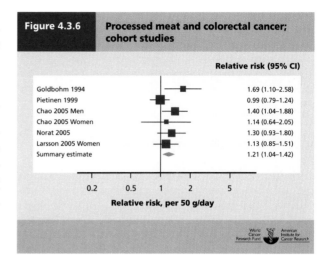

Figure 4.3.6 Processed meat and colorectal cancer; cohort studies

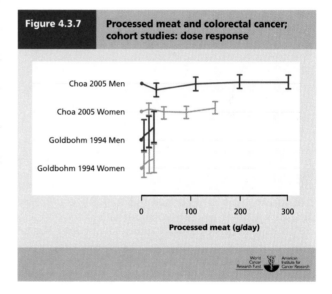

Figure 4.3.7 Processed meat and colorectal cancer; cohort studies: dose response

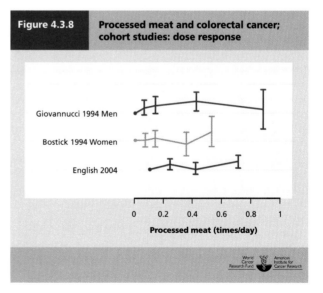

Figure 4.3.8 Processed meat and colorectal cancer; cohort studies: dose response

There is limited evidence, mostly from case-control studies, suggesting that processed meat is a cause of oesophageal cancer.

The Panel is aware that since the conclusion of the SLR, one cohort study[51] has been published. This new information does not change the Panel judgement (see box 3.8).

Lung

Four cohort studies[52 69 95 96] and 10 case-control studies[33 55-57 59 97-104] investigated processed meat and lung cancer.

Three cohort studies reported non-significant increased risk for the highest intake group when compared to the lowest.[69 95 96] One study reported no effect on risk.[52 95] Meta-analysis was possible on two of the studies, giving a summary effect estimate of 1.03 (95% CI 0.92–1.16) per serving/week, with no heterogeneity.[52] All four cohort studies adjusted for smoking.

Six case-control studies reported increased risk for the highest intake group when compared to the lowest,[33 56 57 59 99 100 102-104] which was statistically significant in two.[100 102] Four studies reported non-significant decreased risk.[55 97 98 101] All of the studies adjusted for smoking.

The general mechanisms through which processed meat could plausibly cause cancer are outlined below.

There is limited, inconsistent evidence suggesting that processed meat is a cause of lung cancer.

Stomach cancer

Eight cohort studies,[51 69 105-110] 21 case-control studies,[49 111-132] 1 cross-sectional study,[133] and 1 ecological study[134] investigated processed meat and stomach cancer.

Five cohort studies showed increased risk for the highest intake group when compared to the lowest,[51 106-108 110] which was statistically significant in one.[51] Two studies reported non-significant decreased risk[105 109]; and one showed no effect on risk in men and non-significant decreased risk in women.[69] Meta-analysis was possible on all eight cohort studies, giving a summary effect estimate of 1.02 (95% CI 1.00–1.05) per 20 g/day, with no heterogeneity.

Thirteen case-control studies showed increased risk for the highest intake group when compared to the lowest,[49 113 117 119-121 124-132] which was statistically significant in seven.[120 125 128-132] Three studies showed decreased risk,[118 122 123] which was statistically significant in one[118]; and one showed no effect on risk.[116] Four other studies reported no significant difference between mean intakes in cases and controls.[111 112 114 115] Meta-analysis was possible on nine studies, giving a summary effect estimate of 1.13 (95% CI 1.01–1.25) per 20 g/day, with high heterogeneity.[49 117-119 121 123 128-130]

A dose-response relationship is apparent from case-control but not cohort data.

The single ecological study reports a statistically significant correlation between increased processed meat and stomach cancer risk.[134]

The general mechanisms through which processed meat could plausibly cause cancer are outlined below.

The evidence is inconsistent. There is limited evidence suggesting that processed meat is a cause of stomach cancer.

The Panel is aware that since the conclusion of the SLR, one cohort[135] and two case-control studies[136 137] have been published. This new information does not change the Panel judgement (see box 3.8).

Prostate

Four cohort studies[138-141] and six case-control studies[142-147] investigated processed meat and prostate cancer.

All four cohort studies showed increased risk for the highest intake group when compared to the lowest,[138-141] which was statistically significant in two.[139 141] Meta-analysis was possible on all four cohort studies, giving a summary effect estimate of 1.11 (95% CI 0.995–1.25) per serving/week, with high heterogeneity. Heterogeneity was caused by varying size, not direction, of effect.

Two of these studies reported separately on advanced or aggressive cancer. Both showed increased risk with increasing intake of processed meat,[138 141] which was statistically significant in one.[141] Meta-analysis was possible on both studies, giving a summary effect estimate of 1.09 (95% CI 0.98–1.22) per serving/week, with moderate heterogeneity.

Four case-control studies showed non-significant decreased risk with increasing intake of processed meat[143-145 147]; two showed non-significant increased risk.[142 146] Meta-analysis was possible on five case-control studies, giving a summary effect estimate of 1.01 (95% CI 0.98–1.04) per serving/week, with low heterogeneity.[143-147] The general mechanisms through which processed meat could plausibly cause cancer are outlined below.

There is limited evidence from sparse and inconsistent studies suggesting that processed meat is a cause of prostate cancer.

The Panel is aware that since the conclusion of the SLR, two cohort studies[148 149] have been published. This new information does not change the Panel judgement (see box 3.8).

General mechanisms

Nitrates are produced endogenously at the low pH in the stomach and are added as preservatives to processed meats, both of which may contribute to *N*-nitroso compound production and exposure. *N*-nitroso compounds are suspected mutagens and carcinogens.[150] Many processed meats also contain high levels of salt and nitrite. Some processed meats are also cooked at high temperatures, resulting in the production of heterocyclic amines and polycyclic aromatic hydrocarbons. Red meat contains haem iron. Haem promotes the formation of *N*-nitroso compounds and also contains iron. Free iron can lead to production of free radicals (box 4.3.3).

4.3.5.2 Poultry

The evidence was too limited in amount, consistency, or quality to draw any conclusions.

4.3.5.3 Fish, shellfish

Colorectum

Nineteen cohort studies[8-10 14-18 21 23 69 85 151-161] and 55 case-control studies investigated fish and colorectal cancer.

Nine cohort studies showed decreased risk for the highest intake group when compared to the lowest,[8 15-17 21 69 85 154 157 158 160] which was statistically significant in two.[15 16] Eight studies showed non-significant increased risk.[9 10 18 23 151-153 155 156 159] One study showed no effect on risk[14] and one study reported that there was no statistically significant association.[161] Meta-analysis was possible on seven cohort studies, giving a summary effect estimate of 0.96 (95% CI 0.92–1.00) per serving/week, with low heterogeneity.[8 9 14 18 21 158 160]

Because of the abundant prospective data from cohort studies, case-control studies were not summarised.

Heterogeneity may be partially explained by varying definitions of fish in different studies that included fresh and/or salted or dried fish. It is also possible that high fish intake is associated with low meat intake, which is a potential confounder that has not been adjusted for.

It is biologically plausible that fish n-3 polyunsaturated fatty acids (PUFAs) protect against cancer. Fish oils reduce tumours in animal studies.[162] Likely mechanisms are thought to revolve around their role in reduction of n-6 PUFA-derived eicosanoid biosynthesis (eicosanoids promote inflammation) and direct inhibition of COX-2 (cyclooxygenase-2, an enzyme involved in the production of prostaglandins), which is also implicated in the cancer process (see Chapter 2). This mechanism, though plausible, is not well supported.[163] Alternative suggestions include the relatively high selenium or vitamin D content of fish.

> **A substantial amount of data is available but the results are inconsistent, and residual confounding by meat could not be excluded. There is limited evidence suggesting that eating fish protects against colorectal cancer.**

The Panel is aware that since the conclusion of the SLR, six cohort[28 30 164 165] and two case-control studies[33 166] have been published. This new information does not change the Panel judgement (see box 3.8).

4.3.5.3.1 Cantonese-style salted fish

Nasopharynx

One cohort study[167] and 21 case-control studies[161-188] investigated Cantonese-style salted fish (box 4.3.5) intake in adults and nasopharyngeal cancer. Sixteen case-control studies[168 170-174 177-179 181 188-193] investigated intake in childhood and 10 case-control studies[168 171-174 177 188 189 194 195] investigated intake in infancy (less than 3 years).

Adult intake

The single cohort study showed increased risk for the highest intake group when compared to the lowest. Intake was assessed in the 1960s, 1970s, and 1980s. The p value for trend for the association between each decade's intake and increased risk was < 0.001, 0.014, and 0.21, respectively.

Seventeen of the case-control studies showed increased risk for the highest intake group when compared to the lowest,[169-178 182-188] which was statistically significant in nine.[170 172 173 176 178 182 185-188] One study showed a non-significant decreased risk[168]; three studies reported that there was no association.[179-181] Meta-analysis was possible on nine studies, giving a summary effect estimate of 1.28 (95% CI 1.13–1.44) per serving/ week, with high heterogeneity (figure 4.3.9). Heterogeneity was related to size, and not direction, of effect.

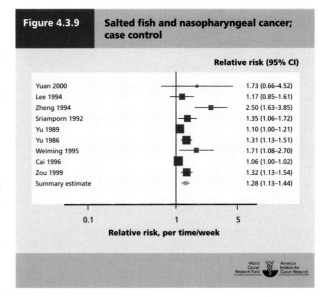

Figure 4.3.9 Salted fish and nasopharyngeal cancer; case control

	Relative risk (95% CI)
Yuan 2000	1.73 (0.66–4.52)
Lee 1994	1.17 (0.85–1.61)
Zheng 1994	2.50 (1.63–3.85)
Sriamporn 1992	1.35 (1.06–1.72)
Yu 1989	1.10 (1.00–1.21)
Yu 1986	1.31 (1.13–1.51)
Weiming 1995	1.71 (1.08–2.70)
Cai 1996	1.06 (1.00–1.02)
Zou 1999	1.32 (1.13–1.54)
Summary estimate	1.28 (1.13–1.44)

Relative risk, per time/week

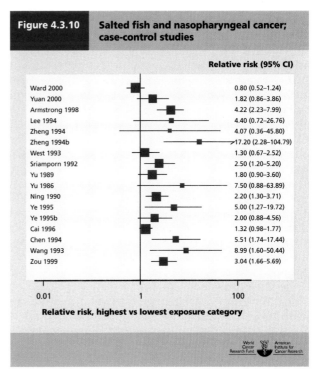

Figure 4.3.10 Salted fish and nasopharyngeal cancer; case-control studies

	Relative risk (95% CI)
Ward 2000	0.80 (0.52–1.24)
Yuan 2000	1.82 (0.86–3.86)
Armstrong 1998	4.22 (2.23–7.99)
Lee 1994	4.40 (0.72–26.76)
Zheng 1994	4.07 (0.36–45.80)
Zheng 1994b	17.20 (2.28–104.79)
West 1993	1.30 (0.67–2.52)
Sriamporn 1992	2.50 (1.20–5.20)
Yu 1989	1.80 (0.90–3.60)
Yu 1986	7.50 (0.88–63.89)
Ning 1990	2.20 (1.30–3.71)
Ye 1995	5.00 (1.27–19.72)
Ye 1995b	2.00 (0.88–4.56)
Cai 1996	1.32 (0.98–1.77)
Chen 1994	5.51 (1.74–17.44)
Wang 1993	8.99 (1.60–50.44)
Zou 1999	3.04 (1.66–5.69)

Relative risk, highest vs lowest exposure category

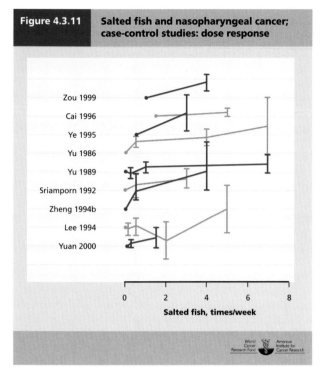

Figure 4.3.11 Salted fish and nasopharyngeal cancer; case-control studies: dose response

Zou 1999
Cai 1996
Ye 1995
Yu 1986
Yu 1989
Sriamporn 1992
Zheng 1994b
Lee 1994
Yuan 2000

0   2   4   6   8

Salted fish, times/week

World Cancer Research Fund • American Institute for Cancer Research

Childhood intake
Fifteen case-control studies that investigated the intake of salted fish at 10 years of age showed increased risk for the highest intake group when compared to the lowest,[168 170 172-174 177-179 181 188-193] which was statistically significant in 8[170 172 173 177-179 188 190] (figure 4.3.10). One study showed a non-significant decreased risk.[171] Meta-analysis was possible on 9 studies,[171 173 174 177 178 181 188-190] giving a summary effect estimate of 1.35 (95% CI 1.14–1.60) per serving/week, with high heterogeneity. Heterogeneity was related to size, and not direction, of effect.

Nine case-control studies that investigated the intake of salted fish at 3 years of age showed increased risk for the highest intake group when compared to the lowest,[171-174 177 188 189 194 195] which was statistically significant in five.[172 173 177 188 195] One study showed no effect on risk.[168] Meta-analysis was possible on five studies,[171 173 174 177 189] giving a summary effect estimate of 1.42 (95% CI 1.11–1.81) per serving/week, with moderate heterogeneity. Heterogeneity was related to size, and not direction, of effect.

A dose-response relationship is apparent from case-control data (figure 4.3.11). Cohort and case-control data suggest a delayed and/or cumulative effect from eating Cantonese-style salted fish.

General mechanisms
Evidence suggests that high intake of nitrate and nitrosamine from salted fish accounts for some of this increased risk of nasopharyngeal cancer development. Nitrosamines are known mutagens and animal carcinogens that induce gene mutation. The N-nitrosamines are a large group of com-

pounds with a common carcinogenic mechanism.[150] Salted fish has been shown to contain N-nitrosamines, with the highest levels in salted fish from areas with the highest mortality from nasopharyngeal cancer.[196 197] The variation in nitrosamine content of salted fish may contribute to heterogeneity in assigning risk to salted fish consumption in different geographic locations. There is also some evidence that genotype interacts with the risk associated with salted fish intake, particularly the gene for the cytochrome P450 enzyme, CYP2E1.[192 198]

> Evidence from several case-control studies is consistent and shows a dose-response effect. There is evidence for plausible mechanisms. Cantonese-style salted fish is probably associated with increased risk of nasopharyngeal cancer.

4.3.5.4 Eggs
The evidence was too limited in amount, consistency, or quality to draw any conclusions.

4.3.5.5 Foods containing vitamin D
Colorectum
Eleven cohort studies[17 24 154 199-210] and 17 case-control studies investigated total vitamin D and/or dietary vitamin D and colorectal cancer. Four cohort studies investigated plasma or serum vitamin D.[22 210-212]

Dietary vitamin D
Twelve estimates from 11 cohort studies reported analyses of the highest intake groups compared to the lowest.[17 154 199-206] Six of these showed non-significant decreased risk[154 199-202 205]; 2 studies reported no effect on risk[17 205]; and 4 studies show non-significant increased risk.[203 204 206] Meta-analysis was possible on 9 studies that investigated dietary vitamin D, giving a summary effect estimate of 0.99 (95% CI 0.97–1.00) per 100 IU/day, with moderate heterogeneity.[17 154 199 202 204-206 209 210]

Serum or plasma vitamin D
All four cohort studies showed non-significant decreased risk for the highest intake groups when compared to the lowest.[22 210-212] Effect estimates were 0.73 (stated as non-significant)[211]; 0.4 (95% CI 1–1.4; serum 25-hydroxyvitamin D) and 1.1 (95% CI 0.4–3.2; serum 1,25 hydroxyvitamin D)[212]; 0.6 (95% CI 0.3–1.1; serum 25-hydroxyvitamin D) and 0.9 (95% CI 0.5–1.7; serum 1,25 hydroxyvitamin D)[210]; and 0.53 (95% CI 0.27–1.04).[22]

Because of the abundant prospective data from cohort studies, case-control studies were not summarised.

The effects of vitamin D and calcium are strongly interrelated because both are growth restraining, both induce differentiation and apoptosis in intestinal cells, and calcium-mediated effects are strongly dependent on vitamin D levels. Data from observational studies are probably hampered by the fact that total levels of the biologically active form are not only dependent on diet but also on supplements and UV exposure of the skin.

The evidence on vitamin D was inconsistent. There is limited evidence suggesting that foods containing vitamin D, or better vitamin D status, protect against colorectal cancer.

The Panel is aware that since the conclusion of the SLR, two case-control studies[166 213] have been published. This new information does not change the Panel judgement (see box 3.8).

4.3.5.6 Foods containing iron
Colorectum

Four cohort studies[214-217] and 23 case-control studies investigated iron intake and colorectal cancer. One cohort study investigated haem iron intake.[218]

The four cohort studies showed increased risk for the highest intake group when compared to the lowest,[214-216 218] which was statistically significant in two.[214 218] Effect estimates were 1.17 (95% CI 0.6–2.3)[216]; 3.35 (95% CI 1.74–6.46; colon cancer)[214]; and 2.18 (95% CI 1.24–3.86; proximal colon cancer).[218] One study reported a non-significant higher intake in cancer cases (18.4 mg) than in controls (17.4 mg).[215] The other reported that mean iron intakes were similar between male colon cancer cases, rectal cancer cases, and male sub-cohort cases (13.2, 13.3, and 13.2 mg per day, respectively), and between female colon cancer cases, rectal cancer cases, and female sub-cohort cases (11.4, 11.6, and 11.7 mg/day, respectively).[217]

Data suggest that the effect may be limited to proximal cancer cases and attenuated in distal cancer. Two studies reported results separately for proximal and distal colon cancer cases.[214-218] The effect estimates for the former were 1.44 (95% CI 1.23–1.69)[214] and 2.18 (95% CI 1.24–3.86),[218] and 1.03 (95% CI 0.8–1.32)[214] and 0.90 (95% CI 0.45–1.81) for the latter.[218]

Because of the abundant prospective data from cohort studies, case-control studies were not summarised.

It is biologically plausible that iron increases colorectal cancer risk due to its catalytic activity on the formation of reactive oxygen species. Haem promotes the formation of *N*-nitroso compounds and also contains iron. Free iron can lead to production of free radicals (box 4.3.3). However, this role has not been confirmed in animal studies. Another hypothesis is that dietary haem induces colonic cytotoxicity and hyperproliferation.[26] Iron overload also activates oxidative responsive transcription factors, proinflammatory cytokines, and iron-induced hypoxia signalling.[83]

The evidence is sparse, of poor quality, and inconsistent. There is limited evidence suggesting that foods containing iron are in general a cause of colorectal cancer. (Also see chapter 4.3.5.1.1 for evidence on red and processed meat, which are classified as convincing causes of colorectal cancer.)

The Panel is aware that since the conclusion of the SLR, two cohort studies[87 219] have been published. This new information does not change the Panel judgement (see box 3.8).

4.3.5.7 Smoked foods
Stomach

Seventeen case-control studies[116 118 220-235] and two ecological studies[236 237] investigated smoked foods and stomach cancer.

Fourteen case-control studies showed increased risk for the highest intake group when compared to the lowest,[118 220 221 224-235] which was statistically significant in 11.[118 224-234] One study reported non-significant decreased risk[222] and 2 studies reported no effect on risk.[116 223] More than half of the effect estimates were greater than 1.5. None of the studies adjusted for infection with *Helicobacter pylori*.

One ecological study reported a statistically significant increased risk with higher intake of smoked foods[236]; the other reported decreased risk, though one constituent of smoked food (3,4-benzopyrene) was associated with increased risk.[237]

Heterogeneity may be partly explained by variation between studies in the definition of smoked foods — some were specific to smoked meats and most included meats.

Smoked foods, particularly meats, may contain polycyclic aromatic hydrocarbons, depending on the fuel burned to produce the smoke.[238] Smoked meats are also often salted or cured, meaning that they are likely to raise endogenous production of *N*-nitroso compounds in the stomach (box 4.3.4).

There is limited evidence from case-control and ecological studies, some of which were of poor quality, that smoked foods are causes of stomach cancer.

The Panel is aware that since the conclusion of the SLR, three case-control studies[136 137 239] have been published. This new information does not change the Panel judgement (see box 3.8).

4.3.5.8 Grilled (broiled) or barbecued (charbroiled) animal foods
Stomach

Three cohort studies[240-242] and 12 case-control studies investigated grilled (broiled) and barbecued (charbroiled) foods and stomach cancer.

Two cohort studies showed increased risk for the highest intake group when compared to the lowest,[240 242] which was statistically significant in one.[242] One study reported a non-significant reduced risk.[241] Effect estimates were 1.67 (p value for trend < 0.05)[242]; 1.77 (95% CI 0.59–5.33) for grilled (broiled) fish and 2.08 (95% CI 0.97–4.46) for grilled (broiled) meat[240]; and 0.84 (95% CI 0.55–1.29).[241] None of the studies adjusted for *H pylori* infection.

Eight case-control studies showed increased risk for the highest intake group when compared to the lowest,[126 129 130 233 243 245-247] which was statistically significant in seven. One study reported a statistically significant decreased risk[121]; two studies reported non-significant decreased risk[220 248]; and one study stated that there was no significant effect on risk.[244]

Charring or cooking meats over open flame generates heterocyclic amines and polycyclic hydrocarbons, which may cause cancer (box 4.3.4).

There is limited, inconsistent evidence, mostly from case-control studies, that grilled (broiled) or barbecued (charbroiled) animal foods are causes of stomach cancer.

4.3.6 Comparison with previous report

The panel responsible for the previous report judged that diets relatively high in red meat were probable causes of colorectal cancer, and noted a pattern whereby red meat was a possible cause of cancers of the pancreas, breast, prostate, and kidney.

The previous report considered methods of production, preservation, processing, and preparation (including cooking). Cured meats were judged to be a possible cause of colorectal cancer; and grilled, barbecued, and fried meats, and other foods to be a possible cause of colorectal cancer; and grilling (broiling) and barbecuing (charbroiling) to be a possible cause of stomach cancer. Processed meat was not identified as such. The evidence on Cantonese-style salted fish was judged to be convincing for nasopharyngeal cancer. The panel noted that the risk was highest when this food is eaten frequently in early childhood. This Report concluded the evidence to be probable, in view of the paucity of prospective data

Since the mid-1990s, the results of cohort studies have strengthened the evidence on red meat and processed meat as causes of colorectal cancer.

4.3.7 Conclusions

The Panel concludes:
The evidence on red meat and processed meat is stronger than in the mid-1990s. Epidemiological evidence on other methods of preserving and preparing meats and other animal foods is sparse, and the overall evidence remains suggestive, at most. The evidence on poultry, fish, and eggs is generally insubstantial.

The evidence that red meats and processed meats are a cause of colorectal cancer is convincing. Cantonese-style salted fish is a probable cause of nasopharyngeal cancer. This finding does not apply to any other type of fish product. Cantonese-style salted fish is also subject to fermentation.

There is limited evidence suggesting that fish, and also foods containing vitamin D, protect against colorectal cancer. There is limited evidence suggesting that red meat is a cause of cancers of the oesophagus, lung, pancreas and endometrium; that processed meat is a cause of cancers of the oesophagus, lung, stomach and prostate; and that foods containing iron are a cause of colorectal cancer. There is also limited evidence that foods that are grilled (broiled), barbecued (charbroiled), and smoked are a cause of stomach cancer. The evidence comes mostly from meat preserved or prepared in these ways.

Meat, as mentioned above, is likely to be relatively high in animal fats. For discussion of the role of animal fats on cancer, see chapter 4.4. Meat may also be energy dense. For discussion on the role of energy-dense foods on weight gain, overweight, and obesity, and the role of weight gain, overweight, and obesity in the risk of some cancers, see Chapters 6 and 8.

4.4 Milk and dairy products

MILK, DAIRY PRODUCTS, AND THE RISK OF CANCER

In the judgement of the Panel, the factors listed below modify the risk of cancer. Judgements are graded according to the strength of the evidence.

	DECREASES RISK		INCREASES RISK	
	Exposure	**Cancer site**	**Exposure**	**Cancer site**
Convincing				
Probable	**Milk[1][4]**	**Colorectum**	**Diets high in calcium[2][3]**	**Prostate**
Limited — suggestive	Milk[1]	Bladder	Milk and dairy products[2] Cheese[4]	Prostate Colorectum
Substantial effect on risk unlikely	None identified			

1   Milk from cows. Most data are from high-income populations, where calcium can be taken to be a marker for milk/dairy consumption. *The Panel judges* that a higher intake of dietary calcium is one way in which milk could have a protective effect.
2   Effect only apparent at high calcium intakes (around 1.5 g/day or more). Evidence for milk and dairy products (but not calcium) was derived only from data for countries with populations that have high calcium and dairy consumption.
3   Includes diets that naturally contain calcium and that contain foods fortified with calcium. See box 4.10.1.
4   Although both milk and cheese are included in the general category of dairy products, their different nutritional composition and consumption patterns may result in different findings.

For an explanation of all the terms used in the matrix, please see chapter 3.5.1, the text of this section, and the glossary.

Milk and products made from milk, such as cheese, butter, ghee, and yoghurt, have been consumed ever since suitable animals were domesticated. Whole milk and cheese and yoghurt made from whole milk have a high proportion of energy from fat and from protein, although the absolute concentrations in liquid milk are lower than those in cheese due to the higher water content. They also contain a number of vitamins, including retinol and riboflavin, and minerals, particularly calcium. In countries where consumption of milk and dairy products is high, these are the main sources of calcium. Low-fat dairy products retain all of the protein, the water-soluble vitamins, and the mineral content. However, the fat-soluble vitamins are significantly reduced. Low-fat milk or whole milk is sometimes fortified with vitamins A and D.

Until the late 19th century, milk from animals was used as a substitute for human milk for feeding infants. Adults did not usually consume such milks; if they did, it was in low amounts. Populations that kept milk-giving animals consumed other dairy products. From the early 20th century, a number of factors were responsible for cow's milk becoming almost a staple food in the USA and some European countries. These included the industrialisation of cattle farming; the identification of milk as a basic food, especially for children; and the development of refrigeration techniques and ultra-heat treated packaging. Dried milk is now a common ingredient in many processed foods.

Overall, *the Panel judges* that the evidence on milk and dairy products, and on calcium, shows that their impact on the risk of cancer varies in different tissues.

The Panel judges as follows:
Milk probably protects against colorectal cancer. There is limited evidence suggesting that milk protects against bladder cancer. There is limited evidence suggesting that cheese is a cause of colorectal cancer. Diets high in calcium are a probable cause of prostate cancer; and there is limited evidence suggesting that high consumption of milk and dairy products is a cause of prostate cancer.

The strongest evidence, corresponding to judgements of 'convincing' and 'probable', shows that milk probably protects against colorectal cancer, and that diets high in calcium are a probable cause of prostate cancer.

Milk and dairy products are important components of diets in some but not all parts of the world. Until recently in history, milk from several ruminant animals was used as a partial substitute for or in addition to human milk; but these milks were usually consumed infrequently and, if at all, later in childhood or by adults. In countries where milk-giving animals were raised, their products were consumed in the form of cheese, butter, ghee, and in fermented form as yoghurts or in combination with alcoholic drinks.

From the late 19th century, consumption of cow's milk greatly increased in the USA, the UK, and some other European countries. This was a result of a massive increase in dairy farming supported by new techniques such as condensation, drying, and cooling. In the 20th century, consumption was further boosted by pasteurisation and doorstep delivery, the decline of breastfeeding, and the common view that modified cow's milk is a suitable food for infants and an excellent food for young children. Dried milk is a mainstay of programmes of food aid to impoverished countries. However, populations living outside North America and northern Europe have until recently consumed little milk as such, and dairy products consumed are in the form of yoghurt or products derived from it. This may be due to the limited capacity to digest lactose beyond infancy observed in these populations. Yoghurt is fermented, which lowers lactose concentration, and is therefore better tolerated.

Reports in the early part of the 20th century of different forms of malnutrition in young children, which documented a requirement for high amounts of animal protein to cure these conditions, supported the categorisation of milk, eggs, and meat as protective foods. By contrast, reports published since the 1960s have identified whole milk and dairy products, which have a high proportion of energy from fat and saturated fatty acids, as foods that contribute to the pathogenesis of coronary heart disease. More recently, some reports concerned with the prevention of osteoporosis in Western populations have recommended high intakes of calcium.

This chapter is concerned with milk and its products. The evidence on milk is on milk from cows, and the evidence on cheese is from all sources. It does not consider human milk or infant formula. For human milk, see chapter 4.11. Nor does it consider soya drinks or other plant-derived alternatives. For soya drinks, see chapter 4.2. For butter, see chapter 4.5.

Calcium is included here because in countries where milk and dairy products are important in diets, these are the main sources of what is a generally high intake of calcium. Dietary calcium also comes from bones when these are consumed (small or tinned fish, for example, and in stews), egg shells, and from some plant foods. In many countries, plant foods are the main source of calcium. See chapters 4.1, 4.2, and 4.4.

4.4.1 Definitions, sources

Milk is produced by all mammal species to suckle their young. It has evolved to be the ideal nourishment for mammalian infants of each species and, in normal conditions, contains all the nutrients they need at that stage of their lives. Although all mammal species produce milk, only a few are employed widely as milk producers, and they are all ruminants. Milk from other species must be modified before feeding to infants to allow for their limited capacity to metabolise and excrete nitrogenous compounds and salts in early life.

Ruminant animals have a large, multichambered stomach that contains microbes, which allows them to ferment cellulose and extract nutrients from green and dried grasses. Some species or breeds (notably European cows) have been bred to produce copious amounts of milk. Around the world, other bovine animals used to supply milk include zebu cows in Asia, water buffalo in Asia and some parts of Europe, and yaks, although usually only in the mountainous regions in Asia. Goats and sheep are also important and widespread milk-producing animals, as well as camels, which live in arid climates around the world. In some areas of the world, other animals such as horses, old- and new-world camels, and reindeer are locally important.

Fresh milk can be consumed raw (untreated) or, as is common in many high-income countries, pasteurised (see chapter 4.9.3). Milk is also commonly processed into a wide variety of foods including cream, concentrated milks, cheese, fats such as butter and ghee, and fermented foods such as yoghurt.

4.4.2 Composition

Milk and dairy products in whole form have a high proportion of energy from fat and protein, and contain some vitamins and minerals.[1] The precise composition varies between species and breeds, and with the nature of their feed. Sheep and yak milks are particularly high in protein; buffalo, sheep, and yak milks are high in fat. Typical whole cow's milk contains 3.4 g protein and 3.6 g fat per 100 g.[1] Reduced fat (semi-skimmed) and low-fat (skimmed) milks are produced from whole milk, and the foods made from these milks have a correspondingly lower fat and fat-soluble vitamin content than those made from whole milk.

Around two thirds of the fatty acids in cow's milk are saturated. Polyunsaturated fatty acids make up less than 4 per cent of milk fat (see chapter 4.5.2). Fat accounts for half of the energy in whole milk. Milk contains all the essential amino acids in the appropriate proportions for humans (see chapter 4.10.1).

The only significant carbohydrate found in milk is the disaccharide lactose. Milk products such as cheese and yoghurt contain varying amounts of lactose. Hard cheeses contain only traces, soft cheeses 2–3 per cent, yoghurts 4 per cent, compared to 5 per cent found in whole milk; this is because cheese and yoghurt have been fermented by bacteria used in the production of these foods.

Milk, cheese, and yoghurt contain high levels of calcium (box 4.4.1). They are also sources of riboflavin and vitamin B12, and full-fat dairy products are sources of retinol, and to a lesser extent, other fat-soluble vitamins. Milk also contains several growth factors and hormones, though these are probably digested in the stomach. However, milk consumption has been shown to elevate circulating levels of insulin-like growth factor.

4.4.3 Consumption patterns

Consumption of milk and dairy products throughout the world is highly variable. The overall global average of around 5 per cent of available dietary energy[2] conceals wide variations. The range is from 10–15 per cent of dietary energy in

Box 4.4.1 **Foods containing calcium**

In countries with high intakes of milk and dairy products, these are the main source of calcium. Most of the epidemiological studies reviewed here are from those countries.

Calcium is found in plant as well as in animal foods, but it is less easily absorbed. Other animal sources include small fish (when eaten with their bones) and meat (when rendered on the bone in stews). Plant sources include green vegetables, nuts, and pulses (legumes).[1 3]

Calcium is the most abundant mineral in the body and is the major mineral constituent of bones. It is central to a variety of functions in the body, such as bone metabolism, nerve and muscle activity, and the control of cell differentiation and proliferation. Calcium metabolism is controlled by various factors, including vitamin D and related hormonal compounds formed by the liver and kidney, necessary for the absorption of calcium from foods, and its regulation in the body.

the USA and some European countries to less than 0.5 per cent in some African and Asian countries.

4.4.4 Interpretation of the evidence

4.4.4.1 General

For general considerations that may affect interpretation of the evidence, see chapters 3.3 and 3.5, and boxes 3.1, 3.2, 3.6 and 3.7

'Relative risk' (RR) is used in this Report to denote ratio measures of effect, including 'risk ratios', 'rate ratios', 'hazard ratios', and 'odds ratios'.

4.4.4.2 Specific

Patterns and ranges of intake. Most studies are carried out in high-income countries where consumption of cow's milk and its products is high, and where the main dairy product consumed is milk.

Classification. Studies usually do not make any distinction between dairy products, such as cheeses from different sources and with different compositions.

4.4.5 Evidence and judgements

The full systematic literature review (SLR) is contained on the CD included with this Report.

4.4.5.1 Milk and dairy products
Prostate
Ten cohort studies,[4-15] 13 case-control studies,[16-29] and 2 ecological studies[30 31] investigated milk and dairy products and prostate cancer; 16 cohort studies,[5-8 10 12 14 32-40] 11 case-control studies,[21 26 27 41-51] and 11 ecological studies[30 31 52-61] investigated milk.

Milk and dairy products
Seven cohort studies showed increased risk with increased intake of milk and dairy products,[4 6 8-11 13 15] which was statistically significant in two.[6 10] Two studies showed non-significant decreased risk[5 12 14]; and one study showed no effect on risk.[7] Meta-analysis was possible on eight studies, giving a summary effect estimate of 1.06 (95% confidence interval (CI) 1.01–1.11) per serving/day, with moderate heterogeneity.[4-12]

Five of these cohort studies reported separately on advanced/aggressive prostate cancer.[5 7 9 10 12] Two studies showed increased risk with increased intake of milk and dairy products,[9 10] which was statistically significant in one.[9] Three studies showed non-significant decreased risk.[5 7 12] Meta-analysis was possible on four studies, giving a summary effect estimate of 1.00 (95% CI 0.94–1.06) per serving/day, with low heterogeneity.[5 7 10 12] The study that could not be included in the meta-analysis was inconsistent with this result, reporting an effect estimate of 2.35 (95% CI 1.29–4.26) per serving/day increase (dry weight).[9]

Eight case-control studies showed increased risk with increased intake of milk and dairy products,[16 19-21 23 24 26 28] which was statistically significant in one.[28] Four studies showed non-significant decreased risk[17 18 22 25 27]; and one study reported that there was no statistically significant effect on risk.[29] Meta-analysis was possible on five relatively high-quality studies, giving a summary effect estimate of 1.03 (95% CI 0.99–1.07) per serving/day, with low heterogeneity.[16-20]

One ecological study showed no significant association, with an age-adjusted correlation coefficient of -0.49.[30] One other ecological study reported no statistically significant effect.[31]

There are many separate exposures being measured within this broad category, which may explain the observed heterogeneity.

A dose-response relationship is apparent from cohort data on all prostate cancer, but not from cohort data on advanced/aggressive prostate cancer or case-control data.

Milk
Six cohort studies showed increased risk with increased intake of milk,[6 8 33 36 37 39] which was statistically significant in one.[6] Three studies showed no effect on risk[32 34 35] and one study showed non-significant decreased risk.[14] The remaining six studies did not report quantified results, but stated results were not statistically significant.[5 7 10 12 38 40] Meta-analysis was possible on eight studies, giving a summary effect estimate of 1.05 (95% CI 0.98–1.14) per serving/day, with low heterogeneity.[6 8 14 32-36]

Six studies reported separately on advanced/aggressive prostate cancer.[7 12 33 36 39 40] Three studies showed increased risk with increased intake of milk, with effect estimates of 1.30 (95% CI 1.04–1.61) per serving/day[36]; 2.8 (in men aged 72.5 years or less, for the highest intake groups compared to the lowest, with no CI reported)[33]; and an increased risk with a p value for trend of 0.005.[39] Three studies did not report quantified results but stated that there was no significant association.[7 12 40]

Seven case-control studies showed increased risk with increased intake of milk,[27] [41-44] [47-51] which was statistically significant in three (including the single relatively high quality study).[41] [43] [44] [47] Two studies showed non-significant decreased risk[21] [45]; one study reported no effect on risk[46] and one study stated that there was no significant association but did not present results.[26] Meta-analysis was possible on six relatively low quality studies, giving a summary effect estimate of 1.08 (95% CI 0.98–1.19) per serving/day, with moderate heterogeneity.[21] [27] [42-45]

Ten ecological studies reported correlations in the direction of increased risk.[31] [52] [54-61] One study did not provide a quantified result, but stated there was no statistically significant association.[53] One study showed a non-significant decreased risk in areas of increased intake.[30]

Milk could plausibly cause prostate cancer through the actions of calcium (see chapter 4.4.5.1.1). Also, consumption of milk increases blood levels of insulin-like growth factor-1, which has been associated with increased prostate cancer risk in some studies.[62] [63]

The evidence is inconsistent from both cohort and case-control studies. There is limited evidence suggesting that milk and dairy products are a cause of prostate cancer.

The Panel is aware that since the conclusion of the SLR, two cohort studies[64] [65] and one case-control study[66] have been published. This new information does not change the Panel judgement (see box 3.8).

4.4.5.1.1 Milk
Colorectum
Thirteen cohort studies[67-82] and 36 case-control studies investigated milk and colorectal cancer. Fifteen cohort studies[72-77] [79] [80] [82-101] and 58 case-control studies investigated dietary calcium.

Milk
Nine cohort studies showed decreased risk with increased intake of milk,[67] [69] [70] [72] [74] [75] [77] [80-82] which was statistically sig-

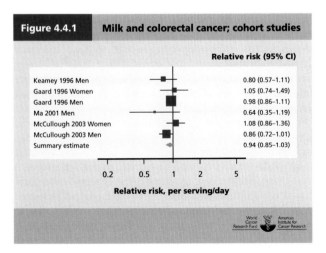

Figure 4.4.1   Milk and colorectal cancer; cohort studies

	Relative risk (95% CI)
Keamey 1996 Men	0.80 (0.57–1.11)
Gaard 1996 Women	1.05 (0.74–1.49)
Gaard 1996 Men	0.98 (0.86–1.11)
Ma 2001 Men	0.64 (0.35–1.19)
McCullough 2003 Women	1.08 (0.86–1.36)
McCullough 2003 Men	0.86 (0.72–1.01)
Summary estimate	0.94 (0.85–1.03)

Relative risk, per serving/day

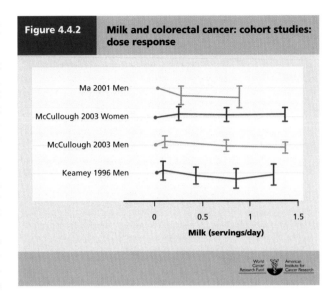

Figure 4.4.2   Milk and colorectal cancer: cohort studies: dose response

Ma 2001 Men
McCullough 2003 Women
McCullough 2003 Men
Keamey 1996 Men

Milk (servings/day)

nificant in two.[67] [80] Two studies showed non-significant increased risk[69] [71] [78] [79] and two studies showed non-significant increased risk in women and non-significant decreased risk in men.[68] [73] [76] Meta-analysis was possible on four studies, giving a summary effect estimate of 0.94 (95% CI 0.85–1.03) per serving/day, with low heterogeneity (figures 4.4.1 and 4.4.2).[72] [73] [76] [81]

In addition, there was a pooled analysis from 10 cohort studies which included 534 536 participants with 4992 cases of colorectal cancer. Milk intake was related to a statistically significant reduced risk of colorectal cancer (relative risk (RR) 0.78; 95% CI 0.69–0.88) for the highest intake group when compared to the lowest.[102]

Dietary calcium
Eleven studies showed decreased risk with increased intake of calcium,[76] [79] [82] [84] [85] [90-93] [99] which was statistically significant in three.[84] [85] [90] One study showed non-significant increased risk[74]; one study showed non-significant increased risk in women and non-significant decreased risk in men[73]; and two studies showed non-significant decreased risk of colon cancer and non-significant increased risk of rectal cancer.[88] [89] Meta-analysis was possible on 10 cohort studies giving a summary effect estimate of 0.98 (95% CI 0.95–1.00) per 200 mg/day, with low heterogeneity (figure 4.4.3).[72] [73] [76] [77] [79] [83] [87] [90] [98] [99] When meta-analysis was restricted to eight studies that reported results separately for colon cancer, a summary effect estimate of 0.95 (95% CI 0.92–0.98) per 200 mg/day was produced, with no heterogeneity.[72] [73] [76] [77] [83] [87] [89] [90]

Dose-response plot
Figure 4.4.4 shows the dose-response curve for dietary calcium intake and colorectal cancer incidence.

In addition, there was a pooled analysis from 10 cohort studies which included 534 536 participants with 4992 cases of colorectal cancer. Dietary calcium intake was related to a statistically significant reduced risk of colorectal cancer (RR 0.86; 95% CI 0.78–0.95) for the highest

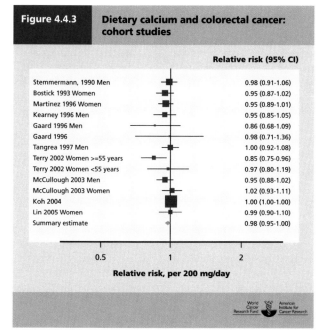

Figure 4.4.3 Dietary calcium and colorectal cancer: cohort studies

Relative risk (95% CI)

Stemmermann, 1990 Men	0.98 (0.91-1.06)
Bostick 1993 Women	0.95 (0.87-1.02)
Martinez 1996 Women	0.95 (0.89-1.01)
Kearney 1996 Men	0.95 (0.85-1.05)
Gaard 1996 Men	0.86 (0.68-1.09)
Gaard 1996	0.98 (0.71-1.36)
Tangrea 1997 Men	1.00 (0.92-1.08)
Terry 2002 Women >=55 years	0.85 (0.75-0.96)
Terry 2002 Women <55 years	0.97 (0.80-1.19)
McCullough 2003 Men	0.95 (0.88-1.02)
McCullough 2003 Women	1.02 (0.93-1.11)
Koh 2004	1.00 (1.00-1.00)
Lin 2005 Women	0.99 (0.90-1.10)
Summary estimate	0.98 (0.95-1.00)

Relative risk, per 200 mg/day

intake group when compared to the lowest.[102]

Because of the abundant prospective data from cohort studies, case-control studies were not summarised.

Dietary calcium intake can be interpreted as a marker of dairy intake only in those populations (usually European, Australian, or from the Americas) that consume relatively regular and large amounts of milk and dairy products. Other dietary sources of calcium include vegetables, nuts, pulses, and fish or meat cooked on the bone (box 4.4.1).

The general mechanisms through which milk could plausibly protect against cancer are outlined below.

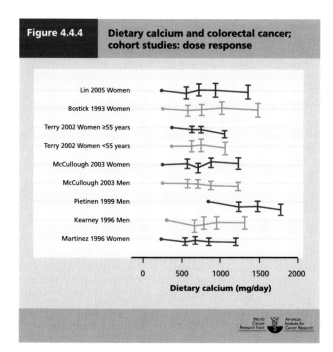

Figure 4.4.4 Dietary calcium and colorectal cancer; cohort studies: dose response

Lin 2005 Women	
Bostick 1993 Women	
Terry 2002 Women ≥55 years	
Terry 2002 Women <55 years	
McCullough 2003 Women	
McCullough 2003 Men	
Pietinen 1999 Men	
Kearney 1996 Men	
Martinez 1996 Women	

Dietary calcium (mg/day)

The evidence on milk from cohort studies is reasonably consistent, supported by stronger evidence from dietary calcium as a dietary marker. There is evidence for plausible mechanisms. Milk probably protects against colorectal cancer.

The Panel is aware that since the conclusion of the SLR, three cohort[80 103 104] and three case-control studies[66 105 106] have been published. This new information does not change the Panel judgement (see box 3.8).

Bladder cancer

Five cohort studies,[34 107-111] 14 case-control studies,[48 112-124] and 1 ecological study[56] investigated milk and bladder cancer.

All five cohort studies showed decreased risk with increased intake of milk,[34 107-111] which was statistically significant in one.[108] Meta-analysis was possible on four studies, giving a summary effect estimate of 0.82 (95% CI 0.67–0.99) per serving/day, with moderate heterogeneity.[34 108-110]

Seven case-control studies showed decreased risk with increased intake of milk,[48 112 115-117 121 122] which was statistically significant in four.[115 117 121 122] Four studies showed non-significant increased risk,[113 114 120 123] and three studies stated that there was no significant association.[118 119 124] Meta-analysis was possible on three relatively high-quality case-control studies, giving a summary effect estimate of 1.00 (95% CI 0.87–1.14) per serving/day, with high heterogeneity.[113-115]

A dose-response relationship is apparent from cohort, but not case-control data.

The single ecological study reported a correlation of 0.45 between milk consumption and death from bladder cancer.[56]

The general mechanisms through which milk could plausibly protect against cancer are outlined below.

The evidence is inconsistent and comes mainly from evidence on dietary calcium. There is limited evidence suggesting that milk protects against bladder cancer.

General mechanisms — milk

The probable effect of milk in reducing cancer risk is likely to be mediated at least in part by calcium. Calcium from diet is an import micronutrient, and intracellular calcium directly influences cell growth and apoptosis. Calcium may also bind to bile and fatty acids, preventing them from damaging the intestinal lining.[125] Milk includes many bioactive constituents, however, which may also play a role.

4.4.5.1.2 Cheese
Colorectum
Eleven cohort studies[67 68 70 72 74 78-80 82 126-128] and 25 case-control studies investigated cheese and colorectal cancer.

Eight cohort studies showed increased risk with increased intake of cheese, none of which was statistically significant.[67 68 70 72 74 79 80 126 127] Two studies reported non-significant decreased risk[78 82] and one study reported that there was no significant association.[128] Two meta-analyses were possible

133

on three and two cohort studies, respectively, giving summary effect estimates of 1.14 (95% CI 0.82–1.58) per serving/day[72 79 126] and 1.11 (95% CI 0.88–1.39) per 50 g/day,[80] [82] both with low heterogeneity.

Because of the abundant prospective data from cohort studies, case-control studies were not summarised.

No specific mechanism has been identified but cheese could plausibly cause colorectal cancer through the indirect mechanisms connected to saturated fats. Saturated fats intake increases insulin production and expression of insulin receptors on colonic cells.[129] Saturated fats can also induce expression of certain inflammatory mediators associated with carcinogenesis.[130]

Epidemiological evidence for cheese intake is consistently in contrast to the probable protective effect from milk.

The evidence is inconsistent. There is limited evidence suggesting that cheese is a cause of colorectal cancer.

The Panel is aware that since the conclusion of the SLR, two cohort studies[66 103 104] and one case-control study[66] have been published. This new information does not change the Panel judgement (see box 3.8).

4.4.5.2 Diets high in calcium
For evidence on calcium supplements, see chapter 4.10.6.4.4.

Calcium is a good marker for dairy intake in Western diets. In areas outside the USA, Europe, and Oceania, dairy products are not as widely consumed and the range of calcium intake is smaller (see also box 4.4.1).

Prostate
Nine cohort studies,[4-8 10 11 131-133] 12 case-control studies,[18 19 23 24 134-144] and 2 ecological studies[145 146] investigated dietary calcium and prostate cancer.

Seven cohort studies showed increased risk with increased intake of dietary calcium,[4-7 10 11 131 133] which was statistically significant in three.[6 10 133] Two studies showed non-significant decreased risk, including the only unadjusted study.[8] [132] Meta-analysis was possible on eight cohort studies, giving a summary effect estimate of 1.27 (95% CI 1.09–1.48) per g/day, with moderate heterogeneity.[5-8 10 11 131-133]

Four of these cohort studies reported separately on advanced/aggressive prostate cancer.[5 7 10 133] Three studies showed increased risk with increased intake of milk and dairy products,[7 10 133] which was statistically significant in one.[133] One study showed non-significant decreased risk.[5] Meta-analysis was possible on all four studies, giving a summary effect estimate of 1.32 (95% CI 1.05–1.64) per g/day, with moderate heterogeneity.[5 7 10 133]

Six case-control studies showed non-significant decreased risk with increased intake of dietary calcium.[18 134 136 138-140 143 144] Five studies showed increased risk,[19 23 24 135 137 141] which was statistically significant in one[19 138]; and one other study showed no effect on risk.[142] Meta-analysis was possible on three relatively high-quality studies, giving a summary effect estimate of 1.16 (95% CI 0.64–2.14) per gram of calcium/day, with high heterogeneity.[18 19 134]

A dose-response relationship was apparent from cohort but not case-control data.

One ecological study from Germany showed a significant increased risk of prostate cancer with higher calcium intakes.[146] Another study from Taiwan reported a non-significant decreased risk with higher calcium intakes.[145]

High calcium intake downregulates the formation of 1,25 dihydroxy vitamin D(3) from vitamin D, thereby increasing cell proliferation in the prostate.[7] Prostate cancer tumours in rats treated with 1,25 dihydroxy vitamin D(3) were significantly smaller and presented smaller numbers of lung metastases.[147]

The evidence, from both cohort and case-control studies, is substantial and consistent with a dose-response relationship. There is evidence for plausible mechanisms. Diets high in calcium are a probable cause of prostate cancer.

The Panel is aware that since the conclusion of the SLR, two cohort studies[64 65] have been published. This new information does not change the Panel judgement (see box 3.8).

4.4.6 Comparison with previous report

The previous report judged that milk and dairy products possibly increase the risk of prostate and kidney cancer. Calcium was judged possibly not to affect the risk of colorectal cancer. Since the mid-1990s, more evidence has emerged on prostate cancer, and that for kidney cancer is now inconclusive.

4.4.7 Conclusions

The Panel concludes:
The evidence on the relationship between milk and dairy products, and also diets high in calcium, and the risk of cancer, points in different directions.

Milk probably protects against colorectal cancer; there is limited evidence suggesting that milk protects against bladder cancer. But there is limited evidence suggesting that cheese is a cause of colorectal cancer.

Diets high in calcium are a probable cause of prostate cancer; there is limited evidence suggesting that high consumption of milk and dairy products is a cause of prostate cancer.

4.5 Fats and oils

FATS, OILS, AND THE RISK OF CANCER

In the judgement of the Panel, the factors listed below modify the risk of cancer. Judgements are graded according to the strength of the evidence.

	DECREASES RISK		INCREASES RISK	
	Exposure	**Cancer site**	**Exposure**	**Cancer site**
Convincing				
Probable				
Limited — suggestive			Total fat	Lung Breast (postmenopause)
			Foods containing animal fats[1]	Colorectum
			Butter	Lung
Substantial effect on risk unlikely		None identified		

1 Includes both foods naturally containing the constituent and foods that have had the constituent added (see Chapter 3).

For an explanation of all the terms used in the matrix, please see chapter 3.5.1, the text of this section, and the glossary.

Fats and oils are the most energy-dense constituents of food supplies and diets. Their contribution to total dietary energy increases with industrialisation and urbanisation. Meat from most industrially bred animals is higher in fat than that from wild animals, and such meat fats, together with fat from milk and dairy products, are a major source of fat in most high-income countries. Many processed foods contain substantial amounts of oils from plant sources. Production and consumption of animal fats and oil from plant sources have greatly increased in recent decades, most of all in China and elsewhere in Asia.

In general, *the Panel judges* that there is only limited evidence suggesting that diets relatively high in fats and oils (in total, or any type) are in themselves a cause of any cancer. This judgement contrasts with those of some earlier reports, which concluded from evidence then available that diets high in fats and oils might be a substantial cause of some cancers. Overall, the evidence does not suggest that diets relatively high in fats and oils might protect against the risk of any cancer.

The Panel judges as follows:
There is limited evidence suggesting that total fat is a cause of lung cancer, and of postmenopausal breast cancer; that animal fat is a cause of colorectal cancer; and that consumption of butter is a cause of lung cancer. *The Panel stresses* that the principal cause of lung cancer is tobacco smoking.

The evidence on fats and oils does not justify any judgement of 'convincing' or 'probable'. For discussion of the role of fats and oils in energy-dense foods and drinks, the effect of energy-dense foods and drinks on weight gain, overweight, and obesity, and the role of weight gain, overweight, and obesity in the risk of some cancers, see Chapters 6 and 8.

Fats or oils may be an intrinsic part of the plant or animal, as contained in the germ of cereals (grains) and the tissues of animals, or extracted and added to food in manufacture, cooking, or at the table.

Production and consumption of fats and oils in general rises with industrialisation and urbanisation, and in particular with the extent to which animal production is intensified, milk and dairy products are consumed, and processed foods include extracted oils. Availability and price are also key factors. In lower-income countries, average population consumption of fat may amount to less than 15 per cent, though usually to 20–30 per cent of total energy; in high-income countries, usually to 30–40 per cent. On a global basis, and most notably in China and elsewhere in Asia, production and consumption of animal fats and plant oils are increasing.

Early reports issued in the context of food insecurity in industrialised countries, including Europe and North America, recommended maintenance and even an increase in consumption of fats and oils. In the second half of the 20th century, reports on fats, oils, and chronic diseases tended to focus on the possible role of diets relatively high in fats and oils in the causation of obesity, type 2 diabetes, coronary heart disease, and cancers of some sites. In recent decades, more attention has been given to issues of the nutritional quality of fats and oils. Distinctions are made between relatively saturated (including hydrogenated) fats, such as from meat, milk, and their products, or from hydrogenated oils in baked goods and many other processed foods; relatively monounsaturated oils, notably olive oil; and relatively polyunsaturated oils, from seeds, nuts, fish, and other sources, some of which — like vitamins — are essential to human health and life. These distinctions are to some extent reflected in the studies reviewed here.

For discussion of the role of fats and oils in energy-dense foods and drinks, the effect of energy-dense foods and drinks on weight gain, overweight, and obesity, and the role of weight gain, overweight, and obesity in the risk of some cancers, see Chapters 6 and 8.

In this Report, fats and oils are classified as foods. This section also covers dietary cholesterol, as well as total fat and individual fatty acids as dietary constituents. Food processes affecting the composition of fats and oils, such as hydrogenation, are also covered here.

4.5.1 Definitions and sources

Dietary fat is mostly made up of triglycerides (three fatty acid molecules attached to a glycerol backbone). Triglycerides are lipids, a class of hydrocarbon-containing organic compounds, which also includes cholesterol. Lipids are used by plants, animals, and humans as a means of storing energy, as structural components of cell membranes, and as precursors of important hormones.

Fatty acids are classified as either 'saturated' or 'unsaturated', depending on their chemical structure (see chapter 4.5.2), and these differences determine their shape and physical properties. Fats high in saturated fatty acids are generally solid at room temperature, whereas those rich in unsaturated fatty acids are liquid. *Trans*-fatty acids, formed in a process called hydrogenation (box 4.5.1), are physically more like saturated fats (harder at lower temperatures), and have similar effects on the body.

The term 'fats' is often used for fats and for oils. Fats can be classified according to their source, use, or chemical composition. Those that are solid or semisolid at ambient temperature are generally high in saturated fatty acids and are often of animal origin; and oils, which are from plant and marine sources, are liquid at ambient temperature in their places of origin. Palm oil and coconut oil, which are relatively high in saturated fatty acids, are semisolid in temperate climates but liquid in the tropics, where coconut and other palm trees grow (also see chapter 4.5.2).

Fats and oils are eaten as part of animal and plant foods, are contained in manufactured foods, used for cooking, and may be added at the table. Animal fats include tallow, lard, and suet, produced as part of the slaughtering process, and butter. Margarine and other fat spreads are made from fish and plant oils. Plant oils are extracted from oily fruits (such as olives), seeds (such as rape and sunflower), nuts (such as walnuts), and other sources.

A small amount of dietary fat is essential to allow absorption of fat-soluble vitamins (A, D, E, and K) and to provide the essential fatty acids that cannot be made by the body. Fat also helps food to taste more interesting and be more palatable, for instance in terms of its texture. Linoleic acid and alpha-linolenic acid are the two essential fatty acids, and are found in vegetables, nuts, and seed oils; lower levels are also found in meat, eggs, and dairy products. Oily fish also contain long-chain unsaturated fatty acids, which influence inflammatory processes in the body.[1] For instance, eicosapentaenoic and docosahexaenoic acids, and related fatty acids, are precursors to prostaglandins, which are hormone-like compounds with diverse effects, including roles in blood vessel dilation and constriction, blood clotting, and inflammation.

Cholesterol is found only in foods of animal origin, such as cheese, butter, meat, seafood, and egg yolks. Most of the cholesterol in the body is manufactured in the liver, rather than coming from these dietary sources.[1] The proportion and types of saturated and unsaturated fatty acids eaten in the diet are more important influences on cholesterol metabolism than the amount of dietary cholesterol.

4.5.2 Composition

The properties of fats and oils are determined by the length and structure of the fatty acids they contain. Liquid oils tend to be higher in unsaturated fatty acids, whereas more solid fats have more saturated fatty acids.

Whether or not a fatty acid is saturated depends on the chemical bonds that join together the chain of carbon atoms that forms the backbone of the molecule. Saturated fatty acids have only single bonds, whereas unsaturated fatty acids have at least one double bond between two adjacent carbon atoms. Monounsaturated fatty acids have only one double bond; polyunsaturated fatty acids have two or more double bonds. The position of the first double bond along the carbon chain is denoted by an 'n'. Thus linoleic acid is 'n-6' and alpha-linolenic acid is 'n-3'. These were previously known as 'omega-6' and 'omega-3' fatty acids.

Saturated fatty acids are long and straight, forming well ordered, relatively solid structures. But each of the double bonds in an unsaturated fatty acid causes the carbon chain to kink; and the more kinks, the less well they pack together, which means they form less solid structures. So, saturated fats are usually solid at room temperature and unsaturated fats are liquid (oils). *Trans*-fatty acids are unsaturated fatty acids formed by a process called hydrogenation, which removes and reconfigures the double bonds, making the carbon chain less kinked. Plant oils can be turned into saturated fats by this process, which, when only partially complete, also leads to production of *trans*-fatty acids (box 4.5.1).

Fats from ruminants (cattle and sheep) contain more saturated fatty acids than pork or poultry fats. Fats from under the skin have a smaller proportion of saturated fatty acids than fats stored around the organs. Beef suet is the hardest culinary fat, while chicken, duck, and

---

> ### Box 4.5.1   Hydrogenation and *trans*-fatty acids
>
> The main single factor that has increased production and consumption of total fat and saturated fatty acids throughout the world, and therefore the energy density of food supplies, is the industrial process of hydrogenation, invented at the beginning of the 20th century.[2] The hydrogenation process was at first used mostly for the manufacture of margarine, but it is now used in the manufacture of many processed foods supplied and consumed throughout the world.
>
> Complete hydrogenation converts the unsaturated fatty acids in oils of plant and marine origin into saturated fatty acids. This process has two commercial benefits.
>
> First, it greatly extends 'shelf-life': oils high in unsaturated fatty acids become rancid, whereas fats high in saturated fatty acids 'keep' for very much longer. Second, it enables conversion of whatever plant and marine oils are cheapest at the time into a uniform, reliable ingredient and product.
>
> Partial hydrogenation produces *trans*-fatty acids, which, although chemically unsaturated, physiologically behave more like saturated fatty acids. For instance, high levels in the diet increase the risk of coronary heart disease. Biscuits and other baked goods may contain as much as 25 per cent or more of their fats in *trans* form. Small amounts of *trans*-fats are also naturally
>
> found in milk and butter.
>
> Because of the evidence on coronary heart disease, regulatory authorities in many countries now require food manufacturers to list *trans*-fatty acid content on nutrition labels of processed foods. Hydrogenated fats found in foods, and labelled as such, are hydrogenated to a variable extent and may therefore contain unspecified amounts of *trans*-fatty acids. This may not be clear on labels where a declaration of *trans*-fatty acid content is not required.
>
> *The Panel notes* that any effect of *trans*-fatty acids specifically on the risk of any cancer is not known.

goose fats are semiliquid at room temperature.

In general, the amount and type of body fat carried by animals and poultry depend on how they live, and this determines the fat content of their meat, unless some of it has been removed during processing. Wild and free-living land animals and birds are lean, and much of their fat is unsaturated; domesticated animals and birds carry more fat, which is higher in saturated fatty acids. Indeed, they are often bred to be more fatty, so that their meat is more succulent.

4.5.3 Consumption patterns

Consumption of total fats and oils varies greatly throughout the world. Average intake of total fat is highest (30–40 per cent of total energy) in most urbanised and industrialised regions such as Europe, North America, Australia, and New Zealand, where people consume relatively more meat and milk and their products. By contrast, fat usually accounts for only 20–30 per cent of total energy in lower-income parts of the world, for instance in Africa, Asia, and Latin America; this may be even lower in rural areas, where people consume low levels of added fats or oils (for instance, from processed foods). However, in general, consumption of fats — and in particular plant oils — is increasing in middle- and low-income countries. (Also see Chapter 1.)

Higher amounts of separated animal fats (as distinct from the fats that are naturally components of foods of animal origin) are consumed in high-income countries. Availability is typically highest in North America, northern Europe, Australia, and New Zealand — as much as 10 per cent in parts of northern Europe, compared with less than 0.5 per cent in much of Africa and Asia.[3]

More plant oils are also consumed in high-income countries; availability is highest in North America, southern Europe and some parts of the Middle East, and lowest in parts of Asia and Africa. Greece has the highest level of consumption — almost 20 per cent of dietary energy — compared with 1.4 per cent in Laos.

Soya bean oil is the most widely consumed oil in the world, particularly in North America, as well as in some Asian and African countries. Sunflower seed oil is the second most widely consumed vegetable oil (particularly in Europe, South Africa, Argentina, Chile, and New Zealand) and palm oil the third (particularly in some African, Asian, and Latin American countries, as well as in Australia). Olive oil is the most widely consumed oil in southern Europe (particularly in Greece, Italy, and Spain). Rapeseed oils are most common in northern Europe and Canada, while groundnut oil is common in some African countries.

The industrial revolution brought significant changes to food supplies, methods of food production, and hence people's diets (see chapter 1.1.3). Before then, it is thought that the amounts of n-6 and n-3 oils in diets had been roughly equal. But with the move to urban–industrial ways of life, vegetable oils (which are predominantly n-6) became cheap and widely available. The ratio of n-6 to n-3 fatty acids is now thought to be between 10 and 20 to 1 in many high-income countries.[4]

The World Health Organization recommends limiting average fat intake for populations to between 15 and 30 per cent of total daily energy intake, and saturated fatty acids to less than 10 per cent.[5] In higher-income countries, fat consumption as a percentage of total energy has been decreasing for some time. However, this is no longer the case in some countries such as the USA, where the percentage of energy from fat has started to increase again.

4.5.4 Interpretation of the evidence

4.5.4.1 General

For general considerations that may affect interpretation of the evidence, see chapters 3.3 and 3.5, and boxes 3.1, 3.2, 3.6 and 3.7.

'Relative risk' (RR) is used in this Report to denote ratio measures of effect, including 'risk ratios', 'rate ratios', 'hazard ratios', and 'odds ratios'.

4.5.4.2 Specific

Some considerations specific to fats and oils are as follows.

Patterns and ranges of intake. In high-income countries where most studies are undertaken, average consumption of fats and oils is relatively high and variation in consumption is not great.

Classification. Studies tend to use classifications relevant to coronary heart disease, some of which may not be relevant to cancer. Thus, they examine not only animal and vegetable fats; meat, fish, and dairy fats; but also saturated and unsaturated fatty acids; monounsaturated and polyunsaturated fatty acids; n-3 and *trans*-fatty acids; and oleic, linoleic, and other individual fatty acids. This makes aggregation and analysis of intakes of fats and oils as a whole, problematic.

Study design. Practically all studies have analysed consumption of fats and oils as an issue of quantity (percentage of total energy intake) rather than nutritional quality (effect of different types of fats and oils). But oils are complex mixtures of nutrients and other bioactive compounds, some of which may have harmful effects on cancer risk and others beneficial effects.

Reporting bias. The use of questionnaires to record consumption of fats and oils may change behaviour. As people become more conscious of what they consume, they tend to under-report true consumption of foods and drinks they regard as unhealthy, including fats and oils. So studies using questionnaires may disproportionately underestimate consumption of fats and oils.

4.5.5 Evidence and judgements

The relationship between the risk of cancer and fat and oil intake may be assessed as weight of fat consumed or adjusted for total energy intake, so that fat is assessed as a proportion of total dietary energy.[6] Where this is the case, this has been stated below.

The full systematic literature review (SLR) is contained on the CD included with this Report.

4.5.5.1 Total fats

Lung

Nine cohort studies,[7-15] 17 case-control studies,[16-32] and 4 ecological studies[33-36] investigated total fat and lung cancer. (Also see chapter 7.4.)

Six cohort studies showed non-significant increased risk for the highest intake group when compared to the lowest.[7 8 10 11 13 14] Three studies showed decreased risk,[9 12 15] which was statistically significant in one.[15] Meta-analysis was possible on two cohort studies, with a summary effect estimate of 1.01 (95% confidence interval (CI) 0.94–1.09) per 10 g fat/day, with high heterogeneity.[11 12] Six of the studies adjusted for smoking, including the two studies in the meta-analysis and not including the statistically significant reduced risk.[7-12]

Pooled analysis from 8 cohort studies (over 430 000 partici-

pants, followed up for 6 to 16 years, more than 3100 lung cancer cases) showed a non-significant increased risk of 1.01 (95% CI 0.98–1.05) per 5 per cent daily energy intake from fat.[37]

Twelve of the case-control studies showed increased risk for the highest intake group when compared to the lowest,[16 17 19-21 23 25 27-29 31 32] which was statistically significant in five.[16 17 19-21 25 31] No studies reported statistically significant reduced risk. Most (12) of these studies adjusted for smoking.[16 19-22 24 25 27 30-32]

The ecological studies reported mixed results, most of which were not statistically significant.[33-35] One study reported a statistically significant decreased risk with increased fat intake.[36]

Although no evidence for plausible mechanisms was found, based on the epidemiological evidence, there is limited evidence suggesting that total fat is a cause of lung cancer.

> **The mixed results from cohort studies contrast with the more consistent results from other studies. Overall, there is limited evidence suggesting that consumption of total fat is a cause of lung cancer.** *The Panel emphasises* **that the principal cause of lung cancer is smoking tobacco.**

Breast (all ages)

Nineteen cohort studies,[38-60] 49 case-control studies,[61-118] and 10 ecological studies[119-128] investigated total fat intake and breast cancer.

Breast (premenopause)

Total fat intake for all ages, and also for premenopausal breast cancer, did not give any overall indication of effect.

Breast (postmenopause)

Nine cohort studies[38 40 43 45 50-52 57-59] and 16 case-control studies[62-65 75 79 85 86 96-98 101 102 109 110 112 116] reported results specifically for postmenopausal breast cancer.

Six cohort studies showed increased risk with increasing fat intake,[38 40 45 50-52 59] which was statistically significant in three.[38 51 52] Three studies reported non-significant reduced risk.[40 43 57 58] Meta-analysis was possible on five cohort studies, giving a summary estimate of 1.06 (95% CI 0.99–1.14) per 20 g/day, with moderate heterogeneity.[38 43 45 50 51]

Pooling project data (7329 invasive postmenopausal breast cancer cases among 351 821 women) showed a reduced risk, with an estimate of 0.96 (95% CI 0.86–1.08) per 25 g increase in energy-adjusted total fat. Menopausal status was not an effect modifier on these data.[129 130]

Eleven case-control studies showed increased risk with increasing fat intake,[62 64 65 75 85 86 96-98 102 109 110 112] which was statistically significant in three.[97 109 112] Five studies showed decreased risk,[63 64 79 101 116] which was statistically significant in one.[64] Meta-analysis was possible on seven control studies, giving a summary estimate of 1.11 (95% CI 1.06–1.16), with no heterogeneity.[62 63 65 75 97 102 109]

There is also evidence on percentage energy from fat. There are four cohort studies[131-134]; three reported decreased risk.[131 133 134] The other study reported non-significant increased risk.[132] There were two case-control studies; both reported a non-significant decreased risk.[135 136]

There is interest in the varying role that different types of individual fatty acids might have on breast cancer risk but there are insufficient data to draw any conclusions. There are mechanistic data connecting polyunsaturated fatty acids and peroxidation.

Higher endogenous oestrogen levels after menopause are a known cause of breast cancer.[137] [138] Dietary fat is relatively well established as a cause of increased endogenous oestrogen production.[139] Low-fat diets are usually associated with high fibre consumption, which may reduce oestrogen concentration by decreasing intestinal reabsorption. In premenopausal women, there is little evidence that serum oestrogen levels are associated either with fat consumption or with breast cancer risk.

An alternative mechanism by which dietary fat could influence steroid hormone levels is that increased serum-free fatty acids could displace oestradiol from serum albumin, thus increasing free oestradiol concentration.[140] However, the serum concentration of sex hormone-binding globulin is a more important determinant of the proportion of oestradiol that can enter the breast epithelial cells. Sex hormone-binding globulin decreases with increasing body mass index and insulin resistance.

Energy-dense diets (among other factors) lower the age of menarche. Early menarche is an established risk factor for breast cancer.

Evidence from prospective epidemiological studies of different types shows inconsistent effects on the whole, while case-control studies show a significant positive association. Mechanistic evidence is speculative. Overall, there is limited evidence suggesting that consumption of total fat is a cause of postmenopausal breast cancer.

4.5.5.1.1 Butter
Lung

Two cohort studies[8] [141] and eight case-control studies[142-149] investigated butter and lung cancer. (Also see chapter 7.4.)

One cohort study showed statistically significant increased risk, with a summary estimate of 1.8 (95% CI 1.0–3.0) for the highest intake group when compared to the lowest.[8] The other cohort study showed non-significant decreased risk in three independent estimates: 0.92 (95% CI 0.65–1.30) for men; 0.90 (95% CI 0.46–1.77) for women; and 0.94 (95% CI 0.62–1.42) for non-smokers.[141] Both studies adjusted for smoking.

Seven case-control studies showed increased risk for the highest intake group when compared to the lowest,[143-149] which was statistically significant in three.[143] [145] [149] One study showed a non-significant decreased risk.[142] Most studies adjusted for smoking.[142] [143] [145-149]

Although no evidence for plausible mechanisms was found, based on the epidemiological evidence, there is limited evidence suggesting that butter is a cause of lung cancer.

There is a limited amount of inconsistent evidence suggesting that consumption of butter is a cause of lung cancer.

4.5.5.2 Foods containing animal fat

The evidence here refers to animal fats as foods, for instance, lard, suet, or dripping, and not to estimated amounts contained within other foods (such as meat and milk and their products, or baked goods).

Colorectum

Five cohort studies investigated animal fats and colorectal cancer.[150-154] (Also see chapter 7.9.)

Three studies showed increased risk with increasing intake of animal fats,[150] [151] [153] which was statistically significant in one,[150] and statistically significant when comparing the second highest intake to the lowest intake group, but not when comparing the highest to lowest, in another study.[151] One study reported no effect on risk[152] and another showed non-significant increased risk in men and non-significant decreased risk in women.[154] Meta-analysis was possible on three studies, giving a summary effect estimate of 1.13 (95% CI 0.92–1.38) per 20 g/day, with moderate heterogeneity.[150] [152] [154]

Because of the abundant prospective data from cohort studies, case-control studies were not summarised.

There is a limited amount of fairly consistent evidence suggesting that consumption of foods containing animal fat is a cause of colorectal cancer.

The Panel is aware that since the conclusion of the SLR, one cohort study[155] has been published. This new information does not change the Panel judgement (see box 3.8).

4.5.6 Comparison with previous report

The panel responsible for the previous report judged it possible that diets relatively high in total fat, and/or in saturated/animal fat, were causes of cancers of the lung, colorectum, breast, endometrium, and prostate. That panel noted a pattern whereby diets relatively high in fat could increase the risk of some cancers, and pointed out that fats and oils are energy-dense, and agreed that energy-dense diets increase the risk of obesity, itself a risk factor for some cancers.

The previous report judged that diets high in dietary cholesterol were a possible cause of cancers of the lung and pancreas. The overall evidence now does not support an association.

Since the mid-1990s, the results of cohort studies have overall tended to weaken the evidence on fats and oils as direct causes of cancer.

4.5.7 Conclusions

The Panel concludes:
Findings from cohort studies conducted since the mid-1990s have made the overall evidence associating fats and oils with the risk of any cancer somewhat less impressive.

There is limited evidence suggesting that total fat is a

cause of lung cancer or postmenopausal breast cancer; that foods containing animal fat are a cause of colorectal cancer; and that butter is a cause of lung cancer. *The Panel stresses that the main cause of lung cancer is smoking tobacco.*

Fats and oils are the most energy-dense constituents of foods. For discussion of the effect of energy-dense foods on weight gain, overweight, and obesity, and the role of weight gain, overweight, and obesity in the risk of some cancers, see Chapters 6, 7, and 8.

4.6 Sugars and salt

SUGARS AND SALT, AND THE RISK OF CANCER

In the judgement of the Panel, the factors listed below modify the risk of cancer. Judgements are graded according to the strength of the evidence.

	DECREASES RISK		INCREASES RISK	
	Exposure	Cancer site	Exposure	Cancer site
Convincing				
Probable			**Salt[1]** **Salted and salty foods**	**Stomach** **Stomach**
Limited — suggestive			Foods containing sugars[2]	Colorectum
Substantial effect on risk unlikely		None identified		

1 'Salt' here means total salt consumption, from processed foods, including salty and salted foods, and also salt added in cooking and at the table.
2 'Sugars' here means all 'non-milk extrinsic' sugars, including refined and other added sugars, honey, and as contained in fruit juices and syrups. It does not include sugars naturally present in whole foods such as fruits. It also does not include lactose as contained in animal or human milk.

For an explanation of all the terms used in the matrix, please see chapter 3.5.1, the text of this section, and the glossary.

Sugars are sweeteners and, in some forms, also a preservative and a bulking agent. Free sugars in the solid state or as syrups are ingredients in many processed foods and drinks. Nutritionally, sugars supply energy and nothing else. Sugars added to food were a luxury until sugar from cane became a major international cash crop, beginning in the 16th century. Consumption of added sugars, from beet as well as cane, and syrups increased rapidly in industrialised countries in the 19th and 20th centuries. High-fructose corn syrups are now also used extensively. Overall consumption of sugars is increasing worldwide, particularly in lower-income countries. In recent decades, and in many countries, consumption of added sugars, notably in the form of sugary drinks, accounts for a substantial proportion of energy intake.

Salt (sodium chloride) is also a preservative. The sodium and chloride in salt are essential nutrients in small amounts. In nature, foods are generally low or very low in sodium. Like sugar, salt historically was scarce and a precious commodity; the Romans paid their labourers in salt, thus the word 'salary' (from 'sal' for salt). Consumption of salt, in the form of many processed, salted, and salty foods, or of salt added in cooking and at table, remains variable. Consumption of salt, and salty and salt-preserved foods, is high in some maritime nations such as Japan, Portugal, and other Portuguese-speaking countries. In inland regions, such as landlocked African countries, consumption has been very low.

Overall, *the Panel judges* that the evidence on salt is confined to stomach cancer, and that on sugars is limited.

The Panel judges as follows:
Salt is a probable cause of stomach cancer. Salt-preserved foods are also a probable cause of stomach cancer. There is limited evidence suggesting that sugars are a cause of colorectal cancer. Within the remit of this Report, the strongest evidence, corresponding to judgements of 'convincing' and 'probable', shows that salt, and also salt-preserved foods, are probably causes of stomach cancer.

'Extrinsic', mainly refined, sugars amount to a substantial part of most industrialised food supplies. Sugars and syrups manufactured from cane, beet, and corn are profitable cash crops and are ingredients in many processed foods and drinks.

There is reason to believe that humans have evolved with a built-in desire for sweet foods. It has also been proposed that humans have a specific appetite for salt that might have evolved because sodium is scarce in nature. In any case, as sugars and salt become readily available and increasingly cheap, consumption tends to rise. In industrialised settings, sugars and salt are mostly consumed, not in food preparation or at the table, but as ingredients of processed foods.

Reports concerned with undernutrition have often, and still do, recommend substantial consumption of sugars and fats; their energy density enables quick weight gain, and the taste preference promotes energy consumption. By contrast, reports concerned with prevention of chronic diseases frequently recommend restraint in consumption of sugars. One reason for this is that sugars are the dietary cause of dental caries. Sugars in the amounts typically consumed in many industrialised countries have also been identified as a cause of obesity, and therefore also indirectly of obesity-related disease. Reports concerned with nutritional deficiencies often recommend the iodisation of salt supplies, to prevent goitre. Reports concerned with the prevention of chronic diseases frequently highlight that salt intakes are usually greatly in excess of requirements, and recommend substantial decreases in salt consumption to prevent hypertension and cardiovascular disease, especially stroke.

For sugared drinks, see chapter 4.7. For the contribution of sugar to weight gain, overweight, and obesity in drinks or through energy density of foods, see Chapter 8. For salted animal products, including Cantonese-style salted fish, see chapter 4.3.

Non-caloric chemical sweeteners are included here.

4.6.1 Definitions, sources

4.6.1.1 Sugars

Sugars here means all sugars in the diet. These are mainly but not only 'extrinsic sugars', which include sucrose (commonly called sugar), maltose, lactose, glucose, and fructose; in foods and drinks, including juices and milk, and in honey and syrups, including high-fructose corn syrup; refined sugars added to food in processing, preparation (cooking), and at the table. 'Intrinsic' sugars are those naturally present in whole foods such as fruits.

Sugars are now cheap and are used widely as sweeteners, preservatives, and bulking agents. They also often have the function of making processed starches, fats, and other ingredients more palatable. Also see box 4.6.1

Sucrose is refined from sugar beet and sugar cane. Maltose and glucose are refined predominantly from corn. High-fructose corn syrup comprises a mixture of glucose with fructose, commonly in close to equal amounts, and is now used in great quantity in food and drink manufacture, particularly in the USA.

The amount of sugars in manufactured foods and drinks varies. Sugared drinks are about 10 per cent by weight added sugars, and up to 100 per cent of their energy comes from sugars. Sugars are often added to fruit juices. Jams and other preserves are about 60 per cent sugars. Cakes, biscuits (cookies), and other baked goods contain starches, fats, and sugars in varying proportions. Most chocolate and much confectionery are high in sugars. It is often supposed that almost all added sugars are contained in obviously sweet foods: this is not so. Breakfast cereals may contain anything from negligible amounts to 50 per cent sugars. Yoghurts may contain anything between 0 to 20 per cent sugars; and ready-to-eat desserts even more. Many canned products include added sugars. Savoury processed foods, such as soups, pickles, bread, and buns, often contain significant amounts of sugars.

| Box 4.6.1 | Sugar, sugars, sugary foods, and drinks |

As indicated in chapter 4.6.4, it is particularly difficult to measure and assess the overall effect of sugars as possible modifiers of the risk of any disease, including cancer. This is partly because of inconsistency in the classification of sugars. Sometimes 'sugar' is equated with sucrose, which has been the chief sugar in human diets, but now is less so. Some studies investigate only 'packet' sugar purchased for use in the home; this is in general a relatively small and diminishing proportion of total sugars consumed. Other studies include sugars as found naturally in fruits and milk.

4.6.1.2 Salt

The term 'salt', in common usage, refers to sodium chloride. It is now a cheap commodity. Like sugar, salt is a preservative and a flavour enhancer. Both salt and sugar trap free water from foods, thus preventing microbial proliferation and spoilage. Salt is found in some rocks and dissolved in seawater, and can be extracted from seawater by evaporation. Both sodium and chloride are essential components of the diet in small amounts.

Usually most salt in diets is contained in processed foods, with only a relatively small amount added in cooking or at the table (box 4.6.2). Some traditional diets include substantial amounts of salt-preserved foods, including salted meat, fish, vegetables, and sometimes also fruits; and also salted foods such as bacon, sausages, and ham, which contain from 3 to 5 g of salt per 100 g. Industrialised diets include many processed foods that are not salt-preserved but contribute substantial amounts of salt to the diet, even if they do not seem salty, as well as more obviously salty foods such as potato crisps (chips), salted nuts, and other salty snack foods. Most of the sodium consumed in urban environments comes from salt added to processed foods, and thus is beyond the control of typical consumers. Many foods such as bread, soups, breakfast cereals, and biscuits may contain substantial amounts of salt; anything from 1 to 4 g per 100 g.

4.6.2 Composition

4.6.2.1 Sugars

Sugars are simple carbohydrates, and provide 3.75 kilocalories per gram (see chapter 4.10.1). Sugars are single molecules such as glucose, fructose, and galactose (monosaccharides), or two molecules bound together (disaccharides) such as sucrose (fructose and glucose), lactose (glucose and galactose), or maltose (two glucose molecules).

The body metabolises different sugars at different rates; for instance, fructose is absorbed and metabolised more slowly than either glucose or sucrose. It is also slightly sweeter than glucose or sucrose, and thus is able to replace them in lower total amounts. Non-caloric chemical sweeteners produce a sweet taste, but are not sugars (box 4.6.3).

There is no dietary requirement for sugars. The World

Box 4.6.2	Salt, and salty, salted, and salt-preserved foods

As indicated in chapter 4.6.4.2, it is difficult to measure salt intake, or the contribution from separate sources (salty, salted, or salt-preserved foods). The most reliable estimates come from measuring the amount of sodium excreted in the urine.

Salt is itself readily identified, although it is sometimes combined in studies with other sodium compounds. Some studies investigate only salt added in cooking or at the table, but this is usually a small proportion of total salt consumption. Results from such studies are liable to produce different results, compared with those from studies that have examined total salt consumption.

It has been thought that any effect of salt on stomach cancer (see chapter 4.6.5.2) is principally the result of regular consumption of salted and salt-preserved foods, rather than salt as such. This is partly because such foods are a substantial part of traditional Japanese and other Asian diets, where incidence of stomach cancer has been and still is high. However, the incidence of this cancer is also high in countries where traditional diets contain substantial amounts of salty as distinct from salt-preserved foods; and the concentration of salt in many processed foods consumed in Europe and North America approaches that of salt-preserved foods.

Box 4.6.3	Chemical sweeteners

Chemical sweeteners such as saccharin, cyclamates, and aspartame have been thought to be possible causes of cancer. This is because some animal studies have shown that very high doses of saccharin, in particular, increase the incidence of bladder cancer in rats. In common with many chemical additives, some sweeteners can be shown to be carcinogenic in experimental settings in massive amounts, far greater than humans could consume in foods and drinks.

The evidence from epidemiological studies does not suggest that chemical sweeteners have a detectable effect on the risk of any cancer.

Health Organization recommends that average consumption of sugars by populations should be less than 10 per cent of total energy.[1]

4.6.2.2 Salt

Pure salt, as sodium chloride, contains no metabolisable energy. Formulated, granulated table salts often include additives, such as anti-caking agents, which prevent salt crystals from sticking together; potassium iodide, included to prevent iodine deficiency; traces of other sodium compounds (carbonate or thiosulphate); and also sugar, to stabilise the potassium iodide. Sea salt may be refined to almost pure sodium chloride, or unrefined, in which case they may include traces of other minerals, algae, and a few salt-tolerant bacteria. Salt may also be flavoured, for example with celery or garlic.

Sodium is essential for the body to function normally. It is a major electrolyte in extracellular fluid. The body's sodium content and its concentration in body fluids are controlled homeostatically to very precise limits; excess sodium is excreted in the urine. Sodium is also involved in regulation of osmolarity, acid-base balance, and the membrane potential of cells. The daily requirement for sodium has been estimated at around 500 mg for adults. On a pragmatic basis, WHO recommends restricting average salt consumption for populations to less than 5 g per day.[1]

4.6.3 Consumption patterns

4.6.3.1 Sugars

Sugars supply on average around 8 per cent of dietary energy worldwide. This figure disguises a wide range of intakes

in different parts of the world. Diets in high-income countries contain roughly twice the amount of sugars as those in lower-income countries. In North America and some European countries, average consumption is around 15–17 per cent of dietary energy, with a fairly wide range around this average. In the USA, in the last decades of the 20th century, many processed foods were reformulated to contain less fat but more sugars. In some parts of Asia, consumption is negligible, although globally sugar supplies are increasing rapidly. Children in high-income countries usually obtain a higher proportion of their daily energy from sugar than adults.[11]

Consumption of sugars has generally increased over the last century, particularly in high-income countries, and also more recently in many countries undergoing economic transition in Asia, Africa, the Middle East, and Latin America.

4.6.3.2 Salt

The use of salt as a preservative has generally decreased as industrial and domestic use of refrigeration has increased (box 4.6.4). But diets containing few salt-preserved foods may nevertheless be high in salt.

The average adult daily intake of salt worldwide varies from less than 6 g to 18 g. Very high levels of intake are found in Japan, some parts of China, Korea, Portugal, Brazil, and other Portuguese-speaking countries, where diets contain substantial amounts of salt-preserved, salt-pickled, salted, or salty foods. The average adult intake is around 9–12 g per day in high-income countries, including Europe and North America.

4.6.4 Interpretation of the evidence

4.6.4.1 General

For general considerations that may affect interpretation of the evidence, see chapters 3.3 and 3.5, and boxes 3.1, 3.2, 3.6 and 3.7.

'Relative risk' (RR) is used in this Report to denote ratio measures of effect, including 'risk ratios', 'rate ratios', 'hazard ratios', and 'odds ratios'.

4.6.4.2 Specific

Classification. Studies of sugars may be of total sugars; of

Box 4.6.4   Refrigeration

Freezing and cooling by use of natural ice and snow is a method of food preservation traditionally available only in cold climates or in winter in temperate climates. Natural ice refrigeration on an industrial scale first developed in the late 19th century, when refrigerated containers used in trains, ships, and then later trucks, greatly increased the production and consumption of red meat. Domestic freezing, chilling, and refrigeration on a mass scale is a phenomenon mostly of the second half of the 20th century.

Today, much perishable food is sold frozen or chilled. Together with the growth of industrial refrigeration, domestic refrigerators began to be used in the USA, Australia, and New Zealand on any scale in the 1920s, and in Europe and Japan mostly since the 1950s. In Japan, for example, households possessing refrigerators increased from 9 per cent in 1960 to 91 per cent in 1970, and 99 per cent in 2004. Supermarkets with freezers, chill cabinets, and domestic refrigerators are now com-

monplace in the cities and towns of tropical countries; poorer rural communities still rely on drying, fermenting, salting, bottling, tinning, and other methods of food preservation, as well as their own gardens and farms. It is unlikely that refrigeration itself has any direct effect on the risk of cancer. Its effects are indirect.

Refrigeration:
- Enables consumption of fresh perishable foods including seasonal vegetables and fruits all year round, as well as of fresh meat.
- Reduces microbial and fungal contamination of perishable foods, notably cereals (grains) and pulses (legumes).
- Reduces the need for and use of salting, smoking, curing, and pickling as methods of preserving vegetables, fruits, and meat.

It can therefore be said that refrigeration (including freezing and chilling) indirectly

influences risk of those cancers, the risk of which is affected by the above factors.

Evidence amounting to a judgement of 'convincing' or 'probable' for such factors is summarised in earlier sections of this chapter, and in Chapter 7, and relates to cancers of the mouth, pharynx, larynx, nasopharynx, oesophagus, lung, stomach, pancreas, liver, and colorectum.

In particular, many studies have noted a reciprocal relationship between use of refrigeration and consumption of salt and foods preserved with salt. Meta-analysis of eight case-control studies[2-9] has shown a significant association between the use of refrigeration (usually as gauged by possession of a domestic refrigerator) and reduced risk of stomach cancer.

The one cohort study[10] identified measured effects in the Netherlands over a 25-year period, in which almost the entire population had access to commercial and domestic refrigeration, and did not find any association.

---

sugars added at the table; of sugary foods and/or drinks; of sucrose; or of added sugars generally; and may or may not include those sugars naturally present in foods. Studies using such varying classifications are difficult to compare. Similarly, studies of salt may be of salt added in cooking and/or at the table; of salty or salted foods; or of salt consumption as a whole. These studies are also difficult to compare. See box 4.6.1 and box 4.6.2.

Measurement. Measurement of salt intake is notoriously difficult, and is best done by measuring the excretion of sodium in urine over a 24-hour period. But this method has only rarely been used.

Study design. See Classification. Also studies may underestimate the amounts of sugars and of salt in foods and drinks consumed outside the home.

Reporting bias. Added sugars are generally regarded as unhealthy, and studies that depend on self-reporting may disproportionately underestimate the consumption of sugars.

4.6.5 Evidence and judgements

The full systematic literature review (SLR) is contained on the CD included with this Report.

The relationship between the intake of sugars and the risk of cancer is often adjusted for total energy intake, meaning that sugars are assessed as a proportion of total dietary energy.[12] Where this is the case, this has been stated.

4.6.5.1 Sugars
Colorectum

One cohort study[13] and 7 case-control studies[14-20] investigated sugars as foods and colorectal cancer. Seven cohort studies[21-27] and 16 case-control studies investigated sugars as nutrients, defined as sucrose or fructose.

Sugars as foods
The single cohort study stated that there was no association between usually adding sugar to cereals and colorectal cancer.[13]

All seven case-control studies showed increased risk with increased sugar intake,[14-20] which was statistically significant in two.[17 18] The classification of 'sugars as foods' varied considerably between studies.

Sugars as nutrients
Four cohort studies reported on total sugar intake.[21 22 25 26] One study reported a non-significant increased risk for the highest intake group when compared to the lowest, with an effect estimate of 1.03 (95% confidence interval (CI) 0.73–1.44).[22] One study reported a non-significant lower sugar intake in cases than controls.[21] Two cohort studies stated that there was no association between sugar intake and risk.[25 26]

Three cohort studies reported on sucrose intake.[23 24 27] Two cohort studies showed non-significant increased risk when comparing the highest intake group against the lowest.[23 27] Effect estimates were 1.45 (95% CI 0.88–2.39)[23] and 1.30 (95% CI 0.99–1.69) in men.[27] One study reported a non-statistically significant decreased risk (0.89 (95% CI 0.72–1.11) in women).[27]

Three cohort studies reported separate results for fructose[23] [24] [27]; one reported a significant increased risk in men of 1.37 (95% CI 1.05–1.78).[27] Two other studies reported non-significant decreased risk.[23] [27]

Because of the abundant prospective data from cohort studies, case-control studies were not summarised.

In most, though not all, animal experiments, sucrose and fructose are associated with increased colonic proliferation and aberrant crypt foci. These sugars may interfere with levels of blood glucose and/or triglycerides, either directly or through hormones like insulin and others (also see Chapter 2).[28]

The evidence is hard to interpret. There is limited evidence suggesting that sugar is a cause of colorectal cancer.

4.6.5.2 Salt
Stomach

Three cohort studies,[10] [29] [30] 21 case-control studies,[2] [4] [31-48] and 12 ecological studies[49-60] investigated total salt use and stomach cancer. Two cohort studies[10] [61] and 13 case-control studies[4] [9] [39] [43] [62-71] investigated salt added at the table; 1 cohort study[72] and 8 case-control studies[4] [39] [73-78] investigated sodium intake.

Total salt use

Two cohort studies showed increased risk with increased salt intake,[10] [30] which was statistically significant in one study in men but not women.[30] One study showed statistically significant decreased risk.[29] Meta-analysis was possible on two cohort studies, giving a summary effect estimate of 1.08 (95% CI 1.00–1.17) per 1 g/day, with moderate heterogeneity (figure 4.6.1). The study that could not be included

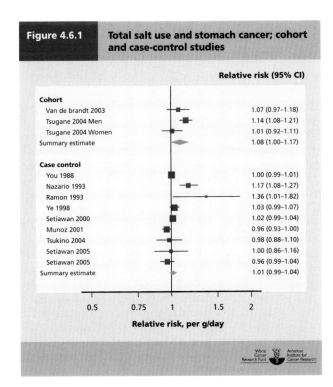

Figure 4.6.1	Total salt use and stomach cancer; cohort and case-control studies

Relative risk (95% CI)

Cohort
Van de brandt 2003	1.07 (0.97–1.18)
Tsugane 2004 Men	1.14 (1.08–1.21)
Tsugane 2004 Women	1.01 (0.92–1.11)
Summary estimate	1.08 (1.00–1.17)

Case control
You 1988	1.00 (0.99–1.01)
Nazario 1993	1.17 (1.08–1.27)
Ramon 1993	1.36 (1.01–1.82)
Ye 1998	1.03 (0.99–1.07)
Setiawan 2000	1.02 (0.99–1.04)
Munoz 2001	0.96 (0.93–1.00)
Tsukino 2004	0.98 (0.88–1.10)
Setiawan 2005	1.00 (0.86–1.16)
Setiawan 2005	0.96 (0.99–1.04)
Summary estimate	1.01 (0.99–1.04)

Relative risk, per g/day

was inconsistent with this summary, with an effect estimate of 0.53 (95% CI 0.31–0.91) for the highest intake group when compared to the lowest; however, this study did not adjust for other factors.[29] The two cohort studies that reported increased risk used much more detailed questionnaires to assess salt intake (150 compared to 27 items). They also adjusted for a greater number of confounders than the study that reported decreased risk.

Twelve of the case-control studies showed increased risk with increased salt intake,[2] [32] [34] [35] [39] [40] [42-46] which was statistically significant in six.[32] [40] [42-45] None of the studies showed statistically significant decreased risk. Most other studies reported either risk estimates close to 1.0 or reported that there was no statistical association. Meta-analysis was possible on eight case-control studies, giving a summary effect estimate of 1.01 (95% CI 0.99–1.04) per 1 g/day, with high heterogeneity (figure 4.6.1).

A dose-response relationship was apparent from cohort but not case-control data.

Seven ecological studies reported increased risk with increased salt intake,[49] [52-55] [57] [58] which was statistically significant in four.[53] [54] [57] [58] The remaining five studies reported either a decreased risk with increased salt intake[50] [56] [59] [60] or no association,[51] none of which was statistically significant. Stomach cancer rates are highest in those areas of the world, such as parts of Asia and Latin America, where diets are traditionally salty due to the regular consumption of meat, fish, vegetables, and other foods preserved by salting, as well as of salty foods.

Salt added at the table

Both cohort studies reported that there was no significant effect, and estimates were close to one (1.0) (95% CI 0.6–1.6)[61] and 0.9 (95% CI 0.56–1.44).[10]

Twelve case-control studies showed increased risk for the highest intake group when compared to the lowest,[4] [9] [39] [43] [62-64] [66-71] which was statistically significant in eight.[4] [9] [43] [62-64] [67] One other study reported similar intakes in cases and control.[65]

Sodium

The single cohort study showed a non-significant decreased risk.[72]

Six case-control studies showed increased risk for the highest intake group when compared to the lowest,[39] [73-77] which was statistically significant in three.[39] [74] [77] Two studies showed decreased risk, which was statistically significant in both.[4] [78] Meta-analysis was possible on five studies, giving a summary effect estimate of 1.18 (95% CI 1.02–1.38) per 1 g/day, with high heterogeneity.[39] [74-76] [78]

Interaction with Helicobacter pylori infection

Two case-control studies that investigated total salt use also investigated the potential for interaction with *H pylori* infection (also see box 7.5.1).[79] [80] One study was suggestive of a multiplicative effect on risk for high salt use and *H pylori* positive status[79]; the other stated that there was no association.[80]

Salt intake may be inversely related to the availability of refrigeration both within and between populations. Salt-preserved foods may be eaten more by those to whom refrigeration is not available.

There is evidence from laboratory experiments that high salt intake damages the lining of the stomach.[81] It has also been shown to increase endogenous *N*-nitroso compound formation.[82] In addition, a high salt diet has been shown to have a synergistic interaction with gastric carcinogens.[82] It may only contribute to gastric cancer in subjects who have *H pylori* infections and are also exposed to a chemical carcinogen.

There is a substantial amount of evidence from studies on total salt use, salt added at the table, and sodium intake. For total salt use, a dose-response relationship was apparent from cohort but not case-control studies. For sodium intake, a dose-response was also apparent from case-control studies. The mechanistic evidence is strong. Salt is a probable cause of stomach cancer.

The Panel is aware that since the conclusion of the SLR, one cohort[83] and two case-control studies[84 85] have been published. This new information does not change the Panel judgement (see box 3.8).

4.6.5.2.1 Salted and salty foods
Stomach

Four cohort studies[86-89], 17 case-control studies[4 6-8 33 41 45 90-99] and 1 ecological study[100] investigated salted or salty foods and stomach cancer.

Three cohort studies showed non-significant increased risk with increased salt intake.[86 88 89] One study reported that there was no association.[87] Meta-analysis was possible on three cohort studies, giving a summary effect estimate of 1.32 (95% CI 0.90–1.95) per one serving/day with

no heterogeneity (figure 4.6.2).

Eleven case-control studies showed increased risk for the highest intake groups when compared to the lowest,[6-8 41 45 91 94-98] which was statistically significant in seven.[6-8 45 94-96] Two studies showed non-significant decreased risk.[4 99] Four studies reported either the same intakes in cases and controls or no statistical association.[33 90 92 93] Meta-analysis was possible on four case-control studies, giving a summary effect estimate of 5.2 (95% CI 2.49–10.83) per one serving/day, with high heterogeneity (figure 4.6.2).

A dose-response relationship is apparent from case-control, but not cohort data (figure 4.6.3).

Heterogeneity may be partly explained by variation between studies in the precise foods being assessed.

The single ecological study showed non-significant decreased risk in areas of increased salt consumption.[100]

The mechanisms through which salt could plausibly cause stomach cancer are given above.

The evidence from both case-control and cohort studies is consistent. A dose-response relationship is apparent from case-control but not cohort studies. There is robust evidence for mechanisms operating in humans. Salted and salty foods are a probable cause of stomach cancer.

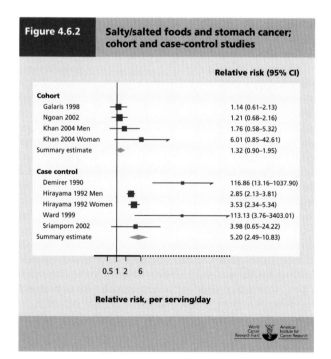

Figure 4.6.2   Salty/salted foods and stomach cancer; cohort and case-control studies

	Relative risk (95% CI)
Cohort	
Galaris 1998	1.14 (0.61–2.13)
Ngoan 2002	1.21 (0.68–2.16)
Khan 2004 Men	1.76 (0.58–5.32)
Khan 2004 Woman	6.01 (0.85–42.61)
Summary estimate	1.32 (0.90–1.95)
Case control	
Demirer 1990	116.86 (13.16–1037.90)
Hirayama 1992 Men	2.85 (2.13–3.81)
Hirayama 1992 Women	3.53 (2.34–5.34)
Ward 1999	113.13 (3.76–3403.01)
Sriamporn 2002	3.98 (0.65–24.22)
Summary estimate	5.20 (2.49–10.83)

Relative risk, per serving/day

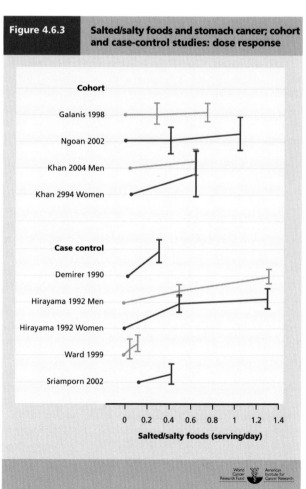

Figure 4.6.3   Salted/salty foods and stomach cancer; cohort and case-control studies: dose response

Cohort: Galanis 1998, Ngoan 2002, Khan 2004 Men, Khan 2994 Women

Case control: Demirer 1990, Hirayama 1992 Men, Hirayama 1992 Women, Ward 1999, Sriamporn 2002

Salted/salty foods (serving/day)

The Panel is aware that since the conclusion of the SLR, two case-control studies[84] [85] have been published. This new information does not change the Panel judgement (see box 3.8).

4.6.6 Comparison with previous report

The judgement of the previous report on sugars and colorectal cancer was in effect similar to that in this Report.

The previous report judged that salt and also salting are probable causes of stomach cancer. This judgement is also much the same as that in this Report.

4.6.7 Conclusions

The Panel concludes:
Salt is a probable cause of stomach cancer. Salted and salty foods are also a probable cause of stomach cancer. There is limited evidence suggesting that sugars are a cause of colorectal cancer.

4.7 Water, fruit juices and other soft drinks, and hot drinks

WATER, FRUIT JUICES, SOFT DRINKS, HOT DRINKS, AND THE RISK OF CANCER

In the judgement of the Panel, the factors listed below modify the risk of cancer. Judgements are graded according to the strength of the evidence.

	DECREASES RISK		INCREASES RISK	
	Exposure	**Cancer site**	**Exposure**	**Cancer site**
Convincing			**Arsenic in drinking water¹**	**Lung**
Probable			**Arsenic in drinking water¹** **Maté²**	**Skin** **Oesophagus**
Limited — suggestive			Arsenic in drinking water¹ Maté² High-temperature drinks	Kidney Bladder Mouth, pharynx, larynx Oesophagus
Substantial effect on risk unlikely		Coffee: pancreas; kidney		

1   The International Agency for Research on Cancer has graded arsenic and arsenic compounds as class 1 carcinogens. The grading for this entry applies specifically to inorganic arsenic in drinking water.
2   As drunk traditionally in parts of South America, scalding hot through a metal straw. Any increased risk of cancer is judged to be caused by epithelial damage resulting from the heat, and not by the herb itself.

For an explanation of all the terms used in the matrix, please see chapter 3.5.1, the text of this section, and the glossary.

Water is essential. Without water, people die in a matter of days. As well as adequate supplies of water, a major public health issue throughout the world is the safety of domestic and other water. Water quality may be compromised by chemical or microbiological contamination.

Fruit juices made from fruits or fruit pulps are often concentrated for storage and transport, then diluted with water to produce the final product. Sugar and other ingredients are frequently added in this final reconstitution process. Soft drinks are usually made from water, sugar, colourings, flavourings, and mixtures of herbs and other ingredients, to give a distinctive taste and character. Consumption of branded, carbonated soft drinks, and cola drinks in particular, has increased greatly in the 20th century, and continues to increase throughout the world. The rise is most marked in lower income groups.

Tea and coffee are now the main hot drinks consumed worldwide. Both contain stimulants and other bioactive constituents, and many people add milk and sugar. A great variety of herbal infusions are also drunk, including maté, the traditional hot drink in parts of South America.

Overall, *the Panel judges* that the direct evidence relating non-alcoholic drinks to cancer is contamination of water supplies with inorganic arsenic and irritation of the oral

cavity by maté, and possibly by other very high-temperature drinks. For evidence relating sugared soft drinks to body fatness, see Chapter 8.

The Panel judges as follows:
The evidence that inorganic arsenic in drinking water is a cause of lung cancer is convincing. Water contaminated in this way is probably a cause of skin cancer. Arsenic and arsenic compounds are recognised carcinogens. There is limited evidence suggesting that water contaminated in this way is a cause of cancers of the kidney and bladder.

Maté, a herbal infusion, as drunk traditionally in parts of Latin America, is probably a cause of oesophageal cancer. Damage caused by the very high temperature of the drink, rather than by the herb itself, is judged to be responsible. There is limited evidence suggesting that maté is a cause of cancers of the mouth, pharynx, and larynx, for the same reason. There is also limited evidence suggesting that high-temperature drinks are a cause of oesophageal cancer.

It is unlikely that coffee has any substantial effect on the risk of cancer either of the pancreas or of the kidney.

Within the remit of this Report, the strongest evidence, corresponding to judgements of 'convincing' or 'probable', shows that inorganic arsenic in drinking water is a cause of lung cancer and probably a cause of skin cancer. Maté is probably a cause of oesophageal cancer. It is unlikely that coffee has any substantial effect on the risk of either cancer of the pancreas or of the kidney.

Chapter 4.7 concerns all non-alcoholic drinks.

Water, including that contained in drinks and foods, is an invariable part of all diets. Bottled spring and mineral waters are consumed by people who can afford them. Juices made from fruits and water, often sweetened (at first with honey and then sugar), have been drunk throughout history. Cordials, squashes, and other drinks made mainly from colourings and flavourings, with some fruit juices, herbs, or other ingredients added, started to become popular from the beginning of the 19th century. Carbonated sweet drinks (sometimes known as sodas) such as cola were first mass-manufactured in the USA and are now commonly consumed throughout the world.

Tea was cultivated and drunk in China for over a thousand years. Then, from the 18th century, it became commonly drunk in Britain, and was cultivated in India and other countries, and drunk in other parts of the world. The original teas were green and drunk without adding milk or sugar. Manufacture of black teas came later; from the 19th century, teas became the main hot stimulant drink in Britain, almost always drunk with milk and often with sugar added. Coffee was cultivated in and exported to many parts of the world from the 19th century; it remains the main cash crop in a number of tropical countries such as Ethiopia and Brazil. Coffee is the main hot stimulant drink in the Americas, many European countries, and also in the Arab world. In some parts of the world, coffee is usually drunk black, with or without sugar; in other countries, milk or cream is often added. Chocolate is also consumed as a beverage.

Reports concerned with infectious diseases, especially of childhood, usually emphasise the importance of safe water supplies. Reports concerned with the prevention of chronic diseases sometimes specify sugared soft drinks as contributors to overweight and obesity. They occasionally recommend substantial consumption of water as healthy in itself and preferable to soft or alcoholic drinks.

Contaminants of water, and also of foods and other drinks, are grouped here with water. High-temperature foods are grouped here with high-temperature drinks.

For the relationship between sugared drinks and body fatness, see Chapter 8.

4.7.1 Definitions, sources

4.7.1.1 Water
Water comes from rain, underground aquifers accessed by wells, springs, and freshwater lakes and rivers.

People cannot live without water, which is vital for the normal functioning of the body. Even mild dehydration (water loss of 1–2 per cent of the body weight) can produce symptoms such as dry mouth and headaches. Stopping all fluid intake may cause death in days, the number depending on

the health of the individual and external conditions such as temperature and humidity.

Water can be used as a vehicle to provide fluoride and can contribute to intakes of essential elements, calcium, iron, and copper, depending on its origin and the piping materials used.

The water content of the body is around 70 per cent: men's bodies contain a higher proportion of water than those of women because women have more body fat, which has minimal amounts of water. Adults produce an average of around 1.5 litres of urine each day and lose an additional litre of water through breathing, from the skin by evaporation or sweating, and in the faeces. Approximately 80 per cent of water intake comes from drinks; food provides the other 20 per cent.

Tap water quality is regulated in most countries based on World Health Organization guidelines for drinking water that includes tap water and bottled water.[1]

Around the world, ground, rain, and river waters are also drunk, often without first being treated to secure safety. More than 1 billion people (around 15 per cent of the world's population) lack access to safe, clean water[2] and are at risk of exposure to water-borne contaminants and infectious diseases. Arsenic, the bacterium *Helicobacter pylori,* and parasitic schistosomes are among the many contaminants that may be found in water supplies. In many low-income countries, access to clean water is limited for the low-income segments of the populations and those living in rural areas.

4.7.1.2 Fruit juices
Fruit juices include liquids extracted from whole or pulped fruits. Commercially prepared fruit juices may be pasteurised to extend shelf-life, and concentrated at source to be reconstituted before packaging, closer to the point of sale.

4.7.1.3 Soft drinks
The term 'soft drinks' is used for a wide range of coloured and flavoured non-alcoholic drinks, usually sold in cans, cartons, or bottles. They may be carbonated (such as cola drinks or lemonade) or still (such as fruit squashes). Some soft drinks are milk-based (milkshakes and yoghurt drinks). Depending on the ingredients, some soft drinks may be marketed with health claims, and are sometimes known as 'functional drinks' (also see box 4.10.2).

4.7.1.4 Hot drinks
The most common hot drinks currently consumed are tea and coffee. These are infusions (brewed using boiling water) usually drunk hot, sometimes very hot (box 4.7.1). Coffee is made from ground, roasted coffee beans — the dried seeds of coffee plant berries. The beans naturally contain caffeine. Decaffeinated coffees are produced by various processes, using water, organic solvents, steam, or by interfering with the expression of the gene coding for caffeine. Instant coffee comprises the soluble solids derived from dried, double-brewed coffee. Coffee is a large bush native to Ethiopia, cultivated in many hot and humid climates. The main coffee-exporting countries are Brazil, Vietnam, and Colombia.

Although many herbal infusions are known as teas, tea is

specifically the infusion of the dried leaves of the plant *Camellia sinensis*. Green tea is made from leaves that have first been cooked, pressed, and dried. To produce black tea, the fresh leaves are withered, rolled repeatedly, allowed to turn deep brown, and then air-dried until they are dark in colour. Tea leaves contain caffeine and theophylline. Decaffeinated teas are produced using similar processes to those used for coffee. Most tea is grown in Asia.

Maté is a type of herbal tea prepared from the dried leaves of the plant *Ilex paraguariensis* that has stimulant properties similar to the other methylxanthine-containing drinks (coffee and tea).

Herbal and other teas are also consumed cold. Iced teas are popular in the USA and some other countries: these are sugared and considered here as soft drinks.

4.7.2 Composition

4.7.2.1 Water

Water is a molecule comprising hydrogen and oxygen: chemically, H_2O. Rainwater may contain traces of air pollutants; water from underground aquifers may contain traces of minerals from surrounding rocks and other surfaces. Ground water may also be contaminated with natural minerals as well as with various industrial and agricultural chemicals, some of which are carcinogenic in laboratory conditions (box 4.7.2). Mineral water from springs and other sources con-

tains higher trace amounts of various minerals and other substances, often detectable to taste. Some spring water is naturally carbonated. Bottled water is either still or carbonated, sometimes artificially. The safety of water in terms of chemical and microbial contamination is well regulated by the WHO programme on chemical safety, but unfortunately, monitoring and surveillance in most countries are limited.

Arsenic residues can arise from agricultural, mining, and industrial practices, or may occur naturally from volcanic activity. WHO guidelines recommend that levels of arsenic in drinking water should not exceed 10 $\mu g/l$.[4] Levels of arsenic in affected areas may range from tens to hundreds, or even thousands, of micrograms per litre. In unaffected areas, levels are typically less than 10 $\mu g/l$. Inorganic arsenic (arsenate or arsenite) is the form that predominantly contaminates drinking water.

Arsenic is classified as a human carcinogen by the International Agency for Research on Cancer. Drinking water contaminated with arsenic is also classed separately as a human carcinogen.[5]

The bacterium *H pylori* is found in water supplies contaminated with faeces. It is an established necessary cause of distal stomach cancer (see box 7.5.1).

Chronic schistosomiasis (infestation with schistosomes) is a known cause of bladder and liver cancer (see chapters 7.16 and 7.8).[6] It is caused by contact with water contaminated by parasite eggs.

Box 4.7.1	High-temperature, and irritant drinks and foods

Constant mechanical irritation of epithelial surfaces causes inflammation, which predisposes to the development of cancer (see Chapter 2). It has also been suggested that foods and drinks with chemically irritant components may be a cause of cancers of those sites with which they come into direct contact. Again, there is not much evidence for this theory, with the possible exception of chilli and stomach cancer (see chapter 4.2).

There is, however, some evidence that some thermally hot (and therefore irritant) drinks are a cause of cancers of those sites with which they come into direct contact. As shown in this section, maté, the herbal infusion, is probably a cause of cancer of the oesophagus, and there is limited evidence suggesting that it is also a cause of other cancers of the oral cavity. This is probably not because of any carcinogen in the herb itself, but because of the way the infusion is traditionally drunk in the pampas region within the southern cone of Latin America, in northern Argentina, Paraguay, and southern Brazil. It is drunk extremely hot from a gourd through a metal straw, which is often kept rested in the mouth, rather like the stem of a tobacco pipe.[3] There is no substantive evidence that maté prepared in the style of tea, loose or in sachets (bags), affects the risk of cancer.

There is also limited evidence suggesting that various other very hot drinks and foods are a cause of cancer of the oesophagus when they are consumed regularly. The implications of this evidence, while so far not strong, suggest that more research may be warranted (see chapter 4.7.5.6).

Box 4.7.2	Contamination of water, and of foods and other drinks

Water contaminants that are causes of cancer are inorganic arsenic (reviewed here) and *Helicobacter pylori* and schistosomes (see Chapter 7).

Many other contaminants of water are identified as or have been thought to be carcinogenic, usually as a result of animal and other experiments, or else as a result of industrial accidents or gross overuse. These include herbicides and pesticides, fertilisers that contain and release nitrates, and disinfectants that also produce potentially toxic contaminants such as chlorinated and brominated organic compounds. They also include chemicals deliberately added to drinking water as public health measures, notably chlorine and fluoride.

These and other industrial, agricultural, and other chemicals are the subject of tests and regulations for toxicity and safety in use. Nevertheless, they are often popularly believed to be significant causes of cancer. This subject is controversial and is likely to remain so.

Currently there is no substantial epidemiological evidence that any of these substances, singly or in combination, as currently regulated and usually consumed in water, or in foods and other drinks, has any significant effect on the risk of any cancer. *The Panel considers* that the evidence is insufficient to conclude that usual intakes of industrial, agricultural, and other chemicals have an effect on the risk of human cancer. Toxicity and carcinogenicity of pollutants as a result of industrial accidents or overuse are outside the scope of this Report.

4.7.2.2 Fruit juices

Bottled or canned or otherwise packaged fruit juices are made from the fruits they contain or from fruit pulp. As well as added water, they usually also contain some added sugars, preservatives, and other additives. They often contain trivial amounts of dietary fibre. Fruit and vegetable juices have different nutritional properties from whole fruits and vegetables. For these reasons, the international 'at least five a day' campaign to encourage people to eat more fruits and vegetables (at least five portions per day) recommends that juices only count as one portion per day, irrespective of the amount consumed.

4.7.2.3 Soft drinks

Soft drinks are made from water, colourings, flavourings, and herbal or other ingredients. They may or may not contain fruit juice. They also contain either sugars or, in 'diet' form, chemical sweeteners (see chapter 4.6 and box 4.6.3). They may or may not be carbonated. The original formulations of cola drinks contained stimulants from the coca and cola plants. Soft drinks may also include yoghurt and other milk derivatives, as yoghurt drinks or fruit 'smoothies', and also added vitamins and minerals. 'Sports' drinks contain sugars, electrolytes, and other additives.

4.7.2.4 Hot drinks

The main hot drinks are tea (usually black tea but also green tea, which is often preferred in China) and coffee. Both contain various antioxidants and phenolic compounds, some of which have been shown to have anti-cancer properties in laboratory conditions.[7] They both also contain caffeine (and the related compound theophylline in tea). There is more caffeine in tea leaves than in coffee beans, but brewed coffee contains more caffeine than brewed tea. Caffeine and theophylline are bioactive, quickening reaction times, relieving fatigue, and stimulating the cardiovascular and central nervous systems.

Tea and coffee, when drunk without adding milk, cream, sugar, lemon, or honey, contain no energy and trivial amounts of some micronutrients; the bioactive chemicals they contain are mentioned above. When these drinks are consumed frequently, both may be substantial dietary sources of some of these bioactive constituents. Thus, coffee is a major source of some antioxidants in the US diet.[8]

4.7.3 Consumption patterns

4.7.3.1 Water

Environmental conditions, health, activity levels, and other factors determine the amount of water needed, but there is no international recommendation for daily consumption. The Institute of Medicine in the USA recommends 2.7 litres per day total water for women and 3.7 litres for men. The UK's Food Standards Agency estimates that most people need to drink at least 1.2 litres of fluids per day. More than half of the world's population has access to drinking water through taps in their homes or outside. Tap water should be regulated to meet international quality guidelines, such as those prepared by WHO.[9]

Most people who do not have access to clean drinking water live in Asia, sub-Saharan Africa, and some parts of Latin America. High concentrations of arsenic in drinking water have been found in areas of Bangladesh, China, and West Bengal (India), and also in more localised areas of Argentina, Australia, Chile, Mexico, Taiwan, China, the USA, and Vietnam. In many of these regions, the drinking water source is groundwater naturally contaminated by arsenic-rich geological formations.[10]

4.7.3.2 Fruit juices

There is little information on the general or local consumption of fruit juices.

4.7.3.3 Soft drinks

In 2004, global consumption of soft drinks was estimated at 480 000 million litres (including bottled water),[11] of which cola and other carbonated drinks accounted for 40 per cent. In terms of sales, carbonated drinks are the largest single category. World sales of cola drinks continue to rise, as do more recently, sales of bottled waters, fruit juices, and 'functional drinks'. The USA is the biggest per capita consumer of soft drinks, followed by Mexico and Chile. The USA alone accounts for more than a 20 per cent share of the global total. Asia is the fastest growing market for soft drinks: sales are increasing at around 3.5 per cent each year.

Average consumption of soft drinks in the USA is around a 12-ounce can (about 350 ml) per person/day. Older children consume about this amount, and sometimes more. Most of these drinks are sugared. At this level, soft drinks contribute a substantial proportion of total sugars intake.

4.7.3.4 Hot drinks

After water, tea and coffee are the most commonly consumed drinks in the world. There are various different methods of preparing these hot drinks depending on culture and personal preference. Coffee consumption is high in northern Europe and North America. Low-income countries export most of the world's coffee; high-income countries consume approximately seven times as much (per capita) as low-income countries.

Average worldwide consumption of tea is around 0.5 kg per person/year; this is exceeded significantly in several Asian countries (notably, China, India, and Japan), and in the UK and Ireland. Worldwide, black tea is the most popular type, although green tea is more commonly drunk in Asia. Maté, as traditionally prepared, is drunk almost exclusively in parts of South America.

4.7.4 Interpretation of the evidence

4.7.4.1 General

For general considerations that may affect interpretation of the evidence, see chapters 3.3 and 3.5, and boxes 3.1, 3.2, 3.6 and 3.7.

'Relative risk' (RR) is used in this Report to denote ratio measures of effect, including 'risk ratios', 'rate ratios', 'hazard ratios', and 'odds ratios'.

4.7.4.2 Specific

Classification. Different types of tea, coffee, and soft drinks are consumed in different cultures. The ways in which tea and coffee are prepared and drunk also vary. For coffee, this includes the degree of roasting, the methods of brewing (which determine the strength and composition), and the different substances added. Similarly, tea may be consumed with or without milk and in different strengths. Associations seen in one population but not another may reflect some aspect of the drink as consumed in that population rather than the drinks themselves. In some studies, fruit juices and bottled waters are included in the definition of soft drinks.

Measurement. Fluid intake is best estimated from urine collection, but this is rarely done. Instead, estimates are usually made from food frequency questionnaires.

Confounding. In interpreting the results of epidemiological studies of all types of drink, confounding by other habits should be considered. For example, heavy consumers of soft drinks, tea, or coffee may also be smokers and drinkers of alcohol.

People who are physically active often consume more liquid than those who are not. Physical activity is therefore a confounder of the relationship between the volume of fluid drunk and cancer risk, but may not be adequately adjusted for.

Reporting bias. Soft and cola drinks are often identified as unhealthy, and studies that depend on self-reporting may disproportionately underestimate consumption.

4.7.5 Evidence and judgements

The full systematic literature review (SLR) is contained on the CD included with this Report.

4.7.5.1 Water

The evidence was too sparse or inconsistent to draw any conclusion about the relationship between water quantity and cancer risk.

4.7.5.1.1 Water-borne contaminants: arsenic

Ecological studies based on known arsenic concentrations in water may be interpreted more robustly than for many other dietary exposures.

Lung

Two cohort studies,[12-17] 2 case-control studies[18][19] and 12 ecological studies[20-30] investigated arsenic in drinking water and lung cancer.

Both cohort studies showed statistically significant increased risk of lung cancer for the highest intake group compared to the lowest.[12-17] Although meta-analysis was not possible, both studies reported that a dose-response relationship was apparent. One study (in Taiwan) based in a population with endemic black foot disease, a manifestation of arsenicosis, reported an effect estimate of 3.29 (95% confidence interval (CI) 1.60–6.78) for average arsenic level in

well water.[13] The other study reported a quantified effect estimate, which was 3.66 (95% CI 1.81–7.03), but this study (based in Japan) did not adjust for smoking.[17]

Both case-control studies showed increased risk of lung cancer for the highest intake group compared to the lowest,[18] [19] which was statistically significant in one.[19] The other study did not report confidence intervals. Effect estimates were 3.01[18] and 8.9 (95% CI 4.0–19.6).[19]

Ecological studies were made in populations from Argentina,[27] Belgium,[21] Chile,[29] China,[23] Switzerland,[20] and Taiwan,[22-26][30] as well as worldwide.[28] Eight studies showed increased risk of lung cancer with increasing levels of arsenic in drinking water,[21-25][27][29][30] which was statistically significant in four.[24][27][29][30] Two studies showed decreased risk,[20][26] which was statistically significant in one.[26] One study reported different inconsistent results for men and women (correlation coefficients of -0.51 for men and 0.07 for women).[28] One study showed that measures to lower arsenic levels in drinking water by using tap water rather than well water were associated with a fall in lung cancer rates in a region of Taiwan with endemic black foot disease.[25]

The general mechanisms through which arsenic could plausibly cause cancer are outlined below. In addition, soluble arsenic in drinking water induces lung cancers in animal models and causes chronic lung disease.[5]

> **The evidence is ample and consistent, both from cohort and case-control as well as ecological studies. There is a dose-response relationship and the effect size is relatively large. There is robust evidence for mechanisms. The evidence that arsenic is a cause of lung cancer is convincing.**

Skin

Two cohort studies,[31][32] 5 case-control studies,[33-37] 1 cross-sectional study,[38] and 11 ecological studies[20][22][24][27][29][30][39-43] investigated arsenic in drinking water and skin cancer.

Both cohort studies showed non-significant increased risk with increasing levels of arsenic in the water[31][32]; however, for one study the increased risk was apparent in women but not in men.[32] Effect estimates were 1.82 (95% CI 0.5–4.66) for women and 0.83 (95% CI 0.17–2.43) for men in Utah,[32] and 1.21 (95% CI 1.00–1.47) per 100 μg/l.[31]

Two case-control studies measured arsenic levels in toe- and fingernails.[36][37] Such measures are less subject to error and bias than some other methods to assess actual exposure to a carcinogen. One study reported a significant increased risk for melanoma with a risk estimate of 1.65 (95% CI 1.27–2.14) per 100 ng/g[36]; the other study reported non-significant increased risk 1.02 (95% CI 0.90–1.17) per 100 ng/g for basal cell carcinoma and 1.12 (95% CI 0.95–1.32) for squamous cell carcinoma.[37]

Two case-control studies that reported on dietary arsenic showed increased risk with increased intake,[33][35] which was statistically significant in one.[33] One study reported a non-significant decreased risk.[34]

The cross-sectional study showed a statistically significant increased risk, with a partially adjusted effect estimate of 5.04 (95% CI 1.07–23.8) for > 0.71 versus 0 parts per million average arsenic content in water.[38]

All 11 ecological studies reported increased risk for skin cancer with increased arsenic exposure,[20 22 24 27 29 30 39-43] which was statistically significant in 4,[24 29 30 40 41] and statistically significant in women but not in men in 1[27]; and significant in men but not women in another study.[20] The effect increased with age (cumulative exposure), where that was measured, and the reported effect estimates were usually large, more than half being greater than 2.5.

The general mechanisms through which arsenic could plausibly cause cancer are outlined below.

The evidence is consistent, from cohort, case-control and ecological studies. There is robust mechanistic evidence. Arsenic is a probable cause of skin cancer.

Kidney

Three cohort studies,[32 44 45] one time-series study,[46] and nine ecological studies[20 22 24 27 29 30 40 47 48] investigated arsenic in drinking water and kidney cancer.

All three cohort studies showed increased risk for the highest intake levels compared to the lowest,[32 44 45] which was statistically significant in one.[45] Effect estimates were 1.49 (95% CI 0.67–3.31; adjusted for smoking),[44] 2.82 (95% CI 1.29–5.36),[45] and 1.13 (women; confidence intervals not reported) and 1.43 (men; confidence intervals not reported).[32]

The single time-series study reported a statistically significant decreased risk in kidney cancer following the installation of a tap water supply system in an arsenic-endemic area of Taiwan.[46]

All nine ecological studies showed increased risk with higher levels of arsenic in drinking water,[20 22 24 27 29 30 40 47 48] which was statistically significant in six.[24 27 30 40 48]

The general mechanisms through which arsenic could plausibly cause cancer are outlined below. In addition, arsenic in drinking water is well absorbed in the gastrointestinal tract, and both inorganic arsenic and its methylated metabolites are excreted in urine.[49] Arsenic can modify the urinary excretion of porphyrins in animals and humans.[50]

The evidence is sparse. There is limited evidence suggesting that arsenic is a cause of kidney cancer.

Bladder

Six cohort studies,[14 17 32 44 45 51] 1 time-series study,[52] 7 case-control studies,[18 53-60] and 11 ecological studies[20 22 24 29 30 40 47 48 61-64] investigated arsenic in drinking water and bladder cancer.

Four cohort studies showed increased risk for the highest intake levels compared to the lowest,[14 17 44 45] which was statistically significant in two.[17 45] One study showed non-significant decreased risk.[32] The single cohort study that measured arsenic levels in finger- or toenails reported an effect estimate of 1.05 (95% CI 0.85–1.29) per 100 ng/g.[51]

Three case-control studies showed increased risk for the highest intake levels compared to the lowest,[18 56-59] which was statistically significant in one.[18] Two studies showed non-significant decreased risk,[53 55] two studies showed no

effect on risk,[54 60] including the single case-control study that measured arsenic levels in finger- or toenails.[60]

Six ecological studies showed increased risk with higher levels of arsenic in drinking water; all were statistically significant.[22 24 29 30 40 62 64] Two studies reported decreased risk,[47 61] which was statistically significant in one.[47] One study showed a non-significant decreased risk in men and a non-significant increased risk in women.[20] Two studies did not provide quantified results.[48 63]

The general mechanisms through which arsenic could plausibly cause cancer are outlined below. In addition, arsenic in drinking water is well absorbed in the gastrointestinal tract, and both inorganic arsenic and its methylated metabolites are excreted in urine.[49] Arsenic can modify the urinary excretion of porphyrins in animals and humans.[50]

The evidence is inconsistent. There is limited evidence suggesting that arsenic is a cause of bladder cancer.

General mechanisms — arsenic
Arsenic is carcinogenic to humans and causes chromosomal abnormalities.[10] It can result in changes in the methylation of oncogenes or tumour-suppressor genes. It also interferes with the activities of several enzymes of the haem biosynthetic pathway. Exposure to arsenite or arsenate results in generation of reduced oxygen species (free radicals) in laboratory animals and human cells. Arsenic biotransformation is thought to deplete cells of reduced glutathione, leading to a state of oxidative stress, characterised by decreased scavenging of free radicals, which can directly damage DNA and induce cell proliferation.[65]

There are several compounds suspected to modulate the chronic environmental toxicity of arsenic –– variables that may either enhance or suppress its genotoxicity and carcinogenicity. Among them are nutritional factors like selenium and zinc, as well as drinking water co-contaminants like antimony.[66]

4.7.5.2 Soft drinks
The evidence was too limited in amount, consistency, or quality to draw any conclusions

4.7.5.3 Fruit juices
The evidence was too limited in amount, consistency, or quality to draw any conclusions.

4.7.5.4 Coffee
Pancreas
Eighteen cohort studies,[67-83] 37 case-control studies,[77 84-119] and 11 ecological studies[120-130] investigated coffee and pancreatic cancer.

Seven cohort studies showed increased risk for the highest intake groups when compared to the lowest,[67 68 71 72 78 80] which was statistically significant in two.[72 80] Seven studies showed non-significant decreased risk.[69 70 73 75 79 81 83] Two studies stated that there was no significant effect on risk.[77 82] One study reported a non-significant increased risk in men and decreased risk in women[76]; and one study reported a non-significant increased risk in women and a non-significant decreased risk in men.[74] Meta-analysis was possible on eight cohort studies, giving a summary effect estimate of 1.00 (95% CI 0.94–1.07) per cup/day, with low heterogeneity (figure 4.7.1).

Some, though not all, of the cohort studies suggest a J-shaped dose-response relationship. An effect at high levels of coffee consumption cannot be excluded.

Case-control studies reported inconsistent results.[77 84-119] Eighteen studies reported increased risk,[84-87 89-91 94 97 99 102-106 112 114 116 119] of which nine were statistically significant.[85 87 94 102 112 114] Eleven studies reported decreased risk,[77 92 93 95]

[96 101 107 109 111 113 118] which was statistically significant in one.[118] Three studies showed no effect on risk[88 98] and one study stated there was no significant effect on risk.[110] Four other studies reported different effects in men and women; however none was statistically significant.[100 108 115 117] Meta-analysis was possible on 26 studies, giving a summary effect estimate of 1.04 (95% CI 1.01–1.07) per cup/day, with moderate heterogeneity (figures 4.7.1 and 4.7.2). Studies that did not adjust for smoking behaviour were more likely to report increased risk. Confounding with smoking could not be excluded.

The ecological studies overall showed an increased mortality between coffee consumption and pancreatic cancer.[120-130] Correlation coefficients ranged from +0.15[122] to +0.59.[124 125]

There is ample evidence, including prospective data, which is consistent and with low heterogeneity, and which fails to show an association. It is unlikely that coffee has any substantial effect on the risk of pancreatic cancer.

Figure 4.7.1	Coffee and pancreatic cancer; cohort and case-control studies

Relative risk (95% CI)

Cohort

	Relative risk (95% CI)
Snowdon 1984	0.98 (0.69–1.40)
Zheng 1993 Men	0.93 (0.81–1.08)
Shibata 1994	1.13 (0.79–1.62)
Stensvold 1994 Men	0.97 (0.83–1.14)
Stensvold 1994 Women	1.08 (0.85–1.37)
Harnack 1997 Women	1.24 (1.02–1.49)
Michaud 2001 Men	0.86 (0.74–1.00)
Michaud 2001 Women	0.96 (0.87–1.07)
Lin 2002 Men	1.14 (0.92–1.41)
Lin 2002 Women	0.86 (0.58–1.26)
Stolzenberg-Solomon 2002 Men	1.05 (0.94–1.17)
Summary estimate	1.00 (0.94–1.07)

Case control

	Relative risk (95% CI)
Elinder 1981	0.85 (0.66–1.09)
MacMahon 1981	1.13 (1.05–1.23)
Wynder 1983 Men	1.01 (0.93–1.10)
Wynder 1983 Women	1.00 (0.90–1.10)
Gold 1985	1.06 (0.89–1.26)
Mack 1986	1.20 (1.07–1.34)
La Vecchia 1987	1.06 (0.89–1.27)
Gorham 1988	1.15 (0.98–1.35)
Falk 1988 Men	1.09 (1.03–1.16)
Falk 1988 Women	1.06 (0.97–1.15)
Clavel 1989 Women	2.00 (1.22–3.28)
Olsen 1989 All respondents	0.97 (0.87–1.08)
Clavel 1989 Men	1.32 (0.91–1.92)
Cuzick 1989	0.93 (0.83–1.05)
Farrow 1990 Men	1.03 (0.94–1.13)
Jain 1991	1.00 (1.00–1.00)
Ghadirian 1991	0.99 (0.93–1.05)
Bueno de Mesquita 1992	0.78 (0.61–1.00)
Stefanati 1992	1.14 (0.80–1.62)
Lyon 1992	1.15 (1.02–1.30)
Zatonski 1993	0.53 (0.27–1.02)
Kalapothaki 1993	0.85 (0.68–1.06)
Sciallero 1993	1.02 (0.84–1.24)
Partanen 1995	0.97 (0.92–1.01)
Gullo 1995	1.25 (1.12–1.40)
Silverman 1998 Men	1.05 (0.98–1.13)
Silverman 1998 Women	1.03 (0.94–1.13)
Villeneuve 2000 Men	1.05 (0.94–1.17)
Villeneuve 2000 Women	0.99 (0.88–1.12)
Kreiger 2001 Women	1.00 (0.77–1.32)
Summary estimate	1.04 (1.01–1.07)

0.5   0.8 1 1.2   2

Relative risk, per cup/day

World Cancer Research Fund   American Institute for Cancer Research

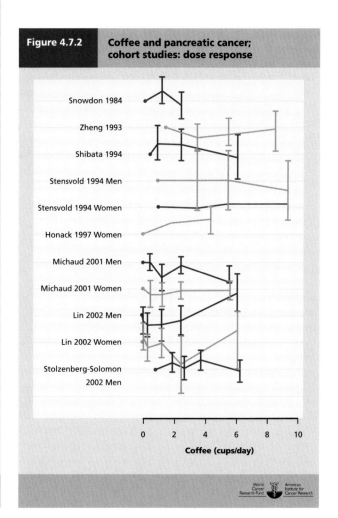

Figure 4.7.2	Coffee and pancreatic cancer; cohort studies: dose response

Snowdon 1984
Zheng 1993
Shibata 1994
Stensvold 1994 Men
Stensvold 1994 Women
Honack 1997 Women
Michaud 2001 Men
Michaud 2001 Women
Lin 2002 Men
Lin 2002 Women
Stolzenberg-Solomon 2002 Men

0   2   4   6   8   10

Coffee (cups/day)

World Cancer Research Fund   American Institute for Cancer Research

Kidney

Five cohort studies,[73 74 131-134] 18 case-control studies,[135-152] and 1 ecological study[153] investigated coffee and kidney cancer.

Two cohort studies showed non-significant decreased risk for the highest intake groups when compared to the lowest.[73 131] One study showed non-significant increased risk[133]; one study stated that there was no association[132 134]; and another study showed non-significant increased risk in women and non-significant decreased risk in men.[74] Effect estimates were 0.15 (95% CI 0.02–1.16),[73] 0.87 (95% CI 0.66–1.16) per cup/day,[131] 2.69 (95% CI 0.89–8.1),[133] and 0.7 (no CI; men) and 1.2 (no CI; women) for highest versus lowest categories of exposure.[74]

The case-control studies reported inconsistent results, only one of which was statistically significant (in women but not in men).[146] Seven studies showed non-significant decreased risk for the highest intake groups when compared to the lowest.[135-138 140 142 143 145] Four studies showed non-significant increased risk[141 144 149 152]; one study reported no effect on risk; four studies stated that there was no association[147 148 150 151]; and two studies showed increased risk in women, which was statistically significant in one,[146] and non-significant decreased risk in men.[139 146] Only four of the best quality case-control studies were able to be meta-analysed, giving a summary estimate of 0.99 (95% CI 0.96–1.01) (figure 4.7.3).

The ecological study reported correlation of incidence of 0.62 for men and 0.4 for women.[153]

There is substantial evidence both from cohort and case-control studies, which is consistent and of low heterogeneity, and which fails to show an association. It is unlikely that coffee has a substantial effect on the risk of kidney cancer.

The Panel is aware that since the conclusion of the SLR, one cohort study[154] has been published. This new information does not change the Panel judgement (see box 3.8).

4.7.5.5 Tea
The evidence was too limited in amount, consistency, or quality to draw any conclusions.

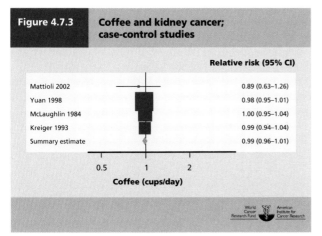

Figure 4.7.3 **Coffee and kidney cancer; case-control studies**

Relative risk (95% CI)

Mattioli 2002	0.89 (0.63–1.26)
Yuan 1998	0.98 (0.95–1.01)
McLaughlin 1984	1.00 (0.95–1.04)
Kreiger 1993	0.99 (0.94–1.04)
Summary estimate	0.99 (0.96–1.01)

Coffee (cups/day)

4.7.5.6 Herbal teas, infusions
4.7.5.6.1 Maté
Oesophagus

Eight case-control studies[155-163] and one ecological study[164] investigated maté and oesophageal cancer.

Seven case-control studies showed increased risk for the highest intake groups when compared to the lowest (figure 4.7.4)[155-159 161-163] which was statistically significant in four.[155 157 159 161] One study showed non-significant decreased risk.[160] Meta-analysis was possible on five studies, all adjusting for smoking, giving a summary effect estimate of 1.16 (95% CI 1.07–1.25) per cup/day, with moderate heterogeneity relating to size but not direction of effect (figure 4.7.5). The two studies not included in the meta-analysis did not adjust for smoking; both reported non-significant increased risk.[156 159]

The single ecological study showed a non-significant relationship between increased maté consumption and oesophageal cancer mortality.[164]

The general mechanisms through which maté could plausibly cause cancer are outlined below.

The evidence, from case-control studies, is consistent and a dose-response relationship is apparent. There is robust evidence for plausible mechanisms. Regular consumption of maté, as drunk in the traditional style in South America, is a probable cause of oesophageal cancer.

Mouth, pharynx, and larynx

Six case-control studies investigated maté and mouth, pharynx, and larynx cancers.[165-170]

All six case-control studies showed increased risk for the highest intake groups when compared to the lowest,[165-170] which was statistically significant in four.[165 167-169]

The general mechanisms through which maté could plausibly cause cancer are outlined below.

The evidence is sparse. There is limited evidence suggesting that maté is a cause of mouth, pharynx, and larynx cancers.

General mechanisms — maté
Maté is typically drunk scalding hot through a metal straw. This produces heat damage in the mouth, pharynx, larynx, and oesophagus. Repeated damage of this nature can lead to cancer (also see Chapter 2). Chemical carcinogenesis from constituents of maté has also been postulated.[171 172]

4.7.5.7 High-temperature foods and drinks
Oesophagus

Three cohort studies[173-176] and 15 case-control studies[162 177-196] investigated hot foods or drinks and oesophageal cancer.

Two cohort studies showed increased risk for consuming high-temperature foods or drinks,[173 174] which was statistically significant in one.[174] The other study stated that there was no association for hot drinks.[175 176] Effect estimates were 1.44 (95% CI 0.91–2.26; hot food),[173] and 1.5 (95% CI 1.1–2.0; men; hot tea) and 1.8 (95% CI 1.1–2.9; women;

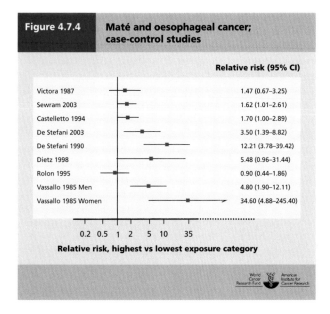

Figure 4.7.4 Maté and oesophageal cancer; case-control studies

Relative risk (95% CI)

Study	RR (95% CI)
Victora 1987	1.47 (0.67–3.25)
Sewram 2003	1.62 (1.01–2.61)
Castelletto 1994	1.70 (1.00–2.89)
De Stefani 2003	3.50 (1.39–8.82)
De Stefani 1990	12.21 (3.78–39.42)
Dietz 1998	5.48 (0.96–31.44)
Rolon 1995	0.90 (0.44–1.86)
Vassallo 1985 Men	4.80 (1.90–12.11)
Vassallo 1985 Women	34.60 (4.88–245.40)

Relative risk, highest vs lowest exposure category

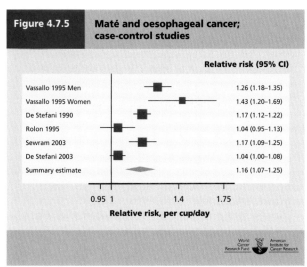

Figure 4.7.5 Maté and oesophageal cancer; case-control studies

Relative risk (95% CI)

Study	RR (95% CI)
Vassallo 1995 Men	1.26 (1.18–1.35)
Vassallo 1995 Women	1.43 (1.20–1.69)
De Stefani 1990	1.17 (1.12–1.22)
Rolon 1995	1.04 (0.95–1.13)
Sewram 2003	1.17 (1.09–1.25)
De Stefani 2003	1.04 (1.00–1.08)
Summary estimate	1.16 (1.07–1.25)

Relative risk, per cup/day

hot tea).[174] Both these studies adjusted for smoking.

Seven case-control studies investigated food temperature[162 178-183 189-191]; seven investigated hot drinks[177 182 184-186 188 192 193]; and four investigated high-temperature hot drinks and soups combined.[191 194-196] For high-temperature food, six studies showed increased risk,[162 178-183 187 189 191] which was statistically significant in three[162 179 180 187 189]; one study showed non-significant decreased risk.[190] For hot drinks, five studies showed increased risk,[177 182 185 186 188] which was statistically significant in four[177 185 186]; two studies showed no significant association[192 193]; one study showed non-significant decreased risk.[184] For hot drinks and soups combined, all four studies showed increased risk,[191 194-196] which was statistically significant in two.[194 195] Several studies did not adjust for smoking or alcohol.[177 180 182 186 194 195]

High-temperature foods and/or drinks produce heat damage in the mouth, pharynx, larynx, and oesophagus.

Repeated damage of this nature can lead to cancer (also see chapter 2.4.1.3).

The evidence is inconsistent. There is limited evidence suggesting that high-temperature drinks are a cause of oesophageal cancer.

4.7.6 Comparison with previous report

Water was not reviewed in the previous report, which had little to say about contaminants in water and did not review arsenic contamination. The previous report did not review soft drinks as such.

The previous report judged that green tea possibly protects against stomach cancer, but this was not supported by the current review. The previous report judged that black tea probably has no relationship with cancers of the stomach, pancreas, and kidney. This time the evidence was judged too limited to draw a clear conclusion. The judgements of the previous report on coffee were practically the same as in this Report, except that the previous report judged that drinking more than five cups per day was a possible cause of bladder cancer. The evidence now indicates that coffee is unlikely to have a substantial effect on risk of this cancer. The previous report judged it possible that maté and other very hot drinks increase the risk of oesophageal cancer. Since the mid-1990s, a greater body of consistent data has been published on maté.

Skin cancer was not reviewed in the previous report.

4.7.7 Conclusions

The Panel concludes:

The evidence that inorganic arsenic in drinking water is a cause of lung cancer is convincing. Water contaminated in this way is probably a cause of skin cancer. There is limited evidence suggesting that water contaminated in this way is a cause of cancers of the kidney and bladder.

Maté is probably a cause of oesophageal cancer when drunk scalding hot through a metal straw, as traditional in parts of South America. The temperature is judged to be responsible for any increased risk of cancer. There is limited evidence suggesting that maté as drunk traditionally is a cause of cancers of the mouth, pharynx, and larynx. There is limited evidence suggesting that high-temperature drinks are a cause of oesophageal cancer.

It is unlikely that coffee has a substantial effect on the risk of cancer either of the pancreas or of the kidney.

4.8 Alcoholic drinks

ALCOHOLIC DRINKS, AND THE RISK OF CANCER

In the judgement of the Panel, the factors listed below modify the risk of cancer. Judgements are graded according to the strength of the evidence.

	DECREASES RISK		INCREASES RISK	
	Exposure	Cancer site	Exposure	Cancer site
Convincing			**Alcoholic drinks**	**Mouth, pharynx and larynx** **Oesophagus** **Colorectum (men)[1]** **Breast (pre- and postmenopause)**
Probable			**Alcoholic drinks**	**Liver[2]** **Colorectum (women)[1]**
Limited — suggestive				
Substantial effect on risk unlikely		Alcoholic drinks (adverse effect): kidney[3]		

1   The judgements for men and women are different because there are fewer data for women. Increased risk is only apparent above a threshold of 30 g/day of ethanol for both sexes.
2   Cirrhosis is an essential precursor of liver cancer caused by alcohol. The International Agency for Research on Cancer has graded alcohol as a class 1 carcinogen for liver cancer. Alcohol alone only causes cirrhosis in the presence of other factors.
3   The evidence was sufficient to judge that alcoholic drinks were unlikely to have an *adverse* effect on the risk of kidney cancer; it was inadequate to draw a conclusion regarding a protective effect.

For an explanation of all the terms used in the matrix, please see chapter 3.5.1, the text of this section, and the glossary.

Many plant and some animal foods can be fermented to produce alcoholic drinks; alcohol has been made this way for thousands of years.

The main alcoholic drinks consumed, in ascending order of alcohol (ethanol) content, are beers and ciders; wines; wines 'fortified' with spirits; and spirits (liquors) and liqueurs. The alcohol content of the many different drinks within each of these categories varies.

Alcoholic drinks induce changes in mood; they also produce physical effects such as loss of coordination. In most countries they are the legal 'intoxicant' of choice, used as a social and professional lubricant; however, certain cultures forbid the drinking of alcohol.

With industrialisation and urbanisation, and the ready availability of alcoholic drinks (which may or may not be taxed), consumption tends to rise.

Alcohol relaxes people's social inhibitions, but it is addictive; dependency on alcohol can seriously affect people's personal and professional lives.

It has been known for a long time that prolonged high consumption of alcohol is a cause of cirrhosis of the liver, though not all people are equally susceptible. Knowledge of its other ill-effects is more recent.

Overall, *the Panel judges* that alcoholic drinks are a cause of cancers of a number of sites and that, in general, the evidence is stronger than it was in the mid-1990s. The evidence does not show any 'safe limit' of intake. The effect is from ethanol, irrespective of the type of drink. Ethanol is classified by the International Agency for Cancer Research as a human carcinogen.

The Panel judges as follows:
The evidence that alcoholic drinks are a cause of cancers of the mouth, pharynx, and larynx, oesophagus, colorectum (men), and breast is convincing. They are probably a cause of liver cancer, and of colorectal cancer in women. It is unlikely that alcoholic drinks have a substantial adverse effect on the risk of kidney cancer.

In final summary, the evidence is that alcoholic drinks are a cause of cancers of the mouth, pharynx, and larynx; the oesophagus; the colorectum in men, and the breast; and probably of liver cancer and colorectal cancer in women. It is unlikely that alcoholic drinks have a substantial adverse effect on the risk of kidney cancer.

Chapter 4.8 concerns all alcoholic drinks.

Alcoholic drinks have been popular in most societies ever

since the effects on mood of the fermented products of plant foods and some animal foods were discovered, probably in Palaeolithic or even earlier times.

Ethanol is the active ingredient in alcoholic drinks; the concentration varies, depending on the type of drink. In the past, beers were made from grains, ciders from fruits, mead from honey, and brews from milk; these were followed by wines, generally made from grapes and with higher concentrations of ethanol. The process of distillation was a later invention, which produced more highly concentrated alcoholic drinks made from grains, fruits, sugar, and other substrates.

Alcohol is liable to be addictive. Its specific effects are to induce a mood of euphoria and disinhibition, which may be dangerous. Much domestic and other violence, and many reckless and violent incidents, and crimes such as arson, wounding, homicide, and car crashes, are alcohol-related.

Reports concerned with food, nutrition, and the prevention of disease have often excluded alcohol. This is because alcohol is also a drug, the impact of which is behavioural and social, as well as biological. More recently, alcoholic drinks have been included in such reports because of the evidence that low to moderate consumption protects against coronary heart disease (but not cerebrovascular disease), and also because of the evidence on cancer, given that ethanol is a human carcinogen.

4.8.1 Definitions and sources

Alcohol is the common term for ethanol, one of a family of alcohols, produced in nature when sugar molecules are broken down to release energy by yeasts. This process of fermentation is used to produce alcoholic drinks. Alcohol is a source of dietary energy (see chapter 4.10.1). It also acts as a drug, affecting both mental and physical responses (alcohol intoxication). Alcoholic drinks include beers, wines, and spirits. Other alcoholic drinks that may be locally important include fermented milks, fermented honey-water (mead), and fermented apples (cider).

Most alcoholic drinks are manufactured industrially. Some are made domestically or illegally, as 'moonshine' or 'hooch'.

4.8.1.1 Beers
Beer, ale, and lager are traditionally produced from barley; today other cereal grains are used. Beer contains between 3 and 7 per cent alcohol. The grain starches are converted to sugars and then fermented by yeasts. The term 'beer' in this Report includes ales and lagers.

4.8.1.2 Wines
Wines are usually produced from grapes and contain between around 9 to 15 per cent alcohol; they are crushed to produce juice and must, which is then fermented. The colour of the grapes and the length of fermentation determine the colour and strength of the final product. Grape vines grow best in temperate regions. Wines can also be produced from other fruits and from rice (sake). Here, wine is taken to mean grape wines. Wines may be fortified with spirits (see chapter 4.8.2.2) to produce drinks of alcohol con-

tent between about 16 and 20 per cent.

4.8.1.3 Spirits/liquors
Spirits are usually produced from cereal grains and sometimes from other plant foods. They are distilled, to give a drink with a higher concentration of ethanol than either beers or wines — around 35–50 per cent or higher. Some of the most globally familiar spirits are brandy (distilled wine), whisky and gin (distilled from grains), rum (from molasses), aguardente also known as cachaça (from sugar), vodka (sometimes from grain, sometimes potatoes), and tequila and mescal (from agave and cactus plants). Spirits and liqueurs are also made from fruits.

4.8.2 Composition

Alcohol has an energy content of 7 kilocalories per gram, and is metabolised in the liver. On average, blood alcohol levels reach a maximum between 30 and 60 minutes after drinking an alcoholic drink, and the body can metabolise 10–15 g alcohol per hour.

Alcohol alters the way the central nervous system functions. Very high alcohol consumption (where blood alcohol reaches 0.4 per cent) can be fatal, as can long-term, regular, high intakes.

4.8.2.1 Beers
There are many varieties of beer, with different compositions. Their alcohol content ranges from around 3 to 7 per cent by volume; beers generally contain a variety of bioavailable phenolic and polyphenolic compounds, which contribute to the taste and colour, many of which have antioxidant properties. Beer is also a source of magnesium, potassium, riboflavin, folate, and other B vitamins.

4.8.2.2 Wines
The composition of wine depends on the grape varieties used, as well as the growing conditions and the wine-making methods, which may vary between vineyards. The alcohol content ranges from around 9 to 15 per cent by volume. Red wines contain high levels of phenolic and polyphenolic compounds (up to a total of around 800–4000 mg/l), particularly resveratrol, derived from the grape skins. Like those in beer, these phenolic compounds add taste and colour. White wines contain fewer phenolics. Red wine has been shown to have antioxidant activity in laboratory experiments. Wine also contains sugars (mainly glucose and fructose), volatile acids (mainly acetic acid), carboxylic acids, and varying levels of calcium, copper, iron, magnesium, potassium, and vitamins B1, B2, B6, and C. Wines may be flavoured with herbs and fortified with spirits (see chapter 4.8.2.3) to produce drinks of alcohol content between about 16 and 20 per cent.

4.8.2.3 Spirits/liquors
The alcohol content of spirits/liquors and liqueurs is usually between 35 and 50 per cent by volume, but can be even higher. Distilled drinks may have herbs and other ingredients added to give them their distinctive character.

4.8.3 Consumption patterns

Much of the information on average consumption of alcoholic drinks, internationally and nationally, is not informative. Within almost all populations, consumption varies widely, usually as a function of availability, price, culture or religion, and dependency. In general, men consume substantially more alcoholic drinks than women. In countries where considerable amounts of alcoholic drinks are produced domestically and by artisanal methods, overall consumption will (if only for this reason) be underestimated. In many countries, alcohol is a public health problem. This is not so much because of the average level of intake, but because a minority of the population, which in high-income countries includes an increasing number of young people, drink alcohol excessively ('binge' drinking).

Worldwide, alcoholic drinks supply an average of 2.3 per cent of total dietary energy. This ranges from around 10 per cent in some northern European countries, to (as recorded) practically zero in Islamic countries. Average consumption is nearly four times higher in high-income compared with low-income countries, and tends to be highest in Europe, North America, and Oceania. Consumption varies within countries: many people do not consume alcoholic drinks, some drink occasionally and others consume 15–25 per cent or more of their dietary energy as alcohol.

Alcoholic drinks are illegal in Islamic countries. In countries where these drinks are legal, there are often restrictions on price and availability to adults, and in particular to young people.

Many countries recommend restriction of alcohol intake for health reasons. In the USA, men are advised not to exceed two drinks per day and women one drink per day. In the UK, the government advises men not to exceed 3–4 units per day and women 2–3 units per day. One US 'drink' is equivalent to about 15 g ethanol, almost two UK units; a unit is 10 ml or 8 g of pure ethanol.

4.8.3.1 Beers
Beers are the most widely consumed alcoholic drinks worldwide. They provide an average of 1 per cent of dietary energy, with a peak of more than 6 per cent in parts of northern Europe. People living in Europe, North America, and Oceania tend to drink the most beer.

4.8.3.2 Wines
Wines provide an average of 0.2 per cent of dietary energy worldwide. They are drunk mainly in Europe, Australasia, and the Americas, with highest levels of consumption in western and southern Europe.

4.8.3.3 Spirits/liquors
There are few data on average consumption of spirits/liquors.

4.8.4 Interpretation of the evidence

4.8.4.1 General
For general considerations that may affect interpretation of the evidence, see chapters 3.3 and 3.5, and boxes 3.1, 3.2, 3.6 and 3.7.

'Relative risk' (RR) is used in this Report to denote ratio measures of effect, including 'risk ratios', 'rate ratios', 'hazard ratios', and 'odds ratios'.

4.8.4.2 Specific
Confounding. At high levels of consumption, the effects of alcohol are heavily confounded by other behaviours, such as smoking tobacco.

Reporting bias. Self-reporting of consumption of alcoholic drinks is liable to underestimate consumption, sometimes grossly, because alcohol is known to be unhealthy and undesirable, and is sometimes drunk secretly. Heavy drinkers usually underestimate their consumption, as do drinkers of illegal or unregulated alcoholic drinks.

Measurement. In recent years, the strength and serving size of some alcoholic drinks have increased. For example, in the UK, wine is commonly served in 250 ml glasses as opposed to the standard 125 or 175 ml glass. In addition, alcohol content of drinks varies widely. Studies that measure consumption in terms of number of drinks may be referring to very different amounts of alcohol (also see box 4.8.1).

4.8.5 Evidence and judgements

The full systematic literature review (SLR) is contained on the CD included with this Report.

4.8.5.1 Alcoholic drinks
There are two different measures of exposure: the number of alcoholic drinks per time period and/or ethanol intake in grams or millilitres per time period. The former measure is likely to be less precise because the size and strength of each drink are unknown.

> **Box 4.8.1   Types of alcoholic drink**
>
> *The Panel judges* that alcoholic drinks are or may be a cause of various cancers, irrespective of the type of alcoholic drink. The causal factor is evidently alcohol (ethanol) itself. There is no significant evidence that alcohol protects against any cancer. The extent to which alcoholic drinks are a cause of various cancers depends on the amount of alcohol drunk.
>
> Epidemiological studies commonly identify the type of alcoholic drink consumed. Some of the evidence reviewed in chapter 4.8.5 does appear to show that some types of drink seem to have different effects. For example, for cancers of the mouth, pharynx, and larynx, the evidence is stronger for consumption of beer and spirits than for wine. Here is the possibility of residual confounding: wine drinkers in many countries tend to have healthier ways of life than beer or spirit drinkers.
>
> Apparent discrepancies in the strength of evidence may also be due partly to variation in the amounts of different types of alcoholic drinks consumed. In general, the evidence suggests similar effects for different types of alcoholic drink.

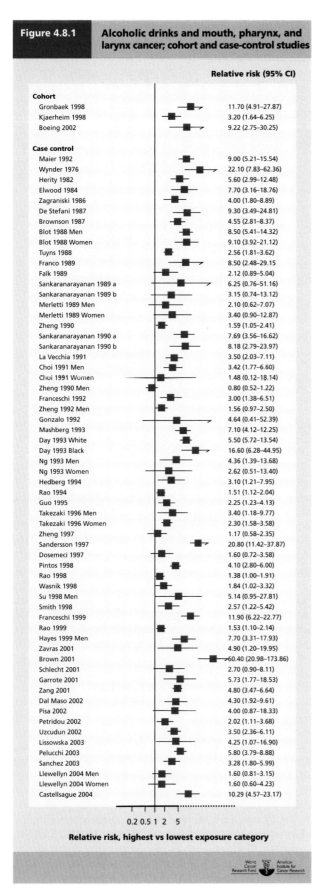

Figure 4.8.1 Alcoholic drinks and mouth, pharynx, and larynx cancer; cohort and case-control studies

Relative risk (95% CI)

Cohort
Gronbaek 1998 — 11.70 (4.91–27.87)
Kjaerheim 1998 — 3.20 (1.64–6.25)
Boeing 2002 — 9.22 (2.75–30.25)

Case control
Maier 1992 — 9.00 (5.21–15.54)
Wynder 1976 — 22.10 (7.83–62.36)
Herity 1982 — 5.60 (2.99–12.48)
Elwood 1984 — 7.70 (3.16–18.76)
Zagraniski 1986 — 4.00 (1.80–8.89)
De Stefani 1987 — 9.30 (3.49–24.81)
Brownson 1987 — 4.55 (2.81–8.37)
Blot 1988 Men — 8.50 (5.41–14.32)
Blot 1988 Women — 9.10 (3.92–21.12)
Tuyns 1988 — 2.56 (1.81–3.62)
Franco 1989 — 8.50 (2.48–29.15)
Falk 1989 — 2.12 (0.89–5.04)
Sankaranarayanan 1989 a — 6.25 (0.76–51.16)
Sankaranarayanan 1989 b — 3.15 (0.74–13.12)
Merletti 1989 Men — 2.10 (0.62–7.07)
Merletti 1989 Women — 3.40 (0.90–12.87)
Zheng 1990 — 1.59 (1.05–2.41)
Sankaranarayanan 1990 a — 7.69 (3.56–16.62)
Sankaranarayanan 1990 b — 8.18 (2.79–23.97)
La Vecchia 1991 — 3.50 (2.03–7.11)
Choi 1991 Men — 3.42 (1.77–6.60)
Choi 1991 Women — 1.48 (0.12–18.14)
Zheng 1990 Men — 0.80 (0.52–1.22)
Franceschi 1992 — 3.00 (1.38–6.51)
Zheng 1992 Men — 1.56 (0.97–2.50)
Gonzalo 1992 — 4.64 (0.41–52.39)
Mashberg 1993 — 7.10 (4.12–12.25)
Day 1993 White — 5.50 (5.72–13.54)
Day 1993 Black — 16.60 (6.28–44.95)
Ng 1993 Men — 4.36 (1.39–13.68)
Ng 1993 Women — 2.62 (0.51–13.40)
Hedberg 1994 — 3.10 (1.21–7.95)
Rao 1994 — 1.51 (1.12–2.04)
Guo 1995 — 2.25 (1.23–4.13)
Takezaki 1996 Men — 3.40 (1.18–9.77)
Takezaki 1996 Women — 2.30 (1.58–3.58)
Zheng 1997 — 1.17 (0.58–2.35)
Sandersson 1997 — 20.80 (11.42–37.87)
Dosemeci 1997 — 1.60 (0.72–3.58)
Pintos 1998 — 4.10 (2.80–6.00)
Rao 1998 — 1.38 (1.00–1.91)
Wasnik 1998 — 1.84 (1.02–3.32)
Su 1998 Men — 5.14 (0.95–27.81)
Smith 1998 — 2.57 (1.22–5.42)
Franceschi 1999 — 11.90 (6.22–22.77)
Rao 1999 — 1.53 (1.10–2.14)
Hayes 1999 Men — 7.70 (3.31–17.93)
Zavras 2001 — 4.90 (1.20–19.95)
Brown 2001 — 60.40 (20.98–173.86)
Schlecht 2001 — 2.70 (0.90–8.11)
Garrote 2001 — 5.73 (1.77–18.53)
Zang 2001 — 4.80 (3.47–6.64)
Dal Maso 2002 — 4.30 (1.92–9.61)
Pisa 2002 — 4.00 (0.87–18.33)
Petridou 2002 — 2.02 (1.11–3.68)
Uzcudun 2002 — 3.50 (2.36–6.11)
Lissowska 2003 — 4.25 (1.07–16.90)
Pelucchi 2003 — 5.80 (3.79–8.88)
Sanchez 2003 — 3.28 (1.80–5.99)
Llewellyn 2004 Men — 1.60 (0.81–3.15)
Llewellyn 2004 Women — 1.60 (0.60–4.23)
Castellsague 2004 — 10.29 (4.57–23.17)

0.2 0.5 1 2 5

Relative risk, highest vs lowest exposure category

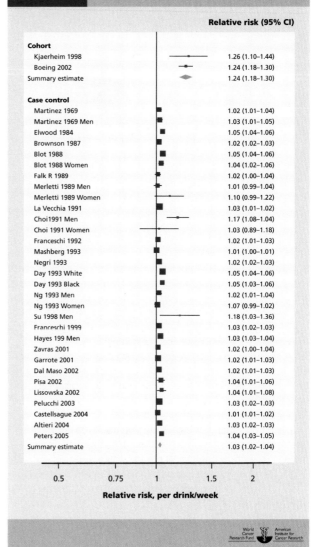

Figure 4.8.2 Alcoholic drinks and mouth, pharynx, and larynx cancer; cohort and case-control studies

Relative risk (95% CI)

Cohort
Kjaerheim 1998 — 1.26 (1.10–1.44)
Boeing 2002 — 1.24 (1.18–1.30)
Summary estimate — 1.24 (1.18–1.30)

Case control
Martinez 1969 — 1.02 (1.01–1.04)
Martinez 1969 Men — 1.03 (1.01–1.05)
Elwood 1984 — 1.05 (1.04–1.06)
Brownson 1987 — 1.02 (1.02–1.03)
Blot 1988 — 1.05 (1.04–1.06)
Blot 1988 Women — 1.04 (1.02–1.06)
Falk R 1989 — 1.02 (1.00–1.04)
Merletti 1989 Men — 1.01 (0.99–1.04)
Merletti 1989 Women — 1.10 (0.99–1.22)
La Vecchia 1991 — 1.03 (1.01–1.02)
Choi1991 Men — 1.17 (1.08–1.04)
Choi 1991 Women — 1.03 (0.89–1.18)
Franceschi 1992 — 1.02 (1.01–1.03)
Mashberg 1993 — 1.01 (1.00–1.01)
Negri 1993 — 1.02 (1.02–1.03)
Day 1993 White — 1.05 (1.04–1.06)
Day 1993 Black — 1.05 (1.03–1.06)
Ng 1993 Men — 1.02 (1.01–1.04)
Ng 1993 Women — 1.07 (0.99–1.02)
Su 1998 Men — 1.18 (1.03–1.36)
Franceschi 1999 — 1.03 (1.02–1.03)
Hayes 199 Men — 1.03 (1.03–1.04)
Zavras 2001 — 1.02 (1.00–1.04)
Garrote 2001 — 1.02 (1.01–1.03)
Dal Maso 2002 — 1.02 (1.01–1.03)
Pisa 2002 — 1.04 (1.01–1.06)
Lissowska 2002 — 1.04 (1.01–1.08)
Pelucchi 2003 — 1.03 (1.01–1.03)
Castellsague 2004 — 1.01 (1.01–1.02)
Altieri 2004 — 1.03 (1.02–1.03)
Peters 2005 — 1.04 (1.03–1.05)
Summary estimate — 1.03 (1.02–1.04)

0.5 0.75 1 1.5 2

Relative risk, per drink/week

Mouth, pharynx, and larynx

Five cohort studies,[1-6] 89 case-control studies,[7-93] and 4 ecological studies[94-97] investigated alcoholic drinks and mouth, pharynx, and larynx cancers.

Total alcoholic drinks

All five cohort studies showed increased risk for the highest intake group when compared to the lowest (figure 4.8.1),[1-6] which was statistically significant in four.[1 2 4 6] Meta-analysis was possible on two studies, giving a summary effect estimate of 1.24 (95% confidence interval (CI) 1.18–1.30) per drink/week, with no heterogeneity (figures 4.8.2 and 4.8.3).[1 2] All cohort studies adjusted for smoking.

Almost all of the case-control studies showed increased risk for the highest intake group when compared to the lowest (figure 4.8.1),[7-19 21-32 34-70 72-93] which was statistically significant in more than half (as can be seen from the high to low

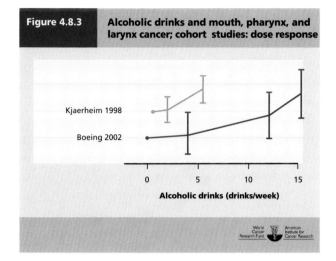

Figure 4.8.3 Alcoholic drinks and mouth, pharynx, and larynx cancer; cohort studies: dose response

Kjaerheim 1998

Boeing 2002

Alcoholic drinks (drinks/week)

Figure 4.8.4 Alcoholic drinks and mouth, pharynx, and larynx cancer; case-control studies: dose response

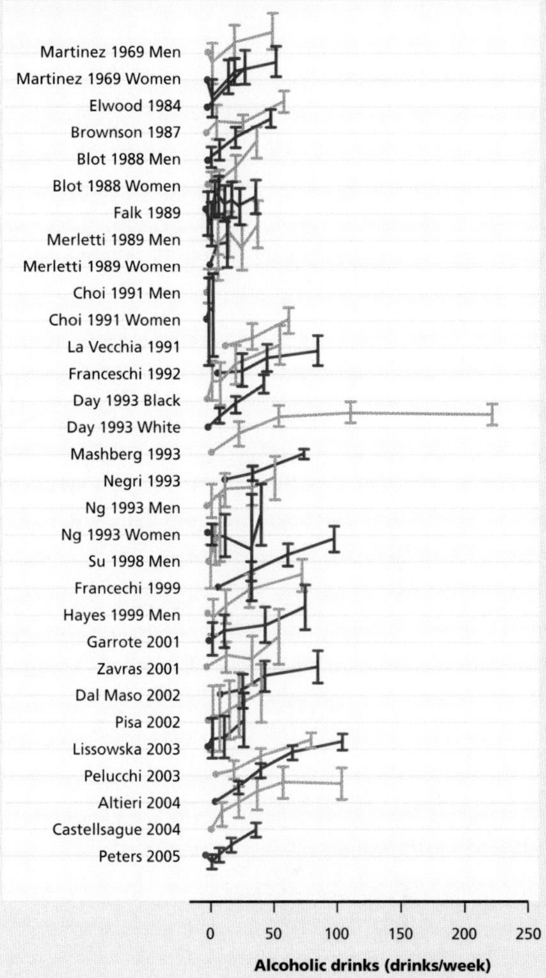

Martinez 1969 Men
Martinez 1969 Women
Elwood 1984
Brownson 1987
Blot 1988 Men
Blot 1988 Women
Falk 1989
Merletti 1989 Men
Merletti 1989 Women
Choi 1991 Men
Choi 1991 Women
La Vecchia 1991
Franceschi 1992
Day 1993 Black
Day 1993 White
Mashberg 1993
Negri 1993
Ng 1993 Men
Ng 1993 Women
Su 1998 Men
Francechi 1999
Hayes 1999 Men
Garrote 2001
Zavras 2001
Dal Maso 2002
Pisa 2002
Lissowska 2003
Pelucchi 2003
Altieri 2004
Castellsague 2004
Peters 2005

Alcoholic drinks (drinks/week)

comparison plot).[8-19 21 23-25 28-32 34-36 40-48 52 54-57 59-67 70 72-75 77-86 89-91 93] No studies reported statistically significant contradictory results. Meta-analysis was possible on 25 studies, giving a summary effect estimate of 1.03 (95% CI 1.02–1.04) per drink/week, with high heterogeneity (figures 4.8.2 and 4.8.4).[17 21 26 27 32 34 35 40-42 52 57 60 62 65 67 69 75 78-80 83-85 89] Heterogeneity related to the size, and not the direction, of effect, and is largely explained by varying design and quality of studies.

A continuous curvilinear dose-response relationship was apparent from cohort and case-control data with no obvious threshold (figures 4.8.3 and 4.8.4).

There was some evidence of publication bias as a result of small studies that did not report a significant association being unpublished. However, such small studies may suffer from issues of quality.

Ecological studies tended to show increased risk with increased consumption.[94-97]

Beers

Two cohort studies,[1 6] 27 case-control studies,[25 26 32 33 36 42 47 58 62 64 65 68 79 83-85 98-105] and 4 ecological studies[94-96 106] reported separately on beer drinking.

Both cohort studies showed statistically significant increased risk with increased intake; both studies adjusted for smoking.[1 6] Almost all case-control studies also showed increased risk,[25 26 32 33 36 42 47 58 62 64 65 68 83-85 98-104] which was statistically significant in many.[36 42 47 62 68 83-85 98-102] Meta-analysis was possible on six case-control studies, giving a summary effect estimate of 1.06 (95% CI 1.03–1.08), with high heterogeneity. Most studies adjusted for smoking. The ecological studies did not show any consistent or statistically significant effect.[94-96 106]

Wines

Twenty-six case-control studies[25 26 32 33 42 58 62 64 65 68 79 83-85 98 99 101 102 104 105 107-109] and four ecological studies[94-96 110] reported separately on wine drinking.

Most of the case-control studies showed increased risk with increased intake,[25 32 33 58 62 64 68 79 84 85 101 102 105 107-109] which

was statistically significant in less than half.[32 33 58 62 68 79 85 108 109] Five studies showed decreased risk,[26 65 83 98 99] which was statistically significant in one.[98 99] Meta-analysis was possible on 11 case-control studies, giving a summary effect estimate of 1.02 (95% CI 1.01–1.03), with high heterogeneity.[32 33 62 68 79 83-85 102 105 109] All studies adjusted for smoking. All four ecological studies showed statistically significant increased risk.[94-96 110]

Spirits

One cohort study,[1] 35 case-control studies,[19 25 26 28 31-33 36 38 42 47 49 50 58 62 64 65 68 79 83-85 98 100-102 104 105 108 109 111-113] and 5 ecological studies[94-96 106 114] reported separately on spirits.

The single cohort study showed a non-significant increased risk with increased intake.[1] Almost all case-control studies showed increased risk, which was statistically significant in many. Meta-analysis was possible on nine case-control studies, giving a summary effect estimate of 1.03 (95% CI 1.04–1.05), with high heterogeneity. Most studies adjusted for smoking. One ecological study reported a significant increased risk; the others tended to show non-significant increased risk in men and non-significant decreased risk in women.

The general mechanisms through which alcohol could plausibly cause cancer are outlined below. In addition, alcohol acts as a synergistic carcinogen with tobacco. Tobacco may induce specific mutations in DNA that are less efficiently repaired in the presence of alcohol. Alcohol may also function as a solvent, enhancing penetration of other carcinogenic molecules into mucosal cells.

There is ample and consistent evidence, both from case-control and cohort studies, with a dose-response relationship. There is robust evidence for mechanisms operating in humans. The evidence that alcoholic drinks are a cause of mouth, pharynx, and larynx cancers is convincing. Alcohol and tobacco together increase the risk of these cancers more than either acting independently. No threshold was identified.

The Panel is aware that since the conclusion of the SLR, one cohort[115] and four case-control studies[116-119] have been published. This new information does not change the Panel judgement (see box 3.8).

Oesophagus

Eight cohort studies,[1 3 120-125] 56 case-control studies,[33 61 67 80 126-182] and 10 ecological studies[2 94 95 114 183-189] investigated alcoholic drinks and oesophageal cancers.

Total alcoholic drinks

Eight cohort studies,[1 3 120-125] 56 case-control studies,[33 61 67 80 126-137 139-182] and 10 ecological studies[2 94 95 114 183-189] reported on total alcoholic drinks.

Six cohort studies showed increased risk for the highest intake group when compared to the lowest (figure 4.8.5),[1 3 120-122 124] which was statistically significant in four,[1 120 122 124] and in men, but not in women in a fifth study.[121] Two studies showed non-significant decreased risk.[123 125] Effect estimates for all studies are shown in the high to low forest plot (figure 4.8.5). Four studies did not adjust for smoking.[122-125]

Most case-control studies showed increased risk for the highest intake group when compared to the lowest (figure 4.8.5),[33 61 67 80 126 128-137 139 141-148 150-166 169 170 172 174 175 177-182] which was statistically significant in 25.[33 61 67 80 128 129 132 133 135 137 139 141 145 147 148 150 152 153 155-166 170 172 174 175 178-180 182]

A few studies showed decreased risk, but none was statistically significant.[140 149 167 168 171 173 176] Meta-analysis was possible on 20 case-control studies, giving a summary effect estimate of 1.04 (95% CI 1.03–1.05) per drink/week, with high heterogeneity (figures 4.8.6 and 4.8.7).[33 61 67 131 133 137 144 149 150 156 157 160 161 170 178-182] Heterogeneity is related predominantly to size, rather than direction, of effect and may

Figure 4.8.5 Alcoholic drinks and oesophageal cancer; cohort and case-control studies

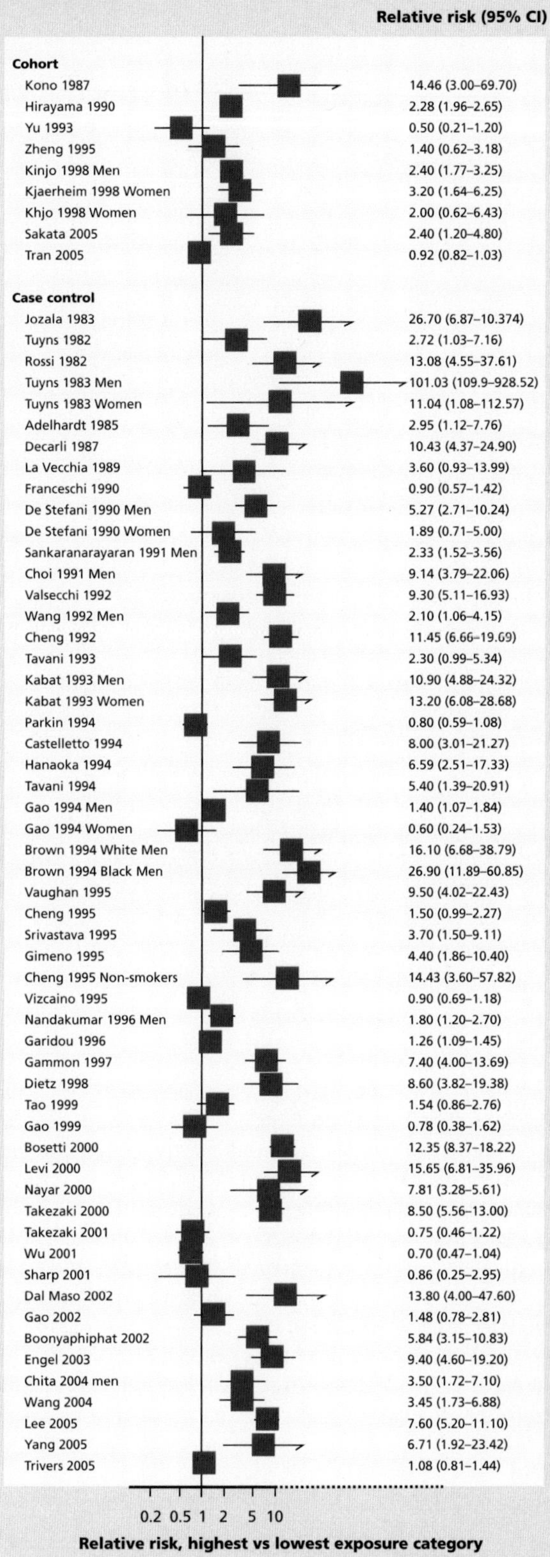

Relative risk (95% CI)

Cohort
Kono 1987	14.46 (3.00–69.70)
Hirayama 1990	2.28 (1.96–2.65)
Yu 1993	0.50 (0.21–1.20)
Zheng 1995	1.40 (0.62–3.18)
Kinjo 1998 Men	2.40 (1.77–3.25)
Kjaerheim 1998 Women	3.20 (1.64–6.25)
Khjo 1998 Women	2.00 (0.62–6.43)
Sakata 2005	2.40 (1.20–4.80)
Tran 2005	0.92 (0.82–1.03)

Case control
Jozala 1983	26.70 (6.87–10.374)
Tuyns 1982	2.72 (1.03–7.16)
Rossi 1982	13.08 (4.55–37.61)
Tuyns 1983 Men	101.03 (109.9–928.52)
Tuyns 1983 Women	11.04 (1.08–112.57)
Adelhardt 1985	2.95 (1.12–7.76)
Decarli 1987	10.43 (4.37–24.90)
La Vecchia 1989	3.60 (0.93–13.99)
Franceschi 1990	0.90 (0.57–1.42)
De Stefani 1990 Men	5.27 (2.71–10.24)
De Stefani 1990 Women	1.89 (0.71–5.00)
Sankaranarayaran 1991 Men	2.33 (1.52–3.56)
Choi 1991 Men	9.14 (3.79–22.06)
Valsecchi 1992	9.30 (5.11–16.93)
Wang 1992 Men	2.10 (1.06–4.15)
Cheng 1992	11.45 (6.66–19.69)
Tavani 1993	2.30 (0.99–5.34)
Kabat 1993 Men	10.90 (4.88–24.32)
Kabat 1993 Women	13.20 (6.08–28.68)
Parkin 1994	0.80 (0.59–1.08)
Castelletto 1994	8.00 (3.01–21.27)
Hanaoka 1994	6.59 (2.51–17.33)
Tavani 1994	5.40 (1.39–20.91)
Gao 1994 Men	1.40 (1.07–1.84)
Gao 1994 Women	0.60 (0.24–1.53)
Brown 1994 White Men	16.10 (6.68–38.79)
Brown 1994 Black Men	26.90 (11.89–60.85)
Vaughan 1995	9.50 (4.02–22.43)
Cheng 1995	1.50 (0.99–2.27)
Srivastava 1995	3.70 (1.50–9.11)
Gimeno 1995	4.40 (1.86–10.40)
Cheng 1995 Non-smokers	14.43 (3.60–57.82)
Vizcaino 1995	0.90 (0.69–1.18)
Nandakumar 1996 Men	1.80 (1.20–2.70)
Garidou 1996	1.26 (1.09–1.45)
Gammon 1997	7.40 (4.00–13.69)
Dietz 1998	8.60 (3.82–19.38)
Tao 1999	1.54 (0.86–2.76)
Gao 1999	0.78 (0.38–1.62)
Bosetti 2000	12.35 (8.37–18.22)
Levi 2000	15.65 (6.81–35.96)
Nayar 2000	7.81 (3.28–5.61)
Takezaki 2000	8.50 (5.56–13.00)
Takezaki 2001	0.75 (0.46–1.22)
Wu 2001	0.70 (0.47–1.04)
Sharp 2001	0.86 (0.25–2.95)
Dal Maso 2002	13.80 (4.00–47.60)
Gao 2002	1.48 (0.78–2.81)
Boonyaphiphat 2002	5.84 (3.15–10.83)
Engel 2003	9.40 (4.60–19.20)
Chita 2004 men	3.50 (1.72–7.10)
Wang 2004	3.45 (1.73–6.88)
Lee 2005	7.60 (5.20–11.10)
Yang 2005	6.71 (1.92–23.42)
Trivers 2005	1.08 (0.81–1.44)

0.2 0.5 1 2 5 10

Relative risk, highest vs lowest exposure category

World Cancer Research Fund / American Institute for Cancer Research

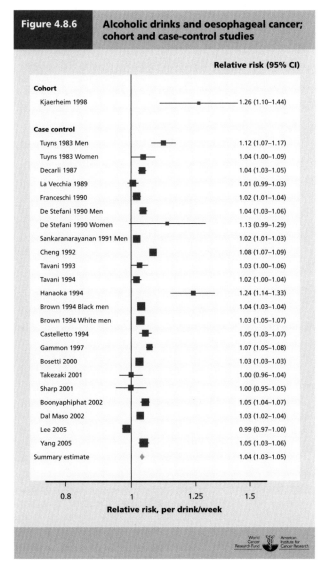

Figure 4.8.6 | **Alcoholic drinks and oesophageal cancer; cohort and case-control studies**

Relative risk (95% CI)

Cohort

| Kjaerheim 1998 | 1.26 (1.10–1.44) |

Case control

Tuyns 1983 Men	1.12 (1.07–1.17)
Tuyns 1983 Women	1.04 (1.00–1.09)
Decarli 1987	1.04 (1.03–1.05)
La Vecchia 1989	1.01 (0.99–1.03)
Franceschi 1990	1.02 (1.01–1.04)
De Stefani 1990 Men	1.04 (1.03–1.06)
De Stefani 1990 Women	1.13 (0.99–1.29)
Sankaranarayanan 1991 Men	1.02 (1.01–1.03)
Cheng 1992	1.08 (1.07–1.09)
Tavani 1993	1.03 (1.00–1.06)
Tavani 1994	1.02 (1.00–1.04)
Hanaoka 1994	1.24 (1.14–1.33)
Brown 1994 Black men	1.04 (1.03–1.04)
Brown 1994 White men	1.03 (1.05–1.07)
Castelletto 1994	1.05 (1.03–1.07)
Gammon 1997	1.07 (1.05–1.08)
Bosetti 2000	1.03 (1.03–1.03)
Takezaki 2001	1.00 (0.96–1.04)
Sharp 2001	1.00 (0.95–1.05)
Boonyaphiphat 2002	1.05 (1.04–1.07)
Dal Maso 2002	1.03 (1.02–1.04)
Lee 2005	0.99 (0.97–1.00)
Yang 2005	1.05 (1.03–1.06)
Summary estimate	1.04 (1.03–1.05)

0.8   1   1.25   1.5

Relative risk, per drink/week

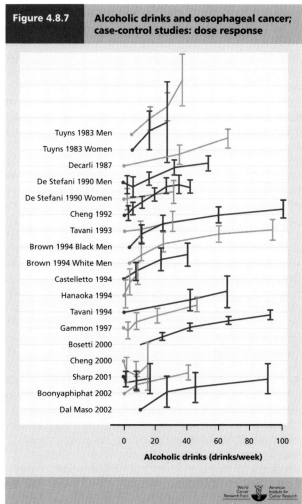

Figure 4.8.7 | **Alcoholic drinks and oesophageal cancer; case-control studies: dose response**

Tuyns 1983 Men
Tuyns 1983 Women
Decarli 1987
De Stefani 1990 Men
De Stefani 1990 Women
Cheng 1992
Tavani 1993
Brown 1994 Black Men
Brown 1994 White Men
Castelletto 1994
Hanaoka 1994
Tavani 1994
Gammon 1997
Bosetti 2000
Cheng 2000
Sharp 2001
Boonyaphiphat 2002
Dal Maso 2002

0   20   40   60   80   100

Alcoholic drinks (drinks/week)

---

be partially explained by the variation in measurement of alcohol intake, variation in the outcome measured (oesophageal or upper aerodigestive tract), or by inadequate adjustment for smoking in some studies. There is a trend for smaller effect estimates from more recent publications, which could be due to improved methods of adjustment for confounders. Not all studies adjusted for smoking.

There is some evidence of publication bias; with smaller studies tending to report larger effects.

The ecological studies were not consistent.[2 94 95 114 183-189] Two reported statistically significant results, both in the direction of increased risk.[94 186]

Beers

One cohort study,[4] 15 case-control studies,[103 129 143 144 159 170 173 176 190-197] and seven ecological studies[94 95 106 184 187 198 199] reported separately on beer drinking.

The single cohort study showed statistically significant increased risk with increased intake after adjustment for

smoking.[4] All case-control studies with the exception of two[173 176] also showed increased risk, which was statistically significant in seven.[103 129 144 159 170 191 193 195-197] Meta-analysis was possible on five case-control studies, giving a summary effect estimate of 1.05 (95% CI 1.03–1.07), with high heterogeneity.[144 159 170 193 197] About half of the studies did not adjust for smoking. The ecological studies were inconsistent and one reported a statistically significant result, which was in the direction of increased risk.[94]

Wines

Ten case-control studies,[143 144 159 161 170 173 190 194 195] one cross-sectional study,[200] and five ecological studies[94 95 106 184 198] reported separately on wine drinking.

All but one of the case-control studies showed increased risk with increased intake,[144] which was statistically significant in seven.[159 161 170 190 195] About half of the studies adjusted for smoking. The single cross-sectional study showed non-significant increased risk.[200] Most ecological

163

studies were in the direction of increased risk.[94 106 184 198]

Spirits

One cohort study,[4] 15 case-control studies,[139 143-145 159 170 173 181 190 191 194-196 201 202] one cross-sectional study,[200] and five ecological studies[94 95 106 184 198] reported separately on spirits.

The single cohort study showed statistically significant increased risk with increased intake after adjustment for smoking.[4] All of the case-control studies also showed increased risk, which was statistically significant in eight.[139 144 145 191 194 195 201 202] Most studies adjusted for smoking. The single cross-sectional study showed non-significant increased risk.[200] The ecological studies were inconsistent and two reported statistically significant results; both were in the direction of increased risk.[94 106]

The general mechanisms through which alcohol could plausibly cause cancer are outlined below. In addition, alcohol acts as a synergistic carcinogen with tobacco. Tobacco may induce specific mutations in DNA that are less efficiently repaired in the presence of alcohol. Alcohol may also function as a solvent, enhancing penetration of other carcinogenic molecules into mucosal cells.

There is ample and consistent evidence, both from cohort and case-control studies, with a dose-response relationship. There is robust evidence for mechanisms operating in humans. The evidence that alcoholic drinks are a cause of oesophageal cancer is convincing. No threshold was identified.

The Panel is aware that since the conclusion of the SLR, one cohort[203] and four case-control studies[204-207] have been published. This new information does not change the Panel judgement (see box 3.8).

Colorectum

Twenty-four cohort studies investigated alcoholic drinks and colorectal cancer.[124 208-235] Thirteen cohort studies[214 216 219 227 230 232 236-251] and 41 case-control studies investigated ethanol intake and colorectal cancer.

Total alcoholic drinks

Eighteen cohort studies showed increased risk for the highest intake group when compared to the lowest,[124 209 210 212-217 220-223 225-228 233-235] which was statistically significant in four.[209 210 216 227] One study showed non-significant increased risk in men and non-significant decreased risk in women.[211 219] Two studies reported no effect on risk[218 231] and three studies reported decreased risk; none was statistically significant.[208 224 229 230 232] Meta-analysis was possible on six cohort studies, giving a summary effect estimate of 1.01 (95% CI 0.95–1.08) per drink/day, with no heterogeneity (figure 4.8.8).

Alcohol (as ethanol)

Eleven of the cohort studies showed increased risk for the highest intake group when compared to the lowest (figure 4.8.9),[214 216 219 227 230 232 237 239-251] which was statistically significant in six.[219 227 230 240 244 245 251] One study reported no

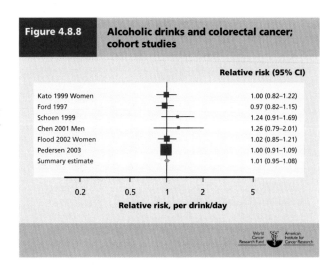

Figure 4.8.8 — Alcoholic drinks and colorectal cancer; cohort studies

Relative risk (95% CI)

	Relative risk (95% CI)
Kato 1999 Women	1.00 (0.82–1.22)
Ford 1997	0.97 (0.82–1.15)
Schoen 1999	1.24 (0.91–1.69)
Chen 2001 Men	1.26 (0.79–2.01)
Flood 2002 Women	1.02 (0.85–1.21)
Pedersen 2003	1.00 (0.91–1.09)
Summary estimate	1.01 (0.95–1.08)

Relative risk, per drink/day

effect on risk for men and non-significant decreased risk for women,[238] and one study reported no statistically significant association.[236] Meta-analysis was possible on nine cohort studies, of which one reported on colorectal cancer and eight reported on colon cancer, giving a summary effect estimate of 1.09 (95% CI 1.03–1.14) per 10 g/day, with moderate heterogeneity(figures 4.8.10 and 4.8.11).

In a separate meta-analysis of nine studies for rectal cancer, the summary effect estimate was 1.06 (95% CI 1.01–1.12) per 10 g/day, with low heterogeneity (figure 4.8.12). It is apparent from the meta-analysis that the reported effect for men was larger and more often statistically significant than for women. Stratified meta-analyses for colorectal cancer gave summary effect estimates of 1.09 (95% CI 1.02–1.15) for seven studies for men, and 1.00 (95% CI 0.89–1.40) for three studies for women. There was no statistically significant difference with cancer site. There was, however, apparent sexual dimorphism, with a larger effect in men than in women, which explains the bulk of the observed heterogeneity.

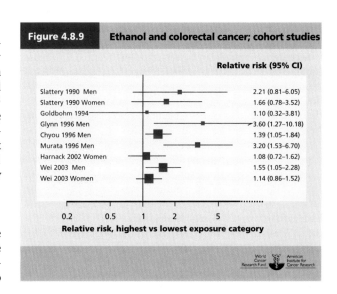

Figure 4.8.9 — Ethanol and colorectal cancer; cohort studies

Relative risk (95% CI)

	Relative risk (95% CI)
Slattery 1990 Men	2.21 (0.81–6.05)
Slattery 1990 Women	1.66 (0.78–3.52)
Goldbohm 1994	1.10 (0.32–3.81)
Glynn 1996 Men	3.60 (1.27–10.18)
Chyou 1996 Men	1.39 (1.05–1.84)
Murata 1996 Men	3.20 (1.53–6.70)
Harnack 2002 Women	1.08 (0.72–1.62)
Wei 2003 Men	1.55 (1.05–2.28)
Wei 2003 Women	1.14 (0.86–1.52)

Relative risk, highest vs lowest exposure category

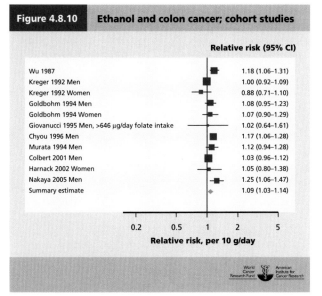

Figure 4.8.10 Ethanol and colon cancer; cohort studies

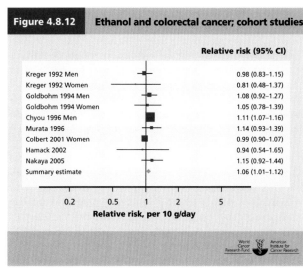

Figure 4.8.12 Ethanol and colorectal cancer; cohort studies

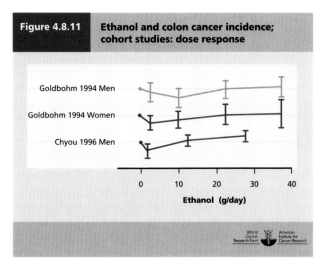

Figure 4.8.11 Ethanol and colon cancer incidence; cohort studies: dose response

When data were analysed separately for drink type (beers, wines, or spirits), they became insufficient to draw any firm conclusions.

Pooled analysis from 8 cohort studies (over 475 000 participants, followed up for 6 to 16 years, more than 4600 colorectal cancer cases) showed a significant increased risk for the highest intake group when compared to the lowest, with an effect estimate of 1.41 (95% CI 1.16–1.72) for those who consumed 45 g/day or greater.[252] No increased risk was observed below intakes of 30 g/day. No significant heterogeneity was observed by sex or cancer site.

In addition, a published meta-analysis of 27 studies reported a statistically significant increased risk, with a summary effect estimate of 1.10 (95% CI 1.05–1.14) per two drinks/day.

Because of the abundant prospective data from cohort studies, case-control studies were not summarized.

The general mechanisms through which alcohol could plausibly cause cancer are outlined below. In addition, the association between alcohol intake and colorectal cancer risk is modified by acetaldehyde dehydrogenase and alcohol dehydrogenase genetic status.[253 254] Alcohol may induce folate deficiency in the colon and rectum, possibly by reducing absorption of folate or by inhibition of critical enzymes. Also, alcohol may disrupt one-carbon metabolism (see Chapter 2). Intestinal bacteria, because of their high alcohol dehydrogenase activity, can oxidise ethanol in colorectal tissue to produce levels of acetaldehyde up to 1000-fold higher than that in blood.

The more elevated risk related to alcohol intake among men compared with women may be because of the generally lower consumption of alcohol among women. That is, it is possible that men exhibit a greater range in the amount of alcohol drunk, which makes effects easier to detect. Also, preferred beverages may differ between the sexes, or there may be hormone-related differences in alcohol metabolism or susceptibility to alcohol.

There is ample and generally consistent evidence from cohort studies. A dose-response is apparent. There is evidence for plausible mechanisms. The evidence that consumption of more than 30 g/day of ethanol from alcoholic drinks is a cause of colorectal cancer in men is convincing, and probably also in women.

The Panel is aware that since the conclusion of the SLR, four cohort[255-258] and four case-control studies[259-262] have been published. This new information does not change the Panel judgement (see box 3.8).

Breast

Eleven cohort studies,[183 263-271] 31 case-control studies[272-310] and 2 ecological studies[311 312] investigated total alcoholic drinks and breast cancer at all ages. Four cohort studies[313-316] and 19 case-control studies[289 302 317-333] investigated alcoholic drinks. Twenty-five cohort studies,[315 334-364] 29 case-control studies,[280 282 317 318 332 333 365-391] and 4 ecological studies[392-395] investigated ethanol intake.

Total alcoholic drinks

Six cohort studies showed increased risk for the highest intake group of total alcoholic drinks when compared to the lowest,[263 264 267-271] which was statistically significant in three.[267 269 270] Three studies showed non-significant decreased risk[265 266]; one study showed no effect on risk.[183] Meta-analysis was possible on three cohort studies, giving a summary effect estimate of 1.07 (95% CI 0.89–1.29) per five times/week, with no heterogeneity (figures 4.8.13 and 4.8.14).[263 271]

Two cohort studies reported separately on premenopausal breast cancer.[264 268] Both showed increased risk for the highest intake group when compared to the lowest, which was statistically significant in one.[268] Three cohort studies reported separately on postmenopausal breast cancer.[264 268 269] Two showed increased risk for the highest intake group when compared to the lowest,[264 269] which was statistically significant in one.[269] The other study showed non-significant decreased risk.[268]

Four additional cohort studies investigated alcoholic drinks.[313-316] All four showed non-significant increased risk for breast cancer at unspecified ages. One study also reported statistically significant increased risk for postmenopausal breast cancer and non-significant decreased risk for premenopausal breast cancer.[315]

Most of the 22 case-control studies that reported on all-age breast cancer and total alcoholic drinks showed increased risk for the highest intake group when compared to the lowest,[273 274 280 282-285 287 288 290 295 297 301-303 305-309 318] which was statistically significant in seven.[273 284 285 306 318] A few studies showed decreased risk, none was statistically significant.[276 291 295 298 302 304] Meta-analysis was possible on 10 case-control studies reporting on breast cancer at all ages, giving a summary estimate of 1.05 (95% CI 1.03–1.07) for an increment of five times/week, with high heterogeneity (figures 4.8.13 and 4.8.14).[274 276 284 286 287 296 306 307] No heterogeneity was apparent with menopausal status. Twelve case-control studies reported separately on premenopausal breast cancer.[272 275 277-279 281 282 292-294 297 299 300 306 310 318] Ten showed increased risk,[272 275 277 279 281 292-294 299 300 306 318] which was statistically significant in two.[272 281 294 299 300 306] One study showed no effect on risk[297] and the other study showed non-significant decreased risk.[278 282 310] Six studies reported separately on postmenopausal breast cancer.[277 278 281 282 289 297 306 310] Five of these showed increased risk,[278 281 282 289 306 310] which was statistically significant in one.[306] The other study reported non-significant decreased risk.[297]

In addition, 19 case-control studies investigated alcoholic drinks.[289 302 318-323 325-331 333] Most showed increased risk for the highest intake group when compared to the lowest, which was statistically significant in six.[302 318 321 323 327 329] Two studies showed non-significant decreased risk[317 324]; one study showed no effect on risk.[332] Four studies reported separate results for premenopausal breast cancer.[318 320 322 333] Of these, two studies showed non-significant increased risk,[318 333] one showed statistically significant increased risk in

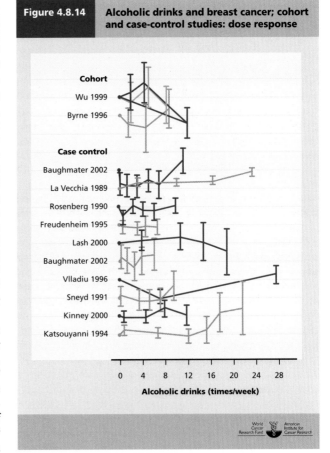

Figure 4.8.13 | **Alcoholic drinks and breast cancer; cohort and case-control studies**

Relative risk (95% CI)

Cohort
Wu 1999	1.38 (0.84–2.26)
Wu 1999	1.08 (0.78–1.50)
Byrne 1996	0.99 (0.77–1.28)
Summary estimate	1.07 (0.89–1.29)

Case control
La Vecchia 1989	1.10 (1.07–1.13)
Baumgartner 2002	1.07 (0.82–1.38)
Katsoyannis 1994	1.05 (0.97–1.12)
Kinney 2000	1.03 (0.92–1.15)
Lash 2000	1.01 (0.86–1.19)
Rosenberg 1990	0.97 (0.86–1.10)
Viladiu 1996	0.97 (0.93–1.11)
Freudenheim 1995	0.94 (0.79–1.13)
Sneyd 1991	0.94 (0.81–1.09)
Baughmater 2002	0.90 (0.79–1.03)
Summary estimate	1.05 (1.03–1.07)

Relative risk, per 5 times/week

Figure 4.8.14 | **Alcoholic drinks and breast cancer; cohort and case-control studies: dose response**

Cohort
Wu 1999
Byrne 1996

Case control
Baughmater 2002
La Vecchia 1989
Rosenberg 1990
Freudenheim 1995
Lash 2000
Baughmater 2002
Vlladiu 1996
Sneyd 1991
Kinney 2000
Katsouyanni 1994

Alcoholic drinks (times/week)

parous women,[322] and one showed non-significant decreased risk.[320] Seven studies reported separately on postmenopausal breast cancer.[289 318 320-322 326 333] All seven studies showed increased risk for the highest intake group when compared to the lowest, which was statistically significant in three,[318] [321 333] and in oestrogen-sensitive cancers in a fourth study.[326]

Both ecological studies showed statistically significant, positive associations.[311 312]

When data were analysed separately for drink type (beers, wines, or spirits), they became insufficient to draw any firm conclusions.

Alcohol (as ethanol)

Twelve cohort studies investigated ethanol intake and all-age breast cancer.[315 336 338-341 343-350 352-354 361-364] Eight cohort studies showed increased risk for the highest intake group when compared to the lowest,[315 336 338-341 343 344 346-348 350 352-354 361] [362] which was statistically significant in six.[338 341 344 350 352 354] [361] Four studies showed decreased risk,[345 349 363 364] which was statistically significant in one.[364] Meta-analysis was possible on nine cohort studies, giving a summary effect estimate of 1.10 (95% CI 1.06–1.14) per 10 g/day, with high heterogeneity (figure 4.8.15). Heterogeneity could be partly explained by differential adjustment for age and reproductive history.

Seven cohort studies reported separately on premenopausal breast cancer.[315 340 343 347 348 352-354 361] Six studies showed increased risk,[340 343 347 348 352-354 361] which was statistically significant in three.[340 348 352] One study showed a non-significant decreased risk.[315] Meta-analysis was possible on five studies, giving a summary estimate of 1.09 (95% CI 1.01–1.17) per 10 g/day, with moderate heterogeneity.[315] [340 343 347 352] Eighteen cohort studies reported separately on postmenopausal breast cancer.[315 334 335 337 339 340 342 347 348 351-361] Fifteen studies showed increased risk,[315 335 337 339 342 347] [348 351 353-361] which was statistically significant in seven.[315 335] [337 339 342 347 357-359] Three studies showed non-significant decreased risk.[334 340 352] Meta-analysis was possible on 11 studies, giving a summary effect estimate of 1.08 (95% CI 1.05–1.10) per 10g/day, with moderate heterogeneity.[315 334 335 339 340 347 352 355 358-360]

Pooled analysis from 6 cohort studies (over 320 000 participants, followed up for up to 11 years, more than 4300 breast cancer cases) showed a significant increased risk with increasing intake, with an effect estimate of 1.09 (95% CI 1.04–1.03) per 10 g/day.[396] No significant heterogeneity was observed by menopausal status.

A separate pooled analysis of 53 case-control studies (more than 58 000 cases and more than 95 000 controls) showed a significant increased risk with increasing intake, with an effect estimate of 7.1 per cent increased risk (95% CI 5.5–8.7%; p < 0.00001) per 10 g/day.[397] No significant heterogeneity was observed by menopausal status.

Eighteen case-control studies investigated ethanol intake and all-age breast cancer.[280 282 317 318 332 365-371 374 378 379 381 383 384 386 387 390 391] Twelve case-control studies showed increased risk for the highest intake group when compared to the lowest,[280 318 332 365 367-369 374 379 381 383 384 386 387 391] which was statistically significant in five.[280 318 368 369 374 381 384] Five studies

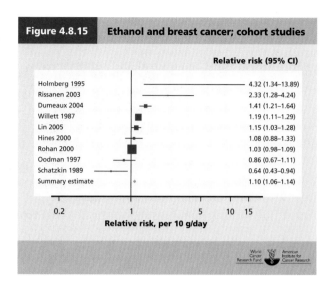

Figure 4.8.15 Ethanol and breast cancer; cohort studies

Relative risk (95% CI)

Holmberg 1995	4.32 (1.34–13.89)
Rissanen 2003	2.33 (1.28–4.24)
Dumeaux 2004	1.41 (1.21–1.64)
Willett 1987	1.19 (1.11–1.29)
Lin 2005	1.15 (1.03–1.28)
Hines 2000	1.08 (0.88–1.33)
Rohan 2000	1.03 (0.98–1.09)
Oodman 1997	0.86 (0.67–1.11)
Schatzkin 1989	0.64 (0.43–0.94)
Summary estimate	1.10 (1.06–1.14)

Relative risk, per 10 g/day

showed decreased risk,[317 366 370 371 378 390] which was statistically significant in one[378]; and one study showed no effect on risk.[282] Meta-analysis was possible on seven case-control studies, giving a summary effect estimate of 1.06 (95% CI 1.04–1.09) per 10 g/day, with moderate heterogeneity (figure 4.8.16).

When case-control data were analysed separately by menopausal status, the meta-analysis for premenopausal breast cancer was consistent with that for all ages (1.08 (95% CI 1.04–1.13) per 10 g/day; nine studies),[317 318 369 373 376 377 380 383 389] but the meta-analysis for postmenopausal breast cancer was not (1.00 (95% CI 0.98–1.01) per 10 g/day; 10 studies).[318 369 372 373 375 380 382 383 385 388]

All four ecological studies showed statistically significant positive associations.[392-395]

The general mechanisms through which alcohol could plausibly cause cancer are outlined below. In addition, most experimental studies in animals have shown that alcohol intake is associated with increased breast cancer risk. Alcohol interferes with oestrogen pathways in multiple ways,

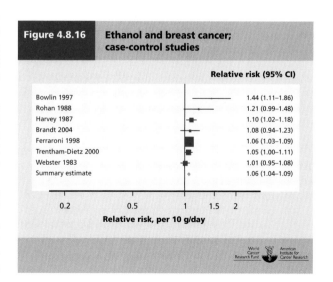

Figure 4.8.16 Ethanol and breast cancer; case-control studies

Relative risk (95% CI)

Bowlin 1997	1.44 (1.11–1.86)
Rohan 1988	1.21 (0.99–1.48)
Harvey 1987	1.10 (1.02–1.18)
Brandt 2004	1.08 (0.94–1.23)
Ferraroni 1998	1.06 (1.03–1.09)
Trentham-Dietz 2000	1.05 (1.00–1.11)
Webster 1983	1.01 (0.95–1.08)
Summary estimate	1.06 (1.04–1.09)

Relative risk, per 10 g/day

influencing hormone levels and oestrogen receptors.[398]

There is an interaction between folate and alcohol affecting breast cancer risk: increased folate status partially mitigates the risk from increased alcohol consumption.[399]

There is ample, generally consistent evidence from case-control and cohort studies. A dose-response relationship is apparent. There is robust evidence for mechanisms operating in humans. The evidence that alcoholic drinks are a cause of premenopausal and postmenopausal breast cancer is convincing. No threshold was identified.

The Panel is aware that since the conclusion of the SLR, one case-control study[400] has been published. This new information does not change the Panel judgement (see box 3.8).

Liver

Fifteen cohort studies[120 208 220 227 401-422] and 33 case-control studies[158 423-460] investigated alcoholic drinks and liver cancer. Fourteen cohort studies[6 120 227 244 403 404 409 410 412 416 422 461-468] and 21 case-control studies[158 427 431 434 436 440 446 452 456 459 469-485] investigated ethanol intake.

Total alcoholic drinks

Data are available from 15 cohort studies.[120 208 220 227 401-422] Eleven cohort studies showed increased risk for the highest intake group when compared to the lowest,[120 220 227 401-404 407-410 413 414 416 417 420 422] which was statistically significant in two.[120 401] Two studies showed non-significant decreased risk.[405 406 412 418 419] Two studies stated that there was no significant difference but did not provide further data.[411 415 421] Heterogeneity is partially explained by differences in whether and how studies have adjusted for hepatitis virus status. The effect estimates of eight studies are given in the high to low comparison forest plot (figure 4.8.17).

Data are available from 33 case-control studies.[158 423-460] Twenty-eight case-control studies showed increased risk for the highest intake group when compared to the lowest,[158 423-432 434-448 451-456 460] which was statistically significant in 12 (one of these studies reported a non-significant decreased risk in women, but a statistically significant increased risk in men[440]).[158 423 427 429-432 434 439 440 442 444 446 447 454-456] Two studies showed non-significant decreased risk.[449] Three studies stated that there was no significant effect on risk.[433 450 457-459] Meta-analysis was possible on five studies, giving a summary effect estimate of 1.18 (95% CI 1.11–1.26) per drink/week, with high heterogeneity (figure 4.8.18).[158 425 434 449 460]

A dose-response relationship is apparent from case-control but not cohort data.

Alcohol (as ethanol)

Ten cohort studies showed increased risk for the highest intake group when compared to the lowest,[6 120 244 403 404 409 410 416 422 461 465-468] which was statistically significant in five (one of these studies reported a non-significant increased risk in women, but a statistically significant increased risk in men[461]).[6 120 244 416 461 465 468] Three studies in men with cirrhosis showed non-significant decreased risk.[227 412 462 463] One

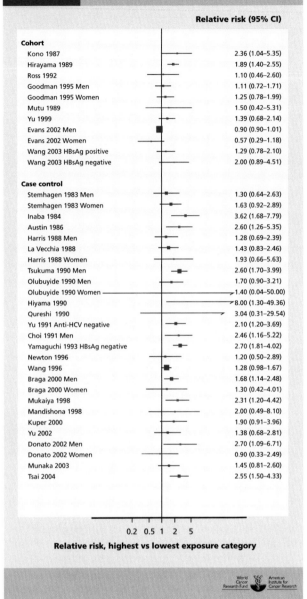

Figure 4.8.17 | **Alcoholic drinks and liver cancer: cohort and case-control studies**

Relative risk (95% CI)

Cohort

Study	RR (95% CI)
Kono 1987	2.36 (1.04–5.35)
Hirayama 1989	1.89 (1.40–2.55)
Ross 1992	1.10 (0.46–2.60)
Goodman 1995 Men	1.11 (0.72–1.71)
Goodman 1995 Women	1.25 (0.78–1.99)
Mutu 1989	1.50 (0.42–5.31)
Yu 1999	1.39 (0.68–2.14)
Evans 2002 Men	0.90 (0.90–1.01)
Evans 2002 Women	0.57 (0.29–1.18)
Wang 2003 HBsAg positive	1.29 (0.78–2.10)
Wang 2003 HBsAg negative	2.00 (0.89–4.51)

Case control

Study	RR (95% CI)
Stemhagen 1983 Men	1.30 (0.64–2.63)
Stemhagen 1983 Women	1.63 (0.92–2.89)
Inaba 1984	3.62 (1.68–7.79)
Austin 1986	2.60 (1.26–5.35)
Harris 1988 Men	1.28 (0.69–2.39)
La Vecchia 1988	1.43 (0.83–2.46)
Harris 1988 Women	1.93 (0.66–5.63)
Tsukuma 1990 Men	2.60 (1.70–3.99)
Olubuyide 1990 Men	1.70 (0.90–3.21)
Olubuyide 1990 Women	1.40 (0.04–50.00)
Hiyama 1990	8.00 (1.30–49.36)
Qureshi 1990	3.04 (0.31–29.54)
Yu 1991 Anti-HCV negative	2.10 (1.20–3.69)
Choi 1991 Men	2.46 (1.16–5.22)
Yamaguchi 1993 HBsAg negative	2.70 (1.81–4.02)
Newton 1996	1.20 (0.50–2.89)
Wang 1996	1.28 (0.98–1.67)
Braga 2000 Men	1.68 (1.14–2.48)
Braga 2000 Women	1.30 (0.42–4.01)
Mukaiya 1998	2.31 (1.20–4.42)
Mandishona 1998	2.00 (0.49–8.10)
Kuper 2000	1.90 (0.91–3.96)
Yu 2002	1.38 (0.68–2.81)
Donato 2002 Men	2.70 (1.09–6.71)
Donato 2002 Women	0.90 (0.33–2.49)
Munaka 2003	1.45 (0.81–2.60)
Tsai 2004	2.55 (1.50–4.33)

0.2 0.5 1 2 5

Relative risk, highest vs lowest exposure category

World Cancer Research Fund / American Institute for Cancer Research

study stated that there was no significant effect on risk.[464] Meta-analysis was possible on six cohort studies, giving a summary effect estimate of 1.10 (95% CI 1.02–1.17) per 10 g/day or 10 ml/day, with no heterogeneity (figure 4.8.19).

Twenty case-control studies showed increased risk for the highest intake group when compared to the lowest,[158 427 431 434 436 440 446 452 456 469 470 472-475 477-479 481-485] which was statistically significant in 12.[158 427 431 434 440 446 456 474 475 477-479 481 483-485] One study showed non-significant decreased risk.[476] Meta-analysis was possible on 14 case-control studies, giving a summary effect estimate of 1.17 (95% CI 1.09–1.25) per 10 g/day or 10 ml/day, with high heterogeneity (figure

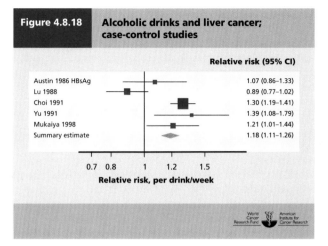

Figure 4.8.18 Alcoholic drinks and liver cancer; case-control studies

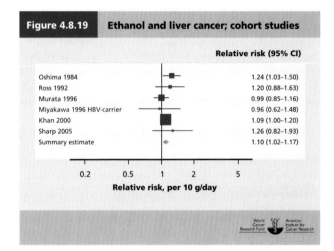

Figure 4.8.19 Ethanol and liver cancer; cohort studies

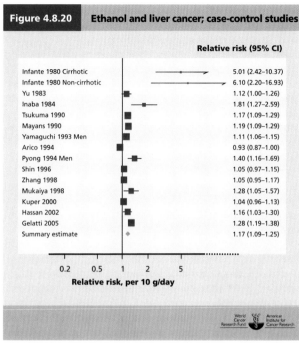

Figure 4.8.20 Ethanol and liver cancer; case-control studies

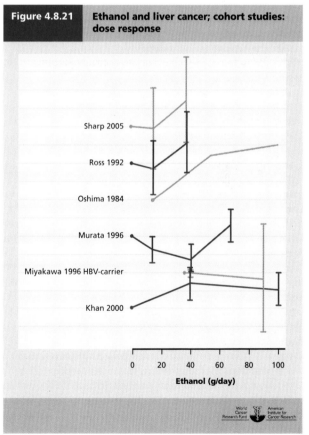

Figure 4.8.21 Ethanol and liver cancer; cohort studies: dose response

4.8.20). Heterogeneity may be due to the inclusion of studies that reported alcoholic behaviour.

A dose-response relationship is apparent from cohort and case-control data (figure 4.8.21).

Beers

Two cohort studies[6][486] and five case-control studies[425][435][444][452][473][479] reported separately on beer drinking.

Both cohort studies showed statistically significant increased risk with increased intake.[6][486] Four case-control studies also showed increased risk,[425][435][444][452][479] which was statistically significant in three.[435][444][452][479] One study reported no effect on risk.[473]

Wines

Three cohort studies[6][410][486] and one case-control study[425] reported separately on wine drinking.

One cohort study showed non-significant increased risk with increased intake.[410] Two studies stated that there was no significant effect on risk.[6][486] The single case-control study showed non-significant increased risk.[425]

Spirits

Two cohort studies[6 486] and five case-control studies[425 444 469 472 479 487] reported separately on spirits.

Both cohort studies showed no significant effect on risk.[6 486] All case-control studies showed increased risk,[425 444 469 472 479 487] which was statistically significant in one[444 479]; and one case-control study showed statistically significant increased risk for consumption of illicit liquor.[487]

Several studies used participants judged to be at high risk of developing liver cancer, that is, people who already had liver cirrhosis. These results are particularly hard to interpret as cirrhosis status affects drinking behaviour. Also the cancer disease path may be different in people with cirrhosis.

Assessment of some studies was hampered by poor exposure assessment, and not all studies adjusted for known confounders such as hepatitis B or C virus.

The general mechanisms through which alcohol could plausibly cause cancer are outlined below. In addition, regular, high levels of alcohol consumption are known to cause liver damage. Tumour promotion has been linked to inflammation in the liver through alcohol-associated fibrosis and hepatitis.[488 489] Alcohol consumption, even at moderate levels, is associated with increases in levels of circulating hepatitis C virus RNA in carriers. Hepatitis C virus infection is highly prevalent among alcoholics with chronic liver disease and appears to accelerate the course of alcoholic liver disease (see chapter 7.8).

There is ample, generally consistent evidence from both cohort and case-control studies. A dose-response relationship is apparent. Alcohol is a cause of cirrhosis that predisposes to liver cancer, but the factors that determine why some people are susceptible to cirrhosis are not known. Alcoholic drinks are a probable cause of liver cancer. No threshold was identified.

The Panel is aware that since the conclusion of the SLR, one case-control study[490] has been published. This new information does not change the Panel judgement (see box 3.8).

Kidney

Three cohort studies[491-493] and 16 case-control studies[308 494-509] investigated alcoholic drinks and kidney cancer. Four cohort studies[6 492 510-513] and five case-control studies[503 504 514-516] investigated ethanol intake.

Total alcoholic drinks

Two cohort studies showed non-significant increased risk for the highest intake group when compared to the lowest.[491 493] One study showed a statistically significant decreased risk.[492] None of the studies was adjusted for smoking; effect estimates were 1.42 (95% CI 0.69–2.9),[493] 1.7 (95% CI 0.8–3.5) for women[491] and 1.2 (95% CI 0.5–2.6) for men,[491] and 0.62 (95% CI 0.41–0.94).[492]

Seven case-control studies showed decreased risk for the highest intake group when compared to the lowest,[308 494 496 499 501-504] of which one was statistically significant[494] and one was statistically significant in women but not in men.[504]

Three studies showed no effect on risk[495 497 509]; three studies stated that there was no significant association[505-507]; two studies showed non-significant increased risk[498 500]; one study showed a non-significant decreased risk in men and a non-significant increased risk in women.[508] Meta-analysis was possible on two studies that adjusted for smoking, giving a summary effect estimate of 0.92 (95% CI 0.71–1.20) per serving/day, with moderate heterogeneity (figure 4.8.22).[496 498]

Alcohol (as ethanol)

All four cohort studies showed decreased risk with increased ethanol intake,[6 492 510-513] which was statistically significant in one.[510 512] Meta-analysis was possible on two unadjusted studies, giving a summary effect estimate of 0.48 (95% CI 0.26–0.90) per serving/day, with no heterogeneity.[492 511]

Three case-control studies showed non-significant decreased risk with increased ethanol intake.[504 514 516] One study showed no effect on risk,[515] and one study stated no significant association.[503] Meta-analysis was possible on two unadjusted studies, giving a summary effect estimate of 0.90 (95% CI 0.77–1.05) per serving/day, with no heterogeneity (figure 4.8.23).[514 515]

There is no known mechanism through which alcohol could decrease kidney cancer risk.

It is unlikely that alcohol increases the risk of kidney cancer, though a protective effect cannot be excluded.

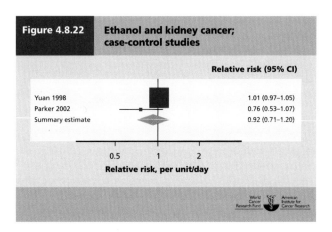

Figure 4.8.22 Ethanol and kidney cancer; case-control studies

Relative risk (95% CI)

	Relative risk (95% CI)
Yuan 1998	1.01 (0.97–1.05)
Parker 2002	0.76 (0.53–1.07)
Summary estimate	0.92 (0.71–1.20)

0.5   1   2

Relative risk, per unit/day

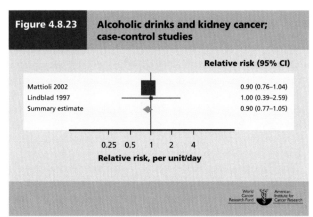

Figure 4.8.23 Alcoholic drinks and kidney cancer; case-control studies

Relative risk (95% CI)

	Relative risk (95% CI)
Mattioli 2002	0.90 (0.76–1.04)
Lindblad 1997	1.00 (0.39–2.59)
Summary estimate	0.90 (0.77–1.05)

0.25   0.5   1   2   4

Relative risk, per unit/day

The Panel is aware that since the conclusion of the SLR, one cohort study[517] has been published. This new information does not change the Panel judgement (see box 3.8).

General mechanisms

Evidence suggests that reactive metabolites of alcohol, such as acetaldehyde, may be carcinogenic. Additionally, the effects of alcohol may be mediated through the production of prostaglandins, lipid peroxidation, and the generation of free-radical oxygen species. Alcohol also acts as a solvent, enhancing penetration of carcinogens into cells. Alcohol has been demonstrated to alter retinoid status in rodent studies and, as a result, cellular growth, cellular differentiation, and apoptosis are adversely altered. For all these pathways, genetic polymorphisms might also influence risk.[398]

Lastly, heavy consumers of alcohol may have diets deficient in essential nutrients, making tissue susceptible to carcinogenesis.

4.8.6 Comparison with previous report

In general, the evidence that alcohol is a cause of a number of cancers has become stronger since the mid-1990s.

The previous report did not find any distinctions between different types of alcoholic drink. This finding is upheld.

The previous report identified a threshold of modest consumption of alcoholic drinks, below which no effect on cancer risk was observed, with the exception of breast cancer. Current evidence does not identify a generally 'safe' threshold.

Current evidence strengthens the previous judgements on colorectal and breast cancers.

4.8.7 Conclusions

The Panel concludes:
Evidence that alcoholic drinks of any type are a cause of various cancers has, on the whole, strengthened.

The evidence that alcoholic drinks are a cause of cancers of the mouth, pharynx, and larynx, oesophagus, colorectum (men), and breast is convincing. They are probably a cause of colorectal cancer in women, and of liver cancer. It is unlikely that alcoholic drinks have a substantial adverse effect on the risk of kidney cancer.

4.9 Food production, preservation, processing, and preparation

Practically all food and drink is changed before it is consumed, for instance by peeling or cooking. The majority of foods and drinks consumed by most people around the world are now modified in many more ways. Products on sale in supermarkets, small shops, and other retail outlets are chilled, pasteurised, canned, bottled, vacuum packed, or otherwise packaged. Most contain a number of ingredients, some of which are also processed. The use of ingredients such as modified starches, added sugars, hydrogenated fats, and also additives used as bulking aids, preservatives, colours, flavours, sweeteners, and for other purposes, is common. In general, rises in consumption of fats, oils, and added sugars occur because of their increased use in processed foods and drinks. Animal and plant products both contain traces of agricultural chemicals. Methods of industrial and domestic food preparation and cooking change the nature of food as eaten.

It is possible that processing and/or preserving methods may alter the nature of food. Different methods of food preservation and processing may be protective, causative, or neutral in their effects on the risk of cancer.

It is for this reason that *the Panel decided* that, as far as practically possible, the evidence on methods of food production, preservation, processing, and preparation (including cooking) should be summarised and judged in the context of the relevant foods and drinks. Most of this evidence is to be found in the previous sections of Chapter 4.

This section summarises other information and findings concerning the ways in which foods and drinks are changed before consumption. These include where data from animal and other experimental studies are not supported by evidence from epidemiological studies. Such studies are often carried out for the purposes of establishing regulations for the safety in use of chemicals known to be toxic, but may use levels of exposure far higher than occur in foods and drinks.

In line with its general criteria for judgement, *the Panel decided* to make no judgements on experimental findings alone that are not supported by epidemiological or other evidence. Nevertheless, *the Panel concurs* that, in general, it seems reasonable to conclude that the changes made to foods and drinks within well regulated, modern food systems, and made to foods and drinks as usually prepared and cooked, are of themselves unlikely to modify the risk of cancer significantly. For this reason, no matrix showing Panel judgements is included in this section.

In line with its general criteria for judgement, *the Panel has decided to* make no judgements on experimental findings from studies using doses of substances at levels far above those found in foods and drinks, many if not most of which are conducted to guide toxicological regulations. *The Panel also concurs* that changes made to processed foods and drinks within well regulated, modern food systems are of themselves unlikely to modify the risk of cancer significantly. For this reason, no matrix showing Panel judgements is included in this section. Those aspects of food production, preservation, processing, and preparation that have been examined in epidemiological as well as experimental settings are discussed and judged in earlier sections of Chapter 4.

This section summarises some of the general methods by which foods and drinks may be changed during their production, preservation, processing, and preparation (including cooking) that may be relevant to the risk of cancer. Almost all foods and drinks are altered — processed, in a general sense of the word — before being consumed.

Reports concerned with the prevention of chronic diseases often mention the added nutritional value of lightly processed cereals (grains), and of vegetables and fruits. But they may not make much distinction between foods and drinks as such, and as modified in production, preservation, processing, and preparation. Previous reports concerned with cancer have concluded that some methods of food and drink modification can produce carcinogens in experimental settings, and that this might reasonably influence cancer risk. Storage conditions that allow contamination of cereals (grains) and other plant foods by aflatoxins, and the preparation of fish Cantonese-style by salting and fermentation, have previously been identified as causes of cancer.

This section covers aspects of food production, preservation, processing, and preparation that are sometimes thought to be relevant to the risk of cancer, but where experimental information (when this exists) is not supported by epidemiological evidence or where there is no such evidence. Where the evidence for foods or drinks is sufficient to judge that they may cause or protect against any cancer, this is summarised and judged in earlier sections of this chapter. For example, see chapter 4.1 for the Panel's findings on aflatoxin contamination; for processed meat and also cooking methods, see chapter 4.3; for salting, see chapter 4.6.

4.9.1 Production

Modern food systems (box 4.9.1) involve various aspects of food production that have some potential to modify the risk of cancer. A clear benefit of these systems of production, distribution, and retail sale, with chilling used at all stages, is the all-year round supply of fresh vegetables and fruits (see chapter 4.2).

The industrialised farming methods that are part of most modern food systems in most countries use various technologies to maximise production. These include the use of fertilisers, pesticides, and herbicides on food crops; and of veterinary drugs in rearing livestock and in aquaculture. Fertilisers play a part in determining nutrient levels in plants, as well as potentially modifying concentrations of other bioactive microconstituents. Residues of these and other chemicals applied to crops are washed from soils by the rain and can contaminate water supplies. See boxes 4.9.2 and 4.9.3.

Methods or consequences of food production, where epidemiological evidence shows or suggests an effect on the risk of cancer, are summarised and judged earlier in this chapter. These are fungal contamination (chapter 4.1), hot drinks and foods (chapter 4.7), and arsenic contamination (chapter 4.7).

Box 4.9.1 Food systems

Food systems involve the production, preservation, processing, and preparation (including cooking) of food. Gatherer–hunters take food as it is found in nature and modify it by the use of fire. Pastoralists modify the animals that are a source of their food through breeding. Agriculture improves plants for human food use, by selective breeding and planting, and animals too are subject to selective breeding. In Egypt, selectively bred wheat was ground into flour, kneaded with water and other ingredients, and baked into bread as early as 4000 years ago.

Thousands of years before industrialisation, most food and drink consumed by the majority of people was modified in some way in its production. This included preservation by drying, and later other methods such as salting, fermenting, pickling, curing, spicing, and freezing in cold climates; and various methods of preparation and cooking, including boiling and roasting.

Food systems were transformed as part of the industrial and later, the technological revolution. But this was not the point at which foods and drinks became modified for the first time. Rather, many new processes were developed such as sterile bottling and canning. Then, beginning in the late 19th century, steel roller mills were devised for the mass-manufacture of white flour and thus white bread; refrigerated transport using railways and ships made possible the industrial production and international export of meat and dairy products. In the 20th century, commercialisation of the hydrogenation process to turn liquid oils into solid fats made margarine manufacture a big business, and the mass manufacture of soft drinks developed.

What is now known as 'conventional' farming, making extensive use of chemical fertilisers, herbicides, and pesticides, and feed concentrates for animals, developed mainly in the second half of the 20th century. More recent developments in food systems include the use of containers to transport foods and drinks nationally and internationally; the development of supermarkets, of which the biggest are now transnational; and the increasing concentration of food producers, manufacturers, retailers, and caterers.

4.9.1.1 Pesticides and herbicides

The use of synthetic pesticides and herbicides has increased vastly since the middle of the 20th century. Nearly 2500 tonnes of these chemicals were used worldwide in 2001.[1]

The chlorinated pesticide dichloro-diphenyl-trichloroethane (DDT) has been banned from use in many countries. Other organochlorine pesticides are now largely being replaced with organophosphorus and carbamate pesticides. These newer types are less persistent in the environment, and have not been found to be carcinogenic in experimental settings.

In many countries, the use of pesticides and herbicides is regulated to minimise residues in foods and drinks, and there are internationally recommended maximum residue limits (box 4.9.3). The use of persistent organic pollutants (organochlorine pesticides, furans, dioxins, and polychlorinated biphenyls) will be banned by 2025 under the United Nations Environment Programme's Stockholm Convention, which entered into force in May 2004.

Many of these contaminants have the potential to accumulate within food systems, and residues of pesticides and herbicides that have been banned from use, or are being phased out, may still be present in foods eaten today. Some contaminants, such as heavy metals and persistent organic compounds, tend to be deposited in fatty tissues and are not easily metabolised or excreted. They accumulate in living creatures, in amounts higher than background levels (for instance, in the soil). Dietary exposure increases with each step up the food chain, as predators consume prey contaminated with these residues.

There are theoretical grounds for concern, which are constantly reviewed by international and national regulatory bodies. However, there is no epidemiological evidence that current exposures are causes of cancers in humans, and so the Panel has made no judgements. Nevertheless, a precautionary approach is wise for women of reproductive age, since vulnerability during embryonic phases of development is increased, and early exposure may result in increased risk at later stages in life.

4.9.1.2 Veterinary drugs

Industrial animal production, as distinct from 'organic' farming (box 4.9.2), requires constant use of antimicrobial drugs to treat and prevent infectious diseases, and promote growth. Residues of these antimicrobials can be found in foods and drinks, normally at levels lower than internationally recommended maximum residue limits (box 4.9.3). When antimicrobials have been found to be carcinogenic in animals, their licence for that use has been withdrawn.

Hormonal anabolic agents are used in animal husbandry in some countries, including the USA, to prevent and terminate pregnancy in cows and to promote growth. Their use has been banned in other countries as well as in the European Union. Hormones designed to stimulate milk production include bovine somatotropin and porcine somatotropin. Many hormones have been found to be multisite carcinogens in experimental settings.[2] These include oestrogens, classed as group 1, human carcinogens, by the International Agency for Research on Cancer (IARC), prog-

'Organic' farming

So-called 'organic' farming is essentially a reversion to, or revival of, methods of agriculture that were the standard until the introduction of farming systems dependent on chemical fertilisers, pesticides, and biocides, in the second half of the 20th century.

Organic farming avoids or largely excludes the use of synthetic fertilisers and pesticides, plant growth regulators, and livestock feed additives. Farmers tend to rely on crop rotation, crop residues, animal manures, and mechanical cultivation to maintain soil productivity, and to supply plant nutrients and control weeds, insects, and other pests. Organic farming is intended to be indefinitely sustainable.

This type of farming has become well established within Europe and is expanding at a steady rate. More than 10 per cent of farms in Austria, Switzerland, and several other countries use organic methods.

The retail market for organic farming in high-income countries has grown about 20 per cent each year since the early 1990s due to increasing consumer demand. Production and distribution have become correspondingly large scale. The variety and availability of processed organic food has increased dramatically, and the cost — which was initially high — is continuing to fall.

Claims that foods produced by organic methods are biologically or nutritionally superior to food produced by intensive methods are not supported by clinical or epidemiological evidence, but some food compositional data indicates higher concentrations of some constituents like vitamin C and dietary fibre. There is evidence that organic products contain fewer residues from chemicals employed in conventional agriculture. However, the subject remains a matter of controversy.

estins (IARC group 2B, possible human carcinogens), and also testosterone (IARC group 1, human carcinogens).

The toxicity of antimicrobial drugs is constantly reviewed by international and national regulatory bodies. *The Panel notes* the findings on hormonal anabolic agents and also the lack of epidemiological evidence. Because there is no supporting epidemiological or other evidence, the Panel made no judgements.

4.9.1.3 Genetic modification

Plant breeding is a process of genetic exchange which is often undertaken with the purpose of acquiring traits that are either beneficial to humans or increase yield. More recently, the use of new technologies of genetic modification, intrinsic to agriculture and animal husbandry from their beginnings, has raised great public interest and controversy. Many crops are now genetically modified by means of gene transfer within and between species. Potential uses of modern genetic modification technology in food production include changing nutritional composition (for example, beta-carotene in 'golden rice'); increasing the hardiness of crops; improving pest or disease resistance; and increasing herbicide tolerance in crop plants (to allow the use of generic herbicides).

Not all genetic modifications include transgenes, in which a gene from one species is transferred across species, or even

kingdoms — that is to say, from plants to animals. Some genetic modifications involve only inactivating existing genes. For example, tomatoes have been genetically modified to render inactive the enzyme that softens the tomato once ripe; thus, the tomato remains hard despite being ripe. This is beneficial for transport and storage purposes.

The production and use of transgenic and genetically modified foods for humans or animal consumption are regulated in most but not all countries. The regulations require that all genetically modified foods be of equivalent safety as the food they are replacing, both nutritionally and toxicologically.

Any effect of genetically modified foods on risk of human disease might be a result of changes in the types of chemical pesticides or herbicides used, rather than of genetic modification itself. Genetically modified crops may require less use of pesticides and herbicides.

Any effect of modern methods of genetic modification of foods on the risk of cancer is unknown. Because there is no supporting epidemiological or other evidence, the Panel made no judgements.

There is too little evidence to draw any conclusion about the association between methods of production and risk of cancer.

4.9.2 Preservation

Methods of preserving foods have probably been in use since before recorded history began. Gatherer–hunter and peasant–agricultural food systems (see chapter 1.1) include various techniques to preserve foods, which remain in use, such as drying, underground storage, fermenting, smoking, and salting. A range of other methods of preservation accompanies, and is part of, industrialisation and urbanisation. These include canning, bottling, refrigeration, heat treatment, and irradiation.

Methods of food preservation, where epidemiological evidence shows or suggests an effect on the risk of cancer, are summarised and judged earlier in this chapter. These are refrigeration (box 4.6.4); processing meat ('processed meat' refers to red meats preserved by smoking, curing, or salting, or by the addition of chemicals, see box 4.3.1 in chapter 4.3); preserving fish Cantonese-style (see box 4.3.5 in chapter 4.3); and salting (chapter 4.6).

4.9.2.1 Drying

Drying is an ancient method used to preserve cereals (grains), pulses (legumes), fruits, and other plant foods. It is also used to preserve meat and fish, often as part of another preservation process such as salting (see box 4.3.5 in chapter 4.3). Freeze-drying, where the food is frozen and the water extracted, has been in commercial use since the mid-20th century, and is used to preserve fruits, herbs, meat, fish, milk, eggs, coffee, and other foods.

4.9.2.2 Fermenting

Fermentation is an ancient method used to preserve many foods and drinks. It may originally have been discovered by accident, because foods ferment as a result of the action of bacteria or moulds (yeasts). Fermentation has special features. It characteristically changes the sensory and nutritional qualities of foods and drinks: for example, bacterial fermentation turns milk into yoghurt and cabbage into kimchi (a staple food in Korea) and sauerkraut. Fermentation by yeasts turns sugar into alcohol, and so is an essential part of the process by which cereals (grains), vegetables, fruits, and other plant foods are the basis for beers, wine, and spirits.

4.9.2.3 Canning, bottling
Bottling and canning were first developed around 1800. The process involves heating or cooking fruits, vegetables, meats, and other foods in containers, then sealing them while still hot. Glass bottles were first used, and then cans.

4.9.2.4 Pasteurisation
Heat can be used to preserve milk and fruit juices by pasteurisation, which kills many micro-organisms. This involves various methods of rapid heating to a specific temperature, maintaining that temperature for a set period of time, followed by rapid cooling.

4.9.2.5 Chemical preservation
Chemical preservative additives are added to perishable processed foods. Antimicrobials inhibit the growth of bacteria and fungi. Antioxidants reduce the rate at which lipids are oxidised through exposure to air, which leads to rancidity. A third type blocks the natural ripening processes that continue to occur in plant foods following harvest. The most commonly used antimicrobial preservatives are benzoates, nitrites (see box 4.3.2 in chapter 4.3), and sulphites. There are internationally specified limits for levels of chemical preservatives in foods and drinks.

4.9.2.6 Irradiation
Irradiation was first patented at the beginning of the 20th century as a means of preserving food using ionising radiation. The process has been tested extensively, but there is considerable public suspicion over the safety of irradiated foods. For example, 2-alkylcyclobutanones, which interact with DNA in laboratory settings, are found exclusively in irradiated foods.

Methods of preservation tend to improve food security and enable more reliable availability of food, but may have adverse effects too. Some methods of food preservation such as drying are almost certainly benign, and others like fermentation may have some beneficial effects. The toxicity of preservatives and preservation methods is constantly reviewed by international and national regulatory bodies. Because experimental data are not supported by epidemiological or other evidence, the Panel made no judgements.

There is too little evidence to draw any conclusion about the association between methods of preservation and risk of cancer.

4.9.3 Processing

Food processing transforms basic ingredients into manufactured foods and drinks. In the broad sense of the word, food production, processing, preservation, and preparation are methods of processing. The term 'processing' here is used to refer to techniques and technologies other than methods of preservation that are used by manufacturers of industrialised processed foods. The processes that take place in kitchens (commercial or domestic) are considered in chapter 4.9.4.

Methods of food processing, where there is evidence that they may affect the risk of cancer, are summarised and judged earlier in this chapter. These are hydrogenation (chapter 4.5); refining (chapters 4.1 and 4.6); and the production of alcohol by fermentation (chapter 4.8).

4.9.3.1 Additives
Many if not most processed foods contain additives. These may be synthetic, 'nature-identical', or natural. As well as preservatives, these include bulking aids, colours, flavours, solvents, and many other categories. For general issues of toxicity in use, see box 4.9.3. Additives mentioned here are some of those where issues of carcinogenicity have arisen (also see box 4.9.4).

Flavours
Alkenylbenzenes are a group of naturally occurring flavours, some of which have been found to cause liver cancer in

Box 4.9.3	Regulation of additives and contaminants

Any chemicals that have a useful function in the production, processing, or preservation of foods or drinks may nevertheless be toxic, and possibly mutagenic or carcinogenic. For this reason, food additives and contaminants, such as traces of chemicals used in industrial agricultural production, are subject to international and national surveillance and regulations.

They are a cause for concern and vigilance because some, and in particular agricultural chemicals, are known to be toxic in experimental settings, though at levels well above those found in foods and drinks.

There is little epidemiological evidence on the possible effects of contaminants and additives as present in foods and drinks.

Because contaminants and additives are subject to international and national regulation, there is a vast amount of toxicological information from experiments on laboratory animals and other settings. Failing any other method, it seems reasonable to observe the effects of food additives and contaminants on laboratory animals at levels greatly in excess of any likely to be present in foods and drinks; and based on several assumptions and judgements, to set limits for safety in use. When such limits are used as regulatory limits, they are also subject to surveillance and special investigation when any chemical present in foods and drinks seems to be a cause for special concern.

This area remains controversial. Theoretically, it would be ideal if food supplies contained no trace of any toxic substance, including those that are or may be mutagenic or carcinogenic. However, some foods in nature contain carcinogens and the issue is not confined to methods of industrial food processing.

Box 4.9.4 Water fluoridation

In the early 1940s, people who lived where drinking water supplies had higher naturally occurring fluoride levels were found to have less dental caries than people who lived in areas with lower naturally occurring fluoride levels. This finding is supported by more recent studies.[5]

Where natural fluoride levels are low, fluoride compounds are sometimes added to water supplies in order to reduce dental caries in the general population.

Most cities in the USA now fluoridate their water supplies; most of Europe does not. The advisability of fluoridation is disputed: fluoride can have adverse effects at doses not much above that recommended for prevention of dental caries, and excess can cause dental fluorosis and bone fragility.

Studies in experimental animals have identified an increased risk of osteosarcomas (bone cancers) when exposed to water containing high concentrations of fluoride. A report published in the USA in 2006 considered all the available evidence on fluoride and osteosarcoma and found the overall evidence to be tentative and mixed, and made no recommendations for revising current available fluoride levels in drinking water.[6] A study published later in 2006 suggested an association between drinking fluoridated water and osteosarcoma in adolescent men.[7] However, preliminary analysis of a second set of cases from the same study does not replicate the findings.[8] The US Centers for Disease Control and Prevention continues to support community water fluoridation as a safe and effective public health measure to prevent and control tooth decay.

These findings are not the basis for any judgement.[9]

rodents at levels vastly higher than normal human dietary intakes.[3]

Colours

About 50 colour compounds are permitted for use in foods.[4] The number varies in different countries. Various azo dyes and other colours found to be carcinogenic in experimental settings have been withdrawn from use.

Those dyes now regulated for use in food are judged by UN and other expert committees not to be carcinogenic in the amounts found in foods and drinks. The xanthene colour erythrosine and ammonia caramel (a class 3 carcinogen, according to IARC) cause cancers in rats given high doses, but are judged to be safe as now used.[10]

Solvents

Around 20 solvents are permitted for food use.[4] Two — dichloromethane and trichloroethylene — once used widely for decaffeinating coffee and tea, have been classified by IARC as possibly and probably carcinogenic to humans, respectively. The Joint FAO/WHO Expert Committee on Food Additives has recommended that use of these solvents should be restricted, and that levels in food should be as low as technologically possible.[10] These solvents are now generally not used for decaffeination.

4.9.3.2 Packaging

Foods and drinks can become contaminated with traces of chemicals that migrate from packaging materials such as plastic wrappings and bottles, and metal cans. Migration from food-contact materials can occur during the processing, storage, and preparation of food. The polymers used in plastic packaging are biologically inert, but their monomers such as vinyl chloride, acrylonitrile, and acrylamide can and do migrate into foods. Plasticisers such as phthalates, used in the manufacture of these polymers, can also migrate into foods and drinks. These are mutagenic or carcinogenic in experimental animals. Nonylphenol and bisphenol-A, used in packaging, mimic the action of oestrogens in the body. Synthetic oestrogens in the diet are not readily excreted and may therefore accumulate in the body.

The potential effects of industrial food-processing methods and of additives and contaminants in foods and drinks on carcinogenicity are constantly reviewed by international and national regulatory bodies. In view of the lack of supporting epidemiological or other evidence, the Panel made no judgements. There is too little evidence to draw any conclusion about the association between methods of preservation and risk of cancer.

4.9.4 Preparation

'Preparation' here means domestic cooking or the cooking done in industrial kitchens, by caterers for indirect or direct sale.

Methods of food preparation, where epidemiological evidence shows or suggests an effect on the risk of cancer, are summarised and judged earlier in this chapter. These are grilling (broiling) and barbecuing (charbroiling) animal foods (chapter 4.3), and carcinogenic compounds generated by cooking these foods in a flame or at very high temperatures (see box 4.3.4 in chapter 4.3), and 'fast foods' (Chapter 8).

4.9.4.1 Industrial cooking

Ready-to-heat and ready-to-eat dishes sold in supermarkets and other retail outlets are a massively increasing market. Like 'fast foods' sold for immediate consumption, these are usually energy dense (see Chapter 8). Intense and prolonged industrial cooking of starch-based foods such as crisps (chips), French fries (chips), and other snack foods, generates acrylamides, classified by IARC as 'probably carcinogenic to humans'. At the time when this Report was completed, acrylamides were the subject of special surveillance and study.

4.9.4.2 Steaming, boiling, stewing

These are methods of cooking at up to 100°C. Some labile water-soluble vitamins are destroyed or lost in this process.

4.9.4.3 Baking, roasting

These are methods of cooking at up to 200°C, but not on a direct flame. During baking, the high temperatures are usually reached only on the surface of the food, while the inner parts often remain below 100°C. Traditional forms of roasting usually involve basting foods with oils or fats.

4.9.4.4 Microwaving

Microwaving exposes food to temperatures up to 200°C. Microwaves are a form of electromagnetic radiation. They cause vibration of water molecules, which produces heat. There is no evidence that microwaves have any specific effect on food composition beyond that of heat.

4.9.4.5 Frying, grilling (broiling), barbecuing (charbroiling)

Also see box 4.3.4 in chapter 4.3. Frying, grilling (broiling), and barbecuing (charbroiling) generate temperatures of up to 400°C, and sometimes use a direct flame to cook food. These methods create high levels of carcinogenic compounds. For any cooking involving wood fires, the type of wood used can also be an important factor in determining which chemicals contaminate the food. Hardwoods such as oak and hickory burn cleanly; others such as mesquite generate copious quantities of polycyclic aromatic hydrocarbons.

Because of the experimental evidence of carcinogen production, it is prudent not to consume burned or charred foods frequently or in large amounts. Industrial food preparation methods are regulated. Because there is no supporting epidemiological or other evidence, the Panel made no judgements.

There is too little evidence to draw any conclusion about the association between methods of preparation and risk of cancer.

4.9.5 Interpretation of the evidence

4.9.5.1 General

For general considerations that may affect interpretation of the evidence, see chapters 3.3 and 3.5, and boxes 3.1, 3.2, 3.6 and 3.7.

Aspects of food production, preservation, processing, and preparation (including cooking), where epidemiological evidence enables judgements to be made, are summarised, with Panel judgements, in previous sections of this chapter.

4.9.5.2 Specific

Measurement. It is practically impossible to measure small amounts of additives and trace amounts of contaminants in foods and drinks except by analysis. Epidemiological studies using usual methods of dietary assessment are therefore generally uninformative.

Terminology. The terms used for different types of cooking vary around the world. 'Broiling' in the USA is called 'grilling' in other countries. 'Barbecuing' may mean grilling in flame or slow cooking near smoking embers. Results of studies in these areas need to be interpreted with care, given that carcinogenic compounds are particularly generated when meat and other animal and plant foods are cooked in a flame, and even more so when they are burned or charred.

Study design. Practically all studies of the topics covered in this section are laboratory experiments on animals. They are commonly carried out to assess toxicity to determine safety in use, as a basis for food safety regulations. The relevance of such work to the actual levels consumed of substances identified in this section is obscure. Also, it is commonly agreed, as in this Report, that information from animal and other experimental settings, which is unsupported by evidence from epidemiological studies, is not a sound basis for firm judgements.

Confounding. Studies commonly report the difficulty in separating out specific methods of processing or cooking, when foods are characteristically processed and prepared in a number of different ways.

4.9.6 Evidence and judgements

The Panel decided to make no judgements on experimental findings of toxicity that are not supported by epidemiological or other evidence.

The evidence considered by the Panel is in the systematic literature review (SLR). Because the Panel made no judgement on the isolated experimental data, this evidence is not summarised separately here.

The full SLR is contained on the CD included with this Report.

4.9.7 Comparison with previous report

In general, the previous report found that information from animal and other experimental settings unsupported by epidemiological evidence, was not a basis for judgement. In this respect, the view of the Panel responsible for this Report is similar. The findings of the previous report on food additives, microbial contaminants, salt and salted foods, salted fish (Cantonese-style), cured meats, and the grilling and barbecuing of meat, fish, and other foods, were all contained in a chapter on food processing. The previous panel's judgements were mostly similar to those made here, with the important exception of processed meat, which was not considered separately from smoked and cured meats by the previous report. The judgements of this Report on these subjects are made in previous sections of this chapter.

4.9.8 Conclusions

The Panel concludes:
The Panel decided to make no judgements on isolated experimental findings that were not supported by epidemiological or other evidence.

It is not possible to make any definitive judgement in the absence of epidemiological evidence. Nevertheless, *the Panel concurs* that, in general, it seems reasonable to conclude that the changes made to foods and drinks within well regulated, modern food systems, and those made to foods and drinks as usually prepared and cooked, are of themselves unlikely to modify the risk of cancer significantly.

There are important exceptions to this tentative conclusion

and in these cases, the Panel's judgements and conclusions are found in the relevant earlier sections of this chapter. These judgements and conclusions are made in those sections wherever epidemiological and other evidence justifies a judgement of a protective or causative effect, using the agreed criteria, for aspects of food production (including contamination), processing, preservation, and preparation (including cooking).

4.10 Dietary constituents and supplements

DIETARY CONSTITUENTS AND SUPPLEMENTS, AND THE RISK OF CANCER

In the judgement of the Panel, the factors listed below modify the risk of cancer. Judgements are graded according to the strength of the evidence.

	DECREASES RISK		INCREASES RISK	
	Exposure	**Cancer site**	**Exposure**	**Cancer site**
Convincing			**Beta-carotene supplements**[1]	**Lung**
Probable	**Calcium**[2] **Selenium**[3]	**Colorectum** **Prostate**		
Limited — suggestive	Retinol[4] Alpha-tocopherol[2] Selenium[3]	Skin[5] Prostate Lung[3] Colorectum[6]	Retinol supplements[1] Selenium supplements[2]	Lung Skin
Substantial effect on risk unlikely		Beta-carotene[7]: prostate; skin (non-melanoma)		

1   The evidence is derived from studies using high-dose supplements (20 mg/day for beta-carotene; 25 000 international units/day for retinol) in smokers.
2   The evidence is derived from studies using supplements at a dose of 200 µg/day.
3   The evidence is derived from studies using supplements at 200 µg/day. Selenium is toxic at high doses.
4   The evidence is derived from studies using supplements at a dose of 25 000 international units/day.
5   Applies only to squamous cell carcinoma.
6   The evidence is derived from studies using supplements at a dose of 200 µg/day. Selenium is toxic at high doses.
7   The evidence is derived from studies using supplements (at doses of 20, 30, 50 mg for prostate, and doses of 30, 50 mg/day for skin), and foods containing beta-carotene: see chapter 4.2.

For an explanation of all the terms used in the matrix, please see chapter 3.5.1, the text of this section, and the glossary.

Nutritional science conventionally divides foods and drinks into their chemical constituent parts, such as water, carbohydrates, fats, proteins, vitamins, and minerals. Their biological functions are then explored, singly or in combination. It is now increasingly agreed by the nutrition science community that research and also public health can additionally benefit from a more integrated approach, in which the emphasis is placed on foods and drinks. In this Report, the evidence, its summaries, and the Panel's judgements are food-based, wherever possible.

Here, the evidence on macronutrients, micronutrients (isolated in the form of supplements), and bioactive constituents of plant foods (also known as phytochemicals) is summarised and judged.

Overall, *the Panel judges* that the evidence that dietary macronutrients specifically affect the risk of cancer is unimpressive. The evidence, based on observational data and randomised controlled trials of supplements, that certain vitamins and minerals affect the risk of specific cancers is, in some cases, impressive.

The Panel judges as follows:
The evidence that high-dose beta-carotene supplements are a cause of lung cancer in tobacco smokers is convincing. There is limited evidence suggesting that high-dose retinol supplements are a cause of lung cancer in tobacco smokers.

Calcium probably protects against colorectal cancer. At specific doses, selenium probably protects against prostate cancer.

It is unlikely that beta-carotene has a substantial effect on the risk of either prostate cancer or non-melanoma skin cancer.

There is limited evidence suggesting that retinol at specific doses protects against squamous cell carcinoma of the skin. There is also limited evidence suggesting that alpha-tocopherol protects against prostate cancer, and that selenium at specific doses protects against colorectal and lung cancer. There is limited evidence suggesting that selenium supplements are a cause of skin cancer.

Within the remit of this Report, the strongest evidence,

corresponding to judgements of 'convincing' or 'probable', shows that high-dose beta-carotene supplements in tobacco smokers are a cause of lung cancer; that calcium probably protects against colorectal cancer; and that selenium probably protects against prostate cancer. It is unlikely that beta-carotene, or foods containing it, have a substantial effect on the risk of either prostate or skin (non-melanoma) cancer. *The Panel emphasises* that this evidence and these judgements relate to these micronutrients only at the specified doses.

Nutrition science in its conventional form as a biological discipline was created in the early 19th century following the identification of carbohydrates, fats, and proteins. As nutrients, these all supply energy and are essential for tissue structure and function, and physical and mental growth and development. Later research has divided these macronutrients into many constituent parts such as monosaccharides and polysaccharides (including non-starch polysaccharides or 'dietary fibre'); saturated and unsaturated fatty acids (which themselves have many fractions); and amino acids. Many of these constituents of the main nutrients are known to have different metabolic, physiological, biochemical, and other effects, in isolation or combination.

Beginning in the early 20th century, a series of substances that do not supply energy were identified also as being vital to life, typically in very small amounts: these are vitamins, minerals, and trace elements. More recently a large number of other substances that are not nutrients, in the sense of being essential components of metabolic processes or cell structure, have been identified as bioactive. Because these are contained in plants, they are commonly known as phytochemicals.

Reports concerned with specifying recommended dietary (or daily) amounts or reference values for nutrients, by their nature, are structured accordingly. Compilations of the chemical composition of foods, used as standard references in epidemiological studies of food, nutrition, and the risk of diseases including cancer, also specify macro- and micro-constituents of foods and drinks, to varied degrees of completeness and accuracy.

Reports concerned with nutritional deficiencies characteristically make recommendations for the relevant micro-constituents. Increasingly though, they often now make recommendations for dietary patterns, diets, and foods and drinks that are high in the microconstituents with which they are concerned. So a report on vitamin A deficiency may specify foods high in carotenoids and retinol, and may also recommend methods of agriculture that emphasise such foods. Reports concerned with prevention of chronic diseases were initially structured in terms of dietary constituents, with only secondary reference to foods. But following a general international agreement that food-based dietary guidelines are more useful, and often better reflect the science, such reports now give more emphasis to foods and drinks, both in their analysis of evidence and in their recommendations.

The policy of this Report is to always emphasise foods and drinks. Thus, earlier sections of this chapter include summaries and judgements of the evidence on dietary fibre, vitamins, minerals, and trace elements as contained in foods, and also on fats, oils, sugars, salt, and alcohol as foods. Also see chapters 4.1 to 4.8. This section is concerned with macronutrients and micronutrients as such, and with non-nutrient bioactive constituents of food (phytochemicals).

4.10.1 Macronutrients

Chemically, macronutrients are classified as carbohydrates, fats, and proteins, and these categories have many sub-classifications. Diets need to include adequate amounts of macronutrients for physical and mental growth and development, and for maintenance of normal tissue structure and function. All macronutrients supply energy. Alcohol also supplies energy, but there is no requirement for it. Also see chapter 4.8.

4.10.1.1 Carbohydrates

Carbohydrates consist of monosaccharide sugars, or larger molecules of these units joined together: disaccharides (two units), oligosaccharides (a few), or polymers (many). For instance, glucose is a monosaccharide and starch is a polymer of glucose units. Polysaccharides are sometimes called 'complex' carbohydrates and sugars 'simple' carbohydrates.

Carbohydrates are generally the largest single source of energy in diets. They supply around 4 kilocalories per gram. They form part of important structural components in the body and, in the form of glucose, are the principal and preferred energy source for metabolism. They also play major roles in several essential cellular and physiological processes. Non-starch polysaccharides are the characterising feature of dietary fibre.

Glycaemic index and glycaemic load are terms used to characterise foods and diets based on their effects on blood glucose levels. Also see box 4.1.3 in chapter 4.1.

Cereals (grains) and products made from them (such as breads, pastas, and breakfast cereals), as well as starchy roots and tubers, are all high in carbohydrates. These foods contain a mixture of complex and simple carbohydrates and other nutrients. Until recently, starches have been the main source of carbohydrate in human diets. With industrialisation and urbanisation, sugars have been added in increasing quantities in food preparation and as an ingredient in processed foods. Diets consumed in some high-income countries now may contain roughly as much carbohydrate in the form of sugars as they do starches. Diets high in complex carbohydrates are usually associated with lower prevalence of obesity, heart disease, and type 2 diabetes.

For summaries and judgements on dietary fibre, see chapter 4.1. For summaries and judgements on sugars, see chapter 4.6. For food processing, see chapter 4.9.

4.10.1.2 Fat

Fats in diets are mostly made up from triglycerides — three fatty acid molecules attached to a glycerol backbone. Triglycerides are lipids, a class of organic compounds characterised by their solubility in organic solvents (such as ether and chloroform); they are usually insoluble in water. The body stores excess energy as lipids in the form of body fat (also known as adipose tissue). Lipids also form part of the structural components of cellular membranes as well as being precursors of important hormones.

Dietary fats include solid fats and liquid oils. Their physical form at a particular temperature is determined by the chemical structure of their constituent fatty acids. Fats with a high proportion of 'saturated' fatty acids are solid or semi-solid at ambient temperatures; those with a higher amount of 'unsaturated' fatty acids are more likely to be oils. The different degrees of saturation produce various effects in the body. Diets high in saturated fatty acids (and also *trans*-fatty acids) (see chapter 4.5 and box 4.5.1) increase circulating blood concentrations of cholesterol and the risk of cardiovascular disease. The World Health Organization recommends limiting total fat to between 15 and 30 per cent of total daily energy intake and saturated fatty acids to less than 10 per cent.[1]

Fats are the most concentrated energy source, supplying around 9 kcal per gram. They also carry the fat-soluble vitamins (see chapter 4.10.2.1). The body can make all but two of the fatty acids it needs — linoleic acid and alpha-linolenic acid, known as the 'essential' fatty acids. Both are found in vegetables, nuts, and seeds and their oils, in varying quantities. They are also found in meat, eggs, and dairy products, but at lower levels. The long-chain fatty acids found in oily fish (eicosapentaenoic and docosahexaenoic acids) can be made to a limited extent in the body, where they play a role in inflammation.[2] These and related fatty acids are precursors to prostaglandins; these hormone-like compounds have other diverse effects, including roles in blood vessel dilation and constriction, blood clotting, and transmission of nerve impulses.

Nuts, seeds, meat, oily fish, whole milk and dairy products, cooking oils and fats, spreadable fats, and a wide range of manufactured foods all contain varying amounts and types of fats. Those from animal sources usually have a higher proportion of saturated fatty acids, and these are common in processed foods.

For summaries and judgements on fats and oils as foods, see chapter 4.5. For summaries and judgements on foods that are or may be high in fats, see chapters 4.3 and 4.4.

4.10.1.3 Proteins

Proteins are large organic molecules made up of amino acids arranged in a chain. Short chains are called peptides, for instance di- and tripeptides (made up of two and three amino acids respectively). Longer chains are known as oligopeptides, and long chains as polypeptides. Proteins are fundamental structural and functional elements within every cell in the body.

Many proteins are enzymes that catalyse biochemical reactions and are vital to metabolism. Others have structural or mechanical functions, such as the proteins in the cytoskeleton, which give cells their shape and strength. They are also important in cell signalling, immune responses, cell adhesion, and the cell cycle.

Proteins supply around 4 kcal per gram. They are digested into their constituent amino acids, which are then absorbed into the blood. The body has the ability to make some amino acids, but others, so called essential amino acids, must be obtained from foods and drinks.

Dietary sources of protein include meats, milk and cheese, pulses (legumes), nuts, and cereals (grains) and products made from them, such as breads. Animal proteins from eggs, milk, and meat contain all the essential amino acids in the proportions needed by humans; soya protein is the only plant food to do so. Other plant protein sources have differing proportions of various essential amino acids, so diets without animal foods or soya need to include a variety of plant protein sources to provide enough of the essential amino acids.

For summaries and judgements on foods that contain proteins, see chapters 4.1, 4.2, 4.3, and 4.4.

4.10.2 Micronutrients

Micronutrients are essential constituents of diets needed in small quantities compared with macronutrients, and are not sources of energy. These are vitamins, minerals, and trace elements. Deficiency of any dietary constituents classified as a micronutrient causes debility, disease, and eventually death.

Many processed foods are 'fortified' with synthetic vitamins and minerals (box 4.10.1). Others contain various microconstituents such as phytochemicals, and sometimes other ingredients such as bacteria and 'prebiotic' polysaccharides; these products are sometimes termed 'functional foods' (box 4.10.2). Both types of product are often marketed with health claims relating to these added constituents or to the whole food.

4.10.2.1 Vitamins

Vitamins are organic molecules, classed as fat- or water-soluble, that are needed for metabolism but cannot be made in the body and so must be supplied in the diet. They have different specific functions in the body. For example, vitamin K is needed for blood clotting and vitamin C for the production of collagen in connective tissue.

Vitamins A (retinol), D, E, and K are fat-soluble and can only be digested, absorbed, and transported in conjunction with dietary fats. So they are found mainly in fatty foods such as liver and oily fish, milk and dairy products, animal fats (such as butter), and vegetable oils. The main sources of vitamin A are plant foods containing the retinol precursors known as carotenoids, which are converted by the body to retinol (see box 4.2.1 in chapter 4.2). Preformed retinol, which is absorbed better than carotenes in plant foods, is found only in animal products, of which liver is a particularly rich source. Fat-soluble vitamins are stored in the liver and in body fat stores. For this reason, they do not need to be consumed every day. For the same reason, some are toxic in high doses.

Vitamin C and the B vitamins are water-soluble. The B group includes thiamin (vitamin B1), riboflavin (B2), niacin (B3), pyridoxine (vitamin B6), biotin, pantothenic acid,

Box 4.10.1 Food fortification

Food 'fortification' refers to the addition of nutrients, often in synthetic form, to foods, so that the food contains more of the nutrients added. The term 'enrichment' is sometimes also used.

The United Nations and other international organisations are responsible for major food fortification programmes, designed in particular to reduce rates of deficiency of vitamin A, iodine, iron, and other nutrients, mostly within low-income countries. But common foods have been fortified in many countries since the early 20th century. For example, in some countries margarine and other fat spreads, or milk, have been fortified with vitamins A and D. White flour, and therefore white bread and other products made from it, is commonly fortified with some B vitamins, and also sometimes with calcium and iron.

The term 'fortification' in these and other examples may refer to the partial replacement of nutrients otherwise absent or depleted by food-processing methods. Or it may refer to the addition of nutrients to levels not found in the food in whole form; for example, the addition of calcium to white bread in the UK is to levels higher than those found in wholegrain breads; and salt may not contain iodine.

Many common processed foods and drinks, including some that would otherwise be low in nutrients, are now fortified with various combinations of synthetic nutrients. These include breakfast cereals, biscuits (cookies) and other baked goods, dried milk, milk-based products, and soft drinks, and even confectionery. Many such products are designed to be consumed by children.

In an increasing number of countries, the nutrients consumed in fortified foods and drinks amount to a substantial and growing proportion of total consumption of these nutrients. For example, since 1998 in the USA, grain has been fortified with folic acid, the synthetic equivalent of folate, as a public health measure designed to reduce the incidence of neural tube defects in the fetus. As a result, it is estimated that over one third of all intake of this nutrient in the USA comes from this source, as well as from fortified breakfast cereals.[3]

folate, and cobalamin (vitamin B12). Excess amounts of water-soluble vitamins are generally not toxic because they are excreted in the urine rather than stored in the body. This also means that they generally have to be consumed more frequently than fat-soluble vitamins. Plant foods are important sources of water-soluble vitamins: for example, cereals (grains), vegetables, fruits, some roots and tubers, and pulses (legumes). They can be destroyed by heat or exposure to the air, or lost by leaching during cooking, for instance when vegetables are boiled (see chapter 4.9.4).

4.10.2.2 Minerals, trace elements

Minerals are inorganic substances. Most foods contain significant amounts of one or more minerals, and these compounds have many specific functions in the body. Some are essential components of enzymes and other proteins (as 'cofactors', such as iron). They are also involved in maintaining normal cell function (sodium, potassium, calcium), and for structure (calcium in bones and teeth). Others include magnesium, phosphorus, and sulphur.

Trace elements are minerals needed by the body in very small amounts. Whether a mineral is defined as a trace element is somewhat arbitrary: iron, zinc, and copper are minerals that may or may not be identified as trace elements. Others include iodine, selenium, chromium, fluoride, boron, cobalt, manganese, molybdenum, and silicon.

4.10.3 Phytochemicals

Phytochemicals are bioactive constituents of plant foods not identified as nutrients because they are not essential in the sense of being vital to life itself. Unlike vitamins and minerals, people do not suffer diseases when their diets are low in phytochemicals. However, consuming them may have beneficial effects on health or active roles in the prevention of diseases. Also see box 4.2.2 in chapter 4.2.

Box 4.10.2 Functional foods

Functional foods are so-called because they are believed or claimed to have special qualities, such as promoting well-being or protecting against disease. What marks them out from 'normal' foods is that they are specifically formulated, manufactured, and marketed as being 'functional' in specified ways, for which claims are made. Some fortified products, such as breakfast cereals and yoghurts, are positioned as functional foods.

The ingredients in functional foods claimed to have special qualities may be added fractions of macronutrients, such as amino acids or fatty acids, or vitamins, minerals, or trace elements. Very often the 'functional' ingredients will be known or claimed to be bioactive in other ways: these include phytochemicals, herbal extracts, and commensal bacteria.

Various phytochemicals have been shown to have anti-oxidant, anti-carcinogenic, anti-inflammatory, immunomodulatory, and antimicrobial effects in laboratory experiments. But it is not yet clear whether consuming these compounds produces these or other effects in the body.

Phytochemicals have various chemical structures and are grouped into families on this basis. They include flavonoids, isoflavones (phytoestrogens), glucosinolates, terpenes, organosulphur compounds, saponins, capsaicinoids, and phytosterols. Many vegetables, fruits, pulses (legumes), herbs, and teas are high in phytochemicals.

4.10.4 Supplements

Vitamins, minerals, trace elements, and other bioactive substances are available as supplements, usually in pill or powder form. These began to be manufactured and marketed after their functions were identified, and claims made for their general benefits in prevention of disease and promotion of well-being.

Many dietary supplements are classed as foods, although

Box 4.10.3 Levels of supplementation

The effects of bioactive substances vary with the quantities consumed. The amounts of nutrients and other substances in diets depend on the nature and quantity of the foods and drinks that taken together make up diets.

The amounts of nutrients and other substances contained in dietary supplements, in this context usually referred to as doses, may or may not be at levels that can be found in diets. Lower amounts, at levels about the same as those that can be found in diets, are known as 'physiological doses'. Higher amounts, at levels above any that can be found in diets, are known as 'pharmacological doses', or sometimes as 'mega-doses'.

Evidence from trials and studies using supplements are often difficult to compare. One reason for this is that both human and animal studies use supplements in different combinations and concentrations. A nutrient that has one effect at a relatively low or physiological dose may have a different effect at a higher or pharmacological dose. For instance, a nutrient that may evidently be protective at a lower or physiological dose may be toxic or pathogenic at a higher dose.

Randomised controlled trials using various doses of micronutrients have produced evidence of the effects of these supplements in modification of the risk of cancers of some sites. This evidence is summarised and judged in chapter 4.10.6.

---

some may be regulated medicinal products. Manufacturers of food supplements may market their products using health claims, although in some countries such as the UK, medicinal claims that the product can prevent, cure, or treat a disease may not be made. Herbal products may be permitted to make certain claims based on their history of being used for a particular condition. The regulatory status of dietary supplements varies from country to country.

Some nutrients such as water-soluble vitamins have been thought to be harmless at pharmacological doses; but there is now evidence, including some summarised and judged in this Report, that this is not always the case. Other nutrients, including fat-soluble vitamins and all minerals and trace elements, are known to be toxic at pharmacological doses; some of these, selenium being one example, are known to be toxic at relatively low pharmacological levels (also see box 4.10.3).

Expert reports issued by United Nations agencies and national governments specify levels of nutrients agreed to protect against deficiency diseases, and also (sometimes) agreed to be safe in use.

Many people take dietary supplements. Their use is higher in high-income countries. In the UK, 35 per cent of respondents reported taking dietary supplements. Around 50 per cent of people in the USA take supplements in some form.

4.10.5 Interpretation of the evidence

4.10.5.1 General
For general considerations that may affect interpretation of the evidence, see chapters 3.3 and 3.5, and boxes 3.1, 3.2, 3.6 and 3.7.

'Relative risk' (RR) is used in this Report to denote ratio measures of effect, including 'risk ratios', 'rate ratios', 'hazard ratios', and 'odds ratios'.

4.10.5.2 Specific
These specific points apply only to trials using micronutrient supplements.

Measurement. The results of supplement trials can be assumed only to apply to levels and forms of the micronutrient present in the supplement.

Study design. Randomised controlled trials (RCTs) using nutrient supplements provide strong evidence. But the evidence can only be taken to apply to supplements at the doses and in the form given, under the specific experimental conditions. The doses used in trials are often pharmacological, in which case they cannot be taken as directly relevant to the nutrients as contained in foods and diets. Supplements in synthetic forms are sometimes but not always chemically identical to the nutrient as found in food, and so may have different biochemical effects. This may also be because of the level of the dose, because the nutrient is given in isolation or separated from the nutritional matrix as found in foods, or for other reasons.

Confounding. In trials using supplements given in combinations, it is not possible to attribute any effect to an individual nutrient.

4.10.6 Evidence and judgements

The full systematic literature review (SLR) is contained on the CD included with this Report.

4.10.6.1 Carbohydrates
For the evidence on foods containing carbohydrate, including dietary fibre, see chapter 4.1. For the evidence on sugars as a food, see chapter 4.6.

4.10.6.2 Fats
For the evidence on foods containing substantial amounts of fats and oils, see chapters 4.3 and 4.4. For the evidence on fats and oils as foods, see chapter 4.5.

4.10.6.3 Proteins
The evidence from the SLRs did not suggest that proteins specifically modify the risk of cancers of any sites. For the evidence on foods containing protein, see chapters 4.1, 4.3, and 4.4.

4.10.6.4 Vitamin supplements
The evidence presented here is derived from studies of vitamins and beta-carotene (a vitamin A precursor) in supplement form only. Microconstituents in supplement form may have very different effects according to form, dosage, combination with other nutrients, interaction with diets as a whole, and other factors.

4.10.6.4.1 Retinol

Skin

Two RCTs investigated retinol supplements and skin cancer (table 4.10.1).[4][5]

Both trials included only participants at risk of developing non-melanoma skin cancer. The retinoid skin cancer prevention (actinic keratoses) trial (SKICAP-AK) included people with a history of precancerous lesions (actinin keratoses); the retinoid skin cancer prevention (squamous cell carcinoma/basal cell carcinoma) trial (SKICAP-S/B) included people with a history of non-melanoma skin cancer. SKICAP-AK showed non-significant increased risk for basal cell carcinoma, with an effect estimate of 1.14 (95% confidence interval (CI) 0.91–1.43), but it did show a statistically significant decreased risk for squamous cell carcinoma 0.68 (95% CI 0.51–0.92), comparing intervention to placebo.[5] SKICAP-S/B produced no evidence of effect for either basal cell carcinoma (106 cases intervention group: 110 cases placebo group) or squamous cell carcinoma (41 cases each in intervention and placebo group).[4]

Meta-analysis was possible on both trials, giving summary effect estimates of 1.10 (95% CI 0.90–1.34) for basal cell carcinoma and 0.93 (95% CI 0.70–1.23) for squamous cell carcinoma.

The mechanism of anti-tumour action of the retinoids is not completely known but retinol is known to bind to cell receptors with promotion of differentiation, alteration of membranes, and immunological adjuvant effects.[6]

The evidence is sparse and studies were conducted on a narrowly defined population group (people at risk of developing skin cancer). There is limited evidence suggesting that retinol supplements protect against squamous cell skin cancer.

The Panel is aware that since the conclusion of the SLR, one case-control study[7] has been published. This new information does not change the Panel judgement (see box 3.8).

Lung

Two trials (one an RCT, the other a non-randomised trial),[8-11] two cohort studies,[12][13] and two case-control studies[14][15] investigated retinol or vitamin A supplements and lung cancer (table 4.10.2).

The single RCT was the Beta-Carotene and Retinol Efficacy Trial (CARET) trial (table 4.10.2) among current and former smokers (some of whom were asbestos workers) who were given retinyl palmitate and beta-carotene, or placebo. It showed statistically significant increased risk of all lung cancers in the treated subjects, with an effect estimate of 1.28 (95% CI 1.04–1.57). The risk of death from lung cancers was 1.46 (95% CI 1.07–2.00).[9] The risk was especially elevated in those who had the intervention as well as exposure to either asbestos or heavy smoking, although neither subgroup analysis was statistically significant. At follow-up (5 years after trial termination), the effect was reduced and no longer statistically significant, with an effect estimate of 1.12 (95% CI 0.97–1.31).[8]

The other trial, which was not randomised, gave retinol or beta-carotene to asbestos-exposed people and used a matched comparison group, giving an adjusted effect estimate of 0.67 (95% CI 0.33–1.37).[11]

One cohort study was stratified according to smoking status (current, former, and never).[12] In current smokers, high-dose vitamin A supplements (synthetic beta-carotene or retinol) were associated with an increased risk, with an effect estimate of 3.42 (with no CI or value for trend reported), when compared to no supplements. Men who never smoked showed a non-significant decreased risk.[12] The other cohort study showed no effect on risk for men and non-significant decreased risk in women. Effect estimates were 1.0 (95% CI 0.66–1.51) for men and 0.65 (95% CI 0.39–1.06) for women, when comparing supplement use to non-use.[13] One case-control study showed a non-significant increased risk with supplement use,[14] the other showed no effect on risk.[15]

It is possible that the potential protective associations present at dietary intake amounts of vitamins are lost or reversed by pharmacological supplementation and the higher levels that this may supply.

The evidence is sparse and inconsistent. There is limited evidence suggesting that high-dose retinol

Table 4.10.1	Retinol supplements and skin cancer; trials			
Trial name	**Number of participants**	**Intervention**	**Length of intervention**	**Length of follow-up**
SKICAP-AK Moon 1997	2297 with moderate risk of skin cancer	25000 IU retinol or placebo daily	5 years	3.8 years
SKICAP-S/B Levine 1997	525 with high risk of skin cancer	25000 IU retinol, 5–10 mg isotretinoin or placebo daily	3 years	3 years

Table 4.10.2	Vitamin A supplements and lung cancer; trials			
Trial name	**Number of participants**	**Intervention**	**Length of intervention**	**Length of follow-up**
Beta-Carotene and Retinol Efficacy Trial (CARET) Goodman 2004 Omenn 1996	18 314 at high risk of developing lung cancer	30 mg beta-carotene and 25 000 IU retinyl palmitate	4 years (trial ended early)	5 years
Western Perth asbestos workers Musk 1998	1203 participants, 996 comparison subjects	Annual supplies of vitamin A (either synthetic beta-carotene or retinol), help in quitting smoking, and dietary advice	Maximum of 4 years	–

supplements are a cause of lung cancer in current smokers.

4.10.6.4.2 Beta-carotene

Lung

Five RCTs[8-10 16-20] and one cohort study[21] investigated beta-carotene supplements and lung cancer (table 4.10.3).

Four studies showed increased risk with a beta-carotene intervention,[16 17 19 20] which was statistically significant in two (during the trial, not at follow-up; smokers).[8-10 16 17] One study showed a non-significant decreased risk.[18] Meta-analysis was possible on three trials, giving a summary effect estimate of 1.10 (95% CI 0.89–1.36) for beta-carotene supplementation versus none, with moderate heterogeneity (figure 4.10.1). Two trials could not be included in the meta-analysis. One trial reported an effect estimate of 1.50 (95% CI 0.43–5.28) for those taking beta-carotene compared to those taking retinol from a total of 10 lung cancers in all participants.[20] The other RCT was the CARET trial (table 4.10.3) among current and former smokers (some of whom were asbestos workers) who were given retinyl palmitate and beta-carotene, or placebo. It showed statistically significant increased risk of all lung cancers in the treated subjects, with an effect estimate of 1.28 (95% CI 1.04–1.57). The risk of death from lung cancers was 1.46 (95% CI 1.07–2.00).[9] The risk was especially elevated in those who had the intervention as well as exposure to either asbestos or heavy smoking, although neither subgroup analysis was statistically

Figure 4.10.1 Beta-carotene supplements and lung cancer; trials

Relative risk (95% CI)

	Relative risk (95% CI)
Virtamo 2003 (ATBC) Men	1.17 (1.02–1.34)
Cook 2000 (PHS) Men	0.90 (0.68–1.18)
Lee 1999 (Women's Health Study)	1.43 (0.83–2.48)
Summary estimate	1.10 (0.89–1.36)

Relative risk, intervention group vs control group

significant. At follow-up (five years after trial termination), the effect was reduced and no longer statistically significant, with an effect estimate of 1.12 (95% CI 0.97–1.31).[8]

One cohort study showed non-significant increased risk for beta-carotene supplementation compared to none in women. The other study showed non-significant decreased risk in men. Effect estimates were 1.23 (95% CI 0.55–2.76; women) and 0.82 (95% CI 0.36–1.85; men).[21]

There is a marked interaction between beta-carotene, heavy smoking and genotype.[22 23] When beta-carotene supplementation among those without the glutathione-S-transferase variant GSTM1 who smoked more than 42 cigarettes per day was compared to beta-carotene supplementation among those without GSTM1 who smoked less than 37 cigarettes per day, a RR of 6.01 (95% CI 1.90–19.08) was observed.[22] After adjusting for age and smoking habits, an RR of 3 (95% CI 1.3–7.1) was observed for the Arg/Arg genotype when 545 $\mu g/l$ of serum beta-carotene was compared to 45 μg g/l.[23] Glutathione-S transferase 1 and 2 are carcinogen-detoxifying enzymes. People without or with less active forms of these enzymes, due to genetic variation, are less able to metabolise toxins than others and have higher risk of cancer, particularly if they are smokers or exposed to regular doses of toxins through another source.

It is possible that the protective association present at dietary intake amounts of carotenoids is lost or reversed by pharmacological supplementation and the higher levels that this may supply. In one animal study, low-dose beta-carotene was protective against smoking-induced changes in p53, while high doses promoted these changes.[24] A second explanation could be the complex nature of naturally occurring carotenoids and the possibility that the protective associations are not due to the specific agent used in supplement studies, but rather to other carotenoids present in dietary exposure[25] or other associated dietary or health related behaviours.

There is strong evidence from good quality trials, consistent with cohort studies. An interaction between smoking, genetics, and beta-carotene is apparent. The evidence that beta-carotene supplements cause lung cancer in current smokers is convincing.

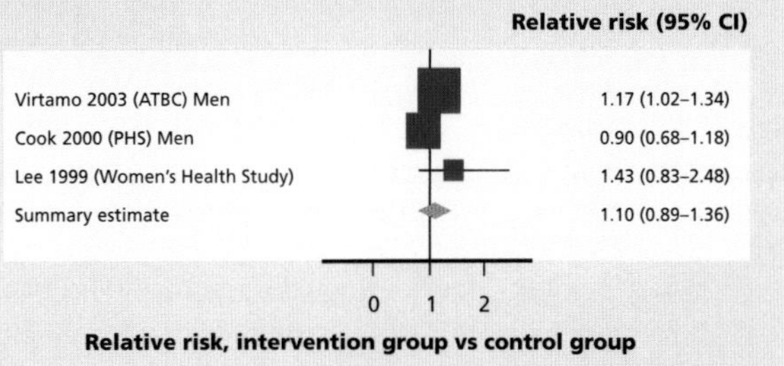

Table 4.10.3 Beta-carotene supplements and lung cancer; trials

Trial name	Number of participants	Intervention	Length of intervention	Length of follow-up
Physicians' Health Study (PHS) Cook 2000	22 071	50 mg beta-carotene taken on alternate days	13 years	–
Women's Health Study (WHS) Lee 1999	39 876	50 mg of beta-carotene taken on alternate days	2 years	4 years
ATBC study (male smokers) Virtamo 2003 Albanes 1996	29 133	20 mg of beta-carotene only or with 50 mg of alpha-tocopherol	5–8 years	6–8 years
Western Perth asbestos workers de Klerk 1998	1024	30 mg/day beta-carotene or 25 000 IU/day retinol	Up to 5 years	–
Beta-Carotene and Retinol Efficacy Trial (CARET) Goodman 2004 Omenn 1996	18 314 at high risk of developing lung cancer	30 mg beta-carotene and 25 000 IU retinyl palmitate	4 years (trial ended early)	5 years

Table 4.10.4	Beta-carotene supplements and prostate cancer; trials			
Trial name	Number of participants	Intervention	Length of intervention	Length of follow-up
Beta-Carotene and Retinol Efficacy Trial (CARET) Omenn 1996 Goodman 2004	18 314 at high risk of developing lung cancer	30 mg beta-carotene and 25 000 IU retinyl palmitate	4 years (trial ended early)	5 years
Physicians' Health Study (PHS) Cook 2000	22 071	50 mg beta-carotene taken on alternate days	13 years	–
ATBC Study (male smokers) Virtamo 2003 Heinonen 1998	29 133	20 mg of beta-carotene only or with 50 mg of alpha-tocopherol	5–8 years	6–8 years

Table 4.10.5	Beta-carotene supplements and skin cancer; trials			
Trial name	Number of participants	Intervention	Length of intervention	Length of follow-up
Nambour Skin Cancer Prevention Trial Green 1999	1621	Four treatment groups: daily application of sunscreen and beta-carotene supplementation (30 mg per day); sunscreen plus placebo tablets; beta-carotene only; or placebo only	4.5 years	–
Beta-Carotene Trial Greenberg 1990	1805 (with history of non-melanoma skin cancer)	50 mg daily	5 years	1–5 years
Physicians' Health Study (PHS) Frieling 2000 Hennekens 1999	22 071	50 mg beta-carotene taken on alternate days	12 years	
Women's Health Study (WHS) Lee 1999	39 876	50 mg of beta-carotene taken on alternate days	2 years	4 years

Prostate

See also chapter 4.2.5.3 for evidence on foods containing beta-carotene. Three RCTs[9 10 16 18 26] and two cohort studies[27 28] investigated beta-carotene supplements (table 4.10.4).

Two trials showed a non-significant increased risk for beta-carotene supplementation compared to none[9 10 16]; the other showed no effect on risk.[18] Effect estimates were 1.26 (95% CI 0.98–1.62) for the 1985 to 1993 follow-up period,[16] 1.01 (95% CI 0.80–1.27),[9 10] and 1.0 (95% CI 0.9–1.1).[18]

One cohort study showed a non-significant increased risk for beta-carotene supplementation compared to none[27]; the other stated that there was no significant association.[28] The single reported effect estimate was 1.17 (95% CI 0.85–1.61).[27]

There is no evidence for any mechanism of action.

There is strong evidence from good quality trials, and from cohort studies, which consistently fails to demonstrate a protective effect. Beta-carotene supplements are unlikely to have a substantial protective effect against prostate cancer. The evidence is too limited to draw a conclusion on a harmful effect.

Skin

See also chapter 4.2.5.3 for evidence on foods containing beta-carotene. Four RCTs[19 29-32] and one cohort study[33] investigated beta-carotene supplements (table 4.10.5).

Non-melanoma skin cancer

Three RCTs investigated non-melanoma skin cancer as an outcome.[29 31 32] Two trials showed non-significant increased risk for beta-carotene supplementation compared to none[31 32]; one trial showed a non-significant decreased risk.[29] The results are shown in the forest plot, separated for basal cell carcinoma and squamous cell carcinoma (figure 4.10.2). Meta-analysis was possible on all three trials, giving a

summary effect estimate of 1.00 (95% CI 0.94–1.07) for basal cell carcinoma and 1.01 (95% CI 0.95–1.06) for squamous cell carcinoma.

The single cohort study showed a non-significant decreased risk for beta-carotene supplementation compared to none. The effect estimate was 0.42 (95% CI 0.12–1.47).[33]

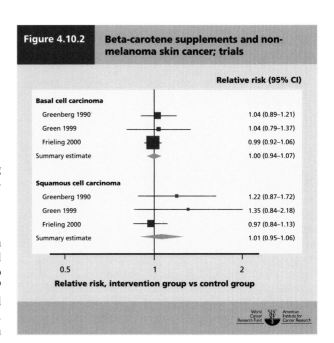

Figure 4.10.2 Beta-carotene supplements and non-melanoma skin cancer; trials

Relative risk (95% CI)

Basal cell carcinoma
Greenberg 1990 — 1.04 (0.89–1.21)
Green 1999 — 1.04 (0.79–1.37)
Frieling 2000 — 0.99 (0.92–1.06)
Summary estimate — 1.00 (0.94–1.07)

Squamous cell carcinoma
Greenberg 1990 — 1.22 (0.87–1.72)
Green 1999 — 1.35 (0.84–2.18)
Frieling 2000 — 0.97 (0.84–1.13)
Summary estimate — 1.01 (0.95–1.06)

0.5   1   2

Relative risk, intervention group vs control group

Melanoma skin cancer

The Women's Health Study[19] and Physicians' Health Study[30] investigated melanoma skin cancer as an outcome. Both trials stated that there was no significant effect from beta-carotene supplementation compared to none.[19 30]

There is no evidence for any mechanism of action.

There is strong evidence from good quality trials that consistently fail to show an effect. It is unlikely that beta-carotene has a substantial effect on the risk of non-melanoma skin cancer.

4.10.6.4.3 Alpha-tocopherol
Prostate

One RCT investigated alpha-tocopherol supplements and prostate cancer (table 4.10.6).[16 26]

The ATBC (Alpha-Tocopherol Beta-Carotene) trial was a large RCT of male smokers given 50 mg of alpha-tocopherol and 20 mg of beta-carotene (see table 4.10.6 for details). It showed a statistically significant decreased risk for alpha-tocopherol supplements, with an effect estimate of 0.66 (95% CI 0.52–0.86) for use compared to non-use. Prostate cancer was not a prior-stated outcome for this trial.[16 26]

Data on dietary, serum, or supplemental vitamin E or alpha-tocopherol levels were suggestive of decreased risk, though generally not statistically significant. Data on gamma-tocopherol provided evidence of an association with decreased risk.

Vitamin E exists in eight different forms or isomers: four tocopherols and four tocotrienols. There is an alpha, beta, gamma, and delta form of each. Each form has slightly different biological properties but all are antioxidants. Alpha-tocopherol is thought to be the most biologically active isomer of vitamin E. It inhibits proliferation, can directly activate certain enzymes, and exerts transcriptional control on several genes.[34] Vitamin E has also been shown to inhibit the growth of human prostate tumours induced in mice.[35]

The evidence is sparse. There is limited evidence that alpha-tocopherol supplements protect against prostate cancer in smokers.

Table 4.10.6	Alpha-tocopherol supplements and prostate cancer; trials			
Trial name	Number of participants	Intervention	Length of intervention	Length of follow-up
ATBC Study (male smokers) Virtamo 2003 Heinonen 1998	29 133	20 mg of beta-carotene only or with 50 mg of alpha-tocopherol	5–8 years	6–8 years

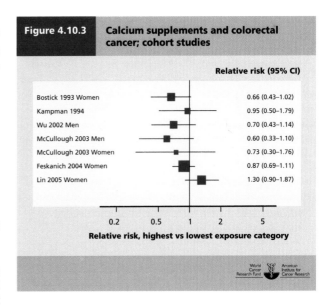

Figure 4.10.3 — Calcium supplements and colorectal cancer; cohort studies

Relative risk (95% CI)

	Relative risk (95% CI)
Bostick 1993 Women	0.66 (0.43–1.02)
Kampman 1994	0.95 (0.50–1.79)
Wu 2002 Men	0.70 (0.43–1.14)
McCullough 2003 Men	0.60 (0.33–1.10)
McCullough 2003 Women	0.73 (0.30–1.76)
Feskanich 2004 Women	0.87 (0.69–1.11)
Lin 2005 Women	1.30 (0.90–1.87)

0.2   0.5   1   2   5

Relative risk, highest vs lowest exposure category

4.10.6.4.4 Calcium
Colorectum

Seven cohort studies investigated calcium supplements and colorectal cancer.[36-43] Three trials[44-49] and four cohort studies[50-53] investigated calcium supplements and colorectal adenomas.

Six cohort studies showed decreased risk for calcium supplements when compared to none,[36-41 43] which was statistically significant in one.[40] One study showed non-significant increased risk.[42] The effect estimates can be seen in the forest plot, apart from one study which reported an effect estimate of 0.76 (95% CI 0.56–0.98) for the highest intake group compared to the lowest (figure 4.10.3).[43]

Pooled analysis from 10 cohort studies (with over 534 000 participants followed up for 6 to 16 years, 4992 cases of colorectal cancer) presented results for calcium from food sources and total calcium which includes supplements. A larger effect was seen for total calcium (0.78, 95% CI 0.69–0.88) than for calcium from food sources (0.86, 95% CI 0.78–0.95).[54]

Because of the abundant prospective data from cohort studies, case-control studies were not summarised.

Adenomas

Two RCTs showed decreased risk of adenomas with calcium supplementation,[44-48] which was statistically significant in one.[44-47] Effect estimates were 0.81 (95% CI 0.67–0.99; 1200 mg calcium; adenoma incidence)[44] and 0.66 (95% CI 0.38–1.17; 4 g calcium; adenoma recurrence).[48]

One additional trial showed a reduced risk of new adenoma growth during a 3-year intervention of a daily mixture of beta-carotene 15 mg, vitamin C 150 mg, vitamin E 75 mg, selenium 101 μg, and calcium (1.6 g daily) as carbonate (p value 0.035), though with no statistically significant effect on the growth of pre-existing adenomas.[49]

Three cohort studies showed decreased risk with calcium supplementation,[50-52] which was statistically significant for one.[50] One study reported no significant association.[53] Meta-analysis was possible on two of these studies, giving a summary effect estimate of 0.91 (95% CI 0.85–0.98) per 200 mg/day.[50] [52] The other study that gave quantified results reported an effect of 0.76 (95% CI 0.42–1.38).[51]

Calcium is an import micronutrient and intracellular calcium is a pervasive second messenger acting on many cellular functions, including cell growth. It has been widely demonstrated that calcium has direct growth-restraining, and differentiation- and apoptosis-inducing action, on normal and tumour colorectal cells.[55]

There is generally consistent evidence from several cohort studies, and evidence from trials for colorectal adenomas. There is evidence for plausible mechanisms. Calcium probably protects against colorectal cancer.

4.10.6.4.5 Selenium
Prostate

One RCT[56] [57] and two cohort studies[27] [58] investigated selenium supplements and prostate cancer (table 4.10.7).

The RCT was conducted in men with a history of skin cancers. Prostate cancer was not a prior stated outcome and was assessed as a secondary endpoint. Out of 974 participants, approximately half were randomised to receive 200 μg of selenium daily. There were 13 cases of prostate cancer in the selenium group and 35 cases in the control group, giving an effect estimate of 0.37 (95% CI 0.20–0.70) for supplement use compared to non-use, after a mean of 4.5 years of the intervention and a mean of 6.5 years follow-up.[56] The effect was strongest in those with the lowest levels of selenium at the start of the trial.[57]

Both cohort studies showed non-significant decreased risk with selenium supplementation.[27] [58] Effect estimates were 0.94 (95% CI 0.57–1.55)[27] and 0.91 (95% CI 0.57–1.48)[58] for use versus non-use.

Dietary selenium data are supportive of an effect (see chapter 4.2.5.8).

The general mechanisms through which selenium could plausibly protect against cancer are outlined below. In addition, selenoproteins are involved in testosterone production, which is an important regulator of both normal and abnormal prostate growth.

There is strong evidence from trials and cohort studies. Selenium probably protects against prostate cancer.

Table 4.10.8	Selenium supplements and lung cancer; trials			
Trial name	Number of participants	Intervention	Length of intervention	Length of follow-up
NPC Trial Reid 2002	1312 people with a history of non-melanoma skin cancers	200 μg selenium daily (primary endpoint was skin cancer)	Mean 4.5 years	Mean 7.9 years

Lung

One RCT investigated selenium supplements and lung cancer (table 4.10.8).[59]

The Nutritional Prevention of Cancer (NPC) Trial consisted of more than 1300 participants enrolled from several dermatology practices who were treated with 200 μg of selenium. The trial showed a non-significant decreased risk with supplementation, with an effect estimate of 0.74 (95% CI 0.44–1.24) after a mean of 4.5 years of the intervention and a mean of 7.9 years follow-up, adjusted for age and smoking. Subgroup analysis indicated that this risk differed according to baseline plasma selenium level, with an effect estimate of 0.42 (95% CI 0.18–0.96) for those in the lowest tertile compared to no apparent effectiveness for individuals in the higher tertiles of plasma selenium.[59] This suggests that selenium supplementation may decrease cancer risk in those who are deficient in dietary selenium, but that this effect may not extend to those whose intake of selenium is within the recommended levels.

The general mechanisms through which selenium could plausibly protect against cancer are outlined below.

The evidence is sparse. There is limited evidence suggesting that selenium protects against lung cancer.

Skin

One RCT[60-62] and one cohort study[33] investigated selenium supplements and skin cancer (table 4.10.9).

The Nutritional Prevention of Cancer Trial (see above) showed a non-statistically significant increased risk of total non-melanoma skin cancer with supplementation, with an effect estimate of 1.18 (95% CI 0.49–2.85). Subgroup analysis showed an effect estimate of 1.14 (95% CI 0.93–1.39) for

Table 4.10.7	Selenium supplements and prostate cancer; trials			
Trial name	Number of participants	Intervention	Length of intervention	Length of follow-up
NPC Trial Clark 1998 Duffield-Lillico 2003	974 men with a history of non-melanoma skin cancers	200 μg selenium daily (primary endpoint was skin cancer)	Mean 4.5 years	Mean 6.5 years

Table 4.10.9	Selenium supplements and skin cancer; trials			
Trial name	Number of participants	Intervention	Length of intervention	Length of follow-up
NPC Trial Combs 1997 Clark 1996 Duffield-Lillico 2002	1312 people with a history of non-melanoma skin cancers	200 μg selenium daily (primary endpoint was skin cancer)	Mean 4.5 years	Mean 6.4 years

squamous cell carcinoma and 1.10 (95% CI 0.95–1.28) for basal cell carcinoma.[61]

The single cohort study stated that there was no statistically significant association.[33]

The evidence is sparse and no plausible mechanisms have been identified. There is limited evidence suggesting that selenium supplements are a cause of skin cancer.

Colorectum

One RCT[60][62] and one cohort study[63] investigated selenium supplements and colorectal cancer (table 4.10.10).

The single trial included 1312 participants who were randomised to receive 200 μg selenium or a placebo. There were 8 colorectal cancer cases in the intervention group and 19 in the control group, giving an effect estimate of 0.36 (p value for trend 0.025) for use versus non-use.[60] A hazard ratio of 0.46 (95% CI 0.21–1.02) is given after a further 2.5 years follow-up.[62]

The single cohort study showed non-significant decreased risk, with an effect estimate of 0.60 (95% CI 0.27–1.32) for use versus non-use.[63]

Dietary selenium data are supportive of an effect (see chapter 4.2.5.8).

The general mechanisms through which selenium could plausibly protect against cancer are outlined below.

The evidence is sparse. There is limited evidence to suggest that selenium protects against colorectal cancer.

General mechanisms

Dietary selenium deficiency has been shown to cause a lack of selenoprotein expression. Twenty-five selenoproteins have been identified in animals, and a number of these have important anti-inflammatory and antioxidant properties.[64] Four are glutathione peroxidises, which protect against oxidative damage to lipids, lipoproteins, and DNA. These enzymes are rapidly degraded during selenium deprivation. Three are thioredoxin reductases and, amongst other functions, these regenerate oxidised ascorbic acid to its active antioxidant form.

Selenoproteins appear to reach their maximal levels relatively easily at normal dietary selenium intake and not to increase with selenium supplementation. It is,

however, plausible that supraphysiological amounts of selenium might affect programmed cell death, DNA repair, carcinogen metabolism, immune system, and anti-angiogenic effects.[65]

4.10.7 Comparison with previous report

This Report associates nutrients and dietary constituents with foods and drinks wherever possible; and findings and judgements on these as contained in foods and drinks are found in previous sections of this chapter. The previous report included a whole chapter on dietary constituents. It found that starch (probably when it is the staple of poverty diets) possibly protected against colorectal cancer but was possibly a cause of stomach cancer. The evidence from the SLRs undertaken for this Report did not reproduce these findings.

The previous report noted that trials using supplements of various micronutrients such as beta-carotene, vitamin E, and multiple vitamins and minerals had produced mixed results. But it did not make formal judgements as a result of these trials, although one of the report's recommendations was that dietary supplements are probably unnecessary, and possibly unhelpful, for reducing cancer risk. RCTs published since the mid-1990s have strengthened the evidence on the relationship of some dietary supplements and the risk of cancers of some sites.

For comparisons with the previous report concerning dietary constituents here identified as foods (such as sugars, fats and oils, and alcohol) or foods which contain certain constituents (such as dietary fibre, vitamins, minerals, and trace elements), see chapters 4.1 to 4.8.

4.10.8 Conclusions

The Panel concludes:

The evidence that the use of high-dose beta-carotene supplements in tobacco smokers is a cause of lung cancer is convincing. There is limited evidence suggesting that high-dose retinol supplements are a cause of lung cancer in this group. The principal cause of lung cancer is smoking tobacco.

Calcium probably protects against colorectal cancer. At specific doses, selenium probably protects against prostate cancer.

There is limited evidence suggesting that retinol at specific doses protects against squamous cell carcinoma of the skin. There is also limited evidence suggesting that alpha-tocopherol protects against prostate cancer; and also that selenium at specific doses protects against colorectal cancer (at a level of 200 μg/day, the dose used in the studies on which this judgement is based).

There is limited evidence suggesting that selenium supplements are a cause of skin cancer. It is unlikely that beta-carotene supplements, or foods containing it, have a substantial effect on the risk of either prostate cancer or skin (non-melanoma) cancer.

Table 4.10.10	Selenium supplements and colorectal cancer; trials			
Trial name	Number of participants	Intervention	Length of intervention	Length of follow-up
NPC Trial Combs 1997 Duffield-Lillico 2002	1312 people with a history of non-melanoma skin cancers	200 μg selenium daily (primary endpoint was skin cancer)	Mean 4.5 years	Mean 6.4 years

189

4.11 Dietary patterns

The nature, quality, quantities, and proportions of different foods and drinks in diets, and the frequency with which they are habitually consumed, constitute dietary patterns. Populations, communities, and families may share similar dietary patterns, which are determined by various factors such as the ecological niche they inhabit, physical environments in which they live, or by tradition, culture, religion, or choice. Dietary patterns, as well as patterns of physical activity, have co-evolved with humans over millennia and are intimately related to long-term survival of the species within a given environment. The changes in environment including diets and activity patterns over the past century are likely to have affected the risk of chronic diseases, including cancer. Indeed, the impact of food and nutrition on health is not generally determined by individual foods and drinks, specific dietary constituents, or the ways in which foods are modified, for example by processing or cooking. No food or drink is an elixir and few are poisons, unless they are contaminated with pathogenic micro-organisms. It is dietary patterns, with physical activity levels and other factors that influence nutritional requirements, that determine nutritional status and other health outcomes that are of interest to this Report.

Dietary patterns are difficult to characterise and are an infrequent subject for epidemiological and experimental investigations which, by their reductionist approach, typically address specific foods and dietary components. This precisely focused approach may overlook the significance of diets as a whole. There is now increasing interest in the examination of the impact of dietary patterns on well-being and disease outcomes, including the risk of cancer.

The Panel notes that existing studies of specific dietary patterns use different definitions and that the evidence they have produced is unclear. Currently, given the agreed criteria for grading evidence in this Report, no judgements can be made on any possible relationship between dietary patterns, as defined in the literature, and the risk of cancer. For this reason, no matrix showing Panel judgements is included in this section. However, a narrative summary provides an analysis of existing evidence relating dietary patterns and cancer-related outcomes.

For most populations at most times, food systems determine dietary patterns; traditionally, these systems have themselves been largely determined by climate and terrain. Until recently in history, diets have been mostly made up from locally available plant and animal sources, as gathered, hunted, reared, cultivated, preserved, processed, prepared, and consumed. The current dietary patterns of subsistence farmers around the world, in East Africa, Mexico, India, and China for instance, differ mostly not as a matter of communal or family choice, but because different staple crops flourish in different parts of the world. The same applies to communities that live near rivers, lakes, and seas: their dietary patterns are different from those of inland populations largely because fish and seafood are available. Traditional diets in the territories on or close to the Mediterranean littoral are typically high in vegetables, fruits, fish, and seafood. The dietary patterns of pastoralist populations, especially those living in Arctic climates, are high in meat and animal foods. The extreme example of imposed dietary patterns are 'poverty' or 'deficiency' diets, consumed by impoverished communities.

One characteristic of human civilisation is food culture: the development of dietary patterns throughout or within societies as part of general culture. It is thought that dietary patterns have acquired a cultural dimension based on the fact that they have evolved with human populations providing advantages for survival within a given ecological setting. Thus food cultures sometimes have become an expression of some system of belief.

Dietetics, in its original form as a general philosophy of the well-led life, was developed in Greece and then later in western Europe (for example, by the School of Salerno, from the 12th century). Scholars and teachers of dietetics recommended various dietary regimes, which involved dietary patterns selected as a matter of choice. These were often simple or frugal, and not just for personal well-being and freedom from disease, but also as an expression of virtue.[1] More recently, people began to adopt certain dietary patterns in the belief that these could protect against disease.

The urban–industrial food systems that generate the foods and drinks now purchased and consumed by most people in the world are characterised by the increased use of technology in production, manufacture, processing, distribution, and sale. Another key feature is globalisation. Spices have been transported from Asia to Europe for thousands of years; sugar has been shipped around the world for half a millennium; similarly, the export of tropical fruits, meat, and tea became subject to major intercontinental trade in the 19th century. Very many if not most foods, or their ingredients, now travel long distances before reaching their point of sale. Globalised food systems are now shaping dietary patterns in all continents.[2] [3]

This chapter summarises some of the dietary patterns that might modify the risk of cancer. Breastfeeding is also mentioned here in this context. For evidence and judgement on lactation, see Chapter 6; on being breastfed in relation to weight gain, overweight, and obesity, see Chapter 8.

4.11.1 Traditional and industrial dietary patterns

Dietary patterns are determined by many factors. This first group includes some traditional and industrial dietary patterns, determined mainly by climate and terrain, material resources, technology, and culture.

4.11.1.1 Mediterranean

The traditional food systems of the territories on or near the Mediterranean littoral, in southern-most Europe, the Middle East, and northern-most Africa, are the fount of a number of great cuisines. These were developed by peoples, often from the East, who settled in successive waves within what is now Spain, southern France and Italy, former Yugoslavia, Greece, Turkey, Cyprus, Crete, Lebanon, Israel, Palestine, Egypt, Libya, Algeria, Tunisia, and Morocco. The Mediterranean dietary patterns that have since evolved generally have some common aspects.

Traditional Mediterranean diets are broadly characterised by high consumption of breads and other cereal foods usually made from wheat, and of vegetables and fruits, fish, cheese, olive oil, tree nuts (almonds and walnuts), and (in non-Islamic countries) wine. Extensive use is made of many herbs and spices. Meat is also consumed, but often only on relatively special occasions or in small amounts in combination with other foods in everyday dishes. Coffee, drunk with added sugar (in modern times), is the traditional hot drink. Desserts may also be sweet but overall consumption of sugar is low.

Since the second half of the 20th century, much attention has been given to the 'Mediterranean' diet. This interest is because of evidence associating the dietary patterns of the populations living in this region with low incidence of coronary heart disease.[4] It is usually thought that this association is causal, and that the reasons include high consumption of fresh foods, dietary fibre, vegetables, fruits, and fish; modest consumption of alcoholic drinks; and low intakes of saturated fatty acids. In addition, historically, habitual levels of physical activity have been high.

Recommendations published since the early 1980s on food, nutrition, and the prevention of cancer have similarities with those for the prevention of coronary heart disease. Mediterranean dietary patterns might therefore also be protective against cancer, either generally or of specific sites.

Traditional Mediterranean dietary patterns are gradually becoming less common as the food supplies of the countries of the Mediterranean littoral become increasingly 'western' or 'globalised'.

4.11.1.2 Asian

Traditional Asian cuisines are very diverse. But traditional Asian dietary patterns do have some qualities in common, certainly those of southern and eastern Asian countries including India, Sri Lanka, Thailand, Cambodia, Vietnam, China, and Korea.

Such traditional Asian dietary patterns are of low energy density. The staple cereal (grain) is usually rice, which is also usually the main source of energy. Traditionally, rice paddy is often also used to breed fish. The amounts of vegetables, fruits, and fish in diets vary; consumption is relatively low in impoverished communities, and often high in those that are more prosperous. In the more affluent centres of civilisation, traditional Indian and Chinese cuisines have been and often remain extremely diverse. But they are almost always made up mainly from foods of plant origin, again with very extensive use of herbs and spices. As in the Mediterranean region, large amounts of meat are usually reserved for special occasions. Japan is a maritime nation, and so the traditional dietary pattern is high in fish and seafood and in salt and salt-preserved foods. The maritime regions of other Asian countries have the same dietary patterns. Traditionally, most alcoholic drinks consumed in Asia are made from grains. Most foods are cooked at low temperatures (steaming, boiling), although some high-temperature methods are also used (stir-frying, deep-frying, roasting). Tea is the traditional hot drink in China, India, Sri Lanka, and Japan. Consumption of fat and sugars is traditionally low.

As with Mediterranean dietary patterns, and probably for broadly the same nutritional reasons, traditional southern and eastern Asian dietary patterns are associated with relatively low rates of obesity, type 2 diabetes, coronary heart disease, and some cancers. However, those that are high in salt are associated with elevated rates of hypertension and stroke. Traditional Asian dietary patterns remain the norm in rural and impoverished regions of southern and eastern Asia, but are now gradually becoming increasingly 'western' or 'globalised' in the urban and more prosperous parts of these countries.

These generalisations do not apply to the countries of northern Asia, including those of the former USSR.

4.11.1.3 Plant-based

Plant-based diets are mainly but not necessarily solely made up from foods of plant origin. Characteristically, cereals (whole or minimally processed grains) and other starchy foods, vegetables and fruits, pulses (legumes), herbs and spices, plant oils, and other foods and ingredients of plant origin are the basis of almost all everyday foods and meals. Meat, poultry, fish, milk and dairy products, animal fats, and other foods and ingredients of animal origin are consumed, usually in small amounts on normal days, but often abundantly on special and feast days. Consumption of alcoholic drinks is also usually reserved for special social occasions.

It is estimated that the dietary patterns of most of the world's population — perhaps around 4 billion people — are plant-based. Traditional Mediterranean and southern and eastern Asian dietary patterns (summarised above) are plant-based, as are the dietary patterns of most rural communities in middle- and low-income countries. Most populations that consume plant-based diets do not do so from choice, but because for them, animals are valuable and animal foods are relatively costly. In some traditions (see chapters 4.11.1.1 and 4.11.1.2), plant-based or vegetarian diets are consumed as an expression of philosophy of life or of religion. These cultures, teachings, or faiths often also include periodic periods of fasting.

The nutritional profiles of plant-based dietary patterns are very variable, depending largely on the degree of variety of the foods consumed, though their energy density is generally low. Traditional plant-based cuisines from all over the world combine cereals (grains) and other starchy foods with beans and other pulses (legumes) as the staple foods. When food supplies are secure they are generally adequate in energy, and also in protein, unless reliant on very low-protein starchy staples such as cassava (manioc). Plant-based diets may be of relatively low energy density, but not necessarily so. Most of the fatty acids in plant-based diets are unsaturated. Levels of vitamins, minerals, trace elements, and phytochemicals vary, again depending on the degree of variety in diets.

Obesity, type 2 diabetes, coronary heart disease, cancers of some sites, and other chronic diseases have been rare or uncommon in those parts of the world where traditional dietary patterns are plant-based. Such diets are now commonly advocated and consumed by health-conscious people in high-income countries, partly on this basis. These diets are also increasingly popular because of the epidemiological and other evidence that components of plant-based dietary patterns are potentially protective against various chronic diseases including some cancers.

4.11.1.4 'Western'

The dietary patterns sometimes classified as 'western' have been generated by industrialised food systems, at first in western Europe, then in the USA. These patterns have also evolved in countries settled mostly by British and western European peoples, including those of the white populations of South Africa, Australia, New Zealand, and enclaves elsewhere in the world. This broad generalisation does not apply to some countries of Latin America, but in general represents the emerging dominant pattern observed in urban centres of the region.

'Western' dietary patterns are energy dense, and are increasingly made up from processed foods.[5] They are high in meat, milk and other dairy products, fatty or sugary foods such as processed meats, pastries, baked goods, confectionery, sugared and often also alcoholic drinks, with variable amounts of vegetables and fruits. The starchy staple foods are usually breads, cereal products, or potatoes. A feature of the global 'nutrition transition' (see chapter 1.2.1) is that 'western' dietary patterns are becoming 'exported' globally with accelerating speed.

'Western' diets defined in this way are associated with overweight and obesity, type 2 diabetes, cardiovascular disease, stroke, some cancers, and other chronic diseases. However, the term 'western diet' is potentially confusing: variations of such diets consumed within 'western' countries can and do have very different nutritional profiles.

4.11.2 Cultural dietary patterns

These dietary patterns are strongly influenced by cultural factors. These include ethical and religious beliefs, and beliefs about health. The distinction is somewhat arbitrary: these patterns are also influenced by climate and terrain, material resources, and technology.

4.11.2.1 Vegetarian and vegan diets

Plant-based dietary patterns need not be vegetarian, except in a loose sense; but vegetarian diets are generally plant-based. The distinction is more one of attitude than nutritional profile. Typically, vegetarians are at least as concerned about the ethics and environmental effects of consuming (and producing) animal foods as they are with their own well-being and protection against disease.

There are many types of vegetarian dietary patterns, and all exclude red meat and processed meat made from red meat. However, people whose intention is to be vegetarian may occasionally eat these meats; and many if not most will consume some foods containing ingredients derived from animals that supply red meat, perhaps inadvertently.

Lacto-ovo vegetarians consume milk and dairy products and also eggs. Vegans consume no foods of animal origin, although some are stricter than others about what they eat. People who avoid red meats may consume poultry and fish, and are sometimes termed 'semi-vegetarian'. The dietary practices of a number of religions are plant-based or vegetarian. Hindus are often vegetarian. Jains are vegan. Rastafarians are semi-vegetarian. Zen macrobiotic food is mostly vegetarian, although the main emphasis is on whole foods. For Seventh-day Adventists, see chapter 4.11.5.5.

Taken together, vegetarian dietary patterns are heterogeneous, as is the nutritional profile of most types of vegetarian diets. Studies of some vegetarians have identified lower rates of obesity and cardiovascular disease, and all-cause mortality. But people who are the subjects of such studies in high-income countries, who are vegetarian as a matter of belief or choice, are frequently of higher socioeconomic status compared with the general population. They are also less likely to smoke and more likely to be physically active (also see chapter 4.11.5.4).

4.11.2.2 Religious

Seventh-day Adventists are a Christian denomination of about 14 million people who, among other ways of life as part of their faith, are sparing in their consumption of meat and meat products; about half are lacto-ovo vegetarians. Most avoid hot condiments and spices, tea and coffee, and alcoholic drinks. Smoking is proscribed. The effect of Seventh-day Adventist ways of life on well-being and health has been the subject of a large number of studies. Rates of chronic diseases are generally lower among Adventists, and this is usually attributed to be their generally healthy ways of life.

Several other religions enjoin their adherents to refrain from consumption of certain foods or beverages — for instance, Islam forbids consumption of pork and alcohol, Judaism pork and other foods, and Hinduism beef.

4.11.2.3 'Healthy'

People who are conscious of the effects of food and nutrition on well-being, and on the risk of disease, may choose to consume 'healthy' diets. Such diets are featured in very many popular television programmes, newspapers, magazines, and books. However, there are as many 'healthy' dietary patterns as there are concepts of what constitutes a healthy diet; and for many people a 'healthy' diet is seen as a diet regime designed to reduce excess body fat. In the USA, the 'Healthy Diet Indicator'[6] and also the 'Healthy Eating Index' are used to assess how well people adhere to the Dietary Guidelines for Americans.

4.11.3 Other dietary patterns

4.11.3.1 Meal frequency

One hypothesis about food, nutrition, and cancer is that risk may be modified by meal patterns. The times of day at which food is eaten vary greatly in different populations. Gatherer–hunters and pastoralists often consume most of their food once a day only, or may not eat large amounts of food every day. Settled agriculturalists may consume two meals at different times of the day, depending on their work.

In urban settings, having three meals a day has been a common pattern. Some may be light meals and some more substantial, but the time of day at which each type is eaten varies in different parts of the world, and also within countries. Some people choose to eat lighter meals or snacks more frequently throughout the day, rather than having three meals. A feature of globalised food supplies and other aspects of modern cultures is the decline of the family meal; instead, an increasing amount of food is eaten alone in the form of quick meals or snacks, in fast-food outlets, in the street, or at home.

4.11.3.2 Breastfeeding

Being breastfed is a type of dietary pattern for infants. In fact it is the only pattern for healthy individuals based on a single food which provides all known essential nutrients for a given period of life. For a general summary of lactation and breastfeeding, see chapter 6.3. For being breastfed, see Chapter 8.

4.11.4 Interpretation of the evidence

4.11.4.1 General

For general considerations that may affect interpretation of the evidence, see chapters 3.3 and 3.5, and boxes 3.1, 3.2, 3.6 and 3.7.

'Relative risk' (RR) is used in this Report to denote ratio measures of effect, including 'risk ratios', 'rate ratios', 'hazard ratios', and 'odds ratios'.

4.11.4.2 Specific

Classification. A major limitation with most studies of dietary patterns is that there is no general agreement on just what constitutes any dietary pattern. For example, 'healthy' diets vary substantially; different types of diets are termed 'vegetarian'; and there are various types of 'Mediterranean' diet. In general, there is considerable scope for variation within any dietary pattern.

Confounding. Patterns of diet are interrelated with other habitual behaviour that may affect the risk of cancer, such as smoking or physical activity; people who habitually consume any type of diet for the sake of their health or for reasons of belief, may also modify other aspects of their way of life. This is likely to confound results that appear to show associations with the risk of cancer.

Study design. The analysis of conventional epidemiological studies tends to focus on specific foods and drinks and specific aspects of diets, rather than the overall pattern.

Reporting bias. People who habitually consume or who try to follow types of diets in the belief that these are healthy may, in studies relying on self-reporting, provide inaccurate records. They may overestimate their consumption of foods like vegetables, fruits, and other foods they believe to be healthy, and underestimate or fail to report consumption of foods and drinks they believe to be unhealthy. This type of reporting bias is a general issue with studies relying on self-reporting, but may be a special issue here. Studies of specific dietary patterns undertaken by scientists who themselves follow these patterns may be seen as biased for this reason.

4.11.5 Evidence and judgements

Epidemiological research concerned with food, nutrition, and the risk of cancer, characteristically examines individual foods and dietary constituents.

There is a growing body of epidemiological work on dietary patterns; these were within the terms of reference of the systematic literature reviews (SLRs) whose findings are the primary basis for the Panel judgements in this Report. However, the evidence on dietary patterns examined in this way, relative to cancers of individual sites, does not permit conclusions to be drawn and *the Panel decided* not to make any judgements. Also see chapter 4.11.4.2.

In the case of dietary patterns, evidence from the SLRs has been supplemented by an informal narrative literature review, and the results are summarised here.

The full SLR is contained on the CD included with this Report.

4.11.5.1 Mediterranean dietary patterns

In a Swedish cohort study, a 2-point increase in a 'Mediterranean' diet score was associated with a 16% (95% confidence interval (CI) 1%–29%) reduced risk of cancer mortality in women aged 40–49, but not among younger women.[7]

An intervention trial investigated the recurrence of colorectal adenomas. This showed that the 'Mediterranean' diet (characterised by high consumption of vegetables, fruit, lean meat, fish, and olive oil) was associated with a reduced risk of recurrence of colorectal adenomas in women (RR 0.30 (95% CI 0.09–0.98), but not in men. [8]

4.11.5.2 Asian dietary patterns

A Japanese cohort study[9] showed significant associations between certain dietary patterns and the risk of stomach cancer. These were for a 'traditional' Japanese dietary pattern in men (RR 2.88, 95% CI 1.76–4.72) and in women (RR 2.40, 95% CI 1.76–4.72); and for a 'healthy' dietary pattern in women (RR 0.56, 95% CI 0.32–0.96) but not in men. There was no association found with the 'western' dietary pattern. In the same Japanese cohort,[10] 'traditional' and 'western' dietary patterns were both positively associated with colon cancer risk in women, but not in men: 'traditional' RR 2.06 (95% CI 1.10–3.84) and 'western' RR 2.06 (95% CI 1.10–4.45).

The narrative review did not identify any other studies on Asian dietary patterns and the risk of cancer.

For evidence and judgements on salt, salting, and salted food, and the risk of stomach cancer, see chapter 4.6 and chapter 7.5.

4.11.5.3 'Western' dietary patterns

The narrative review identified several studies that have used data from large cohorts, mostly undertaken in the USA, to derive various types of 'western' dietary patterns from dietary intake information. This is done by combining key components of diets into what is then identified as types of dietary pattern that may be related to the risk of cancer risk. Some case-control and ecological studies have also been carried out.

Analysis of data from the Health Professionals Follow-Up Study found no association between a 'western' dietary pattern and prostate cancer risk. In the study, this pattern was characterised as being high in refined cereals (grains), red and processed meats, fat, and sweets.[11] Similarly, for breast cancer, another large cohort study reported no association between a 'western' dietary pattern and breast cancer risk.[12]

A 'drinker' dietary pattern, characterised as being high in beer, wine, and spirits, was identified as being associated with a moderately increased risk of breast cancer (RR 1.27, 95% CI 1.06–1.52).

A case-control study from Uruguay reported an association with increased breast cancer risk and a 'western' diet; associations with decreased risk were found for 'traditional', 'stew', and 'healthy' dietary patterns.[13] Another case-control study from Uruguay reported an association with increased stomach cancer risk and a 'starchy' pattern; associations with decreased risk were found for 'healthy' and 'mixed' patterns.[14]

A Swedish case-control study found that a diet high in meat, red meat, high-fat dairy products, high-fat gravy, and sweets was significantly associated with increased risk of gastric cardia adenocarcinoma and oesophageal adenocarcinoma. It also found that a 'drinker' pattern (high intakes of beer, spirits/liquor, and French fries) was significantly associated with the risk of squamous cell carcinoma of the oesophagus.[15]

One of the first studies to investigate diet and cancer using factor analysis was a Japanese study looking at gallbladder/biliary tract cancer mortality using data collected between 1958 and 1975.[16] Western-style diets high in foods with high levels of fats and proteins were associated with decreased risk. For breast cancer mortality in Japan, another ecological study found that westernised diets high in both animal and saturated fats were associated with increased risk.[17]

Another Japanese cohort study showed no association between a western dietary pattern and stomach cancer risk.[9] For colon cancer risk in the same Japanese cohort, 'western' as well as 'traditional' dietary patterns were associated with increased colon cancer risk in women, RR 2.06 (95% CI 1.10–3.84) and RR 2.06 (95% CI 1.10–4.45) respectively, but not in men.[10]

Three dietary patterns were identified from analysis of a Swedish cohort: 'healthy', including wholegrains, vegetables, fruits, tomatoes, poultry, and fish; 'western', including refined grains, fried potato, meat, processed meat, high-fat dairy products, margarine/butter, sweets and soft drinks; and 'drinker', including beer, wine, spirits, and snacks. The only pattern significantly associated with increased risk of renal cell carcinoma was the 'drinker' pattern (RR 0.56, 95% CI 0.34–0.95).[18]

An analysis of the Nurses' Health Study cohort also showed no evidence of an association between breast cancer risk and either a 'prudent' or a 'western' dietary pattern.[19] Similarly, no associations were reported between these dietary patterns and pancreatic cancer in a US cohort study.[20]

Two 'western' dietary patterns were identified from a US cohort. These were a 'prudent' type, characterised as being high in wholegrains, vegetables, fruits, low-fat dairy products, poultry, and fish; and a 'typical' type, characterised as being high in refined cereals (grains), red and processed meats, high-fat dairy products, sweets, and desserts. Neither was associated with overall breast cancer risk. However, the typical western pattern was associated with higher risk of breast cancer among smokers (RR 1.44, 95% CI 1.02–2.03).[21]

A Canadian case-control study identified an association between prostate cancer risk and a 'processed' dietary pattern, characterised as being high in refined cereals (grains), white bread, onions and tomatoes, red meat, processed meat, organ meats, vegetable oil and juice, soft drinks, and bottled water. No significant associations were found with 'healthy living', 'traditional western', or 'beverages' patterns.[22]

A case-control study conducted in central Italy identified a 'vitamin-rich' as well as a 'traditional' dietary pattern; both were strongly associated with decreased risk of stomach cancer.[23]

For colon cancer, a case-control study reported a protective effect of a 'prudent' western dietary pattern and increased risk with a 'typical' western pattern.[24] Another reported a protective effect of a western 'physical activity' pattern.[25]

Analysis of data from the French European Prospective Investigation into Cancer and Nutrition (EPIC) cohort showed a significant association between two 'western' dietary patterns and increased risk of colorectal cancer. The first, RR 1.39 (95% CI 1.00–1.94), included cereal products, potatoes, processed meat, eggs, cheese, butter, sweets, cakes, pizzas and pies, and sandwiches. The second was a 'drinker' pattern, RR 1.42 (95% CI 1.10–1.83), including processed meat, alcoholic beverages, sandwiches, and snacks. A 'meat-eater' pattern, including meat, poultry, and margarine, was non-significantly associated with increased risk of colorectal cancer, RR 1.58 (95% CI 0.98–2.53).[26]

In an Italian cohort study, four dietary patterns were identified: 'western', 'canteen', 'prudent', and 'salad vegetables'. The 'salad vegetables' pattern was associated with lower risk of breast cancer, (RR 0.66, 95% CI 0.47–0.95).[27] Another US cohort study reported no association between either a 'vegetable–fish/poultry–fruit' or a 'beef/pork–starch' pattern and postmenopausal breast cancer. But it found a significant association with decreased risk of invasive breast cancer and a 'traditional southern' pattern, including legumes, salad, and a low intake of mayonnaise salad dressing (RR 0.78, 95% CI 0.65–0.95).[28]

In the Netherlands Cohort Study on Diet and Cancer, factor analysis identified five types of western dietary patterns. Both the 'salad vegetables' and the 'sweet foods' patterns were associated with decreased risk of lung cancer: RR 0.75 (95% CI 0.55–1.01) and RR 0.62 (95% CI 0.43–0.89), respectively. The other three patterns were not significantly associated with lung cancer risk. These were 'pork, processed meats, and potatoes', 'brown for white bread substitution', and 'cooked vegetables'.[29]

One study found that associations between dietary patterns and colorectal cancer were not consistent across European countries. As part of the Dietary Patterns and Cancer (DIETSCAN) project, factor analysis of three European cohorts identified five dietary patterns. Two of these, 'vegetables' and 'pork, processed meats, and potatoes', were common across all three cohorts. The second dietary pattern was associated with increased risk of colon cancer in one cohort of women (RR 1.62, 95% CI 1.12–2.34), and with increased risk of rectal cancer in one cohort of men (RR 2.21, 95% CI 1.07–4.57). Neither pattern was associated with the risk of colorectal cancer in the third cohort.[30]

For thyroid cancer, a case-control study showed that various western dietary patterns of 'fruits', 'raw vegetables', and 'mixed raw vegetables and fruits' were associated with reduced risk of thyroid cancer (RR 0.68, 0.71, and 0.73, respectively). However, a pattern of 'fish and cooked vegetables' was associated with an increased risk (RR 2.79).[31]

Another case-control study showed that a 'dessert' pattern and a 'beef' pattern were associated with increased risk of kidney cancer. A 'juices' factor was associated with increased risk of this cancer in men and an 'unhealthy' pattern with increased risk in women.[32]

One case-control study from Uruguay reported an association with increased risk of oral and pharyngeal cancers and a 'stew' pattern, characterised by cooked vegetables, potato and sweet potato, and boiled meat. It also found a decreased risk of these cancers associated with a 'vegetables and fruits' pattern, characterised by raw vegetables, citrus fruits, other fruits, liver, fish, and desserts.[33]

A case-control study of pancreatic cancer risk showed no association with 'western' and western 'drinker' patterns, but an association with decreased risk and a 'fruits and vegetables' pattern.[34]

A Canadian case-control study found that four dietary patterns were associated with increased risk of kidney cancer: a 'dessert' pattern in both men and women; a 'beef' pattern and a 'juices' pattern in men; and an 'unhealthy' pattern among women.

4.11.5.4 Vegetarian dietary patterns

The narrative review identified several studies that have investigated the relationship between vegetarian diets and the risk of cancer. These often did not adjust for potentially confounding factors. One study found that when adjusted for age only, women who said they consumed vegetarian diets seemed to increase the risk of breast cancer (1.65, 95% CI 1.01–2.7) (vegetarian versus non-vegetarian).[35]

Plausible biological mechanisms have been identified by which vegetarian diets might specifically reduce the risk of cancers of the colon, breast, and prostate (also see chapter 4.2). Any effect of vegetarian diets is likely to be due not only to the exclusion of meat, but also to the inclusion of a larger number and wider range of plant foods, containing an extensive variety of potential cancer-preventive substances.

4.11.5.5 Seventh-day Adventist diets

The SLRs identified a number of cohort studies on the relationship between Seventh-day Adventist diets — and also general ways of life — and the risk of cancer. Two investigated oesophageal cancer,[36 37] seven stomach cancer,[37-43] two kidney cancer,[37 42] one breast cancer[44] and three prostate cancer.[37 41 45] For oesophageal, kidney, breast and prostate cancer, results were mixed and usually not statistically significant, although they were slightly suggestive of reduced risk.

For stomach cancer, meta-analysis of five cohort studies[37-40] [42] gave a summary effect estimate of 0.60 (95% CI 0.44–0.80), with low heterogeneity, with non-included studies also reporting reduced risks. None of the studies that reported reduced risk was adjusted for known confounding factors such as smoking.

As not smoking is a feature of Seventh-day Adventism, *the Panel concluded* that data on the dietary patterns associated with this faith are limited and no conclusion can be reached for any cancer site.

No conclusions can be based on this evidence, because the data are too limited and not comparable across studies.

4.11.5.6 Meal frequency

The SLRs identified 20 case-control studies[46-65] that investigated irregular eating and stomach cancer. All but 1 reported increased risk estimates and 15 were statistically significant. Meta-analysis of 16 case-control studies[50-65] gave a summary effect estimate of 2.76 (95% CI 2.10–3.64) for irregular as opposed to regular eating (p < 0.001), but with high heterogeneity.

However, the reference period was generally some years before cancer diagnosis. Irregular eating can be taken to mean frequent snacking or small meals, or missing main meals. But none of these studies defined 'irregular eating' or quantified the frequency with which meals might be skipped.

Eight case-control studies investigated meal frequency and colorectal cancer.[66-80] Most showed increased risks with increased frequency of meals. Meta-analysis of 11 estimates from 7 of these studies[67-69 76 78-80] gave a summary effect estimate of 1.10 (95% CI 1.02–1.19), with high heterogeneity.

This evidence is also unclear. No cohort studies have been identified as examining meal frequency. People who have stomach or colorectal problems are likely to eat irregularly. There is also high probability of confounding, as regular eating patterns are associated with generally healthy behaviour.

The significance of these findings on meal frequency and stomach and colorectal cancer is unclear, in part because of the high probability of confounding. For this reason, no judgement is made.

4.11.5.7 Being breastfed

The SLRs produced no evidence on any relationship between having been breastfed and the risk of cancer in adult life. However, the reviews did produce evidence on the relationship between lactation and cancer in women, and also between having been breastfed and the risk of overweight and obesity in childhood and thereafter. See chapters 6.3.3 and 8.8.3.

4.11.6 Comparison with previous report

The previous report reviewed evidence on vegetarian and mostly-vegetarian dietary patterns of various types, including Seventh-day Adventist and macrobiotic diets. The report concluded that various types of vegetarian dietary pattern seem to decrease the incidence of cancer in general, as well as of some specific sites. It also concluded that semi-vegetarian diets that include small amounts of meat and foods of animal origin may also be beneficial. This conclusion was not made as a formal judgement.

The previous report identified 'poverty' or 'deficiency' patterns of diet. These are monotonous, very high in refined cereal foods (such as rice), with only small amounts of other foods. This was partly in response to its finding that refined cereals (grains) were a possible cause of oesophageal cancer and that starch was a possible cause of stomach cancer. In explanation, the panel responsible for that report concluded that any increase in the risk of cancer here was likely to be caused by poverty/deficiency dietary patterns, not by the specific food or dietary constituent.

The first recommendation of the previous report was in effect for: 'nutritionally adequate and varied diets, based primarily on foods of plant origin'. This was based partly on the evidently protective effects of vegetables and fruits, and also on the general balance of evidence. The panel emphasised that 'plant-based diets' do and may include relatively modest amounts of foods of animal origin.

4.11.7 Conclusions

The Panel concludes:
Currently, no firm judgements can be made on any possible relationship between dietary patterns and the risk of cancer.

CHAPTER 5

Physical activity

Physical activity is any form of movement using skeletal muscles. Until very recently in history, people necessarily engaged in regular, moderate, and at least occasional vigorous, physical activity. However, with urbanisation and industrialisation, general levels of physical activity have declined. Machines now do most of the work previously done by hand; driving and using public transport have largely replaced walking and cycling. While people in higher income countries and in urban settings in most countries may engage in some active forms of recreation, they remain largely inactive, and many spend much time in sedentary recreations, such as watching television and using home computers.

In general, *the Panel judges* that the evidence on physical activity and the risk of cancer, which has continued to accumulate since the early 1990s, shows or suggests that regular, sustained physical activity protects against cancers of some sites. These include colon cancer and female hormone-related cancers, independently of other factors such as body fatness.

The Panel judges as follows. The evidence that physical activity protects against colon cancer is convincing. Physical activity probably protects against postmenopausal breast cancer; the evidence suggesting that it protects against premenopausal breast cancer is limited. Physical activity probably protects against cancer of the endometrium. The evidence suggesting that physical activity protects against cancers of the lung and pancreas is limited.

The Panel is impressed by the overall consistency of the evidence and *concludes* that relatively high levels of physical activity protect, or may protect, against cancers of the colon, breast (postmenopause), and endometrium. To prevent these cancers, the overall evidence supports the message that the more physically active people are the better; however, this excludes extreme levels of activity.

The Panel also agrees that since physical activity protects against overweight, weight gain, and obesity, it also protects against cancers for which the risk is increased by these factors (see Chapter 8).

The evidence assembled for this Report gives an account of the beneficial effects of higher compared to lower levels of physical activity. However, *the Panel further agrees* that the evidence can equally be interpreted as showing that sedentary ways of life increase or may increase the risk of these cancers. Most people in urbanised, industrialised, and mechanised settings throughout the world now lead these sedentary ways of life.

Finally, *the Panel agrees* that the evidence assembled and judged in this chapter supports the general hypothesis that people have evolved and adapted to be physically active throughout life. *The Panel also agrees*, therefore, that sedentary ways of life are unhealthy. It is aware of current trends and also projections (summarised in Chapter 1) showing that average physical activity levels are continuing to decrease throughout the world.

Within the remit of this Report, the strongest evidence, corresponding to judgements of 'convincing' and 'probable', shows that physical activity of all types protects against cancers of the colon, and also of the breast (postmenopause) and endometrium.

This chapter does not address the social or environmental (or underlying and basic) determinants of physical activity and its general decline; this is the subject of an associated report to be published in late 2008.

PHYSICAL ACTIVITY, AND THE RISK OF CANCER

In the judgement of the Panel, physical activity[1] modifies the risk of the following cancers. Judgements are graded according to the strength of the evidence.

	DECREASES RISK	INCREASES RISK
Convincing	Colon[2]	
Probable	Breast (postmenopause) Endometrium	
Limited — suggestive	Lung Pancreas Breast (premenopause)	
Substantial effect on risk unlikely	None identified	

1 Physical activity of all types: occupational, household, transport, and recreational.
2 Much of the evidence reviewed grouped colon cancer and rectal cancer together as 'colorectal' cancer. *The Panel judges* that the evidence is stronger for colon than for rectum.

For an explanation of the terms used in the matrix, please see chapter 3.5.1, the text of this chapter, and the glossary.

World Cancer Research Fund   American Institute for Cancer Research

Since the emergence of *Homo sapiens* around 250 000 years ago, and until very recently in history, people have usually been regularly physically active from early childhood throughout life unless prevented by disability or infirmity. Gatherer–hunter (and pastoral) and peasant–agricultural communities have to be physically active to sustain their ways of life. This includes building and maintaining dwellings; raising families; seeking food security and feeding infants, dependants, the disabled, and elders; and travelling to find water, game, precious items, and better land. Walking, as well as activities undertaken with hand tools such as gathering, hunting, growing, harvesting, grinding, cooking, cleaning, building, and fighting, all require a regular and substantial amount of energy from food.

Throughout history, manual workers in and around cities have also been physically active, by the nature of their occupations. These range from those who built pyramids in Egypt, Mexico, and elsewhere, and fortifications in Asia, Latin America, and Europe, to the working-class labourers of industrialised countries. Such labourers built houses, sewers, bridges, canals, railways, roads, served in armies and navies, and worked in mines and factories, 'by the sweat of their brow', and still do so, throughout the world.

In modern times, the story of urbanisation and of industrialisation is one in which machines are increasingly used to do the work previously done by hand. Early factory and farm machinery still involved sustained, moderate or vigorous physical activity, as did housework; and most people walked or (later) cycled to work. In the first half of the 20th century, most occupations in high-income countries required physical activity and only a minority of households owned cars or televisions. In middle- and low-income countries at that time, almost all occupations were physically active.

In the second half of the 20th century this all began to change, at first gradually and then more rapidly. Now, at the beginning of the 21st century, most occupations in urban areas throughout the world are sedentary. Household tasks are mostly mechanised; much food is purchased already prepared; most journeys (even short ones) are made by car or public transport; and for young people, television viewing and the use of computers have often largely replaced active recreation.

In public health terms, given the known benefits of regular, sustained physical activity, this shift in whole populations from being active to sedentary is one of the most ominous phenomena of recent decades. This is not confined to high-income countries or urban areas. The ways of life of most people in most countries are now sedentary, with the major exception of peasant farmers and manual labourers, mostly in Asia and Africa but also elsewhere.

General levels of physical activity in high-income countries, and more recently in most other countries, have dropped and continue to drop. It is in this special context that the Panel commissioned systematic literature reviews (SLRs) of the primary evidence on physical activity and cancer.

5.1 Definitions

Physical activity is any movement using skeletal muscles. For people with sedentary ways of life, light physical activity includes standing, walking around an office or home, and shopping and food preparation. Recreation time may involve light, moderate, or vigorous physical activity depending on the nature and intensity of activities, hobbies, and pursuits. Most people with active ways of life are moderately or vigorously physically active at work (manual labour) or at home (household work by hand), and are moderately physically active in transport (walking, riding, and cycling). People with sedentary occupations can be as physically active as people engaged in manual labour, but usually only if they engage in regular moderate and occasional vigorous physical activity away from work.[1]

Sitting, standing, and other light physical activity intrinsic to normal waking life, such as stretching, fidgeting, and maintaining posture, are all forms of physical activity.

Exercise and other forms of physical training are types of recreational physical activity. These may be aerobic, such as running, cycling, dancing, and other activities that increase oxygen uptake and improve cardiovascular function, among other things; or anaerobic, such as resistance training using weights, which increases muscle strength and mass.[1]

Physical activity increases energy expenditure and so is a factor in energy balance (see chapter 8.3.3). The intensity of physical activity can be categorised according to the degree to which it increases energy expenditure above basal metabolism. A table showing the intensity of physical activity involved in different forms of movement is included in Chapter 12.

5.2 Types and levels of physical activity

5.2.1 Types of physical activity

Conventionally, and for the purposes of this Report, overall physical activity is classified into four types. These are:
- Occupational (at work)
- Household (in the home)
- Transport (such as travelling to and from work)
- Recreational (leisure).

Much of the evidence summarised and judged below uses these classifications. They also highlight differences between various ways of life. Populations and communities where physical activity at work and at home depends on hand tools and walking (or riding or cycling) are overall physically active or very active, even without recreational activity. Conversely, people whose ways of life at work and at home are sedentary, and who use mechanised transport, will be overall sedentary, unless they engage in substantial amounts of moderate and perhaps some vigorous physical recreational activity away from work. In general, in high-income countries recreational activity accounts for a greater proportion of an overall lower level of physical activity.[2]

Physical activity can also be classified by intensity: vigorous, moderate, light, or sedentary (see boxes 5.1 and 5.2). It is the combination of frequency, intensity, and duration that determines total physical activity levels. A person may use the same total amount of energy in 1 hour of light physical activity as they do in 30 minutes of moderate activity or 20 minutes of vigorous activity.

5.2.2 Levels of physical activity

For many years, planners responsible for keeping specified population groups (such as builders, soldiers, schoolchildren, or office workers) healthy and productive have compiled estimates of the food or energy needed by these groups. Such estimates consistently show that some people need almost as much energy from food for physical activity as they do for the basic functions of vital organs and the assimilation of food. These are people who are moderately physically active for roughly half of their waking day, are engaged in light work or sitting or resting for most of the rest of their waking hours, and are occasionally vigorously physically active.[4]

In physically active populations where energy from food is not freely available, people tend to be lean, and also small. Below critical levels, as has been observed in Asia and in Europe, food scarcity makes regular, sustained physical work difficult and even impossible.[5 6]

5.2.2.1 Energy costs of ways of life

The energy requirements of healthy adults are determined largely by their habitual physical activity levels (PALs). PALs are the ratio of a person's daily total energy expenditure (TEE) to their basal energy expenditure, and thus take into account the greater energy required for performing the same task with a higher body mass.[2 7]

A sustained PAL of 1.2 corresponds roughly to a bedridden state. People whose occupations are exceptionally active, such as miners, woodcutters, soldiers, and athletes, may need more energy for physical activity than for their basic functions. This translates into habitual PALs above 2.0. Such unusual people are mostly young adults, and these levels of physical activity are not sustained throughout life. PALs above 2.4 can only be sustained over a long period of time by unusually physically fit people. Also see Chapter 12.

In general, in high-income countries in the first decade of the 21st century, average levels of physical activity usually account for about 20 to 30 per cent of TEE, but for extreme-

---

The total amount of energy a person uses during a particular activity is determined by a combination of the duration and intensity of the activity. Metabolic equivalents (METs) describe intensity relative to a person's resting metabolic rate. The energy costs of any particular activity vary, depending on a person's basal energy expenditure and their age, sex, size, skill, and level of fitness. MET values take these factors into account.

High total energy expenditure can be produced by performing low-intensity activity for a long duration or high-intensity activity for a shorter duration. However, these two different types of activity may have different physiological effects. The intensity of physical activity is therefore sometimes stratified into levels, such as vigorous (≥ 6 METs), moderate (3–5.9 METs), or light (<3 METs). METs can be used to describe the intensity of single activities, equivalent to the physical activity ratio (PAR), or the overall level of activity over a day, equivalent to the physical activity level (PAL).

Vigorous physical activity can also be defined as that which increases heart and breathing rates up to 80 per cent or more of their maximum (the point at which anaerobic metabolism is needed to provide energy). Moderate physical activity increases heart rate to around 60–75 per cent of its maximum (and the energy requirement can usually be met by aerobic metabolism using the body's stores of glycogen and then fats). Light physical activity has only minor effects on heart and breathing rates. Sedentary activity (or inactivity) involves no noticeable effort: heart and breathing rates are not raised perceptibly above 'resting' levels.[3] Also see 5.2.2.1.

| Box 5.2 | Sedentary ways of life |

The evidence judged in this chapter shows that higher rather than lower levels of physical activity protect, or may protect, against a number of cancers. Most studies of physical activity are carried out in high-income countries with low average levels of occupational, household, and transport physical activity (characterised as sedentary ways of life).

What are now regarded as high levels of physical activity in urbanised and industrialised settings correspond roughly to what were average levels of physical activity in most (including high-income) countries until well into the second half of the 20th century.[4] Since then, occupations have generally become more sedentary: machines do more household work; more people drive or ride in cars or buses than cycle or walk; and for children as well as adults, active recreation has been largely replaced by watching television or other sedentary pursuits.

This Report has a global perspective, and *the Panel agrees* that the evidence assessed in this chapter can, with equal validity, be judged inversely. This means that relatively low levels of physical activity — as now typical in high-income countries and in urban–industrial settings in all continents and most countries throughout the world — are or may be a cause of cancers of the colon, breast (postmenopause), and endometrium. Also, these low levels are, or may be, a cause of weight gain, overweight, or obesity, which themselves are causes of some cancers. The evidence judged in this chapter supports the general theory that the human species has evolved and adapted to be physically active throughout life, and therefore that sedentary ways of life are unhealthy.

Evidence that sedentary ways of life increase the risk of diseases other than cancer is summarised in Chapters 8 and 10.

---

ly sedentary people this may be as little as 15 per cent.[289] See box 5.2.

The combined contribution of multiple types of physical activity can also be characterised in terms of metabolic equivalent (MET)-hours. METs are usually converted to MET-hours per day or per week, which are calculated as the sum of the MET level for each activity multiplied by the duration the activity was performed.

5.3 Interpretation of the evidence

5.3.1 General
For general considerations, see chapters 3.3 and 3.5 and boxes 3.1, 3.2, 3.6, and 3.7. Relative risk (RR) is used in this Report to denote ratio measures of effect, including risk ratios, rate ratios, hazard ratios, and odds ratios.

5.3.2 Specific
Some considerations specific to physical activity are as follows.

Patterns and ranges. Large studies of physical activity are mainly undertaken in high-income countries. Such studies tend to pay most attention to voluntary recreational activity and may therefore have limited relevance to populations in lower-income countries. In these countries, overall activity levels may be higher and physical activity is mostly of the type classed as occupational, household, or transport.

The evidence summarised in section 5.4 of this chapter generally suggests that the more physically active people are, the better, but with one cautionary note. At levels well above what people at any level of fitness are accustomed to, and well above the ranges reviewed in this Report, vigorous physical activity has a suppressive effect on immune function. This not only increases vulnerability to infectious agents but also to DNA damage. Also see chapter 2.4.1.3.

Classification. There is currently no generally agreed classification of different levels of overall physical activity, with quantified degrees of activity corresponding to terms such as 'active' and 'sedentary'.

Measurement. Physical activity is rarely measured precisely. Ideally, studies would record the frequency, intensity, and duration of people's physical activity over an extended period — day and night. But studies are generally not designed to obtain this information. Objective measures such as pedometers and microcomputer sensors are not often used in large studies. Instead, questionnaires are most frequently used.

Terminology. Analysis of studies shows that what is meant by and included as 'physical activity' varies.

Study design. Different methods of measuring physical activity are reported in the literature, making comparison between studies difficult.

Confounding. In high-income countries, people who are physically active also tend to be health conscious and so, for example, are more likely to be non-smokers and to choose diets they believe to be healthy. This may confound findings that show associations with the risk of cancer.

Reporting bias. Questionnaires measure some forms of physical activity more accurately than others. Thus, people tend to recall vigorous and recreational, and other voluntary activities, with relative accuracy. However, these activities are generally performed for relatively short periods of time and may amount to a smaller than perceived proportion of a person's total physical activity.

5.4 Evidence and judgements

Studies examining physical activity and cancer were included in the SLRs. There is evidence, both epidemiological and mechanistic, that physical activity may protect against cancer

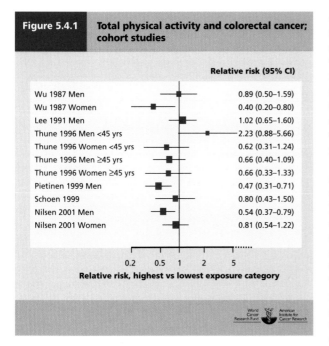

Figure 5.4.1 Total physical activity and colorectal cancer; cohort studies

Relative risk (95% CI)

Wu 1987 Men	0.89 (0.50–1.59)
Wu 1987 Women	0.40 (0.20–0.80)
Lee 1991 Men	1.02 (0.65–1.60)
Thune 1996 Men <45 yrs	2.23 (0.88–5.66)
Thune 1996 Women <45 yrs	0.62 (0.31–1.24)
Thune 1996 Men ≥45 yrs	0.66 (0.40–1.09)
Thune 1996 Women ≥45 yrs	0.66 (0.33–1.33)
Pietinen 1999 Men	0.47 (0.31–0.71)
Schoen 1999	0.80 (0.43–1.50)
Nilsen 2001 Men	0.54 (0.37–0.79)
Nilsen 2001 Women	0.81 (0.54–1.22)

0.2 0.5 1 2 5

Relative risk, highest vs lowest exposure category

in general. Large studies carried out in the USA have shown that physical inactivity is associated with higher overall cancer incidence and mortality.[10-12] These studies are supported by studies on animals.[13] Mechanistic reasons why physical activity may protect against cancer (or why sedentary living may promote cancer) include healthier levels of circulating hormones and the ability of the more active body to consume more food and nutrients without gaining weight (see Chapter 2). Mechanisms by which physical activity may protect against colorectal cancer and female hormone-related cancers are summarised in the following sections.

Evidence from the literature on physical activity and cancer in general indicates that the relationship between physical activity and health is continuous: that is, there does not appear to be a threshold below or above which no effect is found.[14 15] This implies that, in general, the more physically active people are, the better, within the range examined. *The Panel agrees* that this general judgment is supported by the evidence on physical activity and cancer, which is summarised, assessed, and judged below.

The full SLRs are contained on the CD included with this Report.

5.4.1 Colorectal
Eleven cohort studies investigated total physical activity and colon or colorectal cancer.[16-26] Twelve cohort studies investigated occupational physical activity[21 25 27-36] and 24 investigated recreational activity.[10 17 21 25-27 29 30 34 37-51] Five cohort studies investigated frequency of physical activity,[10 16 26 50 52] and seven investigated intensity of physical activity.[22 26 34 37 46 51 53] Case-control studies that investigated physical activity can be found in the full SLRs. Also see chapter 7.9.

Total physical activity
Of the 11 cohort studies considered, 8[16-22 26] reported

decreased risk for the highest physical activity groups when compared to the lowest. This was significant overall in three studies[17-19] and in two additional studies in men but not in women.[16 26] One cohort study reported non-significant increased risk for the lowest physical activity groups when compared to the highest.[25] Meta-analysis was not possible on these studies due to the heterogeneity with which physical activity was measured. Six studies were included in a highest versus lowest analysis, shown in figure 5.4.1. Three studies investigated cancer of the rectum, with mixed results.[17 18 21]

Occupational
Of the 12 cohort studies considered, 6 compared highest to lowest occupational activity groups.[21 25 27-30] All reported decreased risk, which was significant in two[27 30] and borderline significant in one.[25] Six cohort studies compared sedentary occupational activity to high occupational activity[31-36] and all reported increased risk for sedentary activity. This was significant in three studies.[32 33 35] Five studies that investigated colorectal cancer are included in a highest versus lowest plot, shown in figure 5.4.2. Five studies that investigated rectal cancer are examined in a separate highest versus lowest plot, shown in figure 5.4.3.

Recreational
Of the 24 cohort studies considered, 22 compared highest to lowest physical activity groups. All but two of these studies reported decreased risk, which was significant in seven studies.[21 25 26 30 38 41 46] The Health Professionals Follow-Up Study reported an RR of 0.53 (95% confidence interval (CI) 0.32–0.88) comparing men in the highest quintile of physical activity to men in the lowest quintile, with evidence of a dose-response relationship (p for trend = 0.03). In the highest quintile, men reported a median of 47 MET-hours of activity a week; in the lowest quintile, the median was 0.9 MET-hours.[41]

Five studies examined rectal cancer separately, comparing highest with lowest physical activity groups: two reported non-significant decreased risk,[25 27] one reported significant increased risk,[30] and two reported non-significant increased risk.[30 41] Fourteen studies that examined colorectal cancer are included in a highest versus lowest plot, shown in figure 5.4.4.

A published meta-analysis of 19 cohort studies reported significant decreased risk of colon cancer for men with high levels of occupational activity, and also for men and women with high levels of recreational activity. Nine of these studies examined dose response; a significant inverse trend was reported in six studies. Physical activity was not associated with decreased risk of cancer of the rectum.[54]

Walking
Two cohort studies examined measures of walking. A significant increased risk was found in men who reported a 'slower walking pace than others' compared to those who said they had a 'faster walking pace than others'.[39] In a study that examined time spent walking, decreased risk was reported in men who walked for more than 60 minutes a day compared to men who walked for less than 20 minutes a day, but this was not significant.[51]

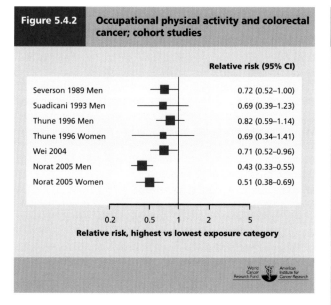

Figure 5.4.2 Occupational physical activity and colorectal cancer; cohort studies

Relative risk (95% CI)

Severson 1989 Men	0.72 (0.52–1.00)
Suadicani 1993 Men	0.69 (0.39–1.23)
Thune 1996 Men	0.82 (0.59–1.14)
Thune 1996 Women	0.69 (0.34–1.41)
Wei 2004	0.71 (0.52–0.96)
Norat 2005 Men	0.43 (0.33–0.55)
Norat 2005 Women	0.51 (0.38–0.69)

Relative risk, highest vs lowest exposure category

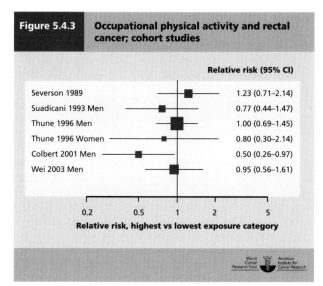

Figure 5.4.3 Occupational physical activity and rectal cancer; cohort studies

Relative risk (95% CI)

Severson 1989	1.23 (0.71–2.14)
Suadicani 1993 Men	0.77 (0.44–1.47)
Thune 1996 Men	1.00 (0.69–1.45)
Thune 1996 Women	0.80 (0.30–2.14)
Colbert 2001 Men	0.50 (0.26–0.97)
Wei 2003 Men	0.95 (0.56–1.61)

Relative risk, highest vs lowest exposure category

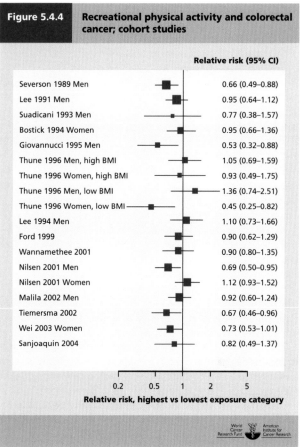

Figure 5.4.4 Recreational physical activity and colorectal cancer; cohort studies

Relative risk (95% CI)

Severson 1989 Men	0.66 (0.49–0.88)
Lee 1991 Men	0.95 (0.64–1.12)
Suadicani 1993 Men	0.77 (0.38–1.57)
Bostick 1994 Women	0.95 (0.66–1.36)
Giovannucci 1995 Men	0.53 (0.32–0.88)
Thune 1996 Men, high BMI	1.05 (0.69–1.59)
Thune 1996 Women, high BMI	0.93 (0.49–1.75)
Thune 1996 Men, low BMI	1.36 (0.74–2.51)
Thune 1996 Women, low BMI	0.45 (0.25–0.82)
Lee 1994 Men	1.10 (0.73–1.66)
Ford 1999	0.90 (0.62–1.29)
Wannamethee 2001	0.90 (0.80–1.35)
Nilsen 2001 Men	0.69 (0.50–0.95)
Nilsen 2001 Women	1.12 (0.93–1.52)
Malila 2002 Men	0.92 (0.60–1.24)
Tiemersma 2002	0.67 (0.46–0.96)
Wei 2003 Women	0.73 (0.53–1.01)
Sanjoaquin 2004	0.82 (0.49–1.37)

Relative risk, highest vs lowest exposure category

intensity of physical activity,[34] and another study reported no association.[53]

Mechanisms

There are a number of mechanisms by which physical activity may protect against colorectal cancer. These include a reduction in insulin resistance, the beneficial effect of physical activity on body fatness (see Chapter 6), the effects on endogenous steroid hormone metabolism, and reduced gut transit time.[55 56]

There is abundant epidemiological evidence from prospective studies showing lower risk of colorectal cancer with higher overall levels of physical activity, as well as with greater frequency and intensity, and there is evidence of a dose-response effect. There is little heterogeneity, except that the effect is not as clear for rectal cancer as it is for colon cancer. There is plausible evidence for mechanisms operating in humans. The evidence that higher levels of physical activity, within the range studied, protects against colon cancer, is convincing.

The Panel is aware that since the conclusion of the SLR, four cohort[56A–56D] and four case control studies[56E-56H] have been published. This new information does not change the Panel judgement (see box 3.8).

Frequency

Of the five cohort studies assessed, three reported decreased risk for the highest frequency of physical activity when compared to the lowest.[16 26 50] In two of these studies, this finding was significant in men but not in women.[16 26] One study reported non-significant increased risk comparing highest with lowest frequency of activity.[44] Another study, comparing lowest with highest frequency of activity, reported non-significant increased risk in women but no association in men.[10]

Intensity

Six cohort studies investigated intensity of physical activity, of which five reported an association between increased intensity and decreased risk. Four reported decreased risk comparing high with low intensity of physical activity,[26 37 46 51] which was significant in all but one study.[51] One study reported a significant increased risk comparing low with high

5.4.2 Breast

Six cohort[57-62] studies and eight case-control studies[63-70] investigated total physical activity and breast cancer. Five cohort studies[10 71-74] and seven case-control studies[75-81] investigated occupational activity. Fourteen cohort studies[10 58 72 74 82-91] and 11 case-control studies[67 76 77 81 92-98] investigated recreational activity. Also see chapter 7.10.

5.4.2.1 Menopause status unspecified
Total physical activity
Two cohort studies[59 60] and four case-control studies[64-66 70] did not specify menopausal status.

One cohort study reported non-significant increased risk for the highest activity group when compared to the lowest.[59] The other reported non-significant decreased risk.[60]

All four case-control studies reported decreased risk for the highest activity group when compared to the lowest. This was significant in one study[66] and in a second study in Hispanic (but not in non-Hispanic) women.[70]

Occupational
Five cohort studies[10 71-74] and two case-control studies[76 81] did not specify menopausal status.

Two cohort studies reported decreased risk comparing high with low physical activity[72 74]; this was significant in one study.[72] Another cohort study reported a borderline increased risk comparing sedentary activity with high activity,[73] and two analyses of the NHANES Epidemiologic Follow-up Study reported no significant associations.[10 71]

Both case-control studies reported non-significant decreased risk for the highest activity group when compared to the lowest.[76 81]

Recreational
Six cohort studies[72 74 82 86 87 89] and six case-control studies[76 81 92-94 98] did not specify menopausal status.

Three cohort studies reported decreased risk for the highest activity group when compared to the lowest[72 82 87]; this was significant in one study.[72] Two studies reported no asso-

ciation[74 86] and one study reported non-significant increased risk.[89] The effect estimates were RR 0.63 (95% CI 0.42–0.95),[72] RR 0.80 (95% CI 0.58–1.12),[87] RR 0.73 (95% CI 0.46–1.14),[82] RR 1.0 (95% CI 0.64–1.54),[74] and RR 1.24 (95% CI 0.83–1.82).[89]

All six case-control studies reported decreased risk with increased physical activity, which was significant in five studies.[76 81 92 93 98] Meta-analysis was possible on these five studies, giving a summary effect estimate of RR 0.90 (95% CI 0.88–0.93) per 7 MET-hours per week (figure 5.4.5), with high heterogeneity. The heterogeneity was related to the size but not the direction of effect.

Mechanisms
There are a number of mechanisms by which physical activity may protect against breast cancer in general. These include the beneficial effect of physical activity on body fatness (see Chapter 6), effects on endogenous steroid hormone metabolism, and a possible strengthening of the immune system. Physical activity may reduce levels of circulating oestrogens and androgens.

The Panel's judgment is given not on breast cancer in general, but separately for premenopausal and postmenopausal breast cancer. See 5.4.2.2 and 5.4.2.3.

5.4.2.2 Premenopause
Total physical activity
Two cohort studies[58 61] and six case-control studies[64-69] reported results for premenopausal breast cancer.

One cohort study reported non-significant but slightly increased risk for the highest activity group when compared to the lowest (RR 1.04; 95% CI 0.82–1.33).[58] The other study reported no association.[61]

Five case-control studies reported decreased risk for the highest activity group when compared to the lowest[64 66 67 69 77]; this was significant in two.[66 69] One study reported non-significant increased risk.[68]

Occupational
Three cohort studies[10 72 73] and six case-control studies[75-80] reported results for premenopausal breast cancer.

Two cohort studies reported decreased risk for the highest activity group compared to the lowest[10 72]; this was significant in one study (RR 0.48; 95% CI 0.24–0.95).[72] One study reported that there was no association.[73]

Two case-control studies reported non-significant decreased risk for the highest activity group when compared to the lowest.[75 76] No associations were reported in the other four studies.[77-80]

Recreational
Four cohort studies[58 72 82 84] and six case-control studies[67 76 77 81 95 96] reported results for premenopausal breast cancer.

Two cohort studies reported non-significant decreased risk for the highest activity group when compared to the lowest.[58 72] Two studies reported non-significant increased risk.[82 84] The effect estimates were RR 0.71 (95% CI 0.45–1.12),[58] RR 0.53 (95% CI 0.25–1.14),[72] RR 1.19 (95% CI 0.43–3.3),[84] and RR 1.83 (95% CI 0.77–4.31).[82]

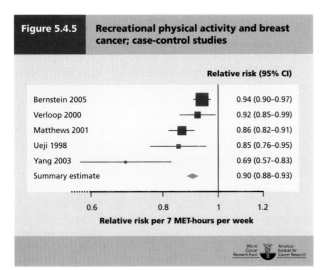

Figure 5.4.5 Recreational physical activity and breast cancer; case-control studies

Relative risk (95% CI)

Study		Relative risk (95% CI)
Bernstein 2005		0.94 (0.90–0.97)
Verloop 2000		0.92 (0.85–0.99)
Matthews 2001		0.86 (0.82–0.91)
Ueji 1998		0.85 (0.76–0.95)
Yang 2003		0.69 (0.57–0.83)
Summary estimate		0.90 (0.88–0.93)

Relative risk per 7 MET-hours per week

Four case-control studies[76 81 95 96] reported decreased risk with increased physical activity; this was significant in two studies,[81 95] neither of which could be included in the meta-analysis. One study reported no association with risk,[67] and another reported non-significant increased risk.[77] Meta-analysis was possible on four case-control studies,[67 76 77 96] giving a summary effect estimate of 1.00 (95% CI 0.97–1.04) per 7 MET-hour per week, with low heterogeneity.

There is ample evidence from prospective studies, but it is inconsistent. There is limited evidence suggesting that physical activity protects against premenopausal breast cancer.

5.4.2.3 Postmenopause
Total physical activity
Two cohort studies[57 62] and six case-control studies[64 66 67 69 70 77] reported results for postmenopausal breast cancer.

Both cohort studies reported decreased risk for the highest activity group when compared to the lowest.[57 62] Effect estimates were RR 0.43 (95% CI 0.19–0.96)[62] and RR 0.20 (95% CI 0.5–1.0),[57] comparing highly active with inactive women.

Five case-control studies reported decreased risk for the highest activity group when compared to the lowest[64 66 67 70 77]; this was significant in three studies.[66 70 77] One study reported non-significant increased risk.[69]

Occupational
Five cohort studies[10 72-74 85] and four case-control studies[75 77-79] reported results for postmenopausal breast cancer.

All five cohort studies reported decreased risk for the highest activity group when compared to the lowest; this was significant in one study.[73] The effect estimates were RR 0.85 (95% CI 0.57–1.28)[74] and RR 0.78 (95% CI 0.52–1.18)[72] for high compared to low occupational activity. The effect estimates were RR 1.5 (95% CI 0.70–2.80)[10] and RR 1.3 (95% CI 1.1–1.7),[73] comparing sedentary to non-sedentary occupations.

Three case-control studies reported decreased risk for the highest activity group when compared to the lowest[75 77 79];

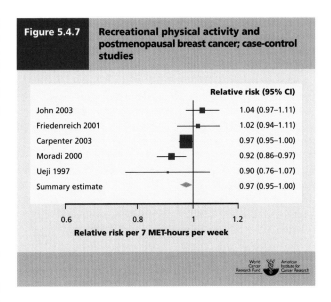

Figure 5.4.7 Recreational physical activity and postmenopausal breast cancer; case-control studies

	Relative risk (95% CI)
John 2003	1.04 (0.97–1.11)
Friedenreich 2001	1.02 (0.94–1.11)
Carpenter 2003	0.97 (0.95–1.00)
Moradi 2000	0.92 (0.86–0.97)
Ueji 1997	0.90 (0.76–1.07)
Summary estimate	0.97 (0.95–1.00)

Relative risk per 7 MET-hours per week

this was significant in one study.[79] One study reported significant increased risk.[78]

Recreational
Eleven cohort studies[10 72 74 82-85 87 88 90 91] and six case-control studies[67 76 77 81 94 97] reported results for postmenopausal breast cancer.

Nine cohort studies reported decreased risk for the highest activity group when compared to the lowest[10 72 82-85 87 88 90]; this was significant in two.[82 84] Two of the studies reported non-significant increased risk.[74 91] Meta-analysis was possible on three studies, giving a summary effect estimate of RR 0.97 (95% CI 0.95–0.99) per 7 MET-hours per week, with no heterogeneity. This is shown in figure 5.4.6.

Meta-analysis was possible on five of the case-control studies, giving a summary effect estimate of RR 0.97 (95% CI 0.95–1.00) per 7 MET-hours per week, with moderate heterogeneity. This is shown in figure 5.4.7.

There is ample evidence from prospective studies showing lower risk of postmenopausal breast cancer with higher levels of physical activity, with a dose-response relationship, although there is some heterogeneity. There is little evidence on frequency, duration, or intensity of activity. There is robust evidence for mechanisms operating in humans. Physical activity probably protects against postmenopausal breast cancer.

The Panel is aware that since the conclusion of the SLR, one case-control study[98A] has been published. This new information does not change the Panel judgement (see box 3.8).

5.4.3 Endometrium
Two cohort studies[99 100] and four case-control studies[101-104] investigated total physical activity and cancer of the endometrium. Three cohort studies[105-107] and 10 case-control studies[102-104 108-114] investigated occupational activity. Four cohort studies[107 115-117] and 10 case-control studies

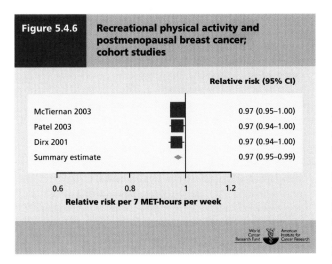

Figure 5.4.6 Recreational physical activity and postmenopausal breast cancer; cohort studies

	Relative risk (95% CI)
McTiernan 2003	0.97 (0.95–1.00)
Patel 2003	0.97 (0.94–1.00)
Dirx 2001	0.97 (0.94–1.00)
Summary estimate	0.97 (0.95–0.99)

Relative risk per 7 MET-hours per week

investigated recreational activity.[102-104] [108-111] [118-120] Also see chapter 7.12.

Total physical activity

One cohort study reported non-significant decreased risk for the highest activity group when compared to the lowest (RR 0.8; 95% CI 0.5–1.1).[99] The other study reported no association when comparing any vigorous activity to none (RR 0.99; 95% CI 0.8–1.2).[121]

All four case-control studies reported decreased risk for the highest activity group when compared to the lowest; this was significant in one.[101]

Occupational

All three cohort studies reported significant decreased risk for the highest activity group when compared to the lowest. Effect estimates are shown in figure 5.4.8.

Seven case-control studies reported decreased risk for the highest activity group when compared to the lowest,[102] [104] [109-111] [113] [114] statistically significant in three.[102] [104] [113] Three studies reported non-significant increased risk.[103] [108] [112] All three cohort studies and eight of the case-control studies were included in a highest versus lowest analysis, most of which showed reduced risk with highwe activity (figure 5.4.8).

Recreational

Three cohort studies reported decreased risk for the highest activity group when compared to the lowest[107] [115] [116]; this was significant in two studies.[115] [116] One study reported non-significant increased risk.[117] See figure 5.4.9.

Nine case-control studies reported decreased risk for

Figure 5.4.9 | **Recreational physical activity and endometrial cancer; cohort and case-control studies**

Relative risk (95% CI)

Cohort

	Relative risk (95% CI)
Terry 1999	0.10 (0.03–0.39)
Folsom 2003	1.05 (0.83–1.32)
Furberg 2003	0.71 (0.34–1.49)
Schouten 2004	0.54 (0.34–0.85)

Case control

Levi 1993	0.53 (0.25–1.11)
Sturgeon 1993	0.83 (0.49–1.41)
Hirose 1996	0.60 (0.38–0.94)
Olsen 1997	0.67 (0.42–1.08)
Jain 2000	0.64 (0.45–0.91)
Moradi 2000	0.77 (0.59–1.00)
Littman 2001	0.83 (0.59–1.16)
Matthews 2005	0.76 (0.51–1.14)
Trentham-Dietz 2006	0.65 (0.49–0.86)

Relative risk, highest vs lowest exposure category

the highest activity group when compared to the lowest,[102] [104] [108-111] [118-120] statistically significant in three.[109] [119] [120] These studies are included in figure 5.4.9. Another study (not included in this figure) reported no significant association.[103]

Mechanisms

As with breast cancer, there are a number of mechanisms by which physical activity may protect against cancer of the endometrium. These include the beneficial effect of physical activity on body fatness (see Chapter 6); effects on endogenous steroid hormone metabolism; and a possible strengthening of the immune system. Also, high levels of physical activity are associated with lower levels of circulating oestrogens and androgens in postmenopausal women.[14]

> There is generally consistent evidence, mostly from case-control studies, showing lower risk of cancer of the endometrium with higher levels of physical activity. There is evidence for mechanisms operating in humans. Physical activity probably protects against cancer of the endometrium.

5.4.4 Lung

Five cohort studies investigated total physical activity[25] [51] [122-124] and two investigated non-recreational activity.[10] [125] Four cohort studies[25] [126-128] and two case-control studies[112] [129] investigated occupational activity. Eleven cohort studies[10] [25] [51] [126-128] [130-134] and four case-control studies[135-138] investigated recreational activity. Another two cohort studies investigated a physical activity measure that did not fit into

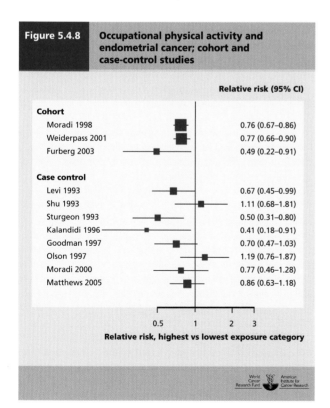

Figure 5.4.8 | **Occupational physical activity and endometrial cancer; cohort and case-control studies**

Relative risk (95% CI)

Cohort

	Relative risk (95% CI)
Moradi 1998	0.76 (0.67–0.86)
Weiderpass 2001	0.77 (0.66–0.90)
Furberg 2003	0.49 (0.22–0.91)

Case control

Levi 1993	0.67 (0.45–0.99)
Shu 1993	1.11 (0.68–1.81)
Sturgeon 1993	0.50 (0.31–0.80)
Kalandidi 1996	0.41 (0.18–0.91)
Goodman 1997	0.70 (0.47–1.03)
Olson 1997	1.19 (0.76–1.87)
Moradi 2000	0.77 (0.46–1.28)
Matthews 2005	0.86 (0.63–1.18)

Relative risk, highest vs lowest exposure category

these categories.[31 126] Also see chapter 7.4.

Total physical activity

Four of the five cohort studies reported decreased risk for the highest activity group compared to the lowest[25 51 123 124]; this was significant in two.[123 124] The other study reported non-significant decreased risk in people under the age of 63, RR 0.84 (95% CI 0.69–1.03) per 20 hours a week; and non-significant increased risk in people aged 63 and over, RR 1.11 (95% CI 0.95–1.29) per 20 hours a week.[122] The effect estimates were RR 0.61 (95% CI 0.41–0.89),[123] RR 0.74 (95% CI 0.59–0.93),[124] RR 0.70 (95% CI 0.48–1.01),[25] and RR 0.76 (95% CI 0.40–1.43),[51] comparing highest to lowest activity groups. All cohort studies were adjusted for smoking.

Non-recreational activity

Two cohort studies reported increased risk with inactivity (sedentary living)[10 125]; this was significant in one.[10] In one study of men, the effect estimate was RR 2.0 (95% CI 1.2–3.5)[10]; in the other study, the estimates were RR 1.26 (95% CI 0.71–2.24) for men and RR 1.41 (95% CI 0.59–3.35) for women.[125] Both studies were adjusted for smoking.

Other physical activity

Two cohort studies reported on other measures of physical activity.[31 126] The Whitehall Study in England reported non-significant increased risk of lung cancer mortality comparing low to high transport-related physical activity.[31] The other study reported decreased risk in both men and women, which was significant in men, comparing high to low occupational and recreational activity combined.[126] Both studies were adjusted for smoking.

Occupational

Two cohort studies reported non-significant increased risk for the highest activity group to the lowest.[127 128] The effect estimates were RR 1.23 (95% CI 0.95–1.59) in a cohort of male non-smokers in Finland,[127] and RR 1.13 (95% CI 0.63–2.05) for men and 1.80 (95% CI 0.75–4.31) for women in the second cohort.[128] Another two cohort studies reported non-significant decreased risk comparing high to low activity.[25 126] The effect estimates were RR 0.88 (95% CI 0.62–1.22) in a cohort of men and women,[25] and in another cohort were RR 0.79 (95% CI 0.30–2.12) for women and RR 0.99 (95% CI 0.70–1.41) for men.[126] All studies were adjusted for smoking.

One case-control study reported non-significant increased risk for the highest activity group when compared to the lowest[112]; the other reported non-significant decreased risk.[129]

Recreational

Ten cohort studies reported decreased risk comparing the highest activity group compared to the lowest[25 51 126-128 130-134]; this was significant in five studies. One study reported non-significant increased risk.[10] Effect estimates were RR 1.11 (95% CI 0.71–1.74),[10] RR 0.90 (95% CI 0.83–0.97),[128] RR 0.97 (95% CI 0.88–1.07),[127] RR 0.27 (95% CI 0.15–0.49, unadjusted for smoking),[130] RR 0.45 (95% CI 0.17–1.18),[131] RR 0.80 (95% CI 0.71–0.90),[132] RR 0.50 (95% CI 0.29–0.87, unadjusted for smoking),[134] RR 0.73 (95% CI 0.54–0.98),[126] RR 0.81 (95% CI 0.58–1.13),[51] and RR 0.8 (95% CI

0.6–1.06).[25] One study reported that mean hours per week of sports activity were lower in cases (0.70) than in controls (1.10).[133] The exposure examined varied, with some studies analysing leisure-time activities, sports, or exercise, and one examining endurance skiers. All but the two studies specified above were adjusted for smoking.

All four case-control studies reported a significant decreased risk comparing high to low levels of activity.[135-138]

Mechanisms

No mechanisms were identified by which physical activity might have a specific effect on the risk of lung cancer. The possibility could not be dismissed that people with pulmonary disease, who are at increased risk of lung cancer, might reduce their level of physical activity.

The association between physical activity and lung cancer is complex. Unlike many other cancers, lung cancer is not positively associated with body mass index (BMI). *The Panel is aware* that the observed association between physical activity and lung cancer may be a reflection of reverse causation due to chronic lung disease.

> **There is evidence from prospective and case-control studies showing lower risk of lung cancer with higher levels of physical activity, but there is no evidence of plausible mechanisms. The relationship between activity, BMI, and lung cancer makes the evidence difficult to interpret. There is limited evidence suggesting that physical activity protects against lung cancer.**

The Panel is aware that since the conclusion of the SLR, one cohort study[138A] has been published. This new information does not change the Panel judgement (see box 3.8).

5.4.5 Pancreas

Three cohort studies[44 139 140] and one case-control study[141] investigated total physical activity and pancreatic cancer. Three cohort studies[139 142 143] and two case-control studies[129 144] investigated occupational activity. Nine cohort studies[31 139 140 142 145-149] and three case-control studies[150-152] investigated recreational activity. Four cohort studies (in three publications) investigated walking,[140 145 146] while two investigated transportation activity.[140 145] Five cohort studies (in four publications)[140 146 149 153] and one case-control study[141] investigated vigorous activity. Four cohort studies (in three publications)[140 145 146] and one case-control study[141] investigated moderate activity. Also see chapter 7.6.

Total physical activity

Two cohort studies reported non-significant decreased risk for the highest activity group compared to the lowest.[44 139] Another cohort study reported non-significant increased risk.[140] The single case-control study reported decreased risk, significant in men but not women.[141]

Occupational

One cohort study reported significant increased risk for people who reported that they felt 'worn out' after work.[139] One study stated they found no significant association[143]; and one study reported non-significant decreased risk for moderate or heavy work compared to sedentary jobs.[142] Both case-control studies reported decreased risk for the highest activity group when compared to the lowest[129 144]; this was significant in one study.[144]

Recreational

Five cohort studies reported non-significant decreased risk for the highest activity group when compared to the lowest.[139 142 145-147] Four cohort studies reported non-significant increased risk.[31 140 148 149] Meta-analysis was possible on three cohort studies, giving a summary effect estimate of RR 0.98 (95% CI 0.91–1.05) per 10 MET-hours per week, with no heterogeneity. All three case-control studies reported decreased risk for the highest activity group compared to the lowest[150-152]; this was significant in one.[150]

Walking

Three cohort studies reported decreased risk for the highest activity group compared to the lowest[140 146]; this was significant in two.[146] The effect estimates were RR 0.48 (95% CI 0.24–0.97) for women in the Nurses' Health Study[146]; RR 0.45 (95% CI 0.26–0.80) for men in the Health Professionals Follow-up Study[146]; and RR 0.99 (95% CI 0.64–1.51) in a study of pancreatic cancer mortality.[140] The Whitehall Study reported increased risk of pancreatic cancer mortality for slow compared to fast walkers (RR 1.1; 95% CI 0.20–5.10).[145]

Vigorous

Three cohort studies reported non-significant decreased risk for the highest activity group compared to the lowest.[140 146 149] Two studies reported non-significant increased risk.[146 153] The single case-control study reported non-significant decreased risk.[141]

Moderate

Two cohort studies reported increased risk for the highest activity group compared to the lowest[140 149]; this was significant in one.[149] Two cohort studies reported decreased risk,[146] which was significant in one.[146] The single case-control study reported non-significant increased risk in men and no association in women.[141]

Mechanisms

Mechanisms by which physical activity may protect against cancer of the pancreas include reduced insulin resistance and reduced gut transit time, which has beneficial effects on bile content and secretion and general pancreatic activity.[154]

There is evidence from prospective studies showing lower risk of pancreatic cancer with higher levels of various types of physical activity, but it is rather inconsistent. There is limited evidence suggesting that physical activity protects against pancreatic cancer.

The Panel is aware that since the conclusion of the SLR, one cohort study[154A] has been published. This new information does not change the Panel judgement (see box 3.8).

5.4.6 Prostate

Two studies showed that higher levels of physical activity were associated with lower risk specifically of advanced or aggressive prostate cancer.[155 156] Also see chapter 7.14.

In the Health Professionals Follow-Up Study, a strong inverse association between vigorous physical activity and advanced prostate cancer was seen in men 65 years or older: RR 0.33 (95% CI 0.17–0.62) for more than 29 MET-hours compared to none. No association was seen in younger men.[155]

In the American Cancer Society Cancer Prevention Study II Nutrition Cohort, high levels of recreational physical activity were associated with decreased risk of aggressive prostate cancer: RR 0.69 (95% CI 0.52–0.92) for more than 35 MET-hours per week compared to no physical activity. No association was found between recreational physical activity and overall prostate cancer.[156]

Mechanisms

Several mechanisms have been proposed for how physical activity may decrease the risk of prostate cancer. Exercise may reduce prostate cancer risk by reducing levels of testosterone and insulin. Acute exercise may promote the formation of free radicals. In people who exercise consistently, this may induce the production of enzymes, such as superoxide dismutase, that protect against oxidative stress. These enzymes may also protect against cancer, since dietary antioxidants have been linked to reduced cancer risk.

The Panel has noted **the evidence presented here that physical activity is associated with reduced risk of advanced or aggressive cancer of the prostate, but has not made a formal judgement.**

5.5 Comparison with previous report

The panel responsible for the previous report judged that the evidence that physical activity protects against cancer of the colon was convincing. Evidence for cancer of the rectum was judged to be unimpressive. Physical activity was judged to be possibly protective against cancers of the lung and of the breast. The previous report mentioned epidemiological, experimental, and mechanistic evidence suggesting that physical activity is generally protective against cancer, and in particular against colon cancer and female hormone-related cancers. The panel responsible for that report also concluded that all types of physical activity were probably beneficial and that people should remain physically active throughout life.

5.6 Conclusions

The Panel concludes:
The evidence that physical activity protects against colon cancer is convincing. Physical activity probably protects against postmenopausal breast cancer, whereas the evidence suggesting that it protects against premenopausal breast cancer is limited. Physical activity probably protects against can-

cer of the endometrium. The evidence suggesting that physical activity protects against cancers of the lung and pancreas is limited.

The Panel notes the overall consistency of the evidence. *The Panel emphasises* that, taken together, the evidence suggests that all types and degrees of physical activity are or may be protective, excluding extreme levels of activity: the evidence for any specific type or degree of physical activity is limited. The evidence is consistent with the message that the more physically active people are, the better.

The Panel also agrees that physical activity, which promotes healthy weight, would be expected to protect against cancers whose risk is increased by overweight, weight gain, and obesity, and conversely that sedentary living increases or may increase the risk of the specified cancers (see Chapters 6 and 8). Most people in urbanised and industrialised settings, not only in high-income countries but throughout the world, now lead sedentary ways of life.

CHAPTER 6

Body composition, growth, and development

The size and shape of the human body, the rates at which humans grow from conception to adult life, and human physical and mental development are all determined by interrelated genetic and environmental, including nutritional, factors.

Specifically, human nutrition, the degree to which the body's needs are met by the nature, quality, and quantity of the foods consumed, has a fundamental effect on health and well-being, and also on the body's ability to resist diseases. These include not only infectious diseases but also chronic diseases, one of which is cancer.

The Panel decided that the evidence apparent in the literature concerned with body composition, growth, and development, including breastfeeding (lactation), was likely to prove of special interest. For this reason, the independent systematic literature reviews, on which the evidence and judgements in this chapter are based, have covered these areas more thoroughly than has previously been attempted.

The three related sections of this chapter pay special attention to degree of body fatness, rates of growth and their outcomes, and also to lactation in relation to the risk of cancer throughout the life course. The first of these sections, which focuses on body composition, is complemented by Chapter 8 on determinants of weight gain, overweight, and obesity.

The findings of the systematic literature reviews are summarised and judged within each section. The matrices that are part of the introduction of each section display the Panel's judgements, which are developed or qualified when necessary in footnotes. Introductory passages also summarise relevant context. Other passages review issues of interpretation of the literature and compare the findings of this with the previous report. For convenience, and also throughout this Report, the Panel's summary judgements are repeated at the end of each section.

The picture that emerges is impressive: much more so than that based on the evidence gathered in the mid-1990s using the then agreed methodology. Its implications are also impressive. Some of the most persuasive evidence in the whole field of food, nutrition, and physical activity indicates that the basis for prevention of cancer should be a whole life course approach, starting at the beginning of life, or even in maternal preparation for pregnancy.

6.1 Body fatness

BODY FATNESS, AND THE RISK OF CANCER

In the judgement of the Panel, the factors listed below modify the risk of cancer. Judgements are graded according to the strength of the evidence.

	DECREASES RISK		INCREASES RISK	
	Exposure	Cancer site	Exposure	Cancer site
Convincing			**Body fatness**	**Oesophagus[1]** **Pancreas** **Colorectum** **Breast (postmenopause)** **Endometrium** **Kidney**
			Abdominal fatness	**Colorectum**
Probable	**Body fatness**	**Breast (premenopause)**	**Body fatness**	**Gallbladder[2]**
			Abdominal fatness	**Pancreas** **Breast (postmenopause)** **Endometrium**
			Adult weight gain	**Breast (postmenopause)**
Limited — suggestive			Body fatness Low body fatness	Liver Lung
Substantial effect on risk unlikely		None identified		

1 For oesophageal adenocarcinomas only.
2 Directly and indirectly, through the formation of gallstones.

For an explanation of all the terms used in the matrix, please see chapter 3.5.1, the text of this section, and the glossary.

A key reason for the success of *Homo sapiens* is our adaptability. Humans have evolved to survive and flourish in almost all environments and circumstances which, during the 250 000 years of our species' existence, have usually included occasional or regular food scarcity and insecurity. We have built-in defences against starvation: our own stores of fat that are used in times of need.

Food insecurity remains endemic, particularly in Africa and Asia. But many people in the world now have access to more than enough to eat and drink and are also relatively physically inactive (see Chapter 5). As a result, stores of body fat tend to increase. What is now a pandemic of overweight and obesity can be seen as a response to circumstances of plenty. One consequence, in the context of reduction in rates of nutritional deficiencies and infections of childhood and early life, and the ageing of human populations, is an increase in the rates of chronic diseases. These include cancer.

Overall, *the Panel judges* that evidence on the degree of body fatness and the risk of cancers of a number of sites is strong and generally consistent. *The Panel emphasises* that the risk of cancer is modified, not only by obesity, as usually defined, but by overweight as well, and even by degrees of body fatness generally regarded as healthy.

The Panel judges as follows:
The evidence that greater body fatness is a cause of adenocarcinoma of the oesophagus, and cancers of the pancreas, colorectum, breast (postmenopause), endometrium, and kidney, is convincing. Greater body fatness is probably a cause of cancer of the gallbladder. There is limited evidence suggesting that greater body fatness is a cause of liver cancer. The evidence that greater abdominal (central) fatness is a cause of colorectal cancer is convincing; and greater abdominal fatness is probably a cause of cancers of the pancreas, breast (postmenopause), and endometrium. By contrast, greater body fatness probably protects against premenopausal breast cancer.

The Panel notes that there is limited evidence suggesting that low body fatness (underweight) is a cause of lung cancer, but residual confounding with smoking and lung disease cannot be ruled out.

See Chapter 8 for judgements on physical activity and sedentary ways of life, the energy density of foods and drinks, breastfeeding, other factors, and the risk of weight gain, overweight, and obesity.

Within the remit of this Report, the strongest evidence, corresponding to judgements of 'convincing' and 'probable', shows that greater body fatness and greater abdominal fatness are causes of cancer of the colorectum; that greater body fatness is additionally a cause of cancers of the oesophagus (adenocarcinoma), pancreas, breast (postmenopause), endometrium, and kidney; and (probably) gallbladder. It also shows that greater abdominal fatness is probably a cause of cancers of the pancreas, breast (postmenopause), and endometrium; but that greater body fatness probably protects against premenopausal breast cancer.

Body fatness and organ mass and composition, commonly assessed by body size measurements, are key factors influencing health and well being throughout the life course.

The main concern of nutrition science, since its beginnings and until the mid-20th century, has been to protect populations against the consequences of malnutrition in the 'classic' sense of the word. That is undernutrition, which increases vulnerability to infectious diseases, especially in infancy and childhood, and results in people who are small and weak, unable to be productive, and with low life expectancy.[1] This remains a central public health priority for middle- and low-income countries.[2]

In the final two decades of the 20th century and into this century, a different and imperative public health nutrition concern has emerged: weight gain, overweight, and obesity. At first, it was generally assumed that societies whose babies are big, whose children grow fast, and whose adults are heavy and tall, were healthy. Compared to societies with inadequate nutrition and poor public health provision, such populations are indeed physically stronger, more productive, have longer lives, and are generally healthier.

This said, since the 1980s, a series of reports based on a rapidly increasing evidence base have concluded that populations of high-income countries, and now also populations of many middle- and low-income countries, are becoming overweight to an extent that is bad for health. These countries are almost exclusively those experiencing social, economic, and nutritional transition. The nutritional transition is characterised by a shift from 'traditional' diets that are low in fat and high in fibre to high-energy 'Western' diets that are high in fat and low in fibre. It is now generally accepted that obesity, but also overweight short of obesity, increases the risk of a number of major chronic diseases including insulin resistance, hyperlipidaemia, hypertension and stroke, type 2 diabetes, and coronary heart disease, as well as cancers of some sites.[3] In this chapter, the evidence on body fatness and cancer is summarised and judged. Also see Chapter 8.

In this Report, the term 'body fatness' refers to the degree of body fatness across the whole range, not only the conventional categories of overweight and obesity.

6.1.1 Definitions and patterns

6.1.1.1 Body fatness

Excess energy from food is stored as fat in the body in adipose tissue. The amount of this body tissue varies more from person to person than any other type (such as muscle, bone, or blood). The size and location of these fat stores also vary considerably between populations, people, and over the course of a person's life. Excess body fat is a cause of a number of chronic diseases and reduces life expectancy (also see Chapter 8).

Since the 1980s, typical body compositions have changed, with a worldwide increase in average body fatness and in overweight and obesity. This change is most notable in high-income countries, and in industrial and urban environments in many if not most countries (see chapters 1.1.3 and 1.2.2). In several low-income countries, high levels of body fatness exist alongside undernutrition in the same communities and even in the same families.[3]

Body fatness is difficult to measure directly or accurately. However, because body fatness is the most variable determinant of weight, several weight-based measures are used as markers of body fatness. The most common is the body mass index (BMI), a measure of weight adjusted for height. BMI is calculated as weight in kilograms divided by height in metres squared (kg/m^2). In most circumstances, BMI has been shown to be reliably linked to body fatness.[4] But this method does not always provide an accurate measure: unusually muscular and lean people (such as manual workers and power athletes) have a relatively high BMI, even if they have relatively little body fat. See table 6.1.1 and also Chapter 8.

A BMI of between 18.5 and 24.9 is generally regarded as 'healthy' or 'normal' (healthy or normal body fatness). This is roughly equivalent to 15–20 per cent body fat in adult men and 25–30 per cent in adult women.[5] The 'underweight' or 'thin' range is a BMI below 18.5 (low body fatness). Above 25 (high body fatness), there are common gradings for overweight, obesity, and extreme ('morbid') obesity. The risk of type 2 diabetes and high blood pressure increases with BMI with no clear threshold, but with a marked increase in risk as BMI approaches 25.[3] The ideal average BMI for populations has been estimated to be 21–22.[6]

The principal cut-off points shown in table 6.1.1 have been agreed by the World Health Organization and are based on the risks associated with being underweight, overweight, or obese (see Chapter 8). However, the healthy ranges of BMI vary between populations. The additional cut-off points take this into account and are recommended for reporting purposes, with a view to facilitating international comparisons.

The principal BMI cut-offs are based on data primarily derived from populations of European origin living in high-income countries, so they may not apply globally. Different

Table 6.1.1	The international classification of adult underweight, overweight, and obesity

A body mass index (BMI) of between 18.5 and 24.9 is generally regarded as 'acceptable' or 'normal'. The 'underweight' or 'thin' range is a BMI of below 18.5. Above 25, the common gradings for overweight and obesity are as shown below:

Classification	BMI (kg/m²)	
	Principal cut-off points	Additional cut-off points
Underweight	**<18.50**	**<18.50**
Severe thinness	<16.00	<16.00
Moderate thinness	16.00–16.99	16.00–16.99
Mild thinness	17.00–18.49	17.00–18.49
Normal range	**18.50–24.99**	**18.50–22.99**
		23.00–24.99
Overweight	**≥25.00**	**≥25.00**
		25.00–27.49
		27.50–29.99
Obese	**≥30.00**	**≥30.00**
Obese class I	30.00–34.99	30.00–32.49
		32.50–34.99
Obese class II	35.00–39.99	35.00–37.49
		37.50–39.99
Obese class III	≥40.00	≥40.00

Adapted with permission from WHO.[3]

BMI cut-off points have been proposed to classify overweight and obesity in different populations, due to different body composition and the relation of BMI to risk in these populations. However, these have not become universally accepted.[7][8] A WHO expert consultation on BMI in Asian populations recommended that the principal BMI cut-off points (table 6.1.1) should be retained as the international classification.[9] However, it also recommended that additional cut-off points of 23, 27.5, 32.5, and 37.5 kg/m² should be added to the international classification and, for reporting purposes, countries should use all categories (that is, 18.5, 23, 25, 27.5, 30, and 32.5 kg/m²; and in many populations, 35, 37.5, and 40 kg/m²) with a view to facilitating international comparisons. The principal and additional cut-off points are shown in table 6.1.1.

At equivalent BMIs, many Asian populations have a higher body fat content, whereas Maori people and Pacific Islanders have more lean tissue and less fat.[4][10][11] Many Asian expert groups and health ministries now define the upper limit of 'acceptable' as a BMI of below 23, whereas the equivalent cut-off point for China is 24. It is unlikely that the excess risk in these populations at relatively low BMIs reflects only differences in body fat — there are probably other related metabolic changes, for instance, those induced by fetal and early childhood nutritional differences. WHO has recognised that Asian populations may choose a BMI cut-off of 23 because of the greater susceptibility of these groups of people to type 2 diabetes and perhaps other complications of excess weight gain.[9] Mexican people have also been shown to be at greater risk, so Latin American populations may also be considered as more sensitive to the effects of weight gain than white people of European origin.[12]

6.1.1.2 Body fat distribution

Fat is not distributed equally around the body. It accumulates subcutaneously (beneath the skin) around the muscles of the upper arm, buttocks, belly, hips, and thighs. It also accumulates intra-abdominally or viscerally (around the organs). Fat stores can be categorised as 'peripheral' (not around the trunk) or 'abdominal' (also called 'central'). The pattern of fat stores is determined largely by genetic factors, with a typically different pattern in men and women, which tends to change with age. Women tend to store more subcutaneous fat around their hips, buttocks, and thighs than men, producing a body profile known as a 'pear shape' (or 'gynoid' pattern of fat distribution). Men are more likely to store fat around their abdomen, producing an 'apple shape' (or 'android' pattern).

The size of peripheral fat stores can be used as a measure of total body fatness, although the proportion of total to abdominal fat varies between people. Waist circumference is a measure that includes both subcutaneous and the more metabolically active intra-abdominal fat stores. The size of intra-abdominal fat stores predicts the risk of chronic diseases, such as metabolic disorders and cardiovascular disease, better than overall indicators of body fatness, such as subcutaneous fat measures or BMI.[13] The size of these fat stores also influences several hormone systems, such as insulin, as well as those involved in the body's response to inflammation, both of which may play a role in cancer processes (box 2.4).[14][15]

Crude estimates of excess abdominal fat can be made by measuring either waist circumference or by calculating the ratio of this measurement to hip circumference (the 'waist to hip' ratio), although this ratio is no longer recommended as a useful indicator of abdominal obesity. Waist circumference is a better single indicator. As is the case for BMI, the cut-off points for excess waist measurements for Asian and Mexican populations are usually lower than those suggested by WHO as suitable for people of European origin. This is because these non-white populations have a greater risk of disease with only modest increases in intra-abdominal fat. The WHO reference values for waist circumferences of 94 cm (37 inches) in men and 80 cm (31.5 inches) in women (on a population basis) are based on their rough equivalence to a BMI of around 25, whereas waist circumferences of 102 cm (40.2 inches) in men and 88 cm (34.6 inches) in women are equivalent to a BMI of around 30.[16][17] For Asian populations, cut-offs for waist circumferences of 90 cm for men and 80 cm for women have been proposed.[18]

6.1.1.3 Adult weight gain

Increases in body weight during adulthood depend mostly on accumulation of fat rather than lean tissue, and therefore any change may better reflect fatness than adult attained weight itself, which is more dependent on lean mass. For this reason, evidence of associations specifically between weight gain in adulthood and cancers was sought in the systematic literature reviews that informed the Panel's judgements.

6.1.2 Interpretation of the evidence

6.1.2.1 General
For general considerations that may affect interpretation of the evidence, see chapters 3.3 and 3.5, and boxes 3.1, 3.2, 3.6 and 3.7.

6.1.2.2 Specific
Some considerations specific to body fatness are as follows.

Classification. The system of classifying underweight, 'normal' weight, overweight, and degrees of obesity as discrete ranges of BMI, is in general use. However, as shown in this chapter and also Chapter 8, the relationship between body fatness and cancer is continuous across the range of BMI. For this reason, the Panel has chosen to use the term 'body fatness' rather than 'overweight' or 'obesity'.

Measurement. BMI is not a perfect marker of body fatness. More precise techniques such as underwater weighing, magnetic resonance imaging, computerised tomography, or dual energy X-ray absorptiometry are rare in large-scale epidemiological studies due to their difficulty and expense. Abdominal fatness is usually measured either using the waist to hip ratio or the waist circumference alone. There is a lack of consensus on how abdominal fatness is best measured, and measurement error is more likely than for some other anthropometric measures such as height and weight. The currently proposed maximum 'cut-off' points for 'healthy' waist circumferences (94 cm or 37 inches for men; 80 cm or 31.5 inches for women) and for 'healthy' waist to hip ratios (1.0 for men; 0.8 for women) are based almost exclusively on studies of cardiovascular or type 2 diabetes risk in white populations in high-income countries. It is not known whether they can be applied to other ethnic groups or outcomes. The relationship between waist circumference and the size of intra-abdominal fat stores (as opposed to subcutaneous abdominal fat stores) may vary between different ethnic groups.[18] As body fatness tends to increase with age in most populations, and is characteristically higher in women than in men, it is important that studies take into account both age and sex. Measurement of change in weight tends to be more precise than static measures such as weight or BMI.

Reporting bias. Objective measures of height and weight, and therefore BMI, are reliable. However, many studies rely on self-reporting, which is liable to introduce bias. Although reported and actual weights are correlated, weight tends to be under-reported, especially by overweight and obese people. BMIs calculated from self-reported data will therefore tend to be lower than from more objective measures.

6.1.3 Evidence and judgements

The full systematic literature review (SLR) is contained on the CD included with this Report.

There are several general mechanisms through which body fatness and abdominal fatness could plausibly influence cancer risk. For example, increasing body fatness raises the inflammatory response, increases circulating oestrogens, and decreases insulin sensitivity. The physiological effects of obesity are described in more detail in Chapter 8. The effects of body fatness-related hormonal changes and inflammation on cancer processes are detailed in box 2.4. Additional site-specific mechanisms are described with the evidence for each cancer site in the following sections.

6.1.3.1 Body fatness
Oesophagus
Three cohort studies[19-21] and eight case-control studies[22-29] investigated body fatness (as measured by BMI) and oesophageal adenocarcinomas.

All three cohort studies showed increased risk for the highest body fatness, as measured by BMI, when compared to the lowest (figure 6.1.1); this was statistically significant in both sexes in one study[21] and in men but not women in two others.[19 20] Effect estimates were 2.58 in men (95% confidence interval (CI) 1.81–3.68; p < 0.001) and 2.06 in women (95% CI 1.25–3.39; p = 0.002)[21]; 2.40 in men (95% CI 1.30–4.42) and 1.57 in women (95% CI 0.51–4.84)[20]; and 1.76 in men (95% CI 1.03–3.02) and 2.13 in women (95% CI 0.97–4.71).[19] The latter study was adjusted for smoking and alcohol but the other two were not.

Seven case-control studies[22-25 27-29] showed increased risk for the highest body fatness group, as measured by BMI, when

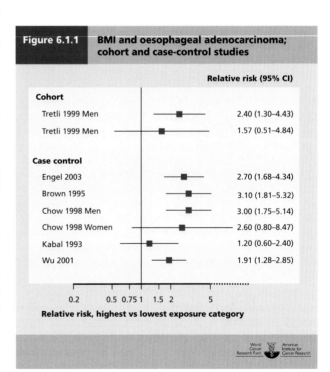

| Figure 6.1.1 | BMI and oesophageal adenocarcinoma; cohort and case-control studies |

Relative risk (95% CI)

Cohort

| Tretli 1999 Men | 2.40 (1.30–4.43) |
| Tretli 1999 Men | 1.57 (0.51–4.84) |

Case control

Engel 2003	2.70 (1.68–4.34)
Brown 1995	3.10 (1.81–5.32)
Chow 1998 Men	3.00 (1.75–5.14)
Chow 1998 Women	2.60 (0.80–8.47)
Kabal 1993	1.20 (0.60–2.40)
Wu 2001	1.91 (1.28–2.85)

0.2   0.5 0.75 1   1.5 2   5

Relative risk, highest vs lowest exposure category

compared to the lowest (figure 6.1.1). This was statistically significant in five studies,[22-24 28 29] and in men but not women in a sixth.[25] One study showed non-significant decreased risk.[26] Meta-analysis was possible on four case-control studies (all of which showed increased risk), giving an effect estimate of 1.11 (95% CI 1.07–1.15) per kg/m[2], with moderate heterogeneity (figure 6.1.2). This would produce an increased risk of 55 per cent for each 5 kg/m[2], assuming a linear relationship, although a curvilinear dose-response relationship cannot be ruled out.

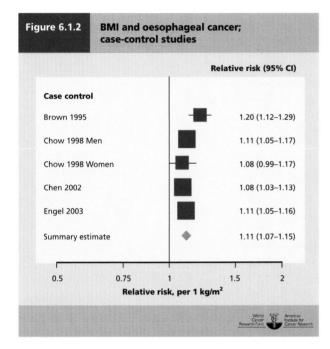

Figure 6.1.2 **BMI and oesophageal cancer; case-control studies**

Relative risk (95% CI)

Case control

Brown 1995	1.20 (1.12–1.29)
Chow 1998 Men	1.11 (1.05–1.17)
Chow 1998 Women	1.08 (0.99–1.17)
Chen 2002	1.08 (1.03–1.13)
Engel 2003	1.11 (1.05–1.16)
Summary estimate	1.11 (1.07–1.15)

Relative risk, per 1 kg/m[2]

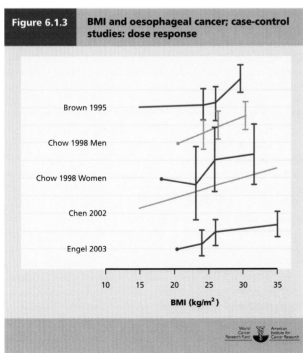

Figure 6.1.3 **BMI and oesophageal cancer; case-control studies: dose response**

BMI (kg/m[2])

A dose-response relationship is apparent from case-control data (figure 6.1.3). Cohort data show a statistically significant trend in men and are suggestive of a similar trend in women.

Studies that investigated body fatness, as measured by BMI, and all types of oesophageal cancer or squamous cell carcinomas showed inconsistent results. Only when results were stratified by cancer type did a consistent pattern emerge, and then only for adenocarcinomas.

An association between body fatness and increased risk of oesophageal adenocarcinoma is consistent, with known geographical and time trends for both BMI and adenocarcinomas.

The general mechanisms through which body fatness could plausibly influence cancer risk are outlined in 6.1.3 (also see box 2.4).

The epidemiology is consistent, with evidence of a dose-response relationship. There is evidence for plausible mechanisms that operate in humans. The evidence that greater body fatness is a cause of oesophageal adenocarcinoma is convincing.

The Panel is aware that since the conclusion of the SLR, two cohort[30 31] and five case-control studies[32-36] have been published. This new information does not change the Panel judgement (see box 3.8).

Pancreas

Twenty-three cohort studies[37-58] and 15 case-control studies[59-73] investigated body fatness (as measured by BMI) and pancreatic cancer.

Thirteen cohort studies showed increased risk with increased body fatness,[37 38 40 43 44 46 47 49 51 54 55 57] which was statistically significant in four.[47 49 54 55] Two studies showed increased risk in both sexes[42 50]; this was statistically significant in women but not in men in one study,[42] and in men but not women in the other.[50] One study showed increased risk in both black and white men, which was significant for white men only.[56] Two studies showed non-significant increased risk in women and non-significant decreased risk in men.[45 52] One study showed statistically significant increased risk in men and non-significant decreased risk in women.[39] Three studies showed non-significant decreased risk[41 48 53] and one study stated that there was no significant association.[58] Meta-analysis was possible on 17 cohort studies, giving a summary effect estimate of 1.14 (95% CI 1.07–1.22) per 5 kg/m[2], with moderate heterogeneity (figure 6.1.4). Most studies adjusted for smoking, with no apparent difference between people who smoked and those that did not.

Five case-control studies showed increased risk with increased body fatness,[62-66] which was statistically significant in one,[66] and in men but not women in another study.[64] Five studies showed decreased risk,[61 68-71] which was statistically significant in one.[69] Two studies showed non-significant decreased risk in men and a non-significant increased risk in women.[59 72] One study showed a statistically significant increased risk in men and a non-significant decreased risk in women.[67] One study showed non-significant decreased

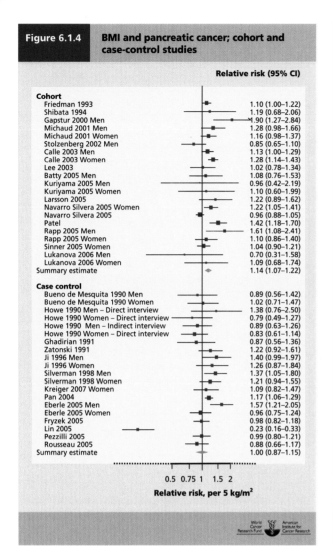

Figure 6.1.4 BMI and pancreatic cancer; cohort and case-control studies

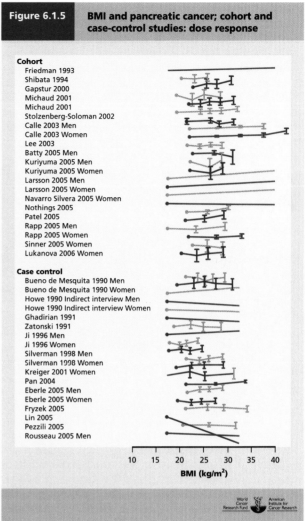

Figure 6.1.5 BMI and pancreatic cancer; cohort and case-control studies: dose response

risk in both sexes when interviewed indirectly, a non-significant decreased risk in women when interviewed directly, and a non-significant increased risk in men.[60] One study stated that there was no significant association.[73] Meta-analysis was possible on 13 case-control studies, giving a summary effect estimate of 1.00 (95% CI 0.87–1.15) per 5 kg/m^2, with high heterogeneity (figure 6.1.4).

A dose-response relationship was apparent from cohort but not case-control data (figure 6.1.5). Although meta-analysis assumes a linear relationship, some cohort studies are suggestive of a curvilinear relationship, though not conclusively so.

The general mechanisms through which body fatness could plausibly influence cancer risk are outlined in 6.1.3 (also see box 2.4).

There is ample epidemiological evidence, which is generally consistent, and there is a dose-response relationship. There is evidence for plausible mechanisms that operate in humans. The evidence that greater body fatness is a cause of pancreatic cancer is convincing.

The Panel is aware that since the conclusion of the SLR, two cohort studies[30][74] have been published. This new information does not change the Panel judgement (also see box 3.8).

Colorectum

Sixty cohort studies[42][45][50][54-58][75-142] and 86 case-control studies investigated body fatness (as measured by BMI) and cancers of the colon and rectum.

Most of the cohort studies showed increased risk with increased body fatness,[42][45][50][54][56-58][75][77][80-82][84-88][91-100][102-104][106][108-115][118-120][122][124-127][132][137][139][142] which was statistically significant in approximately half of these studies.[42][50][54][56-58][75][77][84-88][92-95][99][103][104][109][111][114][115][118-120][124][126][127][132][137][139][142] Relatively few studies showed lower risk with increased body fatness[76][83][90][107][116]; this was statistically significant in only one.[83] One study showed no effect on risk[78] and three stated that there was no association.[79][89][101] Meta-analysis was possible on 28 cohort studies, giving a summary effect estimate of 1.03 (95% CI 1.02–1.04) per kg/m^2, with moderate heterogeneity (figure 6.1.6). This would produce an increased risk of 15 per cent for each 5 kg/m^2, assuming a

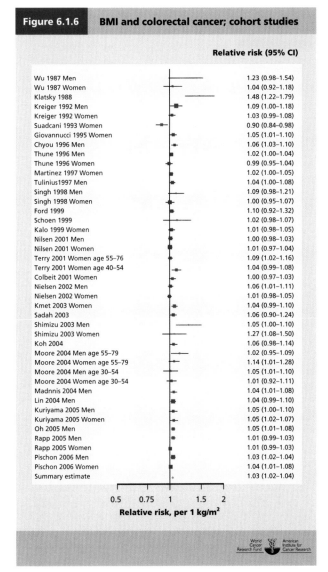

Figure 6.1.6 BMI and colorectal cancer; cohort studies

Relative risk (95% CI)

	Relative risk (95% CI)
Wu 1987 Men	1.23 (0.98–1.54)
Wu 1987 Women	1.04 (0.92–1.18)
Klatsky 1988	1.48 (1.22–1.79)
Kreiger 1992 Men	1.09 (1.00–1.18)
Kreiger 1992 Women	1.03 (0.99–1.08)
Suadcani 1993 Women	0.90 (0.84–0.98)
Giovannucci 1995 Women	1.05 (1.01–1.10)
Chyou 1996 Men	1.06 (1.03–1.10)
Thune 1996 Men	1.02 (1.00–1.04)
Thune 1996 Women	0.99 (0.95–1.04)
Martinez 1997 Women	1.02 (1.00–1.05)
Tulinius 1997 Men	1.04 (1.00–1.08)
Singh 1998 Men	1.09 (0.98–1.21)
Singh 1998 Women	1.00 (0.95–1.07)
Ford 1999	1.10 (0.92–1.32)
Schoen 1999	1.02 (0.98–1.07)
Kalo 1999 Women	1.01 (0.98–1.05)
Nilsen 2001 Men	1.00 (0.98–1.03)
Nilsen 2001 Women	1.01 (0.97–1.04)
Terry 2001 Women age 55–76	1.09 (1.02–1.16)
Terry 2001 Women age 40–54	1.04 (0.99–1.08)
Colbeit 2001 Women	1.00 (0.97–1.03)
Nielsen 2002 Men	1.06 (1.01–1.11)
Nielsen 2002 Women	1.01 (0.98–1.05)
Kmet 2003 Women	1.04 (0.99–1.10)
Sadah 2003	1.06 (0.90–1.24)
Shimizu 2003 Men	1.05 (1.00–1.10)
Shimizu 2003 Women	1.27 (1.08–1.50)
Koh 2004	1.06 (0.98–1.14)
Moore 2004 Men age 55–79	1.02 (0.95–1.09)
Moore 2004 Women age 55–79	1.14 (1.01–1.28)
Moore 2004 Men age 30–54	1.05 (1.01–1.10)
Moore 2004 Women age 30–54	1.01 (0.92–1.11)
Madnnis 2004 Men	1.04 (1.01–1.08)
Lin 2004 Men	1.04 (0.99–1.10)
Kuriyama 2005 Men	1.05 (1.00–1.10)
Kuriyama 2005 Women	1.05 (1.02–1.07)
Oh 2005 Men	1.05 (1.01–1.08)
Rapp 2005 Men	1.01 (0.99–1.03)
Rapp 2005 Women	1.01 (0.99–1.03)
Pischon 2006 Men	1.03 (1.02–1.04)
Pischon 2006 Women	1.04 (1.01–1.08)
Summary estimate	1.03 (1.02–1.04)

0.5   0.75   1   1.5   2

Relative risk, per 1 kg/m²

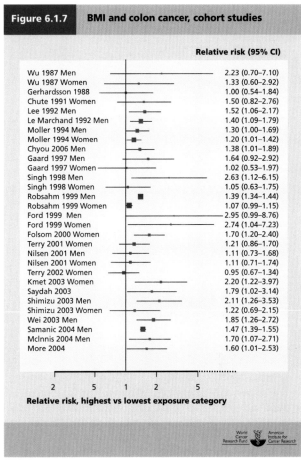

Figure 6.1.7 BMI and colon cancer, cohort studies

Relative risk (95% CI)

	Relative risk (95% CI)
Wu 1987 Men	2.23 (0.70–7.10)
Wu 1987 Women	1.33 (0.60–2.92)
Gerhardsson 1988	1.00 (0.54–1.84)
Chute 1991 Women	1.50 (0.82–2.76)
Lee 1992 Men	1.52 (1.06–2.17)
Le Marchand 1992 Men	1.40 (1.09–1.79)
Moller 1994 Men	1.30 (1.00–1.69)
Moller 1994 Women	1.20 (1.01–1.42)
Chyou 2006 Men	1.38 (1.01–1.89)
Gaard 1997 Men	1.64 (0.92–2.92)
Gaard 1997 Women	1.02 (0.53–1.97)
Singh 1998 Men	2.63 (1.12–6.15)
Singh 1998 Women	1.05 (0.63–1.75)
Robsahm 1999 Men	1.39 (1.34–1.44)
Robsahm 1999 Women	1.07 (0.99–1.15)
Ford 1999 Men	2.95 (0.99–8.76)
Ford 1999 Women	2.74 (1.04–7.23)
Folsom 2000 Men	1.70 (1.20–2.40)
Terry 2001 Women	1.21 (0.86–1.70)
Nilsen 2001 Men	1.11 (0.73–1.68)
Nilsen 2001 Women	1.11 (0.71–1.74)
Terry 2002 Women	0.95 (0.67–1.34)
Kmet 2003 Women	2.20 (1.22–3.97)
Saydah 2003	1.79 (1.02–3.14)
Shimizu 2003 Men	2.11 (1.26–3.53)
Shimizu 2003 Women	1.22 (0.69–2.15)
Wei 2003 Men	1.85 (1.26–2.72)
Samanic 2004 Men	1.47 (1.39–1.55)
McInnis 2004 Men	1.70 (1.07–2.71)
More 2004	1.60 (1.01–2.53)

.2   .5   1   2   5

Relative risk, highest vs lowest exposure category

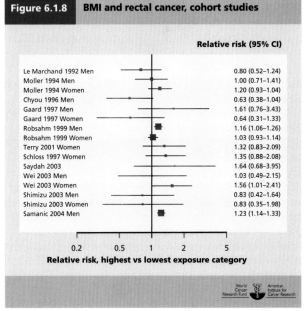

Figure 6.1.8 BMI and rectal cancer, cohort studies

Relative risk (95% CI)

	Relative risk (95% CI)
Le Marchand 1992 Men	0.80 (0.52–1.24)
Moller 1994 Men	1.00 (0.71–1.41)
Moller 1994 Women	1.20 (0.93–1.04)
Chyou 1996 Men	0.63 (0.38–1.04)
Gaard 1997 Men	1.61 (0.76–3.43)
Gaard 1997 Women	0.64 (0.31–1.33)
Robsahm 1999 Men	1.16 (1.06–1.26)
Robsahm 1999 Women	1.03 (0.93–1.14)
Terry 2001 Women	1.32 (0.83–2.09)
Schloss 1997 Women	1.35 (0.88–2.08)
Saydah 2003	1.64 (0.68–3.95)
Wei 2003 Men	1.03 (0.49–2.15)
Wei 2003 Women	1.56 (1.01–2.41)
Shimizu 2003 Men	0.83 (0.42–1.64)
Shimizu 2003 Women	0.83 (0.35–1.98)
Samanic 2004 Men	1.23 (1.14–1.33)

0.2   0.5   1   2   5

Relative risk, highest vs lowest exposure category

linear relationship, although a curvilinear dose-response relationship cannot be ruled out.

When stratified according to cancer site, data suggest a larger increased risk and are more consistent for colon cancer (figure 6.1.7) than for rectal cancer (figure 6.1.8), or for colorectal cancer as a whole (figure 6.1.6). A clear dose-response relationship was apparent from cohort data for colorectal cancer (figure 6.1.9).

Because of the abundant prospective data from cohort studies, case-control studies were not summarised.

The general mechanisms through which body fatness could plausibly influence cancer risk are outlined in 6.1.3 (also see box 2.4).

There is abundant and consistent epidemiological evidence with a clear dose response, and evidence for plausible mechanisms that operate in humans. The evidence that greater body fatness is a cause of colorectal cancer is convincing.

The Panel is aware that since the conclusion of the SLR, seven cohort[30 31 52 143-146] and two case-control studies[147 148] have been published. This new information does not change the Panel judgement (also see box 3.8).

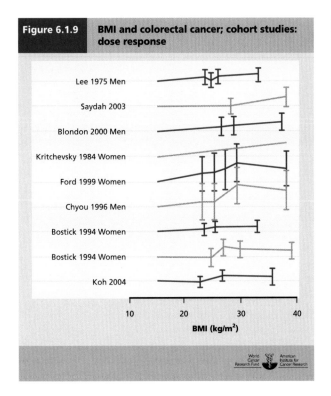

Figure 6.1.9 — BMI and colorectal cancer; cohort studies: dose response

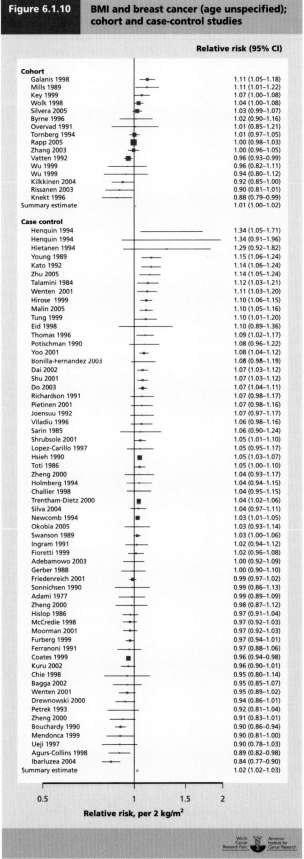

Figure 6.1.10 — BMI and breast cancer (age unspecified); cohort and case-control studies

Breast

Forty-three cohort studies,[42 45 50 122 149-204] 156 case-control studies,[66 205-359] and 2 ecological studies[360 361] investigated body fatness (as measured by BMI) and breast cancer.

Age unspecified

Twenty-six cohort studies[45 50 152-154 161 162 164 166 168 171 172 179 181 188 191 192 194-197 201-204] and 73 case-control studies investigated body fatness,[66 205 207-209 211-215 219 221 222 224 225 228-230 232 234-236 238-240 243-245 251 252 254 255 257 259-261 263-267 269 270 273 276-278 281 282 285 289-292 294-296 298-301 304-306 309 310 313 314 316-319 321-326 329 332 334-337 341-344 347-356 359] (as measured by BMI) and breast cancer at all ages, or where menopausal status was unspecified.

Sixteen cohort studies showed increased risk with increased body fatness,[45 50 152-154 162 164 166 168 171 173 179 181 184 186 188 191 192 201 203 204] which was statistically significant in three.[162 171 179 201] Eight studies showed decreased risk,[161 172 173 184 186 194-197 202] which was statistically significant in two.[173 196 197] Two studies showed no effect on risk.[50 204] Meta-analysis was possible on 16 cohort studies, giving a summary effect estimate of 1.01 (95% CI 1.00–1.02) per 2 kg/m², with moderate heterogeneity (figure 6.1.10).

Forty-seven case-control studies showed increased risk with increased body fatness[66 208 211 213 215 221 222 224 230 232 235 236 239 240 251 252 254 255 257 260 261 265-267 269 276 277 281 282 285 294-296 298-301 305 306 309 310 313 314 316-319 323-326 329 332 334-337 341 343 344 347-350 352-356 359]; this was statistically significant in 22[66 208 211 222 230 232 235 254 255 269 277 285 295 296 298 316-318 329 332 334 336 337 341 349 352 353 359]; 4 studies showed no effect on risk[207 245 278 351]; and the remaining 22 showed decreased risk,[205 209 212 214 219 225 228 229 234 238 243 244 259 263 264 270 273 289-292 304 321 322 342 349] which was statistically significant in 4 studies.[214 263 264 291] One of these studies showed significant increased risk with increased body fatness in Hispanic-American people but non-significant decreased risks among white-American people.[349] Meta-analysis was possible on 62 case-control studies, giving a summary effect estimate of 1.02 (95% CI 1.02–1.03) per 2 kg/m^2, with high heterogeneity (figure 6.1.10).

The two ecological studies showed no consistent association.[360 361]

Postmenopause

Twenty-four cohort studies[42 45 50 122 149-151 155-159 162 163 165 167 169 170 174 175 178 180 182-185 187-195 199 200] and 56 case-control studies investigated body fatness,[66 205-208 214 220 224-227 231 233 237 239 241 242 244 246-250 253-259 261-263 268 271 274 275 279-283 286-288 293 295-297 302 304 308 311 315 321 322 327 329 331 333 336-341 345 349 352 357-359] (as measured by BMI) and postmenopausal breast cancer.

Nineteen cohort studies showed increased risk with increased body fatness,[42 45 50 122 149 151 155-159 162 163 165 167 174 175 180 183-185 187-194 199 200] which was statistically significant in seven.[42 45 149 158 162 163 174 175 180 183 189 192] Five studies showed decreased risk,[150 169 170 178 182 195] which was statistically significant in one.[150] Meta-analysis was possible on 17 studies, giving a summary effect estimate of 1.03 (95% CI 1.01–1.04) per 2 kg/m^2, with high heterogeneity (figure 6.1.11). This would produce an increased risk of 8 per cent for each 5 kg/m^2, assuming a linear relationship, although a curvilinear dose-response relationship cannot be ruled out. Heterogeneity may be explained partially by failure to adjust for hormone replacement therapy (HRT) use. Three major studies that reported results stratified for HRT status all found statistically significant increased risk with increasing body fatness only in women not taking HRT.

Pooled analysis from seven cohort studies (more than 337 000 participants, followed up for up to 11 years, with more than 4300 breast cancer cases) showed a significant

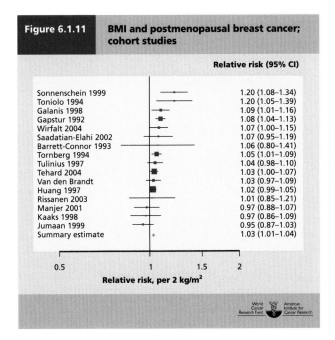

Figure 6.1.11	BMI and postmenopausal breast cancer; cohort studies

Relative risk (95% CI)

Sonnenschein 1999	1.20 (1.08–1.34)
Toniolo 1994	1.20 (1.05–1.39)
Galanis 1998	1.09 (1.01–1.16)
Gapstur 1992	1.08 (1.04–1.13)
Wirfalt 2004	1.07 (1.00–1.15)
Saadatian-Elahi 2002	1.07 (0.95–1.19)
Barrett-Connor 1993	1.06 (0.80–1.41)
Tornberg 1994	1.05 (1.01–1.09)
Tulinius 1997	1.04 (0.98–1.10)
Tehard 2004	1.03 (1.00–1.07)
Van den Brandt	1.03 (0.97–1.09)
Huang 1997	1.02 (0.99–1.05)
Rissanen 2003	1.01 (0.85–1.21)
Manjer 2001	0.97 (0.88–1.07)
Kaaks 1998	0.97 (0.86–1.09)
Jumaan 1999	0.95 (0.87–1.03)
Summary estimate	1.03 (1.01–1.04)

Relative risk, per 2 kg/m^2

Figure 6.1.12	BMI and postmenopausal breast cancer; case-control studies

Relative risk (95% CI)

Chie 1996	1.31 (0.80–2.13)
Hu 1997	1.25 (0.95–1.63)
Zhu 1996	1.21 (0.89–1.64)
Hirose 2003	1.18 (1.13–1.24)
Park 2000	1.18 (1.13–1.24)
Hansen 1997	1.17 (0.95–1.43)
Rattanamongkolg 2002	1.15 (1.05–1.25)
Zhu 2005	1.15 (1.01–1.30)
Yoo 2001	1.14 (1.08–1.21)
Talamini 1984	1.13 (1.02–1.25)
Tung 1999	1.13 (1.01–1.25)
Lopez-Carrillo 1997	1.13 (0.97–1.32)
Graham 1991	1.11 (1.04–1.19)
Chow 2005	1.10 (1.01–1.19)
Magnusson 1998	1.09 (1.06–1.12)
Rosenburg 1990	1.08 (0.99–1.18)
Trentham-Dietz 2000	1.08 (1.06–1.10)
Toti 1986	1.08 (1.02–1.14)
Harris 1992	1.08 (1.00–1.16)
Taioli 1995	1.07 (1.01–1.16)
Kohlmeier 1997	1.07 (1.01–1.13)
Li 2000	1.06 (1.00–1.13)
Newcomb 1999	1.06 (1.04–1.09)
Shoff 2000	1.06 (1.04–1.09)
Swanson 1989	1.06 (1.01–1.11)
Trentham-Dietz 1997	1.06 (1.04–1.08)
Dorn 2003	1.06 (1.01–1.11)
Carpenter 2003	1.06 (1.02–1.10)
Li 2003	1.06 (1.01–1.10)
Hsieh 1990	1.05 (1.03–1.07)
Fioretti 1999	1.05 (0.97–1.13)
Franceschi 1996	1.05 (1.02–1.07)
Terry 2002	1.05 (1.02–1.07)
Ng 1997	1.04 (0.94–1.16)
Hall 2000	1.04 (0.96–1.13)
Adebamowo 2003	1.04 (0.94–1.15)
Van't Veer 1989	1.04 (0.88–1.22)
Marubini 1988	1.03 (0.91–1.17)
Helmrich 1983	1.03 (0.99–1.06)
McCann 2004	1.02 (0.99–1.05)
Adami 1977	1.01 (0.91–1.13)
Hislop 1986	1.01 (0.92–1.10)
Hall 2000	1.00 (0.96–1.04)
Sonnichsen 1990	1.00 (0.98–1.02)
Friedenreich 2002	1.00 (0.96–1.04)
Petrek 1993	0.97 (0.85–1.11)
De Vasconcelos 2001	0.94 (0.85–1.03)
Adams-Campbell 1996	0.90 (0.83–0.98)
Summary estimate	1.05 (1.05–1.06)

Relative risk, per 2 kg/m^2

increased risk of postmenopausal breast cancer with increased body fatness. The effect estimate was 1.07 (95% CI 1.02–1.11) per 4 kg/m^2.[362]

Most case-control studies showed increased risk with increased body fatness,[66 205 207 208 220 224-227 233 237 239 241 246-250 253-258 261 262 271 274 275 279-283 286-288 293 295-297 302 308 311 315 327 329 331 333 336-341 345 349 352 357-359] which was statistically significant in approximately half of these studies.[66 220 227 233 237 241 246 253-258 261 275 280 283 293 295 296 302 308 315 329 333 336 338-341 352 359] Meta-analysis was possible on 48 studies, giving a summary effect estimate of 1.05 (95% CI 1.05–1.06) per 2 kg/m^2, with moderate heterogeneity (figure 6.1.12). This would produce an increased risk of 13 per cent for each 5 kg/m^2, assuming a linear relationship, although a curvilinear dose-response

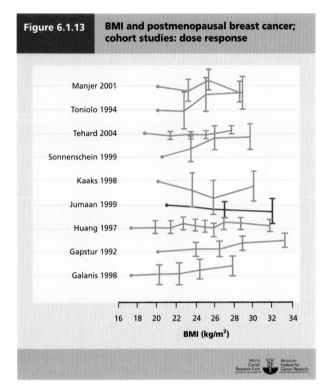

Figure 6.1.13 | BMI and postmenopausal breast cancer; cohort studies: dose response

Figure 6.1.14 | BMI and premenopausal breast cancer; case-control studies: dose response

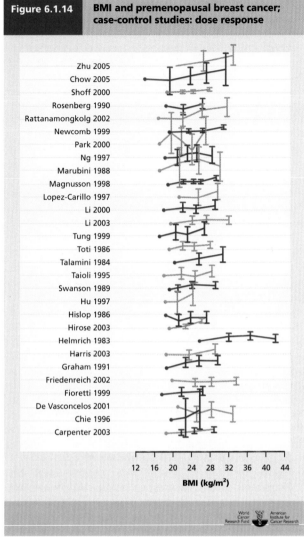

relationship cannot be ruled out. Heterogeneity may be partially explained by differential adjustment between studies.

A dose-response relationship is apparent from cohort and case-control data (figure 6.1.13, figure 6.1.14).

The general mechanisms through which body fatness could plausibly influence cancer risk are outlined in 6.1.3 (also see box 2.4).

There is abundant and consistent epidemiological evidence and a clear dose response, with robust evidence for mechanisms operating in humans. The evidence that greater body fatness is a cause of postmenopausal breast cancer is convincing.

The Panel is aware that since the conclusion of the SLR, one cohort[363] and one case-control study[364] have been published. This new information does not change the Panel judgement (also see box 3.8).

Premenopause

Twenty cohort studies[45 122 149 150 155 162 167 170 174-178 184 185 188-192 195-198] and 59 case-control studies[66 205-208 210 214 216-218 223-227 231 233 237 239 241 242 247-250 253-259 261-263 268 269 272 281 282 284 286-290 293 297 302-304 306-308 311 312 320-322 324-330 336-341 343-346 349 352 357-359] investigated body fatness (as measured by BMI) and premenopausal breast cancer.

Thirteen cohort studies showed decreased risk with increased body fatness,[45 149 150 167 170 174-176 184 185 189 191 192 195-198] which was statistically significant in seven.[149 150 167 176 184 192 195-198] Four studies showed non-significant increased risk.[155 162 188 190] Three studies showed no effect on risk.[122]

[177 178] Meta-analysis was possible on 14 studies, giving a summary effect estimate of 0.94 (95% CI 0.92–0.95) per 2 kg/m², with moderate heterogeneity (figure 6.1.15). This would produce a decreased risk of 15 per cent for each 5 kg/m², assuming a linear relationship, although a curvilinear dose response cannot be ruled out.

Egger's test for publication bias suggested some over-representation of studies showing a protective effect on premenopausal breast cancer of increasing BMI.

Pooled analysis from 7 cohort studies (more than 337 000 participants, followed up for up to 11 years, with more than 4300 breast cancer cases) showed a significant decreased risk of premenopausal breast cancer with increased body fatness. The effect estimate was 0.89 (95% CI 0.81–0.97) per 4 kg/m².[365]

Most case-control studies showed decreased risk with increased body fatness,[205 206 214 216-218 223-225 231 233 237 239 241 242 247-250 259 262 263 268 281 282 284 286-290 293 297 302-304 311 324-328 330 338-341 349] which was statistically significant in approximately one third of these studies.[214 218 223 231 237 250 262 268 303 304 326 327 330]

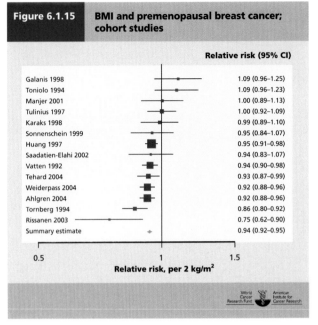

Figure 6.1.15 | BMI and premenopausal breast cancer; cohort studies

	Relative risk (95% CI)
Galanis 1998	1.09 (0.96–1.25)
Toniolo 1994	1.09 (0.96–1.23)
Manjer 2001	1.00 (0.89–1.13)
Tulinius 1997	1.00 (0.92–1.09)
Karaks 1998	0.99 (0.89–1.10)
Sonnenschein 1999	0.95 (0.84–1.07)
Huang 1997	0.95 (0.91–0.98)
Saadatien-Elahi 2002	0.94 (0.83–1.07)
Vatten 1992	0.94 (0.90–0.98)
Tehard 2004	0.93 (0.87–0.99)
Weiderpass 2004	0.92 (0.88–0.96)
Ahlgren 2004	0.92 (0.88–0.96)
Tornberg 1994	0.86 (0.80–0.92)
Rissanen 2003	0.75 (0.62–0.90)
Summary estimate	0.94 (0.92–0.95)

Relative risk, per 2 kg/m²

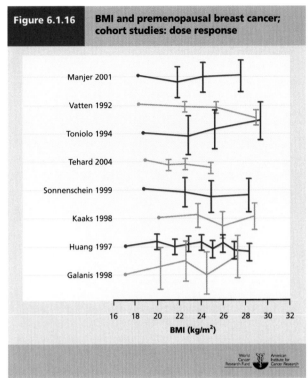

Figure 6.1.16 | BMI and premenopausal breast cancer; cohort studies: dose response

Manjer 2001, Vatten 1992, Toniolo 1994, Tehard 2004, Sonnenschein 1999, Kaaks 1998, Huang 1997, Galanis 1998

BMI (kg/m²)

Meta-analysis was possible on 51 case-control studies,[205-208 216 218 223 226 231 233 239 241 242 247-250 256 258 259 261 262 272 281 282 284 286-290 297 302-304 306-308 311 312 320-322 324-329 336 338-341 343-346 352 357 359] giving a summary effect estimate of 0.97 (95% CI 0.96–0.97) per 2 kg/m², with moderate heterogeneity.

A dose-response relationship was apparent from cohort (figure 6.1.16) and case-control data.

There is no single, well-established mechanism through which body fatness could prevent premenopausal breast cancer. According to the oestrogen plus progesterone theory, overweight premenopausal women would be protected because they would be more frequently anovulatory and therefore less exposed to endogenous progesterone. However, this theory is not well supported by recent studies, which suggest that natural progesterone could be protective.[365] Normal levels of natural progesterone are likely to be protective and women who are well nourished, or perhaps overnourished, who may become slightly overweight in adulthood, may be protected by their natural fertile condition. Another possible mechanism is that the increased adipose tissue-derived oestrogen levels in overweight children could induce early breast differentiation and eliminate some targets for malignant transformation.[366] Anovulation and abnormal hormone profiles are commonly associated with obesity.[367] The age-specific pattern of association of breast cancer with BMI, therefore, is largely explained by its relationship with endogenous sex hormone levels.

Breast cancer diagnosed postmenopause is much more common. Therefore, throughout life, a decreased risk of premenopausal breast cancer would be expected to be outweighed by an increased risk of postmenopausal breast cancer (also see chapter 7.10).

There is a substantial amount of consistent epidemiological evidence, with a dose response, but the mechanistic evidence is speculative. Greater body fatness probably protects against premenopausal breast cancer.

The Panel is aware that since the conclusion of the SLR, one cohort[363] and one case-control study[364] have been published. This new information does not change the Panel judgement (also see box 3.8).

Endometrium

Twenty-three cohort studies,[45 50 52 55 122 137 168 192 368-385] 41 case-control studies,[254 386-455] and 2 cross-sectional studies[456-458] investigated body fatness (as measured by BMI) and endometrial cancer. Three cohort studies[168 376 382] and 6 case-control studies[254 409 416 422 424 425 441] investigated BMI measured as a young adult.

Twenty-two cohort studies showed increased risk with increased body fatness,[50 52 55 122 137 168 192 368-370 373-377 380-383] which was statistically significant in 16.[384] One small study showed non-significant decreased risk.[376 382] Meta-analysis was possible on 15 cohort studies, giving a summary effect estimate of 1.52 (95% CI 1.35–1.72) per 5 kg/m², with high heterogeneity (figure 6.1.17).

Nearly all of the case-control studies showed increased risk with increased body fatness, most of which were statistically significant.[254 387-390 392 394-409 411-438 440-443 446 453 454] One

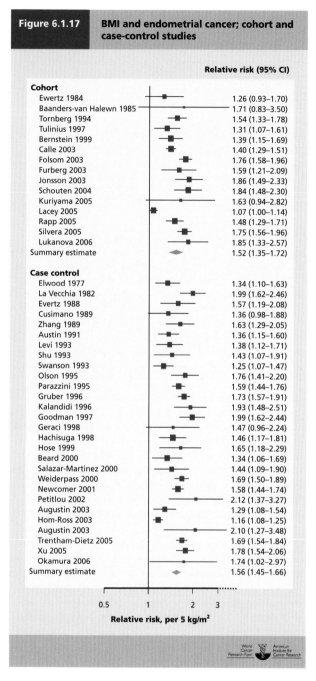

Figure 6.1.17 BMI and endometrial cancer; cohort and case-control studies

Relative risk (95% CI)

Cohort
Ewertz 1984	1.26 (0.93–1.70)
Baanders-van Halewn 1985	1.71 (0.83–3.50)
Tornberg 1994	1.54 (1.33–1.78)
Tulinius 1997	1.31 (1.07–1.61)
Bernstein 1999	1.39 (1.15–1.69)
Calle 2003	1.40 (1.29–1.51)
Folsom 2003	1.76 (1.58–1.96)
Furberg 2003	1.59 (1.21–2.09)
Jonsson 2003	1.86 (1.49–2.33)
Schouten 2004	1.84 (1.48–2.30)
Kuriyama 2005	1.63 (0.94–2.82)
Lacey 2005	1.07 (1.00–1.14)
Rapp 2005	1.48 (1.29–1.71)
Silvera 2005	1.75 (1.56–1.96)
Lukanova 2006	1.85 (1.33–2.57)
Summary estimate	1.52 (1.35–1.72)

Case control
Elwood 1977	1.34 (1.10–1.63)
La Vecchia 1982	1.99 (1.62–2.46)
Evertz 1988	1.57 (1.19–2.08)
Cusimano 1989	1.36 (0.98–1.88)
Zhang 1989	1.63 (1.29–2.05)
Austin 1991	1.36 (1.15–1.60)
Levi 1993	1.38 (1.12–1.71)
Shu 1993	1.43 (1.07–1.91)
Swanson 1993	1.25 (1.07–1.47)
Olson 1995	1.76 (1.41–2.20)
Parazzini 1995	1.59 (1.44–1.76)
Gruber 1996	1.73 (1.57–1.91)
Kalandidi 1996	1.93 (1.48–2.51)
Goodman 1997	1.99 (1.62–2.44)
Geraci 1998	1.47 (0.96–2.24)
Hachisuga 1998	1.46 (1.17–1.81)
Hose 1999	1.65 (1.18–2.29)
Beard 2000	1.34 (1.06–1.69)
Salazar-Martinez 2000	1.44 (1.09–1.90)
Weiderpass 2000	1.69 (1.50–1.89)
Newcomer 2001	1.58 (1.44–1.74)
Petitlou 2002	2.12 (1.37–3.27)
Augustin 2003	1.29 (1.08–1.54)
Hom-Ross 2003	1.16 (1.08–1.25)
Augustin 2003	2.10 (1.27–3.48)
Trentham-Dietz 2005	1.69 (1.54–1.84)
Xu 2005	1.78 (1.54–2.06)
Okamura 2006	1.74 (1.02–2.97)
Summary estimate	1.56 (1.45–1.66)

0.5   1   2   3

Relative risk, per 5 kg/m²

World Cancer Research Fund / American Institute for Cancer Research

Figure 6.1.18 BMI and endometrial cancer; cohort studies: dose response

Baanders-van Halewijn 1985
Ewertz 1984
Calle 2003
Bernstein 1999
Jonsson 2003
Folsom 2003
Silvera 2005
Rapp 2005
Lukanova 2006
Lacey 2005
Kuriyama 2005
Furberg 2003

10   20   30   40   50

BMI (kg/m²)

World Cancer Research Fund / American Institute for Cancer Research

evidence of effect modification by menopause, smoking, or oestrogen-use status.

Both cross-sectional studies reported an association between higher BMI and increased risk of endometrial cancer.[456-458]

The general mechanisms through which body fatness could plausibly influence cancer risk are outlined in 6.1.3 (also see box 2.4).

BMI as a young adult

All three cohort studies showed increased risk with increased body fatness, which was statistically significant in two.[376 382] Meta-analysis was possible on all three cohort studies, giving a summary effect estimate of 1.31 (95% CI 1.12–1.54) per 5 kg/m², with no heterogeneity.[168 376 382]

Four case-control studies showed non-significant increased risk with increased body fatness,[409 416 424 425 441] and two showed non-significant decreased risk.[254 422] Meta-analysis was possible on all six case-control studies, giving a summary effect estimate of 1.10 (95% CI 0.95–1.27) per 5 kg/m², with low heterogeneity.[254 409 416 422 424 425 441]

A dose-response relationship was apparent from cohort but not case-control data.

There is abundant consistent epidemiological evidence with a clear dose response, and robust evidence for mechanisms operating in humans. The evidence that greater body fatness is a cause of endometrial cancer is convincing.

study showed no effect on risk after adjustment for waist circumference, but the unadjusted result showed a statistically significant increased risk.[455] No studies showed decreased risk with increased body fatness. Meta-analysis was possible on 28 case-control studies, giving a summary effect estimate of 1.56 (95% CI 1.45–1.66) per 5 kg/m², with high heterogeneity (figure 6.1.17). Heterogeneity was predominantly the result of variation in the size of effect, rather than direction of effect.

A dose-response relationship is apparent from cohort and case-control data (figures 6.1.17 and 6.1.18). There was no

The Panel is aware that since the conclusion of the SLR, one cohort study[146] and one case control study[459] have been published. This new information does not change the Panel judgement (also see box 3.8).

Kidney

Seventeen cohort studies[42 45 57 122 279 460-473] and 20 case-control studies[66 474-502] investigated body fatness (as measured by BMI) and kidney cancer.

Fifteen cohort studies showed increased risk with increased body fatness[42 45 57 122 279 460-468 470-472]; this was statistically significant in seven studies,[57 122 460 461 465 466 468 472] and in women but not men in another.[42] Two studies stated that there was no statistically significant association.[469 473] No cohort studies showed decreased risk. Meta-analysis was possible on seven cohort studies that adjusted for smoking, giving a summary effect estimate of 1.31 (95% CI 1.24–1.39) per 5 kg/m^2, with low heterogeneity (figure 6.1.19).

Eighteen case-control studies[66 474-493 495-497 499-502] showed increased risk with increased body fatness; this was statistically significant in 14 studies,[66 474 476-478 480-483 485 487 488 490-493 495-497 500] and in men but not women in another.[501] One study showed no effect on risk[498] and another (where the controls were not drawn from the same population as the cases, making it a relatively low-quality study) showed a non-significant decreased risk.[494] Meta-analysis was possible on two case-control studies that adjusted for smoking and eight unadjusted case-control studies. This gave summary effect estimates of 2.05 (95% CI 1.43–2.92) per 5 kg/m^2, with low heterogeneity, and 1.42 (95% CI 1.17–1.72) per 5 kg/m^2, with high heterogeneity, respectively (figure 6.1.19).

A dose-response relationship is apparent from cohort and case-control data (figure 6.1.20).

The general mechanisms through which body fatness could plausibly influence cancer risk are outlined in 6.1.3

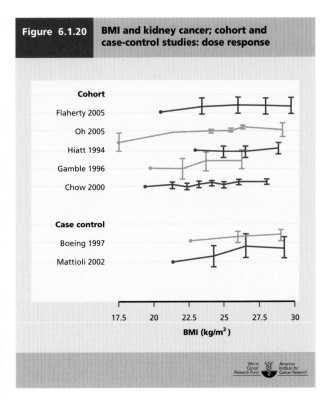

Figure 6.1.20 | **BMI and kidney cancer; cohort and case-control studies: dose response**

and box 2.4; in addition, laboratory studies point to a potential role for insulin and leptin in renal cell carcinoma.[503 504]

There is abundant and consistent epidemiological evidence with a dose-response relationship and evidence of plausible mechanisms. The evidence that greater body fatness is a cause of kidney cancer is convincing.

The Panel is aware that since the conclusion of the SLR, three cohort studies[30 52 142] and one case-control study[505] have been published. This new information does not change the Panel judgement (also see box 3.8).

Gallbladder

Five cohort studies,[42 45 56 58 141 201] seven case-control studies,[506-514] and two cross-sectional studies[515-517] investigated body fatness (as measured by BMI) and gallbladder cancer.

Most cohort studies showed increased risk with increased body fatness. For two studies, results for the whole cohort showed statistically significant increased risk.[42 201] One study reported significant increased risk for women and non-significant increased risk for men,[141] while another reported statistically significant increased risk for women and non-significant decreased risk for men.[45] One study reported a significant increased risk for white men and a non-significant decreased risk for black men.[56] Meta-analysis was possible on four cohort studies, giving a summary effect estimate of 1.23 (95% CI 1.15–1.32) per 5 kg/m^2, with moderate heterogeneity (figure 6.1.21).

Most case-control studies showed increased risk with increased body fatness,[506 507 509 510 513 514] which was

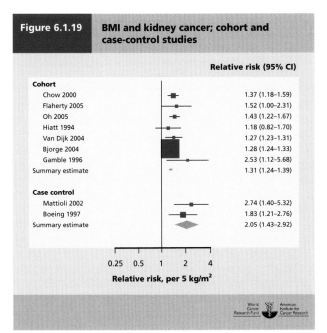

Figure 6.1.19 | **BMI and kidney cancer; cohort and case-control studies**

	Relative risk (95% CI)
Cohort	
Chow 2000	1.37 (1.18–1.59)
Flaherty 2005	1.52 (1.00–2.31)
Oh 2005	1.43 (1.22–1.67)
Hiatt 1994	1.18 (0.82–1.70)
Van Dijk 2004	1.27 (1.23–1.31)
Bjorge 2004	1.28 (1.24–1.33)
Gamble 1996	2.53 (1.12–5.68)
Summary estimate	1.31 (1.24–1.39)
Case control	
Mattioli 2002	2.74 (1.40–5.32)
Boeing 1997	1.83 (1.21–2.76)
Summary estimate	2.05 (1.43–2.92)

Relative risk, per 5 kg/m^2

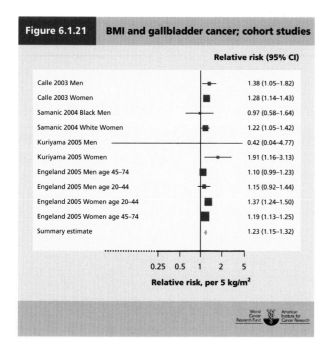

Figure 6.1.21 BMI and gallbladder cancer; cohort studies

Relative risk (95% CI)

Calle 2003 Men	1.38 (1.05–1.82)
Calle 2003 Women	1.28 (1.14–1.43)
Samanic 2004 Black Men	0.97 (0.58–1.64)
Samanic 2004 White Women	1.22 (1.05–1.42)
Kuriyama 2005 Men	0.42 (0.04–4.77)
Kuriyama 2005 Women	1.91 (1.16–3.13)
Engeland 2005 Men age 45–74	1.10 (0.99–1.23)
Engeland 2005 Men age 20–44	1.15 (0.92–1.44)
Engeland 2005 Women age 20–44	1.37 (1.24–1.50)
Engeland 2005 Women age 45–74	1.19 (1.13–1.25)
Summary estimate	1.23 (1.15–1.32)

0.25 0.5 1 2 5

Relative risk, per 5 kg/m^2

World Cancer Research Fund / American Institute for Cancer Research

statistically significant in three.[506 510 513] Two studies showed decreased risk,[511 512] which was statistically significant in one.[512] One study showed no effect on risk in men, but a statistically significant increased risk in women.[508] Meta-analysis was possible on all seven case-control studies,[506-514] giving a summary effect estimate of 1.19 (95% CI 0.81–1.75) per 5 kg/m^2, with high heterogeneity. Heterogeneity could be at least partly attributed to differences in the study participants' ethnicity or sex, or to the number of adjustments made in the study. In addition, there was variation according to whether BMI was derived from direct measurements or self-reports of weight and height, as well as in the outcome measured. For example, one cohort and one case-control study reported biliary tract cancer as opposed to gallbladder cancer specifically, and some studies reported incidence while others reported mortality.

The general mechanisms through which body fatness could plausibly influence cancer risk are outlined in 6.1.3 (also see box 2.5). In addition, obesity is a known cause of gallstone formation and having gallstones increases the risk of gallbladder cancer (see chapter 7.7), possibly through bile cholesterol supersaturation leading to cholesterol-based gallstones. High cholesterol in the bile is not necessarily related to dietary cholesterol — it can also be caused by insulin resistance, which can be caused by obesity. Insulin resistance can independently increase cholesterol synthesis in the liver and decrease cholesterol absorption.[518] Bile cholesterol levels are also gender-linked: women excrete more cholesterol in bile than men.

Owing to the link between gallstones and gallbladder cancer, *the Panel reviewed* the dietary causes of having gallstones, especially in relation to body fatness. BMI increased the risk of having gallstones in a linear fashion.[519] Waist circumference was associated with gallstone risk in men, independently of BMI,[520] and insoluble fibre in the diet showed

a protective effect.[521] Gallstone formation is strongly associated with dieting, especially where it involves rapid weight loss — such as seen with very low-energy diets and bariatric surgery.[522 523] Rapid weight loss is also a common feature of weight cycling. Weight cycling is associated with obesity and independently associated with gallstones; people who are more severe weight cyclers have a higher risk of gallstones.[524]

There is a substantial amount of generally consistent epidemiological evidence with some evidence of a dose response. There is evidence for several plausible mechanisms. Greater body fatness is a probable cause of gallbladder cancer, directly and also indirectly through the formation of gallstones.

Liver

Six cohort studies[42 44 54-57 525] and two case-control studies investigated body fatness[526 527] (as measured by BMI), or obesity, and liver cancer.

Five cohort studies showed increased risk for the highest body fatness group compared to the lowest.[42 44 54 55 57] This was statistically significant in two studies,[54 57] and in men but not women in another two.[42 55] One cohort study showed a statistically significant increased risk in white men and a significant decreased risk in black men.[56] Effect estimates were 1.68 in women (95% CI 0.93–3.04) and 4.52 in men (95% CI 2.94–6.94)[42]; 1.44 in white men (95% CI 1.28–1.61) and 0.68 in black men (95% CI 0.49–0.94)[56]; 1.56 in men (95% CI 1.15–2.12)[57]; 3.88 in men (95% CI 0.96–15.69)[44]; 1.9 in both sexes (95% CI 1.5–2.5)[54]; and 1.70 in women (95% CI 0.95–3.05) and 3.60 in men (95% CI 2.08–6.24).[55]

Neither case-control study showed any statistically significant association.[526 527]

The general mechanisms through which body fatness could plausibly influence cancer risk are outlined in 6.1.3 (also see box 2.4).

The epidemiological evidence shows some inconsistencies, and the mechanistic evidence is speculative. There is limited evidence suggesting that greater body fatness is a cause of liver cancer.

The Panel is aware that since the conclusion of the SLR, two cohort studies[30 528] have been published. This new information does not change the Panel judgement (see box 3.8).

Lung

Twenty-one cohort studies,[42 57 76 88 122 144 529-545] 24 case-control studies,[546-573] and 1 ecological study[574] investigated body fatness (as measured by BMI) and lung cancer.

Twenty cohort studies showed decreased risk with increased body fatness[42 57 76 88 122 529-545]; this was statistically significant in 12 studies,[42 76 122 531 533-535 540 542 543 545] and in women but not men in another study.[536] One study showed no effect on risk.[144] Meta-analysis was possible on 14 cohort studies,[57 88 122 144 530 532 534 535 537 538 540 543-545] giving a summary effect estimate of 0.98 (95% CI 0.98–0.99) per kg/m^2, with high heterogeneity. This would produce a decreased risk of

5 per cent for each 5 kg/m², assuming a linear relationship, although a curvilinear dose-response relationship cannot be ruled out. When meta-analysis was restricted to the 10 studies that adjusted for smoking, the effect estimate and CIs remained the same, but with low heterogeneity.[57 88 144 530 534 537 538 540 544] Heterogeneity was caused by variation in the size but not the direction of the effect.

Begg's and Egger's tests suggested publication bias; that is, the smaller the study, the stronger the protective association observed. Smaller studies, with results of weak or no association, appear to have been less likely to be published.

Twenty-two case-control studies showed decreased risk with increased body fatness,[546-560 562-570 572 573] which was statistically significant in nine.[548 550 551 553 557 563 564 566 567 570 572] Two studies showed increased risk,[561 571] which was statistically significant in one.[561] Meta-analysis was possible on 10 case-control studies,[546 550 554 555 557 566-568 570 572] giving a summary effect estimate of 0.98 (95% CI 0.98–0.99) per kg/m², with low heterogeneity. The effect estimate was unchanged when three studies that did not adjust for smoking were excluded from the analysis.[546 568 572]

The single ecological study showed a non-significant association between increased body fatness and decreased risk.[574]

Smoking is the principal cause of lung cancer and may also be associated with lower BMI. There is a high potential for confounding due to cigarette smoking, and residual confounding is therefore possible. In addition, it is possible that people with undiagnosed lung cancer may lose weight, so giving a spurious association (reverse causation).

There is no known mechanism through which greater body fatness could plausibly protect against lung cancer, or through which low body fatness could increase risk.

Although the epidemiological evidence suggests an inverse relationship, this could be caused by confounding by cigarette smoking or reverse causation due to weight loss from undiagnosed cancer. There is limited evidence suggesting that low body fatness is a cause of lung cancer.

6.1.3.2 Abdominal fatness
Colorectum
Seven cohort studies[87 92 97 115 118 137 142] and two case-control studies investigated waist circumference and colorectal cancer. Six cohort studies[82 87 92 97 115 137 142] and four case-control studies investigated waist to hip ratio.

Waist circumference
All seven cohort studies showed increased risk with increased waist circumference, which was statistically significant in six.[87 97 115 118 137 142] Meta-analysis was possible on four cohort studies, giving a summary effect estimate of 1.05 (95% CI 1.03–1.07) per 2.5 cm (1 inch), with moderate heterogeneity (figure 6.1.22). Both case-control studies reported increased risk with increased waist circumference.

Waist to hip ratio
All six cohort studies showed increased risk with increased waist to hip ratio, which was statistically significant in

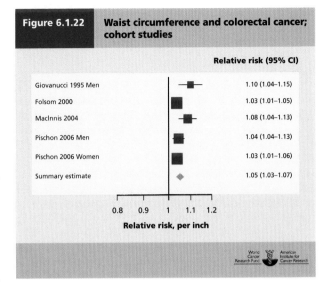

Figure 6.1.22 | **Waist circumference and colorectal cancer; cohort studies**

Relative risk (95% CI)

	Relative risk (95% CI)
Giovanucci 1995 Men	1.10 (1.04–1.15)
Folsom 2000	1.03 (1.01–1.05)
MacInnis 2004	1.08 (1.04–1.13)
Pischon 2006 Men	1.04 (1.04–1.13)
Pischon 2006 Women	1.03 (1.01–1.06)
Summary estimate	1.05 (1.03–1.07)

Relative risk, per inch

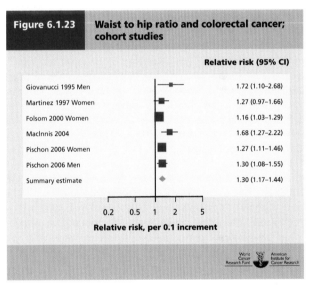

Figure 6.1.23 | **Waist to hip ratio and colorectal cancer; cohort studies**

Relative risk (95% CI)

	Relative risk (95% CI)
Giovanucci 1995 Men	1.72 (1.10–2.68)
Martinez 1997 Women	1.27 (0.97–1.66)
Folsom 2000 Women	1.16 (1.03–1.29)
MacInnis 2004	1.68 (1.27–2.22)
Pischon 2006 Women	1.27 (1.11–1.46)
Pischon 2006 Men	1.30 (1.08–1.55)
Summary estimate	1.30 (1.17–1.44)

Relative risk, per 0.1 increment

five.[87 97 115 137 142] Meta-analysis was possible on five cohort studies, giving a summary effect estimate of 1.30 (95% CI 1.17–1.44) per ratio increment of 0.1, with moderate heterogeneity (figure 6.1.23). Most case-control studies reported increased risk with increased waist circumference.

Because of the abundant prospective data from cohort studies, case-control studies were not summarised.

The general mechanisms through which body fatness and abdominal fatness could plausibly influence cancer risk are outlined in 6.1.3 (also see box 2.4). Many of these, such as increased circulating oestrogens and decreased insulin sensitivity, are particularly associated with abdominal rather than overall body fatness.

There is ample, consistent epidemiological evidence with a clear dose response and robust evidence for mechanisms that operate in humans. The evidence that abdominal fatness is a cause of colorectal cancer is convincing.

The Panel is aware that since the conclusion of the SLR, three cohort studies[31 142 143] have been published. This new information does not change the Panel judgement (see box 3.8).

Pancreas

Three cohort studies investigated waist circumference and pancreatic cancer.[46 74] Two cohort studies investigated waist to hip ratio[51 74] and one investigated patterns of weight gain.[49]

Waist circumference

All three cohort studies showed increased risk with increased waist circumference, which was statistically significant in one. Effect estimates were 1.32 (95% CI 0.73–2.37) per 20 cm (7.9 inches) in women,[46] 1.74 (95% CI 1.00–3.01) per 20 cm (7.9 inches) in men,[46] and 1.13 (95% CI 1.01–1.26) per 10 cm (3.9 inches).[74] The latter study was published after the cut-off date for inclusion in the SLR. However, *the Panel was aware of the study and agreed* to include it in its consideration of this exposure.

Waist to hip ratio

Both cohort studies showed increased risk with increased waist circumference, which was statistically significant in one. Effect estimates were 1.12 (95% CI 0.81–1.55; high versus low)[51] and 1.24 (95% CI 1.04–1.48) per ratio increment of 0.1.[74] The latter study was published after the cut-off date for inclusion in the SLR. However, *the Panel was aware of the study and agreed* to include it in its consideration of this exposure.

Patterns of weight gain

The single cohort study showed a statistically significant increased risk with a self-reported tendency to abdominal (central) weight gain, when compared to peripheral weight gain. The effect estimate was 1.45 (95% CI 1.02–2.07).[49]

The general mechanisms through which abdominal fatness could plausibly influence cancer risk are outlined in 6.1.3 (also see box 2.4).

There is a substantial amount of epidemiological evidence, generally consistent, and there is evidence for plausible mechanisms. Abdominal fatness is a probable cause of pancreatic cancer.

Breast (postmenopause)

Eight cohort studies[157 159 170 174 180 187 199 575-577] and three case-control studies[207 242 304] investigated waist circumference and postmenopausal breast cancer. Eight cohort studies[157 159 163 170 174 180 187 189 199 575 576] and eight case-control studies[241 242 247 248 297 304 308 321] investigated waist to hip ratio.

Waist circumference

All eight cohort studies showed increased risk with increased waist circumference, which was statistically significant in two.[157 180 199] Meta-analysis was possible on four cohort studies,[159 170 575 577] giving a summary effect estimate of 1.05 (95% CI 1.00–1.10) per 8 cm (3.1 inches), with no heterogeneity.

All three case-control studies showed increased risk with increased waist circumference, which was statistically significant in two.[207 242]

Waist to hip ratio

Six cohort studies showed increased risk with increased waist to hip ratio,[157 159 163 170 174 180 187 199 575] which was statistically significant in four.[163 170 187 199 575] Two studies showed non-significant decreased risk.[189 576] Meta-analysis was possible on five cohort studies, giving a summary effect estimate of 1.19 (95% CI 1.10–1.28) per ratio increment of 0.1, with moderate heterogeneity (figure 6.1.24).

Five case-control studies showed increased risk with increased waist to hip ratio,[242 247 297 308 321] which was statistically significant in three.[242 297 308] Three studies showed non-significant decreased risk.[241 248 304] Meta-analysis was possible on seven case-control studies, giving a summary effect estimate of 1.07 (95% CI 1.00–1.14) per ratio increment of 0.1, with moderate heterogeneity (figure 6.1.24).

The general mechanisms through which abdominal fatness could plausibly influence cancer risk are outlined in 6.1.3 (also see box 2.4). Many of these, such as increased circulating oestrogens and decreased insulin sensitivity, are particularly associated with abdominal rather than overall body fatness.

There is a substantial amount of epidemiological evidence but some inconsistency. There is robust evidence for mechanisms that operate in humans. Abdominal fatness is a probable cause of postmenopausal breast cancer.

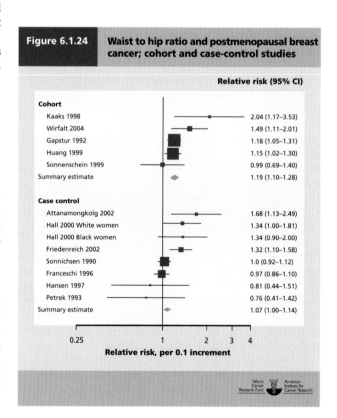

Figure 6.1.24	Waist to hip ratio and postmenopausal breast cancer; cohort and case-control studies

Relative risk (95% CI)

Cohort

	Relative risk (95% CI)
Kaaks 1998	2.04 (1.17–3.53)
Wirfalt 2004	1.49 (1.11–2.01)
Gapstur 1992	1.18 (1.05–1.31)
Huang 1999	1.15 (1.02–1.30)
Sonnenschein 1999	0.99 (0.69–1.40)
Summary estimate	1.19 (1.10–1.28)

Case control

Attanamongkolg 2002	1.68 (1.13–2.49)
Hall 2000 White women	1.34 (1.00–1.81)
Hall 2000 Black women	1.34 (0.90–2.00)
Friedenreich 2002	1.32 (1.10–1.58)
Sonnichsen 1990	1.0 (0.92–1.12)
Franceschi 1996	0.97 (0.86–1.10)
Hansen 1997	0.81 (0.44–1.51)
Petrek 1993	0.76 (0.41–1.42)
Summary estimate	1.07 (1.00–1.14)

Relative risk, per 0.1 increment

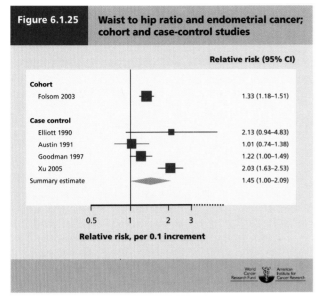

Figure 6.1.25 **Waist to hip ratio and endometrial cancer; cohort and case-control studies**

Relative risk (95% CI)

Cohort	
Folsom 2003	1.33 (1.18–1.51)

Case control	
Elliott 1990	2.13 (0.94–4.83)
Austin 1991	1.01 (0.74–1.38)
Goodman 1997	1.22 (1.00–1.49)
Xu 2005	2.03 (1.63–2.53)
Summary estimate	1.45 (1.00–2.09)

Relative risk, per 0.1 increment

Endometrium

One cohort study[137] and four case-control studies[419 455 578 579] investigated waist circumference and endometrial cancer. One cohort study[137 368 373 374 376] and six case-control studies[388 404 423 424 446 455 578-580] investigated waist to hip ratios.

Waist circumference

The single cohort study showed a statistically significant increased risk for the highest waist circumference group when compared to the lowest. The effect estimate was 4.2 (95% CI 2.8–6.2).[137]

All four case-control studies showed statistically significant increased risk for the highest waist circumference group when compared to the lowest.[419 455 578 579] Three studies adjusted for BMI.[419 455 579]

Waist to hip ratio

The single cohort study showed a statistically significant increased risk for the highest waist circumference group when compared to the lowest.[137 368 373 374 376] The effect estimate was 1.96 (95% CI 1.43–2.71) or 1.33 (95% CI 1.18–1.51) per ratio increment of 0.1 (figure 6.1.25).[373] An earlier report from the same study adjusted for BMI, which reduced the effect estimate and made it non-significant: 1.2 (95% CI 0.8–1.9; high versus low).[137]

Five case-control studies showed increased risk with increased waist to hip ratio,[388 404 423 424 455 578 579] which was statistically significant in two.[404 423 424 455 578 580] One study showed non-significant decreased risk.[446] Meta-analysis was possible on four case-control studies, giving a summary effect estimate of 1.45 (95% CI 1.00–2.09) per ratio increment of 0.1, with high heterogeneity (figure 6.1.25). All four of these case-control studies were adjusted for BMI.

The general mechanisms through which abdominal fatness could plausibly influence cancer risk are outlined in 6.1.3 (also see box 2.4). Many of these, such as increased circulating oestrogens and decreased insulin sensitivity, are particularly associated with abdominal rather than overall body fatness.

> There is a substantial amount of generally consistent epidemiological evidence, but limited prospective data. There is evidence for plausible mechanisms. Greater abdominal fatness is a probable cause of cancer of the endometrium.

6.1.3.3 Adult weight gain
Breast (postmenopause)

Seven cohort studies[158 159 167 193 576 581-586] and 17 case-control studies[217 220 225 231 241 242 255 274 280 283 315 318 327 338 339 349 359 587-591] investigated adult weight gain and postmenopausal breast cancer.

All seven cohort studies showed increased risk with increasing amounts of weight gained in adulthood, which was statistically significant in two.[159 167 581 583 586] Two cohort studies stratified results according to whether or not participants were using HRT.[158 576 584] Both studies showed a statistically significant increased risk in women not using HRT. Studies of weight gain and premenopausal breast cancer showed no overall effect on risk.

The full SLR is contained on the CD included with this Report.

Thirteen case-control studies showed increased risk with increasing amounts of weight gained in adulthood,[217 220 225 231 241 242 255 280 283 315 318 327 338 339 349 587 589-591] which was statistically significant in 11.[217 220 242 255 280 283 315 318 338 339 349 587 589-591] No studies reported significant decreased risk. Meta-analysis was possible on six case-control studies, giving a summary effect estimate of 1.05 (95% CI 1.04–1.07) per 5 kg (11 lbs) gained, with high heterogeneity (figure 6.1.26).

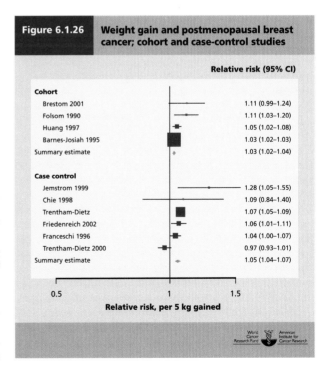

Figure 6.1.26 **Weight gain and postmenopausal breast cancer; cohort and case-control studies**

Relative risk (95% CI)

Cohort	
Brestom 2001	1.11 (0.99–1.24)
Folsom 1990	1.11 (1.03–1.20)
Huang 1997	1.05 (1.02–1.08)
Barnes-Josiah 1995	1.03 (1.02–1.03)
Summary estimate	1.03 (1.02–1.04)

Case control	
Jemstrom 1999	1.28 (1.05–1.55)
Chie 1998	1.09 (0.84–1.40)
Trentham-Dietz	1.07 (1.05–1.09)
Friedenreich 2002	1.06 (1.01–1.11)
Franceschi 1996	1.04 (1.00–1.07)
Trentham-Dietz 2000	0.97 (0.93–1.01)
Summary estimate	1.05 (1.04–1.07)

Relative risk, per 5 kg gained

Heterogeneity may be explained by failure to separate postmenopausal participants using HRT.

There is ample, consistent epidemiological evidence from both cohort and case-control studies. A dose response was apparent from case-control and cohort studies. Adult weight gain is a probable cause of postmenopausal breast cancer.

6.1.4 Comparison with previous report

The previous report used different terminology. It concluded that the evidence that 'high body mass' was a cause of cancer of the endometrium was convincing, and that high body mass was probably a cause of cancers both of the breast (postmenopause) and the kidney. In the previous report, the evidence that high body mass was a cause of cancers of the colon and gallbladder was judged to be possible. Since that time, several cohort studies and other epidemiological and other evidence have greatly strengthened the evidence on body fatness, and specifically on overweight and obesity. Also, the distinction between adenocarcinomas and squamous cell carcinomas has identified a clear relationship between body fatness and adenocarcinomas of the oesophagus. The previous report did not make any judgements specifically on abdominal fatness.

The previous report did not include judgements on body fatness and pancreatic cancer, although it did conclude that high energy intake was a possible cause of this cancer.[592] It also noted data from correlation and animal studies suggesting that high energy intake might increase the risk of cancer in general, without making any judgement.

6.1.5 Conclusions

The Panel concludes:
The evidence that greater body fatness is a cause of cancers of various sites is more impressive now than it was in the mid-1990s.

The evidence that greater body fatness is a cause of cancers of the oesophagus (adenocarcinoma), pancreas, colorectum, breast (postmenopause), endometrium, and kidney is convincing. Greater body fatness is probably a cause of gallbladder cancer, both directly, and indirectly through the formation of gallstones. There is also limited evidence suggesting that greater body fatness is a cause of liver cancer. The evidence that abdominal fatness is a cause of colorectal cancer is convincing; and abdominal fatness is probably a cause of cancers of the pancreas, breast (postmenopause), and endometrium. By contrast, greater body fatness probably protects against cancer of the breast diagnosed before the menopause. *The Panel notes* that there is limited evidence suggesting that low body fatness (underweight) is a cause of cancer of the lung, but residual confounding with smoking and lung disease cannot be ruled out. See chapters 7.4 and 7.10, and Chapter 8 for discussion of the role of energy density in weight gain, overweight, and obesity.

6.2 Growth and development

GROWTH AND DEVELOPMENT, AND THE RISK OF CANCER

In the judgement of the Panel, the factors listed below modify the risk of cancer. Judgements are graded according to the strength of the evidence.

	DECREASES RISK		INCREASES RISK	
	Exposure	**Cancer site**	**Exposure**	**Cancer site**
Convincing			**Adult attained height[1]**	**Colorectum** **Breast (postmenopause)**
Probable			**Adult attained height[1]**	**Pancreas** **Breast (premenopause)** **Ovary**
			Greater birth weight	**Breast (premenopause)**
Limited — suggestive			Adult attained height[1]	Endometrium
Substantial effect on risk unlikely		None identified		

1   Adult attained height is unlikely to directly modify the risk of cancer. It is a marker for genetic, environmental, hormonal, and also nutritional factors affecting growth during the period from preconception to completion of linear growth (see 6.2.1.3).

For an explanation of all the terms used in the matrix, please see chapter 3.5.1, the text of this section, and the glossary.

World Cancer Research Fund / American Institute for Cancer Research

Growth in childhood is a predictor of age at sexual maturity and eventual adult attained height. Food quantity and quality, and the extent of infections and infestations during crucial periods of growth, are critical in determining speed of growth. Rate of growth has metabolic and hormonal effects, which can trigger lifelong consequences.

Since the recognition of the vital importance of nutrition to human health and welfare, public health nutrition policy has emphasised the need for birth weights and rates of growth within ranges defined as those most likely to ensure physical and mental development in childhood, and good health in adult life. Such policies are essential. New standards based on the 'ideal' pattern of growth of healthy, breastfed infants have now been agreed by the World Health Organization.

Overall, *the Panel judges* that evidence on the factors that lead to greater adult attained height, or its consequences, and the risk of cancers of a number of sites, is strong, consistent, and impressive. *The Panel emphasises* that greater adult attained height, meaning how tall people are as adults, is unlikely directly to modify the risk of cancer. It is a marker for genetic, environmental, hormonal, and nutritional factors affecting growth during the period from preconception to completion of linear growth.

The Panel concludes:
The evidence that the factors that lead to greater adult attained height, or its consequences, increase the risk of

cancers of the colorectum and breast (postmenopause) is convincing; and they probably also increase the risk of cancers of the pancreas, breast (premenopause), and ovary.

There is limited evidence suggesting that the factors that lead to greater adult attained height, or its consequences, increase the risk of endometrial cancer.

In addition, the factors that lead to greater birth weight, or its consequences, are probably a cause of premenopausal breast cancer.

A major question for future research is: what are the factors that determine height in adult life? And, given the theme of this Report, what is the relative importance of genetic and environmental factors, what is the role of nutrition, and when in the life course are nutritional factors most relevant? Weighing such evidence, given that adequate birth weight and growth are essential for good health in infancy and childhood, and throughout life, is a major challenge for the biological and nutritional sciences.

Within the remit of this Report, the strongest evidence, corresponding to judgements of 'convincing' and 'probable', shows that the factors that lead to greater adult attained height, or its consequences, are a cause of cancers of the colorectum and breast (postmenopause), and probably also of cancers of the pancreas, breast (premenopause), and ovary. In addition, the factors that lead to greater birth weight, or its consequences, probably increase the risk of premenopausal breast cancer.

Linear growth, from preconception to adulthood, influences health and well-being throughout life, as do body composition and shape.

Standards for birth weight and growth developed by expert panels for relevant United Nations agencies, and approved by UN member states, form the basis for national, municipal, and local paediatric health policies and programmes throughout the world. The WHO/UNU Multicentre Growth Reference Study (MGRS) of healthy, breastfed children is the basis for the WHO 2006 growth standards for children aged 0–5 years.[593]

However, no growth standard has been validated in terms of lifelong risk for chronic diseases, including cancer. As with body weight (see chapter 6.1), policies and programmes concerned with the physical and mental development of infants and children, and growth until adulthood, have focused on the need to protect populations against the consequences of inadequate nutrition and retarded growth. This remains a central public health priority for middle- and low-income countries.

In the 1990s, increasing concern, based on emerging evidence, was expressed by the scientific community in this field.[594] The concern has been that the agreed standards had 'overshot the mark' for optimum growth and health. For several reasons, the agreed growth standards for the first period of life seemed to have been set unnecessarily and unhelpfully high. This perception was heightened by evidence of rapidly increasing rates of childhood overweight and obesity, which tend to track into adult life (see box 8.3). As a result, new standards based on breastfed children were agreed and ratified, and issued in 2005, as guides to optimum growth.[593]

This is the general context in which the Panel has examined the evidence on growth and development, and the risk of cancer.

6.2.1 Definitions and patterns

Growth increases metabolic capacity and also the ability to cope with environmental challenge. From a single cell at conception, human growth progresses through embryogenesis and fetal development, involving cellular multiplication and differentiation in both structure and function. At birth, the body's tissues and organs are highly organised and regulated. The timing and order of these processes are determined by the selective expression of genes, which is both innate and modifiable by the wider environment, including the availability of oxygen, energy, and nutrients. Nutrients also act by regulating hormones, growth factors, binding proteins, and receptors, and their activity.

For every tissue or organ, adverse environmental influences during critical periods of development, such as limited energy or nutrients, can restrict development and future capacity for function. The timing, severity, and duration of any adverse exposure will determine the extent and pattern of any restriction in capacity.

Growth can be divided into three phases: fetal–infant, childhood, and puberty.[595] During the first period, growth is most sensitive to the availability of energy and nutrients. Brain growth is protected more effectively than growth in stature, which is protected more effectively than weight. So the timing of an adverse influence on growth tends to be reflected in a person's body shape, both as a child and as an adult. For instance, for lean tissue to be deposited efficiently and effectively, the appropriate pattern of nutrients must be available in a timely way.

If any nutrients are limited but energy intake is adequate — or more than adequate — a person will be predisposed to excess body fatness. This is because their energy intake will exceed the nutrients available in the body for laying down lean tissue, so the excess energy is stored as fat. People who were of low birth weight have a greater tendency to store fat, in particular abdominally.

6.2.1.1 Birth weight

A baby's size and shape at birth indicates the extent and quality of intra-uterine growth and development. Birth weight can be measured simply and reliably, whereas head circumference, which marks growth of the brain, and length, which marks linear growth, are more difficult to measure reliably. Within the usual range, heavier (and longer) babies tend to become taller children and adults.

Birth weight predicts the risk of death and of various diseases in infancy and later in life. Very low birth weight — less than 2.5 kg (5.5 lbs) for boys and 2.4 kg (5.3 lbs) for girls — increases the risk of perinatal death and disease, or death in infancy and young childhood, usually because of increased vulnerability to infection and infestation. It is well established, at least in high-income countries, that smaller size at birth, and at 1 year of age, predicts increased risk of chronic disease such as cardiovascular disease and type 2 diabetes during adult life.[596] This is due to a reduced capacity to cope with the stress of environmental challenges, such as a poor diet (including excess energy) and physical inactivity. Very high birth weight may also be associated with increased risk — for instance, maternal diabetes or poor glucose homeostasis can cause higher birth weight as well as increased risk of diabetes in the infant.[597] These findings have been shown to be independent of smoking or socioeconomic status, although they may be accentuated in the presence of these additional stress factors.[598]

The extent to which body fatness is a factor in any relationship between low birth weight and disease in later life remains unclear. The associations described above are strongest when low birth weight, or restricted fetal growth, is followed by rapid growth during early childhood.[599-602] Such effects can be experimentally induced in animals, lending weight to the observed associations in humans being causal.

6.2.1.2 Infant and prepubertal growth

The fetal–infant growth phase slows during the second half of the first year of life. The childhood phase of growth becomes established at 6–18 months. Any delay in the onset of this growth phase tends to lead to shorter stature during childhood. Over an extended period of time, growth in height and weight is a smooth process, although there may be growth spurts or times of little change over shorter periods. Growth, through the formation of new tissue, requires a dietary supply of energy (about 5 kilocalories per gram of new tissue) and macronutrients such as amino acids and fatty acids, as well as vitamins, minerals, and trace elements. Each individual factor is vital; if any are limited they will constrain normal growth and development.

At any age, therefore, normal development requires appropriate genetic, hormonal, and nutritional factors to support growth. These in turn require adequate quantity and quality of food, and minimal exposure to food and environmental toxicants, infection, and psychosocial stress. As an infant gets older, the body is increasingly able to cope with environmental challenge.

The pattern and timing of any nutrient shortfall determines the pattern of constrained growth. Patterns of growth failure are highly variable, comprising the differential effects on linear growth (stunting), weight (underweight and wasting), or on specific tissues. Thus stunting may be due to a period of slow growth or a delay to the onset of the childhood phase of growth. If growth has been constrained as the result of an adverse circumstance, which is then removed, there is a drive towards returning to the growth pattern established previously or to the genetically determined growth pattern. This 'catch-up' growth may be in height or weight, or some combination of the two; the term is often used without defining what type of growth is involved. However, 'catch-up' in linear growth after malnutrition is rare beyond the first 2–3 years of life.

In the first 6 months of life, infants who are breastfed and then weaned appropriately to mixed diets grow differently from those fed on formula. This is partly related to the increased risk of infection for formula-fed infants and partly due to the different compositions of human milk and formula feed. Normal child growth (under optimal environmental conditions) from birth to 5 years is specified in the WHO Child Growth Standards.[593]

Throughout the world, particularly in high- and middle-income countries, and in urban areas generally, childhood obesity and type 2 diabetes are becoming more common. Childhood overweight and obesity often persists into adult life. This exposes people to the hormonal and physiological consequences of being overweight or obese earlier in adult life, increasing their risk of related health problems at a relatively young age (also see box 8.3).

6.2.1.3 Adult attained height
Genetic and early life environmental factors, even before birth, are important in determining adult height. The environmental determinants of height attained in adulthood are highlighted by the variation between generations in adoption and migrant studies, where children are moved from a poor or limited nutritional background to an area of high or even overnutrition.[603] Adult height is also linked to birth weight, rate of growth, and age of puberty. Periods of peak growth (such as in infancy and adolescence) are particularly important in determining adult height.

Adult height increases as populations become less vulnerable to undernutrition, infestation, and infection, and as food supplies become more secure; it continues to increase when food is abundant (also see chapter 1.1). This trend has now slowed or even stopped in most high-income countries. Increases in height between generations are generally due to increased leg, rather than spine, length. Leg length is linked to prepubertal growth, particularly to infancy (below the age of 5); after this age, trunk growth becomes more prominent.[604 605]

Growth hormones, insulin-like growth factors, and sex hormone binding proteins all define the biological activity of the respective hormones. These in turn impact on height, growth, sexual maturation (boxes 6.2.1 and 6.2.2), fat storage, and many processes relevant to cancer (box 2.4). It is therefore plausible that nutritional factors that impinge on height could also influence cancer risk, with adult height acting as a marker of that early life experience, in the same way that taller people have a decreased risk of cardiovascular diseases, at least in high-income countries.[606-608]

Therefore, both birth weight and adult attained height are markers of an aggregated fetal and childhood experience; they are clearly also surrogates for important nutritional exposures, which impact on several hormonal and metabolic axes, and which influence cancer risk (also see Chapter 2).

6.2.2. Interpretation of the evidence

6.2.2.1 General
For general considerations that may affect interpretation of the evidence, see chapters 3.3 and 3.5, and boxes 3.1, 3.2, 3.6 and 3.7.

6.2.2.2 Specific
Some considerations specific to growth and development are as follows.

Measurement. Weight at birth is usually recalled accurately by parents. As well as full height, proxy measures may be used in some studies, including leg length, sitting height, or a ratio of these two. The ratio between overall height and limb length varies with genetic background and nutritional experience over the life course.

6.2.3 Evidence and judgements

The full systematic literature review (SLR) is contained on the CD included with this Report.

As indicated in 6.2.1.3, there are several general mechanisms through which the factors that lead to greater adult attained height, or its consequences, could plausibly influence cancer risk. However, adult attained height is unlikely to directly modify the risk of cancer. It is a marker for genetic, environmental, hormonal, and also nutritional factors affecting growth during the period from preconception to completion of linear growth. For example, adult height is the result of several stages of growth from fetal life through childhood. These are all influenced by nutrition, particularly in infancy, which in turn affects hormone levels, and there-

Box 6.2.1   Sexual maturity

Sexual maturity is the biological capability to have children. In girls, this is characterised by ovulatory cycles and/or menarche, the onset of menstruation. In boys, pubertal stages are less easy to characterise, and indirect markers (secondary sex characteristics) are used, such as the age of appearance of pubic hair. As a consequence, there are more data for sexual maturation in girls than boys.

There is considerable variation in the age of sexual maturity, both between and among populations. In high-income countries, the average age of menarche ranges from 12–13 years; this has dropped by around 3 years over the last 150 years, although the change has now generally

halted.[609] In low-income countries, and particularly among the most disadvantaged populations, the average age of menarche may be as high as 16.[610] These trends show the impact of environmental influences on age at menarche.

Adrenal sex hormone production normally rises at around 6 years of age (adrenarchy) and coincides with a rise in BMI (adiposity rebound). Growth hormone, insulin-like growth factors, and sex hormone binding proteins all define the biological activity of the respective hormones.

Children with an early adiposity rebound have earlier sexual maturation and higher risk of later obesity.

Nutrition, birth weight, rates of growth, body fatness, and age of sexual maturity are all connected. The effects of these factors may be different in either sex, with increased body fatness lowering the age at menarche but slowing male sexual maturation.[611] Conversely, early menarche increases the risk of adult obesity.

Undernutrition delays the onset of puberty in both boys and girls.[612] Regular, intense physical activity can delay menarche or cause menstruation to stop in later life. The combination of low birth weight and rapid growth in early childhood also accelerates the development of sexual maturity.

---

fore many processes relevant to cancer (box 2.4). Site-specific mechanisms are described with the evidence for each cancer site.

6.2.3.1 Adult attained height
Colorectum

Twenty-one cohort studies[58 80 82-84 87 88 91 93 108 109 115 117 119 120 124 126 133 140 142 621-625] and 16 case-control studies investigated adult attained height and cancer of the colon and rectum.

Eighteen cohort studies showed increased risk with increased adult attained height[58 80 82-84 87 88 109 115 117 120 124 126 142 622-625]; this was statistically significant in six,[58 80 87 124 623 624] and in another study in men, but not in women.[108 119 621] One study showed non-significant increased risk in men and no effect on risk in women.[140] Two studies showed no effect on risk.[91 93 133] Meta-analysis was possible on 12 cohort studies, giving a summary effect estimate of 1.09

(95% CI 1.06–1.12) per 5 cm (2 inches), with no heterogeneity (figure 6.2.1).

A dose-response relationship was apparent from cohort data.

Because of the abundant prospective data from cohort studies, case-control studies were not summarised.

The general mechanisms through which the factors that lead to greater adult attained height, or its consequences, could plausibly influence cancer risk are outlined in 6.2.1.3 (also see box 2.4). Many of these, such as early-life nutrition, altered hormone profiles, and the rate of sexual maturation, could plausibly increase cancer risk

There is ample prospective epidemiological evidence, which is consistent, and there is a clear dose response, with evidence for plausible mechanisms operating in humans. The evidence that factors that lead to greater

---

Box 6.2.2   Age at menarche and risk of breast cancer

Early menarche is an established risk factor for breast cancer. From pooling project data, based on information from 322 647 women, 4827 breast cancer cases occurred during follow-up, and the fully adjusted risk due to late menarche (at 15 years or above compared with under 12 years of age) was 0.72 (95% confidence interval (CI) 0.62–0.82).[613]

A meta-analysis of 21 epidemiological studies (including both case-control and cohort) reported a risk reduction of about 9 per cent (95% CI 7–11) for each additional year of age at menarche. There was also a statistically significant gradient of risk when breast cancer was diagnosed early or before menopause, and a risk of about 4 per cent (95% CI 2–5) for later diagnoses.[614]

A large cohort study (100 000 partici-

pants) reported a 7 per cent per year decrease in breast cancer risk with increasing age of menarche for premenopause cases (p < 0.05). Compared to those who had their first period at 11 or younger, women experiencing menarche at 15 years or older had a risk of 0.66 (95% CI 0.45–0.97). There was no statistically significant effect for postmenopause cases.[615]

Menarche marks the start of the cyclic production of oestrogen by the ovaries. Therefore early menarche means that a woman is exposed to more oestrogen over the course of her lifetime.[616] This is likely to be the mechanism by which age at menarche influences breast cancer risk. As well as a longer lifetime exposure to oestrogen, early menarche may be associated with increased oestrogen levels during the

whole period of adolescence and early adulthood.[617]

The first onset of breast development in girls occurs about two years before menarche. The years preceding menarche are characterised by a sharp increase in adrenal androgens and the associated appearance of the first pubic and axillary hairs, and the first enlargement of the breasts. At this age, adrenal androgens play an important role in inducing hypothalamic changes leading to menarche.[618] In adulthood, both before and after menopause, high serum androgens levels are associated with increased breast cancer risk.[619 620] Consequently, nutritional exposures in early life that influence sexual maturation in women are also likely to have an indirect impact on later breast cancer risk.

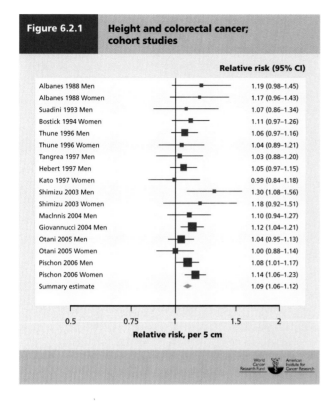

Figure 6.2.1 Height and colorectal cancer; cohort studies

Relative risk (95% CI)

		Relative risk (95% CI)
Albanes 1988 Men		1.19 (0.98–1.45)
Albanes 1988 Women		1.17 (0.96–1.43)
Suadini 1993 Men		1.07 (0.86–1.34)
Bostick 1994 Women		1.11 (0.97–1.26)
Thune 1996 Men		1.06 (0.97–1.16)
Thune 1996 Women		1.04 (0.89–1.21)
Tangrea 1997 Men		1.03 (0.88–1.20)
Hebert 1997 Men		1.05 (0.97–1.15)
Kato 1997 Women		0.99 (0.84–1.18)
Shimizu 2003 Men		1.30 (1.08–1.56)
Shimizu 2003 Women		1.18 (0.92–1.51)
MacInnis 2004 Men		1.10 (0.94–1.27)
Giovannucci 2004 Men		1.12 (1.04–1.21)
Otani 2005 Men		1.04 (0.95–1.13)
Otani 2005 Women		1.00 (0.88–1.14)
Pischon 2006 Men		1.08 (1.01–1.17)
Pischon 2006 Women		1.14 (1.06–1.23)
Summary estimate		1.09 (1.06–1.12)

Relative risk, per 5 cm

Figure 6.2.2 Height and breast cancer (age unspecified); cohort and case-control studies

Relative risk (95% CI)

Cohort

		Relative risk (95% CI)
Nilsen 2001		1.44 (1.10–1.88)
Hoyer 1998		1.17 (1.00–1.36)
Palmer 2001		1.15 (1.03–1.29)
Galanis 1998		1.13 (1.02–1.24)
Vatten 1992		1.13 (1.06,–1.20)
Tulinius 1997		1.10 (1.05–1.15)
Tornberg 1988		1.10 (1.05–1.15)
Palmer 2001		1.10 (1.04–1.16)
Tryggvadottir 2002		1.09 (1.03–1.15)
Nilsen 2001		1.09 (0.79–1.50)
Goodman 1997		1.03 (0.88–1.21)
Key 1999		1.01 (0.90–1.13)
Overvad 1991		1.00 (0.77–1.31)
Kilkinnen 2004		1.00 (0.85–1.17)
Drake 2001		1.00 (0.87–1.14)
Nilsen 2001		0.99 (0.72–1.38)
Wu 2005		0.98 (0.83–1.15)
Nilsen 2001		0.95 (0.68–1.32)
Nilsen 2001		0.80 (0.58–1.10)
Summary estimate		1.09 (1.07–1.12)

Case control

Bruning 1992		1.22 (1.06–1.42)
Ziegler 1996		1.18 (1.06–1.31)
Ueji 1997		1.15 (0.93–1.41)
Lebamowo 2003		1.15 (1.03–1.28)
Hu 1997		1.12 (0.95–1.31)
Challier 1998		1.11 (0.98–1.25)
Wenten 2001		1.08 (0.94–1.25)
Swanson 1989		1.08 (1.03–1.14)
Shu 2001		1.08 (1.00–1.15)
Hirose 1999		1.06 (1.01–1.11)
Adami 1977		1.05 (0.89–1.25)
Hsieh 1990		1.04 (0.91–1.07)
Wenten 2001		1.03 (0.91–1.17)
Silva 2004		1.03 (0.90–1.17)
Yoo 2001		1.02 (0.93–1.11)
McCredie 1998		1.02 (0.95–1.09)
Hislop 1986		1.02 (0.93–1.11)
Tung 1999		1.02 (0.88–1.17)
Drewnowski 2000		1.01 (0.85–1.20)
Zhang 1996		0.99 (0.96–1.02)
Chie 1998		0.97 (0.79–1.18)
Potischman 1990		0.96 (0.80–1.16)
Kato 1992		0.95 (0.86–1.05)
Bouchardy 1990		0.94 (0.88–1.01)
Toti 1986		0.89 (0.82–0.97)
Sarlin 1985		0.88 (0.58–1.34)
Summary estimate		1.03 (1.01–1.04)

Relative risk, per 5 cm

adult attained height, or its consequences, are a cause of colorectal cancer is convincing. The causal factor is unlikely to be tallness itself, but factors that promote linear growth in childhood.

The Panel is aware that since the conclusion of the SLR, three cohort studies[31 141 145] have been published. This new information does not change the Panel judgement (see box 3.8).

Breast
Thirty-three cohort studies,[122 150 151 155-157 161 162 164 166 168 170-172 174-176 178 180 181 183 185-187 189-191 193 196 198-200 203 577 626-637] 56 case-control studies,[205 206 208 214 217 218 220 221 224 225 231 234 241 242 247 248 253 254 256 257 259 261 262 269 272 274 279 280 283 290 297 303 304 306 308 312-314 318 319 323-327 331 333 336 338 339 341 342 346 349 352 588 638-647] and 3 ecological studies[361 625 648] investigated adult attained height and breast cancer.

Age unspecified
Twenty cohort studies[122 150 161 162 164 166 168 171 172 181 186 191 196 203 627-630 632 634-637] and 29 case-control studies[205 208 214 218 221 224 225 234 248 254 259 261 262 269 290 297 306 313 314 318 319 323 324 336 341 342 349 352 638 641 646 647] investigated adult attained height and breast cancer at all ages, or unspecified menopausal status.

Thirteen cohort studies showed increased risk with greater adult attained height,[122 161 162 164 168 171 191 196 628 629 632 634-637] which was statistically significant in nine.[122 161 162 168 191 196 632 634-637] Four studies showed no effect on risk,[172 181 186 630] and two showed decreased risk,[150 166 203 627] which was statistically significant in one study.[150] Another study showed varying effects in different age groups.[633] Meta-analysis was possible on 14 cohort studies, giving a summary effect esti-

mate of 1.09 (95% CI 1.07–1.12) per 5 cm (2 inches), with low heterogeneity (figure 6.2.2).

Twenty-two case-control studies showed increased risk with greater adult attained height,[205 208 218 221 224 234 248 254 259 261 262 290 297 318 319 323 324 341 342 349 352 638 641 647] which was statistically significant in seven.[208 218 224 261 297 324 647] Seven studies showed decreased risk,[214 225 269 306 313 314 336 646] which was statistically significant in one.[336] Meta-analysis was possible on 25 case-control studies, giving a summary effect estimate of 1.03 (95% CI 1.01–1.04) per 5 cm (2 inches), with moderate heterogeneity (figure 6.2.2).

A dose-response relationship was apparent from cohort and case-control data.

All three ecological studies showed increased risk with greater adult attained height.[361 625 648]

Postmenopause

Twenty-two cohort studies[122 151 155-157 162 168 170-172 174 175 178 180 183 185 187 189-191 193 199 200 577 626 631 634 636 637] and 34 case-control studies[205 206 208 214 217 220 224 225 231 241 242 247 253 256 257 259 261 274 280 283 297 304 308 318 327 331 333 338 339 341 352 588 638-640 642 643 646 647] investigated adult attained height and postmenopausal breast cancer.

Twenty-one cohort studies showed increased risk with greater adult attained height,[122 151 155-157 162 168 170-172 174 175 178 180 183 185 187 189-191 193 577 626 631 634 636 637] which was statistically significant in 12.[122 155 162 168 171 172 175 178 183 191 193 577 626 631 636] One study showed no effect on risk.[200] Meta-analysis was possible on 15 cohort studies, giving a summary effect estimate of 1.11 (95% CI 1.09–1.13) per 5 cm (2 inches), with no heterogeneity (figure 6.2.3).

Pooled analysis from 7 cohort studies (more than 337 000 participants, followed up for up to 11 years, with more than 4300 breast cancer cases) showed a statistically significant increased risk of postmenopausal breast cancer with greater adult attained height. The effect estimate was 1.07 (95% CI 1.03–1.12) per 5 cm (2 inches).[362]

Twenty-two case-control studies showed increased risk with greater adult attained height,[205 208 214 217 224 231 242 253 256 257 259 261 279 280 283 297 318 331 338 339 352 588 638-640 642 643 647] which was statistically significant in 11.[208 217 224 253 256 261 297 318 338 339 639] Nine studies showed non-significant decreased risk.[206 220 225 241 274 304 327 333 341 646] Two studies showed no effect on risk.[308] Another study showed non-significant increased risk in white women and no effect on risk in black women.[247] Meta-analysis was possible on 27 case-control studies, giving a summary effect estimate of 1.02 (95% CI 1.01–1.03) per 5 cm (2 inches), with high heterogeneity (figure 6.2.3).

A dose-response relationship was apparent from cohort and from case-control data.

The general mechanisms through which the factors that lead to greater adult attained height, and its consequences, could plausibly influence cancer risk are outlined in 6.2.1.3 (also see box 2.5). Many of these, such as early-life nutrition, altered hormone profiles, and the rate of sexual maturation, could plausibly increase cancer risk.

There is abundant prospective epidemiological evidence, which is generally consistent, with a clear dose response, and evidence for plausible mechanisms operating in humans. The evidence that factors that lead to greater adult attained height, or its consequences, are a cause of postmenopausal breast cancer is convincing. The causal factor is unlikely to be

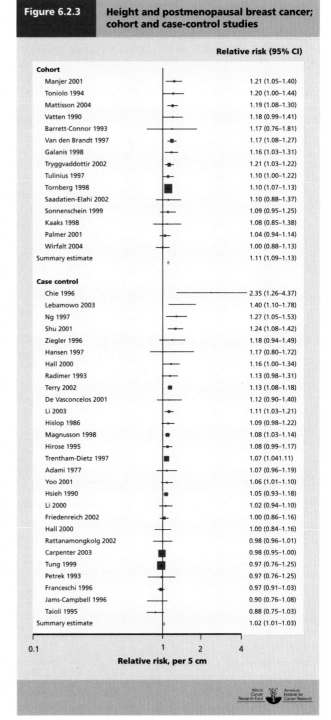

Figure 6.2.3 | **Height and postmenopausal breast cancer; cohort and case-control studies**

tallness itself, but factors that promote linear growth in childhood.

The Panel is aware that since the conclusion of the SLR, one cohort study[649] has been published. This new information does not change the Panel judgement (see box 3.8).

Premenopause

Seventeen cohort studies[122 155 162 170 175 176 178 185 189-191 196 198 626 631 634 636 637] and 38 case-control studies[205 206 208 214 217 224 225 231 241 242 247 248 253 256 257 259 261 272 290 297 303 304 308 312 318 324-327 339 341 346 352 588 638 640 644-647] investigated adult attained height and premenopausal breast cancer.

Eleven cohort studies showed increased risk with greater

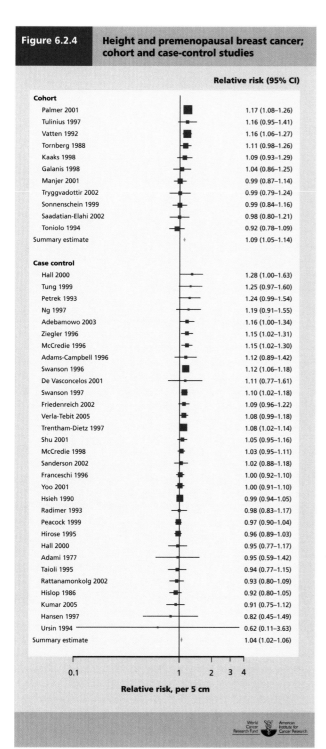

Figure 6.2.4 | **Height and premenopausal breast cancer; cohort and case-control studies**

Relative risk (95% CI)

Cohort

	Relative risk (95% CI)
Palmer 2001	1.17 (1.08–1.26)
Tulinius 1997	1.16 (0.95–1.41)
Vatten 1992	1.16 (1.06–1.27)
Tornberg 1988	1.11 (0.98–1.26)
Kaaks 1998	1.09 (0.93–1.29)
Galanis 1998	1.04 (0.86–1.25)
Manjer 2001	0.99 (0.87–1.14)
Tryggvadottir 2002	0.99 (0.79–1.24)
Sonnenschein 1999	0.99 (0.84–1.16)
Saadatian-Elahi 2002	0.98 (0.80–1.21)
Toniolo 1994	0.92 (0.78–1.09)
Summary estimate	1.09 (1.05–1.14)

Case control

	Relative risk (95% CI)
Hall 2000	1.28 (1.00–1.63)
Tung 1999	1.25 (0.97–1.60)
Petrek 1993	1.24 (0.99–1.54)
Ng 1997	1.19 (0.91–1.55)
Adebamowo 2003	1.16 (1.00–1.34)
Ziegler 1996	1.15 (1.02–1.31)
McCredie 1996	1.15 (1.02–1.30)
Adams-Campbell 1996	1.12 (0.89–1.42)
Swanson 1996	1.12 (1.06–1.18)
De Vasconcelos 2001	1.11 (0.77–1.61)
Swanson 1997	1.10 (1.02–1.18)
Friedenreich 2002	1.09 (0.96–1.22)
Verla-Tebit 2005	1.08 (0.99–1.18)
Trentham-Dietz 1997	1.08 (1.02–1.14)
Shu 2001	1.05 (0.95–1.16)
McCredie 1998	1.03 (0.95–1.11)
Sanderson 2002	1.02 (0.88–1.18)
Franceschi 1996	1.00 (0.92–1.10)
Yoo 2001	1.00 (0.91–1.10)
Hsieh 1990	0.99 (0.94–1.05)
Radimer 1993	0.98 (0.83–1.17)
Peacock 1999	0.97 (0.90–1.04)
Hirose 1995	0.96 (0.89–1.03)
Hall 2000	0.95 (0.77–1.17)
Adami 1977	0.95 (0.59–1.42)
Taioli 1995	0.94 (0.77–1.15)
Rattanamonkolg 2002	0.93 (0.80–1.09)
Hislop 1986	0.92 (0.80–1.05)
Kumar 2005	0.91 (0.75–1.12)
Hansen 1997	0.82 (0.45–1.49)
Ursin 1994	0.62 (0.11–3.63)
Summary estimate	1.04 (1.02–1.06)

0.1   1   2   3   4

Relative risk, per 5 cm

World Cancer Research Fund / American Institute for Cancer Research

adult attained height,[122 155 162 170 175 176 191 196 626 631 634 637] which was statistically significant in two.[196 634 637] Six studies showed non-significant decreased risk.[178 185 189 190 198 636] Meta-analysis was possible on 11 cohort studies, giving a summary effect estimate of 1.09 (95% CI 1.05–1.14) per 5 cm (2 inches), with low heterogeneity (figure 6.2.4).

Pooled analysis from 7 cohort studies (more than 337 000 participants, followed up for up to 11 years, with more than 4300 breast cancer cases) showed a non-significant increased risk of premenopausal breast cancer with greater adult attained height. The effect estimate was 1.02 (95% CI 0.96–1.10) per 5 cm (2 inches).[362]

Twenty-three case-control studies showed increased risk with greater adult attained height,[206 208 214 217 224 231 242 247 256 257 290 297 304 312 318 324-326 339 341 346 638 644 646 647] which was statistically significant in five.[217 290 325 326 339] Thirteen studies showed non-significant decreased risk.[205 225 248 253 259 261 272 303 308 327 640 645] Two studies showed no effect on risk.[241 352 588] Meta-analysis was possible on 31 case-control studies, giving a summary effect estimate of 1.04 (95% CI 1.02–1.06) per 5 cm (2 inches), with moderate heterogeneity (figure 6.2.4).

A dose-response relationship was apparent from cohort and from case-control data.

The general mechanisms through which factors associated with adult attained height could plausibly cause cancer are outlined in 6.2.1.3 (also see box 2.5). Many of these, such as early-life nutrition, altered hormone profiles, and the rate of sexual maturation, could plausibly increase cancer risk.

There are fewer data for premenopausal than for postmenopausal breast cancer. The epidemiological evidence is generally consistent with a dose response and evidence for plausible mechanisms. Greater adult attained height or factors that lead to it are probably a cause of premenopausal breast cancer. The causal factor is unlikely to be tallness itself, but factors that promote linear growth in childhood.

The Panel is aware that since the conclusion of the SLR, one cohort study[649] has been published. This new information does not change the Panel judgement (see box 3.8).

Pancreas

Eight cohort studies,[40 41 53 58 122 650-652] 12 case-control studies,[60-63 67 70 73 653-657] and 1 ecological study[625] investigated adult attained height and pancreatic cancer.

Six cohort studies showed increased risk with greater adult attained height,[40 41 53 122 650 652] which was statistically significant in one.[40] One study showed no effect on risk.[651] Another stated that there was no significant association.[58] Meta-analysis was possible on six cohort studies, giving a summary effect estimate of 1.11 (95% CI 1.05–1.17) per 5 cm (2 inches), with low heterogeneity (figure 6.2.5).

*The Panel is aware of a further study, published after the conclusion of the SLR, from the European Prospective Investigation into Cancer and Nutrition. This reported a statistically significant increased risk for the highest adult

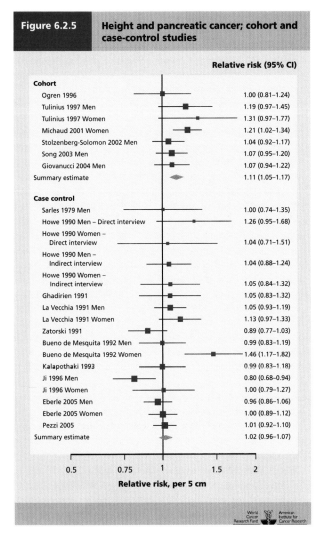

Figure 6.2.5 Height and pancreatic cancer; cohort and case-control studies

Relative risk (95% CI)

Cohort

Ogren 1996	1.00 (0.81–1.24)
Tulinius 1997 Men	1.19 (0.97–1.45)
Tulinius 1997 Women	1.31 (0.97–1.77)
Michaud 2001 Women	1.21 (1.02–1.34)
Stolzenberg-Solomon 2002 Men	1.04 (0.92–1.17)
Song 2003 Men	1.07 (0.95–1.20)
Giovanucci 2004 Men	1.07 (0.94–1.22)
Summary estimate	1.11 (1.05–1.17)

Case control

Sarles 1979 Men	1.00 (0.74–1.35)
Howe 1990 Men – Direct interview	1.26 (0.95–1.68)
Howe 1990 Women – Direct interview	1.04 (0.71–1.51)
Howe 1990 Men – Indirect interview	1.04 (0.88–1.24)
Howe 1990 Women – Indirect interview	1.05 (0.84–1.32)
Ghadirien 1991	1.05 (0.83–1.32)
La Vecchia 1991 Men	1.05 (0.93–1.19)
La Vecchia 1991 Women	1.13 (0.97–1.33)
Zatorski 1991	0.89 (0.77–1.03)
Bueno de Mesquita 1992 Men	0.99 (0.83–1.19)
Bueno de Mesquita 1992 Women	1.46 (1.17–1.82)
Kalapothaki 1993	0.99 (0.83–1.18)
Ji 1996 Men	0.80 (0.68–0.94)
Ji 1996 Women	1.00 (0.79–1.27)
Eberle 2005 Men	0.96 (0.86–1.06)
Eberle 2005 Women	1.00 (0.89–1.12)
Pezzi 2005	1.01 (0.92–1.10)
Summary estimate	1.02 (0.96–1.07)

0.5   0.75   1   1.5   2

Relative risk, per 5 cm

Figure 6.2.6 Height and pancreatic cancer; cohort studies: dose response

Ogren 1996
Tulinius 1997 Men
Tulinius 1997 Women
Michaud 2001 Women
Stolzenberg-Solomon 2002 Men
Song 2003 Men
Giovannucci 2004 Men

155 160 165 170 175 180

Height (cm)

altered hormone profiles, and the rate of sexual maturation, could plausibly increase cancer risk.

> **There is ample prospective epidemiological evidence, though there is some inconsistency. There is evidence for a dose-response relationship and evidence for plausible mechanisms. Greater adult attained height or factors that lead to it are probably a cause of pancreatic cancer. The causal factor is unlikely to be tallness itself, but factors that promote linear growth in childhood.**

Ovary

Seven cohort studies,[168 658-663] nine case-control studies,[254 657 664-670] and two ecological studies[625 671] investigated adult attained height and ovarian cancer.

All seven cohort studies showed increased risk with greater adult attained height, which was statistically significant in four.[168 659 661 663] Meta-analysis was possible on three cohort studies, giving a summary effect estimate of 1.15 (95% CI 1.08–1.21) per 10 cm (3.9 inches), with low heterogeneity (figure 6.2.7).

Seven case-control studies showed non-significant increased risk with greater adult attained height.[254 664 666-670] Two studies showed decreased risk,[657 665] which was statistically significant in one.[665] Meta-analysis was possible on seven case-control studies, giving a summary effect estimate of 0.96 (95% CI 0.87–1.05) per 10 cm (3.9 inches), with moderate heterogeneity (figure 6.2.7). Heterogeneity originated from one relatively large hospital-based study. The confidence intervals of all other studies were large and overlapped the null effect.

A dose-response relationship was apparent from cohort

attained height group when compared to the lowest, with an effect estimate of 1.74 (95% CI 1.20–2.52).[74]

Five case-control studies showed increased risk with greater adult attained height,[60 61 70 654 657] which was statistically significant in women, but not men, in one.[654] Four studies showed decreased risk,[62 63 67 655] which was statistically significant in men, but not women, in one.[63] Two studies showed no effect on risk[653 656] and another stated that there was no significant association.[73] Meta-analysis was possible on 10 case-control studies, giving a summary effect estimate of 1.02 (95% CI 0.96–1.07) per 5 cm (2 inches), with moderate heterogeneity (figure 6.2.5).

A dose-response relationship was apparent from cohort data (figure 6.2.6), but not from case-control data.

The single ecological study showed an association between greater adult attained height and increased pancreatic cancer incidence, which was statistically significant in men.[625]

The general mechanisms through which the factors that lead to greater adult attained height, and its consequences, could plausibly influence cancer risk are outlined in 6.2.1.3 (also see box 2.4). Many of these, such as early-life nutrition,

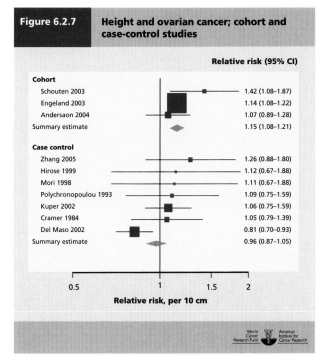

Figure 6.2.7 | **Height and ovarian cancer; cohort and case-control studies**

Relative risk (95% CI)

Cohort
Schouten 2003	1.42 (1.08–1.87)
Engeland 2003	1.14 (1.08–1.22)
Andersaon 2004	1.07 (0.89–1.28)
Summary estimate	1.15 (1.08–1.21)

Case control
Zhang 2005	1.26 (0.88–1.80)
Hirose 1999	1.12 (0.67–1.88)
Mori 1998	1.11 (0.67–1.88)
Polychronopoulou 1993	1.09 (0.75–1.59)
Kuper 2002	1.06 (0.75–1.59)
Cramer 1984	1.05 (0.79–1.39)
Del Maso 2002	0.81 (0.70–0.93)
Summary estimate	0.96 (0.87–1.05)

Relative risk, per 10 cm

data, but not from case-control data.

Both ecological studies showed an association between greater adult attained height and increased cancer incidence.[625] [671]

The general mechanisms through which the factors that lead to greater adult attained height, and its consequences, could plausibly influence cancer risk, are outlined in 6.2.1.3 (also see box 2.4). Many of these, such as early-life nutrition, altered hormone profiles, and the rate of sexual maturation, could plausibly increase cancer risk.

There is some inconsistency, but the better quality epidemiological data show a clearer effect, with a dose-response relationship. There is evidence for plausible mechanisms operating in humans. Adult attained height or factors that lead to it are probably a cause of ovarian cancer. The causal factor is unlikely to be tallness itself, but factors that promote linear growth in childhood.

The Panel is aware that since the conclusion of the SLR, one cohort study[672] and one case-control study[673] have been published. This new information does not change the Panel judgement (see box 3.8).

Endometrium

Ten cohort studies,[168] [369] [371] [372] [375] [379] [382] [385] [674] [675] 16 case-control studies,[254] [389] [396] [402] [404] [409] [416] [419] [420] [422-424] [434-437] [446] [453] [578] [579] [657] [676] [677] and one ecological study[625] investigated adult attained height and endometrial cancer.

Seven cohort studies showed increased risk with greater adult attained height,[168] [369] [372] [375] [379] [382] [674] which was statistically significant in one.[379] One study showed significant

increased risk for postmenopausal women and non-significant decreased risk for premenopausal women.[371] One study showed non-significant increased risk for metastatic endometrial cancer and non-significant decreased risk for non-metastatic endometrial cancer.[675] One study reported no significant difference but gave no further information.[385] Meta-analysis was possible on four cohort studies,[372] [375] [382] [674] giving a summary effect estimate of 1.17 (95% CI 0.96–1.42) per 10 cm (3.9 inches), with no heterogeneity.

Eight of the case-control studies showed increased risk with greater adult attained height,[254] [389] [396] [404] [416] [420] [422] [435-437] [446] [453] [579] [676] [677] which was statistically significant in one.[435] Two studies that showed decreased risk, which was not statistically significant in either case.[402] [434] [578] Five other studies reported non-significant associations.[409] [419] [423] [424] [657] Meta-analysis was possible on 11 case-control studies,[254] [402] [416] [419] [420] [422] [435] [436] [455] [579] [676] giving a summary effect estimate of 1.10 (95% CI 1.00–1.21) per 10 cm (3.9 inches), with moderate heterogeneity.

The general mechanisms through which the factors that lead to greater adult attained height, or its consequences, could plausibly influence cancer risk are outlined in 6.2.1.3 (also see box 2.4). Many of these, such as early-life nutrition, altered hormone profiles, and the rate of sexual maturation, could plausibly increase cancer risk.

Although there is generally consistent evidence for prospective epidemiological data, there is some inconsistency in the evidence between cohort and case-control studies, and the mechanistic evidence is speculative. There is limited evidence that greater adult attained height or factors that lead to it are a cause of endometrial cancer. The causal factor is unlikely to be tallness itself, but factors that promote linear growth in childhood.

6.2.3.2 Greater birth weight
Breast (premenopause)

Six cohort studies[150] [319] [678-681] and four case-control studies[312] [644] [682] [683] investigated birth weight and premenopausal breast cancer.

All six cohort studies showed increased risk with greater birth weight, which was statistically significant in three.[150] [679] [680] Meta-analysis was possible on four cohort studies, giving a summary effect estimate of 1.08 (95% CI 1.04–1.13) per kg (2.2 lbs), with high heterogeneity (figure 6.2.8).

Three case-control studies showed increased risk with greater birth weight,[644] [682] [683] which was statistically significant in one.[682] Another study showed non-significant decreased risk.[312]

The general mechanisms through which the factors that lead to greater birth weight, or its consequences, could plausibly influence cancer risk are outlined in 6.2.1.1. Many of these, such as long-term programming of hormonal systems, could plausibly increase cancer risk.

There is general consistency amongst the relatively few epidemiological studies, with some evidence for a dose response. The mechanistic evidence is speculative.

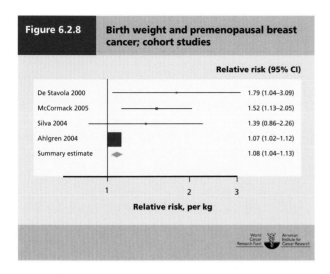

Figure 6.2.8 Birth weight and premenopausal breast cancer; cohort studies

	Relative risk (95% CI)
De Stavola 2000	1.79 (1.04–3.09)
McCormack 2005	1.52 (1.13–2.05)
Silva 2004	1.39 (0.86–2.26)
Ahlgren 2004	1.07 (1.02–1.12)
Summary estimate	1.08 (1.04–1.13)

Relative risk, per kg

ly to directly modify the risk of cancer. It is a marker for genetic, environmental, hormonal, and also nutritional factors affecting growth during the period from preconception to completion of linear growth.

The factors that lead to greater birth weight, or its consequences, are probably a cause of premenopausal breast cancer.

Greater birth weight or factors that lead to greater birth weight are probably a cause of premenopausal breast cancer.

The Panel is aware that since the conclusion of the SLR, one cohort[363] and one case-control study[684] have been published. This new information does not change the Panel judgement (see box 3.8).

6.2.4 Comparison with previous report

The previous report used different terminology from this Report. It concluded that the evidence that rapid growth leads to earlier menarche (itself an established risk factor for breast cancer), and that greater adult attained height increases the risk of breast cancer, was convincing. It also concluded that greater adult height was a possible cause of colorectal cancer.

In general, evidence that the factors that lead to greater adult attained height, or its consequences, increase the risk of cancers of some sites, including colorectal and breast, has become stronger since the mid-1990s.

6.2.5 Conclusions

The Panel concludes:
The evidence that the factors that lead to greater adult attained height (meaning relative tallness), or its consequences, are a cause of cancers of various sites, is more impressive now than it was in the mid-1990s.

The evidence that the factors that lead to greater adult attained height, or its consequences, increase the risk of colorectal cancer and postmenopausal breast cancer is convincing; and they probably increase the risk of cancers of the pancreas, breast (premenopause), and ovary. There is limited evidence suggesting that the factors that lead to adult attained height, or its consequences, increase the risk of endometrial cancer. Greater adult attained height is unlike-

6.3 Lactation

LACTATION, AND THE RISK OF CANCER

In the judgement of the Panel, the factors listed below modify the risk of cancer. Judgements are graded according to the strength of the evidence.

	DECREASES RISK		INCREASES RISK	
	Exposure	**Cancer site**	**Exposure**	**Cancer site**
Convincing	**Lactation**	**Breast (pre- and postmenopause)**		
Probable				
Limited — suggestive	Lactation	Ovary		
Substantial effect on risk unlikely		None identified		

For an explanation of all the terms used in the matrix, please see chapter 3.5.1, the text of this section, and the glossary.

World Cancer Research Fund / American Institute for Cancer Research

Human milk is the natural, complete food for infants until around 6 months of age. There is no completely adequate substitute. Breastfeeding is natural both for the mother and her child, although some women find that they are unable to or do not want to breastfeed. Lactation is the process by which the mother produces her milk.

The Panel judges as follows:
Evidence on lactation, breastfeeding by the mother, and her risk of breast cancer at all ages thereafter, is strong and consistent. It is supported by strong evidence for plausible biological mechanisms.

The Panel concludes that lactation protects against both premenopausal and postmenopausal breast cancer. An implication of this finding, together with those in the earlier sections of this chapter, and also as summarised and judged in Chapter 8, is that more emphasis should be given to factors acting throughout the life course that modify the risk of cancer. There is limited evidence suggesting that lactation protects against cancer of the ovary.

Within the remit of this Report, the strongest evidence, corresponding to the judgement of 'convincing', shows that lactation — breastfeeding by the mother — protects her against breast cancer at all ages thereafter.

Human milk gives infants the best start in life. The view sometimes expressed in the past, that infant formula may in normal circumstances be a complete substitute for human milk, is no longer held.[685-687]

The main focus of attention on breastfeeding and human milk, throughout almost all of the last century, has been on its benefits for the infant and young child during the period of breastfeeding, and then into the stage of weaning, and perhaps up to 5 years of age. This remains a central part of public health nutrition science, policy, and practice.[687]

It is only recently that researchers and those concerned with public health policies have paid substantial attention to the effects of being breastfed on the health of the child in later life, and on the effects of lactation on the health of the mother.[687 688] Thus, the previous report did not investigate what was then the small evidence base on breastfeeding and cancer risk (see 6.3.4).

As shown in the previous two sections of this chapter, it is becoming increasingly evident that early-life environment, including food and nutrition, is of fundamental importance to health and well-being throughout the life course. This has important implications for overall judgements and recommendations designed to promote health and prevent disease, and for public policy. These aspects are discussed in Part 3 of this Report, and in an accompanying report on policy implications, to be published in late 2008.[689]

6.3.1 Definition and patterns

In this Report, the term 'lactation' refers to the process by which the mother produces milk to breastfeed. While lactating women may express their milk for their own or another child, or for storage in human milk banks, lactation is usually synonymous with breastfeeding.

Breastfeeding provides a complete source of nourishment for newborns and young infants, and human milk also contains immunologically active components. The UN global strategy for infant and young child feeding recommends

239

exclusive breastfeeding up to 6 months for the health of both mother and child.[687]

A mother's breasts change during pregnancy to prepare for lactation, although milk is not produced until after the baby is born. Pituitary hormones promote milk production after birth, with suckling acting as the stimulus to let down milk and to continue its production. During breastfeeding, menstruation reduces and often stops (amenorrhea). In almost all mammals, including humans, lactation induces a period of infertility, which increases birth spacing. Babies tend to be weaned earlier in high-income countries. It is recommended that solid foods are not introduced until the infant is around 6 months old. With decreased suckling, lactation slows and then stops, and this is usually accompanied by a return to normal menstruation.

Breastfeeding was almost universal at the beginning of the 20th century. It declined in the mid-1900s, but has been increasing since the 1970s.[690] However, disparity remains with socioeconomic status of mothers.[691] In some low-income countries, high socioeconomic class or education level of mothers is associated with reduced breastfeeding, whereas the opposite is true in many high-income countries.[692] Older mothers and those educated to a higher level are more likely to breastfeed in high-income countries.[693 694]

In Africa, more than 95 per cent of infants are breastfed, often for a long duration, although exclusivity is low and the rising prevalence of HIV may reduce breastfeeding.[695] Also see chapter 4.11.

6.3.2 Interpretation of the evidence

6.3.2.1 General
For general considerations that may affect interpretation of the evidence, see chapters 3.3 and 3.5, and boxes 3.1, 3.2, 3.6 and 3.7.

6.3.2.2 Specific
Some considerations specific to breastfeeding and lactation are as follows.

Patterns and ranges of duration. Most studies have been carried out in high-income countries where, since the second half of the 20th century and until recently, duration of breastfeeding — exclusive or not — has usually been brief. Therefore the findings of these studies may be of limited relevance to areas of the world where breastfeeding practices differ.

Classification. Reports (as distinct from studies) concerned with chronic diseases have not usually considered breastfeeding or other factors specific to infancy and childhood, despite what is now the general agreement that the outcomes of early life experience tend to track into adult life. Also, there is no agreed classification for duration and exclusivity of breastfeeding.

Measurement. Studies reporting on breastfeeding use the term with different meanings. Some studies have simply distinguished between 'ever' and 'never', which means that

results from minimal amounts of breastfeeding — exclusive or not — are combined with results from extended and exclusive breastfeeding.

6.3.3 Evidence and judgements

The full systematic literature review (SLR) is contained on the CD included with this Report.

The principal mechanism through which lactation or breastfeeding could plausibly influence cancer risk is the hormonal influence of the associated period of amenorrhea and infertility. This decreases lifetime exposure to menstrual cycles and therefore alters hormone levels, particularly androgens, which can influence cancer risk (box 2.4). Site-specific mechanisms are described with the evidence for each cancer site discussed below.

Breast
One cohort study[636 696] and 37 case-control studies[207 208 219 244 249 254 264 294-297 302 354 355 591 697-720] investigated ever having breastfed, as compared to never having breastfed, and breast cancer. Five cohort studies[164 177 721-724] and 55 case-control studies[213 215 216 229 232 244 246 254 262 273 279 281 290-292 295 296 299-302 306 312 318 335 337 340 349 355 356 697 699 701-705 707 712-714 717 725-748] investigated the total duration of lactation.

Ever compared to never
The single cohort study showed a statistically significant decreased risk for ever having breastfed when compared to never. The effect estimate, which was adjusted for reproductive factors, was 0.95 (95% CI 0.91–0.99) per month of breastfeeding, based on 1120 cases (age unspecified). A statistically significant decreased risk was observed for premenopausal breast cancer, 0.76 (95% CI 0.59–0.99) per month of breastfeeding, but not for postmenopausal breast cancer, 0.96 (95% CI 0.91–1.01) per month of breastfeeding.[636 696]

Twenty-eight case-control studies investigated breast cancer (age unspecified).[207 208 219 244 254 264 294 295 354 355 591 697 700 703-708 710-713 715-720] Twenty-four of these showed decreased risk for ever having breastfed when compared to never,[207 208 219 244 254 264 294 295 302 354 355 591 700 703-707 710-713 715-720] which was statistically significant in 10 studies.[244 264 294 707 713 716 717 719 720] Four studies showed non-significant increased risk.[219 302 697 708]

Sixteen case-control studies investigated premenopausal breast cancer.[207 208 244 249 295 297 355 698 699 701 702 705 707 709 712 714 716 718] Fourteen of these showed decreased risk for ever having breastfed when compared to never,[244 249 295 297 355 698 701 702 705 707 709 712 714 716 718] which was statistically significant in four.[295 297 698 714 716] Two studies showed non-significant increased risk.[207 208 699]

Fourteen case-control studies investigated postmenopausal breast cancer.[244 296 355 698 699 701 702 707 709 712-714 716 718] Ten of these showed decreased risk for ever having breastfed when compared to never,[244 249 295 296 355 698 701 702 705 707 709 712-714 716 718] which was statistically significant in six.[296 698 701 707 716] Four studies showed non-significant increased risk.[249 295 699 705]

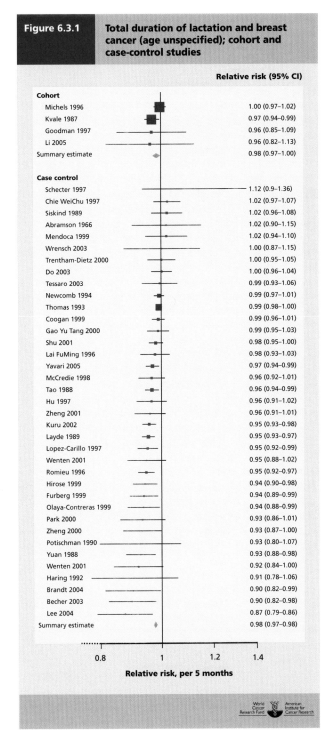

Figure 6.3.1 Total duration of lactation and breast cancer (age unspecified); cohort and case-control studies

Relative risk (95% CI)

Cohort

		Relative risk (95% CI)
Michels 1996		1.00 (0.97–1.02)
Kvale 1987		0.97 (0.94–0.99)
Goodman 1997		0.96 (0.85–1.09)
Li 2005		0.96 (0.82–1.13)
Summary estimate		0.98 (0.97–1.00)

Case control

Schecter 1997		1.12 (0.9–1.36)
Chie WeiChu 1997		1.02 (0.97–1.07)
Siskind 1989		1.02 (0.96–1.08)
Abramson 1966		1.02 (0.90–1.15)
Mendoca 1999		1.02 (0.94–1.10)
Wrensch 2003		1.00 (0.87–1.15)
Trentham-Dietz 2000		1.00 (0.95–1.05)
Do 2003		1.00 (0.96–1.04)
Tessaro 2003		0.99 (0.93–1.06)
Newcomb 1994		0.99 (0.97–1.01)
Thomas 1993		0.99 (0.98–1.00)
Coogan 1999		0.99 (0.96–1.01)
Gao Yu Tang 2000		0.99 (0.95–1.03)
Shu 2001		0.98 (0.95–1.00)
Lai FuMing 1996		0.98 (0.93–1.03)
Yavari 2005		0.97 (0.94–0.99)
McCredie 1998		0.96 (0.92–1.01)
Tao 1988		0.96 (0.94–0.99)
Hu 1997		0.96 (0.91–1.02)
Zheng 2001		0.96 (0.91–1.01)
Kuru 2002		0.95 (0.93–0.98)
Layde 1989		0.95 (0.93–0.97)
Lopez-Carillo 1997		0.95 (0.92–0.99)
Wenten 2001		0.95 (0.88–1.02)
Romieu 1996		0.95 (0.92–0.97)
Hirose 1999		0.94 (0.90–0.98)
Furberg 1999		0.94 (0.89–0.99)
Olaya-Contreras 1999		0.94 (0.88–0.99)
Park 2000		0.93 (0.86–1.01)
Zheng 2000		0.93 (0.87–1.00)
Potischman 1990		0.93 (0.80–1.07)
Yuan 1988		0.93 (0.88–0.98)
Wenten 2001		0.92 (0.84–1.00)
Haring 1992		0.91 (0.78–1.06)
Brandt 2004		0.90 (0.82–0.99)
Becher 2003		0.90 (0.82–0.98)
Lee 2004		0.87 (0.79–0.86)
Summary estimate		0.98 (0.97–0.98)

0.8 1 1.2 1.4

Relative risk, per 5 months

World Cancer Research Fund / American Institute for Cancer Research

Total duration

Four cohort studies showed decreased risk with increased total duration of lactation,[164 177 721-723] which was statistically significant in two.[177 721] One study showed no effect on risk.[724] Meta-analysis was possible on four cohort studies, giving a summary effect estimate of 0.98 (95% CI 0.97–1.00) per 5 months of total breastfeeding, with no heterogeneity

(figure 6.3.1). There was no clear difference when results were stratified according to menopause status.

Pooled analysis from 47 epidemiological studies in 30 countries (more than 50 000 controls and nearly 97 000 breast cancer cases) showed a statistically significant decreased risk breast cancer with duration of lactation. There was an estimated reduction in risk of 4.3 per cent (95% CI 2.9–5.8; p < 0.0001). Menopausal status was not an effect modifier.[749]

Forty-four case-control studies investigated breast cancer (age unspecified).[215 229 232 244 254 262 273 281 290-292 295 299-302 306 318 335 337 340 349 355 356 697 703-705 707 712 713 717 725-727 730 734-738 740-745 747 748] Thirty-five of these showed decreased risk with increased total duration of lactation,[215 229 244 254 262 273 281 290 295 299-302 306 318 335 337 349 355 356 703-705 707 713 717 725-727 729 734 736 737 742-745 747 748] which was statistically significant in 18 studies.[215 244 254 273 281 300 337 349 705 707 713 717 726 727 736 737 743 747 748] Six studies showed non-significant increased risk[291 292 697 730 735 738 740 741] and three studies showed no effect of risk.[232 340 712] Meta-analysis was possible on 37 case-control studies, giving a summary effect estimate of 0.98 (95% CI 0.97–0.98) per 5 months of total breastfeeding, with moderate heterogeneity (figure 6.3.1).

Twenty-six case-control studies investigated pre-menopausal breast cancer.[216 244 254 281 290 295 312 337 355 699 701 702 705 707 712-714 728-732 739 741 743 745 746 748] Twenty-four studies showed decreased risk with increased total duration of lactation,[216 244 254 281 290 295 312 337 355 699 701 702 705 707 712-714 728 729 731 732 739 743 745 746 748] which was statistically significant in eight.[254 295 707 713 714 732 739 745 746] One study showed no effect on risk[741] and one study reported non-significant increased risk.[730] Meta-analysis was possible on 19 case-control studies, giving a summary effect estimate of 0.98 (95% CI 0.97–0.98) per 5 months of total breastfeeding, with moderate heterogeneity.[216 244 254 281 295 312 355 701 702 712-714 729-732 741 743 745 746 748]

Twenty-three case-control studies investigated post-menopausal breast cancer.[213 216 244 246 254 279 281 295 296 337 355 699 701 702 705 707 712-714 728 730 731 739 741 743 748] Fourteen showed decreased risk with increased total duration of lactation,[213 216 244 246 279 281 296 337 355 699 701 705 707 713 714 728 745 746 748] which was statistically significant in three.[213 337 701 707] Two studies showed no effect on risk[739 743] and seven reported non-significant increased risk.[254 295 702 712 730 741 745 746] Meta-analysis was possible on 18 case-control studies, giving a summary effect estimate of 0.99 (95% CI 0.98–1.00) per 5 months of total breastfeeding, with low heterogeneity.[244 246 254 279 281 296 355 701 702 712 714 730 731 739 741 743 745 746]

The general mechanisms through which lactation could plausibly protect against cancer are outlined in 6.3.3. In addition to the hormonal effects of amenorrhea, the strong exfoliation of the breast tissue during lactation, and the massive epithelial apoptosis at the end of breastfeeding, could contribute to risk decrease by elimination of cells with potential initial DNA damage.

There is abundant epidemiological evidence from both prospective and case-control studies, which is consistent and shows a dose-response relationship.

There is robust evidence for plausible mechanisms that operate in humans. The evidence that lactation protects against both premenopausal and postmenopausal breast cancer is convincing.

Ovary

One cohort study[750] and 10 case-control studies[254 751-760] investigated lactation and ovarian cancer.

The single cohort study showed non-significant decreased risk with increased total duration of lactation. The effect estimate was 0.79 (95% CI 0.25–2.56) for five or more children breastfed compared with never breastfeeding. However, this study was relatively small, with only 97 cases.[750]

Seven case-control studies showed decreased risk with increased total duration of lactation,[254 753 754 756-760] which was statistically significant in three.[753 756 759 760] Three studies showed non-significant increased risk.[751 752 755] Meta-analysis was possible on six case-control studies, giving a summary effect estimate of 0.96 (95% CI 0.93–0.99) per 6 months of total breastfeeding, with high heterogeneity (figure 6.3.2).

A dose-response relationship is apparent from case-control data, but cohort data are insufficient.

As described in 6.3.2, substantial heterogeneity could be expected when assessing breastfeeding when, for example, exclusivity of breastfeeding is not always assessed.

The general mechanisms through which lactation could plausibly protect against cancer are outlined in 6.3.3. There is evidence that the reduced number of menstrual cycles associated with breastfeeding protects against some cancers.

There are sparse prospective epidemiological data, though some evidence for a dose response. The mechanistic evidence is speculative. There is limited evidence suggesting that lactation protects against ovarian cancer.

The Panel is aware that since the conclusion of the SLR, one case-control study[761] has been published. This new information does not change the Panel judgement (see box 3.8).

6.3.4 Comparison with previous report

The previous report noted evidence that breastfeeding (meaning lactation) protected against breast cancer, but it did not review the literature or make a judgement.

6.3.5 Conclusions

The Panel concludes:

The evidence on lactation and breast cancer — the most common female hormone-related cancer — is impressive. Much of this has been published since the mid-1990s.

The evidence that lactation protects against breast cancer, at all ages, is convincing. There is limited evidence suggesting that lactation protects against ovarian cancer.

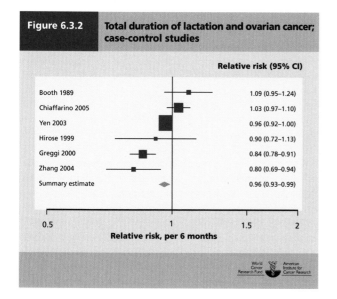

Figure 6.3.2 — Total duration of lactation and ovarian cancer; case-control studies

Relative risk (95% CI)

Study	Relative risk (95% CI)
Booth 1989	1.09 (0.95–1.24)
Chiaffarino 2005	1.03 (0.97–1.10)
Yen 2003	0.96 (0.92–1.00)
Hirose 1999	0.90 (0.72–1.13)
Greggi 2000	0.84 (0.78–0.91)
Zhang 2004	0.80 (0.69–0.94)
Summary estimate	0.96 (0.93–0.99)

Relative risk, per 6 months

CHAPTER 7

Cancers

Every year an estimated 11 million people are diagnosed with cancer (excluding skin cancers) and nearly 7 million people are recorded as dying from cancer. Projections for 2030 predict that these figures will double. Cancer is increasing at rates faster than the increase in global population. It is becoming more common in high-income but also — and most of all — in middle- and low-income countries, absolutely and also relative to other diseases.

The scientific community is convinced that inherited high susceptibility to cancer accounts for only a small proportion of cases. Although we are all more or less susceptible to various diseases, most adult cancers are caused mainly by environmental factors. This means that most cancers are at least in theory preventable.

One important cause of cancer is smoking, or other exposure to, tobacco. Infection, infestation, solar radiation, and other factors are also important. Food and nutrition, physical activity, body composition, and other associated factors are also individually and collectively important modifiers of cancer risk. But there is a difference. Smoking and exposure to tobacco, and these other factors, are all causes of cancer. By contrast, this and the previous chapters show that food and nutrition, and physical activity can protect against cancer. When we are able to do so, we can choose ways of life that protect both ourselves and the next generation against cancer. So our nutritional state — what we eat and drink, how active we are, and how much body fat we carry — not only as adults but also from and before birth, vitally affects our risk of many cancers.

This chapter follows those on foods and drinks, physical activity, and body composition, growth, and development. Its purpose is to summarise the evidence derived from independently commissioned and presented systematic literature reviews (SLRs), and the Panel's judgements and conclusions, as they relate to cancers of 17 sites. Together, these amount to roughly 80 per cent of the incidence of, and deaths from, all cancers worldwide. Evidence on a number of other cancers is also summarised briefly, based on narrative reviews.

The sequence of the sections of this chapter corresponds roughly with the body's systems, or with sites that have anatomical, metabolic, hormonal, or other features in common, and generally follows the sequence of the previous report.

The structure of all the sections, where evidence derives from these systematic reviews, is identical. After brief introductions, matrices display the Panel's judgements. In this chapter, the Panel's judgements also include the 'Limited — no conclusion' category, where evidence is, in the Panel's view, of such poor quality, or too sparse, confused, or conflicting, to allow a conclusion. Footnotes to these matrices include important explanations or qualifications.

Then follow subsections on trends, incidence, and survival; pathogenesis; and other established causes. The next subsection concerns interpretation of the evidence, in which issues and problems related to specific cancer sites are summarised.

'Evidence and judgements' are the central subsections throughout this chapter. Here, the evidence from the SLRs, reported more extensively with graphics in Chapters 4, 5, and 6, is also summarised. The sequence of these subsections is the same as that of Chapters 4–6. The strongest evidence on protection from cancer comes first, followed by the strongest evidence on causation, and so on. Within each passage, summaries of the statistically most powerful epidemiological studies come first, followed by other epidemiological studies, and then summaries of the experimental literature and evidence of biological plausibility. This is followed by the Panel's judgements, which take into account matters of quality and interpretation.

Then follows a subsection comparing the judgements of this Report with those of the previous report, with indications of why these differ when they do. All sections conclude with the Panel's judgements for each cancer site.

7.1 Mouth, pharynx, and larynx

Cancers of the mouth, pharynx, and larynx, taken together, are the seventh most commonly occurring types of cancer worldwide. These cancers are three times more common in men than in women. Over 550 000 cases were recorded in 2002, accounting for around 5 per cent of cancer cases overall. In general, the rates of these cancers are decreasing. These cancers tend to recur. Survival rates are variable and average around 50 per cent at 5 years. Cancers of the mouth, pharynx, and larynx are the seventh most common cause of death from cancer.

Overall, *the Panel judges* that food and nutrition play an important role in the prevention and causation of cancers of the mouth, pharynx, and larynx.

The Panel judges as follows:
The evidence that alcoholic drinks are a cause of cancers of the mouth, pharynx, and larynx is convincing. The risk is multiplied when drinkers of alcohol also smoke tobacco.

Non-starchy vegetables, fruits, and also foods containing carotenoids probably protect against these cancers.

There is limited evidence suggesting that maté, a herbal infusion traditionally drunk scalding hot through a metal straw in parts of South America, is a cause of oral cancer.

The main single cause of these cancers is smoking tobacco. It has been estimated that up to half of these cancers are preventable by appropriate diets and associated factors.

In final summary, the strongest evidence, corresponding to judgements of "convincing" and "probable", shows that alcoholic drinks are a convincing cause of these cancers; and that non-starchy vegetables, fruits, and foods containing carotenoids are probably protective.

There are several different tissues and organs in and around the mouth, pharynx, and larynx. These include the lips, the tongue, the inside lining of the cheeks (buccal mucosa), the floor of the mouth, the gums (gingiva), the palate, and the salivary glands. The pharynx (or throat) is the muscular cavity leading from the nose and mouth to the larynx, which includes the vocal cords.

Ninety per cent of cancers of the mouth, pharynx, and larynx are squamous cell carcinomas, the type discussed here. Cancers of the oropharynx (including the tonsils) and the hypopharynx are also included. For cancer of the nasopharynx, the cavity from the back of the mouth to the nose, see 7.2.

FOOD, NUTRITION, PHYSICAL ACTIVITY, AND CANCERS OF THE MOUTH, PHARYNX, AND LARYNX

In the judgement of the Panel, the factors listed below modify the risk of cancers of the mouth, pharynx, and larynx. Judgements are graded according to the strength of the evidence.

	DECREASES RISK	INCREASES RISK
Convincing		**Alcoholic drinks**
Probable	**Non-starchy vegetables[1]** **Fruits[1]** **Foods containing carotenoids[2]**	
Limited — suggestive		Maté[3]
Limited — no conclusion	Cereals (grains) and their products; starchy roots, tubers, and plantains; dietary fibre; pulses (legumes); meat; poultry; fish; eggs; milk and dairy products; total fat; animal fats; plant oils; coffee; tea; frying; grilling (broiling) and barbecuing (charbroiling); protein; vitamin A; retinol; thiamin; riboflavin; niacin; folate; vitamin C; vitamin E; calcium; iron; selenium; body fatness; energy intake	
Substantial effect on risk unlikely	None identified	

1 Judgements on vegetables and fruits do not include those preserved by salting and/or pickling.
2 Includes both foods naturally containing the constituent and foods which have the constituent added (see chapter 3.5.3).
3 As drunk traditionally in parts of South America, scalding hot through a metal straw. Any increased risk of cancer is judged to be caused by epithelial damage resulting from the heat, and not by the herb itself.

For an explanation of all the terms used in the matrix, please see chapter 3.5.1, the text of this section, and the glossary.

7.1.1 Trends, incidence, and survival

Rates of cancers of the mouth and pharynx (age adjusted) are stable or decreasing in many high-income countries. There was a sharp increase between 1950 and 1980 in several European countries, such as Germany and France, although this has since reached a plateau and started to decrease. Laryngeal cancer rates appear to have been generally stable or decreasing since 1970.[1]

Age-adjusted incidence rates of oral cancers range from 20–40 per 100 000 people in parts of south-central Asia, Europe, Oceania, and southern Africa, to less than 3 per 100 000 in parts of eastern Asia, northern and western Africa, and Central America. Pharyngeal cancers (other than those of the nasopharynx) follow broadly similar incidence patterns, although the overall incidence is lower, with highs of more than 10 per 100 000 in south-central Asia and western Europe, to a low of less than 1 per 100 000 in northern Africa. Age-adjusted incidence rates of laryngeal cancer range from more than 10 per 100 000 in South America, south-central and western Asia, and southern, central, and western Europe to less than 1 per 100 000 in many African countries.[2] Rates are higher in men than in women by approximately three to one.[2] In the USA, rates are higher among African-American people than in white people.[3]

Risk increases with age, and diagnoses of these three types of cancer are most common in people aged 50 or over.[4]

Although cure rates are high for early-stage cancers of the mouth, pharynx, and larynx, second primary tumours are relatively common at these sites.[5] More than 60 per cent of patients do not seek medical advice until the disease is at an advanced stage; in these cases, long-term survival rates are poor, especially if the cancer site is inaccessible.[4] Five-year survival rates are around 60 per cent in the USA and 50 per cent in the UK.[3 6] These cancers account for just over 5 per cent of all cancer incidence, but just under 5 per cent of all cancer deaths.[2] Also see box 7.1.1.

7.1.2 Pathogenesis

Mouth, pharynx, and larynx cancers, like other types, are the result of genetic alterations that lead to small, localised lesions in the mucous membranes that grow in an abnormal way (dysplasia). These lesions may then progress to carcinoma in situ, and then become invasive cancers.

Exposure to carcinogens, such as those in tobacco, can be prolonged and consistent. The mouth and pharynx are directly exposed to both inhaled carcinogens and those that are ingested by drinking and chewing — including, in the case of chewing tobacco and betel quid, when it is spat out after chewing. Chronic damage and inflammation caused by stomach acid are also implicated; some studies have found that laryngopharyngeal reflux (where stomach acid flows upwards to the larynx and/or pharynx) is associated with laryngeal cancers.[7 8]

Cancers of the mouth, pharynx, and larynx frequently show multiple, independent, malignant foci — with second primary cancers occurring relatively frequently. This phenomenon occurs when an entire region of tissue is repeatedly exposed to carcinogens. Around 90 per cent of oral cancers occur after exposure to tobacco or alcohol, or a combination of both.[9]

7.1.3 Other established causes

7.1.3.1 General
(Also see chapter 2.4.)
Throughout this chapter, this section lists factors outside the scope of this Report, identified as established causes of cancer by the World Health Organization International Agency for Research on Cancer, and other authoritative bodies. These factors are as listed in chapter 2.4: tobacco use; infectious agents; radiation; industrial chemicals; and some medications. Other diseases may also increase the risk of cancer. In the same way, life events that modify the risk of cancer — causative and protective — are also included.

'Established' effectively means 'beyond reasonable doubt' — roughly the equivalent of the judgement of 'convincing' used in this Report. Occasionally, authoritative findings that perhaps fall short of 'established' are also included here.

Where possible, a note of interactive or multiplicative effects with food, nutrition, and the other factors covered by this Report is added, as is any indication of scale or relative importance. The factors here are almost all causative, whereas much of the evidence on food, nutrition, physical activity, and related factors shows or suggests protection against cancer.

7.1.3.2 Specific

Other diseases. There is substantial evidence that gastric reflux increases the risk of oral cancers.

Box 7.1.1   Cancer incidence and survival

The cancer incidence rates and figures given in this Report are those reported by cancer registries, now established in many countries. These registries record cases of cancer that have been diagnosed. However, many cases of cancer are not identified or recorded: some countries do not have cancer registries; regions of some countries have few or no records; records in countries suffering war or other disruption are bound to be incomplete; and some people with cancer do not consult a physician. Altogether, this means that the actual incidence of cancer is higher than the figures given here.

The cancer survival rates given in this chapter and elsewhere are usually overall global averages. Survival rates are generally higher in high-income countries and other parts of the world where there are established services for screening and early detection of cancer and well established treatment facilities. Survival also is often a function of the stage at which a cancer is detected and diagnosed. The symptoms of some internal cancers are often evident only at a late stage, which accounts for relatively low survival rates. In this context, 'survival' means that the person with diagnosed cancer has not died 5 years after diagnosis. Also see chapter 9.

Tobacco use. Smoking, and other use of and exposure to tobacco, is the most important cause of oral cancers, including those of the mouth, pharynx, and larynx. These factors are estimated to cause around 60 per cent per cent of all laryngeal cancers. While alcoholic drinks are an independent cause of these cancers, risk is multiplied if drinkers smoke tobacco and if smokers drink .[10] Chewing of betel quid (with or without added tobacco) also causes oral cancers.[11]

Infection and infestation. Human papilloma viruses (HPVs) are a cause of oral cancers.[12-14]

7.1.4 Interpretation of the evidence

7.1.4.1 General
For general considerations that may affect interpretation of the evidence, see chapters 3.3 and 3.5, and boxes 3.1, 3.2, 3.6 and 3.7.

'Relative risk' is used in this Report to denote ratio measures of effect, including 'risk ratios', 'rate ratios', 'hazard ratios', and 'odds ratios'.

7.1.4.2 Specific
Considerations specific to cancers of the mouth, pharynx, and larynx include:

Classification. Some studies did not report separately on cancers of the mouth, pharynx, or larynx, but grouped these cancers with others as 'head and neck cancers' or 'upper aerodigestive tract cancers'. The term 'head and neck cancer' includes all of these sites plus cancers of the middle ear, the nasal cavity, and the paranasal sinuses. The term 'upper aerodigestive tract cancer' includes all head and neck cancers and oesophageal cancer (see 7.3).

Confounding. High-quality studies adjust for smoking but may still be subject to residual confounding. Because of the size of the effect of smoking, and the tendency for the diets of smokers to be low in vegetables and fruits, and for smokers to have relatively lower body mass indices, residual confounding is a particular concern for these exposures. Wherever possible, detailed stratification of the data according to smoking status was obtained.

7.1.5 Evidence and judgements

In total, 238 publications were included in the systematic literature review (SLR) for cancers of the mouth, pharynx, and larynx. Fuller summaries of the epidemiological, experimental, and mechanistic evidence are in Chapters 4–6.

The full SLR is contained on the CD included with this Report.

7.1.5.1 Non-starchy vegetables
(Also see chapter 4.2.5.1.)
A total of 31 case-control studies and 3 ecological studies examined non-starchy vegetables. Other groupings examined were non-starchy vegetables and fruits (in combination) (1 cohort, 6 case-control); raw vegetables (23 case-control); cruciferous vegetables (1 cohort, 14 case-control, and 1 ecological); green, leafy vegetables (1 cohort, 10 case-control); carrots (3 cohort, 18 case-control); and tomatoes (1 cohort, 12 case-control). Most of the studies for the exposures grouped under non-starchy vegetables showed a decreased risk with increased intake. Meta-analysis showed a 28 per cent decreased risk per 50 g per day (figure 4.2.2). The dose-response relationship suggested that the greatest effect was produced by the first increment; that is, that some vegetable consumption confers a protective effect compared with none (figure 4.2.3). However, it is not clear that the effect continues in a linear fashion. It is possible that this is an artificial phenomenon produced by residual confounding due to smoking. There is some unexplained heterogeneity.

This is a wide and disparate category, and many different plant food constituents are represented that could contribute to a protective effect of non-starchy vegetables. These include dietary fibre, carotenoids, folate, selenium, glucosinolates, dithiolthiones, indoles, coumarins, ascorbate, chlorophyll, flavonoids, allylsulphides, flavonoids, and phytoestrogens, some of which are potentially antioxidants. Antioxidants trap free radicals and reactive oxygen molecules, protecting against oxidation damage. It is difficult to unravel the relative importance of each constituent and is likely that any protective effect may result from a combination of influences on several pathways involved in carcinogenesis.

A substantial amount of consistent evidence on non-starchy vegetables, including specific subtypes mostly from case-control studies, shows a dose-response relationship. There is evidence for plausible mechanisms. Non-starchy vegetables probably protect against mouth, pharynx, and larynx cancers.

The Panel is aware that since the conclusion of the SLR, two cohort[15][16] and two case-control studies[17][18] have been published. This new information does not change the Panel judgement. Also see box 3.8.

7.1.5.2 Fruits
(Also see chapter 4.2.5.2.)
A total of 1 cohort study, 35 case-control studies, and 2 ecological studies investigated fruits. Other groupings examined were citrus fruits (1 cohort, 23 case-control, 1 ecological), and non-starchy vegetables and fruits (in combination) (1 cohort, 6 case-control). Most studies showed decreased risk. Meta-analysis showed a 18 per cent decreased risk per 100 g per day for general fruits, or 24 per cent per 50 g per day for citrus fruits (figures 4.2.17 and 4.2.18). The dose-response relationship suggested that the greatest effect was produced by the first increment; that is, that some fruit consumption confers a protective effect compared to none. However, it is not clear that the effect continues in a linear fashion (figures 4.2.19 and 4.2.20). It is possible that this is an artificial phenomenon produced by residual confounding due to smoking.

Studies that reported on combined intake of non-starchy vegetables and fruits showed evidence of an association with decreased risk (see 7.1.5.1).

Fruits are sources of vitamin C and other antioxidants such as carotenoids, phenols, and flavonoids, as well as other potentially bioactive phytochemicals. Antioxidants trap free radicals and reactive oxygen molecules, protecting against oxidation damage. It is difficult to unravel the relative importance of each constituent, and is likely that any protective effect may result from a combination of influences on several pathways involved in carcinogenesis.

The evidence, including that on fruit subtypes, though mostly from case-control studies, is consistent, with a dose-response relationship. There is evidence for plausible mechanisms. Fruits probably protect against mouth, pharynx, and larynx cancers.

The Panel is aware that since the conclusion of the SLR, two cohort studies[15 16] and one case-control study[18] have been published. This new information does not change the Panel judgement. Also see box 3.8.

7.1.5.3 Foods containing carotenoids
(Also see chapter 4.2.5.3.)
Two cohort studies investigated total serum carotenoids, 10 case-control studies investigated pro-vitamin A carotenoids, and 2 case-control studies investigated total dietary carotenoids. Other groupings examined were dietary alpha-carotene (1 cohort); serum alpha-carotene (3 cohort); dietary beta-carotene (1 cohort, 7 case-control); serum beta-carotene (3 cohort, 2 case-control); dietary lycopene (1 cohort, 4 case-control); and serum lycopene (1 cohort, 1 case-control). All of the serum studies and most of the dietary studies showed decreased risk with increased measures of carotenoids. Meta-analysis was not possible. Information comes predominantly from dietary sources, not supplements; therefore no effect can be attributed to carotenoids separate from foods.

In trials, carotenoids have been effective at reducing cellular damage within the mouth, which may act as a precursor to cancers in this region. Carotenoids are antioxidants. Oxidative damage is linked to the formation of tumours through several mechanisms. Oxidative stress damages DNA. This might be prevented or limited by dietary antioxidants found in fruits and vegetables.

There is a considerable amount of evidence, and though it is for different carotenoid types, it is generally consistent, with a dose-response relationship. There is evidence for plausible mechanisms. Foods containing carotenoids probably protect against mouth, pharynx, and larynx cancers.

The Panel is aware that since the conclusion of the SLR, one cohort study[15] has been published. This new information does not change the Panel judgement. Also see box 3.8.

7.1.5.4 Maté
(Also see chapter 4.7.5.6.1.)
Six case-control studies were examined. All reported increased risk from drinking maté, which was statistically significant in four.

There is some biological plausibility. Maté is a herbal infusion traditionally drunk very hot through a metal straw. This produces heat damage in the mouth, pharynx, and larynx. Repeated damage of this nature could lead to cancer. Chemical carcinogenesis from constituents of maté has also been postulated.[19 20]

The evidence is sparse. There is limited evidence suggesting that maté is a cause of mouth, pharynx, and larynx cancers.

7.1.5.5 Alcoholic drinks
(Also see chapter 4.8.5.1.)
Five cohort studies, 89 case-control studies, and 4 ecological studies investigated alcoholic drinks. All cohort studies and nearly all case-control studies showed increased risk. Meta-analysis of cohort data showed a 24 per cent increased risk per drink/week; case-control data showed a 3 per cent increased risk per drink/week (figure 4.8.2). The cohort studies showed a curvilinear dose-response relationship.

It is biologically highly plausible that alcoholic drinks are a cause of mouth, pharynx, and larynx cancers. IARC classifies alcohol as a Class 1 carcinogen. Reactive metabolites of alcohol such as acetaldehyde can be carcinogenic. There is also an interaction with smoking. Tobacco may induce specific mutations in DNA that are less efficiently repaired in the presence of alcohol. Alcohol may also function as a solvent, enhancing penetration of other carcinogenic molecules into mucosal cells. Additionally, the effects of alcohol may be mediated through the production of prostaglandins, lipid peroxidation, and the generation of free radical oxygen species. High consumers of alcohol may also have diets low in essential nutrients, making tissues susceptible to carcinogenesis.

There is ample and consistent evidence, both from case-control and cohort studies, with a dose-response relationship. There is robust evidence for mechanisms operating in humans. The evidence that alcoholic drinks are a cause of mouth, pharynx, and larynx cancers is convincing. Alcohol and tobacco together increase the risk of these cancers more than either acting independently. No threshold was identified.

The Panel is aware that since the conclusion of the SLR, one cohort[15] and four case-control studies[21-24] have been published. This new information does not change the Panel judgement. Also see box 3.8.

7.1.5.6 Other exposures
Other exposures were evaluated. However, the data were either of too low quality, too inconsistent, or the number of studies too few to allow conclusions to be reached. These were as follows: cereals (grains) and their products; starchy

roots, tubers, and plantains; pulses (legumes); foods containing dietary fibre; meat; poultry; fish; eggs; milk and dairy products; total fat; foods containing animal fat; plant oils; coffee; tea; frying, grilling (broiling), and barbecuing; protein; vitamin A; retinol; thiamin; riboflavin; niacin; folate; vitamin C; vitamin E; iron; calcium; selenium; energy intake; and body fatness.

Fourteen case-control studies examined body fatness, as measured by body mass index (BMI). Meta-analysis produced a statistically significant decreased risk with increased BMI, and a dose-response relationship, but reverse causality was implicated. That is, cancers of the mouth, pharynx, and larynx cause significant weight loss, often before diagnosis. Smoking is also associated with low BMI. For these reasons, the data were judged insufficient to allow any conclusion to be drawn.

7.1.6 Comparison with previous report

The main differences between this Report and the previous report are summarised here, together with any reasons for these differences. When the findings here and in the previous report are similar, this is usually not mentioned. Minor differences are not always mentioned.

7.1.6.1 General
The criteria used by the previous report for gauging the strength of the evidence were not identical to the criteria used for this Report. In particular, a judgement of 'convincing' causal association was not conditional on supportive evidence from prospective studies. This Report does make that requirement. It also emphasises the special importance of randomised controlled trials when applied appropriately, especially where the results are positive. In these respects, the criteria used for this Report are more stringent. See box 3.8 in chapter 3.

7.1.6.2 Specific
The previous report separated cancers of the mouth and pharynx from cancer of the larynx. The panel responsible for the previous report judged the evidence that vegetables and fruits protect against cancers of the mouth and pharynx to be convincing. It also judged that these foods probably protect against cancer of the larynx. Vitamin C was judged to be possibly protective against cancers of the mouth and larynx. There is still little information from cohort studies, which weakens the evidence base.

Evidence accumulated since the mid-1990s confirms the previous judgement that the evidence that alcoholic drinks are a cause of oral cancers is convincing. And in the previous report, the evidence that maté is a cause of oral cancers was judged possible for cancers of the mouth and pharynx.

7.1.7 Conclusions

The Panel concludes:
The evidence that alcoholic drinks are a cause of cancers of

the mouth, pharynx, and larynx is convincing. The risk is multiplied when drinkers of alcohol also smoke tobacco.

Non-starchy vegetables, fruits, and foods containing carotenoids probably protect against these cancers.

There is limited evidence suggesting that maté, a herbal infusion, when drunk scalding hot through a metal straw, as is traditional in some parts of South America, is a cause of oral cancer.

The main cause of these cancers is smoking and other use of and exposure to tobacco.

7.2 Nasopharynx

Cancer of the nasopharynx is the 23rd most common type of cancer worldwide. About 80 000 cases were recorded in 2002, accounting for less than 1 per cent overall. In most parts of the world, this cancer is rare. It is relatively common on and near the southern Chinese littoral, and among communities who have migrated from that part of China to other countries. It is twice as common in men as in women. It is the 20th most common cause of death from cancer.

Overall, *the Panel judges* that there is a specific role for Cantonese-style salted fish in the causation of cancer of the nasopharynx.

The Panel judges as follows:
Cantonese-style salted fish is probably a cause of nasopharyngeal cancer. This judgement does not apply to fish salted or fermented by any other method.

There is limited evidence suggesting that non-starchy vegetables and fruits protect against this cancer.

Other causes of this cancer include tobacco smoking and infection with the Epstein-Barr virus.

In final summary, the strongest evidence, corresponding to judgements of "convincing" and "probable", shows that Cantonese-style salted fish is a probable cause of this cancer.

The nasopharynx is the top portion of the pharynx, the muscular cavity leading from the nose and mouth to the larynx.

Cancers in this area arise predominantly from epithelial cells, with squamous cell carcinomas being the most common. Carcinomas constitute 75–90 per cent of nasopharyngeal cancers in low-risk populations, and virtually 100 per cent in high-risk populations.[25] Nasopharyngeal squamous cell carcinomas are included here; other types are not.

FOOD, NUTRITION, PHYSICAL ACTIVITY, AND CANCER OF THE NASOPHARYNX

In the judgement of the Panel, the factors listed below modify the risk of cancer of the nasopharynx. Judgements are graded according to the strength of the evidence.

	DECREASES RISK	INCREASES RISK
Convincing		
Probable		Cantonese-style salted fish[1]
Limited — suggestive	Non-starchy vegetables[2] Fruits[2]	
Limited — no conclusion	Cereals (grains) and their products; nuts and seeds; herbs, spices, and condiments; meat; fish; shellfish and seafood; eggs; plant oils; tea; alcohol; salted plant food; Chinese-style pickled cabbage; pickled radish; pickled mustard leaf; Chinese-style preserved salted eggs; fermented tofu and soya products	
Substantial effect on risk unlikely	None identified	

1 This style of preparation is characterised by treatment with less salt than typically used, and fermentation during the drying process due to relatively high outdoor temperature and moisture levels. This conclusion does not apply to fish prepared (or salted) by other means.
2 Judgements on vegetables and fruits do not include those preserved by salting and/or pickling.

For an explanation of all the terms used in the matrix, please see chapter 3.5.1, the text of this section, and the glossary.

World Cancer Research Fund   American Institute for Cancer Research

---

7.2.1 Trends, incidence, and survival

Age-adjusted rates of nasopharyngeal cancer are decreasing in areas of high incidence, such as Hong Kong and Singapore.[25]

This cancer is predominantly a disease of low-income countries, with overall rates more than three times higher in middle- to low- than in high-income countries. Incidence is also higher in certain ethnic groups — for instance Chinese and also Malay and Filipino people living in south-eastern Asia.

Around the world, age-adjusted incidence rates range from 20–30 per 100 000 people in parts of Hong Kong and south-eastern Asia, to less than 1 per 100 000 across most of the Americas and Europe.

This cancer also occurs in northern Africa, parts of the Middle East, and Micronesia and Polynesia. However, the highest rates are among Cantonese people who live in the central region of Guangdong Province in southern China, which includes Hong Kong.[25] Migrant populations from this province carry the risk levels of the original population, but this decreases over generations.[26] Rates are approximately twice as high in men as in women.[2]

The age profile of nasopharyngeal cancer is different in areas of high compared with low incidence. Risk increases with age in most of the world, but in Guangdong Province it peaks between the ages of 45 and 54. In populations where there is a moderate incidence of this cancer, risk peaks in young adults.[25] Overall 5-year survival rates are around 50 per cent.[27] Also see box 7.1.1.

There are two variants of nasopharyngeal squamous cell carcinoma: keratinising and non-keratinising. The non-keratinising variant can be further divided into differentiated or undifferentiated. In North America, the proportions of each are 25, 12, and 63 per cent, respectively. In southern China, the distribution is different: 2, 3, and 95 per cent.[27]

Box 7.2.1 Epstein-Barr virus

Most adults are infected with the Epstein-Barr virus, but relatively few will ever develop the cancers of which this virus is a contributory or necessary cause. Other factors beyond infection with the virus are needed to lead to the development of cancer. Environmental factors including some dietary factors are thought to render precancerous epithelial cells sensitive to Epstein-Barr virus infection, which then triggers malignancy.[29]

Epstein-Barr virus is a DNA virus of the herpes family. It primarily infects B lymphocytes (white blood cells that produce antibodies), though it can also infect epithelial cells. Infection usually occurs in childhood and does not usually produce symptoms, but in adults it can cause infectious mononucleosis or glandular fever. It is particularly associated with undifferentiated nasopharyngeal carcinoma, the most prevalent type.[30] [31]

In nasopharyngeal carcinoma, all of the tumour cells carry viral DNA in a monoclonal form. This means that Epstein-Barr virus infection must have occurred quite early in the cancer process, before rapid growth.[32] It is not normally possible to detect Epstein-Barr virus infection in non-cancerous nasopharyngeal cells.[31]

7.2.2 Pathogenesis

Variation in the distribution of keratinising squamous cell carcinoma and the two forms of non-keratinising carcinoma in North America and southern China, together with the different age profiles in the two regions, suggests that different disease paths may occur in high-incidence populations.

Patches of dysplasia are the first recognisable precancerous lesions; latent infection with the Epstein-Barr virus (see box 7.2.1) leads to severe dysplasia. The subsequent genetic and chromosomal changes in these lesions lead to invasive carcinoma.[28]

7.2.3 Other established causes

(Also see chapter 2.4 and 7.1.3.1.)

Tobacco use. Smoking tobacco is a cause of nasopharyngeal cancer.

Occupational exposure. Occupational exposure to formaldehyde is also a cause of this cancer.[33-35]

Infectious agents. Epstein-Barr virus infection is a cause of nasopharyngeal cancer (see box 7.2.1).[30] It may be necessary but is not a sufficient cause.

7.2.4 Interpretation of the evidence

7.2.4.1 General
For general considerations that may affect interpretation of the evidence, see chapters 3.3 and 3.5, and boxes 3.1, 3.2, 3.6 and 3.7.

'Relative risk' is used in this Report to denote ratio measures of effect, including 'risk ratios', 'rate ratios', 'hazard ratios', and 'odds ratios'.

7.2.4.2 Specific
Considerations specific to cancer of the nasopharynx and to Cantonese-style salted fish, include:

Classification. The term 'salted' is an incomplete and perhaps misleading term, given that the fish is also fermented. See the footnote of the matrix for this section, and also 7.2.5.3.

Confounding. It is not possible to exclude a genetic component. Those at highest risk are Cantonese-speaking communities living in or originally from Guangdong Province.

Production, preservation, processing, preparation. The method of salting or the type of fish salted varies between regions. The presence of nitrates and nitrosamines (see box 4.3.2) in the fish also varies.

7.2.5 Evidence and judgements

In total, 74 publications were included in the SLR for nasopharyngeal cancer. Fuller summaries of the epidemiological, experimental, and mechanistic evidence are to be found in Chapters 4–6.

The full SLR is contained on the CD included with this Report.

7.2.5.1 Non-starchy vegetables
(Also see chapter 4.2.5.1.)

Five case-control studies and two ecological studies investigated non-starchy vegetables; a further four case-control studies investigated green vegetables. Preserved vegetables were excluded from all categories. Nearly all of the studies showed decreased risk with increased intake.

This is a wide and disparate category, and many different plant food constituents are represented that could contribute to a protective effect of non-starchy vegetables. These include dietary fibre, carotenoids, folate, selenium, glucosinolates, dithiolthiones, indoles, coumarins, ascorbate, chlorophyll, flavonoids, allylsulphides, flavonoids, and phytoestrogens, some of which are potentially antioxidants. Antioxidants trap free radicals and reactive oxygen molecules, protecting against oxidation damage. It is difficult to unravel the relative importance of each constituent and it is likely that any protective effect may result from a combination of influences on several pathways involved in carcinogenesis.

The evidence on non-starchy vegetables is sparse but generally consistent. There is limited evidence suggesting that non-starchy vegetables protect against nasopharyngeal cancer.

7.2.5.2 Fruits
(Also see chapter 4.2.5.2.)

Six case-control studies investigated general fruits and a further five case-control studies investigated citrus fruits. Preserved fruits were excluded from all categories. Most of the studies for general fruits and all of the studies for citrus fruits showed a decreased risk.

This is a wide and disparate category, and many different plant food constituents are represented that could contribute to a protective effect of fruits. These include dietary fibre, carotenoids, folate, selenium, glucosinolates, dithiolthiones, indoles, coumarins, ascorbate, chlorophyll, flavonoids, allyl-sulphides, flavonoids, and phytoestrogens, some of which are potentially antioxidants. Antioxidants trap free radicals and reactive oxygen molecules, protecting against oxidation damage. It is difficult to unravel the relative importance of each constituent and likely that a protective effect may result from a combination of influences on several pathways involved in carcinogenesis. In addition, some components of citrus fruits have been shown directly to inhibit Epstein-Barr virus activation.[36]

The evidence, from case-control studies only, is sparse. There is limited evidence suggesting that fruits protect against nasopharyngeal cancer.

7.2.5.3 Cantonese-style salted fish

(Also see chapter 4.3.5.3.1.)
One cohort study and 21 case-control studies of adult diets were examined. The single cohort study and most of the case-control studies showed increased risk with higher intake. Meta-analysis showed a 28 per cent increased risk per time eaten per week (figure 4.3.9). There is some heterogeneity, not all readily explained. Childhood diet data implicate an increased risk with early-life exposure.

Cantonese-style salted fish is dried in natural conditions outdoors. As prepared on the southern Chinese littoral, it is characterised by treatment with less salt than used on the northern littoral; it is also subject to fermentation during the drying process in the warm, damp climate of southern China.

The high content of nitrate and nitrosamines may account for some of the increased risk associated with salted fish intake. Nitrosamines are known mutagens and animal carcinogens that induce gene mutation. The direct role of nitrosamines in the carcinogenic process is supported by the increased risk for nasopharyngeal cancer development in people who have a variant allele of CYP2E1. This enzyme is expressed in the nasopharynx and is involved in the metabolic activation of nitrosamines to carcinogenic adducts.[37] Additional evidence has suggested a component of salted fish may contain Epstein-Barr virus-activating substances, although the specific agents of action have not been identified.[38]

Evidence from several case-control studies is consistent and shows a dose-response effect. There is evidence for plausible mechanisms. Cantonese-style salted fish is probably a cause of nasopharyngeal cancer.

7.2.5.4 Other exposures

Other exposures were evaluated. However, the data were either of too low quality, too inconsistent, or the number of studies too few to allow conclusions to be reached. These were as follows: cereals (grains) and their products; nuts and seeds; meat; fish; shellfish and seafood; eggs; herbs, spices, and condiments; tea; alcohol; plant oils; salted plant foods; Chinese-style pickled cabbage; pickled radish; pickled mustard leaf; Chinese-style preserved salted eggs; and fermented tofu/soya products.

7.2.6 Comparison with previous report

7.2.6.1 General
See 7.1.6.1, and box 3.8.

7.2.6.2 Specific
The previous report judged the evidence that Cantonese-style salted fish is a cause of nasopharyngeal cancer to be convincing. No further cohort studies have been conducted since the mid-1990s.

7.2.7 Conclusions

The Panel concludes:
Cantonese-style salted fish is probably a cause of nasopharyngeal cancer. This does not apply to fish salted or fermented by any other method.

There is limited evidence suggesting that non-starchy vegetables, and also fruits, protect against this cancer.

7.3 Oesophagus

Cancer of the oesophagus is the eighth most common type of cancer worldwide. Around 460 000 cases occurred in 2002, accounting for over 4 per cent overall. There are two common types of oesophageal cancer, adenocarcinoma and squamous cell carcinoma, which have different patterns of occurrence. In general this cancer is not increasing, except for adenocarcinomas, which are increasing in high-income countries. Oesophageal cancer is twice as common in men as in women. It is usually fatal and is the sixth most common cause of death from cancer.

Overall, *the Panel judges* that food and nutrition and body fatness play an important role in the prevention and causation of cancer of the oesophagus.

The Panel judges as follows:
The evidence that alcoholic drinks are a cause of cancer of the oesophagus is convincing. The risk is multiplied when drinkers of alcohol also smoke tobacco. The evidence that greater body fatness is a cause of oesophageal adenocarcinoma is also convincing. Maté, a herbal infusion, when drunk scalding hot through a metal straw, as is traditional in parts of South America, is probably a cause of this cancer.

Non-starchy vegetables, fruits, and foods containing beta-carotene and/or vitamin C probably protect against oesophageal cancer.

There is limited evidence suggesting that foods containing dietary fibre, folate, pyridoxine, or vitamin E protect against this cancer, and that red meat, processed meat, and high-temperature drinks are causes of this cancer.

See chapter 8 for evidence and judgements on factors that modify the risk of body fatness, including physical activity and sedentary ways of life, the energy density of foods and drinks, and breastfeeding.

Other causes of this cancer include smoking tobacco and chewing betel quid. It has been estimated that most cases of oesophageal cancer are preventable by appropriate diets and associated factors, together with not smoking.

In final summary, the strongest evidence, corresponding to judgements of "convincing" and "probable", shows that alcoholic drinks and body fatness are a cause of this cancer (adenocarcinoma only); that non-starchy vegetables, fruits, and foods containing beta-carotene and/or vitamin C are probably protective; and that maté, as traditionally drunk in parts of South America, is probably a cause of this cancer.

The oesophagus is the muscular tube through which food passes from the pharynx to the stomach.

The oesophagus is lined over most of its length by squamous epithelial cells, where squamous cell carcinomas occur. The portion just above the gastric junction (where the oesophagus meets the stomach) is lined by columnar

---

FOOD, NUTRITION, PHYSICAL ACTIVITY, AND CANCER OF THE OESOPHAGUS

In the judgement of the Panel, the factors listed below modify the risk of cancer of the oesophagus. Judgements are graded according to the strength of the evidence.

	DECREASES RISK	INCREASES RISK
Convincing		**Alcoholic drinks** **Body fatness[1]**
Probable	**Non-starchy vegetables[2]** **Fruits[2]** **Foods containing beta-carotene[3]** **Foods containing vitamin C[3]**	**Maté[4]**
Limited — suggestive	Foods containing dietary fibre[3] Foods containing folate[3] Foods containing pyridoxine[3 5] Foods containing vitamin E[3]	Red meat[6] Processed meat[7] High-temperature drinks
Limited — no conclusion	Cereals (grains) and their products; starchy roots, tubers, and plantains; pulses (legumes); soya and soya products; herbs, spices, and condiments; poultry; fish; eggs; milk and dairy products; total fat; saturated fatty acids; monounsaturated fatty acids; polyunsaturated fatty acids; sugary foods and drinks; salt; salting; fermenting; pickling; smoked and cured foods; nitrates and nitrites; frying; grilling (broiling) and barbecuing (charbroiling); protein; vitamin A; retinol; thiamin; riboflavin; calcium; iron; zinc; pro-vitamin A carotenoids; beta-cryptoxanthin; Seventh-day Adventist diets; adult attained height; energy intake	
Substantial effect on risk unlikely	None identified	

1   For oesophageal adenocarcinomas only.
2   Judgements on vegetables and fruits do not include those preserved by salting and/or pickling.
3   Includes both foods naturally containing the constituent and foods which have the constituent added (see chapter 3.5.3). Dietary fibre is contained in plant foods (see box 4.1.2 and chapter 4.2).
4   As drunk traditionally in parts of South America, scalding hot through a metal straw. Any increased risk of cancer is judged to be caused by epithelial damage resulting from the heat, and not by the herb itself.
5   Vitamin B6.
6   The term 'red meat' refers to beef, pork, lamb, and goat from domesticated animals.
7   The term 'processed meat' refers to meats preserved by smoking, curing, or salting, or addition of chemical preservatives.

For an explanation of all the terms used in the matrix, please see chapter 3.5.1, the text of this section, and the glossary.

epithelial cells, from which adenocarcinomas can develop.[4] Adenocarcinoma of the oesophagus shows similarities with adenocarcinoma of the gastric cardia (see 7.5). Each type accounts for around half of all cases and both types are included in this Report.

7.3.1 Trends, incidence, and survival

Age-adjusted rates of oesophageal squamous cell carcinomas are generally declining, although in some high-income regions, overall rates of oesophageal cancer are increasing. For instance, the incidence of oesophageal adenocarcinoma is rising rapidly in Europe and North America.[39] In the USA, adenocarcinomas in white men increased fivefold between 1974 and the end of the 20th century, making it the fastest increasing cancer studied in that country.[40]

Oesophageal cancer is, however, mainly a disease of low-income countries, occurring around four times more commonly in low- to middle- than in high-income countries. Around the world, age-adjusted incidence rates range from more than 20 per 100 000 people in parts of eastern and southern Africa and eastern and south-central Asia to less than 5 per 100 000 in northern, western, and middle Africa, Central America, and south-eastern Asia. Localised peaks in incidence have been reported to exceed 100 per 100 000. For instance, in rural Linxian, China, oesophageal cancer is the leading cause of death.[41] In the USA, rates are higher among African-American people than in white people. Worldwide, rates are higher in men than in women, by around five to two. In most populations, risk increases with age, with few cases diagnosed in people under 40.

Oesophageal cancer does not usually produce symptoms at the early stages, so the disease is generally at an advanced stage when diagnosed. Survival rates are poor: around 10 per cent at 5 years.[3 6] This type of cancer accounts for a little over 4 per cent of all cancer incidence, but almost 6 per cent of all cancer deaths worldwide. Also see box 7.1.1.

7.3.2 Pathogenesis

The epithelial cells lining the oesophagus are exposed directly to carcinogens in food. Repeated exposures, for instance, to burns from very high-temperature drinks or irritation from the direct action of alcohol, may cause inflammation.

The role of irritation and inflammation in the development of oesophageal cancer is supported by the finding that gastro-oesophageal reflux (where stomach acid flows upwards to the oesophagus) increases the risk of adenocarcinomas by as much as 40-fold.[42] Barrett's oesophagus is a probable intermediate stage between gastro-oesophageal reflux disease, with repeated gastro-oesophageal reflux, and developing oesophageal adenocarcinoma.[43] Barrett's oesophagus is an acquired condition in which squamous cells are replaced by columnar epithelial cells; autopsy studies suggest that it usually remains undiagnosed.[44] The increasing use of endoscopes to investigate abdominal symptoms has resulted in the earlier detection of a small proportion of ade-

nocarcinomas in people with Barrett's oesophagus.[4]

Some people have an abnormally strong lower oesophageal sphincter (a condition called oesophageal achalasia), which means swallowed food is retained in the oesophagus. It causes a 15-fold increase in the risk of squamous cell carcinomas, which may be due to chronic irritation of the lining of the oesophagus or its increased contact with food-borne carcinogens.[45 46]

Tylosis A is the late-onset, inherited familial disease where the outer horny layer of the skin thickens, affecting the palms and soles (hyperkeratosis). Palmar and plantar hyperkeratosis is the single proven genetic abnormality associated with a 25 per cent lifetime incidence of squamous cell cancer of the oesophagus.[47]

7.3.3 Other established causes

(Also see chapter 2.4 and 7.1.3.1.)

Other diseases. Gastric reflux and oesophageal achalasia both increase the risk of, and thus can be seen as a cause of, this cancer. Barrett's oesophagus can be seen as a precancerous condition.

Tobacco use. Smoking is a cause both of oesophageal squamous cell carcinoma and of adenocarcinomas, increasing the risk approximately twofold.[10 39] Smoking is estimated to cause around 40 per cent of all cases. Chewing betel quid (on its own and also with tobacco quid) is also a cause of oesophageal cancers.[11]

Infectious agents. HPV (see box 7.13.1) is also a cause of this cancer, and is estimated to be a cause of almost 25 per cent of squamous cell carcinomas. Like other infectious agents, it may be a necessary cause but is not a sufficient cause. It may also play a role in the divergent geographical distributions of this cancer.[48]

7.3.4 Interpretation of the evidence

7.3.4.1 General

For general considerations that may affect interpretation of the evidence, see chapters 3.3 and 3.5, and boxes 3.1, 3.2, 3.6 and 3.7.

'Relative risk' is used in this Report to denote ratio measures of effect, including 'risk ratios', 'rate ratios', 'hazard ratios', and 'odds ratios'.

7.3.4.2 Specific

Considerations specific to cancer of the oesophagus include:

Classification. There are different types of oesophageal cancer. Squamous cell carcinomas have different geographical and time trends from adenocarcinomas. Each follows a different disease path, and may have different associated risk factors. However, there were only sufficient data to conduct separate analyses for body fatness. Therefore the ratio of squamous cell carcinomas to adenocarcinomas in each study is a potential cause of heterogeneity in all other summaries. The oesophageal-gastric junction and gastric cardia are also lined with columnar epithelial cells. Cancers in these areas are often grouped with oesophageal cancers, although they may also be classed as stomach cancers (see 7.5).[4] Different approaches or definitions in different studies are another potential source of heterogeneity.

Confounding. Smoking is the main single cause of this cancer. High-quality studies adjust for smoking.

7.3.5 Evidence and judgements

In total, 262 publications were included in the SLR for oesophageal cancer. Fuller summaries of the epidemiological, experimental, and mechanistic evidence are to be found in Chapters 4–6.

The full SLR is contained on the CD included with this Report.

7.3.5.1 Foods containing dietary fibre
(Also see chapter 4.1.5.3.)
One cohort study, nine case-control studies, and two ecological studies investigated dietary fibre. Most were suggestive of a relationship with decreased oesophageal cancer incidence. Data come predominantly from dietary sources, not supplements; therefore no specific effect can be attributed specifically to dietary fibre itself, which is interpreted simply as a marker of consumption of foods containing it.

It is not clear whether there is an as yet unknown mechanism through which dietary fibre could exert a direct effect on oesophageal cancer, or whether the effect is mediated through other constituents of the foods (such as cereals (grains), vegetables, and fruits) that contain dietary fibre.

> There is limited evidence, from sparse and inconsistent case-control studies only, suggesting that foods containing dietary fibre protect against oesophageal cancer.

7.3.5.2 Non-starchy vegetables
(Also see chapter 4.2.5.1.)
A total of 5 cohort studies, 37 case-control studies, and 6 ecological studies investigated non-starchy vegetables. Other groupings examined were vegetable and fruit consumption (combined) (8 case-control), raw vegetables (16 case-control), cruciferous vegetables (1 cohort, 5 case-control), allium vegetables (1 cohort, 8 case-control), green, leafy vegetables (1 cohort, 11 case-control), and tomatoes (1 cohort, 9 case-control). All of the studies of raw vegetables and most of the other studies showed decreased risk with increased intake. Meta-analysis of case-control data showed a 31 per cent decreased risk per 50 g of raw vegetables per day (figures 4.2.6 and 4.2.7). Raw vegetables have a more consistent definition than non-starchy vegetables, which may include preserved vegetables and a variety of cooking methods, leading to increased heterogeneity.

This is a wide and disparate category, and many different plant food constituents are represented that could contribute to a protective effect of non-starchy vegetables. These include dietary fibre, carotenoids, folate, selenium, glucosinolates, dithiolthiones, indoles, coumarins, ascorbate, chlorophyll, flavonoids, allylsulphides, flavonoids, and phytoestrogens, some of which are potentially antioxidants. Antioxidants trap free radicals and reactive oxygen molecules, protecting against oxidation damage. It is difficult to unravel the relative importance of each constituent and it is likely that any protective effect may result from a combination of influences on several pathways involved in carcinogenesis.

> There is more evidence, including on vegetable subtypes, from case-control studies than from cohort studies, but both are moderately consistent, and there is some evidence for a dose-response relationship. There is evidence for plausible mechanisms (see chapter 4.2.5.1). Non-starchy vegetables probably protect against oesophageal cancer.

The Panel is aware that since the conclusion of the SLR, one cohort[49] and two case-control studies[17 50] have been published. This new information does not change the Panel judgement. Also see box 3.8.

7.3.5.3 Fruits
(Also see chapter 4.2.5.2.)
A total of 4 cohort studies, 36 case-control studies, and 7 ecological studies investigated fruits; and 1 cohort study, 16 case-control studies, and 1 ecological study investigated citrus fruits. All of the cohort studies and most of the other studies showed decreased risk with increased intake. Meta-analysis of case-control data showed a 22 per cent decreased risk per 50 g of fruit per day, and 30 per cent decreased risk per 50 g of citrus fruit per day (figures 4.2.22 and 4.2.24). A dose-response relationship was apparent. Heterogeneity could not be fully explained.

Fruits are sources of vitamin C and other antioxidants, such as carotenoids, phenols, and flavonoids, as well as other potentially bioactive phytochemicals. Antioxidants trap free radicals and reactive oxygen molecules, protecting against oxidation damage.

It is difficult to unravel the relative importance of each constituent and it is likely that any protective effect may result from a combination of influences on several pathways involved in carcinogenesis.

> The evidence, including that on fruit subtypes, though mostly from case-control studies, is consistent, with a dose-response relationship. There is evidence for plausible mechanisms. Fruits probably protect against oesophageal cancer.

The Panel is aware that since the conclusion of the SLR, one cohort[49] and two case-control studies[50 51] have been published. This new information does not change the Panel judgement. Also see box 3.8.

7.3.5.4 Foods containing folate

(Also see chapter 4.2.5.4.)

Eight case-control studies investigated dietary folate and two case-control studies investigated red-cell and plasma folate. All studies showed a relationship with decreased cancer incidence. Data come predominantly from dietary sources, not supplements; therefore no effect can be attributed to folate separate from foods.

Folate plays an important role in the synthesis, repair, and methylation of DNA. Abnormal DNA methylation has been linked to aberrant gene expression and to cancers at several sites. Folate may also reduce HPV proliferation in cells.

The evidence, from case-control studies only, is sparse. There is limited evidence suggesting that folate protects against oesophageal cancer.

The Panel is aware that since the conclusion of the SLR, one case-control study[52] has been published. This new information does not change the Panel judgement. Also see box 3.8.

7.3.5.5 Foods containing pyridoxine (vitamin B6)

(Also see chapter 4.2.5.5.)

Six case-control studies investigated foods containing pyridoxine and oesophageal cancer.

All six studies showed a relationship between pyridoxine consumption and reduced risk of oesophageal cancer, with none reporting contrary results.

Together with folate and cobalamin (vitamin B12), vitamin B6 is involved in one-carbon metabolism and is important for DNA synthesis, repair, and methylation.

The evidence, from case-control studies only, was sparse. There is limited evidence suggesting that pyridoxine protects against oesophageal cancer.

The Panel is aware that since the conclusion of the SLR, one case-control study[52] has been published. This new information does not change the Panel judgement. Also see box 3.8.

7.3.5.6 Foods containing vitamin C

(Also see chapter 4.2.5.6.)

One cohort study, 19 case-control studies, and 3 ecological studies investigated vitamin C. The single cohort study and nearly all of the case-control studies showed decreased risk with increased intake.

Vitamin C traps free radicals and reactive oxygen molecules, protecting DNA from mutagenic attack, protecting against lipid peroxidation, reducing nitrates, and stimulating the immune system.

A substantial amount of consistent evidence is available, both from cohort and from case-control studies. Foods containing vitamin C probably protect against oesophageal cancer.

The Panel is aware that since the conclusion of the SLR, one case-control study[53] has been published. This new information does not change the Panel judgement. Also see box 3.8.

7.3.5.7 Foods containing vitamin E

(Also see chapter 4.2.5.7.)

One cohort study, nine case-control studies, and one ecological study investigated dietary vitamin E; three cohort studies and four case-control studies investigated serum vitamin E. All cohort studies and most case-control studies showed decreased risk with increased intake; serum case-control data were inconsistent.

Vitamin E is a family of eight compounds collectively referred to as tocopherols. They can act as antioxidants and free radical scavengers; however, few animal studies support an anti-cancer effect.

Much of the evidence on vitamin E, mostly from case-control studies, was of poor quality. There is limited evidence suggesting that foods containing vitamin E protect against oesophageal cancer.

7.3.5.8 Foods containing beta-carotene

(Also see chapter 4.2.5.3.)

Ten case-control studies investigated dietary beta-carotene; three cohort studies and one case-control study investigated serum beta-carotene; and one cohort study and three case-control studies investigated dietary pro-vitamin A carotenoids. Most of these studies showed a relationship with decreased risk.

Data come predominantly from dietary sources, not supplements; therefore no effect can be attributed to carotenoids separate from foods.

Carotenoids are antioxidants, which can prevent lipid oxidation and related oxidative stress. Some, such as beta-carotene, are also pro-vitamin A carotenoids.

There is a substantial amount of consistent evidence available from both cohort and case-control studies. Foods containing beta-carotene probably protect against oesophageal cancer.

7.3.5.9 Red meat

(Also see chapter 4.3.5.1.1.)

Twelve case-control studies investigated red meat. Most were suggestive of increased risk.

There are several potential underlying mechanisms for a positive association of red meat consumption with oesophageal cancer, including the generation of potentially carcinogenic N-nitroso compounds (see box 4.3.2). Some meats are also cooked at high temperatures, resulting in the production of heterocyclic amines and polycyclic aromatic hydrocarbons (see box 4.3.4). Red meat contains haem iron. Free iron can lead to the production of free radicals (see box 4.3.3).

There is limited evidence, from case-control studies, some of which were poor quality, suggesting that red meat is a cause of oesophageal cancer.

The Panel is aware that since the conclusion of the SLR, one cohort study[54] has been published. This new information does not change the Panel judgement. Also see box 3.8.

7.3.5.10 Processed meat

(Also see chapter 4.3.5.1.2.)

Two cohort studies and eight case-control studies investigated processed meat. Both cohort studies were suggestive of increased risk; case-control data were inconsistent. The definition of processed meat varies (see box 4.3.1), which may increase heterogeneity.

Nitrates are produced endogenously in gastric acid and are added as preservatives to processed meats (see box 4.3.2). This may contribute to production of N-nitroso compounds and increased exposure. These compounds are suspected mutagens and carcinogens.[55]

Many processed meats also contain high levels of salt and nitrite. Meats cooked at high temperatures can contain heterocyclic amines and polycyclic aromatic hydrocarbons (see box 4.3.4). Haem promotes the formation of N-nitroso compounds and also contains iron. Free iron can lead to the production of free radicals (see box 4.3.3).

There is limited evidence, mostly from case-control studies, suggesting that processed meat is a cause of oesophageal cancer.

The Panel is aware that since the conclusion of the SLR, one cohort study[54] has been published. This new information does not change the Panel judgement. Also see box 3.8.

7.3.5.11 Maté

(Also see chapter 4.7.5.6.1.)

Eight case-control studies and one ecological study investigated maté. Most were suggestive of an increased incidence with higher maté consumption. Meta-analysis of case-control data showed a 16 per cent increased risk per cup/day (figure 4.7.5). A dose-response relationship was apparent.

There is some biological plausibility. Maté is a tea-like beverage typically drunk very hot through a metal straw. This produces heat damage in the oesophagus. Repeated damage of this nature can lead to cancer (see chapter 2.4.1.3). Chemical carcinogenesis from constituents of maté has also been postulated.[19 20]

The evidence from case-control studies is consistent and a dose-response relationship is apparent. There is robust evidence for plausible mechanisms. Regular consumption of maté, as drunk in the traditional style in South America, is a probable cause of oesophageal cancer.

7.3.5.12 High-temperature foods and drinks

(Also see chapter 4.7.5.7.)

Three cohort studies and 15 case-control studies investigated high-temperature foods and drinks. Most were suggestive of a relationship between them and increased incidence of oesophageal cancer but many were inadequately adjusted for alcohol and smoking.

High-temperature foods and drinks can produce heat damage in the oesophagus. Repeated damage of this nature can predispose to the development of oesophageal cancer.

The evidence is inconsistent. There is limited evidence suggesting that high-temperature drinks are a cause of oesophageal cancer.

The Panel is aware that since the conclusion of the SLR, two case-control studies[50 51] have been published. This new information does not change the Panel judgement. Also see box 3.8.

7.3.5.13 Alcoholic drinks

(Also see chapter 4.8.5.1.)

Eight cohort studies, 56 case-control studies, and 10 ecological studies investigated alcoholic drinks. Most studies showed a relationship between increased consumption and increased cancer incidence. Meta-analysis of case-control data showed a 4 per cent increased risk per drink/week (figure 4.8.6). A dose-response relationship is apparent from case-control data, with no clear threshold.

It is biologically highly plausible that alcoholic drinks are a cause of oesophageal cancer. Reactive metabolites of alcohol such as acetaldehyde can be carcinogenic. Tobacco may induce specific mutations in DNA that are less efficiently repaired in the presence of alcohol. Alcohol may also function as a solvent, enhancing penetration of other carcinogenic molecules into mucosal cells. Additionally, the effects of alcohol may be mediated through the production of prostaglandins, lipid peroxidation, and the generation of free radical oxygen species. Lastly, heavy consumers of alcohol may have diets low in essential nutrients, making tissues susceptible to carcinogenesis.

There is ample and consistent evidence, both from cohort and case-control studies, with a dose-response relationship. There is robust evidence for mechanisms operating in humans. The evidence that alcoholic drinks are a cause of oesophageal cancer is convincing. No threshold was identified.

The Panel is aware that since the conclusion of the SLR, one cohort[56] and four case-control studies[50 51 53 57] have been published. This new information does not change the Panel judgement. Also see box 3.8.

7.3.5.14 Body fatness

(Also see chapter 6.1.3.1.)

A sufficient number of studies investigated BMI to allow squamous cell carcinomas and adenocarcinomas to be analysed separately. While results were inconsistent for squamous cell carcinomas and for all oesophageal cancers, adenocarcinomas, when analysed separately, showed a consistent increased risk with greater BMI. Three cohort studies and eight case-control studies investigated body fatness, as measured by BMI and adenocarcinomas. All of the cohort studies and most of the case-control studies showed increased risk with increased BMI. Meta-analysis of case-control data showed a 55 per cent increased risk per 5 kg/m^2 (figure 6.1.2). A dose-response relationship is apparent. This is consistent with known geographical and time trends for both BMI and adenocarcinomas.

It is biologically plausible that body fatness is a cause of oesophageal cancer. High body fatness is associated with increased gastro-oesophageal reflux and Barrett's oesophagus. It also directly affects levels of many circulating hormones, such as insulin, insulin-like growth factors, and oestrogens, creating an environment that encourages carcinogenesis and discourages apoptosis (see box 2.4) Body fatness stimulates the body's inflammatory response, which may contribute to the initiation and progression of several cancers (see chapter 2.4.1.3).

> **The epidemiology is consistent with evidence of a dose-response relationship. There is evidence for plausible mechanisms that operate in humans. The evidence that greater body fatness is a cause of oesophageal adenocarcinoma is convincing.**

The Panel is aware that since the conclusion of the SLR, two cohort[58][59] and five case-control studies[51][53][60-62] have been published. This new information does not change the Panel judgement. Also see box 3.8.

7.3.5.15 Other exposures
Other exposures were evaluated. However, the data were either too sparse, too inconsistent, or the number of studies too few to allow conclusions to be reached. These were as follows: cereals (grains) or their products; starchy roots, tubers, and plantains; pulses (legumes); soya and soya products; herbs, condiments or spices; poultry; fish; eggs; milk and dairy products; sugary foods and drinks; fermenting; pickling; salt; salting; smoked and cured foods; nitrates and nitrites; frying, grilling (broiling), and barbecuing; total fat; saturated fatty acids; monounsaturated fatty acids; polyunsaturated fatty acids; protein; vitamin A; retinol; pro-vitamin A carotenoids; beta-cryptoxanthin; thiamin; riboflavin; iron; calcium; zinc; energy intake; adult attained height; and Seventh-day Adventist diets.

7.3.6 Comparison with previous report

7.3.6.1 General
See section 7.1.6.1 of this chapter, and box 3.8 in chapter 3.

7.3.6.2 Specific
The previous report judged the evidence that vegetables and fruits protect against oesophageal cancer to be convincing. Data published since then have been somewhat less consistent.

At the time of the previous report, the evidence on body fatness was unclear, because data on adenocarcinomas was inadequate and not analysed separately.

The previous report judged it possible that carotenoids or vitamin C protect against this cancer. The evidence base for foods containing these nutrients is now stronger. The previous report judged it possible that maté and other very hot drinks cause oesophageal cancer. The evidence on maté is now stronger.

7.3.7 Conclusions

The Panel concludes:
The evidence that alcoholic drinks and body fatness (adenocarcinomas only) are causes of cancer of the oesophagus is convincing. The risk is multiplied when drinkers of alcohol also smoke tobacco.

Non-starchy vegetables, fruits, and foods containing beta-carotene and/or vitamin C probably protect against oesophageal cancer.

Maté, a herbal infusion, when drunk scalding hot through a metal straw as is traditional in South America, is probably a cause of this cancer.

There is limited evidence suggesting that foods containing dietary fibre, folate, pyridoxine, or vitamin E protect against this cancer; and that red meat, processed meat, and high temperature drinks are causes of this cancer.

7.4 Lung

Cancer of the lung is the most common type of cancer worldwide (excluding non-melanoma skin cancer). Around 1.4 million cases were recorded in 2002, accounting for over 12 per cent of all cancers. Three-quarters of all cases occur in men. The disease is most common in high-income countries and is increasing in some low-income countries such as China. It is almost always fatal, and is the chief cause of death from cancer: nearly 18 per cent of all deaths from cancer are from this type.

Overall, *the Panel emphasises* that the principal cause of lung cancer is smoking tobacco.

The Panel judges as follows:
The evidence that arsenic in drinking water and (in smokers only) pharmacological doses of beta-carotene are a cause of this cancer is convincing.

Fruits, and also foods containing carotenoids, probably protect against lung cancer.

There is limited evidence suggesting that non-starchy vegetables, selenium and foods containing it, foods containing quercetin, and physical activity protect against lung cancer.

There is also limited evidence suggesting that red meat, processed meat, total fat, butter, pharmacological doses of retinol (smokers only), and low body fatness are causes of lung cancer.

In final summary, the strongest evidence, corresponding to judgements of "convincing" and "probable", shows that arsenic in drinking water and pharmacological doses of beta-carotene (smokers only) are causes of lung cancer; and that fruits and foods containing carotenoids probably protect against this cancer.

The lungs are part of the aerodigestive system. They contain hundreds of lobules, and each lobule contains a bronchiole, its branches, and clusters of alveoli. This is where carbon dioxide (a product of respiration) is removed from the blood and replaced with oxygen, to fuel further respiration, producing energy.

About 90–95 per cent of lung cancers are either small-cell carcinoma or non-small-cell carcinoma. The latter has three major subtypes: squamous cell carcinoma, adenocarcinoma, and large-cell carcinoma.[4] Squamous cell carcinomas account for 30–35 per cent, adenocarcinomas 30–45 per cent, and large-cell carcinomas about 9 per cent of all lung cancers. Small cell lung cancer (SCLC) accounts for 10–15 per cent of all lung cancers; this form is considered a distinct clinical pathological entity due to its characteristic aggressive biology, diffuse nature, propensity for early metastasis, and overall poor prognosis. Mesothelioma, which affects the pleura (layer of cells covering the lung and chest cavity), is almost always caused by previous exposure to asbestos.

FOOD, NUTRITION, PHYSICAL ACTIVITY, AND CANCER OF THE LUNG

In the judgement of the Panel, the factors listed below modify the risk of cancer of the lung. Judgements are graded according to the strength of the evidence.

	DECREASES RISK	INCREASES RISK
Convincing		**Arsenic in drinking water[1]** **Beta-carotene supplements[2]**
Probable	**Fruits[3]** **Foods containing carotenoids[4]**	
Limited — suggestive	Non-starchy vegetables[3] Foods containing selenium[4] Foods containing quercetin[4] Selenium[5] Physical activity[6]	Red meat[7] Processed meat[8] Total fat Butter Retinol supplements[2] Low body fatness
Limited — no conclusion	Cereals (grains) and their products; starchy tubers; dietary fibre; pulses (legumes); poultry; fish; eggs; milk and dairy products; total fat; animal fats; plant oils; soft drinks; coffee; tea; alcohol; preservation, processing, and preparation; carbohydrate; protein vitamin A; thiamin; riboflavin; niacin; vitamin B6; folate; vitamin C; vitamin E; multivitamins; calcium; copper; iron; zinc; pro-vitamin A carotenoids; lycopene; flavonoids; culturally-defined diets; body size, shape, and composition (except low body fatness); energy intake	
Substantial effect on risk unlikely	None identified	

1. The International Agency for Research on Cancer has graded arsenic and arsenic compounds as Class 1 carcinogens. The grading for this entry applies specifically to inorganic arsenic in drinking water.
2. The evidence is derived from studies using high-dose supplements (20 mg/day for beta-carotene; 25 000 international units/day for retinol) in smokers.
3. Judgements on vegetables and fruits do not include those preserved by salting and/or pickling.
4. Includes both foods naturally containing the constituent and foods which have the constituent added (see chapter 3.5.3).
5. The evidence is derived from studies using supplements at a dose of 200 µg/day.
6. Physical activity of all types: occupational, household, transport, and recreational.
7. The term 'red meat' refers to beef, pork, lamb, and goat from domesticated animals.
8. The term 'processed meat' refers to meats preserved by smoking, curing, or salting, or addition of chemical preservatives.

For an explanation of all the terms used in the matrix, please see chapter 3.5.1, the text of this section, and the glossary.

7.4.1 Trends, incidence, and survival

Smoking and other exposure to tobacco smoke are the principal causes of lung cancer. The trend and incidence patterns are explained largely by these exposures. Age-adjusted rates of lung cancer are decreasing in many high-income countries due to decreased smoking. Global and regional trends in incidence have mirrored the prevalence of smoking, with a time lag of around 35 years.[63] Lung cancer was rare until the end of the 19th century, with only 140 cases reported in the world literature before 1898, and only 374 by 1912.[63] Incidence peaked in most high-income countries in the second half of the 20th century, and later for women than men.

The relative incidence of the various types of lung cancer is gradually changing. Between 1980 and 2000, the proportion of squamous cancers decreased as the proportion of adenocarcinomas increased, possibly due to changes in smoking habits or products.[64] Adenocarcinoma is now the most frequently diagnosed type in the USA and Japan; while it is also showing signs of increasing in Europe, squamous cell carcinoma continues to be the predominant type.

Lung cancer is mainly a disease of high-income countries, where the smoking epidemic began earlier, and overall rates are nearly double those in middle- to low-income countries. Around the world, age-adjusted incidence ranges from more than 60 per 100 000 people in North America and across much of Europe, to less than 5 per 100 000 in much of middle Africa. Within Europe, rates are highest in eastern European countries. In the USA, rates are higher among African-American people than in white people. Worldwide, rates are higher in men than in women, by around three to one. The incidence of lung cancer increases with age. Rates will continue to rise in middle- and low-income countries as tobacco smoking increases.

The early stages of lung cancer do not usually produce symptoms, so the disease is generally at an advanced stage when it is diagnosed. Survival rates are poor, around 10 per cent at 5 years, and are usually higher in women than men.[3 6] SCLC has a worse prognosis than non-SCLC (a survival rate of only around 5 per cent at 5 years), because SCLC has a tendency to metastasise (spread) early, and surgery is not usually successful.[4 65] Lung cancer accounts for somewhat over 12 per cent of all cancer incidence, but for nearly 18 per cent of all cancer deaths. Also see box 7.1.1.

7.4.2 Pathogenesis

Carcinogens in tobacco smoke, or other inhaled particles such as coal tar or asbestos, can interact directly with the DNA of lung cells. Because the whole lung is exposed to inhaled carcinogens, several sites may accumulate different cancerous changes, leading to multiple cancers originating in different types of cell.[4]

Inflammation may also play a role in the development of lung cancer, with cancerous changes occurring as a response to chronic exposure to irritants and repeated injury. Columnar epithelial cells are replaced with stratified squamous epithelial cells, which may also increase cancer risk.

The division of these new cells increases, and this eventually is followed by dysplasia of the lung mucosa. When this process involves the full thickness of the mucosa, these dysplastic lesions become carcinoma in situ. Further invasion to the depth of the basement membrane, and the subsequent infiltration of the underlying stroma by malignant cells, signals invasive cancer. This process may take 10–20 years.[4]

People with adenocarcinomas may have an associated history of chronic lung disease, such as scleroderma, rheumatoid disease, sarcoidosis, or tuberculosis.[4]

7.4.3 Other established causes

(Also see chapter 2.4 and section 7.1.3.1.)

Tobacco use. Smoking is the principal cause of lung cancer; it is estimated to be responsible for 85 per cent of all types of this cancer.[66] In populations with a history of long-term cigarette use, the proportion has reached 90 per cent.[10] Involuntary exposure to tobacco smoke ('passive smoking') is also a cause of lung cancer, including in people who have never smoked.[10]

Industrial chemicals. Carcinogens that are causes of lung cancer include aluminium; arsenic; asbestos (both lung cancer and mesothelioma); chloromethyl methyl ether and/or bis-chloromethyl ether; coal-tar fumes; erionite (mesothelioma); pollutants from iron and steel founding; untreated mineral oils; mustard gas; soot; talc containing asbestiform tremolite; and vinyl chloride.[67]

7.4.4 Interpretation of the evidence

7.4.4.1 General
For general considerations that may affect interpretation of the evidence, see chapters 3.3 and 3.5, and boxes 3.1, 3.2, 3.6 and 3.7.

'Relative risk' is used in this Report to denote ratio measures of effect, including 'risk ratios', 'rate ratios', 'hazard ratios', and 'odds ratios'.

7.4.4.2 Specific
Considerations specific to cancer of the lung include:

Measurement. Due to low survival rates, both incidence and mortality can be assessed. Low survival times and rates decrease the reliability of case-control studies, which often rely on proxy reporting.

Confounding. Smoking tobacco is the predominant cause of lung cancer, and smokers tend also to have less healthy diets, more sedentary ways of life, and to be leaner than non-smokers. Therefore a central task in assessing the results of dietary studies is to evaluate the degree to which observed associations in smokers may be due to confounding/residual confounding by cigarette smoking; that is, not a direct result of the dietary exposure examined. A high proportion of the studies assessed below are appropriately adjusted for smoking.

7.4.5 Evidence and judgements

In total, 561 publications were included in the SLR for lung cancer. Fuller summaries of the epidemiological, experimental, and mechanistic evidence are to be found in Chapters 4–6.

The full SLR is contained on the CD included with this Report.

7.4.5.1 Non-starchy vegetables
(Also see chapter 4.2.5.1.)
A total of 17 cohort studies, 27 case-control studies, and 6 ecological studies investigated total vegetables. Other groupings examined were non-starchy vegetables specifically (3 cohort, 1 case-control); green, leafy vegetables, excluding cruciferous (5 cohort, 17 case-control); non-starchy root vegetables and tubers (2 cohort); and carrots (6 cohort, 21 case-control, 1 ecological). Most studies showed decreased risk with increased intake. Data are particularly consistent when stratified for carrots. A pooled analysis of 8 cohort studies (more than 430 000 participants, followed up for 6–16 years, with more than 3200 lung cancer cases) showed a non-significant decreased risk for the groups that ate the most vegetables. There was considerable heterogeneity, not all readily explained.

This is a wide and disparate category, and many different plant food constituents are represented that could contribute to a protective effect of non-starchy vegetables. These include dietary fibre, carotenoids, folate, selenium, glucosinolates, dithiolthiones, indoles, coumarins, ascorbate, chlorophyll, flavonoids, allylsulphides, flavonoids, and phytoestrogens, some of which are potentially antioxidants. Antioxidants trap free radicals and reactive oxygen molecules, protecting against oxidation damage. It is difficult to unravel the relative importance of each constituent and it is likely that any protective effect may result from a combination of influences on several pathways involved in carcinogenesis.

A substantial amount of evidence is available but some studies were not adjusted for smoking. A dose response is apparent from both cohort and case-control studies. There is limited evidence suggesting that non-starchy vegetables protect against lung cancer.

7.4.5.2 Fruits
(Also see chapter 4.2.5.2.)
Twenty-five cohort studies, 32 case-control studies, and 7 ecological studies investigated fruit consumption. Most of these showed decreased risk with increased intake. Meta-analysis of cohort data showed a 6 per cent decreased risk per 80 g serving/day; meta-analysis of case-control data showed a 20 per cent decreased risk per serving/day (figure 4.2.25). A pooled analysis of 8 cohort studies (more than 430 000 participants, followed up for 6–16 years, with more than 3200 lung cancer cases) showed a 23 per cent decreased risk for the groups that ate the most fruit. There is considerable heterogeneity, perhaps explained by the broad and disparate nature of this category.

Fruits are sources of vitamin C and other antioxidants, such as carotenoids, phenols, and flavonoids, as well as other potentially bioactive phytochemicals. Antioxidants trap free radicals and reactive oxygen molecules, protecting against oxidation damage. In addition, flavonoids found in fruit directly inhibit the expression of a cytochrome P450 enzyme. This helps to metabolise toxins and has been associated with increased risk of lung cancer, primarily in smokers.[68] It is difficult to unravel the relative importance of each constituent, and it is likely that any protective effect may result from a combination of influences on several pathways involved in carcinogenesis.

The evidence is ample and consistent. A dose-response relationship is apparent from both cohort and case-control studies and there is evidence for plausible mechanisms operating in humans. The evidence that fruits protect against lung cancer is convincing.

The Panel is aware that since the conclusion of the SLR, one case-control study[69] has been published. This new information does not change the Panel judgement. Also see box 3.8.

7.4.5.3 Foods containing carotenoids
(Also see chapter 4.2.5.3.)
A total of 11 cohort studies, 16 case-control studies, and 1 ecological study investigated total dietary carotenoids; 4 cohort studies and 5 case-control studies investigated serum or plasma carotenoids. Other groupings examined were dietary beta-cryptoxanthin (7 cohort, 8 case-control, 1 ecological), and serum/plasma beta-cryptoxanthin (6 cohort, 1 case-control). Nearly all cohort studies and most case-control studies showed decreased risk with increased intake. Meta-analysis of cohort data showed a 2 per cent decreased risk per 1 mg dietary carotenoid intake per day, or per 10 μg beta-cryptoxanthin intake per day (figure 4.2.28). A pooled analysis of 7 cohort studies (almost 400 000 participants, followed up for 7–16 years, with more than 3100 lung cancer cases) showed a 24 per cent decreased risk for the groups that consumed the most beta-cryptoxanthin. Several case-control studies did not adjust for smoking. Data come predominantly from dietary sources, not supplements; therefore no effect can be attributed to carotenoids separate from foods.

Carotenoids are antioxidants, which can prevent lipid oxidation and related oxidative stress. Some, such as beta-carotene, are also pro-vitamin A carotenoids.

There is a substantial amount of evidence available from both cohort and case-control studies. A clear dose-response relationship is apparent from cohort studies. Foods containing carotenoids probably protect against lung cancer.

7.4.5.4 Foods containing selenium
(Also see chapter 4.2.5.8.)
Two cohort studies, 2 case-control studies, and 2 ecological studies investigated dietary selenium; 10 cohort studies, 7 case-control studies, and 4 ecological studies investigated

plasma or serum selenium; and 3 cohort studies investigated selenium levels in nails. Most studies showed decreased risk with increased intake. Meta-analysis of cohort data on plasma or serum selenium produced evidence of decreased risk with a clear dose-response relationship.

Dietary selenium deficiency has been shown to cause a lack of selenoprotein expression. Twenty-five selenoproteins have been identified in animals and a number of these have important anti-inflammatory and antioxidant properties. Four are glutathione peroxidases, which protect against oxidative damage to biomolecules such as lipids, lipoproteins, and DNA. Three are thioredoxin reductases and, among other functions, these regenerate oxidised ascorbic acid to its active antioxidant form.

The evidence available is sparse. There is limited evidence to suggest that foods containing selenium protect against lung cancer.

7.4.5.5 Foods containing quercetin

(Also see chapter 4.2.5.9.)
Two cohort studies and three case-control studies investigated quercetin intake. Both cohort studies showed statistically significant decreased risk for the highest intake groups. Data from case-control studies were more heterogeneous.

Quercetin is a flavonoid which directly inhibits expression of a cytochrome P450 enzyme that helps to metabolise toxins, resulting in decreased DNA damage in laboratory experiments.[70]

The evidence available is sparse and inconsistent. There is limited evidence suggesting that foods containing quercetin protect against lung cancer.

7.4.5.6 Red meat

(Also see chapter 4.3.5.1.1.)
One cohort study and nine case-control studies investigated red meat. The single cohort study and most of the case-control studies showed increased risk with increased intake.

Red meat contains haem iron (see box 4.3.3). Free iron can lead to the production of free radicals. When cooked at high temperatures, red meat can also contain heterocyclic amines and polycyclic aromatic hydrocarbons (see box 4.3.4).

There is limited evidence, mostly from inconsistent case-control studies, suggesting that red meat is a cause of lung cancer.

7.4.5.7 Processed meat

(Also see chapter 4.3.5.1.2.)
Four cohort studies and 10 case-control studies investigated processed meat, most of which showed increased risk with increased intake.

N-nitroso compounds are suspected mutagens and carcinogens that are found in processed meats, and produced in the stomach from nitrates, including those used to preserve meats.[55] Many processed meats also contain high levels of salt and nitrite (see box 4.3.2). When cooked at high temperatures, meats can also contain heterocyclic amines and polycyclic aromatic hydrocarbons (see box 4.3.4). Haem promotes the formation of N-nitroso compounds and also contains iron. Free iron can lead to production of free radicals (see box 4.3.3).

There is limited, inconsistent evidence suggesting that processed meat is a cause of lung cancer.

7.4.5.8 Total fat

(Also see chapter 4.5.5.1.)
Nine cohort studies, 17 case-control studies, and 4 ecological studies investigated total fat intake. Most studies showed increased risk with increased intake, although cohort data were less suggestive of an effect, and few studies were statistically significant. No evidence for plausible mechanisms was found.

The mixed results from cohort studies contrast with the more consistent results from other studies. Overall, there is limited evidence suggesting that consumption of total fat is a cause of lung cancer. _The Panel emphasises_ that the principle cause of lung cancer is smoking tobacco.

7.4.5.9 Butter

(Also see chapter 4.5.5.1.1.)
Two cohort studies and eight case-control studies investigated butter consumption. Most studies showed increased risk with increased intake, but cohort data were inconsistent. No evidence for plausible mechanisms was found.

There is a limited amount of inconsistent evidence suggesting that consumption of butter is a cause of lung cancer.

7.4.5.10 Arsenic in drinking water

(Also see chapter 4.7.5.1.1.)
Two cohort studies, 2 case-control studies, and 12 ecological studies investigated arsenic in drinking water. All cohort and case-control studies, and most ecological studies, showed a relationship between increased levels of arsenic in drinking water and increased incidence. Meta-analysis was not possible, but effect estimates tended to be large (an increased risk of over 300 per cent for the highest levels).

Soluble arsenic in drinking water induces lung cancers in animal models.[71] In humans, arsenic is a chromosomal mutagen (an agent that induces mutations involving more than one gene, typically large deletions or rearrangements). It can also act as a synergistic co-mutagen. Arsenic exposure also causes chronic lung disease.[71] The Joint FAO/WHO Expert Committee on Food Additives has set a provisional tolerable weekly intake of 0.015 mg/kg of body weight.[72]

The evidence is ample and consistent, from cohort and case-control as well as ecological studies. There is a dose-response relationship, and the effect size is relatively large. There is robust evidence for mechanisms. The evidence that arsenic in drinking water is a cause of lung cancer is convincing.

7.4.5.11 Retinol supplements (in smokers)

(Also see chapter 4.10.6.4.1.)

Two trials (one randomised controlled, one non-randomised), two cohort studies, and two case-control studies investigated retinol or retinol supplements. The single randomised controlled trial, performed in current and former smokers only, showed a statistically significant increased risk with a high-dose supplement. There was a suggestion of further elevated incidence in heavy smokers and asbestos workers. The non-randomised trial was inconclusive. One cohort, also stratified by smoking status, showed a relationship with increased incidence only in current smokers. All other studies failed to stratify by smoking status and were inconclusive.

It is possible that some protective effect present at dietary intake amounts of vitamins is lost or reversed by the higher levels supplied by pharmacologic supplementation.

The evidence is sparse and inconsistent. There is limited evidence suggesting that high-dose vitamin A supplements are a cause of lung cancer in current smokers.

7.4.5.12 Beta-carotene supplements (in smokers)

(Also see chapter 4.10.6.4.2.)

Four randomised controlled trials and two cohort studies investigated beta-carotene supplements. Of these, one randomised controlled trial was performed in smokers. This study showed a statistically significant increased risk of 17 per cent with a daily 20 mg beta-carotene supplement. It also suggested that heavy smoking elevated the risk further. Other trials and studies, either in non-smokers or not stratified according to smoking status, were inconclusive.

There is a marked interaction between beta-carotene, heavy smoking, and glutathione *S*-transferase (GST) genotype. GST is a carcinogen-detoxifying enzyme (see chapter 2.5). Beta-carotene supplementation among people without GSTM1 (one of the variants of the GST gene) who smoked more than 42 cigarettes per day was compared to beta-carotene supplementation among those without GSTM1 who smoked less than 37 cigarettes per day. A relative risk of 6.01 (95% confidence interval 1.90–19.08) was observed.

It is possible that a protective association present at dietary intake amounts of carotenoids is lost or reversed by the higher levels that pharmacological supplementation may supply. In one animal study, low-dose beta-carotene was protective against smoking-induced changes in the tumour-suppressor p53 gene (see box 2.2), while high doses promoted these changes.[73] A second explanation could relate to disturbance of the complex nature of naturally occurring carotenoids. It is possible that the protective associations are not due to the specific agent used in supplement studies, but rather to other carotenoids present in dietary exposure,[74] or other associated dietary or health-related behaviour.

There is strong evidence from good-quality trials, consistent with cohort studies. An interaction between smoking, genotype, and beta-carotene is apparent. The evidence that beta-carotene supplements cause lung cancer in current smokers is convincing.

7.4.5.13 Selenium supplements

(Also see chapter 4.10.6.4.5.)

One randomised controlled trial investigated selenium supplements and lung cancer.

The single trial of more than 1300 participants given 200 μg/day of selenium for 13 years showed a non-significant decreased risk with supplementation, adjusted for age and smoking. Subgroup analysis indicated that this risk differed according to baseline plasma selenium level, with a statistically significant decreased risk for those with the lowest initial plasma selenium. This is suggestive that selenium supplementation may decrease cancer risk in those who have poor selenium status, but that this effect may not extend to those who do not.

Dietary selenium deficiency has been shown to cause a lack of selenoprotein expression. Twenty-five selenoproteins have been identified in animals and a number of these have important anti-inflammatory and antioxidant properties. Four are glutathione peroxidases, which protect against oxidative damage to biomolecules such as lipids, lipoproteins, and DNA. Three are thioredoxin reductases and, among other functions, these regenerate oxidised ascorbic acid to its active antioxidant form.

The evidence is sparse. There is limited evidence suggesting that selenium protects against lung cancer.

7.4.5.14 Physical activity

(Also see chapter 5.4.4.)

In total, 5 cohort studies investigated total physical activity; 2 cohort studies investigated non-recreational activity; 4 cohort studies and 2 case-control studies investigated occupational activity; and 11 cohort studies and 4 case-control studies investigated recreational activity. Overall, most studies showed decreased risk with increased physical activity. No studies showed a statistically significant increased risk. Of the categories analysed, consistent protective relationships were reported for total physical activity, non-recreational activity, and recreational activity. Increased heterogeneity in occupational physical activity may be due to either the extreme variation in exposure definition, or the generally lower levels of occupational activity, meaning that, as a percentage of daily activity, occupational activity is of reduced importance in many high-income countries (where these studies were generally performed).

Sustained, moderate physical activity raises metabolic rate and increases maximal oxygen uptake. In the long term, regular periods of such activity increase the body's metabolic efficiency and capacity (the amount of work that it can perform), as well as reducing blood pressure and insulin resistance.

There is evidence from prospective and case-control studies showing lower risk of lung cancer with higher levels of physical activity, but there is no evidence of plausible mechanisms. The relationship between activity, BMI, and lung cancer makes the evidence difficult to interpret. There is limited evidence suggesting that physical activity protects against lung cancer.

The Panel is aware that since the conclusion of the SLR, one cohort study[75] has been published. This new information does not change the Panel judgement. Also see box 3.8.

7.4.5.15 Body fatness

(Also see chapter 6.1.3.1.)

Twenty-one cohort studies, 24 case-control studies, and 1 ecological study investigated body fatness, as measured by BMI. Nearly all of the cohort and case-control studies showed decreased risk with increased BMI. Meta-analysis of cohort and case-control data provided evidence of a statistically significant reduced risk, with no heterogeneity in cohort data.

Smoking is the principal cause of lung cancer and may also be associated with lower BMI. There is a high potential for confounding due to tobacco smoking, and residual confounding is therefore possible. In addition, it is possible that people with undiagnosed lung cancer may lose weight, so giving a spurious association (reverse causation).

There is no known mechanism through which greater body fatness could plausibly protect against lung cancer, or through which low body fatness could increase risk.

Although the epidemiological evidence suggests an inverse relationship, this could be caused by confounding by cigarette smoking or reverse causation due to weight loss from undiagnosed cancer. There is limited evidence suggesting that low body fatness is a cause of lung cancer.

7.4.5.16 Other exposures

Other exposures were evaluated. However, the data were either of too low quality, too inconsistent, or the number of studies too few to allow conclusions to be reached. These were as follows: cereals (grains) or their products; starchy tubers; pulses (legumes); meat; poultry; fish; eggs; animal fats; milk and dairy products; soft drinks; coffee; tea; alcohol; processing, preservation, and preparation; carbohydrate; dietary fibre; total fat; protein; vitamin A; retinol; pro-vitamin A carotenoids; lycopene; thiamin; riboflavin; niacin; vitamin B6; folate; vitamin C; vitamin E; multivitamins; iron; zinc; copper; calcium; selenium; flavonoids; energy intake; plant oils; body size, shape, and composition (except low body fatness); and culturally defined diets.

7.4.6 Comparison with previous report

7.4.6.1 General

See section 7.1.6.1 of this chapter, and box 3.8 in chapter 3.

7.4.6.2 Specific

The previous report judged the evidence that vegetables and fruits protect against lung cancer to be convincing. Evidence, particularly from cohort studies published since the mid-1990s, is more consistent for fruits than for vegetables.

The findings of the previous report for carotenoids, and for pharmaceutical doses of beta-carotene given to smokers, were identical to the current findings (for foods containing carotenoids), although the previous report did not include a matrix entry for beta-carotene supplements. The previous report did not review arsenic.

7.4.7 Conclusions

The Panel concludes:

The evidence that arsenic in drinking water and (in smokers only) pharmacological doses of beta-carotene are causes of lung cancer is convincing.

Fruits, and also foods containing carotenoids, probably protect against lung cancer.

There is limited evidence suggesting that non-starchy vegetables, selenium and foods containing it, foods containing quercetin, and physical activity protect against lung cancer.

There is also limited evidence suggesting that red meat, processed meat, total fat, butter, pharmacological doses of retinol (in smokers only), and low body fatness are causes of lung cancer.

Smoking tobacco is the main cause of lung cancer.

7.5 Stomach

Cancer of the stomach is the fourth most common type of cancer worldwide. Almost one million cases were recorded in 2002. Two out of three cases occur in men. Overall, it is decreasing rapidly in high-income countries, but remains very common elsewhere in the world. It is usually fatal and is the second most common cause of death from cancer.

Overall, *the Panel judges* that food and nutrition play an important role in the prevention and causation of stomach cancer.

The Panel judges as follows:
Non-starchy vegetables, including specifically allium vegetables, as well as fruits probably protect against stomach cancer.

Salt, and also salt-preserved foods, are probably causes of this cancer.

There is limited evidence suggesting that pulses (legumes), including soya and soya products, and also foods containing selenium protect against stomach cancer.

There is also limited evidence suggesting that chilli, processed meat, smoked foods, and grilled (broiled) and barbecued (charbroiled) animal foods are causes of stomach cancer.

Infection with the bacterium *Helicobacter pylori* is established as a necessary cause of almost all cases of stomach cancer. It has been estimated that most cases of this cancer are preventable by appropriate diets and associated factors.

In final summary, the strongest evidence, corresponding to judgements of "convincing" and "probable",shows that non-starchy vegetables, allium vegetables, and fruits protect against stomach cancer; and that salt and also salt-preserved foods are causes
of this cancer.

The stomach is the sac-like part of the digestive system between the oesophagus and the small intestine. The body of the stomach is lined by a mucous membrane consisting of columnar epithelial cells and glands, surrounded by muscle.

There are two main types of stomach cancer. Distal gastric cancers (those of the lower portion of the stomach) are the predominant type. The other type is cancer of the gastric cardia or of the gastro-oesophageal junction.[4] The latter are sometimes grouped with oesophageal adenocarcinomas.

Distal gastric cancers may be classified depending on their appearance under the microscope as intestinal or diffuse (from mucus-producing cells). The former is more common and predominates in areas of high incidence; the latter has a poorer prognosis, tends to occur at a younger age, and may also occur in the cardia.[76] More than 95 per cent of gastric cancers are adenocarcinomas.[77]

FOOD, NUTRITION, PHYSICAL ACTIVITY, AND CANCER OF THE STOMACH

In the judgement of the Panel, the factors listed below modify the risk of cancer of the stomach. Judgements are graded according to the strength of the evidence.

	DECREASES RISK	INCREASES RISK
Convincing		
Probable	**Non-starchy vegetables**[1] **Allium vegetables**[1] **Fruits**[1]	**Salt**[2] **Salted and salty foods**
Limited — suggestive	Pulses (legumes)[3] Foods containing selenium[4]	Chilli[1] Processed meat[5] Smoked foods[6] Grilled (broiled) or barbecued (charbroiled) animal foods[6]
Limited — no conclusion	Cereals (grains) and their products; dietary fibre; potatoes; starchy roots, tubers, and plantains; nuts and seeds; herbs, spices, and condiments; meat (unprocessed); poultry; eggs; milk and dairy products; fats and oils; total fat; fatty acid composition; cholesterol; sugars; sugar (sucrose); fruit juices; coffee; tea; alcohol; dietary nitrate and nitrite, *N*-nitrosodimethylamine; drying or dried food; protein; thiamin; riboflavin; vitamin C; vitamin D; multivitamin/mineral supplements; calcium; iron; selenium supplements; carotenoids; culturally defined diets; meal frequency; eating speed; body fatness; energy intake	
Substantial effect on risk unlikely	None identified	

1 Judgements on vegetables and fruits do not include those preserved by salting and/or pickling.
2 'Salt' here means total salt consumption, from processed foods, including salty and salted foods, and also salt added in cooking and at the table.
3 Including soya and soya products.
4 Includes both foods naturally containing the constituent and foods which have the constituent added (see chapter 3.5.3).
5 The term 'processed meat' refers to meats preserved by smoking, curing, or salting, or addition of chemical preservatives.
6 The evidence is mostly from meats preserved or cooked in these ways.

For an explanation of all the terms used in the matrix, please see chapter 3.5.1, the text of this section, and the glossary.

7.5.1 Trends, incidence, and survival

Age-adjusted rates of stomach cancer are decreasing, and in 2002 (in many countries) were half what they were 30 years earlier. However, during the same period, two types of cancer affecting the upper (proximal) section of the stomach — those of the gastro-oesophageal junction and gastric cardia

— increased, notably in high-income countries.[78] The decline in stomach cancer incidence is likely to have been due partly to the increased availability of refrigeration (see box 4.6.4). This has had the effect of increasing availability and consumption of fresh foods such as vegetables and fruits, and decreasing consumption of foods preserved by salt and other relevant methods.[79 80]

Age-adjusted incidence rates range from more than 60 per 100 000 people in Japan and other countries in eastern Asia, to less than 10 per 100 000 in much of Africa and North America. Chile and other Latin American countries, as well as Portugal and eastern Europe, have moderately high rates of 30 per 100 000. Rates are also higher in some ethnic groups, for instance, Asian and Pacific Islanders living in the USA, and African-American, and Hispanic-American people; rates are also twice as high in men as women. Rates of different types of stomach cancer also vary, both geographically and between ethnic groups. Cancers affecting the lower (distal) section of the stomach are most common in low- to middle-income countries and in people of African origin; proximal tumours are predominant in high-income countries and in white people.[78] Risk increases with age; stomach cancer is rarely diagnosed in people under 50.

The 5-year survival rate for stomach cancer is approximately 20 per cent.[3 6] Survival rates are higher in countries which have screening programmes that lead to early detection, and where distal cancer (which has a better prognosis) predominates.[81] Stomach cancer accounts for nearly 9 per cent of all cancer incidence, but somewhat over 10 per cent of all cancer deaths worldwide. Also see box 7.1.1.

7.5.2 Pathogenesis

Changes in the stomach mucosa, brought about by a variety of environmental factors and ageing, can eventually lead to atrophic gastritis. The chronic form of this condition, and the resulting changes in the characteristics of the stomach cells, appear to be precursor conditions to the development of distal stomach cancer.[4] Food carcinogens can also potentially interact directly with the epithelial cells that line the stomach. However, cancer can also develop without these precursors, particularly when the bacterium *H pylori* is present in the stomach (see box 7.5.1).[81]

Three independent cohort studies have shown the progression of gastritis from the non-atrophic to the atrophic form. Epidemiological studies of atrophic gastritis have also shown an association with dietary factors, especially a high intake of salt (mostly in the form of salty and salted foods).[90]

N-nitrosamines are known carcinogens produced in the stomach from nitrate in foods, and via nitrite from endogenous nitric oxide production in chronic inflammation (see box 4.3.2). They may be potential causes of stomach cancer[92] (see chapter 2.4.2.6).

Cancers of the gastric cardia show many similarities to oesophageal cancer (see 7.3.1). There is a clear association between Barrett's oesophagus and adenocarcinoma of the lower (distal) oesophagus and of the gastric cardia, caused by chronic acid damage.

Box 7.5.1 *Helicobacter pylori*

H pylori is a bacterium that lives in the human stomach. Infection does not usually produce symptoms, and spreads through saliva and faecal material. Prevalence increases with age, but differs dramatically among populations.[82] In the USA, prevalence is less than 20 per cent at 20 years old and about 50 per cent at 50 years, which may be typical of high-income countries,[83] while in Korea, it is 50 per cent at 5 years and 90 per cent at 20 years, and in Japan it reaches 85 per cent by middle age.[84]

H pylori colonises the gastric mucosa and elicits both inflammatory and immune lifelong responses, including the release of various bacterial and host-dependent cytotoxic substances.[85] *H pylori* infection greatly reduces the bioavailability of vitamin C. This may play a role in the development of stomach cancer in the presence of dietary and other factors that are a cause of this cancer. In studies of precancerous lesions or gastric atrophy, eradication of *H pylori* promoted regression of these cancer precursors.[86-88]

Some people develop stomach cancer without apparent infection with *H pylori*. Reported percentages of non-cardia cancers that test positive for *H pylori* range from approximately 60 to 95 per cent, averaging around 86 per cent,[89] but those with distal stomach cancer who test negative for *H pylori* may have undergone a loss of infection associated with the atrophic gastritis, and consequently a decline in antibody titre. It can be regarded as a necessary cause for those stomach cancers arising in the distal region of the stomach.[90]

The longer the time of infection, and the greater the impact on the gastric mucosa, the more likely it is that stomach cancer will develop and take a severe form. The exact site of the cancer is most likely to be where the mucosa is most affected.[91] Those who develop extensive gastritis and gastric atrophy are at increased risk of developing cancer.[81]

The diffuse type of distal stomach cancers (those that develop from mucus-producing cells) show some genetic predisposition, with an increased risk for people with blood group A. Genetic predisposition is thought to be a factor in 5–10 per cent of diffuse cancers.[93] Stomach cancer is part of the spectrum of cancers associated with the germ line mismatch repair (MMR) gene alterations that give rise to hereditary nonpolyposis colorectal cancer (HNPCC).[77] Also see chapter 7.9.2.

7.5.3 Other established causes

(Also see chapter 2.4 and 7.1.3.1.)

Infection and infestation. The bacterium *H pylori* is an important cause of distal stomach cancers (see box 7.5.1). Also, Epstein-Barr virus is carcinogenic to humans and has been linked to stomach cancers (particularly gastric lymphoepithelial carcinomas and a smaller proportion of gastric adenocarcinomas) in some studies.[30]

Industrial chemicals. Industrial exposure to ethylene oxide is carcinogenic to humans and has led to increased risk of stomach cancer in some studies.[94]

7.5.4 Interpretation of the evidence

7.5.4.1 General
For general considerations that may affect interpretation of the evidence, see chapters 3.3 and 3.5, and boxes 3.1, 3.2, 3.6 and 3.7.

'Relative risk' is used in this Report to denote ratio measures of effect, including 'risk ratios', 'rate ratios', 'hazard ratios', and 'odds ratios'.

7.5.4.2 Specific
Considerations specific to cancer of the stomach include the following.

Classification. Most evidence relates to distal stomach cancers, although cancers of the gastric cardia and gastro-oesophageal junction might be included in an outcome of 'stomach cancer'. It is now well recognised that proximal and distal stomach cancers are quite different, but relatively few studies stratified results on the basis of subsite. For many early studies, most stomach cancer was probably distal in origin, so the lack of stratification was less important. As the incidence and overall proportion of proximal cancer have increased in recent years in high-income countries, there is a greater likelihood that the general term 'stomach cancer' will represent a combination of the two subsites and therefore results will be less informative.

Measurement. Owing to low survival rates, both incidence and mortality can be assessed. Low survival times and rates decrease the reliability of case-control studies, which often rely on proxy reporting.

Confounding. *H pylori* infection is a necessary cause of distal stomach cancer. This has only been established relatively recently. Only recent studies have incorporated *H pylori* status into their design and have adjusted or stratified for infection.

7.5.5 Evidence and judgements

In total, 722 publications were included in the SLR for stomach cancer. Fuller summaries of the epidemiological, experimental, and mechanistic evidence are to be found in Chapters 4–6.

The full SLR is contained on the CD included with this Report.

7.5.5.1 Non-starchy vegetables
(Also see chapter 4.2.5.1.)
A total of 10 cohort studies, 45 case-control studies, and 19 ecological studies investigated total vegetables. Other groupings examined were green-yellow vegetables (11 cohort, 21 case-control, 8 ecological); green, leafy vegetables (6 cohort, 13 case-control, 2 ecological); tomatoes (3 cohort, 19 case-control); white or pale vegetables (2 cohort, 6 case-control); raw vegetables (6 cohort, 25 case-control, 3 ecological); or non-starchy vegetables and fruits (5 cohort, 6 case-control).

Most studies showed decreased risk with increased intake. However, cohort data were less consistent than case-control data. Meta-analysis of cohort data showed a 19 per cent decreased risk per 50 g green-yellow vegetables/day; no other subcategory analyses were statistically significant. Case-control data showed a 15 per cent decreased risk per 50 g vegetables/day (figures 4.2.8. and 4.2.9); a 21 per cent decreased risk per 50 g green-yellow vegetables/day; a 57 per cent decreased risk per 50 g green, leafy vegetables/day; a 30 per cent decreased risk per 50 g tomatoes/day; and a 25 per cent decreased risk per 50 g raw vegetables/day (figure 4.2.12). There was unexplained heterogeneity.

This is a wide and disparate category, and many different plant food constituents are represented that could contribute to a protective effect of non-starchy vegetables. These include dietary fibre, carotenoids, folate, selenium, glucosinolates, dithiolthiones, indoles, coumarins, ascorbate, chlorophyll, flavonoids, allylsulphides, flavonoids, and phytoestrogens, some of which are potentially antioxidants. Antioxidants trap free radicals and reactive oxygen molecules, protecting against oxidation damage. It is difficult to unravel the relative importance of each constituent and it is likely that any protective effect may result from a combination of influences on several pathways involved in carcinogenesis.

A substantial amount of evidence is available, including on specific subtypes, particularly green-yellow vegetables, with a dose-response relationship in case-control, but not cohort, data. There is evidence for plausible mechanisms. Non-starchy vegetables probably protect against stomach cancer.

The Panel is aware that since the conclusion of the SLR, one case-control study[95] has been published. This new information does not change the Panel judgement. Also see box 3.8.

7.5.5.2 Allium vegetables
(Also see chapter 4.2.5.1.1.)
A total of 2 cohort studies, 27 case-control studies, and 2 ecological studies investigated allium vegetables; and 1 cohort study, 16 case-control studies, and 2 ecological studies investigated garlic. There was also one relevant intervention study that combined allitridium (a garlic extract containing triallylsulphides) and selenium supplements. Most of the studies showed decreased risk with increased intake. Meta-analysis of cohort data showed a 23 per cent decreased risk per 50 g allium vegetables/day. Meta-analysis of case-control data showed a 20 per cent decreased risk per 50 g allium vegetables/day (figure 4.2.14), and a 59 per cent decreased risk per serving of garlic/day. The single trial of combined selenium and allitridium supplements showed a statistically significant decreased risk in men but not women, after 5 years of follow-up.

Allium vegetables, particularly garlic, have antibiotic properties. Although this may act directly against *H pylori*, studies in humans have not shown this effect. It is also possible that antibacterial effects of garlic might inhibit the secondary colonisation of the stomach after *H pylori*-induced atrophy. At present, there is no evidence to support or refute this idea.

The evidence, though not copious and mostly from case-control studies, is consistent, with a dose-response relationship. There is evidence for plausible mechanisms. Allium vegetables probably protect against stomach cancer.

7.5.5.3 Fruits

(Also see chapter 4.2.5.2.)

Sixteen cohort studies, 51 case-control studies, and 23 ecological studies investigated fruits. Most studies showed decreased risk with increased intake, but there was unexplained heterogeneity. Cohort studies suggested a non-significant relationship with decreased risk. Meta-analysis of case-control data showed a 17 per cent decreased risk per 50 g fruits per day (figure 4.2.27).

Fruits are sources of vitamin C and other antioxidants, such as carotenoids, phenols, and flavonoids, as well as other potentially bioactive phytochemicals. Antioxidants trap free radicals and reactive oxygen molecules, protecting against oxidation damage. In addition, flavonoids found in fruits directly inhibit the expression of a cytochrome P450 enzyme, which helps to metabolise toxins and has been associated with increased risk of lung cancer, primarily in smokers.[68] It is difficult to unravel the relative importance of each constituent and it is likely that a protective effect may result from a combination of influences on several pathways involved in carcinogenesis.

The evidence is ample and more consistent, with a dose-response relationship, for case-control studies than for cohorts. There is evidence for plausible mechanisms. Fruits probably protect against stomach cancer.

The Panel is aware that since the conclusion of the SLR, three case-control studies[95-97] have been published. This new information does not change the Panel judgement. Also see box 3.8.

7.5.5.4 Pulses (legumes) including soya and soya products

(Also see chapter 4.2.5.10.)

A total of 3 cohort studies, 22 case-control studies, and 16 ecological studies investigated pulses (legumes) and stomach cancer; and 2 cohort studies, 9 case-control studies, and 2 ecological studies investigated soya and soya products. All of the cohort studies and most of the case-control studies showed decreased risk with increased intake. Ecological studies showed decreased risk for soya and soya products, but were inconsistent for pulses (legumes).

Meta-analysis of cohort studies showed a non-significant relationship with decreased risk. Meta-analysis of case-control studies produced evidence for a relationship with decreased risk.

Pulses (legumes), particularly soya, contain high levels of isoflavones that have shown anti-cancer properties in laboratory experiments. Saponins and other bioactive constituents of soya (and to a lesser extent, other pulses) may also have anti-cancer properties, although these are less well demonstrated.

The evidence, mostly from case-control studies, is inconsistent. There is limited evidence suggesting that pulses (legumes), including soya and soya products, protect against stomach cancer.

7.5.5.5 Foods containing selenium

(Also see chapter 4.2.5.8.)

One case-control study and 5 ecological studies investigated dietary selenium; 3 cohort studies, 9 case-control studies and 3 ecological studies investigated blood selenium; and 1 cohort study and 1 case-control study investigated selenium in toenails or hair. All of the studies for blood, nail, or hair selenium levels showed decreased risk with increased selenium intake. Meta-analysis of cohort data showed a non-significant decreased risk, and meta-analysis of case-control data produced statistically significant evidence of decreased risk.

Dietary selenium deficiency has been shown to cause a lack of selenoprotein expression. Twenty-five selenoproteins have been identified in animals and a number of these have important anti-inflammatory and antioxidant properties. Four are glutathione peroxidases, which protect against oxidative damage to biomolecules such as lipids, lipoproteins, and DNA. Three are thioredoxin reductases, which, among other functions, regenerate oxidised ascorbic acid to its active antioxidant form. Selenoproteins with powerful antioxidant activity may provide protection against the inflammatory effect of *H pylori* that can lead to gastric cancer in infected individuals.

A substantial amount of evidence was available on selenium, from dietary questionnaires as well as blood, nails, and hair, mostly from case-control studies. There is limited evidence suggesting that foods containing selenium protect against stomach cancer.

7.5.5.6 Chilli

(Also see chapter 4.2.5.12.1.)

Fourteen case-control studies investigated chilli use. Most of these reported increased risk with increased use, although results were heterogeneous and data were not suitable for meta-analysis.

Anecdotally, chilli may be used to disguise 'off' flavours in foods, so these data may be confounded by socioeconomic status, the availability of refrigeration, and *H pylori* infection.

Some constituents of chilli are irritants, which could therefore plausibly increase inflammation in the stomach (also see chapter 2.4.1.3).

The evidence, from case-control studies only, is inconsistent. There is limited evidence suggesting that chilli is associated with an increased risk of stomach cancer.

7.5.5.7 Processed meat

(Also see chapter 4.3.5.1.2.)

Eight cohort studies, 21 case-control studies, 1 cross-sectional study, and 1 ecological study investigated processed meat. Most of these showed increased risk with higher intake. Meta-analysis of cohort data showed a non- significant relationship with increased risk. Meta-analysis of case-control data produced evidence of a statistically significant dose-response relationship. Heterogeneity is likely to be caused by the diverse nature of definitions for processed meat in different studies.

Nitrates are produced endogenously in gastric acid, and are added as preservatives to processed meats. They may contribute to N-nitroso compound production and exposure. N-nitroso compounds are suspected mutagens and carcinogens (see box 4.3.2).[55] Many processed meats also contain high levels of salt and nitrite. Meats cooked at high temperatures can contain heterocyclic amines and polycyclic aromatic hydrocarbons (see box 4.3.4). Haem promotes the formation of N-nitroso compounds and also contains iron. Free iron can lead to the production of free radicals (see box 4.3.3).

The evidence is inconsistent. There is limited evidence suggesting that processed meat is a cause of stomach cancer.

The Panel is aware that since the conclusion of the SLR, one cohort[98] and two case-control studies[95 99] have been published. This new information does not change the Panel judgement. Also see box 3.8.

7.5.5.8 Smoked foods
(Also see chapter 4.3.5.7.)
Seventeen case-control studies and two ecological studies investigated smoked foods. Most of these showed increased risk with increased intake, with none reporting statistically significant reduced risk.

Definitions of smoked foods varied between studies, although most included smoked meats and/or fish. Smoked foods are often salted. High rates of mortality from stomach cancer are found in countries such as Iceland, Hungary, and Latvia, where diets include a regular intake of meat and/or fish preserved by smoking.

Smoked foods, particularly meats, may contain polycyclic aromatic hydrocarbons, depending on the fuel burned to produce the smoke.[100] (Also see box 4.3.4.) Smoked meats are also often salted or cured, meaning that they are likely to raise endogenous production of N-nitroso compounds in the stomach (see box 4.3.2). These are suspected causes of stomach cancer.

There is limited evidence from case-control and ecological studies, some of which were of poor quality, that smoked foods are causes of stomach cancer.

The Panel is aware that since the conclusion of the SLR, three case-control studies[95 96 99] have been published. This new information does not change the Panel judgement. Also see box 3.8.

7.5.5.9 Grilled (broiled) or barbecued (charbroiled) animal foods
(Also see chapter 4.3.5.8.)
Three cohort studies and 12 case-control studies investigated grilled (broiled) or barbecued (charbroiled) foods (these were predominantly meats or fish, although not all studies specified the foods studied). Most studies showed increased risk with increased intake.

Cooking methods involving grilling above a heat source and barbecuing can produce marked differences in levels of carcinogens in foods cooked in these ways (see chapter 4.9.4). For example, fat dripping on hot surfaces can form polycyclic aromatic hydrocarbons and heterocyclic amines (see box 4.3.4), while oven grilling prevents this from happening, resulting in much lower levels of these compounds in the cooked foods.

There is limited, inconsistent evidence, mostly from case-control studies, that grilled (broiled) or barbecued (charbroiled) animal foods are causes of stomach cancer.

7.5.5.10 Salt
(Also see chapter 4.6.5.2.)
Three cohort studies, 21 case-control studies, and 12 ecological studies investigated total salt use. Other groupings examined were salt added at the table (2 cohort, 13 case-control) and sodium intake (1 cohort, 8 case-control). Most studies showed increased risk with increased intake, but there is some unexplained heterogeneity. Meta-analysis of case-control data showed an 18 per cent increased risk per gram of sodium per day; the meta-analyses for total salt indicated increased risk but were not statistically significant (figure 4.6.1).

Assessment of salt intake is complicated as the small proportion added during preparation or at the table is very variable and difficult to quantify. Higher-quality studies, which are better adjusted, tend to report a greater or more significant effect. However, residual confounding is possible: salt intake may be inversely related to the availability of refrigeration in a population, and so to socioeconomic status, which is itself related to stomach cancer risk.

Salt has been shown to directly damage the stomach lining in animal trials. It has also been shown to increase endogenous N-nitroso compound formation (see box 4.3.2). Salt may enhance the action of carcinogens in the stomach. In addition, salt intake may facilitate H pylori infection.[101]

There is a substantial amount of evidence from studies on total salt use, salt added at the table, and sodium intake. For total salt use, a dose-response relationship was apparent from cohort but not case-control studies. For sodium intake, a dose response was also apparent from case-control studies. The mechanistic evidence is strong. Salt is a probable cause of stomach cancer.

The Panel is aware that since the conclusion of the SLR, one cohort[102] and two case-control studies[95 99] have been published. This new information does not change the Panel judgement. Also see box 3.8.

7.5.5.11 Salted and salty foods
(Also see chapter 4.6.5.2.1.)
Four cohort studies, 17 case-control studies, and 1 ecological study investigated salty or salted foods. Nearly all of the

studies showed increased risk with increased intake. Meta-analysis of cohort data showed a non-significant increased risk; meta-analysis of case-control data showed a 5.2-fold increased risk per serving per day (figure 4.6.2). Heterogeneity may be partly explained by variation between studies in the precise foods being assessed.

As stated above, assessment of salt intake is complicated. Again, higher-quality studies report a greater or more significant effect.

Again, salt has been shown to directly damage the stomach lining in animal trials. It has also been shown to increase endogenous N-nitroso compound formation (see box 4.3.2).

The evidence, both from case-control and cohort studies, is consistent. A dose-response relationship is apparent from case-control but not cohort studies. There is robust evidence for mechanisms operating in humans. Salted and salty foods are probable causes of stomach cancer.

The Panel is aware that since the conclusion of the SLR, two case-control studies[95] [99] have been published. This new information does not change the Panel judgement. Also see box 3.8.

7.5.5.12 Other exposures

Other exposures were evaluated. However, the data were either of too low quality, too inconsistent, or the number of studies too few to allow conclusions to be reached. These were as follows: cereals (grains) and their products; starchy roots, potatoes, and other tubers; plantains; nuts and seeds; herbs, spices, and condiments; meat; poultry; eggs; fats and oils; milk and dairy products; sugar; fruit juices; coffee; tea; alcohol; nitrosodimethylamine/dietary nitrate/nitrite; drying or dried food; dietary fibre; sugars; total fat; fatty acid composition; cholesterol; protein; carotenoids; thiamin; riboflavin; vitamin C; vitamin D; multivitamin/mineral supplements; selenium supplements; iron; calcium; energy intake; body fatness; culturally defined diets; meal frequency; and eating speed.

7.5.6 Comparison with previous report

7.5.6.1 General
See 7.1.6.1, and box 3.8.

7.5.6.2 Specific
The previous report judged the evidence that vegetables and fruits protect against stomach cancer to be convincing. Since then, the evidence from cohort studies has been rather equivocal, whereas evidence from case-control studies remains strong and consistent. Previously, the compounds found in allium vegetables were judged possibly to protect against stomach cancer; more recent evidence for allium vegetables is stronger.

The previous report found the evidence that refrigeration protects against stomach cancer to be convincing. Also see box 4.6.4.

Before the mid-1990s there were no published trials of selenium supplements. Two trials are now available, as well as increased numbers of cohort and case-control studies, but the evidence is still limited and only suggestive of a protective effect.

7.5.7 Conclusions

The Panel concludes:
Non-starchy vegetables, and specifically allium vegetables, as well as fruits probably protect against stomach cancer.

Salt and salt-preserved foods are probably causes of this cancer.

There is limited evidence suggesting that pulses (legumes) including soya and soya products and foods containing selenium protect against stomach cancer.

There is also limited evidence suggesting that chilli, processed meat, smoked foods, and grilled (broiled) and barbecued (charbroiled) animal foods are causes of stomach cancer.

Infection with the bacterium *H pylori* is a necessary but not sufficient cause of stomach cancer.

7.6 Pancreas

Cancer of the pancreas is the thirteenth most common type of cancer worldwide. About 230 000 cases were recorded in 2002, accounting for around 2 per cent of cancers overall. The incidence is somewhat more common in men than in women. It is generally increasing, particularly in high-income countries, where it is most frequent. It is rare in Africa and Asia. This cancer is almost always fatal and is the ninth most common cause of cancer death.

Overall, *the Panel is impressed* by the strength of the evidence that body fatness, abdominal fatness, and the factors that lead to greater adult attained height, or its consequences, are causes of cancer of the pancreas.

The Panel judges as follows:
The evidence that body fatness is a cause of cancer of the pancreas is convincing; abdominal fatness is probably a cause of this cancer.

Foods containing folate probably protect against this cancer.

The factors that lead to greater adult attained height, or its consequences, are probably a cause of pancreatic cancer.

It is unlikely that coffee has any substantial effect on the risk of this cancer.

There is limited evidence suggesting that fruits and physical activity protect against this cancer, and that red meat is a cause of this cancer.

See chapter 8 for evidence and judgements on factors that modify the risk of body fatness and abdominal fatness, including physical activity and sedentary ways of life, the energy density of foods and drinks, and breastfeeding.

Tobacco smoking is an established cause of this cancer.

In final summary, the strongest evidence, corresponding to judgements of "convincing" and "probable", shows that body fatness and (probably) abdominal fatness are both causes of cancer of the pancreas, and that the factors that lead to greater adult attained height, or its consequences, are probably also a cause of this cancer. Foods containing folate are probably protective. It is unlikely that coffee has any substantial effect on the risk of this cancer.

The pancreas is an elongated gland located behind the stomach. It contains two types of tissue, exocrine and endocrine. The exocrine pancreas produces digestive enzymes that are secreted into the small intestine. Cells in the endocrine pancreas produce hormones including insulin and glucagon, which influence glucose metabolism.

Over 95 per cent of pancreatic cancers are adenocarcinomas of the exocrine pancreas, the type included in this Report.

FOOD, NUTRITION, PHYSICAL ACTIVITY, AND CANCER OF THE PANCREAS

In the judgement of the Panel, the factors listed below modify the risk of cancer of the pancreas. Judgements are graded according to the strength of the evidence.

	DECREASES RISK	INCREASES RISK
Convincing		**Body fatness**
Probable	**Foods containing folate[1]**	**Abdominal fatness** **Adult attained height[2]**
Limited — suggestive	Fruits[3] Physical activity[4]	Red meat[5]
Limited — no conclusion	Cereal (grains) and their products; dietary fibre; vegetables; pulses (legumes); soya and soya products; processed meat; poultry; fish; eggs; milk and dairy products; total fat; butter; plant oils; margarine; cholesterol; sugar (sucrose); black tea; green tea; alcohol; nitrate and nitrite; total carbohydrate; folic acid supplements; vitamin C; vegetarianism; age at menarche; lactation; energy intake	
Substantial effect on risk unlikely	Coffee	

1 Includes both foods naturally containing the constituent and foods which have the constituent added (see chapter 3.5.3).
2 Adult attained height is unlikely directly to modify the risk of cancer. It is a marker for genetic, environmental, hormonal, and also nutritional factors affecting growth during the period from preconception to completion of linear growth (see chapter 6.2.1.3).
3 Judgements on vegetables and fruits do not include those preserved by salting and/or pickling.
4 Physical activity of all types: occupational, household, transport, and recreational.
5 The term 'red meat' refers to beef, pork, lamb, and goat from domesticated animals.

For an explanation of all the terms used in the matrix, please see chapter 3.5.1, the text of this section, and the glossary.

7.6.1 Trends, incidence, and survival

Age-adjusted rates of pancreatic cancer have been generally stable since the 1970s, following an approximate three-fold rise over the preceding 50 years in the countries for which data are available.[103 104]

This is mainly a disease of high-income countries, where overall rates are nearly three times higher than in middle- and low-income countries. Around the world, age-adjusted incidence rates range from 10–15 per 100 000 people in parts of northern, central, and eastern Europe to less than 1 per 100 000 in areas of Africa and Asia, although rates are relatively high in some countries in these areas, for example, Japan and Korea. In the USA, rates are higher among African-American people than in white people.[3] The risk of pancreatic cancer increases with age, with most diagnoses made in people between the ages of 60 and 80.

The early stages of this cancer do not usually produce symptoms, so the disease is generally advanced when it is diagnosed. Survival rates are therefore low — around 4 per cent at 5 years. This cancer accounts for around 2 per cent of all cancer incidence, but somewhat over 3 per cent of all cancer deaths.[4] Also see box 7.1.1.

7.6.2 Pathogenesis

The ductal cells in the head of the pancreas are exposed to pancreatic secretions, as well as bile, and environmental carcinogens can reach these cells through those fluids or in the blood (see 7.7).

The pancreas is relatively inaccessible to routine medical examination, so the progression of this cancer through precursor lesions is not well understood. However, inflammation is implicated in this process through chronic pancreatitis, which is a risk factor for pancreatic cancer. The role of infection with *H pylori* (see box 7.5.1) is the subject of ongoing research.[105] Conditions that lead to high insulin levels in pancreatic secretions, such as insulin resistance and type 2 diabetes, may increase the risk of this cancer.[106]

More than 90 per cent of pancreatic cancer cases are sporadic (due to spontaneous rather than inherited mutations), although a family history increases risk, particularly where more than one family member is involved.[105] Around 75–90 per cent of pancreatic cancer cases involve a point mutation in the K-ras oncogene[107] (see box 2.2 in chapter 2).

7.6.3 Other established causes

(Also see chapters 2.4 and 7.1.3.1.)

Tobacco use. Approximately 25 per cent of cases of pancreatic cancer are attributable to tobacco smoking.

7.6.4 Interpretation of the evidence

7.6.4.1 General
For general considerations that may affect interpretation of the evidence, see chapters 3.3 and 3.5, and boxes 3.1, 3.2, 3.6 and 3.7.

'Relative risk' is used in this Report to denote ratio measures of effect, including 'risk ratios', 'rate ratios', 'hazard ratios', and 'odds ratios'.

7.6.4.2 Specific
Considerations specific to cancer of the pancreas include:

Measurement. Owing to very low survival rates, both incidence and mortality can be assessed. Low survival times and

rates decrease the reliability of case-control studies, which often rely on proxy reporting.

Confounding. High-quality studies adjust for smoking.

7.6.5 Evidence and judgements

In total, 318 publications were included in the SLR for this cancer. Fuller summaries of the epidemiological, experimental, and mechanistic evidence are in Chapters 4–6.

The full SLR is contained on the CD included with this Report.

7.6.5.1 Fruits
(Also see chapter 4.2.5.2.)
Six cohort studies, 16 case-control studies, and 8 ecological studies investigated fruits. All cohort studies and most other studies showed decreased risk with increased intake. Meta-analysis of cohort data showed a non-significant decreased risk. Meta-analysis of case-control data showed a statistically significant decreased risk.

Fruits are sources of vitamin C and other antioxidants, such as carotenoids, phenols, and flavonoids, as well as other potentially bioactive phytochemicals. Antioxidants trap free radicals and reactive oxygen molecules, protecting against oxidation damage. In addition, flavonoids found in fruit directly inhibit the expression of the cytochrome P450 enzyme, which helps to metabolise toxins and has been associated with increased risk of lung cancer, primarily in smokers.[68] It is difficult to unravel the relative importance of each constituent and is likely that a protective effect may result from a combination of influences on several pathways involved in carcinogenesis.

> **The evidence is inconsistent. There is limited evidence suggesting that fruits protect against pancreatic cancer.**

The Panel is aware that since the conclusion of the SLR, one cohort study[108] has been published. This new information does not change the Panel judgement. Also see box 3.8.

7.6.5.2 Foods containing folate
(Also see chapter 4.2.5.4.)
Three cohort studies, two case-control studies, and one ecological study investigated folate from foods and/or folic acid from supplements. Meta-analysis of all three cohort studies showed a non-significant decreased risk, with high heterogeneity. When stratified according to the source, both dietary studies showed a non-significant decreased risk, and three studies of supplements showed a non-significant increased risk. One cohort study also analysed serum folate levels, showing a significant decreased risk of 55 per cent for the highest levels compared with the lowest. Both the case-control studies and the ecological study showed decreased risk with increased intake. Folic acid supplements do not show a protective effect.

Folate plays an important role in the synthesis and repair of DNA. There is a known interaction between folate and alcohol and the risk of some cancers (see chapter 4.8). Folate intake is strongly correlated with intake of non-starchy polysaccharide or dietary fibre.

> The evidence available is sparse but a dose-response relationship was apparent from cohort studies. There is limited evidence suggesting that foods containing folate protect against pancreatic cancer.

The Panel is aware that since the conclusion of the SLR, one cohort study[109] has been published. This new information does not change the Panel judgement. Also see box 3.8.

7.6.5.3 Red meat

(Also see chapter 4.3.5.1.1.)
Seven cohort studies and four case-control studies investigated red meat. Nearly all of the studies showed increased risk with increased intake.

Red meat contains haem iron. Free iron can lead to the production of free radicals (see box 4.3.3). When cooked at high temperatures, red meat can also contain heterocyclic amines and polycyclic aromatic hydrocarbons (see box 4.3.4).

> Evidence from cohort studies is less consistent than that from case-control studies. There is limited evidence suggesting that red meat is a cause of pancreatic cancer.

The Panel is aware that since the conclusion of the SLR, one cohort study[110] has been published. This new information does not change the Panel judgement. Also see box 3.8.

7.6.5.4 Coffee

(Also see chapter 4.7.5.4.)
Eighteen cohort studies, 37 case-control studies, and 11 ecological studies investigated coffee. Analysis of cohort data showed an effect estimate close to null with low heterogeneity. Data for case-control studies were less consistent.

> There is ample evidence, including prospective data, which is consistent and with low heterogeneity, and which fails to show an association. It is unlikely that coffee has a substantial effect on the risk of pancreatic cancer.

7.6.5.5 Physical activity

(Also see chapter 5.4.5.)
A total of three cohort studies and one case-control study investigated total physical activity; three cohort studies and two case-control studies investigated occupational activity; and nine cohort studies and three case-control studies investigated recreational activity. Several studies also examined walking and transportation. Most of the studies showed decreased risk with increased physical activity, though there was heterogeneity in the direction of effect and no clear dose-response relationship.

Sustained moderate physical activity raises the metabolic rate and increases maximal oxygen uptake. In the long term, regular periods of such activity increase the body's metabolic

efficiency and capacity (the amount of work that it can perform), as well as reducing blood pressure and insulin resistance. In addition, low levels of physical activity decrease gastrointestinal transit times. This alters bile content and secretion, as well as affecting pancreatic activity.[111]

> There is evidence from prospective studies showing lower risk of pancreatic cancer with higher levels of various types of physical activity, but it is rather inconsistent. There is limited evidence suggesting that physical activity protects against pancreatic cancer.

The Panel is aware that since the conclusion of the SLR, one cohort study[112] has been published. This new information does not change the Panel judgement. Also see box 3.8.

7.6.5.6 Body fatness

(Also see chapter 6.1.3.1.)
Twenty-three cohort studies and 15 case-control studies investigated body fatness, as measured by BMI. Most cohort studies showed increased risk with increased body fatness, but case-control studies were inconsistent. Meta-analysis of cohort data showed a 14 per cent increased risk per 5 kg/m^2 (figure 6.1.4). Heterogeneity appeared to be explained by a number of studies failing to adjust for smoking, which is separately associated with both BMI and pancreatic cancer.

It is biologically plausible that body fatness is a cause of pancreatic cancer. There is an established connection between increasing BMI or body fatness and insulin resistance and diabetes. The risk of this cancer is increased in people with insulin resistance or diabetes. It also directly affects levels of many circulating hormones, such as insulin, insulin-like growth factors, and oestrogens, creating an environment that encourages carcinogenesis and discourages apoptosis (see box 2.4). Body fatness stimulates the inflammatory response, which may contribute to the initiation and progression of several cancers (see chapter 2.4.1.3).

> There is ample epidemiological evidence, which is generally consistent, and there is a dose-response relationship. There is evidence for plausible mechanisms that operate in humans. The evidence that greater body fatness is a cause of pancreatic cancer is convincing.

The Panel is aware that since the conclusion of the SLR, two cohort studies[58][112] have been published. This new information does not change the Panel judgement. Also see box 3.8.

7.6.5.7 Abdominal fatness

(Also see chapter 6.1.3.2.)
Three cohort studies investigated waist circumference, two cohort studies investigated waist to hip ratio, and one cohort study investigated patterns of weight gain, all of which showed increased risk with increasing measures of abdominal fatness. Half of all studies were statistically significant.

The general mechanisms through which abdominal fatness could plausibly cause cancer are outlined in chapter 6.1.3 (also see box 2.4). The hormonal and other biological effects of being overweight or obese are outlined in chapter 8. Many of these, such as increased circulating oestrogens and decreased insulin sensitivity, are associated with abdominal fatness independently of overall body fatness.

> **There is a substantial amount of epidemiological evidence that is generally consistent, and there is evidence for plausible mechanisms. Abdominal fatness is a probable cause of pancreatic cancer.**

The Panel is aware that since the conclusion of the SLR, one cohort study[112] has been published. This new information does not change the Panel judgement. Also see box 3.8.

7.6.5.8 Adult attained height

(Also see chapter 6.2.3.1.)

Eight cohort studies, 12 case-control studies, and 1 ecological study investigated adult attained height. Most cohort studies and the single ecological study showed increased risk with greater adult attained height. Case-control studies were inconsistent. Meta-analysis of cohort data showed an 11 per cent increased risk per 5 cm of height (figure 6.2.5). There was considerable heterogeneity in case-control data, not all readily explained. However, the cohort studies showed a linear dose-response relationship (figure 6.2.6).

The general mechanisms through which the factors that lead to greater adult attained height, or its consequences, could plausibly influence cancer risk are outlined in chapter 6.2.1.3 (for more detail see box 2.4). Many of these, such as early-life nutrition, altered hormone profiles, and the rate of sexual maturation, could plausibly increase cancer risk.

> **There is ample prospective epidemiological evidence, though there is some inconsistency. There is evidence for a dose-response relationship, and evidence for plausible mechanisms. The factors that lead to greater adult attained height, or its consequences, are probably a cause of pancreatic cancer. The causal factor is unlikely to be tallness itself, but factors that promote linear growth in childhood.**

The Panel is aware that since the conclusion of the SLR, one cohort study[112] has been published. This new information does not change the Panel judgement. Also see box 3.8.

7.6.5.9 Other exposures

Other exposures were evaluated. However, the data were either of too low quality, too inconsistent, or the number of studies too few to allow conclusions to be reached. These were as follows: cereals (grains) and their products; vegetables; pulses (legumes); soya and soya products; processed meat; poultry; fish; eggs; milk and dairy products; butter; margarine; black tea; green tea; alcoholic drinks; nitrate/nitrite; total carbohydrate; dietary fibre; sucrose; total fat; cholesterol; folic acid supplements; plant oils; energy intake; age at menarche; vegetarianism; and lactation.

In the case of alcoholic drinks, although low-to-moderate levels of drinking were unlikely to have an effect on risk, it could not be excluded that heavy drinking might have an effect.

7.6.6 Comparison with previous report

7.6.6.1 General

See 7.1.6.1, and box 3.8 in chapter 3.

7.6.6.2 Specific

Apart from vegetables and fruits, the strongest evidence and judgements here are remarkably different from the previous report. Much of the evidence on body fatness, abdominal fatness, attained adult height (tallness), and physical activity is recent.

7.6.7 Conclusions

The Panel concludes:

The evidence that body fatness is a cause of cancer of the pancreas is convincing; abdominal fatness is probably a cause of this cancer.

Foods containing folate (but not folic acid supplements) probably protect against pancreatic cancer.

The factors that lead to greater adult attained height, or its consequences, are probably a cause of this cancer. Greater height is unlikely to directly modify the risk of cancer; it is a marker for genetic, environmental, hormonal, and also nutritional factors affecting growth during the period from preconception to completion of linear growth.

It is unlikely that coffee has any substantial effect on risk. There is limited evidence suggesting that fruits and also physical activity protect against this cancer, and that red meat is a cause of this cancer.

7.7 Gallbladder

Cancer of the gallbladder accounts for somewhat over 2 per cent of all cancer incidence and rates are generally declining. The highest rates occur in eastern Asia and eastern Europe, but it is rare in Africa. This cancer is usually fatal and is the 17th most common cause of cancer death.

The Panel judges as follows:
Body fatness is probably a cause of cancer of the gallbladder and people with gallstones are more likely to develop gallbladder cancer.

See chapter 8 for evidence and judgements on factors that modify the risk of body fatness, including physical activity and sedentary ways of life, the energy density of foods and drinks, and breastfeeding.

In final summary, the strongest evidence, corresponding to judgements of "convincing" and "probable", shows that body fatness is probably a cause of gallbladder cancer, both directly and indirectly, through the formation of gallstones.

The gallbladder is a small sac-like organ that forms part of the biliary tract. Bile, produced in the liver, flows into the gallbladder, where it is stored and concentrated until released into the small intestine.

More than 90 per cent of gallbladder cancers are adeno-carcinomas, while only a small proportion are squamous cell carcinomas.[4]

FOOD, NUTRITION, PHYSICAL ACTIVITY, AND CANCER OF THE GALLBLADDER

In the judgement of the Panel, the factors listed below modify the risk of cancer of the gallbladder. Judgements are graded according to the strength of the evidence.

	DECREASES RISK	INCREASES RISK
Convincing		
Probable		**Body fatness[1]**
Limited — suggestive		
Limited — no conclusion		Peppers (capsicums); fish; coffee; tea; alcohol; vitamin C.
Substantial effect on risk unlikely		None identified

1   Directly and indirectly, through the formation of gallstones.

For an explanation of all the terms used in the matrix, please see chapter 3.5.1, the text of this section, and the glossary.

World Cancer Research Fund / American Institute for Cancer Research

7.7.1 Trends, incidence, and survival

Age-adjusted rates of gallbladder cancer are decreasing.[1] Even in many of the countries where incidence had been relatively high, such as in eastern Asia and eastern Europe, rates have decreased and continued to fall, following a dramatic rise in the 1970s and 1980s.

There is no clear geographical pattern to the distribution of gallbladder cancer. Age-adjusted incidence rates range from 5–10 per 100 000 people in parts of eastern Asia and eastern Europe to less than 1 per 100 000 in parts of Africa. In the USA, rates are higher among both Native- and Hispanic-American people than in white people.[113] Around most of the world, gallbladder cancer is slightly more common in women than men. In Japan and Korea, this trend is reversed, with around 60 per cent of cases in men.[103] Risk increases with age, with more than two thirds of cases occurring in people aged 65 years or older.[114]

Gallbladder cancer is usually advanced at diagnosis. Survival rates are poor: at 5 years less than 12 per cent for advanced disease, but this is much higher (by up to 20 per cent) when the cancer is caught early. Gallbladder cancer accounts for just over 2 per cent of all cancer incidence, and the same proportion of all cancer deaths. Also see box 7.1.1.

7.7.2 Pathogenesis

The pathogenesis of gallbladder cancer is not well understood, partly because it is often diagnosed at a late stage.

Having gallstones increases the risk of this cancer. The associated inflammation decreases the speed at which bile empties from the gallbladder; gallstones may also have a direct effect by blocking the transit of bile.[115] Gallstones, like gallbladder cancers, are more common in women than men, and the risk of cancer is proportional to the size of the gallstones.[116] However, other factors must also be involved: in high-income countries up to 1 person in 10 has gallstones (many asymptomatic),[117] whereas gallbladder cancer is diagnosed in only around 1 in 50 000.

Many toxins, whether they come from diet, smoke inhalation, or other environmental sources (and their metabolic products) are excreted and concentrated in the bile.

Early stages of the disease include plaque-like lesions and small ulcerations in the mucosal lining of the gallbladder, which are associated with chronic inflammation (cholecystitis). This may progress to carcinoma in situ, and then to invasive tumours. This process probably takes at least 20 years (cholecystitis is seldom seen in people under 40), hence the age profile of gallbladder cancer. Chronic inflammation caused by other factors (such as in 'porcelain gallbladder' or from chronic bacterial infection) may be a necessary stage in the development of gallbladder cancer, although the evidence is not conclusive.[4] [118] [119]

A congenital deformity to the pancreatic ducts is associated with most gallbladder cancers in eastern Asia.[120] This may account for the different epidemiology in this region, and could imply a distinct pathogenesis with different risk factors. Mutations of the tumour-suppressor p53 gene are frequent in gallbladder cancers (see box 2.2).[121]

7.7.3 Other established causes

(Also see chapter 2.4 and 7.1.3.1 of this chapter.)

Other diseases. Having gallstones increases the risk of gallbladder cancer and can be identified as a cause of this cancer.

Other causes are not established; see 7.7.2.

7.7.4 Interpretation of the evidence

7.7.4.1 General
For general considerations that may affect interpretation of the evidence, see chapters 3.3 and 3.5, and boxes 3.1, 3.2, 3.6 and 3.7.

'Relative risk' is used in this Report to denote ratio measures of effect, including 'risk ratios', 'rate ratios', 'hazard ratios', and 'odds ratios'.

7.7.4.2 Specific
Considerations specific to cancer of the gallbladder include:

Confounding. Having gallstones increases the risk of gallbladder cancer. Exposures with an apparent link to gallbladder cancer may act indirectly, through gallstones, or directly, either after gallstone formation or in their absence. It is not yet possible to separate these effects. See 7.7.7.

7.7.5 Evidence and judgements

In total, 48 publications were included in the SLR for gallbladder cancer. Fuller summaries of the epidemiological, experimental, and mechanistic evidence are to be found in Chapters 4–6.

The full SLR is contained on the CD included with this Report.

7.7.5.1 Body fatness
(Also see chapter 6.1.3.1.)
Five cohort studies, seven case-control studies, and two cross-sectional studies investigated body fatness, as measured by BMI. Most studies showed increased risk with increased body fatness. Meta-analysis of cohort data showed a 23 per cent increased risk per 5 kg/m^2; meta-analysis of

case-control data showed a 19 per cent increased risk per 5 kg/m^2. Heterogeneity could be partly attributed to differences in the study participants' ethnicity or sex, or to the number of adjustments made in the study.

Body fatness directly affects levels of many circulating hormones, such as insulin, insulin-like growth factors, and oestrogens, creating an environment that encourages carcinogenesis and discourages apoptosis (see box 2.4). It also stimulates the body's inflammatory response, which may contribute to the initiation and progression of several cancers (see chapter 2.4.1.3). In addition, obesity is a known cause of gallstone formation, and having gallstones increases the risk of gallbladder cancer, possibly through bile cholesterol supersaturation.

Because having gallstones is a cause of gallbladder cancer, *the Panel also reviewed* the dietary causes of gallstones, especially in relation to body fatness. Having a relatively high BMI increases the risk of gallstones in a linear fashion; waist circumference is associated with gallstone risk in men, independently of BMI. Gallstone formation is associated with repeated dieting, especially where it involves rapid weight loss, such as that from very low-energy diets and bariatric surgery.

> **There is a substantial amount of generally consistent epidemiological evidence with some evidence of a dose-response relationship. There is evidence for several plausible mechanisms. Greater body fatness is a probable cause of gallbladder cancer, directly and also indirectly through the formation of gallstones.**

7.7.5.2 Other exposures
Other exposures were evaluated. However, the data were either of too low quality, too inconsistent, or the number of studies too few to allow conclusions to be reached. These included capsicums, fish, coffee, tea, alcohol, and vitamin C.

7.7.6 Comparison with previous report

7.7.6.1 General
See 7.1.6.1, and box 3.8 of chapter 3.

7.7.6.2 Specific
Since publication of the previous report, the evidence that body fatness is an indirect and a direct cause of gallbladder cancer has strengthened.

7.7.7 Conclusions

The Panel concludes:
Greater body fatness is probably a cause of cancer of the gallbladder. People with gallstones are more likely to develop gallbladder cancer.

7.8 Liver

Cancer of the liver is the sixth most common type of cancer worldwide. Around 625 000 cases were recorded in 2002, accounting for around 6 per cent of all cancers. About half of all cases occur in China, and it is more common in middle- and low-income countries. It is almost always fatal, and is the third most common cause of death from cancer, accounting for around 9 per cent of all deaths.

Overall, *the Panel notes* that toxic compounds are the main causes of primary liver cancer related to foods and drinks.

The Panel judges as follows:
The evidence that aflatoxins, which contaminate mostly cereals (grains) and pulses (legumes) stored in hot, wet conditions, are a cause of liver cancer is convincing. Alcoholic drinks are probably a direct cause of this cancer. There is limited evidence suggesting that fruits are protective, and that body fatness is a cause of this cancer.

Other causes of this cancer include infection with hepatitis viruses B or C, the development of cirrhosis from any cause, and infestation with liver flukes.

In final summary, the strongest evidence, corresponding to judgements of "convincing" and "probable", shows that aflatoxins, and probably alcoholic drinks, are causes of liver cancer.

The liver is the body's largest organ. It processes and stores nutrients, and produces cholesterol and proteins such as albumin, clotting factors, and the lipoproteins that carry cholesterol. It also secretes bile and performs many metabolic functions, including detoxification of several classes of carcinogen.

Different types of tumour occur in the liver. Each has potentially different causes and natural history. Around 75–90 per cent of liver cancers are hepatocellular carcinoma. This starts in hepatocytes, which are the commonest type of liver cell, and has various subtypes. Cholangiocarcinomas account for 10–20 per cent of primary liver cancers. These cancers start in the small bile ducts (tubes that carry bile to the gallbladder) within the liver. Hepatoblastoma and angiosarcoma are less common types of liver cancer. Hepatocellular carcinoma is the main type included here. Secondary tumours of the liver are not included.

FOOD, NUTRITION, PHYSICAL ACTIVITY, AND CANCER OF THE LIVER

In the judgement of the Panel, the factors listed below modify the risk of cancer of the liver. Judgements are graded according to the strength of the evidence.

	DECREASES RISK	INCREASES RISK
Convincing		**Aflatoxins¹**
Probable		**Alcoholic drinks²**
Limited — suggestive	Fruits³	Body fatness
Limited — no conclusion	Cereals (grains) and their products¹; non-starchy vegetables; peanuts (groundnuts)¹; fish; salted fish; water source; coffee; tea	
Substantial effect on risk unlikely	None identified	

1   Foods that may be contaminated with aflatoxins include cereals (grains), and also pulses (legumes), seeds, nuts, and some vegetables and fruits (see chapter 4.2).
2   Cirrhosis is an essential precursor of liver cancer caused by alcohol. The International Agency for Research on Cancer has graded alcohol as a Class 1 carcinogen for liver cancer. Alcohol alone only causes cirrhosis in the presence of other susceptibility factors.
3   Judgements on vegetables and fruits do not include those preserved by salting and/or pickling.

For an explanation of all the terms used in the matrix, please see chapter 3.5.1, the text of this section, and the glossary.

7.8.1 Trends, incidence, and survival

Age-adjusted rates of liver cancer are either increasing or stable in most countries for which data are available.[6][122] However, a recent report on trends in the USA between 1975 and 2001 suggested that these increases may now be reversing.[3]

This is predominantly a disease of middle- to low-income countries, where overall rates are more than double those in high-income countries. Around the world, age-adjusted incidence rates range from more than 40 per 100 000 people in eastern Asia and parts of Africa to less than 5 per 100 000 in the Americas and northern Europe.[2] In the USA, rates are higher among African-American and Hispanic-American people, and Asian and Pacific Islanders, than in white people.[3] Globally, rates are higher in men than women by five to two.

Risk tends to increase with age, although the disease develops at a younger age (typically around the age of 40, or below) in people living in Asia and Africa compared with those in high-income countries.[123]

Box 7.8.1 Hepatitis viruses

Hepatitis B and hepatitis C viruses are causes of liver cancer. The former appears to act directly by damaging cells and their DNA. The latter shows an indirect effect, mediated by cirrhosis. For both, there is potential for nutrition status to have an effect at several stages: susceptibility to and duration of infection, liver damage, DNA damage, and cancer progression.[129]

Around 7–8 per cent of the world's population is estimated to be infected with hepatitis B virus. It is mostly spread by blood and sexual transmission. In endemic areas, the carrier rate may be 10–20 per cent.[130] It is often acquired at birth or in childhood, and is endemic in areas of Africa and Asia. Chronic hepatitis B virus carriers have a 100-fold greater chance of developing liver cancer than non-carriers. Those infected in adulthood have a lower risk of this cancer than those infected in childhood because there is less time for the virus to cause inflammation.[130] Vaccination against hepatitis B virus has been shown to reduce the prevalence of liver cancer by 60 per cent.[131]

Liver cancer in hepatitis B virus carriers is not necessarily connected with cirrhosis: up to 40 per cent of associated liver cancer cases are non-cirrhotic. Hepatitis B virus carries its genetic code as DNA rather than RNA. Viral DNA can insert itself into liver cells and alter their DNA.

Around 3 per cent of the world's population is estimated to be infected with hepatitis C virus. It is more prevalent in high-income countries. Approximately 80 per cent of these infections become chronic, of which 15–20 per cent develops into cirrhosis. Of those, 1–4 per cent develops into liver cancer each year. Interruption of the sequence of chronic hepatitis developing into cirrhosis prevents liver cancer. Also, there is an interaction between hepatitis C virus infection, liver cancer risk, and consumption of alcoholic drinks.[132] There is no vaccine against hepatitis C. It is mostly spread by blood.

The early stages of liver cancer do not usually produce symptoms, so the disease is generally advanced when it is diagnosed. Survival rates are poor: at 5 years, approximately 5 per cent.[124] This cancer accounts for almost 6 per cent of all cancer incidence, but around 9 per cent of all cancer deaths.[2] Also see box 7.1.1.

7.8.2 Pathogenesis

Liver cancer generally follows cirrhosis, so any cause of cirrhosis — either viral (see box 7.8.1) or chemical — is likely to increase cancer risk. Approximately 80 per cent of hepatocellular carcinoma cases develop in cirrhotic livers.[123]

As for cancers at most sites, accumulated sequential changes (see chapter 2.5), specifically in mature hepatocytes, lead to the development of dysplastic nodules; over the course of around 5 years, 30 per cent may develop into tumours.[125] Hepatocellular carcinoma cells show numerous genetic changes, perhaps accumulated during cellular proliferation, which is part of the normal liver repair process.[126] The hepatitis B virus-related type (see box 7.8.1) appears to be more genetically unstable than others.[127] [128]

The liver is a common site for metastasis of tumours originating in other organs.

7.8.3 Other established causes

(Also see chapter 2.4 and 7.1.3.1.)

Other diseases. Cirrhosis of the liver increases the risk of, and so can be seen as a cause of, liver cancer.

Infection and infestation. Chronic viral hepatitis is a cause of liver cancer (see box 7.8.1).[130] Infestation with liver flukes is a cause of cholangiocarcinoma.

Medication. Oral contraceptives containing high doses of oestrogen and progesterone may be a cause of this cancer.[90] [133]

7.8.4 Interpretation of the evidence

7.8.4.1 General
For general considerations that may affect interpretation of the evidence, see chapters 3.3 and 3.5, and boxes 3.1, 3.2, 3.6 and 3.7.

'Relative risk' is used in this Report to denote ratio measures of effect, including 'risk ratios', 'rate ratios', 'hazard ratios', and 'odds ratios'.

7.8.4.2 Specific
Considerations specific to cancer of the liver include:

Classification. Most of the data is on hepatocellular carcinoma, the most well characterised (and most common) form of liver cancer. However, different outcomes are reported for unspecified primary liver cancer, compared with hepatocellular carcinoma or cholangiocarcinoma. This suggests different causation and so may therefore be a cause of heterogeneity.

Confounding. Hepatitis B and C viruses are possible confounders or effect modifiers; high-quality studies adjust for them. Not all studies do so.

Measurement. Owing to low survival rates, both incidence and mortality can be assessed. Low survival times and rates decrease the reliability of case-control studies, which often rely on proxy reporting.

7.8.5 Evidence and judgements

In total, 273 publications were included in the SLR for liver cancer. Fuller summaries of the epidemiological, experimental, and mechanistic evidence are to be found in Chapters 4–6.

The full SLR is contained on the CD included with this Report.

7.8.5.1 Fruits
(Also see chapter 4.2.5.2.)
One cohort study and five case-control studies investigated fruits. The cohort study and most of the case-control stud-

ies showed decreased risk with increased fruit intake. No studies showed statistically significant increased risk.

Fruits are sources of vitamin C and other antioxidants, such as carotenoids, phenols, and flavonoids, as well as other potentially bioactive phytochemicals. Antioxidants trap free radicals and reactive oxygen molecules, protecting against oxidation damage.

In addition, flavonoids found in fruit directly inhibit the expression of a cytochrome P450 enzyme, which helps to metabolise toxins and has been associated with increased risk of lung cancer, primarily in smokers.[68] It is difficult to unravel the relative importance of each constituent and is likely that a protective effect may result from a combination of influences on several pathways involved in carcinogenesis.

The evidence is sparse and inconsistent. There is limited evidence suggesting that fruits protect against liver cancer.

The Panel is aware that since the conclusion of the SLR, one case-control study[134] has been published. This new information does not change the Panel judgement. Also see box 3.8.

7.8.5.2 Aflatoxins

(Also see chapter 4.1.5.4.)

Five cohort studies and seven case-control studies investigated biomarkers of exposure to aflatoxins. All of the cohort studies and most of the case-control studies showed increased risk with elevated measures of exposure. Most cohort studies showed significant dose-response relationships, although the variety of measures used prevented meta-analysis. Effect estimates ranged from a three- to sevenfold increased risk for the highest measures of exposure.

There is strong mechanistic evidence through the metabolic product of aflatoxin B1, which is known to be genotoxic and is formed in the liver. It directly damages DNA, forming adducts. The activity of GST enzymes can result in lower levels of adducts with varying efficiency between genotypes. There is clear and consistent evidence that GST-positive genotypes protect against the increased risk of liver cancer from hepatitis infection combined with aflatoxin exposure. This supports a causal role for aflatoxin B1 in hepatocellular carcinoma.

The evidence is ample and consistent and is supported by strong evidence for mechanisms operating in humans. A dose-response relationship is apparent from both cohort and case-control studies. The evidence that aflatoxins and aflatoxin-contaminated foods are a cause of liver cancer is convincing.

7.8.5.3 Alcoholic drinks

(Also see chapter 4.8.5.1.)

A total of 15 cohort studies and 33 case-control studies investigated alcoholic drinks, and 14 cohort studies and 21 case-control studies investigated total ethanol intake. Most studies showed increased risk with increased alcohol intake, with none reporting statistically significant decreased risk. Meta-

analysis of cohort data showed a 10 per cent increased risk per 10 g ethanol/day. Meta-analysis of case-control data showed an 18 per cent increased risk per drink/week, or a 17 per cent increased risk per 10 g ethanol/day (figures 4.8.18–4.8.19).

Heterogeneity in case-control studies may be explained by alcoholic behaviour, by proxy reporting, or by failure to adjust for hepatitis virus status. Several studies used participants judged to be at high risk of developing liver cancer (people who already had liver cirrhosis). These results are particularly difficult to interpret as cirrhosis status affects drinking behaviour. Also, the cancer disease path may be different in people with cirrhosis.

It is biologically highly plausible that alcoholic drinks are a cause of liver cancer. Reactive metabolites of alcohol such as acetaldehyde can be carcinogenic. DNA mutations may be less efficiently repaired in the presence of alcohol. Alcohol may also function as a solvent, enhancing penetration of other carcinogenic molecules into cells. Additionally, the effects of alcohol may be mediated through the production of prostaglandins, lipid peroxidation, and the generation of free radical oxygen species. Lastly, heavy consumers of alcohol may have diets low in essential nutrients, making tissues susceptible to carcinogenesis. In addition, regular, high levels of alcohol consumption are known to cause liver damage. Tumour promotion has been linked to inflammation in the liver through alcohol-associated fibrosis and hepatitis. Alcohol consumption, even at moderate levels, is associated with increases in levels of circulating hepatitis C virus RNA in carriers of this infection. This infection is highly prevalent among alcoholics with chronic liver disease, and appears to accelerate the course of alcoholic liver disease.

There is ample, generally consistent evidence from both cohort and case-control studies. A dose-response relationship is apparent. Alcohol is a cause of cirrhosis, which predisposes to liver cancer, but the factors that determine why some people are susceptible to cirrhosis are not known. Alcoholic drinks are a probable cause of liver cancer. No threshold was identified.

The Panel is aware that since the conclusion of the SLR, one case-control study[135] has been published. This new information does not change the Panel judgement. Also see box 3.8.

7.8.5.4 Body fatness

(Also see chapter 6.1.3.1.)

Six cohort studies and two case-control studies investigated body fatness, as measured by BMI, or obesity. All cohort studies showed increased risk with increased body fatness, except in one subgroup of African-American men. There was substantial heterogeneity and none of the studies adjusted for hepatitis virus status. The two case-control studies provided no clear evidence of any effect.

Body fatness directly affects levels of many circulating hormones, such as insulin, insulin-like growth factors, and oestrogens, creating an environment that encourages carcinogenesis and discourages apoptosis (see box 2.4). It stimulates the body's inflammatory response, which may contribute to the initiation and progression of several cancers (see chapter 2.4.1.3).

> **The epidemiological evidence shows some inconsistencies and the mechanistic evidence is speculative. There is limited evidence suggesting that greater body fatness is a cause of liver cancer.**

The Panel is aware that since the conclusion of the SLR, two cohort studies[58][136] have been published. This new information does not change the Panel judgement. Also see box 3.8.

7.8.5.5 Other exposures

Other exposures were evaluated. However, the data were either of too low quality, too inconsistent, or the number of studies too few to allow conclusions to be reached. These were as follows: cereals (grains) and their products; non-starchy vegetables; peanuts; fish; salted fish; water source; coffee; and tea.

In cases of cereals (grains) and peanuts, there are data connecting these foods to liver cancer, but *the Panel judges* that any causative factor is likely to be aflatoxins.

7.8.6 Comparison with previous report

7.8.6.1 General
See 7.1.6.1, and box 3.8 in chapter 3.

7.8.6.2 Specific
Since publication of the previous report, the evidence that aflatoxin contamination of food is a cause of liver cancer is stronger and now justifies a judgement of 'convincing'.

7.8.7 Conclusions

The Panel concludes:
The evidence is convincing that aflatoxins, which contaminate mostly cereals (grains) and pulses (legumes), usually as a result of long storage in hot, wet conditions, are a cause of liver cancer.

Alcoholic drinks are probably a cause of liver cancer.

There is limited evidence suggesting that fruits are protective, and that body fatness is a cause of this cancer.

7.9 Colon and rectum

Cancers of the colon and rectum are the third most common type worldwide. Around 1 million cases were recorded in 2002, accounting for around 9 per cent overall. Rates of this cancer increase with industrialisation and urbanisation. It has been much more common in high-income countries but is now increasing in middle- and low-income countries. It remains relatively uncommon in Africa and much of Asia. It is somewhat more common in men than in women. It is fatal in just under half of all cases and is the fourth most common cause of death from cancer.

Overall, *the Panel judges* that food and nutrition have a highly important role in the prevention and causation of cancers of the colon and rectum (here termed colorectum).

The Panel judges as follows:
The evidence that physical activity protects against colorectal cancer is convincing, although the evidence is stronger for colon than for rectum. The evidence that red meat, processed meat, substantial consumption of alcoholic drinks (in men), body fatness and abdominal fatness, and the factors that lead to greater adult attained height, or its consequences, are causes of colorectal cancer is convincing. Substantial consumption of alcoholic drinks is probably a cause of this cancer in women. Foods containing dietary fibre, and garlic, milk, and calcium probably protect against this cancer.

There is limited evidence suggesting that non-starchy vegetables, fruits, foods containing folate, fish, foods containing vitamin D, and selenium and foods containing it protect against colorectal cancer, and that foods containing iron, cheese, foods containing animal fats, and foods containing sugars are causes of this cancer.

See chapter 8 for evidence and judgements on factors that modify the risk of body fatness and abdominal fatness, including physical activity and sedentary ways of life, the energy density of foods and drinks, and breastfeeding.

It has been estimated that this cancer is mostly preventable by appropriate diets and associated factors.

In final summary, the strongest evidence, corresponding to judgements of "convincing" and "probable", shows that physical activity protects against colorectal cancer. The evidence also shows that red meat and processed meat, substantial consumption of alcoholic drinks (by men and probably by women), body fatness and abdominal fatness, and the factors that lead to greater adult attained height, or its consequences, are causes of this cancer. Foods containing dietary fibre, and also garlic, milk, and calcium, probably protect against this cancer.

FOOD, NUTRITION, PHYSICAL ACTIVITY, AND CANCERS OF THE COLON AND THE RECTUM

In the judgement of the Panel, the factors listed below modify the risk of cancers of the colon and the rectum. Judgements are graded according to the strength of the evidence.

	DECREASES RISK	INCREASES RISK
Convincing	**Physical activity**[1][2]	**Red meat**[3][4] **Processed meat**[4][5] **Alcoholic drinks (men)**[6] **Body fatness** **Abdominal fatness** **Adult attained height**[7]
Probable	**Foods containing dietary fibre**[8] **Garlic**[9] **Milk**[10][11] **Calcium**[12]	**Alcoholic drinks (women)**[6]
Limited — suggestive	Non-starchy vegetables[9] Fruits[9] Foods containing folate[8] Foods containing selenium[8] Fish Foods containing vitamin D[8][13] Selenium[14]	Foods containing iron[4][8] Cheese[10] Foods containing animal fats[8] Foods containing sugars[15]
Limited — no conclusion	Cereals (grains) and their products; potatoes; poultry; shellfish and other seafood; other dairy products; total fat; fatty acid composition; cholesterol; sugar (sucrose); coffee; tea; caffeine; total carbohydrate; starch; vitamin A; retinol; vitamin C; vitamin E; multivitamins; non-dairy sources of calcium; methionine; beta-carotene; alpha-carotene; lycopene; meal frequency; energy intake	
Substantial effect on risk unlikely	None identified	

1. Physical activity of all types: occupational, household, transport, and recreational.
2. Much of the evidence reviewed grouped colon cancer and rectal cancer together as 'colorectal' cancer. *The Panel judges* that the evidence is stronger for colon than for rectum.
3. The term 'red meat' refers to beef, pork, lamb, and goat from domesticated animals.
4. Although red and processed meats contain iron, the general category of 'foods containing iron' comprises many other foods, including those of plant origin.
5. The term 'processed meat' refers to meats preserved by smoking, curing, or salting, or addition of chemical preservatives.
6. The judgements for men and women are different because there are fewer data for women. Increased risk is only apparent above a threshold of 30 g/day of ethanol for both sexes.
7. Adult attained height is unlikely directly to modify the risk of cancer. It is a marker for genetic, environmental, hormonal, and also nutritional factors affecting growth during the period from preconception to completion of linear growth (see chapter 6.2.1.3).
8. Includes both foods naturally containing the constituent and foods which have the constituent added (see chapter 3.5.3). Dietary fibre is contained in plant foods (see box 4.1.2 and chapter 4.2).
9. Judgements on vegetables and fruits do not include those preserved by salting and/or pickling.
10. Although both milk and cheese are included in the general category of dairy products, their different nutritional composition and consumption patterns may result in different findings.
11. Milk from cows. Most data are from high-income populations, where calcium can be taken to be a marker for milk/dairy consumption. *The Panel judges* that a higher intake of dietary calcium is one way in which milk could have a protective effect.
12. The evidence is derived from studies using supplements at a dose of 1200 mg/day.
13. Found mostly in fortified foods and animal foods.
14. The evidence is derived from studies using supplements at a dose of 200 µg/day. Selenium is toxic at high doses.
15. 'Sugars' here means all 'non-milk extrinsic' sugars, including refined and other added sugars, honey, and as contained in fruit juices and syrups. It does not include sugars naturally present in whole foods such as fruits. It also does not include lactose as contained in animal or human milks.

For an explanation of all the terms used in the matrix, please see chapter 3.5.1, the text of this section, and the glossary.

The colon is the lower part of the intestinal tract. It extends from the caecum to the rectum. In the colon, water and salts are absorbed from undigested foods, and muscles move the waste products towards the rectum. The colon contains a vast population of many types of bacteria, which have potentially important functions. These include the fermentation of unabsorbed carbohydrate (non-starch polysaccharides and resistant starch) to release energy and short chain fatty acids that influence the health of the colonic mucosa. It may also be infected with harmful types of bacteria. The colon is lined with mucous membranes, and also contains lymphoid cells that form part of the body's immune defences.

Approximately 95 per cent of colorectal cancers are adenocarcinomas. Other types of cancer that can occur here include mucinous carcinomas and adenosquamous carcinomas.[4] Adenocarcinomas are covered here. A systematic review of colorectal adenomas was conducted to understand the contribution of food, nutrition, and physical activity to the pathogenesis of colorectal cancer, and contributed to interpretation of the underlying mechanisms.

7.9.1 Trends, incidence, and survival

There is no clear trend in global age-adjusted rates of colorectal cancer. There has, however, been a rapid increase in rates in high-income countries that have recently made the transition from a relatively low-income economy, such as Japan, Singapore, and eastern European countries. Rates have at least doubled in many of these countries since the mid-1970s.[137] Colorectal cancer is mainly a disease of high-income countries, where overall rates are nearly four times higher than in middle- to low-income countries. Around the world, age-adjusted incidence rates range from more than 40 per 100 000 people in North America, parts of Europe, Australia, New Zealand, and Japan to less than 5 per 100 000 in much of Africa, Central America, and parts of Asia.[2] In the USA, rates are higher among African-American people than in white people.[3] This disease is slightly more common in men than in women, by seven to five. Risk increases with age until old age, when it levels off.[6]

Colorectal cancer often produces symptoms at an early enough stage to make it treatable, meaning that survival rates are relatively high. In addition, regular screening is common in some countries such as the USA. The 5-year overall survival rate averages 50 per cent, with 55 per cent in high-income countries and 39 per cent in middle- to low-income countries.[124] This cancer accounts for somewhat over 9 per cent of all cancer incidence, but around 8 per cent of all cancer deaths. Also see box 7.1.1.

7.9.2 Pathogenesis

Carcinogens ingested as part of, or with, foods and drinks can interact directly with the cells that line the colon and rectum if they are not metabolised or absorbed in the small intestine. Colorectal cancer can also develop from a background of inflammatory bowel disease (ulcerative colitis or Crohn's disease).[138]

Between 5 and 10 per cent of colorectal cancers are a consequence of recognised hereditary conditions. The two major ones are familial adenomatous polyposis (FAP) and HNPCC[139] (also see 7.5.2). A further 20 per cent of cases occur in people who have a family history of colorectal cancer.[139] People with FAP develop a large number of adenomas at a relatively young age; if left untreated, nearly all will develop colorectal cancer by the time they reach 40.[140]

On average, people develop HNPCC in their mid-40s[140]; having this form of the disease increases the risk of a number of other gastrointestinal cancers. HNPCC involves mutations in DNA repair genes, a recognised step in the development of many colorectal cancers.

There are two characterised pathways to colorectal cancer, although they are likely to be linked — the 'gatekeeper' and the 'caretaker' pathways.[141] The gatekeeper pathway is involved in 85 per cent of sporadic colorectal cancers, and is the one associated with FAP.[140] It involves the disruption of genes that regulate growth, and for colorectal cancer, the key one is the tumour-suppressor gene APC. The caretaker pathway is characterised by disruption to genes that maintain genetic stability. It leads to 15 per cent of sporadic cancers, and is involved in the development of HNPCC.[140] Several tumour-suppressor genes are mutated in this pathway[142] (also see box 2.2 in chapter 2).

7.9.3 Other established causes

(Also see chapter 2.4 and 7.1.3.1.)

Other diseases. Inflammatory bowel disease (Crohn's disease and ulcerative colitis) increase the risk of, and so may be seen as a cause of, colon cancer.

Medication. Non-steroidal anti-inflammatory drugs such as aspirin and hormone replacement therapy in postmenopausal women have been shown to decrease colon cancer risk.[143] [144]

7.9.4 Interpretation of the evidence

7.9.4.1 General
For general considerations that may affect interpretation of the evidence, see chapters 3.3 and 3.5, and boxes 3.1, 3.2, 3.6 and 3.7.

'Relative risk' is used in this Report to denote ratio measures of effect, including 'risk ratios', 'rate ratios', 'hazard ratios', and 'odds ratios'.

7.9.4.2 Specific
Considerations specific to colorectal cancer include:

Classification. Cancers in different parts of the colon and in the rectum could have different pathogeneses and different causal agents.

7.9.5 Evidence and judgements

In total, 752 publications were included in the SLR for cancers of the colon and rectum. Fuller summaries of the epidemiological, experimental, and mechanistic evidence are to be found in Chapters 4–6.

The full SLR is contained on the CD included with this Report.

7.9.5.1 Foods containing dietary fibre
(Also see chapter 4.1.5.3.)
Sixteen cohort studies and 91 case-control studies investigated dietary fibre. Most studies showed decreased risk with

increased intake. Meta-analysis of cohort data showed a 10 per cent decreased risk per 10 g/day (see figure 4.1.1). Heterogeneity may be caused by variation in the definition of dietary fibre between studies. A pooled analysis of 8100 colorectal cancer cases among 730 000 participants, followed up for 6–20 yeas, showed a non-significant decreased risk for the groups that consumed the most dietary fibre. Data come predominantly from dietary sources, not supplements; therefore no effect can be attributed specifically to fibre, which is interpreted simply as a marker of consumption of foods containing it, although specific mechanisms have been identified.

Fibre exerts several effects in the gastrointestinal tract, but the precise mechanisms for its probable protective role are still not clearly understood. Fibre dilutes faecal content, decreases transit time, and increases stool weight. Fermentation products, especially short-chain fatty acids, are produced by the gut flora from a wide range of dietary carbohydrates and mucins that reach the colon. Short-chain fatty acids, such as butyrate, induce apoptosis, cell cycle arrest, and differentiation in experimental studies. Fibre intake is also strongly correlated with intake of folate, though adjusting for this often does not affect the risk reduction attributed to fibre.

A clear dose-response relationship is apparent from generally consistent cohort studies, supported by evidence for plausible mechanisms, but residual confounding could not be excluded. Foods containing dietary fibre probably protect against colorectal cancer.

The Panel is aware that since the conclusion of the SLR, seven cohort studies[145-151] and one case-control study[152] have been published. This new information does not change the Panel judgement. Also see box 3.8.

7.9.5.2 Non-starchy vegetables
(Also see chapter 4.2.5.1.)
Seventeen cohort studies and 71 case-control studies investigated non-starchy vegetables. Although meta-analysis of cohort data produced no evidence of an association, a comparison of the groups with the highest intakes against those with the lowest was suggestive of an association.

This is a wide and disparate category, and many different plant food constituents are represented that could contribute to a protective effect of non-starchy vegetables. These include dietary fibre, carotenoids, folate, selenium, glucosinolates, dithiolthiones, indoles, coumarins, ascorbate, chlorophyll, flavonoids, allylsulphides, flavonoids, and phytoestrogens, some of which are potentially antioxidants. Antioxidants trap free radicals and reactive oxygen molecules, protecting against oxidation damage. It is difficult to unravel the relative importance of each constituent and it is likely that any protective effect may result from a combination of influences on several pathways involved in carcinogenesis.

A substantial amount of evidence is available but it is inconsistent. There is limited evidence suggesting that non-starchy vegetables protect against colorectal cancer.

The Panel is aware that since the conclusion of the SLR, three case-control studies[17][152][154] have been published. This new information does not change the Panel judgement. Also see box 3.8.

7.9.5.3 Garlic
(Also see chapter 4.2.5.1.2.)
Two cohort studies and six case-control studies investigated garlic. All studies reported decreased risk with increased intake, with none reporting contrary results. Most studies did not reach statistical significance, and meta-analysis was not possible.

There is considerable preclinical evidence with model carcinogens and transplantable tumours that supports an anti-cancer effect of garlic and some of its allyl sulphur components. Animal studies demonstrate that allyl sulphides effectively inhibit colon tumour formation, and also can inhibit cell growth in laboratory experiments.

The evidence, though not copious and mostly from case-control studies, is consistent, with a dose-response relationship. There is evidence for plausible mechanisms. Garlic probably protects against colorectal cancer.

The Panel is aware that since the conclusion of the SLR, one case-control study[17] has been published. This new information does not change the Panel judgement. Also see box 3.8.

7.9.5.4 Fruits
(Also see chapter 4.2.5.2.)
Twenty cohort studies and 57 case-control studies investigated fruits. More than half of the cohort studies showed decreased risk with increased intake. Meta-analysis of cohort data produced no clear evidence of an overall association. However, stratification by sex did show a statistically significant decreased risk with increased intake among women, but not men.

This difference could be hormone-related, speculating a connection with the protective effects observed in postmenopausal women provided by hormone replacement therapy. Another possibility is that this could be artefactual: men may have not reported their diets as accurately as women.

Because of the abundant prospective data from cohort studies, case-control studies were not summarised.

Fruits are sources of vitamin C and other antioxidants, such as carotenoids, phenols, and flavonoids, as well as other potentially bioactive phytochemicals. Antioxidants trap free radicals and reactive oxygen molecules, protecting against oxidation damage. In addition, flavonoids found in fruit directly inhibit the expression of a cytochrome P450 enzyme, which helps to metabolise toxins and has been associated with increased risk of lung cancer, primarily in smokers.[68] It is difficult to unravel the relative importance of each constituent and it is likely that a protective effect may result from a combination of influences on several pathways involved in carcinogenesis.

There is a substantial amount of evidence but it is inconsistent. There is limited evidence suggesting that fruits protect against colorectal cancer.

The Panel is aware that since the conclusion of the SLR, one cohort[147 153 155] and five case control studies[152 154 156-158] have been published. This new information does not change the Panel judgement. Also see box 3.8.

7.9.5.5 Foods containing folate
(Also see chapter 4.2.5.4.)
Nine cohort studies investigated dietary folate and two cohort studies investigated serum folate. Most studies showed decreased risk with increased intake. Meta-analysis of cohort data produced evidence of decreased risk with a clear dose-response relationship. Both studies that investigated serum folate levels, which may be a more accurate and precise measure than dietary estimates, showed decreased risk for colon cancer, but not rectal cancer; this was statistically significant in one study. Data come predominantly from dietary sources, not supplements; therefore no effect can be attributed specifically to folate, which is interpreted simply as a marker of consumption of foods containing it.

Folate plays an important role in the synthesis, repair, and methylation of DNA. Abnormal DNA methylation has been linked to aberrant gene expression and also to cancers at several sites. Folate may also reduce HPV proliferation in cells (also see box 7.13.1). In addition, folate intake is also strongly correlated with intake of dietary fibre, which probably protects against colorectal cancer (see 7.9.5.1).

The evidence from cohort studies is plentiful, with a dose-response relationship, but there is unexplained inconsistency. Residual confounding from dietary fibre is possible. There is limited evidence suggesting that foods containing folate protect against colorectal cancer.

The Panel is aware that since the conclusion of the SLR, four cohort[159-163] and two case control studies[152 164] have been published. This new information does not change the Panel judgement. Also see box 3.8.

7.9.5.6 Foods containing selenium
(Also see chapter 4.2.5.8.)
Fifteen case-control studies investigated dietary selenium, all of which showed decreased risk with increased intake. Meta-analysis of case-control data produced evidence of decreased risk with increased serum selenium levels, showing a clear dose-response relationship.

Dietary selenium deficiency has been shown to cause a lack of selenoprotein expression. Twenty-five selenoproteins have been identified in animals, and a number of these have important anti-inflammatory and antioxidant properties. Four are glutathione peroxidases, which protect against oxidative damage to biomolecules such as lipids, lipoproteins, and DNA. Three are thioredoxin reductases, which regenerate oxidised ascorbic acid to its active antioxidant form, among other functions.

A substantial amount of data was available, from case-control studies only. There is limited evidence suggesting that foods containing selenium protect against colorectal cancer.

7.9.5.7 Red meat
(Also see chapter 4.3.5.1.1.)
Sixteen cohort and 71 case-control studies investigated red meat. Nearly all cohort studies showed increased risk with higher intake. Meta-analysis of cohort data showed a 43 per cent increased risk per time consumed/week (figure 4.3.2) or a 15 per cent increased risk per 50 g/day (figure 4.3.3). Heterogeneity could not be fully explained but some studies could have included processed meats in the 'red meat' category.

There are several potential underlying mechanisms for a positive association of red meat consumption with colorectal cancer, including the generation of potentially carcinogenic *N*-nitroso compounds (see box 4.3.2). Some meats are also cooked at high temperatures, resulting in the production of heterocyclic amines and polycyclic aromatic hydrocarbons (see box 4.3.4). Red meat contains haem iron. Free iron can lead to the production of free radicals (see box 4.3.3).

A substantial amount of data from cohort and case-control studies showed a dose-response relationship, supported by evidence for plausible mechanisms operating in humans. Red meat is a convincing cause of colorectal cancer.

The Panel is aware that since the conclusion of the SLR, six cohort[165-173] and four case-control studies[154 156 157 174] have been published. This new information does not change the Panel judgement. Also see box 3.8.

7.9.5.8 Processed meat
(Also see chapter 4.3.5.1.2.)
Fourteen cohort studies and 44 case-control studies investigated processed meat. Nearly all cohort studies showed increased risk with higher intake. Meta-analysis of cohort data showed a 21 per cent increased risk per 50 g/day (figure 4.3.6). Heterogeneity was low and explained by the disparity in category definitions between studies, as well as by improved adjustment for confounders in recent studies.

Nitrates are both produced endogenously in gastric acid and added as preservatives to processed meats. They may contribute to *N*-nitroso compound production and exposure. These compounds are suspected mutagens and carcinogens (see box 4.3.2).[55] Many processed meats also contain high levels of salt and nitrite. Meats cooked at high temperatures can contain heterocyclic amines and polycyclic aromatic hydrocarbons (see box 4.3.4). Haem promotes the formation of *N*-nitroso compounds and also contains iron. Free iron can lead to production of free radicals (see box 4.3.3).

There is a substantial amount of evidence, with a dose-response relationship apparent from cohort studies. There is strong evidence for plausible mechanisms operating in humans. Processed meat is a convincing cause of colorectal cancer.

The Panel is aware that since the conclusion of the SLR, five cohort[153 165-169 171 173 175] and two case-control studies[154 157] have been published. This new information does not change the Panel judgement. Also see box 3.8.

7.9.5.9 Fish

(Also see chapter 4.3.5.3.)

Nineteen cohort studies and 55 case-control studies investigated fish. Most cohort studies showed decreased risk with higher intake. Meta-analysis showed a non-significant decreased risk. Heterogeneity may be partially explained by varying definitions of fish in different studies to include fresh and/or salted and dried fish. Also, high fish intake may be associated with low meat intake, which is a potential confounder that has not been adjusted for.

Because of the abundant prospective data from cohort studies, case-control studies were not summarised.

It is biologically plausible that long-chain fish n-3 polyunsaturated fatty acids (PUFAs) protect against cancer (see chapter 2.4.1.3). Fish oils reduce tumours in animal studies.[176] Likely mechanisms are thought to include their role in reduction of n-6 PUFA-derived eicosanoid biosynthesis (eicosanoids influence inflammation) and direct inhibition of cyclo-oxygenase-2, also implicated in the cancer process This mechanism, though plausible, is not well supported.[177] Alternative suggestions include the relatively high selenium or vitamin D content of fish.

A substantial amount of data is available but the results are inconsistent, and residual confounding by meat could not be excluded. There is limited evidence suggesting that eating fish protects against colorectal cancer.

The Panel is aware that since the conclusion of the SLR, six cohort[147 165 167-169 171 178] and two case-control studies[152 154] have been published. This new information does not change the Panel judgement. Also see box 3.8.

7.9.5.10 Foods containing vitamin D

(Also see chapter 4.3.5.5.)

Eleven cohort studies and 17 case-control studies investigated total vitamin D and/or dietary vitamin D. Four cohort studies investigated plasma or serum vitamin D. Most of the studies of intake, and all of the studies of plasma or serum vitamin D, showed decreased risk as measures of intake increased.

The effects of vitamin D and calcium are strongly interrelated because both are growth restraining, both induce differentiation and apoptosis in intestinal cells, and calcium-mediated effects are strongly dependent on vitamin D levels. Data from observational studies were limited by the fact that levels of the biologically active form are not only dependent on diet but also on supplements, and ultraviolet (UV) exposure of the skin.

The evidence on vitamin D was inconsistent. There is limited evidence suggesting that foods containing vitamin D or vitamin D status protect against colorectal cancer.

The Panel is aware that since the conclusion of the SLR, two case-control studies[152 179] have been published. This new information does not change the Panel judgement. Also see box 3.8.

7.9.5.11 Foods containing iron

(Also see chapter 4.3.5.6.)

Four cohort studies and 23 case-control studies investigated iron intake. All cohort studies showed increased risk with increased intake, which was statistically significant in two.

It is biologically plausible that iron increases colorectal cancer risk due to its catalytic activity on the formation of reactive oxygen species. However, this role has not been confirmed in animal studies. Another hypothesis relates to dietary haem, which can induce colonic cytotoxicity and hyperproliferation.[180] Iron overload also activates oxidative responsive transcription factors, pro-inflammatory cytokines and iron-induced hypoxia signalling.[181] Also see box 4.3.3.

The evidence is sparse, of poor quality, and inconsistent. There is limited evidence suggesting that foods containing iron are in general a cause of colorectal cancer. (Also see chapter 4.3 for evidence specifically on red and processed meat, which are classified as convincing causes of colorectal cancer.)

The Panel is aware that since the conclusion of the SLR, two cohort studies[175 182] have been published. This new information does not change the Panel judgement. Also see box 3.8.

7.9.5.12 Milk

(Also see chapter 4.4.5.1.2.)

Thirteen cohort studies and 36 case-control studies investigated milk; 15 cohort studies and 58 case-control studies investigated dietary calcium. Most cohort studies showed decreased risk with increased intake. A pooled analysis of 10 cohort studies (nearly 5000 colorectal cancer cases among more than 530 000 participants) showed a 15 per cent decreased risk for the groups that drank the most milk, and a 14 per cent decreased risk for the groups with the highest dietary calcium intakes.[183]

Most of the evidence used here comes from Western countries, where dietary calcium intake can be taken as a marker for dairy consumption.

Any effect of milk in reducing colorectal cancer risk is likely to be mediated at least in part by calcium, which has direct growth-restraining and differentiation- and apoptosis-inducing actions on normal and tumour colorectal cells.[184] Milk includes many bioactive constituents, which may also play a role.

The evidence on milk from cohort studies is reasonably consistent, supported by stronger evidence from dietary calcium, as a dietary marker. There is evidence for plausible mechanisms. Milk probably protects against colorectal cancer.

The Panel is aware that since the conclusion of the SLR, three cohort[185-188] and three case-control studies[154 158 189] have been published. This new information does not change the Panel judgement. Also see box 3.8.

7.9.5.13 Cheese

(Also see chapter 4.4.5.1.2.)

Eleven cohort studies and 25 case-control studies investigated cheese. Most cohort studies showed increased risk with increased intake. Meta-analysis showed a non-significant increased risk.

The potential mechanisms for the association of cheese with cancers of the colon and rectum are unclear. Saturated fatty acids can induce expression of inflammatory mediators and stimulate increased insulin production.

The evidence is inconsistent. There is limited evidence suggesting that cheese is a cause of colorectal cancer.

The Panel is aware that since the conclusion of the SLR, two cohort studies[185-188] and one case-control study[189] have been published. This new information does not change the Panel judgement. Also see box 3.8.

7.9.5.14 Foods containing animal fats

(Also see chapter 4.5.5.2.)

Five cohort studies investigated animal fats. Most studies showed increased risk with increased intake but there is potential for residual confounding. Meta-analysis of cohort data showed a non-significant increased risk.

Diets high in fat lead to increased levels of bile acids in the colon. Bile acids are metabolised by the bacterial flora to deoxycholic acid, which can promote cancer in rodents. The conversion of bile acids to secondary bile acids such as deoxycholic acid is decreased by the lower pH induced by short-chain fatty acids produced in diets high in non-starch polysaccharides. Also, deoxycholic acid is less soluble at a lower pH, which may limit its adverse effects.[190]

There is a limited amount of fairly consistent evidence suggesting that consumption of foods containing animal fats is a cause of colorectal cancer.

The Panel is aware that since the conclusion of the SLR, one cohort study[167] has been published. This new information does not change the Panel judgement. Also see box 3.8.

7.9.5.15 Foods containing sugars

(Also see chapter 4.6.5.1.)

A total of one cohort study and seven case-control studies investigated sugars as foods. Seven cohort studies and 16 case-control studies investigated sugars as nutrients, defined as total sugar, sucrose, or fructose. Most studies showed increased risk with increased total sugars, sucrose, or fructose intake. Data were particularly suggestive for fructose.

In most, though not all, animal experiments, sucrose and fructose are associated with increased colonic proliferation and aberrant crypt foci, which are precursors of colon cancers (see chapter 2).

The evidence is sparse and inconsistent. There is limited evidence suggesting that foods containing sugars are a cause of colorectal cancer.

7.9.5.16 Alcoholic drinks

(Also see chapter 4.8.5.1.)

Twenty-four cohort studies investigated alcoholic drinks; 13 cohort studies and 41 case-control studies investigated ethanol intake. Nearly all cohort studies showed increased risk with increased intake, with none reporting statistically significant contrary results. Meta-analysis of cohort data showed a 9 per cent increased risk per 10 g ethanol/day (figure 4.8.10). A pooled analysis of more than 4600 colorectal cancer cases among more than 475 000 participants, followed up for 6–16 years, showed a 41 per cent increased risk for the groups that drank the most alcohol.[191] There was some suggestion of sexual dimorphism, with a possibly greater effect in men than in women. This more elevated risk may be because of the generally higher consumption of alcohol among men. Also, men and women may prefer different types of alcoholic drinks, there may be hormone-related differences in alcohol metabolism, or susceptibility to alcohol may exist. Data also suggested a 'J'-shaped dose-response relationship, with low intake being associated with lower risk compared with no intake.

Because of the abundant prospective data from cohort studies, case-control studies were not summarised.

Reactive metabolites of alcohol such as acetaldehyde can be carcinogenic. There is also an interaction with smoking. Tobacco may induce specific mutations in DNA that are less efficiently repaired in the presence of alcohol. Alcohol may also function as a solvent, enhancing penetration of other carcinogenic molecules into mucosal cells. Additionally, the effects of alcohol may be mediated through the production of prostaglandins, lipid peroxidation, and the generation of free radical oxygen species. Lastly, high consumers of alcohol may have diets low in essential nutrients, making tissues susceptible to carcinogenesis.

There is ample and generally consistent evidence from cohort studies. A dose-response relationship is apparent. There is evidence for plausible mechanisms. The evidence that consumption of more than about 30 g per day of ethanol from alcoholic drinks is a cause of colorectal cancer in men is convincing; and it is probably a cause in women.

The Panel is aware that since the conclusion of the SLR, four cohort studies[159 192-194] and four case-control studies[154 195-197] have been published. This new information does not change the Panel judgement. Also see box 3.8.

7.9.5.17 Calcium

(Also see chapter 4.10.6.4.4.)

Seven cohort studies investigated calcium supplements. All but one reported decreased risk with calcium supplementation. A pooled analysis of 10 cohort studies (nearly 5000 colorectal cancer cases among more than 530 000 participants, followed up for 6–16 years) showed a 22 per cent decreased risk for the groups with the highest calcium intakes (dietary and supplemental sources).[183] In addition, two randomised controlled trials and four cohort studies investigated calcium supplements and the risk of adenomas. Both trials and most of the cohort studies showed decreased risk with supplementation.

Because of the abundant prospective data from cohort studies, case-control studies were not summarised.

Calcium from diet is an important nutrient; intracellular calcium is a pervasive second messenger acting on many cellular functions including cell growth. Calcium has direct growth-restraining and differentiation- and apoptosis-inducing actions on normal and tumour colorectal cells.[184]

There is generally consistent evidence from several cohort studies, and evidence from trials for colorectal adenomas. There is evidence for plausible mechanisms. Calcium probably protects against colorectal cancer.

7.9.5.18 Selenium

(Also see chapter 4.10.6.4.5.)
One randomised controlled trial and one cohort study investigated selenium supplements. The trial showed a statistically significant decreased risk with a daily supplement of 200 g of selenium. This was a relatively small study (1321 participants; 8 cases in the supplement group and 19 in the control group) and colorectal cancer was a secondary outcome. The cohort study showed non-significant decreased risk.

Dietary selenium deficiency has been shown to cause a lack of selenoprotein expression. Twenty-five selenoproteins have been identified in animals and a number of these have important anti-inflammatory and antioxidant properties. Four are glutathione peroxidases, which protect against oxidative damage to biomolecules such as lipids, lipoproteins, and DNA. Three are thioredoxin reductases and, among other functions, these regenerate oxidised ascorbic acid to its active antioxidant form.

The evidence is sparse. There is limited evidence to suggest that selenium protects against colorectal cancer.

7.9.5.19 Physical activity

(Also see chapter 5.4.1.)
Eleven cohort studies investigated total physical activity; 12 cohort studies investigated occupational physical activity; and 24 cohort studies investigated recreational activity. Most studies reported an association between increased physical activity and decreased cancer risk. Most studies were unsuitable for meta-analysis due to the disparate measures used to assess physical activity. The data also suggested that the effect was reduced or removed for rectal cancer. The evidence, overall, was broad and consistent. A published meta-analysis of 19 cohort studies reported a statistically significant decreased risk for physical activity for colon cancer, but not for rectal cancer.

Sustained moderate physical activity raises the metabolic rate and increases maximal oxygen uptake. In the long term, regular periods of such activity increase the body's metabolic efficiency and capacity (the amount of work that it can perform), as well as reducing blood pressure and insulin resistance. In addition, physical activity increases gut motility.

There is abundant epidemiological evidence from prospective studies showing lower risk of colorectal cancer with higher overall levels of physical activity, as well as with greater frequency and intensity, and there is evidence of a dose-response effect. There is little heterogeneity, except that the effect is not as clear for rectal cancer as it is for colon cancer. There is plausible evidence for mechanisms operating in humans. The evidence that higher levels of physical activity, within the range studied, protect against colon cancer is convincing.

The Panel is aware that since the conclusion of the SLR, four cohort[198-201] and four case-control studies[154 202-204] have been published. This new information does not change the Panel judgement. Also see box 3.8.

7.9.5.20 Body fatness

(Also see chapter 6.1.3.1.)
Sixty cohort studies and 86 case-control studies investigated body fatness, as measured by BMI. Most of the cohort studies showed increased risk with increased body fatness. Meta-analysis of cohort data showed a 15 per cent increased risk per 5 kg/m² (figure 6.1.6). Heterogeneity is explained partially by sexual and geographical differences, and also by cancer site. When stratified according to cancer site, data are more consistent and suggest a larger increased risk for colon cancer (figure 6.1.7) than for rectal cancer (figure 6.1.8).

Because of the abundant prospective data from cohort studies, case-control studies were not summarised.

Body fatness directly affects levels of many circulating hormones, such as insulin, insulin-like growth factors, and oestrogens, creating an environment that encourages carcinogenesis and discourages apoptosis. It also stimulates the body's inflammatory response, which may contribute to the initiation and progression of several cancers. Also see chapter 6.1.3 and box 2.4.

There is abundant and consistent epidemiological evidence with a clear dose-response relationship, and evidence for plausible mechanisms that operate in humans. The evidence that greater body fatness is a cause of colorectal cancer is convincing.

The Panel is aware that since the conclusion of the SLR, 15 cohort[58 59 151 205-215] and 2 case-control studies[216-218] have been published. This new information does not change the Panel judgement. Also see box 3.8.

7.9.5.21 Abdominal fatness

(Also see chapter 6.1.3.2.)
Seven cohort studies and two case-control studies investigated waist circumference; six cohort studies and four case-control studies investigated waist to hip ratio. All cohort studies showed increased risk with either increased waist circumference or increased waist to hip ratio. Meta-analysis was possible on four cohort studies measuring waist circumference and five cohort studies measuring waist to hip ratio. This showed a 5 per cent increased risk per inch of waist cir-

cumference, or a 30 per cent increased risk per 0.1 increment of waist to hip ratio (figures 6.1.22 and 6.1.23).

The general mechanisms through which abdominal fatness could plausibly influence cancer risk are outlined in chapter 6.1.3 (for more detail see box 2.4). The hormonal and other biological effects of being overweight or obese are outlined in chapter 8. Many of these, such as increased circulating oestrogens and decreased insulin sensitivity, are associated with abdominal fatness independently of overall body fatness.

> **There is ample consistent epidemiological evidence with a clear dose-response relationship and robust evidence for mechanisms that operate in humans. The evidence that abdominal fatness is a cause of colorectal cancer is convincing.**

The Panel is aware that since the conclusion of the SLR, three cohort studies[146 205 209] *have been published. This new information does not change the Panel judgement. Also see box 3.8.*

7.9.5.22 Adult attained height

(Also see chapter 6.2.3.1.)

Twenty-one cohort studies and 16 case-control studies investigated adult attained height. Most cohort studies showed increased risk with increased height. Meta-analysis of cohort data showed a 9 per cent increased risk per 5 cm of height (figure 6.2.1).

Because of the abundant prospective data from cohort studies, case-control studies were not summarised.

The general mechanisms through which the factors that lead to greater adult attained height, or its consequences, could plausibly influence cancer risk are outlined in chapter 6.2.1.3 (for more detail see box 2.4). Many of these, such as early-life nutrition, altered hormone profiles, and the rate of sexual maturation, could plausibly increase cancer risk.

> **There is ample prospective epidemiological evidence, which is consistent, and there is a clear dose-response relationship, with evidence for plausible mechanisms operating in humans. The evidence that the factors that lead to greater adult attained height, or its consequences, are a cause of colorectal cancer is convincing. The causal factor is unlikely to be tallness itself, but factors that promote linear growth in childhood.**

The Panel is aware that since the conclusion of the SLR, four cohort studies[146 151 206 207 209] *have been published. This new information does not change the Panel judgement. Also see box 3.8.*

7.9.5.23 Other exposures

Other exposures were evaluated. However, the data were either of too low quality, too inconsistent, or the number of studies too few to allow conclusions to be reached. These were as follows: cereals (grains) or their products; potatoes; poultry; shellfish and other seafood; dairy products other than cheese or milk; non-dairy sources of calcium; coffee; caffeine; tea; total carbohydrate; starch; sugar; total fat; fatty acid composition; cholesterol; vitamin A; retinol; beta-carotene; alpha-carotene; lycopene; vitamin C; vitamin E; methionine; multivitamins; meal frequency; and energy intake.

7.9.6 Comparison with previous report

7.9.6.1 General

See 7.1.6.1, and box 3.8 in chapter 3.

7.9.6.2 Specific

The previous report judged the evidence that vegetables protect against colorectal cancer to be convincing. The results of cohort studies since then have generally not been supportive of this judgement.

Evidence that red meat and, in particular, processed meat are causes of colorectal cancer is now stronger.

The previous report noted the evidence showing that greater adult height was a possible cause of colorectal cancer. The evidence now is stronger, as is that for body fatness and for abdominal fatness. The previous report found that frequent meals or snacks possibly increased the risk of colorectal cancer; this was not found here.

The evidence that dietary fibre protects against colorectal cancer is here judged to be stronger than it was previously. Evidence that garlic, milk, and calcium supplements are probably protective was not found previously.

7.9.7 Conclusions

The Panel concludes:

The evidence that physical activity protects against colorectal cancer is convincing, although the evidence is stronger for colon than for rectum.

The evidence that red meat, processed meat, substantial consumption (more than about 30 g per day ethanol) of alcoholic drinks (by men, and probably by women), body fatness and abdominal fatness, and the factors that lead to greater adult attained height, or its consequences, are causes of colorectal cancer is convincing.

Foods containing dietary fibre, as well as garlic, milk, and calcium, probably protect against this cancer.

There is limited evidence suggesting that non-starchy vegetables, fruits, foods containing folate, as well as fish, foods containing vitamin D, and also selenium and foods containing it, protect against colorectal cancer, and that foods containing iron, and also cheese, foods containing animal fats, and foods containing sugars are causes of this cancer.

7.10 Breast

FOOD, NUTRITION, PHYSICAL ACTIVITY, AND CANCER OF THE BREAST (PREMENOPAUSE)

In the judgement of the Panel, the factors listed below modify the risk of cancer of the breast (premenopause). Judgements are graded according to the strength of the evidence.

	DECREASES RISK	INCREASES RISK
Convincing	Lactation	Alcoholic drinks
Probable	Body fatness	Adult attained height[1] Greater birth weight
Limited — suggestive	Physical activity[2]	
Limited — no conclusion	Cereals (grains) and their products; dietary fibre; potatoes; vegetables; fruits; pulses (legumes); soya and soya products; meat; poultry; fish; eggs; milk and dairy products; fats and oils; total fat; vegetable fat; fatty acid composition, *trans*-fatty acids; cholesterol; sugar (sucrose); other sugars; sugary foods and drinks; coffee; tea; carbohydrate; starch; glycaemic index; protein; vitamin A; riboflavin; vitamin B6; folate; vitamin B12; vitamin C; vitamin D; vitamin E; calcium; iron; selenium; carotenoids; isoflavones; dichlorodiphenyldichloroethylene; dichlorodiphenyltrichloroethane; dieldrin; hexachlorobenzene; hexachlorocyclohexane; *trans*-nonachlor; polychlorinated biphenyls; dietary patterns; culturally defined diets; adult weight gain; energy intake; being breastfed	
Substantial effect on risk unlikely	None identified	

1   Adult attained height is unlikely directly to modify the risk of cancer. It is a marker for genetic, environmental, hormonal, and also nutritional factors affecting growth during the period from preconception to completion of linear growth (see chapter 6.2.1.3).
2   Physical activity of all types: occupational, household, transport, and recreational.

For an explanation of all the terms used in the matrix, please see chapter 3.5.1, the text of this section, and the glossary.

FOOD, NUTRITION, PHYSICAL ACTIVITY, AND CANCER OF THE BREAST (POSTMENOPAUSE)

In the judgement of the Panel, the factors listed below modify the risk of cancer of the breast (postmenopause). Judgements are graded according to the strength of the evidence.

	DECREASES RISK	INCREASES RISK
Convincing	Lactation	Alcoholic drinks Body fatness Adult attained height[1]
Probable	Physical activity[2]	Abdominal fatness Adult weight gain
Limited — suggestive		Total fat
Limited — no conclusion	Cereals (grains) and their products; dietary fibre; potatoes; vegetables and fruits; pulses (legumes); soya and soya products; meat; poultry; fish; eggs; milk and dairy products; fats and oils; vegetable fat; fatty acid composition; cholesterol; sugar (sucrose); sugary foods and drinks; coffee; tea; carbohydrate; starch; glycaemic index; protein; vitamin A; riboflavin; vitamin B6; folate; vitamin B12; vitamin C; vitamin D; vitamin E; calcium; iron; selenium; carotenoids; isoflavones; dichlorodiphenyldichloroethylene; dichlorodiphenyltrichloroethane; dieldrin; hexachlorobenzene; hexachlorocyclohexane; *trans*-nonachlor; polychlorinated biphenyls; dietary patterns; culturally defined diets; birth weight; birth length; energy intake; being breastfed	
Substantial effect on risk unlikely	None identified	

1   Adult attained height is unlikely directly to modify the risk of cancer. It is a marker for genetic, environmental, hormonal, and also nutritional factors affecting growth during the period from preconception to completion of linear growth (see chapter 6.2.1.3).
2   Physical activity of all types: occupational, household, transport, and recreational.

For an explanation of all the terms used in the matrix, please see chapter 3.5.1, the text of this section, and the glossary.

Cancer of the breast is the most common cancer in women worldwide. Around 1.15 million cases were recorded in 2002, accounting for around 23 per cent of all cancers in women (11 per cent overall).

Observed rates of this cancer increase with industrialisation and urbanisation, and also with facilities for early detection. It remains much more common in high-income countries but is now increasing rapidly in middle- and low-income countries, including within Africa, much of Asia, and Latin America. Breast cancer is fatal in under half of all cases and is the leading cause of death

from cancer in women (fifth overall), accounting for 14 per cent of all cancer deaths worldwide.

Breast cancer is hormone related, and the factors that modify the risk of this cancer when diagnosed premenopausally and when diagnosed (much more commonly) postmenopausally are not the same.

Overall, *the Panel is impressed* by the pattern of evidence showing the importance of early life events, including food and nutrition, as well as factors that affect hormone status, in modification of the risk of breast cancer.

The Panel judges as follows:

The evidence that lactation protects against breast cancer at all ages is convincing.

Physical activity probably protects against breast cancer postmenopause, and there is limited evidence suggesting that it protects against this cancer diagnosed premenopause. The evidence that alcoholic drinks are a cause of breast cancer at all ages is convincing. The evidence that the factors that lead to greater adult attained height, or its consequences, are a cause of postmenopausal breast cancer is convincing, and these are probably also a cause of breast cancer diagnosed premenopause.

The factors that lead to greater birth weight, or its consequences, are probably a cause of breast cancer diagnosed premenopause. Adult weight gain is probably a cause of postmenopausal breast cancer. The evidence that body fatness is a cause of postmenopausal breast cancer is convincing, and abdominal body fatness is probably also a cause. On the other hand, body fatness probably protects against breast cancer diagnosed premenopause. There is limited evidence suggesting that total dietary fat is a cause of postmenopausal breast cancer.

Life events that protect against breast cancer include late menarche, early pregnancy, bearing children, and early menopause, all of which have the effect of reducing the number of menstrual cycles, and therefore lifetime exposure to oestrogen. The reverse also applies.

See chapter 8 for evidence and judgements on factors that modify the risk of body fatness and abdominal fatness, including physical activity and sedentary ways of life, the energy density of foods and drinks, and breastfeeding.

In final summary, the strongest evidence, corresponding to judgements of "convincing" and "probable", shows that lactation protects against breast cancer; that alcoholic drinks are a cause of this cancer; that the factors that lead to greater adult attained height, or its consequences, are a cause of postmenopausal and probably also premenopausal breast cancer; that factors that lead to greater birth weight, or its consequences, are probably a cause of premenopausal breast cancer; and that abdominal body fatness and adult weight gain are probably a cause of postmenopausal breast cancer. Body fatness is a cause of postmenopausal breast cancer but probably protects against premenopausal breast cancer.

Breast tissue comprises mainly fat, glandular tissue (arranged in lobes), ducts, and connective tissue. Breast tissue develops in response to hormones such as oestrogens, progesterone, insulin, and growth factors. The main periods of development are during puberty, pregnancy, and lactation. The glandular tissue atrophies after menopause.

Breast cancers are almost all carcinomas of the epithelial cells lining the ducts (the channels in the breast that carry milk to the nipple).[219] Premenopausal and postmenopausal breast cancers are considered separately in this Report. Although rare, breast cancer can occur in men, but it is not included here.

7.10.1 Trends, incidence, and survival

Age-adjusted rates of breast cancer in women are increasing in most countries, particularly in areas where the incidence had previously been low, such as Japan, China, and southern and eastern Europe.[124 137]

This is predominantly a disease of high-income countries, where overall rates are nearly three times higher than in middle- to low-income countries. Around the world, age-adjusted incidence rates range from 75–100 per 100 000 women in North America, northern Europe, and Australia, to less than 20 per 100 000 in parts of Africa and Asia.[2] In the USA, rates are higher among white women than those from other ethnic groups, although mortality is highest in black women.[3]

Overall risk doubles each decade until the menopause, when the increase slows down or remains stable. However, breast cancer is more common after the menopause. Studies of women who migrate from areas of low risk to areas of high risk show that rates of breast cancer in migrants assume the rate in the host country within one or two generations. This shows that environmental factors are important in the progression of the disease.[220]

Breast cancers can often be detected at a relatively early stage. In countries that provide or advocate screening, most of these cancers are diagnosed when the disease is still at a localised stage.[221] Survival rates range from more than 90 to less than 50 per cent, depending on the characteristics of the tumour, its size and spread, and the availability of treatment.[4] Average 5-year survival rates are higher in high-income countries: around 73 per cent, compared with 57 per cent in middle- to low-income countries. Breast cancer accounts for nearly 23 per cent of all cancer incidence in women and 14 per cent of all cancer deaths (all sites except for skin (non-melanoma) and in women only). Also see box 7.1.1.

7.10.2 Pathogenesis

Breast tissue, as well as hormones and hormone-receptor status, varies at different stages of life. It is therefore possible that individual risk factors will have different effects at different life stages (see 7.10.5). Early menarche, late menopause, not bearing children, and late (over 30) first pregnancy all increase breast cancer risk.[220 222] The age when breasts develop, and menopause, are both influenced by nutrition, with overnutrition leading to early puberty and late menopause; undernutrition delays puberty and advances menopause (see chapter 6.2).

Hormones play an important role in breast cancer progression because they modulate the structure and growth of epithelial tumour cells.[4] Different cancers vary in hormone sensitivity. Many breast cancers also produce hormones, such as growth factors, that act locally, and these can both stimulate and inhibit the tumour's growth.[223 224]

Between 4 and 9 per cent of breast cancer cases are hereditary, and are usually caused by inherited mutations in either the BRCA1 or BRCA2 gene.[225 226] In addition, growth factor receptor genes, as well as some oncogenes, are overexpressed in many breast cancers[4] (see box 2.2).

7.10.3 Other established causes

(Also see chapter 2.4 and 7.1.3.1.)

Life events. As stated above, lifetime exposure to oestrogen, influenced by early menarche, late natural menopause, not bearing children, and late (over 30) first pregnancy all increase the risk of, and may be seen as causes of, breast cancer.[220] [222] The reverse also applies: late menarche, early menopause, bearing children, and early pregnancy all reduce the risk of, and may be seen as protective against, breast cancer. Age of breast development and menopause are influenced by nutrition, with high-energy diets promoting earlier puberty and late menopause, and low-energy diets delaying puberty and advancing menopause.

Radiation. Ionising radiation exposure from medical treatment such as X-rays, particularly during puberty, increases risk, even at low doses.[227]

Medication. Hormone replacement therapy is a cause of breast cancer. The increased risk appears to disappear a few years after cessation.[144] Oral contraceptives containing both oestrogen and progesterone cause a small, transient, increased risk of breast cancer; the increased risk disappears after cessation.[133]

7.10.4 Interpretation of the evidence

7.10.4.1 General

For general considerations that may affect interpretation of the evidence, see chapters 3.3 and 3.5, and boxes 3.1, 3.2, 3.6 and 3.7.

'Relative risk' is used in this Report to denote ratio measures of effect, including 'risk ratios', 'rate ratios', 'hazard ratios', and 'odds ratios'.

7.10.4.2 Specific

Considerations specific to breast cancer include:

Patterns. The preponderance of data from high-income countries is a special issue with breast cancer. Breast cancer is hormone related, and factors that modify risk have different effects on cancers diagnosed pre- and postmenopause.

Classification. Because of the importance of menopause as an effect modifier, studies should stratify for menopause status. Many do not.

Confounding. Hormone replacement therapy is an important possible confounder in postmenopausal breast cancer. A few studies also reported results separately for different hormone receptor profiles within cancers. High-quality studies adjust for age, number of reproductive cycles, age at which children were born, and the taking of hormone-based medications.

7.10.5 Evidence and judgements

In total, 873 publications were included in the SLR for breast cancer. Fuller summaries of the epidemiological, experimental, and mechanistic evidence are to be found in Chapters 4–6.

The full SLR is contained on the CD included with this Report.

7.10.5.1 Alcoholic drinks

(Also see chapter 4.8.5.1.)

A total of 11 cohort studies, 31 case-control studies, and 2 ecological studies investigated alcoholic drinks; 25 cohort studies, 29 case-control studies, and 4 ecological studies investigated ethanol intake and all-age breast cancer. Further studies investigated the relationship with alcoholic drinks in either pre- or postmenopausal breast cancer. Most studies showed increased risk with increased intake. Meta-analysis of cohort data showed a 10 per cent increased risk per 10 g ethanol/day; meta-analysis of case-control data showed a 5 per cent increased risk per 5 drinks/week, and a 6 per cent increased risk per 10 g ethanol/day (figures 4.8.13, 4.8.15, and 4.8.16). Menopausal status did not significantly alter the association. Two pooled analyses also showed statistically significant increased risks of 9 and 7 per cent per 10 g ethanol/day. The first was based on 6 cohort studies with more than 320 000 participants, followed up for up to 11 years, with more than 4300 breast cancer cases. The other analysed 53 case-control studies, with more than 58 000 cases and more than 95 000 controls.[228] [229]

Reactive metabolites of alcohol, such as acetaldehyde, may be carcinogenic. Additionally, the effects of alcohol may be mediated through the production of prostaglandins, lipid peroxidation, and the generation of free radical oxygen species. Alcohol also acts as a solvent, enhancing penetration of carcinogens into cells. High consumers of alcohol may have diets deficient in essential nutrients, making tissues susceptible to carcinogenesis. In addition, most experimental studies in animals have shown that alcohol intake is associated with increased breast cancer risk. Alcohol interferes with oestrogen metabolism and action in multiple ways, influencing hormone levels and oestrogen receptors.

There is an interaction between folate and alcohol affecting breast cancer risk: increased folate status partially mitigates the risk from increased alcohol consumption.[230]

There is ample, generally consistent evidence from case-control and cohort studies. A dose-response relationship is apparent. There is robust evidence for mechanisms operating in humans. The evidence that alcoholic drinks are a cause of premenopausal and postmenopausal breast cancer is convincing. No threshold was identified.

The Panel is aware that since the conclusion of the SLR, one case-control study[231] has been published. This new information does not change the Panel judgement. Also see box 3.8.

7.10.5.2 Lactation

(Also see chapter 6.3.3.)

One cohort study and 37 case-control studies investigated ever having breastfed as compared to never having breastfed; and 5 cohort studies and 55 case-control studies investigated the total duration of lactation. The single cohort study and most case-control studies showed decreased risk (age unspecified) with ever having breastfed compared with never. Most studies showed decreased risk with increasing duration of breastfeeding. Meta-analysis of case-control data showed a 3 per cent decreased risk per 5 months of total breastfeeding (figure 6.3.1); meta-analysis of cohort data showed a non-significant decreased risk. Pooled analysis from 47 epidemiological studies in 30 countries (more than 50 000 controls and nearly 97 000 breast cancer cases) showed a statistically significant decreased risk of breast cancer of 4.3 per cent for each 12 months of breastfeeding. Menopause status was not an effect modifier.[228] [386]

Lactation is associated with increased differentiation of breast cells and with lower exposure to endogenous sex hormones during amenorrhea accompanying lactation. In addition, the strong exfoliation of breast tissue during lactation, and the massive epithelial apoptosis at the end of lactation, could decrease risk by elimination of cells with potential DNA damage.

> **There is abundant epidemiological evidence from both prospective and case-control studies, which is consistent and shows a dose-response relationship. There is robust evidence for plausible mechanisms that operate in humans. The evidence that lactation protects against both premenopausal and postmenopausal breast cancer is convincing.**

7.10.5.3 Physical activity

(Also see chapter 5.4.2.)

Six cohort studies and 8 case-control studies investigated total physical activity; 5 cohort studies and 7 case-control studies investigated occupational activity; and 14 cohort studies and 11 case-control studies investigated recreational activity.

Menopause age unspecified

Most studies showed decreased risk with increased physical activity. Meta-analysis of case-control data showed a 10 per cent decreased risk per 7 MET-hours recreational activity/week (figure 5.4.5).

Premenopause

Data were inconsistent for most categories, but data on occupational activity were suggestive of decreased risk.

Postmenopause

Nearly all of the cohort studies and most case-control studies showed decreased risk with increased physical activity. Meta-analysis of cohort data showed a 3 per cent decreased risk per 7 MET-hours recreational activity/week (figure 5.4.6).

Sustained moderate physical activity raises the metabolic rate and increases maximal oxygen uptake. In the long term, regular periods of such activity increase the body's metabolic efficiency and capacity (the amount of work that it can perform), as well as reducing blood pressure and insulin resistance. In addition, it decreases levels of oestrogens and androgens in postmenopausal women. Some trials have also shown decreases in circulating oestrogens, increased menstrual cycle length, and decreased ovulation in premenopausal women with a high level of physical activity.

> **Premenopause: There is ample evidence from prospective studies, but it is inconsistent. There is limited evidence suggesting that physical activity protects against premenopausal breast cancer.**

> **Postmenopause: There is ample evidence from prospective studies showing lower risk of postmenopausal breast cancer with higher levels of physical activity, with a dose-response relationship, although there is some heterogeneity. There is little evidence on frequency, duration, or intensity of activity. There is robust evidence for mechanisms operating in humans. Physical activity probably protects against postmenopausal breast cancer.**

The Panel is aware that since the conclusion of the SLR, one case-control study[232] has been published. This new information does not change the Panel judgement. Also see box 3.8.

7.10.5.4 Body fatness

(Also see chapter 6.1.3.1.)

Forty-three cohort studies, more than 100 case-control studies, and 2 ecological studies investigated body fatness, as measured by BMI. When grouped for all ages, data were inconsistent. However, a consistent effect emerged when they were stratified according to menopausal status. Most studies showed a decreased risk for premenopausal breast cancer and an increased risk for postmenopausal breast cancer with increased body fatness. For cancer diagnosed premenopause, meta-analysis of cohort data showed a 15 per cent decreased risk per 5 kg/m^2; meta-analysis of case-control data showed a 15 per cent increased risk per 5 kg/m^2. For cancer diagnosed postmenopause, meta-analysis of cohort data showed an 8 per cent increased risk per 5 kg/m^2; meta-analysis of case-control data showed a 13 per cent increased risk per 5 kg/m^2 (figures 6.1.11–6.1.16).

Two pooled analyses showed statistically significant increased risk for postmenopausal cancer. One of these also showed a statistically significant decreased risk for premenopausal breast cancer. One pooled analysis was based on 7 cohort studies with more than 337 000 participants, followed up for up to 11 years, with more than 4300 breast cancer cases. It showed a 14 per cent decreased risk per 5 kg/m^2 for cancer diagnosed premenopause and a 9 per cent increased risk per 5 kg/m^2 for cancer diagnosed postmenopause. The other pooled analysis, based on 53 case-control studies with more than 58 000 cases and more than 95 000 controls, showed a 19 per cent increased risk per 5 kg/m^2 for postmenopausal breast cancer.[233] [234]

Body fatness directly affects levels of many circulating hormones, such as insulin, insulin-like growth factors, and oestrogens, creating an environment that encourages carcinogenesis and discourages apoptosis (see box 2.4). It also stimulates the body's inflammatory response, which may contribute to the initiation and progression of several cancers (see chapter 2.4.1.3). Adjusting for serum levels of oestradiol diminishes or destroys the association with BMI, suggesting that hormones are a predominant mechanism.[235]

There is no single well established mechanism through which body fatness could prevent premenopausal breast cancer. According to the oestrogen plus progesterone theory, overweight premenopausal women would be protected because they would be more frequently anovulatory, and therefore less exposed to endogenous progesterone. However, this theory is not well supported by recent studies, which suggest that natural progesterone could be protective.[236] Normal levels of natural progesterone are likely to be protective, and well nourished, or perhaps overnourished women, who may become slightly overweight in adulthood, may be protected by their natural fertile condition. Another possible mechanism is that the increased adipose tissue-derived oestrogen levels in overweight children could induce early breast differentiation and eliminate some targets for malignant transformation.[237] Anovulation and abnormal hormone profiles are commonly associated with obesity.[238] The age-specific pattern of association of breast cancer with BMI, therefore, is largely explained by its relationship with endogenous sex hormone levels.

Breast cancer diagnosed postmenopause is much more common. Therefore, throughout life, a decreased risk of premenopausal breast cancer would be expected to be outweighed by an increased risk of postmenopausal breast cancer.

Premenopause: There is a substantial amount of consistent epidemiological evidence with a dose-response relationship, but the mechanistic evidence is speculative. Greater body fatness probably protects against premenopausal breast cancer.

Postmenopause: There is abundant and consistent epidemiological evidence and a clear dose-response relationship with robust evidence for mechanisms operating in humans. The evidence that greater body fatness is a cause of postmenopausal breast cancer is convincing.

The Panel is aware that since the conclusion of the SLR, one cohort[239] and one case-control study[240] have been published. This new information does not change the Panel judgement. Also see box 3.8.

7.10.5.5 Adult attained height
(Also see chapter 6.2.3.1.)
Thirty-three cohort studies, 56 case-control studies, and 3 ecological studies investigated adult attained height.

Age unspecified
Twenty cohort studies and 29 case-control studies investigated adult attained height and breast cancer at all ages, or unspecified menopausal status. Most of the studies showed increased risk. Meta-analysis of cohort data showed a 9 per cent increased risk per 5 cm of height; meta-analysis of case-control data showed a 3 per cent increased risk per 5 cm of height (figure 6.2.2).

Premenopause
Seventeen cohort studies and 38 case-control studies investigated adult attained height and premenopausal breast cancer. Most of the studies showed increased risk. Meta-analysis of cohort data showed a 9 per cent increased risk per 5 cm of height; meta-analysis of case-control data showed a 4 per cent increased risk per 5 cm of height (figure 6.2.4). A pooled analysis of 7 cohort studies (more than 337 000 participants, followed up for up to 11 years, with more than 4300 breast cancer cases) showed a non-significant increased risk with greater adult attained height.[234]

There are fewer data for premenopausal than for postmenopausal breast cancer. The epidemiological evidence is generally consistent, with a dose-response relationship and evidence for plausible mechanisms. The factors that lead to greater adult attained height, or its consequences, are probably a cause of premenopausal breast cancer. The causal factor is unlikely to be tallness itself, but factors that promote linear growth in childhood.

Postmenopause
Twenty-two cohort studies and 34 case-control studies investigated adult attained height and postmenopausal breast cancer. Nearly all of the cohort studies and most of the case-control studies showed increased risk, with no studies showing statistically significant contrary results. Meta-analysis of cohort data showed an 11 per cent increased risk per 5 cm of height; meta-analysis of case-control data showed a 2 per cent increased risk per 5 cm of height (figure 6.2.3). A pooled analysis of 7 cohort studies (more than 337 000 participants, followed up for up to 11 years, with more than 4300 breast cancer cases) showed a statistically significant 7 per cent increased risk per 5 cm of height.[234] The ecological studies provided supporting data.

The general mechanisms through which the factors that lead to greater adult attained height, or its consequences, could plausibly influence cancer risk are outlined in chapter 6.2.1.3 (for more detail see box 2.4). Many of these, such as early-life nutrition, altered hormone profiles, and the rate of sexual maturation, could plausibly increase cancer risk.

There is abundant prospective epidemiological evidence, which is generally consistent, with a clear dose-response relationship, and evidence for plausible mechanisms operating in humans. The evidence that the factors that lead to greater adult attained height, or its consequences, are a cause of postmenopausal breast cancer is convincing. The causal factor is unlikely to be tallness itself, but factors that promote linear growth in childhood.

The Panel is aware that since the conclusion of the SLR, one cohort study[241] has been published. This new information does not change the Panel judgement. Also see box 3.8.

7.10.5.6 Abdominal fatness (postmenopause)

(Also see chapter 6.1.3.2.)

Eight cohort studies and three case-control studies investigated waist circumference and postmenopausal breast cancer; eight cohort studies and eight case-control studies investigated waist to hip ratio. All of the waist-circumference studies and most of those on waist to hip ratio showed increased risk with increased measures of abdominal fatness. Meta-analysis of cohort data showed a 19 per cent increased risk per 0.1 increment in waist to hip ratio (figure 6.1.24).

The general mechanisms through which abdominal fatness could plausibly cause cancer are outlined in chapter 6.1.3 (for more detail see box 2.4). The hormonal and other biological effects of being overweight or obese are outlined in chapter 8. Many of these, such as increased levels of circulating oestrogens and decreased insulin sensitivity, are associated with abdominal fatness independently of overall body fatness.

There is a substantial amount of epidemiological evidence but some inconsistency. There is robust evidence for mechanisms that operate in humans. Abdominal fatness is a probable cause of postmenopausal breast cancer.

7.10.5.7 Adult weight gain (postmenopause)

(Also see chapter 6.1.3.3.)

Seven cohort studies and 17 case-control studies investigated adult weight gain and postmenopausal breast cancer. Nearly all of the studies showed increased risk with increased weight gain in adulthood. Meta-analysis of case-control data showed a 5 per cent increased risk per 5 kg gained (figure 6.1.26). Heterogeneity may be explained by failure to separate postmenopausal participants taking hormone replacement therapy.

Body fatness directly affects levels of many circulating hormones, such as insulin, insulin-like growth factors, and oestrogens, creating an environment that encourages carcinogenesis and discourages apoptosis (see chapter 2.7.1.3). It also stimulates the body's inflammatory response, which may contribute to the initiation and progression of several cancers.

There is ample, consistent epidemiological evidence from both cohort and case-control studies. A dose-response relationship was apparent from case-control and cohort studies. Adult weight gain is a probable cause of postmenopausal breast cancer.

7.10.5.8 Greater birth weight (premenopause)

(Also see chapter 6.2.3.2.)

Six cohort studies and four case-control studies investigated birth weight. All cohort studies and most case-control studies showed increased risk with greater birth weight, with none reporting statistically significant contrary results.

Meta-analysis of cohort data showed an 8 per cent increased risk per kg (figure 6.2.8).

The general mechanisms through which the factors that lead to greater birth weight, or its consequences, could plausibly influence cancer risk are outlined in chapter 6.2.1.1. Many of these, such as long-term programming of hormonal systems, could plausibly increase cancer risk. Greater birth weight raises circulating maternal oestrogen levels and may increase insulin-like growth factor (IGF)-1 activity; low birth weight raises both fetal and maternal levels of IGF-1 binding protein. The action of both oestrogens and IGF-1 are thought to be important in fetal growth and mammary gland development, and play a central, synergistic role in the initiation and promotion of breast cancer.[242] Animal experiments also provide evidence that exposure to oestrogens during fetal and early postnatal development can increase the risk of mammary cancers.[243]

There is general consistency amongst the relatively few epidemiological studies, with some evidence for a dose-response relationship. The mechanistic evidence is speculative. The factors that lead to greater birth weight, or its consequences, are probably a cause of premenopausal breast cancer.

The Panel is aware that since the conclusion of the SLR, one cohort study[239] and one case-control study[244] have been published. This new information does not change the Panel judgement. Also see box 3.8.

7.10.5.9 Total fat (postmenopause)

(Also see chapter 4.5.5.1.)

Nine cohort studies and 16 case-control studies investigated total fat intake and postmenopausal breast cancer. Most studies showed increased risk with increased intake. Meta-analysis of cohort data showed a non-significant increased risk; meta-analysis of case-control data showed a statistically significant increased risk. A pooled analysis (more than 350 000 participants and more than 7300 breast cancer cases) showed an overall non-significant decreased risk with increased fat intake. Menopausal status did not significantly alter the result.[245]

Higher endogenous oestrogen levels after menopause are a known cause of breast cancer.[235 246] Dietary fat may also increase endogenous oestrogen production.[247]

Evidence from prospective epidemiological studies of different types on the whole shows inconsistent effects, while case-control studies show a significant positive association. Mechanistic evidence is speculative. Overall, there is limited evidence suggesting that consumption of total fat is a cause of postmenopausal breast cancer.

7.10.5.10 Other exposures

For premenopausal breast cancer, other exposures were evaluated. However, the data were either of too low quality, too inconsistent, or the number of studies too few to allow conclusions to be reached. These were as follows: cereals (grains) and their products; potatoes; vegetables; fruits; pulses (legumes); soya and soya products; meat; poultry; fish; eggs; fats and oils; vegetable fat; sugar; sugary foods and drinks; milk and dairy products; coffee; tea; carbohydrate; starch; dietary fibre; sugars; total fat; fatty acid composition; *trans*-fatty acids; cholesterol; protein; vitamin A; carotenoids; folate; riboflavin; vitamin B6; cobalamin; vitamin C; vitamin D; vitamin E; iron; calcium; selenium; isoflavones; dieldrin; *trans*-nonachlor; dichlorodiphenyl-trichloroethane; dichlorodiphenyldichloroethylene; polychlorinated biphenyls; hexachlorocyclohexane; hexachlorobenzene; energy intake; adult weight gain; adult attained height; dietary patterns; culturally defined diets; glycaemic index; and being breastfed.

For postmenopausal breast cancer other exposures were evaluated. However, the data were either of too low quality, too inconsistent, or the number of studies too few to allow conclusions to be reached. These were as follows: cereals (grains) and their products; potatoes; vegetables and fruits; pulses; soya and soya products; meat; poultry; fish; eggs; fats and oils; sugar; sugary drinks and foods; milk and dairy products; coffee; tea; carbohydrate; starch; dietary fibre; vegetable fat; fatty acid composition; cholesterol; protein; vitamin A and carotenoids; riboflavin; vitamin B6; vitamin B12; folate; vitamin C; vitamin D; vitamin E; isoflavones; iron; calcium; selenium; dieldrin; *trans*-nonachlor; dichloro-diphenyltrichloroethane; dichlorodiphenyldichloroethylene; polychlorinated biphenyls; hexachlorocyclohexane; hexachlorobenzene; energy intake; birth length; culturally defined diets; dietary patterns; glycaemic index; being breastfed; and birth weight.

There is considerable speculation around a biologically plausible interaction of soya and soya products with breast cancer development, due to their high phytoestrogen content. Data on pulses (legumes) were sparse and inconsistent, and there were insufficient studies available on soya consumption to allow a conclusion to be reached.

7.10.6 Comparison with previous report

7.10.6.1 General
See 7.1.6.1, and box 3.8.

7.10.6.2 Specific
One of the most striking differences between the two reports is the finding here on lactation. The previous report mentioned studies indicating that breastfeeding may protect against breast cancer, but it did not review or judge this evidence.

The previous report found that high body mass probably increases the risk for breast cancer diagnosed after the menopause, while this Report found the evidence for body fatness to be convincing. While the previous report made no judgement on high body mass and premenopausal breast cancer, this Report found that greater body fatness probably decreases the risk. The previous report judged the evidence to be convincing that rapid growth, together with greater adult height, are causes of breast cancer. This Report does not make a judgement on rates of growth. The previous report did not make judgments on birth weight.

The previous report judged it probable that vegetables and fruits decrease breast cancer risk. Cohort findings since then have been equivocal.

7.10.7 Conclusions

The Panel concludes:

The evidence that lactation protects against breast cancer at all ages therafter is convincing. Physical activity probably protects against postmenopausal breast cancer, and there is limited evidence suggesting that it protects against premenopausal breast cancer. The evidence that alcoholic drinks are a cause of breast cancer at all ages is convincing. The evidence that the factors that lead to greater attained adult height or its consequences are a cause of postmenopausal breast cancer is convincing; these are probably a cause of premenopausal breast cancer.

The factors that lead to greater birth weight or its consequences are probably a cause of breast cancer diagnosed premenopause. Adult weight gain is probably a cause of postmenopausal breast cancer. The evidence that body fatness is a cause of postmenopausal breast cancer is convincing, and abdominal body fatness is probably a cause of this cancer. On the other hand, body fatness probably protects against breast cancer diagnosed premenopause. There is limited evidence suggesting that total dietary fat is a cause of postmenopausal breast cancer.

7.11 Ovary

Ovarian cancer is the seventh most common cancer in women (and the 16th most common cancer overall) worldwide. Around 200 000 cases were recorded in 2002, accounting for around 4 per cent of all new cases of cancer in women (2 per cent overall). It is most frequent in high-income countries. This cancer is usually fatal, and is the seventh most common cause of cancer death in women worldwide (15th overall).

The Panel judges as follows:
The factors that lead to greater adult attained height, or its consequences, are probably a cause of cancer of the ovary. There is limited evidence suggesting that non-starchy vegetables, and also lactation, protect against this cancer.

Life events that protect against ovarian cancer include late menarche, bearing children, and early menopause, all of which have the effect of reducing the number of menstrual cycles, and therefore lifetime exposure to oestrogen.

In final summary, the strongest evidence, corresponding to judgements of "convincing" and "probable", shows that the factors that lead to greater adult attained height, or its consequences, are probably a cause of cancer of the ovary.

The ovaries are the sites of egg production in women. They are also the main source of the hormones oestrogen and progesterone.

There are three types of ovarian tissue that can produce cancers: epithelial cells, which cover the ovary; stromal cells, which produce hormones; and germ cells, which become eggs. Many different types of ovarian cancers can occur. About 85–90 per cent of ovarian cancers are carcinomas,[4] the type included here.

FOOD, NUTRITION, PHYSICAL ACTIVITY, AND CANCER OF THE OVARY

In the judgement of the Panel, the factors listed below modify the risk of cancer of the ovary. Judgements are graded according to the strength of the evidence.

	DECREASES RISK	INCREASES RISK
Convincing		
Probable		**Adult attained height[1]**
Limited — suggestive	Non-starchy vegetables[2] Lactation	
Limited — no conclusion	Dietary fibre; fruits; pulses (legumes); meat; poultry; fish; eggs; milk and dairy products; total fat; cholesterol; coffee; tea; alcohol; carbohydrate; lactose; protein; vitamin A; folate; vitamin C; vitamin E; recreational activity; body fatness; abdominal fatness; weight change; energy intake	
Substantial effect on risk unlikely	None identified	

1 Adult attained height is unlikely directly to modify the risk of cancer. It is a marker for genetic, environmental, hormonal, and also nutritional factors affecting growth during the period from preconception to completion of linear growth (see chapter 6.2.1.3).
2 Judgements on vegetables and fruits do not include those preserved by salting and/or pickling.

For an explanation of all the terms used in the matrix, please see chapter 3.5.1, the text of this section, and the glossary.

7.11.1 Trends, incidence, and survival

There is no clear global trend in ovarian cancer incidence. Rates appear to be high in high-income countries, and rising in countries undergoing economic transition.[137] For instance in Japan, there was a fourfold increase in the age-adjusted mortality rate (from 0.9 to 3.6 per 100 000 women) between 1950 and 1997.[248]

Ovarian cancer rates are nearly three times higher in high- than in middle- to low-income countries. Around the world, age-adjusted incidence rates range from more than 10 per 100 000 women in Europe and North America, to less than 5 per 100 000 in parts of Africa and Asia. But rates are relatively high elsewhere in Asia, for example in Singapore and the Philippines.[2] In the USA, rates are higher among white women than in those from other ethnic groups; rates are also higher in Jewish women of Ashkenazi descent.[3 249]

Risk increases with age, although the rate of increase slows after the menopause, with most ovarian cancers occurring after menopause. Only 10–15 per cent of cases occur before the menopause, although germ cell cancers peak in women aged between 15 and 35.[4]

Ovarian cancer often has no symptoms at the early stages, so the disease is generally advanced when it is diagnosed. The 5-year survival rate ranges from approximately 30 to 50 per cent.[3 6] This cancer accounts for about 7 per cent of all cancer incidence and 4 per cent of cancer deaths in women worldwide. Also see box 7.1.1.

7.11.2 Pathogenesis

The pathogenesis of this disease is not well characterised, although various mechanisms have been suggested. Over many cycles of ovulation, the ovarian surface epithelium undergoes repeated disruption and repair. The epithelial cells are stimulated to proliferate, which increases the probability of spontaneous mutations. Alternatively, following ovulation, these cells may become trapped within the connective tissue surrounding the ovary, which can lead to the formation of inclusion cysts. If this happens, the epithelial cells are subjected to a unique pro-inflammatory microenvironment, which may increase the rate of DNA damage.

Most ovarian cancers occur spontaneously, although 5–10 per cent of cases develop due to a genetic predisposition.[104] The latter, involving dysfunctional BRCA1 or BRCA2 genes (see chapter 2.4.1.1), produces high-grade carcinomas, with a poorer prognosis.[250]

7.11.3 Other established causes

(Also see chapter 2.4 and 7.1.3.1.)

Life events. The risk of ovarian cancer is affected by the number of menstrual cycles during a woman's lifetime. Not bearing children increases the risk of, and may be seen as a cause of, ovarian cancer. The reverse also applies: bearing children reduces the risk of, and may be seen as protective against, ovarian cancer.[251-253] There is also substantial evidence that, as with breast cancer, early menarche and late natural menopause increase the risk of, and may be seen as causes of, ovarian cancer. The reverse also applies: late menarche and early menopause reduce the risk of, and may be seen as protective against, ovarian cancer.[251-253]

Medication. Oral contraceptives protect against this cancer.[133]

7.11.4 Interpretation of the evidence

7.11.4.1 General
For general considerations that may affect interpretation of the evidence, see chapters 3.3 and 3.5, and boxes 3.1, 3.2, 3.6 and 3.7.

'Relative risk' is used in this Report to denote ratio measures of effect, including 'risk ratios', 'rate ratios', 'hazard ratios', and 'odds ratios'.

7.11.4.2 Specific
Considerations specific to cancer of the ovary include:

Patterns. Because ovarian cancer is hormone related, factors that modify risk might have different effects at different times of life. If so, this might partly explain heterogeneous results.

Confounding. High-quality studies adjust for age, number of reproductive cycles, age at which children were born, and the taking of hormone-based medications.

Classification. There are different histological subtypes of ovarian cancer, which may have independent risk factors and disease progression patterns. Most studies combine these subtypes.

7.11.5 Evidence and judgements

In total, 187 publications were included in the SLR for ovarian cancer. Fuller summaries of the epidemiological, experimental, and mechanistic evidence are to be found in Chapters 4–6.

The full SLR is contained on the CD included with this Report.

7.11.5.1 Non-starchy vegetables
(Also see chapter 4.2.5.1.)
A total of five cohort studies, eight case-control studies, and two ecological studies investigated non-starchy vegetables; three cohort studies and two case-control studies investigated green, leafy vegetables. All showed decreased risk with increased intake, with none reporting contrary results. Meta-analysis of cohort data showed a statistically significant decreased risk for non-starchy vegetables, with a clear dose-response relationship. A pooled analysis of 12 cohort studies (more than 560 000 participants, followed up for 7–22 years, with more than 2100 ovarian cancer cases) showed a non-significant decreased risk for the highest intake group of non-starchy vegetables.[254]

This is a wide and disparate category, and many different plant food constituents are represented that could contribute to a protective effect of non-starchy vegetables. These include dietary fibre, carotenoids, folate, selenium, glucosinolates, dithiolthiones, indoles, coumarins, ascorbate, chlorophyll, flavonoids, allylsulphides, flavonoids, and phytoestrogens, some of which are potentially antioxidants. Antioxidants trap free radicals and reactive oxygen molecules, protecting against oxidation damage. It is difficult to unravel the relative importance of each constituent and it is likely that any protective effect may result from a combination of influences on several pathways involved in carcinogenesis.

> **Evidence from cohort and case-control studies is sparse. There is limited evidence suggesting that non-starchy vegetables protect against ovarian cancer.**

The Panel is aware that since the conclusion of the SLR, one case-control study[17] has been published. This new information does not change the Panel judgement. Also see box 3.8.

7.11.5.2 Adult attained height
(Also see chapter 6.2.3.1.)
Seven cohort studies, nine case-control studies, and two ecological studies investigated adult attained height. All cohort studies and most other studies showed increased risk with greater adult attained height. Meta-analysis of cohort data showed an 8 per cent increased risk per 5 cm of height (figure 6.2.7); meta-analysis of case-control data showed no statistically significant relationship. Heterogeneity in the latter was derived almost entirely from one study.

The general mechanisms through which the factors that lead to greater adult attained height, or its consequences, could plausibly influence cancer risk are outlined in chapter 6.2.1.3 (see box 2.4). Many of these, such as early-life nutrition, altered hormone profiles, and the rate of sexual maturation, could plausibly increase cancer risk.

> **There is some inconsistency, but the better quality epidemiological data show a clearer effect, with a dose-response relationship. There is evidence for plausible mechanisms operating in humans. The factors that lead to greater adult attained height, or its consequences, are probably a cause of ovarian cancer. The causal factor is unlikely to be tallness itself, but factors that promote linear growth in childhood.**

The Panel is aware that since the conclusion of the SLR, one cohort study[255] and one case-control study[256] have been published. This new information does not change the Panel judgement. Also see box 3.8.

7.11.5.3 Lactation

(Also see chapter 6.3.3.)
One cohort study and 10 case-control studies investigated lactation, most of which showed an association with reduced risk. Meta-analysis of case-control data showed statistically significant decreased risk with increased accumulated lifetime duration of breastfeeding, with a clear dose-response relationship. Substantial heterogeneity is partially explained by variation in the assessment of breastfeeding when, for example, exclusivity of breastfeeding is not always assessed.

Lactation delays the return of menstruation and ovulation after childbirth. The general mechanisms through which lactation could plausibly protect against cancer are outlined in chapter 6.3.3. There is evidence that the reduced number of menstrual cycles associated with breastfeeding protect against some cancers.

> **There are sparse prospective epidemiological data, though some evidence for a dose-response relationship. The mechanistic evidence is speculative. There is limited evidence suggesting that lactation protects against ovarian cancer.**

The Panel is aware that since the conclusion of the SLR, one case-control study[257] has been published. This new information does not change the Panel judgement. Also see box 3.8.

7.11.5.4 Other exposures

Other exposures were evaluated. However, the data were either of too low quality, too inconsistent, or the number of studies too few to allow conclusions to be reached. These were as follows: pulses (legumes); fruits; meat; poultry; fish; eggs; milk and dairy products; coffee; tea; alcohol; carbohydrate; dietary fibre; lactose; total fat; cholesterol; protein; vitamin A; folate; vitamin C; vitamin E; recreational activity; energy intake; body fatness; weight change; and abdominal fatness.

7.11.6 Comparison with previous report

7.11.6.1 General

See 7.1.6.1, and box 3.8 in chapter 3.

7.11.6.2 Specific

The finding here on adult attained height is new.

7.11.7 Conclusions

The Panel concludes:

The factors that lead to greater adult attained height, or its consequences, are probably a cause of cancer of the ovary.

There is limited evidence suggesting that non-starchy vegetables, and also lactation, protect against this cancer.

7.12 Endometrium

Endometrial cancer is the eighth most common cancer in women (and the 17th most common cancer overall) worldwide. Around 200 000 cases were recorded in 2002, accounting for around 4 per cent of all new cases of cancer in women (2 per cent overall). It is most frequent in high-income countries. Around three quarters of women with this cancer survive for 5 years. It is the 13th most common cause of cancer death in women worldwide (21st overall).

Overall, *the Panel is impressed* by the pattern of evidence showing the importance of physical activity and body fatness, as well as factors that affect hormone status, in modification of the risk of endometrial cancer.

The Panel judges as follows:
The evidence that body fatness is a cause of cancer of the endometrium is convincing; abdominal fatness is probably a cause. Physical activity probably protects against this cancer. There is limited evidence suggesting that non-starchy vegetables protect against endometrial cancer, and that red meat, and also the factors that lead to greater adult attained height, or its consequences, are causes of this cancer.

Life events that protect against endometrial cancer include bearing children and early menopause, which have the effect of reducing the number of menstrual cycles and therefore lifetime exposure to oestrogens. The reverse also applies.

See chapter 8 for evidence and judgements on factors that modify the risk of body fatness and abdominal fatness, including physical activity and sedentary ways of life, the energy density of foods and drinks, and breastfeeding.

In final summary, the strongest evidence, corresponding to judgements of "convincing" and "probable", shows that body fatness and probably abdominal fatness are causes of endometrial cancer, and that physical activity is protective.

FOOD, NUTRITION, PHYSICAL ACTIVITY, AND CANCER OF THE ENDOMETRIUM

In the judgement of the Panel, the factors listed below modify the risk of cancer of the endometrium. Judgements are graded according to the strength of the evidence.

	DECREASES RISK	INCREASES RISK
Convincing		**Body fatness**
Probable	**Physical activity[1]**	**Abdominal fatness**
Limited — suggestive	Non-starchy vegetables[2]	Red meat[3] Adult attained height[4]
Limited — no conclusion	Cereals (grains) and their products; dietary fibre; fruits; pulses (legumes); soya and soya products; poultry; fish; eggs; milk and dairy products; total fat; animal fats; saturated fatty acids; cholesterol; coffee; alcohol; carbohydrates; protein; retinol; vitamin C; vitamin E; beta-carotene; lactation; energy intake	
Substantial effect on risk unlikely	None identified	

1 Physical activity of all types: occupational, household, transport, and recreational.
2 Judgements on vegetables and fruits do not include those preserved by salting and/or pickling.
3 The term 'red meat' refers to beef, pork, lamb, and goat from domesticated animals.
4 Adult attained height is unlikely directly to modify the risk of cancer. It is a marker for genetic, environmental, hormonal, and also nutritional factors affecting growth during the period from preconception to completion of linear growth (see chapter 6.2.1.3).

For an explanation of all the terms used in the matrix, please see chapter 3.5.1, the text of this section, and the glossary.

The endometrium is the lining of the uterus. It is subject to a process of cyclical change during the fertile years of a woman's life.

The majority of cancers that occur in the body of the womb are endometrial cancers, mostly adenocarcinomas,[4] the type included here.

7.12.1 Trends, incidence, and survival

Age-adjusted rates of endometrial cancer are increasing in countries undergoing transition from low- to high-income economies, although there is no clear, overall trend in high-income countries.

This is mainly a disease of high-income countries, where overall rates are nearly five times higher than in middle- to low-income countries. Around the world, age-adjusted incidence rates range from more than 15 per 100 000 women in North America and parts of Europe to less than 5 per 100 000 in most of Africa and Asia. In the USA, rates are higher in white women than among those from other ethnic groups, although mortality rates are higher in black women.[3 258] Risk increases with age, with most diagnoses made postmenopause.

Endometrial cancer often produces symptoms at relatively early stages, so the disease is generally diagnosed early. At around 73 per cent, the overall 5-year survival rate is relatively high, although it is lower in middle- than in high-income countries (67 compared with 82 per cent).[124 259] Endometrial cancer accounts for almost 2 per cent of all cancer incidence (around 4 per cent in women), but just under 1 per cent of all cancer deaths (nearly 2 per cent in women). Also see box 7.1.1.

7.12.2 Pathogenesis

Type 1 endometrial tumours are oestrogen driven, account for around 80 per cent of endometrial cancers, and have a favourable prognosis.[260] They follow a clear development pathway, starting with endometrial hyperplasia (an increase in the number of cells), and are relatively well differentiated. Type 2 tumours are less common, accounting for around 10 per cent of endometrial cancers. Most are associated with endometrial atrophy (wasting), tend to metastasise, and have a less favourable prognosis.

Up to 70 per cent of endometrial cancers are reported in women who have no recognised risk factors — such as those that might disrupt endocrine (hormone) processes.[4] Some studies have shown that polycystic ovary syndrome and insulin sensitivity, which are both components of metabolic syndrome, may play a role in the pathogenesis of endometrial cancer, perhaps through hormonal disruption.[261]

The tumour-suppressor gene PTEN is also involved in the development of endometrial cancers.[260] Also see also box 2.2.

7.12.3 Other established causes

(Also see chapter 2.4 and 7.1.3.1.)

Life events. Not bearing children increases the risk of, and may be seen as a cause of, endometrial cancer.[262] The reverse also applies: bearing children reduces the risk of, and may be seen as protective against, endometrial cancer.[258-261] There is also substantial evidence that, as with breast and ovarian cancer, late natural menopause increases the risk of, and may be seen as a cause of, endometrial cancer. The reverse also applies: early menopause reduces the risk of, and may be seen as protective against, this cancer.[133]

Medication. Oral contraceptives protect against this cancer.[133] Oestrogen-only hormone replacement therapy is a cause of this cancer,[144] as is tamoxifen.

7.12.4 Interpretation of the evidence

7.12.4.1 General
For general considerations that may affect interpretation of the evidence, see chapters 3.3 and 3.5, and boxes 3.1, 3.2, 3.6 and 3.7.

'Relative risk' is used in this Report to denote ratio measures of effect, including 'risk ratios', 'rate ratios', 'hazard ratios', and 'odds ratios'.

7.12.4.2 Specific
Considerations specific to cancer of the endometrium include:

Patterns. Because endometrial cancer is hormone related, factors that modify risk might have different effects at different times of life.

Confounding. High-quality cohort studies eliminate women who have had hysterectomies from 'at-risk' populations. High-quality case-control studies assess the levels of hysterectomies in control groups.

7.12.5 Evidence and judgements

In total, 282 publications were included in the SLR for endometrial cancer. Fuller summaries of the epidemiological, experimental, and mechanistic evidence are to be found in Chapters 4–6.

The full SLR is contained on the CD included with this Report.

7.12.5.1 Non-starchy vegetables
(Also see chapter 4.2.5.1.)
Ten case-control studies investigated non-starchy vegetables, and seven case-control studies investigated cruciferous vegetables. Most studies showed decreased risk with increased intake. Meta-analysis of case-control data produced evidence of decreased risk with non-starchy or cruciferous vegetable intake, with a clear dose-response relationship. There were no cohort data.

This is a wide and disparate category, and many different plant food constituents are represented that could contribute to a protective effect of non-starchy vegetables. These include dietary fibre, carotenoids, folate, selenium, glucosinolates, dithiolthiones, indoles, coumarins, ascorbate, chlorophyll, flavonoids, allylsulphides, flavonoids, and phytoestrogens, some of which are potentially antioxidants. Antioxidants trap free radicals and reactive oxygen molecules, protecting against oxidation damage.

It is difficult to unravel the relative importance of each constituent and it is likely that any protective effect may result from a combination of influences on several pathways involved in carcinogenesis.

> Evidence comes from case-control studies only. There is limited evidence suggesting that non-starchy vegetables protect against endometrial cancer.

7.12.5.2 Red meat
(Also see chapter 4.3.5.1.1.)
One cohort study and seven case-control studies investigated red meat. Most studies showed increased risk with higher intake. Meta-analysis of case-control data produced evidence of increased risk with higher intake, with a clear dose-response relationship.

There are several potential underlying mechanisms for a positive association of red meat consumption with endometrial cancer, including the generation of potentially carcinogenic N-nitroso compounds (see box 4.3.2).

Some meats are also cooked at high temperatures, resulting in the production of heterocyclic amines and polycyclic aromatic hydrocarbons (see box 4.3.4). Red meat contains haem iron. Free iron can lead to the production of free radicals (see box 4.3.3).

The evidence, mostly from case-control studies, is sparse. There is limited evidence suggesting that red meat is a cause of endometrial cancer.

The Panel is aware that since the conclusion of the SLR, one case-control study[263] has been published. This new information does not change the Panel judgement. Also see box 3.8.

7.12.5.3 Physical activity

(Also see chapter 5.4.3.)

Two cohort studies and 4 case-control studies investigated total physical activity; 3 cohort studies and 10 case-control studies investigated occupational activity; and 4 cohort studies and 10 case-control studies investigated recreational activity. Nearly all of the cohort studies and most of the other studies showed decreased risk with increased physical activity. Although meta-analysis was not possible due to the wide variety in measures used, comparisons of high with low activity levels showed a consistent association with decreased risk (figures 5.4.8 and 5.4.9).

Sustained moderate physical activity raises the metabolic rate and increases maximal oxygen uptake. In the long term, regular periods of such activity increase the body's metabolic efficiency and capacity (the amount of work that it can perform), as well as reducing blood pressure and insulin resistance. In addition, physical activity has been found to affect serum levels of oestradiol, oestrone, and androgens in postmenopausal women, even after adjusting for BMI. More generally, effects on oestrogen metabolism may operate directly, or through decreasing body fat stores. Physical activity is also known to have favourable effects on insulin resistance, which may also result in decreased risk of endometrial cancer. Physical activity also results in decreased risk of diabetes and high blood pressure, which are risk factors for endometrial cancer.

There is generally consistent evidence, mostly from case-control studies, showing lower risk of cancer of the endometrium with higher levels of physical activity. There is evidence for mechanisms operating in humans. Physical activity probably protects against cancer of the endometrium.

7.12.5.4 Body fatness

(Also see chapter 6.1.3.1.)

Twenty-three cohort studies, 41 case-control studies and 2 cross-sectional studies investigated body fatness, as measured by BMI. Three cohort studies and six case-control studies investigated BMI as a young adult. Nearly all of the studies showed increased risk with increased body fatness, more than half of which were statistically significant. Meta-analysis of cohort data showed an overall 52 per cent increased risk per 5 kg/m^2, or a 31 per cent increased risk per 5 kg/m^2 as a young adult; meta-analysis of case-control data showed an overall 56 per cent increased risk per 5 kg/m^2, with a non-significant increased risk for BMI as a young adult (figures 6.1.17 and 6.1.18). Heterogeneity existed in the size, but not direction, of the effect.

Body fatness directly affects levels of many circulating hormones, such as insulin, insulin-like growth factors, and oestrogens, creating an environment that encourages carcinogenesis and discourages apoptosis (see box 2.4). It also stimulates the body's inflammatory response, which may contribute to the initiation and progression of several cancers (see chapter 2.4.1.3).

There is abundant, consistent epidemiological evidence with a clear dose-response relationship, and robust evidence for mechanisms operating in humans. The evidence that greater body fatness is a cause of endometrial cancer is convincing.

The Panel is aware that since the conclusion of the SLR, one cohort study[215] and one case-control study[264] have been published. This new information does not change the Panel judgement. Also see box 3.8.

7.12.5.5 Abdominal fatness

(Also see chapter 6.1.3.2.)

One cohort study and four case-control studies investigated waist circumference; one cohort study and six case-control studies investigated waist to hip ratio. Both cohort studies and most case-control studies showed statistically significant increased risk with increased abdominal fatness. Meta-analysis of case-control data showed a non-significant increased risk.

The general mechanisms through which abdominal fatness could plausibly cause cancer are outlined in chapter 6.1.3 (for more detail see box 2.4). The hormonal and other biological effects of being overweight or obese are outlined in chapter 8. Many of these, such as increased circulating oestrogens and decreased insulin sensitivity, are associated with abdominal fatness independently of overall body fatness.

There is a substantial amount of generally consistent epidemiological evidence, but limited prospective data. There is evidence for plausible mechanisms. Greater abdominal fatness is a probable cause of endometrial cancer.

7.12.5.6 Adult attained height

(Also see chapter 6.2.3.1.)

Ten cohort studies, 16 case-control studies and 1 ecological study investigated adult attained height. Most studies showed increased risk with greater adult attained height. Meta-analysis of cohort and case-control data showed non-significant increased risk.

The general mechanisms through which the factors that lead to greater adult attained height, or its consequences, could plausibly influence cancer risk are outlined in chapter 6.2.1.3 (for more detail see box 2.4). Many of these, such as early-life nutrition, altered hormone profiles, and the rate of sexual maturation, could plausibly increase cancer risk.

Although there is generally consistent evidence for prospective epidemiological data, there is some inconsistency in the evidence between cohort and case-control studies, and the mechanistic evidence is speculative. There is limited evidence that greater adult attained height, or the factors that lead to it, are a cause of endometrial cancer. The causal factor is unlikely to be tallness itself, but factors that promote linear growth in childhood.

7.12.5.7 Other exposures

Other exposures were evaluated. However, the data were either of too low quality, too inconsistent, or the number of studies too few to allow conclusions to be reached. These were as follows: cereals (grains) and their products; fruits; pulses (legumes); tofu and soya; poultry; fish; eggs; milk and dairy products; coffee; alcohol; carbohydrates; dietary fibre; total fat; animal fats; saturated fatty acids; cholesterol; protein; retinol; beta-carotene; vitamin C; vitamin E; energy intake; and lactation.

7.12.6 Comparison with previous report

7.12.6.1 General

See 7.1.6.1, and box 3.8 in chapter 3.

7.12.6.2 Specific

The finding here on physical activity is new. The evidence on body fatness and on abdominal fatness (not considered separately in the previous report's matrices) has strengthened.

7.12.7 Conclusions

The Panel concludes:

The evidence that body fatness is a cause of cancer of the endometrium is convincing; abdominal fatness is probably also a cause.

Physical activity probably protects against this cancer.

There is limited evidence suggesting that non-starchy vegetables protect against endometrial cancer, and that red meat, and also the factors that lead to greater adult attained height, or its consequences, are causes of this cancer.

7.13 Cervix

Cervical cancer is the second most common cancer in women worldwide. Around half a million cases were recorded in 2002, accounting for around 10 per cent of all new cases of cancer in women (5 per cent overall). It is most common in Africa, some parts of Asia including India, and in Latin America. It is most common in relatively young women. Five-year survival rates are around 50 per cent. It is the third most common cause of cancer death in women.

Overall, *the Panel notes* that food and nutrition and associated factors are not significant factors in modification of the risk of cancer of the cervix, although general nutritional status may affect a woman's vulnerability to infection.

Life events that protect against cervical cancer include having relatively few sexual partners. The reverse also applies. Infection with HPV is a necessary cause of this cancer, and smoking tobacco increases risk.

The Panel judges as follows:
There is limited evidence suggesting that carrots protect against cervical cancer.

In final summary, there is no strong evidence, corresponding to judgements of "convincing" and "probable", to conclude that any aspect of food, nutrition, and physical activity modifies the risk of cervical cancer.

The cervix is the neck of the womb. The part of the cervix inside the cervical canal is called the endocervix. The part on the outside is the ectocervix. Most cervical cancers start where these two parts meet. There are two main types, squamous cell carcinoma and adenocarcinoma. Occasionally, mixed carcinomas, with features of both types, occur. Approximately 80 per cent of cervical cancers are squamous cell carcinomas, with most of the rest being adenocarcinomas.[265] Both types of cervical cancer are covered in this Report.

7.13.1 Trends, incidence, and survival

Age-adjusted rates of cervical cancer are decreasing, particularly in high- and middle-income countries, although there are insufficient data to derive trends in low-income countries. In high-income countries, the incidence of adenocarcinomas has increased since the 1970s, both absolutely and relative to squamous cell carcinomas. The prevalence appears to be increasing disproportionately in young women.[266]

Cervical cancer is predominantly a disease of low-income countries, with overall rates nearly twice as high in middle- to low- as in high-income countries. Around the world, age-adjusted incidence rates range from more than 40 per 100 000 women in parts of Africa, South America, and Melanesia, to less than 10 per 100 000 in North America and parts of Asia. However, rates are relatively high elsewhere

FOOD, NUTRITION, PHYSICAL ACTIVITY, AND CANCER OF THE CERVIX

In the judgement of the Panel, the factors listed below modify the risk of cancer of the cervix. Judgements are graded according to the strength of the evidence.

	DECREASES RISK	INCREASES RISK
Convincing		
Probable		
Limited — suggestive	Carrots[1]	
Limited — no conclusion	Non-starchy vegetables; fruits; milk; retinol; vitamin E; alcoholism[2]; body fatness; adult attained height.	
Substantial effect on risk unlikely	None identified	

1 Judgements on vegetables and fruits do not include those preserved by salting and/or pickling.
2 Although data suggest that alcoholism is related to increased risk, *the Panel concludes* that this is likely to be due to factors other than alcohol intake itself.

For an explanation of all the terms used in the matrix, please see chapter 3.5.1, the text of this section, and the glossary.

in Asia, for example in India and Bangladesh. In the USA, rates are higher among both African-American and Hispanic-American women than in white women. The incidence of many cancers rises with age, but cervical cancer peaks in younger women, between the ages of 30 and 45.[6] However, mortality does not follow the same pattern, and rises with age. Most women in high-income countries, and to varying degrees in other countries, have access to preventive screening programmes that are designed to detect precancerous lesions. If these are identified and removed, the incidence of this cancer is reduced. After a screening programme was implemented in the UK in 1988, cervical cancer incidence (age-standardised rate) has fallen by nearly 60 per cent.[6] It is generally well accepted that better access to cervical screening programmes worldwide would decrease both the incidence and mortality rates for this cancer.[267] More recently vaccination against HPV has become a preventive option.

The overall 5-year survival rate is approximately 50 per cent: 61 per cent in high-income countries compared with 41 per cent in middle- to low-income countries.[124] This cancer accounts for somewhat over 4 per cent of all cancer incidence (around 10 per cent in women) but only around 4 per cent of all cancer deaths (just over 9 per cent in women). Also see box 7.1.1.

7.13.2 Pathogenesis

Virtually all cervical cancers are associated with HPV infection (see box 7.13.1), and a woman's nutrition status may influence her susceptibility to this infection.[268] However, the majority of women with HPV do not develop cervical cancer. Therefore, HPV infection is a necessary but not a sufficient cause of cervical cancer. Women become susceptible to developing cervical cancer following HPV infection, but other environmental factors are required for the cancer to develop.

These factors may include toxins such as polycyclic aromatic hydrocarbons (see box 4.3.4) from tobacco smoke, food, or other environmental sources, which have been found in the mucus lining the cervix.[269]

Box 7.13.1	**Human papilloma viruses**

Human papilloma viruses (HPVs) are common. They infect squamous epithelia and generate warts. They are passed by direct contact; genital HPV infections are sexually transmitted. HPV infection rates are higher in women who have had a higher number of sexual partners (particularly male partners); do not use barrier methods of contraception; and who started having sex at a younger age.

There are more than 100 types of HPV. All can interfere with host-cell machinery that prevents cells from growing and replicating excessively, which are some of the cellular mechanisms that help protect the body against cancer development. Low-risk HPVs cause genital warts; high-risk HPVs cause squamous intra-epithelial lesions that can progress to invasive squamous cell carcinoma. The majority of human cervical cancers are associated with high-risk HPV infections. Four subtypes of this virus account for 80 per cent of all cervical cancer.

HPV infection tends to remain dormant, and with repeated infection, the HPV genome becomes integrated within the host cell genome and some cells may become cancerous.

Most HPV infections do not become persistent, and most persistent HPV infections do not lead to cancer. However, HPV infection is demonstrably present in 99 per cent of women with cervical cancer, and may be present but undetected in the remainder. HPV is a necessary while not sufficient cause of cervical cancer.

There are several stages at which foods or nutrition status could influence progression. Dietary factors influence susceptibility to infection; infection can alter nutrition status; diet may affect the likelihood of infections becoming persistent; and dietary factors have been shown to alter DNA stability and repair. Unfortunately, there is a shortage of epidemiological evidence specific to HPV at each of these stages. There is some limited evidence that eating vegetables and fruits can protect against persistence.[268] There is also evidence that folate can reduce persistence and independently reduce the risk of precancerous lesions in high-risk-HPV infected women.[270-272]

7.13.3 Other established causes

(Also see chapter 2.4 and 7.1.3.1.)

Life events. Early sexual experience and a relatively high number of sexual partners increase the risk and severity of HPV infection, and may be seen as indirect causes of cervical cancer.[220] [222]

Tobacco use. Smoking tobacco makes a woman twice as likely to develop cervical cancer.[10] Tobacco by-products have been found in the cervical mucus of women who smoke. The effect of smoking is independent of that of viral infection.[10] [273]

Infectious agents. HPV infection (see box 7.13.1) is a necessary but not sufficient cause of cervical cancer.[273] [274]

Medication. Dethylstilboestrol (a synthetic oestrogen, now withdrawn) used by women during pregnancy is a cause of vaginal and cervical clear-cell adenocarcinoma in their daughters.[275]

7.13.4 Interpretation of the evidence

7.13.4.1 General
For general considerations that may affect interpretation of the evidence, see chapters 3.3 and 3.5, and boxes 3.1, 3.2, 3.6 and 3.7.

'Relative risk' is used in this Report to denote ratio measures of effect, including 'risk ratios', 'rate ratios', 'hazard ratios', and 'odds ratios'.

7.13.4.2 Specific
Considerations specific to cancer of the cervix include:

Confounding. High-quality studies adjust for HPV infection. Early studies that failed to adjust for HPV status have reduced validity.

7.13.5 Evidence and judgements

In total, 154 publications were included in the SLR for cervical cancer. Fuller summaries of the epidemiological, experimental, and mechanistic evidence are to be found in Chapters 4–6.

The full SLR is contained on the CD included with this Report.

7.13.5.1 Carrots
(Also see chapter 4.2.5.1.3.)
Five case-control studies and one ecological study investigated carrots. All of the case-control studies showed decreased risk for the highest levels of intake compared with the lowest, statistically significant in three. The case-control studies all used hospital-based controls and none adjusted for HPV status. The single ecological study showed non-significant increased risk with high intake of carrots.

Some carotenoids, including beta-carotene and alpha-carotene, which are found at high levels in carrots, are precursors of vitamin A. They also have properties independent of their pro-vitamin A activity. Carotenoids are recognised antioxidants, and low blood levels of dietary antioxidants are associated with HPV persistence.[276]

The evidence, from case-control studies only, is sparse but consistent. There is limited evidence suggesting that carrots protect against cervical cancer.

7.13.5.2 Other exposures
Other exposures were evaluated. However, the data were either of too low quality, too inconsistent, or the number of studies too few to allow conclusions to be reached. These were as follows: non-starchy vegetables; fruits; milk; retinol; vitamin E; alcoholism; body fatness; and adult attained height.

Although data suggest that alcoholism is related to increased risk, *the Panel concludes* that this is likely to be due to factors other than alcohol intake itself.

7.13.5.3 Exposures as related to non-invasive cancer outcomes
The following exposures were evaluated. However, the data were either too sparse, too inconsistent, or the number of studies too few to allow conclusions to be reached: vitamin A (as beta-carotene, alpha-carotene, or retinol); folate; vitamin C; vitamin E; and lycopene.

7.13.6 Comparison with previous report

7.13.6.1 General
See 7.1.6.1, and box 3.8 in chapter 3.

7.13.6.2 Specific
The previous report found that vegetables and fruits, and carotenoids (not carrots specifically), and also vitamins C and E possibly protect against cervical cancer.

7.13.7 Conclusions

The Panel concludes:
There is limited evidence suggesting that carrots protect against cervical cancer. The evidence is too limited to conclude that any aspect of food, nutrition, and physical activity directly modifies the risk of this cancer.

7.14 Prostate

Prostate cancer is the second most common cancer in men (and the sixth most common cancer overall) worldwide. Around 680 000 cases were recorded in 2002, accounting for around 12 per cent of all new cases of cancer in men (6 per cent overall). It is most commonly diagnosed in high-income countries, where screening is common. Five-year survival rates are around 60 per cent. It is the sixth most common cause of cancer death in men worldwide.

Overall, *the Panel notes* the impressive recent evidence from cohort studies and trials demonstrating effects, or absence of effect, of specific foods and nutrients on prostate cancer.

The Panel judges as follows:
Foods containing lycopene, as well as selenium or foods containing it, probably protect against prostate cancer. Foods containing calcium are a probable cause of this cancer. It is unlikely that beta-carotene (whether from foods or supplements) has a substantial effect on the risk of this cancer. There is limited evidence suggesting that pulses (legumes) including soya and soya products, foods containing vitamin E, and alpha-tocopherol supplements are protective; and that processed meat, and milk and dairy products are a cause of this cancer.

In final summary, the strongest evidence, corresponding to judgements of "convincing" and "probable", shows that foods containing lycopene, as well as selenium or foods containing it, probably protect against prostate cancer, and that foods containing calcium are a probable cause of this cancer. It is unlikely that beta-carotene (whether from foods or supplements) has a substantial effect on the risk of this cancer.

The prostate is a walnut-sized gland in men that surrounds the top of the urethra; it produces seminal fluid. Its growth and function are controlled by male hormones such as testosterone.

Almost all prostate cancers are adenocarcinomas,[4] the type included here.

7.14.1 Trends, incidence, and survival

Age-adjusted incidence rates of prostate cancer increased dramatically between 1988 and 1992.[137] This was largely because of the increased availability of screening for prostate-specific antigen (PSA) in men without symptoms of the disease. This test leads to the detection of many prostate cancers that are small and/or would otherwise remain unrecognised, and which may or may not develop further into higher stage disease (see 7.14.2). Rates were already increasing before the availability of PSA testing, and have continued to increase in middle-income countries where screening is still not widely available.[124] This suggests that prostate cancer is influenced

---

FOOD, NUTRITION, PHYSICAL ACTIVITY, AND CANCER OF THE PROSTATE

In the judgement of the Panel, the factors listed below modify the risk of cancer of the prostate. Judgements are graded according to the strength of the evidence.

	DECREASES RISK	INCREASES RISK
Convincing		
Probable	Foods containing lycopene[1 2] Foods containing selenium[1] Selenium[3]	Diets high in calcium[4 5]
Limited — suggestive	Pulses (legumes)[6] Foods containing vitamin E[1] Alpha-tocopherol[7]	Processed meat[8] Milk and dairy products[5]
Limited — no conclusion	Cereals (grains) and their products; dietary fibre; potatoes; non-starchy vegetables; fruits; meat; poultry; fish; eggs; total fat; plant oils; sugar (sucrose); sugary foods and drinks; coffee; tea; alcohol; carbohydrate; protein; vitamin A; retinol; thiamin; riboflavin; niacin; vitamin C; vitamin D; gamma-tocopherol; vitamin supplements; multivitamins; iron; phosphorus; zinc; other carotenoids; physical activity; energy expenditure; vegetarian diets; Seventh-day Adventist diets; body fatness; abdominal fatness; birth weight; energy intake	
Substantial effect on risk unlikely	Beta-carotene[1 9]	

1   Includes both foods naturally containing the constituent and foods which have the constituent added (see chapter 3.5.3).
2   Mostly contained in tomatoes and tomato products. Also fruits such as grapefruit, watermelon, guava, and apricot.
3   The evidence is derived from studies using supplements at a dose of 200 µg/day. Selenium is toxic at high doses.
4   Includes diets that naturally contain calcium and that contain foods fortified with calcium. See box 4.10.1.
5   Effect only apparent at high calcium intakes (around 1.5 g/day or more). Evidence for milk and dairy products (but not calcium) was derived only from countries with populations that have high calcium and dairy consumption.
6   Including soya and soya products.
7   The evidence is derived from studies using supplements at a dose of 50 mg/day.
8   The term 'processed meat' refers to meats preserved by smoking, curing, or salting, or addition of chemical preservatives.
9   The evidence is derived from studies using supplements at doses of 20, 30, and 50 mg/day.

For an explanation of all the terms used in the matrix, please see chapter 3.5.1, the text of this section, and the glossary.

by environmental factors. Although screening is increasingly popular in many high-income countries, its value, for example in reducing mortality, is controversial. There has been a decline in incidence and mortality in several high-income countries since the 1990s although rates remain higher than those recorded before screening became available. This trend may be due to elimination of early stage disease and improved treatment.[277]

Prostate cancer is mainly a disease of high-income countries, where overall rates are nearly six times higher than in middle- to low-income countries. Around the world, age-adjusted incidence rates range from more than 100 per 100 000 men in North America, parts of the Caribbean, and Oceania, to less than 10 per 100 000 in Melanesia and much of Asia.[2] This wide range is partly, but not entirely, attributable to the increased availability of screening in high-income countries. In the USA, rates are higher among African-American men than in white men.[3]

Risk increases with age, rising sharply after 40. In most high-income countries, incidence in men below 40 is typically less than 1 per 100 000, rising to more than 1000 per 100 000 in those aged 65 and over.[278]

Average survival for prostate cancer is relatively high worldwide, although markedly more so in high-income countries. The 5-year survival rate is approximately 60 per cent overall: 76 per cent in high-income countries compared with 45 per cent in middle- to low-income countries.[124] This cancer accounts for around 6 per cent of all cancer incidence (nearly 12 per cent in men) but around 3 per cent of all cancer deaths (almost 6 per cent in men; all sites except for non-melanoma skin). Also see box 7.1.1.

7.14.2 Pathogenesis

The disease usually develops slowly and dysplastic lesions may precede cancer by many years or even decades. Extrapolations from autopsy studies suggest that most men would have prostate cancer if they lived to be more than 100.[278] The number of prostate cancers found incidentally at autopsy, which had been asymptomatic and not a cause of death, suggests that small, localised prostate cancers can remain unrecognised for many years before progressing to a clinically significant form. Men are more likely to die with, rather than from, prostate cancer.[279 280]

The increased prostate cancer incidence in first-degree male relatives of women who have early onset breast cancer suggests a genetic predisposition.[281] Some studies propose that this may be linked to the BRCA genes.[282]

Growth factors, particularly IGF, as well as androgens have also been implicated in the development of prostate cancers. Serum levels of IGF-1 can be associated with prostate cancer independently of PSA levels.[283] High levels of testosterone promote cell differentiation, which could protect against the development of this cancer. Therefore, declining levels of this hormone in older age may contribute to the development of this cancer.[284]

7.14.3 Other established causes

(Also see chapter 2.4 and 7.1.3.1.)

There are no other established causes of prostate cancer.

7.14.4 Interpretation of the evidence

7.14.4.1 General
For general considerations that may affect interpretation of the evidence, see chapters 3.3 and 3.5, and boxes 3.1, 3.2, 3.6 and 3.7.

'Relative risk' is used in this Report to denote ratio measures of effect, including 'risk ratios', 'rate ratios', 'hazard ratios', and 'odds ratios'.

7.14.4.2 Specific
Considerations specific to cancer of the prostate include:

Confounding. Screening is associated with relatively high socioeconomic status and also with 'health-conscious' behaviour such as taking exercise or following dietary guidelines. High-quality studies adjust for these factors. Some case-control studies use cases that have been detected by screening. If so, it is important that control groups are also from a screened population.

7.14.5 Evidence and judgements

In total, 558 publications were included in the SLR for prostate cancer. Fuller summaries of the epidemiological, experimental, and mechanistic evidence are to be found in Chapters 4–6.

The full SLR is contained on the CD included with this Report.

7.14.5.1 Pulses (legumes) including soya and soya products
(Also see chapter 4.2.5.10.)
A total of 3 cohort studies, 11 case-control studies, and 6 ecological studies investigated pulses (legumes); 4 cohort studies, 4 case-control studies, and 2 ecological studies investigated soya and soya products. Most studies showed decreased risk with increased intake. Meta-analysis of case-control data produced evidence of an association with legume intake, with a clear dose-response relationship.

Pulses (legumes), particularly soya foods, contain various compounds that may have anti-cancer effects. These compounds could plausibly influence oestrogen metabolism. In addition, phytoestrogens in pulses and soya can have an androgenic effect, potentially inhibiting testosterone-induced growth of the prostate.

The evidence, mostly from case-control studies, is inconsistent. There is limited evidence suggesting that pulses (legumes), including soya and soya products, protect against prostate cancer.

7.14.5.2 Processed meat

(Also see chapter 4.3.5.1.2.)

Four cohort studies and six case-control studies investigated processed meat. All cohort studies reported increased risk with higher intake; and most case-control studies also showed this effect.

Nitrates are both produced endogenously in gastric acid and added as preservatives to processed meats (box 4.3.2). They may contribute to N-nitroso compound production and exposure. These compounds are suspected mutagens and carcinogens.[55]

Many processed meats also contain high levels of salt and nitrite. Meats cooked at high temperatures can contain heterocyclic amines and polycyclic aromatic hydrocarbons (box 4.3.4). Haem promotes the formation of N-nitroso compounds and also contains iron. Free iron can lead to production of free radicals (box 4.3.3).

> **There is limited evidence from sparse and inconsistent studies suggesting that processed meat is a cause of prostate cancer.**

The Panel is aware that since the conclusion of the SLR, two cohort studies[285 286] have been published. This new information does not change the Panel judgement. Also see box 3.8.

7.14.5.3 Milk and dairy products

(Also see chapter 4.4.5.1.)

A total of 10 cohort studies, 13 case-control studies, and 2 ecological studies investigated milk and dairy foods; 16 cohort studies, 11 case-control studies, and 11 ecological studies investigated milk. Most of the studies showed increased risk with increased intake. Meta-analysis of cohort data produced evidence of a clear dose-response relationship between advanced/aggressive cancer risk with milk intake, and between all prostate cancer risk and milk and dairy products.

Most other meta-analyses show non-significant increased risk. Ecological studies consistently report a relationship in the direction of increased risk between milk or dairy consumption and prostate cancer.

High calcium intake downregulates the formation of 1,25-dihydroxy vitamin D3 from vitamin D, thereby increasing cell proliferation in the prostate.[287] Prostate cancer tumours in rats treated with 1,25-dihydroxy vitamin D3 were significantly smaller, and presented smaller numbers of lung metastases.[288] Also, consumption of milk increases blood levels of IGF-1, which has been associated with increased prostate cancer risk in some studies.[283 289]

> **The evidence is inconsistent from both cohort and case-control studies. There is limited evidence suggesting that milk and dairy products are a cause of prostate cancer.**

The Panel is aware that since the conclusion of the SLR, two cohort studies[290 291] and one case-control study[189] have been published. This new information does not change the Panel judgement. Also see box 3.8.

7.14.5.4 Diets high in calcium

(Also see chapter 4.4.5.2.)

Nine cohort studies, 12 case-control studies, and 2 ecological studies investigated dietary calcium. Most cohort studies showed increased risk with increased calcium intake; case-control studies were inconsistent. Meta-analysis of cohort data showed an increased risk of 27 per cent per g/day; meta-analysis of cohort data on advanced or aggressive prostate cancer showed an increased risk of 32 per cent per g/day. Meta-analyses of case-control data showed non-significant increased risk.

Calcium can be taken to be a marker for dairy intake in high-income populations. In areas outside the USA, Europe, and Oceania, dairy products are not as widely consumed, and the range of calcium intakes is smaller.

High calcium intake downregulates the formation of 1,25-dihydroxy vitamin D3 from vitamin D, thereby increasing cell proliferation in the prostate.[287] Prostate cancer tumours in rats treated with 1,25-dihydroxy vitamin D3 were significantly smaller and presented fewer lung metastases.[288]

> **The evidence, from both cohort and case-control studies, is substantial and consistent, with a dose-response relationship. There is evidence for plausible mechanisms. Diets high in calcium are a probable cause of prostate cancer.**

The Panel is aware that since the conclusion of the SLR, two cohort studies[290 291] have been published. This new information does not change the Panel judgement. Also see box 3.8.

7.14.5.5 Foods containing selenium

(Also see chapter 4.2.5.8.)

A total of 1 cohort study, 7 case-control studies, and 2 ecological studies investigated dietary selenium; 12 cohort studies and 4 case-control studies investigated serum or plasma selenium; and 3 cohort studies, 3 case-control studies, and 1 ecological study investigated levels in nails. Most studies, including all of those that reported separately on advanced/aggressive prostate cancer, showed decreased risk with increased intake. Meta-analysis of cohort data on advanced or aggressive prostate cancer showed a decreased risk of 13 per cent per 10 μg selenium/litre of serum or plasma (figure 4.2.37), or 20 per cent per 100 ng selenium per g of nail clippings. Meta-analyses of cohort data that included all prostate cancer diagnoses showed non-significant decreased risk. Case-control studies were inconsistent.

Dietary selenium deficiency has been shown to cause a lack of selenoprotein expression. Twenty-five selenoproteins have been identified in animals, and a number of these have important anti-inflammatory and antioxidant properties. Four are glutathione peroxidases, which protect against oxidative damage to biomolecules such as lipids, lipoproteins, and DNA. Three are thioredoxin reductases; among other functions, these regenerate oxidised ascorbic acid to its active antioxidant form.

In addition, selenoproteins are involved in testosterone production, which is an important regulator of both normal and abnormal prostate growth.

The evidence from cohort and case-control studies is
consistent, with a dose-response relationship. There is
evidence for plausible mechanisms. Foods containing
selenium probably protect against prostate cancer.

7.14.5.6 Foods containing lycopene
(Also see chapter 4.2.5.3.)
A total of 5 cohort studies, 9 case-control studies, and 3 ecological studies investigated tomatoes; 3 cohort studies and
14 case-control studies investigated dietary lycopene; and 6
cohort studies and 2 case-control studies investigated serum
or plasma lycopene. Most of the studies showed decreased
risk with increased intake. Studies of cumulative lycopene
intake, or of tomato sauce products (from which lycopene is
highly bioavailable), showed statistically significant
decreased risk. Meta-analysis of cohort data on serum or
plasma lycopene, which are likely to be more precise and
accurate than dietary assessments, showed a 4 per cent
decreased risk per 10 μg lycopene/litre.

Lycopene is best absorbed from vegetables and fruits that
contain it after they are cooked and pureed. The best measures, that take the degree of absorption into account, are
therefore from studies on tomato sauce or serum/plasma
lycopene. The Panel also gave emphasis to studies on
advanced or aggressive cancers, which may be better linked
to prognosis than studies that include early stage or
unrecognised disease.

Lycopene is the most potent carotenoid antioxidant, has
an antiproliferative effect, reduces plasma low-density
lipoprotein cholesterol, improves immune function, and
reduces inflammation.

There is a substantial amount of consistent evidence,
in particular on tomato products, from both cohort and
case-control studies. There is evidence for plausible
mechanisms. Foods containing lycopene probably
protect against prostate cancer.

*The Panel is aware that since the conclusion of the SLR, two
cohort studies[292][293] and one case-control study[294] have been
published. This new information does not change the Panel
judgement. Also see box 3.8.*

7.14.5.7 Selenium
(Also see chapter 4.10.6.4.5.)
One randomised controlled trial and two cohort studies
investigated selenium supplements. The randomised controlled trial was conducted in 974 men with a history of skin
cancers, randomised to receive a daily supplement of 200 μg
selenium or a placebo. Prostate cancer was not a prior stated outcome, and was assessed as a secondary endpoint. The
trial showed a 63 per cent decreased risk from selenium supplementation. Both cohort studies showed non-significant
decreased risk with selenium supplementation.

Dietary selenium deficiency has been shown to cause a
lack of selenoprotein expression. Twenty-five selenoproteins
have been identified in animals and a number of these have
important anti-inflammatory and antioxidant properties.
Four are glutathione peroxidases, which protect against

oxidative damage to biomolecules such as lipids, lipoproteins, and DNA. Three are thioredoxin reductases; among
other functions, these regenerate oxidised ascorbic acid to
its active antioxidant form. In addition, selenoproteins are
involved in testosterone production, which is an important
regulator of both normal and abnormal prostate growth.

There is strong evidence from trials and cohort studies.
Selenium probably protects against prostate cancer.

7.14.5.8 Foods containing vitamin E
(Also see chapter 4.2.5.7.)
A total of 2 cohort studies, 13 case-control studies, and 1 ecological study investigated dietary vitamin E; and 4 cohort
studies and 1 case-control study investigated serum vitamin
E. Other groupings examined were serum or plasma alpha-
tocopherol (8 cohort, 2 case-control) and serum gamma-
tocopherol (6 cohort, 1 case-control). Most studies showed
decreased risk with increased intake. Meta-analysis of
cohort data on serum gamma-tocopherol produced evidence
of an association with decreased risk, with a clear dose-
response relationship.

Vitamin E is an antioxidant that has been reported to prevent DNA damage, enhance DNA repair, prevent lipid peroxidation, and prevent activation of carcinogens such as
nitrosamines. Vitamin E protects vitamin A and selenium in
the body. In addition to acting as a free-radical scavenger,
vitamin E enhances the body's immune response, which may
play a role in cancer defences.

The evidence on vitamin E, mostly from case-control
studies, was inconsistent. There is limited evidence
suggesting that foods containing vitamin E protect
against prostate cancer.

*The Panel is aware that since the conclusion of the SLR, two
cohort studies[293][295] have been published. This new information
does not change the Panel judgement. Also see box 3.8.*

7.14.5.9 Beta-carotene
(Also see chapters 4.2.5.3 and 4.10.6.4.2.)
Six cohort studies and 21 case-control studies investigated
dietary beta-carotene; 10 cohort studies and 5 case-control
studies investigated serum or plasma beta-carotene; 3 randomised controlled trials and 2 cohort studies investigated
beta-carotene supplements. Meta-analyses of 6 cohort studies and 15 case-control studies that investigated beta-
carotene from food and 7 cohort studies that investigated
serum or plasma beta-carotene produced evidence for there
being no association with prostate cancer risk. One randomised controlled trial produced evidence of no association; the other two showed that it was unlikely that
beta-carotene reduced incidence, but did not exclude an
effect of increasing incidence.

There is strong evidence from good quality trials
and from cohort studies, which consistently fail
to demonstrate a protective effect. Beta-carotene
supplements are unlikely to have a substantial

protective effect against prostate cancer. The evidence is too limited to draw a conclusion on a harmful effect. It is unlikely that beta-carotene or foods containing it have a substantial effect on the risk of prostate cancer.

The Panel is aware that since the conclusion of the SLR, two cohort studies[293][295] have been published. This new information does not change the Panel judgement. Also see box 3.8.

7.14.5.10 Alpha-tocopherol (vitamin E)
(Also see chapter 4.10.6.4.3.)
One randomised controlled trial investigated alpha-tocopherol supplements and prostate cancer. The large randomised controlled trial of male smokers given daily supplements of 50 mg of alpha-tocopherol and 20 mg of beta-carotene showed a statistically significant 34 per cent decreased risk for alpha-tocopherol supplements. Prostate cancer was not a prior-stated outcome for this trial.

Vitamin E exists in eight different forms (isomers): four tocopherols and four tocotrienols. There is an alpha, beta, gamma, and delta form of each. Each form has slightly different biological properties but all are antioxidants. Alpha-tocopherol is thought to be the most biologically active isomer of vitamin E. It inhibits cell proliferation, can directly activate certain enzymes, and exerts transcriptional control on several genes. Vitamin E may have a direct effect on prostate growth by decreasing cellular concentrations of testosterone, which could impair differentiation.

The evidence is sparse. There is limited evidence that alpha-tocopherol supplements protect against prostate cancer in smokers.

7.14.5.11 Other exposures
Other exposures were evaluated. However, the data were either of too low quality, too inconsistent, or the number of studies too few to allow conclusions to be reached. These were as follows: culturally defined diets (vegetarian, Seventh-day Adventist); cereals (grains) and their products; potatoes; fruit and (non-starchy) vegetables; poultry; meat; fish; eggs; all fats; plant oils; sugar; confectionery; dietary fibre; fat; protein; carbohydrate; coffee; tea; alcoholic drinks; vitamin supplements; multivitamins; vitamin A; retinol; carotenoids; thiamine; riboflavin; niacin; vitamin C; vitamin D; vitamin E from foods; iron; zinc; phosphorus; physical activity; energy intake; energy expenditure; body composition; size and shape; and birth weight.

7.14.6 Comparison with previous report

7.14.6.1 General
See 7.1.6.1, and box 3.8 in chapter 3.

7.14.6.2 Specific
The findings here on foods containing lycopene and/or calcium, and on selenium or foods containing it, are new,

reflecting the recent intense research interest in prostate cancer, including randomised controlled supplementation trials.

7.14.7 Conclusions

The Panel concludes:
Foods containing lycopene, as well as selenium and foods containing it, probably protect against prostate cancer. Diets high in calcium are a probable cause of this cancer. It is unlikely that beta-carotene (whether from foods or supplements) has a substantial effect on the risk of this cancer. There is limited evidence suggesting that pulses (legumes) including soya and soya products, foods containing vitamin E, and alpha-tocopherol supplements are protective, and that processed meat, and milk and dairy products are a cause of this cancer.

7.15 Kidney

Cancer of the kidney is the 15th most common type worldwide. Around 200 000 cases were recorded in 2002, accounting for around 2 per cent of all cancers. Average overall survival rates are around 50 per cent at 5 years. It is the 16th most common cause of death from cancer.

Overall, *the Panel is impressed* by the pattern of evidence showing the importance of body fatness as a cause of cancer of the kidney.

The Panel judges as follows:
The evidence that body fatness is a cause of this cancer is convincing. It is unlikely that coffee has a substantial effect, or that alcoholic drinks have an adverse effect, on the risk of this cancer. There is limited evidence suggesting that arsenic in drinking water is a cause of this cancer.

Smoking is a cause of cancer of the kidney.

In final summary, the strongest evidence, corresponding to judgements of "convincing" and "probable",shows that greater body fatness is a cause of kidney cancer; and that it is unlikely that coffee has a substantial effect, or alcoholic drinks an adverse effect, on the risk of this cancer.

The kidneys are at the back of the abdomen and outside the peritoneal cavity. They filter waste products and water from the blood, producing urine, which empties into the bladder through the ureter. They are also important endocrine organs concerned with salt and water metabolism, and convert vitamin D to its active form.

Renal cell carcinoma is the most common kidney cancer, accounting for approximately 85 per cent. The majority of these are adenocarcinomas,[4] the type included here. Kidney cancers also include transition cell carcinomas of the renal pelvis, sarcomas, and Wilms' tumour (nephroblastoma), a childhood cancer. This section refers mainly to renal cell carcinomas; some studies also examined transitional cell carcinomas.

7.15.1 Trends, incidence, and survival

Age-adjusted rates of kidney cancer are increasing worldwide. Rates have doubled in many high-income countries since the mid-1970s, with some of the largest increases in countries in eastern Europe, for example, that are undergoing profound economic transition.[137]

This is mainly a disease of high-income countries, where rates are nearly five times higher overall than in middle- to low-income countries. Around the world, age-adjusted incidence rates range from 10–20 per 100 000 people in North America, parts of Europe, and Australia to less than 2 per 100 000 in parts of Africa.[2] In the USA, rates are higher among African-American people than in white people. Globally, rates are higher in men than in women, by five to three.[3] Risk increases with age, with most diagnoses made

---

FOOD, NUTRITION, PHYSICAL ACTIVITY, AND CANCER OF THE KIDNEY

In the judgement of the Panel, the factors listed below modify the risk of cancer of the kidney. Judgements are graded according to the strength of the evidence.

	DECREASES RISK	INCREASES RISK
Convincing		**Body fatness**
Probable		
Limited — suggestive		Arsenic in drinking water[1]
Limited — no conclusion	Cereals (grains) and their products; vegetables; fruits; meat; poultry; fish; eggs; milk and dairy products; total fat; soft drinks; tea; alcoholic drinks (protective effect)[2]; carbohydrate; protein; vitamin A; retinol; vitamin C; vitamin E; beta-carotene; flavonol; Seventh-day Adventist diets; physical activity; body fatness at age 18–20; weight at age 18–20; birth weight; adult attained height; age at menarche; energy intake.	
Substantial effect on risk unlikely	Coffee; alcoholic drinks (adverse effect)[2]	

1 The International Agency for Research on Cancer has graded arsenic and arsenic compounds as Class 1 carcinogens. The grading for this entry applies specifically to inorganic arsenic in drinking water.
2 The evidence was sufficient to judge that alcoholic drinks were unlikely to have an *adverse* effect on the risk of kidney cancer; but it was inadequate to draw a conclusion regarding a protective effect.

For an explanation of all the terms used in the matrix, please see chapter 3.5.1, the text of this section, and the glossary.

---

in people between the ages of 60 and 80.[296]

Kidney cancer is diagnosed at an early stage in more than half of cases. The 5-year survival rate is about 95 per cent for early stage cancers, and about 20 per cent at the most advanced stages.[296] Overall, 5-year survival rates are more than 50 per cent in high-income countries, but lower in middle- to low-income countries.[3][6] This cancer accounts for almost 2 per cent of all cancer incidence, and somewhat over 1 per cent of all cancer deaths. Also see box 7.1.1.

7.15.2 Pathogenesis

Urine contains many waste products from food, drinks, and other environmental sources, and some of these are potential carcinogens, such as carcinogens from cigarette smoke, and may play a role in kidney cancer.

It is not clear whether benign renal adenomas are a precursor of renal cell carcinoma. They are similar histologically and are frequently distinguished predominantly by their size.

Most adult kidney cancers are sporadic renal cell carcinomas, which can be divided into two main types. The conventional (or clear cell) type accounts for 75 per cent; 12 per cent of cases are of the papillary form,[296] which are less likely to metastasise. In 60 per cent of conventional carcinoma cases, there is a mutation in the von Hippel–Lindau tumour suppressor gene (VHL) (see box 2.2).[297] VHL disease is also a cause of some familial kidney cancers.

7.15.3 Other established causes

(Also see chapter 2.4 and 7.1.3.1.)

Tobacco use. Smoking is a cause of kidney cancer, increasing the risk approximately twofold.[10] The association is stronger for cancers of the renal pelvis.[298]

Medication. Analgesics containing phenacetin are a cause of cancer of the renal pelvis.[299] Dialysis is a cause of kidney cancer, perhaps through its role in the development of acquired renal cystic disease.[300 301]

7.15.4 Interpretation of the evidence

7.15.4.1 General
For general considerations that may affect interpretation of the evidence, see chapters 3.3 and 3.5, and boxes 3.1, 3.2, 3.6 and 3.7.

'Relative risk' is used in this Report to denote ratio measures of effect, including 'risk ratios', 'rate ratios', 'hazard ratios', and 'odds ratios'.

7.15.4.2 Specific
Considerations specific to cancer of the kidney include:

Classification. The subtype of kidney cancer may also be important. Papillary renal cell carcinomas may follow a different disease path from other renal cell carcinomas. Some studies also included transitional cell carcinomas or looked at both renal and urinary tract tumours.

Confounding. High-quality studies adjust for smoking.

7.15.5 Evidence and judgements

In total, 187 publications were included in the SLR for kidney cancer. Fuller summaries of the epidemiological, experimental, and mechanistic evidence are to be found in Chapters 4–6.

The full SLR is contained on the CD included with this Report.

7.15.5.1 Arsenic in drinking water
(Also see chapter 4.7.5.1.1.)
Three cohort studies, one time-series study, and nine ecological studies investigated arsenic in drinking water. All studies showed increased risk for the highest intake levels

compared with the lowest. Effect sizes, particularly from ecological studies in areas of high exposure levels, tend to be relatively large.

Arsenic is carcinogenic to humans and causes chromosomal abnormalities.[217] Arsenic biotransformation is thought to lead to a state of oxidative stress. In addition, arsenic in drinking water is well absorbed in the gastrointestinal tract, and both inorganic arsenic and its methylated metabolites are excreted in urine. Arsenic can modify the urinary excretion of porphyrins in animals and humans.

> **The evidence is sparse. There is limited evidence suggesting that arsenic in drinking water is a cause of kidney cancer.**

7.15.5.2 Coffee
(Also see chapter 4.7.5.4.)
Five cohort studies, 18 case-control studies, and 1 ecological study investigated coffee. None of the cohort studies and only 1 of the case-control studies reported a statistically significant association. Meta-analysis of case-control data produced evidence of no association.

> **There is substantial evidence, both from cohort and case-control studies, which is consistent and of low heterogeneity, and which fails to show an association. It is unlikely that coffee has a substantial effect on the risk of kidney cancer.**

The Panel is aware that since the conclusion of the SLR, one cohort study[302] has been published. This new information does not change the Panel judgement. Also see box 3.8.

7.15.5.3 Alcoholic drinks
(Also see chapter 4.8.5.1.)
A total of 3 cohort studies and 16 case-control studies investigated alcoholic drinks; 4 cohort and 5 case-control studies investigated ethanol intake. Studies showed no consistent direction of effect. Meta-analysis of cohort data on ethanol produced evidence of a dose-response relationship with decreased risk; cohort data on alcoholic drinks were heterogeneous. Meta-analyses of case-control data showed non-significant decreased risk.

> **It is unlikely that alcoholic drinks increase the risk of kidney cancer, though a protective effect cannot be excluded.**

The Panel is aware that since the conclusion of the SLR, one cohort study[302] has been published. This new information does not change the Panel judgement. Also see box 3.8.

7.15.5.4 Body fatness
(Also see chapter 6.1.3.1.)
Seventeen cohort studies and 20 case-control studies investigated body fatness, as measured by BMI. Nearly all of them showed increased risk with increased body fatness, with none showing a statistically significant decreased risk. Meta-analysis of cohort data showed a 31 per cent increased risk

per 5 kg/m²; meta-analysis of case-control data showed a 205 (adjusted for smoking) or 42 (unadjusted) per cent increased risk per 5 kg/m² (figures 6.1.19 and 6.1.20). There was little heterogeneity in the former two analyses; the heterogeneity in the latter could be partially explained by failure to adjust for smoking.

Body fatness directly affects levels of many circulating hormones, such as insulin, insulin-like growth factors, and oestrogens, creating an environment that encourages carcinogenesis and discourages apoptosis (box 2.4). It also stimulates the body's inflammatory response, which may contribute to the initiation and progression of several cancers (see chapter 2.4.1.3). In addition, laboratory studies point to a potential role for insulin and leptin in renal cell carcinoma.[303] [304]

> There is abundant and consistent epidemiological evidence with a dose-response relationship and evidence of plausible mechanisms. **The evidence that greater body fatness is a cause of kidney cancer is convincing.**

The Panel is aware that since the conclusion of the SLR, three cohort studies[58] [213] [305] and one case-control study[306] have been published. This new information does not change the Panel judgement. Also see box 3.8.

7.15.5.5 Other exposures
Other exposures were evaluated. However, the data were either of too low quality, too inconsistent, or the number of studies too few to allow conclusions to be reached. These were as follows: cereals (grains) or their products; vegetables; fruits; meat; poultry; fish; eggs; milk and dairy products; soft drinks; tea; alcoholic drinks (protective effect); carbohydrate; total fat; protein; vitamin A; retinol; beta-carotene; vitamin C; vitamin E; flavonol; physical activity; energy intake; body fatness at age 18–20; weight at age 18–20; age at menarche; adult attained height; birth weight; and Seventh-day Adventist diets.

7.15.6 Comparison with previous report

7.15.6.1 General
See 7.1.6.1, and box 3.8.

7.15.6.2 Specific
The previous report judged that high body mass is probably a cause of kidney cancer. Since then the evidence for body fatness has become stronger.

7.15.7 Conclusions

The Panel concludes:
The evidence that body fatness is a cause of kidney cancer is convincing. It is unlikely that coffee has a substantial effect, or alcoholic drinks an adverse effect, on the risk of this cancer. There is limited evidence suggesting that arsenic in drinking water is a cause of this cancer.

7.16 Bladder

Cancer of the bladder is the 10th most common type worldwide. Around 350 000 cases were recorded in 2002, accounting for around 3 per cent of all cancers. It is most common in high-income countries. Rates are much higher in men than in women. Overall rates of this cancer are not changing much. Average overall survival rates vary depending on how soon the cancer is detected. It is the 11th most common cause of death from cancer.

Overall, *the Panel notes* the evidence that food, nutrition, and physical activity are not significant factors in the development of cancer of the bladder.

The Panel judges as follows:
There is limited evidence suggesting that milk protects against bladder cancer; and that arsenic in drinking water is a cause.

Smoking tobacco and schistosomiasis are other causes of this cancer.

In final summary, the evidence is too limited to conclude that any aspect of food, nutrition, and physical activity directly modifies the risk of bladder cancer.

The bladder is a sac-like organ that is the reservoir for urine. The inside of the bladder is lined by transitional epithelial cells known as the urothelium.

The term 'urothelial cancers' includes predominantly transition cell carcinomas of the bladder and cancers of the upper part of the urinary tract. Transitional cell carcinoma is the most common form, accounting for more than 90 per cent of bladder cancers, the type mainly included here. Other types (in order of incidence) include squamous cell carcinomas, adenocarcinomas, and small cell cancers.[4]

7.16.1 Trends, incidence, and survival

There is no clear global trend in bladder cancer incidence. While rates increased in many countries during the 20th century, this rise has generally slowed since the mid-1980s or stopped.[137] However, there are exceptions, such as in Japan and countries in eastern Europe that are in economic transition.

Bladder cancer is predominantly a disease of high-income countries, where overall rates are slightly more than three times higher than in middle- to low-income countries. Around the world, age-adjusted incidence rates range from 20–30 per 100 000 men in southern and western Europe and North America to less than 1 per 100 000 in much of Middle Africa and Asia.[2] It is five times more common in men than in women, and risk increases with age. In northern Africa and parts of Asia, where schistosomiasis (a parasitic disease, also known as bilharzia) is prevalent, bladder cancer rates are high and squamous cell carcinomas of the bladder are

FOOD, NUTRITION, PHYSICAL ACTIVITY, AND CANCER OF THE BLADDER

In the judgement of the Panel, the factors listed below modify the risk of cancer of the bladder. Judgements are graded according to the strength of the evidence.

	DECREASES RISK	INCREASES RISK
Convincing		
Probable		
Limited — suggestive	Milk[1]	Arsenic in drinking water[2]
Limited — no conclusion	Cereals (grains) and their products; vegetables; fruits; pulses (legumes); meat; poultry; fish; eggs; total fat; butter; dietetic foods; soft drinks; diet drinks; fruit juices; coffee; tea; caffeine; alcohol; chlorinated surface water; total fluid intake; sweeteners; frying; carbohydrate; protein; vitamin A; folate; vitamin C; vitamin E; multivitamin supplements; selenium; beta-carotene; alpha-carotene; lycopene; beta-cryptoxanthin; lutein; zeaxanthin; flavonoids; physical activity; body fatness; energy intake	
Substantial effect on risk unlikely	None identified	

1 Milk from cows. Most data are from high-income populations, where calcium can be taken to be a marker for milk/dairy consumption. *The Panel judges* that a higher intake of dietary calcium is one way in which milk could have a protective effect.
2 The International Agency for Research on Cancer has graded arsenic and arsenic compounds as Class 1 carcinogens. The grading for this entry applies specifically to inorganic arsenic in drinking water.

For an explanation of all the terms used in the matrix, please see chapter 3.5.1, the text of this section, and the glossary.

the most common type. In Egypt, it is the most common cancer among men and the third most common among women.[307] In the USA, rates are higher in white people than among other ethnic groups.[3]

Five-year survival rates vary according to the stage of the cancer when it is diagnosed. They range from 63 to 88 per cent in cases of superficial bladder carcinoma, and from 47 to 63 per cent in muscle-invasive bladder cancer.[4] However, recurrence rates for this cancer are relatively high.[308] This disease accounts for just over 3 per cent of all cancer incidence, and around 2 per cent of all cancer deaths. Also see box 7.1.1.

7.16.2 Pathogenesis

Dietary carcinogens, as well as those from tobacco smoke or other environmental sources, are often excreted in the urine,

so the bladder lining is exposed to these toxins.

Urothelial cell carcinomas start as superficial bladder carcinomas. The majority have low rates of progression, although they can occur at multiple sites. Low-risk lesions may never progress, but they have a poor prognosis if they become invasive cancers.

The superficial lesion that carries the highest risk, carcinoma in situ, progresses to invasive cancer in more than 50 per cent of cases if it is not treated. These high-risk lesions are often found with multiple papillary tumours, but because they may involve different molecular changes, they are likely to have a different natural history to low-risk lesions.[308]

Squamous cell carcinoma may be caused by chronic inflammation, for instance from latent schistosomiasis, chronic infections, or long-term catheter use.

Mutations in the tumour-suppressor p53 gene, as well as abnormalities in chromosome 9, are common in invasive bladder cancer (see box 2.2). Inherited mutations of two other genes, GSTM1 (glutathione S-transferase null) and NAT2 (n-acetyltransferase; slow acetylation) also cause bladder cancer. NAT2 interacts with cigarette smoke, and may be responsible for 20–46 per cent of bladder cancers.[309]

7.16.3 Other established causes

(Also see chapter 2.4 and 7.1.3.1.)

Tobacco use. Smoking is a major cause of bladder cancer. It is estimated that more than half of all cases in men and around a third in women are caused by smoking.[10] [310]

Infection and infestation. Infestation with schistosomes (particularly *Schistosoma haematobium*) is a cause of bladder cancer, particularly squamous cell carcinomas.[311] This is estimated to be responsible for 10 per cent of bladder cancer cases in middle- and low-income countries, and 3 per cent of cases overall.[312]

Industrial chemicals. Occupational exposure to aromatic amines, such as 2-naphthylamine (used in dyes), also increases the risk of bladder cancer.[313]

7.16.4 Interpretation of the evidence

7.16.4.1 General
For general considerations that may affect interpretation of the evidence, see chapters 3.3 and 3.5, and boxes 3.1, 3.2, 3.6 and 3.7.

'Relative risk' is used in this Report to denote ratio measures of effect, including 'risk ratios', 'rate ratios', 'hazard ratios', and 'odds ratios'.

7.16.4.2 Specific
Considerations specific to cancer of the bladder include:

Confounding. High-quality studies adjust for smoking.

7.16.5 Evidence and judgements

In total, 349 publications were included in the SLR for bladder cancer. Fuller summaries of the epidemiological, experimental, and mechanistic evidence are to be found in Chapters 4–6.

The full SLR is contained on the CD included with this Report.

7.16.5.1 Milk
(Also see chapter 4.4.5.1.1.)
Five cohort studies, 14 case-control studies, and 1 ecological study investigated milk. All of the cohort studies and half of the case-control studies showed decreased risk with increased intake of milk. Meta-analysis of cohort data produced evidence of an association with decreased risk, with a clear dose-response relationship. Meta-analysis of case-control data was inconclusive.

The possible effect of milk in reducing bladder cancer risk is likely to be mediated at least in part by calcium, which has direct growth-restraining and differentiation- and apoptosis-inducing actions on normal and tumour cells.[184] However, milk includes many bioactive constituents, which may also play a role.

The evidence is inconsistent and comes mainly from evidence on dietary calcium. There is limited evidence suggesting that milk protects against bladder cancer.

7.16.5.2 Arsenic in drinking water
(Also see chapter 4.7.5.1.1.)
Six cohort studies, 1 time-series study, 7 case-control studies, and 11 ecological studies investigated arsenic in drinking water. Most studies showed increased risk for groups with the highest intakes when compared with the lowest.

Soluble arsenic in drinking water induces lung cancers in experimental animal models.[71] In humans, arsenic is a chromosomal mutagen (an agent that induces mutations involving more than one gene, typically large deletions or rearrangements). It can also act as a synergistic co-mutagen. Arsenic exposure also causes chronic lung disease.[71] These mechanisms may also apply to bladder cancer. The Joint FAO/WHO Expert Committee on Food Additives has set a provisional tolerable weekly intake of 0.015 mg per kg body weight.[72]

The evidence is inconsistent. There is limited evidence suggesting that arsenic is a cause of bladder cancer.

7.16.5.3 Other exposures
Other exposures were evaluated. However, the data were either of too low quality, too inconsistent, or the number of studies too few to allow conclusions to be reached. These were as follows: cereals (grains) and their products; vegetables; fruits; pulses (legumes); meat; poultry; fish; eggs; butter; dietetic foods; soft drinks; diet drinks; fruit juices; coffee; caffeine; tea; alcohol; chlorinated surface water; sweeteners; frying; carbohydrate; total fat; protein; vitamin A; beta-carotene; alpha-carotene; lycopene; beta-cryptoxanthin; lutein; zeaxanthin; folate; vitamin C; vitamin E; selenium; multivitamin supplements; flavonoids; energy intake; physical activity; body fatness; and total fluid intake.

7.16.6 Comparison with previous report

7.16.6.1 General
See 7.1.6.1, and box 3.8.

7.16.6.2 Specific
The previous report judged that vegetables and fruits probably protect against bladder cancer. As with other sites, the evidence for these foods is now considered to be weaker, in this case, very much so. The previous finding that coffee (more than five cups per day) is a possible cause of bladder cancer was not found here.

7.16.7 Conclusions

The Panel concludes:
There is limited evidence suggesting that milk protects against bladder cancer and that arsenic in drinking water is a cause.

7.17 Skin

Cancer of the skin in its various forms is the most common type of cancer worldwide. Around 90 per cent of all skin cancers are non-melanoma. Around 4 million cases were recorded in 2002, but it is likely that many cases are not referred, and this cancer is not included in the rankings in this Report. Around 160 000 cases of melanoma skin cancer were recorded in 2002, accounting for around 1.5 per cent of all cancers. Skin cancers are more common in high-income countries and among light-skinned people. Overall rates of this cancer are increasing. Survival rates of melanoma are high and also depend on access to treatment. Five-year survival rates for non-melanoma skin cancer are more than 99 per cent. Melanoma is the 22nd most common cause of death from cancer.

Overall, *the Panel emphasises* that the main cause of skin cancer is over-exposure to radiation from sunlight.

The Panel judges as follows:
Arsenic in drinking water is probably a cause of skin cancer. There is limited evidence suggesting that retinol protects against squamous cell carcinomas of the skin, and that selenium is a cause of skin cancer. It is unlikely that beta-carotene or foods containing it have a substantial effect on the risk of non-melanoma skin cancer.

In final summary, the strongest evidence, corresponding to judgements of "convincing" and "probable", shows that arsenic in drinking water is probably a cause of skin cancer. It is unlikely that beta-carotene or foods containing it have a substantial effect on the risk of non-melanoma skin cancer.

The skin is the outer covering of the body. There are two main types of skin cancer: melanoma and non-melanoma. Non-melanoma is more common. The most common non-melanoma tumours are basal cell carcinoma and squamous cell carcinoma, which together account for 90 per cent of skin cancers.[4] Melanomas are nearly always pigmented and usually develop from pigmented lesions such as moles. Melanoma accounts for 4 per cent of skin cancers. Other skin cancers such as Kaposi's sarcoma and cutaneous lymphomas are not included here.

7.17.1 Trends, incidence, and survival

Age-adjusted rates of both melanoma and non-melanoma skin cancers are increasing. Rates have doubled since the mid-1950s in many high-income countries, particularly those that already had high rates. This trend is restricted to countries where a high proportion of the population is fair-skinned.[137] The incidence of non-melanoma skin cancer is also increasing.[4] It is estimated that there are more than a million new cases each year in the USA alone,[314] and in Australia the reported incidence is even higher.[315]

FOOD, NUTRITION, PHYSICAL ACTIVITY, AND CANCER OF THE SKIN

In the judgement of the Panel, the factors listed below modify the risk of cancer of the skin. Judgements are graded according to the strength of the evidence.

	DECREASES RISK	INCREASES RISK
Convincing		
Probable		**Arsenic in drinking water[1]**
Limited — suggestive	Retinol[2]	Selenium supplements[3]
Limited — no conclusion	Potatoes; non-starchy vegetables; fruits; fish; eggs; milk; total fat; cholesterol; coffee; tea; alcohol; protein; vitamin A; retinol (foods); folate; vitamin C; vitamin D; vitamin E; multivitamins; selenium; carotenoids; beta-carotene (melanoma); alpha-carotene; lycopene; physical activity; body fatness; energy intake	
Substantial effect on risk unlikely	Beta-carotene[4] (non-melanoma)	

1 The International Agency for Research on Cancer has graded arsenic and arsenic compounds as Class 1 carcinogens. The grading for this entry applies specifically to inorganic arsenic in drinking water.
2 The evidence is derived from studies using supplements at a dose of 25 000 international units/day. Applies only to squamous cell carcinoma.
3 The evidence is derived from studies using supplements at a dose of 200 µg/day.
4 The evidence is derived from studies using supplements at doses of 30, and 50 mg/day, and from foods containing beta-carotene. See chapter 4.2.

For an explanation of all the terms used in the matrix, please see chapter 3.5.1, the text of this section, and the glossary.

Skin cancer is mainly a disease of high-income countries, where overall melanoma rates are more than 10 times higher than in middle- to low-income countries. Age-adjusted incidence rates range from more than 30 per 100 000 people in Australia and New Zealand to less than 1 per 100 000 across much of Africa and Asia. Rates are relatively high (around 15 per 100 000) in North America, Israel, and many northern European countries.[2] In the USA, rates are higher in white people than among other ethnic groups.[3] Non-melanoma skin cancer is the most common cancer in the world, and correlates with lighter skin colour and accumulated sun exposure.[316]

Although both melanoma and non-melanoma skin cancer incidence increases with age, melanoma causes a disproportionate number of cancers in young and middle-aged people.[317] Melanomas are most common on exposed areas of the body, and are relatively rare on areas that are usually covered by clothing.

Despite the considerably higher incidence of non-melanoma skin cancer compared with melanoma (around 20 to 1 in the USA), this less common type accounts for 79 per cent of skin cancer deaths.[318] The 5-year survival rate is between 80 and 90 per cent in high-income countries, but just over half that in middle- to low-income countries.[124] This difference is partly due to a different, prevalent type of melanoma (acral melanoma, on the soles of the feet), which has a poorer prognosis. Melanoma accounts for somewhat over 1 per cent of all cancer incidence, but only around 0.5 per cent of all cancer deaths. Non-melanoma skin cancers are almost never fatal.[319] Also see box 7.1.1.

7.17.2 Pathogenesis

The skin changes with age and is affected by hormonal influences and exposure to the sun and wind. Skin pigmentation varies between individuals and its structure also differs, depending, for instance, on whether it covers the lips, the soles of the feet, or the eyelids. All of these aspects influence skin cancer risk. Both melanoma and non-melanoma skin cancers are thought to be caused largely by UV irradiation mainly from sunlight. There is a clear relationship between accumulated sun exposure and non-melanoma skin cancer, but melanoma is more common in office workers than in outdoor workers, suggesting that damage from episodic exposure and extreme occasional sun damage (blistering sunburn) may be more important.[4] The role of sun damage is supported by the association between measures of sun sensitivity and skin cancer incidence, which is higher in people who have freckles and skin that burns without tanning, more moles, blue eyes, and red hair.[320] [321]

UV-damaged cells are usually removed by apoptosis (programmed cell death, see chapter 2.5.2) in a process involving the p53 protein. However, in non-melanoma skin cancer, the p53 tumour-suppressor gene is often damaged by UVB irradiation, so faulty cells are not removed from the skin. Both UVB and UVA irradiation also have direct and indirect effects on the cutaneous immune system, lowering the skin's cell-mediated immunity,[322] which is another factor that may influence carcinogenesis.

People who have a family history of melanoma may be predisposed to this type of skin cancer, although only one major inherited mutation has been found, and less than 2 per cent of melanomas are attributable to this inherited mutation.[323]

7.17.3 Other established causes

(Also see chapter 2.4 and 7.1.3.1.)

Radiation. Over-exposure to UV radiation (mainly from sunlight) is the chief cause of both non-melanoma and melanoma skin cancers.[324] In the case of melanoma, the main cause is episodic skin exposure involving severe sunburn, particularly in fair-skinned white people.[317]

Medication. Immune suppression in organ-transplant and

AIDS patients is also associated with an increased risk of skin cancer (in addition to Kaposi's sarcomas).[325]

Infection and infestation. HPV can cause squamous cell carcinomas, especially in immune-compromised people.[325]

7.17.4 Interpretation of the evidence

7.17.4.1 General
For general considerations that may affect interpretation of the evidence, see chapters 3.3 and 3.5, and boxes 3.1, 3.2, 3.6 and 3.7.

'Relative risk' is used in this Report to denote ratio measures of effect, including 'risk ratios', 'rate ratios', 'hazard ratios', and 'odds ratios'.

7.17.4.2 Specific
Considerations specific to cancer of the skin include:

Classification. Melanoma and non-melanoma cancers may have different causes; this would explain heterogeneity in studies that do not distinguish between these two types of skin cancer. Non-melanoma skin cancer cases are commonly not recorded by cancer registries, and are therefore underestimated in many reports.

Confounding. High-quality studies adjust for sun exposure and distinguish between cancer types.

7.17.5 Evidence and judgements

In total, 167 publications were included in the SLR for skin cancer. Fuller summaries of the epidemiological, experimental, and mechanistic evidence are in Chapters 4–6.

The full SLR is contained on the CD included with this Report.

7.17.5.1 Arsenic in drinking water
(Also see chapter 4.7.5.1.1.)

Two cohort studies, 5 case-control studies, 1 cross-sectional study, and 11 ecological studies investigated arsenic in drinking water. Nearly all studies showed an association between increased arsenic and skin cancer. Two case-control studies used toenail and fingernail measurements, which are thought to be more reliable than dietary estimates. These studies both showed increased risk, which was statistically significant in one. The single cross-sectional study and all ecological studies showed increased risk, with several reporting relatively large and statistically significant effect estimates.

Soluble arsenic in drinking water induces lung cancers in experimental animal models.[71] In humans, arsenic is a chromosomal mutagen (an agent that induces mutations involving more than one gene, typically large deletions or rearrangements). It can also act as a synergistic co-mutagen. Arsenic exposure also causes chronic lung disease.[71] These mechanisms may also be applicable to skin cancer. The Joint FAO/WHO Expert Committee on Food Additives has set a provisional tolerable weekly intake of 0.015 mg per kg body weight.[72]

The evidence is consistent, from cohort, case-control, and ecological studies. There is robust mechanistic evidence. Arsenic in drinking water is a probable cause of skin cancer.

7.17.5.2 Retinol

(Also see chapter 4.10.6.4.1.)

Two randomised controlled trials investigated retinol supplements. Both trials included only participants at risk of developing non-melanoma skin cancer, and both gave results stratified according to this type. While neither trial reported a statistically significant association to basal cell carcinoma, one of the two studies did report a statistically significant relationship with decreased squamous cell carcinoma risk.

The mechanism of anti-tumour action of the retinoids is not completely understood, but retinol is known to bind to cell receptors with promotion of differentiation, alteration of membranes, and immunological adjuvant effects.[326]

The evidence is sparse and studies were conducted on a narrowly defined population group (people at risk of developing skin cancer). There is limited evidence suggesting that retinol supplements protect against squamous cell skin cancer.

The Panel is aware that since the conclusion of the SLR, one case-control study[327] has been published. This new information does not change the Panel judgement. Also see box 3.8.

7.17.5.3 Selenium supplements

(Also see chapter 4.10.6.4.5.)

One randomised controlled trial and one cohort study investigated selenium supplements. The trial showed a statistically significant increased risk of total non-melanoma skin cancer with daily supplementation of 200 μg selenium. Subgroup analysis indicated that this risk might differ according to cancer type, with a statistically significant increased risk for squamous cell carcinoma but not basal cell carcinoma. The single cohort study stated that there was no statistically significant association.

No plausible mechanisms for how selenium might increase risk of skin cancer have been suggested.

The evidence is sparse, and no plausible mechanisms have been identified. There is limited evidence suggesting that selenium supplements are a cause of skin cancer.

7.17.5.4 Beta-carotene (non-melanoma)

(Also see chapters 4.2.5.3 and 4.10.6.4.2)

Four randomised controlled trials and one cohort study investigated beta-carotene supplements; two cohort studies and seven case-control studies investigated dietary beta-carotene; three cohort studies and one case-control study investigated beta-carotene from food and supplements combined; and eight cohort studies and three case-control studies investigated serum or plasma beta-carotene.

All three randomised controlled trials that investigated beta-carotene supplement interventions against placebo with respect to non-melanoma skin cancer reported results very close to null. Meta-analysis of the three trials produced evidence of no association. Two trials that investigated beta-carotene supplement interventions against placebo with respect to melanoma stated that there was no association with risk.

Meta-analysis of cohort data on plasma or serum beta-carotene and non-melanoma skin cancer, and cohort data that investigated the same exposure in melanoma, showed no clear association. No clear association was shown with dietary beta-carotene.

There is strong evidence from good quality trials that consistently fail to show an effect. It is unlikely that beta-carotene has a substantial effect on the risk of non-melanoma skin cancer. It is unlikely that foods containing beta-carotene have any substantial effect on the risk of non-melanoma skin cancer.

7.17.5.5 Other exposures

Other exposures were evaluated. However, the data were either of too low quality, too inconsistent, or the number of studies too few to allow conclusions to be reached. These were as follows: potatoes; non-starchy vegetables; fruits; fish; eggs; milk; coffee; tea; alcohol; foods containing selenium; total fat; cholesterol; protein; vitamin A; retinol (foods); beta-carotene (melanoma); alpha-carotene; carotenes; lycopene; folate; vitamin C; vitamin D; vitamin E; multivitamins; physical activity; energy intake; and body fatness.

7.17.6 Comparison with previous report

Skin cancers were not reviewed in the previous report.

7.17.7 Conclusions

The Panel concludes:

Arsenic in drinking water is probably a cause of skin cancer. There is limited evidence suggesting that retinol protects against squamous cell carcinomas of the skin and that selenium is a cause of skin cancer. It is unlikely that beta-carotene or foods containing it have a substantial effect on the risk of non-melanoma skin cancer. The main cause of skin cancer is over-exposure to UV radiation from sunlight.

7.18 Other cancers

The Panel also considered other cancers, not generally recognised to have a relationship to food, nutrition, and physical activity. These are cancers of the thyroid gland and testis, and cancers of the lymphoid and haemopoietic systems, the musculoskeletal system, and the nervous systems.

Five narrative reviews were commissioned. This method was not systematic, and *the Panel decided* not to make any judgements regarding the causality of any associations in the text or matrices.

Some of the evidence that emerged may merit more thorough investigation and further studies.

The Panel noted as follows:
Some of these cancers are known to have as established causes other diseases, tobacco use, radiation, infection, or industrial chemicals, or else not to have established causes. Some details are given in the following sections. From the reviews commissioned, some evidence emerges.

Thyroid cancer. Non-cruciferous, non-starchy vegetables and fish show an association with decreased risk. Body fatness and adult attained height show an association with increased risk.

Lymphoid and haemopoietic cancers. Vegetables and fruits are associated with decreased risk. Alcoholic drinks have an association with decreased risk. Meat, total fat, and body fatness are associated with increased risk. Milk and dairy products show an association with increased risk of non-Hodgkin's lymphoma.

Other cancers. The evidence on food, nutrition, physical activity, and cancers of the musculoskeletal and nervous systems is too limited to draw any conclusions.

7.18.1 Thyroid

Thyroid cancer is the 21st most common type worldwide. An estimated 141 000 cases occurred in 2002, accounting for just over 1 per cent overall. This cancer type is the 23rd most common cause of cancer death. It is more common in high-income countries, with rates more than twice those of middle- to low-income countries.

Thyroid cancer is not usually fatal, with a 5-year survival rate of approximately 70 per cent.[2] It is increasing in incidence worldwide, although this may be partly explained by changing diagnostic practices.[124 137]

Thyroid cancer rates peak between the ages of 25 and 55, then decline and rise again in the elderly. This cancer is more common in women than in men. Also see box 7.1.1.

Differentiated carcinomas account for 94 per cent of these cancers (80 per cent papillary and 14 per cent follicular car-

cinomas). Medullary carcinoma and the highly aggressive anaplastic carcinoma comprise the remainder.[4]

Exposure to ionising radiation, especially during childhood, is a cause of this cancer.[328]

7.18.1.1 Evidence
The evidence from the narrative review is summarised below.

7.18.1.1.1 Vegetables
One pooled analysis of 11 case-control studies (2241 cases and 3716 controls) investigated consumption of vegetables. It showed a statistically significant reduced incidence with higher intakes of vegetable other than cruciferous types. Cruciferous vegetables were not significantly associated with reduced incidence.

Vegetables contain many potentially protective substances, including several antioxidants, as well as phytochemicals with antiproliferative capabilities. They are also a rich source of folate, which plays an important role in the synthesis, repair, and methylation of DNA.

7.18.1.1.2 Fish
One pooled analysis of 13 case-control studies (2497 cases and 4337 controls) and 2 case-control studies investigated fish consumption. These were consistent in showing a significantly reduced incidence with increased consumption in areas of endemic iodine deficiency, but none in areas where iodine intakes are high.

Fish is known to be an important natural source of iodine in the diets of different populations, and therefore an association between fish intake and thyroid cancer risk may be mediated by iodine.

7.18.1.1.3 Body fatness
One pooled analysis of 12 case-control studies (cases: 2056 women and 417 men; controls: 3358 women and 965 men) and 1 cohort study investigated BMI or obesity. Obesity was associated with a statistically significant increased incidence in women, with a clear dose-response relationship. No association was observed in men (although this could have been influenced by the relatively small number of cases). The cohort study also showed a relationship with increased incidence.

Body size might affect iodine requirement and therefore, indirectly, influence thyroid cancer risk.

7.18.1.1.4 Adult attained height
One pooled analysis of 12 case-control studies (cases: 2056 women and 417 men; controls: 3358 women and 965 men) investigated adult attained height. Greater height was associated with a statistically significant increased incidence in both women and men, with a clear dose-response relationship. The effect was greater in men than in women.

Body size might affect iodine requirement and therefore, indirectly, influence thyroid cancer risk. The association with height in both men and women may indicate a potential influence of some growth factor or hormone during childhood or adolescence, but the potential role of growth factors on thyroid carcinogenesis is still poorly defined.

7.18.1.2 Conclusions

Thyroid cancer was reviewed in the previous report. It judged that both iodine deficiency (probably) and iodine excess (possibly) were causes of this cancer, and also that vegetables and fruits were possibly protective.

The Panel concludes that the associations identified warrant more investigation into food, nutrition, and thyroid cancer.

7.18.2 Testis

Cancer of the testis is the 19th most common type in men. An estimated 49 000 cases occurred in 2002, accounting for around 0.5 per cent overall. This cancer is increasing worldwide, with rapid rises in many high-income countries and some transition countries.[124] Rates are more than five times higher than in middle- to low-income countries.

Cancer of the testis is usually not fatal where chemotherapy is available, with a 5-year survival rate of more than 90 per cent in high-income countries, but less than 60 per cent in middle- to low-income countries.[2 6] Also see box 7.1.1.

Most (95 per cent) testicular cancers are germ cell cancers, with seminomas being the other main subtype.[4]

The most well established risk factor for testicular cancer is the failure of one testis or both to descend into the normal position during fetal development.[4] Rates peak in young adulthood.

7.18.2.1 Evidence
The evidence from the narrative review is summarised below.

7.18.2.1.1 Milk and dairy products
Five case-control studies, one twin study, and four ecological studies investigated milk and dairy consumption. All ecological studies and two of the case-control studies showed statistically significant relationships between increased milk and dairy consumption and increased testicular cancer incidence.

None of the other studies reported statistically significant associations, although non-significant associations were heterogeneous.

There are no well established mechanisms through which milk could influence testicular cancer development. Milk and dairy products contain fat, protein, and calcium, all of which may have an effect on testicular cancer risk.

7.18.2.2 Conclusions
Cancer of the testis was not reviewed in the previous report.

The Panel concludes that the evidence does not warrant significant investigation into food, nutrition, and testicular cancer.

7.18.3 Lymphoid and haemopoietic system

Cancers of the lympho-haemopoietic system are predominantly lymphomas (Hodgkin's or non-Hodgkin's), leukaemias, and multiple myelomas. These cancers have different non-dietary causes and there is no reason to believe that they might be affected by food, nutrition, and physical activity in the same ways.

If taken together, this group of cancers would be the sixth most common type worldwide. An estimated 749 000 cases occurred in 2002, accounting for around 7 per cent overall. Approximately 48 per cent of these cancers were lymphomas (83 per cent non-Hodgkin's; 17 per cent Hodgkin's), and 40 per cent were leukaemias, with multiple myelomas accounting for the remaining 12 per cent.[2]

Non-Hodgkin's lymphoma is the 11th most common cause of cancer incidence. It is increasing in incidence worldwide.[124] Non-Hodgkin's lymphoma is most frequent in high-income countries, with rates more than twice those of middle- to low-income countries. It is usually fatal, with a 5-year survival rate of less than 35 per cent.[4] This is not a single cancer, but a wide group of cancers (such as Burkitt's lymphoma and diffuse large B-cell lymphoma), each with a distinct geographical distribution, development path, age profile, and prognosis.

Hodgkin's lymphoma is the 25th most common type. It is most frequent in high-income countries, where rates are more than twice those of middle- to low-income countries. It is not usually fatal, with a 5-year survival rate of approximately 75 per cent in high-income countries and less than 60 per cent in middle- to low-income countries.[2 4] This cancer occurs mainly in children, young adults, and the elderly (tending to occur at a younger age or in old age in middle- to low-income countries).[124]

Leukaemias are the 12th most common type and the 10th most common cause of cancer death. They are gradually increasing in incidence worldwide. They are most frequent in high-income countries, with rates more than twice those of middle- to low-income countries. Leukaemias are usually fatal, with a 5-year survival rate of approximately 40 per cent in high-income countries, and less than 20 per cent in middle- to low-income countries.[124] However, childhood leukaemias have a very high survival rate. This is not a single cancer, but a wide group of both acute and chronic leukaemias.

Multiple myeloma is the 24th most common type and the 19th most common cause of cancer death. It is gradually increasing in incidence worldwide, and is most frequent in high-income countries with rates more than three times higher than in middle- to low-income countries. It is usually fatal, with a 5-year survival rate of less than 50 per cent in high-income countries and less than 30 per cent in middle- to low-income countries.[2]

Infection with Epstein-Barr virus (see box 7.2.1) is a risk factor for developing Hodgkin's lymphoma.[329] HIV-1 infection, immune suppression (whatever the cause), and infection with Epstein-Barr and human T-cell leukaemia virus all increase the risk of developing non-Hodgkin's lymphoma.[330]

Tobacco use, infection with human T-cell leukaemia virus, radiation, and benzene are established causes of leukaemia.[10 67 328 331] Exposure to ionising radiation is a cause of multiple myeloma. Also see chapter 2.4.

7.18.3.1 Evidence

The evidence from the narrative review is summarised below.

7.18.3.1.1 Vegetables and fruits

One cohort study and six case-control studies investigated vegetables and fruits. The cohort study and five of the case-control studies showed statistically significant associations with increased vegetable and fruit intake and reduced incidence of lymphoid and haemopoietic cancers. However, the cohort study and two of the case-control studies reported on non-Hodgkin's lymphoma only. The sixth case-control study reported increased incidence with consumption of 'vegetables other than cruciferous, leafy, or yellow/orange'.

Vegetables and fruits contain many potentially protective substances, including several antioxidants, as well as phytochemicals with antiproliferative capabilities. They are also a rich source of folate, which plays an important role in the synthesis, repair, and methylation of DNA.

7.18.3.1.2 Milk and dairy products

One cohort study, nine case-control studies, and one ecological study investigated milk and dairy products, with most reporting on non-Hodgkin's lymphoma. The cohort study, the ecological study, and most of the case-control studies reported statistically significant associations between increased milk and dairy consumption and increased incidence.

There are no well established mechanisms by which milk could increase lymphoma incidence. Hypotheses include calcium restricting the bioavailability of vitamin D (this vitamin promotes differentiation and apoptosis and inhibits cancer cell growth in the laboratory). Alternatively, organochlorines (which are potential carcinogens) may accumulate in dairy fat. A final hypothesis is that bovine leukaemia virus might transmit through milk to humans, although there is no direct evidence for this.

7.18.3.1.3 Meat

One cohort study, seven case-control studies, and one ecological study investigated meat or red meat. The cohort study, the ecological study, and most of the case-control studies showed an association with increased incidence, with several reaching statistical significance. A review article came to the same conclusion.

There are no postulated mechanisms by which meat could increase the incidence of lymphoid and haemopoietic cancers.

7.18.3.1.4 Fish

Two cohort studies and seven case-control studies investigated fish and lymphoid and haematopoietic cancers. Most studies showed a non-significant relationship with reduced incidence. This reached statistical significance in two case-control studies that reported results separately for non-Hodgkin's lymphoma.

One animal study has shown that fish oils can inhibit the formation of lymphoid and haemopoietic cancers.

7.18.3.1.5 Fat

Two cohort studies and four case-control studies investigated fat consumption. All showed statistically significant relationships with increased incidence. One case-control study that reported separately on PUFAs described a significantly reduced incidence for that fatty acid type, while confirming a significant increased incidence for saturated fatty acids.

There are no postulated mechanisms by which fat could increase lymphoid and haemopoietic cancers.

7.18.3.1.6 Alcoholic drinks

One pooled analysis of case-control studies representing 15 175 participants, with 6492 non-Hodgkin's lymphoma cases, showed a statistically significant reduced incidence for this type, particularly Burkitt's lymphoma.

There are no postulated mechanisms by which alcohol could decrease the incidence of lymphoid and haemopoietic cancers.

7.18.3.1.7 Body fatness

Nine cohort studies and 11 case-control studies investigated BMI or obesity and non-Hodgkin's lymphoma, leukaemia, or multiple myeloma. In each case, most studies reported an association with increased incidence, with several reporting statistically significant relationships.

Obesity results in pathological states of inflammation and altered immune responses, both of which are factors that can influence lymphoid and haemopoietic cell function.

7.18.3.2 Conclusions

These cancers were not reviewed in the previous report.

The Panel concludes that more work into mechanisms that might underlie the associations identified is warranted. A more comprehensive and systematic review might also clarify the epidemiology. The different cancer types should be investigated separately unless there is reason to believe that they have common causes.

7.18.4 Musculoskeletal system

Cancers of the musculoskeletal system are a diverse group, including those of the bones, muscles, and related tissues, all around the body. These include liposarcomas, fibrosarcomas, osteosarcomas, and myosarcomas.

These cancers are all uncommon or rare, each accounting for less than 1 per cent — usually much less — of all cancers. There is no reason to think that they have causes in common.

The narrative review did not produce any findings.

Because these cancers are uncommon, any study investigating their possible links with food, nutrition, and physical activity would be unlikely to be fruitful. Because they are diverse, any investigation that grouped all of them together would also be unlikely to show consistent results.

7.18.4.1 Conclusions

These cancers were not reviewed in the previous report.

The Panel concludes that it is unlikely that any further investigation would be warranted.

7.18.5 Nervous system

Cancers of the brain and central nervous system are the 18th most common type worldwide. An estimated 189 000 cases occurred in 2002, accounting for around 2 per cent overall. These cancers are most frequent in high-income countries, with rates more than twice those of middle- to low-income countries. Brain tumours are relatively common among childhood cancers. They are the 13th most common cause of cancer death, and are usually fatal. The overall 5-year survival rate is less than 25 per cent, with higher rates for many brain tumours that occur during childhood, and in high- rather than in middle- to low-income countries.[2] Also see box 7.1.1.

Tumours of neural tissue account for approximately half of these cancers, with most of these being glioblastomas.[4] Meningiomas are the other major type of central nervous system tumour, with sellar tumours, cranial and spinal nerve tumours, central nervous system lymphomas, and other rare brain tumour types comprising the remainder.

The incidence of these cancers appears to be increasing worldwide, although the trend is not entirely clear.[124] The causes of brain and central nervous system cancers have not been well established.

The narrative review did not produce any findings.

Because these cancers are uncommon, any study investigating their possible links with food, nutrition, and physical activity would be unlikely to be fruitful. Because they are diverse, any investigation that grouped all of them together would also be unlikely to show consistent results.

7.18.5.1 Conclusions

These cancers were not reviewed in the previous report.

The Panel concludes that it is unlikely that any further investigation is warranted.

CHAPTER 8

Determinants of weight gain, overweight, and obesity

This chapter examines food, nutrition, and physical activity as factors that modify the risk of weight gain, overweight, and obesity, which themselves influence cancer risk.

The Panel agreed that as for the other systematic literature reviews elsewhere in this Report, a review of the epidemiological literature should be amplified by consideration of established knowledge on mechanisms, including basic thermodynamics and mechanisms of energy input, output, and balance.

As shown in Chapters 6 and 7 of this Report, the evidence that obesity, weight gain, and also overweight short of obesity increase the risk of a number of cancers, is more impressive than was the case in the mid-1990s. Also, it is now generally agreed that the rapid rise in the incidence of overweight and obesity is a public health nutrition emergency worldwide. In most countries in Asia, Latin America, and the Middle East, and some in Africa, chronic diseases including obesity are now more prevalent than nutritional deficiencies and infectious diseases.

The Panel agreed therefore that any comprehensive report on the prevention of cancer must also deal with the prevention of overweight, obesity, and weight gain. Expert reports that inform public health policy on cardiovascular diseases have, for many years, accepted that factors identified as causes of obesity are also causes of cardiovascular diseases. The Panel agrees that the same applies to cancer. So unless there is reason to think otherwise, anything that modifies the risk of weight gain, overweight, and obesity also modifies the risk of those cancers whose risk is increased by weight gain, overweight, and obesity.

The Panel judges that the evidence that regular and sustained physical activity of all types protects against weight gain, overweight, and obesity is convincing. Correspondingly, the evidence that sedentary living is a cause of these conditions is also convincing. Television viewing, a particular form of very sedentary behaviour, which may be associated with snacking on energy-dense foods, is probably also a cause.

Low energy-dense foods — typically foods that are high in fibre and bulky because of their water content — are probably protective. Such foods include cereals (grains), pulses (legumes), and vegetables and fruits, and are also often micronutrient-dense, meaning high in vitamins,

minerals, and other bioactive compounds. Correspondingly, the Panel judges that high energy-dense foods, in particular sugary drinks and 'fast foods', are probably a cause of weight gain, overweight, and obesity. Such foods are typically high in fats and/or sugars, contain little water or dietary fibre, and are often low in micronutrients.

The Panel also judges that sustained breastfeeding probably protects infants and young children against overweight and obesity, which tend to track into later childhood and adult life.

The Panel's conclusions and judgements on the dietary and associated determinants of weight gain, overweight, and obesity also apply to cancers for which the risk is increased by weight gain, overweight, and obesity, unless there is reason to think otherwise.

Within the remit of this Report, the strongest evidence, corresponding to judgements of 'convincing' and 'probable', shows that physical activity of all types protects against weight gain, overweight, and obesity, whereas sedentary living is causative; that low energy-dense foods are probably protective and high energy-dense foods are probably causative; that being breastfed is probably protective; and that sugary drinks, 'fast foods', and television watching are probably causative.

Environmental factors (physical, economic, political, and sociocultural) are extremely important in determining health behaviour, including that which affects body fatness. Such factors are the subject of a further report to be published in late 2008.

FOOD, NUTRITION, PHYSICAL ACTIVITY, AND WEIGHT GAIN, OVERWEIGHT, AND OBESITY

In the judgement of the Panel, the factors listed below modify the risk of weight gain, overweight, and obesity. Judgements are graded according to the strength of the evidence.

Factors that decrease risk promote appropriate energy intake, and those that increase risk promote excess energy intake, relative to the level of energy expenditure.

	DECREASES RISK	INCREASES RISK
Convincing	**Physical activity**	**Sedentary living[1]**
Probable	**Low energy-dense foods[2]** **Being breastfed[4]**	**Energy-dense foods[2 3]** **Sugary drinks[5]** **'Fast foods'[6]** **Television viewing[7]**
Limited — suggestive		
Limited — no conclusion	Refined cereals (grains) and their products; starchy roots, tubers, and plantains; fruits; meat; fish; milk and dairy products; fruit juices; coffee; alcoholic drinks; sweeteners	
Substantial effect on risk unlikely	None identified	

1 Sedentary living comprises both high levels of physical inactivity and low levels of physical activity (in terms of intensity, frequency, and duration). Also see box 5.2.
2 The direct epidemiological evidence for low energy-dense foods is from wholegrain cereals (grains) and cereal products, non-starchy vegetables, and dietary fibre. The direct epidemiological evidence for energy-dense foods is from animal fat and fast foods. These are interpreted as markers of the energy density of diets, based on compelling physiological and mechanistic evidence (box 8.1).
3 Some relatively unprocessed energy-dense foods (which tend to be eaten sparingly), such as nuts, seeds, and some vegetable oils, are valuable sources of nutrients.
4 The evidence relates principally to obesity in childhood, but overweight and obesity in children tend to track into adult life: overweight children are liable to become overweight and obese adults.
5 The evidence relates to all drinks containing added caloric sweeteners, notably sucrose and high-fructose corn syrup. Fruit juices are also sugary drinks and could have similar effects, but the evidence is currently limited.
6 'Fast foods' characteristically are consumed often, in large portions, and are energy dense (box 8.2).
7 Television viewing (box 8.4) is here identified as a sedentary activity (box 5.2). It is also associated with consumption of energy-dense foods (box 8.1). The evidence relates specifically to childhood and adolescence, and is taken also to apply to adults.

For an explanation of all the terms used in the matrix, please see chapter 3.5.1, the text of this section, and the glossary.

colon and rectum, breast (postmenopause), endometrium, and kidney is convincing; and it is probably a cause of cancer of the gallbladder. In addition, the evidence that abdominal fatness is a cause of cancer of the colon is convincing; and it is also probably a cause of cancers of the breast (postmenopause) and endometrium. Body fatness probably protects against breast cancer that becomes evident before the menopause.

Further, rates of overweight and obesity have greatly increased since the 1990s, not only throughout high-income countries, but also in urban and even rural areas of many if not most middle- and many low-income countries; and not only in adults, but also in children and young people. Obesity in both childhood and adult life can now be seen more as a disease of poverty than of affluence. In 2005, the World Health Organization estimated the number of overweight adults (age 15+) to be approximately 1.6 billion, with projections for 2015 increasing this figure to 2.3 billion.[6]

The evidence showing that body fatness is, or probably is, a cause of a number of cancers, as well as a large number of disorders and diseases (see 8.2.2), is impressive; and overweight and obesity are now pandemic, including among children and young people. For these reasons, *the Panel decided to commission this chapter*, and also decided that its assessments and judgements should be based on the same principles underlying their assessments of the links between food, nutrition, and physical activity with specific cancers.

The Panel agrees that any factor related to food, nutrition, and physical activity that increases the risk of weight gain, overweight, and obesity, can also be taken to increase the risk of cancers associated with excess body fatness, unless there is reason to think otherwise. Thus if regular, sustained physical activity of all types and regular consumption of low energy-dense foods protect against weight gain, overweight, and obesity, then they would also be expected to protect indirectly against those cancers identified in Chapter 7 as being associated with body fatness.

Social and environmental (underlying and basic) factors that modify the risk of weight gain, overweight, and obesity are critically important and the subject of an associated report to be published in late 2008.[7]

8.1 Definitions

Humans take in energy from food and drinks, which is used for the body's natural processes and for physical activity. People gain weight if they take in more energy than they use and lose weight if they take in less energy than they use. Excess energy is stored mostly as body fat, laid down at various sites around the body, regardless of whether the excess energy comes from carbohydrates, fats, or proteins, or from ethanol from alcoholic drinks. Conversely, with a deficiency of energy, carbohydrates are initially released in the form of

Recent and current research shows that degree of body fatness (often characterised as overweight and obesity) is a more important cause of cancer than was evident in the mid-1990s.[5] As stated in Chapters 6 and 7, the evidence that body fatness is a cause of cancers of the oesophagus, pancreas,

| Box 8.1 | Energy density |

A concept central to the Panel's thinking, assessments, and judgements in this chapter is that of the energy density of foods and drinks.

Energy density describes the amount of energy per unit weight of foods or diets. The units of measure are kilocalories (kcal) or kilojoules (kJ) per 100 grams (g). The body derives energy from the macronutrients in foods and drinks. The metabolisable energy of carbohydrate and protein is around 4 kcal (17 kJ)/g; of fat, 9 kcal (38 kJ)/g; and of ethanol — from alcoholic drinks — 7 kcal (29 kJ)/g. It follows that of the macronutrients in pure form, fats and oils are the most energy-dense, followed by ethanol; and protein and carbohydrate are least energy-dense.[1] By contrast, dietary fibre generates around 1.5 kcal (6.3 kJ)/g.[2] Water, like all foods and drinks, requires some energy for its absorption and metabolism, but its energy value can, for practical purposes, be counted as nil.

The energy density of foods and diets varies depending on the water content and concentration of the different macronutrients, and of dietary fibre. In general, low energy-dense foods and diets are high in fibre, and also in water. Therefore, in terms of weight, they are relatively 'dilute' in energy-providing macronutrients. Cereals (grains) and vegetables cooked in water, and most fruits, are examples of low energy-dense foods. By contrast, high energy-dense diets tend to contain fewer fibre-rich foods and to be relatively concentrated in macronutrients. Many processed foods are energy dense.

Energy-dense foods are usually high in fats or oils, and/or processed starches and added sugars. 'Fast foods' (box 8.2), certain baked goods, and confectionery are examples of high energy-dense foods. The energy density of meat depends on the amount of fat it contains and how it is cooked. Low energy-dense foods are often high in vitamins and minerals and other bioactive constituents. Processed, high energy-dense foods are often low in micronutrients.

There is no evidence that drinking a lot of water with the consumption of energy-dense foods mimics the intake of low energy-dense foods.

In general, people tend to consume roughly the same amount of food from day to day, measured by bulk and weight. Several human clinical studies have shown that high energy-dense diets can undermine normal appetite regulation — a process that has been termed 'passive over-consumption'.[3][4] Higher energy density diets tend to lead to greater energy intake.

Energy consumed in drinks appears to be less easily recognised by appetite control systems than energy in foods. Drinks by their nature are generally high in water and so, compared to foods, have low energy density. However, altering the energy density of drinks, for instance by adding sugar, nevertheless does influence the overall amount of energy consumed, just as it does for foods, even though the absolute levels of energy density for drinks are lower than that for foods. For this reason, caloric drinks may play a special role in contributing to positive energy balance.

The Panel has given special emphasis to the substantial body of robust experimental evidence, both in humans and in relevant animal models, underpinned by the principles of thermodynamics. To reach its conclusions, the Panel interpreted the epidemiological findings in the light of this experimental evidence. Thus, *the Panel notes* the associations between specific foods and food groups with weight gain, overweight, and obesity, and has interpreted them, in the light of the experimental evidence, as indicating a general effect of energy density rather than as several different specific effects of particular foods and drinks. *The Panel concludes* that energy density is a probable causal factor underlying the observed associations with specific foods and food groups, and therefore has decided that energy density is entered into the matrix as such. Similar principles apply to physical activity although, unlike energy density, epidemiological studies estimate this more directly.

The evidence, compelling on physiological grounds and supported by experimental and observational evidence, is for diets with plenty of low energy-dense foods to limit weight gain; and for diets with substantial amounts of high energy-dense foods to promote weight gain — especially when there is frequent consumption of large portions of energy-dense foods and drinks. Although drinks are characteristically high in water and less energy dense than foods, the same principles apply, within the drink category.

immediately available glycogen, followed by use of body fat and of protein in the form of lean tissue. Balance (no weight loss or gain) is achieved when energy input equals output, over time. When body fat stores increase or decrease, there is an accompanying change in lean body mass, with around three quarters of progressive weight gain or loss representing changes in body fat stores.

As stated in Chapter 6, body mass index (BMI) is the conventional indicator of body fatness, and takes account of both height and weight. BMI is calculated as weight in kilograms divided by height in metres squared (BMI = kg/m^2). This method does not always provide an accurate measure of body fatness. Unusually lean but muscular people have a relatively high BMI, even if they have little fat. The BMI criteria for risk are now supplemented by measures of excess abdominal fat, because this selective accumulation is a particular risk to health. But the BMI method provides a simple measure of body fatness for most people, most of the time.[8] See table 8.1 and also Chapter 6.

8.2 Trends and incidence

Brief summaries of the worldwide trends in BMI are given in Chapter 1. The more historical and detailed perspective that follows provides an important evolutionary context for interpretation of the clinical, epidemiological, and experimental data reviewed.

8.2.1 Human evolution and adaptation

Overweight and obesity became a public health issue only relatively recently in human history. Before industrialisation, underweight and weight loss, leading to debility caused by shortage or deficiency of energy from food, were the main nutritional issues.[10] Food insecurity is still a feature of life for the remaining gatherer–hunter and pastoralist communities, and for many agricultural communities in adverse social or environmental circumstances. Periodic episodes of food shortage are a defining characteristic of any type of nomadic life. It is likely that the human species has evolved

Box 8.2	Fast food

The term 'fast food' is used in lay publications and in common discourse, as well as in the scientific literature. It is also used as a category in research studies of food, nutrition, and the risk of diseases, including cancer. In the literature, the term does not refer to all foods that can be consumed immediately or quickly, and certainly does not refer to foods such as fruits. In general, the term refers to readily available, energy-dense meals, snacks, foods, and drinks. These tend to be consumed often and are frequently offered in large portion sizes. In the literature, the term usually refers to 'fast food' served in transnational restaurants and the many 'fast foods' created in each country and region that imitate those served in such transnational restaurants.

Studies assessed in this chapter (see 8.8) show an association between the consumption of 'fast foods' as defined in the literature and a higher risk of weight gain and obesity. These studies examined people who ate at 'fast-food' restaurants or from takeaway outlets: most of the foods they consumed were high energy-dense products. There is no plausible basis for weight gain being caused by the speed with which a food is prepared or made available. Indeed, many foods can be prepared speedily without also being energy dense. These studies support the Panel's conclusion that the energy density of foods and drinks is an important determinant of body mass.

Table 8.1	Body mass index as a measure of body fatness

A body mass index (BMI) of between 18.5 and 24.9 is generally regarded as 'acceptable' or 'normal'. This is roughly equivalent to 15–20 per cent body fat in adult men and 25–30 per cent in adult women.[1] The 'underweight' or 'thin' range is a BMI of below 18.5. Above 25, the common gradings for overweight and obesity are as follows:

| Classification | BMI (kg/m²) | |
	Principal cut-off points	Additional cut-off points
Normal range	18.50–24.99	18.50–22.99
		23.00–24.99
Overweight	≥25.00	≥25.00
		25.00–27.49
		27.50–29.99
Obese	≥30.00	≥30.00
Obese class I	30.00–34.99	30.00–32.49
		32.50–34.99
Obese class II	35.00–39.99	35.00–37.49
		37.50–39.99
Obese class III	≥40.00	≥40.00

Adapted with permission from WHO[9]

The principal cut-off points have been proposed to classify overweight and obesity. The additional cut-off points are used in some countries as useful public health references.[9] Also see chapter 6.1.1.

and adapted to favour the deposition of body fat in order to survive food shortages.[11] [12]

Famines still occur in regions of the world ravaged by wars and droughts, particularly in Africa. In children, poor maternal nutrition, inadequate and inappropriate feeding of infants and young children, and recurrent infections still cause millions of deaths every year. Therefore it is unlikely that the United Nations Millennium Development Goal, to halve the 1990 global rate of malnutrition in under-5s by 2015, will be achieved.[13] [14]

In the past, people in most settled communities possibly lived a large part of their lives in approximate energy balance, with adults usually remaining lean, neither losing nor gaining much weight from year to year. This pattern is still evident in food-secure agricultural communities in Africa, Asia, and Latin America, as well as in those urban areas where ways of life involve a substantial amount of physical labour and where energy-dense foods are scarce. Historically, being overweight has been seen as a sign of wealth, the ability to provide, and a social advantage. This is still the case in countries where food insecurity remains endemic or is a living memory.

8.2.2 Obesity as a public health issue

Even in the highest-income countries, obesity was uncommon until the 19th century, except among wealthy people who had access to plentiful amounts of food. But with industrialisation and urbanisation in Europe, and then in North America and other countries, issues of food insecurity disappeared, food supplies became more plentiful, and food generally became more energy dense (in particular, increasingly processed and higher in fats and sugars). At the same time, occupations gradually became more sedentary.[15]

Consequently, from the latter part of the 19th century, overweight and obesity were not unusual among middle-aged, middle-class adults in high-income countries; from the middle of the 20th century, they became fairly common in adults in high-income countries. In low-income countries, and even most high-income countries, there has been a rapid increase in the prevalence of obesity in the period from 1990 to the present. The rate of increase of the prevalence of obesity globally has accelerated during this period.[16]

Although obesity was recognised as a public health problem in higher-income countries in the 1970s,[17] [18] until fairly recently it was generally not taken seriously. It was typically seen by health professionals and the public as being caused by bad habits and weak will — obese patients would simply be advised to follow a low-energy diet. Only in the past decade has there been a growing and wide recognition of the significance of the social and environmental forces that influence the quality and quantity of food and drink consumed and physical activity undertaken.[19]

Further, until recently, the causal role of obesity in increasing the risk of other diseases was not well understood. Since the 1980s, however, obesity has increasingly been recognised

Table 8.2	Approximate relative risk of physical health problems associated with obesity	
Relative risk greater than 3	**Relative risk 2–3**	**Relative risk 1–2**
Type 2 diabetes	Coronary heart disease	Cancer
Gallbladder disease	Hypertension	Reproductive hormone abnormalities
Dyslipidaemia	Osteoarthritis (knees)	Polycystic ovary syndrome
Insulin resistance	Hyperuricaemia and gout	Impaired fertility
Breathlessness		Low back pain
Sleep apnoea		Increased risk of anaesthesia complications
		Fetal defects (associated with maternal obesity)

Adapted with permission from WHO[1]

as a disease in itself, and also as a cause of several disorders and diseases (table 8.2). Many people who are obese suffer several of these diseases, disorders, or disabilities. Obese people, women in particular, are also more likely to experience personal, social, and professional difficulties[20] and reduced opportunities for employment and advancement.[21]

Obesity also lowers life expectancy. It is estimated that at 40 years of age, an obese person can expect to live 6 to 7 years less than someone defined as being of 'normal' weight. The UK government has suggested that the average life expectancy of men living in England has fallen because so many are obese.[22][23] It is also now generally accepted that, to a lesser degree, overweight short of obesity as usually defined is a cause of many of these pathologies (table 8.2).[24]

8.2.3 Obesity as a global pandemic

Now, at the beginning of the 21st century, overweight and obesity are common, and their prevalence is increasing rapidly. WHO estimated in 2005 that 1.6 billion adults worldwide were overweight, of whom 300 million were obese.[25] About one sixth of the adult population worldwide was overweight and a further 7 per cent obese. The very rapid rise in overweight and obesity in children, together with a fast and accelerating rise in type 2 diabetes in young people (box 8.3), are particularly striking.

Although the very rapid rise in obesity throughout the world was not expected, there is now general agreement on why obesity has become pandemic. The demographic, nutritional, and epidemiological shifts that affected the populations of the first countries to be industrialised in the 19th century are now occurring worldwide, and at a faster rate. In 1975, of a global population of around 4 billion, about 35 per cent (or 1.4 billion people) lived in cities or urban areas. In 2005, of a global population of 6.5 billion, about 49 per cent (or 3.2 billion people) lived in urban areas: so in three decades the world's urban population has more than doubled. The projections for 2030 are a world population of perhaps 8.2 billion, of which 60 per cent (or 4.9 billion people) will live in urban areas: an increase of over three times the 1975 figure within the space of one lifetime.[34]

Living in cities does not of itself predispose people to weight gain, overweight, and obesity; this depends on how people work and live, and what they eat and drink. Daily

Box 8.3	Body fatness in childhood

Childhood overweight and obesity are becoming increasingly common, not only in high-income countries, but in industrialised areas in most countries around the world.[26] The most widely used definition of childhood obesity is that of Cole et al.[27]

Ten per cent of the world's children were estimated to be overweight in 2000. Recent evidence suggests that this problem affects almost all countries and is escalating.[28] In many countries, an additional 1 per cent of children are becoming overweight or obese every year. From the 1970s to the end of the 1990s, the prevalence of overweight and obesity in children doubled or tripled in several large countries in most regions, such as Canada and the United States in North America; Brazil and Chile in Latin America; Australia and Japan in the Western Pacific region; and Finland, France, Germany, Italy, and Spain in Europe. Projections estimate that by 2010, half of all school-age children will be over-

weight in the Americas, along with some 44 per cent of children in the eastern Mediterranean region, and 35 per cent in the European region (including the countries of the former Soviet Union) and in the western Pacific region.[29]

Children who are overweight are liable to remain overweight as adults or to become obese.[26][30] The likelihood of an overweight or obese child becoming or remaining obese in adulthood is increased by their degree of body fatness and the age at which they are assessed. Below about the age of 10, the degree of overweight or obesity is only partly related to adult fatness, while by 18 years of age, obesity is largely fixed.[30] Even when adults are not overweight, they may retain an increased risk of morbidity and mortality from having been overweight in adolescence.[31]

As with overweight and obesity in adulthood, childhood overweight and obesity are causes of other chronic diseases. Most

of the consequences of obesity take years, or even decades, to become clinically evident, but some are apparent in childhood. Over half of overweight 5–10-year-old children have been reported to have one cardiovascular disease risk factor, such as high blood pressure, hyperlipidaemia, or elevated insulin level.[32] Children who are even only moderately overweight have elevated low-density lipoprotein cholesterol levels. Type 2 diabetes, almost unknown in early life until recently, is rising rapidly in children as obesity increases. Some areas in the USA experienced a 10-fold increase in this form of diabetes in children between the 1980s and 1990s.[33]

Children who experienced growth restriction or very low-energy diets in very early life (and in utero), but who then gained weight rapidly in infancy or early childhood, are especially likely to become obese and to develop type 2 diabetes as children and as adults.

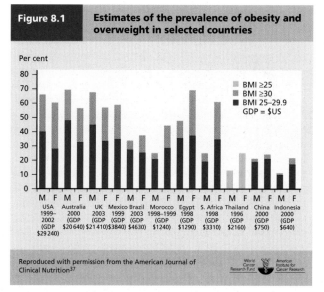

Figure 8.1   **Estimates of the prevalence of obesity and overweight in selected countries**

Reproduced with permission from the American Journal of Clinical Nutrition[37]

Estimates are given by country for men and women, for three BMI ranges: ≥ 25; ≥ 30; and 25–29.9. GDP = gross domestic product per capita ($US). UK = United Kingdom. USA = United States of America.

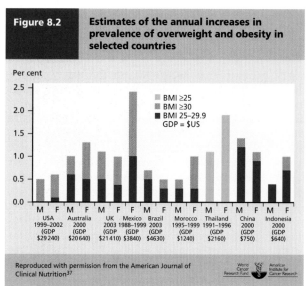

Figure 8.2   **Estimates of the annual increases in prevalence of overweight and obesity in selected countries**

Reproduced with permission from the American Journal of Clinical Nutrition[37]

Estimates are given by country for men and women, for three BMI ranges: ≥ 25; ≥ 30; and 25–29.9. GDP = gross domestic product per capita ($US). UK = United Kingdom. USA = United States of America.

ways of life for non-industrialised populations typically involve relatively high levels of physical activity. This includes manual labour and walking, even when food supplies are secure and plentiful; and staple foods — cereals (grains) or roots and tubers — which are almost always of relatively low energy density (box 8.1). In contrast, ways of life in industrialised cities are more likely to be sedentary. Modern urban food supplies are increasingly processed, with products that are relatively energy dense: low in dietary fibre and relatively high in fats and oils, and refined starches and sugars. Modern urban food supplies also include more meat and energy-dense alcoholic and soft drinks. An additional factor, in what has been termed this 'obesogenic' environment, is the ready availability and low price of very many processed foods and drinks. This makes it easy for poor as well as rich people to consume more energy than their bodies require.[20 35]

Obesity is still more common in high-income countries, where about 22 per cent of the adult population (185 million people) are now obese, compared with less than 4 per cent (115 million people) in middle- to low-income countries.[36] However, of the six countries where more than 60 per cent of the adult population are overweight or obese, while three are higher income (the United States, Australia, and Great Britain), three are lower-income (Mexico, Egypt, and South Africa).[37] In middle- and low-income countries, obesity, and the diseases caused by weight gain leading to obesity, coexist with diseases and disorders of undernutrition in the same communities and families.[38] See figures 8.1 and 8.2.

In general, obesity is more common in women than in men, although more men are overweight.[1] Overweight and obesity rates usually increase up to middle age and then are lower in old age. Obesity rates rise first in cities and urban areas; rural communities are slower to show this increase.[1] Of 38

nationally representative studies among the very lowest income countries, women of child-bearing age were more likely to be overweight than underweight, even in rural areas.[39]

Obesity rates vary with socioeconomic status. In a cross-country analysis, as national income rose, BMI increased rapidly, then flattened, and eventually declined.[40] It increased most rapidly until an annual income of about $US 5000, and peaked at about $US 12 500 for women and $US 17 000 for men. In countries whose gross national product (GNP) per head is less than $US 2500, obesity in women is more common among those with a high income.[41] But even in a number of countries with GNP per capita below $US 2 500, such as China, more women of lower compared to higher socioeconomic status are overweight. As countries use more money (measured by rises in national GNP), obesity is increasingly becoming a disease of the poor.[41]

8.3 Regulation of body fatness

As stated, the physiological cause of weight gain, overweight, and obesity is the consumption of more energy from foods and drinks than is used. Therefore both dietary intake and energy expended, and physical activity, are determinants of energy balance. In particular, the systems responsible for regulating appetite to match energy intake to expenditure are crucial. This section summarises relevant points about thermodynamics and the physiological mechanisms involved in energy intake, expenditure, and balance.

8.3.1 Thermodynamics
The first law of thermodynamics states that energy cannot be created or destroyed, but only transformed. In humans and other animals, energy is supplied by the metabolism of

food, using up oxygen in the process. Of the energy the body liberates from food, about 10 per cent is used in its digestion, absorption, and metabolism.

Energy expenditure can be measured in a calorimeter, a sealed chamber designed for this purpose, either directly as heat production or indirectly by measuring the amounts of oxygen used and carbon dioxide produced. The amount of energy metabolised can then be calculated. Studies using calorimeters prove that the principles of thermodynamics, manifest as energy balance, with weight loss and weight gain as described in this chapter, apply both in humans and in animals.[42] Such studies were the first to prove that restriction of energy from food results in weight loss.[43]

Energy restriction to less than is expended will result in weight loss, independent of the type of macronutrients supplied in the diet. Recent trials,[44-47] however, show that different macronutrients may have different effects on metabolism, independent of their energy content. For instance, low-carbohydrate diets cause the body to metabolise carbohydrate stored in the body as glycogen; the associated water excreted leads to loss of weight but not, unless there is a deficit in total energy, of tissue. Foods high in dietary fibre, such as wholegrain cereals and vegetables, promote satiety and therefore may influence weight regulation by improving appetite regulation and tending to constrain excess energy consumption.[48]

8.3.2 Energy intake and output

Human energy needs comprise the amount of energy used to maintain the body's functions (measured as basal metabolic rate or BMR); to digest and assimilate food (diet-induced thermogenesis); and to provide fuel for physical activity. This energy comes originally from foods and drinks, and is sourced by the body from stores of carbohydrate, fat, and protein.

Human basal energy needs vary largely as a function of the total mass of lean tissue, which in turn relates to sex, size, and age. Physical activity levels vary from day to day, as does energy intake from foods and drinks. Excess intake is stored; these stores are used to meet the needs of a higher output — as a result of extra physical activity, for example. In pre-menopausal women, basal needs vary to some extent with ovulatory and other cyclical hormonal changes.

Usually, body weight and energy stores balance over a month or so. Short-term changes in weight are mostly caused by fluctuations in the body's store of water, not in stored energy. Thus between meals and overnight, the short-term stores of carbohydrate (glycogen in liver and muscles) are mobilised and oxidised, with associated water. This causes weight loss, but mostly of water. Longer-term changes in weight, by contrast, are due to alterations in the body's fat tissue. Therefore substantial daily fluctuations in weight do not reflect changes in energy stores, whereas consistent weight gain (or weight loss) over a substantial period of time does. In undernourished people with negligible fat stores, weight loss reflects loss of lean tissue, used for energy. In sedentary adults who are not undernourished, changes in weight over a period of time reflect changes mainly in the body's stores of fat.

8.3.3 Energy requirement and balance

The energy used to maintain the body's functions (basal metabolism) fuels many physiological processes. These include maintenance of the balance of minerals within cells and the electrical potential difference across membranes. Energy is also required for processes such as DNA repair and the production of new cells, and for the synthesis of proteins and other structural and functional molecules. The assimilation of food involves the production and secretion of various enzymes and hormones that control the flow of nutrient molecules through different metabolic pathways.

The regulation of these interrelated processes depends on factors such as general health, age, and also genetic and other factors that vary between people.[49]

Tissue deposition during growth in childhood, puberty, and pregnancy and lactation, has additional energy costs. Pregnant women have modestly increased energy requirements, but many are less physically active during pregnancy. Lactating women require about an extra daily 750 kcal (3150 kJ) of energy from food.

The major energy cost above BMR comes from physical activity (see Chapter 5).

For any given weight, BMR is largely a function of the proportion of lean body mass to total body mass; this varies with sex and age, and also health and nutrition status. In sedentary adults, lean mass (and so BMR) decreases with age: older adolescents and young adults usually have higher energy requirements than middle-aged and elderly people. This means that as they age, people need to consume less energy from foods and drinks if they are to stay in energy balance and not gain weight.

Energy requirements — the energy expended by the body — vary between people. A small, lean, elderly man weighing 50 kg living in the tropics, who takes only light exercise, might be in energy balance at around 1750 kcal (7350 kJ) per day; whereas a young man weighing 80 kg, who is extremely active as a manual labourer, is likely to need over 3500 kcal (14.6 MJ) per day. A sedentary, elderly woman weighing 55 kg might be in energy balance at 1500 kcal (6300 kJ) per day; whereas a young woman who trains with weights daily might need up to 2750 kcal (11.5 MJ). Positive energy balance means consuming more energy than is expended, in which case, the body will gain weight — mainly as fat, but also as lean tissue, which increases BMR. Negative energy balance means consuming less energy than is expended, in which case the body will lose weight — again mainly fat, but also lean tissue. This, together with other adaptations such as reducing physical activity, tends to mitigate weight loss.

In obesity there is excess stored energy, mainly as fat but also as lean tissue, which leads to increased energy expenditure, so that higher energy intake is needed to maintain energy balance.

As people gain weight and their BMR increases, they need more energy from foods and drinks to maintain their increased weight. Over time, a new balance may be achieved, so that no more weight is gained, or the balance may remain positive even at the heavier weight, so that weight continues to be gained.[50]

8.3.4 Appetite and weight control

Humans have many physiological control systems to help balance energy input and output. Underfeeding leads to increased appetite. Eating a meal normally leads to satiation, a feeling of fullness which stops the eating, and satiety, which inhibits the desire to begin to eat. However, humans vary with regard to the extent to which they are able to maintain body weight over years or decades; some appear to maintain energy balance readily, others can only do so with difficulty. The maintenance of energy balance involves various processes including satiety responses, appetite control systems, and other homeostatic mechanisms. In the main, the control systems are most effective in responding to underfeeding, by increasing appetite, and are less effective at reducing intake with long-term overfeeding. Psychological, social, and cultural factors are important underlying influences on dietary patterns and physical activity.

Control seems to be least effective at relatively low levels of physical activity, meaning that sedentary people tend to gain weight more readily than active people. Conversely, although high levels of physical activity increase energy requirements and appetite, the likelihood of consuming more than is needed is lower. In addition, both increased energy density[51] and portion size appear to promote overconsumption.[52-54]

In rodents, various mechanisms have been identified that affect appetite control and weight. Some of these, involving the hormones leptin and ghrelin, for example, may turn out to be important for humans. But in humans, energy homeostasis is most reliably achieved by relatively active ways of life, together with low energy-dense diets. It is likely, in humans at least, that energy homeostasis operates most effectively within a range of physical activity and so also of energy expenditure, to which humans have evolved since the emergence of *Homo sapiens* about 250 000 years ago, and to which they are adapted.[11 55]

8.4 Other causes

Genetic, social, and environmental factors over the life course influence the prevalence of weight gain, overweight, and obesity. A large number of genes are involved with complex gene–gene and gene–environment interactions. Estimates of the extent to which relative body mass is inherited, derived from studies of identical (monozygotic) twins or adopted children and their biological parents, are consistently high, ranging between 64 and 84 per cent.[56] Correspondingly, relatively high energy intake and/or relatively low energy expenditure, as well as levels of habitual physical activity, also tend to run in families.[57-59]

Genetically determined obesity, such as the single-gene defects that cause Prader-Willi syndrome, Bardet-Biedl syndrome, and congenital leptin deficiency, is rare. Polymorphisms, in particular chromosomal locations linked to obesity in various populations, are now being investigated.[60] The study of genetic determinants of weight gain is tending to show that appetite regulation and spontaneous physical activity, rather than metabolism, have the dominant role.[56]

8.5 Risks of overweight and obesity

The risk of ill health and of death rises with increasing BMI, from a point well below a BMI of 30 (figures 8.3 and 8.4).[61-67]

The effects of overweight and obesity in the USA have been thought to be declining because of improvements in the medical treatment of complications such as high blood pressure, type 2 diabetes, and abnormal blood lipids. But large

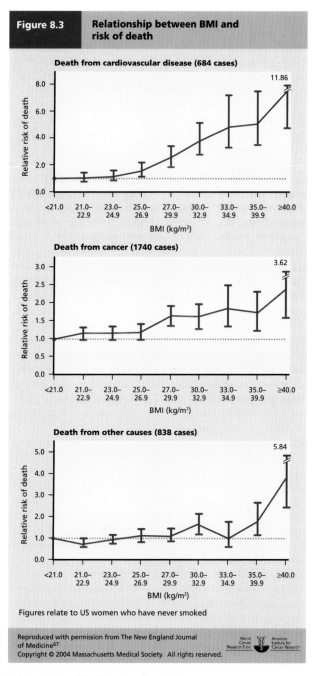

Figure 8.3 Relationship between BMI and risk of death

Death from cardiovascular disease (684 cases)

Death from cancer (1740 cases)

Death from other causes (838 cases)

Figures relate to US women who have never smoked

Relative risks of death were adjusted for: age; presence or absence of a parental history of coronary heart disease; menopausal status and hormone use; physical activity; and alcohol consumption. Bars denote 95% confidence intervals.

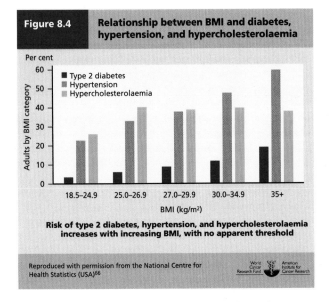

Figure 8.4 Relationship between BMI and diabetes, hypertension, and hypercholesterolaemia

Per cent

- Type 2 diabetes
- Hypertension
- Hypercholesterolaemia

Adults by BMI category

BMI (kg/m²)

Risk of type 2 diabetes, hypertension, and hypercholesterolaemia increases with increasing BMI, with no apparent threshold

Reproduced with permission from the National Centre for Health Statistics (USA)[66]

prospective studies with direct long-term monitoring of US women show increases in death rates when BMI exceeds 25 (except in smokers who tend to be thin and die earlier than non-smokers).[67]

Figure 8.3 shows relative risks for death among women who had never smoked. The monotonic relationship held for deaths from cancer and, more strongly, for deaths from cardiovascular causes. For other deaths, the increased risk in the leanest group was primarily due to chronic obstructive pulmonary disease and cirrhosis.

When death rate is plotted graphically against BMI, U- or J-shaped curves imply that having a low BMI both increases the risk of death and reduces life expectancy. But care needs to be taken to exclude the impact of smoking and of undiagnosed diseases such as cancer, which can lead to unintended weight loss well before a diagnosis is made.[68]

8.6 Method

As already stated (see Chapter 3), a full understanding of the biological factors that modify the risk of chronic diseases such as obesity requires a synthesis of several types of evidence. Each type has advantages and disadvantages, and all contribute to an overall picture. But there are special considerations that need to be taken into account for weight gain, overweight, and obesity.

First, this chapter includes consideration of thermodynamics, and the mechanisms of energy input, output, and balance, to complement evidence from observational and experimental studies. Evidence on the physiological mechanisms, including robust experimental evidence in humans, is abundant. Reliable evidence for mechanisms by which a particular factor affects energy balance is an especially important consideration when assessing and judging evidence on biological causation.

Next, clinical and epidemiological evidence in this area has specific problems. Studies on obese subjects based on their retrospective assessment (recall) of diet and physical activity are prone to serious bias. Also, interventions that may work in the short term are often ineffective in the longer term. Further, even if specific interventions are shown to cause weight loss, they are not necessarily the same factors that caused the weight gain originally. Finally, because of the crucial importance of environmental (economic, social, cultural, and political) factors in determining weight-related behaviour, interventions which focus on individual behaviour in isolation from the environment may fail to show long-term impact.

The Panel therefore decided to exclude data from such studies that are inherently problematic from the systematic literature review (SLR) of the clinical and epidemiological evidence. The literature review included trials or studies that ran for, or included follow-up of, less than a year in the review of underlying mechanisms. These were interpreted as contributing to understanding of mechanisms underpinning regulation of body fatness, though not in themselves as evidence of long-term impact on body fatness. The failure of interventions that are successful in the short term to translate to the long term is probably due to the powerful influences of sociocultural and other environmental factors in determining behaviour. Case-control studies were excluded, due to the special bias inherent in retrospective dietary reports related to weight gain. Trials that prescribed energy-restricted diets as the intervention were also excluded; only trials using ad libitum (unrestricted) diets as the intervention were included. Studies in children under 5 years old were also excluded. The restriction to include only studies in free-living participants means that results from this SLR are relatively robust and generalisable.

8.7 Interpretation of the evidence

Energy balance and body composition

Measuring energy intake and expenditure in free-living participants taking part in prospective observational studies is complex. Interpretation of measures of energy intake per se is problematic, due to inaccuracies in assessment and the complexity of its relationships with body mass and physical activity. Current techniques are not sufficiently precise to reliably detect the small imbalances that lead to weight gain, against a background of much higher levels of total energy intake and expenditure. Studies addressing the effectiveness of interventions designed to encourage weight loss are also difficult to interpret from the point of view of what causes weight gain in the first place. Interventions in free-living populations tend to have relatively low compliance.

Initial weight loss is hard to sustain in the long term, and so long-term studies tend to show less weight loss than predicted by short-term interventions. While the causes of short-term weight loss or maintenance can be identified and understood physiologically, the causes of long-term weight loss or maintenance may be different. Weight-loss trials were included in the review and informed the judgements reported here, but the causes of weight loss are not necessarily the converse of the causes of weight gain and obesity.

Box 8.4	**Television viewing**

The Panel decided to include evidence on television viewing, which is a discrete and measurable pastime associated with obesity. Subjective methods such as diaries or questionnaires, and more objective methods such as accelerometers, pedometers, or heart rate monitoring, can be used to measure relatively complex patterns of physical activity. However, all such methods are prone to imprecision and bias. On the other hand, the time spent on single, simple activities such as viewing television can be recalled more precisely, and it is rela-tively straightforward to measure the num-ber of hours someone spends watching television.

As shown in 8.8.8, watching television is associated with the development of obesi-ty (as well as with metabolic and cardio-vascular pathology). Such adverse effects are unlikely to be caused simply by the act of watching television. Television watching is a sedentary behaviour; the degree of physical inactivity during television watch-ing appears to be profound compared with other sedentary activities such as reading, or sitting and talking. Also, time spent watching television displaces opportunities for more active pursuits and increases exposure to promotion of foods that may promote weight gain. Further, watching television may be accompanied by relatively uninhibited consumption of energy-dense foods, which may be eaten in large portion sizes. Measuring the num-ber of hours someone spends watching television not only measures physical inac-tivity, but also a collection of related behaviour.[70]

Several of the studies that contributed data to this report used self-reported body weight, which correlates well with measured body weight, although under-reporting is com-mon, particularly among more overweight subjects.

Self-reported information on food consumption has also been used; this is prone to similar bias. Consumption of foods or drinks regarded as 'unhealthy', for instance, those con-taining fat, sugars, and alcohol, tend to be under-reported more than others.

Designs and reporting methods vary between studies, mak-ing it difficult to combine data. For most of the exposures assessed, many different measures are used. Study results can, and have been compared, but meta-analysis was not usually possible. Nevertheless, when epidemiological and trial data are interpreted appropriately, and the results are assessed together in the light of biological evidence, this research does identify aspects of food and nutrition, and ways of life such as being physically active, that are the most important deter-minants of overweight, weight gain, and obesity.

Social (including economic and political) and environ-mental factors are important determinants of behaviour, including that which affects body fatness. Such factors are the subject of a further report to be published one year after this Report.

Physical activity

Measurement of physical activity is complex (also see Chapter 5). When exposure measurement is less precise than outcome measurement, the apparent effect is attenuated. Most cohort studies used subjective assessment methods.

Although all studies are prospective, some studies do not allow reverse causality to be excluded. That is, a high BMI at the start of the study may be a cause of decreasing phys-ical activity and may also be independently associated with an increased risk of weight gain. Although many studies adjusted for potential confounders, the complexity of this area makes residual confounding difficult to exclude.

Trials of physical activity interventions and cohort studies that investigated the effects of physical activity on weight gain vary greatly in size, length, follow-up, intervention details, and study design, making comparisons problematic and precluding meta-analysis. In the case of physical activ-ity and obesity, cross-sectional data may also be valuable.[69]

More recent studies report an inverse relationship between physical activity and weight gain. While this could be explained by improvements in study design, publication bias may be present.

Being breastfed

The definition and classification of breastfeeding varied between studies. Some studies included mixed feeding, per-haps in a 'predominantly breastfed' group; some reported mixed feeding separately to exclusive feeding. In other stud-ies, it was unclear what level of exclusiveness was used. The duration of exclusive breastfeeding varied and was not always reported. Intervention trials of the effect of breast-feeding are impossible for practical and ethical reasons. Results may remain confounded, because in high-income countries where most studies are undertaken, mothers from higher socio-economic groups tend to breastfeed for longer periods, and it is difficult to correct for social class completely.

8.8 Evidence and judgements

A total of 207 publications were included in the SLR for the determinants of weight gain, overweight, and obesity. The evidence from these studies is summarised here and is fol-lowed by the Panel's assessments and judgements.

The evidence included observational epidemiology, trials, and mechanistic data, with particularly strong and robust evidence in humans, including data from short-term trials, which were interpreted as evidence of underlying mecha-nisms rather than of long-term impact. Each of these types of evidence is presented according to the particular expo-sures in the matrix. The exposures in the matrix reflect the Panel's interpretation of the causal pathway by which the exposures/interventions might influence the risk of obesity.

The Panel agreed that in the particular case of weight gain, overweight, and obesity, the epidemiological and trial evi-dence on cereals (grains), on vegetables, and on foods high in dietary fibre, should be interpreted in the light of, and as a marker of, their low energy density. It also agreed that, cor-respondingly, epidemiological and trial evidence on animal fats should be interpreted on the basis of their high energy density (box 8.1). Therefore, *the Panel concludes* that the epidemiological associations between specific foods, and weight gain and obesity, were probably due to a general effect of the relative energy density of such foods and drinks rather than any other characteristic.

The full SLR is contained on the CD included with this Report.

8.8.1 Physical activity

Three randomised controlled trials (RCTs)[71-73] and 16 cohort studies[74-89] investigated total physical activity and weight maintenance or change in adults. Nine RCTs investigated combined physical activity and diet interventions in adults.[90-100] Ten cohort studies[101-110] and 1 case-cohort study[111] investigated occupational activity; 19 cohort studies.[73 78 86 87 102 104 106 111-121] and 1 case-cohort study[111] investigated recreational activity in adults; 2 cohort studies investigated household activity[86 122]; 1 cohort study investigated frequency of physical activity in adults[107]; 3 cohort studies investigated intensity of physical activity in adults.[78 102 123] Two long-term RCTs,[124 125] 3 short-term RCTs,[126-128] and 15 cohort studies.[129-145] investigated total physical activity in children, and 4 cohort studies investigated frequency of physical activity in children.[145-148]

Total physical activity in adults

Two trials showed at least one statistically significant decreased measure of weight gain/body fatness with a physical activity intervention.[71 73] One trial showed no effect on weight maintenance.[72] (See table 8.3.)

In the Schmitz trial, at 39 weeks, the intervention group gained significantly more fat-free mass (0.89 kg, p = 0.009) and lost more body fat (1.63 per cent, p = 0.006) compared with controls.[71] There was no statistically significant effect on weight or waist measurements. The Fogelholm trial showed lower weight regain and waist-circumference measures in the moderate walking group than in either the control or high-intensity groups.[73] The Borg trial showed no statistically significant difference to weight maintenance.[72] However, resistance training attenuated the regain of body fat mass during the maintenance phase, though not after follow-up.

Also see 8.8.4, 8.8.5, 8.8.6, and 8.8.7 for dietary interventions.

All nine trials showed a decreased risk of at least one measure of weight gain with interventions that included physical activity and diet advice. This tended to be removed or attenuated as follow-up periods extended past 12 months (table 8.4).

The first Pound of Prevention trial showed that 82 per cent of the intervention group maintained or lost weight, compared with 56 per cent of the control group.[90] The second showed a statistically significant higher weight loss or maintenance in high-income women and men than in low-income women from intervention, but no statistically significant difference overall between intervention and control.[91] At 3 years, there was no statistically significant difference.[92] In the Women's Healthy Lifestyle Project, the intervention group showed statistically significant reductions in weight and waist to hip ratio levels compared with baseline. The control group showed no statistically significant difference.[93 94] In Leermarker's trial,[95] both intervention groups showed statistically significant reductions in weight (-1.6 kg, whereas controls gained 0.2 kg; p < 0.01). (The 54-month follow-up showed statistically significant lower increases in low-density lipoprotein cholesterol in the intervention group than in the control group.[95]) In the Harrell trial, the intervention group showed statistically significant lesser body fat than the control group.[96]

The Patient-centred Assessment and Counselling for Exercise trial showed no difference in BMI, but a non-significant lower percentage of body fat in the intervention group compared with the control group.[97] The Burke trial showed no statistically significant effect on BMI, but fewer individuals in the high-intensity group became overweight or obese.[98] The Pritchard trial showed a statistically significant greater weight loss in the diet than in the exercise group.[99] However, dual energy X-ray absorptiometry scans showed that 60 per cent of weight loss in dieters was fat tissue, compared to 80 per cent in the exercise group, which also showed better preservation of lean tissue. In the King trial, the exercise-focused intervention showed statistically significant better weight maintenance than diet or control.[100]

Cohort studies in adults

All 16 cohort studies showed decreased risk for at least one measure of weight gain, overweight, or obesity with increased physical activity, which was statistically significant in 12.[74-85]

Effect estimates (not all studies reported effect estimates) were a 0.77 per cent decrease in annual percentage change in weight (95% confidence interval (CI) 0.53–1.01) per one-unit increase in physical activity level[89]; a 0.32 kg/m² greater increase in BMI (95% CI 0.19–0.46) for not taking exercise, compared to taking exercise in men, and a 0.30 kg/m² (95% CI 0.16–0.44) for the same comparison in women[85]; a 0.03 kg/m² decrease in BMI (95% CI

Table 8.3	Physical activity interventions in adults			
Author	**Number of participants**	**Intervention**	**Length of intervention**	**Length of follow-up**
Schmitz 2003	56 women	Strength-training programme or control (aimed at weight loss)	15 weeks	6 months
Fogelholm 2000	85 women who had undergone a 12-week very low-calorie diet	Moderate or high-intensity walking programme (aimed at weight-loss maintenance), or control	40 weeks	33 months
Borg 2002	90 men who had undergone a 2-month very low-energy diet	Walking programme, resistance training (aimed at weight-loss maintenance) or control	8 months	31 months

Table 8.4	Diet and physical activity interventions in adults				
Trial	**Number of participants**	**Intervention**		**Length of intervention**	**Length of follow-up**
Pound of Prevention (Forster 1988)	219	Monthly education newsletters, with and without incentives, monitoring postcards, optional education course. Advice on healthy diet and exercise		12 months	–
Pound of Prevention II (Jeffery 1997, 1999)	288 men, 594 high-income women, and 404 low-income women	Newsletters with and without lottery incentives, or control		12 months	3 years
Women's Healthy Lifestyle Project (Kuller 2001, Simkin-Silverman 1995)	535 women	Behavioural programme or control		5 years	6–54 months
Leermarkers 1998	67 sedentary men	Clinic or home-based intervention or control		–	4 months
Harrell 1996	1504 police trainees	'Health and fitness programme' or the usual training		9 weeks	–
Patient-centred Assessment and Counselling for Exercise (Proper 2003) Burke 2003	299 municipal service workers	Intervention or control		9 months	–
	137 couples	High- or low-intensity intervention or control		4 months	12 months
Pritchard 1997	58 overweight men	A worksite programme comparing diet to exercise interventions		–	12 months
King 1989	90 men who had participated in a 1-year weight-loss trial	Comparing diet or exercise programmes against control in maintenance of previous weight loss		–	–

0.005–0.0001; p = 0.049) per 1-unit increase in metabolic equivalent (MET) hours per day[83]; a 0.91 kg decrease in men (95% CI 0.42–1.4) per physical activity score unit and a 2.14 kg decrease in women (95% CI 1.35–2.93)[81]; a 0.12 kg decrease (95% CI 0.07–0.16) per 0.10 MET change in physical activity level[80]; a 0.29 kg decrease (± 0.12 kg; p < 0.02) per log physical activity score in women only[79]; a 0.38 cm decrease in waist circumference (95% CI 0.16–0.60) for an increase in vigorous physical activity from baseline of 25 MET hours per week (this effect was reduced to 0.19 cm (95% CI 0.03–0.35 cm) after controlling for change in BMI)[78]; a 2.98 kg decrease (95% CI 1.41–4.55) per 200 exercise units in white women, and change in physical activity was inversely associated with change in body weight in all four race and sex subgroups (p < 0.0005)[77]; a 0.32 kg decrease (95% CI 0.16–0.48; p < 0.0001) per 1-unit, within-woman increase in sports/exercise scale[86]; a 0.41 kg/m² decrease in current BMI (95% CI 0.02–0.81; p value for trend 0.042) per 1-unit increase in past sport participation[75]; a 1.09 risk of increased BMI (95% CI 1.01–1.17) for the *inactive* group compared with the referent in the overweight, and a 0.95 risk of increased BMI (95% CI 0.91–0.99) in the *average* compared to the *active* reference group in the overweight subgroup.[74] One study showed that the baseline physical activity index was a significant predictor of weight gain (correlation coefficient of 0.39; p value for trend < 0.05) and fat mass gain (correlation coefficient of 0.40; p value for trend < 0.05) when one outlier was removed (weight regain of approximately 40 kg).[82] One study stated that there was a non-significant trend for lower increases in BMI with increased physical activity.[84]

One study showed a non-significant association between increased physical activity energy expenditure (correlation coefficient of -0.03; p value for trend 0.77) and physical activity level (correlation coefficient of -0.03; p value for trend 0.80) and subsequent weight gain.[88]

Other physical activity assessments in adults

Two cohort studies showed a statistically significant decreased risk of weight gain, overweight, or obesity with increased occupational activity[108 110]; two studies showed statistically significant decreased risk in women only[102 105]; four studies showed no significant association[103 104 107 109]; two studies had mixed results[101 106]; and one study showed a statistically significant increased risk (exposure was 'lifting').[111] There was considerable heterogeneity.

Six cohort studies showed a decreased risk of weight gain, overweight, or obesity with increased recreational activity.[73 86 118-121] Six studies showed no significant association[87 102 104 111 115 116]; five studies had mixed results,[78 106 112-114] and one study showed a statistically significant increased risk.[118]

One cohort study showed a statistically significant decreased risk of weight gain, overweight, or obesity with increased household activity.[122] One study showed no significant association.[86]

One cohort study showed no statistically significant association between frequency of physical activity and risk of weight gain, overweight, or obesity.[107]

Two cohort studies showed a statistically significant decreased risk of weight gain, overweight, or obesity with increased frequency of high-intensity physical activity.[78 102] One study showed no significant association.[123]

One cohort study showed a statistically significant decreased risk of weight gain, overweight, or obesity with

Table 8.5	Physical activity interventions in children			
Author	**Number of participants**	**Intervention**	**Length of intervention**	**Length of follow-up**
Mo-Suwan 1998	292 kindergarten children	Randomised by class (n=10) into exercise or control group	29–30 weeks	12 months
Sallis 1993	549 school children (mean age 9.25)	Randomised by school to specialist-led or teacher-led physical activity programme, or control condition	–	18 months
Flores 1995	110 children (mean age 12.6)	Randomised by class to Dance for Health or control conditions	12 weeks	–
Pangrazi 2003	606 children (mean age 9.8)	Randomised by school to usual physical education, PLAY (Promoting Lifetime Activity for Youth) (intervention) and PLAY plus usual physical education and control (no physical education or PLAY)	12 weeks	–
Neumark-Sztainer 2003	201 physically inactive girls (mean age 14.9 (intervention) and 15.8 (control))	Randomised by school to multicomponent physical education class or control. Intervention included 8-week maintenance component of weekly meetings	24 weeks	–

increased number of steps climbed in a day.[87] One study showed a statistically significant decreased risk of weight gain, overweight, or obesity with increased routine, daily physical activity level, and a non-significant decreased risk with change in daily physical activity level.[86]

Both long-term trials showed statistically significant decreased risk of at least one measure of weight gain, overweight, or obesity.[124][125] However, one of the trials also reported statistically significant lower BMIs in the control group (table 8.5).[125]

Two short-term trials showed no statistically significant difference with physical activity interventions.[127][128] One short-term trial showed a decreased risk of weight gain, overweight, or obesity with a dance-based physical activity intervention, which was statistically significant in girls.[126]

The Mo-Suwan trial showed a non-significant decreased prevalence of obesity in the intervention group (p = 0.057). Girls had a statistically significant decreased risk of increasing BMI of 0.32 (95% CI 0.18–0.56); boys had a non-significant increased risk of 1.08 (95% CI 0.62–1.89). At 1 year, the prevalence of obesity (defined by 95th skinfold percentile) decreased by 2.7 per cent in the intervention group and increased by 1.4 per cent in the controls.[124] The Sallis trial showed statistically significant lower BMI at 6 and 12 months (p value for trend < 0.05), but not at 18 months, in the control group. However, boys in the specialist-led group had thinner skinfold measurements at 6 and 12 months, but not at 18 months. Girls in the control group had lower BMI at each time point and this was statistically significant at 18 months (p < 0.01).[125]

The Flores trial showed a decreased risk of weight gain with intervention, which was statistically significant in girls only (BMI change -0.8 kg/m² in intervention and 0.3 kg/m² control). Boys showed similar, though non-significant, trends.[126] The Pangrazi trial showed no statistically significant difference between the intervention and control schools. However, girls showed a statistically significant higher activity in two out of three of the interventions than control girls.[128] The Neumark-Stzainer trial showed no statistically significant difference in BMI between the intervention and control schools, with non-significant improvements in several analyses.[127]

Twelve cohort studies showed decreased risk for at least one measure of weight gain, overweight, or obesity with increased physical activity in children, which was statistically significant in 11 (including the 2 cohort studies that used objective measures to assess physical activity).[132-145] Three studies stated that there was no statistically significant association.[129-131]

General mechanisms

The general mechanisms through which physical activity could plausibly protect against weight gain, overweight, and obesity are outlined in 8.3 and in Chapter 5. In addition, an important physiological consequence of physical activity is fat oxidation, although this effect may be attenuated in obese people. Regular exercise has been shown to increase fat oxidation in both healthy and obese people, a mechanism that is thought to occur as a result of improved insulin sensitivity,[149] although this effect may be attenuated in obese people. Evidence has shown that physical activity could potentially influence appetite control by: increasing the sensitivity of satiety signals; altering food choice or macronutrient preference; and modifying the pleasure response to food, which may elevate hunger, food intake, and body weight. Short- and medium-term studies have, however, shown that individuals can tolerate substantial negative energy balance during sustained physical activity, thus resulting in weight loss. Eventually, food intake will increase to compensate for the exercise-induced energy loss, although the degree of compensation may vary greatly between individuals.[150]

The epidemiological evidence on physical activity is substantial and consistent. There is robust mechanistic evidence, particularly in relation to its impact on

appetite regulation and energy balance. Overall, the evidence that all types of physical activity protect against weight gain, overweight, and obesity is convincing. It has this effect by promoting appropriate energy intake. Conversely, the evidence can be interpreted as showing that sedentary living is a cause of weight gain, overweight, and obesity.

The Panel is aware that since the conclusion of the SLR, nine RCTs[151-159] and four cohort studies[160-163] have been published. This new information does not change the Panel judgement (see box 3.8).

8.8.2 Sedentary living

One RCT investigated physical inactivity in children[164] (see table 8.6) and three cohort studies investigated physical inactivity in adults.[87 122 165] In addition, one RCT[164] and 16 cohort studies[129 143 147 166-178] investigated television viewing. These data are summarised separately in 8.8.8. Television viewing is a behaviour that usually involves being highly sedentary, although other activities, such as snacking, are also associated with it (see box 8.4).

Sedentary living involves a high level of inactivity, with low levels of activity. The data reviewed here relate to physical inactivity, which is only one component of sedentary living. Somebody who is inactive for considerable periods of time might also engage in regular, moderate, or vigorous physical activity at other times, and therefore not be sedentary. The strong mechanistic evidence on the effects of sedentary living, particularly in an environment with easy access to frequent, large portions of high energy-dense foods, contribute to the Panel's judgement on sedentary living.

The single trial showed no significant relationship between sedentary living and BMI. Post-intervention, BMI was unchanged, but behaviour such as the number of children watching more than 2 hours of television per day was significantly lower in the intervention group, as was total number of hours watched.[164]

Two cohort studies showed increased risk of weight gain with increased sitting time.[122 165] One study stated that there was no statistically significant relationship.[87] Effect estimates were 1.28 (95% CI 1.04–1.58) for the risk of becoming obese in those sitting at work, or away from home, or driving for more than 40 hours per week compared with less than 1 hour a week; 1.11 (95% CI 0.85–1.45) in those who spent > 40 hours a week sitting at home compared with 0–1 hours per week[122]; and 0.80 (95% CI 0.70–0.91) for the likelihood of weight maintenance (vs weight gain) with a low (< 33

hours per week) compared with high (≥ 52 hours per week) sitting time.[165]

The general mechanisms through which sedentary living could plausibly cause weight gain, overweight, and obesity are outlined above and in Chapter 5.

The epidemiological evidence that sedentary living causes weight gain, overweight, and obesity is relatively sparse, but there is robust mechanistic evidence in humans. *The Panel concludes* that the evidence that sedentary living causes weight gain, overweight, and obesity is convincing.

The Panel is aware that since the conclusion of the SLR, one cohort study[179] and one case-control study[180] have been published. This new information does not change the Panel judgement (see box 3.8).

8.8.3 Being breastfed

Two published SLRs[181 182] and three subsequent cohort studies[98 171 183] investigated being breastfed.

The larger literature review included 61 studies that investigated being breastfed and later risk of obesity, of which 43 were cohort studies, 15 were cross-sectional studies, and 3 were case-control studies.[182] It showed a statistically significant decreased risk of obesity with breastfeeding. Meta-analysis was possible on 28 studies, giving a summary effect estimate of 0.87 (95% CI 0.85–0.89) for breastfeeding compared with formula feeding.

Only two studies looked at adult obesity; the rest assessed obesity in those under 18 years. This effect was attenuated, but still statistically significant, when only the six studies that adjusted for parental obesity, maternal smoking, and social class were included, with an effect estimate of 0.93 (95% CI 0.88–0.99).[182]

The smaller literature review included 28 studies that investigated being breastfed and risk of obesity in later childhood.[181] It showed a statistically significant decreased risk of obesity with breastfeeding. Meta-analysis was possible on nine studies (two cohort studies and seven cross-sectional studies), giving an adjusted summary effect estimate of 0.78 (95% CI 0.71–0.85) for breastfeeding compared with not. The assessment of exposure to breastfeeding differed between studies. One study compared children who were mostly or only breastfed in their first 6 months with those who were mostly or only formula-fed, while most of the studies compared children who were never breastfed with children always breastfed. Again, the effect was attenuated when only maximally adjusted studies were included.

All three cohort studies published after the conclusion of the above-mentioned literature reviews showed decreased risk of obesity with breastfeeding.[98 171 183] However, the effect was not statistically significant when fully adjusted in two studies,[171 183] and one study showed a decreased risk of obesity, which was statistically significant in adolescence but not adulthood.[98] Effect estimates

Table 8.6	**Sedentary behaviour interventions in children**			
Author	**Number of participants**	**Intervention**	**Length of intervention**	**Length of follow-up**
Dennison 2004	176 children from middle-income families (mean age 4.0)	Randomised by daycare centre (n=18) into intervention that addressed nutrition, reducing sedentary behaviours, or control group	12 weeks	–

were 0.70 (95% CI 0.54–0.91; minimally adjusted) but 1.22 (95% CI 0.87–1.71) in the final model[171]; and 0.15 (95% CI 0.03–0.72) for being obese in adolescence and 0.34 (95% CI 0.12–1.01) for being obese in adulthood.[98] One study reported a regression coefficient of -0.30 (95% CI -0.053 to -0.007; p value for trend 0.012) and BMI at age 8 years after adjustment for sex.[183] The study stated that breastfeeding was not a statistically significant predictor of BMI after multivariate adjustment.

General mechanisms

Exclusively breastfed children show different growth patterns from those of formula-fed infants (also see chapter 6.2). Breastfed infants consume less total energy and less protein than formula-fed infants.[184] It is possible that the bioactive factors in human milk could modulate energy metabolism, a process in which leptin (present in human milk but not formula) may be implicated. Alternatively, the effect of elevated protein intake and plasma insulin concentrations in formula-fed babies could stimulate fat deposition and early adipocyte development.

The epidemiological and mechanistic evidence that being breastfed protects against overweight and obesity is substantial and generally consistent. While there are some issues to do with measurement and confounding, there is evidence for plausible mechanisms. Being breastfed is probably protective. The epidemiological evidence relates to childhood overweight and obesity; overweight children tend to become obese adults.

The Panel is aware that since the conclusion of the SLR, three cohort studies[185-187] have been published. This new information does not change the Panel judgement (see box 3.8).

8.8.4 Low energy-dense foods

The Panel decided to group the epidemiological evidence on foods that are low in energy (box 8.1) into this general category. This decision was informed by the mechanistic evidence.

Nutrition interventions

Fourteen randomised controlled trials investigated dietary interventions and weight loss, and prevention of weight gain, overweight, or obesity.[45 188-200] Most trials increased the proportion of low energy-dense foods and drinks in people's diets. However, the stated aims of trials varied and some may not be directly relevant. In particular, low-carbohydrate diets seem to lead to energy reduction with high energy density, but the long-term health impact of such diets is not known (see table 8.7).

All trials showed that restricted energy diets decreased the risk of weight gain, overweight, and obesity. All trials also showed that increasing the consumption of low energy-dense foods and decreasing the consumption of high energy-dense foods in diets decreased risk of weight gain, overweight, and obesity. Some found that these varied approaches were more

effective than general energy restriction; some did not. Most trials with sufficient follow-up periods also showed that weight loss was not commonly maintained after the intervention ended.

The Matvienko trial showed no significant difference from analysis of the whole dataset, although participants with higher initial BMI showed improved weight maintenance with intervention, with statistically significant weight gain in the control group.[200] The Epstein trial showed non-significant weight loss in both intervention groups, with a non-significantly greater weight loss in the decreased fat and sugar group.[199] The Swinburn trial showed statistically significant weight loss with the low-fat diet at one year, but no significant difference at five years.[195] The Flemming trial showed statistically significant weight loss with the low-fat diet and calorie-controlled interventions.[197] The Dansinger trial showed statistically significant weight loss for all diets and no significant difference between them.[198] The Harvey-Berino trial showed statistically significant greater weight loss with calorie restriction than with the low-fat diet.[196] The Jeffery trial showed statistically significant greater weight loss with the low-fat diet at the end of the intervention; after follow-up, both groups had returned to their original weights.[194] The Sheppard trial showed statistically significant greater weight loss in the low-fat diet group.[193] The Shah trial showed no statistically significant difference in weight loss between the low-fat and low-calorie diets.[192] The Foster trial showed statistically significant greater weight loss for the low carbohydrate diet at three and six months, but a non-significant greater weight loss at one year.[45] The Stern trial showed a non-significant greater weight loss with the low-carbohydrate diet than the calorie-restricted diet.[191] The Ebbeling trial showed statistically significant greater weight loss with the reduced glycaemic load trial.[190] The Simkin-Silverman trial showed statistically significant greater weight loss and/or maintenance for the intervention group.[189] The Toubro trial showed no significant difference between the two weight-loss regimes, but did show statistically significant maintenance (less regained weight) in the ad libitum maintenance regime than in the fixed energy group.[188]

8.8.4.1 Wholegrain cereals and cereal products

Four cohort studies investigated wholegrain cereals and cereal products.

All four cohort studies showed decreased risk of weight gain and/or obesity for the highest intake group when compared with the lowest, which was statistically significant in two.[201-204] The two statistically significant results were both from studies that investigated all food sources of wholegrains. Effect estimates for higher wholegrain intake were 0.81 (95% CI 0.73–0.91; p value for trend 0.0002) for obesity and 0.77 (95% CI 0.59–1.01; p value for trend 0.03) for major weight gain[204]; decreased weight gain with greater total wholegrain intake (p value for trend < 0.0001)[203]; regression coefficients of -0.07 (95% CI -0.30 to 0.17) for men and -0.20 (95% CI -0.49 to 0.09) for women for the relationship between wholegrain bread intake and waist circumference[202]; and 0.91 (95% CI 0.79–1.05; p value for trend 0.13) for the relationship between wholegrain break-

Table 8.7	Nutrition interventions			
Author	Number of participants	Intervention	Length of intervention	Length of follow-up
Matvienko 2001	40 female young adults	Nutrition education	4 months	16 months
Epstein 2001	26 children with at least one obese parent – and their families	Increased vegetables and fruits of decreased fat and sugar intake	12 months	–
Dansinger 2005	160 adults with one obesity-related comorbidity	Low-carbohydrate diet, low-fat diet, calorie restriction, and macronutrient balance	12 months	–
Flemming 2002	100 otherwise healthy overweight or obese adults	High, moderate, and low-fat diet compared with a calorie-controlled group	12 months	–
Harvey-Berino 1999	80 otherwise healthy overweight or obese adults	Low-fat diet or low-calorie diet	24 weeks	–
Swinburn 2001	103 adults with one obesity-related comorbidity	Low-fat diet or general dietary advice	12 months	5 years
Jeffery 1995	74 moderately obese but otherwise healthy women	Low-fat diet or low-calorie intervention	18 months	–
Sheppard 1991	303 women at increased risk of breast cancer	Low-fat diet or other intervention	12 months	–
Shah 1996	122 overweight but otherwise healthy women (data only available for 75)	Low-fat diet or low-calorie diet	6 months	12 months
Foster 2003	63 obese but otherwise healthy people	Low-carbohydrate diet (Atkins) compared with low-calorie diet	6 months	12 months
Stern 2004	87 obese adults	Low-carbohydrate diet or calorie-restricted diet	12 months	–
Ebbeling 2003	14 obese adolescents/ young adults	Reduced glycaemic load diet compared with reduced energy and reduced-fat diet	6 month intensive phase + 6 month maintenance phase	–
Simkin-Silverman 1998	489 women, 50% were not over or underweight at baseline	Meetings led by behavioural psychologists and nutritionists compared with control	18 months	–
Toubro 1997	43	First randomised to rapid or slow weight-loss programmes, then re-randomised to a fixed energy or ad lib maintenance programme	12 months	–

fast cereal intake and risk of being overweight.[201]

Definitions of wholegrain foods remain contentious (see box 4.1.1).

Wholegrains (consisting of the grain endosperm, germ, and bran) provide an abundant source of dietary fibre, resistant starch, phytoestrogens, antioxidants, and other micronutrients (see chapter 4.1). The primary mechanism for an effect on weight gain is through low-energy density. However, there are other mechanisms through which wholegrains may have a physiological effect on weight gain. For instance, several studies have demonstrated a positive relation between wholegrain consumption and improved blood insulin profiles, which could provide an indirect mechanism.

Wholegrain cereals and cereal products are assessed here as high-fibre foods and as a marker for low energy-dense foods. For this reason, no separate judgement is made for wholegrain cereals and cereal products.

8.8.4.2 Foods containing dietary fibre

Six cohort studies investigated foods containing fibre, four in adults and two in children.[115 173 203-206]

Five cohort studies showed decreased risk of weight gain and/or obesity for the highest intake group when compared with the lowest,[115 203-206] which was statistically significant in three.[203-205] One study (in children) showed a non-significant decreased risk in boys and a non-significant increased risk in girls.[173] Of the two studies that showed non-significant decreased risk, one investigated the relationship between infant diets and adolescent obesity.[206] Effect estimates in adults were 0.51 (95% CI 0.39–0.67; p value for trend < 0.0001) for overweight and 0.66 (95% CI 0.58–0.74; p value for trend < 0.0001) for obesity[204]; p value for trend ≥ 0.001 for weight gain (no effect estimate)[205]; 0.39 standard deviation (SD) g per day weight change (± 0.2) for the highest intake group and 1.4 SD g per day weight change (± 0.2) for the lowest, p value for trend < 0.0001[203]; and the univariate model (adjusted for retirement (yes/no); type of job (sedentary or active); interaction between retirement and type of job; age; smoking; and the base level of the behaviour) showed a regression coefficient of -0.31, p value for trend < 0.01, and the multivariable model (additionally adjusted for all other behaviours examined, including physical activity and dietary variables) showed a regression coefficient of -0.17, p value for trend 0.10.[115] Effect estimates in children were 0.78 (95% CI 0.60–1.02) for adolescent obesity with the highest intake group of fibre foods at 3 years old[206]; and regression coefficients of 0.0011 (95% CI -0.0073 to 0.0095; p value for trend 0.80) in girls and -0.0046 (95% CI -0.014 to 0.0046; p value for trend 0.320) in boys.[173]

Residual confounding is possible, as indicated by the maximally adjusted cohort study above. People whose diets are high in fibre from food often also have other habits regarded as healthy, which may be difficult to characterise precisely. On the other hand, there is considerable evidence for a specific effect of dietary fibre on satiety and on mechanisms relating to appetite regulation, such as gastric emptying.[48]

Fibre from food has a low energy density, as it is not digested in the small bowel and can only undergo partial fermentation in the large bowel. Fibre consumption may increase satiation by increasing chewing, slowing gastric emptying and elevating stomach distension, and stimulation of cholecystokinin. The increased viscosity of soluble fibre can reduce the overall rate and extent of digestion, which may also result in reduced energy from protein and fat and a blunted post-prandial glycaemic and insulinaemic response to carbohydrates. Fibre-induced delayed absorption and the resultant presence of macronutrients in the distal small intestine, known as the ileal brake, mediate the release of several gut hormones.[207]

The evidence on foods containing dietary fibre is assessed here as a marker for low energy-dense foods, although there are specific mechanisms beyond energy density. For this reason, no separate judgement is made for dietary fibre.

8.8.4.3 Non-starchy vegetables
Five cohort studies investigated non-starchy vegetables, four in adults and one in children.[114 208-211]

All five cohort studies showed decreased risk of weight gain and/or obesity for the highest group of non-starchy vegetables intake when compared with the lowest, which was statistically significant in two.[114 210] Effect estimates in adults were 0.84 (95% CI 0.75–0.93; p value for trend < 0.0001) for becoming obese and 0.76 (95% CI 0.59–0.99; p value for trend 0.01) for major weight gain[210]; -0.12 kg/m² mean change in BMI (95% CI -0.22 to -0.02; p value for trend 0.012)[114]; regression coefficient of -0.05 (95% CI -1.24 to -0.63) with change in BMI[211]; and 0.99 (95% CI 0.87–1.13) for weight gain.[209] Weight and height were measured in the two statistically significant studies, and were self-reported in the two non-significant studies. The study in children showed a statistically significant decreased risk of raised BMI z-scores in boys (regression coefficient of -0.003, 95% CI -0.004 to -0.001) but no relationship in girls.[208]

Increased consumption of non-starchy vegetables, which are generally low in energy density, may result in a compensatory decrease in the consumption of more energy-dense foods. Most non-starchy vegetables tend to have a low glycaemic index and contain soluble dietary fibre, which may

result in slowed gastric emptying and increased satiety. Fruits and vegetables contain high concentrations of a range of important micronutrients such as antioxidants and phytoestrogens that may also have a beneficial influence upon the energy homeostatic pathways.

Non-starchy vegetables are assessed here as high fibre foods and as a marker for low energy-dense foods. For this reason, no separate judgement is made for non-starchy vegetables.

Overall, the epidemiological evidence that low energy-dense foods protect against weight gain, overweight, and obesity is substantial and generally consistent. The mechanistic evidence, particularly that on appetite regulation and energy balance, is compelling. Taking all types of evidence together, low energy-dense foods probably protect against weight gain, overweight, and obesity. They have this effect by promoting appropriate energy intake.

The Panel is aware that since the conclusion of the SLR, two RCTs,[212 213] three cohort studies,[179 214 215] and one case-cohort study[216] have been published. This new information does not change the Panel judgement (see box 3.8).

8.8.5 Energy-dense foods
The Panel decided to group the epidemiological evidence on foods that are high in energy (box 8.1) into this general category. This decision was informed by the mechanistic evidence.

In addition to the evidence summarised below, several of the trials reviewed in 8.8.4 investigated the effect of reducing intake of energy-dense foods and drinks, which generally decreased the risk of weight gain during the intervention. The evidence on sugary drinks and 'fast foods' are also relevant to the judgement for this general category (see 8.8.6 and 8.8.7).

8.8.5.1 Animal fats
Three cohort studies investigated animal fats, two in adults and one in children.[211 217 218]

All three cohort studies showed increased risk of weight gain for the highest intake group when compared to the lowest, which was statistically significant in one study,[218] and in one analysis of data on children.[217] Regression coefficients in adults were 0.0032 (95% CI 0.0063–0.00006) linking animal fat intake and increased risk of weight gain (height and weight were self-reported)[218]; and 4.85 (95% CI -3.5 to 13.2; p value for trend 0.26) linking animal fat intake and weight change (measured).[211] The study in children (recording animal fat intake from 1 to 7 years of age) showed a statistically significant greater weight at 7 years for the highest intake group of 29.3 kg (SD±2.0) compared with 23.7 kg (SD±1.2) in the lowest (p value for trend < 0.05).[217] When animal fat intake was measured as g/1000 kcal, g/kg body weight, or compared to Roher index (weight in g × 100/height in cm³), no statistically significant difference was apparent.

As the most energy-dense macronutrient, there are several

plausible mechanisms by which dietary fat could lead to positive energy balance and obesity. The efficiency of nutrient use is higher for fat than carbohydrate or protein. When energy balance is positive and fat is being stored, the storage of this fat only requires a small degree of oxidation (approximately 3 per cent of the energy stored). The high energy density of fat may promote passive overconsumption. Prolonged consumption of a high-fat diet may desensitise the individual to a number of appetite controls. The palatability of fat may induce voluntary overconsumption.

The evidence on animal fats is assessed here as a marker for energy-dense foods. For this reason, no separate judgement is made for animal fats.
High energy-dense foods are probably a cause of weight gain, overweight, and obesity, particularly when large portion sizes are consumed regularly. They have this effect by promoting excess energy intake. Also see entries on sugary drinks (8.8.6), 'fast foods' (8.8.7), and television viewing (8.8.8).

The Panel is aware that since the conclusion of the SLR, one cohort[219] and one case-control study[180] have been published. This new information does not change the Panel judgement (see box 3.8).

8.8.6 Sugary drinks
The evidence on sugary drinks is reviewed separately due to its independent effect on body fatness. It also contributes to the judgement on energy-dense foods and drinks.

One RCT[220] and four cohort studies investigated sugary drinks.[115 221-223] Two cohort studies were in adults[115 223]; the trial and two other cohort studies were in children.[221 222]

The single trial included 644 children randomised by class to receive teaching sessions to discourage consumption of sugary, carbonated drinks or to control. After 12 months, change in BMI z-score was non-significantly lower in the intervention group, with a change of 0.7 (SD 0.2) compared with 0.8 (SD 0.3) in the control group.[220]

Three cohort studies showed increased risk of weight gain when frequency of sugary drink intake increased,[115 222 223] which was statistically significant in two.[115 222] One study showed no association.[221] This study was in children, and investigated intake of 'fruit drinks', but excluded fruit juice, soda (fizzy drinks), or diet soda. The effect estimates for the two adult studies were mean weight gain of 4.69 kg for 1991 to 1995 and 4.20 kg for 1995 to 1999 in women who increased their sugar-sweetened soft drink consumption, and 1.34 kg and 0.15 kg in women who decreased their consumption[223]; regression coefficients of 0.20 (p value for trend < 0.01) for the univariate model relating weight gain to increase in intake of sugar-sweetened soft drinks and 0.12 (p value for trend 0.05) for the multivariable model (this study also reported a statistically significant relationship with increased waist circumference).[115] The cohort study in children that reported an effect estimate showed that BMI increased by 0.24 kg/m^2 (95% CI 0.10–0.30; p value for trend 0.03) per sugary drink (not including fruit juice)/day and the effect estimate for the frequency of obesity was 1.60

(95% CI 1.14–2.24; p value for trend 0.02), also per drink/day.[222]

There is considerable variation in the definition of 'sugary drinks' between studies. The study that reported no association excluded fizzy drinks.

Studies have demonstrated that, when consumed as part of a soft drink, the energy from sugars may not be compensated for in the same way as when consumed as part of a solid meal.[224] Limited studies have shown that in adults, short-term (10-week) intake of sugar-sweetened foods and drinks (of which 80% were drinks) promoted weight gain, whilst consumption of artificially sweetened foods resulted in weight loss.[28]

The epidemiological and mechanistic evidence that drinks containing added sugars, including sucrose and high-fructose corn syrup, are a cause of weight gain, overweight, and obesity is substantial and consistent. Sugary drinks probably cause weight gain, overweight, and obesity. Like energy-dense foods and drinks, they have this effect by promoting excess energy intake.

The Panel is aware that since the conclusion of the SLR, one RCT,[225] one cohort,[226] and one case-control study[180] have been published. This new information does not change the Panel judgement (see box 3.8).

8.8.7 'Fast foods'
The evidence on 'fast foods' is reviewed separately due to their independent effect on body fatness. It also contributes to the judgement on energy-dense foods and drinks.

Six cohort studies investigated 'fast foods' (see box 8.2), four in adults and two in children.[165 227-231]

All six cohort studies showed increased risk of weight gain with increased intake of 'fast foods', which was statistically significant in four,[165 227 229 230] and in women but not men in an additional study.[231] Effect estimates in adults were a regression coefficient of 0.85 (95% CI 0.43–1.27; p value for trend < 0.05) in low-income women and 0.39 (95% CI 0.15–0.64; p value for trend < 0.05) for the association between number of 'fast-food meals' per week and BMI[231]; a 0.85 (95% CI 0.75–0.96) chance of maintaining weight (equivalent to a 15 per cent increased risk of weight gain)[165]; a weight gain of 1.72 kg (95% CI 0.52–2.92; p value for trend 0.005) greater for black people who visited 'fast-food restaurants' frequently compared to those who visited infrequently, and 1.84 kg (95% CI 0.86–2.82; p value for trend < 0.0013) greater for the same comparison in white people[230]; and a 0.72 kg (95% CI 0.33–1.11; p value for trend < 0.01) greater weight gain for people who visited fast-food restaurants more than twice a week compared to those who visited infrequently.[229] One study in children showed a statistically significant greater increase in BMI z-scores of 0.82 for those who ate food from quick-service outlets more than twice a week compared to 0.28 for those who never ate quick-service foods (p value for trend 0.0023).[227] One study in children stated that there was a statistically significant association between increased 'takeaway food' intake and BMI at the age of 8, but that after multivariable adjustment there was no statistically significant relationship.[228]

The energy density of a food reflects the energy content per unit weight (box 8.1). Many of the highly consumed processed and 'fast foods' have a high energy density, often due to a high content of fat and refined starches and sugars and a correspondingly low water content.[232]

> **The evidence that 'fast foods' as defined in the literature are a cause of weight gain, overweight, and obesity is strong and consistent. This epidemiological evidence reinforces the Panel's judgement on energy-dense foods. Other factors are that 'fast foods' are promoted vigorously, are cheap, and are often available in large portion sizes at low cost. 'Fast foods' probably cause weight gain, overweight, and obesity. They have this effect by promoting excess energy intake.**

The Panel is aware that since the conclusion of the SLR, two cohort studies[226 233] and one case-control study[180] have been published. This new information does not change the Panel judgement (see box 3.8).

8.8.8 Television viewing

The evidence on television viewing is reviewed separately due to its independent effect on body fatness. It also contributes to the judgement on sedentary living (8.8.2) and may be a marker for other behaviour, such as consumption of energy-dense foods (box 8.1).[70]

One RCT[234] and 16 cohort studies[129 143 147 166-178] investigated television viewing, all in children, adolescents, or young adults. Some studies grouped other sedentary leisure-time activities, such as playing videogames, together with television viewing.

The single RCT showed a statistically significant decreased risk of body fatness with decreased television viewing. The trial included 198 children randomised by school into an intervention or control group for six months. The intervention aimed to reduce television, videotape, and videogame use with supporting lessons, encouragement not to eat meals whilst watching television, and a seven hours per week television budget. The intervention group showed a 0.45 kg/m^2 greater decrease in BMI (95% CI -0.73 to -0.17) than the control group. Statistically significant greater decreases were also seen in skinfold measurement, waist circumference, and waist to hip ratio. The intervention group showed statistically significant fewer hours of television viewing (p value for trend < 0.001) and fewer meals eaten in front of the television (p value for trend < 0.02).[234]

Ten cohort studies showed increased risk of weight gain and/or obesity with increased television viewing,[143 166-168 170-175] which were statistically significant in nine.[143 166-168 170-174] Four studies stated that there was no significant association[129 176-178] and an additional study found an association with videogame-playing in girls but not boys, but no association with television viewing.[147] One study showed a non-significant decreased risk.[169] Effect estimates (four studies did not report effect estimates) were a regression coefficient of 0.029 (p value for trend < 0.001) for the relationship between

hours spent watching television and the risk of obesity (as defined by triceps skinfolds on or above the 85th percentile) and 0.14 (p value for trend < 0.001) for triceps skinfolds on or above the 95th percentile[174]; regression coefficients of 0.037 (95% CI 0.011–0.058; p value for trend 0.001) for the relationship between time spent watching television or playing videogames in girls and 0.038 (95% CI 0.018–0.059; p value for trend 0.001) for the same relationship in boys[173]; correlation coefficient of 0.14 (95% CI 0.01–0.27; p value for trend < 0.05) for the relationship between time spent watching television and subscapular skinfold thickness (as a measure of body fatness)[143]; a regression coefficient of 0.054 (p value for trend 0.82) for the relationship between television viewing and BMI[175]; a regression coefficient of 0.48 (standard error 0.19; p value for trend 0.012) for relationship between television viewing in adolescence and BMI at 26 years in a maximally adjusted model[167]; a regression coefficient of 0.47 (SE 0.21; p value for trend 0.02) for the relationship between television viewing and BMI[166]; a regression coefficient of 0.19 (p value for trend < 0.01) for the relationship between time spent watching television or playing videogames and BMI[172]; an effect estimate of 1.55 (95% CI 1.13–2.12) for the group that watched the most television when compared to the lowest.[171] Watching television or videos, playing computer games, or listening to audio tapes was a positive predictor of body fat in 2 out of 4 models investigating variables related to percentage body fat at age 8 years[170]; a regression coefficient of 0.05 (95% CI 0.02–0.07; p value for trend < 0.01) for the relationship between time spent watching television and BMI[168]; and a BMI of 19.5 kg/m^2 (95% CI 19.3–19.7) in the group that watched the most television compared to a BMI of 19.6 kg/m^2 (95% CI 19.4–19.9) in the group that watched the least.[169]

> **Television viewing is a form of very sedentary behaviour. The epidemiological evidence is mostly consistent and generally free of methodological issues. Results from the intervention trial are impressive, and there is evidence of a dose-response relationship. Television viewing may also be associated with consumption of energy-dense foods and drinks. Studies were of children and adolescents, but these can be taken to apply also to adults. Given that television viewing is a sedentary behaviour, the mechanistic evidence, particularly that on energy input, output, and turnover, is compelling. Television viewing is probably a cause of weight gain, overweight, and obesity. It has this effect by promoting an energy intake in excess of the relatively low level of energy expenditure.**

8.8.9 Other exposures

The following exposures were evaluated: total fat, refined cereals (grains)/cereal products, starchy roots, tubers and plantains, fruits, fruit juices, fish, milk and dairy products, alcoholic drinks, sweeteners, and coffee. However, the data were either too low quality, too inconsistent, or the number of studies too few to allow conclusions to be reached.

8.9 Comparison with previous report

The panel responsible for the previous report made recommendations on body mass and on weight gain, based on the evidence that high body mass increases the risk of some cancers (also see Chapter 6). The report did not review the determinants of weight gain, overweight, and obesity.

8.10 Conclusions

The Panel concludes:

Throughout this Report, our conclusions and judgements derive from a balance of different types of evidence, including epidemiological, clinical trial, and mechanistic data (as set out in Chapter 3). Compared to evidence on the factors that modify the risk of cancer, there is more and better evidence from clinical trials, and less from observational epidemiology, while there is a large and robust body of experimental evidence in humans on mechanisms of energy balance. Factors that increase (or decrease) risk of weight gain do this through promoting (or discouraging) excess energy intake. The interaction of energy density of diets and level of physical activity is fundamental.

In light of this, we have taken an integrated approach in our interpretation of the evidence relating to weight gain, overweight, and obesity, much of which has focused on specific foods, drinks, and dietary constituents. The various foods and dietary constituents have therefore been interpreted in the context of the energy density of foods and diets.

The evidence showing that regular, sustained physical activity of all types protects against weight gain, overweight, and obesity is convincing. Being breastfed is probably protective. While the evidence is from studies of infants and young children, childhood overweight and obesity tend to track into adult life. Low energy-dense foods, especially those containing dietary fibre, are probably also protective.

The evidence that sedentary living is a cause of weight gain, overweight, and obesity is convincing. Energy-dense foods are probably also a cause. Sugary drinks (those containing added caloric sweeteners, notably sucrose and high-fructose corn syrup); 'fast foods' (which are readily available and may be energy dense and frequently consumed, often in large portions); and television viewing (a sedentary behaviour associated with consumption of energy-dense foods) are all probable causes of weight gain, overweight, and obesity.

The evidence reviewed in this chapter does not include the important role played by sociocultural and other environmental factors, which will be the subject of a further report to be published in late 2008. Nevertheless, given the evidence summarised in Chapter 7 on the role of body fatness in causing various cancers, the factors identified here should be considered to be additional, indirect causes of those cancers.

CHAPTER 9

Cancer survivors

Cancer survivors are people who are living with a diagnosis of cancer, including those who have recovered.

Awareness of cancer survival has increased greatly since the 1990s. So has the number of people living with a diagnosis of cancer. The total number of recorded cancer survivors in the world in 2002 was estimated to be just under 25 million, and by 2050 may approach 70 million.

The term 'cancer survivor' covers a very wide variety of circumstances. Thus, the needs of people currently undergoing therapy are likely to be different from those of people whose metabolic functions have been altered as a result of therapy and from those of people who are evidently fully recovered and whose functions are intact.

Nevertheless, the *Panel accepts* the validity of the concept of cancer survivor, *welcomes* the rising con-sciousness that cancer is a disease best spoken of and dealt with openly, and *agrees* that the best way to improve quality of life and increase the chances of prolonged life and recovery from cancer is when cancer survivors take responsibility for themselves, supported by associates, friends, and family, while always also consulting their professional advisors and making best use of available medical care sys-tems and qualified social support.

Correspondingly, *we the Panel collectively have accepted a special responsibility* to give our best advice, having examined the evidence derived from systematic reviews of the scientific literature done according to our agreed methodology, and also from our knowledge of the whole range of evidence and consideration of the precautionary principle and best clinical and public health practice.

Research on food, nutrition, physical activity, and cancer survival is at an early stage. Overall, *the Panel agrees* that it is not possible to make judge-ments that apply specifically to cancer survivors, based on the evidence reviewed for this Report. The available evidence on cancer survivors has a number of limitations: it is of variable quality; it is difficult to interpret; and it has not yet produced any impres-sive results. Definite general judgements are made more problematic because of differences in the health of cancer survivors at various stages;

between cancers of various sites; and between the effects of the many types of conventional and other therapies used.

The Panel notes as follows:
Regular physical activity and other measures that control body weight may help prevent recurrence, at least of breast cancer. In any case, when able to do so, cancer survivors are likely to gain general health benefit, and a sense of control over their circumstances, from regular physical activity.

The evidence does not support the use of high-dose supplements of microconstituents as a means of improving outcome in people with a diagnosis of cancer. Cancer survivors should consult their physician and/or a qualified nutrition professional, who can evaluate the safety and efficacy of specific dietary supplements, and counsel an appropriate action based on current research relevant to their particular clinical situation.

In summary, evidence that some aspects of food, nutrition, or physical activity specifically modify the condition of cancer survivors is emerging, but is not yet sufficiently developed to enable the Panel to make judgements that apply specifically to cancer survivors, as distinct from people without cancer.

The concept of 'cancer survivor' first gained currency in the USA in the 1990s, particularly among advocacy groups formed to give information, advice, and support to people with cancer. The term here refers to people living with a diagnosis of cancer, including those believed to have recovered.

Consciousness of cancer survival has increased greatly since the 1990s, especially in high-income countries. This is only partly because of the increase in numbers. Another reason is that cancer is increasingly a disease spoken of openly, and seen less as the visitation of a death sentence.

Cancer survivors, and their families and friends, are increasingly determined to take responsibility for living with cancer. They do this individually and collectively, usually in collaboration with their medical and surgical advisors, and often with practitioners offering complementary and alternative therapies, regimens, and advice.

Cancer survivors as an overall group, together with those who are closest to them, are especially concerned to learn about and act on helpful recommendations. These should be least likely to do harm, and most likely to help limit the progress of the cancer. They should also help prevent a recurrence of that or another cancer, and help prevent other diseases, as well as improve the quality of survivors' lives. This places a special responsibility on professionals in this field, to consider carefully what can be recommended.

The Panel's recommendations for cancer survivors are in Part 3, Chapter 12.

9.1 Definitions

The term 'cancer survivors' denotes all people who are living with a diagnosis of cancer, and those who have recovered from the disease. In this definition, then, cancer survival begins at the point of diagnosis.

Cancer survivors include the following population groups; these are often not discrete, because people may fall into several of the groups below.

After diagnosis, before treatment
- People with cancer who have chosen to have treatment
- People with cancer who choose to have no treatment.

During treatment
- People being treated with modern conventional therapies
  - Radiation

- Chemotherapy
- Surgery
- Combinations of radiation, chemotherapy, and surgery.

- People treated with therapies that are alternative or complementary to conventional ones (box 9.1), usually as well as, but sometimes instead of, conventional therapies
  - Naturopathy
  - Radical diets (very low fat, raw food, other)
  - Energy restriction
  - Orthomolecular nutrition (including all forms of supplementation)
  - Gerson therapy, Hoxsey therapy, antineoplastons, Coley's toxins, other
  - Traditional therapies (Ayurvedic, Chinese herbal, other)
  - Combinations of these, with or without conventional therapy
  - Other.

After treatment
- People whose treatment has been said to be successful, and who have undamaged metabolic functions
- People whose treatment has been said to be successful, and who have damaged metabolic functions
  - People who have had parts of their digestive tract surgically removed (mouth, oesophagus, stomach, small intestine, colon)
  - As above, also with colostomy, ileostomy
  - Other.

People with secondary cancer or cancer of a different site
- Where treatment has been unsuccessful, and who have undamaged metabolic functions
- Where treatment has been unsuccessful, and who have damaged metabolic functions
  - Those who have had parts of their digestive tract surgically removed (mouth, oesophagus, stomach, small intestine, colon)
  - As above, also with colostomy, ileostomy
  - Other
- People with metastasised or disseminated cancer, with or without cachexia
- People with terminal cancer.

After recovery
- People who are alive 5–10 years after successful treatment
- People who are alive 10+ years after successful treatment (including those who had cancer as a child).

The definition of 'cancer survivor' here does not include people living with a diagnosis of a benign tumour, or tumours defined as premalignant, such as premalignant cervical lesions or polyps in the colon.

'Cancer survivors' as defined here also does not include those living with people who are living with a diagnosis of cancer. Sometimes this wider definition is used, and from the public, community, and family health points of view, issues that concern cancer survivors are also of vital importance to their partners, family members, and close friends.[1] Such loved ones are most likely to want to know what to do, and will seek professional guidance, both for the person with diagnosed cancer, and also for themselves and family members.

This becomes most important practically when decisions need to be made about family shopping and meal preparation, and eating out. Should the family member with cancer be treated differently? Or should the whole family follow the same recommendations and advice? These are not questions of direct professional concern to cancer researchers, but do concern physicians, and other health professionals, whose responsibility includes passing on authoritative recommendations, or else giving the best available advice and guidance.

9.2 Occurrence

The number of cancer survivors has greatly increased in recent decades, especially in high-income countries. This is partly because the general prevalence of cancer continues to rise, within a world population that is also rising. In addition, screening programmes for common cancers are identifying many more cases, usually at relatively early stages. As already stated, the rapid rise in the recorded incidence of prostate cancer in recent years is largely because of increased use of methods of detection (see chapter 7.14.1). Also, for some cancers, medical and surgical treatments and follow-up care are increasing the time that people live with cancer; these interventions are also improving rates of recovery. In the USA, estimates of the number of cancer survivors have increased from around 3 million (1.5 per cent of the population) in 1970 to over 10 million (close to 4 per cent of the population) in 2002. The absolute number of cancer survivors aged 65 years and older is predicted to double in the USA by the year 2050.[1]

Calculations of the type made in the USA have not been made in Europe as a whole. European Union countries together now have a larger population than the USA, but given the overall differences between the two (somewhat lower rates of screening, detection, and years of survival after diagnosis in Europe), a rough guess of 5 million European survivors (or 1 per cent of the population) seems reasonable.[2] In 2002, the total number of recorded cancer survivors in the world was estimated to be just under 25 million.[3]

If prevalence of, and survival with, cancer worldwide con-

tinues to increase, and follows predictions made in the USA, and given a further increasing global population, the number of recorded cancer survivors worldwide in 2025 will approach 50 million, and in 2050 will approach 70 million. Such projections may be conservative, and also do not take into account people with cancer that is not diagnosed or recorded.

Among cancer survivors in the USA in 2002, the most common cancer diagnosed was breast cancer among women (22 per cent), prostate cancer among men (18 per cent), and colorectal cancer among men and women combined (10 per cent).[1] These figures are not proportional to incidence rates because the average time of survival after diagnosis of different cancers varies. In Europe, breast cancer was the most prevalent cancer in women (34 per cent), followed by colorectal cancer (10 per cent). In men, colorectal cancer (15 per cent), prostate cancer (12 per cent), and lung cancer (10 per cent) were most prevalent.[2]

9.3 Interpretation of the evidence

9.3.1 General
For general considerations that may affect interpretation of the evidence, see chapters 3.3 and 3.5, and boxes 3.1, 3.2, 3.6 and 3.7.

9.3.2 Specific
Nature of the field. The main problem faced by reviews of cancer survivors, as indicated in 9.1, is the scale and heterogeneity of the field. The interventions reviewed were studied in people with a number of different cancers, at different stages, and for different outcomes.

Classification. There are many groups of cancer survivors. Some have been diagnosed but have not yet received treatment. Others are undergoing treatments that have damaging effects and which, for some, have damaged the physical function of the body. Others have been overtly free from cancer for several or many years. As yet, there are no generally agreed classifications of cancer survivors, or the different stages of cancer survival, which makes comparisons of studies problematic.

Study design. Studies should take into account and report the stage of treatment participants are at, and give details of this treatment. Studies need to have sufficient statistical power to address the research question being examined.

Confounding. Clinical and pathological characteristics of the cancer, such as tissue of origin, stage at diagnosis, and specific molecular characteristics, are the strongest predictors of outcome, and are powerful confounding factors, especially in observational studies. Cancer treatments and their consequences may change the effects of interventions in ways that are not well understood. Different cancers may be modified in different ways by food, nutrition, and physical activity.

This complexity is increased by the effects of treatment and the disease itself, both of which can affect food consumption, digestion, absorption, and metabolism, and

Box 9.1	Conventional and unconventional therapies

Conventional medicine is also known as modern or Western medicine. It is allopathic, meaning that it relies on diagnosis of disease, by examinations and tests, and treatment. With cancer, treatment includes surgery, chemotherapy, and radiotherapy. Conventional medicine is based on investigation of the biology (including anatomy, physiology, and biochemistry) of body organs, tissues, and cells. It includes an understanding of the pathological processes that lead to disease, and testing of interventions for efficacy and safety. Conventional practitioners undergo externally validated and structured education and training programmes, and continuing professional development, and they are subject to statutory regulation.

Complementary and alternative medicine includes many diverse medical and healthcare systems, practices, and products — some traditional, some modern. Training and regulation of providers exist, but often vary between therapies and nations. Some orthodox scientific evidence is available regarding some of these therapies, although the efficacy of many remains unclear and often controversial.

These therapies include mind–body interventions, such as meditation; biologically based treatments, such as radical nutritional regimens, micronutrient supplements, and herbal products; manipulative and body-based techniques, such as massage and osteopathy; 'energy therapies', such as the use of magnets or

therapeutic touch; and alternative medical systems, such as traditional Chinese and Ayurvedic medicine.

'Integrative medicine' is a recent approach that uses some complementary and alternative therapies within conventional medicine. Physical activity programmes and dietary interventions are commonly used in integrative medicine, together with counselling.

Cancer survivors should consult their physician or qualified health professional before initiating any therapies that are alternative or complementary to conventional therapies. Cancer survivors should keep all of the health professionals involved in providing any treatment fully informed of their choices in these areas.

---

also a person's physical condition or behaviour. This is particularly important for studies that relate body fatness to cancer risk, as cancer often causes weight loss. In some cases, surgery may have been performed to remove parts of the gastrointestinal tract affected by cancer. Cancer often results in loss of appetite, and cancer treatments may cause nausea or a decreased ability to absorb nutrients from food.[4] An important strength of randomised trials, provided they are sufficiently large, is that confounding variables, both known and unknown, will on average be distributed equally between the treatment and control groups, and will therefore not bias the study results (also see chapter 3.1.6).

9.4 Evidence and judgements

A systematic literature review (SLR) was undertaken to assess the role of food, nutrition, and physical activity in the case of cancer survivors. This review addressed the efficacy of nutritional and physical activity interventions in cancer survivors in relation to mortality, disease-free survival, cancer recurrence, secondary cancers, quality of life, and adverse effects of treatment regimens.[5]

This SLR was designed differently from those on the causes of cancer in people assumed to be free from the disease, and used as the bases for judgements in previous chapters. This decision was taken because the focus of the research questions was not on causation, but on the efficacy of particular interventions. In addition, people with cancer are in a clinical situation and will often be receiving, or will have received, medical, surgical, or other treatments that may affect their nutritional status; this limits the value of some kinds of observational evidence.

For these and other reasons, it was decided in the case of cancer survivors to give pre-eminence to randomised controlled trials (RCTs), which are least likely to be confounded, and are best suited to investigate the relatively short-term efficacy of specific interventions. The review undertaken was

of 53 nutritional intervention trials and 23 physical activity trials. It assessed the quality of all the studies reviewed, including the size of the study populations; the length of the interventions and of the follow-up programmes; the methods used to ensure randomisation; and the methods of statistical analysis.

There were usually insufficient numbers of any type of study to allow useful combining of data for meta-analysis. Overall, data were also insufficient to allow for separate analyses of survivors before, during, and after treatment. The Panel's standard criteria used to grade the strength of evidence, and the matrices used to record the Panel's judgements, used in previous chapters, were not used in the case of cancer survivors.

A narrative review of observational studies was also conducted. As stated above, these are less suited in the study of efficacy of treatments, and so in studies of cancer survivors their results should be treated with caution. Also see 9.3.

The full SLR is contained on the CD included with this Report.

9.4.1 Randomised controlled trials
9.4.1.1 'Healthy' diets

Food-based RCTs were defined as those using interventions that offered advice about 'healthy eating' (variously defined) or specific diets such as high-fibre diets and/or weight-loss programmes. Twelve trials met the criteria for inclusion in the review of food-based interventions. Study designs tended to be of poor quality, and insufficient information was available about the methods used for randomisation and blinding. Duration of interventions varied between seven weeks and three years.

Small trials conducted in Russia, the Netherlands, and Poland reported on the effects of 'healthy diet' interventions for breast cancer survivors, either during or after treatment, and cancer recurrence. A reduced fat and energy diet decreased the recurrence of breast cancer in the Russian study.[6] A study conducted both in the Netherlands and in

| Box 9.2 | Use of supplements by cancer survivors |

In the USA and in other high-income countries, the use of supplements in physiological (low dose) and also pharmacological (high dose) amounts is common among the general population and also among cancer survivors.

At least 50 per cent of the US population take vitamin and mineral supplements.[52] Supplement use among US cancer survivors has been shown in two studies published in 2004 to be similar to the average, but high-dose supplements may be more commonly used by cancer survivors.[53 54] Survivors are also reported to be high users of complementary and alternative medicines and other treatments.[55] Several hundred web sites promote high-dose supplements with unsupported claims that they are active cancer cures or can prevent recurrence.

Poland examined the effect of dietary advice and psychological support to achieve weight loss, but no significant effect on breast cancer recurrence was reported, perhaps because of the small size and limited power of the study.[7]

Six trials reported on the effect of 'healthy diets' on 'quality of life'. Of these, one study of people surviving breast, ovary, prostate, or testicular cancers showed a positive effect, in a programme that combined general dietary information with physical training and coping skills.[8] A study of people surviving head and neck or gastrointestinal cancers showed a beneficial effect with a programme of dietary counselling compared to usual care.[9] The other studies reported no effect.[10-13]

Only one trial investigated food-based interventions and side-effects of treatment. This study found that individual nutritional advice, adapted to the patient's own needs and tastes, reduced adverse effects from radiotherapy in people with head and neck cancers.[14]

Three small trials examined food-based interventions and all-cause mortality. The studies were conducted in survivors of non-melanoma skin cancer,[15] colorectal or lung cancer,[16] and breast, ovary, prostate, or testicular cancer.[8] None of the trials reported a significant association between the intervention and all-cause mortality.

No conclusions can be derived from these results.

The Panel is aware of two large, multicentre, randomised trials of breast cancer survivors, the WINS study, published in 2006, and the WHEL study, published in 2007. The WINS trial tested a dietary intervention to reduce fat intake in over 2000 women with early stage breast cancer. After 5 years of follow-up, the women in the intervention group had a 24 per cent reduced risk of recurrence compared with the control group (relative risk 0.76, 95% CI 0.60–0.98).[17] However, these findings cannot be easily translated into recommendations for breast cancer survivors, for several reasons. First, women in the intervention group had more extensive surgical procedures. Also, they lost weight during the trial and it is possible that weight loss was responsible for their improved outcome. Finally, dietary fat reduction was most beneficial in women with oestrogen- or progesterone-receptor negative tumours, a finding that may be due to chance.[18]

The WHEL study tested the effect of a dietary intervention high

in vegetables, fruits, and dietary fibre, and low in fat, in over 3000 women with early stage breast cancer. After 7.3 years of follow-up, there was no difference in breast cancer recurrence, new breast cancer, or all-cause mortality between the intervention and control groups.[19] Unlike the WINS study, in the WHEL study women in both the intervention group and the control group experienced small increases in weight, and this may partially account for the different results in these two trials.

9.4.1.2 Supplements

Data from 39 RCTs were assessed. The review included trials on supplements of retinol,[20-26] beta-carotene,[27-30] vitamin B6,[31 32] vitamin C,[31 32] multivitamins,[27 33 34] vitamin E,[35-37] selenium,[35-38] and isoflavones.[39 40] Additionally, single trials of each of evening primrose oil,[41] glutamine,[42] and N-acetylcysteine[26] and nine trials of commercial supplements were reviewed.[43-51] Also see box 9.2.

Trial quality and number of participants tended to be higher in supplement trials than in the dietary-intervention trials. Compliance was monitored in the majority of trials, and placebos were usually given to the control group. However, the controls in all seven retinol trials and in five of the nine commercial supplement interventions were given 'usual treatment' or an 'unrestricted' diet.

There was considerable variation in the methods and length and type of intervention used, and the overall quality of many studies was poor. Furthermore, the disparate vitamins and other bioactive substances used in these studies make comparison difficult. Results were null or non-significant in almost all cases.

Trials where data were sufficient and the exposures were homogeneous enough to allow meta-analysis included those examining retinol and all-cause or cancer mortality. Comparing the intervention to usual treatment, the summary estimate from four trials that examined all-cause mortality was 0.97 (95% CI 0.83–1.13)[23-26]; from three trials that examined cancer mortality, the summary estimate was 0.92 (95% CI 0.65–1.31).[23 24 26]

One small trial of bladder cancer survivors showed a significant reduction in cancer recurrence. This trial compared supplementation with a multivitamin plus a high-dose combination of vitamins A, B6, C, and E and zinc against a multivitamin alone.[33]

A larger trial designed to test the effect of 200 micrograms per day of selenium supplementation on recurrent non-melanoma skin cancer showed no effect on skin cancer, but a protective effect on prostate cancer.[36 37]

Fifteen trials investigated types of supplementation and side-effects of cancer treatment. One small study reported higher treatment toxicity in survivors of haematological cancers with vitamin A supplementation (as retinol or beta-carotene).[23] No significant results were reported in the other studies.[27 29 31 32 34 35 38-40 48 56-58]

The evidence from this review of trials does not show that micronutrient supplements have any benefits in cancer survivors. High-dose supplements may be harmful. Some micronutrients and other bioactive compounds are known to be toxic at high doses.

9.4.1.3 Physical activity

Twenty-three physical activity RCTs met the criteria for inclusion in the review. Interventions ranged from simple advice to increase physical activity, to enrolment in supervised exercise programmes. These were mostly small trials and of short duration. In half of the studies, compliance levels were unclear, and the majority failed to record physical activity levels in the control group, which severely limits their value.

Only three of the physical activity intervention trials reported on mortality or cancer recurrence.[8 59 60] None of these studies reported significant effects.

Twenty trials investigated quality of life outcomes with physical activity interventions. Nine of these trials were in survivors of haematological cancer,[61] lung cancer,[62] prostate cancer,[63] and in a combination of cancers.[8 12 64-68] Eleven trials were in breast cancer survivors.[62-73] Two of the interventions in these trials included nutrition components.[12 64]

The physical activity interventions, assessment instruments, and outcomes studied were varied. The interventions included many types of supervised or home-based exercise programmes. Several studies assessed well-being and quality of life using a version of the Functional Assessment of Cancer Therapy scale,[69] although other questionnaires and scales were also used. Quality of life outcomes included a range of measures of physical, functional, and emotional well-being, as well as measures of physical fitness.

Of the 20 physical activity trials that investigated quality of life, 18 reported a benefit from the intervention on at least one of the outcome measures reported in the study. None of the trials reported harmful effects of the physical activity interventions on any of the outcomes studied.

Taken together, these trials provide some evidence for the benefit of physical activity on post-treatment quality of life in cancer survivors.

9.4.2 Observational data

Three reviews that examined data from 26 observational cohort or case-control studies met the criteria for inclusion in the review of observational data.[70-72]

All of these compared breast cancer outcomes in cancer survivors to 'body fatness', as measured by body mass index (BMI) (see chapter 6.1). The results of these studies were generally consistent. An overall increased risk of mortality with increasing BMI was reported, although there was some heterogeneity in study results.

Of 21 studies that followed cases for at least 5 years, 12 showed statistically significant associations between higher BMI and worse outcome, while others showed insignificant results or were null. One study found that mortality risk decreased as BMI increased. Physical activity was associated with an enhanced quality of life in cancer survivors.

While this information suggests that higher body fatness before diagnosis leads to a worse outcome, and also that physical activity may be beneficial in breast cancer survivors, it is nevertheless insufficient to justify any firm judgement on body fatness specifically in relation to cancer survivors.

The Panel is aware of two large observational studies that investigated physical activity in breast cancer survivors. A study of nearly 3000 breast cancer survivors in the Nurses' Health Study reported reduced risk of breast cancer mortality in women who were physically active, compared with sedentary women.[73] In a second study of over 1200 women, physical activity measured before diagnosis of breast cancer was associated with reduced all-cause mortality; this association was statistically significant in women who were overweight or obese at diagnosis.[74]

9.5 Comparison with the previous report

The previous report did not include any review, assessment, or recommendations directed at cancer survivors. The panel responsible for that report stated that its recommendations were especially important for population groups and people most susceptible to cancer.

9.6 Conclusions

The Panel concludes:

Research into the effects of food, nutrition, and physical activity in cancer survivors is in its early stages. For this reason, and also because of the scale and heterogeneity of the field, the evidence reviewed here is inconclusive.

Regular physical activity and other measures that control weight may help prevent recurrence of breast cancer and improve quality of life. When able to do so, cancer survivors may gain general health benefit and a sense of control over their circumstances from regular physical activity.

The evidence does not support the use of high-dose supplements of microconstituents as a means of improving outcomes in people with a diagnosis of cancer.

Cancer survivors should consult their physician and/or a qualified nutrition professional who can evaluate the safety and efficacy of specific dietary supplements, and offer advice based on current research relevant to their particular clinical situation.

As with all the chapters in Part 2 of this Report, the Panel's recommendations for cancer survivors are in Part 3, Chapter 12.

CHAPTER 10

Findings of other reports

The assessments and judgements made by the Panel shown in the preceding chapters are based on evidence from systematic literature reviews of original research studies, compiled according to specified criteria, on food, nutrition, physical activity, and the risk of cancer. However, the Panel recognises that recommendations on food, nutrition, and physical activity are also made in relation to other diseases. These include recommendations designed to control and prevent chronic diseases other than cancer, and those designed to influence the dietary and activity patterns of populations and individuals. Recommendations that address nutritional adequacy (prevention of deficiencies), and prevention and management of infectious diseases (vulnerability to which is affected by nutritional status) should also be taken into account.

The Panel has therefore decided that its recommendations designed to control and prevent the incidence of cancer, made in the following chapters, should take into account the judgements and recommendations of authoritative reports related to the prevention and control of other diseases. Any potential conflicts that might arise between its own recommendations and others that cover the same aspects of food, nutrition, and physical activity are identified in this chapter.

As stated in its title, the present Report has a global perspective. The importance of dietary issues related to chronic diseases, relative to those for nutritional adequacy and infectious diseases, varies both between countries and between subpopulations within countries. The approach taken by this Report, to consider recommendations from other reports, is particularly relevant for those parts of the world now suffering the 'double burden' of endemic deficiencies and infection — especially of infancy and childhood — as well as increasing incidence of cancers of various sites, and of other chronic diseases. Nevertheless, people, as well as public health authorities, need integrated messages. In Chapter 12 we state whether any recommendation is affected as a result of the findings of other such reports.

This chapter has also assembled the findings of other recent reports on food, nutrition, physical activity, and cancer. These show where judgements and recommendations are consistent, and where they have changed, as science has developed and as views on relative weight of evidence from different types of research have evolved. In addition, comparisons have been made in Chapters 4 to 7 between the findings of this Report and the previous report, published in 1997.

Dietary guidelines produced by expert bodies have been part of national and international public health nutrition policies since the early 20th century. At first, the recommended dietary intakes for the planning of food supplies were designed to prevent specific nutritional deficiencies. From the 1960s, a different type of guidance began to emerge, designed to prevent food and nutrition-related chronic diseases, including heart disease and cancer.

A previous review analysed the findings of 100 expert reports published between 1961 and 1991 that include guidelines and recommendations to prevent various chronic diseases.[1] Some of the landmark reports produced over this period are 'The Causes of Cancer',[2] 'The US Surgeon General's Report on Nutrition and Health',[3] 'Nutritional Goals for Health in Latin America',[4] 'Medical Aspects of Dietary Fibre' published by the Royal College of Physicians of London,[5] and 'Diet and Health' and 'Diet, Nutrition, and Cancer' published by the US National Research Council.[6 7] Towards the end of this 30-year period, dietary guidelines to prevent chronic diseases tended to move the emphasis away from dietary constituents (such as saturated fat or vitamins). Instead, the focus shifted to foods and drinks, and sometimes to dietary patterns as a whole.

The 1961–1991 review[1] shows consistent agreement on the types of diet recommended to protect against obesity, cardiovascular disease (CVD), cancer of a number of sites, type 2 diabetes, gut disorders and diseases, osteoporosis, dental caries, and other chronic diseases. Compared with diets typically consumed in high-income countries, the recommended diets are high in wholegrain or minimally processed cereals (grains), vegetables and fruits, and are therefore high in dietary fibre and bioactive microconstituents, relatively high in fish, and contain lean meat. These recommended diets are also correspondingly low in total fat and saturated fatty acids, sugars, and salt; fatty and salty foods; sugary foods and drinks in general; and alcoholic drinks. The review also shows that the expert reports consistently recommend regular, sustained, physical activity.

However, almost without exception, expert reports on chronic diseases treated these issues independently to those of nutritional adequacy (and the prevention of nutritional deficiencies), or of the prevention and management of infectious diseases, notably of infancy and childhood, and vice versa. The separate consideration of these issues usually reflected the focus either on national concerns in high-income societies, or the specific interests of specialists.

10.1 Method

This chapter is based on a systematic review of secondary literature that examines recommendations for dietary and physical activity produced since 1990 for the prevention of a number of diseases. Therefore, this chapter carries forward the work of the 1961–1991 review. The purpose is to give an account of the recommendations of other reports and not to assess the evidence therein. The full systematic literature review is contained on the CD included with this Report.

10.1.1 Diseases and exposures

The diseases in this present review are categorised as nutritional deficiencies, infectious diseases, chronic diseases other than cancer, and cancer. These are diseases identified by the United Nations and other authoritative bodies as being causally linked with food, nutrition, and physical activity. They are also identified as significant contributors to the global burden of preventable disease in terms of prevalence and cost.

The 'exposures' covered in this review are those identified in the report that preceded this one[8] as convincing or probable modifiers of cancer risk — together with those judged by other reports to justify a recommendation designed to prevent or control other diseases. The reports analysed include recommendations on relevant foods and drinks (including food production, preservation, processing, and preparation), and dietary constituents, physical activity, and energy balance.

10.1.2 Reports reviewed

The reports reviewed were published between 1990 and 31 December 2004 in the English language. To be included in the review, reports needed to:
- Involve an expert panel
- Include an original review of relevant literature
- Include explicit disease-specific conclusions and recommendations
- Base their conclusions on published peer-reviewed literature specified as a bibliography.

This approach eliminated reports that simply restated previous recommendations. It also ensured that the review included only reports with the main aim of developing or updating nutrition-related recommendations. Reports commissioned by industry, business-interest organisations, or other interested parties were excluded.

The criteria used for and timing of this review meant that some important reports were not included. *The Panel is aware* of these exclusions and has supplemented the text where such an omission would have given an incomplete picture.

Of more than 10 000 documents identified initially by database searches, applying these criteria reduced the number to 207. All of these reports were read and 94 were included in the review: 16 reports from international organisations,[8-23] 39 from North American organisations,[24-62] 22 from the European Union,[63-84] 14 from Australasia,[85-98] 2 from India,[99 100] and 1 report from South Africa.[101] The recommendations in the 113 that were finally excluded are generally consistent with those in the included reports.

The Panel is aware that other important reports have been published, which were either published subsequent to the review for this chapter or did not meet the criteria for inclusion. The organisations that produced these reports are: the American Cancer Society,[102] the International Agency for Research on Cancer,[103] the National Institute for Health and Clinical Excellence,[104] and the US Department of Health and Human Services and the Department of Agriculture,[105] and the National Heart, Lung and Blood Institute and the World Health Organization.[106 106B] The recommendations from these reports were also taken into consideration during the formulation of the recommendations for this Report.

10.2 Interpretation of the data

Some caution is needed when interpreting the information presented here. Most of the reports included have been commissioned by and for high-income countries and so reflect the nutrition concerns of such countries. Producing these reports is expensive and is likely to be beyond the means of most individual middle- and low-income countries. Where a recommendation is made for diets high in vegetables and fruits, for example, this means high in relation to the diets typical of high-income countries. Meeting such recommendations might mean increases in intake in some countries and maintaining already high intakes in others. Recommendations for vegetables and fruits usually do not include potatoes, which are generally grouped with roots and tubers (see chapter 4.1.1).

Many of these reports are concerned with what are now pandemic diseases of the circulatory system (ischaemic heart and cerebrovascular diseases and their determinants such as obesity, high levels of blood fats, and high blood pressure). Fewer reports are concerned specifically with cancer or diseases of other systems of the body, although an increasing number now link obesity with type 2 diabetes, and cancer.

Only a minority of the reports reviewed attempt to be comprehensive, and the terms of reference of these reports may be limited. For example, of the 15 reports addressing cancer, just 4 are concerned solely with cancers in general. Of the rest, 4 focus on chronic diseases including cancer, 2 are concerned only with colorectal cancer, 2 with vitamin supplementation, 1 with oral health, 1 with children's health, and 1 with fats and oils. Also, some reports on cancer do not review alcohol, food additives and contaminants, or breast-feeding. For such reasons, most reports say nothing about many of the aspects of food, nutrition, and physical activity addressed in this Report. The summary below states where there is significant disagreement between reports. *The Panel decided* not to include a tabulated summary of the recommendations from reports on cancer because, in view of our own Report, this would be non-contributory.

Until recently, few reports have used a systematic approach to assess the prevention of nutritional deficiencies in general. Although it has been established that vulnerability to infectious diseases — especially of infancy and childhood — is crucially affected by nutritional status, only in the past few years has there been an extensive analysis and a coherent approach to the recognition of the role of individual micronutrients such as vitamin A, zinc, and selenium in reducing life-threatening infections, for example, of the respiratory and gastrointestinal tracts, which continue to exact a huge burden of disability and premature death.

Many reports concerned with food, nutrition, and physical activity also stress the importance of not smoking or using tobacco. This information is not included here.

10.3 Nutritional deficiencies

10.3.1 Background

Undernutrition and hunger remain common in parts of the world where populations are impoverished and food is insecure, largely for social (including political and economic) and environmental reasons. Global rates of malnutrition (inadequate energy intake) and micronutrient deficiencies remain high, especially in low-income countries.

Many diseases are caused by deficiencies of specific or combined essential nutrients. These diseases, when severe and prolonged, can be fatal. In the 1990s, relevant UN agencies specified that certain micronutrient deficiencies were the most important global public health problems.[107 108] Those identified included deficiencies of iron (causing anaemia, lassitude, and learning difficulties), iodine (causing goitre and cretinism), and vitamin A (causing xerophthalmia, impaired night vision, and eventually blindness).

Infants, young children, and pregnant and lactating women have been, and remain, the main focus of recommendations designed to prevent and control nutritional deficiencies. Recommendations for combating specific deficiencies include programmes of salt iodisation (iodine); consumption of foods containing readily absorbable iron, including meat and other foods of animal origin (iron); and consumption of foods high in carotenoids or retinol (vitamin A). Supplementation and fortification are also recommended.[107 108] Other recommendations continue to promote exclusive breastfeeding, as well as the supply of adequate and varied weaning foods (preferably indigenous or local), and water and food free from infectious agents.

A number of trials and systematic analyses have assessed the value of interventions with micronutrients. The results are sometimes different when tested in African, Asian, or Latin American children, and this probably reflects the different prevailing nutritional conditions. The results emphasise the importance of ensuring that micronutrient intakes are adequate and that dietary factors that enhance micronutrient status form an important part of the diet of both children and adults, with particular attention being paid to women before and during pregnancy.

10.3.2 Introduction

Few reports concerning nutritional deficiencies qualified for inclusion in this review. Of the 95 included, 2 make recommendations on preventing rickets,[28] [52] 4 on preventing iron deficiency anaemia,[11] [13] [51] [92] and 4 on preventing vitamin A deficiency.[14] [19] [21] [79] These reports come from 10 different organisations: 1 from Europe, 6 from international agencies, and 3 from North America. No reports were included whose recommendations relate to malnutrition in general, or to iodine deficiency.

10.3.3 Foods and drinks

Vegetables, fruits, pulses (legumes), nuts, seeds, herbs, and spices. Three reports recommended that various vegetables and fruits — being those high in vitamin C and folates — should be included with meals to boost iron absorption and hence prevent iron deficiency anaemia.[11] [13] [51] Another report recommended that the complementary diets of infants and young children should include vegetables and fruits high in vitamin A to prevent vitamin A deficiency.[21]

Meat, fish, and eggs. One report recommended including foods that are high in absorbable iron, such as lean meat, to prevent iron deficiency anaemia.[51]

Dietary constituents and supplements. For vitamin C, folic acid, and iron, see chapter 4.10. Also, one report recommended that after the age of 6 months, infants receiving breastmilk or cow's milk as their main drink, or those consuming less than 500 ml/day of infant or follow-on formula, should receive a vitamin A supplement to prevent vitamin A deficiency.[79] Two reports include recommendations for vitamin A supplementation,[14] [19] and two recommended vitamin D to prevent rickets.[28] [52]

Breastfeeding. One report recommended that mothers should breastfeed exclusively for the first 4–6 months of their child's life to prevent iron deficiency in the child.[19]

10.3.4 Comparison of reports

One difference in emphasis between these reports and those on cancer (and other reports not included in the review) is the stress given to the importance of extended, exclusive breastfeeding (see 10.4.3), and the importance of safe water supplies.

Differences in recommendations for supplementation of diets of infants and young children are not substantial.

An apparent difference between these reports, and those on cancer and other chronic diseases, is the recommendation to consume meat as a source of absorbable iron to prevent anaemia. However, only modest amounts are proposed,

and reports on cancer and other chronic diseases do not recommend diets without red meat.

The Panel agrees that these matters of emphasis and considerations should be taken into account in its recommendations. See Chapter 12. Also see the Panel's conclusions in 10.7.

10.4 Infectious diseases

10.4.1 Background

Vulnerability to a number of common infectious diseases is affected by nutritional status; this is especially important in infants and young children.[109] Interaction between nutrition and infection occurs with 'classic' malnutrition — inadequate energy from food — and also with deficiencies of a range of vitamins and minerals. Relevant diseases include diarrhoeal diseases, respiratory infections, measles, whooping cough, and chickenpox.[109] On a global basis, rates of dangerous infectious diseases — especially of infancy and childhood — remain high, particularly in low-income countries. Conversely, repeated infections impair nutritional status, particularly during childhood.

The usual recommendations in previous reports concerning food, nutrition, and infectious diseases of infants and young children have been for exclusive breastfeeding, adequate and varied weaning foods (preferably indigenous or local), and water and food supplies free from infectious agents.[107]

10.4.2 Introduction

Few reports concerned with infections qualified for inclusion in the review. Of the 95 reports accepted, 3 included recommendations for the prevention or management of diarrhoea,[10] [17] [91] 3 for the management of HIV and AIDS,[9] [12] [25] 1 for the management of measles,[85] and 1 for respiratory diseases.[91] These 7 reports were published by 6 organisations: 2 from Australasia, 3 from international agencies, and 1 from North America. No reports were found that make dietary recommendations to help prevent or manage dysentery, malaria, or tuberculosis.

10.4.3 Foods and drinks

Cereals (grains), roots, tubers, and plantains. One report recommended that people with HIV or AIDS should include staple foods with every meal.[9] This report specified refined starchy foods such as white rice, maize meals, white bread, noodles, and potatoes to avoid gastric aggravation.[9]

Vegetables, fruits, pulses (legumes), nuts, seeds, herbs, and spices. One report recommended that people with HIV or AIDS should eat a wide variety of vegetables, fruits, and pulses (legumes) every day.[9]

Meat, fish, and eggs. One report recommended that people with HIV or AIDS should eat meat, poultry, and fish regularly.[9] It advised that meat should be cooked thoroughly, and foods containing raw eggs avoided, to prevent diarrhoea.[9]

Milk and dairy products. One report recommended that people with HIV or AIDS should consume milk products regularly.[9]

Fats and oils. One report recommended that people with HIV or AIDS should include fats and oils in their diet to maintain their weight.[9]

Salt and sugar. One report recommended that people with HIV or AIDS should include sugar and sugary foods in their diet to maintain their weight.[9]

Water, fruit juices, soft drinks, and hot drinks. One report recommended that people with HIV or AIDS should drink plenty of clean and safe water. If in doubt, and during an episode of diarrhoea, water should be boiled before use, and coffee and tea avoided.[9]

Food production, processing, preservation, and preparation. Also see 10.5.3. Two reports made recommendations on preventing diarrhoea: contaminated food and drink should be avoided; clean utensils should be used during preparation and serving; and food should be stored safely and served immediately after preparation.[10 17] One of these reports also recommended that foods should be covered and refrigerated where possible, for the same reason.[17] Similarly, another report recommended storing fresh food and leftovers in a cool place or a refrigerator.[9] Two reports recommended that foods should be cooked thoroughly and leftovers reheated to a high temperature to prevent diarrhoea.[9 17]

Dietary constituents and supplements. One report recommended that some people with measles should receive vitamin A supplements.[85]

Breastfeeding. Three reports recommended that women should breastfeed exclusively for the first 4–6 months of their child's life to prevent the child having diarrhoea.[10 17 91] Of these, one further advised non-exclusive breastfeeding up to 2 years of age and beyond if possible.[17] Another report made the same recommendation to prevent respiratory disease in the infant.[91] Two reports recommended that women infected with HIV should avoid breastfeeding where possible to prevent transmission of the virus to their child, and should cease breastfeeding as soon as is feasible.[12 25] One report recommended that clean, nutritious weaning foods should be introduced to an infant at 4–6 months of age, beginning initially with soft mashed foods to prevent the child having diarrhoea.[17]

10.4.4 Physical activity

One report recommended that people with HIV or AIDS should take light exercise.[9]

10.4.5 Comparison of reports

As with reports on nutritional deficiencies, one difference in emphasis between these reports and those on cancer is the stress given to the importance of extended, exclusive breastfeeding and the importance of safe water supplies.

The Panel agrees that these matters of emphasis should be taken into account in its recommendations. On the important issue of mothers with HIV or AIDS, *the Panel endorses* the position of the WHO that 'exclusive breastfeeding is recommended for HIV-infected women for the first 6 months of life unless replacement feeding is acceptable, feasible, affordable, sustainable and safe for them and their infants before that time'. Also see Chapter 12.

Many of the specific recommendations to protect against deficiencies and infections in these reports (and others) are in harmony with those designed to prevent chronic diseases; few are inconsistent. On salt and the prevention of goitre, and meat/iron and the prevention of deficiency, and the promotion of physical and mental health, see 10.5.7.

The recommendations made by the Panel in Chapter 12, when these take into account prevention of nutritional deficiencies and infectious diseases, are based additionally on the expert judgement of Panel members experienced in these areas. Many such reports were excluded by the criteria for inclusion for systematic review. These usually emphasise the need for food security — the constant availability of adequate, appropriate, and nourishing food. This fundamental priority does not contradict the findings of reports concerned with chronic diseases. Similarly, reports concerned with deficiencies and infections, especially of infancy and childhood, emphasise the need for safe water (and safe water supply and reliable sewage systems). This also does not contradict the findings of reports concerned with chronic diseases.

10.5 Chronic diseases other than cancer

10.5.1 Background

In general, chronic diseases such as obesity, type 2 diabetes, and cardiovascular disease (CVD), as well as some cancers, appear to have been uncommon, even in older people, until recent history. With urbanisation and industrialisation, they have become more prevalent, even among younger people. It is now generally accepted that the main causes of chronic diseases are environmental factors, including inappropriate food and nutrition, and physical inactivity.

Expert reports concerning the impact of unbalanced food and nutrition on the risk of chronic diseases began to appear in the 1970s.[110] At first, these were concerned mostly with coronary heart disease (CHD), which had become the most common cause of total and premature mortality in various high-income countries. Later reports began to consider other chronic diseases, or chronic diseases in general. For example, a report published by WHO in 1990 considered that a number of diseases could be prevented by appropriate food and nutrition. These include cerebrovascular disease, CHD, dental caries, type 2 diabetes, obesity, osteoporosis, various cancers, and various gut disorders.[111]

Forty-two reports published mostly in high-income countries between 1973 and 1988 were reviewed in 1990.[111] These made recommendations for reducing the risk of chronic diseases. They proposed that changes in consumption of certain foods and drinks were causing the rise in chronic diseases, as was physical inactivity. They identified foods and drinks relatively concentrated in total fat and saturated fatty acids, sugar and salt, and alcohol, as well as diets low in relatively unprocessed grains and other starchy foods, vegetables and fruits, and dietary fibre. Later reports noted that obesity and type 2 diabetes in particular were becoming more common in middle-income countries, and that these diseases were no longer 'diseases of affluence'.

More or less the same dietary recommendations were made for the prevention of all of these chronic diseases, including cancer.[1] For high-income countries, this has been summarised as diets with: 'moderately low levels of fat, with special emphasis on restriction of saturated fatty acids and cholesterol; high levels of complex carbohydrates; only moderate levels of protein, especially animal protein; and only low levels of added sugars'.[7]

Global population average nutrient goals for the prevention of chronic diseases were published by WHO in 1990 as follows: total fats 15–30 per cent, saturated fats 0–10 per cent, and polyunsaturated fatty acids 3–7 per cent of total energy intake; cholesterol 0–300 g/day; sugar 0–10 per cent of total energy intake; salt less than 6 g/day; starch/complex carbohydrates 50–70 per cent of total energy intake; dietary fibre 27–40 g/day; and dietary protein 10–15 per cent of total energy intake.[111]

10.5.2 Introduction

This section presents the recommendations made since 1990 on chronic diseases other than cancer. Of the 95 reports reviewed, 60 made recommendations relating to the prevention of obesity, type 2 diabetes, or CVD. These were produced by 34 different organisations: 6 from Australasia, 10 from Europe, 2 from India, 2 from international agencies, 13 from North America, and 1 from South Africa. Of these, 33 discussed the prevention of CVD in general,[16 22 30 32 34 36 37 39-47 57 61-63 68 69 71 72 77 78 80 84 91 92 94 97 98] 24 the prevention of CHD,[8 22 24 26 30 35 36 53 62 64 66 73 75 81 88 91-93 95-97 99-101] 14 the prevention of type 2 diabetes,[22 30 31 45 53 57 62 69 76 77 88 89 91 92] 8 the prevention of dyslipidaemia,[16 30 53 57 77 87 91 98] 16 the prevention of hypertension,[16 22 30 34 36 44 46 56 57 62 69 71 88 91 92 98] 12 the prevention of overweight/obesity,[8 16 18 22 27 53 62 69 76 91 92 98] and 11 the prevention of stroke,[30 36 38 40 42 62 70 77 88 91 111] Nine reports included recommendations to prevent osteoporosis[22 23 33 48 58 59 88 91 92] and 10 to prevent dental caries.[22 49 50 52 53 65 69 74 91 92] Two reports referred to the prevention of skeletal disorders in general[30 82] and 3 to the prevention of dental diseases in general.[62 79 88] These have been produced by 16 different organisations: 1 from Australasia, 4 from Europe, 1 from an international agency, and 10 from North America. Some 5 reports made recommendations to prevent gut diseases and disorders, produced by 4 organisations: 2 from Australasia, 1 from Europe, and 1 from North America. Of these, 3 referred to the prevention of constipation,[9 60 91] 2 to the prevention of diverticular disease,[91 92] and 1 to the prevention of Crohn's disease[92] and ulcerative colitis.[92] Recommendations regarding food intolerances were found in 4 reports,[79 86 91 92] of which 1 was concerned with lactose intolerance[88] and 1 with coeliac disease.[92]

10.5.3 Foods and drinks

Cereals (grains), roots, tubers, and plantains. Fourteen reports recommended including wholegrain cereals in the diet.[16 18 24 36 40 41 43 66 70 78 91 92 95 98] Four of these recommended that people should consume 3–6 servings per day to prevent CVD,[36 40 78 98] and those at risk of CVD should eat 6–12 servings per day.[98] Three recommended that people should limit their intake of refined carbohydrates, particularly from cereals (grains).[36 41 98]

Vegetables, fruits, pulses (legumes), nuts, seeds, herbs, and spices. Sixteen reports recommended consuming relatively high amounts of vegetables and fruits[22 35 36 40 69 70 73 75 77 78 80 91 92 95 98 100] with 13 recommending at least 400 g per day (at least 5 servings).[22 35 36 40 69 73 75 77 78 83 95 98 100] Eleven reports recommended the consumption of pulses (legumes).[16 22 24 36 37 41 43 70 88 91 98]

Meat, fish, and eggs. Eight reports recommended that consumption of red meat should be moderated and lean meat preferred (unspecified amount).[16 24 40 41 66 78 98 101] Seven reports recommended including fish in the diet.[16 24 41 43 66 80 91] Nine reports recommended consuming oily fish.[22 39 40 72 78 80 91 93 98] Eleven reports recommended that people should consume 1–3 servings of fish a week.[22 30 39 40 70 72 78 83 93 96 98] Two reports recommended that egg consumption should be limited.[16 98]

Fats and oils. Twenty-five reports recommended that total dietary fat intake should be limited.[8 22 24 26 34 35 46 53 56 62 64 69 70 77 78 80 84 87 89 91 94 98-101] Thirty-three reports recommended that intake of saturated fatty acids should be limited.[8 16 22 24 26 30 31 34-36 40 41 43 53 56 62 63 66 69 70 76-78 80 88 89 91 94 95 98-101] Three reports recommended that dietary fat intake should not be restricted in children under 2 years of age.[26 41 83] Seven reports recommended moderate intake of polyunsaturated fatty acid.[24 30 35 66 70 80 93] One report recommended that if total fat intake is restricted, people who are inactive and overweight should still include some polyunsaturated fatty acids in their diet to prevent CHD.[98] One report recommended that n-6 fatty acids should form 5–8 per cent of energy intake to prevent stroke,[70] while another suggested they should form 4–8 per cent to prevent CVD.[69] One report recommended that to prevent CHD, linoleic acid should make up no more than 10 per cent of total energy, at a ratio of between 5:1 and 10:1 with alpha-linolenic acid.[8] Five reports recommended the consumption of n-3 fatty acids.[70 72 80 91 93] Two reports recommended that eicosapentaenoic acid and docosahexaenoic acid should be included in the diet.[23 39] Nine reports recommended restricting intake of *trans*-fatty acids.[22 30 36 40 41 43 69 83 98] Three reports recommended restricting the combined intake of *trans*- and saturated fatty acids.[93 97 98] Four reports recommended limiting the intake of hydrogenated, vegetable, and partially hydrogenated fats.[24 62 66 91] Three reports recommended restricting myristic acid intake (including coconut products).[66 91 101]

Salt and sugar. Twenty reports recommended that salt intake should be limited to no more than 6 g/day for adults,[16 30 35 36 40 41 44 46 56 62 63 69-71 73 80 88 91 98 100] while another recommended that people should consume less than 5 g/day.[22] Ten reports recommended that people should limit their sodium intake.[30 40 41 44 46 56 59 66 80 88] Seven reports recommended that consumption of sugary foods should be limited,[36 41 62 69 91 92 98] with six specifying the prevention of dental disease.[22 62 65 74 79 92] Four of these reports made this recommendation only in relation to dental disease.[22 65 74 79] Ten reports recommended that the proportion of energy in the diet from sugar should be limited (either total, added, or non-milk extrinsic sugars).[36 41 53 62 73 87 91 92 98 101]

Milk and dairy products. Eleven reports recommended that low-fat dairy products should be chosen in preference to high-fat versions.[16 24 36 40 41 46 56 66 83 98 101]

Water, fruit juices, soft drinks, and hot drinks. Three reports recommended that water should be chosen as a drink to prevent overweight/obesity and dental damage.[22 65 92] One report recommended that individuals (particularly older people) should consume between 1.5 and 2 litres of water each day to prevent constipation.[60] One report recommended that people with HIV or AIDS should drink plenty of fluids to prevent constipation.[9] Three reports recommended that people should limit their consumption of sugary drinks to prevent dental damage.[22 65 92] Three reports recommended against using sugary drinks in babies' bottles to prevent dental damage.[49 65 92] Two recommended that people should limit their caffeine intake to no more than four cups of coffee per day to prevent osteoporosis.[48 59] One report recommended that caffeine should be eliminated to prevent constipation.[60]

Alcoholic drinks. Sixteen reports recommended that men should drink no more than two alcoholic drinks per day and that women should drink no more than one.[22 31 36 40 44 46 56 62 70 73 75 77 88 91 96 97] Two reports recommended that people with dyslipidaemia should limit their intake of alcoholic drinks.[64 96] Five reports recommended that if people choose to drink, they should do so only with meals.[40 56 62 70 91] Five reports recommended that alcohol intake should be limited.[34 44 64 96 99] Three reports recommended that men should drink no more than 21 units of alcohol/week (equivalent to three drinks a day), and women no more than 14 (equivalent to two drinks a day).[73 75 76] One report recommended avoiding high intakes of alcohol to prevent osteoporosis.[23] Two reports recommended that alcohol should be eliminated completely to prevent constipation[60] and stroke.[70]

Food production, processing, preservation, and preparation. Also see 10.4.3. Two reports recommended that food should be grilled (broiled) or steamed, rather than fried.[62 101]

Dietary constituents and supplements. Eight reports recommended that carbohydrates should provide between 45 and 65 per cent of total energy intake as part of a healthy diet.[24 53 63 64 69 80 87 99] Three reports recommended including complex carbohydrates in the diet.[16 87 99] Fifteen reports recommended a diet relatively high in dietary fibre.[9 16 35 36 40 41 53 60 63 64 69 70 95 98 101] Sixteen recommended restricting dietary

cholesterol intake.[8 16 24 26 30 35 36 40 43 62 63 66 70 78 80 93] Thirteen reports recommended that 'at risk' groups, and also people with type 2 diabetes, should limit dietary cholesterol to less than 200 mg/day to prevent CVD.[30 34-36 40 41 43 44 46 63 64 99 101] These groups of people include those at risk of or with pre-existing CVD, or those with elevated levels of low-density lipoprotein (LDL) cholesterol. Two reports recommended that there should be no restriction of dietary cholesterol for children under 2 years of age.[26 80] One report recommended that more than 400 micrograms/day of folate should be consumed to prevent CVD.[98] Three reports recommended the consumption of vitamin D to prevent osteoporosis,[22 48 59] and another made this recommendation for preventing skeletal disorders in general.[82] One report recommended that children with inflammatory bowel disease should have at least 400 international units (IU) of vitamin D per day to prevent osteoporosis.[58] Another report recommended that vitamin D intakes for people with gastrointestinal diseases should be 800 IU/day to prevent osteoporosis.[33] Various reports recommended that people should ensure that they have an adequate intake of calcium,[16 22 30 33 46 48 58 59 70 82] potassium,[22 46 56 80] and magnesium.[46 70] Three recommended that people should brush their teeth with a fluoride toothpaste to prevent dental damage.[50 65 74] With regard to supplements, one report recommended against the use of antioxidant supplements to prevent CVD,[43] while two recommended against beta-carotene supplements.[61 73] One report recommended against using vitamin E supplements to prevent CHD,[61 73] and another to prevent CVD.[47]

Breastfeeding. One report recommended that women should breastfeed to prevent dyslipidaemia in the infant.[87] Two gave this advice as a means of preventing overweight/obesity in the infant,[27 92] and one of these specified exclusive breastfeeding for 6 months.[92] Four reports recommended that women should breastfeed exclusively for 6 months to prevent food intolerance in the infant,[27 79 91 92] of which two made this recommendation to prevent Crohn's disease,[27 92] and ulcerative colitis.[27 92] One report also recommended breastfeeding as a way of reducing the risk or delaying the onset of coeliac disease[92] in the infant.

10.5.4 Physical activity

Twenty-four reports recommended that people should undertake at least 30 minutes of moderate intensity physical activity on most days of the week.[16 22 30 33-36 40 43 45 56 57 62 64 68 69 73 76 78 80 89 96 97 101] One of these recommended 60 minutes/day of moderate, or 30 minutes/day of vigorous activity,[69] while two reports recommended 60 minutes/day of moderate activity.[22 53] Three reports recommended that children and adolescents should perform 60 minutes of activity on most days of the week.[16 41 62] Seventeen reports recommended that people should be physically active for general good health and to prevent chronic diseases.[9 16 23 27 30 34 40-42 59 62 64 75 77 82 88 91] Two reports recommended that weight-bearing activity should be included to prevent skeletal disorders including osteoporosis.[59 82] Four reports recommended that people, especially children, should limit sedentary activities.[27 41 62 82]

10.5.5 Growth, development, body composition

Two reports recommended that people should avoid being underweight to prevent skeletal disorders, including osteoporosis.[23 82]

10.5.6 Weight gain, overweight, obesity

Fifteen reports recommended that a body mass index (BMI) of less than 25 is healthy.[35 36 38 40 41 43 46 56 62 69 80 91 96 98 101] Eight of these reports specified a BMI range of 18.5–24.9.[35 38 40 43 46 56 62 91] Two reports recommended a BMI range of 18.5–23 for Asian people.[99 100] Twelve reports recommended that people should achieve and maintain a healthy weight.[16 18 23 34 41 46 62 69 82 91 98 111] Six reports recommended that people should lose weight if they have a BMI of 25 or above.[34 40 44 46 77 78] One report recommended that people who are overweight or obese should lose 5–10 kg to prevent CHD.[73] One recommended that overweight people at risk of type 2 diabetes should lose 5–10 per cent of their bodyweight to prevent this disease.[31] Nine reports recommended that men maintain a waist circumference of no more than 40 inches (102 cm) and women no more than 35 inches (89 cm).[34-36 40 43 44 78 89 98] Two recommended that Asian men should have a waist to hip ratio of not more than 0.88; for Asian women this should not exceed 0.85.[99 100] Three reports recommended that people should limit their intake of energy-dense foods.[36 62 89]

10.5.7 Comparison of reports

There is one significant difference between the reports that focus specifically on cancer (see 10.6) and those concerned with chronic diseases other than cancer. The discussion in a number of these reports noted the evident protective effect of modest alcohol consumption against CHD (but not cerebrovascular disease or other chronic diseases). However, no report included in this review explicitly recommended the consumption of alcoholic drinks.

There are some significant differences — at least in emphasis — between reports that make recommendations to prevent chronic diseases other than cancer, and those that make recommendations for preventing cancer specifically. Reports concerned with preventing chronic diseases other than cancer, particularly CVD, give more prominence to the importance of diets high in cereals (grains) — preferably wholegrain or minimally processed — as well as diets high in vegetables, fruits, and fish. High-fat milk and dairy products are judged to increase the risk of CVD, but these foods are not thought to be a major factor in the development of cancer.

The iodisation of salt supplies, which is necessary to prevent goitre, need not be in conflict with recommendations on maximum levels of salt intake. Recommendations to limit consumption of red meat need not conflict with recommendations for iron intake to prevent clinical and subclinical deficiency, and to promote physical and mental development.

The Panel agrees that these differences and considerations be taken into account in its recommendations which, when they are based partly on findings on diseases other than cancer, are clearly identified as such. See Chapter 12.

In general, *the Panel notes* the impressive consistency of findings apparent from a systematic review of expert reports published since 1990 on food, nutrition, physical activity, and the prevention of chronic diseases, which reinforce the findings of earlier, less formally conducted work. The main evidence-based recommendations made by expert reports on cancer, and by reports on chronic diseases other than cancer, are mostly harmonious and often practically identical. This includes reports on obesity, type 2 diabetes, CVD, and disorders of the digestive system, osteoporosis, and dental diseases.

10.6 Cancer

10.6.1 Background

Throughout recorded history, cancer has been attributed — at least in part — to food and nutrition, as well as to other environmental factors. Until the beginning of the 20th century, high consumption of meat and salt, and low consumption of bulky plant foods, vegetables, and fruits were thought to increase the risk of cancer in general. In the first two thirds of the 20th century, a series of laboratory and ecological studies found that energy restriction protected against cancer in laboratory animals, and that diets low in fibre and high in meat, fat, salt, salty foods, and/or alcoholic drinks seemed to increase the risk of some cancers in particular.[15]

From the late 1970s, reports began to be published that summarised the scientific literature on food, nutrition, and cancer, and provided dietary recommendations for the prevention of cancer. Between 1977 and 1989, 12 such reports were published in, or for, Canada (1), Europe (2), Japan (1), Latin America (1), and USA (7). These reports have been reviewed previously.[1] They tended to recommend relatively high consumption of cereals (grains), vegetables, and fruits (and so of dietary fibre and micronutrients); relatively low consumption of red meat, and smoked and cured meats; low consumption of salted and salty foods; low or no consumption of alcoholic drinks; maintenance of a healthy body weight; and regular physical activity.

10.6.2 Introduction

Following this work, this section presents the recommendations made for controlling and preventing cancer since 1990. The order of the passages below follows that of the contents of the present Report. Overall, of the 95 reports reviewed, 15 include recommendations on preventing cancer. These reports have been produced by 12 different organisations: 1 from Australasia, 3 from Europe, 5 in or for North America, and 3 from international agencies. There are no such reports from middle- or low-income countries. Of the 15 reports, 12 present recommendations relating to the prevention of cancer in general[8 15 22 29 47 61 62 67 83 88 91 92] and 11 of these also make recommendations on preventing site-specific cancers. These include cancers of the bladder (3)[15 88 91]; breast (7)[15 29 62 67 88 91 92]; 2 for cervix, endometrium, kidney, larynx, liver, nasopharynx, oesophagus, pancreas, and stomach[15 67]; colon and rectum (9)[15 20 29 62 67 88 90-92]; lung (3)[15 47 67]; mouth/pharynx (3)[15 65 67]; and 1 for ovary and prostate.[15] The recommendations summarised in this section (10.6) are for preventing cancer in general, unless stated otherwise.

355

Table 10.1	Recommendations to prevent food-related diseases

The table below summarises recommendations from reports published since 1991 for the management, control, and prevention of chronic diseases, nutritional deficiencies, and relevant infectious diseases. Recommendations related to cancer are not included here. Unless indicated otherwise, there is no disagreement between reports. To present the findings of the review more easily, recommendations have only been included if they are made in three or more reports. However, *the Panel does not intend* this as a measure of the quality of the recommendations themselves. For more detailed information, please refer to the appropriate sections in this chapter.

EXPOSURE	RECOMMENDATIONS	TO PREVENT OR MANAGE
Cereals (grains), roots, tubers, and plantains	Include wholegrain cereals in the diet (unspecified amount)	CVD,[36 41 43 78 98] CHD[16 24 66 91 92 95]
	Suggested intake of 3–6 or more servings/day of wholegrain cereals	CVD[36 40 78 98]
	Foods high in iron should be eaten in combination with foods that enhance rather than inhibit iron absorption: cereals (grains) should be consumed with meals of low iron content, and foods high in ascorbic acid, such as tubers, should be included with meals	Iron deficiency anaemia[11 13 51]
Vegetables, fruits, pulses (legumes), nuts, seeds, herbs, and spices	Include 400 g (5 or more servings)/day of vegetables and fruits	CVD,[36 40 69 77 78 80 98 111] CHD,[35 40 73 75 95 100 111] hypertension[35 36 73 95 100 111]
	Include pulses (legumes) in the diet (unspecified amount)	CVD,[36 41 43 91 98] CHD[16 24 88]
	Foods high in ascorbic acid, such as orange juice, carrots, and cauliflower, should be included with meals	Iron deficiency anaemia[11 13 51]
Meat, fish, and eggs	Red meat consumption should be moderated and lean meat preferred (unspecified amount)	CVD,[16 40 41 78 98] CHD[24 66 101]
	Include fish in the diet (unspecified amount)	CVD,[16 41 43 80] CHD[24 66 91]
	Consume between 1 and 3 servings/week of fish	CVD,[39 40 72 78 80 98] CHD[22 30 40 93 96]
	Choose oily fish (unspecified amount)	CVD,[39 40 72 78 80 98] CHD[22 36 91 93]
Fats and oils	Limit intake of hydrogenated/partially hydrogenated vegetable oils and hard margarines (unspecified amount)	CHD[24 62 66 91]
	Total dietary fat intake should be limited (unspecified amount)	CVD[46 77 84]
	Total dietary fat to provide no more than 35% of total energy	CHD,[8 53 66] overweight/obesity[22 53 69]
	Total dietary fat to provide no more than 30% of total energy	CVD,[22 69 78] CHD[24 26 34 35 62 64 101]
	Dietary fat intake should not be restricted	In children under 2 years of age[26 41 80]
	Limit/reduce intake of saturated fats (unspecified amount)	CHD[53 88 98]
	Intake of saturated fat should be no more than 10% of energy	CVD[16 22 36 40 41 63 69 78 80 94] CHD[8 24 26 62 66 91 92 95 101]
	Intake of saturated fat should be no more than 7% of energy	CVD,[34 36 41 43 44] CHD,[35 99 100] people with, or at risk of, CVD or with elevated LDL cholesterol (including those with diabetes)[31 34-36 40 41 43 44]
	Intake of saturated fatty acid intake should be limited (unspecified amount)	CHD[53 88 98]
	Restrict intake of myristic acid (including coconut products)	CHD[66 91 101]
	Limit intake of dietary cholesterol to <300 mg/day	CVD,[16 36 40 43 63 78] CHD[8 24 26 35 62 66 93]
	Limit intake of dietary cholesterol to <200 mg/day	CVD in people with diabetes, people at risk of, or with pre-existing, CVD or those with elevated LDL cholesterol,[34 36 41 43 44 63] CHD in people with diabetes, people at risk of, or with pre-existing, CVD or those with elevated LDL cholesterol[35 64 101]
	Limit intake of polyunsaturated fatty acids to no more than 10% of energy	CHD[24 66 93 101]
	Limit intake of *trans*-fatty acids (unspecified amount)	CVD[36 40 41 43 98]

Table 10.1   Continued

EXPOSURE	RECOMMENDATIONS	TO PREVENT OR MANAGE
Salt and sugar	Limit intake of sodium to no more than 100 mmol/day	Hypertension[30 46 56 80 88]
	Limit/reduce sodium intake (unspecified amount)	CVD in children at risk of CVD and in adults with hypertension[40 41 44 46]
	Limit/reduce consumption of salt and salted foods to no more than 6 g of salt/day	CVD,[16 36 40 41 63 69 71 80 91] CHD,[35 73 80 100] hypertension,[30 46 56 62 69 71 80 88 91 98] stroke[40 70 80]
	Limit the proportion of energy in the diet from sugar (unspecified amount)	CVD,[36 41 98] overweight/obesity[62 91 92]
	Limit consumption of sugary foods (unspecified amount)	CVD,[36 41 98] overweight/obesity[62 69 91 92]
	Avoid consumption of sugary foods and drinks between meals	Dental caries[22 65 74 92]
	Limit sugar intake	Dental caries[22 65 74 91 92]
Milk and dairy products	Eat low-fat versions of dairy products in preference to high-fat versions	CVD,[16 36 40 43 46 80 98] CHD[24 66 101]
Water, fruit juices, soft drinks, and hot drinks	Avoid using sugary drinks in baby bottles	Dental disease[49 65 92]
Alcoholic drinks	Limit intake of alcoholic drinks to two drinks for men and one drink for women per day	CVD,[22 36 40 44 46 77 97] CHD,[31 73 75 88 96] hypertension,[31 46 56 62 91] stroke[31 40 62 70 77 91]
	If drinking, do so only with meals	Hypertension,[56 62 91] stroke[40 62 70 91]
Food production, processing, preservation, and preparation	Limit/reduce intake of refined carbohydrates/grain products and foods	CVD[36 41 98]
Dietary constituents and supplements	Include fibre in the diet (unspecified amount)	CVD[36 69 98]
	Brush teeth with fluoride toothpaste twice daily	Dental caries[50 65 74]
	Ensure an adequate intake of vitamin D	Osteoporosis[22 48 59]
	Ensure an adequate intake of calcium	Osteoporosis[22 33 48 58 59 88]
Dietary patterns	Encourage exclusive breastfeeding for first 4–6 months	Diarrhoea[10 17 91]
	Women should breastfeed exclusively for 6 months	Food intolerances in the infant[27 79 91 92]
Physical activity	Be physically active	CVD,[30 34 40-42 44] CHD,[64 75 88 91] osteoporosis[23 59 88]
	Minimum of 30 minutes of moderate-intensity physical activity on most days of the week	CVD[16 22 34 36 40 43 45 57 62 68 78 80] CHD[22 35 64 73 96 97 101] type 2 diabetes[22 30 31 57 62 69 76 89] hypertension[16 56 57 62] overweight/obesity[16 57 62 69]
	60 minutes of physical activity for children and adolescents on most days of the week	CVD[16 41 62]
Weight gain, overweight, and obesity	Achieve/maintain a healthy weight (unspecified)	Type 2 diabetes[22 62 69 91] hypertension[34 46 62 98]
	Achieve/maintain a BMI of 18.5–24.9 kg/m²	Stroke,[38 40 62] hypertension[46 56 91]
	If BMI is ≥25 kg/m², lose weight	CVD[34 40 44 46 77 78]
	Achieve/maintain a waist circumference of no more than 35 inches (89 cm) for women and 40 inches (102 cm) for men	CVD[34-36 40 43 44 78 89 98]

BMI, body mass index; CHD, coronary heart disease; CVD, cardiovascular disease; LDL, low density lipoprotein

10.6.3 Foods and drinks

Cereals (grains), roots, tubers, and plantains. Six reports recommended diets high in cereals (grains),[15 20 29 90-92] with some emphasising relatively unprocessed grains. One recommended 600–800 g/day of a variety of cereals (grains), pulses (legumes), roots, tubers, and plantains, stating that this is based more on the evidence for other chronic diseases.[15]

Vegetables, fruits, pulses (legumes), nuts, seeds, herbs, and spices. Nine reports recommended diets relatively high in vegetables and fruits,[15 20 22 29 65 67 83 90 91] with five specifying five or more portions a day.[15 22 29 67 83] One report recommended the consumption of five portions of vegetables and two portions of fruits each day.[91] Four reports recommended diets relatively high in pulses (legumes).[15 29 88 91]

Meat, fish, and eggs. Five reports recommended limiting red meat[15 20 22 29 83]; two of these advised opting for lean varieties.[22 29] Three reports recommended that meat should be baked, grilled (broiled), or poached rather than fried or flame grilled (charbroiled).[15 22 29] One recommended minimal intake of smoked and cured meats.[15] Four recommended choosing poultry[15 20 22 29] and fish.[15 20 22 29] One recommended limiting Cantonese-style fermented salted fish.[22]

Fats and oils. Three reports recommended limiting total fat intake: upper limits vary between 15 and 30 per cent,[15] 25 and 30 per cent,[15 90] and 30 and 35 per cent.[8] Two recommended restricting saturated fatty acid intake to 10 per cent or less of total energy intake.[8 67] One recommended limiting animal fats,[15] and another limiting linoleic acid.[53]

Salt and sugar. Two reports recommended that consumption of salt, salty, and salted foods should be limited to a total intake of less than 6 g of salt/day.[15 22] Two reports recommended limiting sugars and refined carbohydrates.[15 29] One of these advised limiting sugars to less than 10 per cent of total energy intake.[15]

Water, fruit juices, soft drinks, and hot drinks. One report recommended drinking plenty of water to prevent cancers of the colon and rectum and bladder.[91] Two reports recommended limiting sugars and syrups from sources such as soft drinks.[15 29] Another recommended avoiding very hot and scalding drinks.[22]

Alcoholic drinks. Six reports recommended limiting alcoholic drinks.[15 22 29 62 91 92] When an amount was specified, this was usually a maximum of 1–2 drinks per day.

Food production, processing, preservation, and preparation. (Also see meat, fish, and eggs.) Two reports recommended avoiding contaminants (in particular aflatoxins and mycotoxins).[15 22] One of these recommended that perishable foods should be refrigerated.[15]

Dietary constituents and supplements. One report recommended diets high in dietary fibre/non-starch polysaccharides.[83] Another recommended 1000–1200 mg/day of calcium to prevent colorectal cancer.[90] Two stated that dietary supplements are unnecessary and possibly even harmful.[15 83]

10.6.4 Physical activity

Ten reports recommended regular, sustained physical activity.[15 20 22 29 62 67 83 88 90 91] Those that specify the intensity and duration, recommend moderate physical activity for around 30–60 minutes per day.

10.6.5 Growth, development, body composition

One report recommended that women should breastfeed exclusively to prevent them from developing breast cancer — ideally until the child is 6 months old.[91]

10.6.6 Weight gain, overweight, obesity

Five reports recommended maintaining a BMI of between 18.5 and 24.9.[15 29 67 83 91] One of these advised that people should not gain more than 5 kg during their adult life.[15] One report recommended avoiding energy-dense foods.[29]

10.6.7 Comparison of reports

There is no substantial disagreement between any of these reports. *The Panel also notes* the general consistency with its own findings and recommendations.

10.7 Conclusions

The Panel concludes:

We are impressed by the similarity of the conclusions and recommendations in all types of expert report reviewed here. For reports that recommended diets high in cereals (grains) (preferably relatively unrefined), and in vegetables and fruits, and pulses (legumes), no conflicting recommendations were found. These reports also include recommendations for diets low in red and processed meats; and correspondingly high in dietary fibre and micronutrients, including bioactive microconstituents; and low in fats, saturated fatty acids, added sugars, salt, and alcoholic drinks.

We are also impressed by the consistency between reports on deficiencies and infections that stress the vital importance of extended, exclusive breastfeeding for the sake of the child; and reports on chronic diseases that make the same recommendation, for the sake of both children and mothers. We are also impressed by the agreement of the reports on the benefits of all forms of regular, sustained physical activity, and the corresponding risks of sedentary ways of life. Evidence on micronutrient supplements is less clear. We consider this largely reflects the clinical needs of populations vulnerable to deficiencies.

CHAPTER 11

Research issues

The evidence of causal relationships between food, nutrition, physical activity, body composition, and cancer is and always will be incomplete. New methods of research, and new issues to study, are always being developed. However, this ongoing work does not mean that the response to every question is 'more research is needed'. The previous chapters in this Report show that in many areas, the evidence of causal relationships is already strong enough to justify public health goals and personal recommendations, which are specified in Chapter 12. This chapter outlines future strategic research directions that the Panel sees as especially promising to build on this current base of knowledge.

In many areas, as shown in the matrices introducing each section of Chapter 7, the evidence may be suggestive but inconclusive. These particular areas are those in which new efforts to answer research questions may be most likely to result in findings that can advance scientific knowledge or change public health practice. The research directions identified here are often cross-cutting and interdisciplinary. These could increase understanding of the cancer process, and provide new evidence to clarify and strengthen the recommendations made in Chapter 12.

There are also many fields of study that are only now beginning to be explored. These include exposures in early life including before birth that affect birth weight, growth in childhood, age at menarche, and attained adult height. They also include interactions between food and nutrition and other factors, notably smoking, inflammation, and infectious agents. There is as yet relatively little epidemiological research on broad patterns of diets, and the inter-relationship between elements of diets: more understanding here will enable recommendations to be made with increasing confidence.

More needs to be known about the levels of exposure that are critical as modifiers of cancer risk, and the extent to which risk is decreased or increased at different levels. In some areas, understanding will be improved by general agreement on the nature and definition of exposures; examples include physical activity,

processed meat, and breastfeeding.

Until recently, epidemiological and experimental research studies were typically carried out separately, and with different objectives. But to be convincing, epidemiological evidence, however consistent, needs to be supported by concrete evidence of biological mechanisms. A promising development is an increased tendency for epidemiologists and basic scientists to work as team members, to mutual benefit. Future research should encourage this.

One broad category of research, not reviewed for this Report, concerns the underlying social (including economic and political) and broad environmental determinants of patterns of food, nutrition, and physical activity. This area is also critical to the successful translation of the knowledge of the causes of cancer into improved health. This crucially important aspect of research is contained in a separate report dedicated to this topic to be published in late 2008.

11.1 Principles

The principles applied when identifying the research questions specified here are as follows:

Interdisciplinary
The research directions discussed here are focused not on issues that are specific to separate disciplines, such as epidemiology or cancer biology, but on interdisciplinary issues and questions that concern the relationships between cancer and food, nutrition, physical activity, and obesity.

Important
The benefit of conducting more research where the evidence is already convincing and well understood is likely to be small. Research that investigates areas where the evidence is unclear is likely to be of especial value.

Research is also of most value when the results have a large potential impact on the overall burden of disease. This may be because the exposure under consideration has a potentially profound effect on cancer risk or because the cancer site in question is particularly common.

Innovative
Research questions need to be practical and yet innovative, which implies that they should not be constrained by conventional wisdom. More innovative research is needed. Investigators should be imaginative and collaborate across disciplines, and be willing to engage in research programmes most likely to benefit public health.

Box 11.1 Updating the evidence

Research findings continue to accumulate. This evidence needs to be identified, analysed, and interpreted. The World Cancer Research Fund International, together with the American Institute for Cancer Research, the organisations responsible for commissioning this Report, have now commissioned a process of continuous updating of the literature. This will be the basis for periodic updates of this Report's findings. The process will continue to make use of systematic literature reviews and is being overseen by an international expert steering group, including members of the Panel responsible for this Report.

11.2 Research issues

How can the evidence for specific nutritional or physical activity exposures in relation to cancer be strengthened?

Exposures judged 'probable' or 'limited — suggestive' in the matrices of this Report are most promising as a focus of further research when evidence is scant. Examples of such exposures include calcium and dairy products as related to cancer of the prostate; vitamin D and cancer of the colon; folate and cancers of the oesophagus, pancreas, and colorectum; and selenium and cancers of the lung, colorectum, and prostate. Those already judged convincing, by their very nature, are less likely to be influenced by new research. Also, people are increasingly using non-traditional therapies, and these should also be a topic for more systematic research.

Study design options include pooling of prospective data (especially for rarer cancers), longer follow-up of existing cohorts, investigations with biomarker measurements of intake and biomarker endpoints, and new randomised controlled trials (RCTs).

For exposures where strong evidence exists of a causal relationship, what are the effect sizes with respect to timing, dose, and duration of exposure?

The evidence currently available for various exposures and cancer risk is limited in terms of timing, dose, duration, and size of effect. This kind of evidence is important for healthcare providers and policy-makers to make informed decisions on public health programmes, and for people to make better-informed choices.

Study design options include pooling of prospective data (especially for less common cancers), longer follow-up of existing cohorts, and obtaining more information on early life dietary exposures. This research direction applies to a number of the questions addressed in this Report. For example, more information on timing, dose, and duration of exposure is needed on the effects of body size and fatness at different times of life in relation to future risk of breast cancer and colorectal cancer; the effects of timing, dose, and duration of use of alcohol and breast cancer risk; and detailed dose-response information on red meat and processed meat in relation to colorectal and other cancers.

How do environmental and genetic factors modify the effects of exposures on cancer risk?

Further investigation into the presence of effect modification is needed to deepen understanding of risk among different population groups and to help health professionals and policy-makers provide more precise recommendations. Factors that should be studied as potential effect modifiers include tobacco, exogenous hormones, medications (such as non-steroidal anti-inflammatory drugs), metabolising genes, genes associated with various cancers, and other food, nutrition, and body composition exposures.

What mechanisms link foods and drinks, dietary constituents, or other nutritional and physical activity factors to cancer risk?

There is general agreement that nutritional factors, body composition, and physical activity are important determinants of cancer risk. However, it has been difficult to identify with confidence the precise pathways whereby such exposures influence the process of cancer development. Inevitably, the impact of nutrition will ultimately be at the level of DNA and gene expression, but the ways in which this occurs, either via genetic mutation or epigenetic events, is only now beginning to be explored. There are many nutritional factors for which epidemiological data suggest that a relationship exists, but where complete understanding of the biological pathways is lacking. Examples include adiposity, physical activity, height, red meat, processed meat, vegetables, alcoholic drinks, lactation, arsenic, dairy products, and whole grains.

Dietary constituents that are especially favourable to this type of mechanistic investigation include beta-carotene, calcium, vitamin D, folate, selenium, polycyclic aromatic hydrocarbons, and dietary fibre. Intermediate biological mechanisms potentially relevant to mechanistic understanding include inflammation, insulin resistance, growth factors, oxidation, gut flora, hormonal changes, and various cellular metabolic and molecular processes. Such mechanisms may vary by the histopathological and molecular characteristics of the tumours. Intermediate markers may clarify questions of causation and serve as surrogate endpoints for observational and intervention studies.

Study designs that may be useful to examine these questions include human metabolic studies with cancer-related endpoints and metabolic studies added onto existing nutrient RCTs. Intermediate endpoints should be incorporated into large, prospective, observational or intervention studies to better understand their links to both nutritional factors and cancer endpoints.

Increasingly with greater understanding of the interplay of nutritional state and genetic expression, programmes of study that incorporate elements of different disciplines and technologies should illuminate the fundamental processes underpinning diet–cancer links.

Which genetic polymorphisms and nutritional exposures that influence gene expression are useful for understanding the relationship between nutrition or physical activity and cancer?

Certain genetic polymorphisms (genetic variants that appear in at least 1 per cent of the population) may increase, while others may decrease, the extent to which nutritional factors affect cancer risk. Studying gene–nutrient interactions is likely to yield better results as technology allows the simultaneous examination of multiple gene–nutrient interactions, and as better systems evolve for synthesising the large amounts of data that are generated by these newer techniques.

Genetic make up can impact the extent to which our bodies respond to nutritional factors. Also, genes express themselves (or switch on) to varying degrees depending on the nutritional environment. Understanding the extent to which nutrients affect gene expression in such a way as to impact on both cancer risk itself and the nutrient/cancer risk relationship is very important.

Examples of gene–nutrient interactions include N-acetyl transferase and meat. In certain cases, genetic polymorphisms (for example, MTHFR 677 TT for low folate intake and LCT — lactase persistence — for dairy food intake) can act as proxies for nutritional exposures. This can be examined using a Mendelian randomisation study design, controlling for confounding factors. For example, the effects of folate may be demonstrated by looking at the differences in cancer outcome between people who have the MTHFR gene variant that mimics low folate intake (MTHFR 677 TT) and people who do not. Carrying this form of the gene is unlikely to be related to other potential confounding factors such as smoking or socioeconomic status.

Does weight loss in overweight or obese people reduce cancer risk?

Body fatness and weight gain increase the risk of several cancers. But the effects of weight loss on cancer risk are poorly understood. Study design options for investigating this question include model systems with caloric restriction and weight loss, human metabolic studies with intermediate endpoints, and cohort studies with explicit inquiries about intentional weight loss.

What are the relevant milestones in the timing of growth and development that affect cancer risk and how can they be modified by food, nutrition, and physical activity?

Critical periods for exposure to factors that lead to increased cancer risk during the life course should be identified. For example, high birth weight and rapid growth in height during adolescence are both associated with an increased risk of breast cancer. Some countries have extensive child and adolescent growth data that can be examined in relation to cancer outcomes using registries.

How can factors related to food production, processing, preservation, and cooking methods, which may affect cancer risk, best be studied in humans?

Current methods used to produce food are changing faster than at any other point in history. It is most important to understand how old and new methods might affect the risk of cancer. In addition to changes in agricultural practices, both rapid urbanisation and economic globalisation have transformed food systems. Methods used to evaluate the changes in cancer risk that might be tied to these new patterns need to be developed. Relevant factors may include exogenous hormone administration in the production of meat, production of heterocyclic amines and polycyclic aromatic hydrocarbons by high-temperature cooking, use of food additives, use of pesticides, novel processing methods, and storage conditions.

How do food, nutrition, body composition, and physical activity affect outcomes in cancer survivors?

The extent to which cancer survivors are similar to or different from people without cancer, in terms of the extent to which their cancer risk is sensitive to changes in diet, body composition, and physical activity, needs to be investigated.

A number of further questions arise:
- Are any effects of food, nutrition, and physical activity additive?
- Are the type and the progression of the cancer important in this regard?
- Is the extent to which cancer survivors have had exposure to chemotherapeutic or radiological treatment important?

There are two broad contexts for these questions: do diet, nutrition, or physical activity before diagnosis affect outcome after treatment? And do changes in these after diagnosis and treatment affect outcome?

In addition to RCTs among survivors, existing cohort studies can examine some of these questions since there are now fairly large numbers of cancer survivors in some cohorts. Pooling of the data from these studies could be valuable. Good information on clinical–pathological factors and treatments is necessary in observational studies because these potentially confounding factors affect cancer prognosis and may be related to nutritional exposures.

How do relationships between food, nutrition, and physical activity and cancer risk differ in various parts of the world?

In areas of the world where patterns of cancer and patterns of diet are different, the relationship between nutrition and cancer risk can also vary. For example, in middle- and low-income countries, the inverse relation between body mass and premenopausal breast cancer is usually not seen. It could be that there are factors such as genes, body composition, or physical activity that modify the effect of body mass on cancer risk in some populations.

How can measures of food, nutrition, physical activity, and body composition, as they relate to cancer risk, be improved?

Better ways of characterising and measuring the short- and long-term exposures most relevant to determining cancer risk are needed. These may include incorporating new instruments in prospective studies, whether internet-based or telephone-based recalls, dietary records, with, if possible, strong validation studies using biomarkers. Also, additional development of intake biomarkers, where feasible, and their incorporation in large prospective studies would be helpful.

Finally, expanded investigation of dietary indexes and patterns, which have the potential to capture the effect of multiple, interconnected dietary factors, may further enhance our understanding of nutrition and cancer.

Part 3

Recommendations

3

Introduction to Part 3

The culmination of the five-year process resulting in this Report is Chapter 12, in which the Panel's public health goals and personal recommendations are specified. These are preceded by a statement of the principles that have guided the Panel in its thinking.

The goals and recommendations are based on judgements made by the Panel in Part 2, as shown in the introductory matrices. Such judgements are of a 'convincing' or 'probable' causal effect, either of decreased or increased risk.

Judgements of 'convincing' or 'probable' generally justify goals and recommendations. These are proposed as the basis for public policies and for personal choices that, if effectively implemented, will be expected to reduce the incidence of cancer for people, families, and communities.

Eight general and two special goals and recommendations are specified. In each case a general recommendation is followed by public health goals and personal recommendations, together with footnotes when further explanation or clarification is required. These are all shown in boxed text. The accompanying text includes a summary of the evidence; justification of the goals and recommendations; and guidance on how to achieve them.

Reliable judgements are carefully derived from good evidence. But specific public health and personal goals and recommendations do not automatically follow from the evidence, however strong and consistent. The process of moving from evidence to judgements and to recommendations has been one of the Panel's main responsibilities, and has involved much discussion and debate until final agreement has been reached. The goals and recommendations here have been unanimously agreed.

Food, nutrition, body composition, and physical activity also affect the risk of diseases other than cancer. Informed by the findings of other reports summarised in Chapter 10, the goals and recommendations have therefore been agreed with an awareness of their wider public health implications.

The goals and recommendations are followed by the Panel's conclusions on the dietary patterns most likely to protect against cancer. As conventionally undertaken, epidemiological and experimental studies are usually sharply focused. In order to discern the 'big picture' of healthy and protective diets, it is necessary to integrate a vast amount of detailed information. This also has been part of the Panel's task.

The main focus of this Report is on nutritional and other biological and associated factors that modify the risk of cancer. *The Panel is aware* that, as with other diseases, the risk of cancer is critically influenced by social, cultural, economic, and ecological factors. Thus the foods and drinks that people consume are not purely because of personal choice; often opportunities to access adequate food or to undertake physical activity can be constrained, either for reasons of ill health or geography, economics, or equally powerfully, by culture.

There is a limit to what can be achieved by individuals, families, communities, and health professionals.

Identifying not only the nutritional and associated factors that affect the risk of cancer but also the deeper factors enables a wider range of policy recommendations and options to be identified. This is the subject of a separate report to be published in late 2008.

The members of the Panel and supporting secretariat, and the executives of the WCRF global network responsible for commissioning this Report, have been constantly reminded of the importance of their work during its five-year duration. The public health goals and personal recommendations of the Panel that follow are offered as a significant contribution towards the prevention and control of cancer throughout the world.

CHAPTER 12

Public health goals and personal recommendations

This Report is concerned with food, nutrition, physical activity, body composition, and the prevention of cancer, worldwide. Chapter 12 is the culmination of the Report. It explains the principles that guide the Panel's decisions; lists and explains the Panel's recommendations to prevent cancer; and identifies appropriate dietary patterns. The recommendations are in the form of a series of general statements; public health goals designed to be used by health professionals; and recommendations for people — as communities, families, and individuals — who can also be guided by the goals. Footnotes are included when needed for further explanation or clarity.

Most cancer is preventable. The risk of cancers is often influenced by inherited factors. Nevertheless, it is generally agreed that the two main ways to reduce the risk of cancer are achievable by most well informed people, if they have the necessary resources. These are not to smoke tobacco and to avoid exposure to tobacco smoke; and to consume healthy diets and be physically active, and to maintain a healthy weight. Other factors, in particular infectious agents, and also radiation, industrial chemicals, and medication, affect the risk of some cancers.

The Panel notes that previous reports have attributed roughly one third of the world's cancer burden to smoking and exposure to tobacco, and roughly another one third to a combination of inappropriate food and nutrition, physical inactivity, and overweight and obesity. By their nature, these estimates are approximations, but *the Panel judges* that avoidance of tobacco in any form, together with appropriate food and nutrition, physical activity, and body composition, have the potential over time to reduce much and perhaps most of the global burden of cancer. This is in the context of general current trends towards decreased physical activity and increased body fatness, and projections of an increasing and ageing global population.

The recommendations here are derived from the evidence summarised and judged in Part 2 of this Report. They have also taken into account relevant dietary and associated recommendations made in other reports commissioned by United Nations agencies and other authoritative international and national organisations, designed to promote nutritional adequacy and prevent cardiovascular and other chronic diseases. They therefore contribute to diets that are generally protective, and that also provide adequate energy and nutrients. The recommendations can therefore be the basis for policies, programmes, and choices that should prevent cancer, and also protect against deficiency diseases, infections especially of early life, and other chronic diseases.

Throughout its work, the Panel has also been conscious that enjoyment of food and drink is a central part of family and social life, and that food systems that generate adequate, varied, and delicious diets are one central part of human civilisation. From the cultural and culinary, as well as the nutritional point of view, the recommendations here amount to diets similar to cuisines already well established and enjoyed in many parts of the world.

12.1 Principles

The recommendations presented in this chapter are designed as the basis for policies, programmes, and personal choices to reduce the incidence of cancer in general. These are guided by a number of separate principles and also by one overall principle, which is, that taken together, the recommendations provide an integrated approach to establishing healthy patterns of diet and physical activity, and healthy ways of life.

In order to be useful both for health professionals who advise on cancer, and for people who are interested in reducing their own risk of cancer, the recommendations are quantified wherever possible and appropriate. See box 12.1.

12.1.1 Integrated

The Panel, in making its recommendations, has been concerned to ensure that most people in most situations throughout the world will be able to follow its advice. The recommendations are framed to emphasise aspects of food and nutrition, physical activity, and body composition that protect against cancer. They are also integrated with existing advice on promoting healthy ways of life, such as that to prevent other diseases. At the same time, the Panel has given special attention to making recommendations that can form the basis for rational policies, effective programmes, and healthy personal choices.

12.1.2 Broad based

In assessing the evidence, making its judgements, and in framing its recommendations, the Panel has, where appropriate, chosen to take a broad view. It has also agreed to base its advice on foods and whole diets rather than on specific nutrients. Thus, recommendations 4 and 5 concern plant foods and animal foods in general, while their specific public health goals and personal recommendations are mostly concerned with vegetables and fruits, and then with red meat and processed meat, where the evidence on cancer is strongest.

The same applies to physical activity. The evidence shows that all types and degrees of physical activity protect or probably protect against some common cancers. Recommendation 2 therefore does not specify any particular physical activity (of which sport and exercise are one type). Rather, it recommends sustained physical activity as part of active ways of life. What type of physical activity is most appropriate and enjoyable depends on individual abilities and preferences, as well as the settings in which populations, communities, families, and individuals live.

The Panel has taken the same approach in considering the recommendations altogether. As a whole, the recommendations contribute to whole diets and overall levels of physical activity most likely to prevent cancer. This does not imply one particular diet, or a specific form of physical activity, but rather key elements designed to be incorporated into existing and traditional diets and ways of life around the world. This is emphasised in section 12.3 of this chapter, on patterns of food, nutrition, and physical activity.

12.1.3 Global

This Report has a global perspective. It is therefore appropriate that the recommendations here are for people and populations all over the world; that they apply to people irrespective of their state of health or their susceptibility to cancer; and that they include cancer survivors.

Some factors that modify the risk of cancer are more common, and so of more concern, in some parts of the world than others. It is possible that such factors might become more widespread, but the recommendations on them in this Report are in the context of their current local importance.

Just as people's susceptibility to cancer varies, so will the extent to which they will benefit from following these recommendations, though most people can expect to benefit to some extent from each of them.

Recommendations for whole populations are usually now identified as also being of importance for people who, while not being clinically symptomatic, have known risk factors for disease. People at higher risk of various cancers include smokers and people regularly exposed to tobacco smoke; people infected with specific micro-organisms; overweight and obese people; sedentary people; people with high intakes of alcoholic drinks; people who are immunosuppressed; and those with a family history of cancer. Such people are often at higher risk of diseases other than cancer. *The Panel agrees* that the recommendations here apply to these people.

They also apply to cancer survivors, meaning people living with a diagnosis of cancer, including those identified as having recovered from cancer (see Chapter 9). This is subject to important qualifications, stated in the special recommendations for this group of people.

12.1.4 Cancer in general

This Report is concerned with the prevention of cancer in general. Evidence for particular cancer sites provided the building blocks. A key task for the Panel was to take this specific evidence and formulate recommendations that would, in general, lead to a lower burden from cancer regardless of site.

This broad approach is appropriate from the public health point of view. International agencies, national governments, other policy-makers, health professionals, and people within communities and families, and also as individuals, want to know how to prevent cancer in general.

12.1.5 Designed to have major impact

Every case of cancer is important. But the responsibility of those concerned with public health is to encourage policies, programmes, and choices that will have the greatest impact.

For this reason, the Panel has paid special attention to the more common cancers; cancers where there is the most clear-cut evidence of modification of risk by food, nutrition, physical activity, and body composition; and cancers that may most readily be prevented by achievable recommendations. Special attention has also been paid to those aspects of food and nutrition, physical activity, and body composition that seem most likely to prevent cancers of a number of sites.

FOOD, NUTRITION, PHYSICAL ACTIVITY, AND THE PREVENTION OF CANCER
OVERVIEW OF THE PANEL'S KEY JUDGEMENTS

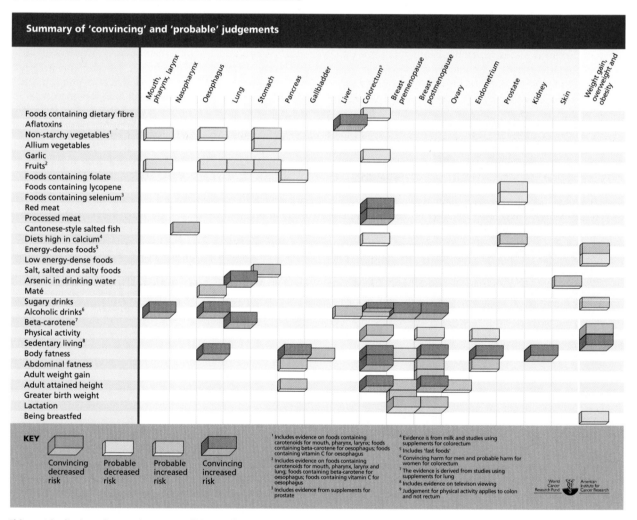

This matrix displays the Panel's most confident judgements on the strength of the evidence causally relating food, nutrition, and physical activity to the risk of cancer. It is a synthesis of all the matrices introducing the text of Chapters 4, 5, 6, 7, and 8 of this Report, but shows only judgements of 'convincing' and 'probable', on which the following recommendations are based. It does not show a detailed breakdown of the individual foods, drinks, and their constituents. The full matrix, which also includes judgements of 'limited — suggestive', is on the fold-out section, which can be found inside the back cover of this Report.

In this matrix, the columns correspond to the cancer sites that are the subject of Chapter 7 and body fatness that is the subject of Chapter 8. The rows correspond to factors that the Panel judges to be 'convincing' or 'probable', either as protective against or causative of cancer of the sites specified, or of weight gain, overweight, or obesity. Such judgements usually justify public health goals and personal recommendations. The strength of the evidence is shown by the height of the blocks in this matrix — see the key.

Box 12.1 Quantification

Public health professionals who advise on preventing cancer, including those responsible for planning food supplies or exercise programmes (for example, for schools, hospitals, or canteens), or those working in clinical settings, need to be able to give specific, actionable, and relevant advice that includes prevention of cancer.

To do this they need to know how much of what foods and drinks, what levels of body fatness, and how much physical activity are most likely to protect against cancer. So do people in general, as members of communities and families, as well as individuals. For these reasons, the personal and public health goals in each of the recommendations are quantified wherever possible.

Translation of an overall body of current evidence into quantified recommendations is a challenge for all expert panels responsible for recommendations designed to guide public policy, and professional and personal decisions. This process is not and cannot be 'an exact science'. Within any population, people differ from one another, and there are differences between populations as well. A single, numerical recommendation is not able to encompass these differing needs and so will necessarily be imprecise.

Furthermore, the evidence rarely shows a clear point above or below which risk changes suddenly. Rather, there is usually a continuous relationship between the exposure, be it body fatness, physical activity, or level of consumption of a food or drink, and cancer risk. The shape of this 'dose response' may vary — sometimes it is a straight line, or it may be curved, for instance J-shaped or U-shaped. All of these

factors need to be taken into account. The quantified recommendations are therefore based on the evidence but are also a matter of judgement.

For example, the evidence on alcoholic drinks and breast cancer, as shown in chapters 4.8 and 7.10, does not show any 'safe threshold'. The risk evidently increases, albeit modestly, at any level of intake of any alcoholic drink. And there is no nutritional need to consume alcohol. So in this case, the appropriate recommendation based solely on the evidence for breast cancer would be not to consume alcoholic drinks; the quantified recommendation would be zero.

However, the integrated approach that guides these recommendations means that the Panel has taken into account evidence for a likely protective effect of modest amounts of alcohol against coronary heart disease, and has not made this recommendation based only on the evidence for cancer (see recommendation 6).

In addition, in some cases, there is evidence for adverse effects unrelated to cancer risk that might help to quantify recommendations. Physical activity is a case in point. The evidence, as shown in Chapters 5 and 7, shows that high levels of all types of physical activity protect or may protect against some cancers, and also that low levels increase the risk of these cancers. But there is also evidence (not derived from the systematic literature reviews), that above certain high levels, which vary depending on people's general state of fitness, physical activity can provoke an undesirable inflammatory response.

The Panel also used such an approach in considering the minimum limit for healthy

body mass index, which does not derive from the evidence on cancer. The implication is that upper as well as lower limits may need to be recommended.

These quantified recommendations are also guided by the ranges of foods and drinks, physical activity, and body composition identified in the studies whose results, taken together, form the basis for the Panel's judgements. High and low limits can be set by simply following the ranges in the studies themselves, mostly cohort studies.

The case for doing this is quite strong; this prospective evidence provides a robust basis for defining the dose response. On the other hand, many studies have been carried out among populations who have only a rather narrow range of dietary intakes, levels of physical activity, and degree of body fatness, which makes detection of associations difficult. Further, these ranges may not themselves be optimal, and this makes it difficult to define what is healthy. In such cases, a recommended range based only on the results of such studies would be flawed. Ecological studies, which often address a much wider range of intakes, were also part of this review and, though not central to the judgement of causality, nevertheless inform the quantification of the recommendations.

As well as considering the evidence from studies on cancer, the Panel, in common with others, has also used its collective knowledge of other relevant considerations in making the quantified recommendations in this chapter. It has also taken into account the ranges of intake of foods and drinks, and the ranges of advisable body composition and physical activity recommended in other reports.

12.1.6 Prevention of other diseases taken into account

Chapter 10 of this Report is based on a systematic review of secondary sources — other reports — on other diseases where the risk is modified by food and nutrition and related factors. These diseases are nutritional deficiencies; relevant infectious diseases, especially diarrhoea and respiratory infections of early childhood; and chronic diseases other than cancer.

As stated above, the recommendations here are designed to prevent cancer as a whole. For similar reasons of public health, the Panel, in considering and judging the secondary evidence presented in Chapter 10, has made sure that the recommendations here take the prevention of other diseases into account.

Often recommendations to prevent cancer are much the same as recommendations to control or prevent other diseases. When this is evidently so, the Panel has stated

that its recommendations are supported or reinforced. Occasionally, recommendations to prevent other diseases include factors that evidently do not apply to cancer: for example, saturated fatty acids, contained mostly in animal foods, are accepted to be a cause of coronary heart disease, but have no special relevance to the risk of cancer.

There are also some cases where recommendations to prevent other diseases conflict, or seem to conflict, with those for cancer. One example is alcoholic drinks. While no report on cardiovascular disease has ever recommended consumption of alcoholic drinks, low levels of consumption of alcoholic drinks are likely to protect against coronary heart disease; whereas there is no evidence that alcoholic drinks at any level of consumption have any benefit for any cancer. In cases like this, the Panel's recommendations may be modified to take such a conflict into account; this is clearly indicated in the recommendations.

12.1.7 Challenging

The Panel emphasises that food and life should be enjoyed. *The Panel recognises* that for many people, these recommendations will involve change. People tend to enjoy ways of life that they have become used to. However, when they change, people often enjoy their new ways of life as much or more. *The Panel is aware* of the importance of aspirational goals and recommendations. To achieve substantial public and personal health gain, some of these need to be challenging.

For many populations and people, especially in industrialised or urban settings, achieving all of these recommendations will not be easy. Levels of physical activity within societies that are basically sedentary, and energy density of diets, are often well outside the ranges recommended here. But *the Panel believes* that populations and people who achieve these recommendations will not only reduce their risk of cancer, as well as of other diseases, but are also likely to improve their positive health and well-being.

Sometimes it may take time for people to achieve changes. The Panel has taken this into account when applying the evidence to framing these recommendations. See box 12.2.

Some people will not be able to follow some or all of these recommendations because of their situation or circumstances. For such people, the recommendations as stated here may be unattainable, but working towards them will also reduce the risk of cancer, although to a lesser degree.

Box 12.2 Making gradual changes

The evidence reviewed by the Panel more often than not does not show thresholds of food and drink consumption, body fatness, or physical activity below or above which the risk of cancer suddenly changes. In such cases, any change in the exposure would be expected to lead to a change in cancer risk, whatever the starting level, and no single point lends itself to being an obvious recommended level. Recommendations might then simply state 'the less the better' or 'the more the better'. However, while that would be faithful to the evidence, it is less helpful for people trying to implement change — the question arises of how much more or less, or of what level should be a target.

These judgements take account of several factors — the range of foods and drinks consumed, the level of physical activity or degree of body fatness found in the studies reviewed, or the possibility of adverse effects at particularly high or low levels, but also the precise nature of the relationship between them and the risk of cancer. In some cases, this may be a relatively straight line, in others it may be curved, for instance either U-shaped or J-shaped. Therefore the Panel has chosen to make quantified recommendations that in its judgement would result in a real health gain, and are achievable yet challenging. However, it would be wrong to interpret this as meaning that any movement towards them, but which did not reach them, was valueless. On the contrary, these recommendations should act as a spur to change of any amount. While it is true that a smaller change than recommended would lead to less reduction in risk, any change at all would nevertheless provide at least some benefit.

A perceived inability to achieve the targets should not be a disincentive to making changes to move in that direction. So a change from eating two portions of vegetables daily to three, or a reduction in body mass index from 29 to 27, while not meeting the goals, would nevertheless be valuable.

12.2   Goals and recommendations

The Panel's goals and recommendations, the culmination of five years of work, are guided by the principles above. They are based on the best available evidence, which has been identified, collected, analysed, displayed, summarised, and judged systematically, transparently, and independently. The public health goals are for populations and are therefore principally for health professionals; the recommendations are for people, as communities, families, and individuals. The eight general recommendations are followed by two special recommendations. Together they are designed to be integrated and to contribute to healthy dietary patterns, healthy ways of life, and general well-being.

The Panel emphasises that the setting of recommendations is not and cannot be 'an exact science'. Recommendations derive from judgements based on the best evidence but that evidence and those judgements may still not be such that only one possible recommendation would follow. Several aspects of recommendations designed to improve health can be questioned. *The Panel believes* nevertheless that its recommendations are as firmly based as the science currently allows, and therefore represent a sound base for developing policy and action.

The 10 recommendations here derive from the evidence on food, nutrition, and physical activity but not on their wider socioeconomic, cultural, and other determinants. *The Panel is aware* that patterns of diet and physical activity, as well as the risk of diseases such as cancer, are also crucially influenced by social and environmental factors. These broader factors, and recommendations designed as the basis for policies and programmes that can create healthier societies and environments, are the subject of a further report to be published in late 2008.

The Panel has agreed that its recommendations normally derive from evidence that justifies judgements of 'convincing' and 'probable', as shown in the top halves of the matrices in the chapters and sections of Part 2. This means that the evidence is sufficiently strong to make recommendations designed as the basis for public health policies and programmes. Therefore judgements that evidence is 'limited — suggestive' do not normally form the basis for recommendations.

As shown in the following pages, the goals and recommendations themselves are boxed. They begin with a general statement. This is followed by the public health goals and the personal recommendations, together with any necessary footnotes. These footnotes are an integral part of the recommendations. The boxed texts are followed by passages summarising the relevant judgements made by the Panel. Then the specifications made in the public health goals and personal recommendations are explained. This is followed by passages of further clarification and qualification as necessary: in special circumstances, the points made here are also

RECOMMENDATIONS

BODY FATNESS
Be as lean as possible within the
normal range of body weight

PHYSICAL ACTIVITY
Be physically active as part of everyday life

FOODS AND DRINKS THAT PROMOTE WEIGHT GAIN
Limit consumption of energy-dense foods
Avoid sugary drinks

PLANT FOODS
Eat mostly foods of plant origin

ANIMAL FOODS
Limit intake of red meat and avoid processed meat

ALCOHOLIC DRINKS
Limit alcoholic drinks

PRESERVATION, PROCESSING, PREPARATION
Limit consumption of salt
Avoid mouldy cereals (grains) or pulses (legumes)

DIETARY SUPPLEMENTS
Aim to meet nutritional needs through diet alone

BREASTFEEDING
Mothers to breastfeed; children to be breastfed

CANCER SURVIVORS
Follow the recommendations for cancer prevention

integral to the recommendations. Finally, guides showing how people can sustain the recommendations are included.

The public health goals are for populations and so are primarily for health professionals, and are quantified where appropriate. 'Population' includes the world population, national populations, and population groups such as schoolchildren, hospital patients, and staff who eat in canteens, generally or in specific settings. The personal recommendations are for people as communities, families, and as individuals. This allows for the fact that decisions on the choice of foods and drinks are often taken communally or within families, or by the family members responsible for buying and preparing meals and food, as well as by individuals. Personal recommendations are best followed in conjunction with public health goals. For example, the recommendation that people walk briskly for at least 30 minutes every day is to enable them to increase their average physical activity level (PAL) by about 0.1.

The Panel concludes that the evidence that high body fatness and also physical inactivity are causes of a number of cancers, including common cancers, is particularly strong. For this reason, the first three sets of goals and recommendations are designed as a basis for policies, programmes, and choices whose purpose is to maintain healthy body weights and to sustain physical activity, throughout life. The remaining five general recommendations are not in any order of priority; instead, they follow the order that their subjects appear in the chapters in Part 2. After the eight general recommendations, there are two special recommendations, one on breastfeeding and one for cancer survivors, that are targeted at specific groups of people.

These goals and recommendations are concerned with food and nutrition, physical activity, and body fatness. Other factors that modify the risk of cancer outside the remit of this Report, such as smoking, infectious agents, radiation, industrial chemicals, and medication, are specified in Chapter 2 and throughout Chapter 7.

The Panel emphasises the importance of not smoking and of avoiding exposure to tobacco smoke.

Greater birth weight, and adult attained height

The evidence that the factors that lead to greater adult attained height, or its consequences, increase the risk of cancers of the colorectum and breast (postmenopause) is convincing; and they probably also increase the risk of cancers of the pancreas, breast (premenopause) and ovary. In addition, the factors that lead to greater birth weight, or its consequences, are probably a cause of premenopausal breast cancer. Also see chapter 6.

The Panel has agreed that height and birth weight are themselves unlikely directly to modify the risk of cancer. They are markers for genetic, environmental, hormonal, and nutritional factors affecting growth during the period from preconception to completion of linear growth. However, the precise mechanisms by which they operate are currently unclear. In addition, they are known to have different associations with other chronic diseases such as cardiovascular disease. For these reasons, they are not the subject of recommendations in this chapter.

Understanding the factors that influence growth, and how they might modify the risk of cancer and other chronic diseases, is an important question for future research, including the relative importance of genetic and environmental factors, and when in the life course nutritional factors might be most relevant. Identifying optimal growth trajectories that protect health not only in childhood but also throughout life is a major challenge for the research and public health communities.

RECOMMENDATION 1

BODY FATNESS

Be as lean as possible within the normal range[1] of body weight

PUBLIC HEALTH GOALS

Median adult body mass index (BMI) to be between 21 and 23, depending on the normal range for different populations[2]

The proportion of the population that is overweight or obese to be no more than the current level, or preferably lower, in 10 years

---

PERSONAL RECOMMENDATIONS

Ensure that body weight through childhood and adolescent growth projects[3] towards the lower end of the normal BMI range at age 21

Maintain body weight within the normal range from age 21

Avoid weight gain and increases in waist circumference throughout adulthood

---

[1] 'Normal range' refers to appropriate ranges issued by national governments or the World Health Organization
[2] To minimise the proportion of the population outside the normal range
[3] 'Projects' in this context means following a pattern of growth (weight and height) throughout childhood that leads to adult BMI at the lower end of the normal range. Such patterns of growth are specified in International Obesity Task Force and WHO growth reference charts

---

Evidence

The evidence that overweight and obesity increase the risk of a number of cancers is now even more impressive than in the mid-1990s. Since that time, rates of overweight and obesity, in adults as well as in children, have greatly increased in most countries.

The evidence that greater body fatness is a cause of cancers of the colorectum, oesophagus (adenocarcinoma), endometrium, pancreas, kidney, and breast (postmenopause) is convincing. It is a probable cause of cancer of the gallbladder. Body fatness probably protects against premenopausal breast cancer, but increases the risk of breast cancer overall. This is because postmenopausal breast cancer is more common. The evidence that abdominal (central) fatness is a cause of cancer of the colorectum is convincing; and it is a probable cause of cancers of the pancreas and endometrium, and of postmenopausal breast cancer. Adult weight gain is a probable cause of postmenopausal breast cancer. Greater birth weight is a probable cause of premenopausal breast cancer. Also see Chapters 6 and 7.

Justification

Maintenance of a healthy weight throughout life may be one of the most important ways to protect against cancer. This will also protect against a number of other common chronic diseases.

Weight gain, overweight, and obesity are now generally much more common than in the 1980s and 1990s. Rates of overweight and obesity doubled in many high-income countries between 1990 and 2005. In most countries in Asia and Latin America, and some in Africa, chronic diseases including obesity are now more prevalent than nutritional deficiencies and infectious diseases.

Being overweight or obese increases the risk of some cancers. Overweight and obesity also increase the risk of conditions including dyslipidaemia, hypertension and stroke, type 2 diabetes, and coronary heart disease. Overweight in childhood and early life is liable to be followed by overweight and obesity in adulthood. Further details of evidence and judgements can be found in Chapters 6 and 8. Maintenance of a healthy weight throughout life may be one of the most important ways to protect against cancer.

Public health goals

The points here are additional to those made in the footnotes to the goals above.

> Median adult BMI for different populations to be between 21 and 23, depending on the normal range

To date, the range of normal weight has been usually identified as a BMI between 18.5 and 24.9; overweight and obesity has been identified as a BMI of 25 or over 30, respectively. However, the evidence that is the basis for this Report does not show any threshold at a BMI of 25. The relationship between BMI and risk of disease varies between different populations (see chapter 8.4), and so the median population BMI that accompanies lowest risk will vary. *The Panel therefore recommends* that the population median lies between 21 and 23, which allows for this variation. Within any population, the range of individual BMIs will vary around this.

> The proportion of the population that is overweight or obese to be no more than the current level, or preferably lower, in 10 years

The context for this goal, which like the others specified here is designed as a guide for national and other population policies, is the current general rapid rise in overweight and obesity. The goal proposes a time-frame. Policy-makers are encouraged to frame specific goals according to their own circumstances. The implications of the goal for countries where there is a current increasing trend are that over the 10-year period, the increase would stop, and then rates of overweight and obesity would begin to drop.

While it is clear that obesity itself is a cause of some cancers and of other diseases, it is also a marker for dietary and physical activity patterns that independently lead to poor health.

Box 12.3 — Height, weight, and ranges of body mass index (BMI)

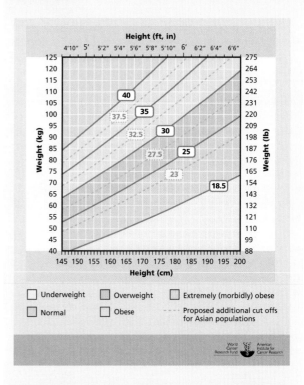

In the chart above, a BMI between 18.5 and 25 is highlighted. A BMI between 18.5 and 25 has conventionally been regarded as normal or healthy. BMIs under 18.5 represent underweight, which is unhealthy; BMIs between 25 and 30 are called overweight; BMIs over 30 are called obesity; and BMIs over 40 are designated as extremely (morbidly) obese.

However, different cut-off points for overweight and obesity have been agreed in some countries; these cut-offs usually specify overweight at BMI less than 25, and obesity at BMI less than 30. Such specifications should be used for and by people living in those countries. These are shown in dotted lines.

BMI is calculated using weight and height. Using the graph above, a person who is 170 cm tall and weighs 68 kg has a BMI within the normal range. To calculate BMI, divide weight (kg) by height (m) squared. Therefore, a person who is 1.7 m tall and who weighs 68 kg has a BMI of 23.5.

It should be noted that BMI should be interpreted with caution, as in some cases it may be misleading, for instance in muscular people such as manual workers and some athletes, and older people, children, or people less than 5 feet tall (152 cm).

Personal recommendations

The points here are additional to those made in the footnotes to the recommendations above.

Ensure that body weight through childhood and adolescent growth projects towards the lower end of the normal BMI range at age 21

Maintain body weight within the normal range from age 21

These two related recommendations emphasise the importance of prevention of excess weight gain, overweight, and obesity, beginning in early life — indeed, in infancy and childhood. As stated, the normal range of BMI is within 18.5 to 25, with some variation between countries; where the agreed range is different this should be used as the guide. See box 12.3.

These recommendations do not mean that all healthy people within the normal range of BMI need necessarily aim to lower their BMI. However, people who have gained weight, even within the normal range, are advised to aim to return to their original weight.

People above the normal range of BMI are recommended to lose weight to approach the normal range. See 'Guidance' and also recommendations 2 and 3.

Avoid weight gain and increases in waist circumference throughout adulthood

There may be specific adverse effects from gaining weight during adulthood (see chapter 6.1.1.3), and so maintenance of weight within the normal range throughout adult life is recommended.

The World Health Organization reference values for waist circumferences of 94 cm (37 inches) in men and 80 cm (31.5 inches) in women (on a population basis) are based on their rough equivalence to a BMI of around 25, whereas waist circumferences of 102 cm (40.2 inches) in men and 88 cm (34.6 inches) in women are equivalent to a BMI of around 30. For Asian populations, cut-offs for waist circumferences of 90 cm (35.4 inches) for men and 80 cm (31.5 inches) for women have been proposed.

Guidance

This overall recommendation can best be achieved by being physically active throughout life, and by choosing diets based on foods that have low energy density and avoiding sugary drinks.

People who are already outside the normal BMI range should seek advice from appropriately qualified professionals with a view to returning towards the normal range. However, for weight control, recommendations 1, 2, and 3 can be followed.

RECOMMENDATION 2

PHYSICAL ACTIVITY

Be physically active as part of everyday life

PUBLIC HEALTH GOALS

The proportion of the population that is sedentary[1] to be halved every 10 years

Average physical activity levels (PALs)[1] to be above 1.6

PERSONAL RECOMMENDATIONS

Be moderately physically active, equivalent to brisk walking,[2] for at least 30 minutes every day

As fitness improves, aim for 60 minutes or more of moderate, or for 30 minutes or more of vigorous, physical activity every day[2][3]

Limit sedentary habits such as watching television

---

[1] The term 'sedentary' refers to a PAL of 1.4 or less. PAL is a way of representing the average intensity of daily physical activity. PAL is calculated as total energy expenditure as a multiple of basal metabolic rate
[2] Can be incorporated in occupational, transport, household, or leisure activities
[3] This is because physical activity of longer duration or greater intensity is more beneficial

---

Evidence

The evidence that physical activity of all types protects against cancer and also against obesity, and therefore indirectly those cancers whose risk is increased by obesity, has continued to accumulate since the early 1990s.

The evidence that physical activity protects against colon cancer is convincing. It probably protects against postmenopausal breast cancer and endometrial cancer. Also see Chapter 5.

The evidence that physical activity protects against weight gain, overweight, and obesity is convincing. The evidence that sedentary living increases the risk of weight gain, overweight, and obesity is also convincing. Television viewing, a form of very sedentary behaviour, is probably a cause of weight gain, overweight, and obesity. Also see Chapter 8.

Justification

Most populations, and people living in industrialised and urban settings, have habitual levels of activity below levels to which humans are adapted.

With industrialisation, urbanisation, and mechanisation, populations and people become more sedentary. As with overweight and obesity, sedentary ways of life have been usual in high-income countries since the second half of the 20th century. They are now common if not usual in most countries.

All forms of physical activity protect against some cancers, as well as against weight gain, overweight, and obesity; correspondingly, sedentary ways of life are a cause of these cancers and of weight gain, overweight, and obesity. Weight gain, overweight, and obesity are also causes of some cancers independently of the level of physical activity. Further details of evidence and judgements can be found in Chapters 5, 6, and 8.

The evidence summarised in Chapter 10 also shows that physical activity protects against other diseases and that sedentary ways of life are causes of these diseases.

Public health goals

The points here are additional to those made in the footnotes to the goals above.

> The proportion of the population that is sedentary to be halved every 10 years

As above, the context for this goal, which like the others specified here is designed as a guide for national and other population policies, is the current general rapid rise in sedentary ways of life. Again as above, the goal proposes a time-frame. Its achievement will require leadership from governments, city planners, school boards, and others. Policy-makers are encouraged to frame goals according to their specific circumstances.

The recommendation takes account of the magnitude of health gain expected from moving, even modestly, from sedentary ways of life, compared to increasing the level of activity for already active people.

> Average physical activity levels to be above 1.6

Average PALs for people in high income populations are between around 1.4 and 1.6. PALs for people in the normal range of BMI often average around 1.6. *The Panel emphasises* that the goal is to move above a PAL of 1.6. Levels of 1.7 and more are readily achieved by active and fit people. See Chapter 5.

Personal recommendations

The points here are additional to those made in the footnotes to the recommendations above.

> Be moderately physically active, equivalent to brisk walking for at least 30 minutes every day

> As fitness improves, aim for 60 minutes or more of moderate, or for 30 minutes or more of vigorous, physical activity every day

These recommendations are linked. The first derives from the evidence on cancer. The second derives from the evidence on overweight and obesity, themselves a cause of some cancers. In making these two recommendations, the Panel also recognises that for people who have been habitually sedentary for some time, a first recommendation, which is also meant to be intermediary, is sensible. Levels of activity above those recommended here are likely to be additionally beneficial, unless excessive, which may lead to an acute inflammatory response indicated by muscle pain and vulnerability to infections.

> Limit sedentary habits such as watching television

Watching television is a form of very sedentary behaviour. Children may commonly watch television for more than three hours a day, and are often also exposed to heavy marketing of foods that are high in energy and of sugary drinks on television.

Table 12.1 — **How to achieve a healthy physical activity level (PAL)**

This table provides guidance on the impact of specific periods of activity on overall physical activity levels. Increasing activity can be achieved in many different ways. See Chapter 5.

The table lists some examples of the effect on average daily PAL of doing different activities for different periods of time. The estimates are approximate and rounded.

So for a person with a PAL of 1.6, an extra 30 minutes daily of moderate activity would increase PAL to around 1.7.

Category	Increase in daily PAL (for an hour of activity *a week*)	Increase in daily PAL (for 20 minutes of activity *a day*)	Increase in daily PAL (for 30 minutes of activity *a day*)	Increase in daily PAL (for 40 minutes of activity *a day*)	Increase in daily PAL (for an hour of activity *a day*)
Sedentary					
Lying down quietly	0	0	0	0	0
Light					
Walking slowly, light gardening, housework	0.01	0.03	0.05	0.06	0.09
Moderate					
Walking briskly, cycling, dancing, swimming	0.03	0.07	0.10	0.13	0.20
Vigorous					
Running, tennis, football	0.07	0.17	0.25	0.35	0.50

Guidance

Most people can readily build regular moderate, and some vigorous, physical activity into their everyday lives.

Moderate physical activity can readily be built into everyday life. It is not necessary to devote a continuous half hour every day to moderate activity. With walking as an example, walk briskly all or part of the way to and from work, or on local errands, or at school; take a break for a walk in the middle of the day or the evening; use stairs rather than the elevator. The same applies to other moderate activities.

The best choice of vigorous physical activity is that which is most enjoyable for the family or the individual — be it swimming, running, dancing, rowing, cycling, hill walking, aerobic workouts, or team games such as football and badminton. Resistance and balance training are also beneficial. Some sports and recreations such as golf are not vigorously active. A good test that activity is vigorous is that it involves sweating and raises heart rate to 60–80 per cent of its maximum.

People whose work is sedentary should take special care to build moderate and vigorous physical activity into their everyday lives.

It is also important to avoid long periods of sedentary behaviour, such as watching television. This behaviour is also often associated with consumption of energy-dense food and sugary drinks.

A common misconception is that sport or exercise is the only way in which to be physically active. Physical activity includes that involved with transport (such as walking and cycling), household (chores, gardening), and occupation (manual and other active work), as well as recreational activity.

See table 12.1 for guidance on how to achieve and maintain a healthy PAL. This table provides guidance on the impact of specific periods of activity on overall PALs. Increasing activity can be achieved in many different ways.

The table lists some examples of the effect on average daily PAL of doing different activities for different periods of time. The estimates are approximate and rounded. So for a person with a PAL of 1.6, an extra 30 minutes daily of moderate activity would increase their PAL to around 1.7.

RECOMMENDATION 3

FOODS AND DRINKS THAT PROMOTE WEIGHT GAIN

**Limit consumption of energy-dense foods[1]
Avoid sugary drinks[2]**

PUBLIC HEALTH GOALS

Average energy density of diets[3] to be lowered towards 125 kcal per 100 g

Population average consumption of sugary drinks[2] to be halved every 10 years

---

PERSONAL RECOMMENDATIONS

Consume energy-dense foods[1] [4] sparingly

Avoid sugary drinks[2]

Consume 'fast foods'[5] sparingly, if at all

---

[1] Energy-dense foods are here defined as those with an energy content of more than about 225–275 kcal per 100 g
[2] This principally refers to drinks with added sugars. Fruit juices should also be limited
[3] This does not include drinks
[4] Limit processed energy-dense foods (also see recommendation 4). Relatively unprocessed energy-dense foods, such as nuts and seeds, have not been shown to contribute to weight gain when consumed as part of typical diets, and these and many vegetable oils are valuable sources of nutrients
[5] The term 'fast foods' refers to readily available convenience foods that tend to be energy-dense and consumed frequently and in large portions

Evidence

Evidence shows that foods and diets that are high in energy, particularly those that are highly processed, and sugary drinks, increase the risk of overweight and obesity. Some foods low in energy density probably protect against some cancers.

Energy-dense foods and sugary drinks probably promote weight gain, especially when consumed frequently and in large portions. Correspondingly, low energy-dense foods, (often relatively unprocessed) probably protect against weight gain, overweight, and obesity. Specific types of low energy-dense foods, such as vegetables and fruits and foods containing dietary fibre, probably protect against some cancers. Also see recommendation 4, Chapter 8, and box 12.4.

Justification

Consumption of energy-dense foods and sugary drinks is increasing worldwide and is probably contributing to the global increase in obesity.

This overall recommendation is mainly designed to prevent and to control weight gain, overweight, and obesity. Further details of evidence and judgements can be found in Chapter 8.

'Energy density' measures the amount of energy (in kcal or kJ) per weight (usually 100 g) of food. Food supplies that are mainly made up of processed foods, which often contain substantial amounts of fat or sugar, tend to be more energy-dense than food supplies that include substantial amounts of fresh foods. Taken together, the evidence shows that it is not specific dietary constituents that are problematic, so much as the contribution these make to the energy density of diets.

Because of their water content, drinks are less energy-dense than foods. However, sugary drinks provide energy but do not seem to induce satiety or compensatory reduction in subsequent energy intake, and so promote overconsumption of energy and thus weight gain.

Public health goals

The points here are additional to those made in the footnotes to the goals above.

Average energy density of diets to be lowered towards 125 kcal per 100 g

Diets appropriately low in energy density are identified as supplying around 125 kcal (or 525 kJ) per 100 g, excluding any drinks. These of course will include foods whose energy density is higher than this average.

Population average consumption of sugary drinks to be halved every 10 years

The context for this goal, which like others specified here is designed as a guide for national and other population policies, is the current general rapid rise in weight gain, overweight, and obesity, especially in children and young people, and the rapid rise in consumption of sugary drinks. As above, the goal proposes a time-frame. Achievement of this challenging goal implies support from regulatory authorities and from manufacturers of sugary drinks. Policy-makers are encouraged to frame goals according to their specific circumstances.

Personal recommendations

The points here are additional to those made in the footnotes to the recommendations above.

Consume energy-dense foods sparingly

Energy-dense foods are here defined as those supplying more than about 225–275 kcal (950–1150 kJ) per 100 g. Foods naturally high in dietary fibre or water, such as vegetables and fruits, and cereals (grains) prepared without fats and oils, are usually low in energy density. Non-starchy vegetables, roots and tubers, and fruits provide roughly between 10 and 100 kcal per 100 g, and cereals (grains) and pulses (legumes) between about 60 and 150 kcal per 100 g. Breads and lean meat, poultry, and fish usually provide between about 100 and 225 kcal per 100 g. Most foods containing substantial amounts of fats, oils, or added sugars, including many 'fast foods' as defined here, as well as many pre-prepared dishes and snacks, baked goods, desserts, and confectionery, are high in energy density.

This recommendation does not imply that all energy-dense foods should be avoided. Some, such as certain oils of plant origin, nuts, and seeds, are important sources of nutrients; their consumption has not been linked with weight gain, and by their nature they tend to be consumed sparingly.

Avoid sugary drinks

This recommendation is especially targeted at soft drinks (including colas, sodas, and squashes) with added sugars. Consumption of such drinks, including in 'super-sizes', has greatly increased in many countries. The evidence that such drinks 'fool' the human satiety mechanism, thereby promoting weight gain, is impressive. They are best not drunk at all. The implication of this recommendation is to prefer water. Low-energy soft drinks, and coffee and tea (without added sugar), are also preferable. Fruit juices, even with no added sugar, are likely to have the same effect and may promote weight gain, and so they should not be drunk in large quantities.

Consume 'fast foods' sparingly, if at all

As already stated, 'fast foods' does not refer to all foods (and drinks) that are readily available for consumption. The term refers to readily available convenience foods that tend to be energy-dense, and that are often consumed frequently and in large portions. Most of the evidence on 'fast foods' is from studies of such foods, such as burgers, fried chicken pieces, French fries (chips), and fatty or sugary drinks, as served in international franchised outlets.

Guidance

Foods and diets that are low in energy density, and avoidance of sugary drinks, are the best choices, in particular for people who lead generally sedentary lives.

The recommendation above can be best achieved by replacing energy-dense foods, such as fatty and sugary processed foods and 'fast foods', with those of low energy density, such as plant foods including non-starchy vegetables, fruits, and relatively unprocessed cereals (grains) (see recommendation 4), and replacing sugary drinks with unsweetened drinks such as water, and unsweetened tea or coffee.

The total energy content of diets is related not only to the energy density of individual foods consumed, but also to the frequency with which they are eaten and the portion size. The physical capacity of the human stomach and digestive system is limited. In general, people usually consume roughly the same amount of food from day to day, measured by weight. Energy-dense diets can undermine normal appetite regulation and therefore lead to greater energy intake.

Sugary drinks are a particular problem as these can be drunk in large quantities without a feeling of satiety. By replacing these foods and drinks with those of low energy density, such as vegetables and fruits, relatively unprocessed cereals (grains) and pulses (legumes), water and non-caloric drinks, the risk of weight gain is reduced, which therefore would be expected to reduce the risk of developing some cancers.

RECOMMENDATION 4

PLANT FOODS

Eat mostly foods of plant origin

PUBLIC HEALTH GOALS

Population average consumption of non-starchy[1]
vegetables and of fruits to be at least 600 g (21 oz) daily[2]

Relatively unprocessed cereals (grains) and/or pulses
(legumes), and other foods that are a natural source of
dietary fibre, to contribute to a population average
of at least 25 g non-starch polysaccharide daily

PERSONAL RECOMMENDATIONS

Eat at least five portions/servings
(at least 400 g or 14 oz) of a variety[2] of
non-starchy vegetables and of fruits every day

Eat relatively unprocessed cereals (grains)
and/or pulses (legumes) with every meal[3]

Limit refined starchy foods

People who consume starchy roots or tubers[4]
as staples also to ensure intake of sufficient
non-starchy vegetables, fruits, and pulses (legumes)

[1] This is best made up from a range of various amounts of non-starchy vegetables
and fruits of different colours including red, green, yellow, white, purple, and
orange, including tomato-based products and allium vegetables such as garlic
[2] Relatively unprocessed cereals (grains) and/or pulses (legumes) to contribute to
an average of at least 25 g non-starch polysaccharide daily
[3] These foods are low in energy density and so promote healthy weight
[4] For example, populations in Africa, Latin America, and the Asia-Pacific region

Evidence

**The evidence that diets high in vegetables and fruits protect
against cancer is overall less compelling than in the mid-
1990s. However, vegetables and fruits, and other foods containing dietary fibre, probably protect against a number of
cancers.**

Non-starchy vegetables probably protect against cancers of
the mouth, pharynx, larynx, oesophagus, and stomach.
Allium vegetables in particular probably protect against cancer of the stomach. Garlic probably protects against cancers
of the colon and rectum. Fruits probably protect against cancers of the mouth, pharynx, larynx, oesophagus, lung, and
stomach. Also see chapter 4.2.

Foods containing dietary fibre probably protect against
cancers of the colorectum. Foods containing folate probably
protect against cancer of the pancreas. Foods containing

carotenoids probably protect against cancers of the mouth,
pharynx, larynx, and lung; foods containing beta-carotene
probably protect against oesophageal cancer; and foods containing lycopene probably protect against prostate cancer.
Foods containing vitamin C probably protect against
oesophageal cancer; and foods containing selenium probably protect against prostate cancer. It is unlikely that foods
containing beta-carotene have a substantial effect on the risk
of cancers of the prostate or skin (non-melanoma). It cannot be confidently assumed that the effects of these foods
can be attributed to the nutrient specified, which may be acting as a marker for other constituents in the foods. Also see
chapter 4.2.

Justification
**An integrated approach to the evidence shows that most
diets that are protective against cancer are mainly made up
from foods of plant origin.**

Higher consumption of several plant foods probably protects
against cancers of various sites. What is meant by 'plant-
based' is diets that give more emphasis to those plant foods
that are high in nutrients, high in dietary fibre (and so in
non-starch polysaccharides), and low in energy density.

Non-starchy vegetables, and fruits, probably protect
against some cancers. Being typically low in energy density,
they probably also protect against weight gain. Further
details of evidence and judgements can be found in
Chapters 4 and 8.

Non-starchy vegetables include green, leafy vegetables,
broccoli, okra, aubergine (eggplant), and bok choy, but not,
for instance, potato, yam, sweet potato, or cassava. Non-
starchy roots and tubers include carrots, Jerusalem artichokes, celeriac (celery root), swede (rutabaga), and
turnips.

The goals and recommendations here are broadly similar
to those that have been issued by other international and
national authoritative organisations (see Chapter 10). They
derive from the evidence on cancer and are supported by evidence on other diseases. They emphasise the importance of
relatively unprocessed cereals (grains), non-starchy vegetables and fruits, and pulses (legumes), all of which contain
substantial amounts of dietary fibre and a variety of micronutrients, and are low or relatively low in energy density. These,
and not foods of animal origin, are the recommended centre for everyday meals.

Public health goals
The points here are additional to those made in the footnotes
to the goals above.

Population average consumption of non-starchy
vegetables and of fruits to be at least 600 g (21 oz) daily

This goal represents amounts well above average population
intakes in almost all parts of the world. Non-starchy vegetables exclude starchy roots and tubers (such as potatoes
and potato products).

In populations where most people consume at least 400 g

of vegetables and fruits daily (see below), the average consumption is likely to correspond roughly to at least 600 g per day.

> Relatively unprocessed cereals (grains) and/or pulses (legumes), and other foods that are a natural source of dietary fibre, to contribute to a population average of at least 25 g non-starch polysaccharide daily

All cereals (grains) and pulses (legumes) undergo some form of processing before they can be consumed. Cooking is a form of processing. This goal is designed to emphasise the value of wholegrains, and generally of plant foods naturally containing substantial amounts of dietary fibre. This does not include processed foods with forms of dietary fibre added, for which evidence of a protective effect is lacking. A total of 25 g of non-starch polysaccharide is roughly equivalent to 32 g of dietary fibre. Also see box 4.1.2 in chapter 4.1.

Personal recommendations
The points here are additional to those made in the footnotes to the recommendations above.

> Eat at least five portions/servings (at least 400 g or 14 oz) of a variety of non-starchy vegetables and of fruits every day

> Eat relatively unprocessed cereals (grains) and/or pulses (legumes) with every meal

> Limit refined starchy foods

These three linked recommendations also relate to the public health goals above. It is likely that there is further protective benefit from consuming more than five portions/servings of non-starchy vegetables and fruits. The recommendation on relatively unprocessed cereals (grains) and pulses (legumes) is designed to ensure that these become a feature of all meals. Refined starchy foods include products made from white flour such as bread, pasta, pizza; white rice; and also foods that are fatty and sugary, such as cakes, pastries, biscuits (cookies), and other baked goods.

> People who consume starchy roots and tubers as staples to ensure intake of sufficient non-starchy vegetables, fruits, and pulses (legumes)

In many parts of the world, traditional food systems are based on roots or tubers, such as cassava, sweet potato, yam, or taro. Traditional food systems should be protected: as well as their cultural value, and their suitability to local climate and terrain, they are often nutritionally superior to the diets that tend to displace them. However, monotonous traditional diets, especially those that contain only small amounts of non-starchy vegetables, fruits, and pulses (legumes), are likely to be low in nutrients, which may increase susceptibility to infection and so be relevant to the risk of some cancers.

Other plant foods

Some plant foods are not the subject of goals or recommendations.

Nuts, seeds, plant oils. The evidence on nuts, seeds, and plant oils, and the risk of cancer, is not substantial. However, nuts and seeds are sources of dietary fibre, essential fatty acids, and vitamins and minerals. Though they are energy-dense, and so should be eaten sparingly, they have not been associated with weight gain. Similarly, modest amounts of appropriate plant oils can be used as the primary form of fat for use in cooking and food preparation. See chapter 4.2.

Sugars. Sugars and also syrups in their various forms are refined from cane, beet, or corn. The evidence on sugary drinks is strong enough to generate goals and recommendations (3, above). The evidence suggesting that foods containing substantial amounts of added sugars increase the risk of colorectal cancer is limited, and so the Panel has made no recommendation. However, the general implication of the goals and recommendations made here is that consumption of foods containing added sugars would be limited. See chapter 4.6.

Guidance
Maintaining plant-based diets is easily done by planning meals and dishes around plant foods rather than meat and other foods of animal origin.

Meat and other animal foods became centrepieces of meals as a result of industrialisation, one consequence of which is that meat becomes cheap. As stated above, foods of plant origin are recommended to be the basis of all meals. A healthy plate is one that is at least two thirds full of plant foods; and instead of processed cereals and grains, wholegrain versions are better choices.

As stated in recommendation 3, vegetables and fruits are generally low in energy density. Therefore, by consuming the amount of vegetables and fruits recommended above, and limiting the amount of energy-dense foods consumed, people can reduce their risk of cancer directly, as well as the risk of overweight and obesity.

One portion of vegetables or fruits is approximately 80 g or 3 oz. If consuming the recommended amount of vegetables and fruits stated above, average consumption will be at least 400 g or 14 oz per day.

RECOMMENDATION 5

ANIMAL FOODS

**Limit intake of red meat[1] and
avoid processed meat[2]**

PUBLIC HEALTH GOAL

Population average consumption of red meat
to be no more than 300 g (11 oz) a week,
very little if any of which to be processed

PERSONAL RECOMMENDATION

People who eat red meat[1]
to consume less than 500 g (18 oz) a week,
very little if any to be processed[2]

[1] 'Red meat' refers to beef, pork, lamb, and goat from domesticated animals
including that contained in processed foods
[2] 'Processed meat' refers to meat preserved by smoking, curing or salting, or
addition of chemical preservatives, including that contained in processed foods

Evidence

**The evidence that red meat, and particularly processed
meat, is a cause of colorectal cancer is stronger now than it
was in the mid-1990s.**

The evidence that red meat is a cause of colorectal cancer is
convincing. The evidence that processed meat is a cause of
colorectal cancer is also convincing. Cantonese-style salted
fish (see chapter 4.3, box 4.3.5, and also box 12.5) is a probable cause of nasopharyngeal cancer: this conclusion does
not apply to fish prepared (or salted) by other means. Milk
from cows probably protects against colorectal cancer. Diets
high in calcium are a probable cause of prostate cancer; this
effect is only apparent at high calcium intakes (around 1.5
g per day or more). Also see chapters 4.3 and 4.4.

Justification

**An integrated approach to the evidence also shows that
many foods of animal origin are nourishing and healthy if
consumed in modest amounts.**

People who eat various forms of vegetarian diets are at low
risk of some diseases including some cancers, although it is
not easy to separate out these benefits of the diets from other
aspects of their ways of life, such as not smoking, drinking
little if any alcohol, and so forth. In addition, meat can be
a valuable source of nutrients, in particular protein, iron,
zinc, and vitamin B12. *The Panel emphasises* that this overall recommendation is not for diets containing no meat —
or diets containing no foods of animal origin. The amounts
are for weight of meat as eaten. As a rough conversion, 300
g of cooked red meat is equivalent to about 400–450 g raw

weight, and 500 g cooked red meat to about 700–750 g raw
weight. The exact conversion will depend on the cut of meat,
the proportions of lean and fat, and the method and degree
of cooking, so more specific guidance is not possible.

Red or processed meats are convincing or probable causes of some cancers. Diets with high levels of animal fats are
often relatively high in energy, increasing the risk of weight
gain. Further details of evidence and judgements can be
found in Chapters 4 and 8.

Public health goal
The points here are additional to those made in the footnotes
to the goal above.

Population average consumption of red meat
to be no more than 300 g (11 oz) a week,
very little if any of which to be processed

This goal is given in terms of weekly consumption to encourage perception that red meat need not be a daily food. The
goal of 300 g or 11 oz a week corresponds to the level of
consumption of red meat at which the risk of colorectal cancer can clearly be seen to rise. The evidence on processed
meat is even more clear-cut than that on red meat, and the
data do not show any level of intake that can confidently be
shown not to be associated with risk.

Other animal foods

Many animal foods are not the subject of goals or recommendations.

Poultry, fish. The evidence on poultry and the risk of cancer is
not substantial. The evidence suggesting that fish protects
against colorectal cancer is limited. (Cantonese-style salted fish
is a special case — see chapter 4.3.) However, people who eat
flesh foods are advised to prefer poultry, and all types of fish, to
red meat. Flesh from wild animals, birds, and fish, whose nutritional profiles are different from those of domesticated and
industrially reared creatures, is also preferred. See chapter 4.3.

Eggs. The evidence on eggs and the risk of cancer is not substantial. There is no basis for recommending avoidance of eggs
to prevent cancer. See chapter 4.3.

Milk, cheese, other dairy products. The evidence on cow's milk,
cheese, and foods high in calcium, and the risk of cancer, is
hard to interpret. The evidence on colorectal cancer and on prostate
cancer seems to be in conflict. After long discussion, the Panel
chose to make no recommendations here. See chapter 4.4.

Animal fats. The evidence suggesting that animal fats are a cause
of colorectal cancer is limited. Animal fats are high in energy and
the Panel integrated the limited evidence suggesting that animal fats are a cause of overweight and obesity into its findings
on energy-dense foods. The implication is that it is best to limit
consumption of animal fats, as part of meat and also as contained in processed foods, in part because of the relation with
cardiovascular disease. See chapter 4.5.

Personal recommendation
The points here are additional to those made in the footnotes to the recommendation above.

> People who regularly eat red meat
> to consume less than 500 g (18 oz) a week,
> very little if any to be processed

This recommendation relates to the goal above. In populations where most people consume less than 500 g (18 oz) a week, the population average is likely to correspond to no more than roughly 300 g (11 oz) a week.

Guidance
There are many ways to enjoy meat and other animal foods as part of plant-based diets.

For those who eat flesh foods, the amount of red meat consumed can be limited by choosing poultry and fish instead. It is better also to consume the lean parts of red meat.

It is best that processed meats are avoided. They are generally energy-dense and can also contain high levels of salt (see recommendation 7). They also tend to be preserved by smoking, curing, or salting, or with the addition of chemical preservatives. Some of these methods of preservation are known to generate carcinogens; while the epidemiological evidence that these are causes of cancer is limited, it is a wise precaution to avoid them. Processed meat includes ham, bacon, pastrami, and salami. Sausages, frankfurters, and 'hot dogs', to which nitrates/nitrites or other preservatives are added, are also processed meats. Minced meats sometimes, but not always, fall inside this definition if they are preserved chemically. The same point applies to 'hamburgers'. Fresh meats that have simply been minced or ground and then shaped and cooked are not considered to be 'processed'.

Substantial amounts of meat are not needed to sustain adequate consumption of protein and iron. All flesh foods are high in protein, and for people who consume varied diets without any flesh foods, more than adequate protein can be derived from a mixture of pulses (legumes) and cereals (grains). Iron is present in many plant foods, as well as in meat.

RECOMMENDATION 6

ALCOHOLIC DRINKS
Limit alcoholic drinks[1]

PUBLIC HEALTH GOAL

Proportion of the population drinking more than the recommended limits to be reduced by one third every 10 years[1][2]

PERSONAL RECOMMENDATION

If alcoholic drinks are consumed, limit consumption to no more than two drinks a day for men and one drink a day for women[1][2][3]

[1] This recommendation takes into account that there is a likely protective effect for coronary heart disease
[2] Children and pregnant women not to consume alcoholic drinks
[3] One 'drink' contains about 10–15 grams of ethanol

Evidence
The evidence that all types of alcoholic drink are a cause of a number of cancers is now stronger than it was in the mid-1990s.

The evidence that alcoholic drinks are a cause of cancers of the mouth, pharynx, and larynx, oesophagus, and breast (pre- and postmenopausal) is convincing. The evidence that alcoholic drinks are a cause of colorectal cancer in men is convincing. Alcoholic drinks are a probable cause of liver cancer, and of colorectal cancer in women. It is unlikely that alcoholic drinks have a substantial adverse effect on the risk of kidney cancer. Also see chapter 4.8.

Justification
The evidence on cancer justifies a recommendation not to drink alcoholic drinks. Other evidence shows that modest amounts of alcoholic drinks are likely to reduce risk of coronary heart disease.

The evidence does not show a clear level of consumption of alcoholic drinks below which there is no increase in risk of the cancers it causes. This means that, based solely on the evidence on cancer, even small amounts of alcoholic drinks should be avoided. Further details of evidence and judgements can be found in Chapter 4. In framing the recommendation here, the Panel has also taken into account the evidence that modest amounts of alcoholic drinks are likely to protect against coronary heart disease, as described in Chapter 10.

The evidence shows that all alcoholic drinks have the same effect. Data do not suggest any significant difference depending on the type of drink. This recommendation therefore covers all alcoholic drinks, whether beers, wines, spirits (liquors), or other alcoholic drinks. The important factor is the amount of ethanol consumed.

The Panel emphasises that children and pregnant women should not consume alcoholic drinks.

Public health goal

The points here are additional to those made in the footnotes to the goal above.

> Proportion of the population drinking
> more than the recommended limits to be
> reduced by one third every 10 years

The context for this goal, which like the others specified here is designed as a guide for national and other population policies, is the current common rise in regular and heavy consumption of alcoholic drinks, including among young people. The focus of the goal is especially on those consuming above the recommended limits, rather than regular modest drinkers. Again as above, the goal proposes a timeframe. Achievement of this goal requires substantial support from regulatory authorities, the manufacturers of alcoholic drinks, and from the owners of bars and other locations where alcoholic drinks are sold and consumed. Policy-makers are encouraged to frame goals according to their specific circumstances.

Personal recommendation

The points here are additional to those made in the footnotes to the recommendation above.

> If alcoholic drinks are consumed,
> limit consumption to no more than two drinks
> a day for men and one drink a day for women

Modest consumption of alcoholic drinks has been shown to be protective against coronary heart disease compared to no drinking, with higher levels of drinking in some cases showing increased risk. Nevertheless, no authoritative body has made specific recommendations for alcohol consumption to avoid coronary heart disease because of the adverse biological, behavioural, physical, social, and other effects of higher levels of consumption.

For those who do consume alcoholic drinks, no more than two drinks per day (men) and no more than one drink per day (women) are the recommended limits. These limits are expressed as amounts per day, because occasional heavy drinking (say, at weekends) while at other times alcoholic drinks are not consumed, is particularly likely to lead to adverse outcomes.

Guidance

For those people who choose to consume alcoholic drinks, the Panel endorses the advice of other authoritative bodies. These generally advise an upper limit of around two drinks per day for men and one for women.

RECOMMENDATION 7

PRESERVATION, PROCESSING, PREPARATION

**Limit consumption of salt[1]
Avoid mouldy cereals (grains) or pulses (legumes)**

PUBLIC HEALTH GOALS

Population average consumption of salt from all sources to be less than 5 g (2 g of sodium) a day

Proportion of the population consuming more than 6 g of salt (2.4 g of sodium) a day to be halved every 10 years

Minimise exposure to aflatoxins from mouldy cereals (grains) or pulses (legumes)

PERSONAL RECOMMENDATIONS

Avoid salt-preserved, salted, or salty foods; preserve foods without using salt[1]

Limit consumption of processed foods with added salt to ensure an intake of less than 6 g (2.4 g sodium) a day

Do not eat mouldy cereals (grains) or pulses (legumes)

[1] Methods of preservation that do not or need not use salt include refrigeration, freezing, drying, bottling, canning, and fermentation

Evidence

Some methods of food preservation, processing, and preparation affect the risk of cancer. The strongest evidence concerns processed meats, preserved by salting, smoking, pickling, addition of chemicals, and other methods (see recommendation 5, above); salt from all sources; and salt-preserved foods.

Salt and salt-preserved foods are probably a cause of stomach cancer: see chapter 4.6.

The Panel judges that refrigeration, while not likely to have any direct effect on the risk of cancer, indirectly protects against some cancers because it affects consumption of foods which themselves influence the risk of cancer. For instance, it may increase the availability and nutrient content of fresh, perishable foods (vegetables and fruits; meat; milk; see chapters 4.2, 4.3, and 4.4); and decrease the need for processed foods (preserved by salting, smoking, curing, and pickling; see chapters 4.3 and 4.9). Also see recommendations 4 and 5, and box 4.6.4 in chapter 4.6.

Some plant foods, notably cereals (grains) and pulses (legumes), may be contaminated with aflatoxins, produced by moulds (fungi) during storage in hot and humid conditions. The evidence that aflatoxins are a cause of liver cancer is convincing. Also see chapter 4.1.

Justification

The strongest evidence on methods of food preservation, processing, and preparation shows that salt and salt-preserved foods are probably a cause of stomach cancer, and that foods contaminated with aflatoxins are a cause of liver cancer.

Salt is necessary for human health and life itself, but at levels very much lower than those typically consumed in most parts of the world. At the levels found not only in high-income countries but also in those where traditional diets are high in salt, consumption of salty foods, salted foods, and salt itself, is too high. The critical factor is the overall amount of salt.

Microbial contamination of foods and drinks and of water supplies, remains a major public health problem worldwide. Specifically, the contamination of cereals (grains) and pulses (legumes) with aflatoxins, produced by some moulds when such foods are stored for too long in warm temperatures is an important public health problem, and not only in tropical countries.

Salt and salt-preserved foods are a probable cause of some cancers. Aflatoxins are a convincing cause of liver cancer. Further details of evidence and judgements can be found in Chapter 4.

Public health goals
The points here are additional to those made in the footnotes to the goal above.

Population average consumption of salt from all sources to be less than 5 g (2 g of sodium) a day

Proportion of the population consuming more than 6 g of salt (2.4 g of sodium) a day to be halved every 10 years

The reason for these linked goals, which like the others specified above are designed as a guide for national and other population policies, is the very high consumption of salt in most countries. Again as above, one of the goals proposes a time-frame. This time-frame implies a continuing effort into the future to achieve levels that might seem difficult within a single decade. Its achievement implies support from regulatory authorities and from the manufacturers of salty and salted foods. Policy-makers are encouraged to frame goals according to their specific circumstances.

Minimise exposure to aflatoxins from mouldy cereals (grains) or pulses (legumes)

Personal recommendations
The points here are additional to those made in the footnotes to the recommendations above.

Avoid salt-preserved, salted, or salty foods; preserve foods without using salt

Limit consumption of processed foods with added salt to ensure an intake of less than 6 g (2.4 g sodium) a day

For most people, these two linked recommendations are designed to reduce salt consumption substantially. Usually most salt in diets is contained in processed foods. Some such foods are obviously salty. Others, bread for example, usually do not taste salty, but bread and other cereal products are a major source of salt in high-income countries, together with many other industrially processed foods that may not appear 'salty'. When preserving foods at home, methods that minimise use of salt are recommended. Avoid the use of salt at table.

Do not eat mouldy cereals (grains) or pulses (legumes)

The prudent approach is to avoid consumption of any cereals (grains) or pulses (legumes) that may have been stored

Other methods of preservation and preparation

Most methods of food preservation, processing, and preparation are not the subject of goals or recommendations. Some of these are of public interest and some are mentioned here.

Drying, fermenting, canning, bottling. There is no good evidence that these methods of food preservation in themselves have any effect on the risk of cancer. When they do not involve the use of salt, they are preferable to methods that do add salt. See chapter 4.9.

Refrigeration. The epidemiological evidence associating use of refrigeration with reduction of the risk of stomach cancer is substantial. The previous report judged this evidence to be convincing. The Panel responsible for this Report judged that the effect of refrigeration as such on cancer risk was not likely to be directly causative. Nevertheless, the benefits of industrial and domestic freezing, refrigeration, and chilling include availability of perishable foods, including vegetables and fruits, all year round, protection against microbial contamination, and reduced need to preserve food by salting. In these respects, refrigeration is beneficial. Also see box 4.6.4 in chapter 4.6.

Additives, contaminants. There is little epidemiological evidence on any relationship between food additives and contaminants, whose use is subject to regulation, and the risk of cancer. Also see chapter 4.9.

Steaming, boiling, stewing, baking, roasting, frying, grilling (broiling), barbecuing (charbroiling). While evidence suggesting that grilled (broiled) and barbecued (charbroiled) animal foods are a cause of stomach cancer is limited, there is evidence from experimental settings showing that carcinogens are formed when meats, animal foods, and some other foods are cooked at very high temperatures, and most of all when they are exposed to direct flame. While the epidemiological evidence that these are causes of cancer is limited, it is a wise precaution to avoid foods cooked in this way. This effect is not found when foods are cooked by use of boiling water. Also see chapter 4.9.

for a relatively long time in warm, ambient temperatures, even if they show no visible signs of mould.

Guidance

At all stages in the food chain, from production to purchase and storage ready for food preparation, prefer methods of food preservation, processing, and preparation that keep perishable foods relatively fresh, and that do not involve the use of salt.

Salt is just one way to add savour to foods. Many herbs and spices can be used instead. After a period of time of limiting the use of salt, taste sensitivity to it increases, preference decreases, and the natural savour of food becomes apparent. Food labels give some guidance. Products advertised as 'reduced salt' may still be high in salt.

Keep food fresh by use of refrigeration. Discard food showing signs of mould (other than those such as some cheeses manufactured by use of benign moulds).

RECOMMENDATION 8

DIETARY SUPPLEMENTS

Aim to meet nutritional needs through diet alone[1]

PUBLIC HEALTH GOAL

Maximise the proportion of the population achieving nutritional adequacy without dietary supplements

---

PERSONAL RECOMMENDATION

Dietary supplements are not recommended for cancer prevention

---

[1] This may not always be feasible. In some situations of illness or dietary inadequacy, supplements may be valuable

---

Evidence

Randomised controlled trials have produced strong evidence that high-dose supplements of some nutrients modify the risk of some cancers.

The evidence that high-dose beta-carotene supplements are a cause of lung cancer in smokers is convincing. Calcium probably protects against cancers of the colorectum. Selenium in high doses probably protects against prostate cancer. It is unlikely that beta-carotene, or foods fortified with this constituent, have a substantial effect on the risk of cancers of the prostate or skin (non-melanoma). Also see chapters 4.2 and 4.10.

Justification

The evidence shows that high-dose nutrient supplements can be protective or can cause cancer. The studies that demonstrate such effects do not relate to widespread use among the general population, in whom the balance of risks and benefits cannot confidently be predicted. A general recommendation to consume supplements for cancer prevention might have unexpected adverse effects. Increasing the consumption of the relevant nutrients through the usual diet is preferred.

The recommendations of this Report, in common with its general approach, are food based. Vitamins, minerals, and other nutrients are assessed in the context of the foods and drinks that contain them. *The Panel judges* that the best source of nourishment is foods and drinks, not dietary supplements. There is evidence that high-dose dietary supplements can modify the risk of some cancers. Although some studies in specific, usually high-risk, groups have shown evidence of cancer prevention from some supplements, this finding may not apply to the general population. Their level of benefit may be different, and there may be unexpected and uncommon adverse effects. Therefore it is unwise to recommend widespread supplement use as a means of cancer prevention. Further details of evidence and judgements can be found in Chapter 4.

In general, for otherwise healthy people, inadequacy of intake of nutrients is best resolved by nutrient-dense diets and not by supplements, as these do not increase consumption of other potentially beneficial food constituents. *The Panel recognises* that there are situations when supplements are advisable. See box 12.4.

Public health goal
The points here are additional to that in the footnote above.

> Maximise the proportion of the population achieving
> nutritional adequacy without dietary supplements

In many parts of the world, nutritional inadequacy is endemic. In cases of crisis, it is necessary to supply supplements of nutrients to such populations or to fortify food to ensure at least minimum adequacy of nutritional status. The best approach is to protect or improve local food systems so that they are nutritionally adequate. The same applies in high-income countries, where impoverished communities and families, vulnerable people including those living alone, the elderly, and the chronically ill or infirm, are also liable to be

consuming nutritionally inadequate diets. In such cases of immediate need, supplementation is necessary. See box 12.4.

Personal recommendation
The points here are additional to that in the footnote above.

> Dietary supplements are not recommended
> for cancer prevention

This recommendation applies to self-administration of low (physiological) as well as high (pharmacological) doses of supplements, unless on the advice of a qualified health professional who can assess potential risks and benefits.

Guidance
Choose nutrient-rich foods and drinks instead of dietary supplements.

This can be done by following all the recommendations made here, in the context of appropriate general recommendations on food, nutrition, physical activity, and body composition, designed to protect against disease and to promote health and well-being.

Box 12.4 When supplements are advisable

The Panel judges that the use of supplements as possible protection against colorectal and prostate cancer should not be routinely recommended.

In general, as already stated, with secure food supplies and access to a variety of foods and drinks, when people follow the recommendations here in the context of general dietary recommendations, supplements are normally unnecessary. Furthermore, in diets, nutrients are present in combinations often not found in 'multi'-supplements, and with other bioactive substances.

The Panel recognises, however, that dietary supplements, in addition to varied diets, may at times be beneficial for specific population groups. Examples include vitamin B12 for people over the age of 50 who have difficulty absorbing naturally occurring vitamin B12, folic acid supplements for women who may become or are pregnant, and vitamin D supplements for people who are not exposed to sufficient sunlight or some people (such as the elderly or people with dark skin) who do not synthesise adequate vitamin D from sunlight.

The Panel advises against self-administration of supplements as protection against specific cancers. The findings on calcium and selenium apply in specific settings and specific doses. A recommendation for routine consumption in the general population might show a different balance of risks and benefits. Advice for individuals whose particular circumstances have been assessed is best given in a clinical setting in consultation with an appropriately qualified professional.

SPECIAL RECOMMENDATION 1

BREASTFEEDING

Mothers to breastfeed; children to be breastfed[1]

PUBLIC HEALTH GOAL

The majority of mothers to breastfeed
exclusively, for six months[2] [3]

PERSONAL RECOMMENDATION

Aim to breastfeed infants exclusively[2]
up to six months and continue
with complementary feeding thereafter[3]

[1] Breastfeeding protects both mother and child
[2] 'Exclusively' means human milk only, with no other food or drink, including water
[3] In accordance with the UN Global Strategy on Infant and Young Child Feeding

Evidence

The evidence on cancer supports the evidence on well-being, positive health, and prevention of other diseases: at the beginning of life, human milk is best.

The evidence that lactation protects the mother against breast cancer at all ages is convincing. There is limited evidence suggesting that lactation protects the mother against cancer of the ovary. Having been breastfed probably protects children against overweight and obesity, and therefore those cancers for which weight gain, overweight, and obesity are a cause. Overweight and obesity in children tend to track into adult life. Also see recommendation 1 and chapters 6.3, 7.10, and 8.

Justification

The evidence on cancer as well as other diseases shows that sustained, exclusive breastfeeding is protective for the mother as well as the child.

This is the first major report concerned with the prevention of cancer to make a recommendation specifically on breastfeeding, to prevent breast cancer in mothers, and to prevent overweight and obesity in children. Further details of evidence and judgements can be found in Chapters 6 and 8.

Other benefits of breastfeeding for mothers and their children are well known. Breastfeeding protects against infections in infancy, protects the development of the immature immune system, protects against other childhood diseases, and is vital for the development of the bond between mother and child. It has many other benefits. Breastfeeding is especially vital in parts of the world where water supplies are not safe and where impoverished families do not readily have the money to buy infant formula and other infant and young child foods.

This recommendation has a special significance. While derived from the evidence on being breastfed, it also indicates that policies and actions designed to prevent cancer need to be directed throughout the whole life course, from the beginning of life.

Public health goal
The points here are additional to those made in the footnotes to the goal above.

The majority of mothers to breastfeed
exclusively, for six months

Sustained, exclusive breastfeeding was the norm until the development and marketing of infant formulas, which largely replaced breastfeeding in high-income and then in most countries by the second half of the 20th century.

While the practice of breastfeeding and exclusive breastfeeding has been increasing in many countries in recent decades, in most countries now only a minority of mothers exclusively breastfeed their babies until four months, and an even smaller number until six months.

This is the context for this goal, which like the others specified here, is designed as a guide for national and other population policies. It does not imply that in any population where over half of all mothers breastfeed exclusively for six months that the ultimate goal has been reached: the greater the proportion, the better. Its achievement will require increased support from regulatory authorities and from the manufacturers of infant formulas. Policy-makers are encouraged to frame goals according to their specific circumstances.

The Panel emphasises the importance of exclusive breastfeeding (other than vitamin drops where locally recommended), with no other sustenance, including water.

There are special situations where breastfeeding is recommended with caution or is not advised. The main special situation is when mothers have HIV/AIDS. On this, the UN Global Strategy as revised in late 2006 states: 'Exclusive breastfeeding is recommended for HIV-infected women for the first six months of life unless replacement feeding is acceptable, feasible, affordable, sustainable, and safe for them and their infants before that time.'

Personal recommendation
The points here are additional to those made in the footnotes to the recommendations above.

Aim to breastfeed infants exclusively
up to six months and continue
with complementary feeding thereafter

This and the population goal are references to the UN Global Strategy on Infant and Young Child Feeding, which is endorsed by the Panel. None of the phrasing of the goals and recommendations here is designed to modify the Strategy, which allows for special circumstances, including those in which mothers are not able to breastfeed their babies or may otherwise be well advised not to do so.

Guidance

On breastfeeding, the Panel endorses the UN Global Strategy on Infant and Young Child Feeding.

It is universally agreed, by UN agencies, national governments, health professionals, civil society organisations, and the infant formula and milk industries, that human milk is the best food for infants and young children. Therefore, this Report recommends that mothers breastfeed exclusively, for six months, as recommended in the Strategy.

SPECIAL RECOMMENDATION 2

CANCER SURVIVORS[1]

**Follow the recommendations
for cancer prevention[2]**

RECOMMENDATIONS

All cancer survivors[3] to receive nutritional care
from an appropriately trained professional

If able to do so, and unless otherwise advised,
aim to follow the recommendations for
diet, healthy weight, and physical activity[2]

---

[1] Cancer survivors are people who are living with a diagnosis of cancer, including those who have recovered from the disease
[2] This recommendation does not apply to those who are undergoing active treatment, subject to the qualifications in the text
[3] This includes all cancer survivors, before, during, and after active treatment

---

Evidence

The available evidence on cancer survivors has limitations. It is of variable quality; it is difficult to interpret; and it has not yet produced impressive results. The evidence for this review does not include the active treatment period.

The term 'cancer survivor' denotes people in a very wide range of circumstances. It is unlikely that specific recommendations based on evidence applying to any one group of people would apply to all cancer survivors.

In no case is the evidence specifically on cancer survivors clear enough to make any firm judgements or recommendations that apply to cancer survivors as a whole, or to those who are survivors of any specific cancer.

Justification

Subject to the qualifications made here, *the Panel has agreed that its recommendations apply also to cancer survivors. There may be specific situations where this advice may not apply, for instance, where treatment has compromised gastrointestinal function.*

If possible, when appropriate, and unless advised otherwise by a qualified professional, the recommendations of this Report also apply to cancer survivors. The Panel has made this judgement based on its examination of the evidence, including that specifically on cancer survivors, and also on its collective knowledge of the pathology of cancer and its interactions with food, nutrition, physical activity, and body composition. In no case is the evidence specifically on cancer survivors clear enough to make any firm judgements or recommendations to cancer survivors. Further details of evidence and judgements can be found in Chapter 9.

Treatment for many cancers is increasingly successful, and so cancer survivors increasingly are living long enough to develop new primary cancers or other chronic diseases. The recommendations in this Report would also be expected to reduce risk of those conditions, and so can also be recommended on that account.

Recommendations

In the special circumstances of cancer survivors, who until they have recovered from the disease are in a clinical setting, *the Panel decided* not to separate public health goals and personal recommendations. The points here are additional to those made in the footnotes above.

All cancer survivors to receive nutritional care from an appropriately trained professional

The circumstances of cancer survivors vary greatly. Given the increased importance of food, nutrition, physical activity, and body composition in cancer survival, people who have received a diagnosis of cancer should consult an appropriately trained health professional as soon as possible. The advice received will be designed to take their personal situation and circumstances into account.

People who are undergoing surgical, chemical, or radiotherapy for cancer are likely to have special nutritional requirements; as are people after treatment whose ability to consume or metabolise food has been altered by treatment; and people in the later stages of cancer whose immediate need is to arrest or slow down weight loss. These are all clinical situations where the advice of an appropriately trained health professional is essential.

The evidence does not support the use of high-dose supplements of microconstituents as a means of improving outcome. Cancer survivors should consult their physician and/or a qualified nutrition professional, who can evaluate the safety and efficacy of specific dietary supplements, and counsel appropriate action based on current research relevant to their particular clinical situation.

All cancer survivors to aim to follow the recommendations for diet, healthy weight, and physical activity

This general approach is for cancer survivors who are able, and have not been advised otherwise, to follow the recommendations of this Report.

There is growing evidence that physical activity and other measures that control weight may help to prevent cancer recurrence, particularly breast cancer. These findings are in line with the recommendations of this Report. Cancer survivors are also likely to gain health benefit, and a sense of control, from regular physical activity at levels that they can sustain.

Guidance

The general purpose of the recommendations made in this Report is to 'stop cancer before it starts'. Crucial support will be given to cancer survivors who decide to follow the overall recommendations made in this chapter, when the people living closest to them also make this choice. As well as giving crucial support and improving the quality of life of the cancer survivor, they will also be reducing their own risk of cancer.

12.3 Patterns of food, nutrition, and physical activity

Those responsible for reports such as this are faced with a number of challenges. Information, even from high-income countries where most research is carried out, is incomplete and often patchy, and that from many countries is fragmentary. Most modern research in the nutritional and other biological sciences is highly focused. Many researchers address not just what foods affect the risk of disease, but what specific agent or agents in the food are responsible, or the exact biological pathway involved. The amount of data produced by such studies is multiplying and its sheer volume can obscure the general view needed as a basis for public health goals and personal recommendations.

As a result, until relatively recently, expert reports concerned with the prevention of disease tended to frame their conclusions and recommendations in terms of specific dietary constituents being the most relevant factors modifying the risk of disease. Thus, since the 1960s, reports concerned with prevention of coronary heart disease have recommended cuts in consumption of saturated fats and of dietary cholesterol. Such recommendations, while staying closer to the science as usually carried out, and of value to planners of food supplies and in the formulation of manufactured food, are less effective as ways of encouraging healthy choices of foods and drinks. People consume foods and drinks, rather than nutrients.

Also, what people eat and drink and how they behave are only partly a matter of choice. Many other factors are involved including income, climate, and culture. Although food supplies are now becoming increasingly globalised, the people of South India are not likely to move to meat-based diets, nor will most people in the USA adopt lentils as staple foods.

More recently, some reports have adopted a food-based approach to the prevention of disease and the promotion of well-being. This has presented the expert panels responsible for reports such as this one with another challenge. This is to review, assess, and judge the evidence in ways that respect its nature, yet at the same time also seek to discern 'the bigger picture'. A further challenge is to identify healthy patterns of food, nutrition, and physical activity that allow for — indeed encourage — the diversity both of traditional and modern food systems and cuisines.

12.3.1 The integrated approach

Since its work began, five years before publication of this Report, the Panel has used a broad, integrative approach. This, while largely derived from conventional 'reductionist' research, has sought to find patterns of consumption of foods and drinks, degrees of physical activity, and scale of body composition that lead to recommendations designed to prevent cancer at personal and population levels.

This approach has proved to work. As recommendation 2 indicates, meticulous examination of the many studies on physical activity and the risk of cancer shows that all types of activity — occupational, transport, domestic, recreational — do or may protect against some cancers. The type of activity is evidently unimportant. Given the general tendency of populations living in industrialised and urbanised societies to become increasingly sedentary, this enables clear recommendations designed to encourage increased levels of physical activity.

At a more detailed level, the same point applies to alcoholic drinks, as indicated in recommendation 6. Many studies have been undertaken to examine the relationship of beer, wine, and spirits (liquor) to the risk of cancer — and to other diseases. Taken all together, these show that it is alcoholic drinks in general — which is to say, the amount of ethanol consumed — that are or may be a cause of some cancers. Again, this enables the framing of clear recommendations that take into account the effect of modest amounts of alcoholic drinks on the risk of coronary heart disease.

Recommendations 3, 4, and 5 also show how the integrated approach stays with the science and, by looking for patterns, can create broad public and personal health messages. After particularly careful discussions, *the Panel agreed* that a key factor determining vulnerability to weight gain, overweight, and obesity, and thus to those cancers whose risk is increased in these ways, is not so much specific foods, drinks, or nutrients, but the relative energy density of diets. This is not an obvious conclusion from the studies whose results form the basis for this judgement. Up to now, epidemiologists have rarely used energy density as a concept in the design of their studies.

Comparably, the vast amount of evidence on specific foods and drinks does indeed show a more general pattern with vegetables and fruits, and with red and processed meat. In framing recommendations 4 and 5, *the Panel agreed* that recommendations on these types of food should be seen in the broader context of plant and animal foods. This is not a new conclusion. Plant-based diets, which is to say diets within which foods of plant origin are more central than is typical in industrialised and urbanised settings, are now commonly recognised as protective against some cancers. Again, the judgement requires qualification, as has been done in the footnotes and text. Many foods of animal origin are nourishing, and only the evidence on red meat and on processed meat is strong enough to justify specific recommendations. Nevertheless, with such precautions, *the Panel has agreed* that dietary patterns in which foods of plant origin are more central, with red meat less so, are protective.

12.3.2 Nutritional patterns

The recommendations made in this Report do not specify every major type of food and drink. In this sense they do not, taken together, amount to whole diets. Nevertheless, combined with the text that accompanies them, they are likely to promote the nutritional adequacy of diets and healthy body composition. For this and other reasons, they will also be expected to help prevent nutritional deficiencies and related infectious diseases.

Thus, a diet based on these recommendations is likely to have modest fat content (through limiting energy-dense foods), especially in saturated fatty acids (limiting red and processed meat); to be relatively high in starch and fibre (from emphasis on relatively unprocessed plant foods including cereals (grains)), while being low in sugar (due to limiting energy-dense foods and sugary drinks). Overall, the macronutrient profile is likely to be similar to that recommended in authoritative reports concerned more gener-ally with prevention of other chronic diseases.

A number of the positive recommendations derive from evidence on foods that contribute various micronutrients to the diet. These, including relatively unprocessed cereals (grains), vegetables and fruits, and pulses (legumes), as well as various foods of animal origin, would be expected to supply ample vitamin A (mostly in the form of carotenoids), folate, other B vitamins including vitamin B12, vitamin C, vitamin E, selenium, iron, zinc, potassium, and indeed sodium.

12.3.3 Integration with national recommendations

In national settings, the recommendations of this Report will be best used in combination with recommendations issued by governments or on behalf of nations, designed to prevent chronic and other diseases. Also see box 12.5.

In the Panel's judgement, based on its collective knowledge of food, nutrition, physical activity, and disease prevention, and also experience of national contexts, the recommendations here are likely to be harmonious with those designed to prevent disease in specific countries, which take local and national dietary patterns, food cultures, and social and other circumstances into account.

Box 12.5 Regional and special circumstances

The goals and recommendations specified in 12.2 are generally relevant worldwide.

In three cases, evidence that is strong enough to be the basis for goals and recommendations is of importance only in discrete geographical regions. That is not to say that if the same foods or drinks were consumed elsewhere they would not have the same effect, but rather that currently, people in the rest of the world do not consume them. These are the herbal drink maté, probably a cause of oesophageal cancer; Cantonese-style salted fish, probably a cause of nasopharyngeal cancer; and contamination of water supplies with arsenic, a cause of lung cancer and (probably) skin cancer. *The Panel considers* that detailed goals and recommendations in these cases are most appropriately set by local and/or regional regulatory authorities, other policy-makers, and health professionals in the countries affected.

Maté

As stated in chapter 4.7 and elsewhere, maté is a herbal infusion originally cultivated and drunk by the original inhabitants in Argentina, Uruguay, and Rio Grande do Sul in Brazil, where it is now adopted as a staple drink. Reports on the prevention of cancer have identified maté as a cause or possible cause of cancers of the oral cavity

and oesophagus. The product is commonly available in supermarkets in many countries, but the evidence shows that the causal factor is maté drunk very hot through a metal straw often left resting on the lip, the form traditional within Latin America. It is probable that the cause of cancer is not the herb but the thermic effect.

RECOMMENDATION

Avoid consumption of maté as drunk in parts of Latin America, very hot and through a metal straw.

Cantonese-style salted fish

Cantonese-style salted fish, as stated in chapter 4.3 and elsewhere, is part of the traditional diet consumed by people living around the Pearl River Delta region in southern China, and has been given to children, even as part of a weaning diet. This style of fish is prepared with less salt than used on the northern Chinese littoral, is allowed to ferment, and so is eaten in a decomposed state. While it is also consumed by communities of emigrants from the Pearl River Delta in other countries, this particular preparation of fish is not otherwise an issue, and there is no good evidence that other forms of preserved fish affect the risk of cancer.

RECOMMENDATIONS

Avoid consumption of Cantonese-style salted fish.

Children not to eat this type of fish.

Arsenic in water

Contamination of water supplies with arsenic is a different type of special case. This may happen as a result of release of industrial effluents, and also because of geological and other environmental circumstances. High concentrations of arsenic in drinking water have been found in areas of Bangladesh, China, and West Bengal (India); and also in more localised areas of Argentina, Australia, Chile, Mexico, Taiwan, China, the USA, and Vietnam. Arsenic is classed as a carcinogen by the International Agency for Research on Cancer.

RECOMMENDATIONS

Avoid use of any source of water that may be contaminated with arsenic.

Authorities to ensure that safe water supplies are available where such contamination occurs.

12.3.4 General patterns

The Panel has not been able to base its recommendations on general patterns of food and nutrition, as stated above, on evidence specifically directed towards that question. Reasons for this, as summarised in chapter 4.9, are that relatively few epidemiological studies examine diets in an integrated form; and of these, most do not define the nature of such diets in a way that can be compared with other studies. Those that do, such as studies of Seventh-day Adventists, often examine the effects of whole ways of life, including factors that may confound findings specifically on food, nutrition, and physical activity.

For the future, *the Panel recommends* that protocols be agreed to enable well conducted epidemiological studies to be carried out on patterns of food, nutrition, and of physical activity, using agreed definitions and methods that allow comparisons and detailed analyses.

A number of traditional and more modern food systems generate a variety of climatically and culturally appropriate, delicious, and nourishing cuisines that are harmonious with the recommendations made here. These include the many traditional cuisines of the Mediterranean littoral, and of South-East and East Asia, and some diets devised since the industrialisation and internationalisation of food systems. The latter are often adaptations of traditional diets, enjoyed by people in higher income countries as part of generally healthy ways of life.

12.3.5 Health, well-being, and ways of life

Throughout our work we, the members of this Panel, have been aware that prevention of cancer through changes to food and nutrition, physical activity, and body composition is a major global, regional, and national task; and also that this work is one part of a greater task, to prevent disease and to promote well-being throughout the world, sustainably and equitably.

As part of this task, integrated and comprehensive programmes should be developed on cancer prevention, together with prevention of other chronic diseases, such as type 2 diabetes, cardiovascular diseases, osteoporosis, other chronic diseases, and also nutrient deficiencies and relevant infectious diseases, especially of early childhood. This approach, broader than any now undertaken within the UN system, would need to be coordinated by relevant international and national organisations.

All reports on the prevention of cancer must emphasise the fundamental importance of tobacco control, as we do here. The one habit that most unequivocally is a cause of cancer is smoking, and other use of and exposure to tobacco. Partly because of its addictive nature, and for other reasons, tobacco smoking is not a simple matter of personal choice. Its reduction requires vigilant commitment from governments and civil society at all levels.

In general, ways of life — patterns of behaviour within societies — are never just personal matters. In this Report, we have concentrated our attention on nutritional and associated factors that affect the risk of cancer, and our goals and recommendations here for populations and for people are framed accordingly. An associated report to be published in late 2008 will deal with the social and environmental factors that influence the risk of cancer, with appropriate recommendations.

Appendices

APPENDIX A

Project process

How this Report has been achieved

This Report follows, develops, and replaces *Food, Nutrition and the Prevention of Cancer: a global perspective,* the first report commissioned by the World Cancer Research Fund together with the American Institute for Cancer Research, which was published in 1997.

In 2001, WCRF and AICR agreed that it was time to commission a new report. Since the mid 1990s, the amount of scientific literature on this subject has dramatically increased. New methods of analysing and assessing evidence have been developed, facilitated by advances in electronic technology. There is more evidence, in particular on overweight and obesity and on physical activity. Examining food, nutrition, and physical activity in relation to cancer survivors is a new field of study. The need for a new report was obvious, and a multilevel process involving global collaboration was put in place.

Commissioning this Report

The goal of this second Report, *Food, Nutrition, Physical Activity, and the Prevention of Cancer: a Global Perspective,* has been to identify, review, and assess all the relevant research to date. It has used the most meticulous methods for assessment and review in order to generate a comprehensive series of recommendations on food, nutrition, and physical activity suitable for all societies and designed to reduce the risk of cancer. The process has also been devised as the basis for a continuous review that will keep the evidence updated into the future.

The process was organised into overlapping stages, designed to ensure objectivity and transparency as well as separation between the collection of evidence and the business of assessing and judging it. First, an expert task force developed a method for systematic review of the voluminous scientific literature. Second, research teams collected and reviewed the literature based upon this methodology. Third, an expert Panel assessed and judged this evidence and agreed recommendations. The results are published in this Report.

The whole project has taken six years, with the launch and distribution of the second Report taking place in November 2007.

Agreeing the methodology

As a first stage, WCRF International developed an appropriate method for collecting, synthesising, analysing, and reporting the evidence. In 2002, a Methodology Task Force of experts in nutrition, cancer, epidemiology, methodology, and statistics was convened. This Task Force drew on the accumulated experience of existing techniques to develop a unique new process. The methodology is described in a *Systematic Literature Review Specification Manual,* which contains the instructions for conducting the systematic reviews.

The methods specified in the manual were tested at two centres, one in the USA and the other in the UK, and as a result the manual was modified. It has formed the basis of all the reviews of the literature on food, nutrition, physical activity, and the risk of cancer for all relevant cancer sites and on weight gain, overweight, and obesity.

Reviewing the literature

WCRF International then invited scientific centres to bid for the work of systematic literature review (SLR), and contracted with nine institutions in Europe and North America to conduct reviews of the literature on all cancer sites where evidence of links with food, nutrition, and associated factors was already apparent, as well as that on determinants of overweight and obesity, and on authoritative reports concerned with other diseases. The project team from each centre included expertise in epidemiology, nutrition, cancer, mechanisms, statistics, and project management. Teams have been supported by a review coordinator — a member of the WCRF International Secretariat. All reviews have included the relevant epidemiological and experimental literature.

Using the specification manual to ensure a comprehensive and consistent approach to the analysis plus a common format for displaying the evidence, each centre undertook one or more SLRs and produced a report on the evidence for each cancer site. The reports were subject to peer review both at the initial protocol stage and when the reports were submitted in complete form. They were then revised before being summarised and submitted to the Panel. The systematic reviews present the findings of the review teams based on the agreed protocol. They stop short of assessing or judging the strength and implications of the evidence.

Judging the evidence

The Panel of 21 experts was convened by WRCF International in 2003 to develop the second Report. Members of the Panel come from all the main continents and from 11 countries. Its collective expertise includes nutrition, cancer, obesity, other chronic diseases, physical activity, epidemiology, biochemistry, statistics, public health, and public policy. The Panel includes members of the Panel from the first WCRF/AICR report and relevant World Health Organization expert consultations, as well as observers from the Methodology Task Force and the Mechanisms Working Group and from six relevant United Nations and other international organisations. The Panel convened twice a year for three- or four-day meetings between 2003 and 2007.

The Panel has been responsible for assessing the evidence from the SLRs, for agreeing judgements based on their assessments, and for agreeing a comprehensive set of recommendations. The Panel has also been responsible for identifying issues arising from this work that would be appropriate topics for future research.

For the next stage, the Panel, supplemented by additional expertise, examined the evidence on the determinants of dietary and activity patterns, and of obesity, and the effectiveness of interventions from personal to population level. Publication of this separate report is due in late 2008.

Managing the project

The second Report was commissioned by WCRF International and has been funded and published by WCRF/AICR. WCRF International set up a multilevel process to manage the project, and an Executive Team was established with the specific responsibility of directing it.

Executive Team:	Executive body responsible for Report. Composed of WCRF International and AICR executives and advisors.
Secretariat:	Manages the whole report process.
Advisory Group:	Guides the Executive Team and the Panel on policy and strategic and technical issues

The Secretariat has included WCRF International staff in the UK, AICR staff in the USA, and consultants, including in the following positions:

Project Director:	Overall responsibility for the report and its scientific content. Chair of Executive Team.
Chief Editor:	Responsible for editorial quality of the report. Chair of Advisory Group.
Project Manager:	Responsible for day-to-day management of the project; Chair of Secretariat.
Chapter Managers:	Drive progress on chapters of the report.

In addition to the work of producing the second Report, a Communications Strategy Group from within the WCRF global network was set up to be responsible for all aspects of the promotion of the report before, during, and after its launch in November 2007.

Keeping up to date

This Report is meant to guide future scientific research, cancer prevention education programmes, and health policy around the world. It provides a solid evidence base for policy-makers, health professionals, researchers, and informed and interested people to draw on and work with.

WCRF International has been mindful that the literature is continually expanding, and has commissioned a continuous review of the evidence. This process will be overseen by an expert panel convened by WCRF International, responsible for assessing and judging the updated evidence as a basis for recommendations and action to prevent cancer worldwide.

Process for the second Expert Report

Peer Reviewers
Review protocol and end product developed by Literature Review Teams

Panel
Interpretation of the evidence
Development of recommendations
Final report content

Methodology Task Force
Develop methodology (specification manual) to be used in reviews

Systematic Literature Review Teams
Perform reviews on link between food, nutrition and cancer

Advisory Group
Guidance and feedback to Literature Review Teams

NEW EXPERT REPORT

STAGE 1   STAGE 2   STAGE 3

World Cancer Research Fund   American Institute for Cancer Research

The first WCRF/AICR Expert Report

In September 1997, the World Cancer Research Fund and its affiliate in the USA, the American Institute for Cancer Research, jointly published *Food, Nutrition and the Prevention of Cancer: a global perspective*.

On publication, this 670-page WCRF/AICR report, in its distinctive blue cover, and with its accompanying summary, was immediately recognised as the most authoritative and influential in its field. It became the standard text worldwide for policy-makers in government at all levels, for civil society and health professional organisations, and in teaching and research for centres of academic excellence.

Responsibility for the first report and its conclusions and recommendations was taken by a panel of scientists convened by WCRF/AICR, chaired by Professor John Potter. Panel members came from Africa, Asia (India, China, Japan) and Latin America, as well as Europe and the USA. The collective knowledge of the panel included nutrition, cancer, other chronic diseases, energy balance, epidemiology, biochemistry, toxicology, statistics, public health, and public policy.

Official observers came from the World Health Organization, the International Agency for Research on Cancer, the Food and Agriculture Organization of the United Nations, and the US National Cancer Institute. The Panel, supported by a WCRF Secretariat, held a series of seven three-day meetings between 1993 and 1997.

Special features

The first report had a number of special features, adapted and developed in this second Report. All its findings were introduced and summarised in plain language, to make the science and its significance as clear and accessible as possible. This facilitated its use as a tool for policy-makers at all levels from international government to municipalities, schools, and hospitals, as well as the standard basis for academic teaching and practice.

The panel responsible for the first report concluded that worldwide, around 4 million deaths each year are preventable by adoption of its recommendations. Part of the purpose of the report was to show that prevention of cancer by means of food, nutrition, and associated factors is as feasible and crucial as prevention of coronary heart disease. Its recommendations take into account prevention of other chronic diseases, and also prevention of nutritional deficiencies and food-related infectious diseases.

The conclusions of the first report were based on method-ical reviews of the epidemiological, experimental, and other relevant expert literature. The judgements of the panel were presented in the form of matrices, adapted for this second Report. This matrix approach, in which judgements such as 'convincing' and 'probable' were displayed according to common specified criteria on the relative strength of evidence, was pioneered in the first WCRF/AICR report.

The 14 recommendations of the 1997 report are food based. Taken together, they amount to whole diets judged to give the best protection against cancer, other chronic diseases, and also other food-related diseases. The first report also included a chapter on the public policy implications of its recommendations. As part of the second Report process, this aspect is the subject of a separate report to be published in late 2008.

Impact and influence

WCRF/AICR has a special commitment to ensure that the work for which it is responsible has a global impact and that its reports are placed in the right hands. Accordingly, over 30 000 copies of the first report and of its summary have been distributed throughout the world, to policy-makers in government, to health professional and civil society organisations, to scientists responsible for research and prevention, and to all other qualified and interested people.

In addition, the report and its summary have been translated or adapted for a number of regions and countries, including Latin America, China, Japan, India, Germany, France, Italy, and the Asia-Pacific region.

The report has had a powerful impact on cancer prevention at all levels. Governments and authoritative organisations around the world use it to shape public health policy. The 2003 WHO report, *Diet, Nutrition and the Prevention of Chronic Diseases*, the scientific basis for the WHO Global Strategy on Diet, Physical Activity and Health, adapted the methods pioneered by WCRF to classify the strength of scientific evidence and to display evidence-based judgements in the form of matrices.

Research scientists use the first report as a basis for their work. Academics and public health educators use it as the pre-eminent textbook. Having set the agenda in its field, it is frequently cited in the academic and professional literature and at international scientific conferences. It has stimulated debate about how best to engage in a systematic and objective interpretation of the scientific data on food, nutrition, and the prevention of cancer.

Directly, and also indirectly through its influence on professionals, it guides communities, families, and individuals throughout the world as they make choices about their food and nutrition, physical activity, and weight management. The report has also been used as the basis for the research, education, and associated programmes of the WCRF global network in the USA, the UK, the Netherlands, China (Hong Kong), and France, which together distribute tens of millions of brochures and newsletters each year to assist their supporters and to fulfil their missions.

The first report laid solid foundations for this second Report, which has developed its methods and made use of the latest electronic technology in compiling, displaying, and assessing the evidence. The overall purpose of both reports has been, and will remain, that of WCRF and AICR: to prevent cancer, worldwide.

The World Cancer Research Fund global network

Since its foundation in 1982, the World Cancer Research Fund global network has been dedicated to the prevention of cancer. All the members of the global network have the same mission: to prevent cancer worldwide.

Cancer is a global disease. Some types of cancer are more common in the higher income countries of Europe, North America, and elsewhere. Other types are more common in Africa and Asia and other lower-income parts of the world; and as shown in Chapter 1 of this Report, these are among the many compelling reasons why it is necessary to study cancer from a global perspective in order to understand how best to prevent cancer in any one country.

The WCRF global network consists of WCRF International and its member organisations. These are national charities based in the USA, the UK, the Netherlands, France, and Hong Kong.

Each member organisation is supported by donations from the public and is independent of government. Each is a separate legal entity, responsible to its own board and accountable to the donors who support it. All member organisations determine their own programmes, which are designed to be most effective in national and local environments. Through national education and research programmes, a primary goal of the WCRF global network is to help promote changes that will decrease rates of cancer incidence. WCRF International provides each member with financial, operational, and scientific services and support.

Education

The extensive education programmes of the global network encourage and enable individuals, families, and communities to make healthy choices. Until 2007, these were based on the six *Diet and Health Guidelines for Cancer Prevention*, developed from the recommendations made in the first expert report published in 1997 (see Appendix B).

All the global network's education programmes reflect the most current research and the latest scientific agreements. A prime purpose of this second Report is to provide the basis for the WCRF global network's education programmes from 2007.

All network member organisations produce a wide variety of publications. Collectively, these are the most extensive in their field. They include a quarterly newsletter, booklets, brochures, and leaflets covering many themes, from the latest information on antioxidants to suggestions for the quick preparation of healthy meals. The emphasis is on easy tips

and support for individuals and their families to adopt healthy ways of life. Public seminars and specific materials for dieticians, scientists, parents, and children all ensure that relevant information reaches these specific groups in appropriate formats and language. National websites provide an immediate and interactive communication tool with the facility for nutrition hot lines, recipe corners, and daily tips, in addition to access to the wide range of educational materials.

Research

The global network funds research worldwide on the role of food, nutrition, physical activity, and associated factors in the causation and prevention of cancer. There are two research grant programmes within the network. One is operated by WCRF International in London; the other is based with the American Institute for Cancer Research, a member of the network, in Washington, DC. The programmes support epidemiological studies and basic laboratory research. In 2007, the cumulative research funding by all members of the WCRF global network amounts to over $US 105 million, supporting almost 800 projects and involving over a thousand scientists from 23 countries.

The research issues raised in Chapter 11 of this Report will be the basis for setting new research priorities for the global network.

Global impact

In its first year in 1982, AICR, with the agreement of the US National Academy of Sciences, reprinted the pioneering NAS report on *Diet, Nutrition and Cancer* and distributed it to policy-makers, opinion-formers, and health professionals throughout the USA. The findings and recommendations of the NAS report became the first basis for the education and other programmes of AICR.

Following the foundation of WCRF in the UK in 1990, the decision was taken to commission a new report with a global perspective. This work took five years. The result was the first report, published by WCRF together with AICR in 1997 (see Appendix B). With the development of the global network, the science in the field, and new understanding of the causes of cancer, the decision was taken in 2001 to commission this second Report, which has also been a five-year task. This Report will enable the global network to deliver the most current and reliable advice on food, nutrition, physical activity, body composition, and associated factors, in order to reduce the risk of cancer. It replaces the 1997 report as the leading work of reference and basis for action in the field, throughout the world.

The global network is already committed to continue this work by continuous updating and evaluation of the scientific evidence. This commitment means that the network is now able to offer the best and most reliable advice now and also in the future.

The global network is also proud of its work done in association with United Nations and other authoritative international and national organisations. This work is concerned with the prevention of cancer, and also the prevention of other diseases. The methods and findings of the first and now this Report are offered as a basis for the work of other organisations that are also committed to the prevention of disease and the promotion of health and well-being, worldwide.

Our membership

World Cancer Research Fund International is the association that coordinates the global network. The greatest impact can be achieved when allied organisations work together. Founded in 1999 and based in London and the USA, WCRF International maximises the potential of each member organisation, and strengthens their work. The commissioning and funding of this Report, and provision of the secretariat, is an example of all members of the global network combining together. This has required collaboration on a global basis, in the interests of the network and all its members, and to further their joint mission.

Founded in 1982, The *American Institute for Cancer Research* was the first organisation to focus exclusively on the link between diet and cancer, and became the first member of the WCRF global network. Located in Washington, DC, AICR is now one of the largest cancer charities in the USA, funding scientific research and offering a wide range of education programmes.

World Cancer Research Fund UK became the second member of the global network when it was established in 1990. Based in London, it is the UK's leading charity in the field of diet, nutrition, and cancer prevention, and is responsible for raising awareness of the diet and cancer link among scientists, public health officials, media, and the general public.

Wereld Kanker Onderzoek Fonds (WCRF NL) began work in 1994 in the Netherlands as the third member of the global network. Based in Amsterdam, it is the only Dutch char-

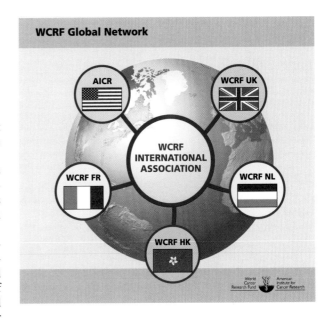

WCRF Global Network

ity specialising in cancer prevention by means of food, nutrition, physical activity, and associated factors, and has already made a major contribution to the acceptance of this message in the Netherlands.

World Cancer Research Fund Hong Kong (WCRF HK) began work in 2002. As traditional Chinese diets have been replaced by more western diets, patterns of cancer incidence are changing. WCRF HK is playing a vital role, especially in working with government health departments in Hong Kong, to disseminate education and research programmes on cancer prevention.

Fonds Mondial de Recherche contre le Cancer (WCRF FR), founded in 2004, is the latest member of the WCRF global network. Based in Paris, WCRF FR is building its research and education programmes, working with like-minded organisations to disseminate the vital information to help people to make healthy choices and so reduce their risk of cancer.

From its beginnings in the early 1980s, the WCRF global network has consistently been a pioneer and a leader of research and education on food, nutrition, physical activity, and the prevention of cancer. The network has a special commitment to creation of the most reliable science-based recommendations and their translation into messages that form the basis for action by professionals, communities, families, and individuals.

This work is being done for these organisations in the USA, the UK, the Netherlands, France, and Hong Kong, and on behalf of people in all countries. The global network will remain one of the leaders of the international cancer prevention movement, in the broader context of better personal and public health, worldwide.

Glossary

Terms here are defined in the context of this Report. Some terms may have other meanings in other contexts.

Absorption
The movement of **nutrients** and other food constituents from the gut into the blood.

Acid-base balance
The appropriate acidity of the blood and tissues. Abnormal acid-base balance may indicate a change in respiratory or metabolic status.

Adduct (see **DNA adduct**)

Adenocarcinoma
Cancer of glandular **epithelial** cells.

Adenosine triphosphate (ATP)
The principal molecule used for storage and transfer of **energy** in metabolic processes.

Adipose tissue
Body fat. Tissue comprising mainly cells (adipocytes) containing triglyceride. It acts as an **energy** reserve, provides insulation and protection, and secretes metabolically active **hormones**.

Adiposity rebound
The age at which **body mass index** (BMI) increases after reaching a nadir at around 4–6 years of age. Earlier age of adiposity rebound has been linked to later development of **obesity**.

Adjustment
A statistical tool for taking into account the effect of known **confounders** (see box 3.1).

Adrenarche
The period, typically between age 6 and 10 years, characterised by an increase in secretion of **androgens** from the adrenal cortex.

Aerobic metabolism
The normal process of producing **ATP** as a source of **energy** using oxygen.

Aflatoxins
Naturally-occurring **mycotoxins** that are produced by many species of *Aspergillus*, a fungus, most notably *Aspergillus flavus* and *Aspergillus parasiticus*. Aflatoxins are toxic and carcinogenic to animals, including humans (see box 4.1.4).

Age-adjusted incidence
The number of events in a population, usually expressed per 100,000 people, over a defined period of time, adjusted for the varying proportion of people in each age group between populations and over time. It allows for comparisons between countries with different age structures (see box 7.1.1).

Alpha-linolenic acid
An essential n-3 **polyunsaturated fatty acid** (C18:3 n3).

Amenorrhoea
The absence of menstruation.

Amino acid
An **organic compound** containing an amino group and a carboxylic acid group. The basic building blocks of proteins such as **enzymes**.

Anaerobic metabolism
The process of producing **ATP** as a source of **energy** without oxygen, resulting in lactic acid accumulation.

Androgen
Any masculinising sex **hormone**, such as **testosterone**.

Angiogenesis
The process of generating new blood vessels.

Antioxidants
Any substance that inhibits oxidation or traps or quenches **reactive oxygen species** generated during metabolism.

Anthropometric measures
Measures of body dimensions.

ATP (see **adenosine triphosphate**)

Basal energy expenditure (see **basal metabolic rate**)

Basal metabolic rate (BMR)
The amount of **energy** required to maintain the essential body functions in resting and fasting conditions, expressed as megajoules, kilojoules, or kilocalories per minute, hour, or day.

Begg's test
A statistical test for small study effects such as **publication bias**.

Beta-glucans
Non-starch polysaccharides composed of glucose subunits linked in such a way as to render them indigestible by pancreatic amylase. A major component of the cell wall polysaccharides of oats (see non-starch polysaccharides and **dietary fibre**).

Bias
In epidemiology, deviation of an observed result from the true value in a particular direction (systematic error) due to factors pertaining to the observer or to study design or analysis. See also **selection bias**.

Bile
A greenish-yellow fluid secreted by the liver and stored in the gallbladder. Bile plays an important role in the intestinal **absorption** of fats. Bile contains **cholesterol**, bile salts, and waste products such as bilirubin.

Biliary tract
The biliary tract includes the **bile** ducts within the liver, the common bile duct, which connects the liver and gallbladder to the small intestine, and the cystic duct, which connects the gallbladder to the common bile duct.

Bioavailability
The degree to which a **nutrient** (or other substance) can be absorbed and used by the body.

BMI (see **body mass index**)

BMR (see **basal metabolic rate**)

Body mass index (BMI)
Body weight expressed in kilograms divided by the square of height expressed in metres (BMI = kg/m²). It provides an indirect measure of body fatness. Also called Quetelet's Index.

Caffeine
An alkaloid found in coffee, tea, kola nuts, chocolate, and other foods that acts as a stimulant and a diuretic.

Cancer survivor
Any person who has received a diagnosis of cancer

Cantonese-style salted fish
Fish that has been treated with varying amounts of salt and dried in natural conditions outdoors. It is characterised by treatment with less salt than typically used and is also subject to **fermentation** during the drying process due to relatively high outdoor temperature and moisture levels (see box 4.3.5).

Carcinogen
Any substance or agent capable of causing cancer.

Carcinoma
Malignant tumour derived from **epithelial** cells, usually with the ability to spread into the surrounding tissue (invasion) and produce secondary tumours (**metastases**).

Carcinoma in situ
The first stage of carcinoma in which the **malignant** tumour has not spread beyond the **epithelium**.

Cardiovascular disease
A group of diseases that involve the heart and/or blood vessels (arteries and veins). While the term technically refers to any disease that affects the cardiovascular system, it is usually used to refer to those related to atherosclerosis.

Case-control study
An epidemiological study in which the participants are chosen based on their disease or condition (cases) or lack of it (controls) to test whether past or recent history of an **exposure** such as smoking, genetic profile, alcohol consumption, or dietary intake is associated with the risk of disease (see box 3.4).

CE
Common Era — the period of measured time beginning with the year one on the Gregorian calendar. The notations CE and BCE (Before Common Era) are alternative notations for AD and BC, respectively.

Cell cycle
The sequence of stages that a cell passes through between one cell division and the next.

Cell signalling
Mechanisms whereby cells send messages to, or respond to external stimuli from, other cells.

Cerebrovascular disease
A group of diseases of the brain due to damage to the blood vessels, in which an area of the brain is transiently or permanently affected by ischaemia or bleeding.

Cholesterol
The principal sterol in animal tissues, synthesised in the body; an essential component of cell membranes and the **precursor** of the **steroid hormones** and vitamin D.

Chromatin
Mass of genetic material in the nucleus of a cell, composed of **DNA** and proteins that condense to form chromosomes.

Chronic disease
A disease that develops or persists over a long period of time. Includes noncommunicable diseases such as cancer, **cardiovascular disease**, and **diabetes**, and some infectious diseases such as tuberculosis.

CI (see **confidence interval**)

Coeliac disease
Intolerance to the gliadin fraction of the protein gluten from wheat, rye, and barley. The villi of the small intestine atrophy and **nutrient absorption** from food is poor. Stools are often bulky and contain a large amount of unabsorbed fat.

Cohort study
A study of a (usually large) group of people whose characteristics are recorded at recruitment (and sometimes later), followed up for a period of time during which outcomes of interest are noted. Differences in the frequency of outcomes (such as disease) within the cohort are calculated in relation to different levels of **exposure** to factors of interest, for example smoking, alcohol consumption, diet, and **exercise**. Differences in the likelihood of a particular outcome are presented as the **relative risk** comparing one level of exposure to another (see box 3.4).

Compliance
The extent to which people such as study participants follow an allocated treatment programme.

Computed tomography (CT)
A form of X-ray that produces cross-sectional or other images of the body.

Confidence interval (CI)
A measure of the uncertainty in an estimate, usually reported as 95% confidence interval (CI), which is the range of values within which there is a 95% chance that the true value lies. For example the effect of smoking on the **relative risk** of lung cancer in one study may be expressed as 10 (95% CI 5–15). This means that in this particular analysis, the estimate of the relative risk was calculated as 10, and that there is a 95% chance that the true value lies between 5 and 15.

Confounder
A variable, within a specific epidemiological study, that is associated with an **exposure**, is also a risk factor for the disease, and is not in the causal pathway from the exposure to the disease. If not adjusted for, this factor may distort the apparent exposure–disease relationship. An example is that smoking is related both to coffee drinking and to risk of lung cancer and thus, unless accounted for (controlled) in studies, might make coffee drinking appear falsely as a possible cause of lung cancer (see box 3.1).

Confounding factor (see **confounder**)

Confounding variable (see **confounder**)

Cretinism
Underactivity of the thyroid gland (hypothyroidism) in infancy, resulting in poor growth, severe mental retardation, and deafness.

CT (see **computed tomography**)

Curing
Various preservation and flavouring processes, especially of meat or fish, by the addition of a combination of salt, sugar, and either **nitrate** or **nitrite**. Curing processes often involve **smoking**. The addition of saltpetre (sodium nitrate) gives a pinkish colour to meat. Bacteria convert the nitrates in cured meats to nitrites and **nitrosamines**, which are potentially carcinogenic to humans (see box 4.3.2).

Cytotoxic
Poisonous to living cells.

Deoxyribonucleic acid (DNA)
The double-stranded, helical molecular chain found within the nucleus of each cell that carries the genetic information.

DEXA (see **dual energy X-ray absorptiometry**)

Diabetes mellitus
A metabolic disorder involving impaired metabolism of glucose due either to failure of secretion of the **hormone insulin** (type 1 diabetes) or to impaired responses of tissues to insulin (type 2 diabetes), which results in complications including kidney failure, blindness, and increased risk of **cardiovascular disease**.

Dietary fibre
Constituents of plant cell walls that are not digested in the small intestine. Several methods of analysis are used, which identify different components. The many constituents that are variously included in the definitions have different chemical and physiological features that are not easily defined under a single term. The different analytical methods do not generally characterise the physiological impact of foods or diets. **Non-starch polysaccharides** are a consistent feature and are fermented by colonic bacteria to produce **energy** and short chain **fatty acids** including butyrate. The term dietary fibre is increasingly seen as a concept describing a particular aspect of some dietary patterns (see box 4.1.2).

Dietary supplement
A substance, often in tablet or capsule form, which is consumed in addition to the usual diet. Dietary supplements typically refer to vitamins or **minerals**, though **phytochemicals** or other substances may be included.

Differentiation
The process of development of cells to take on the structural and functional characteristics specific to a particular tissue. Also, the degree to which tumour cells have the structure or function of the organ from which the tumour arose. Tumours can be described as well, moderately, or poorly differentiated: well-differentiated tumours appear similar to the cells of the organ in which they arose; poorly differentiated tumours do not. The degree of differentiation is often of prognostic significance.

Disaccharide
A carbohydrate composed of two **monosaccharides**.

Diverticular disease
The presence of pouch-like hernias (diverticula) through the muscle layer of the colon, associated with a low intake of **dietary fibre** and high intestinal pressure due to straining. Faecal matter may be trapped in these diverticula, causing them to become inflamed, causing pain and diarrhoea (diverticulitis).

DNA (see **deoxyribonucleic acid**)

DNA adducts
DNA adducts are compounds formed by the reaction of a chemical with DNA, which may damage the DNA. If repaired, some adducts can be excreted and measured in the urine as a marker of DNA damage. If not repaired, DNA may function abnormally and may therefore be a stage in carcinogenesis.

Docosahexaenoic acid (DHA)
A long-chain n-3 **polyunsaturated fatty acid** (C22:6 n3).

Dose response
A term derived from pharmacology that describes the degree to which an effect changes with the level of an **exposure**, for instance the intake of a drug or food (see box 3.2).

Double bond
A covalent bond between two carbon atoms each with one hydrogen atom, for instance in **fatty acids**.

Dual energy X-ray absorptiometry (DEXA)
A means of measuring the density of different body tissues such as bone or fat, using two X-ray beams with differing energy levels.

Dyslipidaemia
Any disorder of lipoprotein metabolism resulting in abnormal plasma concentrations or forms of lipoprotein, such as high total or **low-density lipoprotein** (LDL) **cholesterol** or triglyceride, and low high-density lipoprotein (HDL) cholesterol concentrations.

Dysplasia
Abnormal development of the cells of a tissue.

Ecological study
A study in which differences in patterns of **exposure**, for instance in consumption of a particular **nutrient** or food, are compared at aggregate level, with populations (rather than individuals) as the unit of analysis (see box 3.4).

Egger's test
A statistical test for small study effects such as **publication bias**.

Eicosapentaenoic acid (EPA)
A long-chain n-3 **polyunsaturated fatty acid** (C20:5 n3).

Effect modifier/effect modification
Effect modification (or effect-measure modification) occurs when a measure of effect for an **exposure** changes over levels of another variable (the modifier) (see box 3.6).

Emulsifier
A substance that promotes the formation of a stable mixture, or emulsion, of two substances that do not normally mix well (for example oil and water).

Endocrine
Referring to organs or glands that secrete **hormones** into the blood.

Energy
Energy, measured as calories or joules, is required for all metabolic processes. Fats, carbohydrates, proteins, and alcohol from foods and drinks release energy when they are metabolised in the body.

Energy adjustment
The use of statistical methods to 'adjust' intakes of a dietary factor under study for total **energy** intake (see box 3.7).

Energy balance
The state in which the total **energy** absorbed from foods and drinks equals total energy expended. Also the degree to which intake exceeds expenditure (positive energy balance) or expenditure exceeds intake (negative energy balance).

Enzyme
A protein that acts as a catalyst in living organisms, promoting chemical reactions and regulating the rate at which they proceed.

Epidemic
A widespread or rapidly spreading disease that affects many individuals in a population at the same time, markedly in excess of the number normally expected.

Epigenetic
Relating to the control of **gene expression** through mechanisms that do not depend on changes in the nucleotide sequence of **DNA**, for example through methylation of DNA or acetylation of histone.

Epithelial (see **epithelium**)

Epithelial-mesenchymal transition (EMT)
A disorder of cell **differentiation** where cells assume a mesenchymal rather than an **epithelial phenotype**. Cancer cells may have phenotypic similarities to EMT.

Epithelium
The layer of cells covering internal and external surfaces of the body, including the skin and mucous membranes lining body cavities such as the lung, gut, and urinary tract.

Essential amino acid
An amino acid that is required for normal cellular structure and metabolic function but which humans cannot synthesise and so must obtain from food.

Evidence
Information that helps to determine whether a proposal or belief is true or valid, or false or invalid.

Exercise
A type of **physical activity**, often deliberate such as sport, which improves fitness or health.

Exposure
A factor to which an individual may be exposed to varying degrees, such as intake of a food, level or type of **physical activity**, or aspect of body composition.

Extracellular fluid
All body fluid not contained within cells. Includes the fluid in blood vessels (plasma) and between cells (interstitial fluid).

Factor analysis
A statistical technique used to examine the structure underlying the interactions between several variables.

Fat-free mass
The mass of all body tissue excluding the **lipid** components.

Fatty acid
A carboxylic acid with a carbon chain of varying length, which may be either saturated (no **double bonds**) or unsaturated (one or more double bonds). Three fatty acids attached to a **glycerol** backbone make up a triglyceride, the usual form of fat in foods and **adipose tissue**.

Fermentation
The anaerobic metabolic breakdown of molecules such as glucose. Fermentation yields **energy** in the form of lactate, acetate, ethanol, or other simple product.

Fetal programming (see **programming**)

Food systems
The interconnected agricultural, ecological, economic, social, cultural, and technological systems involved in food production, distribution, and consumption.

Forest plot
A simple visual representation of the amount of variation between the results of the individual studies in a **meta-analysis**. Their construction begins with plotting the observed **exposure** effect of each individual study, which is represented as the centre of a square. Horizontal lines run through this to show the 95% **confidence interval**. Different sized squares may be plotted for each of the individual studies, the size of the box increasing with the size of the study and the weight that it takes in the analysis. The overall summary estimate of effect and its confidence interval can also be added to the bottom of this plot, if appropriate, and this is represented as a diamond. The centre of the diamond is the pooled summary estimate and the horizontal tips are the confidence intervals (see box 3.3).

Fortification
The deliberate addition of **nutrients** to foods or drinks as a means of increasing the level of intake in a population (see box 4.10.1).

Functional food
Any food, similar in appearance to conventional food, claiming to have specific physiological effects that benefit health and/or reduce the risk of disease. Products are sometimes sold in medicinal forms (see box 4.10.2).

Gene expression
The active production of the **RNA** and protein that are coded for by a particular gene. In any cell, not all genes are expressed (see **epigenetic**).

Genetic modification
The manipulation of a living organism's genetic material by eliminating, modifying, or adding copies of specific genes, often from other organisms. Also known as 'genetic engineering'.

Germ cell (see **germ line**)

Germ line
Eggs and sperm and the cells that develop into them, through which genetic information is passed from generation to generation.

Genotype
The genetic makeup of a cell or organism.

GH (see **growth hormone**)

Gleason score
A quantitative measure of the degree of **differentiation** of prostate cancers. High Gleason scores, representing aggressive disease, are associated with poor prognoses. **Whitemore and Jewett scales** are used to assess prostate cancer stage.

Glycaemic index
A system for ranking foods containing carbohydrates according to the effect of a standard amount on blood glucose levels. Foods that raise the blood sugar the most have the highest glycaemic index (see box 4.1.3).

Glycaemic load
The **glycaemic index** of a food multiplied by the number of grams of carbohydrate in the serving of food (see box 4.1.3).

Glycerol
A three-carbon molecule that forms the backbone of triglyceride in fats (see **fatty acid**).

Goitre
Enlargement of the thyroid gland, seen as a swelling in the neck; may be hypothyroid, with low production of thyroid **hormone**, euthyroid (normal levels), or hyperthyroid (excessive production). Deficiency of iodine is one cause.

Gross domestic product
The total market value of all the goods and services produced within a nation in a given year.

Growth hormone (GH)
Also known as somatotropin, a **hormone** secreted by the pituitary gland that stimulates secretion of growth factors from the liver and so also protein synthesis and growth of the long bones in the legs and arms. It also promotes the breakdown and use of **fatty acids**, rather than glucose, as an **energy** source.

Haem
The part of the organic molecule haemoglobin in red blood cells containing iron to which oxygen binds for transport around the body.

Herbicide
A pesticide used to kill or control the growth of unwanted plants. Selective herbicides kill certain targets while leaving a desired crop relatively unharmed. Non-selective herbicides kill every plant with which they come into contact.

Heterocyclic amines
A family of compounds formed from protein and sugars in meat, chicken, and fish cooked at very high temperatures by grilling (broiling) or frying that have potential carcinogenic effects (see box 4.3.4).

Heterogeneity
A measure of difference between the results of different studies addressing a similar question. In **meta-analysis**, the degree of heterogeneity may be calculated statistically using the I^2 test.

High fructose corn syrup (HFCS)
A form of corn syrup that has undergone enzymatic processing in order to increase its fructose content. Used to sweeten soft drinks, juices, ice cream, and many other processed foods, especially in the USA (see box 4.6.1).

High-income countries
Countries with a gross average annual national product of more than an agreed figure per head (in 2006 this was more than $US 10 726). This term is less judgemental and more descriptive than 'economically developed' countries.

Homeostasis
The maintenance of biological conditions in a stable state.

Hormone
A substance secreted by specialised cells that affects the structure and/or function of other cells or tissues in another part of the body.

Hydrogenation
The process by which unsaturated **fatty acids** in vegetable oils are made more saturated by the addition of hydrogen. This makes liquid oils more solid at room temperature and more resistant to oxidation, for instance in the manufacture of margarines. Incomplete hydrogenation can lead to the formation of *trans*-fatty acids (see box 4.5.1).

Hyperkeratosis
Excessive thickening of the outer horny layer of the skin, affecting the palms and soles.

Hyperplasia
An increase in the number of cells in a tissue.

Hypertension
High blood pressure; a risk factor for **cardiovascular** and kidney disease.

Hypoxia
Abnormally low levels of oxygen in blood or tissues.

IARC
International Agency for Research on Cancer (www.iarc.fr).

IGF binding proteins
Proteins that bind to insulin-like growth factors (which are implicated in the cancer process, see Chapter 2) in the bloodstream.

Immune response
The production of antibodies or specialised cells in response to foreign proteins or other substances.

Incidence rates
The number of new cases of a condition appearing during a specified period of time expressed relative to the size of the population, for example 60 new cases of breast cancer per 100 000 women per year.

Inflammation
The immunologic response of tissues to injury or infection. Inflammation is characterised by accumulation of white blood cells that produce several bioactive chemicals, causing redness, pain, and swelling.

Inflammatory bowel disease
A term used to describe Crohn's disease and **ulcerative colitis**: both are characterised by chronic **inflammation** of the gut.

Insulin
A protein **hormone** secreted by the pancreas that promotes the uptake and utilisation of glucose, particularly in the liver and muscles. Inadequate secretion of, or tissue response to, insulin leads to **diabetes mellitus**.

Intrinsic sugars
Sugars naturally integrated into the cellular structure of foods, for example those present in unprocessed fruits and vegetables.

Intra-abdominal fat
Also known as visceral fat. Fat stored within the abdomen surrounding the internal organs (see **adipose tissue**).

In utero
In the uterus; refers to events that occur before birth.

Invasive cancer
Tumours that spread into surrounding healthy tissue.

Iron-deficiency anaemia
A low blood concentration of haemoglobin due to a deficiency of iron, due either to unusually high demands or low intake or impaired **absorption**.

Irradiation
Exposure to ionising radiation. Food irradiation is used to disinfest, sterilise, or preserve food.

Jewett scale (see **Whitemore and Jewett scales**)

K-ras
One of a class of genes (proto-oncogenes) which when mutated can malfunction to become an **oncogene**, promoting the transformation of normal cells into cancer cells (see box 2.2).

Lactation
The production and secretion of milk by the mammary glands.

Lacto-ovo-vegetarian diet
A vegetarian diet characterised by the inclusion of eggs and dairy products, but no other animal products.

Latency
The period of time between the onset of a disease process and its detection or clinical appearance.

Lean body mass
The mass of those parts of the body that are not **adipose tissue**. Lean body mass includes some **lipid** and is not synonymous with **fat-free mass**.

Lesion
A general term for any abnormality of cells or tissues, including those due to cancerous change.

Linoleic acid
An essential n-6 **polyunsaturated fatty acid** (C18:2 n6).

Lipids
Naturally occurring organic molecules that are insoluble in water, including triglycerides; **fatty acids**; phospholipids; lipoproteins; carotenoids; **cholesterol**, which is a **precursor** of **steroid hormones** and vitamin D; and the other fat-soluble vitamins A, E, and K. Lipids are an essential component of cell membranes and many metabolic processes.

Low-density lipoprotein (LDL) cholesterol
A class of lipoproteins that is the major carrier of cholesterol in the blood in humans. A high blood LDL cholesterol concentration is a cause of coronary artery disease.

Low-income countries
Countries with a gross average annual national product of less than an agreed figure per head (in 2006 this was $US 875). This term is less judgemental and more descriptive than 'economically developing' countries.

Lymphocyte
Several types of white blood cell, part of the immune system, found in the blood and lymph glands.

Macronutrient
Those **nutrient** components of the diet that provide **energy**: carbohydrate, fat, and protein; ethanol also provides energy but is not a nutrient.

Magnetic resonance imaging (MRI)
A technique that produces images of parts of the body using analysis of the behaviour of water molecules within body tissues when placed in a strong magnetic field.

Malignant
A tumour with the capacity to spread to surrounding tissue or to other sites in the body.

Melanoma
Malignant tumour of the skin derived from the pigment-producing cells (melanocytes).

Membrane potential
The difference in electrical charge across the cell membrane.

Menarche
The beginning of menstruation (see boxes 6.1 and 6.2).

MET (see **metabolic equivalent**)

Meta-analysis
The process of using statistical methods to combine the results of different studies.

Metabolic equivalent (MET)
One MET equals the **resting metabolic rate**, measured as the rate of oxygen consumption, which is approximately 3.5 millilitres of oxygen per kilogram body weight per minute. Equivalent to **physical activity ratio** (see box 5.1).

Metabolic syndrome
A common cluster of a variety of several risk factors for **cardiovascular disease** including **insulin** resistance, abdominal **obesity**, high blood pressure, and abnormal blood **lipids**.

Metastasis
The spread of **malignant** cancer cells to distant locations around the body from the original site.

Micronutrients
Vitamins and **minerals** present in foods and required in the diet for normal body function in small quantities, conventionally of less than 1 g/day (see box 4.2.3).

Migrant study
A study of people who migrate from one country to other countries with different environments and cultural backgrounds. The experience, such as mortality or disease incidence, of the migrant group is compared with that of people in their current country of residence and in their country of origin.

Mineral
An inorganic compound in food required by the body for normal function, such as calcium, magnesium, and iron.

Monosaccharide
Simple sugar consisting of a single sugar molecule, such as glucose, fructose, and galactose. They form the basis of **disaccharides** such as sucrose, and of **oligosaccharides**, starch, and **non-starch polysaccharides**.

MRI (see **magnetic resonance imaging**)

Mucosal
Relating to mucous membranes.

Mutagens
Chemical compounds or physical agents capable of inducing genetic mutations.

Mycotoxins
Toxins produced by fungi (moulds), especially *Aspergillus flavus* under tropical conditions and *Penicillium* and *Fusarium* species under temperate conditions (see box 4.1.4).

Neoplasm
A benign or **malignant** tumour.

Nested case-control study
A **case-control study** in which cases and controls are drawn from the population of a **cohort study**; often used for studies of prospectively collected information or biological samples.

Neurotransmitter
A chemical secreted by one nerve cell that stimulates a response in a neighbouring nerve cell.

Night blindness
A condition in which a person has impaired vision in the dark, characteristic of vitamin A deficiency.

Nitrate
A salt containing the nitrate ion, which contains nitrogen and oxygen in proportion 1:3 (NO_3). Derived from decomposing organic material such as manure, plants, and human waste, and a component of chemical fertilisers (see box 4.3.2).

Nitrite
A salt containing the nitrite ion, which contains nitrogen and oxygen in proportion 1:2 (NO_2). Sodium nitrite is added to many **processed meats**. Nitrites are also formed in the body from **nitrates** in plant foods that are eaten. When consumed, nitrites can lead to the generation of *N*-**nitroso compounds**, some of which are known **carcinogens** (see box 4.3.2).

Nitrosamines
A group of chemicals formed by the reaction of **nitrites** with amines; some nitrosamines are **carcinogens** (see box 4.3.2).

N-**nitroso compound** (see **nitrosamines**)

Non-caloric sweetener
A food additive that replicates the sweetness of sugar but with negligible food **energy** (see box 4.6.2).

Non-exercise activity thermogenesis (NEAT)
The **energy** used in non-conscious or **spontaneous physical activity**, such as fidgeting and posture maintenance.

Non-milk extrinsic sugars
Sugars not present within the cellular structure of foods, apart from those in milk or milk products. For example those added to foods or in juices, syrups, or honey.

Non-starch polysaccharide
A carbohydrate comprising at least 10 simple sugar molecules; a major component of plant cell walls and the principal analytic fraction characterising **dietary fibre** (see box 4.1.2).

Nucleic acid
The four building blocks of **DNA** – guanine, thymine, cytosine, and adenine.

Nutrient
A substance present in food and required by the body for maintenance of normal structure and function, and for growth and development. Nutrients include **macronutrients** (fat, protein, and carbohydrate), which provide **energy** as well as performing metabolic and structural functions, and **micronutrients** (vitamins and **minerals**), which do not provide energy but are necessary for normal metabolic function.

Obesity
Excess body fat to a degree that increases the risk of various diseases. Conventionally defined as a **BMI** of 30 kg/m^2 or more. Different cut-off points have been proposed for specific populations.

Odds ratio
A measure of the risk of an outcome such as cancer, associated with an **exposure** of interest, used in **case-control studies**; approximately equivalent to the **relative risk**.

Oligosaccharide
A compound comprising between 2 and 10 simple sugar molecules (**monosaccharides**).

Oncogene
A gene whose protein product contributes to the transformation of normal cells into cancer cells. Oncogenes result from the mutation of normal genes called proto-oncogenes (see box 2.2).

Organic compounds
Any member of a large class of chemical compounds whose molecules contain carbon (and other elements), with exception of carbides, carbonates, and carbon oxides. Most occur naturally only in the bodies and products of living organisms.

Organic farming
Agricultural production system without or with only limited use of pesticides, synthetic fertilisers, growth regulators, and livestock feed additives (see box 4.9.2).

Osteomalacia
A disease due to vitamin D deficiency characterised by inadequate bone mineralisation, pain, and increased bone fragility.

Osteoporosis
Loss of the tissues of bone (bone cells, mineral, and protein) to an extent that increases the risk of fracture.

Oxidative damage
Damage to cells or structures in cells caused by oxidation, either by chemicals or by radiation. Some oxidants are generated in the normal course of metabolism. Oxidation of **DNA** is one cause of mutation.

p53
A protein central to regulation of cell growth. Mutations of the p53 gene are important causes of cancer (see **oncogene** and box 2.2).

Pasteurisation
Partial **sterilisation** of foods at a temperature that destroys microorganisms such as bacteria, viruses, moulds, yeast, and protozoa without major changes in the chemistry of the food.

Pathogenesis
The origin and development of disease. The mechanisms by which causal factors increase the risk of disease.

Pedometer
An instrument that records the number of steps taken.

Peer review
The scrutiny of scientific papers by one or more suitably qualified scientists.

Pentosan
A **polysaccharide** composed of pentose sugars (with a ring comprising 5 carbon atoms), for example arabans or xylans.

Phenotype
The characteristics displayed by an organism; this depends on both the **genotype** and environmental factors.

Phosphorylation
Addition of phosphate groups to hydroxyl groups on proteins, catalysed by a protein kinase with **ATP** as phosphate donor. A key process in **cell signalling** and **energy** transfer.

Physical activity
Any movement using skeletal muscles.

Physical activity level (PAL)
Energy expenditure per day as a multiple of **basal metabolic rate** (BMR) (see box 5.2).

Physical activity ratio (PAR)
The **energy** cost of an activity per minute divided by the energy cost of **basal metabolic rate** per minute. Thus, the energy cost of sitting at rest is about 1.2; for walking at a normal pace, 4; and for jogging, 7.

Phytochemicals
Compounds found in plants not required for normal structure or function, which may modify physiological functions and influence health (see box 4.2.1).

Point estimate
An estimate that is reported as a single value. The precision of a point estimate is indicated by the width of the **confidence interval** that surrounds it.

Point mutation
Mutation of a single **DNA** base in a gene often leading to a single peptide change in a protein, which can influence its function.

Polycyclic aromatic hydrocarbons
A family of chemical compounds, including several known **carcinogens**, formed by incomplete combustion of organic substances such as wood, coal, diesel, fat, or tobacco (see box 4.3.4).

Polymorphisms
Common variations (more than 1 per cent of the population) in the **DNA** sequence of a gene.

Polyphenol
Any of a group of chemical substances found in plants that have more than one phenol group per molecule; includes tannins, lignins, and flavonoids.

Polysaccharide
A polymer composed of multiple subunits of **monosaccharides** (simple sugars) linked together.

Polyunsaturated fatty acids
Fatty acids containing two or more **double bonds**.

Pooled analysis (see **pooling**)

Pooling
In epidemiology, a type of study where original individual-level data from two or more original studies are obtained, combined, and re-analysed.

Positive energy balance (see **energy balance**)

Prebiotic
Dietary carbohydrate that reaches the colon, where it promotes growth of beneficial bacterial flora (see box 4.10.2).

Precursor
A chemical compound from which another compound is formed.

Processed meat
Meat (usually **red meat**) preserved by **smoking**, **curing**, or salting, or by the addition of preservatives. Definitions vary between countries and studies as to what precisely is included (see box 4.3.1).

Programming
The process whereby events happening during fetal life (fetal programming), such as growth restriction, or in infancy can permanently affect the structure and function of particular organs, and so also metabolic processes. Combined with other factors, this can in turn alter the response to environmental **exposures** and so susceptibility to disease.

Promoter region
The region of **DNA** in a gene which initiates the **transcription** of DNA to **RNA** when the **enzyme** RNA polymerase binds to it.

Prostaglandins
A range of **hormones** derived from essential **fatty acids**. Among many other processes, they influence blood pressure and **inflammation**.

Publication bias
A **bias** in the overall balance of **evidence** in the published literature due to selective publication. Not all studies carried out are published, and those that are may differ from those that are not. Publication bias can be tested for with either **Begg's** or **Egger's tests**.

Randomised controlled trial (RCT)
A study in which a comparison is made between one intervention (often a treatment or prevention strategy) and another (control). Sometimes the control group receives an inactive agent (a placebo). Groups are randomised to one intervention or the other, so that any difference in outcome between the two groups can be ascribed with confidence to the intervention. Neither investigators nor subjects usually know to which condition they have been randomised; this is called 'double-blinding' (see box 3.4).

RCT (see **randomised controlled trial**)

Reactive oxygen species
Oxygen-containing radical or reactive ion that oxidises DNA (removes electrons); can be hydroxyl radical (OH-), hydrogen peroxide (H_2O_2) or superoxide radical (O_2-).

Red meat
Meat from domesticated cattle, pigs, sheep, and goats; not poultry and fish or meat from wild animals.

Refined sugars
Sugars obtained by purification from plants which contain it, principally sugar cane or beet.

Relative risk (RR)
The ratio of the rate of disease or death among people exposed to a factor, compared to the rate among the unexposed, usually used in **cohort studies** (see **odds ratio**).

Resting metabolic rate
Metabolic rate in a fasting subject sitting quietly (also see **basal metabolic rate**).

Reverse causation
The situation when an abnormal level of an **exposure** is caused by the cancer or its treatment, rather than the other way round. For example if cancer causes weight loss, then the finding that low **BMI** is associated with increased risk may reflect weight loss due to cancer rather than low weight causing cancer.

Ribonucleic acid (RNA)
The molecule created by RNA polymerase from **DNA** (**transcription**) which carries the genetic message to ribosomes (**translation**), where proteins are made.

Rickets
Malformation of the bones in growing children due to deficiency of vitamin D. In adults the equivalent is **osteomalacia**.

RNA (see **ribonucleic acid**)

Salt iodisation
The practice of **fortifying** salt with iodide as a means of ensuring adequate iodine intake.

Satiation
The development of fullness during eating that limits the size of a meal consumed (see **satiety**).

Satiety
The suppression of appetite after eating that inhibits the starting of eating (see **satiation**).

Saturated fatty acids
Fatty acids that do not contain any **double bonds**.

Selection bias
Bias arising from the procedures used to select study participants and from factors influencing participation.

Single bond
A covalent bond between two carbon atoms, each with two hydrogen atoms, for instance in **saturated fatty acids**.

Single nucleotide polymorphism (SNP)
DNA sequence variation where a single nucleotide in the DNA is altered. SNPs account for 90% of all human genetic variation (see **polymorphism** and **point mutation**).

SLR (see **systematic literature review**)

Smoking (foods)
Smoking is the process of **curing**, cooking, or seasoning food by exposing it for long periods of time to the smoke from a wood fire. 'Hot smoking' is a process that can be used to fully cook raw meats or fish, while 'cold smoking' is an hours- or days-long process that is generally used to preserve or flavour foods (usually meats or fish, but sometimes cheeses, vegetables, fruits).

SNP (see **single nucleotide polymorphism**)

Socioeconomic status
A combined product of social and economic status reflecting education level, personal wealth, class, and associated factors.

Solvent
Substances (usually liquid) capable of dissolving or dispersing one or more other substances.

Spontaneous physical activity (see **non-exercise activity thermogenesis**)

Squamous cell carcinoma
A **malignant** cancer derived from squamous **epithelial** cells.

Stabiliser
One of a number of food additives, such as agar or pectin (used in jam, for example), that give foods a firmer texture. While they are not true **emulsifiers**, they help to stabilise emulsions.

Statistical significance
The probability that any observed result might not have occurred by chance. In most epidemiologic work, a study result whose probability is less than 5% ($p < 0.05$) is considered sufficiently unlikely to have occurred by chance to justify the designation 'statistically significant' (see **confidence interval**).

Stem cell
A cell that can self-renew or give rise to a lineage of more differentiated cells.

Sterilisation
The destruction of bacteria or other microorganisms by heat, radiation, or chemical means.

Steroid hormone
One of several **hormones** derived from **cholesterol** and having a central effect on growth and metabolism.

Supplement (see **dietary supplement**)

Systematic literature review (SLR)
A means of compiling and assessing published **evidence** that addresses a scientific question with a predefined protocol and transparent methods (see box 3.5).

Testosterone
An androgenic **steroid hormone** and the principal male sex **hormone**.

Thermodynamics
The branch of physics concerned with the study of energy and its conversion between different forms.

Thermogenesis
The process of heat production. In adults, arising from the metabolic processes during the digestion and assimilation of food and during shivering.

Tocotrienol
A form of vitamin E.

Total energy expenditure
The **energy** expended in a 24-hour period by an individual or a group of individuals. It reflects the average amount of energy spent in a typical day, but may not be the exact amount of energy spent each and every day.

Transcription
Synthesis of **RNA** from **DNA** by the **enzyme** RNA polymerase.

Transition cultures
Countries in the process of changing from one predominant social/cultural structure to another, for instance moving from lower-income to higher-income status with the accompanying changes that this implies.

Translation
The process by which **RNA** carries the genetic message from **DNA** to generate proteins in the ribosome.

Tumour suppressor gene
A gene whose protein product inhibits tumour formation (see also **oncogene** and box 2.2).

UICC
International Union Against Cancer (www.uicc.org).

Ulcerative colitis
A disease causing chronic **inflammation** of the large intestine (colon). Together with another disease of inflammation of the intestines called Crohn's disease, referred to as **inflammatory bowel disease**.

Underwater weighing
A method for estimating the proportions of body fat and lean mass. By comparing weight underwater with weight on land, and taking account of the different densities of fat and lean tissue, the proportions of fat and lean can be calculated.

UVA/UVB
Ultraviolet light of different wavelengths. UVA has relatively long wave lengths, UVB relatively short.

Visceral fat (see **intra-abdominal fat**)

Waist to hip circumference ratio (WHR)
A measure of body shape indicating fat distribution.

Weight cycling
Repeated abnormal losses and regains of weight, often the result of repeated diet regimes.

Whitemore and Jewett scales
A scale used to describe the stage of prostate cancer.

WHO
World Health Organization (www.who.int).

Wholegrain
Cereal grain that retains the bran and germ as well as the endosperm, in contrast to refined grains that retain only the endosperm. All components of the grain are retained in their usual proportions, though the term 'wholegrain' may apply to products that include other constituents, so that the complete product comprises less than 100% wholegrain (see box 4.1.1).

WHR (see **waist to hip circumference ratio**)

References

Chapter 1

1. Food and Agriculture Organization of the United Nations. *FAOSTAT. http://apps.fao.org.* 2003.
2. Adair LS, Popkin BM. Are child eating patterns being transformed globally? *Obes Res* 2005;13:1281-99.
3. Statistics South Africa. *South Africa census. www.statssa.gov.za/publications/P0302/P 03022006.pdf.* 2006.
4. Australian Bureau of Statistics. *National Nutritional Survey: Selected Highlights. http://www.abs.gov.au/AUSSTATS/abs@.n sf/ProductsbyTopic.* 1995.
5. Shisana O, Rehle T, Simbayi LC, et al., editors. *South African National HIV Prevalence, HIV Incidence, Behaviour and Communication Survey, 2005.* Cape Town: Human Sciences Research Council Press, 2006.
6. Barquera S, Rivera JA, Espinosa-Montero J, et al. Energy and nutrient consumption in Mexican women 12-49 years of age: analysis of the National Nutrition Survey 1999. *Salud Publica Mex* 2003;45 Suppl 4:S530-9.
7. Barquera S, Rivera JA, Safdie M, et al. Energy and nutrient intake in preschool and school age Mexican children: National Nutrition Survey 1999. *Salud Publica Mex* 2003;45 Suppl 4:S540-50.
8. Bergman P, Hauser G. Biosocial and nutritional effects on body composition in young adults from Wroclaw, Poland. *J Biosoc Sci* 2006;38:721-34.
9. Boing AF, Peres MA, Antunes JL. Mortality from oral and pharyngeal cancer in Brazil: trends and regional patterns, 1979-2002. *Rev Panam Salud Publica* 2006;20:1-8.
10. Bourne LT, Lambert EV, Steyn K. Where does the black population of South Africa stand on the nutrition transition? *Public Health Nutr* 2002;5:157-62.
11. de Vries E, Steliarova-Foucher E, Spatz A, et al. Skin cancer incidence and survival in European children and adolescents (1978-1997). Report from the Automated Childhood Cancer Information System project. *Eur J Cancer* 2006;42:2170-82.
12. Deuffic-Burban S, Mohamed MK, Larouze B, et al. Expected increase in hepatitis C-related mortality in Egypt due to pre-2000 infections. *J Hepatol* 2006;44:455-61.
13. DiSipio T, Rogers C, Newman B, et al. The Queensland Cancer Risk Study: Behavioural risk factor results. *Aust N Z J Public Health* 2006;30:375-82.
14. Du S, Lu B, Zhai F, et al. A new stage of the nutrition transition in China. *Public Health Nutr* 2002;5:169-74.
15. Galal OM. The nutrition transition in Egypt: obesity, undernutrition and the food consumption context. *Public Health Nutr* 2002;5:141-8.
16. Haley MM. Changing consumer demand for meat: The US Example, 1970-2000. In: Regmi A, editor. *Changing Structure of Global Food Consumption and Trade.* Washington DC, 2001.
17. Hemminki K, Li X, Czene K. Cancer risks in first-generation immigrants to Sweden. *Int J Cancer* 2002;99:218-28.
18. Hernandez B, Cuevas-Nasu L, Shamah-Levy T, et al. Factors associated with overweight and obesity in Mexican school-age children: results from the National Nutrition Survey 1999. *Salud Publica Mex* 2003;45 Suppl 4:S551-7.
19. Hoare J, Henderson L, Bates C, et al. *The National Diet and Nutrition Survey: adults aged 19 to 64 years. http://www.food.gov.uk/multimedia/pdfs /ndnsprintedreport.pdf.* 2004.
20. International Agency for Research on Cancer. *Globocan 2002. http://www-dep.iarc.fr/.* 2006.
21. Jaime PC, Monteiro CA. Fruit and vegetable intake by Brazilian adults, 2003. *Cad Saude Publica* 2005;21 Suppl:19-24.
22. Kaatsch P, Steliarova-Foucher E, Crocetti E, et al. Time trends of cancer incidence in European children (1978-1997): report from the Automated Childhood Cancer Information System Project. *Eur J Cancer* 2006;42:1961-71.
23. Katanoda K, Matsumura Y. National Nutrition Survey in Japan: its methodological transition and current findings. *J Nutr Sci Vitaminol (Tokyo)* 2002;48:423-32.
24. Kruger HS, Puoane T, Senekal M, et al. Obesity in South Africa: challenges for government and health professionals. *Public Health Nutr* 2005;8:491-500.
25. Labadarios D, Steyn NP, Maunder E, et al. The National Food Consumption Survey (NFCS): South Africa, 1999. *Public Health Nutr* 2005;8:533-43.
26. Li D, Premier R. Cuisine: Hangzhou foods and their role in community health and nutrition. *Asia Pac J Clin Nutr* 2004;13:141-6.
27. Liu Y, Zhai F, Popkin BM. Trends in eating behaviours among Chinese children (1991-1997). *Asia Pac J Clin Nutr* 2006;15:72-80.
28. Monteiro CA, Conde WL, Popkin BM. Is obesity replacing or adding to undernutrition? Evidence from different social classes in Brazil. *Public Health Nutr* 2002;5:105-12.
29. Moreno LA, Sarria A, Popkin BM. The nutrition transition in Spain: a European Mediterranean country. *Eur J Clin Nutr* 2002;56:992-1003.
30. Office for National Statistics. *National Statistics Online. www.statistics.gov.uk.* 2006.
31. Nielsen SJ, Popkin BM. Changes in beverage intake between 1977 and 2001. *Am J Prev Med* 2004;27:205-10.
32. Palacio-Mejia LS, Rangel-Gomez G, Hernandez-Avila M, et al. Cervical cancer, a disease of poverty: mortality differences between urban and rural areas in Mexico. *Salud Publica Mex* 2003;45 Suppl 3:S315-25.
33. Parsons TJ, Manor O, Power C. Changes in diet and physical activity in the 1990s in a large British sample (1958 birth cohort). *Eur J Clin Nutr* 2005;59:49-56.
34. Pollack SL. Consumer demand for fruit and vegetables: The US example. *Changing Structure of global food consumption and trade.* Washington DC: United States Department of Agriculture, 2001.
35. Prynne CJ, Paul AA, Mishra GD, et al. Changes in intake of key nutrients over 17 years during adult life of a British birth cohort. *Br J Nutr* 2005;94:368-76.
36. Rivera JA, Sepulveda Amor J. Conclusions from the Mexican National Nutrition Survey 1999: translating results into nutrition policy. *Salud Publica Mex* 2003;45 Suppl 4:S565-75.
37. Sekula W, Nelson M, Figurska K, et al. Comparison between household budget survey and 24-hour recall data in a nationally representative sample of Polish households. *Public Health Nutr* 2005;8:430-9.
38. Serra-Majem L, MacLean D, Ribas L, et al. Comparative analysis of nutrition data from national, household, and individual levels: results from a WHO-CINDI collaborative project in Canada, Finland, Poland, and Spain. *J Epidemiol Community Health* 2003;57:74-80.
39. Shetty PS. Nutrition transition in India. *Public Health Nutr* 2002;5:175-82.
40. Steptoe A, Wardle J, Cui W, et al. Trends in smoking, diet, physical exercise, and attitudes toward health in European university students from 13 countries, 1990-2000. *Prev Med* 2002;35:97-104.

41. Joint United Nations Programme on HIV/AIDS. *Report on the global AIDS epidemic 2006.* *http://www.unaids.org/en/HIV_data/200 6GlobalReport/default.asp.* 2006.

42. Vainio H, Bianchini F, editors. *IARC Handbooks of Cancer Prevention, Weight Control and Physical Activity.* Lyon: International Agency for Research on Cancer, World Health Organization, 2002.

43. Vainio H, Bianchini F, editors. *IARC Handbooks of Cancer Prevention, Fruit and Vegetables.* Lyon: International Agency for Research on Cancer, World Health Organization, 2003.

44. Vorster HH, Margetts BM, Venter CS, et al. Integrated nutrition science: from theory to practice in South Africa. *Public Health Nutr* 2005;8:760-5.

45. Waskiewicz A, Piotrowski W, Sygnowska E, et al. Did favourable trends in food consumption observed in the 1984-2001 period contribute to the decrease in cardiovascular mortality? Pol-MONICA Warsaw Project. *Kardiol Pol* 2006;64:16-23; discussion 4-5.

46. World Health Organization. *WHO Global Infobase.* *http://www.who.int/ncd_surveillance/inf obase/web/InfoBasePolicyMaker/Reports /reportListCountries.aspx.* 2006.

47. Yamaguchi K. Overview of cancer control programs in Japan. *Jpn J Clin Oncol* 2002;32 Suppl:S22-31.

47A. Sproston K, Primatesa P, editors. *Health Survey for England 2002.* London: Department of Health, 2003.

47B. Rosenbaum S, Skinner R, Knight I, et al. A survey of heights and weights of adults in Great Britain, 1980. *Ann Hum Biol* 1985;12:115-27.

48. Eaton SB. The ancestral human diet: what was it and should it be a paradigm for contemporary nutrition? *Proc Nutr Soc* 2006;65:1-6.

49. Cohen M. History, diet and hunter-gatherers. In: Kiple K, Ornelas K, editors. *The Cambridge World History of Food.* Cambridge: Cambridge University Press, 2000.

50. Eaton B, Shostak M, Konner M. The stone age diet. *The Paleolithic Prescription.* New York: Harper and Row, 1988.

51. Eaton SB, Shostak M, Konner M. The first fitness formula. *The Paleolithic Prescription.* New York: Harper and Row, 1988.

52. Zimmerman M. An experimental study of mummification pertinent to the antiquity of cancer. *Cancer 1970* 1977;40:1358-62.

53. Schaefer O. Eskimos (Inuit). In: Trowell H, Burkitt D, editors. *Western Diseases: Their Emergence and Prevention.* London: Edward Arnold, 1981.

54. Messer E. Maize. In: Kiple K, Ornelas K, editors. *The Cambridge World History of Food*: Cambridge University Press, 2000.

55. Miller N, Wetterstrom W. The beginnings of agriculture: the ancient Near East. In: Kiple K, Ornelas K, editors. *The Cambridge World History of Food.* Cambridge: Cambridge University Press, 2000.

56. Jacob H. Bread in the ancient world. *Six Thousand Years of Bread. Its Holy and Unholy History.* New York: The Lyons Press, 1997.

57. Miller N, Wetterstrom W, Roger D, et al. Food and drink around the world. In: Kiple K, Ornelas K, editors. *The Cambridge World History of Food.* Cambridge: Cambridge University Press, 2000.

58. Sinnett P, Whyte M, Williams E, et al. Peasant Agriculturalists. In: Trowell H, Burkitt D, editors. *Western Diseases: Their Emergence and Prevention.* London: Edward Arnold, 1981.

59. McMichael AJ. Infectious disease: humans and microbes co-evolving. In: Press CU, editor. *Human Frontiers, Environments and Disease. Past Patterns, Uncertain Futures.* Cambridge, 2001.

60. Proctor R. A question of civilization? *Cancer Wars. How Politics Shapes What We Know And Don't Know About Cancer.* New York: Basic Books, 1995.

61. Seymour J. Of industrial man: the land. *The Ultimate Heresy.* Bideford, Devon: Green Books, 1989.

62. Nestle M. The Mediterannean (diets and disease prevention). In: Kiple K, Ornelas K, editors. *The Cambridge World History of Food.* Cambridge: Cambridge University Press, 2000.

63. Popkin BM. The nutrition transition: an overview of world patterns of change. *Nutr Rev* 2004;62:S140-3.

64. Pollan M. Industrial. *The Omnivore's Dilemma. The Search for a Prefect Meal in a Fast Food World.* London: Bloomsbury, 2006.

65. Shallenberger R, Wretlind A, Page L. Sugars in food: occurance and usage. In: Sipple H, McNutt K, editors. *Sugars in Nutrition. A Nutrition Association Monograph.* New York: New York Academy Press, 1974.

66. Giedion S. Mechanization encounters the organic. *Mechanization takes Command.* Oxford: Oxford University Press, 1948.

67. Hoffmann W. 100 years of the margarine industry. In: van Stuyvenberg A, editor. *Margarine. An Economic, Social and Scientific History, 1869-1969.* Liverpool: Liverpool University Press, 1969.

68. Quandt S. Infant and child nutrition. In: Kiple K, Ornelas K, editors. *The Cambridge World History of Food.* Cambridge: Cambridge University Press, 2000.

69. Hollingsworth D. The application of the newer knowledge of nutrition. In: Drummond J, Wilbraham A, editors. *The Englishman's Food. Five Centuries of English Diet.* London, 1991.

70. Food and Agriculture Organization of the United Nations. *Globalization of Food Systems in Developing Countries: Impact on Food Security and Nutrition.* Rome, 2004.

71. Cordain L, Eaton SB, Sebastian A, et al. Origins and evolution of the Western diet: health implications for the 21st century. *Am J Clin Nutr* 2005;81:341-54.

72. Fogel RW. Reconsidering Expectations of Economic Growth After World War II from the Perspective of 2004. *International Monetary Fund (IMF) Staff Papers* 2005;52.

73. Committee on Diet Nutrition and Cancer, Assembly of Life Sciences, National Research Council (US). *Diet, Nutrition and Cancer.* Washington, DC: National Academy Press, 1982.

74. Committee on Diet and Health, Food and Nutrition Board, Commission on Life Sciences, et al. *Diet and Health: Implications for Reducing Chronic Disease Risk.* Washington, DC: National Academy Press, 1989.

75. World Health Organization. *Diet, Nutrition and the Prevention of Chronic Diseases.* Geneva: WHO, 1990.

76. Hawkes C. The role of foreign direct investment in the nutrition transition. *Public Health Nutr* 2005;8:357-65.

77. Hawkes C. Uneven dietary development: linking the policies and processes of globalization with the nutrition transition, obesity and diet-related chronic diseases. *Global Health* 2006;2:4.

78. Yach D, Hawkes C, Gould CL, et al. The global burden of chronic diseases: overcoming impediments to prevention and control. *JAMA* 2004;291:2616-22.

79. Kuhnlein HV, Johns T. Northwest African and Middle Eastern food and dietary

change of indigenous peoples. *Asia Pac J Clin Nutr* 2003;12:344-9.

80. Kuhnlein HV, Receveur O, Soueida R, et al. Arctic indigenous peoples experience the nutrition transition with changing dietary patterns and obesity. *J Nutr* 2004;134:1447-53.

81. World Health Organization. *WHO Nutrition. www.WHO:int/nutrition/ topics/3-foodconsumption/en/print.html.* 2006.

82. Popkin BM. The shift in stages of the nutrition transition in the developing world differs from past experiences. *Public Health Nutr* 2002;5:205-14.

83. Popkin BM. Global nutrition dynamics: the world is shifting rapidly toward a diet linked with noncommunicable diseases. *Am J Clin Nutr* 2006;84:289-98.

84. Wu Y. Overweight and obesity in China. *BMJ* 2006;333:362-3.

85. Bell AC, Ge K, Popkin BM. Weight gain and its predictors in Chinese adults. *Int J Obes* 2001;25:1079-86.

86. Wang Y, Mi J, Shan XY, et al. Is China facing an obesity epidemic and the consequences? The trends in obesity and chronic disease in China. *Int J Obes (Lond)* 2007;31:177-88.

87. Silventoinen K, Sans S, Tolonen H, et al. Trends in obesity and energy supply in the WHO MONICA Project. *Int J Obes Relat Metab Disord* 2004;28:710-8.

88. Department of Health. *Forecasting obesity to 2010.* http://www.dh.gov.uk/PublicationsAndSt atistics/Publications/PublicationsStatistics /PublicationsStatisticsArticle/fs/en?CONT ENT_ID=4138630&chk=XVZ/60. 2006.

89. Mendez MA, Monteiro CA, Popkin BM. Overweight exceeds underweight among women in most developing countries. *Am J Clin Nutr* 2005;81:714-21.

90. Popkin BM. An overview on the nutrition transition and its health implications: the Bellagio meeting. *Public Health Nutr* 2002;5:93-103.

91. Bull F, Armstrong TP, Dixon T, et al. Physical inactivity. In: Ezzati M, Lopez A, Rodgers A, et al., editors. *Comparative quantification of health risks: global and regional burden of disease.* Geneva: World Health Organization, 2004.

92. National Center for Chronic Disease Prevention and Health Promotion. *Physical Activity and Health. A report of the Surgeon General.* http://www.cdc.gov/nccdphp/sgr/sgr.htm. 1999.

93. Mackay J, Jemal A, Lee N, et al. *The Cancer Atlas:* American Cancer Society, 2006.

94. Parkin DM, Bray F, Ferlay J, et al. Global cancer statistics, 2002. *CA Cancer J Clin* 2005;55:74-108.

95. Parkin DM. International variation. *Oncogene* 2004;23:6329-40.

96. Parkin DM, Whelan SL, Ferlay J, et al. Cancer Incidence in Five Continents, Vol I to VIII. *IARC CancerBase* 2005;7.

97. Key TJ, Allen NE, Spencer EA, et al. The effect of diet on risk of cancer. *Lancet* 2002;360:861-8.

98. Doll R, Peto R. The causes of cancer: quantitative estimates of avoidable risks of cancer in the United States today. *J Natl Cancer Inst* 1981;66:1191-308.

99. Kolonel LN, Hinds MW, Hankin JH. Cancer patterns among migrant and native-born Japanese in Hawaii in relation to smoking, drinking and dietary habits. *In: Gelboin, H.V. et al (eds) Genetic and Environmental factors in Experimental and Human Cancer. Tokyo: Japan Sci Soc Press pp 327-340 1980.*

100. McMichael AJ, McCall MG, Hartshorne JM, et al. Patterns of gastro-intestinal cancer in European migrants to Australia: the role of dietary change. *Int J Cancer* 1980;25:431-7.

101. McMichael AJ, Giles GG. Cancer in migrants to Australia: extending the descriptive epidemiological data. *Cancer Res* 1988;48:751-6.

102. Yavari P, Hislop TG, Bajdik C, et al. Comparison of cancer incidence in Iran and Iranian immigrants to British Columbia, Canada. *Asian Pac J Cancer Prev* 2006;7:86-90.

103. Nelson NJ. Migrant studies aid the search for factors linked to breast cancer risk. *J Natl Cancer Inst* 2006;98:436-8.

104. Flood DM, Weiss NS, Cook LS, et al. Colorectal cancer incidence in Asian migrants to the United States and their descendants. *Cancer Causes Control* 2000;11:403-11.

105. Hemminki K, Li X. Cancer risks in second-generation immigrants to Sweden. *Int J Cancer* 2002;99:229-37.

106. Zagorsky JL. Health and wealth. The late-20th century obesity epidemic in the U.S. *Econ Hum Biol* 2005;3:296-313.

Chapter 2

1. Craig WJ. Phytochemicals: guardians of our health. *J Am Diet Assoc* 1997;97:S199-204.

2. Finley JW. Bioavailability of selenium from foods. *Nutr Rev* 2006;64:146-51.

3. McNaughton SA, Marks GC. Development of a food composition database for the estimation of dietary intakes of glucosinolates, the biologically active constituents of cruciferous vegetables. *Br J Nutr* 2003;90:687-97.

4. Finley JW. Proposed criteria for assessing the efficacy of cancer reduction by plant foods enriched in carotenoids, glucosinolates, polyphenols and selenocompounds. *Ann Bot (Lond)* 2005;95:1075-96.

5. Milner JA. Molecular targets for bioactive food components. *J Nutr* 2004;134:2492S-8S.

6. Barker DJ. The fetal and infant origins of adult disease. *BMJ* 1990;301:1111.

7. Jackson AA, Bhutta ZA, Lumbiganon P. Nutrition as a preventative strategy against adverse pregnancy outcomes. Introduction. *J Nutr* 2003;133:1589S-91S.

8. Bertram C, Trowern AR, Copin N, et al. The maternal diet during pregnancy programs altered expression of the glucocorticoid receptor and type 2 11beta-hydroxysteroid dehydrogenase: potential molecular mechanisms underlying the programming of hypertension in utero. *Endocrinology* 2001;142:2841-53.

9. Lillycrop KA, Phillips ES, Jackson AA, et al. Dietary protein restriction of pregnant rats induces and folic acid supplementation prevents epigenetic modification of hepatic gene expression in the offspring. *J Nutr* 2005;135:1382-6.

10. Khaw KT, Wareham N, Luben R, et al. Glycated haemoglobin, diabetes, and mortality in men in Norfolk cohort of European prospective investigation of cancer and nutrition (EPIC-Norfolk). *BMJ* 2001;322:15-8.

11. Barnard RJ, Aronson WJ, Tymchuk CN, et al. Prostate cancer: another aspect of the insulin-resistance syndrome? *Obes Rev* 2002;3:303-8.

12. Uauy R, Solomons N. Diet, nutrition, and the life-course approach to cancer prevention. *J Nutr* 2005;135:2934S-45S.

13. Calle EE, Kaaks R. Overweight, obesity and cancer: epidemiological evidence and proposed mechanisms. *Nat Rev Cancer* 2004;4:579-91.

14. Lane DP. Cancer. p53, guardian of the genome. *Nature* 1992;358:15-6.

15. Birch JM. Li-Fraumeni syndrome. *Eur J Cancer* 1994;30A:1935-41.

16. Dashwood RH, Myzak MC, Ho E. Dietary HDAC inhibitors: time to rethink weak ligands in cancer chemoprevention? *Carcinogenesis* 2006;27:344-9.

17. Esquela-Kerscher A, Slack FJ. Oncomirs – microRNAs with a role in cancer. *Nat Rev Cancer* 2006;6:259-69.

18. Romney SL, Ho GY, Palan PR, et al. Effects of beta-carotene and other factors on outcome of cervical dysplasia and human papillomavirus infection. *Gynecol Oncol* 1997;65:483-92.

19. Kim YI, Giuliano A, Hatch KD, et al. Global DNA hypomethylation increases progressively in cervical dysplasia and carcinoma. *Cancer* 1994;74:893-9.

20. Giovannucci E. Epidemiologic studies of folate and colorectal neoplasia: a review. *J Nutr* 2002;132:2350S-5S.

21. Jordan CT, Guzman ML, Noble M. Cancer stem cells. *N Engl J Med* 2006;355:1253-61.

22. Polyak K, Hahn WC. Roots and stems: stem cells in cancer. *Nat Med* 2006;12:296-300.

23. Al-Hajj M, Wicha MS, Benito-Hernandez A, et al. Prospective identification of tumorigenic breast cancer cells. *Proc Natl Acad Sci USA* 2003;100:3983-8.

24. Hemmati HD, Nakano I, Lazareff JA, et al. Cancerous stem cells can arise from pediatric brain tumors. *Proc Natl Acad Sci USA* 2003;100:15178-83.

25. Singh SK, Clarke ID, Terasaki M, et al. Identification of a cancer stem cell in human brain tumors. *Cancer Res* 2003;63:5821-8.

26. Bapat SA, Mali AM, Koppikar CB, et al. Stem and progenitor-like cells contribute to the aggressive behavior of human epithelial ovarian cancer. *Cancer Res* 2005;65:3025-9.

27. Collins AT, Berry PA, Hyde C, et al. Prospective identification of tumorigenic prostate cancer stem cells. *Cancer Res* 2005;65:10946-51.

28. Ricci-Vitiani L, Lombardi DG, Pilozzi E, et al. Identification and expansion of human colon-cancer-initiating cells. *Nature* 2007;445:111-5.

29. Houghton J, Stoicov C, Nomura S, et al. Gastric cancer originating from bone marrow-derived cells. *Science* 2004;306:1568-71.

30. Nkondjock A, Shatenstein B, Maisonneuve P, et al. Specific fatty acids and human colorectal cancer: an overview. *Cancer Detect Prev* 2003;27:55-66.

31. Roynette CE, Calder PC, Dupertuis YM, et al. n-3 polyunsaturated fatty acids and colon cancer prevention. *Clin Nutr* 2004;23:139-51.

32. Hoeijmakers JH. Genome maintenance mechanisms for preventing cancer. *Nature* 2001;411:366-74.

33. Larsen NB, Rasmussen M, Rasmussen LJ. Nuclear and mitochondrial DNA repair: similar pathways? *Mitochondrion* 2005;5:89-108.

34. Gonzalez C, Najera O, Cortes E, et al. Hydrogen peroxide-induced DNA damage and DNA repair in lymphocytes from malnourished children. *Environ Mol Mutagen* 2002;39:33-42.

35. Wei Q, Shen H, Wang LE, et al. Association between low dietary folate intake and suboptimal cellular DNA repair capacity. *Cancer Epidemiol Biomarkers Prev* 2003;12:963-9.

36. Collins AR, Harrington V, Drew J, et al. Nutritional modulation of DNA repair in a human intervention study. *Carcinogenesis* 2003;24:511-5.

37. Astley SB, Elliott RM, Archer DB, et al. Evidence that dietary supplementation with carotenoids and carotenoid-rich foods modulates the DNA damage: repair balance in human lymphocytes. *Br J Nutr* 2004;91:63-72.

38. Tomasetti M, Alleva R, Borghi B, et al. In vivo supplementation with coenzyme Q10 enhances the recovery of human lymphocytes from oxidative DNA damage. *Faseb J* 2001;15:1425-7.

39. Seo YR, Sweeney C, Smith ML. Selenomethionine induction of DNA repair response in human fibroblasts. *Oncogene* 2002;21:3663-9.

40. Kiss I, Sandor J, Ember I. Allelic polymorphism of GSTM1 and NAT2 genes modifies dietary-induced DNA damage in colorectal mucosa. *Eur J Cancer Prev* 2000;9:429-32.

41. Arab L, Steck-Scott S, Fleishauer AT. Lycopene and the lung. *Exp Biol Med (Maywood)* 2002;227:894-9.

42. Aguiar M, Masse R, Gibbs BF. Regulation of cytochrome P450 by posttranslational modification. *Drug Metab Rev* 2005;37:379-404.

43. van Rees BP, Ristimaki A. Cyclooxygenase-2 in carcinogenesis of the gastrointestinal tract. *Scand J Gastroenterol* 2001;36:897-903.

44. Hein DW. Molecular genetics and function of NAT1 and NAT2: role in aromatic amine metabolism and carcinogenesis. *Mutat Res* 2002;506-507:65-77.

45. Sheweita SA, Tilmisany AK. Cancer and phase II drug-metabolizing enzymes. *Curr Drug Metab* 2003;4:45-58.

46. Lee JS, Surh YJ. Nrf2 as a novel molecular target for chemoprevention. *Cancer Lett* 2005;224:171-84.

47. Fujita K. Food-drug interactions via human cytochrome P450 3A (CYP3A). *Drug Metabol Drug Interact* 2004;20:195-217.

48. Harris RZ, Jang GR, Tsunoda S. Dietary effects on drug metabolism and transport. *Clin Pharmacokinet* 2003;42:1071-88.

49. Okey AB, Boutros PC, Harper PA. Polymorphisms of human nuclear receptors that control expression of drug-metabolizing enzymes. *Pharmacogenet Genomics* 2005;15:371-9.

50. Davis CD, Milner J. Frontiers in nutrigenomics, proteomics, metabolomics and cancer prevention. *Mutat Res* 2004;551:51-64.

51. Hayes JD, Flanagan JU, Jowsey IR. Glutathione transferases. *Annu Rev Pharmacol Toxicol* 2005;45:51-88.

52. Seow A, Yuan JM, Sun CL, et al. Dietary isothiocyanates, glutathione S-transferase polymorphisms and colorectal cancer risk in the Singapore Chinese Health Study. *Carcinogenesis* 2002;23:2055-61.

53. Sheweita SA. Drug-metabolizing enzymes: mechanisms and functions. *Curr Drug Metab* 2000;1:107-32.

54. Hubner RA, Houlston RS. MTHFR C677T and colorectal cancer risk: A meta-analysis of 25 populations. *Int J Cancer* 2007;120:1027-35.

55. Le Marchand L. Meat intake, metabolic genes and colorectal cancer. *IARC Sci Publ* 2002;156:481-5.

56. Brennan P, Hsu CC, Moullan N, et al. Effect of cruciferous vegetables on lung cancer in patients stratified by genetic status: a mendelian randomisation approach. *Lancet* 2005;366:1558-60.

57. Weinberg ED. The role of iron in cancer. *Eur J Cancer Prev* 1996;5:19-36.

58. McCord JM. Iron, free radicals, and oxidative injury. *Semin Hematol* 1998;35:5-12.

59. Huang X. Iron overload and its association with cancer risk in humans: evidence for iron as a carcinogenic metal. *Mutat Res* 2003;533:153-71.

60. Lewin MH, Bailey N, Bandaletova T, et al. Red meat enhances the colonic formation of the DNA adduct O6-carboxymethyl guanine: implications for colorectal cancer risk. *Cancer Res* 2006;66:1859-65.

61. Talalay P, Fahey JW. Phytochemicals from cruciferous plants protect against cancer by modulating carcinogen metabolism. *J Nutr* 2001;131:3027S-33S.

62. Kojima T, Tanaka T, Mori H. Chemoprevention of spontaneous endometrial cancer in female Donryu rats by dietary indole-3-carbinol. *Cancer Res* 1994;54:1446-9.

63. Kang ZC, Tsai SJ, Lee H. Quercetin inhibits benzo[a]pyrene-induced DNA adducts in human Hep G2 cells by altering cytochrome P-450 1A1 gene expression. *Nutr Cancer* 1999;35:175-9.

64. Goodman GE, Thornquist MD, Balmes J, et al. The Beta-Carotene and Retinol Efficacy Trial: incidence of lung cancer and cardiovascular disease mortality during 6-year follow-up after stopping beta-carotene and retinol supplements. *J Natl Cancer Inst* 2004;96:1743-50.

65. UK Food Standards Agency. *Safe Upper Levels for Vitamins and Minerals.* http://www.food.gov.uk/multimedia/pdfs/vitmin2003.pdf. 2003.

66. Hursting SD, Lavigne JA, Berrigan D, et al. Calorie restriction, aging, and cancer prevention: mechanisms of action and applicability to humans. *Annu Rev Med* 2003;54:131-52.

67. Stattin P, Lukanova A, Biessy C, et al. Obesity and colon cancer: does leptin provide a link? *Int J Cancer* 2004;109:149-52.

68. Chang S, Hursting SD, Contois JH, et al. Leptin and prostate cancer. *Prostate* 2001;46:62-7.

69. The Endogenous Hormones and Breast Cancer Collaborative Group. Endogenous sex hormones and breast cancer in postmenopausal women: reanalysis of nine prospective studies. *J Natl Cancer Inst* 2002;94:606-16.

70. Kaaks R, Lukanova A, Kurzer MS. Obesity,

endogenous hormones, and endometrial cancer risk: a synthetic review. *Cancer Epidemiol Biomarkers Prev* 2002;11:1531-43.

71. Rexrode KM, Pradhan A, Manson JE, et al. Relationship of total and abdominal adiposity with CRP and IL-6 in women. *Ann Epidemiol* 2003;13:674-82.

72. Loffreda S, Yang SQ, Lin HZ, et al. Leptin regulates proinflammatory immune responses. *Faseb J* 1998;12:57-65.

73. Le Roith D, Bondy C, Yakar S, et al. The somatomedin hypothesis: 2001. *Endocr Rev* 2001;22:53-74.

74. Doll R, Peto R. The causes of cancer: quantitative estimates of avoidable risks of cancer in the United States today. *J Natl Cancer Inst* 1981;66:1191-308.

75. World Health Organization and International Agency for Research on Cancer. *World Cancer Report*. Lyon: IARC Press, 2003.

76. Coussens LM, Werb Z. Inflammation and cancer. *Nature* 2002;420:860-7.

77. Smyth MJ, Dunn GP, Schreiber RD. Cancer immunosurveillance and immunoediting: the roles of immunity in suppressing tumor development and shaping tumor immunogenicity. *Adv Immunol* 2006;90:1-50.

78. Zitvogel L, Tesniere A, Kroemer G. Cancer despite immunosurveillance: immunoselection and immunosubversion. *Nat Rev Immunol* 2006;6:715-27.

79. Miura S, Tsuzuki Y, Hokari R, et al. Modulation of intestinal immune system by dietary fat intake: relevance to Crohn's disease. *J Gastroenterol Hepatol* 1998;13:1183-90.

80. Tlaskalova-Hogenova H, Tuckova L, Lodinova-Zadnikova R, et al. Mucosal immunity: its role in defense and allergy. *Int Arch Allergy Immunol* 2002;128:77-89.

81. Hanna MK, Kudsk KA. Nutritional and pharmacological enhancement of gut-associated lymphoid tissue. *Can J Gastroenterol* 2000;14 Suppl D:145D-51D.

82. Kudsk KA. Current aspects of mucosal immunology and its influence by nutrition. *Am J Surg* 2002;183:390-8.

83. Gleeson M, Nieman DC, Pedersen BK. Exercise, nutrition and immune function. *J Sports Sci* 2004;22:115-25.

84. Kubena KS, McMurray DN. Nutrition and the immune system: a review of nutrient-nutrient interactions. *J Am Diet Assoc* 1996;96:1156-64; quiz 65-6.

85. Levi RS, Sanderson IR. Dietary regulation of gene expression. *Curr Opin Gastroenterol* 2004;20:139-42.

86. Wieringa FT, Dijkhuizen MA, West CE, et al. Reduced production of immunoregulatory cytokines in vitamin A- and zinc-deficient Indonesian infants. *Eur J Clin Nutr* 2004;58:1498-504.

87. Marcos A, Nova E, Montero A. Changes in the immune system are conditioned by nutrition. *Eur J Clin Nutr* 2003;57 Suppl 1:S66-9.

88. Trikha M, Corringham R, Klein B, et al. Targeted anti-interleukin-6 monoclonal antibody therapy for cancer: a review of the rationale and clinical evidence. *Clin Cancer Res* 2003;9:4653-65.

89. Dijsselbloem N, Vanden Berghe W, De Naeyer A, et al. Soy isoflavone phyto-pharmaceuticals in interleukin-6 affections. Multi-purpose nutraceuticals at the crossroad of hormone replacement, anti-cancer and anti-inflammatory therapy. *Biochem Pharmacol* 2004;68:1171-85.

90. Petersen AM, Pedersen BK. The anti-inflammatory effect of exercise. *J Appl Physiol* 2005;98:1154-62.

91. Nieman DC. Nutrition, exercise, and immune system function. *Clin Sports Med* 1999;18:537-48.

92. Stickel F, Schuppan D, Hahn EG, et al. Cocarcinogenic effects of alcohol in hepatocarcinogenesis. *Gut* 2002;51:132-9.

93. Bowlus CL. The role of iron in T cell development and autoimmunity. *Autoimmun Rev* 2003;2:73-8.

94. Latunde-Dada GO, Young SP. Iron deficiency and immune responses. *Scand J Immunol Suppl* 1992;11:207-9.

95. Ekiz C, Agaoglu L, Karakas Z, et al. The effect of iron deficiency anemia on the function of the immune system. *Hematol J* 2005;5:579-83.

96. Bosetti C, Negri E, Trichopoulos D, et al. Long-term effects of oral contraceptives on ovarian cancer risk. *Int J Cancer* 2002;102:262-5.

97. Genazzani A. *Hormone Replacement Therapy and Cancer: The Current Status of Research and Practice*. New York: Parthenon, 2002.

98. Hannaford P, Elliott A. Use of exogenous hormones by women and colorectal cancer: evidence from the Royal College of General Practitioners' Oral Contraception Study. *Contraception* 2005;71:95-8.

99. Collaborative Group on Hormonal Factors in Breast Cancer. Breast cancer and breastfeeding: collaborative reanalysis of individual data from 47 epidemiological studies in 30 countries, including 50302 women with breast cancer and 96973 women without the disease. *Lancet* 2002;20:187-95.

100. Smith JS, Green J, Berrington de Gonzalez A, et al. Cervical cancer and use of hormonal contraceptives: a systematic review. *Lancet* 2003;361:1159-67.

101. Lacey JV, Jr., Mink PJ, Lubin JH, et al. Menopausal hormone replacement therapy and risk of ovarian cancer. *JAMA* 2002;288:334-41.

102. Pike MC, Pearce CL, Wu AH. Prevention of cancers of the breast, endometrium and ovary. *Oncogene* 2004;23:6379-91.

103. Mackay J, Eriksen M, Shafey O. *The Tobacco Atlas*. 2nd ed. Atlanta: American Cancer Society, 2006.

104. Mackay J, Jemal A, Lee N, et al. *The Cancer Atlas*. Atlanta: American Cancer Society, 2006.

105. Nishikawa A, Mori Y, Lee IS, et al. Cigarette smoking, metabolic activation and carcinogenesis. *Curr Drug Metab* 2004;5:363-73.

106. Alberg A. The influence of cigarette smoking on circulating concentrations of antioxidant micronutrients. *Toxicology* 2002;180:121-37.

107. Piyathilake CJ, Henao OL, Macaluso M, et al. Folate is associated with the natural history of high-risk human papillomaviruses. *Cancer Res* 2004;64:8788-93.

108. Moller P, Loft S. Oxidative DNA damage in human white blood cells in dietary antioxidant intervention studies. *Am J Clin Nutr* 2002;76:303-10.

109. Hites RA, Foran JA, Schwager SJ, et al. Global assessment of polybrominated diphenyl ethers in farmed and wild salmon. *Environ Sci Technol* 2004;38:4945-9.

110. Davies S. Subsequent malignant neoplasms in survivors of childhood cancer: Childhood Cancer Survivor Study (CCSS) studies. *Pediatr Blood Cancer* 2007;48:727-30.

111. Hanahan D, Weinberg RA. The hallmarks of cancer. *Cell* 2000;100:57-70.

112. Sharpless NE, DePinho RA. Cancer: crime and punishment. *Nature* 2005;436:636-7.

113. Bohnsack BL, Hirschi KK. Nutrient regulation of cell cycle progression. *Annu Rev Nutr* 2004;24:433-53.

114. Lotan R. Aberrant expression of retinoid receptors and lung carcinogenesis. *J Natl Cancer Inst* 1999;91:989-91.

115. Palan PR, Chang CJ, Mikhail MS, et al. Plasma concentrations of micronutrients during a nine-month clinical trial of beta-carotene in women with precursor cervical cancer lesions. *Nutr Cancer* 1998;30:46-52.

116. Butterworth C, Jr., Hatch K, Gore H, et al. Improvement in cervical dysplasia associated with folic acid therapy in users of oral contraceptives. *Am J Clin Nutr*, 1982:73-82.

117. Abu J, Batuwangala M, Herbert K, et al. Retinoic acid and retinoid receptors: potential chemopreventive and therapeutic role in cervical cancer. *Lancet Oncol* 2005;6:712-20.

118. Chen C, Kong AN. Dietary cancer-chemopreventive compounds: from signaling and gene expression to pharmacological effects. *Trends Pharmacol Sci* 2005;26:318-26.

119. Li N, Sun Z, Han C, et al. The chemopreventive effects of tea on human oral precancerous mucosa lesions. *Proc Soc Exp Biol Med* 1999;220:218-24.

120. Strauss L, Santti R, Saarinen N, et al. Dietary phytoestrogens and their role in hormonally dependent disease. *Toxicol Lett* 1998;102-103:349-54.

121. Adlercreutz H. Phyto-oestrogens and cancer. *Lancet Oncol* 2002;3:364-73.

122. Niculescu MD, Pop EA, Fischer LM, et al. Dietary isoflavones differentially induce gene expression changes in lymphocytes

from postmenopausal women who form equol as compared with those who do not. *J Nutr Biochem* 2006;18:380-90.

123. Lamprecht S, Lipkin M. Cellular mechanisms of calcium and vitamin D in the inhibition of colorectal carcinogenesis. *Ann NY Acad Sci* 2001;952:73-87.

124. Sesink AL, Termont DS, Kleibeuker JH, et al. Red meat and colon cancer: the cytotoxic and hyperproliferative effects of dietary heme. *Cancer Res* 1999;59:5704-9.

125. Knowles LM, Milner JA. Possible mechanism by which allyl sulfides suppress neoplastic cell proliferation. *J Nutr* 2001;131:1061S-6S.

126. Rao CV, Hirose Y, Indranie C, et al. Modulation of experimental colon tumorigenesis by types and amounts of dietary fatty acids. *Cancer Res* 2001;61:1927-33.

127. Gupta RA, Tan J, Krause WF, et al. Prostacyclin-mediated activation of peroxisome proliferator-activated receptor delta in colorectal cancer. *Proc Natl Acad Sci USA* 2000;97:13275-80.

128. Price PT, Nelson CM, Clarke SD. Omega-3 polyunsaturated fatty acid regulation of gene expression. *Curr Opin Lipidol* 2000;11:3-7.

129. Novak TE, Babcock TA, Jho DH, et al. NF-kappa B inhibition by omega-3 fatty acids modulates LPS-stimulated macrophage TNF-alpha transcription. *Am J Physiol Lung Cell Mol Physiol* 2003;284:L84-9.

130. Collett ED, Davidson LA, Fan YY, et al. n-6 and n-3 polyunsaturated fatty acids differentially modulate oncogenic Ras activation in colonocytes. *Am J Physiol Cell Physiol* 2001;280:C1066-75.

131. Chapkin RS, Clark AE, Davidson LA, et al. Dietary fiber differentially alters cellular fatty acid-binding protein expression in exfoliated colonocytes during tumor development. *Nutr Cancer* 1998;32:107-12.

132. LeRoith D, Baserga R, Helman L, et al. Insulin-like growth factors and cancer. *Ann Intern Med* 1995;122:54-9.

133. Yakar S, Leroith D, Brodt P. The role of the growth hormone/insulin-like growth factor axis in tumor growth and progression: lessons from animal models. *Cytokine Growth Factor Rev* 2005;16:407-20.

134. Fenton JI, Hord NG, Lavigne JA, et al. Leptin, insulin-like growth factor-1, and insulin-like growth factor-2 are mitogens in ApcMin/+ but not Apc+/+ colonic epithelial cell lines. *Cancer Epidemiol Biomarkers Prev* 2005;14:1646-52.

135. Grimm JJ. Interaction of physical activity and diet: implications for insulin-glucose dynamics. *Public Health Nutr* 1999;2:363-8.

136. McTiernan A, Sorensen B, Yasui Y, et al. No effect of exercise on insulin-like growth factor 1 and insulin-like growth factor binding protein 3 in postmenopausal women: a 12-month randomized clinical trial. *Cancer Epidemiol Biomarkers Prev* 2005;14:1020-1.

137. Schmitz KH, Ahmed RL, Yee D. Effects of a 9-month strength training intervention on insulin, insulin-like growth factor (IGF)-I, IGF-binding protein (IGFBP)-1, and IGFBP-3 in 30-50-year-old women. *Cancer Epidemiol Biomarkers Prev* 2002;11:1597-604.

138. Colbert LH, Mai V, Perkins SN, et al. Exercise and intestinal polyp development in APCMin mice. *Med Sci Sports Exerc* 2003;35:1662-9.

139. Thompson HJ, Zhu Z, Jiang W. Dietary energy restriction in breast cancer prevention. *J Mammary Gland Biol Neoplasia* 2003;8:133-42.

140. Zhu Z, Jiang W, McGinley J, et al. Effects of dietary energy repletion and IGF-1 infusion on the inhibition of mammary carcinogenesis by dietary energy restriction. *Mol Carcinog* 2005;3:170-6.

141. Mawson A, Lai A, Carroll JS, et al. Estrogen and insulin/IGF-1 cooperatively stimulate cell cycle progression in MCF-7 breast cancer cells through differential regulation of c-Myc and cyclin D1. *Mol Cell Endocrinol* 2005;229:161-73.

142. Wood JG, Rogina B, Lavu S, et al. Sirtuin activators mimic caloric restriction and delay ageing in metazoans. *Nature* 2004;430:686-9.

143. Fischer U, Schulze-Osthoff K. Apoptosis-based therapies and drug targets. *Cell Death Differ* 2005;12 Suppl 1:942-61.

144. Mihara M, Erster S, Zaika A, et al. p53 has a direct apoptogenic role at the mitochondria. *Mol Cell* 2003;11:577-90.

145. Thompson HJ, Zhu Z, Jiang W. Weight control and breast cancer prevention: are the effects of reduced energy intake equivalent to those of increased energy expenditure? *J Nutr* 2004;134:3407S-11S.

146. Salganik RI, Albright CD, Rodgers J, et al. Dietary antioxidant depletion: enhancement of tumor apoptosis and inhibition of brain tumor growth in transgenic mice. *Carcinogenesis* 2000;21:909-14.

147. Albright CD, Salganik RI, Van Dyke T. Dietary depletion of vitamin E and vitamin A inhibits mammary tumor growth and metastasis in transgenic mice. *J Nutr* 2004;134:1139-44.

148. Watson WH, Cai J, Jones DP. Diet and apoptosis. *Annu Rev Nutr* 2000;20:485-505.

149. Khan H, Afaq F, Mukhtar H. Apoptosis by dietary factors: the suicide solution for delaying cancer growth. *Carcinogenesis* 2007;28:233-9.

150. Sun S, Hail N, Lotan R. Apoptosis as a novel target for cancer chemoprevention. *J Natl Cancer Inst* 2004;96:662-72.

151. Gunawardena K, Murray DK, Meikle AW. Vitamin E and other antioxidants inhibit human prostate cancer cells through apoptosis. *Prostate* 2000;44:287-95.

152. Takahashi H, Kosaka N, Nakagawa S. alpha-Tocopherol protects PC12 cells from hyperoxia-induced apoptosis. *J Neurosci Res* 1998;52:184-91.

153. Folkman J. Fundamental concepts of the angiogenic process. *Curr Mol Med* 2003;3:643-51.

154. Cao Y, Cao R. Angiogenesis inhibited by drinking tea. *Nature* 1999;398:381.

155. Rose DP, Connolly JM. Regulation of tumor angiogenesis by dietary fatty acids and eicosanoids. *Nutr Cancer* 2000;37:119-27.

156. Matsuura N, Miyamae Y, Yamane K, et al. Aged garlic extract inhibits angiogenesis and proliferation of colorectal carcinoma cells. *J Nutr* 2006;136:842S-6S.

157. Bailey AP, Shparago M, Gu JW. Exercise increases soluble vascular endothelial growth factor receptor-1 (sFlt-1) in circulation of healthy volunteers. *Med Sci Monit* 2006;12:CR45-50.

158. Roomi MW, Ivanov V, Kalinovsky T, et al. Inhibition of matrix metalloproteinase-2 secretion and invasion by human ovarian cancer cell line SK-OV-3 with lysine, proline, arginine, ascorbic acid and green tea extract. *J Obstet Gynaecol Res* 2006;32:148-54.

159. Hahn T, Szabo L, Gold M, et al. Dietary administration of the proapoptotic vitamin E analogue {alpha}-tocopheryloxyacetic acid inhibits metastatic murine breast cancer. *Cancer Res* 2006;66:9374-8.

Chapter 3

1. Parkin DM, Whelan SL, Ferlay J, et al., editors. *Cancer Incidence in Five Continents, Volume VIII*. Lyon: IARC, 2002.

2. Carroll KK. Experimental evidence of dietary factors and hormone-dependent cancers. *Cancer Res* 1975;35:3374-83.

3. Doll R, Peto R. *The Causes of Cancer*. Oxford: Oxford University Press, 1981.

4. National Academy of Sciences. *Diet, Nutrition, and Cancer*. Washington, DC: National Academy Press, 1982.

5. Committee on Diet and Health, Food and Nutrition Board, Committee on Life Sciences, National Research Council. *Diet and Health: Implications for Reducing Chronic Disease Risk*. Washington, DC: National Academy Press, 1989.

6. Kinlen LJ. Fat and cancer. *Br Med J (Clin Res Ed)* 1983;286:1081-2.

7. Braam LA, Ocke MC, Bueno-de-Mesquita HB, et al. Determinants of obesity-related underreporting of energy intake. *Am J Epidemiol* 1998;147:1081-6.

8. Heerstrass DW, Ocke MC, Bueno-de-Mesquita HB, et al. Underreporting of energy, protein and potassium intake in relation to body mass index. *Int J Epidemiol* 1998;27:186-93.

9. Goris AH, Westerterp-Plantenga MS, Westerterp KR. Undereating and underrecording of habitual food intake in obese men: selective underreporting of fat intake. *Am J Clin Nutr* 2000;71:130-4.

10. Johansson G, Wikman A, Ahren AM, et al. Underreporting of energy intake in repeated 24-hour recalls related to gender, age, weight status, day of interview, educational level, reported food intake, smoking habits and area of living. *Public Health Nutrition* 2001;4:919-27.

11. Asbeck I, Mast M, Bierwag A, et al. Severe underreporting of energy intake in normal weight subjects: use of an appropriate standard and relation to restrained eating. *Public Health Nutrition* 2002;5:683-90.

12. Ferrari P, Slimani N, Ciampi A, et al. Evaluation of under- and overreporting of energy intake in the 24-hour diet recalls in the European Prospective Investigation into Cancer and Nutrition (EPIC). *Public Health Nutrition* 2002;5:1329-45.

13. Horner NK, Patterson RE, Neuhouser ML, et al. Participant characteristics associated with errors in self-reported energy intake from the Women's Health Initiative food-frequency questionnaire. *Am J Clin Nutr* 2002;76:766-73.

14. Tooze JA, Subar AF, Thompson FE, et al. Psychosocial predictors of energy underreporting in a large doubly labeled water study. *Am J Clin Nutr* 2004;79:795-804.

15. Rothman KJ. *Epidemiology: An Introduction*. New York: Oxford University Press, 2002.

16. Last JM, editor. *A Dictionary of Epidemiology*. 4th ed. New York: Oxford University Press, 2001.

17. Willett WC. *Nutritional Epidemiology*. New York: Oxford University Press, 1990.

18. Wacholder S, McLaughlin JK, Silverman DT, et al. Selection of controls in case-control studies. I. Principles. *Am J Epidemiol* 1992;135:1019-28.

19. Wacholder S, Silverman DT, McLaughlin JK, et al. Selection of controls in case-control studies. III. Design options. *Am J Epidemiol* 1992;135:1042-50.

20. Wacholder S, Silverman DT, McLaughlin JK, et al. Selection of controls in case-control studies. II. Types of controls. *Am J Epidemiol* 1992;135:1029-41.

21. Riboli E, Kaaks R. The EPIC Project: rationale and study design. European Prospective Investigation into Cancer and Nutrition. *Int J Epidemiol* 1997;26 Suppl 1:S6-14.

22. Riboli E, Hunt KJ, Slimani N, et al. European Prospective Investigation into Cancer and Nutrition (EPIC): study populations and data collection. *Public Health Nutrition* 2002;5:1113-24.

23. Belanger CF, Hennekens CH, Rosner B, et al. The nurses' health study. *Am J Nurs* 1978;78:1039-40.

24. Belanger C, Speizer FE, Hennekens CH, et al. The nurses' health study: current findings. *Am J Nurs* 1980;80:1333.

25. Speizer FE, Willett W, Colditz GA. *The Nurses' Health Study*. http://www.channing.harvard.edu/nhs/index.html. 2007.

26. Albanes D, Heinonen OP, Taylor PR, et al. Alpha-tocopherol and beta-carotene supplements and lung cancer incidence in the alpha-tocopherol, beta-carotene cancer prevention study: effects of base-line characteristics and study compliance. *J Natl Cancer Inst* 1996;88:1560-70.

27. Higgins JP, Thompson SG, Deeks JJ, et al. Measuring inconsistency in meta-analyses. *Br Med J* 2003;327:557-60.

28. Beaglehole R, Bonita R, Kjellström T. *Basic epidemiology*. Geneva: World Health Organization, 1993.

29. Diet, nutrition and the prevention of chronic diseases. *World Health Organ Tech Rep Ser* 2003;916:i-viii, 1-149, backcover.

30. Rothman KJ, Greenland S. *Modern Epidemiology*. 2nd ed. Philadelphia: Lippincott-Raven, 1998.

31. van den Brandt PA, Spiegelman D, Yaun SS, et al. Pooled analysis of prospective cohort studies on height, weight, and breast cancer risk. *Am J Epidemiol* 2000;152:514-27.

32. Moshfegh A, Perloff B, Raper N, et al. New methods for national nutrition monitoring in the United States [abstract]. *XIVth International Congress of Dietetics*, 2004.

33. Rosner B, Willett WC. Interval estimates for correlation coefficients corrected for within-person variation: implications for study design and hypothesis testing. *Am J Epidemiol* 1988;127:377-86.

34. Willett WC, Sampson L, Stampfer MJ, et al. Reproducibility and validity of a semiquantitative food frequency questionnaire. *Am J Epidemiol* 1985;122:51-65.

35. Day N, McKeown N, Wong M, et al. Epidemiological assessment of diet: a comparison of a 7-day diary with a food frequency questionnaire using urinary markers of nitrogen, potassium and sodium. *Int J Epidemiol* 2001;30:309-17.

36. Kipnis V, Midthune D, Freedman L, et al. Bias in dietary-report instruments and its implications for nutritional epidemiology. *Public Health Nutrition* 2002;5:915-23.

37. Kipnis V, Midthune D, Freedman LS, et al. Empirical evidence of correlated biases in dietary assessment instruments and its implications. *Am J Epidemiol* 2001;153:394-403.

38. Kipnis V, Subar AF, Midthune D, et al. Structure of dietary measurement error: results of the OPEN biomarker study. *Am J Epidemiol* 2003;158:14-21; discussion 22-6.

39. Schoeller DA. Measurement of energy expenditure in free-living humans by using doubly labeled water. *J Nutr* 1988;118:1278-89.

40. Kaaks RJ. Biochemical markers as additional measurements in studies of the accuracy of dietary questionnaire measurements: conceptual issues. *Am J Clin Nutr* 1997;65:1232S-9S.

41. Bingham SA. Biomarkers in nutritional epidemiology. *Public Health Nutrition* 2002;5:821-7.

42. Satia JA, King IB, Morris JS, et al. Toenail and plasma levels as biomarkers of selenium exposure. *Ann Epidemiol* 2006;16:53-8.

43. Hunter DJ, Morris JS, Chute CG, et al. Predictors of selenium concentration in human toenails. *Am J Epidemiol* 1990;132:114-22.

44. Kipnis V, Freedman LS, Brown CC, et al. Interpretation of energy adjustment models for nutritional epidemiology. *Am J Epidemiol* 1993;137:1376-80.

45. Brown CC, Kipnis V, Freedman LS, et al. Energy adjustment methods for nutritional epidemiology: the effect of categorization. *Am J Epidemiol* 1994;139:323-38.

46. Wacholder S, Schatzkin A, Freedman LS, et al. Can energy adjustment separate the effects of energy from those of specific macronutrients? *Am J Epidemiol* 1994;140:848-55.

47. Bingham SA, Day NE. Using biochemical markers to assess the validity of prospective dietary assessment methods and the effect of energy adjustment. *Am J Clin Nutr* 1997;65:1130S-7S.

48. Willett WC, Howe GR, Kushi LH. Adjustment for total energy intake in epidemiologic studies. *Am J Clin Nutr* 1997;65:1220S-8S; discussion 1229S-31S.

49. Ries L, Harkins D, Krapcho M, et al., editors. *SEER Cancer Statistics Review, 1975-2003*. Bethesda: National Cancer Institute, 2006.

50. Black RJ, Bray F, Ferlay J, et al. Cancer incidence and mortality in the European Union: cancer registry data and estimates of national incidence for 1990. *Eur J Cancer* 1997;33:1075-107.

51. Fritz AG, Percy C, Jack A, et al., editors. *International Classification of Diseases for Oncology*. Geneva: World Health Organization, 2000.

52. Hill AB. The environment and disease: association or causation? *Proc R Soc Med* 1965;58:295-300.

53. US Surgeon General's Advisory Committee on Smoking and Health. *Smoking and Health: Report of the Advisory Committee to the Surgeon General of the Public Health Service*. Washington, DC: US Department of Health, Education, and Welfare, 1964.

Chapter 4

Chapter 4.1

1. Burkitt DP, Trowell HC. Dietary fibre and western diseases. *Ir Med J* 1977;70:272-7.

2. Trowell H, Burkitt D. Physiological role of dietary fiber: a ten-year review. *ASDC J Dent Child* 1986;53:444-7.

3. World Health Organization. 2003. *Diet, Nutrition and the Prevention of Chronic Diseases: Report of a Joint WHO/FAO Expert Consultation*. In: WHO Technical Report Series no 916. http://www.who.int/entity/dietphysicalactivity/publications/trs916/download/en/index.html.

4. World Health Organization. 1990. *Diet, Nutrition, and the Prevention of Chronic Diseases. Report of a WHO Study Group*. In: WHO Technical Report Series no 797.

5. International Agency for Research on Cancer. 2002. *Some Traditional Herbal Medicines, Some Mycotoxins, Naphthalene and Styrene*. In: IARC Monogr Eval Carcinog Risks Hum no 82. http://monographs.iarc.fr/ENG/Monographs/vol82/volume82.pdf.

6. Food and Agriculture Organization of the United Nations, World Health Organization, United Nations Environment Programme International. 1999. *Third Joint FAO/WHO/UNEP International Conference on Mycotoxins*. ftp://ftp.fao.org/es/esn/food/meetings/mycotoxins_report_en.pdf.

7. Bingham S. Food components and mechanisms of interest in cancer and diet in relation to their measurement. *Eur J Clin Nutr* 1993;47 Suppl 2:S73-7.

8. Englyst HN, Kingman SM, Cummings JH. Classification and measurement of nutritionally important starch fractions. *Eur J Clin Nutr* 1992;46 Suppl 2:S33-50.

9. Norat T, Bingham S, Ferrari P, et al. Meat, fish, and colorectal cancer risk: the European Prospective Investigation into cancer and nutrition. *J Natl Cancer Inst* 2005;97:906-16.

10. Mathers JC. Pulses and carcinogenesis: potential for the prevention of colon, breast and other cancers. *Br J Nutr* 2002;88 Suppl 3:S273-9.

11. Voorrips LE, Goldbohm RA, van Poppel G, et al. Vegetable and fruit consumption and risks of colon and rectal cancer in a prospective cohort study: The Netherlands Cohort Study on Diet and Cancer. *Am J Epidemiol* 2000;152:1081-92.

12. Tangrea J, Helzlsouer K, Pietinen P, et al. Serum levels of vitamin D metabolites and the subsequent risk of colon and rectal cancer in Finnish men. *Cancer Causes Control* 1997;8:615-25.

13. Wong HL, Seow A, Arakawa K, et al. Vitamin D receptor start codon polymorphism and colorectal cancer risk: effect modification by dietary calcium and fat in Singapore Chinese. *Carcinogenesis* 2003;24:1091-5.

14. Koh WP, Yuan JM, van den Berg D, et al. Interaction between cyclooxygenase-2 gene polymorphism and dietary n-6 polyunsaturated fatty acids on colon cancer risk: The Singapore Chinese Health Study. *Br J Cancer* 2004;90:1760-4.

15. Tjonneland AM, Overvad K, Bingham SA, et al. Dietary fibers protect against colorectal cancer among the participants in the European Prospective Investigation into Cancer and Nutrition (EPiC) study. *Ugeskr Laeger* 2004;166:2458-60.

16. Sellers TTA, Bazyk AAE, Bostick RRM, et al. Diet and risk of colon cancer in a large prospective study of older women: an analysis stratified on family history (Iowa, United States). *Cancer Causes Control* 1998;9:357-67.

17. Michels KB, Fuchs CS, Giovannucci E, et al. Fiber intake and incidence of colorectal cancer among 76,947 women and 47,279 men. *Cancer Epidemiol Biomarkers Prev* 2005;14:842-9.

18. Wark PA, Weijenberg MP, van 't Veer P, et al. Fruits, vegetables, and hMLH1 protein-deficient and -proficient colon cancer: The Netherlands cohort study. *Cancer Epidemiol Biomarkers Prev* 2005;14:1619-25.

19. Heilbrun LK, Nomura A, Hankin JH, et al. Diet and colorectal cancer with special reference to fiber intake. *Int J Cancer* 1989;44:1-6.

20. Bostick RM, Potter JD, Sellers TA, et al. Relation of calcium, vitamin D, and dairy food intake to incidence of colon cancer among older women. The Iowa Women's Health Study. *Am J Epidemiol* 1993;137:1302-17.

21. Konings EJ, Goldbohm RA, Brants HA, et al. Intake of dietary folate vitamers and risk of colorectal carcinoma: results from The Netherlands Cohort Study. *Cancer* 2002;95:1421-33.

22. Sanjoaquin MA, Appleby PN, Thorogood M, et al. Nutrition, lifestyle and colorectal cancer incidence: a prospective investigation of 10998 vegetarians and non-vegetarians in the United Kingdom. *Br J Cancer* 2004;90:118-21.

23. Wu AH, Paganini Hill A, Ross RK, et al. Alcohol, physical activity and other risk factors for colorectal cancer: a prospective study. *Br J Cancer* 1987;55:687-94.

24. Colbert LH, Hartman TJ, Malila N, et al. Physical activity in relation to cancer of the colon and rectum in a cohort of male smokers. *Cancer Epidemiol Biomarkers Prev* 2001;10:265-8.

25. McCullough ML, Robertson AS, Chao A, et al. A prospective study of whole grains, fruits, vegetables and colon cancer risk. *Cancer Causes Control* 2003;14:959-70.

26. Mai V, Flood A, Peters U, et al. Dietary fibre and risk of colorectal cancer in the Breast Cancer Detection Demonstration Project (BCDDP) follow-up cohort. *Int J Epidemiol* 2003;32:234-9.

27. Higginbotham S, Zhang ZF, Lee IM, et al.

Dietary glycemic load and risk of colorectal cancer in the Women's Health Study. *J Natl Cancer Inst* 2004;96:229-33.

28. Bingham SA, Day NE, Luben R, et al. Dietary fibre in food and protection against colorectal cancer in the European Prospective Investigation into Cancer and Nutrition (EPIC): an observational study. *Lancet* 2003;361:1496-501.

29. Steinmetz KA, Kushi LH, Bostick RM, et al. Vegetables, fruit, and colon cancer in the Iowa Women's Health Study. *Am J Epidemiol* 1994;139:1-15.

30. Pietinen P, Malila N, Virtanen M, et al. Diet and risk of colorectal cancer in a cohort of Finnish men. *Cancer Causes Control* 1999;10:387-96.

31. Glynn SA, Albanes D, Pietinen P, et al. Colorectal cancer and folate status: a nested case-control study among male smokers. *Cancer Epidemiol Biomarkers Prev* 1996;5:487-94.

32. Giovannucci E. Intake of fat, meat and fiber in relation to risk of colon cancer in men. *Cancer Res* 1994;54:2390-7.

33. Fuchs CS, Giovannucci EL, Colditz GA, et al. Dietary fiber and the risk of colorectal cancer and adenoma in women. *N Engl J Med* 1999;340:169-76.

34. Terry P, Giovannucci E, Michels KB, et al. Fruit, vegetables, dietary fiber and risk of colorectal cancer. *J Natl Cancer Inst* 2001;93:525-33.

35. Willett WC, Stampfer MJ, Colditz GA, et al. Relation of meat, fat, and fiber intake to the risk of colon cancer in a prospective study among women. *N Engl J Med* 1990;323:1664-72.

36. Kato I, Akhmedkhanov A, Koenig K, et al. Prospective study of diet and female colorectal cancer: the New York University Women's Health Study. *Nutr Cancer* 1997;28:276-81.

37. Gaard M, Tretli S, Loken EB. Dietary factors and risk of colon cancer: a prospective study of 50,535 young Norwegian men and women. *Eur J Cancer Prev* 1996;5:445-54.

38. Park Y, Hunter DJ, Spiegelman D, et al. Dietary fiber intake and risk of colorectal cancer: a pooled analysis of prospective cohort studies. *JAMA* 2005;294:2849-57.

39. Giovannucci E, Rimm EB, Stampfer MJ, et al. Intake of fat, meat, and fiber in relation to risk of colon cancer in men. *Cancer Res* 1994;54:2390-7.

40. Cummings JH. Dietary fibre and large bowel cancer. *Proc Nutr Soc* 1981;40:7-14.

41. Bowers K, Albanes D, Limburg P, et al. A prospective study of anthropometric and clinical measurements associated with insulin resistance syndrome and colorectal cancer in male smokers. *Am J Epidemiol* 2006;164:652-64.

42. Otani T, Iwasaki M, Ishihara J, et al. Dietary fiber intake and subsequent risk of colorectal cancer: the Japan Public Health Center-based prospective study. *Int J Cancer* 2006;119:1475-80.

43. Shin A, Li H, Shu XO, et al. Dietary intake of calcium, fiber and other micronutrients in relation to colorectal cancer risk: results from the Shanghai Women's Health Study. *Int J Cancer* 2006;119:2938-42.

44. Lin J, Zhang SM, Cook NR, et al. Dietary intakes of fruit, vegetables, and fiber, and risk of colorectal cancer in a prospective cohort of women (United States). *Cancer Causes Control* 2005;16:225-33.

45. MacInnis RJ, English DR, Haydon AM, et al. Body size and composition and risk of rectal cancer (Australia). *Cancer Causes Control* 2006;17:1291-7.

46. Bingham SA, Norat T, Moskal A, et al. Is the association with fiber from foods in colorectal cancer confounded by folate intake? *Cancer Epidemiol Biomarkers Prev* 2005;14:1552-6.

47. Wakai K, Hirose K, Matsuo K, et al. Dietary risk factors for colon and rectal cancers: a comparative case-control study. *J Epidemiol* 2006;16:125-35.

48. Kasum CM, Jacobs DR, Jr., Nicodemus K, et al. Dietary risk factors for upper aerodigestive tract cancers. *Int J Cancer* 2002;99:267-72.

49. Tzonou A, Lipworth L, Kalandidi A, et al. Dietary factors and the risk of endometrial cancer: a case - control study in Greece. *Br J Cancer* 1996;73:1284-90.

50. Chen H, Tucker KL, Graubard BI, et al. Nutrient intakes and adenocarcinoma of the esophagus and distal stomach. *Nutr Cancer* 2002;42:33-40.

51. Terry P, Lagergren J, Ye W, et al. Inverse association between intake of cereal fiber and risk of gastric cardia cancer. *Gastroenterology* 2001;120:387-91.

52. Soler M, Bosetti C, Franceschi S, et al. Fiber intake and the risk of oral, pharyngeal and esophageal cancer. *Int J Cancer* 2001;91:283-7.

53. Mayne ST, Risch HA, Dubrow R, et al. Nutrient intake and risk of subtypes of esophageal and gastric cancer. *Cancer Epidemiol Biomarkers Prev* 2001;10:1055-62.

54. De Stefani E, Ronco A, Mendilaharsu M, et al. Diet and risk of cancer of the upper aerodigestive tract - II. Nutrients. *Oral Oncol* 1999;35:22-6.

55. Zhang ZF, Kurtz RC, Yu GP, et al. Adenocarcinomas of the esophagus and gastric cardia: the role of diet. *Nutr Cancer* 1997;27:298-309.

56. Brown LM, Swanson CA, Gridley G, et al. Adenocarcinoma of the esophagus: role of obesity and diet. *J Natl Cancer Inst* 1995;87:104-9.

57. Tavani A, Negri E, Franceschi S, et al. Risk factors for esophageal cancer in women in northern Italy. *Cancer* 1993;72:2531-6.

58. Kabat GC, Ng SK, Wynder EL. Tobacco, alcohol intake, and diet in relation to adenocarcinoma of the esophagus and gastric cardia. *Cancer Causes Control* 1993;4:123-32.

59. Liaw Y-P, Huang Y-C, Lo P-Y, et al. Nutrient intakes in relation to cancer mortality in Taiwan. *Nutr. Res.* 2003;23:1597-606.

60. Sichieri R, Everhart JE, Mendonça GAS. Diet and mortality from common cancers in Brazil: an ecological study. *Cad Saude Publica* 1996;12:53-9.

61. Tzonou A, Lipworth L, Garidou A, et al. Diet and risk of esophageal cancer by histologic type in a low-risk population. *Int J Cancer* 1996;68:300-4.

62. Terry P, Lagergren J, Hansen H, et al. Fruit and vegetable consumption in the prevention of oesophageal and cardia cancers. *Eur J Cancer Prev* 2001;10:365-9.

63. Sun CA, Wang LY, Chen Chien J, et al. Genetic polymorphisms of glutathione S-transferases M1 and T1 associated with susceptibility to aflatoxin-related hepatocarcinogenesis among chronic hepatitis B carriers: a nested case-control study. *Carcinogenesis* 2001;22:1289-94.

64. Chen CJ, Yu MW, Liaw YF, et al. Chronic hepatitis B carriers with null genotypes of glutathione S-transferase M1 and T1 polymorphisms who are exposed to aflatoxin are at increased risk of hepatocellular carcinoma. *Am J Hum Genet* 1996;59:128-34.

65. Yu MW, Lien JP, Chiu YH, et al. Effect of aflatoxin metabolism and DNA adduct formation on hepatocellular carcinoma among chronic hepatitis B carriers in Taiwan. *J Hepatol* 1997;27:320-30.

66. Wang LY, Hatch M, Chen CJ, et al. Aflatoxin exposure and risk of hepatocellular carcinoma in Taiwan. *Int J Cancer* 1996;67:620-5.

67. Sun Z, Lu P, Gail MH, et al. Increased risk of hepatocellular carcinoma in male hepatitis B surface antigen carriers with chronic hepatitis who have detectable urinary aflatoxin metabolite M1. *Hepatology* 1999;30:379-83.

68. Ross RK, Yuan JM, Yu MC, et al. Urinary aflatoxin biomarkers and risk of hepatocellular carcinoma. *Lancet* 1992;339:943-6.

69. Qian GS, Ross RK, Yu MC, et al. A follow-up study of urinary markers of aflatoxin exposure and liver cancer risk in Shanghai, People's Republic of China. *Cancer Epidemiol Biomarkers Prev* 1994;3:3-10.

70. Chen CJ, Wang LY, Lu SN, et al. Elevated aflatoxin exposure and increased risk of hepatocellular carcinoma. *Hepatology* 1996;24:38-42.

71. Lunn RM, Zhang Yu J, Wang LW, et al. p53 mutations, chronic hepatitis B virus infection, and aflatoxin exposure in hepatocellular carcinoma in Taiwan. *Cancer Res* 1997;57:3471-7.

72. Tsuboi S, Kawamura K, Cruz ML, et al. Aflatoxin B1 and primary hepatocellular carcinoma in Japan, Indonesia and the Philippines. (Detection aflatoxin B1 in human serum and urine samples). *ICMR Annals* 1984;4:175-85.

73. Srivatanakul P, Parkin DM, Khlat M, et al. Liver-cancer in Thailand. 2. A case-control study of hepatocellular-carcinoma. *Int J Cancer* 1991;48:329-32.

74. Salamat LA, Tsuboi S. Dietary aflatoxin: a

possible factor in the etiology of primary liver cancer. *ICMR Annals* 1985;5:131-8.

75. Ragab W, Kohail H. The possible association of dietary aflatoxin with the incidence of primary hepatic tumours. *J Med Res Inst* 1996;16:165-70.

76. Parkin DM, Srivatanakul P, Khlat M, et al. Liver-cancer in Thailand. I. A case-control study of cholangiocarcinoma. *Int J Cancer* 1991;48:323-8.

77. Mandishona E, MacPhail AP, Gordeuk VR, et al. Dietary iron overload as a risk factor for hepatocellular carcinoma in Black Africans. *Hepatology* 1998;27:1563-6.

78. Bulatao Jayme J, Almero EM, Castro MC, et al. A case-control dietary study of primary liver cancer risk from aflatoxin exposure. *Int J Epidemiol* 1982;11:112-9.

79. Abaza H, El Mallah S, El Kady A, et al. Mycotoxins and hepatocellular carcinoma (HCC) in Egypt. *J Trop Med* 1993;2:33-40.

80. Eaton DL, Ramsdell HS, Neal G. Biotransformation of aflatoxins. In: Eaton DL, Groopman JD, editors. *The Toxicology of Aflatoxins: Human Health, Veterinary and Agricultural Significance*. San Diego: Academic Press, 1994.

81. Luch A. Nature and nurture - lessons from chemical carcinogenesis. *Nat Rev Cancer* 2005;5:113-25.

Chapter 4.2

1. Kuhnlein HV. Promoting the nutritional and cultural benefits of traditional food systems of Indigenous People. *Forum Nutr* 2003;56:222-3.

2. Cannon G. *Food and Health: the Experts Agree. An analysis of One Hundred Authoritative Scientific Reports on Food, Nutrition and Public Health Published Throughout the World in Thirty Years, Between 1961 and 1991*. London: Consumers' Association, 1992.

3. World Cancer Research Fund, American Institute for Cancer Research. *Food, Nutrition and the Prevention of Cancer: a Global Perspective*. Washington, DC: AICR, 1997.

4. World Health Organization. 2003. *Diet, Nutrition and the Prevention of Chronic Diseases: Report of a Joint WHO/FAO Expert Consultation*. In: WHO Technical Report Series no 916. http://www.who.int/entity/dietphysicalactivity/publications/trs916/download/en/index.html.

5. Davidson A. *The Penguin Companion to Food*. Revised ed. Harmondsworth: Penguin Books, 2002.

6. McCreight JD, Ryder EJ, editors. *XXVI International Horticultural Congress: Advances in Vegetable Breeding*. Toronto: International Society for Horticultural Science, 2004.

7. Aggarwal BB, Ichikawa H. Molecular targets and anticancer potential of indole-3-carbinol and its derivatives. *Cell Cycle* 2005;4:1201-15.

8. Pool-Zobel BL. Inulin-type fructans and reduction in colon cancer risk: review of experimental and human data. *Br J Nutr* 2005;93 Suppl 1:S73-90.

9. Jakubikova J, Sedlak J. Garlic-derived organosulfides induce cytotoxicity, apoptosis, cell cycle arrest and oxidative stress in human colon carcinoma cell lines. *Neoplasma* 2006;53:191-9.

10. McGee H. *McGee on Food and Cooking*. London: Hodder and Stoughton, 2004.

11. Lee HY, Oh SH, Woo JK, et al. Chemopreventive effects of deguelin, a novel Akt inhibitor, on tobacco-induced lung tumorigenesis. *J Natl Cancer Inst* 2005;97:1695-9.

12. Dewanto V, Wu X, Adom KK, et al. Thermal processing enhances the nutritional value of tomatoes by increasing total antioxidant activity. *J Agric Food Chem* 2002;50:3010-4.

13. Arab L, Steck S. Lycopene and cardiovascular disease. *Am J Clin Nutr* 2000;71:1691S-5S; discussion 6S-7S.

14. Song K, Milner JA. Heating garlic inhibits its ability to suppress 7, 12-dimethylbenz(a)anthracene-induced DNA adduct formation in rat mammary tissue. *J Nutr* 1999;129:657-61.

15. Leklem JE. Vitamin B-6. In: Shils M, Olson JA, Shike M, et al., editors. *Nutrition in Health and Disease*. 9th ed. Baltimore: Williams & Wilkins, 1999.

16. Geissler C, Powers H, editors. *Human Nutrition*. 11th ed. London: Elsevier Churchill Livingstone, 2005.

17. Food and Agriculture Organization of the United Nations. *FAOSTAT*. http://faostat.fao.org/site/345/default.aspx. 2006.

18. Morabia A, Wynder EL. Dietary habits of smokers, people who never smoked, and exsmokers. *Am J Clin Nutr* 1990;52:933-7.

19. McPhillips JB, Eaton CB, Gans KM, et al. Dietary differences in smokers and nonsmokers from two southeastern New England communities. *J Am Diet Assoc* 1994;94:287-92.

20. Ursin G, Ziegler RG, Subar AF, et al. Dietary patterns associated with a low-fat diet in the national health examination follow-up study: identification of potential confounders for epidemiologic analyses. *Am J Epidemiol* 1993;137:916-27.

21. De Stefani E, Correa P, Oreggia F, et al. Risk factors for laryngeal cancer. *Cancer* 1987;60:3087-91.

22. Notani PN, Jayant K. Role of diet in upper aerodigestive tract cancers. *Nutr Cancer* 1987;10:103-13.

23. Franco EL, Kowalski LP, Oliveira BV, et al. Risk factors for oral cancer in Brazil: a case-control study. *Int J Cancer* 1989;43:992-1000.

24. Gridley G, McLaughlin JK, Block G, et al. Diet and oral and pharyngeal cancer among blacks. *Nutr Cancer* 1990;14:219-25.

25. Oreggia F, De Stefani E, Correa P, et al. Risk factors for cancer of the tongue in Uruguay. *Cancer* 1991;67:180-3.

26. Franceschi S, Bidoli E, Baron AE, et al. Nutrition and cancer of the oral cavity and pharynx in north-east Italy. *Int J Cancer* 1991;47:20-5.

27. Zheng W, Blot WJ, Shu XO, et al. Risk factors for oral and pharyngeal cancer in Shanghai, with emphasis on diet. *Cancer Epidemiol Biomarkers Prev* 1992;1:441-8.

28. Zheng W, Blot WJ, Shu XO, et al. Diet and other risk factors for laryngeal cancer in Shanghai, China. *Am J Epidemiol* 1992;136:178-91.

29. Zheng T, Boyle P, Willett WC, et al. A case-control study of oral cancer in Beijing, People's Republic of China. Associations with nutrient intakes, foods and food groups. *Eur J Cancer B Oral Oncol* 1993;29B:45-55.

30. De Stefani E, Oreggia F, Ronco A, et al. Salted meat consumption as a risk factor for cancer of the oral cavity and pharynx: a case-control study from Uruguay. *Cancer Epidemiol Biomarkers Prev* 1994;3:381-5.

31. Esteve J, Riboli E, Pequignot G, et al. Diet and cancers of the larynx and hypopharynx: the IARC multi-center study in southwestern Europe. *Cancer Causes Control* 1996;7:240-52.

32. Chatenoud L, La Vecchia C, Franceschi S, et al. Refined-cereal intake and risk of selected cancers in Italy. *Am J Clin Nutr* 1999;70:1107-10.

33. De Stefani E, Boffetta P, Ronco AL, et al. Dietary patterns and risk of cancer of the oral cavity and pharynx in Uruguay. *Nutr Cancer* 2005;51:132-9.

34. Crosignani P, Russo A, Tagliabue G, et al. Tobacco and diet as determinants of survival in male laryngeal cancer patients. *Int J Cancer* 1996;65:308-13.

35. Kune GA, Kune S, Field B, et al. Oral and pharyngeal cancer, diet, smoking, alcohol, and serum vitamin A and beta-carotene levels: a case-control study in men. *Nutr Cancer* 1993;20:61-70.

36. Takezaki T, Hirose K, Inoue M, et al. Tobacco, alcohol and dietary factors associated with the risk of oral cancer among Japanese. *Jpn J Cancer Res* 1996;87:555-62.

37. Levi F, Pasche C, La Vecchia C, et al. Food groups and risk of oral and pharyngeal cancer. *Int J Cancer* 1998;77:705-9.

38. Franceschi S, Favero A, Conti E, et al. Food groups, oils and butter, and cancer of the oral cavity and pharynx. *Br J Cancer* 1999;80:614-20.

39. De Stefani E, Boffetta P, Oreggia F, et al. Plant foods and risk of laryngeal cancer: A case-control study in Uruguay. *Int J Cancer* 2000;87:129-32.

40. De Stefani E, Deneo-Pellegrini H, Mendilaharsu M, et al. Diet and risk of cancer of the upper aerodigestive tract - I. Foods. *Oral Oncol* 1999;35:17-21.

41. Garrote LF, Herrero R, Reyes RM, et al. Risk factors for cancer of the oral cavity and oro-pharynx in Cuba. *Br J Cancer* 2001;85:46-54.

42. Bosetti C, La Vecchia C, Talamini R, et al. Food groups and laryngeal cancer risk: a case-control study from Italy and

Switzerland. *Int J Cancer* 2002;100:355-60.

43. Rajkumar T, Sridhar H, Balaram P, et al. Oral cancer in Southern India: the influence of body size, diet, infections and sexual practices. *Eur J Cancer Prev* 2003;12:135-43.

44. Marchioni DL, Fisberg RM, do Rosario M, et al. Diet and cancer of oral cavity and pharynx: a case-control study in Sao Paulo, Brazil. *IARC Sci Publ* 2002;156:559-61.

45. Gaudet MM, Olshan AF, Poole C, et al. Diet, GSTM1 and GSTT1 and head and neck cancer. *Carcinogenesis* 2004;25:735-40.

46. Lissowska J, Pilarska A, Pilarski P, et al. Smoking, alcohol, diet, dentition and sexual practices in the epidemiology of oral cancer in Poland. *Eur J Cancer Prev* 2003;12:25-33.

47. McLaughlin JK, Gridley G, Block G, et al. Dietary factors in oral and pharyngeal cancer. *J Natl Cancer Inst* 1988;80:1237-43.

48. Day GL, Blot WJ, Austin DF, et al. Racial differences in risk of oral and pharyngeal cancer: alcohol, tobacco, and other determinants. *J Natl Cancer Inst* 1993;85:465-73.

49. Franceschi S, Barra S, La Vecchia C, et al. Risk factors for cancer of the tongue and the mouth. A case-control study from northern Italy. *Cancer* 1992;70:2227-33.

50. Sanchez MJ, Martinez C, Nieto A, et al. Oral and oropharyngeal cancer in Spain: influence of dietary patterns. *Eur J Cancer Prev* 2003;12:49-56.

51. Koo LC, Mang OW, Ho JH. An ecological study of trends in cancer incidence and dietary changes in Hong Kong. *Nutr Cancer* 1997;28:289-301.

52. Schrauzer GN. Cancer mortality correlation studies. II. Regional associations of mortalities with the consumptions of foods and other commodities. *Med Hypotheses* 1976;2:39-49.

53. Knox EG. Foods and diseases. *Br J Prev Soc Med* 1977;31:71-80.

54. Boeing H. Alcohol and risk of cancer of the upper gastrointestinal tract: first analysis of the EPIC data. *IARC Sci Publ* 2002;156:151-4.

55. Zatonski W, Becher H, Lissowska J, et al. Tobacco, alcohol, and diet in the etiology of laryngeal cancer: a population-based case-control study. *Cancer Causes Control* 1991;2:3-10.

56. Brown LM, Gridley G, Diehl SR, et al. Family cancer history and susceptibility to oral carcinoma in Puerto Rico. *Cancer* 2001;92:2102-8.

57. Llewellyn CD, Linklater K, Bell J, et al. An analysis of risk factors for oral cancer in young people: a case-control study. *Oral Oncol* 2004;40:304-13.

58. Franceschi S, Bidoli E, La Vecchia C, et al. Tomatoes and risk of digestive-tract cancers. *Int J Cancer* 1994;59:181-4.

59. De Stefani E, Oreggia F, Rivero S, et al. Salted meat consumption and the risk of laryngeal cancer. *Eur J Epidemiol* 1995;11:177-80.

60. Takezaki T, Shinoda M, Hatooka S, et al. Subsite-specific risk factors for hypopharyngeal and esophageal cancer (Japan). *Cancer Causes Control* 2000;11:597-608.

61. Maier H, Tisch M. Epidemiology of laryngeal cancer: results of the Heidelberg case-control study. *Acta Otolaryngol Suppl* 1997;527:160-4.

62. De Stefani E, Oreggia F, Boffetta P, et al. Tomatoes, tomato-rich foods, lycopene and cancer of the upper aerodigestive tract: a case-control in Uruguay. *Oral Oncol* 2000;36:47-53.

63. Tavani A, Gallus S, La Vecchia C, et al. Diet and risk of oral and pharyngeal cancer. An Italian case-control study. *Eur J Cancer Prev* 2001;10:191-5.

64. Uzcudun AE, Retolaza IR, Fernandez PB, et al. Nutrition and pharyngeal cancer: results from a case-control study in Spain. *Head Neck* 2002;24:830-40.

65. Pisa FE, Barbone F. Diet and the risk of cancers of the lung, oral cavity and pharynx, and larynx: a population-based case-control study in north-east Italy. *IARC Sci Publ* 2002;156:141-3.

66. Kjaerheim K, Gaard M, Andersen A. The role of alcohol, tobacco, and dietary factors in upper aerogastric tract cancers: a prospective study of 10,900 Norwegian men. *Cancer Causes Control* 1998;9:99-108.

67. Lee KY, Lee C, Park YS, et al. A study of relation between dietary vitamin A intake and serum vitamin A levels and cancer risk in Korea. *Korean J Nutr* 1985;18:301-11.

68. Hebert JR, Landon J, Miller DR. Consumption of meat and fruit in relation to oral and esophageal cancer: a cross-national study. *Nutr Cancer* 1993;19:169-79.

69. Kapil U, Singh P, Bahadur S, et al. Assessment of risk factors in laryngeal cancer in India: a case-control study. *Asian Pac J Cancer Prev* 2005;6:202-7.

70. Zheng W, Sellers TA, Doyle TJ, et al. Retinol, antioxidant vitamins, and cancers of the upper digestive tract in a prospective cohort study of postmenopausal women. *Am J Epidemiol* 1995;142:955-60.

71. Kasum CM, Jacobs DR, Jr., Nicodemus K, et al. Dietary risk factors for upper aerodigestive tract cancers. *Int J Cancer* 2002;99:267-72.

72. La Vecchia C, Negri E, D'Avanzo B, et al. Dietary indicators of oral and pharyngeal cancer. *Int J Epidemiol* 1991;20:39-44.

73. La Vecchia C, Negri E, D'Avanzo B, et al. Dietary indicators of laryngeal cancer risk. *Cancer Res* 1990;50:4497-500.

74. Fioretti F, Bosetti C, Tavani A, et al. Risk factors for oral and pharyngeal cancer in never smokers. *Oral Oncol* 1999;35:375-8.

75. Nishimoto IN, Pintos J, Schlecht NF, et al. Assessment of control selection bias in a hospital-based case-control study of upper aero-digestive tract cancers. *J Cancer Epidemiol Prev* 2002;7:131-41.

76. Maserejian NN, Giovannucci E, Rosner B, et al. Prospective study of fruits and vegetables and risk of oral premalignant lesions in men. *Am J Epidemiol* 2006;164:556-66.

77. Boeing H, Dietrich T, Hoffmann K, et al. Intake of fruits and vegetables and risk of cancer of the upper aero-digestive tract: the prospective EPIC-study. *Cancer Causes Control* 2006;17:957-69.

78. Galeone C, Pelucchi C, Levi F, et al. Onion and garlic use and human cancer. *Am J Clin Nutr* 2006;84:1027-32.

79. Kreimer AR, Randi G, Herrero R, et al. Diet and body mass, and oral and oropharyngeal squamous cell carcinomas: analysis from the IARC multinational case-control study. *Int J Cancer* 2006;118:2293-7.

80. Guo W, Blot WJ, Li JY, et al. A nested case-control study of oesophageal and stomach cancers in the Linxian nutrition intervention trial. *Int J Epidemiol* 1994;23:444-50.

81. Hirayama T. [A large scale cohort study on the effect of life styles on the risk of cancer by each site]. *Gan No Rinsho* 1990;Spec No:233-42.

82. Yu Y, Taylor PR, Li JY, et al. Retrospective cohort study of risk-factors for esophageal cancer in Linxian, People's Republic of China. *Cancer Causes Control* 1993;4:195-202.

83. Tran GD, Sun XD, Abnet CC, et al. Prospective study of risk factors for esophageal and gastric cancers in the Linxian general population trial cohort in China. *Int J Cancer* 2005;113:456-63.

84. Li JY, Ershow AG, Chen ZJ, et al. A case-control study of cancer of the esophagus and gastric cardia in Linxian. *Int J Cancer* 1989;43:755-61.

85. Bosetti C, La Vecchia C, Talamini R, et al. Food groups and risk of squamous cell esophageal cancer in northern Italy. *Int J Cancer* 2000;87:289-94.

86. Gao YT, McLaughlin JK, Gridley G, et al. Risk factors for esophageal cancer in Shanghai, China. II. Role of diet and nutrients. *Int J Cancer* 1994;58:197-202.

87. De Stefani E, Munoz N, Esteve J, et al. Mate drinking, alcohol, tobacco, diet, and esophageal cancer in Uruguay. *Cancer Res* 1990;50:426-31.

88. Launoy G, Milan C, Day NE, et al. Diet and squamous-cell cancer of the oesophagus: a French multicentre case-control study. *Int J Cancer* 1998;76:7-12.

89. Negri E, La Vecchia C, Franceschi S, et al. Vegetable and fruit consumption and cancer risk. *Int J Cancer* 1991;48:350-4.

90. Rolon PA, Castellsague X, Benz M, et al. Hot and cold mate drinking and esophageal cancer in Paraguay. *Cancer Epidemiol Biomarkers Prev* 1995;4:595-605.

91. Sammon AM. Protease inhibitors and carcinoma of the esophagus. *Cancer* 1998;83:405-8.

92. Sammon AM. A case-control study of diet and social factors in cancer of the esophagus in Transkei. *Cancer*

1992;69:860-5.

93. Su W, Han XY, Wang YP, et al. Joint risks in a case-control study of esophageal cancer in Shanxi Province, People's Republic of China. *Tohoku J Exp Med* 1994;174:177-80.

94. Tzonou A, Lipworth L, Garidou A, et al. Diet and risk of esophageal cancer by histologic type in a low-risk population. *Int J Cancer* 1996;68:300-4.

95. De Stefani E, Brennan P, Boffetta P, et al. Vegetables, fruits, related dietary antioxidants, and risk of squamous cell carcinoma of the esophagus: a case-control study in Uruguay. *Nutr Cancer* 2000;38:23-9.

96. Cheng KK, Sharp L, McKinney PA, et al. A case-control study of oesophageal adenocarcinoma in women: a preventable disease. *Br J Cancer* 2000;83:127-32.

97. Levi F, Pasche C, Lucchini F, et al. Food groups and oesophageal cancer risk in Vaud, Switzerland. *Eur J Cancer Prev* 2000;9:257-63.

98. Nayar D, Kapil U, Joshi YK, et al. Nutritional risk factors in esophageal cancer. *J Assoc Physicians India* 2000;48:781-7.

99. Terry P, Lagergren J, Hansen H, et al. Fruit and vegetable consumption in the prevention of oesophageal and cardia cancers. *Eur J Cancer Prev* 2001;10:365-9.

100. Onuk MD, Oztopuz A, Memik F. Risk factors for esophageal cancer in eastern Anatolia. *Hepatogastroenterology* 2002;49:1290-2.

101. Xibib S, Meilan H, Moller H, et al. Risk factors for oesophageal cancer in Linzhou, China: a case-control study. *Asian Pac J Cancer Prev* 2003;4:119-24.

102. Hung HC, Huang MC, Lee JM, et al. Association between diet and esophageal cancer in Taiwan. *J Gastroenterol Hepatol* 2004;19:632-7.

103. Cook-Mozaffari PJ, Azordegan F, Day NE, et al. Oesophageal cancer studies in the Caspian Littoral of Iran: results of a case-control study. *Br J Cancer* 1979;39:293-309.

104. Ziegler RG, Morris LE, Blot WJ, et al. Esophageal cancer among black men in Washington, D.C. II. Role of nutrition. *J Natl Cancer Inst* 1981;67:1199-206.

105. Tuyns AJ, Riboli E, Doornbos G, et al. Diet and esophageal cancer in Calvados (France). *Nutr Cancer* 1987;9:81-92.

106. Ren A, Han X. [Dietary factors and esophageal cancer: a case-control study]. *Zhonghua Liu Xing Bing Xue Za Zhi* 1991;12:200-4.

107. Hu J, Nyren O, Wolk A, et al. Risk factors for oesophageal cancer in northeast China. *Int J Cancer* 1994;57:38-46.

108. Soler M, Bosetti C, Franceschi S, et al. Fiber intake and the risk of oral, pharyngeal and esophageal cancer. *Int J Cancer* 2001;91:283-7.

109. Takezaki T, Gao CM, Wu JZ, et al. Dietary protective and risk factors for esophageal and stomach cancers in a low-epidemic area for stomach cancer in

Jiangsu Province, China: comparison with those in a high-epidemic area. *Jpn J Cancer Res* 2001;92:1157-65.

110. Zhang W, An F, Lin H. [A case-control study on the risk factors of esophageal cancer in Jieyang City of Guangdong in China]. *Zhonghua Liu Xing Bing Xue Za Zhi* 2001;22:442-5.

111. Chen H, Ward MH, Graubard BI, et al. Dietary patterns and adenocarcinoma of the esophagus and distal stomach. *Am J Clin Nutr* 2002;75:137-44.

112. Li K, Yu P. Food groups and risk of esophageal cancer in Chaoshan region of China: a high-risk area of esophageal cancer. *Cancer Invest* 2003;21:237-40.

113. Brown LM, Blot WJ, Schuman SH, et al. Environmental factors and high risk of esophageal cancer among men in coastal South Carolina. *J Natl Cancer Inst* 1988;80:1620-5.

114. De Stefani E, Boffetta P, Deneo-Pellegrini H, et al. The role of vegetable and fruit consumption in the aetiology of squamous cell carcinoma of the oesophagus: a case-control study in Uruguay. *Int J Cancer* 2005;116:130-5.

115. Yang CX, Wang HY, Wang ZM, et al. Risk factors for esophageal cancer: a case-control study in South-western China. *Asian Pac J Cancer Prev* 2005;6:48-53.

116. Howell MA. Factor analysis of international cancer mortality data and per capita food consumption. *Br J Cancer* 1974;29:328-36.

117. Hara N, Sakata K, Nagai M, et al. Statistical analyses on the pattern of food consumption and digestive-tract cancers in Japan. *Nutr Cancer* 1984;6:220-8.

118. Sichieri R, Everhart JE, Mendonça GAS. Diet and mortality from common cancers in Brazil: an ecological study. *Cad Saude Publica* 1996;12:53-9.

119. Zhuo XG, Watanabe S. Factor analysis of digestive cancer mortality and food consumption in 65 Chinese counties. *J Epidemiol* 1999;9:275-84.

120. Pottern LM, Morris LE, Blot WJ, et al. Esophageal cancer among black men in Washington, D.C. I. Alcohol, tobacco, and other risk factors. *J Natl Cancer Inst* 1981;67:777-83.

121. Mettlin C, Graham S, Priore R, et al. Diet and cancer of the esophagus. *Nutr Cancer* 1981;2:143-7.

122. Yu MC, Garabrant DH, Peters JM, et al. Tobacco, alcohol, diet, occupation, and carcinoma of the esophagus. *Cancer Res* 1988;48:3843-8.

123. Engel LS, Chow WH, Vaughan TL, et al. Population attributable risks of esophageal and gastric cancers. *J Natl Cancer Inst* 2003;95:1404-13.

124. Brown LM, Swanson CA, Gridley G, et al. Adenocarcinoma of the esophagus: role of obesity and diet. *J Natl Cancer Inst* 1995;87:104-9.

125. Zhang ZF, Kurtz RC, Yu GP, et al. Adenocarcinomas of the esophagus and gastric cardia: the role of diet. *Nutr Cancer* 1997;27:298-309.

126. Sharp L, Chilvers CE, Cheng KK, et al. Risk factors for squamous cell carcinoma of the oesophagus in women: a case-control study. *Br J Cancer* 2001;85:1667-70.

127. Nakachi K, Imai K, Hoshiyama Y, et al. The joint effects of two factors in the aetiology of oesophageal cancer in Japan. *J Epidemiol Community Health* 1988;42:355-64.

128. Castelletto R, Castellsague X, Munoz N, et al. Alcohol, tobacco, diet, mate drinking, and esophageal cancer in Argentina. *Cancer Epidemiol Biomarkers Prev* 1994;3:557-64.

129. Gao CM, Takezaki T, Ding JH, et al. Protective effect of allium vegetables against both esophageal and stomach cancer: a simultaneous case-referent study of a high-epidemic area in Jiangsu Province, China. *Jpn J Cancer Res* 1999;90:614-21.

130. Terry P, Lagergren J, Wolk A, et al. Reflux-inducing dietary factors and risk of adenocarcinoma of the esophagus and gastric cardia. *Nutr Cancer* 2000;38:186-91.

131. Graham S, Marshall J, Haughey B, et al. Nutritional epidemiology of cancer of the esophagus. *Am J Epidemiol* 1990;131:454-67.

132. Cheng KK, Day NE, Duffy SW, et al. Pickled vegetables in the aetiology of oesophageal cancer in Hong Kong Chinese. *Lancet* 1992;339:1314-8.

133. Cheng KK, Duffy SW, Day NE, et al. Oesophageal cancer in never-smokers and never-drinkers. *Int J Cancer* 1995;60:820-2.

134. Srivastava M, Kapil U, Chattopadhyaya TK, et al. Nutritional risk factors in carcinoma esophagus. *Nutr Res* 1995;15:177-85.

135. Phukan RK, Chetia CK, Ali MS, et al. Role of dietary habits in the development of esophageal cancer in Assam, the north-eastern region of India. *Nutr Cancer* 2001;39:204-9.

136. Tavani A, Negri E, Franceschi S, et al. Risk factors for esophageal cancer in women in northern Italy. *Cancer* 1993;72:2531-6.

137. Tao X, Zhu H, Matanoski GM. Mutagenic drinking water and risk of male esophageal cancer: a population-based case-control study. *Am J Epidemiol* 1999;150:443-52.

138. Wang M, Guo C, Li M. [A case-control study on the dietary risk factors of upper digestive tract cancer]. *Zhonghua Liu Xing Bing Xue Za Zhi* 1999;20:95-7.

139. Chitra S, Ashok L, Anand L, et al. Risk factors for esophageal cancer in Coimbatore, southern India: a hospital-based case-control study. *Indian J Gastroenterol* 2004;23:19-21.

140. Gonzalez CA, Pera G, Agudo A, et al. Fruit and vegetable intake and the risk of stomach and oesophagus adenocarcinoma in the European Prospective Investigation into Cancer and Nutrition (EPIC-EURGAST). *Int J Cancer* 2006;118:2559-66.

141. Decarli A, Liati P, Negri E, et al. Vitamin A and other dietary factors in the etiology of esophageal cancer. *Nutr Cancer* 1987;10:29-37.

142. Tavani A, Negri E, Franceschi S, et al. Risk factors for esophageal cancer in lifelong nonsmokers. *Cancer Epidemiol Biomarkers Prev* 1994;3:387-92.

143. Yokoyama A, Kato H, Yokoyama T, et al. Esophageal squamous cell carcinoma and aldehyde dehydrogenase-2 genotypes in Japanese females. *Alcohol Clin Exp Res* 2006;30:491-500.

144. Chyou PH, Nomura AM, Hankin JH, et al. A case-cohort study of diet and stomach cancer. *Cancer Res* 1990;50:7501-4.

145. Kneller RW, McLaughlin JK, Bjelke E, et al. A cohort study of stomach cancer in a high-risk American population. *Cancer* 1991;68:672-8.

146. Botterweck AA, van den Brandt PA, Goldbohm RA. A prospective cohort study on vegetable and fruit consumption and stomach cancer risk in The Netherlands. *Am J Epidemiol* 1998;148:842-53.

147. Hirvonen T, Virtamo J, Korhonen P, et al. Flavonol and flavone intake and the risk of cancer in male smokers (Finland). *Cancer Causes Control* 2001;12:789-96.

148. McCullough ML, Robertson AS, Jacobs EJ, et al. A prospective study of diet and stomach cancer mortality in United States men and women. *Cancer Epidemiol Biomarkers Prev* 2001;10:1201-5.

149. Fujino Y, Tamakoshi A, Ohno Y, et al. Prospective study of educational background and stomach cancer in Japan. *Prev Med* 2002;35:121-7.

150. Kobayashi M, Tsubono Y, Sasazuki S, et al. Vegetables, fruit and risk of gastric cancer in Japan: a 10-year follow-up of the JPHC Study Cohort I. *Int J Cancer* 2002;102:39-44.

151. Crane PS, Rhee SU, Seel DJ. Experience with 1,079 cases of cancer of the stomach seen in Korea from 1962 to 1968. *Am J Surg* 1970;120:747-51.

152. Haenszel W, Kurihara M, Segi M, et al. Stomach cancer among Japanese in Hawaii. *J Natl Cancer Inst* 1972;49:969-88.

153. Ye EC. [Case-control study of 100 gastric cancer cases]. *Chung Hua Yu Fang I Hsueh Tsa Chih* 1981;15:107-9.

154. Funakoshi N, Kanoh T, Uchino H, et al. Gastric cancer and diet. The analysis of the epidemiological survey in Tango district of Kyoto prefecture. *Naika Hokan* 1983;30:175-81.

155. Ren TS. [Case-control study of gastric cancer in ten rural counties in China]. *Chung Hua Liu Hsing Ping Hsueh Tsa Chih* 1985;6:29-32.

156. Correa P, Fontham E, Pickle LW, et al. Dietary determinants of gastric cancer in south Louisiana inhabitants. *J Natl Cancer Inst* 1985;75:645-54.

157. Risch HA, Jain M, Choi NW, et al. Dietary factors and the incidence of cancer of the stomach. *Am J Epidemiol* 1985;122:947-59.

158. Yi Y. Analysis of etiological factors on gastric cancer in Fuzhou City China. *Chinese Journal of Epidemiology* 1986;7:48-50.

159. You WC, Blot WJ, Chang YS, et al. Diet and high risk of stomach cancer in Shandong, China. *Cancer Res* 1988;48:3518-23.

160. De Stefani E, Boffetta P, Mendilaharsu M, et al. Dietary nitrosamines, heterocyclic amines, and risk of gastric cancer: a case-control study in Uruguay. *Nutr Cancer* 1998;30:158-62.

161. De Stefani E, Correa P, Boffetta P, et al. Dietary patterns and risk of gastric cancer: a case-control study in Uruguay. *Gastric Cancer* 2004;7:211-20.

162. De Stefani E, Correa P, Boffetta P, et al. Plant foods and risk of gastric cancer: a case-control study in Uruguay. *Eur J Cancer Prev* 2001;10:357-64.

163. De Stefani E, Correa P, Fierro L, et al. Alcohol drinking and tobacco smoking in gastric cancer. A case-control study. *Rev Epidemiol Sante Publique* 1990;38:297-307.

164. Boeing H, Jedrychowski W, Wahrendorf J, et al. Dietary risk factors in intestinal and diffuse types of stomach cancer: a multicenter case-control study in Poland. *Cancer Causes Control* 1991;2:227-33.

165. Cai L. [A case-control study of stomach cancer in Changle, Fujian Province - by the risk state analysis]. *Chung Hua Liu Hsing Ping Hsueh Tsa Chih* 1991;12:15-9.

166. Sanchez-Diez A, Hernandez-Mejia R, Cueto-Espinar A. Study of the relation between diet and gastric cancer in a rural area of the Province of Leon, Spain. *Eur J Epidemiol* 1992;8:233-7.

167. Boeing H, Frentzel-Beyme R, Berger M, et al. Case-control study on stomach cancer in Germany. *Int J Cancer* 1991;47:858-64.

168. Memik F, Nak SG, Gulten M, et al. Gastric carcinoma in northwestern Turkey: epidemiologic characteristics. *J Environ Pathol Toxicol Oncol* 1992;11:335-8.

169. Ren D, Jin J, Wang D, et al. The nutritional factors related to gastric cancer in Tianjin. *Ying Yang Xue Bao* 1992;14:325-8.

170. Wang R. [The epidemiological study of subtype risk factors of gastric cancer]. *Chung Hua Liu Hsing Ping Hsueh Tsa Chih* 1993;14:295-9.

171. Hansson LE, Nyren O, Bergstrom R, et al. Diet and risk of gastric cancer. A population-based case-control study in Sweden. *Int J Cancer* 1993;55:181-9.

172. Ramon JM, Serra L, Cerdo C, et al. Dietary factors and gastric cancer risk. A case-control study in Spain. *Cancer* 1993;71:1731-5.

173. Inoue M, Tajima K, Hirose K, et al. Life-style and subsite of gastric cancer - joint effect of smoking and drinking habits. *Int J Cancer* 1994;56:494-9.

174. Cornee J, Pobel D, Riboli E, et al. A case-control study of gastric cancer and nutritional factors in Marseille, France. *Eur J Epidemiol* 1995;11:55-65.

175. Gajalakshmi CK, Shanta V. Lifestyle and risk of stomach cancer: a hospital-based case-control study. *Int J Epidemiol* 1996;25:1146-53.

176. López-Carrillo L, Lopez-Cervantes M, Ramirez-Espitia A, et al. Alcohol consumption and gastric cancer in Mexico. *Cad Saude Publica* 1998;14:25-32.

177. Ye W, Yi Y, Luo R. [A case-control study on diet and gastric cancer]. *Chung Hua Yu Fang I Hsueh Tsa Chih* 1998;32:100-2.

178. Ji BT, Chow WH, Yang G, et al. Dietary habits and stomach cancer in Shanghai, China. *Int J Cancer* 1998;76:659-64.

179. Ward MH, L¢pez-Carrillo L. Dietary factors and the risk of gastric cancer in Mexico City. *Am J Epidemiol* 1999;149:925-32.

180. Mathew A, Gangadharan P, Varghese C, et al. Diet and stomach cancer: a case-control study in South India. *Eur J Cancer Prev* 2000;9:89-97.

181. Cai L, Yu SZ, Zhang ZF. Helicobacter pylori infection and risk of gastric cancer in Changle County, Fujian Province, China. *World J Gastroenterol* 2000;6:374-6.

182. Munoz N, Plummer M, Vivas J, et al. A case-control study of gastric cancer in Venezuela. *Int J Cancer* 2001;93:417-23.

183. Sriamporn S, Setiawan V, Pisani P, et al. Gastric cancer: the roles of diet, alcohol drinking, smoking and *Helicobacter pylori* in northeastern Thailand. *Asian Pac J Cancer Prev* 2002;3:345-52.

184. Kim HJ, Chang WK, Kim MK, et al. Dietary factors and gastric cancer in Korea: a case-control study. *Int J Cancer* 2002;97:531-5.

185. Xibin S, Moller H, Evans HS, et al. Residential environment, diet and risk of stomach cancer: a case-control study in Linzhou, China. *Asian Pac J Cancer Prev* 2002;3:167-72.

186. Suh S, Koo B, Choi Y, et al. [The nutritional intakes of the stomach cancer patients in the Daegu and Gyeongbuk areas, Korea]. *Korean J Comm Nutr* 2003;8:202-19.

187. Sipetic S, Tomic-Kundakovic S, Vlajinac H, et al. [Diet and gastric cancer]. *Vojnosanit Pregl* 2003;60:697-705.

188. Hara M, Hanaoka T, Kobayashi M, et al. Cruciferous vegetables, mushrooms, and gastrointestinal cancer risks in a multicenter, hospital-based case-control study in Japan. *Nutr Cancer* 2003;46:138-47.

189. López-Carrillo L, Lopez-Cervantes M, Robles-Diaz G, et al. Capsaicin consumption, *Helicobacter pylori* positivity and gastric cancer in Mexico. *Int J Cancer* 2003;106:277-82.

190. Fei S, Xiao S. [Diet and gastric cancer: a case-control study in Shanghai urban districts]. *Chin J Gastroenterol* 2003;8:143-7.

191. Lissowska J, Gail MH, Pee D, et al. Diet and stomach cancer risk in Warsaw, Poland. *Nutr Cancer* 2004;48:149-59.

192. Lagiou P, Samoli E, Lagiou A, et al. Flavonoids, vitamin C and adenocarcinoma of the stomach. *Cancer*

Causes Control 2004;15:67-72.

193. Boccia S, Persiani R, La Torre G, et al. Sulfotransferase 1A1 polymorphism and gastric cancer risk: a pilot case-control study. *Cancer Lett* 2005;229:235-43.

194. Nan HM, Park JW, Song YJ, et al. Kimchi and soybean pastes are risk factors of gastric cancer. *World J Gastroenterol* 2005;11:3175-81.

195. Setiawan VW, Yu GP, Lu QY, et al. Allium vegetables and stomach cancer risk in China. *Asian Pac J Cancer Prev* 2005;6:387-95.

196. Hayashi K, Watanabe Y, Uozumi G, et al. An epidemiological study on intestinal metaplasia of stomach analysis of correlation with atrophic gastritis and dietary habits. *J Kyoto Prefect Univ Med* 1985;94:883-8.

197. Maruchi N, Aoki S, Tsuda K, et al. Relation of food consumption to cancer mortality in Japan, with special reference to international figures. *Gann* 1977;68:1-13.

198. Koifman S, Koifman RJ. Stomach cancer incidence in Brazil: an ecologic study with selected risk factors. *Cad Saude Publica* 1997;13:85-92.

199. Vutuc C, Kunze M, Gredler B. [Mortality of gastric, large intestine and rectal cancer and food consumption in Austria (1953-1974)]. *Wien Med Wochenschr* 1977;127:170-2.

200. Tominaga S, Ogawa H, Kuroishi T. Usefulness of correlation analyses in the epidemiology of stomach cancer. *Natl Cancer Inst Monogr* 1982;62:135-40.

201. Inaba Y, Takagi H, Yanai H. [Correlation study of cancer mortality and food consumption]. *Gan No Rinsho* 1986;32:567-75.

202. Shimada A. [Regional differences in gastric cancer mortality and eating habits of people]. *Gan No Rinsho* 1986;32:692-8.

203. Llopis A, Morales M, Rodriguez R. Digestive cancer in relation to diet in Spain. *J Environ Pathol Toxicol Oncol* 1992;11:169-75.

204. Nasu K, Oguni I, Kanaya S, et al. Differences in food intake and nutritional status between the areas with low and high standardized mortality ratio for stomach cancer in Shizouka Prefecture. *Jap J Nutr* 1992;50:133-44.

205. Vioque J, Egea CM, Porta M. Stomach cancer mortality in Spain: an ecological analysis of diet, altitude, latitude, and income. *J Epidemiol Community Health* 1995;49:441-2.

206. Azevedo LF, Salgueiro LF, Claro R, et al. Diet and gastric cancer in Portugal - a multivariate model. *Eur J Cancer Prev* 1999;8:41-8.

207. Jansen MC, Bueno-De-Mesquita HB, Rasanen L, et al. Consumption of plant foods and stomach cancer mortality in the seven countries study. Is grain consumption a risk factor? Seven Countries Study Research Group. *Nutr Cancer* 1999;34:49-55.

208. Takezaki T, Gao CM, Ding JH, et al. Comparative study of lifestyles of residents in high and low risk areas for gastric cancer in Jiangsu Province, China; with special reference to allium vegetables. *J Epidemiol* 1999;9:297-305.

209. Cai L, Yu SZ, Ye WM, et al. Fish sauce and gastric cancer: an ecological study in Fujian Province, China. *World J Gastroenterol* 2000;6:671-5.

210. Hirayama T. Does daily intake of green-yellow vegetables reduce the risk of cancer in man? An example of the application of epidemiological methods to the identification of individuals at low risk. *IARC Sci Publ* 1982:531-40.

211. Hirayama T. [Primary cancer prevention by life style modification]. 1989;35:163-70.

212. Inoue M, Tajima K, Kobayashi S, et al. Protective factor against progression from atrophic gastritis to gastric cancer - data from a cohort study in Japan. *Int J Cancer* 1996;66:309-14.

213. Kato I, Tominaga S, Matsumoto K. A prospective study of stomach cancer among a rural Japanese population: a 6-year survey. *Jpn J Cancer Res* 1992;83:568-75.

214. Khan MM, Goto R, Kobayashi K, et al. Dietary habits and cancer mortality among middle aged and older Japanese living in Hokkaido, Japan by cancer site and sex. 2004;5:58-65.

215. Ngoan LT, Mizoue T, Fujino Y, et al. Dietary factors and stomach cancer mortality. *Br J Cancer* 2002;87:37-42.

216. Sauvaget C, Nagano J, Hayashi M, et al. Vegetables and fruit intake and cancer mortality in the Hiroshima/Nagasaki Life Span Study. *Br J Cancer* 2003;88:689-94.

217. Sauvaget C, Lagarde F, Nagano J, et al. Lifestyle factors, radiation and gastric cancer in atomic-bomb survivors (Japan). *Cancer Causes Control* 2005;16:773-80.

218. Yatsuya H, Toyoshima H, Tamakoshi A, et al. Individual and joint impact of family history and *Helicobacter pylori* infection on the risk of stomach cancer: a nested case-control study. *Br J Cancer* 2004;91:929-34.

219. Goiriena De Gandarias FJ, Santidrian MI, Barranquero AM. Etiopathogenic study of cancer of the digestive tract in Biscay Spain with special emphasis on the role played by diet and consumption of alcohol and tobacco. *Rev Sanid Hig Publica (Madr)* 1987;62:1411-30.

220. Hu JF. [Risk analysis of fuzzy states in data of case-control study for stomach cancer in Heilongjiang Province]. *Zhonghua Zhong Liu Za Zhi* 1989;11:28-30.

221. Burr ML, Holliday RM. Fruit and stomach cancer. *J Hum Nutr Diet* 1989;2:273-7.

222. Jedrychowski W, Maugeri U, Jedrychowska I, et al. The analytic epidemiologic study on occupational factors and stomach cancer occurrence. *G Ital Med Lav* 1990;12:3-8.

223. Demirer T, Icli F, Uzunalimoglu O, et al. Diet and stomach cancer incidence. A case-control study in Turkey. *Cancer*

1990;65:2344-8.

224. Lee HH, Wu HY, Chuang YC, et al. Epidemiologic characteristics and multiple risk factors of stomach cancer in Taiwan. *Anticancer Res* 1990;10:875-81.

225. Kato I, Tominaga S, Ito Y, et al. A comparative case-control analysis of stomach cancer and atrophic gastritis. *Cancer Res* 1990;50:6559-64.

226. Hoshiyama Y, Sasaba T. A case-control study of stomach cancer and its relation to diet, cigarettes, and alcohol consumption in Saitama Prefecture, Japan. *Cancer Causes Control* 1992;3:441-8.

227. Youm PY, Kim SH. [A case-control study on dietary and other factors related to stomach cancer incidence]. *Korean J Nutr* 1998;31:62-71.

228. Watabe K, Nishi M, Miyake H, et al. Lifestyle and gastric cancer: a case-control study. *Oncol Rep* 1998;5:1191-4.

229. Hamada GS, Kowalski LP, Nishimoto IN, et al. Risk factors for stomach cancer in Brazil (II): a case-control study among Japanese Brazilians in Sao Paulo. *Jpn J Clin Oncol* 2002;32:284-90.

230. Nishimoto IN, Hamada GS, Kowalski LP, et al. Risk factors for stomach cancer in Brazil (I): a case-control study among non-Japanese Brazilians in Sao Paulo. *Jpn J Clin Oncol* 2002;32:277-83.

231. Ito LS, Inoue M, Tajima K, et al. Dietary factors and the risk of gastric cancer among Japanese women: a comparison between the differentiated and non-differentiated subtypes. *Ann Epidemiol* 2003;13:24-31.

232. Zickute J, Strumylaite L, Dregval L, et al. [Vegetables and fruits and risk of stomach cancer]. *Medicina (Kaunas)* 2005;41:733-40.

233. Wong BC, Ching CK, Lam SK, et al. Differential north to south gastric cancer-duodenal ulcer gradient in China. China Ulcer Study Group. *J Gastroenterol Hepatol* 1998;13:1050-7.

234. Nagai M, Hashimoto T, Yanagawa H, et al. Relationship of diet to the incidence of esophageal and stomach cancer in Japan. *Nutr Cancer* 1982;3:257-68.

235. Kato I, Tominaga S, Kuroishi T. Per capita foods/nutrients intake and mortality from gastrointestinal cancers in Japan. *Jpn J Cancer Res* 1987;78:453-9.

236. Kneller RW, Guo WD, Hsing AW, et al. Risk factors for stomach cancer in sixty-five Chinese counties. *Cancer Epidemiol Biomarkers Prev* 1992;1:113-8.

237. Imaizumi Y. Longitudinal gompertzian analysis of mortality from stomach cancer in Japan, 1950-1993. *Mech Ageing Dev* 1995;85:133-45.

238. Corella D, Cortina P, Guillen M, et al. Dietary habits and geographic variation in stomach cancer mortality in Spain. *Eur J Cancer Prev* 1996;5:249-57.

239. Tominaga S, Kuroishi T. An ecological study on diet/nutrition and cancer in Japan. *Int J Cancer* 1997;Suppl:10-6.

240. Tsubono Y, Kobayashi M, Tsugane S. Food consumption and gastric cancer

mortality in five regions of Japan. *Nutr Cancer* 1997;27:60-4.

241. Tokui N, Yoshimura T, Fujino Y, et al. Dietary habits and stomach cancer risk in the JACC Study. *J Epidemiol* 2005;15 Suppl 2:S98-108.

242. Jedrychowski W, Boeing H, Popiela T, et al. Dietary practices in households as risk factors for stomach cancer: a familial study in Poland. *Eur J Cancer Prev* 1992;1:297-304.

243. Tuyns AJ, Kaaks R, Haelterman M, et al. Diet and gastric cancer. A case-control study in Belgium. *Int J Cancer* 1992;51:1-6.

244. Acheson ED, Doll R. Dietary factors in carcinoma of the stomach: a study of 100 cases and 200 controls. *Gut* 1964;5:126-31.

245. Tajima K, Tominaga S. Dietary habits and gastro-intestinal cancers: a comparative case-control study of stomach and large intestinal cancers in Nagoya, Japan. *Jpn J Cancer Res* 1985;76:705-16.

246. Li XX. [Case-control study of gastric cancer in high-incidence areas]. *Chinese Journal of Epidemiology* 1986;7:340-2.

247. Buiatti E, Palli D, Decarli A, et al. A case-control study of gastric cancer and diet in Italy. *Int J Cancer* 1989;44:611-6.

248. Graham S, Haughey B, Marshall J, et al. Diet in the epidemiology of gastric cancer. *Nutr Cancer* 1990;13:19-34.

249. Moon HK. Diet and stomach cancer: a case-control study in Korea. *Korean J Epidemiol* 1991;13:33-51.

250. Gonzalez CA, Sanz JM, Marcos G, et al. Dietary factors and stomach cancer in Spain: a multi-centre case-control study. *Int J Cancer* 1991;49:513-9.

251. Jarebinski M, Adanja B, Vlajinac H, et al. [Epidemiologic-anamnestic study of stomach cancer in relation to nutrition]. *Vojnosanit Pregl* 1994;51:309-13.

252. Appleby PN, Key TJ, Burr ML, et al. Mortality and fresh fruit consumption. *IARC Sci Publ* 2002;156:131-3.

253. Galanis DJ, Kolonel LN, Lee J, et al. Intakes of selected foods and beverages and the incidence of gastric cancer among the Japanese residents of Hawaii: a prospective study. *Int J Epidemiol* 1998;27:173-80.

254. Kato I, Tominaga S, Ito Y, et al. A prospective study of atrophic gastritis and stomach cancer risk. *Jpn J Cancer Res* 1992;83:1137-42.

255. Graham S, Schotz W, Martino P. Alimentary factors in the epidemiology of gastric cancer. *Cancer* 1972;30:927-38.

256. Jedrychowski W, Popiela T, Tobiasz-Adamczyk B, et al. [Dietary factors and laxatives in the epidemiology of stomach cancer]. *Nowotwory* 1981;30:353-60.

257. Jedrychowski W, Wahrendorf J, Popiela T, et al. A case-control study of dietary factors and stomach cancer risk in Poland. *Int J Cancer* 1986;37:837-42.

258. Coggon D, Barker DJ, Cole RB, et al. Stomach cancer and food storage. *J Natl Cancer Inst* 1989;81:1178-82.

259. Lee JK, Park BJ, Yoo KY, et al. Dietary factors and stomach cancer: a case-control study in Korea. *Int J Epidemiol* 1995;24:33-41.

260. Huang XE, Tajima K, Hamajima N, et al. Effect of life styles on the risk of subsite-specific gastric cancer in those with and without family history. *J Epidemiol* 1999;9:40-5.

261. Huang XE, Hirose K, Wakai K, et al. Comparison of lifestyle risk factors by family history for gastric, breast, lung and colorectal cancer. *Asian Pac J Cancer Prev* 2004;5:419-27.

262. Takezaki T, Gao CM, Wu JZ, et al. hOGG1 Ser(326)Cys polymorphism and modification by environmental factors of stomach cancer risk in Chinese. *Int J Cancer* 2002;99:624-7.

263. Suh S, Koo B, Choi Y, et al. [Lifestyle and eating behaviors of the stomach cancer patients in Daegu and Kyungpook areas in Korea]. *Korean J Nutr* 2002;35:380-93.

264. Lee SA, Kang D, Shim KN, et al. Effect of diet and *Helicobacter pylori* infection to the risk of early gastric cancer. *J Epidemiol* 2003;13:162-8.

265. Terry P, Nyren O, Yuen J. Protective effect of fruits and vegetables on stomach cancer in a cohort of Swedish twins. *Int J Cancer* 1998;76:35-7.

266. Dalgat DM, Aliev RG, Gireev GI, et al. [Epidemiology of stomach cancer in Dagestan]. *Vopr Onkol* 1974;20:76-82.

267. López-Carrillo L, Torres-Lopez J, Galvan-Portillo M, et al. *Helicobacter pylori*-CagA seropositivity and nitrite and ascorbic acid food intake as predictors for gastric cancer. *Eur J Cancer* 2004;40:1752-9.

268. Graham S, Lilienfe AM, Tidings JE. Dietary and purgation factors in epidemiology of gastric cancer. *Cancer* 1967;20:2224-34.

269. Hoey J, Montvernay C, Lambert R. Wine and tobacco: risk factors for gastric cancer in France. *Am J Epidemiol* 1981;113:668-74.

270. Trichopoulos D, Ouranos G, Day NE, et al. Diet and cancer of the stomach: a case-control study in Greece. *Int J Cancer* 1985;36:291-7.

271. La Vecchia C, Negri E, Decarli A, et al. A case-control study of diet and gastric cancer in northern Italy. *Int J Cancer* 1987;40:484-9.

272. Ward MH, Pan WH, Cheng YJ, et al. Dietary exposure to nitrite and nitrosamines and risk of nasopharyngeal carcinoma in Taiwan. *Int J Cancer* 2000;86:603-9.

273. Yuan JM, Wang XL, Xiang YB, et al. Preserved foods in relation to risk of nasopharyngeal carcinoma in Shanghai, China. *Int J Cancer* 2000;85:358-63.

274. Ning JP, Yu MC, Wang QS, et al. Consumption of salted fish and other risk factors for nasopharyngeal carcinoma (NPC) in Tianjin, a low-risk region for NPC in the People's Republic of China. *J Natl Cancer Inst* 1990;82:291-6.

275. Ye W, Yingnan Yi, Tianshu Zhou, Rutao Lin. A case-control study on risk condition of nasopharyngeal carcinoma in Southern area of Fujian Province. *J Fujian Med College* 1995;29:179-82.

276. Wang X, Chunyan Lin, Xiwen Sun, Yubo Shi, Yanjie Liu, Xudong Dai. The relationship between nasopharyngeal cancer and dietary as well as environmental factors in Heilongjiang province. *J China Oncol* 1993;15:75-6.

277. Guo Y, Futian L, Wenqin J, et al. Study on incidence factors of nasopharyngeal Carcinoma in Situ using small area analysis model. *Ai Zheng* 2001;20:1272-5.

278. Armstrong RW, Imrey PB, Lye MS, et al. Nasopharyngeal carcinoma in Malaysian Chinese: salted fish and other dietary exposures. In: 12, editor. *Int J Cancer*, 1998:228-35.

279. Chen DL, Huang TB. A case-control study of risk factors of nasopharyngeal carcinoma. *Cancer Lett* 1997;117:17-22.

280. Huang T, Chen D, Zhang J, et al. The comparison of risk factors of nasopharyngeal cancer between Northen and Southern China. *Ai Zheng* 1997;16:324-5.

281. Farrow DC, Vaughan TL, Berwick M, et al. Diet and nasopharyngeal cancer in a low-risk population. *Int J Cancer* 1998;78:675-9.

282. Alavanja MC, Dosemeci M, Samanıc C, et al. Pesticides and lung cancer risk in the agricultural health study cohort. *Am J Epidemiol* 2004;16:876-85.

283. Breslow RA, Graubard BI, Sinha R, et al. Diet and lung cancer mortality: a 1987 National Health Interview Survey cohort study. *Cancer Causes Control* 2000;11:419-31.

284. Chow WH, Schuman LM, McLaughlin JK, et al. A cohort study of tobacco use, diet, occupation, and lung cancer mortality. *Cancer Causes Control* 1992;3:247-54.

285. Feskanich D, Ziegler RG, Michaud DS, et al. Prospective study of fruit and vegetable consumption and risk of lung cancer among men and women. *J Natl Cancer Inst* 2000;92:1812-23.

286. Holick CN, Michaud DS, Stolzenberg-Solomon R, et al. Dietary carotenoids, serum beta-carotene, and retinol and risk of lung cancer in the alpha-tocopherol, beta-carotene cohort study. *Am J Epidemiol* 2002;156:536-47.

287. Jansen MC, Bueno-de-Mesquita HB, Feskens EJ, et al. Quantity and variety of fruit and vegetable consumption and cancer risk. *Nutr Cancer* 2004;48:142-8.

288. Knekt P, Jarvinen R, Seppanen R, et al. Dietary antioxidants and the risk of lung cancer. *Am J Epidemiol* 1991;134:471-9.

289. Knekt P, Jarvinen R, Teppo L, et al. Role of various carotenoids in lung cancer prevention. *J Natl Cancer Inst* 1999;91:182-4.

290. Liu Y, Sobue T, Otani T, et al. Vegetables, fruit consumption and risk of lung cancer among middle-aged Japanese men and women: JPHC Study. *Cancer Causes Control* 2004;15:349-57.

291. Miller AB. Vegetables and fruits and lung cancer. *IARC Sci Publ* 2002;156:85-7.

292. Miller AB, Altenburg HP, Bueno-de-Mesquita B, et al. Fruits and vegetables and lung cancer: Findings from the European Prospective Investigation into Cancer and Nutrition. *Int J Cancer* 2004;108:269-76.

293. Neuhouser ML, Patterson RE, Thornquist MD, et al. Fruits and vegetables are associated with lower lung cancer risk only in the placebo arm of the beta-carotene and retinol efficacy trial (CARET). *Cancer Epidemiol Biomarkers Prev* 2003;12:350-8.

294. Ocke MC, Bueno-de-Mesquita HB, Feskens EJ, et al. Repeated measurements of vegetables, fruits, beta-carotene, and vitamins C and E in relation to lung cancer. The Zutphen Study. *Am J Epidemiol* 1997;145:358-65.

295. Ratnasinghe D, Forman MR, Tangrea JA, et al. Serum carotenoids are associated with increased lung cancer risk among alcohol drinkers, but not among non-drinkers in a cohort of tin miners. *Alcohol Alcohol* 2000;35:355-60.

296. Shibata A, Paganini-Hill A, Ross RK, et al. Dietary beta-carotene, cigarette smoking, and lung cancer in men. *Cancer Causes Control* 1992;3:207-14.

297. Skuladottir H, Tjoenneland A, Overvad K, et al. Does insufficient adjustment for smoking explain the preventive effects of fruit and vegetables on lung cancer? *Lung Cancer* 2004;45:1-10.

298. Stahelin HB, Gey KF, Eichholzer M, et al. Plasma antioxidant vitamins and subsequent cancer mortality in the 12-year follow-up of the prospective Basel Study. *Am J Epidemiol* 1991;133:766-75.

299. Steinmetz KA, Potter JD, Folsom AR. Vegetables, fruit, and lung cancer in the Iowa Women's Health Study. *Cancer Res* 1993;53:536-43.

300. Voorrips LE, Goldbohm RA, Verhoeven DT, et al. Vegetable and fruit consumption and lung cancer risk in the Netherlands Cohort Study on diet and cancer. *Cancer Causes Control* 2000;11:101-15.

301. Agudo A, Esteve MG, Pallares C, et al. Vegetable and fruit intake and the risk of lung cancer in women in Barcelona, Spain. *Eur J Cancer* 1997;33:1256-61.

302. Alavanja MC, Brownson RC, Benichou J. Estimating the effect of dietary fat on the risk of lung cancer in nonsmoking women. *Lung Cancer* 1996;14 Suppl 1:S63-74.

303. Axelsson G, Rylander R. Diet as risk for lung cancer: a Swedish case-control study. *Nutr Cancer* 2002;44:145-51.

304. Biscevic A, Ustamujic A. Relative effects of nutrients on carcinogenesis. *Med Arh* 2004;58:347-50.

305. Caicoya M. [Lung cancer and vegetable consumption in Asturias, Spain. A case control study]. *Med Clin (Barc)* 2002;119:206-10.

306. Candelora EC, Stockwell HG, Armstrong AW, et al. Dietary intake and risk of lung cancer in women who never smoked. *Nutr Cancer* 1992;17:263-70.

307. Darby S, Whitley E, Doll R, et al. Diet, smoking and lung cancer: a case-control study of 1000 cases and 1500 controls in South-West England. *Br J Cancer* 2001;84:728-35.

308. De Stefani E, Brennan P, Boffetta P, et al. Diet and adenocarcinoma of the lung: a case-control study in Uruguay. *Lung Cancer* 2002;35:43-51.

309. De Stefani E, Brennan P, Ronco A, et al. Food groups and risk of lung cancer in Uruguay. *Lung Cancer* 2002;38:1-7.

310. Dorgan JF, Ziegler RG, Schoenberg JB, et al. Race and sex differences in associations of vegetables, fruits, and carotenoids with lung cancer risk in New Jersey (United States). *Cancer Causes Control* 1993;4:273-81.

311. Fontham ET, Pickle LW, Haenszel W, et al. Dietary vitamins A and C and lung cancer risk in Louisiana. *Cancer* 1988;62:2267-73.

312. Forman MR, Yao SX, Graubard BI, et al. The effect of dietary intake of fruits and vegetables on the odds ratio of lung cancer among Yunnan tin miners. *Int J Epidemiol* 1992;21:437-41.

313. Hu J, Mao Y, Dryer D, et al. Risk factors for lung cancer among Canadian women who have never smoked. *Cancer Detect Prev* 2002;26:129-38.

314. Jain M, Burch JD, Howe GR, et al. Dietary factors and risk of lung cancer: results from a case-control study, Toronto, 1981-1985. *Int J Cancer* 1990;45:287-93.

315. Kalandidi A, Katsouyanni K, Voropoulou N, et al. Passive smoking and diet in the etiology of lung cancer among non-smokers. *Cancer Causes Control* 1990;1:15-21.

316. Ko YC, Lee CH, Chen MJ, et al. Risk factors for primary lung cancer among non-smoking women in Taiwan. *Int J Epidemiol* 1997;26:24-31.

317. Kubik AK, Zatloukal P, Tomasek L, et al. Lung cancer risk among Czech women: a case-control study. *Prev Med* 2002;34:436-44.

318. Lagiou P, Samoli E, Lagiou A, et al. Flavonoid intake in relation to lung cancer risk: case-control study among women in Greece. *Nutr Cancer* 2004;49:139-43.

319. MacLennan R, Da Costa J, Day NE, et al. Risk factors for lung cancer in Singapore Chinese, a population with high female incidence rates. *Int J Cancer* 1977;20:854-60.

320. Marchand JL, Luce D, Goldberg P, et al. Dietary factors and the risk of lung cancer in New Caledonia (South Pacific). *Nutr Cancer* 2002;42:18-24.

321. Mohr DL, Blot WJ, Tousey PM, et al. Southern cooking and lung cancer. *Nutr Cancer* 1999;35:34-43.

322. Nyberg F, Agrenius V, Svartengren K, et al. Dietary factors and risk of lung cancer in never-smokers. *Int J Cancer* 1998;78:430-6.

323. Pierce RJ, Kune GA, Kune S, et al. Dietary and alcohol intake, smoking pattern, occupational risk, and family history in lung cancer patients: results of a case-control study in males. *Nutr Cancer* 1989;12:237-48.

324. Pillow PC, Hursting SD, Duphorne CM, et al. Case-control assessment of diet and lung cancer risk in African Americans and Mexican Americans. *Nutr Cancer* 1997;29:169-73.

325. Rachtan J. Dietary habits and lung cancer risk among Polish women. *Acta Oncol* 2002;41:389-94.

326. Ruano-Ravina A, Figueiras A, Dosil-Diaz O, et al. A population-based case-control study on fruit and vegetable intake and lung cancer: a paradox effect? *Nutr Cancer* 2002;43:47-51.

327. Stefani ED, Boffetta P, Deneo-Pellegrini H, et al. Dietary antioxidants and lung cancer risk: a case-control study in Uruguay. *Nutr Cancer* 1999;34:100-10.

328. Swanson CA, Brown CC, Sinha R, et al. Dietary fats and lung cancer risk among women: the Missouri Women's Health Study (United States). *Cancer Causes Control* 1997;8:883-93.

329. Wu-Williams AH, Dai XD, Blot W, et al. Lung cancer among women in north-east China. *Br J Cancer* 1990;62:982-7.

330. Ziegler RG, Mason TJ, Stemhagen A, et al. Carotenoid intake, vegetables, and the risk of lung cancer among white men in New Jersey. *Am J Epidemiol* 1986;123:1080-93.

331. Lan L, Ding Y. Study on serum vitamin A beta carotene and immune function in lung cancer. *Ying Yang Xue Bao* 1990;12:228-32.

332. Khlat M, Bouchardy C, Parkin DM. [Cancer mortality in immigrants from the Near East in Australia]. *Rev Epidemiol Sante Publique* 1993;41:208-17.

333. Le Marchand L, Hankin JH, Bach F, et al. An ecological study of diet and lung cancer in the South Pacific. *Int J Cancer* 1995;63:18-23.

334. Mulder I, Jansen MC, Smit HA, et al. Role of smoking and diet in the cross-cultural variation in lung-cancer mortality: the Seven Countries Study. Seven Countries Study Research Group. *Int J Cancer* 2000;88:665-71.

335. Taioli E, Nicolosi A, Wynder EL. Possible role of diet as a host factor in the aetiology of tobacco-induced lung cancer: an ecological study in southern and northern Italy. *Int J Epidemiol* 1991;20:611-4.

336. Smith-Warner SA, Spiegelman D, Yaun SS, et al. Fruits, vegetables and lung cancer: a pooled analysis of cohort studies. *Int J Cancer* 2003;107:1001-11.

337. Jansen MC, Bueno-de-Mesquita HB, Rasanen L, et al. Cohort analysis of fruit and vegetable consumption and lung cancer mortality in European men. *Int J Cancer* 2001;92:913-8.

338. Knekt P, Jarvinen R, Seppanen R, et al. Dietary flavonoids and the risk of lung cancer and other malignant neoplasms. *Am J Epidemiol* 1997;146:223-30.

339. Kvale G, Bjelke E, Gart JJ. Dietary habits and lung cancer risk. *Int J Cancer*

1983;31:397-405.

340. Ozasa K, Watanabe Y, Ito Y, et al. Dietary habits and risk of lung cancer death in a large-scale cohort study (JACC Study) in Japan by sex and smoking habit. *Jpn J Cancer Res* 2001;92:1259-69.

341. Speizer FE, Colditz GA, Hunter DJ, et al. Prospective study of smoking, antioxidant intake, and lung cancer in middle-aged women (USA). *Cancer Causes Control* 1999;10:475-82.

342. Bond GG, Thompson FE, Cook RR. Dietary vitamin A and lung cancer: results of a case-control study among chemical workers. *Nutr Cancer* 1987;9:109-21.

343. Gao CM, Tajima K, Kuroishi T, et al. Protective effects of raw vegetables and fruit against lung cancer among smokers and ex-smokers: a case-control study in the Tokai area of Japan. *Jpn J Cancer Res* 1993;84:594-600.

344. Harris RW, Key TJ, Silcocks PB, et al. A case-control study of dietary carotene in men with lung cancer and in men with other epithelial cancers. *Nutr Cancer* 1991;15:63-8.

345. Mayne ST, Janerich DT, Greenwald P, et al. Dietary beta carotene and lung cancer risk in U.S. nonsmokers. *J Natl Cancer Inst* 1994;86:33-8.

346. Pawlega J, Rachtan J, Dyba T. Evaluation of certain risk factors for lung cancer in Cracow (Poland) - a case-control study. *Acta Oncol* 1997;36:471-6.

347. Pisani P, Berrino F, Macaluso M, et al. Carrots, green vegetables and lung cancer: a case-control study. *Int J Epidemiol* 1986;15:463-8.

348. Sankaranarayanan R, Varghese C, Duffy SW, et al. A case-control study of diet and lung cancer in Kerala, south India. *Int J Cancer* 1994;58:644-9.

349. Suzuki I, Hamada GS, Zamboni MM, et al. Risk factors for lung cancer in Rio de Janeiro, Brazil: a case-control study. *Lung Cancer* 1994;11:179-90.

350. Ziegler RG, Colavito EA, Hartge P, et al. Importance of alpha-carotene, beta-carotene, and other phytochemicals in the etiology of lung cancer. *J Natl Cancer Inst* 1996;88:612-5.

351. Axelsson G, Liljeqvist T, Andersson L, et al. Dietary factors and lung cancer among men in west Sweden. *Int J Epidemiol* 1996;25:32-9.

352. Brennan P, Fortes C, Butler J, et al. A multicenter case-control study of diet and lung cancer among non-smokers. *Cancer Causes Control* 2000;11:49-58.

353. Dai XD, Lin CY, Sun XW, et al. The etiology of lung cancer in nonsmoking females in Harbin, China. *Lung Cancer* 1996;14 Suppl 1:S85-91.

354. Koo LC. Dietary habits and lung cancer risk among Chinese females in Hong Kong who never smoked. *Nutr Cancer* 1988;11:155-72.

355. Kreuzer M, Heinrich J, Kreienbrock L, et al. Risk factors for lung cancer among nonsmoking women. *Int J Cancer* 2002;100:706-13.

356. Mettlin C. Milk drinking, other beverage habits, and lung cancer risk. *Int J Cancer* 1989;43:608-12.

357. Rachtan J. A case-control study of lung cancer in Polish women. *Neoplasma* 2002;49:75-80.

358. Rachtan J, Sokolowski A. Risk factors for lung cancer among women in Poland. *Lung Cancer* 1997;18:137-45.

359. Hsing AW, McLaughlin JK, Chow WH, et al. Risk factors for colorectal cancer in a prospective study among U.S. white men. *Int J Cancer* 1998;77:549-53.

360. Shibata A, Paganini Hill A, Ross RK, et al. Intake of vegetables, fruits, beta-carotene, vitamin C and vitamin supplements and cancer incidence among the elderly: a prospective study. *Br J Cancer* 1992;66:673-9.

361. Giovannucci E, Rimm EB, Stampfer MJ, et al. Intake of fat, meat, and fiber in relation to risk of colon cancer in men. *Cancer Res* 1994;54:2390-7.

362. Steinmetz KA, Kushi LH, Bostick RM, et al. Vegetables, fruit, and colon cancer in the Iowa Women's Health Study. *Am J Epidemiol* 1994;139:1-15.

363. Michels KB, Edward G, Joshipura KJ, et al. Prospective study of fruit and vegetable consumption and incidence of colon and rectal cancers. *J Natl Cancer Inst* 2000;92:1740-52.

364. Terry P, Giovannucci E, Michels KB, et al. Fruit, vegetables, dietary fiber and risk of colorectal cancer. *J Natl Cancer Inst* 2001;93:525-33.

365. Colbert LH, Hartman TJ, Malila N, et al. Physical activity in relation to cancer of the colon and rectum in a cohort of male smokers. *Cancer Epidemiol Biomarkers Prev* 2001;10:265-8.

366. McCullough ML, Robertson AS, Chao A, et al. A prospective study of whole grains, fruits, vegetables and colon cancer risk. *Cancer Causes Control* 2003;14:959-70.

367. Sato Y, Tsubono Y, Nakaya N, et al. Fruit and vegetable consumption and risk of colorectal cancer in Japan: The Miyagi Cohort Study. *Public Health Nutr* 2005;8:309-14.

368. Kato I, Akhmedkhanov A, Koenig K, et al. Prospective study of diet and female colorectal cancer: the New York University Women's Health Study. *Nutr Cancer* 1997;28:276-81.

369. Pietinen P, Malila N, Virtanen M, et al. Diet and risk of colorectal cancer in a cohort of Finnish men. *Cancer Causes Control* 1999;10:387-96.

370. Schoen RE, Tangen CM, Kuller LH, et al. Increased blood glucose and insulin, body size, and incident colorectal cancer. *J Natl Cancer Inst* 1999;91:1147-54.

371. Bueno de Mesquita HB, Ferrari P, Riboli E. Plant foods and the risk of colorectal cancer in Europe: preliminary findings. *IARC Sci Publ* 2002;156:89-95.

372. Flood A, Velie EM, Chaterjee N, et al. Fruit and vegetable intakes and the risk of colorectal cancer in the Breast Cancer Detection Demonstration Project follow-up cohort. *Am J Clin Nutr* 2002;75:936-43.

373. Sanjoaquin MA, Appleby PN, Thorogood M, et al. Nutrition, lifestyle and colorectal cancer incidence: a prospective investigation of 10998 vegetarians and non-vegetarians in the United Kingdom. *Br J Cancer* 2004;90:118-21.

374. Lin J, Zhang SM, Cook NR, et al. Dietary intakes of fruit, vegetables, and fiber, and risk of colorectal cancer in a prospective cohort of women (United States). *Cancer Causes Control* 2005;16:225-33.

375. Tiemersma EW, Kampman E, Bueno de Mesquita HB, et al. Meat consumption, cigarette smoking, and genetic susceptibility in the etiology of colorectal cancer: results from a Dutch prospective study. *Cancer Causes Control* 2002;13:383-93.

376. Voorrips LE, Goldbohm RA, van Poppel G, et al. Vegetable and fruit consumption and risks of colon and rectal cancer in a prospective cohort study: The Netherlands Cohort Study on Diet and Cancer. *Am J Epidemiol* 2000;152:1081-92.

377. Thun MJ, Calle EE, Namboodiri MM, et al. Risk factors for fatal colon cancer in a large prospective study. *J Natl Cancer Inst* 1992;84:1491-500.

378. Wark PA, Weijenberg MP, van 't Veer P, et al. Fruits, vegetables, and hMLH1 protein-deficient and -proficient colon cancer: The Netherlands cohort study. *Cancer Epidemiol Biomarkers Prev* 2005;14:1619-25.

379. Sellers TTA, Bazyk AAE, Bostick RRM, et al. Diet and risk of colon cancer in a large prospective study of older women: an analysis stratified on family history (Iowa, United States). *Cancer Causes Control* 1998;9:357-67.

380. Wakai K, Hirose K, Matsuo K, et al. Dietary risk factors for colon and rectal cancers: a comparative case-control study. *J Epidemiol* 2006;16:125-35.

381. Fairfield KM, Hankinson SE, Rosner BA, et al. Risk of ovarian carcinoma and consumption of vitamins A, C, and E and specific carotenoids: a prospective analysis. *Cancer* 2001;92:2318-26.

382. Kushi LH, Mink PJ, Folsom AR, et al. Prospective study of diet and ovarian cancer. *Am J Epidemiol* 1999;149:21-31.

383. Larsson SC, Holmberg L, Wolk A, et al. Fruit and vegetable consumption in relation to ovarian cancer incidence: the Swedish mammography cohort. *Br J Cancer* 2004;90:2167-70.

384. Mommers M, Schouten LJ, Goldbohm RA, et al. Consumption of vegetables and fruits and risk of ovarian carcinoma: results from the Netherlands Cohort Study on Diet and Cancer. *Cancer* 2005;104:1512-9.

385. Schulz M, Lahmann PH, Boeing H, et al. Fruit and vegetable consumption and risk of epithelial ovarian cancer: the European Prospective Investigation into Cancer and Nutrition. *Cancer Epidemiol Biomarkers Prev* 2005;14:2531-5.

386. Bosetti C, Negri E, Franceschi S, et al. Diet and ovarian cancer risk: a case-control study in Italy. *Int J Cancer* 2001;93:911-5.

387. McCann SE, Freudenheim JL, Marshall JR, et al. Risk of human ovarian cancer is related to dietary intake of selected nutrients, phytochemicals and food groups. *J Nutr* 2003;133:1937-42.

388. McCann SE, Moysich KB, Mettlin C. Intakes of selected nutrients and food groups and risk of ovarian cancer. *Nutr Cancer* 2001;39:19-28.

389. Pan SY, Ugnat AM, Mao Y, et al. A case-control study of diet and the risk of ovarian cancer. *Cancer Epidemiol Biomarkers Prev* 2004;13:1521-7.

390. Shu XO, Gao YT, Yuan JM, et al. Dietary factors and epithelial ovarian cancer. *Br J Cancer* 1989;59:92-6.

391. Tavani A, Bosetti C, Dal Maso L, et al. Influence of selected hormonal and lifestyle factors on familial propensity to ovarian cancer. *Gynecol Oncol* 2004;92:922-6.

392. Zhang M, Yang ZY, Binns CW, et al. Diet and ovarian cancer risk: a case-control study in China. *Br J Cancer* 2002;86:712-7.

393. Ganmaa D, Sato A. The possible role of female sex hormones in milk from pregnant cows in the development of breast, ovarian and corpus uteri cancers. *Med Hypotheses* 2005;65:1028-37.

394. Rose DP, Boyar AP, Wynder EL. International comparisons of mortality rates for cancer of the breast, ovary, prostate, and colon, and per capita food consumption. *Cancer* 1986;58:2363-71.

395. Engle A, Muscat JE, Harris RE. Nutritional risk factors and ovarian cancer. *Nutr Cancer* 1991;15:239-47.

396. La Vecchia C, Decarli A, Negri E, et al. Dietary factors and the risk of epithelial ovarian cancer. *J Natl Cancer Inst* 1987;79:663-9.

397. Koushik A, Hunter DJ, Spiegelman D, et al. Fruits and vegetables and ovarian cancer risk in a pooled analysis of 12 cohort studies. *Cancer Epidemiol Biomarkers Prev* 2005;14:2160-7.

398. Shu XO, Zheng W, Potischman N, et al. A population-based case-control study of dietary factors and endometrial cancer in Shanghai, People's Republic of China. *Am J Epidemiol* 1993;137:155-65.

399. Potischman N, Swanson CA, Brinton LA, et al. Dietary associations in a case-control study of endometrial cancer. *Cancer Causes Control* 1993;4:239-50.

400. Levi F, Franceschi S, Negri E, et al. Dietary factors and the risk of endometrial cancer. *Cancer* 1993;71:3575-81.

401. Tzonou A, Lipworth L, Kalandidi A, et al. Dietary factors and the risk of endometrial cancer: a case - control study in Greece. *Br J Cancer* 1996;73:1284-90.

402. Goodman MT, Wilkens LR, Hankin JH, et al. Association of soy and fiber consumption with the risk of endometrial cancer. *Am J Epidemiol* 1997;146:294-306.

403. Jain MG, Howe GR, Rohan TE. Nutritional factors and endometrial cancer in Ontario, Canada. *Cancer Control* 2000;7:288-96.

404. McCann SE, Freudenheim JL, Marshall JR, et al. Diet in the epidemiology of endometrial cancer in western New York (United States). *Cancer Causes Control* 2000;11:965-74.

405. Littman AJ, Beresford SA, White E. The association of dietary fat and plant foods with endometrial cancer (United States). *Cancer Causes Control* 2001;12:691-702.

406. Petridou E, Kedikoglou S, Koukoulomatis P, et al. Diet in relation to endometrial cancer risk: a case-control study in Greece. *Nutr Cancer* 2002;44:16-22.

407. Tao MH, Xu WH, Zheng W, et al. A case-control study in Shanghai of fruit and vegetable intake and endometrial cancer. *Br J Cancer* 2005;92:2059-64.

408. Barbone F, Austin H, Partridge EE. Diet and endometrial cancer: a case-control study. *Am J Epidemiol* 1993;137:393-403.

409. Terry P, Wolk A, Vainio H, et al. Fatty fish consumption lowers the risk of endometrial cancer: a nationwide case-control study in Sweden. *Cancer Epidemiol Biomarkers Prev* 2002;11:143-5.

410. Goodman MT, Hankin JH, Wilkens LR, et al. Diet, body size, physical activity, and the risk of endometrial cancer. *Cancer Res* 1997;57:5077-85.

411. Boone CW, Kelloff GJ, Malone WE. Identification of candidate cancer chemopreventive agents and their evaluation in animal models and human clinical trials: a review. *Cancer Res* 1990;50:2-9.

412. Lampe JW, Chen C, Li S, et al. Modulation of human glutathione S-transferases by botanically defined vegetable diets. *Cancer Epidemiol Biomarkers Prev* 2000;9:787-93.

413. Dorant E, van den Brandt PA, Goldbohm RA, et al. Consumption of onions and a reduced risk of stomach carcinoma. *Gastroenterology* 1996;110:12-20.

414. Gonzalez CA, Pera G, Agudo A, et al. Fruit and vegetable intake and the risk of stomach and oesophagus adenocarcinoma in the European Prospective Investigation into Cancer and Nutrition (EPIC-EURGAST). *Int J Cancer* 2006;118:2559-66.

415. Csendes A, Medina E, Gaete MC, et al. [Gastric cancer: an epidemiologic and dietary study in 100 patients and 100 controls]. *Rev Med Chil* 1976;104:761-5.

416. You WC. [A study on the relationship between consumption of allium vegetables and gastric cancer]. *Chung Hua Yu Fang I Hsueh Tsa Chih* 1988;22:321-3.

417. Hu JF, Zhang SF, Jia EM, et al. Diet and cancer of the stomach: a case-control study in China. *Int J Cancer* 1988;41:331-5.

418. Chen K, Jiao D, Lu L, et al. A case-control study on diet and stomach cancer in a high incidence area of stomach cancer. *Ying Yang Xue Bao* 1992;14:150-4.

419. Garcia-Closas R, Gonzalez CA, Agudo A, et al. Intake of specific carotenoids and flavonoids and the risk of gastric cancer in Spain. *Cancer Causes Control* 1999;10:71-5.

420. Xu HX. [Relation between the diet of the residents and the incidence of gastric cancer in Yantai District]. *Chung Hua Liu Hsing Ping Hsueh Tsa Chih* 1985;6:245-7.

421. You WC, Blot WJ, Chang YS, et al. Allium vegetables and reduced risk of stomach cancer. *J Natl Cancer Inst* 1989;81:162-4.

422. Li H, Chen XL, Li HQ. Polymorphism of CYPIA1 and GSTM1 genes associated with susceptibility of gastric cancer in Shandong Province of China. *World J Gastroenterol* 2005;11:5757-62.

423. Li H, Li HQ, Wang Y, et al. An intervention study to prevent gastric cancer by micro-selenium and large dose of allitridum. *Chin Med J (Engl)* 2004;117:1155-60.

424. Zheng GH, Li H, Fan WT, et al. [Study on the long-time effect on allitridum and selenium in prevention of digestive system cancers]. *Zhonghua Liu Xing Bing Xue Za Zhi* 2005;26:110-2.

425. Graham DY, Anderson SY, Lang T. Garlic or jalapeno peppers for treatment of Helicobacter pylori infection. *Am J Gastroenterol* 1999;94:1200-2.

426. Iimuro M, Shibata H, Kawamori T, et al. Suppressive effects of garlic extract on Helicobacter pylori-induced gastritis in Mongolian gerbils. *Cancer Lett* 2002;187:61-8.

427. Franceschi S, Parpinel M, La Vecchia C, et al. Role of different types of vegetables and fruit in the prevention of cancer of the colon, rectum, and breast. *Epidemiology* 1998;9:338-41.

428. Gong Y, Ji B, Gao Y, et al. The nutritional epidemiology of rectal cancer in a population-based case-control study in Shanghai. *Ying Yang Xue Bao* 1993;15:309-17.

429. Hu JF, Liu YY, Yu YK, et al. Diet and cancer of the colon and rectum: a case-control study in China. *Int J Epidemiol* 1991;20:362-7.

430. Le Marchand L, Hankin JH, Wilkens LR, et al. Dietary fiber and colorectal cancer risk. *Epidemiology* 1997;8:658-65.

431. Levi F, Pasche C, La Vecchia C, et al. Food groups and colorectal cancer risk. *Br J Cancer* 1999;79:1283-7.

432. Yang G, Gao Y, Ji B. [Dietary factors and cancer of the colon and rectum in a population based case-control study in Shanghai]. *Zhonghua Liu Xing Bing Xue Za Zhi* 1994;15:299-303.

433. Yang G, Gao Y, Ji B. [Comparison of risk factors between left and right-sided colon cancer]. *Zhongguo Yi Xue Ke Xue Yuan Xue Bao* 1994;16:63-8.

434. Yang G, Ji B, Gao Y. Diet and nutrients as risk factors of colon cancer: a population-based case control study in Shanghai. *Ying Yang Xue Bao* 1993;14:373-9.

435. Kamal-Fouad K, Kishk N. Cancer colon:

occupational and nutritional association. *J Med Res Inst* 2002;23:80-94.

436. Xiao D, Lew KL, Kim YA, et al. Diallyl trisulfide suppresses growth of PC-3 human prostate cancer xenograft in vivo in association with Bax and Bak induction. *Clin Cancer Res* 2006;12:6836-43.

437. Chu Q, Lee DT, Tsao SW, et al. S-allylcysteine, a water-soluble garlic derivative, suppresses the growth of a human androgen-independent prostate cancer xenograft, CWR22R, under in vivo conditions. *BJU Int* 2007;99:925-32.

438. Shukla Y, Kalra N. Cancer chemoprevention with garlic and its constituents. *Cancer Lett* 2007;247:167-81.

439. Milner JA. Preclinical perspectives on garlic and cancer. *J Nutr* 2006;136:827S-31S.

440. La Vecchia C, Decarli A, Fasoli M, et al. Dietary vitamin A and the risk of intraepithelial and invasive cervical neoplasia. *Gynecol Oncol* 1988;30:187-95.

441. La Vecchia C, Franceschi S, Decarli A, et al. Dietary vitamin A and the risk of invasive cervical cancer. *Int J Cancer* 1984;34:319-22.

442. Hirose K, Hamajima N, Takezaki T, et al. Smoking and dietary risk factors for cervical cancer at different age group in Japan. *J Epidemiol* 1998;8:6-14.

443. Marshall JR, Graham S, Byers T, et al. Diet and smoking in the epidemiology of cancer of the cervix. *J Natl Cancer Inst* 1983;70:847-51.

444. Rajkumar T, Franceschi S, Vaccarella S, et al. Role of paan chewing and dietary habits in cervical carcinoma in Chennai, India. *Br J Cancer* 2003;88:1388-93.

445. Guo WD, Hsing AW, Li JY, et al. Correlation of cervical cancer mortality with reproductive and dietary factors, and serum markers in China. *Int J Epidemiol* 1994;23:1127-32.

446. Giuliano AR, Papenfuss M, Nour M, et al. Antioxidant nutrients: associations with persistent human papillomavirus infection. *Cancer Epidemiol Biomarkers Prev* 1997;6:917-23.

447. Chyou PH, Nomura AMY, Stemmermann GN. Diet, alcohol, smoking and cancer of the upper aerodigestive tract: a prospective study among Hawaii Japanese men. *Int J Cancer* 1995;60:616-21.

448. Maier H, Dietz A, Gewelke U, et al. Tobacco and alcohol and the risk of head and neck cancer. *Clin Investig* 1992;70:320-7.

449. Yang T, Xie X, Xie M, et al. [A comparative study on the risk factors for the incidence of tongue cancer]. *Hunan Yi Ke Da Xue Xue Bao* 1998;23:141-2.

450. Gallus S, Bosetti C, Franceschi S, et al. Laryngeal cancer in women: tobacco, alcohol, nutritional, and hormonal factors. *Cancer Epidemiol Biomarkers Prev* 2003;12:514-7.

451. Gridley G, McLaughlin JK, Block G, et al.

Vitamin supplement use and reduced risk of oral and pharyngeal cancer. *Am J Epidemiol* 1992;135:1083-92.

452. Toporcov TN, Antunes JL, Tavares MR. Fat food habitual intake and risk of oral cancer. *Oral Oncol* 2004;40:925-31.

453. Hanaoka T, Tsugane S, Ando N, et al. Alcohol consumption and risk of esophageal cancer in Japan: a case-control study in seven hospitals. *Jpn J Clin Oncol* 1994;24:241-6.

454. Victora CG, Munoz N, Day NE, et al. Hot beverages and oesophageal cancer in southern Brazil: a case-control study. *Int J Cancer* 1987;39:710-6.

455. Gimeno SG, de Souza JM, Mirra AP, et al. [Risk factors for cancer of the esophagus: a case control study in a metropolitan area of south-eastern Brazil]. *Rev Saude Publica* 1995;29:159-65.

456. Wolfgarten E, Rosendahl U, Nowroth T, et al. Coincidence of nutritional habits and esophageal cancer in Germany. *Onkologie* 2001;24:546-51.

457. Yanai H, Inaba Y, Takagi H, et al. Multivariate analysis of cancer mortalities for selected sites in 24 countries. *Environ Health Perspect* 1979;32:83-101.

458. Guo WD, Li JY, Blot WJ, et al. Correlations of dietary intake and blood nutrient levels with esophageal cancer mortality in China. *Nutr Cancer* 1990;13:121-7.

459. Barone J, Taioli E, Hebert JR, et al. Vitamin supplement use and risk for oral and esophageal cancer. *Nutr Cancer* 1992;18:31-41.

460. Wu M, Zhao JK, Hu XS, et al. Association of smoking, alcohol drinking and dietary factors with esophageal cancer in high- and low-risk areas of Jiangsu Province, China. *World J Gastroenterol* 2006;12:1686-93.

461. Fraser GE, Beeson WL, Phillips RL. Diet and lung cancer in California Seventh-day Adventists. *Am J Epidemiol* 1991;133:683-93.

462. Fu YY, Takezaki T, Tajima K. [Risk factors of lung cancer - follow-up studies in Nagoya Japan]. *Zhonghua Liu Xing Bing Xue Za Zhi* 1997;18:328-30.

463. Knekt P. Vitamin E and smoking and the risk of lung cancer. *Ann N Y Acad Sci* 1993;686:280-7; discussion 7-8.

464. Kromhout D. Essential micronutrients in relation to carcinogenesis. *Am J Clin Nutr* 1987;45:1361-7.

465. Olson JE, Yang P, Schmitz K, et al. Differential association of body mass index and fat distribution with three major histologic types of lung cancer: evidence from a cohort of older women. *Am J Epidemiol* 2002;156:606-15.

466. Takezaki T, Inoue M, Kataoka H, et al. Diet and lung cancer risk from a 14-year population-based prospective study in Japan: with special reference to fish consumption. *Nutr Cancer* 2003;45:160-7.

467. Wang LD, Hammond EC. Lung cancer, fruit, green salad and vitamin pills. *Chin Med J (Engl)* 1985;98:206-10.

468. Alavanja MC, Field RW, Sinha R, et al. Lung cancer risk and red meat consumption among Iowa women. *Lung Cancer* 2001;34:37-46.

469. Hu J, Johnson KC, Mao Y, et al. A case-control study of diet and lung cancer in northeast China. *Int J Cancer* 1997;71:924-31.

470. Ozturk O, Isbir T, Yaylim I, et al. GST M1 and CYP1A1 gene polymorphism and daily fruit consumption in Turkish patients with non-small cell lung carcinomas. *In Vivo* 2003;17:625-32.

471. Shimizu H, Morishita M, Mizuno K, et al. A case-control study of lung cancer in nonsmoking women. *Tohoku J Exp Med* 1988;154:389-97.

472. Xu Z, Brown LM, Pan GW, et al. Cancer risks among iron and steel workers in Anshan, China. Part II: Case-control studies of lung and stomach cancer. *Am J Ind Med* 1996;30:7-15.

473. Sone Y, Sakamoto N, Suga K, et al. Comparison of diets among elderly female residents in two suburban districts in Chiang Mai Province, Thailand, in dry season - survey on high- and low-risk districts of lung cancer incidence. *Appl Human Sci* 1998;17:49-56.

474. Tomioka F, Wakasugi H. Study on food intake patterns in Korea. *Jpn J Health Hum Ecol* 1995;61:317-28.

475. Kang ZC, Tsai SJ, Lee H. Quercetin inhibits benzo[a]pyrene-induced DNA adducts in human Hep G2 cells by altering cytochrome P-450 1A1 gene expression. *Nutr Cancer* 1999;35:175-9.

476. Alexandrov K, Cascorbi I, Rojas M, et al. CYP1A1 and GSTM1 genotypes affect benzo[a]pyrene DNA adducts in smokers' lung: comparison with aromatic/hydrophobic adduct formation. *Carcinogenesis* 2002;23:1969-77.

477. Le Marchand L, Murphy SP, Hankin JH, et al. Intake of flavonoids and lung cancer. *J Natl Cancer Inst* 2000;92:154-60.

478. Rylander R, Axelsson G. Lung cancer risks in relation to vegetable and fruit consumption and smoking. *Int J Cancer* 2006;118:739-43.

479. Haenszel W, Kurihara M, Locke FB, et al. Stomach cancer in Japan. *J Natl Cancer Inst* 1976;56:265-74.

480. Wu-Williams AH, Yu MC, Mack TM. Life-style, workplace, and stomach cancer by subsite in young men of Los Angeles County. *Cancer Res* 1990;50:2569-76.

481. Yu GP, Hsieh CC. Risk factors for stomach cancer: a population-based case-control study in Shanghai. *Cancer Causes Control* 1991;2:169-74.

482. Falcao JM, Dias JA, Miranda AC, et al. Red wine consumption and gastric cancer in Portugal: a case-control study. *Eur J Cancer Prev* 1994;3:269-76.

483. Kolonel LN, Nomura AM, Hirohata T, et al. Association of diet and place of birth with stomach cancer incidence in Hawaii Japanese and Caucasians. *Am J Clin Nutr* 1981;34:2478-85.

484. Lucchin L, Masciullo C, Perina P, et al.

[Correlation between nutrition and tumours in Alto Adige: critical considerations]. *Clinica Dietologica* 1994;21:77-83.

485. Meyer F. [Relationship between diet and carcinoma of stomach, colon, rectum, and pancreas in France]. *Gastroenterol Clin Biol* 1977;1:971-82.

486. Peri L, Pietraforte D, Scorza G, et al. Apples increase nitric oxide production by human saliva at the acidic pH of the stomach: a new biological function for polyphenols with a catechol group? *Free Radic Biol Med* 2005;39:668-81.

487. Fei SJ, Xiao SD. Diet and gastric cancer: a case-control study in Shanghai urban districts. *Chin J Dig Dis* 2006;7:83-8.

488. Phukan RK, Narain K, Zomawia E, et al. Dietary habits and stomach cancer in Mizoram, India. *J Gastroenterol* 2006;41:418-24.

489. Campos F, Carrasquilla G, Koriyama C, et al. Risk factors of gastric cancer specific for tumor location and histology in Cali, Colombia. *World J Gastroenterol* 2006;12:5772-9.

490. Zheng X, Yan L, Nilsson B, et al. Epstein-Barr virus infection, salted fish and nasopharyngeal carcinoma. A case-control study in southern China. *Acta Oncol* 1994;33:867-72.

491. Armstrong RW, Kannan Kutty M, Armstrong MJ. Self-specific environments associated with nasopharyngeal carcinoma in Selangor, Malaysia. *Soc Sci Med* 1978;12:149-56.

492. Huang Z, Jiang Y, Fang Y. An epidemiological study on risk factors of nasopharyngeal carcinoma in Guangxi province. *Ind Occup Dis* 2002;28:193-6.

493. Iwase Y, Takemura Y, Ju-ichi M, et al. Inhibitory effect of Epstein-Barr virus activation by Citrus fruits, a cancer chemopreventor. *Cancer Lett* 1999;139:227-36.

494. Stolzenberg-Solomon RZ, Pietinen P, Taylor PR, et al. Prospective study of diet and pancreatic cancer in male smokers. *Am J Epidemiol* 2002;155:783-92.

495. Shibata A, Mack TM, Paganini-Hill A, et al. A prospective study of pancreatic cancer in the elderly. *Int J Cancer* 1994;58:46-9.

496. Mills PK, Beeson WL, Abbey DE, et al. Dietary habits and past medical history as related to fatal pancreas cancer risk among Adventists. *Cancer* 1988;61:2578-85.

497. Chan JM, Wang F, Holly EA. Vegetable and fruit intake and pancreatic cancer in a population-based case-control study in the San Francisco bay area. *Cancer Epidemiol Biomarkers Prev* 2005;14:2093-7.

498. Olsen GW, Mandel JS, Gibson RW, et al. A case-control study of pancreatic cancer and cigarettes, alcohol, coffee and diet. *Am J Public Health* 1989;79:1016-9.

499. Bueno de Mesquita HB, Maisonneuve P, Runia S, et al. Intake of foods and nutrients and cancer of the exocrine pancreas: a population-based case-control study in The Netherlands. *Int J Cancer* 1991;48:540-9.

500. Mizuno S, Watanabe S, Nakamura K, et al. A multi-institute case-control study on the risk factors of developing pancreatic cancer. *Jpn J Clin Oncol* 1992;22:286-91.

501. Lyon JL, Slattery ML, Mahoney AW, et al. Dietary intake as a risk factor for cancer of the exocrine pancreas. *Cancer Epidemiol Biomarkers Prev* 1993;2:513-8.

502. Anderson KE, Kadlubar FF, Kulldorff M, et al. Dietary intake of heterocyclic amines and benzo(a)pyrene: associations with pancreatic cancer. *Cancer Epidemiol Biomarkers Prev* 2005;14:2261-5.

503. Falk RT, Pickle LW, Fontham ET, et al. Life-style risk factors for pancreatic cancer in Louisiana: a case-control study. *Am J Epidemiol* 1988;128:324-36.

504. Voirol M, Infante F, Raymond L, et al. [Nutritional profile of patients with cancer of the pancreas]. *Schweiz Med Wochenschr* 1987;117:1101-4.

505. Howe GR, Jain M, Miller AB. Dietary factors and risk of pancreatic cancer: results of a Canadian population-based case-control study. *Int J Cancer* 1990;45:604-8.

506. Ji BT, Chow WH, Gridley G, et al. Dietary factors and the risk of pancreatic cancer: a case-control study in Shanghai China. *Cancer Epidemiol Biomarkers Prev* 1995;4:885-93.

507. Ohba S, Nishi M, Miyake H. Eating habits and pancreas cancer. *Int J Pancreatol* 1996;20:37-42.

508. Soler M, Chatenoud L, La Vecchia C, et al. Diet, alcohol, coffee and pancreatic cancer: final results from an Italian study. *Eur J Cancer Prev* 1998;7:455-60.

509. Silverman DT, Swanson CA, Gridley G, et al. Dietary and nutritional factors and pancreatic cancer: a case-control study based on direct interviews. *J Natl Cancer Inst* 1998;90:1710-9.

510. Zhang Y, Cantor KP, Lynch CF, et al. Occupation and risk of pancreatic cancer: a population-based case-control study in Iowa. *J Occup Environ Med* 2005;47:392-8.

511. Mori M, Hariharan M, Anandakumar M, et al. A case-control study on risk factors for pancreatic diseases in Kerala, India. *Hepatogastroenterology* 1999;46:25-30.

512. Benhamou S, Clavel F, Rezvani A, et al. [Relation between mortality in cancer of the pancreas and food and tobacco consumption in France]. *Biomed Pharmacother* 1982;36:389-92.

513. Kato I, Tajima K, Kuroishi T, et al. Latitude and pancreatic cancer. *Jpn J Clin Oncol* 1985;15:403-13.

514. Vioque J, Gonzalez SL, Cayuela DA. [Cancer of the pancreas: an ecologic study]. *Med Clin (Barc)* 1990;95:121-5.

515. Corella PD, Cortina GP, Coltell SO. [Nutritional factors and geographic differences in pancreatic cancer mortality in Spain]. *Rev Sanid Hig Publica (Madr)* 1994;68:361-76.

516. Larsson SC, Hakansson N, Naslund I, et al. Fruit and vegetable consumption in relation to pancreatic cancer risk: a prospective study. *Cancer Epidemiol Biomarkers Prev* 2006;15:301-5.

517. Sauvaget C, Kasagi F, Waldren CA. Dietary factors and cancer mortality among atomic-bomb survivors. *Mutat Res* 2004;551:145-52.

518. Parkin DM, Srivatanakul P, Khlat M, et al. Liver-cancer in Thailand. I. A case-control study of cholangiocarcinoma. *Int J Cancer* 1991;48:323-8.

519. Kuper H, Tzonou A, Lagiou P, et al. Diet and hepatocellular carcinoma: a case-control study in Greece. *Nutr Cancer* 2000;38:6-12.

520. Yu SZ, Huang XE, Koide T, et al. Hepatitis B and C viruses infection, lifestyle and genetic polymorphisms as risk factors for hepatocellular carcinoma in Haimen, China. *Jpn J Cancer Res* 2002;93:1287-92.

521. Lam KC, Yu MC, Leung JW, et al. Hepatitis B virus and cigarette smoking: risk factors for hepatocellular carcinoma in Hong Kong. *Cancer Res* 1982;42:5246-8.

522. Kweon S, Park KA, Choi H. Chemopreventive effect of garlic powder diet in diethylnitrosamine-induced rat hepatocarcinogenesis. *Life Sci* 2003;73:2515-26.

523. Kweon S, Kim Y, Choi H. Grape extracts suppress the formation of preneoplastic foci and activity of fatty acid synthase in rat liver. *Exp Mol Med* 2003;35:371-8.

524. Shukla Y, Arora A. Suppression of altered hepatic foci development by curcumin in wistar rats. *Nutr Cancer* 2003;45:53-9.

525. Shukla Y, Kalra N, Katiyar S, et al. Chemopreventive effect of indole-3-carbinol on induction of preneoplastic altered hepatic foci. *Nutr Cancer* 2004;50:214-20.

526. Talamini R, Polesel J, Montella M, et al. Food groups and risk of hepatocellular carcinoma: a multicenter case-control study in Italy. *Int J Cancer* 2006;119:2916-21.

527. Kojima M, Wakai K, Tamakoshi K, et al. Diet and colorectal cancer mortality: results from the Japan collaborative cohort study. *Nutr Cancer* 2004;50:23-32.

528. Singh PN, Fraser GE. Dietary risk factors for colon cancer in a low-risk population. *Am J Epidemiol* 1998;148:761-74.

529. Phillips RL. Role of life-style and dietary habits in risk of cancer among seventh-day adventists. *Cancer Res* 1975;35:3513-22.

530. Tsubono Y, Otani T, Kobayashi M, et al. No association between fruit or vegetable consumption and the risk of colorectal cancer in Japan. *Br J Cancer* 2005;92:1782-4.

531. Turner F, Smith G, Sachse C, et al. Vegetable, fruit and meat consumption and potential risk modifying genes in relation to colorectal cancer. *Int J Cancer* 2004;112:259-64.

532. Juarranz Sanz M, Soriano Llora T, Calle Puron ME, et al. [Influence of the diet on the development of colorectal cancer in a population of Madrid]. *Rev Clin Esp* 2004;204:355-61.

533. Kuriki K, Hamajima N, Chiba H, et al. Increased risk of colorectal cancer due to interactions between meat consumption and the CD36 gene A52C polymorphism among Japanese. *Nutr Cancer* 2005;51:170-7.

534. Padayatty SJ, Katz A, Wang Y, et al. Vitamin C as an antioxidant: evaluation of its role in disease prevention. *J Am Coll Nutr* 2003;22:18-35.

535. Fountoulakis A, Martin IG, White KL, et al. Plasma and esophageal mucosal levels of vitamin C: role in the pathogenesis and neoplastic progression of Barrett's esophagus. *Dig Dis Sci* 2004;49:914-9.

536. Liu RH, Liu J, Chen B. Apples prevent mammary tumors in rats. *J Agric Food Chem* 2005;53:2341-3.

537. Nomura AM, Ziegler RG, Stemmermann GN, et al. Serum micronutrients and upper aerodigestive tract cancer. *Cancer Epidemiol Biomarkers Prev* 1997;6:407-12.

538. Zheng W, Blot WJ, Diamond EL, et al. Serum micronutrients and the subsequent risk of oral and pharyngeal cancer. *Cancer Res* 1993;53:795-8.

539. Tavani A, Negri E, Franceschi S, et al. Attributable risk for laryngeal cancer in northern Italy. *Cancer Epidemiol Biomarkers Prev* 1994;3:121-5.

540. Bidoli E, Bosetti C, La Vecchia C, et al. Micronutrients and laryngeal cancer risk in Italy and Switzerland: a case-control study. *Cancer Causes Control* 2003;14:477-84.

541. Mackerras D, Buffler PA, Randall DE, et al. Carotene intake and the risk of laryngeal cancer in coastal Texas. *Am J Epidemiol* 1988;128:980-8.

542. Freudenheim JL, Graham S, Byers TE, et al. Diet, smoking, and alcohol in cancer of the larynx: a case-control study. *Nutr Cancer* 1992;17:33-45.

543. Negri E, Franceschi S, Bosetti C, et al. Selected micronutrients and oral and pharyngeal cancer. *Int J Cancer* 2000;86:122-7.

544. Rossing MA, Vaughan TL, McKnight B. Diet and pharyngeal cancer. *Int J Cancer* 1989;44:593-7.

545. Knekt P, Aromaa A, Maatela J, et al. Serum micronutrients and risk of cancers of low incidence in Finland. *Am J Epidemiol* 1991;134:356-61.

546. Drozdz M, Gierek T, Jendryczko A, et al. Zinc, vitamins A and E, and retinol-binding protein in sera of patients with cancer of the larynx. *Neoplasma* 1989;36:357-62.

547. Abiaka C, Al-Awadi F, Gulshan S, et al. Plasma concentrations of alpha-tocopherol and urate in patients with different types of cancer. *J Clin Pharm Ther* 2001;26:265-70.

548. De Stefani E, Ronco A, Mendilaharsu M, et al. Diet and risk of cancer of the upper aerodigestive tract - II. Nutrients. *Oral Oncol* 1999;35:22-6.

549. Negri E, La Vecchia C, Franceschi S, et al. Attributable risk for oral cancer in northern Italy. *Cancer Epidemiol Biomarkers Prev* 1993;2:189-93.

550. Bandera EV, Freudenheim JL, Marshall JR, et al. Diet and alcohol consumption and lung cancer risk in the New York State Cohort (United States). *Cancer Causes Control* 1997;8:828-40.

551. Bandera EV, Freudenheim JL, Marshall JR, et al. Impact of losses to follow-up on diet/alcohol and lung cancer analyses in the New York State Cohort. *Nutr Cancer* 2002;42:41-7.

552. Michaud DS, Feskanich D, Rimm EB, et al. Intake of specific carotenoids and risk of lung cancer in 2 prospective US cohorts. *Am J Clin Nutr* 2000;72:990-7.

553. Shekelle RB, Lepper M, Liu S, et al. Dietary vitamin A and risk of cancer in the Western Electric study. *Lancet* 1981;2:1185-90.

554. Wright ME, Mayne ST, Stolzenberg-Solomon RZ, et al. Development of a comprehensive dietary antioxidant index and application to lung cancer risk in a cohort of male smokers. *Am J Epidemiol* 2004;160:68-76.

555. Yong LC, Brown CC, Schatzkin A, et al. Intake of vitamins E, C, and A and risk of lung cancer. The NHANES I epidemiologic followup study. First National Health and Nutrition Examination Survey. *Am J Epidemiol* 1997;146:231-43.

556. Bandera EV, Freudenheim JL, Graham S, et al. Alcohol consumption and lung cancer in white males. *Cancer Causes Control* 1992;3:361-9.

557. Cheng TJ, Christiani DC, Xu X, et al. Increased micronucleus frequency in lymphocytes from smokers with lung cancer. *Mutat Res* 1996;349:43-50.

558. Garcia J, Atalah E, Urteaga C, et al. [Dietary carotene intake and lung cancer among men from Santiago]. *Rev Med Chil* 1995;123:51-60.

559. Samet JM, Skipper BJ, Humble CG, et al. Lung cancer risk and vitamin A consumption in New Mexico. *Am Rev Respir Dis* 1985;131:198-202.

560. Wright ME, Mayne ST, Swanson CA, et al. Dietary carotenoids, vegetables, and lung cancer risk in women: the Missouri women's health study (United States). *Cancer Causes Control* 2003;14:85-96.

561. Ziegler RG, Mason TJ, Stemhagen A, et al. Dietary carotene and vitamin A and risk of lung cancer among white men in New Jersey. *J Natl Cancer Inst* 1984;73:1429-35.

562. Connett JE, Kuller LH, Kjelsberg MO, et al. Relationship between carotenoids and cancer. The Multiple Risk Factor Intervention Trial (MRFIT) Study. *Cancer* 1989;64:126-34.

563. Ito Y, Wakai K, Suzuki K, et al. Serum carotenoids and mortality from lung cancer: a case-control study nested in the Japan Collaborative Cohort (JACC) study. *Cancer Sci* 2003;94:57-63.

564. Ito Y, Wakai K, Suzuki K, et al. Lung cancer mortality and serum levels of carotenoids, retinol, tocopherols, and folic acid in men and women: a case-control study nested in the JACC Study. *J Epidemiol* 2005;15 Suppl 2:S140-9.

565. Ito Y, Kurata M, Hioki R, et al. Cancer mortality and serum levels of carotenoids, retinol, and tocopherol: a population-based follow-up study of inhabitants of a rural area of Japan. *Asian Pac J Cancer Prev* 2005;6:10-5.

566. Yuan JM, Ross RK, Chu XD, et al. Prediagnostic levels of serum beta-cryptoxanthin and retinol predict smoking-related lung cancer risk in Shanghai, China. *Cancer Epidemiol Biomarkers Prev* 2001;10:767-73.

567. Burgaz S, Torun M, Yardim S, et al. Serum carotenoids and uric acid levels in relation to cancer. *J Clin Pharm Ther* 1996;21:331-6.

568. LeGardeur BY, Lopez A, Johnson WD. A case-control study of serum vitamins A, E, and C in lung cancer patients. *Nutr Cancer* 1990;14:133-40.

569. Luo X. [Vitamin nutritional status of a high lung cancer risk population]. *Zhonghua Zhong Liu Za Zhi* 1991;13:257-60.

570. Stam J, Strankinga WF, Fikkert JJ, et al. Vitamins and lung cancer. *Lung* 1990;168 Suppl:1075-81.

571. Tominaga K, Saito Y, Mori K, et al. An evaluation of serum microelement concentrations in lung cancer and matched non-cancer patients to determine the risk of developing lung cancer: a preliminary study. *Jpn J Clin Oncol* 1992;22:96-101.

572. Rohan TE, Jain M, Howe GR, et al. A cohort study of dietary carotenoids and lung cancer risk in women (Canada). *Cancer Causes Control* 2002;13:231-7.

573. Voorrips LE, Goldbohm RA, Brants HA, et al. A prospective cohort study on antioxidant and folate intake and male lung cancer risk. *Cancer Epidemiol Biomarkers Prev* 2000;9:357-65.

574. Le Marchand L, Hankin JH, Kolonel LN, et al. Intake of specific carotenoids and lung cancer risk. *Cancer Epidemiol Biomarkers Prev* 1993;2:183-7.

575. Comstock GW, Alberg AJ, Huang HY, et al. The risk of developing lung cancer associated with antioxidants in the blood: ascorbic acid, carotenoids, alpha-tocopherol, selenium, and total peroxyl radical absorbing capacity. *Cancer Epidemiol Biomarkers Prev* 1997;6:907-16.

576. Goodman GE, Schaffer S, Omenn GS, et al. The association between lung and prostate cancer risk, and serum micronutrients: results and lessons learned from beta-carotene and retinol efficacy trial. *Cancer Epidemiol Biomarkers Prev* 2003;12:518-26.

577. Ratnasinghe DL, Yao SX, Forman M, et al. Gene-environment interactions between the codon 194 polymorphism of XRCC1 and antioxidants influence lung cancer risk. *Anticancer Res* 2003;23:627-32.

578. Bakker Schut TC, Puppels GJ, Kraan YM, et al. Intracellular carotenoid levels measured by Raman microspectroscopy: comparison of lymphocytes from lung

cancer patients and healthy individuals. *Int J Cancer* 1997;74:20-5.

579. Mannisto S, Smith-Warner SA, Spiegelman D, et al. Dietary carotenoids and risk of lung cancer in a pooled analysis of seven cohort studies. *Cancer Epidemiol Biomarkers Prev* 2004;13:40-8.

580. Abnet CC, Qiao YL, Dawsey SM, et al. Prospective study of serum retinol, beta-carotene, beta-cryptoxanthin, and lutein/zeaxanthin and esophageal and gastric cancers in China. *Cancer Causes Control* 2003;14:645-55.

581. Jendryczko A, Drozdz M, Pardela M, et al. [Vitamins A and E and vitamin A-binding proteins in the blood serum of patients with esophageal cancer]. *Przegl Lek* 1989;46:632-5.

582. Valsecchi MG. Modelling the relative risk of esophageal cancer in a case-control study. *J Clin Epidemiol* 1992;45:347-55.

583. Mayne ST, Risch HA, Dubrow R, et al. Nutrient intake and risk of subtypes of esophageal and gastric cancer. *Cancer Epidemiol Biomarkers Prev* 2001;10:1055-62.

584. Smith AH, Waller KD. Serum beta-carotene in persons with cancer and their immediate families. *Am J Epidemiol* 1991;133:661-71.

585. Franceschi S, Bidoli E, Negri E, et al. Role of macronutrients, vitamins and minerals in the aetiology of squamous-cell carcinoma of the oesophagus. *Int J Cancer* 2000;86:626-31.

586. Terry P, Lagergren J, Ye W, et al. Antioxidants and cancers of the esophagus and gastric cardia. *Int J Cancer* 2000;87:750-4.

587. Chen H, Tucker KL, Graubard BI, et al. Nutrient intakes and adenocarcinoma of the esophagus and distal stomach. *Nutr Cancer* 2002;42:33-40.

588. Platz EA, De Marzo AM, Erlinger TP, et al. No association between pre-diagnostic plasma C-reactive protein concentration and subsequent prostate cancer. *Prostate* 2004;59:393-400.

589. Schuurman AG, Goldbohm RA, Dorant E, et al. Vegetable and fruit consumption and prostate cancer risk: a cohort study in The Netherlands. *Cancer Epidemiol Biomarkers Prev* 1998;7:673-80.

590. Giovannucci E, Rimm EB, Liu Y, et al. A prospective study of tomato products, lycopene, and prostate cancer risk. *J Natl Cancer Inst* 2002;94:391-8.

591. Giovannucci E, Ascherio A, Rimm EB, et al. Intake of carotenoids and retinol in relation to risk of prostate cancer. *J Natl Cancer Inst* 1995;87:1767-76.

592. Mills PK, Beeson WL, Phillips RL, et al. Cohort study of diet, lifestyle, and prostate cancer in Adventist men. *Cancer* 1989;64:598-604.

593. Mills PK, Beeson WL, Phillips RL, et al. Cancer incidence among California Seventh-day Adventists, 1976-1982. *Am J Clin Nutr* 1994;59:1136S-42S.

594. Hsing AW, McLaughlin JK, Schuman LM, et al. Diet, tobacco use, and fatal prostate cancer: results from the Lutheran Brotherhood Cohort Study. *Cancer Res* 1990;50:6836-40.

595. Hodge AM, English DR, McCredie MRE, et al. Foods, nutrients and prostate cancer. *Cancer Causes Control* 2004;15:11-20.

596. Vogt TM, Mayne ST, Graubard BI, et al. Serum lycopene, other serum carotenoids, and risk of prostate cancer in US Blacks and Whites. *Am J Epidemiol* 2002;155:1023-32.

597. Kolonel LN, Hankin JH, Whittemore AS, et al. Vegetables, fruits, legumes and prostate cancer: a multiethnic case-control study. *Cancer Epidemiol Biomarkers Prev* 2000;9:795-804.

598. Norrish AE, Jackson RT, Sharpe SJ, et al. Prostate cancer and dietary carotenoids. *Am J Epidemiol* 2000;151:119-23.

599. Jain MG, Hislop GT, Howe GR, et al. Plant foods, antioxidants, and prostate cancer risk: findings from case-control studies in Canada. *Nutr Cancer* 1999;34:173-84.

600. Villeneuve PJ, Johnson KC, Kreiger N, et al. Risk factors for prostate cancer: results from the Canadian National Enhanced Cancer Surveillance System. The Canadian Cancer Registries Epidemiology Research Group. *Cancer Causes Control* 1999;10:355-67.

601. Key TJ, Silcocks PB, Davey GK, et al. A case-control study of diet and prostate cancer. *Br J Cancer* 1997;76:678-87.

602. Jian L, Du CJ, Lee AH, et al. Do dietary lycopene and other carotenoids protect against prostate cancer? *Int J Cancer* 2005;113:1010-4.

603. Sonoda T, Nagata Y, Mori M, et al. A case-control study of diet and prostate cancer in Japan: possible protective effect of traditional Japanese diet. *Cancer Sci* 2004;95:238-42.

604. Tzonou A, Signorello LB, Lagiou P, et al. Diet and cancer of the prostate: a case-control study in Greece. *Int J Cancer* 1999;80:704-8.

605. Hayes RB, Ziegler RG, Gridley G, et al. Dietary factors and risks for prostate cancer among blacks and whites in the United States. *Cancer Epidemiol Biomarkers Prev* 1999;8:25-34.

606. Le Marchand L, Hankin JH, Kolonel LN, et al. Vegetable and fruit consumption in relation to prostate cancer risk in Hawaii: a reevaluation of the effect of dietary beta-carotene. *Am J Epidemiol* 1991;133:215-9.

607. Lagiou A, Trichopoulos D, Tzonou A, et al. Are there age-dependent effects of diet on prostate cancer risk? *Soz Praventivmed* 2001;46:329-34.

608. Rao AV, Fleshner N, Garwal S. Serum and tissue lycopene and biomarkers of oxidation in prostate cancer patients: a case-control study. *Nutr Cancer* 1999;33:159-64.

609. Ganmaa D, Li XM, Wang J, et al. Incidence and mortality of testicular and prostatic cancers in relation to world dietary practices. *Int J Cancer* 2002;98:262-7.

610. Grant WB. An ecologic study of dietary links to prostate cancer. *Altern Med Rev* 1999;4:162-9.

611. Grant WB. A multicountry ecologic study of risk and risk reduction factors for prostate cancer mortality. *Eur Urol* 2004;45:271-9.

612. Platz EA, Leitzmann MF, Hollis BW, et al. Plasma 1,25-dihydroxy- and 25-hydroxyvitamin D and subsequent risk of prostate cancer. *Cancer Causes Control* 2004;15:255-65.

613. Schuurman AG, Goldbohm RA, Brants HA, et al. A prospective cohort study on intake of retinol, vitamins C and E, and carotenoids and prostate cancer risk (Netherlands). *Cancer Causes Control* 2002;13:573-82.

614. Parker AS, Cerhan JR, Putnam SD, et al. A cohort study of farming and risk of prostate cancer in Iowa. *Epidemiology* 1999;10:452-5.

615. Yoshizawa K, Willett WC, Morris SJ, et al. Study of prediagnostic selenium level in toenails and the risk of advanced prostate cancer. *J Natl Cancer Inst* 1998;90:1219-24.

616. McCann SE, Ambrosone CB, Moysich KB, et al. Intakes of selected nutrients, foods, and phytochemicals and prostate cancer risk in Western New York. *Nutr Cancer* 2005;53:33-41.

617. Cohen JH, Kristal AR, Stanford JL. Fruit and vegetable intakes and prostate cancer risk. *J Natl Cancer Inst* 2000;92:61-8.

618. Sanderson M, Coker AL, Logan P, et al. Lifestyle and prostate cancer among older African-American and Caucasian men in South Carolina. *Cancer Causes Control* 2004;15:647-55.

619. Lu QY, Hung JC, Heber D, et al. Inverse associations between plasma lycopene and other carotenoids and prostate cancer. *Cancer Epidemiol Biomarkers Prev* 2001;10:749-56.

620. Deneo-Pellegrini H, De Stefani E, Ronco A, et al. Foods, nutrients and prostate cancer: a case-control study in Uruguay. *Br J Cancer* 1999;80:591-7.

621. van Gils CH, Bostick RM, Stern MC, et al. Differences in base excision repair capacity may modulate the effect of dietary antioxidant intake on prostate cancer risk: an example of polymorphisms in the XRCC1 gene. *Cancer Epidemiol Biomarkers Prev* 2002;11:1279-84.

622. Norrish AE, Jackson RT, Sharpe SJ, et al. Men who consume vegetable oils rich in monounsaturated fat: their dietary patterns and risk of prostate cancer (New Zealand). *Cancer Causes Control* 2000;11:609-15.

623. Norrish AE, Skeaff CM, Arribas GL, et al. Prostate cancer risk and consumption of fish oils: a dietary biomarker-based case-control study. *Br J Cancer* 1999;81:1238-42.

624. Bosetti C, Talamini R, Montella M, et al. Retinol, carotenoids and the risk of prostate cancer: a case-control study from Italy. *Int J Cancer* 2004;112:689-92.

625. Meyer F, Bairati I, Fradet Y, et al. Dietary energy and nutrients in relation to

preclinical prostate cancer. *Nutr Cancer* 1997;29:120-6.

626. Huang HY, Alberg AJ, Norkus EP, et al. Prospective study of antioxidant micronutrients in the blood and the risk of developing prostate cancer. *Am J Epidemiol* 2003;157:335-44 [published erratum: *Am J Epidemiol* 2003;157:1126].

627. Gann PH, Ma J, Giovannucci E, et al. Lower prostate cancer risk in men with elevated plasma lycopene levels: results of a prospective analysis. *Cancer Res* 1999;59:1225-30.

628. Wu K, Erdman JW, Jr., Schwartz SJ, et al. Plasma and dietary carotenoids, and the risk of prostate cancer: a nested case-control study. *Cancer Epidemiol Biomarkers Prev* 2004;13:260-9.

629. Nomura AM, Stemmermann GN, Lee J, et al. Serum micronutrients and prostate cancer in Japanese Americans in Hawaii. *Cancer Epidemiol Biomarkers Prev* 1997;6:487-91.

630. Comstock GW, Helzlsouer KJ, Bush TL. Prediagnostic serum levels of carotenoids and vitamin E as related to subsequent cancer in Washington County, Maryland. *Am J Clin Nutr* 1991;53:260S-4S.

631. Heber D, Lu QY. Overview of mechanisms of action of lycopene. *Exp Biol Med (Maywood)* 2002;227:920-3.

632. Stram DO, Hankin JH, Wilkens LR, et al. Prostate cancer incidence and intake of fruits, vegetables and related micronutrients: the multiethnic cohort study (United States). *Cancer Causes Control* 2006;17:1193-207.

633. Kirsh VA, Mayne ST, Peters U, et al. A prospective study of lycopene and tomato product intake and risk of prostate cancer. *Cancer Epidemiol Biomarkers Prev* 2006;15:92-8.

634. Goodman M, Bostick RM, Ward KC, et al. Lycopene intake and prostate cancer risk: effect modification by plasma antioxidants and the XRCC1 genotype. *Nutr Cancer* 2006;55:13-20.

635. Woodson K, Tangrea JA, Lehman TA, et al. Manganese superoxide dismutase (MnSOD) polymorphism, alpha-tocopherol supplementation and prostate cancer risk in the alpha-tocopherol, beta-carotene cancer prevention study (Finland). *Cancer Causes Control* 2003;14:513-8.

636. Daviglus ML, Dyer AR, Persky V, et al. Dietary beta-carotene, vitamin C, and risk of prostate cancer: results from the Western Electric Study. *Epidemiology* 1996;7:472-7.

637. Andersson SO, Wolk A, Bergstrom R, et al. Energy, nutrient intake and prostate cancer risk: a population-based case-control study in Sweden. *Int J Cancer* 1996;68:716-22.

638. Ghadirian P, Lacroix A, Maisonneuve P, et al. Nutritional factors and prostate cancer: a case-control study of French Canadians in Montreal, Canada. *Cancer Causes Control* 1996;7:428-36.

639. West DW, Slattery ML, Robison LM, et al.

Adult dietary intake and prostate cancer risk in Utah: a case-control study with special emphasis on aggressive tumors. *Cancer Causes Control* 1991;2:85-94.

640. Kolonel LN, Yoshizawa CN, Hankin JH. Diet and prostatic cancer: a case-control study in Hawaii. *Am J Epidemiol* 1988;127:999-1012.

641. Talamini R, Franceschi S, La Vecchia C, et al. Diet and prostatic cancer: a case-control study in northern Italy. *Nutr Cancer* 1992;18:277-86.

642. Ohno Y, Yoshida O, Oishi K, et al. Dietary beta-carotene and cancer of the prostate: a case-control study in Kyoto, Japan. *Cancer Res* 1988;48:1331-6.

643. Rohan TE, Howe GR, Burch JD, et al. Dietary factors and risk of prostate cancer: a case-control study in Ontario, Canada. *Cancer Causes Control* 1995;6:145-54.

644. Ross RK, Shimizu H, Paganini-Hill A, et al. Case-control studies of prostate cancer in blacks and whites in southern California. *J Natl Cancer Inst* 1987;78:869-74.

645. La Vecchia C, Negri E, D'Avanzo B, et al. Dairy products and the risk of prostatic cancer. *Oncology* 1991;48:406-10.

646. Mettlin C, Selenskas S, Natarajan N, et al. Beta-carotene and animal fats and their relationship to prostate cancer risk. A case-control study. *Cancer* 1989;64:605-12.

647. Oishi K, Okada K, Yoshida O, et al. A case-control study of prostatic cancer with reference to dietary habits. *Prostate* 1988;12:179-90.

648. Yoshida O, Okada K, Oishi K, et al. [A case-control study of prostatic cancer - with reference to dietary history]. *Gan No Rinsho* 1986;32:591-6.

649. Cook NR, Stampfer MJ, Ma J, et al. Beta-carotene supplementation for patients with low baseline levels and decreased risks of total and prostate carcinoma. *Cancer* 1999;86:1783-92.

650. Weinstein SJ, Wright ME, Pietinen P, et al. Serum alpha-tocopherol and gamma-tocopherol in relation to prostate cancer risk in a prospective study. *J Natl Cancer Inst* 2005;97:396-9.

651. Knekt P, Aromaa A, Maatela J, et al. Serum vitamin A and subsequent risk of cancer: cancer incidence follow-up of the Finnish Mobile Clinic Health Examination Survey. *Am J Epidemiol* 1990;132:857-70.

652. Meyer F, Galan P, Douville P, et al. Antioxidant vitamin and mineral supplementation and prostate cancer prevention in the SU.VI.MAX trial. *Int J Cancer* 2005;116:182-6.

653. Hayes RB, Bogdanovicz JF, Schroeder FH, et al. Serum retinol and prostate cancer. *Cancer* 1988;62:2021-6.

654. Davies TW, Treasure FP, Welch AA, et al. Diet and basal cell skin cancer: results from the EPIC-Norfolk cohort. *Br J Dermatol* 2002;146:1017-22.

655. McNaughton SA, Marks GC, Gaffney P, et al. Antioxidants and basal cell carcinoma of the skin: a nested case-control study. *Cancer Causes Control* 2005;16:609-18.

656. Vinceti M, Pellacani G, Malagoli C, et al. A population-based case-control study of diet and melanoma risk in northern Italy. *Public Health Nutr* 2005;8:1307-14.

657. Millen AE, Tucker MA, Hartge P, et al. Diet and melanoma in a case-control study. *Cancer Epidemiol Biomarkers Prev* 2004;13:1042-51.

658. Hakim IA, Harris RB. Joint effects of citrus peel use and black tea intake on the risk of squamous cell carcinoma of the skin. *BMC Dermatology*, 2001:3.

659. Hakim IA, Harris RB, Ritenbaugh C. Citrus peel use is associated with reduced risk of squamous cell carcinoma of the skin. *Nutr Cancer* 2000;37:161-8.

660. Kirkpatrick CS, White E, Lee JA. Case-control study of malignant melanoma in Washington State. II. Diet, alcohol, and obesity. *Am J Epidemiol* 1994;139:869-80.

661. Naldi L, Gallus S, Tavani A, et al. Risk of melanoma and vitamin A, coffee and alcohol: a case-control study from Italy. *Eur J Cancer Prev* 2004;13:503-8.

662. Sahl WJ, Glore S, Garrison P, et al. Basal cell carcinoma and lifestyle characteristics. *Int J Dermatol* 1995;34:398-402.

663. Bain C, Green A, Siskind V, et al. Diet and melanoma. An exploratory case-control study. *Ann Epidemiol* 1993;3:235-8.

664. Feskanich D, Willett WC, Hunter DJ, et al. Dietary intakes of vitamins A, C, and E and risk of melanoma in two cohorts of women. *Br J Cancer* 2003;88:1381-7.

665. Fung TT, Hunter DJ, Spiegelman D, et al. Vitamins and carotenoids intake and the risk of basal cell carcinoma of the skin in women (United States). *Cancer Causes Control* 2002;13:221-30.

666. Fung TT, Spiegelman D, Egan KM, et al. Vitamin and carotenoid intake and risk of squamous cell carcinoma of the skin. *Int J Cancer* 2003;103:110-5.

667. Schaumberg DA, Frieling UM, Rifai N, et al. No effect of beta-carotene supplementation on risk of nonmelanoma skin cancer among men with low baseline plasma beta-carotene. *Cancer Epidemiol Biomarkers Prev* 2004;13:1079-80.

668. Karagas MR, Greenberg ER, Nierenberg D, et al. Risk of squamous cell carcinoma of the skin in relation to plasma selenium, alpha-tocopherol, beta-carotene, and retinol: a nested case-control study. *Cancer Epidemiol Biomarkers Prev* 1997;6:25-9.

669. Hsueh YM, Chiou HY, Huang YL, et al. Serum beta-carotene level, arsenic methylation capability, and incidence of skin cancer. *Cancer Epidemiol Biomarkers Prev* 1997;6:589-96.

670. Breslow RA, Alberg AJ, Helzlsouer KJ, et al. Serological precursors of cancer: malignant melanoma, basal and squamous cell skin cancer, and prediagnostic levels of retinol, beta-carotene, lycopene, alpha-tocopherol, and selenium. *Cancer Epidemiol Biomarkers Prev* 1995;4:837-42.

671. Wald NJ, Thompson SG, Densem JW, et al.

Serum beta-carotene and subsequent risk of cancer: results from the BUPA Study. *Br J Cancer* 1988;57:428-33.

672. Dorgan JF, Boakye NA, Fears TR, et al. Serum carotenoids and alpha-tocopherol and risk of nonmelanoma skin cancer. *Cancer Epidemiol Biomarkers Prev* 2004;13:1276-82.

673. Kune GA, Bannerman S, Field B, et al. Diet, alcohol, smoking, serum beta-carotene, and vitamin A in male nonmelanocytic skin cancer patients and controls. *Nutr Cancer* 1992;18:237-44.

674. Stryker WS, Stampfer MJ, Stein EA, et al. Diet, plasma levels of beta-carotene and alpha-tocopherol, and risk of malignant melanoma. *Am J Epidemiol* 1990;131:597-611.

675. Block G, Patterson B, Subar A. Fruit, vegetables, and cancer prevention: a review of the epidemiological evidence. *Nutr Cancer* 1992;18:1-29.

676. van Poppel G, Goldbohm RA. Epidemiologic evidence for beta-carotene and cancer prevention. *Am J Clin Nutr* 1995;62:1393S-402S.

677. Stolzenberg-Solomon RZ, Pietinen P, Barrett MJ, et al. Dietary and other methyl-group availability factors and pancreatic cancer risk in a cohort of male smokers. *Am J Epidemiol* 2001;153:680-7.

678. Skinner HG, Michaud DS, Giovannucci EL, et al. A prospective study of folate intake and the risk of pancreatic cancer in men and women. *Am J Epidemiol* 2004;160:248-58.

679. Baghurst PA, McMichael AJ, Slavotinek AH, et al. A case-control study of diet and cancer of the pancreas. *Am J Epidemiol* 1991;134:167-79.

680. Stolzenberg-Solomon RZ, Albanes D, Nieto FJ, et al. Pancreatic cancer risk and nutrition-related methyl-group availability indicators in male smokers. *J Natl Cancer Inst* 1999;91:535-41.

681. Larsson SC, Hakansson N, Giovannucci E, et al. Folate intake and pancreatic cancer incidence: a prospective study of Swedish women and men. *J Natl Cancer Inst* 2006;98:407-13.

682. Jaskiewicz K. Oesophageal carcinoma: cytopathology and nutritional aspects in aetiology. *Anticancer Res* 1989;9:1847-52.

683. Jaskiewicz K, Marasas WF, Lazarus C, et al. Association of esophageal cytological abnormalities with vitamin and lipotrope deficiencies in populations at risk for esophageal cancer. *Anticancer Res* 1988;8:711-5.

684. Tan W, Miao X, Wang L, et al. Significant increase in risk of gastroesophageal cancer is associated with interaction between promoter polymorphisms in thymidylate synthase and serum folate status. *Carcinogenesis* 2005;26:1430-5.

685. Piyathilake CJ, Henao OL, Macaluso M, et al. Folate is associated with the natural history of high-risk human papillomaviruses. *Cancer Res* 2004;64:8788-93.

686. Su LJ, Arab L. Nutritional status of folate and colon cancer risk: evidence from NHANES I epidemiologic follow-up study. *Ann Epidemiol* 2001;11:65-72.

687. Giovannucci E, Rimm EB, Ascherio A, et al. Alcohol, low-methionine - low-folate diets, and risk of colon cancer in men. *J Natl Cancer Inst* 1995;87:265-73.

688. Fuchs CS, Willett WC, Colditz GA, et al. The influence of folate and multivitamin use on the familial risk of colon cancer in women. *Cancer Epidemiol Biomarkers Prev* 2002;11:227-34.

689. Larsson SC, Giovannucci E, Wolk A. A prospective study of dietary folate intake and risk of colorectal cancer: modification by caffeine intake and cigarette smoking. *Cancer Epidemiol Biomarkers Prev* 2005;14:740-3.

690. Flood A, Caprario L, Chaterjee N, et al. Folate, methionine, alcohol, and colorectal cancer in a prospective study of women in the United States. *Cancer Causes Control* 2002;13:551-61.

691. Harnack L, Jacobs DR, Jr., Nicodemus K, et al. Relationship of folate, vitamin B-6, vitamin B-12, and methionine intake to incidence of colorectal cancers. *Nutr Cancer* 2002;43:152-8.

692. Konings EJ, Goldbohm RA, Brants HA, et al. Intake of dietary folate vitamers and risk of colorectal carcinoma: results from The Netherlands Cohort Study. *Cancer* 2002;95:1421-33.

693. Terry P, Jain M, Miller AB, et al. Dietary intake of folic acid and colorectal cancer risk in a cohort of women. *Int J Cancer* 2002;97:864-7.

694. Glynn SA, Albanes D, Pietinen P, et al. Colorectal cancer and folate status: a nested case-control study among male smokers. *Cancer Epidemiol Biomarkers Prev* 1996;5:487-94.

695. Kato I, Dnistrian AM, Schwartz M, et al. Serum folate, homocysteine and colorectal cancer risk in women: a nested case-control study. *Br J Cancer* 1999;79:1917-22.

696. Giovannucci E, Stampfer MJ, Colditz GA, et al. Multivitamin use, folate, and colon cancer in women in the Nurses' Health Study. *Ann Intern Med* 1998;129:517-24.

697. Sanjoaquin MA, Allen N, Couto E, et al. Folate intake and colorectal cancer risk: a meta-analytical approach. *Int J Cancer* 2005;113:825-8.

698. de Vogel S, van Engeland M, Luchtenborg M, et al. Dietary folate and APC mutations in sporadic colorectal cancer. *J Nutr* 2006;136:3015-21.

699. Brink M, Weijenberg MP, de Goeij AF, et al. Dietary folate intake and k-ras mutations in sporadic colon and rectal cancer in The Netherlands Cohort Study. *Int J Cancer* 2005;114:824-30.

700. Zhang SM, Moore SC, Lin J, et al. Folate, vitamin B6, multivitamin supplements, and colorectal cancer risk in women. *Am J Epidemiol* 2006;163:108-15.

701. Jiang Q, Chen K, Ma X, et al. Diets, polymorphisms of methylenetetrahydrofolate reductase, and the susceptibility of colon cancer and rectal cancer. *Cancer Detect Prev* 2005;29:146-54.

702. Otani T, Iwasaki M, Hanaoka T, et al. Folate, vitamin B6, vitamin B12, and vitamin B2 intake, genetic polymorphisms of related enzymes, and risk of colorectal cancer in a hospital-based case-control study in Japan. *Nutr Cancer* 2005;53:42-50.

703. Prinz-Langenohl R, Fohr I, Pietrzik K. Beneficial role for folate in the prevention of colorectal and breast cancer. *Eur J Nutr* 2001;40:98-105.

704. Kim YI. Role of folate in colon cancer development and progression. *J Nutr* 2003;133:3731S-9S.

705. Tuyns AJ. Protective effect of citrus fruit on esophageal cancer. *Nutr Cancer* 1983;5:195-200.

706. Kabat GC, Ng SK, Wynder EL. Tobacco, alcohol intake, and diet in relation to adenocarcinoma of the esophagus and gastric cardia. *Cancer Causes Control* 1993;4:123-32.

707. Rogers MA, Vaughan TL, Davis S, et al. Consumption of nitrate, nitrite, and nitrosodimethylamine and the risk of upper aerodigestive tract cancer. *Cancer Epidemiol Biomarkers Prev* 1995;4:29-36.

708. Liaw Y-P, Huang Y-C, Lo P-Y, et al. Nutrient intakes in relation to cancer mortality in Taiwan. *Nutr. Res.* 2003;23:1597-606.

709. Lee KW, Lee HJ, Surh YJ, et al. Vitamin C and cancer chemoprevention: reappraisal. *Am J Clin Nutr* 2003;78:1074-8.

710. Veugelers PJ, Porter GA, Guernsey DL, et al. Obesity and lifestyle risk factors for gastroesophageal reflux disease, Barrett esophagus and esophageal adenocarcinoma. *Dis Esophagus* 2006;19:321-8.

711. Taylor PR, Qiao YL, Abnet CC, et al. Prospective study of serum vitamin E levels and esophageal and gastric cancers. *J Natl Cancer Inst* 2003;95:1414-6.

712. Han P. Levels of vitamin A, E and C in serum of cancer patients. *Chin J Clin Oncol* 1993;20:759-61.

713. Hartman TJ, Albanes D, Pietinen P, et al. The association between baseline vitamin E, selenium, and prostate cancer in the alpha-tocopherol, beta-carotene cancer prevention study. *Cancer Epidemiol Biomarkers Prev* 1998;7:335-40.

714. Ramon JM, Bou R, Romea S, et al. Dietary fat intake and prostate cancer risk: a case-control study in Spain. *Cancer Causes Control* 2000;11:679-85.

715. Lee MM, Wang RT, Hsing AW, et al. Case-control study of diet and prostate cancer in China. *Cancer Causes Control* 1998;9:545-52.

716. Hietanen E, Bartsch H, Bereziat JC, et al. Diet and oxidative stress in breast, colon and prostate cancer patients: a case-control study. *Eur J Clin Nutr* 1994;48:575-86.

717. Allen NE, Morris JS, Ngwenyama RA, et al.

A case-control study of selenium in nails and prostate cancer risk in British men. *Br J Cancer* 2004;90:1392-6.

718. Hsing AW, Comstock GW, Abbey H, et al. Serologic precursors of cancer. Retinol, carotenoids, and tocopherol and risk of prostate cancer. *J Natl Cancer Inst* 1990;82:941-6.

719. Eichholzer M, Stahelin HB, Gey KF, et al. Prediction of male cancer mortality by plasma levels of interacting vitamins: 17-year follow-up of the prospective Basel study. *Int J Cancer* 1996;66:145-50.

720. Eichholzer M, Stahelin HB, Gutzwiller F, et al. Association of low plasma cholesterol with mortality for cancer at various sites in men: 17-y follow-up of the prospective Basel study. *Am J Clin Nutr* 2000;71:569-74.

721. Eichholzer M, Stahelin HB, Ludin E, et al. Smoking, plasma vitamins C, E, retinol, and carotene, and fatal prostate cancer: seventeen-year follow-up of the prospective Basel study. *Prostate* 1999;38:189-98.

722. Willett WC, Polk BF, Underwood BA, et al. Relation of serum vitamins A and E and carotenoids to the risk of cancer. *N Engl J Med* 1984;310:430-4.

723. Knekt P, Aromaa A, Maatela J, et al. Serum vitamin E and risk of cancer among Finnish men during a 10-year follow-up. *Am J Epidemiol* 1988;127:28-41.

724. Helzlsouer KJ, Huang HY, Alberg AJ, et al. Association between alpha-tocopherol, gamma-tocopherol, selenium, and subsequent prostate cancer. *J Natl Cancer Inst* 2000;92:2018-23.

725. Laaksonen DE, Laukkanen JA, Niskanen L, et al. Serum linoleic and total polyunsaturated fatty acids in relation to prostate and other cancers: a population-based cohort study. *Int J Cancer* 2004;111:444-50.

726. Fleshner N, Fair WR, Huryk R, et al. Vitamin E inhibits the high-fat diet promoted growth of established human prostate LNCaP tumors in nude mice. *J Urol* 1999;161:1651-4.

727. Willis MS, Wians FH. The role of nutrition in preventing prostate cancer: a review of the proposed mechanism of action of various dietary substances. *Clin Chim Acta* 2003;330:57-83.

728. Clark LC, Cantor KP, Allaway WH. Selenium in forage crops and cancer mortality in U.S. counties. *Arch Environ Health* 1991;46:37-42.

729. Schrauzer GN, White DA, Schneider CJ. Cancer mortality correlation studies - III: statistical associations with dietary selenium intakes. *Bioinorg Chem* 1977;7:23-31.

730. Goodman GE, Schaffer S, Bankson DD, et al. Predictors of serum selenium in cigarette smokers and the lack of association with lung and prostate cancer risk. *Cancer Epidemiol Biomarkers Prev* 2001;10:1069-76.

731. Kabuto M, Imai H, Yonezawa C, et al. Prediagnostic serum selenium and zinc levels and subsequent risk of lung and stomach cancer in Japan. *Cancer Epidemiol Biomarkers Prev* 1994;3:465-9.

732. Knekt P, Aromaa A, Maatela J, et al. Serum selenium and subsequent risk of cancer among Finnish men and women. *J Natl Cancer Inst* 1990;82:864-8.

733. Knekt P, Marniemi J, Teppo L, et al. Is low selenium status a risk factor for lung cancer? *Am J Epidemiol* 1998;148:975-82.

734. Kornitzer M, Valente F, De Bacquer D, et al. Serum selenium and cancer mortality: a nested case-control study within an age- and sex-stratified sample of the Belgian adult population. *Eur J Clin Nutr* 2004;58:98-104.

735. Menkes MS, Comstock GW, Vuilleumier JP, et al. Serum beta-carotene, vitamins A and E, selenium, and the risk of lung cancer. *N Engl J Med* 1986;315:1250-4.

736. Nomura A, Heilbrun LK, Morris JS, et al. Serum selenium and the risk of cancer, by specific sites: case-control analysis of prospective data. *J Natl Cancer Inst* 1987;79:103-8.

737. Salonen JT, Salonen R, Lappetelainen R, et al. Risk of cancer in relation to serum concentrations of selenium and vitamins A and E: matched case-control analysis of prospective data. *BMJ* 1985;290:417-20.

738. Ujiie S, Kikuchi H. The relation between serum selenium value and cancer in Miyagi, Japan: 5-year follow up study. *Tohoku J Exp Med* 2002;196:99-109.

739. Gromadzinska J, Wasowicz W, Rydzynski K, et al. Oxidative-stress markers in blood of lung cancer patients occupationally exposed to carcinogens. *Biol Trace Elem Res* 2003;91:203-15.

740. Hu JF, Liu YY, Yu YK. [Estimation of latency period of lung cancer]. *Zhonghua Zhong Liu Za Zhi* 1994;16:18-21.

741. Torun M, Aldemir H, Yardim S. Serum selenium levels in various cancer types. *Trace Elem Electrolytes* 1995;12:186-90.

742. Wei HJ, Luo XM, Xing J, et al. [Selenium intake and metabolic study in workers of the Yunnan Tin Mine]. *Zhongguo Yi Xue Ke Xue Yuan Xue Bao* 1987;9:198-201.

743. Zachara BA, Marchaluk-Wisniewska E, Maciag A, et al. Decreased selenium concentration and glutathione peroxidase activity in blood and increase of these parameters in malignant tissue of lung cancer patients. *Lung* 1997;175:321-32.

744. Chen J, Geissler C, Parpia B, et al. Antioxidant status and cancer mortality in China. *Int J Epidemiol* 1992;21:625-35.

745. Lange JH. Reanalysis of epidemiological data for selenium anti-cancer activity. *Toxicol Ind Health* 1991;7:319-25.

746. Nakachi K, Limtrakul P, Sonklin P, et al. Risk factors for lung cancer among Northern Thai women: epidemiological, nutritional, serological, and bacteriological surveys of residents in high- and low-incidence areas. *Jpn J Cancer Res* 1999;90:1187-95.

747. Garland M, Morris JS, Stampfer MJ, et al. Prospective study of toenail selenium levels and cancer among women. *J Natl Cancer Inst* 1995;87:497-505.

748. Hartman TJ, Taylor PR, Alfthan G, et al. Toenail selenium concentration and lung cancer in male smokers (Finland). *Cancer Causes Control* 2002;13:923-8.

749. van den Brandt PA, Goldbohm RA, van 't Veer P, et al. A prospective cohort study on selenium status and the risk of lung cancer. *Cancer Res* 1993;53:4860-5.

750. Vinceti M, Nacci G, Rocchi E, et al. Mortality in a population with long-term exposure to inorganic selenium via drinking water. *J Clin Epidemiol* 2000;53:1062-8.

751. Vlajinac H, Ilic M, Sipetic S, et al. A case-control study of diet and prostate cancer. *J BUON* 2001;6:177-81.

752. Hardell L, Degerman A, Tomic R, et al. Levels of selenium in plasma and glutathione peroxidase in erythrocytes in patients with prostate cancer or benign hyperplasia. *Eur J Cancer Prev* 1995;4:91-5.

753. Schrauzer GN, White DA, Schneider CJ. Cancer mortality correlation studies - IV: associations with dietary intakes and blood levels of certain trace elements, notably Se-antagonists. *Bioinorg Chem* 1977;7:35-56.

754. Shamberger RJ, Rukovena E, Longfield AK, et al. Antioxidants and cancer. I. Selenium in the blood of normals and cancer patients. *J Natl Cancer Inst* 1973;50:863-70.

755. Li HJ, Stampfer MJ, Giovannucci EL, et al. A prospective study of plasma selenium levels and prostate cancer risk. *J Natl Cancer Inst* 2004;96:696-703.

756. Jacobs ET, Giuliano AR, Martinez ME, et al. Plasma levels of 25-hydroxyvitamin D, 1,25-dihydroxyvitamin D and the risk of prostate cancer. *J Steroid Biochem Mol Biol* 2004;89-90:533-7.

757. Brooks JD, Metter EJ, Chan DW, et al. Plasma selenium level before diagnosis and the risk of prostate cancer development. *J Urol* 2001;166:2034-8.

758. Nomura AM, Lee J, Stemmermann GN, et al. Serum selenium and subsequent risk of prostate cancer. *Cancer Epidemiol Biomarkers Prev* 2000;9:883-7.

759. Coates RJ, Weiss NS, Daling JR, et al. Serum levels of selenium and retinol and the subsequent risk of cancer. *Am J Epidemiol* 1988;128:515-23.

760. Peleg I, Morris S, Hames CG. Is serum selenium a risk factor for cancer? *Med Oncol Tumor Pharmacother* 1985;2:157-63.

761. Willett WC, Polk BF, Morris JS, et al. Prediagnostic serum selenium and risk of cancer. *Lancet* 1983;2:130-4.

762. Virtamo J, Valkeila E, Alfthan G, et al. Serum selenium and risk of cancer. A prospective follow-up of nine years. *Cancer* 1987;60:145-8.

763. Criqui MH, Bangdiwala S, Goodman DS, et al. Selenium, retinol, retinol-binding protein, and uric acid. Associations with cancer mortality in a population-based prospective case-control study. *Ann*

Epidemiol 1991;1:385-93.

764. Ringstad J, Jacobsen BK, Tretli S, et al. Serum selenium concentration associated with risk of cancer. *J Clin Pathol* 1988;41:454-7.

765. Salonen JT, Alfthan G, Huttunen JK, et al. Association between serum selenium and the risk of cancer. *Am J Epidemiol* 1984;120:342-9.

766. Vogt TM, Ziegler RG, Graubard BI, et al. Serum selenium and risk of prostate cancer in U.S. blacks and whites. *Int J Cancer* 2003;103:664-70.

767. Tsachev K, Tsvetkov M, Kumanov K, et al. [Serum selenium levels of patients with adenoma and carcinoma of the prostate gland]. *Khirurgiia (Sofiia)* 1987;40:33-5.

768. van den Brandt PA, Zeegers MP, Bode P, et al. Toenail selenium levels and the subsequent risk of prostate cancer: a prospective cohort study. *Cancer Epidemiol Biomarkers Prev* 2003;12:866-71.

769. Ghadirian P, Maisonneuve P, Perret C, et al. A case-control study of toenail selenium and cancer of the breast, colon, and prostate. *Cancer Detect Prev* 2000;24:305-13.

770. Lipsky K, Zigeuner R, Zischka M, et al. Selenium levels of patients with newly diagnosed prostate cancer compared with control group. *Urology* 2004;63:912-6.

771. Morris JS, Rohan T, Soskolne CL, et al. Selenium status and cancer mortality in subjects residing in four Canadian provinces. *J Radio Nucl Chem* 2001;249:421-7.

772. Duffield-Lillico AJ, Dalkin BL, Reid ME, et al. Selenium supplementation, baseline plasma selenium status and incidence of prostate cancer: an analysis of the complete treatment period of the Nutritional Prevention of Cancer Trial. *BJU Int* 2003;91:608-12.

773. Clark LC, Dalkin B, Krongrad A, et al. Decreased incidence of prostate cancer with selenium supplementation: results of a double-blind cancer prevention trial. *Br J Urol* 1998;81:730-4.

774. Redman C, Scott JA, Baines AT, et al. Inhibitory effect of selenomethionine on the growth of three selected human tumor cell lines. *Cancer Lett* 1998;125:103-10.

775. Pathak SK, Sharma RA, Mellon JK. Chemoprevention of prostate cancer by diet-derived antioxidant agents and hormonal manipulation (review). *Int J Oncol* 2003;22:5-13.

776. Qiu JL, Chen K, Wang XB, et al. [A case-control study on the relationship between nutrition and gastric cancer in islanders]. *Chung Hua Liu Hsing Ping Hsueh Tsa Chih* 2004;25 487-91.

777. Shamberger RJ, Tytko S, Willis CE. Antioxidants in cereals and in food preservatives and declining gastric cancer mortality. *Cleve Clin Q* 1972;39:119-24.

778. Shamberger RJ, Tytko SA, Willis CE. Antioxidants and cancer. Part VI.

Selenium and age-adjusted human cancer mortality. *Arch Environ Health* 1976;31:231-5.

779. Chen J. Dietary practices and cancer mortality in China. *IARC Sci Publ* 1991;105:18-21.

780. Saito K, Saito T, Hosokawa T, et al. Blood selenium level and the interaction of copper, zinc and manganese in stomach cancer. *Trace Elem Med* 1984;1:148-52.

781. Burguera JL, Burguera M, Gallignani M, et al. Blood serum selenium in the province of Merida, Venezuela, related to sex, cancer incidence and soil selenium content. *J Trace Elem Electrolytes Health Dis* 1990;4:73-7.

782. Liu XG. [Serum and tissue copper, zinc and selenium levels in patients with gastric carcinoma]. *Chung Hua Chieh Ho Ho Hu Hsi Hsi Chi Ping Tsa Chih* 1991;13:93-6.

783. Pawlowicz Z, Zachara BA, Trafikowska U, et al. Blood selenium concentrations and glutathione peroxidase activities in patients with breast cancer and with advanced gastrointestinal cancer. *J Trace Elem Electrolytes Health Dis* 1991;5:275-7.

784. Scieszka M, Danch A, Machalski M, et al. Plasma selenium concentration in patients with stomach and colon cancer in the Upper Silesia. *Neoplasma* 1997;44:395-7.

785. Beno I, Klvanova J, Magalova T, et al. Blood levels of natural antioxidants in gastric and colorectal precancerous lesions and cancers in Slovakia. *Neoplasma* 2000;47:37-40.

786. Yu SY, Chu YJ, Gong XL, et al. Regional variation of cancer mortality incidence and its relation to selenium levels in China. *Biol Trace Elem Res* 1985;7:21-9.

787. van den Brandt PA, Goldbohm RA, van't Veer P, et al. A prospective cohort study on toenail selenium levels and risk of gastrointestinal cancer. *J Natl Cancer Inst* 1993;85:224-9.

788. Li DG. [A preliminary investigation on the role of selenium and other trace elements in the pathogenesis of gastric cancer]. *Chung Hua Liu Hsing Ping Hsueh Tsa Chih* 1987;8:276-80.

789. Mark SD, Qiao YL, Dawsey SM, et al. Prospective study of serum selenium levels and incident esophageal and gastric cancers. *J Natl Cancer Inst* 2000;92:1753-63.

790. Wei WQ, Abnet CC, Qiao YL, et al. Prospective study of serum selenium concentrations and esophageal and gastric cardia cancer, heart disease, stroke, and total death. *Am J Clin Nutr* 2004;79:80-5.

791. Whanger PD. Selenium and its relationship to cancer: an update dagger. *Br J Nutr* 2004;91:11-28.

792. Fernandez Banares F, Cabre E, Esteve M, et al. Serum selenium and risk of large size colorectal adenomas in a geographical area with a low selenium status. *Am J Gastroenterol* 2002;97:2103-8.

793. Schober SE, Comstock GW, Helsing KJ, et

al. Serologic precursors of cancer. I. Prediagnostic serum nutrients and colon cancer risk. *Am J Epidemiol* 1987;126:1033-41.

794. Wang HH, Wu CC. Clinical evaluation of serum trace elements in colorectal cancer. *Chin J Gastroenterol* 1995;12:9-14.

795. Milde D, Novak O, Stu ka V, et al. Serum levels of selenium, manganese, copper, and iron in colorectal cancer patients. *Biol Trace Elem Res* 2001;79:107-14.

796. Ganther HE. Selenium metabolism, selenoproteins and mechanisms of cancer prevention: complexities with thioredoxin reductase. *Carcinogenesis* 1999;20:1657-66.

797. Combs GF, Jr. Status of selenium in prostate cancer prevention. *Br J Cancer* 2004;91:195-9.

798. Knekt P, Kumpulainen J, Jarvinen R, et al. Flavonoid intake and risk of chronic diseases. *Am J Clin Nutr* 2002;76:560-8.

799. Garcia-Closas R, Agudo A, Gonzalez CA, et al. Intake of specific carotenoids and flavonoids and the risk of lung cancer in women in Barcelona, Spain. *Nutr Cancer* 1998;32:154-8.

800. Haenszel W, Correa P, Cuello C, et al. Gastric cancer in Colombia. II. Case-control epidemiological study of precursor lesions. *J Natl Cancer Inst* 1976;57:1021-6.

801. Zaldivar R. Epidemiology of gastric and colo-rectal cancer in United-States and Chile with particular reference to the role of dietary and nutritional variables, nitrate fertilizer pollution, and N-nitroso compounds. *Zentralbl Bakteriol Mikrobiol Hyg [B]* 1977;164:193-217.

802. Ahn YO. Diet and stomach cancer in Korea. *Int J Cancer* 1997;Suppl 10:7-9.

803. Nagata C, Takatsuka N, Kawakami N, et al. A prospective cohort study of soy product intake and stomach cancer death. *Br J Cancer* 2002;87:31-6.

804. Nagata C. Ecological study of the association between soy product intake and mortality from cancer and heart disease in Japan. *Int J Epidemiol* 2000;29:832-6.

805. Tatsuta M, Iishi H, Baba M, et al. Attenuation by genistein of sodium-chloride-enhanced gastric carcinogenesis induced by N-methyl-N'-nitro-N-nitrosoguanidine in Wistar rats. *Int J Cancer* 1999;80:396-9.

806. Watanabe H, Uesaka T, Kido S, et al. Influence of concomitant miso or NaCl treatment on induction of gastric tumors by N-methyl-N'-nitro-N-nitrosoguanidine in rats. *Oncol Rep* 1999;6:989-93.

807. Li X-M, Liu X-F, Akio S. Relationship between the incidence rates of testicular and prostatic cancers and food consumptions. *Chinese Journal of Cancer Research* 2002;. 14:240-5.

808. Hebert JR, Hurley TG, Olendzki BC, et al. Nutritional and socioeconomic factors in relation to prostate cancer mortality: a cross-national study. *J Natl Cancer Inst* 1998;90:1637-47.

809. Armstrong B, Doll R. Environmental factors and cancer incidence and mortality in different countries, with special reference to dietary practices. *Int J Cancer* 1975;15:617-31.

810. Allen NE, Sauvaget C, Roddam AW, et al. A prospective study of diet and prostate cancer in Japanese men. *Cancer Causes Control* 2004;15:911-20.

811. Hirayama T. Epidemiology of prostate cancer with special reference to the role of diet. *Natl Cancer Inst Monogr* 1979:149-55.

812. Severson RK, Nomura AM, Grove JS, et al. A prospective study of demographics, diet, and prostate cancer among men of Japanese ancestry in Hawaii. *Cancer Res* 1989;49:1857-60.

813. Jacobsen BK, Knutsen SF, Fraser GE. Does high soy milk intake reduce prostate cancer incidence? The Adventist Health Study (United States). *Cancer Causes Control* 1998;9:553-7.

814. Jian L, Zhang DH, Lee AH, et al. Do preserved foods increase prostate cancer risk? *Br J Cancer* 2004;90:1792-5.

815. Lee MM, Gomez SL, Chang JS, et al. Soy and isoflavone consumption in relation to prostate cancer risk in China. *Cancer Epidemiol Biomarkers Prev* 2003;12:665-8.

816. Sung JF, Lin RS, Pu YS, et al. Risk factors for prostate carcinoma in Taiwan: a case-control study in a Chinese population. *Cancer* 1999;86:484-91.

817. Rao AV, Sung MK. Saponins as anticarcinogens. *J Nutr* 1995;125:717S-24S.

818. Yanagihara K, Ito A, Toge T, et al. Antiproliferative effects of isoflavones on human cancer cell lines established from the gastrointestinal tract. *Cancer Res* 1993;53:5815-21.

819. Borges C, Villalobos Perez JJ. [Gastric cancer. I. Epidemiology]. *Rev Invest Clin* 1968;20:11-23.

820. Llanos J, Valdes E. [Cigarette consumption and food habits in patients with peptic ulcer and gastric cancer]. *Rev Med Chil* 1985;113:433-5.

821. López-Carrillo L, Hernandez AM, Dubrow R. Chili pepper consumption and gastric cancer in Mexico: a case-control study. *Am J Epidemiol* 1994;139:263-71.

Chapter 4.3

1. McGee H. *McGee on Food and Cooking*. London: Hodder and Stoughton, 2004.

2. Institute of Environmental Science and Research Limited. 2004. *Nitrates and Nitrites Dietary Exposure and Risk Assessment*.

3. International Agency for Research on Cancer. In preparation. *Ingested Nitrates and Nitrites*. In: IARC Monogr Eval Carcinog Risks Hum no 94. http://monographs.iarc.fr/ENG/Meetings/94-nitratenitrite.pdf.

4. Sugimura T, Wakabayashi K, Nakagama H, et al. Heterocyclic amines: mutagens/carcinogens produced during cooking of meat and fish. *Cancer Sci* 2004;95:290-9.

5. Kazerouni N, Sinha R, Hsu CH, et al. Analysis of 200 food items for benzo[a]pyrene and estimation of its intake in an epidemiologic study. *Food Chem Toxicol* 2001;39:423-36.

6. Ibanez R, Agudo A, Berenguer A, et al. Dietary intake of polycyclic aromatic hydrocarbons in a Spanish population. *J Food Prot* 2005;68:2190-5.

7. Food and Agriculture Organization of the United Nations. *FAOSTAT*. http://faostat.fao.org/site/345/default.aspx. 2006.

8. Bostick RM, Potter JD, Kushi LH, et al. Sugar, meat, and fat intake, and non-dietary risk factors for colon cancer incidence in Iowa women (United States). *Cancer Causes Control* 1994;5:38-52.

9. Willett WC, Stampfer MJ, Colditz GA, et al. Relation of meat, fat, and fiber intake to the risk of colon cancer in a prospective study among women. *N Engl J Med* 1990;323:1664-72.

10. Giovannucci E, Rimm EB, Stampfer MJ, et al. Intake of fat, meat, and fiber in relation to risk of colon cancer in men. *Cancer Res* 1994;54:2390-7.

11. Singh PN, Fraser GE. Dietary risk factors for colon cancer in a low-risk population. *Am J Epidemiol* 1998;148:761-74.

12. Fraser GE. Associations between diet and cancer, ischemic heart disease, and all-cause mortality in non-Hispanic white California Seventh-day Adventists. *Am J Clin Nutr* 1999;70:532S-8S.

13. Jarvinen R, Knekt P, Hakulinen T, et al. Dietary fat, cholesterol and colorectal cancer in a prospective study. *Br J Cancer* 2001;85:357-61.

14. English DR, MacInnis RJ, Hodge AM, et al. Red meat, chicken, and fish consumption and risk of colorectal cancer. *Cancer Epidemiol Biomarkers Prev* 2004;13:1509-14.

15. Norat T, Bingham S, Ferrari P, et al. Meat, fish, and colorectal cancer risk: the European Prospective Investigation into cancer and nutrition. *J Natl Cancer Inst* 2005;97:906-16.

16. Kato I, Akhmedkhanov A, Koenig K, et al. Prospective study of diet and female colorectal cancer: the New York University Women's Health Study. *Nutr Cancer* 1997;28:276-81.

17. Pietinen P, Malila N, Virtanen M, et al. Diet and risk of colorectal cancer in a cohort of Finnish men. *Cancer Causes Control* 1999;10:387-96.

18. Larsson SC, Rafter J, Holmberg L, et al. Red meat consumption and risk of cancers of the proximal colon, distal colon and rectum: the Swedish Mammography Cohort. *Int J Cancer* 2005;113:829-34.

19. Wei EK, Giovannucci E, Wu K, et al. Comparison of risk factors for colon and rectal cancer. *Int J Cancer* 2004;108:433-42.

20. Chen JJ, Stampfer MMJ, Hough HHL, et al. A prospective study of N-acetyltransferase genotype, red meat intake, and risk of colorectal cancer. *Cancer Res* 1998;58:3307-11.

21. Tiemersma EW, Kampman E, Bueno de Mesquita HB, et al. Meat consumption, cigarette smoking, and genetic susceptibility in the etiology of colorectal cancer: results from a Dutch prospective study. *Cancer Causes Control* 2002;13:383-93.

22. Feskanich D, Ma J, Fuchs CS, et al. Plasma vitamin D metabolites and risk of colorectal cancer in women. *Cancer Epidemiol Biomarkers Prev* 2004;13:1502-8.

23. Phillips RL. Role of life-style and dietary habits in risk of cancer among seventh-day adventists. *Cancer Res* 1975;35:3513-22.

24. Sellers TTA, Bazyk AAE, Bostick RRM, et al. Diet and risk of colon cancer in a large prospective study of older women: an analysis stratified on family history (Iowa, United States). *Cancer Causes Control* 1998;9:357-67.

25. Larsson SC, Wolk A. Meat consumption and risk of colorectal cancer: a meta-analysis of prospective studies. *Int J Cancer* 2006;119:2657-64.

26. Sesink AL, Termont DS, Kleibeuker JH, et al. Red meat and colon cancer: the cytotoxic and hyperproliferative effects of dietary heme. *Cancer Res* 1999;59:5704-9.

27. Chao A, Thun MJ, Connell CJ, et al. Meat consumption and risk of colorectal cancer. *Am Med Ass* 2005;293:172-82.

28. Lin J, Zhang SM, Cook NR, et al. Dietary fat and fatty acids and risk of colorectal cancer in women. *Am J Epidemiol* 2004;160:1011-22.

29. Chan AT, Tranah GJ, Giovannucci EL, et al. Prospective study of N-acetyltransferase-2 genotypes, meat intake, smoking and risk of colorectal cancer. *Int J Cancer* 2005;115:648-52.

30. Brink M, Weijenberg MP, de Goeij AF, et al. Meat consumption and K-ras mutations in sporadic colon and rectal cancer in The Netherlands Cohort Study. *Br J Cancer* 2005;92:1310-20.

31. Sato Y, Nakaya N, Kuriyama S, et al. Meat consumption and risk of colorectal cancer in Japan: the Miyagi Cohort Study. *Eur J Cancer Prev* 2006;15:211-8.

32. Oba S, Shimizu N, Nagata C, et al. The relationship between the consumption of meat, fat, and coffee and the risk of colon cancer: a prospective study in Japan. *Cancer Lett* 2006;244:260-7.

33. Huang XE, Hirose K, Wakai K, et al. Comparison of lifestyle risk factors by family history for gastric, breast, lung and colorectal cancer. *Asian Pac J Cancer Prev* 2004;5:419-27.

34. Butler LM, Duguay Y, Millikan RC, et al. Joint effects between UDP-glucuronosyltransferase 1A7 genotype and dietary carcinogen exposure on risk of colon cancer. *Cancer Epidemiol Biomarkers Prev* 2005;14:1626-32.

35. Turner F, Smith G, Sachse C, et al. Vegetable, fruit and meat consumption

and potential risk modifying genes in relation to colorectal cancer. *Int J Cancer* 2004;112:259-64.

36. Juarranz Sanz M, Soriano Llora T, Calle Puron ME, et al. [Influence of the diet on the development of colorectal cancer in a population of Madrid]. *Rev Clin Esp* 2004;204:355-61.

37. Rolon PA, Castellsague X, Benz M, et al. Hot and cold mate drinking and esophageal cancer in Paraguay. *Cancer Epidemiol Biomarkers Prev* 1995;4:595-605.

38. Brown LM, Swanson CA, Gridley G, et al. Adenocarcinoma of the esophagus: role of obesity and diet. *J Natl Cancer Inst* 1995;87:104-9.

39. Zhang ZF, Kurtz RC, Yu GP, et al. Adenocarcinomas of the esophagus and gastric cardia: the role of diet. *Nutr Cancer* 1997;27:298-309.

40. De Stefani E, Deneo-Pellegrini H, Boffetta P, et al. Meat intake and risk of squamous cell esophageal cancer: a case-control study in Uruguay. *Int J Cancer* 1999;82:33-7.

41. De Stefani E, Deneo-Pellegrini H, Mendilaharsu M, et al. Diet and risk of cancer of the upper aerodigestive tract - I. Foods. *Oral Oncol* 1999;35:17-21.

42. De Stefani E, Deneo-Pellegrini H, Ronco AL, et al. Food groups and risk of squamous cell carcinoma of the oesophagus: a case-control study in Uruguay. *Br J Cancer* 2003;89:1209-14.

43. Barone J, Taioli E, Hebert JR, et al. Vitamin supplement use and risk for oral and esophageal cancer. *Nutr Cancer* 1992;18:31-41.

44. Bosetti C, La Vecchia C, Talamini R, et al. Food groups and risk of squamous cell esophageal cancer in northern Italy. *Int J Cancer* 2000;87:289-94.

45. Levi F, Pasche C, Lucchini F, et al. Food groups and oesophageal cancer risk in Vaud, Switzerland. *Eur J Cancer Prev* 2000;9:257-63.

46. Tavani A, La Vecchia C, Gallus S, et al. Red meat intake and cancer risk: a study in Italy. *Int J Cancer* 2000;86:425-8.

47. Yu MC, Garabrant DH, Peters JM, et al. Tobacco, alcohol, diet, occupation, and carcinoma of the esophagus. *Cancer Res* 1988;48:3843-8.

48. Brown LM, Blot WJ, Schuman SH, et al. Environmental factors and high risk of esophageal cancer among men in coastal South Carolina. *J Natl Cancer Inst* 1988;80:1620-5.

49. Ward MH, Sinha R, Heineman EF, et al. Risk of adenocarcinoma of the stomach and esophagus with meat cooking method and doneness preference. *Int J Cancer* 1997;71:14-9.

50. Chen H, Ward MH, Graubard BI, et al. Dietary patterns and adenocarcinoma of the esophagus and distal stomach. *Am J Clin Nutr* 2002;75:137-44.

51. Gonzalez CA, Jakszyn P, Pera G, et al. Meat intake and risk of stomach and esophageal adenocarcinoma within the European Prospective Investigation Into

Cancer and Nutrition (EPIC). *J Natl Cancer Inst* 2006;98:345-54.

52. Breslow RA, Graubard BI, Sinha R, et al. Diet and lung cancer mortality: a 1987 National Health Interview Survey cohort study. *Cancer Causes Control* 2000;11:419-31.

53. Alavanja MC, Brownson RC, Benichou J. Estimating the effect of dietary fat on the risk of lung cancer in nonsmoking women. *Lung Cancer* 1996;14 Suppl 1:S63-74.

54. Alavanja MC, Field RW, Sinha R, et al. Lung cancer risk and red meat consumption among Iowa women. *Lung Cancer* 2001;34:37-46.

55. De Stefani E, Brennan P, Ronco A, et al. Food groups and risk of lung cancer in Uruguay. *Lung Cancer* 2002;38:1-7.

56. De Stefani E, Fontham ET, Chen V, et al. Fatty foods and the risk of lung cancer: a case-control study from Uruguay. *Int J Cancer* 1997;71:760-6.

57. Hu J, Mao Y, Dryer D, et al. Risk factors for lung cancer among Canadian women who have never smoked. *Cancer Detect Prev* 2002;26:129-38.

58. Kubik AK, Zatloukal P, Tomasek L, et al. Dietary habits and lung cancer risk among non-smoking women. *Eur J Cancer Prev* 2004;13:471-80.

59. Marchand JL, Luce D, Goldberg P, et al. Dietary factors and the risk of lung cancer in New Caledonia (South Pacific). *Nutr Cancer* 2002;42:18-24.

60. Sinha R, Kulldorff M, Curtin J, et al. Fried, well-done red meat and risk of lung cancer in women (United States). *Cancer Causes Control* 1998;9:621-30.

61. Swanson CA, Brown CC, Sinha R, et al. Dietary fats and lung cancer risk among women: the Missouri Women's Health Study (United States). *Cancer Causes Control* 1997;8:883-93.

62. Zhou W, Park S, Liu G, et al. Dietary iron, zinc, and calcium and the risk of lung cancer. *Epidemiology* 2005;16:772-9.

63. Stolzenberg-Solomon RZ, Pietinen P, Taylor PR, et al. Prospective study of diet and pancreatic cancer in male smokers. *Am J Epidemiol* 2002;155:783-92.

64. Nothlings U, Wilkens LR, Murphy SP, et al. Meat and fat intake as risk factors for pancreatic cancer: the multiethnic cohort study. *J Natl Cancer Inst* 2005;97:1458-65.

65. Larsson SC, Hakanson N, Permert J, et al. Meat, fish, poultry and egg consumption in relation to risk of pancreatic cancer: a prospective study. *Int J Cancer* 2006;118:2866-70.

66. Michaud DS, Giovannucci E, Willett WC, et al. Dietary meat, dairy products, fat, and cholesterol and pancreatic cancer risk in a prospective study. *Am J Epidemiol* 2003;157:1115-25.

67. Zheng W, McLaughlin JK, Gridley G, et al. A cohort study of smoking, alcohol consumption, and dietary factors for pancreatic cancer (United States). *Cancer Causes Control* 1993;4:477-82.

68. Coughlin SS, Calle EE, Patel AV, et al.

Predictors of pancreatic cancer mortality among a large cohort of United States adults. *Cancer Causes Control* 2000;11:915-23.

69. Khan MM, Goto R, Kobayashi K, et al. Dietary habits and cancer mortality among middle aged and older Japanese living in Hokkaido, Japan by cancer site and sex. 2004;5:58-65.

70. Lyon JL, Slattery ML, Mahoney AW, et al. Dietary intake as a risk factor for cancer of the exocrine pancreas. *Cancer Epidemiol Biomarkers Prev* 1993;2:513-8.

71. Anderson KE, Sinha R, Kulldorff M, et al. Meat intake and cooking techniques: associations with pancreatic cancer. *Mutat Res* 2002;506-507:225-31.

72. Zhang Y, Cantor KP, Lynch CF, et al. Occupation and risk of pancreatic cancer: a population-based case-control study in Iowa. *J Occup Environ Med* 2005;47:392-8.

73. Mainz DL, Black O, Webster PD. Hormonal control of pancreatic growth. *J Clin Invest* 1973;52:2300-4.

74. Summerskill WH, Wolpert E. Ammonia metabolism in the gut. *Am J Clin Nutr* 1970;23:633-9.

75. Zheng W. Dietary intake of energy and animal foods and endometrial cancer incidence. *Am J Epidemiol* 1995;142:388-94.

76. Potischman N, Swanson CA, Brinton LA, et al. Dietary associations in a case-control study of endometrial cancer. *Cancer Causes Control* 1993;4:239-50.

77. Shu XO, Zheng W, Potischman N, et al. A population-based case-control study of dietary factors and endometrial cancer in Shanghai, People's Republic of China. *Am J Epidemiol* 1993;137:155-65.

78. Goodman MT, Hankin JH, Wilkens LR, et al. Diet, body size, physical activity, and the risk of endometrial cancer. *Cancer Res* 1997;57:5077-85.

79. Jain MG, Howe GR, Rohan TE. Nutritional factors and endometrial cancer in Ontario, Canada. *Cancer Control* 2000;7:288-96.

80. McCann SE, Freudenheim JL, Marshall JR, et al. Diet in the epidemiology of endometrial cancer in western New York (United States). *Cancer Causes Control* 2000;11:965-74.

81. Lissner L, Kroon UB, Bjorntorp P, et al. Adipose tissue fatty acids and dietary fat sources in relation to endometrial cancer: a retrospective study of cases in remission, and population-based controls. *Acta Obstet Gynecol Scand* 1993;72:481-7.

82. Xu WH, Dai Q, Xiang YB, et al. Animal food intake and cooking methods in relation to endometrial cancer risk in Shanghai. *Br J Cancer* 2006;95:1586-92.

83. Huang X. Iron overload and its association with cancer risk in humans: evidence for iron as a carcinogenic metal. *Mutat Res* 2003;533:153-71.

84. Flood A, Velie EM, Sinha R, et al. Meat, fat, and their subtypes as risk factors for colorectal cancer in a prospective cohort

of women. *Am J Epidemiol* 2003;158:59-68.

85. Goldbohm RA, van den Brandt PA, van 't Veer P, et al. A prospective cohort study on the relation between meat consumption and the risk of colon cancer. *Cancer Res* 1994;54:718-23.

86. Sato Y, Tsubono Y, Nakaya N, et al. Fruit and vegetable consumption and risk of colorectal cancer in Japan: The Miyagi Cohort Study. *Public Health Nutr* 2005;8:309-14.

87. Balder HF, Vogel J, Jansen MC, et al. Heme and chlorophyll intake and risk of colorectal cancer in the Netherlands cohort study. *Cancer Epidemiol Biomarkers Prev* 2006;15:717-25.

88. Huang XE, Hirose K, Wakai K, et al. Comparison of lifestyle risk factors by family history for gastric, breast, lung and colorectal cancer. *Asian Pac J Cancer Prev* 2004;5:419-27.

89. Kjaerheim K, Gaard M, Andersen A. The role of alcohol, tobacco, and dietary factors in upper aerogastric tract cancers: a prospective study of 10,900 Norwegian men. *Cancer Causes Control* 1998;9:99-108.

90. Chyou PH, Nomura AMY, Stemmermann GN. Diet, alcohol, smoking and cancer of the upper aerodigestive tract: a prospective study among Hawaii Japanese men. *Int J Cancer* 1995;60:616-21.

91. Pottern LM, Morris LE, Blot WJ, et al. Esophageal cancer among black men in Washington, D.C. I. Alcohol, tobacco, and other risk factors. *J Natl Cancer Inst* 1981;67:777-83.

92. Ziegler RG, Morris LE, Blot WJ, et al. Esophageal cancer among black men in Washington, D.C. II. Role of nutrition. *J Natl Cancer Inst* 1981;67:1199-206.

93. Levi F, Pasche C, Lucchini F, et al. Processed meat and the risk of selected digestive tract and laryngeal neoplasms in Switzerland. *Ann Oncol* 2004;15:346-9.

94. Yang CX, Wang HY, Wang ZM, et al. Risk factors for esophageal cancer: a case-control study in South-western China. *Asian Pac J Cancer Prev* 2005;6:48-53.

95. Ozasa K, Watanabe Y, Ito Y, et al. Dietary habits and risk of lung cancer death in a large-scale cohort study (JACC Study) in Japan by sex and smoking habit. *Jpn J Cancer Res* 2001;92:1259-69.

96. Veierod MB, Laake P, Thelle DS. Dietary fat intake and risk of lung cancer: a prospective study of 51,452 Norwegian men and women. *Eur J Cancer Prev* 1997;6:540-9.

97. Bond GG, Thompson FE, Cook RR. Dietary vitamin A and lung cancer: results of a case-control study among chemical workers. *Nutr Cancer* 1987;9:109-21.

98. De Stefani E, Brennan P, Boffetta P, et al. Diet and adenocarcinoma of the lung: a case-control study in Uruguay. *Lung Cancer* 2002;35:43-51.

99. De Stefani E, Fierro L, Correa P, et al. Mate drinking and risk of lung cancer in males: a case-control study from Uruguay.

Cancer Epidemiol Biomarkers Prev 1996;5:515-9.

100. Goodman MT, Hankin JH, Wilkens LR, et al. High-fat foods and the risk of lung cancer. *Epidemiology* 1992;3:288-99.

101. Kreuzer M, Heinrich J, Kreienbrock L, et al. Risk factors for lung cancer among nonsmoking women. *Int J Cancer* 2002;100:706-13.

102. Mettlin C. Milk drinking, other beverage habits, and lung cancer risk. *Int J Cancer* 1989;43:608-12.

103. Mohr DL, Blot WJ, Tousey PM, et al. Southern cooking and lung cancer. *Nutr Cancer* 1999;35:34-43.

104. Pisa FE, Barbone F. Diet and the risk of cancers of the lung, oral cavity and pharynx, and larynx: a population-based case-control study in north-east Italy. *IARC Sci Publ* 2002;156:141-3.

105. Galanis DJ, Kolonel LN, Lee J, et al. Intakes of selected foods and beverages and the incidence of gastric cancer among the Japanese residents of Hawaii: a prospective study. *Int J Epidemiol* 1998;27:173-80.

106. McCullough ML, Robertson AS, Jacobs EJ, et al. A prospective study of diet and stomach cancer mortality in United States men and women. *Cancer Epidemiol Biomarkers Prev* 2001;10:1201-5.

107. Ngoan LT, Mizoue T, Fujino Y, et al. Dietary factors and stomach cancer mortality. *Br J Cancer* 2002;87:37-42.

108. Nomura A, Grove JS, Stemmermann GN, et al. A prospective study of stomach cancer and its relation to diet, cigarettes, and alcohol consumption. *Cancer Res* 1990;50:627-31.

109. van den Brandt PA, Botterweck AA, Goldbohm RA. Salt intake, cured meat consumption, refrigerator use and stomach cancer incidence: a prospective cohort study (Netherlands). *Cancer Causes Control* 2003;14:427-38.

110. Zheng W, Sellers TA, Doyle TJ, et al. Retinol, antioxidant vitamins, and cancers of the upper digestive tract in a prospective cohort study of postmenopausal women. *Am J Epidemiol* 1995;142:955-60.

111. Acheson ED, Doll R. Dietary factors in carcinoma of the stomach: a study of 100 cases and 200 controls. *Gut* 1964;5:126-31.

112. Funakoshi N, Kanoh T, Uchino H, et al. Gastric cancer and diet. The analysis of the epidemiological survey in Tango district of Kyoto prefecture. *Naika Hokan* 1983;30:175-81.

113. Tajima K, Tominaga S. Dietary habits and gastro-intestinal cancers: a comparative case-control study of stomach and large intestinal cancers in Nagoya, Japan. *Jpn J Cancer Res* 1985;76:705-16.

114. Jedrychowski W, Wahrendorf J, Popiela T, et al. A case-control study of dietary factors and stomach cancer risk in Poland. *Int J Cancer* 1986;37:837-42.

115. Goiriena De Gandarias FJ, Santidrian MI, Barranquero AM. Etiopathogenic study

of cancer of the digestive tract in Biscay Spain with special emphasis on the role played by diet and consumption of alcohol and tobacco. *Rev Sanid Hig Publica (Madr)* 1987;62:1411-30.

116. Coggon D, Barker DJ, Cole RB, et al. Stomach cancer and food storage. *J Natl Cancer Inst* 1989;81:1178-82.

117. Buiatti E, Palli D, Decarli A, et al. A case-control study of gastric cancer and diet in Italy. *Int J Cancer* 1989;44:611-6.

118. Moon HK. Diet and stomach cancer: a case-control study in Korea. *Korean J Epidemiol* 1991;13:33-51.

119. Gonzalez CA, Sanz JM, Marcos G, et al. Dietary factors and stomach cancer in Spain: a multi-centre case-control study. *Int J Cancer* 1991;49:513-9.

120. Boeing H, Frentzel-Beyme R, Berger M, et al. Case-control study on stomach cancer in Germany. *Int J Cancer* 1991;47:858-64.

121. Hansson LE, Nyren O, Bergstrom R, et al. Diet and risk of gastric cancer. A population-based case-control study in Sweden. *Int J Cancer* 1993;55:181-9.

122. Inoue M, Tajima K, Hirose K, et al. Life-style and subsite of gastric cancer - joint effect of smoking and drinking habits. *Int J Cancer* 1994;56:494-9.

123. Cornee J, Pobel D, Riboli E, et al. A case-control study of gastric cancer and nutritional factors in Marseille, France. *Eur J Epidemiol* 1995;11:55-65.

124. López-Carrillo L, Lopez-Cervantes M, Ramirez-Espitia A, et al. Alcohol consumption and gastric cancer in Mexico. *Cad Saude Publica* 1998;14:25-32.

125. Youm PY, Kim SH. [A case-control study on dietary and other factors related to stomach cancer incidence]. *Korean J Nutr* 1998;31:62-71.

126. De Stefani E, Boffetta P, Mendilaharsu M, et al. Dietary nitrosamines, heterocyclic amines, and risk of gastric cancer: a case-control study in Uruguay. *Nutr Cancer* 1998;30:158-62.

127. Watabe K, Nishi M, Miyake H, et al. Lifestyle and gastric cancer: a case-control study. *Oncol Rep* 1998;5:1191-4.

128. Ward MH, López-Carrillo L. Dietary factors and the risk of gastric cancer in Mexico City. *Am J Epidemiol* 1999;149:925-32.

129. De Stefani E, Ronco A, Brennan P, et al. Meat consumption and risk of stomach cancer in Uruguay: a case-control study. *Nutr Cancer* 2001;40:103-7.

130. Sipetic S, Tomic-Kundakovic S, Vlajinac H, et al. [Diet and gastric cancer]. *Vojnosanit Pregl* 2003;60:697-705.

131. López-Carrillo L, Lopez-Cervantes M, Robles-Diaz G, et al. Capsaicin consumption, *Helicobacter pylori* positivity and gastric cancer in Mexico. *Int J Cancer* 2003;106:277-82.

132. De Stefani E, Correa P, Boffetta P, et al. Dietary patterns and risk of gastric cancer: a case-control study in Uruguay. *Gastric Cancer* 2004;7:211-20.

133. Nomura A, Yamakawa H, Ishidate T, et al. Intestinal metaplasia in Japan: association with diet. *J Natl Cancer Inst*

1982;68:401-5.

134. Llopis A, Morales M, Rodriguez R. Digestive cancer in relation to diet in Spain. *J Environ Pathol Toxicol Oncol* 1992;11:169-75.

135. Larsson SC, Bergkvist L, Wolk A. Processed meat consumption, dietary nitrosamines and stomach cancer risk in a cohort of Swedish women. *Int J Cancer* 2006;119:915-9.

136. Phukan RK, Narain K, Zomawia E, et al. Dietary habits and stomach cancer in Mizoram, India. *J Gastroenterol* 2006;41:418-24.

137. Strumylaite L, Zickute J, Dudzevicius J, et al. Salt-preserved foods and risk of gastric cancer. *Medicina (Kaunas)* 2006;42:164-70.

138. Cross AJ, Peters U, Kirsh VA, et al. A prospective study of meat and meat mutagens and prostate cancer risk. *Cancer Res* 2005;65:11779-84.

139. Veierod MB, Laake P, Thelle DS. Dietary fat intake and risk of prostate cancer: a prospective study of 25,708 Norwegian men. *Int J Cancer* 1997;73:634-8.

140. Le Marchand L, Kolonel LN, Wilkens LR, et al. Animal fat consumption and prostate cancer: a prospective study in Hawaii. *Epidemiology* 1994;5:276-82.

141. Michaud DS, Augustsson K, Rimm EB, et al. A prospective study on intake of animal products and risk of prostate cancer. *Cancer Causes Control* 2001;12:557-67.

142. McCann SE, Ambrosone CB, Moysich KB, et al. Intakes of selected nutrients, foods, and phytochemicals and prostate cancer risk in Western New York. *Nutr Cancer* 2005;53:33-41.

143. Nowell S, Ratnasinghe DL, Ambrosone CB, et al. Association of SULT1A1 phenotype and genotype with prostate cancer risk in African-Americans and Caucasians. *Cancer Epidemiol Biomarkers Prev* 2004;13:270-6.

144. Bosetti C, Micelotta S, Dal Maso L, et al. Food groups and risk of prostate cancer in Italy. *Int J Cancer* 2004;110:424-8.

145. Deneo-Pellegrini H, De Stefani E, Ronco A, et al. Foods, nutrients and prostate cancer: a case-control study in Uruguay. *Br J Cancer* 1999;80:591-7.

146. Ewings P, Bowie C. A case-control study of cancer of the prostate in Somerset and east Devon. *Br J Cancer* 1996;74:661-6.

147. De Stefani E, Fierro L, Barrios E, et al. Tobacco, alcohol, diet and risk of prostate cancer. *Tumori* 1995;81:315-20.

148. Rodriguez C, McCullough ML, Mondul AM, et al. Meat consumption among Black and White men and risk of prostate cancer in the Cancer Prevention Study II Nutrition Cohort. *Cancer Epidemiol Biomarkers Prev* 2006;15:211-6.

149. Wu K, Hu FB, Willett WC, et al. Dietary patterns and risk of prostate cancer in U.S. men. *Cancer Epidemiol Biomarkers Prev* 2006;15:167-71.

150. Goldman R, Shields PG. Food mutagens. *J Nutr* 2003;133 Suppl 3:965S-73S.

151. Hirayama T. [A large scale cohort study on the effect of life styles on the risk of cancer by each site]. *Gan No Rinsho* 1990;Spec No:233-42.

152. Hsing AW, McLaughlin JK, Chow WH, et al. Risk factors for colorectal cancer in a prospective study among U.S. white men. *Int J Cancer* 1998;77:549-53.

153. Hirayama T. Association between alcohol consumption and cancer of the sigmoid colon: observations from a Japanese cohort study. *Lancet* 1989;2:725-7.

154. Kearney J, Giovannucci E, Rimm EB, et al. Calcium, vitamin D, and dairy foods and the occurrence of colon cancer in men. *Am J Epidemiol* 1996;143:907-17.

155. Knekt P, Jarvinen R, Dich J, et al. Risk of colorectal and other gastro-intestinal cancers after exposure to nitrate, nitrite and N-nitroso compounds: a follow-up study. *Int J Cancer* 1999;80:852-6.

156. Sanjoaquin MA, Appleby PN, Thorogood M, et al. Nutrition, lifestyle and colorectal cancer incidence: a prospective investigation of 10998 vegetarians and non-vegetarians in the United Kingdom. *Br J Cancer* 2004;90:118-21.

157. Kojima M, Wakai K, Tamakoshi K, et al. Diet and colorectal cancer mortality: results from the Japan collaborative cohort study. *Nutr Cancer* 2004;50:23-32.

158. Ma J, Giovannucci E, Pollak M, et al. Milk intake, circulating levels of insulin-like growth factor-I, and risk of colorectal cancer in men. *J Natl Cancer Inst* 2001;93:1330-6.

159. Luchtenborg M, Weijenberg MP, de Goeij AF, et al. Meat and fish consumption, APC gene mutations and hMLH1 expression in colon and rectal cancer: a prospective cohort study (The Netherlands). *Cancer Causes Control* 2005;16:1041-54.

160. Gaard M, Tretli S, Loken EB. Dietary factors and risk of colon cancer: a prospective study of 50,535 young Norwegian men and women. *Eur J Cancer Prev* 1996;5:445-54.

161. Phillips RL, Snowdon DA. Dietary relationships with fatal colorectal cancer among Seventh-Day Adventists. *J Natl Cancer Inst* 1985;74:307-17.

162. Rao CV, Hirose Y, Indranie C, et al. Modulation of experimental colon tumorigenesis by types and amounts of dietary fatty acids. *Cancer Res* 2001;61:1927-33.

163. MacLean CH, Newberry SJ, Mojica WA, et al. Effects of omega-3 fatty acids on cancer risk: a systematic review. *JAMA* 2006;295:403-15.

164. Lin J, Zhang SM, Cook NR, et al. Dietary intakes of fruit, vegetables, and fiber, and risk of colorectal cancer in a prospective cohort of women (United States). *Cancer Causes Control* 2005;16:225-33.

165. Siezen CL, Bueno-de-Mesquita HB, Peeters PH, et al. Polymorphisms in the genes involved in the arachidonic acid-pathway, fish consumption and the risk

of colorectal cancer. *Int J Cancer* 2006;119:297-303.

166. Wakai K, Hirose K, Matsuo K, et al. Dietary risk factors for colon and rectal cancers: a comparative case-control study. *J Epidemiol* 2006;16:125-35.

167. Zou X, Li J, Li J, et al. The preliminary results of epidemiology investigation in the role of Epstein-Barr virus and salty fish in nasopharyngeal carcinoma in Sihu area, Guangdong province. *China Carcinoma* 1994;3:23-5.

168. Ward MH, Pan WH, Cheng YJ, et al. Dietary exposure to nitrite and nitrosamines and risk of nasopharyngeal carcinoma in Taiwan. *Int J Cancer* 2000;86:603-9.

169. Yuan JM, Wang XL, Xiang YB, et al. Preserved foods in relation to risk of nasopharyngeal carcinoma in Shanghai, China. *Int J Cancer* 2000;85:358-63.

170. Armstrong RW, Imrey PB, Lye MS, et al. Nasopharyngeal carcinoma in Malaysian Chinese: salted fish and other dietary exposures. In: 12, editor. *Int J Cancer*, 1998:228-35.

171. Lee HP, Gourley L, Duffy SW, et al. Preserved foods and nasopharyngeal carcinoma: a case-control study among Singapore Chinese. In: 13, editor. *Int J Cancer*, 1994:585-90.

172. Zheng X, Christensson B, Drettner B. Studies on etiological factors of nasopharyngeal carcinoma. *Acta Otolaryngol* 1993;113:455-7.

173. Zheng X, Yan L, Nilsson B, et al. Epstein-Barr virus infection, salted fish and nasopharyngeal carcinoma. A case-control study in southern China. *Acta Oncol* 1994;33:867-72.

174. Zheng YM, Tuppin P, Hubert A, et al. Environmental and dietary risk factors for nasopharyngeal carcinoma: a case-control study in Zangwu County, Guangxi, China. *Br J Cancer* 1994;69:508-14.

175. West S, Hildesheim A, Dosemeci M. Non-viral risk factors for nasopharyngeal carcinoma in the Philippines: results from a case-control study. *Int J Cancer* 1993;55:722-7.

176. Sriamporn S, Vatanasapt V, Pisani P, et al. Environmental risk factors for nasopharyngeal carcinoma: a case-control study in northeastern Thailand. *Cancer Epidemiol Biomarkers Prev* 1992;1:345-8.

177. Yu MC, Huang TB, Henderson BE. Diet and nasopharyngeal carcinoma: a case-control study in Guangzhou, China. *Int J Cancer* 1989;43:1077-82.

178. Ning JP, Yu MC, Wang QS, et al. Consumption of salted fish and other risk factors for nasopharyngeal carcinoma (NPC) in Tianjin, a low-risk region for NPC in the People's Republic of China. *J Natl Cancer Inst* 1990;82:291-6.

179. Armstrong RW, Armstrong MJ. Environmental risk factors and nasopharyngeal carcinoma in Selangor, Malaysia: A cross-ethnic perspective. *Ecol*

Dis 1983;2:185-98.

180. Henderson BE, Louie E, SooHoo Jing J, et al. Risk factors associated with nasopharyngeal carcinoma. *The New England journal of medicine* 1976;295:1101-6.

181. Yang XR, Diehl S, Pfeiffer R, et al. Evaluation of risk factors for nasopharyngeal carcinoma in high-risk nasopharyngeal carcinoma families in Taiwan. *Cancer Epidemiol Biomarkers Prev* 2005;14:900-5.

182. Ye W, Yingnan Yi, Tianshu Zhou, Rutao Lin. A case-control study on risk condition of nasopharyngeal carcinoma in Southern area of Fujian Province. *J Fujian Med College* 1995;29:179-82.

183. Ye W, Yi Y, Lin R, et al. A case-control study for nasopharyngeal carcinoma in Minan prefecture, Fujian province China. *Chronic Diesease Prevention and Control* 1995;3:158-61.

184. Cai L, Yi Y. A matched study with various controls in Nasopharyngeal carcinoma epidemiology in Fujian province. *Journal of Fujian Medical College* 1996;30:199-202.

185. Chen W, Yu L, Wei X, et al. Etiology study of nasopharyngeal cancer in Guanxi Tin mines- relationship between dust exposure and nasopharyngeal cancer. *Industrial Health and Occupational Disease* 1994;20:25-8.

186. Wang X, Chunyan Lin, Xiwen Sun, Yubo Shi, Yanjie Liu, Xudong Dai. The relationship between nasopharyngeal cancer and dietary as well as environmental factors in Heilongjiang province. *J China Oncol* 1993;15:75-6.

187. Zou J, Sun Q, Yuan Y, et al. A case-control study of nasopharyngeal carcinoma among inhabitants in high background radiation areas of Yangjinag, China. *China Journal of Radiology Medicine and Protection* 1999;19:94-.

188. Yu MC, Ho JH, Lai SH, et al. Cantonese-style salted fish as a cause of nasopharyngeal carcinoma: report of a case-control study in Hong Kong. *Cancer Res* 1986;46:956-61.

189. Yu MC, Mo CC, Chong WX, et al. Preserved foods and nasopharyngeal carcinoma: a case-control study in Guangxi, China. *Cancer Res* 1988;48:1954-9.

190. Armstrong RW, Eng AC. Salted fish and nasopharyngeal carcinoma in Malaysia. *Soc Sci Med* 1983;17:1559-67.

191. Na J, Hu M. Case-control study on NCP. *Journal of China Epidemiology* 1988;9:224.

192. Hildesheim A, Anderson LM, Chen CJ, et al. CYP2E1 genetic polymorphisms and risk of nasopharyngeal carcinoma in Taiwan. *J Natl Cancer Inst* 1997;89:1207-12.

193. Lanier A, Bender T, Talbot M, et al. Nasopharyngeal carcinoma in Alaskan Eskimos Indians, and Aleuts: a review of cases and study of Epstein-Barr virus, HLA, and environmental risk factors. *Cancer* 1980;46:2100-6.

194. Jeannel D, Hubert A, de Vathaire F, et al. Diet, living conditions and nasopharyngeal carcinoma in Tunisia—a case-control study. *Int J Cancer* 1990;46:421-5.

195. Geser A, Charnay N, Day NE, et al. Environmental factors in the etiology of nasopharyngeal carcinoma: report on a case-control study in Hong Kong. *IARC Sci Publ* 1978:213-29.

196. Zou X, Li J, Lu S, et al. Volatile N-nitrosamines in salted fish samples from high- and low-risk areas for NPC in China. *Chin Med Sci J* 1992;7:201-4.

197. Zou XN, Lu SH, Liu B. Volatile N-nitrosamines and their precursors in Chinese salted fish - a possible etological factor for NPC in China. *Int J Cancer* 1994;59:155-8.

198. Kongruttanachok N, Sukdikul S, Setavarin S, et al. Cytochrome P450 2E1 polymorphism and nasopharyngeal carcinoma development in Thailand: a correlative study. *BMC Cancer* 2001;1:4.

199. Bostick RM, Potter JD, Sellers TA, et al. Relation of calcium, vitamin D, and dairy food intake to incidence of colon cancer among older women. The Iowa Women's Health Study. *Am J Epidemiol* 1993;137:1302-17.

200. Garland C, Shekelle RB, Barrett Connor E, et al. Dietary vitamin D and calcium and risk of colorectal cancer: a 19-year prospective study in men. *Lancet* 1985;1:307-9.

201. Zheng W, Anderson KE, Kushi LH, et al. A prospective cohort study of intake of calcium, vitamin D, and other micronutrients in relation to incidence of rectal cancer among postmenopausal women. *Cancer Epidemiol Biomarkers Prev* 1998;7:221-5.

202. Martinez ME, Giovannucci EL, Colditz GA, et al. Calcium, vitamin D, and the occurrence of colorectal cancer among women. *J Natl Cancer Inst* 1996;88:1375-82.

203. Jarvinen R, Knekt P, Hakulinen T, et al. Prospective study on milk products, calcium and cancers of the colon and rectum. *Eur J Clin Nutr* 2001;55:1000-7.

204. Terry P, Baron JA, Bergkvist L, et al. Dietary calcium and vitamin D intake and risk of colorectal cancer: a prospective cohort study in women. *Nutr Cancer* 2002;43:39-46.

205. McCullough ML, Robertson AS, Rodriguez C, et al. Calcium, vitamin D, dairy products, and risk of colorectal cancer in the Cancer Prevention Study II Nutrition Cohort (United States). *Cancer Causes Control* 2003;14:1-12.

206. Lin J, Zhang SM, Cook NR, et al. Intakes of calcium and vitamin D and risk of colorectal cancer in women. *Am J Epidemiol* 2005;161:755-64.

207. Giovannucci E, Stampfer MJ, Colditz GA, et al. Multivitamin use, folate, and colon cancer in women in the Nurses' Health Study. *Ann Intern Med* 1998;129:517-24.

208. Kesse E, Boutron Ruault MC, Norat T, et al. Dietary calcium, phosphorus, vitamin D, dairy products and the risk of colorectal adenoma and cancer among French women of the E3N-EPIC prospective study. *Int J Cancer* 2005;117:137-44.

209. Heilbrun LK, Nomura A, Hankin JH, et al. Diet and colorectal cancer with special reference to fiber intake. *Int J Cancer* 1989;44:1-6.

210. Tangrea J, Helzlsouer K, Pietinen P, et al. Serum levels of vitamin D metabolites and the subsequent risk of colon and rectal cancer in Finnish men. *Cancer Causes Control* 1997;8:615-25.

211. Garland CF, Comstock GW, Garland FC, et al. Serum 25-hydroxyvitamin D and colon cancer: eight-year prospective study. *Lancet* 1989;2:1176-8.

212. Braun MM, Helzlsouer KJ, Hollis BW, et al. Colon cancer and serum vitamin D metabolite levels 10-17 years prior to diagnosis. *Am J Epidemiol* 1995;142:608-11.

213. Slattery ML, Neuhausen SL, Hoffman M, et al. Dietary calcium, vitamin D, VDR genotypes and colorectal cancer. *Int J Cancer* 2004;111:750-6.

214. Wurzelmann JI, Silver A, Schreinemachers DM, et al. Iron intake and the risk of colorectal cancer. *Cancer Epidemiol Biomarkers Prev* 1996;5:503-7.

215. Glynn SA, Albanes D, Pietinen P, et al. Colorectal cancer and folate status: a nested case-control study among male smokers. *Cancer Epidemiol Biomarkers Prev* 1996;5:487-94.

216. Kato I, Dnistrian AM, Schwartz M, et al. Iron intake, body iron stores and colorectal cancer risk in women: a nested case-control study. *Int J Cancer* 1999;80:693-8.

217. Konings EJ, Goldbohm RA, Brants HA, et al. Intake of dietary folate vitamers and risk of colorectal carcinoma: results from The Netherlands Cohort Study. *Cancer* 2002;95:1421-33.

218. Lee DH, Anderson KE, Harnack LJ, et al. Heme iron, zinc, alcohol consumption, and colon cancer: Iowa Women's Health Study. *J Natl Cancer Inst* 2004;96:403-7.

219. Chan AT, Ma J, Tranah GJ, et al. Hemochromatosis gene mutations, body iron stores, dietary iron, and risk of colorectal adenoma in women. *J Natl Cancer Inst* 2005;97:917-26.

220. Hoshiyama Y, Sasaba T. A case-control study of single and multiple stomach cancers in Saitama Prefecture, Japan. *Jpn J Cancer Res* 1992;83:937-43.

221. Dalgat DM, Aliev RG, Gireev GI, et al. [Epidemiology of stomach cancer in Dagestan]. *Vopr Onkol* 1974;20:76-82.

222. Jedrychowski W, Popiela T, Tobiasz-Adamczyk B, et al. [Dietary factors and laxatives in the epidemiology of stomach cancer]. *Nowotwory* 1981;30:353-60.

223. Ye EC. [Case-control study of 100 gastric cancer cases]. *Chung Hua Yu Fang I Hsueh Tsa Chih* 1981;15:107-9.

224. Ren TS. [Case-control study of gastric cancer in ten rural counties in China]. *Chung Hua Liu Hsing Ping Hsueh Tsa Chih* 1985;6:29-32.

225. Risch HA, Jain M, Choi NW, et al. Dietary factors and the incidence of cancer of the stomach. *Am J Epidemiol* 1985;122:947-59.

226. Choi NW, Miller AB, Fodor JG, et al. Consumption of precursors of N-nitroso compounds and human gastric cancer. *IARC Sci Publ* 1987;84:492-6.

227. Lee HH, Wu HY, Chuang YC, et al. Epidemiologic characteristics and multiple risk factors of stomach cancer in Taiwan. *Anticancer Res* 1990;10:875-81.

228. Sanchez-Diez A, Hernandez-Mejia R, Cueto-Espinar A. Study of the relation between diet and gastric cancer in a rural area of the Province of Leon, Spain. *Eur J Epidemiol* 1992;8:233-7.

229. Wang R. [The epidemiological study of subtype risk factors of gastric cancer]. *Chung Hua Liu Hsing Ping Hsueh Tsa Chih* 1993;14:295-9.

230. Ramon JM, Serra L, Cerdo C, et al. Dietary factors and gastric cancer risk. A case-control study in Spain. *Cancer* 1993;71:1731-5.

231. Falcao JM, Dias JA, Miranda AC, et al. Red wine consumption and gastric cancer in Portugal: a case-control study. *Eur J Cancer Prev* 1994;3:269-76.

232. Ji BT, Chow WH, Yang G, et al. Dietary habits and stomach cancer in Shanghai, China. *Int J Cancer* 1998;76:659-64.

233. Liu X, Wang Q, Ma J. [A case-control study on the risk factors of stomach cancer in Tianjin City]. *Chung Hua Liu Hsing Ping Hsueh Tsa Chih* 2001;22:362-4.

234. Fei S, Xiao S. [Diet and gastric cancer: a case-control study in Shanghai urban districts]. *Chin J Gastroenterol* 2003;8:143-7.

235. Lissowska J, Gail MH, Pee D, et al. Diet and stomach cancer risk in Warsaw, Poland. *Nutr Cancer* 2004;48:149-59.

236. Rudan I, Vadla D, Strnad M, et al. [The Mediterranean diet and occurrence of malignant tumors of the digestive system in the Croatian islands]. *Lijec Vjesn* 2003;125:60-7.

237. Dungal N, Sigurjonsson J. Gastric cancer and diet. A pilot study on dietary habits in two districts differing markedly in respect of mortality from gastric cancer. *Br J Cancer* 1967;21:270-6.

238. Garcia-Falcon MS, Simal-Gandara J. Polycyclic aromatic hydrocarbons in smoke from different woods and their transfer during traditional smoking into chorizo sausages with collagen and tripe casings. *Food Addit Contam* 2005;22:1-8.

239. Campos F, Carrasquilla G, Koriyama C, et al. Risk factors of gastric cancer specific for tumor location and histology in Cali, Colombia. *World J Gastroenterol* 2006;12:5772-9.

240. Kato I, Tominaga S, Matsumoto K. A prospective study of stomach cancer among a rural Japanese population: a 6-year survey. *Jpn J Cancer Res* 1992;83:568-75.

241. Sauvaget C, Lagarde F, Nagano J, et al. Lifestyle factors, radiation and gastric cancer in atomic-bomb survivors (Japan). *Cancer Causes Control* 2005;16:773-80.

242. Ikeda M, Yoshimoto K, Yoshimura T, et al. A cohort study on the possible association between broiled fish intake and cancer. *Gann* 1983;74:640-8.

243. Hoshiyama Y, Sasaba T. A case-control study of stomach cancer and its relation to diet, cigarettes, and alcohol consumption in Saitama Prefecture, Japan. *Cancer Causes Control* 1992;3:441-8.

244. Graham S, Schotz W, Martino P. Alimentary factors in the epidemiology of gastric cancer. *Cancer* 1972;30:927-38.

245. Wu-Williams AH, Yu MC, Mack TM. Life-style, workplace, and stomach cancer by subsite in young men of Los Angeles County. *Cancer Res* 1990;50:2569-76.

246. Kim HJ, Chang WK, Kim MK, et al. Dietary factors and gastric cancer in Korea: a case-control study. *Int J Cancer* 2002;97:531-5.

247. Suh S, Koo B, Choi Y, et al. [Lifestyle and eating behaviors of the stomach cancer patients in Daegu and Kyungpook areas in Korea]. *Korean J Nutr* 2002;35:380-93.

248. Boccia S, Persiani R, La Torre G, et al. Sulfotransferase 1A1 polymorphism and gastric cancer risk: a pilot case-control study. *Cancer Lett* 2005;229:235-43.

Chapter 4.4

1. McGee H. *McGee on Food and Cooking*. London: Hodder and Stoughton, 2004.

2. Food and Agriculture Organization of the United Nations. *FAOSTAT*. http://faostat.fao.org/site/345/default.aspx. 2006.

3. Davidson A. *The Penguin Companion to Food*. Revised ed. Harmondsworth: Penguin Books, 2002.

4. Platz EA, Leitzmann MF, Hollis BW, et al. Plasma 1,25-dihydroxy- and 25-hydroxyvitamin D and subsequent risk of prostate cancer. *Cancer Causes Control* 2004;15:255-65.

5. Schuurman AG, van den Brandt PA, Dorant E, et al. Animal products, calcium and protein and prostate cancer risk in The Netherlands Cohort Study. *Br J Cancer* 1999;80:1107-13.

6. Tseng M, Breslow RA, Graubard BI, et al. Dairy, calcium, and vitamin D intakes and prostate cancer risk in the National Health and Nutrition Examination Epidemiologic Follow-up Study cohort. *Am J Clin Nutr* 2005;81:1147-54.

7. Rodriguez C, McCullough ML, Mondul AM, et al. Calcium, dairy products, and risk of prostate cancer in a prospective cohort of United States men. *Cancer Epidemiol Biomarkers Prev* 2003;12:597-603.

8. Berndt SI, Carter HB, Landis PK, et al. Calcium intake and prostate cancer risk in a long-term aging study: the Baltimore Longitudinal Study of Aging. *Urology* 2002;60:1118-23.

9. Michaud DS, Augustsson K, Rimm EB, et al. A prospective study on intake of animal products and risk of prostate cancer. *Cancer Causes Control* 2001;12:557-67.

10. Chan JM, Stampfer MJ, Ma J, et al. Dairy products, calcium, and prostate cancer risk in the Physicians' Health Study. *Am J Clin Nutr* 2001;74:549-54.

11. Chan JM, Pietinen P, Virtanen M, et al. Diet and prostate cancer risk in a cohort of smokers, with a specific focus on calcium and phosphorus (Finland). *Cancer Causes Control* 2000;11:859-67.

12. Hsing AW, McLaughlin JK, Schuman LM, et al. Diet, tobacco use, and fatal prostate cancer: results from the Lutheran Brotherhood Cohort Study. *Cancer Res* 1990;50:6836-40.

13. Gann PH, Hennekens CH, Sacks FM, et al. Prospective study of plasma fatty acids and risk of prostate cancer. *J Natl Cancer Inst* 1994;86:281-6.

14. Allen NE, Sauvaget C, Roddam AW, et al. A prospective study of diet and prostate cancer in Japanese men. *Cancer Causes Control* 2004;15:911-20.

15. Rodriguez C, Jacobs EJ, Patel AV, et al. Jewish ethnicity and prostate cancer mortality in two large US cohorts. *Cancer Causes Control* 2002;13:271-7.

16. McCann SE, Ambrosone CB, Moysich KB, et al. Intakes of selected nutrients, foods, and phytochemicals and prostate cancer risk in Western New York. *Nutr Cancer* 2005;53:33-41.

17. Sanderson M, Coker AL, Logan P, et al. Lifestyle and prostate cancer among older African-American and Caucasian men in South Carolina. *Cancer Causes Control* 2004;15:647-55.

18. Hodge AM, English DR, McCredie MRE, et al. Foods, nutrients and prostate cancer. *Cancer Causes Control* 2004;15:11-20.

19. Chan JM, Giovannucci E, Andersson SO, et al. Dairy products, calcium, phosphorous, vitamin D, and risk of prostate cancer (Sweden). *Cancer Causes Control* 1998;9:559-66.

20. Lee MM, Wang RT, Hsing AW, et al. Case-control study of diet and prostate cancer in China. *Cancer Causes Control* 1998;9:545-52.

21. Sonoda T, Nagata Y, Mori M, et al. A case-control study of diet and prostate cancer in Japan: possible protective effect of traditional Japanese diet. *Cancer Sci* 2004;95:238-42.

22. Deneo-Pellegrini H, De Stefani E, Ronco A, et al. Foods, nutrients and prostate cancer: a case-control study in Uruguay. *Br J Cancer* 1999;80:591-7.

23. Tzonou A, Signorello LB, Lagiou P, et al. Diet and cancer of the prostate: a case-control study in Greece. *Int J Cancer* 1999;80:704-8.

24. Hayes RB, Ziegler RG, Gridley G, et al. Dietary factors and risks for prostate cancer among blacks and whites in the United States. *Cancer Epidemiol Biomarkers Prev* 1999;8:25-34.

25. Andersson SO, Baron J, Wolk A, et al. Early life risk factors for prostate cancer: a population-based case-control study in Sweden. *Cancer Epidemiol Biomarkers Prev* 1995;4:187-92.

26. Chen YC, Chiang CI, Lin RS, et al. Diet, vegetarian food and prostate carcinoma among men in Taiwan. *Br J Cancer* 2005;93:1057-61.

27. Ewings P, Bowie C. A case-control study of cancer of the prostate in Somerset and east Devon. *Br J Cancer* 1996;74:661-6.

28. Talamini R, La Vecchia C, Decarli A, et al. Nutrition, social factors and prostatic cancer in a Northern Italian population. *Br J Cancer* 1986;53:817-21.

29. Chaklin AV, Plotnikov SV. [Importance of various factors in the occurrence of prostatic cancer]. *Urol Nefrol (Mosk)* 1984;4:46-51.

30. Colli JL, Colli A. Comparisons of prostate cancer mortality rates with dietary practices in the United States. *Urol Oncol* 2005;23:390-8.

31. Ganmaa D, Li XM, Wang J, et al. Incidence and mortality of testicular and prostatic cancers in relation to world dietary practices. *Int J Cancer* 2002;98:262-7.

32. Gronberg H, Damber L, Damber JE. Total food consumption and body mass index in relation to prostate cancer risk: a case-control study in Sweden with prospectively collected exposure data. *J Urol* 1996;155:969-74.

33. Le Marchand L, Kolonel LN, Wilkens LR, et al. Animal fat consumption and prostate cancer: a prospective study in Hawaii. *Epidemiology* 1994;5:276-82.

34. Ursin G, Bjelke E, Heuch I, et al. Milk consumption and cancer incidence: a Norwegian prospective study. *Br J Cancer* 1990;61:456-9.

35. Severson RK, Nomura AM, Grove JS, et al. A prospective study of demographics, diet, and prostate cancer among men of Japanese ancestry in Hawaii. *Cancer Res* 1989;49:1857-60.

36. Snowdon DA, Phillips RL, Choi W. Diet, obesity, and risk of fatal prostate cancer. *Am J Epidemiol* 1984;120:244-50.

37. Veierod MB, Laake P, Thelle DS. Dietary fat intake and risk of prostate cancer: a prospective study of 25,708 Norwegian men. *Int J Cancer* 1997;73:634-8.

38. Giovannucci E, Ascherio A, Rimm EB, et al. Intake of carotenoids and retinol in relation to risk of prostate cancer. *J Natl Cancer Inst* 1995;87:1767-76.

39. Snowdon DA. Animal product consumption and mortality because of all causes combined, coronary heart disease, stroke, diabetes, and cancer in Seventh-day Adventists. *Am J Clin Nutr* 1988;48:739-48.

40. Hirayama T. Epidemiology of prostate cancer with special reference to the role of diet. *Natl Cancer Inst Monogr* 1979:149-55.

41. Jain MG, Hislop GT, Howe GR, et al. Plant foods, antioxidants, and prostate cancer risk: findings from case-control studies in Canada. *Nutr Cancer* 1999;34:173-84.

42. Bosetti C, Micelotta S, Dal Maso L, et al. Food groups and risk of prostate cancer in Italy. *Int J Cancer* 2004;110:424-8.

43. De Stefani E, Fierro L, Barrios E, et al. Tobacco, alcohol, diet and risk of prostate cancer. *Tumori* 1995;81:315-20.

44. Talamini R, Franceschi S, La Vecchia C, et al. Diet and prostatic cancer: a case-control study in northern Italy. *Nutr Cancer* 1992;18:277-86.

45. Mettlin C, Selenskas S, Natarajan N, et al. Beta-carotene and animal fats and their relationship to prostate cancer risk. A case-control study. *Cancer* 1989;64:605-12.

46. Sung JF, Lin RS, Pu YS, et al. Risk factors for prostate carcinoma in Taiwan: a case-control study in a Chinese population. *Cancer* 1999;86:484-91.

47. La Vecchia C, Negri E, D'Avanzo B, et al. Dairy products and the risk of prostatic cancer. *Oncology* 1991;48:406-10.

48. Mettlin CJ, Schoenfeld ER, Natarajan N. Patterns of milk consumption and risk of cancer. *Nutr Cancer* 1990;13:89-99.

49. Mishina T, Watanabe H, Araki H, et al. [High risk group for prostatic cancer by matched pair analysis]. *Nippon Hinyokika Gakkai Zasshi* 1981;72:1256-79.

50. Mishina T, Watanabe H, Araki H, et al. Epidemiological study of prostatic cancer by matched-pair analysis. *Prostate* 1985;6:423-36.

51. Rotkin ID. Studies in the epidemiology of prostatic cancer: expanded sampling. *Cancer Treat Rep* 1977;61:173-80.

52. Zhang J, Kesteloot H. Milk consumption in relation to incidence of prostate, breast, colon, and rectal cancers: is there an independent effect? *Nutr Cancer* 2005;53:65-72.

53. Li XM, Ganmaa D, Qin LQ, et al. [The effects of estrogen-like products in milk on prostate and testes]. [Chinese]. *Zhong Hua Nan Ke Xue* 2003;9:186-90.

54. Li X-M, Liu X-F, Akio S. Relationship between the incidence rates of testicular and prostatic cancers and food consumptions. *Chinese Journal of Cancer Research* 2002;. 14:240-5.

55. Hebert JR, Hurley TG, Olendzki BC, et al. Nutritional and socioeconomic factors in relation to prostate cancer mortality: a cross-national study. *J Natl Cancer Inst* 1998;90:1637-47.

56. Tominaga S, Kuroishi T. An ecological study on diet/nutrition and cancer in Japan. *Int J Cancer* 1997;Suppl:10-6.

57. Decarli A, La VC. Environmental factors and cancer mortality in Italy: correlational exercise. *Oncology* 1986;43:116-26.

58. Rose DP, Boyar AP, Wynder EL. International comparisons of mortality rates for cancer of the breast, ovary, prostate, and colon, and per capita food consumption. *Cancer* 1986;58:2363-71.

59. Schrauzer GN. Cancer mortality correlation studies. II. Regional associations of mortalities with the consumptions of foods and other commodities. *Med Hypotheses* 1976;2:39-49.

60. Armstrong B, Doll R. Environmental factors and cancer incidence and mortality in different countries, with special reference to dietary practices. *Int J Cancer* 1975;15:617-31.

61. Howell MA. Factor analysis of international cancer mortality data and per capita food consumption. *Br J Cancer* 1974;29:328-36.

62. Chan JM, Stampfer MJ, Giovannucci E, et al. Plasma insulin-like growth factor-I and prostate cancer risk: a prospective study. *Science* 1998;279:563-6.

63. Morris JK, George LM, Wu T, et al. Insulin-like growth factors and cancer: no role in screening. Evidence from the BUPA study and meta-analysis of prospective epidemiological studies. *Br J Cancer* 2006;95:112-7.

64. Giovannucci E, Liu Y, Stampfer MJ, et al. A prospective study of calcium intake and incident and fatal prostate cancer. *Cancer Epidemiol Biomarkers Prev* 2006;15:203-10.

65. Kesse E, Bertrais S, Astorg P, et al. Dairy products, calcium and phosphorus intake, and the risk of prostate cancer: results of the French prospective SU.VI.MAX (Supplementation en Vitamines et Mineraux Antioxydants) study. *Br J Nutr* 2006;95:539-45.

66. Gallus S, Bravi F, Talamini R, et al. Milk, dairy products and cancer risk (Italy). *Cancer Causes Control* 2006;17:429-37.

67. Phillips RL. Role of life-style and dietary habits in risk of cancer among seventh-day adventists. *Cancer Res* 1975;35:3513-22.

68. Phillips RL, Snowdon DA. Dietary relationships with fatal colorectal cancer among Seventh-Day Adventists. *J Natl Cancer Inst* 1985;74:307-17.

69. Hirayama T. [A large scale cohort study on the effect of life styles on the risk of cancer by each site]. *Gan No Rinsho* 1990;Spec No:233-42.

70. Khan MM, Goto R, Kobayashi K, et al. Dietary habits and cancer mortality among middle aged and older Japanese living in Hokkaido, Japan by cancer site and sex. 2004;5:58-65.

71. Hirayama T. Association between alcohol consumption and cancer of the sigmoid colon: observations from a Japanese cohort study. *Lancet* 1989;2:725-7.

72. Kearney J, Giovannucci E, Rimm EB, et al. Calcium, vitamin D, and dairy foods and the occurrence of colon cancer in men. *Am J Epidemiol* 1996;143:907-17.

73. Gaard M, Tretli S, Loken EB. Dietary factors and risk of colon cancer: a prospective study of 50,535 young Norwegian men and women. *Eur J Cancer Prev* 1996;5:445-54.

74. Jarvinen R, Knekt P, Hakulinen T, et al. Prospective study on milk products, calcium and cancers of the colon and rectum. *Eur J Clin Nutr* 2001;55:1000-7.

75. Wu K, Willett WC, Fuchs CS, et al. Calcium intake and risk of colon cancer in women and men. *J Natl Cancer Inst* 2002;94:437-46.

76. McCullough ML, Robertson AS, Rodriguez C, et al. Calcium, vitamin D, dairy products, and risk of colorectal cancer in the Cancer Prevention Study II Nutrition Cohort (United States). *Cancer Causes*

Control 2003;14:1-12.

77. Martinez ME, Giovannucci EL, Colditz GA, et al. Calcium, vitamin D, and the occurrence of colorectal cancer among women. J Natl Cancer Inst 1996;88:1375-82.

78. Sanjoaquin MA, Appleby PN, Thorogood M, et al. Nutrition, lifestyle and colorectal cancer incidence: a prospective investigation of 10998 vegetarians and non-vegetarians in the United Kingdom. Br J Cancer 2004;90:118-21.

79. Lin J, Zhang SM, Cook NR, et al. Intakes of calcium and vitamin D and risk of colorectal cancer in women. Am J Epidemiol 2005;161:755-64.

80. Kesse E, Boutron Ruault MC, Norat T, et al. Dietary calcium, phosphorus, vitamin D, dairy products and the risk of colorectal adenoma and cancer among French women of the E3N-EPIC prospective study. Int J Cancer 2005;117:137-44.

81. Ma J, Giovannucci E, Pollak M, et al. Milk intake, circulating levels of insulin-like growth factor-I, and risk of colorectal cancer in men. J Natl Cancer Inst 2001;93:1330-6.

82. Kampman E, Goldbohm RA, van den Brandt PA, et al. Fermented dairy products, calcium, and colorectal cancer in The Netherlands Cohort Study. Cancer Res 1994;54:3186-90.

83. Bostick RM, Potter JD, Sellers TA, et al. Relation of calcium, vitamin D, and dairy food intake to incidence of colon cancer among older women. The Iowa Women's Health Study. Am J Epidemiol 1993;137:1302-17.

84. Slob IC, Lambregts JL, Schuit AJ, et al. Calcium intake and 28-year gastrointestinal cancer mortality in Dutch civil servants. Int J Cancer 1993;54:20-5.

85. Garland C, Shekelle RB, Barrett Connor E, et al. Dietary vitamin D and calcium and risk of colorectal cancer: a 19-year prospective study in men. Lancet 1985;1:307-9.

86. Zheng W, Anderson KE, Kushi LH, et al. A prospective cohort study of intake of calcium, vitamin D, and other micronutrients in relation to incidence of rectal cancer among postmenopausal women. Cancer Epidemiol Biomarkers Prev 1998;7:221-5.

87. Stemmermann GN, Nomura A, Chyou PH. The influence of dairy and nondairy calcium on subsite large-bowel cancer risk. Dis Colon Rectum 1990;33:190-4.

88. Chyou PH, Nomura AM, Stemmermann GN. A prospective study of colon and rectal cancer among Hawaii Japanese men. Ann Epidemiol 1996;6:276-82.

89. Colbert LH, Hartman TJ, Malila N, et al. Physical activity in relation to cancer of the colon and rectum in a cohort of male smokers. Cancer Epidemiol Biomarkers Prev 2001;10:265-8.

90. Terry P, Baron JA, Bergkvist L, et al. Dietary calcium and vitamin D intake and risk of colorectal cancer: a prospective cohort study in women. Nutr Cancer 2002;43:39-

46.

91. Wei EK, Giovannucci E, Wu K, et al. Comparison of risk factors for colon and rectal cancer. Int J Cancer 2004;108:433-42.

92. Wu AH, Paganini Hill A, Ross RK, et al. Alcohol, physical activity and other risk factors for colorectal cancer: a prospective study. Br J Cancer 1987;55:687-94.

93. Kato I, Akhmedkhanov A, Koenig K, et al. Prospective study of diet and female colorectal cancer: the New York University Women's Health Study. Nutr Cancer 1997;28:276-81.

94. Pietinen P, Malila N, Virtanen M, et al. Diet and risk of colorectal cancer in a cohort of Finnish men. Cancer Causes Control 1999;10:387-96.

95. Heilbrun LK, Hankin JH, Nomura AMY, et al. Colon cancer and dietary fat, phosphorus, and calcium in Hawaiian-Japanese men. Am J Clin Nutr 1986;43:306-9.

96. Heilbrun LK, Nomura A, Hankin JH, et al. Diet and colorectal cancer with special reference to fiber intake. Int J Cancer 1989;44:1-6.

97. Glynn SA, Albanes D, Pietinen P, et al. Colorectal cancer and folate status: a nested case-control study among male smokers. Cancer Epidemiol Biomarkers Prev 1996;5:487-94.

98. Tangrea J, Helzlsouer K, Pietinen P, et al. Serum levels of vitamin D metabolites and the subsequent risk of colon and rectal cancer in Finnish men. Cancer Causes Control 1997;8:615-25.

99. Koh WP, Yuan JM, van den Berg D, et al. Interaction between cyclooxygenase-2 gene polymorphism and dietary n-6 polyunsaturated fatty acids on colon cancer risk: The Singapore Chinese Health Study. Br J Cancer 2004;90:1760-4.

100. Wong HL, Seow A, Arakawa K, et al. Vitamin D receptor start codon polymorphism and colorectal cancer risk: effect modification by dietary calcium and fat in Singapore Chinese. Carcinogenesis 2003;24:1091-5.

101. Sellers TTA, Bazyk AAE, Bostick RRM, et al. Diet and risk of colon cancer in a large prospective study of older women: an analysis stratified on family history (Iowa, United States). Cancer Causes Control 1998;9:357-67.

102. Cho E, Smith-Warner SA, Spiegelman D, et al. Dairy foods, calcium, and colorectal cancer: a pooled analysis of 10 cohort studies. J Natl Cancer Inst 2004;96:1015-22.

103. Larsson SC, Bergkvist L, Wolk A. High-fat dairy food and conjugated linoleic acid intakes in relation to colorectal cancer incidence in the Swedish Mammography Cohort. Am J Clin Nutr 2005;82:894-900.

104. Larsson SC, Bergkvist L, Rutegard J, et al. Calcium and dairy food intakes are inversely associated with colorectal cancer risk in the Cohort of Swedish Men. Am J Clin Nutr 2006;83:667-73; quiz 728-9.

105. Kuriki K, Hamajima N, Chiba H, et al. Increased risk of colorectal cancer due to interactions between meat consumption and the CD36 gene A52C polymorphism among Japanese. Nutr Cancer 2005;51:170-7.

106. Huang XE, Hirose K, Wakai K, et al. Comparison of lifestyle risk factors by family history for gastric, breast, lung and colorectal cancer. Asian Pac J Cancer Prev 2004;5:419-27.

107. Sakauchi F, Mori M, Washio M, et al. Dietary habits and risk of urothelial cancer incidence in the JACC study. J Epidemiol 2005;15:S190-S5.

108. Sakauchi F, Mori M, Washio M, et al. Dietary habits and risk of urothelial cancer death in a large-scale cohort study (JACC Study) in Japan. Nutr Cancer 2004;50:33-9.

109. Michaud DS, Spiegelman D, Clinton SK, et al. Fluid intake and the risk of bladder cancer in men. N Engl J Med 1999;340:1390-7.

110. Chyou PH, Nomura AM, Stemmermann GN. A prospective study of diet, smoking, and lower urinary tract cancer. Ann Epidemiol 1993;3:211-6.

111. Nagano J, Kono S, Preston DL, et al. Bladder-cancer incidence in relation to vegetable and fruit consumption: a prospective study of atomic-bomb survivors. Int J Cancer 2000;86:132-8.

112. Ohashi Y, Nakai S, Tsukamoto T, et al. Habitual intake of lactic acid bacteria and risk reduction of bladder cancer. Urol Int 2002;68:273-80.

113. Wilkens LR, Kadir MM, Kolonel LN, et al. Risk factors for lower urinary tract cancer: the role of total fluid consumption, nitrites and nitrosamines, and selected foods. Cancer Epidemiol Biomarkers Prev 1996;5:161-6.

114. Risch HA, Burch JD, Miller AB, et al. Dietary factors and the incidence of cancer of the urinary bladder. Am J Epidemiol 1988;127:1179-91.

115. Slattery ML, West DW, Robison LM. Fluid intake and bladder cancer in Utah. Int J Cancer 1988;42:17-22.

116. Wakai K, Hirose K, Takezaki T, et al. Foods and beverages in relation to urothelial cancer: case-control study in Japan. Int J Urol 2004;11:11-9.

117. Mettlin C, Graham S. Dietary risk factors in human bladder cancer. Am J Epidemiol 1979;110:255-63.

118. Gremy F, Momas I, Daures JP. [Risk factors in bladder cancer. A case-control study in the department of Herault, France]. Bull Acad Natl Med 1993;177:47-62.

119. Geoffroy-Perez B, Cordier S. Fluid consumption and the risk of bladder cancer: results of a multicenter case-control study. Int J Cancer 2001;93:880-7.

120. Lu CM, Lan SJ, Lee YH, et al. Tea consumption: fluid intake and bladder cancer risk in southern Taiwan. Urology 1999;54:823-8.

121. Nakata S, Sato J, Ohtake N, et al. [Epidemiological study of risk factors for bladder cancer]. Hinyokika Kiyo

1995;41:969-77.

122. Wang L. [1:1 pair matched case-control study on bladder cancer]. *Chung Hua Liu Hsing Ping Hsueh Tsa Chih* 1990;11:352-5.

123. La Vecchia C, Negri E, Decarli A, et al. Dietary factors in the risk of bladder cancer. *Nutr Cancer* 1989;12:93-101.

124. Sullivan JW. Epidemiologic survey of bladder cancer in greater New Orleans. *J Urol* 1982;128:281-3.

125. Newmark HL, Wargovich MJ, Bruce WR. Colon cancer and dietary fat, phosphate, and calcium: a hypothesis. *J Natl Cancer Inst* 1984;72:1323-5.

126. Singh PN, Fraser GE. Dietary risk factors for colon cancer in a low-risk population. *Am J Epidemiol* 1998;148:761-74.

127. Kojima M, Wakai K, Tamakoshi K, et al. Diet and colorectal cancer mortality: results from the Japan collaborative cohort study. *Nutr Cancer* 2004;50:23-32.

128. Willett WC, Stampfer MJ, Colditz GA, et al. Relation of meat, fat, and fiber intake to the risk of colon cancer in a prospective study among women. *N Engl J Med* 1990;323:1664-72.

129. Bruce WR, Wolever TM, Giacca A. Mechanisms linking diet and colorectal cancer: the possible role of insulin resistance. *Nutr Cancer* 2000;37:19-26.

130. Giugliano D, Ceriello A, Esposito K. The effects of diet on inflammation: emphasis on the metabolic syndrome. *J Am Coll Cardiol* 2006;48:677-85.

131. Baron JA, Beach M, Wallace K, et al. Risk of prostate cancer in a randomized clinical trial of calcium supplementation. *Cancer Epidemiol Biomarkers Prev* 2005;14:586-9.

132. Laaksonen DE, Laukkanen JA, Niskanen L, et al. Serum linoleic and total polyunsaturated fatty acids in relation to prostate and other cancers: a population-based cohort study. *Int J Cancer* 2004;111:444-50.

133. Giovannucci E, Rimm EB, Wolk A, et al. Calcium and fructose intake in relation to risk of prostate cancer. *Cancer Res* 1998;58:442-7.

134. Ramon JM, Bou R, Romea S, et al. Dietary fat intake and prostate cancer risk: a case-control study in Spain. *Cancer Causes Control* 2000;11:679-85.

135. Du S, Shi L, Zhang H, et al. [Relationship between dietary nutrients intakes and human prostate cancer]. *Wei Sheng Yen Chiu* 1997;26:122-5.

136. Key TJ, Silcocks PB, Davey GK, et al. A case-control study of diet and prostate cancer. *Br J Cancer* 1997;76:678-87.

137. Tavani A, Bertuccio P, Bosetti C, et al. Dietary intake of calcium, vitamin D, phosphorus and the risk of prostate cancer. *Eur Urol* 2005;48:27-33.

138. Vlajinac H, Ilic M, Sipetic S, et al. A case-control study of diet and prostate cancer. *J BUON* 2001;6:177-81.

139. Vlajinac HD, Marinkovic JM, Ilic MD, et al. Diet and prostate cancer: a case-control study. *Eur J Cancer* 1997;33:101-7.

140. Kaul L, Heshmat MY, Kovi J, et al. The role of diet in prostate cancer. *Nutr Cancer*

1987;9:123-8.

141. Walker M, Aronson KJ, King W, et al. Dietary patterns and risk of prostate cancer in Ontario, Canada. *Int J Cancer* 2005;116:592-8.

142. Tavani A, Gallus S, Franceschi S, et al. Calcium, dairy products, and the risk of prostate cancer. *Prostate* 2001;48:118-21.

143. Ohno Y, Yoshida O, Oishi K, et al. Dietary beta-carotene and cancer of the prostate: a case-control study in Kyoto, Japan. *Cancer Res* 1988;48:1331-6.

144. Oishi K, Okada K, Yoshida O, et al. A case-control study of prostatic cancer with reference to dietary habits. *Prostate* 1988;12:179-90.

145. Liaw Y-P, Huang Y-C, Lo P-Y, et al. Nutrient intakes in relation to cancer mortality in Taiwan. *Nutr. Res.* 2003;23:1597-606.

146. Boing H, Martinez L, Frentzel Beyme R, et al. Regional nutritional pattern and cancer mortality in the Federal Republic of Germany. *Nutr Cancer* 1985;7:121-30.

147. Lokeshwar BL, Schwartz GG, Selzer MG, et al. Inhibition of prostate cancer metastasis in vivo: a comparison of 1,23-dihydroxyvitamin D (calcitriol) and EB1089. *Cancer Epidemiol Biomarkers Prev* 1999;8:241-8.

Chapter 4.5

1. Calder PC. n-3 Polyunsaturated fatty acids, inflammation, and inflammatory diseases. *Am J Clin Nutr* 2006;83:1505S-19S.

2. van Stuyvenberg JH. *Margarine: an Economic, Social and Scientific History, 1869-1969.* Toronto: University of Toronto Press, 1969.

3. Food and Agriculture Organization of the United Nations. *FAOSTAT.* http://faostat.fao.org/site/345/default.as px. 2006.

4. Simopoulos AP. Human requirement for N-3 polyunsaturated fatty acids. *Poult Sci* 2000;79:961-70.

5. World Health Organization. 2003. *Diet, Nutrition and the Prevention of Chronic Diseases: Report of a Joint WHO/FAO Expert Consultation.* In: WHO Technical Report Series no 916. http://www.who.int/entity/dietphysicalac tivity/publications/trs916/download/en/in dex.html.

6. Willett WC, Howe GR, Kushi LH. Adjustment for total energy intake in epidemiologic studies. *Am J Clin Nutr* 1997;65:1220S-8S; discussion 9S-31S.

7. Bandera EV, Freudenheim JL, Marshall JR, et al. Diet and alcohol consumption and lung cancer risk in the New York State Cohort (United States). *Cancer Causes Control* 1997;8:828-40.

8. Knekt P, Seppanen R, Jarvinen R, et al. Dietary cholesterol, fatty acids, and the risk of lung cancer among men. *Nutr Cancer* 1991;16:267-75.

9. Shaten BJ, Kuller LH, Kjelsberg MO, et al. Lung cancer mortality after 16 years in MRFIT participants in intervention and

usual-care groups. Multiple Risk Factor Intervention Trial. *Ann Epidemiol* 1997;7:125-36.

10. Speizer FE, Colditz GA, Hunter DJ, et al. Prospective study of smoking, antioxidant intake, and lung cancer in middle-aged women (USA). *Cancer Causes Control* 1999;10:475-82.

11. Veierod MB, Laake P, Thelle DS. Dietary fat intake and risk of lung cancer: a prospective study of 51,452 Norwegian men and women. *Eur J Cancer Prev* 1997;6:540-9.

12. Wu Y, Zheng W, Sellers TA, et al. Dietary cholesterol, fat, and lung cancer incidence among older women: the Iowa Women's Health Study (United States). *Cancer Causes Control* 1994;5:395-400.

13. Alfano CM, Klesges RC, Murray DM, et al. Physical activity in relation to all-site and lung cancer incidence and mortality in current and former smokers. *Cancer Epidemiol Biomarkers Prev* 2004;13:2233-41.

14. Stahelin HB, Gey KF, Eichholzer M, et al. Plasma antioxidant vitamins and subsequent cancer mortality in the 12-year follow-up of the prospective Basel Study. *Am J Epidemiol* 1991;133:766-75.

15. Stemmermann GN, Nomura AM, Chyou PH, et al. Prospective study of alcohol intake and large bowel cancer. *Dig Dis Sci* 1990;35:1414-20.

16. Alavanja MC, Brownson RC, Benichou J. Estimating the effect of dietary fat on the risk of lung cancer in nonsmoking women. *Lung Cancer* 1996;14 Suppl 1:S63-74.

17. Bandera EV, Freudenheim JL, Graham S, et al. Alcohol consumption and lung cancer in white males. *Cancer Causes Control* 1992;3:361-9.

18. Caicoya M. [Lung cancer and vegetable consumption in Asturias, Spain. A case control study]. *Med Clin (Barc)* 2002;119:206-10.

19. De Stefani E, Brennan P, Boffetta P, et al. Diet and adenocarcinoma of the lung: a case-control study in Uruguay. *Lung Cancer* 2002;35:43-51.

20. De Stefani E, Deneo-Pellegrini H, Mendilaharsu M, et al. Dietary fat and lung cancer: a case-control study in Uruguay. *Cancer Causes Control* 1997;8:913-21.

21. Goodman MT, Kolonel LN, Yoshizawa CN, et al. The effect of dietary cholesterol and fat on the risk of lung cancer in Hawaii. *Am J Epidemiol* 1988;128:1241-55.

22. Hu J, Johnson KC, Mao Y, et al. A case-control study of diet and lung cancer in northeast China. *Int J Cancer* 1997;71:924-31.

23. Huang C, Zhang X, Qiao Z, et al. A case-control study of dietary factors in patients with lung cancer. *Biomed Environ Sci* 1992;5:257-65.

24. Marchand JL, Luce D, Goldberg P, et al. Dietary factors and the risk of lung cancer in New Caledonia (South Pacific). *Nutr Cancer* 2002;42:18-24.

25. Pillow PC, Hursting SD, Duphorne CM, et al. Case-control assessment of diet and lung cancer risk in African Americans and Mexican Americans. *Nutr Cancer* 1997;29:169-73.

26. Scali J, Astre C, Segala C, et al. Relationship of serum cholesterol, dietary and plasma beta-carotene with lung cancer in male smokers. *Eur J Cancer Prev* 1995;4:169-74.

27. Schabath MB, Hernandez LM, Wu X, et al. Dietary phytoestrogens and lung cancer risk. *JAMA* 2005;294:1493-504.

28. Shen H, Wei Q, Pillow PC, et al. Dietary folate intake and lung cancer risk in former smokers: a case-control analysis. *Cancer Epidemiol Biomarkers Prev* 2003;12:980-6.

29. Tan AJ, He SP, Huang MX. [A matched case-control study on the relations between beta-carotene and lung cancer]. *Zhonghua Liu Xing Bing Xue Za Zhi* 1995;16:199-202.

30. Zhou B, Wang T, Sun G, et al. A case-control study of the relationship between dietary factors and risk of lung cancer in women of Shenyang, China. *Oncol Rep* 1999;6:139-43.

31. Mohr DL, Blot WJ, Tousey PM, et al. Southern cooking and lung cancer. *Nutr Cancer* 1999;35:34-43.

32. Swanson CA, Brown CC, Sinha R, et al. Dietary fats and lung cancer risk among women: the Missouri Women's Health Study (United States). *Cancer Causes Control* 1997;8:883-93.

33. Le Marchand L, Hankin JH, Bach F, et al. An ecological study of diet and lung cancer in the South Pacific. *Int J Cancer* 1995;63:18-23.

34. Mulder I, Jansen MC, Smit HA, et al. Role of smoking and diet in the cross-cultural variation in lung-cancer mortality: the Seven Countries Study. Seven Countries Study Research Group. *Int J Cancer* 2000;88:665-71.

35. Schrauzer GN. Cancer mortality correlation studies. II. Regional associations of mortalities with the consumptions of foods and other commodities. *Med Hypotheses* 1976;2:39-49.

36. Tomioka F, Wakasugi H. Study on food intake patterns in Korea. *Jpn J Health Hum Ecol* 1995;61:317-28.

37. Smith-Warner SA, Ritz J, Hunter DJ, et al. Dietary fat and risk of lung cancer in a pooled analysis of prospective studies. *Cancer Epidemiol Biomarkers Prev* 2002;11:987-92.

38. Barrett-Connor E, Friedlander NJ. Dietary fat, calories, and the risk of breast cancer in postmenopausal women: a prospective population-based study. *J Am Coll Nutr* 1993;12:390-9.

39. Bingham SA, Luben R, Welch A, et al. Are imprecise methods obscuring a relation between fat and breast cancer? *Lancet* 2003;362:212-4.

40. Byrne C, Ursin G, Ziegler RG. A comparison of food habit and food frequency data as predictors of breast cancer in the NHANES I/NHEFS cohort. *J Nutr* 1996;126:2757-64.

41. Gaard M, Tretli S, Lken EB. Dietary fat and the risk of breast cancer: a prospective study of 25,892 Norwegian women. *Int J Cancer* 1995;63:13-7.

42. Giovannucci E, Stampfer MJ, Colditz GA, et al. A comparison of prospective and retrospective assessments of diet in the study of breast cancer. *Am J Epidemiol* 1993;137:502-11.

43. Graham S, Zielezny M, Marshall J, et al. Diet in the epidemiology of postmenopausal breast cancer in the New York State Cohort. *Am J Epidemiol* 1992;136:1327-37.

44. Horn-Ross PL, Hoggatt KJ, West DW, et al. Recent diet and breast cancer risk: the California Teachers Study (USA). *Cancer Causes Control* 2002;13:407-15.

45. Howe GR, Friedenreich CM, Jain M, et al. A cohort study of fat intake and risk of breast cancer. *J Natl Cancer Inst* 1991;83:336-40.

46. Jones DY, Schatzkin A, Green SB, et al. Dietary fat and breast cancer in the National Health and Nutrition Examination Survey I Epidemiologic Follow-up Study. *J Natl Cancer Inst* 1987;79:465-71.

47. Kinlen LJ. Meat and fat consumption and cancer mortality: a study of strict religious orders in Britain. *Lancet* 1982;1:946-9.

48. Knekt P, Aromaa A, Maatela J, et al. Serum vitamin A and subsequent risk of cancer: cancer incidence follow-up of the Finnish Mobile Clinic Health Examination Survey. *Am J Epidemiol* 1990;132:857-70.

49. Kushi LH, Potter JD, Bostick RM, et al. Dietary fat and risk of breast cancer according to hormone receptor status. *Cancer Epidemiol Biomarkers Prev* 1995;4:11-9.

50. Kushi LH, Sellers TA, Potter JD, et al. Dietary fat and postmenopausal breast cancer. *J Natl Cancer Inst* 1992;84:1092-9.

51. Mattisson I, Wirfalt E, Wallstrom P, et al. High fat and alcohol intakes are risk factors of postmenopausal breast cancer: a prospective study from the Malmo diet and cancer cohort. *Int J Cancer* 2004;110:589-97.

52. Sieri S, Krogh V, Muti P, et al. Fat and protein intake and subsequent breast cancer risk in postmenopausal women. *Nutr Cancer* 2002;42:10-7.

53. Thiebaut AC, Clavel-Chapelon F. [Fat consumption and breast cancer: preliminary results from the E3N-Epic cohort]. *Bull Cancer (Paris)* 2001;88:954-8.

54. Toniolo P, Riboli E, Shore RE, et al. Consumption of meat, animal products, protein, and fat and risk of breast cancer: a prospective cohort study in New York. *Epidemiology* 1994;5:391-7.

55. Van den Brandt PA, Van't Veer P, Goldbohm RA, et al. A prospective cohort study on dietary fat and the risk of postmenopausal breast cancer. *Cancer Res* 1993;53:75-82.

56. Voorrips LE, Brants HA, Kardinaal AF, et al. Intake of conjugated linoleic acid, fat, and other fatty acids in relation to postmenopausal breast cancer: the Netherlands Cohort Study on Diet and Cancer. *Am J Clin Nutr* 2002;76:873-82.

57. Willett WC, Stampfer MJ, Colditz GA, et al. Dietary fat and the risk of breast cancer. *N Engl J Med* 1987;316:22-8.

58. Willett WC, Hunter DJ, Stampfer MJ, et al. Dietary fat and fiber in relation to risk of breast cancer. An 8-year follow-up. *JAMA* 1992;268:2037-44.

59. Wirfalt E, Mattisson I, Gullberg B, et al. Postmenopausal breast cancer is associated with high intakes of omega6 fatty acids (Sweden). *Cancer Causes Control* 2002;13:883-93.

60. Wolk A, Bergstrom R, Hunter D, et al. A prospective study of association of monounsaturated fat and other types of fat with risk of breast cancer. *Arch Intern Med* 1998;158:41-5.

61. Ames HG, Gee MI, Hawrysh ZJ. Taste perception and breast cancer: evidence of a role for diet. *J Am Diet Assoc* 1993;93:541-6.

62. Aro A, Mannisto S, Salminen I, et al. Inverse association between dietary and serum conjugated linoleic acid and risk of breast cancer in postmenopausal women. *Nutr Cancer* 2000;38:151-7.

63. Bonilla-Fernandez P, Lopez-Cervantes M, Torres-Sanchez LE, et al. Nutritional factors and breast cancer in Mexico. *Nutr Cancer* 2003;45:148-55.

64. Braga C, La Vecchia C, Negri E, et al. Intake of selected foods and nutrients and breast cancer risk: an age- and menopause-specific analysis. *Nutr Cancer* 1997;28:258-63.

65. Challier B, Perarnau JM, Viel JF. Garlic, onion and cereal fibre as protective factors for breast cancer: a French case-control study. *Eur J Epidemiol* 1998;14:737-47.

66. Cooper JA, Rohan TE, Cant EL, et al. Risk factors for breast cancer by oestrogen receptor status: a population-based case-control study. *Br J Cancer* 1989;59:119-25.

67. Dai Q, Shu XO, Jin F, et al. Consumption of animal foods, cooking methods, and risk of breast cancer. *Cancer Epidemiol Biomarkers Prev* 2002;11:801-8.

68. D'Avanzo B, Negri E, Gramenzi A, et al. Fats in seasoning and breast cancer risk: an Italian case-control study. *Eur J Cancer* 1991;27:420-3.

69. De Stefani E, Deneo-Pellegrini H, Mendilaharsu M, et al. Essential fatty acids and breast cancer: a case-control study in Uruguay. *Int J Cancer* 1998;76:491-4.

70. De Stefani E, Ronco A, Mendilaharsu M, et al. Meat intake, heterocyclic amines, and risk of breast cancer: a case-control study in Uruguay. *Cancer Epidemiol Biomarkers Prev* 1997;6:573-81.

71. Do MH, Lee SS, Jung PJ, et al. Intake of dietary fat and vitamin in relation to breast cancer risk in Korean women: a case-control study. *J Korean Med Sci*

2003;18:534-40.

72. Dos Santos Silva I, Mangtani P, McCormack V, et al. Lifelong vegetarianism and risk of breast cancer: a population-based case-control study among South Asian migrant women living in England. Int J Cancer 2002;99:238-44.

73. Ewertz M. Breast cancer in Denmark. Incidence, risk factors, and characteristics of survival. Acta Oncol 1993;32:595-615.

74. Franceschi S, Favero A, Decarli A, et al. Intake of macronutrients and risk of breast cancer. Lancet 1996;347:1351-6.

75. Gerber M, Richardson S, Crastes de Paulet P, et al. Relationship between vitamin E and polyunsaturated fatty acids in breast cancer: nutritional and metabolic aspects. Cancer 1989;64:2347-52.

76. Ghadirian P, Lacroix A, Perret C, et al. Breast cancer risk and nutrient intake among French Canadians in Montreal: A case-control study. Breast 1998;7:108-13.

77. Goodman MT, Nomura AM, Wilkens LR, et al. The association of diet, obesity, and breast cancer in Hawaii. Cancer Epidemiol Biomarkers Prev 1992;1:269-75.

78. Goodstine SL, Zheng TZ, Holford TR, et al. Dietary (n-3)/(n-6) fatty acid ratio: possible relationship to premenopausal but not postmenopausal breast cancer risk in U.S. women. J Nutr 2003;133:1409-14.

79. Graham S, Hellmann R, Marshall J, et al. Nutritional epidemiology of postmenopausal breast cancer in western New York. Am J Epidemiol 1991;134:552-66.

80. Hankin JH, Zhao LP, Wilkens LR, et al. Attributable risk of breast, prostate, and lung cancer in Hawaii due to saturated fat. Cancer Causes Control 1992;3:17-23.

81. Henquin N, Trostler N, Horn Y. Nutritional risk factors and breast cancer in Jewish and Arab women. Cancer Nurs 1994;17:326-33.

82. Hermann S, Linseisen J, Chang-Claude J. Nutrition and breast cancer risk by age 50: A population-based case-control study in Germany. Nutr Cancer 2002;44:23-34.

83. Hietanen E, Bartsch H, Bereziat JC, et al. Diet and oxidative stress in breast, colon and prostate cancer patients: a case-control study. Eur J Clin Nutr 1994;48:575-86.

84. Hirohata T, Nomura AM, Hankin JH, et al. An epidemiologic study on the association between diet and breast cancer. J Natl Cancer Inst 1987;78:595-600.

85. Hirohata T, Shigematsu T, Nomura AM, et al. Occurrence of breast cancer in relation to diet and reproductive history: a case-control study in Fukuoka, Japan. Natl Cancer Inst Monogr 1985;69:187-90.

86. Holmberg L, Ohlander EM, Byers T, et al. Diet and breast cancer risk. Results from a population-based, case-control study in Sweden. Arch Intern Med 1994;154:1805-11.

87. Ingram DM, Nottage E, Roberts T. The role of diet in the development of breast cancer: a case-control study of patients with breast cancer, benign epithelial hyperplasia and fibrocystic disease of the breast. Br J Cancer 1991;64:187-91.

88. Iscovich JM, Iscovich RB, Howe G, et al. A case-control study of diet and breast cancer in Argentina. Int J Cancer 1989;44:770-6.

89. Jakovljevic J, Touillaud MS, Bondy ML, et al. Dietary intake of selected fatty acids, cholesterol and carotenoids and estrogen receptor status in premenopausal breast cancer patients. Breast Cancer Res Treat 2002;75:5-14.

90. Katsouyanni K, Willett W, Trichopoulos D, et al. Risk of breast cancer among Greek women in relation to nutrient intake. Cancer 1988;61:181-5.

91. Katsouyanni K, Trichopoulou A, Stuver S, et al. The association of fat and other macronutrients with breast cancer: a case-control study from Greece. Br J Cancer 1994;70:537-41.

92. Kumar NB, Riccardi D, Cantor A, et al. A case-control study evaluating the association of purposeful physical activity, body fat distribution, and steroid hormones on premenopausal breast cancer risk. Breast J 2005;11:266-72.

93. Landa MC, Frago N, Tres A. Diet and the risk of breast cancer in Spain. Eur J Cancer Prev 1994;3:313-20.

94. Lee MM, Chang IY, Horng CF, et al. Breast cancer and dietary factors in Taiwanese women. Cancer Causes Control 2005;16:929-37.

95. Lee HP, Gourley L, Duffy SW, et al. Dietary effects on breast-cancer risk in Singapore. Lancet 1991;337:1197-200.

96. London SJ, Sacks FM, Stampfer MJ, et al. Fatty acid composition of the subcutaneous adipose tissue and risk of proliferative benign breast disease and breast cancer. J Natl Cancer Inst 1993;85:785-93.

97. McCann SE, Ip C, Ip MM, et al. Dietary intake of conjugated linoleic acids and risk of premenopausal and postmenopausal breast cancer, Western New York exposures and cancer study (WEB study). Cancer Epidemiol Biomarkers Prev 2004;13:1480-4.

98. Miller AB, Kelly A, Choi NW, et al. A study of diet and breast cancer. Am J Epidemiol 1978;107:499-509.

99. Potischman N, Swanson CA, Coates RJ, et al. Dietary relationships with early onset (under age 45) breast cancer in a case-control study in the United States: Influence of chemotherapy treatment. Cancer Causes Control 1997;8:713-21.

100. Potischman N, Coates RJ, Swanson CA, et al. Increased risk of early-stage breast cancer related to consumption of sweet foods among women less than age 45 in the United States. Cancer Causes Control 2002;13:937-46.

101. Pryor M, Slattery ML, Robinson LM, et al. Adolescent diet and breast cancer in Utah. Cancer Res 1989;49:2161-7.

102. Richardson SGMCS. The role of fat, animal protein and some vitamin consumption in breast cancer: a case control study in southern France. Int J Cancer 1991;48:1-9. 44 ref.

103. Ronco A, De Stefanii E, Mendilaharsu M, et al. Meat, fat and risk of breast cancer: a case-control study from Uruguay. Int J Cancer 1996;65:328-31.

104. Santiago E, González MJ, Matos MI, et al. Association between dietary fat and breast cancer in Puerto Rican postmenopausal women attending a breast cancer clinic. P R Health Sci J 1998;17:235.

105. Sarin R, Tandon RK, Paul S, et al. Diet, body fat and plasma lipids in breast cancer. Indian J Med Res 1985;81:493-8.

106. Xiao OS, Jin F, Dai Q, et al. Soyfood intake during adolescence and subsequent risk of breast cancer among Chinese women. Cancer Epidemiol Biomarkers Prev 2001;10:483-8.

107. Shu XO, Jin F, Dai Q, et al. Association of body size and fat distribution with risk of breast cancer among chinese women. Int J Cancer 2001;94:449-55.

108. Toniolo P, Riboli E, Protta F, et al. Calorie-providing nutrients and risk of breast cancer. J Natl Cancer Inst 1989;81:278-86.

109. van't Veer P, Kok FJ, Hermus RJ, et al. Alcohol dose, frequency and age at first exposure in relation to the risk of breast cancer. Int J Epidemiol 1989;18:511-7.

110. Van 't Veer P, van Leer EM, Rietdijk A, et al. Combination of dietary factors in relation to breast-cancer occurrence. Int J Cancer 1991;47:649-53.

111. Van't Veer P, Kok FJ, Brants HA, et al. Dietary fat and the risk of breast cancer. Int J Epidemiol 1990;19:12-8.

112. Wakai K, Dillon DS, Ohno Y, et al. Fat intake and breast cancer risk in an area where fat intake is low: a case-control study in Indonesia. Int J Epidemiol 2000;29:20-8.

113. Witte JS, Ursin G, Siemiatycki J, et al. Diet and premenopausal bilateral breast cancer: a case-control study. Breast Cancer Res Treat 1997;42:243-51.

114. Yu SZ, Lu RF, Xu DD, et al. A case-control study of dietary and nondietary risk factors for breast cancer in Shanghai. Cancer Res 1990;50:5017-21.

115. Yuan JM, Wang QS, Ross RK, et al. Diet and breast cancer in Shanghai and Tianjin, China. Br J Cancer 1995;71:1353-8.

116. Zaridze D, Lifanova Y, Maximovitch D, et al. Diet, alcohol consumption and reproductive factors in a case-control study of breast cancer in Moscow. Int J Cancer 1991;48:493-501.

117. Zheng T, Holford TR, Mayne ST, et al. Lactation and breast cancer risk: a case-control study in Connecticut. Br J Cancer 2001;84:1472-6.

118. Zheng T, Holford TR, Tessari J, et al. Breast cancer risk associated with congeners of polychlorinated biphenyls. Am J Epidemiol 2000;152:50-8.

119. Armstrong B, Doll R. Environmental

factors and cancer incidence and mortality in different countries, with special reference to dietary practices. *Int J Cancer* 1975;15:617-31.

120. Boing H, Martinez L, Frentzel Beyme R, et al. Regional nutritional pattern and cancer mortality in the Federal Republic of Germany. *Nutr Cancer* 1985;7:121-30.

121. Grant WB. An ecologic study of dietary and solar ultraviolet-B links to breast carcinoma mortality rates. *Cancer* 2002;94:272-81.

122. Gray GE, Pike MC, Henderson BE. Breast-cancer incidence and mortality rates in different countries in relation to known risk factors and dietary practices. *Br J Cancer* 1979;39:1-7.

123. Hems G. The contributions of diet and childbearing to breast-cancer rates. *Br J Cancer* 1978;37:974-82.

124. Hursting SD, Thornquist M, Henderson MM. Types of dietary fat and the incidence of cancer at five sites. *Prev Med* 1990;19:242-53.

125. Ishimoto H, Nakamura H, Miyoshi T. Epidemiological study on relationship between breast cancer mortality and dietary factors. *Tokushima J Exp Med* 1994;41:103-14.

126. Kolonel LN, Hankin JH, Lee J, et al. Nutrient intakes in relation to cancer incidence in Hawaii. *Br J Cancer* 1981;44:332-9.

127. Liaw YP, Chen HL, Cheng CW, et al. An international epidemiologic study of breast cancer mortality and total fat intake in postmenopausal women. *Nutr Res* 2005;25:823-34.

128. Rose DP, Boyar AP, Wynder EL. International comparisons of mortality rates for cancer of the breast, ovary, prostate, and colon, and per capita food consumption. *Cancer* 1986;58:2363-71.

129. Hunter DJ, Spiegelman D, Adami HO, et al. Non-dietary factors as risk factors for breast cancer, and as effect modifiers of the association of fat intake and risk of breast cancer. *Cancer Causes Control* 1997;8:49-56.

130. Smith-Warner SA, Spiegelman D, Adami HO, et al. Types of dietary fat and breast cancer: a pooled analysis of cohort studies. *Int J Cancer* 2001;92:767-74.

131. Holmes MD, Hunter DJ, Colditz GA, et al. Association of dietary intake of fat and fatty acids with risk of breast cancer. *JAMA* 1999;281:914-20.

132. Velie E, Kulldorff M, Schairer C, et al. Dietary fat, fat subtypes, and breast cancer in postmenopausal women: a prospective cohort study. *J Natl Cancer Inst* 2000;92:833-9.

133. Wakai K, Tamakoshi K, Date C, et al. Dietary intakes of fat and fatty acids and risk of breast cancer: a prospective study in Japan. *Cancer Sci* 2005;96:590-9.

134. Wirfalt E, Vessby B, Mattisson I, et al. No relations between breast cancer risk and fatty acids of erythrocyte membranes in postmenopausal women of the Malmo Diet Cancer cohort (Sweden). *Eur J Clin Nutr* 2004;58:761-70.

135. Romieu I, Lazcano-Ponce E, Sanchez-Zamorano LM, et al. Carbohydrates and the risk of breast cancer among Mexican women. *Cancer Epidemiol Biomarkers Prev* 2004;13:1283-9.

136. Zhu Z, Parviainen M, Mannisto S, et al. Vitamin E concentration in breast adipose tissue of breast cancer patients (Kuopio, Finland). *Cancer Causes Control* 1996;7:591-5.

137. Key T, Appleby P, Barnes I, et al. Endogenous sex hormones and breast cancer in postmenopausal women: reanalysis of nine prospective studies. *J Natl Cancer Inst* 2002;94:606-16.

138. Kaaks R, Berrino F, Key T, et al. Serum sex steroids in premenopausal women and breast cancer risk within the European Prospective Investigation into Cancer and Nutrition (EPIC). *J Natl Cancer Inst* 2005;97:755-65.

139. Wu AH, Pike MC, Stram DO. Meta-analysis: dietary fat intake, serum estrogen levels, and the risk of breast cancer. *J Natl Cancer Inst* 1999;91:529-34.

140. Bruning PF, Bonfrer JM. Free fatty acid concentrations correlated with the available fraction of estradiol in human plasma. *Cancer Res* 1986;46:2606-9.

141. Ozasa K, Watanabe Y, Ito Y, et al. Dietary habits and risk of lung cancer death in a large-scale cohort study (JACC Study) in Japan by sex and smoking habit. *Jpn J Cancer Res* 2001;92:1259-69.

142. Axelsson G, Liljeqvist T, Andersson L, et al. Dietary factors and lung cancer among men in west Sweden. *Int J Epidemiol* 1996;25:32-9.

143. Bond GG, Thompson FE, Cook RR. Dietary vitamin A and lung cancer: results of a case-control study among chemical workers. *Nutr Cancer* 1987;9:109-21.

144. Brennan P, Fortes C, Butler J, et al. A multicenter case-control study of diet and lung cancer among non-smokers. *Cancer Causes Control* 2000;11:49-58.

145. Darby S, Whitley E, Doll R, et al. Diet, smoking and lung cancer: a case-control study of 1000 cases and 1500 controls in South-West England. *Br J Cancer* 2001;84:728-35.

146. De Stefani E, Fontham ET, Chen V, et al. Fatty foods and the risk of lung cancer: a case-control study from Uruguay. *Int J Cancer* 1997;71:760-6.

147. Goodman MT, Hankin JH, Wilkens LR, et al. High-fat foods and the risk of lung cancer. *Epidemiology* 1992;3:288-99.

148. Pierce RJ, Kune GA, Kune S, et al. Dietary and alcohol intake, smoking pattern, occupational risk, and family history in lung cancer patients: results of a case-control study in males. *Nutr Cancer* 1989;12:237-48.

149. Rachtan J. A case-control study of lung cancer in Polish women. *Neoplasma* 2002;49:75-80.

150. Willett WC, Stampfer MJ, Colditz GA, et al. Relation of meat, fat, and fiber intake to the risk of colon cancer in a prospective study among women. *N Engl J Med* 1990;323:1664-72.

151. Giovannucci E, Rimm EB, Stampfer MJ, et al. Intake of fat, meat, and fiber in relation to risk of colon cancer in men. *Cancer Res* 1994;54:2390-7.

152. Bostick RM, Potter JD, Kushi LH, et al. Sugar, meat, and fat intake, and non-dietary risk factors for colon cancer incidence in Iowa women (United States). *Cancer Causes Control* 1994;5:38-52.

153. Sanjoaquin MA, Appleby PN, Thorogood M, et al. Nutrition, lifestyle and colorectal cancer incidence: a prospective investigation of 10998 vegetarians and non-vegetarians in the United Kingdom. *Br J Cancer* 2004;90:118-21.

154. Goldbohm RA, van den Brandt PA, van 't Veer P, et al. A prospective cohort study on the relation between meat consumption and the risk of colon cancer. *Cancer Res* 1994;54:718-23.

155. Lin J, Zhang SM, Cook NR, et al. Dietary fat and fatty acids and risk of colorectal cancer in women. *Am J Epidemiol* 2004;160:1011-22.

Chapter 4.6

1. World Health Organization. 2003. *Diet, Nutrition and the Prevention of Chronic Diseases: Report of a Joint WHO/FAO Expert Consultation*. In: WHO Technical Report Series no 916. http://www.who.int/entity/dietphysicalactivity/publications/trs916/download/en/index.html.

2. Ye W, Yi Y, Luo R. [A case-control study on diet and gastric cancer]. *Chung Hua Yu Fang I Hsueh Tsa Chih* 1998;32:100-2.

3. Xibin S, Moller H, Evans HS, et al. Residential environment, diet and risk of stomach cancer: a case-control study in Linzhou, China. *Asian Pac J Cancer Prev* 2002;3:167-72.

4. Munoz N, Plummer M, Vivas J, et al. A case-control study of gastric cancer in Venezuela. *Int J Cancer* 2001;93:417-23.

5. Mathew A, Gangadharan P, Varghese C, et al. Diet and stomach cancer: a case-control study in South India. *Eur J Cancer Prev* 2000;9:89-97.

6. Liu X, Wang Q, Ma J. [A case-control study on the risk factors of stomach cancer in Tianjin City]. *Chung Hua Liu Hsing Ping Hsueh Tsa Chih* 2001;22:362-4.

7. Fei S, Xiao S. [Diet and gastric cancer: a case-control study in Shanghai urban districts]. *Chin J Gastroenterol* 2003;8:143-7.

8. Demirer T, Icli F, Uzunalimoglu O, et al. Diet and stomach cancer incidence. A case-control study in Turkey. *Cancer* 1990;65:2344-8.

9. Buiatti E, Palli D, Decarli A, et al. A case-control study of gastric cancer and diet in Italy. *Int J Cancer* 1989;44:611-6.

10. van den Brandt PA, Botterweck AA, Goldbohm RA. Salt intake, cured meat consumption, refrigerator use and stomach cancer incidence: a prospective

cohort study (Netherlands). *Cancer Causes Control* 2003;14:427-38.

11. McGee H. *McGee on Food and Cooking*. London: Hodder and Stoughton, 2004.

12. Willett WC, Howe GR, Kushi LH. Adjustment for total energy intake in epidemiologic studies. *Am J Clin Nutr* 1997;65:1220S-8S; discussion 9S-31S.

13. Phillips RL. Role of life-style and dietary habits in risk of cancer among seventh-day adventists. *Cancer Res* 1975;35:3513-22.

14. Macquart Moulin G, Riboli E, Cornee J, et al. Case-control study on colorectal cancer and diet in Marseilles. *Int J Cancer* 1986;38:183-91.

15. Benito E, Obrador A, Stiggelbout A, et al. A population-based case-control study of colorectal cancer in Majorca. I. Dietary factors. *Int J Cancer* 1990;45:69-76.

16. Bidoli E, Franceschi S, Talamini R, et al. Food consumption and cancer of the colon and rectum in north-eastern Italy. *Int J Cancer* 1992;50:223-9.

17. Franceschi S, Favero A. The role of energy and fat in cancers of the breast and colon-rectum in a southern European population. *Ann Oncol* 1999;10 Suppl 6:61-3.

18. Tuyns AJ, Kaaks R, Haelterman M. Colorectal cancer and the consumption of foods: a case-control study in Belgium. *Nutr Cancer* 1988;11:189-204.

19. Miller AB, Howe GR, Jain M, et al. Food items and food groups as risk factors in a case-control study of diet and colo-rectal cancer. *Int J Cancer* 1983;32:155-61.

20. Slattery ML, Potter JD, Ma KN, et al. Western diet, family history of colorectal cancer, NAT2, GSTM-1 and risk of colon cancer. *Cancer Causes Control* 2000;11:1-8.

21. Chyou PH, Nomura AM, Stemmermann GN. A prospective study of colon and rectal cancer among Hawaii Japanese men. *Ann Epidemiol* 1996;6:276-82.

22. Terry PD, Jain M, Miller AB, et al. Glycemic load, carbohydrate intake, and risk of colorectal cancer in women: a prospective cohort study. *J Natl Cancer Inst* 2003;95:914-6.

23. Bostick RM, Potter JD, Kushi LH, et al. Sugar, meat, and fat intake, and non-dietary risk factors for colon cancer incidence in Iowa women (United States). *Cancer Causes Control* 1994;5:38-52.

24. Higginbotham S, Zhang ZF, Lee IM, et al. Dietary glycemic load and risk of colorectal cancer in the Women's Health Study. *J Natl Cancer Inst* 2004;96:229-33.

25. Roberts Thomson IC, Ryan P, Khoo KK, et al. Diet, acetylator phenotype, and risk of colorectal neoplasia. *Lancet* 1996;347:1372-4.

26. Terry P, Giovannucci E, Michels KB, et al. Fruit, vegetables, dietary fiber and risk of colorectal cancer. *J Natl Cancer Inst* 2001;93:525-33.

27. Michaud DS, Fuchs CS, Liu S, et al. Dietary glycemic load, carbohydrate, sugar, and colorectal cancer risk in men and women. *Cancer Epidemiol Biomarkers Prev* 2005;14:138-47.

28. Poulsen M, Molck AM, Thorup I, et al. The influence of simple sugars and starch given during pre- or post-initiation on aberrant crypt foci in rat colon. *Cancer Lett* 2001;167:135-43.

29. Nagata C, Takatsuka N, Kawakami N, et al. A prospective cohort study of soy product intake and stomach cancer death. *Br J Cancer* 2002;87:31-6.

30. Tsugane S, Sasazuki S, Kobayashi M, et al. Salt and salted food intake and subsequent risk of gastric cancer among middle-aged Japanese men and women. *Br J Cancer* 2004;90:128-34.

31. Csendes A, Medina E, Gaete MC, et al. [Gastric cancer: an epidemiologic and dietary study in 100 patients and 100 controls]. *Rev Med Chil* 1976;104:761-5.

32. Haenszel W, Kurihara M, Locke FB, et al. Stomach cancer in Japan. *J Natl Cancer Inst* 1976;56:265-74.

33. Funakoshi N, Kanoh T, Uchino H, et al. Gastric cancer and diet. The analysis of the epidemiological survey in Tango district of Kyoto prefecture. *Naika Hokan* 1983;30:175-81.

34. Correa P, Fontham E, Pickle LW, et al. Dietary determinants of gastric cancer in south Louisiana inhabitants. *J Natl Cancer Inst* 1985;75:645-54.

35. Goiriena De Gandarias FJ, Santidrian MI, Barranquero AM. Etiopathogenic study of cancer of the digestive tract in Biscay Spain with special emphasis on the role played by diet and consumption of alcohol and tobacco. *Rev Sanid Hig Publica (Madr)* 1987;62:1411-30.

36. You WC, Blot WJ, Chang YS, et al. Diet and high risk of stomach cancer in Shandong, China. *Cancer Res* 1988;48:3518-23.

37. Hu JF, Zhang SF, Jia EM, et al. Diet and cancer of the stomach: a case-control study in China. *Int J Cancer* 1988;41:331-5.

38. Negri E, La Vecchia C, D'Avanzo B, et al. Salt preference and the risk of gastrointestinal cancers. *Nutr Cancer* 1990;14:227-32.

39. Graham S, Haughey B, Marshall J, et al. Diet in the epidemiology of gastric cancer. *Nutr Cancer* 1990;13:19-34.

40. Cai L. [A case-control study of stomach cancer in Changle, Fujian Province - by the risk state analysis]. *Chung Hua Liu Hsing Ping Hsueh Tsa Chih* 1991;12:15-9.

41. Boeing H, Frentzel-Beyme R, Berger M, et al. Case-control study on stomach cancer in Germany. *Int J Cancer* 1991;47:858-64.

42. Ren D, Jin J, Wang D, et al. The nutritional factors related to gastric cancer in Tianjin. *Ying Yang Xue Bao* 1992;14:325-8.

43. Nazario CM, Szklo M, Diamond E, et al. Salt and gastric cancer: a case-control study in Puerto Rico. *Int J Epidemiol* 1993;22:790-7.

44. Ramon JM, Serra L, Cerdo C, et al. Dietary factors and gastric cancer risk. A case-control study in Spain. *Cancer* 1993;71:1731-5.

45. Erkisi M, Colakoglu S, Koksal F, et al. Relationship of *Helicobacter pylori* infection to several malignant and non-malignant gastrointestinal diseases. *J Exp Clin Cancer Res* 1997;16:289-93.

46. Setiawan VW, Zhang ZF, Yu GP, et al. GSTT1 and GSTM1 null genotypes and the risk of gastric cancer: a case-control study in a Chinese population. *Cancer Epidemiol Biomarkers Prev* 2000;9:73-80.

47. Tsukino H, Hanaoka T, Otani T, et al. hOGG1 Ser326Cys polymorphism, interaction with environmental exposures, and gastric cancer risk in Japanese populations. *Cancer Sci* 2004;95:977-83.

48. Setiawan VW, Yu GP, Lu QY, et al. Allium vegetables and stomach cancer risk in China. *Asian Pac J Cancer Prev* 2005;6:387-95.

49. Correa P, Cuello C, Fajardo LF, et al. Diet and gastric cancer: nutrition survey in a high-risk area. *J Natl Cancer Inst* 1983;70:673-8.

50. Koifman S, Koifman RJ. Stomach cancer incidence in Brazil: an ecologic study with selected risk factors. *Cad Saude Publica* 1997;13:85-92.

51. Wong BC, Ching CK, Lam SK, et al. Differential north to south gastric cancer duodenal ulcer gradient in China. China Ulcer Study Group. *J Gastroenterol Hepatol* 1998;13:1050-7.

52. Kono S, Ikeda M, Ogata M. Salt and geographical mortality of gastric cancer and stroke in Japan. *J Epidemiol Community Health* 1983;37:43-6.

53. Hara N, Sakata K, Nagai M, et al. [Geographical difference of mortality of digestive cancers and food consumption]. *Gan No Rinsho* 1984;30:1665-74.

54. Lu JB, Qin YM. Correlation between high salt intake and mortality rates for oesophageal and gastric cancers in Henan Province, China. *Int J Epidemiol* 1987;16:171-6.

55. Tsugane S, Akabane M, Inami T, et al. Urinary salt excretion and stomach cancer mortality among four Japanese populations. *Cancer Causes Control* 1991;2:165-8.

56. Honjo S, Kono S, Yamaguchi M. Salt and geographic variation in stomach cancer mortality in Japan. *Cancer Causes Control* 1994;5:285-6.

57. Imaizumi Y. Longitudinal gompertzian analysis of mortality from stomach cancer in Japan, 1950-1993. *Mech Ageing Dev* 1995;85:133-45.

58. Tominaga S, Kuroishi T. An ecological study on diet/nutrition and cancer in Japan. *Int J Cancer* 1997;Suppl:10-6.

59. Zhuo XG, Watanabe S. Factor analysis of digestive cancer mortality and food consumption in 65 Chinese counties. *J Epidemiol* 1999;9:275-84.

60. Cai L, Yu SZ, Ye WM, et al. Fish sauce and gastric cancer: an ecological study in Fujian Province, China. *World J Gastroenterol* 2000;6:671-5.

61. Nomura A, Grove JS, Stemmermann GN, et

al. A prospective study of stomach cancer and its relation to diet, cigarettes, and alcohol consumption. *Cancer Res* 1990;50:627-31.

62. Tuyns AJ. Salt and gastrointestinal cancer. *Nutr Cancer* 1988;11:229-32.

63. Coggon D, Barker DJ, Cole RB, et al. Stomach cancer and food storage. *J Natl Cancer Inst* 1989;81:1178-82.

64. Boeing H, Jedrychowski W, Wahrendorf J, et al. Dietary risk factors in intestinal and diffuse types of stomach cancer: a multicenter case-control study in Poland. *Cancer Causes Control* 1991;2:227-33.

65. Gonzalez CA, Sanz JM, Marcos G, et al. Dietary factors and stomach cancer in Spain: a multi-centre case-control study. *Int J Cancer* 1991;49:513-9.

66. Falcao JM, Dias JA, Miranda AC, et al. Red wine consumption and gastric cancer in Portugal: a case-control study. *Eur J Cancer Prev* 1994;3:269-76.

67. López-Carrillo L, Lopez-Cervantes M, Ramirez-Espitia A, et al. Alcohol consumption and gastric cancer in Mexico. *Cad Saude Publica* 1998;14:25-32.

68. López-Carrillo L, Lopez-Cervantes M, Ward MH, et al. Nutrient intake and gastric cancer in Mexico. *Int J Cancer* 1999;83:601-5.

69. Nishimoto IN, Hamada GS, Kowalski LP, et al. Risk factors for stomach cancer in Brazil (I): a case-control study among non-Japanese Brazilians in Sao Paulo. *Jpn J Clin Oncol* 2002;32:277-83.

70. Hamada GS, Kowalski LP, Nishimoto IN, et al. Risk factors for stomach cancer in Brazil (II): a case-control study among Japanese Brazilians in Sao Paulo. *Jpn J Clin Oncol* 2002;32:284-90.

71. Sipetic S, Tomic-Kundakovic S, Vlajinac H, et al. [Diet and gastric cancer]. *Vojnosanit Pregl* 2003;60:697-705.

72. Chyou PH, Nomura AM, Hankin JH, et al. A case-cohort study of diet and stomach cancer. *Cancer Res* 1990;50:7501-4.

73. Ward MH, Sinha R, Heineman EF, et al. Risk of adenocarcinoma of the stomach and esophagus with meat cooking method and doneness preference. *Int J Cancer* 1997;71:14-9.

74. Palli D, Russo A, Decarli A. Dietary patterns, nutrient intake and gastric cancer in a high-risk area of Italy. *Cancer Causes Control* 2001;12:163-72.

75. Suh S, Koo B, Choi Y, et al. [The nutritional intakes of the stomach cancer patients in the Daegu and Gyeongbuk areas, Korea]. *Korean J Comm Nutr* 2003;8:202-19.

76. Lissowska J, Gail MH, Pee D, et al. Diet and stomach cancer risk in Warsaw, Poland. *Nutr Cancer* 2004;48:149-59.

77. Qiu JL, Chen K, Wang XB, et al. [A case-control study on the relationship between nutrition and gastric cancer in islanders]. *Chung Hua Liu Hsing Ping Hsueh Tsa Chih* 2004;25 487-91.

78. Kim HJ, Kim MK, Chang WK, et al. Effect of nutrient intake and *Helicobacter pylori* infection on gastric cancer in Korea: a

case-control study. *Nutr Cancer* 2005;52:138-46.

79. Machida-Montani A, Sasazuki S, Inoue M, et al. Association of *Helicobacter pylori* infection and environmental factors in non-cardia gastric cancer in Japan. *Gastric Cancer* 2004;7:46-53.

80. Fontham ET, Ruiz B, Perez A, et al. Determinants of *Helicobacter pylori* infection and chronic gastritis. *Am J Gastroenterol* 1995;90:1094-101.

81. Bergin IL, Sheppard BJ, Fox JG. *Helicobacter pylori* infection and high dietary salt independently induce atrophic gastritis and intestinal metaplasia in commercially available outbred Mongolian gerbils. *Dig Dis Sci* 2003;48:475-85.

82. Takahashi M. [Enhancing effect of a high salt diet on gastrointestinal carcinogenesis]. *Gan No Rinsho* 1986;32:667-73.

83. Shikata K, Kiyohara Y, Kubo M, et al. A prospective study of dietary salt intake and gastric cancer incidence in a defined Japanese population: the Hisayama study. *Int J Cancer* 2006;119:196-201.

84. Strumylaite L, Zickute J, Dudzevicius J, et al. Salt-preserved foods and risk of gastric cancer. *Medicina (Kaunas)* 2006;42:164-70.

85. Phukan RK, Narain K, Zomawia E, et al. Dietary habits and stomach cancer in Mizoram, India. *J Gastroenterol* 2006;41:418-24.

86. Galanis DJ, Kolonel LN, Lee J, et al. Intakes of selected foods and beverages and the incidence of gastric cancer among the Japanese residents of Hawaii: a prospective study. *Int J Epidemiol* 1998;27:173-80.

87. Kato I, Tominaga S, Matsumoto K. A prospective study of stomach cancer among a rural Japanese population: a 6-year survey. *Jpn J Cancer Res* 1992;83:568-75.

88. Khan MM, Goto R, Kobayashi K, et al. Dietary habits and cancer mortality among middle aged and older Japanese living in Hokkaido, Japan by cancer site and sex. 2004;5:58-65.

89. Ngoan LT, Mizoue T, Fujino Y, et al. Dietary factors and stomach cancer mortality. *Br J Cancer* 2002;87:37-42.

90. Gajalakshmi CK, Shanta V. Lifestyle and risk of stomach cancer: a hospital-based case-control study. *Int J Epidemiol* 1996;25:1146-53.

91. Dalgat DM, Aliev RG, Gireev GI, et al. [Epidemiology of stomach cancer in Dagestan]. *Vopr Onkol* 1974;20:76-82.

92. Modan B, Lubin F, Barell V, et al. The role of starches in etiology of gastric cancer. *Cancer* 1974;34:2087-92.

93. Ye EC. [Case-control study of 100 gastric cancer cases]. *Chung Hua Yu Fang I Hsueh Tsa Chih* 1981;15:107-9.

94. Hirayama T. Life-style and cancer: from epidemiological evidence to public behavior change to mortality reduction of target cancers. 1992:65-74.

95. Ji BT, Chow WH, Yang G, et al. Dietary

habits and stomach cancer in Shanghai, China. *Int J Cancer* 1998;76:659-64.

96. Ward MH, Lépez-Carrillo L. Dietary factors and the risk of gastric cancer in Mexico City. *Am J Epidemiol* 1999;149:925-32.

97. Huang XE, Tajima K, Hamajima N, et al. Effect of life styles on the risk of subsite-specific gastric cancer in those with and without family history. *J Epidemiol* 1999;9:40-5.

98. Sriamporn S, Setiawan V, Pisani P, et al. Gastric cancer: the roles of diet, alcohol drinking, smoking and *Helicobacter pylori* in northeastern Thailand. *Asian Pac J Cancer Prev* 2002;3:345-52.

99. Kim HJ, Chang WK, Kim MK, et al. Dietary factors and gastric cancer in Korea: a case-control study. *Int J Cancer* 2002;97:531-5.

100. Nasu K, Oguni I, Kanaya S, et al. Differences in food intake and nutritional status between the areas with low and high standardized mortality ratio for stomach cancer in Shizouka Prefecture. *Jap J Nutr* 1992;50:133-44.

Chapter 4.7

1. World Health Organization. *Guidelines for Drinking-water Quality*. 3rd ed. Geneva: WHO, 2006.

2. World Health Organization, United Nations Children's Fund (UNICEF). 2005. *Water for Life: Making it Happen.* http://www.who.int/entity/water_sanitation_health/waterforlife.pdf.

3. International Agency for Research on Cancer. 1991. *Coffee, Tea, Mate, Methylxanthines and Methylglyoxal.* In: IARC Monogr Eval Carcinog Risks Hum no 51.

4. World Health Organization. *Arsenic in drinking water. Fact sheet no 210.* http://www.who.int/mediacentre/factsheets/fs210/en/index.html. 2006.

5. International Agency for Research on Cancer. 2004. *Some Drinking-water Disinfectants and Contaminants, including Arsenic.* In: IARC Monogr Eval Carcinog Risks Hum no 84. http://monographs.iarc.fr/ENG/Monographs/vol84/volume84.pdf.

6. International Agency for Research on Cancer. 1994. *Schistosomes, Liver Flukes and Helicobacter Pylori.* In: IARC Monogr Eval Carcinog Risks Hum no 61. http://monographs.iarc.fr/ENG/Monographs/vol61/volume61.pdf.

7. Kris-Etherton PM, Hecker KD, Bonanome A, et al. Bioactive compounds in foods: their role in the prevention of cardiovascular disease and cancer. *Am J Med* 2002;113 Suppl 9B:71S-88S.

8. McGee H. *McGee on Food and Cooking.* London: Hodder and Stoughton, 2004.

9. World Health Organization. *Guidelines for Drinking-water Quality*. 3rd ed. Geneva: WHO, 2006.

10. International Agency for Research on Cancer. 2004. *Arsenic in Drinking Water.*

In: IARC Monogr Eval Carcinog Risks Hum no 84.

11. Zenith International. 2005. *Zenith Report on Global Soft Drinks*.

12. Chen CJ, Wu MM, Lee SS, et al. Atherogenicity and carcinogenicity of high-arsenic artesian well water. Multiple risk factors and related malignant neoplasms of blackfoot disease. *Arteriosclerosis* 1988;8:452-60.

13. Chen CL, Hsu LI, Chiou HY, et al. Ingested arsenic, cigarette smoking, and lung cancer risk: a follow-up study in arseniasis-endemic areas in Taiwan. *JAMA* 2004;292:2984-90.

14. Chiou HY, Hsueh YM, Liaw KF, et al. Incidence of internal cancers and ingested inorganic arsenic: a seven-year follow-up study in Taiwan. *Cancer Res* 1995;55:1296-300.

15. Nakadaira H, Endoh K, Katagiri M, et al. Elevated mortality from lung cancer associated with arsenic exposure for a limited duration. *J Occup Environ Med* 2002;44:291-9.

16. Tsuda T, Nagira T, Yamamoto M, et al. Malignant neoplasms among residents who drank well water contaminated by arsenic from a king's yellow factory. *J UOEH* 1989;11 Suppl:289-301.

17. Tsuda T, Babazono A, Yamamoto E, et al. Ingested arsenic and internal cancer: a historical cohort study followed for 33 years. *Am J Epidemiol* 1995;141:198-209.

18. Chen CJ, Chuang YC, You SL, et al. A retrospective study on malignant neoplasms of bladder, lung and liver in blackfoot disease endemic area in Taiwan. *Br J Cancer* 1986;53:399-405.

19. Ferreccio C, Gonzalez C, Milosavjlevic V, et al. Lung cancer and arsenic concentrations in drinking water in Chile. *Epidemiology* 2000;11:673-9.

20. Brueschweiler BJ, Schlatter JR, de Weck D, et al. Occurrence of arsenic in drinking water of the canton of Valais Part II: epidemiological comparison between arsenic concentrations and cancer incidence rates. *Mitt Lebensmitteluntersuchung Hyg* 2005;96:106-17.

21. Buchet JP, Lison D. Mortality by cancer in groups of the Belgian population with a moderately increased intake of arsenic. *Int Arch Occup Environ Health* 1998;71:125-30.

22. Chen CJ, Wang CJ. Ecological correlation between arsenic level in well water and age-adjusted mortality from malignant neoplasms. *Cancer Res* 1990;50:5470-4.

23. Chen CJ, Kuo TL, Wu MM. Arsenic and cancers. *Lancet* 1988;1:414-5.

24. Chen CJ, Chuang YC, Lin TM, et al. Malignant neoplasms among residents of a blackfoot disease-endemic area in Taiwan: high-arsenic artesian well water and cancers. *Cancer Res* 1985;45:5895-9.

25. Chiu HF, Ho SC, Yang CY. Lung cancer mortality reduction after installation of tap-water supply system in an arseniasis-endemic area in Southwestern Taiwan. *Lung Cancer* 2004;46:265-70.

26. Guo HR. Arsenic Level in Drinking Water and Mortality of Lung Cancer (Taiwan). *Cancer Causes Control* 2004;15:171-7.

27. Hopenhayn-Rich C, Biggs ML, Smith AH. Lung and kidney cancer mortality associated with arsenic in drinking water in Cordoba, Argentina. *Int J Epidemiol* 1998;27:561-9.

28. Schrauzer GN, White DA, Schneider CJ. Cancer mortality correlation studies - IV: associations with dietary intakes and blood levels of certain trace elements, notably Se-antagonists. *Bioinorg Chem* 1977;7:35-56.

29. Smith AH, Goycolea M, Haque R, et al. Marked increase in bladder and lung cancer mortality in a region of Northern Chile due to arsenic in drinking water. *Am J Epidemiol* 1998;147:660-9.

30. Tsai SM, Wang TN, Ko YC. Mortality for certain diseases in areas with high levels of arsenic in drinking water. *Arch Environ Health* 1999;54:186-93.

31. Hsueh YM, Chiou HY, Huang YL, et al. Serum beta-carotene level, arsenic methylation capability, and incidence of skin cancer. *Cancer Epidemiol Biomarkers Prev* 1997;6:589-96.

32. Lewis DR, Southwick JW, Ouellet-Hellstrom R, et al. Drinking water arsenic in Utah: a cohort mortality study. *Environ Health Perspect* 1999;107:359-65.

33. Chen YC, Guo YL, Su HJ, et al. Arsenic methylation and skin cancer risk in southwestern Taiwan. *J Occup Environ Med* 2003;45:241-8.

34. Chen YC, Xu L, Guo YL, et al. Genetic polymorphism in p53 codon 72 and skin cancer in southwestern Taiwan. *J Environ Sci Health A Tox Hazard Subst Environ Eng* 2003;38:201-11.

35. Pesch B, Ranft U, Jakubis P, et al. Environmental arsenic exposure from a coal-burning power plant as a potential risk factor for nonmelanoma skin carcinoma: results from a case-control study in the district of Prievidza, Slovakia. *Am J Epidemiol* 2002;155:798-809.

36. Beane Freeman LE, Dennis LK, Lynch CF, et al. Toenail arsenic content and cutaneous melanoma in Iowa. *Am J Epidemiol* 2004;160:679-87.

37. Karagas MR, Stukel TA, Morris JS, et al. Skin cancer risk in relation to toenail arsenic concentrations in a US population-based case-control study. *Am J Epidemiol* 2001;153:559-65.

38. Hsueh YM, Cheng GS, Wu MM, et al. Multiple risk factors associated with arsenic-induced skin cancer: effects of chronic liver disease and malnutritional status. *Br J Cancer* 1995;71:109-14.

39. Guo HR, Yu HS, Hu H, et al. Arsenic in drinking water and skin cancers: cell-type specificity (Taiwan, ROC). *Cancer Causes Control* 2001;12:909-16.

40. Wu MM, Kuo TL, Hwang YH, et al. Dose-response relation between arsenic concentration in well water and mortality from cancers and vascular diseases. *Am J Epidemiol* 1989;130:1123-32.

41. Tseng WP. Effects and dose - response relationships of skin cancer and blackfoot disease with arsenic. *Environ Health Perspect* 1977;19:109-19.

42. Morton W, Starr G, Pohl D, et al. Skin cancer and water arsenic in Lane County, Oregon. *Cancer* 1976;37:2523-32.

43. Tseng WP, Chu HM, How SW, et al. Prevalence of skin cancer in an endemic area of chronic arsenicism in Taiwan. *J Natl Cancer Inst* 1968;40:453-63.

44. Kurttio P, Pukkala E, Kahelin H, et al. Arsenic concentrations in well water and risk of bladder and kidney cancer in Finland. *Environ Health Perspect* 1999;107:705-10.

45. Chiou HY, Chiou ST, Hsu YH, et al. Incidence of transitional cell carcinoma and arsenic in drinking water: a follow-up study of 8,102 residents in an arseniasis-endemic area in northeastern Taiwan. *Am J Epidemiol* 2001;153:411-8.

46. Yang CY, Chiu HF, Wu TN, et al. Reduction in kidney cancer mortality following installation of a tap water supply system in an arsenic-endemic area of Taiwan. *Arch Environ Health* 2004;59:484-8.

47. Hinwood AL, Jolley DJ, Sim MR. Cancer incidence and high environmental arsenic concentrations in rural populations: results of an ecological study. *Int J Environ Health Res* 1999;9:131-41.

48. Chen CJ, Chen CW, Wu MM, et al. Cancer potential in liver, lung, bladder and kidney due to ingested inorganic arsenic in drinking water. *Br J Cancer* 1992;66:888-92.

49. Tchounwou PB, Patlolla AK, Centeno JA. Carcinogenic and systemic health effects associated with arsenic exposure - a critical review. *Toxicol Pathol* 2003;31:575-88.

50. Apostoli P, Sarnico M, Bavazzano P, et al. Arsenic and porphyrins. *Am J Ind Med* 2002;42:180-7.

51. Michaud DS, Wright ME, Cantor KP, et al. Arsenic concentrations in prediagnostic toenails and the risk of bladder cancer in a cohort study of male smokers. *Am J Epidemiol* 2004;160:853-9.

52. Yang CY, Chiu HF, Chang CC, et al. Bladder cancer mortality reduction after installation of a tap-water supply system in an arsenious-endemic area in southwestern Taiwan. *Environ Res* 2005;98:127-32.

53. Bates MN, Rey OA, Biggs ML, et al. Case-control study of bladder cancer and exposure to arsenic in Argentina. *Am J Epidemiol* 2004;159:381-9.

54. Bates MN, Smith AH, Cantor KP. Case-control study of bladder cancer and arsenic in drinking water. *Am J Epidemiol* 1995;141:523-30.

55. Steinmaus C, Yuan Y, Bates MN, et al. Case-control study of bladder cancer and drinking water arsenic in the western United States. *Am J Epidemiol* 2003;158:1193-201.

56. Chen YC, Su HJ, Guo YL, et al. Arsenic

methylation and bladder cancer risk in Taiwan. *Cancer Causes Control* 2003;14:303-10.

57. Chen YC, Su HJ, Guo YL, et al. Interaction between environmental tobacco smoke and arsenic methylation ability on the risk of bladder cancer. *Cancer Causes Control* 2005;16:75-81.

58. Chen YC, Xu L, Guo YL, et al. Polymorphisms in GSTT1 and p53 and urinary transitional cell carcinoma in south-western Taiwan: a preliminary study. *Biomarkers* 2004;9:386-94.

59. Su HJ, Guo L, Lai MD, et al. The NAT2* slow acetylator genotype is associated with bladder cancer in Taiwanese, but not in the black foot disease endemic area population. *Pharmacogenetics* 1998;8:187-90.

60. Karagas MR, Tosteson TD, Morris JS, et al. Incidence of transitional cell carcinoma of the bladder and arsenic exposure in New Hampshire. *Cancer Causes Control* 2004;15:465-72.

61. Lamm SH, Engel A, Kruse MB, et al. Arsenic in drinking water and bladder cancer mortality in the United States: an analysis based on 133 U.S. counties and 30 years of observation. *J Occup Environ Med* 2004;46:298-306.

62. Guo HR, Tseng YC. Arsenic in drinking water and bladder cancer: comparison between studies based on cancer registry and death certificates. *Environ Geochem Health* 2000;22:83-91.

63. Guo HR, Chiang HS, Hu H, et al. Arsenic in drinking water and incidence of urinary cancers. *Epidemiology* 1997;8:545-50.

64. Hopenhayn-Rich C, Biggs ML, Fuchs A, et al. Bladder cancer mortality associated with arsenic in drinking water in Argentina. *Epidemiology* 1996;7:117-24.

65. Buchet J, Lison D. Clues and uncertainties in the risk assessment of arsenic in drinking water. *Food Chem Toxicol* 2000;38:S81-5.

66. Gebel T. Confounding variables in the environmental toxicology of arsenic. *Toxicology* 2000;144:155-62.

67. Stolzenberg-Solomon RZ, Pietinen P, Taylor PR, et al. Prospective study of diet and pancreatic cancer in male smokers. *Am J Epidemiol* 2002;155:783-92.

68. Nomura A, Heilbrun LK, Stemmermann GN. Prospective study of coffee consumption and the risk of cancer. *J Natl Cancer Inst* 1986;76:587-90.

69. Hiatt RA, Klatsky AL, Armstrong MA. Pancreatic cancer, blood glucose and beverage consumption. *Int J Cancer* 1988;41:794-7.

70. Friedman GD, van den Eeden SK. Risk factors for pancreatic cancer: an exploratory study. *Int J Epidemiol* 1993;22:30-7.

71. Shibata A, Mack TM, Paganini-Hill A, et al. A prospective study of pancreatic cancer in the elderly. *Int J Cancer* 1994;58:46-9.

72. Harnack LJ, Anderson KE, Zheng W, et al. Smoking, alcohol, coffee, and tea intake and incidence of cancer of the exocrine pancreas: the Iowa Women's Health Study. *Cancer Epidemiol Biomarkers Prev* 1997;6:1081-6.

73. Jacobsen BK, Bjelke E, Kvale G, et al. Coffee drinking, mortality, and cancer incidence: results from a Norwegian prospective study. *J Natl Cancer Inst* 1986;76:823-31.

74. Stensvold I, Jacobsen BK. Coffee and cancer: a prospective study of 43,000 Norwegian men and women. *Cancer Causes Control* 1994;5:401-8.

75. Michaud DS, Giovannucci E, Willett WC, et al. Coffee and alcohol consumption and the risk of pancreatic cancer in two prospective United States cohorts. *Cancer Epidemiol Biomarkers Prev* 2001;10:429-37.

76. Lin Y, Tamakoshi A, Kawamura T, et al. Risk of pancreatic cancer in relation to alcohol drinking, coffee consumption and medical history: findings from the Japan collaborative cohort study for evaluation of cancer risk. *Int J Cancer* 2002;99:742-6.

77. Elinder CG, Millqvist K, Floderus-Myrhed B, et al. Swedish studies do not support the hypothesis about a connection between coffee and cancer of the pancreas. *Lakartidningen* 1981;78:3676-7.

78. Whittemore AS, Paffenbarger RS, Jr., Anderson K, et al. Early precursors of pancreatic cancer in college men. *J Chronic Dis* 1983;36:251-6.

79. Snowdon DA, Phillips RL. Coffee consumption and risk of fatal cancers. *Am J Public Health* 1984;74:820-3.

80. Hirayama T. Epidemiology of pancreatic cancer in Japan. *Jpn J Clin Oncol* 1989;19:208-15.

81. Zheng W, McLaughlin JK, Gridley G, et al. A cohort study of smoking, alcohol consumption, and dietary factors for pancreatic cancer (United States). *Cancer Causes Control* 1993;4:477-82.

82. Klatsky AL, Armstrong MA, Friedman GD. Coffee, tea, and mortality. *Ann Epidemiol* 1993;3:375-81.

83. Khan MM, Goto R, Kobayashi K, et al. Dietary habits and cancer mortality among middle aged and older Japanese living in Hokkaido, Japan by cancer site and sex. 2004;5:58-65.

84. Gold EB, Gordis L, Diener MD, et al. Diet and other risk factors for cancer of the pancreas. *Cancer* 1985;55:460-7.

85. Mack TM, Yu MC, Hanisch R, et al. Pancreas cancer and smoking, beverage consumption, and past medical history. *J Natl Cancer Inst* 1986;76:49-60.

86. Stefanati A, Saletti C, Califano A, et al. Coffee, alcohol, smoking and risk of cancer of the pancreas: a case-control study. *J Prev Med Hyg* 1992;33:65-70.

87. MacMahon B, Yen S, Trichopoulos D, et al. Coffee and cancer of the pancreas. *N Engl J Med* 1981;304:630-3.

88. Norell SE, Ahlbom A, Erwald R, et al. Diet and pancreatic cancer: a case-control study. *Am J Epidemiol* 1986;124:894-902.

89. Clavel F, Benhamou E, Auquier A, et al. Coffee, alcohol, smoking and cancer of the pancreas: a case-control study. *Int J Cancer* 1989;43:17-21.

90. Cuzick J, Babiker AG. Pancreatic cancer, alcohol, diabetes mellitus and gall-bladder disease. *Int J Cancer* 1989;43:415-21.

91. Pfeffer F, Avilas RH, Vargas F, et al. [Smoking, consumption of alcoholic beverages and coffee as factors associated with the development of cancer of the pancreas]. *Rev Invest Clin* 1989;41:205-8.

92. Olsen GW, Mandel JS, Gibson RW, et al. A case-control study of pancreatic cancer and cigarettes, alcohol, coffee and diet. *Am J Public Health* 1989;79:1016-9.

93. Bueno de Mesquita HB, Maisonneuve P, Moerman CJ, et al. Lifetime consumption of alcoholic beverages, tea and coffee and exocrine carcinoma of the pancreas: a population-based case-control study in The Netherlands. *Int J Cancer* 1992;50:514-22.

94. Lyon JL, Mahoney AW, French TK, et al. Coffee consumption and the risk of cancer of the exocrine pancreas: a case-control study in a low-risk population. 1992;3:164-70.

95. Mizuno S, Watanabe S, Nakamura K, et al. A multi-institute case-control study on the risk factors of developing pancreatic cancer. *Jpn J Clin Oncol* 1992;22:286-91.

96. Kalapothaki V, Tzonou A, Hsieh CC, et al. Tobacco, ethanol, coffee, pancreatitis, diabetes mellitus, and cholelithiasis as risk factors for pancreatic carcinoma. *Cancer Causes Control* 1993;4:375-82.

97. Sciallero S, Bonelli L, Saccomanno S, et al. Socioeconomic characteristics, life style, diabetes, family history of cancer and risk of pancreatic cancer. *Eur J Gastroenterol Hepatol* 1993;5:367-71.

98. Kreiger N, LaCroix J, Sloan M. Hormonal factors and pancreatic cancer in women. *Ann Epidemiol* 2001;11:563-7.

99. Falk RT, Pickle LW, Fontham ET, et al. Life-style risk factors for pancreatic cancer in Louisiana: a case-control study. *Am J Epidemiol* 1988;128:324-36.

100. Wynder EL, Hall NE, Polansky M. Epidemiology of coffee and pancreatic cancer. *Cancer Res* 1983;43:3900-6.

101. Kinlen LJ, McPherson K. Pancreas cancer and coffee and tea consumption: a case-control study. *Br J Cancer* 1984;49:93-6.

102. Goiriena De Gandarias FJ, Santidrian MI, Barranquero AM. Etiopathogenic study of cancer of the digestive tract in Biscay Spain with special emphasis on the role played by diet and consumption of alcohol and tobacco. *Rev Sanid Hig Publica (Madr)* 1987;62:1411-30.

103. La Vecchia C, Liati P, Decarli A, et al. Coffee consumption and risk of pancreatic cancer. *Int J Cancer* 1987;40:309-13.

104. Voirol M, Infante F, Raymond L, et al. [Nutritional profile of patients with cancer of the pancreas]. *Schweiz Med Wochenschr* 1987;117:1101-4.

105. Gorham ED, Garland CF, Garland FC, et al. Coffee and pancreatic cancer in a rural California county. 1988;148:48-53.

106. Farrow DC, Davis S. Risk of pancreatic cancer in relation to medical history and the use of tobacco, alcohol and coffee. *Int J Cancer* 1990;45:816-20.

107. Ghadirian P, Simard A, Baillargeon J. Tobacco, alcohol, and coffee and cancer of the pancreas. A population-based, case-control study in Quebec, Canada. *Cancer* 1991;67:2664-70.

108. Baghurst PA, McMichael AJ, Slavotinek AH, et al. A case-control study of diet and cancer of the pancreas. *Am J Epidemiol* 1991;134:167-79.

109. Jain M, Howe GR, St Louis P, et al. Coffee and alcohol as determinants of risk of pancreas cancer: a case-control study from Toronto. *Int J Cancer* 1991;47:384-9.

110. Cortes Vizcaino C, Sabater Pons A, Calatayud Sarthoud A, et al. A case-control study of cancer of the pancreas. *Oncologia* 1993;16:65-9.

111. Zatonski WA, Boyle P, Przewozniak K, et al. Cigarette smoking, alcohol, tea and coffee consumption and pancreas cancer risk: a case-control study from Opole, Poland. *Int J Cancer* 1993;53:601-7.

112. Gullo L, Pezzilli R, Morselli-Labate AM. Coffee and cancer of the pancreas: an Italian multicenter study. The Italian Pancreatic Cancer Study Group. 1995;11:223-9.

113. Partanen T, Hemminki K, Vainio H, et al. Coffee consumption not associated with risk of pancreas cancer in Finland. *Prev Med* 1995;24:213-6.

114. Kokic NZ, Adanja JB, Vlajinac DH, et al. Case-control study of pancreatic cancer in Serbia, Yugoslavia. 1996;43:353-6.

115. Nishi M, Ohba S, Hirata K, et al. Dose-response relationship between coffee and the risk of pancreas cancer. *Jpn J Clin Oncol* 1996;26:42-8.

116. Silverman DT, Swanson CA, Gridley G, et al. Dietary and nutritional factors and pancreatic cancer: a case-control study based on direct interviews. *J Natl Cancer Inst* 1998;90:1710-9.

117. Villeneuve PJ, Johnson KC, Hanley AJ, et al. Alcohol, tobacco and coffee consumption and the risk of pancreatic cancer: results from the Canadian Enhanced Surveillance System case-control project. Canadian Cancer Registries Epidemiology Research Group. *Eur J Cancer Prev* 2000;9:49-58.

118. Alguacil J, Kauppinen T, Porta M, et al. Risk of pancreatic cancer and occupational exposures in Spain. PANKRAS II Study Group. *Ann Occup Hyg* 2000;44:391-403.

119. Mori M, Hariharan M, Anandakumar M, et al. A case-control study on risk factors for pancreatic diseases in Kerala, India. *Hepatogastroenterology* 1999;46:25-30.

120. Stocks P. Cancer mortality in relation to national consumption of cigarettes, solid fuel, tea and coffee. *Br J Cancer* 1970;24:215-25.

121. Schrauzer GN. Cancer mortality correlation studies. II. Regional associations of mortalities with the consumptions of foods and other commodities. *Med Hypotheses* 1976;2:39-49.

122. Cuckle HS, Kinlen LJ. Coffee and cancer of the pancreas. *Br J Cancer* 1981;44:760-1.

123. Benhamou S, Clavel F, Rezvani A, et al. [Relation between mortality in cancer of the pancreas and food and tobacco consumption in France]. *Biomed Pharmacother* 1982;36:389-92.

124. Benarde MA, Weiss W. Coffee consumption and pancreatic cancer: temporal and spatial correlation. *BMJ* 1982;284:400-2.

125. Binstock M, Krakow D, Stamler J, et al. Coffee and pancreatic cancer: an analysis of international mortality data. *Am J Epidemiol* 1983;118:630-40.

126. Hara N, Sakata K, Nagai M, et al. [Geographical difference of mortality of digestive cancers and food consumption]. *Gan No Rinsho* 1984;30:1665-74.

127. Kato I, Tajima K, Kuroishi T, et al. Latitude and pancreatic cancer. *Jpn J Clin Oncol* 1985;15:403-13.

128. Decarli A, La VC. Environmental factors and cancer mortality in Italy: correlational exercise. *Oncology* 1986;43:116-26.

129. Vioque J, Gonzalez SL, Cayuela DA. [Cancer of the pancreas: an ecologic study]. *Med Clin (Barc)* 1990;95:121-5.

130. Cortes VC, Saiz SC, Gimenez Fernandez FJ, et al. Ecologic correlation of consumption in Spain and pancreas cancer mortality. *Oncologia* 1992;15:190-7.

131. Prineas RJ, Folsom AR, Zhang ZM, et al. Nutrition and other risk factors for renal cell carcinoma in postmenopausal women. *Epidemiology* 1997;8:31-6.

132. Hiatt RA, Tolan K, Quesenberry CP, Jr. Renal cell carcinoma and thiazide use: a historical, case-control study (California, USA). *Cancer Causes Control* 1994;5:319-25.

133. Washio M, Mori M, Sakauchi F, et al. Risk factors for kidney cancer in a Japanese population: findings from the JACC study. *J Epidemiol* 2005;15:S203-S11.

134. Nicodemus KK, Sweeney C, Folsom AR. Evaluation of dietary, medical and lifestyle risk factors for incident kidney cancer in postmenopausal women. *Int J Cancer* 2004;108:115-21.

135. Mucci LA, Lindblad P, Steineck G, et al. Dietary acrylamide and risk of renal cell cancer. *Int J Cancer* 2004;109:774-6.

136. Mattioli S, Truffelli D, Baldasseroni A, et al. Occupational risk factors for renal cell cancer: a case - control study in northern Italy. *J Occup Environ Med* 2002;44:1028-36.

137. Yuan JM, Gago-Dominguez M, Castelao JE, et al. Cruciferous vegetables in relation to renal cell carcinoma. *Int J Cancer* 1998;77:211-6.

138. Kreiger N, Marrett LD, Dodds L, et al. Risk factors for renal cell carcinoma: results of a population-based case-control study. *Cancer Causes Control* 1993;4:101-10.

139. Yu MC, Mack TM, Hanisch R, et al. Cigarette smoking, obesity, diuretic use, and coffee consumption as risk factors for renal cell carcinoma. *J Natl Cancer Inst* 1986;77:351-6.

140. Mclaughlin JK, Mandel JS, Blot WJ, et al. A population-based case-control study of renal cell carcinoma. *J Natl Cancer Inst* 1984;72:275-84.

141. Benhamou S, Lenfant MH, Ory-Paoletti C, et al. Risk factors for renal-cell carcinoma in a French case-control study. *Int J Cancer* 1993;55:32-6.

142. Goodman MT, Morgenstern H, Wynder EL. A case-control study of factors affecting the development of renal cell cancer. *Am J Epidemiol* 1986;124:926-41.

143. Armstrong B, Garrod A, Doll R. A retrospective study of renal cancer with special reference to coffee and animal protein consumption. *Br J Cancer* 1976;33:127-36.

144. Wynder EL, Mabuchi K, Whitmore WF, Jr. Epidemiology of adenocarcinoma of the kidney. *J Natl Cancer Inst* 1974;53:1619-34.

145. Boeing H, Schlehofer B, Wahrendorf J. Diet, obesity and risk for renal cell carcinoma: results from a case control-study in Germany. *Z Ernahrungswiss* 1997;36:3-11.

146. Wolk A, Gridley G, Niwa S, et al. International renal cell cancer study. VII. Role of diet. *Int J Cancer* 1996;65:67-73.

147. Chow WH, Gridley G, Mclaughlin JK, et al. Protein intake and risk of renal cell cancer. *J Natl Cancer Inst* 1994;86:1131-9.

148. Mclaughlin JK, Gao YT, Gao RN, et al. Risk factors for renal-cell cancer in Shanghai, China. *Int J Cancer* 1992;52:562-5.

149. Maclure M, Willett W. A case-control study of diet and risk of renal adenocarcinoma. *Epidemiology* 1990;1:430-40.

150. Asal NR, Risser DR, Kadamani S, et al. Risk factors in renal cell carcinoma: I. Methodology, demographics, tobacco, beverage use, and obesity. *Cancer Detect Prev* 1988;11:359-77.

151. McCredie M, Ford JM, Stewart JH. Risk factors for cancer of the renal parenchyma. *Int J Cancer* 1988;42:13-6.

152. Talamini R, Baron AE, Barra S, et al. A case-control study of risk factor for renal cell cancer in northern Italy. *Cancer Causes Control* 1990;1:125-31.

153. Armstrong B, Doll R. Environmental factors and cancer incidence and mortality in different countries, with special reference to dietary practices. *Int J Cancer* 1975;15:617-31.

154. Lee JE, Giovannucci E, Smith-Warner SA, et al. Total fluid intake and use of individual beverages and risk of renal cell cancer in two large cohorts. *Cancer Epidemiol Biomarkers Prev* 2006;15:1204-11.

155. Vassallo A, Correa P, De Stefani E, et al. Esophageal cancer in Uruguay: a case-control study. *J Natl Cancer Inst* 1985;75:1005-9.

156. Victora CG, Munoz N, Day NE, et al. Hot beverages and oesophageal cancer in

southern Brazil: a case-control study. *Int J Cancer* 1987;39:710-6.

157. De Stefani E, Munoz N, Esteve J, et al. Mate drinking, alcohol, tobacco, diet, and esophageal cancer in Uruguay. *Cancer Res* 1990;50:426-31.

158. Rolon PA, Castellsague X, Benz M, et al. Hot and cold mate drinking and esophageal cancer in Paraguay. *Cancer Epidemiol Biomarkers Prev* 1995;4:595-605.

159. Dietz J, Pardo SH, Furtado CD, et al. [Risk factors related to esophageal cancer in Rio Grande do Sul, Brazil]. *Rev Assoc Med Bras* 1998;44:269-72.

160. Castelletto R, Castellsague X, Munoz N, et al. Alcohol, tobacco, diet, mate drinking, and esophageal cancer in Argentina. *Cancer Epidemiol Biomarkers Prev* 1994;3:557-64.

161. Sewram V, De Stefani E, Brennan P, et al. Mate consumption and the risk of squamous cell esophageal cancer in Uruguay. *Cancer Epidemiol Biomarkers Prev* 2003;12:508-13.

162. De Stefani E, Boffetta P, Deneo-Pellegrini H, et al. The role of vegetable and fruit consumption in the aetiology of squamous cell carcinoma of the oesophagus: a case-control study in Uruguay. *Int J Cancer* 2005;116:130-5.

163. De Stefani E, Deneo-Pellegrini H, Ronco AL, et al. Food groups and risk of squamous cell carcinoma of the oesophagus: a case-control study in Uruguay. *Br J Cancer* 2003;89:1209-14.

164. Sichieri R, Everhart JE, Mendonça GAS. Diet and mortality from common cancers in Brazil: an ecological study. *Cad Saude Publica* 1996;12:53-9.

165. De Stefani E, Correa P, Oreggia F, et al. Risk factors for laryngeal cancer. *Cancer* 1987;60:3087-91.

166. Franco EL, Kowalski LP, Oliveira BV, et al. Risk factors for oral cancer in Brazil: a case-control study. *Int J Cancer* 1989;43:992-1000.

167. Oreggia F, De Stefani E, Correa P, et al. Risk factors for cancer of the tongue in Uruguay. *Cancer* 1991;67:180-3.

168. Pintos J, Franco EL, Oliveira BV, et al. Mate, coffee, and tea consumption and risk of cancers of the upper aerodigestive tract in southern Brazil. *Epidemiology* 1994;5:583-90.

169. Nishimoto IN, Pintos J, Schlecht NF, et al. Assessment of control selection bias in a hospital-based case-control study of upper aero-digestive tract cancers. *J Cancer Epidemiol Prev* 2002;7:131-41.

170. Toporcov TN, Antunes JL, Tavares MR. Fat food habitual intake and risk of oral cancer. *Oral Oncol* 2004;40:925-31.

171. Goldenberg D. Mate: a risk factor for oral and oropharyngeal cancer. *Oral Oncol* 2002;38:646-9.

172. Goldenberg D, Golz A, Joachims HZ. The beverage mate: a risk factor for cancer of the head and neck. *Head Neck* 2003;25:595-601.

173. Chyou PH, Nomura AMY, Stemmermann GN. Diet, alcohol, smoking and cancer of the upper aerodigestive tract: a prospective study among Hawaii Japanese men. *Int J Cancer* 1995;60:616-21.

174. Kinjo Y, Cui Y, Akiba S, et al. Mortality risks of oesophageal cancer associated with hot tea, alcohol, tobacco and diet in Japan. *J Epidemiol* 1998;8:235-43.

175. Tran GD, Sun XD, Abnet CC, et al. Prospective study of risk factors for esophageal and gastric cancers in the Linxian general population trial cohort in China. *Int J Cancer* 2005;113:456-63.

176. Guo W, Blot WJ, Li JY, et al. A nested case-control study of oesophageal and stomach cancers in the Linxian nutrition intervention trial. *Int J Epidemiol* 1994;23:444-50.

177. De Jong UW, Breslow N, Hong JG, et al. Aetiological factors in oesophageal cancer in Singapore Chinese. *Int J Cancer* 1974;13:291-303.

178. Gao YT, McLaughlin JK, Gridley G, et al. Risk factors for esophageal cancer in Shanghai, China. II. Role of diet and nutrients. *Int J Cancer* 1994;58:197-202.

179. Hanaoka T, Tsugane S, Ando N, et al. Alcohol consumption and risk of esophageal cancer in Japan: a case-control study in seven hospitals. *Jpn J Clin Oncol* 1994;24:241-6.

180. Srivastava M, Kapil U, Chattopadhyaya TK, et al. Nutritional risk factors in carcinoma esophagus. *Nutr Res* 1995;15:177-85.

181. Garidou A, Tzonou A, Lipworth L, et al. Life-style factors and medical conditions in relation to esophageal cancer by histologic type in a low-risk population. *Int J Cancer* 1996;68:295-9.

182. Nayar D, Kapil U, Joshi YK, et al. Nutritional risk factors in esophageal cancer. *J Assoc Physicians India* 2000;48:781-7.

183. Phukan RK, Chetia CK, Ali MS, et al. Role of dietary habits in the development of esophageal cancer in Assam, the north-eastern region of India. *Nutr Cancer* 2001;39:204-9.

184. Terry P, Lagergren J, Wolk A, et al. Drinking hot beverages is not associated with risk of esophageal cancers in a Western population. *Br J Cancer* 2001;84:120-1.

185. Sharp L, Chilvers CE, Cheng KK, et al. Risk factors for squamous cell carcinoma of the oesophagus in women: a case-control study. *Br J Cancer* 2001;85:1667-70.

186. Onuk MD, Oztopuz A, Memik F. Risk factors for esophageal cancer in eastern Anatolia. *Hepatogastroenterology* 2002;49:1290-2.

187. Hu J, Nyren O, Wolk A, et al. Risk factors for oesophageal cancer in northeast China. *Int J Cancer* 1994;57:38-46.

188. Gao CM, Takezaki T, Ding JH, et al. Protective effect of allium vegetables against both esophageal and stomach cancer: a simultaneous case-referent study of a high-epidemic area in Jiangsu Province, China. *Jpn J Cancer Res* 1999;90:614-21.

189. Zhang W, An F, Lin H. [A case-control study on the risk factors of esophageal cancer in Jieyang City of Guangdong in China]. *Zhonghua Liu Xing Bing Xue Za Zhi* 2001;22:442-5.

190. Yang CX, Wang HY, Wang ZM, et al. Risk factors for esophageal cancer: a case-control study in South-western China. *Asian Pac J Cancer Prev* 2005;6:48-53.

191. Hung HC, Huang MC, Lee JM, et al. Association between diet and esophageal cancer in Taiwan. *J Gastroenterol Hepatol* 2004;19:632-7.

192. Tavani A, Negri E, Franceschi S, et al. Risk factors for esophageal cancer in women in northern Italy. *Cancer* 1993;72:2531-6.

193. Terry P, Lagergren J, Ye W, et al. Antioxidants and cancers of the esophagus and gastric cardia. *Int J Cancer* 2000;87:750-4.

194. Nakachi K, Imai K, Hoshiyama Y, et al. The joint effects of two factors in the aetiology of oesophageal cancer in Japan. *J Epidemiol Community Health* 1988;42:355-64.

195. Cheng KK, Day NE, Duffy SW, et al. Pickled vegetables in the aetiology of oesophageal cancer in Hong Kong Chinese. *Lancet* 1992;339:1314-8.

196. Cheng KK, Duffy SW, Day NE, et al. Oesophageal cancer in never-smokers and never-drinkers. *Int J Cancer* 1995;60:820-2.

Chapter 4.8

1. Kjaerheim K, Gaard M, Andersen A. The role of alcohol, tobacco, and dietary factors in upper aerogastric tract cancers: a prospective study of 10,900 Norwegian men. *Cancer Causes Control* 1998;9:99-108.

2. Boeing H. Alcohol and risk of cancer of the upper gastrointestinal tract: first analysis of the EPIC data. *IARC Sci Publ* 2002;156:151-4.

3. Zheng W, Sellers TA, Doyle TJ, et al. Retinol, antioxidant vitamins, and cancers of the upper digestive tract in a prospective cohort study of postmenopausal women. *Am J Epidemiol* 1995;142:955-60.

4. Gronbaek M, Becker U, Johansen D, et al. Population based cohort study of the association between alcohol intake and cancer of the upper digestive tract. *BMJ* 1998;317:844-7.

5. Kasum CM, Jacobs DR, Jr., Nicodemus K, et al. Dietary risk factors for upper aerodigestive tract cancers. *Int J Cancer* 2002;99:267-72.

6. Kato I, Nomura AM, Stemmermann GN, et al. Prospective study of the association of alcohol with cancer of the upper aerodigestive tract and other sites. *Cancer Causes Control* 1992;3:145-51.

7. Crosignani P, Russo A, Tagliabue G, et al. Tobacco and diet as determinants of survival in male laryngeal cancer patients. *Int J Cancer* 1996;65:308-13.

8. Maier H, Dietz A, Gewelke U, et al. Tobacco

and alcohol and the risk of head and neck cancer. *Clin Investig* 1992;70:320-7.

9. Wynder EL, Covey LS, Mabuchi K, et al. Environmental factors in cancer of the larynx: a second look. *Cancer* 1976;38:1591-601.

10. Rothman K, Keller A. The effect of joint exposure to alcohol and tobacco on risk of cancer of the mouth and pharynx. *J Chronic Dis* 1972;25:711-6.

11. Bross ID, Coombs J. Early onset of oral cancer among women who drink and smoke. *Oncology* 1976;33:136-9.

12. Graham S, Dayal H, Rohrer T, et al. Dentition, diet, tobacco, and alcohol in the epidemiology of oral cancer. *J Natl Cancer Inst* 1977;59:1611-8.

13. Jafarey NA, Mahmood Z, Zaidi SH. Habits and dietary pattern of cases of carcinoma of the oral cavity and oropharynx. *J Pak Med Assoc* 1977;27:340-3.

14. Herity B, Moriarty M, Bourke GJ, et al. A case-control study of head and neck cancer in the Republic of Ireland. *Br J Cancer* 1981;43:177-82.

15. Herity B, Moriarty M, Daly L, et al. The role of tobacco and alcohol in the aetiology of lung and larynx cancer. *Br J Cancer* 1982;46:961-4.

16. Bruzzi P, Margarino G, Tonetti R, et al. [A controlled-case study on risk factors in tumors of the oral cavity. Perspectives and indications for early diagnosis]. *Minerva Med* 1983;74:19-24.

17. Elwood JM, Pearson JC, Skippen DH, et al. Alcohol, smoking, social and occupational factors in the aetiology of cancer of the oral cavity, pharynx and larynx. *Int J Cancer* 1984;34:603-12.

18. Zagraniski RT, Kelsey JL, Walter SD. Occupational risk factors for laryngeal carcinoma: Connecticut, 1975-1980. *Am J Epidemiol* 1986;124:67-76.

19. De Stefani E, Correa P, Oreggia F, et al. Risk factors for laryngeal cancer. *Cancer* 1987;60:3087-91.

20. Zemla B, Day N, Swiatnicka J, et al. Larynx cancer risk factors. *Neoplasma* 1987;34:223-33.

21. Brownson RC, Chang JC. Exposure to alcohol and tobacco and the risk of laryngeal cancer. *Arch Environ Health* 1987;42:192-6.

22. Mackerras D, Buffler PA, Randall DE, et al. Carotene intake and the risk of laryngeal cancer in coastal Texas. *Am J Epidemiol* 1988;128:980-8.

23. Tuyns AJ, Esteve J, Raymond L, et al. Cancer of the larynx/hypopharynx, tobacco and alcohol: IARC international case-control study in Turin and Varese (Italy), Zaragoza and Navarra (Spain), Geneva (Switzerland) and Calvados (France). *Int J Cancer* 1988;41:483-91.

24. Sankaranarayanan R, Duffy SW, Day NE, et al. A case-control investigation of cancer of the oral tongue and the floor of the mouth in southern India. *Int J Cancer* 1989;44:617-21.

25. Franco EL, Kowalski LP, Oliveira BV, et al. Risk factors for oral cancer in Brazil: a case-control study. *Int J Cancer* 1989;43:992-1000.

26. Merletti F, Boffetta P, Ciccone G, et al. Role of tobacco and alcoholic beverages in the etiology of cancer of the oral cavity/oropharynx in Torino, Italy. *Cancer Res* 1989;49:4919-24.

27. Falk RT, Pickle LW, Brown LM, et al. Effect of smoking and alcohol consumption on laryngeal cancer risk in coastal Texas. *Cancer Res* 1989;49:4024-9.

28. Sankaranarayanan R, Duffy SW, Padmakumary G, et al. Risk factors for cancer of the buccal and labial mucosa in Kerala, southern India. *J Epidemiol Community Health* 1990;44:286-92.

29. Sankaranarayanan R, Duffy SW, Padmakumary G, et al. Tobacco chewing, alcohol and nasal snuff in cancer of the gingiva in Kerala, India. *Br J Cancer* 1989;60:638-43.

30. La Vecchia C, Negri E, D'Avanzo B, et al. Dietary indicators of laryngeal cancer risk. *Cancer Res* 1990;50:4497-500.

31. Zheng TZ, Boyle P, Hu HF, et al. Tobacco smoking, alcohol consumption, and risk of oral cancer: a case-control study in Beijing, People's Republic of China. *Cancer Causes Control* 1990;1:173-9.

32. Franceschi S, Barra S, La Vecchia C, et al. Risk factors for cancer of the tongue and the mouth. A case-control study from northern Italy. *Cancer* 1992;70:2227-33.

33. Franceschi S, Talamini R, Barra S, et al. Smoking and drinking in relation to cancers of the oral cavity, pharynx, larynx, and esophagus in northern Italy. *Cancer Res* 1990;50:6502-7.

34. Choi SY, Kahyo H. Effect of cigarette smoking and alcohol consumption in the aetiology of cancer of the oral cavity, pharynx and larynx. *Int J Epidemiol* 1991;20:878-85.

35. La Vecchia C, Negri E, D'Avanzo B, et al. Dietary indicators of oral and pharyngeal cancer. *Int J Epidemiol* 1991;20:39-44.

36. Freudenheim JL, Graham S, Byers TE, et al. Diet, smoking, and alcohol in cancer of the larynx: a case-control study. *Nutr Cancer* 1992;17:33-45.

37. Zheng W, Blot WJ, Shu XO, et al. Risk factors for oral and pharyngeal cancer in Shanghai, with emphasis on diet. *Cancer Epidemiol Biomarkers Prev* 1992;1:441-8.

38. Zheng W, Blot WJ, Shu XO, et al. Diet and other risk factors for laryngeal cancer in Shanghai, China. *Am J Epidemiol* 1992;136:178-91.

39. Lopez-Abente G, Pollan M, Monge V, et al. Tobacco smoking, alcohol consumption, and laryngeal cancer in Madrid. *Cancer Detect Prev* 1992;16:265-71.

40. Negri E, La Vecchia C, Franceschi S, et al. Attributable risk for oral cancer in northern Italy. *Cancer Epidemiol Biomarkers Prev* 1993;2:189-93.

41. Mashberg A, Boffetta P, Winkelman R, et al. Tobacco smoking, alcohol drinking, and cancer of the oral cavity and oropharynx among U.S. veterans. *Cancer* 1993;72:1369-75.

42. Ng SK, Kabat GC, Wynder EL. Oral cavity cancer in non-users of tobacco. *J Natl Cancer Inst* 1993;85:743-5.

43. Hedberg K, Vaughan TL, White E, et al. Alcoholism and cancer of the larynx: a case-control study in western Washington (United States). *Cancer Causes Control* 1994;5:3-8.

44. Rao DN, Ganesh B, Rao RS, et al. Risk assessment of tobacco, alcohol and diet in oral cancer - a case-control study. *Int J Cancer* 1994;58:469-73.

45. Bundgaard T, Wildt J, Frydenberg M, et al. Case-control study of squamous cell cancer of the oral cavity in Denmark. *Cancer Causes Control* 1995;6:57-67.

46. Guo X, Cheng M, Fei S. A case-control study of the etiology of laryngeal cancer in Liaoning Province. *Chin Med J (Engl)* 1995;108:347-50.

47. Takezaki T, Hirose K, Inoue M, et al. Tobacco, alcohol and dietary factors associated with the risk of oral cancer among Japanese. *Jpn J Cancer Res* 1996;87:555-62.

48. Sanderson RJ, de Boer MF, Damhuis RA, et al. The influence of alcohol and smoking on the incidence of oral and oropharyngeal cancer in women. *Clin Otolaryngol* 1997;22:444-8.

49. Dosemeci M, Gokmen I, Unsal M, et al. Tobacco, alcohol use, and risks of laryngeal and lung cancer by subsite and histologic type in Turkey. *Cancer Causes Control* 1997;8:729-37.

50. Zheng T, Holford T, Chen Y, et al. Risk of tongue cancer associated with tobacco smoking and alcohol consumption: a case-control study. *Oral Oncol* 1997;33:82-5.

51. Rao DN, Desai PB. Risk assessment of tobacco, alcohol and diet in cancers of base tongue and oral tongue - a case control study. *Indian J Cancer* 1998;35:65-72.

52. Su WZ, Ohno Y, Tohnai I, et al. Case-control study of oral cancer in Shenyang, northeastern China. *Int J Clin Oncol* 1998;3:13-8.

53. Wasnik KS, Ughade SN, Zodpey SP, et al. Tobacco consumption practices and risk of oro-pharyngeal cancer: a case-control study in Central India. *Southeast Asian J Trop Med Public Health* 1998;29:827-34.

54. Pintos J, Franco EL, Kowalski LP, et al. Use of wood stoves and risk of cancers of the upper aero-digestive tract: a case-control study. *Int J Epidemiol* 1998;27:936-40.

55. Smith EM, Hoffman HT, Summersgill KS, et al. Human papillomavirus and risk of oral cancer. *Laryngoscope* 1998;108:1098-103.

56. Chatenoud L, La Vecchia C, Franceschi S, et al. Refined-cereal intake and risk of selected cancers in Italy. *Am J Clin Nutr* 1999;70:1107-10.

57. Franceschi S, Levi F, La Vecchia C, et al. Comparison of the effect of smoking and alcohol drinking between oral and pharyngeal cancer. *Int J Cancer* 1999;83:1-4.

58. Fioretti F, Bosetti C, Tavani A, et al. Risk factors for oral and pharyngeal cancer in never smokers. *Oral Oncol* 1999;35:375-

8.

59. Rao DN, Desai PB, Ganesh B. Alcohol as an additional risk factor in laryngopharyngeal cancer in Mumbai - a case-control study. *Cancer Detect Prev* 1999;23:37-44.

60. Hayes RB, Bravo-Otero E, Kleinman DV, et al. Tobacco and alcohol use and oral cancer in Puerto Rico. *Cancer Causes Control* 1999;10:27-33.

61. Takezaki T, Shinoda M, Hatooka S, et al. Subsite-specific risk factors for hypopharyngeal and esophageal cancer (Japan). *Cancer Causes Control* 2000;11:597-608.

62. Zavras AI, Douglass CW, Joshipura K, et al. Smoking and alcohol in the etiology of oral cancer: gender-specific risk profiles in the south of Greece. *Oral Oncol* 2001;37:28-35.

63. Brown LM, Gridley G, Diehl SR, et al. Family cancer history and susceptibility to oral carcinoma in Puerto Rico. *Cancer* 2001;92:2102-8.

64. Schlecht NF, Pintos J, Kowalski LP, et al. Effect of type of alcoholic beverage on the risks of upper aerodigestive tract cancers in Brazil. *Cancer Causes Control* 2001;12:579-87.

65. Garrote LF, Herrero R, Reyes RM, et al. Risk factors for cancer of the oral cavity and oro-pharynx in Cuba. *Br J Cancer* 2001;85:46-54.

66. Zang EA, Wynder EL. Reevaluation of the confounding effect of cigarette smoking on the relationship between alcohol use and lung cancer risk, with larynx cancer used as a positive control. *Prev Med* 2001;32:359-70.

67. Dal Maso L, La Vecchia C, Polesel J, et al. Alcohol drinking outside meals and cancers of the upper aero-digestive tract. *Int J Cancer* 2002;102:435-7.

68. Talamini R, Bosetti C, La Vecchia C, et al. Combined effect of tobacco and alcohol on laryngeal cancer risk: a case-control study. *Cancer Causes Control* 2002;13:957-64.

69. Pisa FE, Barbone F. Diet and the risk of cancers of the lung, oral cavity and pharynx, and larynx: a population-based case-control study in north-east Italy. *IARC Sci Publ* 2002;156:141-3.

70. Petridou E, Zavras AI, Lefatzis D, et al. The role of diet and specific micronutrients in the etiology of oral carcinoma. *Cancer* 2002;94:2981-8.

71. Balaram P, Sridhar H, Rajkumar T, et al. Oral cancer in southern India: the influence of smoking, drinking, paan-chewing and oral hygiene. *Int J Cancer* 2002;98:440-5.

72. Uzcudun AE, Retolaza IR, Fernandez PB, et al. Nutrition and pharyngeal cancer: results from a case-control study in Spain. *Head Neck* 2002;24:830-40.

73. Sanchez MJ, Martinez C, Nieto A, et al. Oral and oropharyngeal cancer in Spain: influence of dietary patterns. *Eur J Cancer Prev* 2003;12:49-56.

74. Gallus S, Bosetti C, Franceschi S, et al. Laryngeal cancer in women: tobacco, alcohol, nutritional, and hormonal factors. *Cancer Epidemiol Biomarkers Prev* 2003;12:514-7.

75. Pelucchi C, Talamini R, Levi F, et al. Fibre intake and laryngeal cancer risk. *Ann Oncol* 2003;14:162-7.

76. Llewellyn CD, Linklater K, Bell J, et al. An analysis of risk factors for oral cancer in young people: a case-control study. *Oral Oncol* 2004;40:304-13.

77. Gaudet MM, Olshan AF, Poole C, et al. Diet, GSTM1 and GSTT1 and head and neck cancer. *Carcinogenesis* 2004;25:735-40.

78. Castellsague X, Quintana MJ, Martinez MC, et al. The role of type of tobacco and type of alcoholic beverage in oral carcinogenesis. *Int J Cancer* 2004;108:741-9.

79. Lissowska J, Pilarska A, Pilarski P, et al. Smoking, alcohol, diet, dentition and sexual practices in the epidemiology of oral cancer in Poland. *Eur J Cancer Prev* 2003;12:25-33.

80. Martinez I. Factors associated with cancer of the esophagus, mouth, and pharynx in Puerto Rico. *J Natl Cancer Inst* 1969;42:1069-94.

81. Hinds MW, Thomas DB, O'Reilly HP. Asbestos, dental X-rays, tobacco, and alcohol in the epidemiology of laryngeal cancer. *Cancer* 1979;44:1114-20.

82. Stevens MH, Gardner JW, Parkin JL, et al. Head and neck cancer survival and life-style change. *Arch Otolaryngol* 1983;109:746-9.

83. Blot WJ, McLaughlin JK, Winn DM, et al. Smoking and drinking in relation to oral and pharyngeal cancer. *Cancer Res* 1988;48:3282-7.

84. Day GL, Blot WJ, Austin DF, et al. Racial differences in risk of oral and pharyngeal cancer: alcohol, tobacco, and other determinants. *J Natl Cancer Inst* 1993;85:465-73.

85. Altieri A, Bosetti C, Gallus S, et al. Wine, beer and spirits and risk of oral and pharyngeal cancer: a case-control study from Italy and Switzerland. *Oral Oncol* 2004;40:904-9.

86. Llewellyn CD, Johnson NW, Warnakulasuriya KA. Risk factors for oral cancer in newly diagnosed patients aged 45 years and younger: a case-control study in Southern England. *J Oral Pathol Med* 2004;33:525-32.

87. De Stefani E, Boffetta P, Deneo-Pellegrini H, et al. Supraglottic and glottic carcinomas: epidemiologically distinct entities? *Int J Cancer* 2004;112:1065-71.

88. Toporcov TN, Antunes JL, Tavares MR. Fat food habitual intake and risk of oral cancer. *Oral Oncol* 2004;40:925-31.

89. Peters ES, McClean MD, Liu M, et al. The ADH1C polymorphism modifies the risk of squamous cell carcinoma of the head and neck associated with alcohol and tobacco use. *Cancer Epidemiol Biomarkers Prev* 2005;14:476-82.

90. De Stefani E, Boffetta P, Ronco AL, et al. Dietary patterns and risk of cancer of the oral cavity and pharynx in Uruguay. *Nutr Cancer* 2005;51:132-9.

91. Kapil U, Singh P, Bahadur S, et al. Assessment of risk factors in laryngeal cancer in India: a case-control study. *Asian Pac J Cancer Prev* 2005;6:202-7.

92. Lu CT, Yen YY, Ho CS, et al. A case-control study of oral cancer in Changhua County, Taiwan. *J Oral Pathol Med* 1996;25:245-8.

93. Merchant A, Husain SS, Hosain M, et al. Paan without tobacco: an independent risk factor for oral cancer. *Int J Cancer* 2000;86:128-31.

94. Razvodovsky YE. Aggregate level time series association between alcohol consumption and cancer mortality rate. *Alcoholism* 2003;39:11-20.

95. Schrauzer GN. Cancer mortality correlation studies. II. Regional associations of mortalities with the consumptions of foods and other commodities. *Med Hypotheses* 1976;2:39-49.

96. de Stefani E, Deneo H, Carzoglio J, et al. [Geographical correlations in laryngeal cancer]. *An Otorrinolaringol Ibero Am* 1984;11:335-44.

97. Lin YS, Jen YM, Wang BB, et al. Epidemiology of oral cavity cancer in Taiwan with emphasis on the role of betel nut chewing. *ORL J Otorhinolaryngol Relat Spec* 2005;67:230-6.

98. Burch JD, Howe GR, Miller AB, et al. Tobacco, alcohol, asbestos, and nickel in the etiology of cancer of the larynx: a case-control study. *J Natl Cancer Inst* 1981;67:1219-24.

99. Olsen J, Sabreo S, Fasting U. Interaction of alcohol and tobacco as risk factors in cancer of the laryngeal region. *J Epidemiol Community Health* 1985;39:165-8.

100. Young TB, Ford CN, Brandenburg JH. An epidemiologic study of oral cancer in a statewide network. *Am J Otolaryngol* 1986;7:200-8.

101. Spitz MR, Fueger JJ, Goepfert H, et al. Squamous cell carcinoma of the upper aerodigestive tract. A case comparison analysis. *Cancer* 1988;61:203-8.

102. Kabat GC, Chang CJ, Wynder EL. The role of tobacco, alcohol use, and body mass index in oral and pharyngeal cancer. *Int J Epidemiol* 1994;23:1137-44.

103. Rogers MA, Vaughan TL, Davis S, et al. Consumption of nitrate, nitrite, and nitrosodimethylamine and the risk of upper aerodigestive tract cancer. *Cancer Epidemiol Biomarkers Prev* 1995;4:29-36.

104. Schildt EB, Eriksson M, Hardell L, et al. Oral snuff, smoking habits and alcohol consumption in relation to oral cancer in a Swedish case-control study. *Int J Cancer* 1998;77:341-6.

105. Huang WY, Winn DM, Brown LM, et al. Alcohol concentration and risk of oral cancer in Puerto Rico. *Am J Epidemiol* 2003;157:881-7.

106. Breslow NE, Enstrom JE. Geographic correlations between cancer mortality rates and alcohol-tobacco consumption in the United States. *J Natl Cancer Inst* 1974;53:631-9.

455

107. De Stefani E, Deneo-Pellegrini H, Mendilaharsu M, et al. Diet and risk of cancer of the upper aerodigestive tract - I. Foods. Oral Oncol 1999;35:17-21.

108. De Stefani E, Correa P, Oreggia F, et al. Black tobacco, wine and mate in oropharyngeal cancer. A case-control study from Uruguay. Rev Epidemiol Sante Publique 1988;36:389-94.

109. Oreggia F, De Stefani E, Correa P, et al. Risk factors for cancer of the tongue in Uruguay. Cancer 1991;67:180-3.

110. Knox EG. Foods and diseases. Br J Prev Soc Med 1977;31:71-80.

111. Olsen GW, Mandel JS, Gibson RW, et al. A case-control study of pancreatic cancer and cigarettes, alcohol, coffee and diet. Am J Public Health 1989;79:1016-9.

112. Zatonski W, Becher H, Lissowska J, et al. Tobacco, alcohol, and diet in the etiology of laryngeal cancer: a population-based case-control study. Cancer Causes Control 1991;2:3-10.

113. Sokic SI, Adanja BJ, Marinkovic JP, et al. Case-control study of risk factors in laryngeal cancer. Neoplasma 1994;41:43-7.

114. Longnecker MP, Wolz M, Parker DA. Ethnicity, distilled spirits consumption and mortality in Pennsylvania. J Stud Alcohol 1981;42:791-6.

115. Maserejian NN, Giovannucci E, Rosner B, et al. Prospective study of fruits and vegetables and risk of oral premalignant lesions in men. Am J Epidemiol 2006;164:556-66.

116. Garavello W, Bosetti C, Gallus S, et al. Type of alcoholic beverage and the risk of laryngeal cancer. Eur J Cancer Prev 2006;15:69-73.

117. Vlajinac HD, Marinkovic JM, Sipetic SB, et al. Case-control study of oropharyngeal cancer. Cancer Detect Prev 2006;30:152-7.

118. Petti S, Scully C. Association between different alcoholic beverages and leukoplakia among non- to moderate-drinking adults: a matched case-control study. Eur J Cancer 2006;42:521-7.

119. Vaezi MF, Qadeer MA, Lopez R, et al. Laryngeal cancer and gastroesophageal reflux disease: a case-control study. Am J Med 2006;119:768-76.

120. Kono S, Ikeda M, Tokudome S, et al. Cigarette smoking, alcohol and cancer mortality: a cohort study of male Japanese physicians. Jpn J Cancer Res 1987;78:1323-8.

121. Kinjo Y, Cui Y, Akiba S, et al. Mortality risks of oesophageal cancer associated with hot tea, alcohol, tobacco and diet in Japan. J Epidemiol 1998;8:235-43.

122. Sakata K, Hoshiyama Y, Morioka S, et al. Smoking, alcohol drinking and esophageal cancer: findings from the JACC Study. J Epidemiol 2005;15 Suppl 2:S212-9.

123. Tran GD, Sun XD, Abnet CC, et al. Prospective study of risk factors for esophageal and gastric cancers in the Linxian general population trial cohort in China. Int J Cancer 2005;113:456-63.

124. Hirayama T. [A large scale cohort study on the effect of life styles on the risk of cancer by each site]. Gan No Rinsho 1990;Spec No:233-42.

125. Yu Y, Taylor PR, Li JY, et al. Retrospective cohort study of risk-factors for esophageal cancer in Linxian, People's Republic of China. Cancer Causes Control 1993;4:195-202.

126. Tao X, Zhu H, Matanoski GM. Mutagenic drinking water and risk of male esophageal cancer: a population-based case-control study. Am J Epidemiol 1999;150:443-52.

127. Bradshaw E, Schonland M. Smoking, drinking and oesophageal cancer in African males of Johannesburg, South Africa. Br J Cancer 1974;30:157-63.

128. Tuyns AJ, Pequignot G, Gignoux M, et al. Cancers of the digestive tract, alcohol and tobacco. Int J Cancer 1982;30:9-11.

129. Adelhardt M, Moller Jensen O, Sand Hansen H. Cancer of the larynx, pharynx, and oesophagus in relation to alcohol and tobacco consumption among Danish brewery workers. Dan Med Bull 1985;32:119-23.

130. Wang HH, Antonioli DA, Goldman H. Comparative features of esophageal and gastric adenocarcinomas: recent changes in type and frequency. Hum Pathol 1986;17:482-7.

131. La Vecchia C, Negri E. The role of alcohol in oesophageal cancer in non-smokers, and of tobacco in non-drinkers. Int J Cancer 1989;43:784-5.

132. Rao DN, Sanghvi LD, Desai PB. Epidemiology of esophageal cancer. Semin Surg Oncol 1989;5:351-4.

133. De Stefani E, Munoz N, Esteve J, et al. Mate drinking, alcohol, tobacco, diet, and esophageal cancer in Uruguay. Cancer Res 1990;50:426-31.

134. Wang YP, Han XY, Su W, et al. Esophageal cancer in Shanxi Province, People's Republic of China: a case-control study in high and moderate risk areas. Cancer Causes Control 1992;3:107-13.

135. Kabat GC, Ng SK, Wynder EL. Tobacco, alcohol intake, and diet in relation to adenocarcinoma of the esophagus and gastric cardia. Cancer Causes Control 1993;4:123-32.

136. Gao YT, McLaughlin JK, Blot WJ, et al. Risk factors for esophageal cancer in Shanghai, China. I. Role of cigarette smoking and alcohol drinking. Int J Cancer 1994;58:192-6.

137. Hanaoka T, Tsugane S, Ando N, et al. Alcohol consumption and risk of esophageal cancer in Japan: a case-control study in seven hospitals. Jpn J Clin Oncol 1994;24:241-6.

138. Brown LM, Silverman DT, Pottern LM, et al. Adenocarcinoma of the esophagus and esophagogastric junction in white men in the United States: alcohol, tobacco, and socioeconomic factors. Cancer Causes Control 1994;5:333-40.

139. Rolon PA, Castellsague X, Benz M, et al. Hot and cold mate drinking and esophageal cancer in Paraguay. Cancer Epidemiol Biomarkers Prev 1995;4:595-605.

140. Vizcaino AP, Parkin DM, Skinner ME. Risk factors associated with oesophageal cancer in Bulawayo, Zimbabwe. Br J Cancer 1995;72:769-73.

141. Srivastava M, Kapil U, Chattopadhyaya TK, et al. Nutritional risk factors in carcinoma esophagus. Nutr Res 1995;15:177-85.

142. Garidou A, Tzonou A, Lipworth L, et al. Life-style factors and medical conditions in relation to esophageal cancer by histologic type in a low-risk population. Int J Cancer 1996;68:295-9.

143. Zhang ZF, Kurtz RC, Sun M, et al. Adenocarcinomas of the esophagus and gastric cardia: medical conditions, tobacco, alcohol, and socioeconomic factors. Cancer Epidemiol Biomarkers Prev 1996;5:761-8.

144. Gammon MD, Schoenberg JB, Ahsan H, et al. Tobacco, alcohol, and socioeconomic status and adenocarcinomas of the esophagus and gastric cardia. J Natl Cancer Inst 1997;89:1277-84.

145. Dietz J, Pardo SH, Furtado CD, et al. [Risk factors related to esophageal cancer in Rio Grande do Sul, Brazil]. Rev Assoc Med Bras 1998;44:269-72.

146. Zambon P, Talamini R, La Vecchia C, et al. Smoking, type of alcoholic beverage and squamous-cell oesophageal cancer in northern Italy. Int J Cancer 2000;86:144-9.

147. Levi F, Pasche C, Lucchini F, et al. Food groups and oesophageal cancer risk in Vaud, Switzerland. Eur J Cancer Prev 2000;9:257-63.

148. Nayar D, Kapil U, Joshi YK, et al. Nutritional risk factors in esophageal cancer. J Assoc Physicians India 2000;48:781-7.

149. Sharp L, Chilvers CE, Cheng KK, et al. Risk factors for squamous cell carcinoma of the oesophagus in women: a case-control study. Br J Cancer 2001;85:1667-70.

150. Boonyaphiphat P, Thongsuksai P, Sriplung H, et al. Lifestyle habits and genetic susceptibility and the risk of esophageal cancer in the Thai population. Cancer Lett 2002;186:193-9.

151. Gao CM, Takezaki T, Wu JZ, et al. Glutathione-S-transferases M1 (GSTM1) and GSTT1 genotype, smoking, consumption of alcohol and tea and risk of esophageal and stomach cancers: a case-control study of a high-incidence area in Jiangsu Province, China. Cancer Lett 2002;188:95-102.

152. Znaor A, Brennan P, Gajalakshmi V, et al. Independent and combined effects of tobacco smoking, chewing and alcohol drinking on the risk of oral, pharyngeal and esophageal cancers in Indian men. Int J Cancer 2003;105:681-6.

153. Wang AH, Sun CS, Li LS, et al. Genetic susceptibility and environmental factors of esophageal cancer in Xi'an. World J Gastroenterol 2004;10:940-4.

154. Jozala E, Infante S, Marchini JS, et al.

[Alcoholism, smoking and epidermoid carcinoma of the middle third of the esophagus: a case-control study]. *Rev Saude Publica* 1983;17:221-5.

155. Rossi M, Ancona E, Mastrangelo G, et al. [Epidemiologic findings in esophageal cancer in the Veneto region]. *Minerva Med* 1982;73:1531-40.

156. Tuyns AJ. Oesophageal cancer in non-smoking drinkers and in non-drinking smokers. *Int J Cancer* 1983;32:443-4.

157. Decarli A, Liati P, Negri E, et al. Vitamin A and other dietary factors in the etiology of esophageal cancer. *Nutr Cancer* 1987;10:29-37.

158. Choi SY, Kahyo H. Effect of cigarette smoking and alcohol consumption in the etiology of cancers of the digestive tract. *Int J Cancer* 1991;49:381-6.

159. Valsecchi MG. Modelling the relative risk of esophageal cancer in a case-control study. *J Clin Epidemiol* 1992;45:347-55.

160. Cheng KK, Day NE, Duffy SW, et al. Pickled vegetables in the aetiology of oesophageal cancer in Hong Kong Chinese. *Lancet* 1992;339:1314-8.

161. Castelletto R, Castellsague X, Munoz N, et al. Alcohol, tobacco, diet, mate drinking, and esophageal cancer in Argentina. *Cancer Epidemiol Biomarkers Prev* 1994;3:557-64.

162. Vaughan TL, Davis S, Kristal A, et al. Obesity, alcohol, and tobacco as risk factors for cancers of the esophagus and gastric cardia: adenocarcinoma versus squamous cell carcinoma. *Cancer Epidemiol Biomarkers Prev* 1995;4:85-92.

163. Cheng KK, Duffy SW, Day NE, et al. Oesophageal cancer in never-smokers and never-drinkers. *Int J Cancer* 1995;60:820-2.

164. Cheng KK, Duffy SW, Day NE, et al. Stopping drinking and risk of oesophageal cancer. *BMJ* 1995;310:1094-7.

165. Gimeno SG, de Souza JM, Mirra AP, et al. [Risk factors for cancer of the esophagus: a case control study in a metropolitan area of south-eastern Brazil]. *Rev Saude Publica* 1995;29:159-65.

166. Nandakumar A, Anantha N, Pattabhiraman V, et al. Importance of anatomical subsite in correlating risk factors in cancer of the oesophagus - report of a case-control study. *Br J Cancer* 1996;73:1306-11.

167. Gao CM, Takezaki T, Ding JH, et al. Protective effect of allium vegetables against both esophageal and stomach cancer: a simultaneous case-referent study of a high-epidemic area in Jiangsu Province, China. *Jpn J Cancer Res* 1999;90:614-21.

168. Cheng KK, Sharp L, McKinney PA, et al. A case-control study of oesophageal adenocarcinoma in women: a preventable disease. *Br J Cancer* 2000;83:127-32.

169. Bosetti C, Franceschi S, Levi F, et al. Smoking and drinking cessation and the risk of oesophageal cancer. *Br J Cancer* 2000;83:689-91.

170. Bosetti C, La Vecchia C, Negri E, et al. Wine and other types of alcoholic beverages and the risk of esophageal cancer. *Eur J Clin Nutr* 2000;54:918-20.

171. Takezaki T, Gao CM, Wu JZ, et al. Dietary protective and risk factors for esophageal and stomach cancers in a low-epidemic area for stomach cancer in Jiangsu Province, China: comparison with those in a high-epidemic area. *Jpn J Cancer Res* 2001;92:1157-65.

172. Lee JM, Lee YC, Yang SY, et al. Genetic polymorphisms of XRCC1 and risk of the esophageal cancer. *Int J Cancer* 2001;95:240-6.

173. Wu MM, Kuo TL, Hwang YH, et al. Dose-response relation between arsenic concentration in well water and mortality from cancers and vascular diseases. *Am J Epidemiol* 1989;130:1123-32.

174. Engel LS, Chow WH, Vaughan TL, et al. Population attributable risks of esophageal and gastric cancers. *J Natl Cancer Inst* 2003;95:1404-13.

175. Chitra S, Ashok L, Anand L, et al. Risk factors for esophageal cancer in Coimbatore, southern India: a hospital-based case-control study. *Indian J Gastroenterol* 2004;23:19-21.

176. Parkin DM, Vizcaino AP, Skinner ME, et al. Cancer patterns and risk factors in the African population of southwestern Zimbabwe, 1963-1977. *Cancer Epidemiol Biomarkers Prev* 1994;3:537-47.

177. Trivers KF, De Roos AJ, Gammon MD, et al. Demographic and lifestyle predictors of survival in patients with esophageal or gastric cancers. *Clin Gastroenterol Hepatol* 2005;3:225-30.

178. Sankaranarayanan R, Duffy SW, Padmakumary G, et al. Risk factors for cancer of the oesophagus in Kerala, India. *Int J Cancer* 1991;49:485-9.

179. Lee CH, Lee JM, Wu DC, et al. Independent and combined effects of alcohol intake, tobacco smoking and betel quid chewing on the risk of esophageal cancer in Taiwan. *Int J Cancer* 2005;113:475-82.

180. Yang CX, Wang HY, Wang ZM, et al. Risk factors for esophageal cancer: a case-control study in South-western China. *Asian Pac J Cancer Prev* 2005;6:48-53.

181. Tavani A, Negri E, Franceschi S, et al. Risk factors for esophageal cancer in women in northern Italy. *Cancer* 1993;72:2531-6.

182. Tavani A, Negri E, Franceschi S, et al. Risk factors for esophageal cancer in lifelong nonsmokers. *Cancer Epidemiol Biomarkers Prev* 1994;3:387-92.

183. Thun MJ, Peto R, Lopez AD, et al. Alcohol consumption and mortality among middle-aged and elderly U.S. adults. *N Engl J Med* 1997;337:1705-14.

184. Kono S, Ikeda M. Correlation between cancer mortality and alcoholic beverage in Japan. *Br J Cancer* 1979;40:449-55.

185. Yanai H, Inaba Y, Takagi H, et al. Multivariate analysis of cancer mortalities for selected sites in 24 countries. *Environ Health Perspect* 1979;32:83-101.

186. Kendell RE. The beneficial consequences of the United Kingdom's declining per capita consumption of alcohol in 1979-82. *Alcohol Alcohol* 1984;19:271-6.

187. Thouez JP, Ghadirian P. [Geographical relations between mortality from cancer of the esophagus, cirrhosis of the liver, alcohol and tobacco: case of the Province of Quebec]. *Soc Sci Med* 1986;22:611-8.

188. Guo WD, Li JY, Blot WJ, et al. Correlations of dietary intake and blood nutrient levels with esophageal cancer mortality in China. *Nutr Cancer* 1990;13:121-7.

189. Macfarlane GJ, Macfarlane TV, Lowenfels AB. The influence of alcohol consumption on worldwide trends in mortality from upper aerodigestive tract cancers in men. *J Epidemiol Community Health* 1996;50:636-9.

190. De Jong UW, Breslow N, Hong JG, et al. Aetiological factors in oesophageal cancer in Singapore Chinese. *Int J Cancer* 1974;13:291-303.

191. Segal I, Reinach SG, de Beer M. Factors associated with oesophageal cancer in Soweto, South Africa. *Br J Cancer* 1988;58:681-6.

192. Sammon AM. Protease inhibitors and carcinoma of the esophagus. *Cancer* 1998;83:405-8.

193. Mettlin C, Graham S, Priore R, et al. Diet and cancer of the esophagus. *Nutr Cancer* 1981;2:143-7.

194. Victora CG, Munoz N, Day NE, et al. Hot beverages and oesophageal cancer in southern Brazil: a case-control study. *Int J Cancer* 1987;39:710-6.

195. Yu MC, Garabrant DH, Peters JM, et al. Tobacco, alcohol, diet, occupation, and carcinoma of the esophagus. *Cancer Res* 1988;48:3843-8.

196. Brown LM, Blot WJ, Schuman SH, et al. Environmental factors and high risk of esophageal cancer among men in coastal South Carolina. *J Natl Cancer Inst* 1988;80:1620-5.

197. Graham S, Marshall J, Haughey B, et al. Nutritional epidemiology of cancer of the esophagus. *Am J Epidemiol* 1990;131:454-67.

198. Chilvers C, Fraser P, Beral V. Alcohol and oesophageal cancer: an assessment of the evidence from routinely collected data. *J Epidemiol Community Health* 1979;33:127-33.

199. Llopis A, Morales M, Rodriguez R. Digestive cancer in relation to diet in Spain. *J Environ Pathol Toxicol Oncol* 1992;11:169-75.

200. Hinds MW, Kolonel LN, Lee J, et al. Associations between cancer incidence and alcohol/cigarette consumption among five ethnic groups in Hawaii. *Br J Cancer* 1980;41:929-40.

201. Vassallo A, Correa P, De Stefani E, et al. Esophageal cancer in Uruguay: a case-control study. *J Natl Cancer Inst* 1985;75:1005-9.

202. Hu J, Nyren O, Wolk A, et al. Risk factors for oesophageal cancer in northeast

China. *Int J Cancer* 1994;57:38-46.

203. Ishikawa A, Kuriyama S, Tsubono Y, et al. Smoking, alcohol drinking, green tea consumption and the risk of esophageal cancer in Japanese men. *J Epidemiol* 2006;16:185-92.

204. Yokoyama A, Kato H, Yokoyama T, et al. Esophageal squamous cell carcinoma and aldehyde dehydrogenase-2 genotypes in Japanese females. *Alcohol Clin Exp Res* 2006;30:491-500.

205. Wu M, Zhao JK, Hu XS, et al. Association of smoking, alcohol drinking and dietary factors with esophageal cancer in high- and low-risk areas of Jiangsu Province, China. *World J Gastroenterol* 2006;12:1686-93.

206. Wu IC, Lu CY, Kuo FC, et al. Interaction between cigarette, alcohol and betel nut use on esophageal cancer risk in Taiwan. *Eur J Clin Invest* 2006;36:236-41.

207. Veugelers PJ, Porter GA, Guernsey DL, et al. Obesity and lifestyle risk factors for gastroesophageal reflux disease, Barrett esophagus and esophageal adenocarcinoma. *Dis Esophagus* 2006;19:321-8.

208. Hirayama T. Mortality in Japanese with life-styles similar to Seventh-Day Adventists: strategy for risk reduction by life-style modification. *Natl Cancer Inst Monogr* 1985;69:143-53.

209. Jacobs EJ, Connell CJ, Patel AV, et al. Multivitamin use and colon cancer mortality in the Cancer Prevention Study II cohort (United States). *Cancer Causes Control* 2001;12:927-34.

210. Hirayama T. Association between alcohol consumption and cancer of the sigmoid colon: observations from a Japanese cohort study. *Lancet* 1989;2:725-7.

211. Williams RR, Sorlie PD, Feinleib M, et al. Cancer incidence by levels of cholesterol. *JAMA* 1981;245:247-52.

212. Pollack ES, Nomura AM, Heilbrun LK, et al. Prospective study of alcohol consumption and cancer. *N Engl J Med* 1984;310:617-21.

213. Klatsky AL, Armstrong MA, Friedman GD, et al. The relations of alcoholic beverage use to colon and rectal cancer. *Am J Epidemiol* 1988;128:1007-15.

214. Stemmermann GN, Nomura AM, Chyou PH, et al. Prospective study of alcohol intake and large bowel cancer. *Dig Dis Sci* 1990;35:1414-20.

215. Suadicani P, Hein HO, Gyntelberg F. Height, weight, and risk of colorectal cancer. An 18-year follow-up in a cohort of 5249 men. *Scand J Gastroenterol* 1993;28:285-8.

216. Giovannucci E, Rimm EB, Ascherio A, et al. Alcohol, low-methionine - low-folate diets, and risk of colon cancer in men. *J Natl Cancer Inst* 1995;87:265-73.

217. Singh PN, Fraser GE. Dietary risk factors for colon cancer in a low-risk population. *Am J Epidemiol* 1998;148:761-74.

218. Pedersen A, Johansen C, Gronbaek M. Relations between amount and type of alcohol and colon and rectal cancer in a Danish population based cohort study.

Gut 2003;52:861-7.

219. Wei EK, Giovannucci E, Wu K, et al. Comparison of risk factors for colon and rectal cancer. *Int J Cancer* 2004;108:433-42.

220. Kjaerheim K, Andersen A, Helseth A. Alcohol abstainers: a low-risk group for cancer - a cohort study of Norwegian teetotalers. *Cancer Epidemiol Biomarkers Prev* 1993;2:93-7.

221. Schoen RE, Tangen CM, Kuller LH, et al. Increased blood glucose and insulin, body size, and incident colorectal cancer. *J Natl Cancer Inst* 1999;91:1147-54.

222. Flood A, Caprario L, Chaterjee N, et al. Folate, methionine, alcohol, and colorectal cancer in a prospective study of women in the United States. *Cancer Causes Control* 2002;13:551-61.

223. Sanjoaquin MA, Appleby PN, Thorogood M, et al. Nutrition, lifestyle and colorectal cancer incidence: a prospective investigation of 10998 vegetarians and non-vegetarians in the United Kingdom. *Br J Cancer* 2004;90:118-21.

224. Sidney S, Friedman GD, Hiatt RA. Serum cholesterol and large bowel cancer. A case-control study. *Am J Epidemiol* 1986;124:33-8.

225. Koh WP, Yuan JM, van den Berg D, et al. Interaction between cyclooxygenase-2 gene polymorphism and dietary n-6 polyunsaturated fatty acids on colon cancer risk: The Singapore Chinese Health Study. *Br J Cancer* 2004;90:1760-4.

226. Chen J, Ma J, Stampfer MJ, et al. Alcohol dehydrogenase 3 genotype is not predictive for risk of colorectal cancer. *Cancer Epidemiol Biomarkers Prev* 2001;10:1303-4.

227. Murata M, Takayama K, Choi BC, et al. A nested case-control study on alcohol drinking, tobacco smoking and cancer. *Cancer Detect Prev* 1996;20:557-65.

228. Hsing AW, McLaughlin JK, Chow WH, et al. Risk factors for colorectal cancer in a prospective study among U.S. white men. *Int J Cancer* 1998;77:549-53.

229. Ford ES. Body mass index and colon cancer in a national sample of adult US men and women. *Am J Epidemiol* 1999;150:390-8.

230. Otani T, Iwasaki M, Yamamoto S, et al. Alcohol consumption, smoking, and subsequent risk of colorectal cancer in middle-aged and elderly Japanese men and women: Japan Public Health Center-based prospective study. *Cancer Epidemiol Biomarkers Prev* 2003;12:1492-500.

231. Kato I, Dnistrian AM, Schwartz M, et al. Serum folate, homocysteine and colorectal cancer risk in women: a nested case-control study. *Br J Cancer* 1999;79:1917-22.

232. Glynn SA, Albanes D, Pietinen P, et al. Alcohol consumption and risk of colorectal cancer in a cohort of Finnish men. *Cancer Causes Control* 1996;7:214-23.

233. Su LJ, Arab L. Nutritional status of folate

and colon cancer risk: evidence from NHANES I epidemiologic follow-up study. *Ann Epidemiol* 2001;11:65-72.

234. Tiemersma EW, Kampman E, Bueno de Mesquita HB, et al. Meat consumption, cigarette smoking, and genetic susceptibility in the etiology of colorectal cancer: results from a Dutch prospective study. *Cancer Causes Control* 2002;13:383-93.

235. Konings EJ, Goldbohm RA, Brants HA, et al. Intake of dietary folate vitamers and risk of colorectal carcinoma: results from The Netherlands Cohort Study. *Cancer* 2002;95:1421-33.

236. Garland C, Shekelle RB, Barrett Connor E, et al. Dietary vitamin D and calcium and risk of colorectal cancer: a 19-year prospective study in men. *Lancet* 1985;1:307-9.

237. Stemmermann GN, Nomura AM, Heilbrun LK. Dietary fat and the risk of colorectal cancer. *Cancer Res* 1984;44:4633-7.

238. Kreger BE, Anderson KM, Schatzkin A, et al. Serum cholesterol level, body mass index, and the risk of colon cancer. The Framingham Study. *Cancer* 1992;70:1038-43.

239. Gapstur SM, Potter JD, Folsom AR. Alcohol consumption and colon and rectal cancer in postmenopausal women. *Int J Epidemiol* 1994;23:50-7.

240. Chyou PH, Nomura AM, Stemmermann GN. A prospective study of colon and rectal cancer among Hawaii Japanese men. *Ann Epidemiol* 1996;6:276-82.

241. Colbert LH, Hartman TJ, Malila N, et al. Physical activity in relation to cancer of the colon and rectum in a cohort of male smokers. *Cancer Epidemiol Biomarkers Prev* 2001;10:265-8.

242. Fuchs CS, Willett WC, Colditz GA, et al. The influence of folate and multivitamin use on the familial risk of colon cancer in women. *Cancer Epidemiol Biomarkers Prev* 2002;11:227-34.

243. Harnack L, Jacobs DR, Jr., Nicodemus K, et al. Relationship of folate, vitamin B-6, vitamin B-12, and methionine intake to incidence of colorectal cancers. *Nutr Cancer* 2002;43:152-8.

244. Nakaya N, Tsubono Y, Kuriyama S, et al. Alcohol consumption and the risk of cancer in Japanese men: the Miyagi cohort study. *Eur J Cancer Prev* 2005;14:169-74.

245. Wu AH, Paganini Hill A, Ross RK, et al. Alcohol, physical activity and other risk factors for colorectal cancer: a prospective study. *Br J Cancer* 1987;55:687-94.

246. Malila N, Virtamo J, Virtanen M, et al. Dietary and serum alpha-tocopherol, beta-carotene and retinol, and risk for colorectal cancer in male smokers. *Eur J Clin Nutr* 2002;56:615-21.

247. Glynn SA, Albanes D, Pietinen P, et al. Colorectal cancer and folate status: a nested case-control study among male smokers. *Cancer Epidemiol Biomarkers Prev* 1996;5:487-94.

248. Feskanich D, Ma J, Fuchs CS, et al. Plasma

vitamin D metabolites and risk of colorectal cancer in women. *Cancer Epidemiol Biomarkers Prev* 2004;13:1502-8.

249. Goldbohm RA, Van den Brandt PA, Van 't Veer P, et al. Prospective study on alcohol consumption and the risk of cancer of the colon and rectum in the Netherlands. *Cancer Causes Control* 1994;5:95-104.

250. Pietinen P, Malila N, Virtanen M, et al. Diet and risk of colorectal cancer in a cohort of Finnish men. *Cancer Causes Control* 1999;10:387-96.

251. Longnecker MMP, Orza MMJ, Adams MME, et al. A meta-analysis of alcoholic beverage consumption in relation to risk of colorectal cancer. *Cancer Causes Control* 1990;1:59.

252. Cho E, Smith-Warner SA, Ritz J, et al. Alcohol intake and colorectal cancer: a pooled analysis of 8 cohort studies. *Ann Intern Med* 2004;140:603-13.

253. Murata M, Tagawa M, Watanabe S, et al. Genotype difference of aldehyde dehydrogenase 2 gene in alcohol drinkers influences the incidence of Japanese colorectal cancer patients. *Jpn J Cancer Res* 1999;90:711-9.

254. Tiemersma EW, Wark PA, Ocke MC, et al. Alcohol consumption, alcohol dehydrogenase 3 polymorphism, and colorectal adenomas. *Cancer Epidemiol Biomarkers Prev* 2003;12:419-25.

255. Jin MJ, Chen K, Song L, et al. The association of the DNA repair gene XRCC3 Thr241Met polymorphism with susceptibility to colorectal cancer in a Chinese population. *Cancer Genet Cytogenet* 2005;163:38-43.

256. Jiang Q, Chen K, Ma X, et al. Diets, polymorphisms of methylenetetrahydrofolate reductase, and the susceptibility of colon cancer and rectal cancer. *Cancer Detect Prev* 2005;29:146-54.

257. Wakai K, Kojima M, Tamakoshi K, et al. Alcohol consumption and colorectal cancer risk: findings from the JACC Study. *J Epidemiol* 2005;15 Suppl 2:S173-9.

258. Chen K, Jiang Q, Ma X, et al. Alcohol drinking and colorectal cancer: a population-based prospective cohort study in China. *Eur J Epidemiol* 2005;20:149-54.

259. Huang XE, Hirose K, Wakai K, et al. Comparison of lifestyle risk factors by family history for gastric, breast, lung and colorectal cancer. *Asian Pac J Cancer Prev* 2004;5:419-27.

260. Kim DH, Ahn YO, Lee BH, et al. Methylenetetrahydrofolate reductase polymorphism, alcohol intake, and risks of colon and rectal cancers in Korea. *Cancer Lett* 2004;216:199-205.

261. Hong YC, Lee KH, Kim WC, et al. Polymorphisms of XRCC1 gene, alcohol consumption and colorectal cancer. *Int J Cancer* 2005;116:428-32.

262. Diergaarde B, Tiemersma EW, Braam H, et al. Dietary factors and truncating APC mutations in sporadic colorectal adenomas. *Int J Cancer* 2005;113:126-32.

263. Byrne C, Ursin G, Ziegler RG. A comparison of food habit and food frequency data as predictors of breast cancer in the NHANES I/NHEFS cohort. *J Nutr* 1996;126:2757-64.

264. Feigelson HS, E. CE, Robertson AS, et al. Alcohol consumption increases the risk of fatal breast cancer (United States). *Cancer Causes Control* 2001;12:895-902.

265. Hoyer AP, Engholm G. Serum lipids and breast cancer risk: a cohort study of 5,207 Danish women. *Cancer Causes Control* 1992;3:403-8.

266. Key TJ, Sharp GB, Appleby PN, et al. Soya foods and breast cancer risk: a prospective study in Hiroshima and Nagasaki, Japan. *Br J Cancer* 1999;81:1248-56.

267. Morch LS, Becker U, Olsen J, et al. [Should the sensible drinking limits for adults be changed?]. *Ugeskr Laeger* 2005;167:3777-9.

268. Petri AL, Tjonneland A, Gamborg M, et al. Alcohol intake, type of beverage, and risk of breast cancer in pre- and postmenopausal women. *Alcohol Clin Exp Res* 2004;28:1084-90.

269. Pike MC, Kolonel LN, Henderson BE, et al. Breast cancer in a multiethnic cohort in Hawaii and Los Angeles: risk factor-adjusted incidence in Japanese equals and in Hawaiians exceeds that in whites. *Cancer Epidemiol Biomarkers Prev* 2002;11:795-800.

270. Vachon CM, Cerhan JR, Vierkant RA, et al. Investigation of an interaction of alcohol intake and family history on breast cancer risk in the Minnesota Breast Cancer Family Study. *Cancer* 2001;92:240-8.

271. Wu K, Helzlsouer KJ, Comstock GW, et al. A prospective study on folate, B12, and pyridoxal 5'-phosphate (B6) and breast cancer. *Cancer Epidemiol Biomarkers Prev* 1999;8:209-17.

272. Althuis MD, Brogan DD, Coates RJ, et al. Breast cancers among very young premenopausal women (United States). *Cancer Causes Control* 2003;14:151-60.

273. Atalah E, Urteaga C, Rebolledo A, et al. [Breast cancer risk factors in women in Santiago, Chile]. *Rev Med Chil* 2000;128:137-43.

274. Baumgartner KB, Annegers JF, McPherson RS, et al. Is alcohol intake associated with breast cancer in Hispanic women? The New Mexico Women's Health Study. *Ethn Dis* 2002;12:460-9.

275. Brinton LA, Potischman NA, Swanson CA, et al. Breastfeeding and breast cancer risk. *Cancer Causes Control* 1995;6:199-208.

276. Freudenheim JL, Marshall JR, Graham S, et al. Lifetime alcohol consumption and risk of breast cancer. *Nutr Cancer* 1995;23:1-11.

277. Freudenheim JL, Ambrosone CB, Moysich KB, et al. Alcohol dehydrogenase 3 genotype modification of the association of alcohol consumption with breast cancer risk. *Cancer Causes Control* 1999;10:369-77.

278. Freudenheim JL, Bonner M, Krishnan S, et al. Diet and alcohol consumption in relation to p53 mutations in breast tumors. *Carcinogenesis* 2004;25:931-9.

279. Haile RW, Witte JS, Ursin G, et al. A case-control study of reproductive variables, alcohol, and smoking in premenopausal bilateral breast cancer. *Breast Cancer Res Treat* 1996;37:49-56.

280. Harvey EB, Schairer C, Brinton LA, et al. Alcohol consumption and breast cancer. *J Natl Cancer Inst* 1987;78:657-61.

281. Hirose K, Tajima K, Hamajima N, et al. A large-scale, hospital-based case-control study of risk factors of breast cancer according to menopausal status. *Jpn J Cancer Res* 1995;86:146-54.

282. Holmberg L, Ohlander EM, Byers T, et al. Diet and breast cancer risk. Results from a population-based, case-control study in Sweden. *Arch Intern Med* 1994;154:1805-11.

283. Hu YH, Nagata C, Shimizu H, et al. Association of body mass index, physical activity, and reproductive histories with breast cancer: a case-control study in Gifu, Japan. *Breast Cancer Res Treat* 1997;43:65-72.

284. Katsouyanni K, Trichopoulou A, Stuver S, et al. Ethanol and breast cancer: an association that may be both confounded and causal. *Int J Cancer* 1994;58:356-61.

285. Kikuchi S, Okamoto N, Suzuki T, et al. [A case control study of breast cancer, mammary cyst and dietary, drinking or smoking habit in Japan]. *Gan No Rinsho* 1990;Spec No:365-9.

286. Kinney AY, Millikan RC, Lin YH, et al. Alcohol consumption and breast cancer among black and white women in North Carolina (United States). *Cancer Causes Control* 2000;11:345-57.

287. Lash TL, Aschengrau A. Alcohol drinking and risk of breast cancer. *Breast J* 2000;6:396-9.

288. Lee KM, Abel J, Ko Y, et al. Genetic polymorphisms of cytochrome P450 19 and 1B1, alcohol use, and breast cancer risk in Korean women. *Br J Cancer* 2003;88:675-8.

289. Lenz SK, Goldberg MS, Labreche F, et al. Association between alcohol consumption and postmenopausal breast cancer: results of a case-control study in Montreal, Quebec, Canada. *Cancer Causes Control* 2002;13:701-10.

290. Marcus PM, Newman B, Millikan RC, et al. The associations of adolescent cigarette smoking, alcoholic beverage consumption, environmental tobacco smoke, and ionizing radiation with subsequent breast cancer risk (United States). *Cancer Causes Control* 2000;11:271-8.

291. Mayberry RM, Stoddard-Wright C. Breast cancer risk factors among black women and white women: similarities and differences. *Am J Epidemiol* 1993;136:1445-56.

292. McCredie MRE, Dite GS, Giles GG, et al. Breast cancer in Australian women under the age of 40. *Cancer Causes Control* 1998;9:189-98.

293. Peacock SL, White E, Daling JR, et al. Relation between obesity and breast cancer in young women. *Am J Epidemiol* 1999;149:339-46.

294. Potischman N, Swanson CA, Coates RJ, et al. Dietary relationships with early onset (under age 45) breast cancer in a case-control study in the United States: Influence of chemotherapy treatment. *Cancer Causes Control* 1997;8:713-21.

295. Rosenberg L, Slone D, Shapiro S, et al. Breast cancer and alcoholic-beverage consumption. *Lancet* 1982;1:267-70.

296. Rosenberg L, Palmer JR, Miller DR, et al. A case-control study of alcoholic beverage consumption and breast cancer. *Am J Epidemiol* 1990;131:6-14.

297. Sneyd MJ, Paul C, Spears GF, et al. Alcohol consumption and risk of breast cancer. *Int J Cancer* 1991;48:812-5.

298. Sturmer T, Wang-Gohrke S, Arndt V, et al. Interaction between alcohol dehydrogenase II gene, alcohol consumption, and risk for breast cancer. *Br J Cancer* 2002;87:519-23.

299. Swanson CA, Coates RJ, Schoenberg JB, et al. Body size and breast cancer risk among women under age 45 years. *Am J Epidemiol* 1996;143:698-706.

300. Swanson CA, Coates RJ, Malone KE, et al. Alcohol consumption and breast cancer risk among women under age 45 years. *Epidemiology* 1997;8:231-7.

301. Tajima K, Hirose K, Ogawa M, et al. [Hospital epidemiology - a comparative case control study of breast and cervical cancers]. *Gan No Rinsho* 1990;Spec No:351-64.

302. Talamini R, La Vecchia C, Decarli A, et al. Social factors, diet and breast cancer in a northern Italian population. *Br J Cancer* 1984;49:723-9.

303. Tavani A, Gallus S, La Vecchia C, et al. Risk factors for breast cancer in women under 40 years. *Eur J Cancer* 1999;35:1361-7.

304. Thorand B, Kohlmeier L, Simonsen N, et al. Intake of fruits, vegetables, folic acid and related nutrients and risk of breast cancer in postmenopausal women. *Public Health Nutr* 1998;1:147-56.

305. Toniolo P, Riboli E, Protta F, et al. Breast cancer and alcohol consumption: a case-control study in northern Italy. *Cancer Res* 1989;49:5203-6.

306. Vecchia C, la Negri E, Parazzini F, et al. Alcohol and breast cancer: update from an Italian case-control study. *Eur J Cancer Clin Oncol* 1989;25:1711-7.

307. Viladiu P, Izquierdo A, de Sanjose S, et al. A breast cancer case-control study in Girona, Spain. Endocrine, familial and lifestyle factors. *Eur J Cancer Prev* 1996;5:329-35.

308. Williams RR, Horm JW. Association of cancer sites with tobacco and alcohol consumption and socioeconomic status of patients: interview study from the Third National Cancer Survey. *J Natl Cancer Inst* 1977;58:525-47.

309. Yim DS, Parkb SK, Yoo KY, et al. Relationship between the Val158Met polymorphism of catechol O-methyl transferase and breast cancer. *Pharmacogenetics* 2001;11:279-86.

310. Zheng T, Holford TR, Zahm SH, et al. Glutathione S-transferase M1 and T1 genetic polymorphisms, alcohol consumption and breast cancer risk. *Br J Cancer* 2003;88:58-62.

311. Anglin L, Mann RE, Smart RG. Changes in cancer mortality rates and per capita alcohol consumption in Ontario, 1963-1983. *Int J Addict* 1995;30:489-95.

312. Guo WD, Chow WH, Zheng W, et al. Diet, serum markers and breast cancer mortality in China. *Jpn J Cancer Res* 1994;85:572-7.

313. Baglietto L, English DR, Gertig DM, et al. Does dietary folate intake modify effect of alcohol consumption on breast cancer risk? Prospective cohort study. *BMJ* 2005;331:807.

314. Colditz GA, Rosner B. Cumulative risk of breast cancer to age 70 years according to risk factor status: data from the Nurses' Health Study. *Am J Epidemiol* 2000;152:950-64.

315. Holmberg L, Baron JA, Byers T, et al. Alcohol intake and breast cancer risk: effect of exposure from 15 years of age. *Cancer Epidemiol Biomarkers Prev* 1995;4:843-7.

316. Hoyer AP, Grandjean P, Jorgensen T, et al. Organochlorine exposure and risk of breast cancer. *Lancet* 1998;352:1816-20.

317. Adami HO, Lund E, Bergstrom R, et al. Cigarette smoking, alcohol consumption and risk of breast cancer in young women. *Br J Cancer* 1988;58:832-7.

318. Bowlin SJ, Leske MC, Varma A, et al. Breast cancer risk and alcohol consumption: results from a large case-control study. *Int J Epidemiol* 1997;26:915-23.

319. Claus EB, Stowe M, Carter D. Breast carcinoma in situ: Risk factors and screening patterns. *J Natl Cancer Inst* 2001;93:1811-7.

320. Fioretti F, Tavani A, Bosetti C, et al. Risk factors for breast cancer in nulliparous women. *Br J Cancer* 1999;79:1923-8.

321. Gallus S, Franceschi S, La Vecchia C. Alcohol, postmenopausal hormones, and breast cancer. *Ann Intern Med* 2003;139:601-2.

322. Hirose K, Tajima K, Hamajima N, et al. Impact of established risk factors for breast cancer in nulligravid Japanese women. *Breast Cancer* 2003;10:45-53.

323. Ibarluzea JM, Fernandez MF, Santa-Marina L, et al. Breast cancer risk and the combined effect of environmental estrogens. *Cancer Causes Control* 2004;15:591-600.

324. Iscovich JM, Iscovich RB, Howe G, et al. A case-control study of diet and breast cancer in Argentina. *Int J Cancer* 1989;44:770-6.

325. Landa MC, Frago N, Tres A. Diet and the risk of breast cancer in Spain. *Eur J Cancer Prev* 1994;3:313-20.

326. Li CI, Malone KE, Porter PL, et al. The relationship between alcohol use and risk of breast cancer by histology and hormone receptor status among women 65-79 years of age. *Cancer Epidemiol Biomarkers Prev* 2003;12:1061-6.

327. Lucena RA, Allam MF, Costabeber IH, et al. Breast cancer risk factors: PCB congeners. *Eur J Cancer Prev* 2001;10:117-9.

328. McElroy JA, Kanarek MS, Trentham-Dietz A, et al. Potential exposure to PCBs, DDT and PBDEs from sport-caught fish consumption in relation to breast cancer risk in Wisconsin. *Environ Health Perspect* 2004;112:156-62.

329. Mendonca GAS, Eluf-Neto J, Andrada-Serpa MJ, et al. Organochlorines and breast cancer: a case-control study in Brazil. *Int J Cancer* 1999;83:596-600.

330. Moorman PG, Ricciuti MF, Millikan RC, et al. Vitamin supplement use and breast cancer in a North Carolina population. *Public Health Nutr* 2001;4:821-7.

331. Okobia MN, Bunker CH, Lee LL, et al. Case-control study of risk factors for breast cancer in Nigerian women: a pilot study. *East Afr Med J* 2005;82:14-9.

332. Webster LA, Layde PM, Wingo PA, et al. Alcohol consumption and risk of breast cancer. *Lancet* 1983;2:724-6.

333. Zaridze D, Lifanova Y, Maximovitch D, et al. Diet, alcohol consumption and reproductive factors in a case-control study of breast cancer in Moscow. *Int J Cancer* 1991;48:493-501.

334. Barrett-Connor E, Friedlander NJ. Dietary fat, calories, and risk of breast cancer in postmenopausal women: a prospective population-based study. *J Am Coll Nutr* 1993;12:390-9.

335. Chen WY, Colditz GA, Rosner B, et al. Use of postmenopausal hormones, alcohol, and risk for invasive breast cancer. *Ann Intern Med* 2002;137:798-804.

336. Colditz GA, Rosner BA, Chen WY, et al. Risk factors for breast cancer according to estrogen and progesterone receptor status. *J Natl Cancer Inst* 2004;96:218-28.

337. Duffy C, Assaf AR, Cyr MG, et al. Alcohol and folate intake and breast cancer risk. *J Gen Intern Med* 2004;19:115.

338. Dumeaux V, Lund E, Hjartaker A. Use of oral contraceptives, alcohol, and risk for invasive breast cancer. *Cancer Epidemiol Biomarkers Prev* 2004;13:1302-7.

339. Feigelson HS, Jonas CR, Robertson AS, et al. Alcohol, folate, methionine, and risk of incident breast cancer in the American Cancer Society Cancer Prevention Study II Nutrition Cohort. *Cancer Epidemiol Biomarkers Prev* 2003;12:161-4.

340. Friedenreich CM, Howe GR, Miller AB, et al. A cohort study of alcohol consumption and risk of breast cancer. *Am J Epidemiol* 1993;137:512-20.

341. Fuchs CS, Stampfer MJ, Colditz GA, et al. Alcohol consumption and mortality among women. *N Engl J Med* 1995;332:1245-50.

342. Gapstur SM, Potter JD, Sellers TA, et al. Increased risk of breast cancer with

alcohol consumption in postmenopausal women. *Am J Epidemiol* 1992;136:1221-31.

343. Garland M, Hunter DJ, Colditz GA, et al. Alcohol consumption in relation to breast cancer risk in a cohort of United States women 25-42 years of age. *Cancer Epidemiol Biomarkers Prev* 1999;8:1017-21.

344. Giovannucci E, Stampfer MJ, Colditz GA, et al. Recall and selection bias in reporting past alcohol consumption among breast cancer cases. *Cancer Causes Control* 1993;4:441-8.

345. Goodman MT, Cologne JB, Moriwaki H, et al. Risk factors for primary breast cancer in Japan: 8-year follow-up of atomic bomb survivors. *Prev Med* 1997;26:144-53.

346. Hines LM, Hankinson SE, Smith-Warner SA, et al. A prospective study of the effect of alcohol consumption and ADH3 genotype on plasma steroid hormone levels and breast cancer risk. *Cancer Epidemiol Biomarkers Prev* 2000;9:1099-105.

347. Horn-Ross PL, Hoggatt KJ, West DW, et al. Recent diet and breast cancer risk: the California Teachers Study (USA). *Cancer Causes Control* 2002;13:407-15.

348. Jain MG, Ferrence RG, Rehm JT, et al. Alcohol and breast cancer mortality in a cohort study. *Breast Cancer Res Treat* 2000;64:201-9.

349. Kilkkinen A, Virtamo J, Vartiainen E, et al. Serum enterolactone concentration is not associated with breast cancer risk in a nested case-control study. *Int J Cancer* 2004;108:277-80.

350. Lin Y, Kikuchi S, Tamakoshi K, et al. Prospective study of alcohol consumption and breast cancer risk in Japanese women. *Int J Cancer* 2005;116:779-83.

351. Mattisson I, Wirfalt E, Wallstrom P, et al. High fat and alcohol intakes are risk factors of postmenopausal breast cancer: a prospective study from the Malmo diet and cancer cohort. *Int J Cancer* 2004;110:589-97.

352. Rissanen H, Knekt P, Jarvinen R, et al. Serum fatty acids and breast cancer incidence. *Nutr Cancer* 2003;45:168-75.

353. Rohan TE, Jain M, Howe GR, et al. Alcohol consumption and risk of breast cancer: a cohort study. *Cancer Causes Control* 2000;11:239-47.

354. Schatzkin A, Jones DY, Hoover RN, et al. Alcohol consumption and breast cancer in the epidemiologic follow-up study of the first National Health and Nutrition Examination Survey. *N Engl J Med* 1987;316:1169-73.

355. Sellers TA, Grabrick DM, Vierkant RA, et al. Does folate intake decrease risk of postmenopausal breast cancer among women with a family history? *Cancer Causes Control* 2004;15:113-20.

356. Sieri S, Krogh V, Muti P, et al. Fat and protein intake and subsequent breast cancer risk in postmenopausal women. *Nutr Cancer* 2002;42:10-7.

357. Stolzenberg-Solomon RZ, Leitzman M, Chang SS, et al. Dietary folate intake, alcohol use and postmenopausal breast cancer risk in the Prostate, Lung, Colorectal, Ovarian (PLCO) Cancer Screening Trial. *Am J Epidemiol* 2004;159:S69-S.

358. Suzuki R, Ye W, Rylander-Rudqvist T, et al. Alcohol and postmenopausal breast cancer risk defined by estrogen and progesterone receptor status: a prospective cohort study. *J Natl Cancer Inst* 2005;97:1601-8.

359. Tjonneland A, Thomsen BL, Stripp C, et al. Alcohol intake, drinking patterns and risk of postmenopausal breast cancer in Denmark: a prospective cohort study. *Cancer Causes Control* 2003;14:277-84.

360. van den Brandt PA, Goldbohm RA, van 't Veer P. Alcohol and breast cancer: results from The Netherlands Cohort Study. *Am J Epidemiol* 1995;141:907-15.

361. Willett WC, Stampfer MJ, Colditz GA, et al. Moderate alcohol consumption and the risk of breast cancer. *N Engl J Med* 1987;316:1174-80.

362. Zhang SM, Willett WC, Selhub J, et al. Plasma folate, vitamin B6, vitamin B12, homocysteine, and risk of breast cancer. *J Natl Cancer Inst* 2003;95:373-80.

363. Zhang Y, Kreger BE, Dorgan JF, et al. Alcohol consumption and risk of breast cancer: the Framingham Study revisited. *Am J Epidemiol* 1999;149:93-101.

364. Schatzkin A, Carter CL, Green SB, et al. Is alcohol consumption related to breast cancer? Results from the Framingham Heart Study. *J Natl Cancer Inst* 1989;81:31-5.

365. Brandt B, Hermann S, Straif K, et al. Modification of breast cancer risk in young women by a polymorphic sequence in the egfr gene. *Cancer Res* 2004;64:7-12.

366. Cade J, Thomas E, Vail A. Case-control study of breast cancer in south east England: nutritional factors. *J Epidemiol Community Health* 1998;52:105-10.

367. Cooper JA, Rohan TE, Cant EL, et al. Risk factors for breast cancer by oestrogen receptor status: a population-based case-control study. *Br J Cancer* 1989;59:119-25.

368. Favero A, Parpinel M, Franceschi S. Diet and risk of breast cancer: major findings from an Italian case-control study. *Biomed Pharmacother* 1998;52:109-15.

369. Ferraroni M, Decarli A, Willett WC, et al. Alcohol and breast cancer risk: a case-control study from northern Italy. *Int J Epidemiol* 1991;20:859-64.

370. Furberg H, Newman B, Moorman P, et al. Lactation and breast cancer risk. *Int J Epidemiol* 1999;28:396-402.

371. Ghadirian P, Lacroix A, Perret C, et al. Breast cancer risk and nutrient intake among French Canadians in Montreal: A case-control study. *Breast* 1998;7:108-13.

372. Graham S, Hellmann R, Marshall J, et al. Nutritional epidemiology of postmenopausal breast cancer in western New York. *Am J Epidemiol*

1991;134:552-66.

373. Harris RE, Wynder EL. Breast cancer and alcohol consumption. A study in weak associations. *JAMA* 1988;259:2867-71.

374. Hebestreit A, Swai B, Krawinkel M. Breast cancer and diet in the Kilimanjaro region of Tanzania. *J Nutr* 2003;133:3852S-S.

375. Kohlmeier L, Simonsen N, van 't Veer P, et al. Adipose tissue trans fatty acids and breast cancer in the European Community Multicenter Study on Antioxidants, Myocardial Infarction, and Breast Cancer. *Cancer Epidemiol Biomarkers Prev* 1997;6:705-10.

376. Kropp S, Becher H, Nieters A, et al. Low-to-moderate alcohol consumption and breast cancer risk by age 50 years among women in Germany. *Am J Epidemiol* 2001;154:624-34.

377. Kumar NB, Riccardi D, Cantor A, et al. A case-control study evaluating the association of purposeful physical activity, body fat distribution, and steroid hormones on premenopausal breast cancer risk. *Breast J* 2005;11:266-72.

378. Lee EO, Ahn SH, You C, et al. Determining the main risk factors and high-risk groups of breast cancer using a predictive model for breast cancer risk assessment in South Korea. *Cancer Nurs* 2004;27:400-6.

379. Lilla C, Koehler T, Kropp S, et al. Alcohol dehydrogenase 1B (ADH1B) genotype, alcohol consumption and breast cancer risk by age 50 years in a German case-control study. *Br J Cancer* 2005;92:2039-41.

380. Mannisto S, Virtanen M, Kataja V, et al. Lifetime alcohol consumption and breast cancer: a case-control study in Finland. *Public Health Nutr* 2000;3:11-8.

381. Mezzetti M, La Vecchia C, Decarli A, et al. Population attributable risk for breast cancer: diet, nutrition, and physical exercise. *J Natl Cancer Inst* 1998;90:389-94.

382. Newcomb PA, Egan KM, Titus-Ernstoff L, et al. Lactation in relation to postmenopausal breast cancer. *Am J Epidemiol* 1999;150:174-82.

383. Rohan TE, McMichael AJ. Alcohol consumption and risk of breast cancer. *Int J Cancer* 1988;41:695-9.

384. Tavani A, Mezzetti M, La Vecchia C, et al. Influence of selected dietary and lifestyle risk factors on familial propensity to breast cancer. *Epidemiology* 1999;10:96-8.

385. Terry P, Rohan TE, Wolk A, et al. Fish consumption and breast cancer risk. *Nutr Cancer* 2002;44:1-6.

386. Toniolo P, Riboli E, Cappa AP. [Diet and breast cancer. A population study in the Vercelli Province]. *Epidemiol Prev* 1990;12:59-61.

387. Trentham-Dietz A, Newcomb PA, Storer BE, et al. Risk factors for carcinoma in situ of the breast. *Cancer Epidemiol Biomarkers Prev* 2000;9:697-703.

388. van't Veer P, Kok FJ, Hermus RJ, et al. Alcohol dose, frequency and age at first

exposure in relation to the risk of breast cancer. *Int J Epidemiol* 1989;18:511-7.

389. Viel JF, Perarnau JM, Challier B, et al. Alcoholic calories, red wine consumption and breast cancer among premenopausal women. *Eur J Epidemiol* 1997;13:639-43.

390. Yoo K, Tajima K, Park S, et al. Postmenopausal obesity as a breast cancer risk factor according to estrogen and progesterone receptor status (Japan). *Cancer Lett* 2001;167:57-63.

391. Zhu K, Davidson NE, Hunter S, et al. Methyl-group dietary intake and risk of breast cancer among African-American women: a case-control study by methylation status of the estrogen receptor alpha genes. *Cancer Causes Control* 2003;14:827-36.

392. Boing H, Martinez L, Frentzel Beyme R, et al. Regional nutritional pattern and cancer mortality in the Federal Republic of Germany. *Nutr Cancer* 1985;7:121-30.

393. Ewertz M, Duffy SW. Incidence of female breast cancer in relation to prevalence of risk factors in Denmark. *Int J Cancer* 1994;56:783-7.

394. Grant WB. An ecologic study of dietary and solar ultraviolet-B links to breast carcinoma mortality rates. *Cancer* 2002;94:272-81.

395. Lagiou P, Trichopoulou A, Henderickx HK, et al. Household budget survey nutritional data in relation to mortality from coronary heart disease, colorectal cancer and female breast cancer in European countries. *Eur J Clin Nutr* 1999;53:328-32.

396. Smith-Warner SA, Spiegelman D, Yaun SS, et al. Alcohol and breast cancer in women: a pooled analysis of cohort studies. *JAMA* 1998;279:535-40.

397. Hamajima N, Hirose K, Tajima K, et al. Alcohol, tobacco and breast cancer - collaborative reanalysis of individual data from 53 epidemiological studies, including 58,515 women with breast cancer and 95,067 women without the disease. *Br J Cancer* 2002;87:1234-45.

398. Dumitrescu RG, Shields PG. The etiology of alcohol-induced breast cancer. *Alcohol* 2005;35:213-25.

399. Boffetta P, Hashibe M. Alcohol and cancer. *Lancet Oncol* 2006;7:149-56.

400. Li CI, Daling JR, Malone KE, et al. Relationship between established breast cancer risk factors and risk of seven different histologic types of invasive breast cancer. *Cancer Epidemiol Biomarkers Prev* 2006;15:946-54.

401. Chen CJ, Wang LY, Lu SN, et al. Elevated aflatoxin exposure and increased risk of hepatocellular carcinoma. *Hepatology* 1996;24:38-42.

402. Ogimoto I, Shibata A, Kurozawa Y, et al. Risk of death due to hepatocellular carcinoma among drinkers and ex-drinkers. Univariate analysis of JACC study data. *Kurume Med J* 2004;51:59-70.

403. Kono S, Ikeda M, Tokudome S, et al. Alcohol and cancer in male Japanese physicians. *J Cancer Res Clin Oncol* 1985;109:82-5.

404. Kono S, Ikeda M, Tokudome S, et al. Alcohol and mortality: a cohort study of male Japanese physicians. *Int J Epidemiol* 1986;15:527-32.

405. Inaba Y, Kikuchi S, Namihisa T, et al. [The effect of smoking and drinking habit on the process from liver cirrhosis to liver cancer]. *Gan No Rinsho* 1990;Spec No:299-304.

406. Inaba Y, Namihisa T, Ichikawa S, et al. [A long-term follow-up study of the histologically confirmed chronic liver diseases in the Juntedo University Hospital]. *Gan No Rinsho* 1989;35:221-6.

407. Yuan JM, Ross RK, Gao YT, et al. Follow up study of moderate alcohol intake and mortality among middle aged men in Shanghai, China. *BMJ* 1997;314:18-23.

408. Tu JT, Gao RN, Zhang DH, et al. Hepatitis B virus and primary liver cancer on Chongming Island, People's Republic of China. *Natl Cancer Inst Monogr* 1985;69:213-5.

409. Nishiuchi M, Shinji Y. [Increased incidence of hepatocellular carcinoma in abstinent patients with alcoholic cirrhosis]. *Gan To Kagaku Ryoho* 1990;17:1-6.

410. Goodman MT, Moriwaki H, Vaeth M, et al. Prospective cohort study of risk factors for primary liver cancer in Hiroshima and Nagasaki, Japan. *Epidemiology* 1995;6:36-41.

411. Tanaka K, Sakai H, Hashizume M, et al. A long-term follow-up study on risk factors for hepatocellular carcinoma among Japanese patients with liver cirrhosis. *Jpn J Cancer Res* 1998;89:1241-50.

412. Evans AA, Chen G, Ross EA, et al. Eight-year follow-up of the 90,000-person Haimen City cohort: I. hepatocellular carcinoma mortality, risk factors, and gender differences. *Cancer Epidemiol Biomarkers Prev* 2002;11:369-76.

413. Wang LY, Hatch M, Chen CJ, et al. Aflatoxin exposure and risk of hepatocellular carcinoma in Taiwan. *Int J Cancer* 1996;67:620-5.

414. Wang LY, You SL, Lu SN, et al. Risk of hepatocellular carcinoma and habits of alcohol drinking, betel quid chewing and cigarette smoking: a cohort of 2416 HBsAg-seropositive and 9421 HBsAg-seronegative male residents in Taiwan. *Cancer Causes Control* 2003;14:241-50.

415. Kato I, Tominaga S, Ikari A. The risk and predictive factors for developing liver cancer among patients with decompensated liver cirrhosis. *Jpn J Clin Oncol* 1992;22:278-85.

416. Thygesen LC, Albertsen K, Johansen C, et al. Cancer incidence among Danish brewery workers. *Int J Cancer* 2005;116:774-8.

417. Hirayama T. A large-scale cohort study on risk factors for primary liver cancer, with special reference to the role of cigarette smoking. *Cancer Chemother Pharmacol* 1989;23 Suppl:S114-7.

418. London WT, Evans AA, McGlynn K, et al. Viral, host and environmental risk factors for hepatocellular carcinoma: a prospective study in Haimen City, China. *Intervirology* 1995;38:155-61.

419. Sakoda LC, Graubard BI, Evans AA, et al. Toenail selenium and risk of hepatocellular carcinoma mortality in Haimen City, China. *Int J Cancer* 2005;115:618-24.

420. Yu MW, Horng IS, Hsu KH, et al. Plasma selenium levels and risk of hepatocellular carcinoma among men with chronic hepatitis virus infection. *Am J Epidemiol* 1999;150:367-74.

421. Meng W, Tang JG, Shen FM, et al. Nested case-control study on risk factors of hepatocellular carcinoma. *Fudan Univ J Med Sci* 2002;29:368-71.

422. Ross RK, Yuan JM, Yu MC, et al. Urinary aflatoxin biomarkers and risk of hepatocellular carcinoma. *Lancet* 1992;339:943-6.

423. Chalasani N, Baluyut A, Ismail A, et al. Cholangiocarcinoma in patients with primary sclerosing cholangitis: a multicenter case-control study. *Hepatology* 2000;31:7-11.

424. Kuper H, Lagiou P, Mucci LA, et al. Risk factors for cholangiocarcinoma in a low risk Caucasian population. *Soz Praeventivmed* 2001;46:182-5.

425. Austin H, Delzell E, Grufferman S, et al. A case-control study of hepatocellular carcinoma and the hepatitis B virus, cigarette smoking, and alcohol consumption. *Cancer Res* 1986;46:962-6.

426. La Vecchia C, Negri E, Decarli A, et al. Risk factors for hepatocellular carcinoma in northern Italy. *Int J Cancer* 1988;42:872-6.

427. Tsukuma H, Hiyama T, Oshima A, et al. A case-control study of hepatocellular carcinoma in Osaka, Japan. *Int J Cancer* 1990;45:231-6.

428. Qureshi H, Zuberi SJ, Jafarey NA, et al. Hepatocellular carcinoma in Karachi. *J Gastroenterol Hepatol* 1990;5:1-6.

429. Yu MW, You SL, Chang AS, et al. Association between hepatitis C virus antibodies and hepatocellular carcinoma in Taiwan. *Cancer Res* 1991;51:5621-5.

430. Chen CJ, Liang KY, Chang AS, et al. Effects of hepatitis B virus, alcohol drinking, cigarette smoking and familial tendency on hepatocellular carcinoma. *Hepatology* 1991;13:398-406.

431. Yamaguchi G. Hepatocellular carcinoma and its risk factors - their annual changes and effects on the age at onset. *Kurume Med J* 1993;40:33-40.

432. Braga C, La Vecchia C, Negri E, et al. Attributable risks for hepatocellular carcinoma in northern Italy. *Eur J Cancer* 1997;33:629-34.

433. La Vecchia C, Negri E, Cavalieri d'Óro L, et al. Liver cirrhosis and the risk of primary liver cancer. *Eur J Cancer Prev* 1998;7:315-20.

434. Mukaiya M, Nishi M, Miyake H, et al. Chronic liver diseases for the risk of hepatocellular carcinoma: a case-control study in Japan. Etiologic association of alcohol consumption, cigarette smoking and the development of chronic liver

diseases. *Hepatogastroenterology* 1998;45:2328-32.

435. Mandishona E, MacPhail AP, Gordeuk VR, et al. Dietary iron overload as a risk factor for hepatocellular carcinoma in Black Africans. *Hepatology* 1998;27:1563-6.

436. Kuper H, Tzonou A, Kaklamani E, et al. Tobacco smoking, alcohol consumption and their interaction in the causation of hepatocellular carcinoma. *Int J Cancer* 2000;85:498-502.

437. Kuper H, Tzonou A, Lagiou P, et al. Diet and hepatocellular carcinoma: a case-control study in Greece. *Nutr Cancer* 2000;38:6-12.

438. Omer RE, Verhoef L, Van't Veer P, et al. Peanut butter intake, GSTM1 genotype and hepatocellular carcinoma: a case-control study in Sudan. *Cancer Causes Control* 2001;12:23-32.

439. Tsai JF, Chuang LY, Jeng JE, et al. Betel quid chewing as a risk factor for hepatocellular carcinoma: a case-control study. *Br J Cancer* 2001;84:709-13.

440. Donato F, Tagger A, Gelatti U, et al. Alcohol and hepatocellular carcinoma: the effect of lifetime intake and hepatitis virus infections in men and women. *Am J Epidemiol* 2002;155:323-31.

441. Yu SZ, Huang XE, Koide T, et al. Hepatitis B and C viruses infection, lifestyle and genetic polymorphisms as risk factors for hepatocellular carcinoma in Haimen, China. *Jpn J Cancer Res* 2002;93:1287-92.

442. Yu H, Harris RE, Kabat GC, et al. Cigarette smoking, alcohol consumption and primary liver cancer: a case-control study in the USA. *Int J Cancer* 1988;42:325-8.

443. Munaka M, Kohshi K, Kawamoto T, et al. Genetic polymorphisms of tobacco- and alcohol-related metabolizing enzymes and the risk of hepatocellular carcinoma. *J Cancer Res Clin Oncol* 2003;129:355-60.

444. Yuan JM, Govindarajan S, Arakawa K, et al. Synergism of alcohol, diabetes, and viral hepatitis on the risk of hepatocellular carcinoma in blacks and whites in the U.S. *Cancer* 2004;101:1009-17.

445. Buckley JD, Sather H, Ruccione K, et al. A case-control study of risk factors for hepatoblastoma. A report from the Childrens Cancer Study Group. *Cancer* 1989;64:1169-76.

446. Inaba Y, Maruchi N, Matsuda M, et al. A case-control study on liver cancer with special emphasis on the possible aetiological role of schistosomiasis. *Int J Epidemiol* 1984;13:408-12.

447. Hiyama T, Tsukuma H, Oshima A, et al. [Liver cancer and life style - drinking habits and smoking habits]. *Gan No Rinsho* 1990;Spec No:249-56.

448. Newton R, Ngilimana PJ, Grulich A, et al. Cancer in Rwanda. *Int J Cancer* 1996;66:75-81.

449. Lu SN, Lin TM, Chen CJ, et al. A case-control study of primary hepatocellular carcinoma in Taiwan. *Cancer* 1988;62:2051-5.

450. Wang A. [An epidemiologic study on the etiology of primary hepatocellular carcinoma in Shaanxi]. *Zhonghua Liu Xing Bing Xue Za Zhi* 1993;14:208-11.

451. Wang ZJ, Zhou YP, Cheng B. [An epidemiologic study on the aetiological factors of primary liver cancer in Shunde City of Guangdong province]. *Zhonghua Liu Xing Bing Xue Za Zhi* 1996;17:141-4.

452. Stemhagen A, Slade J, Altman R, et al. Occupational risk factors and liver cancer. A retrospective case-control study of primary liver cancer in New Jersey. *Am J Epidemiol* 1983;117:443-54.

453. Olubuyide IO, Bamgboye EA. A case-controlled study of the current role of cigarette smoking and alcohol consumption in primary liver cell carcinoma in Nigerians. *Afr J Med Med Sci* 1990;19:191-4.

454. Fukuda K, Shibata A, Hirohata I, et al. A hospital-based case-control study on hepatocellular carcinoma in Fukuoka and Saga prefectures, Northern Kyushu, Japan. *Jpn J Cancer Res* 1993;84:708-14.

455. Tsai JF, Jeng JE, Chuang LY, et al. Habitual betel quid chewing and risk for hepatocellular carcinoma complicat ing cirrhosis. *Medicine (Baltimore)* 2004;83:176-87.

456. Gelatti U, Covolo L, Franceschini M, et al. Coffee consumption reduces the risk of hepatocellular carcinoma independently of its aetiology: a case-control study. *J Hepatol* 2005;42:528-34.

457. Lam KC, Yu MC, Leung JW, et al. Hepatitis B virus and cigarette smoking: risk factors for hepatocellular carcinoma in Hong Kong. *Cancer Res* 1982;42:5246-8.

458. Lin J. [A study on aetiological factors of primary hepato-carcinoma in Tianjin China]. *Zhonghua Liu Xing Bing Xue Za Zhi* 1991;12:346-9.

459. Tanaka K, Hirohata T, Takeshita S. Blood transfusion, alcohol consumption, and cigarette smoking in causation of hepatocellular carcinoma: a case-control study in Fukuoka, Japan. *Jpn J Cancer Res* 1988;79:1075-82.

460. Yu MC, Tong MJ, Govindarajan S, et al. Nonviral risk factors for hepatocellular carcinoma in a low-risk population, the non-Asians of Los Angeles County, California. *J Natl Cancer Inst* 1991;83:1820-6.

461. Jee SH, Ohrr H, Sull JW, et al. Cigarette smoking, alcohol drinking, hepatitis B, and risk for hepatocellular carcinoma in Korea. *J Natl Cancer Inst* 2004;96:1851-6.

462. Miyakawa H, Sato C, Izumi N, et al. Hepatitis C virus infection in alcoholic liver cirrhosis in Japan: its contribution to the development of hepatocellular carcinoma. *Alcohol Alcohol Suppl* 1993;1a:85-90.

463. Miyakawa H, Izumi N, Marumo F, et al. Roles of alcohol, hepatitis virus infection, and gender in the development of hepatocellular carcinoma in patients with liver cirrhosis. *Alcohol Clin Exp Res* 1996;20:91a-4a.

464. Sun Z, Lu P, Gail MH, et al. Increased risk of hepatocellular carcinoma in male hepatitis B surface antigen carriers with chronic hepatitis who have detectable urinary aflatoxin metabolite M1. *Hepatology* 1999;30:379-83.

465. Khan KN, Yatsuhashi H. Effect of alcohol consumption on the progression of hepatitis C virus infection and risk of hepatocellular carcinoma in Japanese patients. *Alcohol Alcohol* 2000;35:286-95.

466. Sharp GB, Lagarde F, Mizuno T, et al. Relationship of hepatocellular carcinoma to soya food consumption: a cohort-based, case-control study in Japan. *Int J Cancer* 2005;115:290-5.

467. Dutta U, Byth K, Kench J, et al. Risk factors for development of hepatocellular carcinoma among Australians with hepatitis C: a case-control study. *Aust N Z J Med* 1999;29:300-7.

468. Oshima A, Tsukuma H, Hiyama T, et al. Follow-up study of HBs Ag-positive blood donors with special reference to effect of drinking and smoking on development of liver cancer. *Int J Cancer* 1984;34:775-9.

469. Parkin DM, Srivatanakul P, Khlat M, et al. Liver-cancer in Thailand. I. A case-control study of cholangiocarcinoma. *Int J Cancer* 1991;48:323-8.

470. Shin HR, Lee CU, Park HJ, et al. Hepatitis B and C virus, Clonorchis sinensis for the risk of liver cancer: a case-control study in Pusan, Korea. *Int J Epidemiol* 1996;25:933-40.

471. Colloredo Mels G, Paris B, Bertone V, et al. [Primary hepatocarcinoma. Epidemiologic case-control study in the province of Bergamo]. *Minerva Med* 1986;77:297-306.

472. Srivatanakul P, Parkin DM, Khlat M, et al. Liver-cancer in Thailand. 2. A case-control study of hepatocellular-carcinoma. *Int J Cancer* 1991;48:329-32.

473. Tanaka K, Hirohata T, Takeshita S, et al. Hepatitis B virus, cigarette smoking and alcohol consumption in the development of hepatocellular carcinoma: a case-control study in Fukuoka, Japan. *Int J Cancer* 1992;51:509-14.

474. Cordier S, Le TB, Verger P, et al. Viral infections and chemical exposures as risk factors for hepatocellular carcinoma in Vietnam. *Int J Cancer* 1993;55:196-201.

475. Pyong SJ, Tsukuma H, Hiyama T. Case-control study of hepatocellular carcinoma among Koreans living in Osaka, Japan. *Jpn J Cancer Res* 1994;85:674-9.

476. Arico S, Corrao G, Torchio P, et al. A strong negative association between alcohol consumption and the risk of hepatocellular carcinoma in cirrhotic patients. A case-control study. *Eur J Epidemiol* 1994;10:251-7.

477. Zhang JY, Wang X, Han SG, et al. A case-control study of risk factors for hepatocellular carcinoma in Henan, China. *Am J Trop Med Hyg* 1998;59:947-51.

478. Tagger A, Donato F, Ribero ML, et al. Case-control study on hepatitis C virus (HCV) as a risk factor for hepatocellular carcinoma: the role of HCV genotypes and the synergism with hepatitis B virus and alcohol. Brescia HCC Study. *Int J Cancer* 1999;81:695-9.

479. Hassan MM, Hwang LY, Hatten CJ, et al. Risk factors for hepatocellular carcinoma: synergism of alcohol with viral hepatitis and diabetes mellitus. *Hepatology* 2002;36:1206-13.

480. Donato F, Gelatti U, Tagger A, et al. Intrahepatic cholangiocarcinoma and hepatitis C and B virus infection, alcohol intake, and hepatolithiasis: a case-control study in Italy. *Cancer Causes Control* 2001;12:959-64.

481. Yu MC, Mack T, Hanisch R, et al. Hepatitis, alcohol consumption, cigarette smoking, and hepatocellular carcinoma in Los Angeles. *Cancer Res* 1983;43:6077-9.

482. Infante F, Voirol M, Brahime Reteno O, et al. [Alcohol, tobacco and food consumption in liver cancer and cirrhosis. Preliminary results]. *Schweiz Med Wochenschr* 1980;110:875-6.

483. Bulatao Jayme J, Almero EM, Castro MC, et al. A case-control dietary study of primary liver cancer risk from aflatoxin exposure. *Int J Epidemiol* 1982;11:112-9.

484. Mayans MV, Calvet X, Bruix J, et al. Risk factors for hepatocellular carcinoma in Catalonia, Spain. *Int J Cancer* 1990;46:378-81.

485. Hardell L, Bengtsson NO, Jonsson U, et al. Aetiological aspects on primary liver cancer with special regard to alcohol, organic solvents and acute intermittent porphyria - an epidemiological investigation. *Br J Cancer* 1984;50:389-97.

486. Prior P. Long-term cancer risk in alcoholism. *Alcohol Alcohol* 1988;23:163-71.

487. Mohamed AE, Kew MC, Groeneveld HT. Alcohol consumption as a risk factor for hepatocellular carcinoma in urban southern African blacks. *Int J Cancer* 1992;51:537-41.

488. Bartsch H, Nair J. Chronic inflammation and oxidative stress in the genesis and perpetuation of cancer: role of lipid peroxidation, DNA damage, and repair. *Langenbecks Arch Surg* 2006;391:499-510.

489. Seitz HK, Stickel F. Risk factors and mechanisms of hepatocarcinogenesis with special emphasis on alcohol and oxidative stress. *Biol Chem* 2006;387:349-60.

490. Franceschi S, Montella M, Polesel J, et al. Hepatitis viruses, alcohol, and tobacco in the etiology of hepatocellular carcinoma in Italy. *Cancer Epidemiol Biomarkers Prev* 2006;15:683-9.

491. Hiatt RA, Tolan K, Quesenberry CP, Jr. Renal cell carcinoma and thiazide use: a historical, case-control study (California, USA). *Cancer Causes Control* 1994;5:319-25.

492. Rashidkhani B, Akesson A, Lindblad P, et al. Alcohol consumption and risk of renal cell carcinoma: a prospective study of Swedish women. *Int J Cancer* 2005;117:848-53.

493. Washio M, Mori M, Sakauchi F, et al. Risk factors for kidney cancer in a Japanese population: findings from the JACC study. *J Epidemiol* 2005;15:S203-S11.

494. Hu J, Mao Y, White K, et al. Overweight and obesity in adults and risk of renal cell carcinoma in Canada. *Soz Praventivmed* 2003;48:178-85.

495. Mucci LA, Dickman PW, Steineck G, et al. Dietary acrylamide and cancer of the large bowel, kidney, and bladder: absence of an association in a population-based study in Sweden. *Br J Cancer* 2003;88:84-9.

496. Parker AS, Cerhan JR, Lynch CF, et al. Gender, alcohol consumption, and renal cell carcinoma. *Am J Epidemiol* 2002;155:455-62.

497. Augustsson K, Skog K, Jagerstad M, et al. Dietary heterocyclic amines and cancer of the colon, rectum, bladder, and kidney: a population-based study. *Lancet* 1999;353:703-7.

498. Yuan JM, Gago-Dominguez M, Castelao JE, et al. Cruciferous vegetables in relation to renal cell carcinoma. *Int J Cancer* 1998;77:211-6.

499. Pelucchi C, La Vecchia C, Negri E, et al. Alcohol drinking and renal cell carcinoma in women and men. *Eur J Cancer Prev* 2002;11:543-5.

500. Goodman MT, Morgenstern H, Wynder EL. A case-control study of factors affecting the development of renal cell cancer. *Am J Epidemiol* 1986;124:926-41.

501. Wynder EL, Mabuchi K, Whitmore WF, Jr. Epidemiology of adenocarcinoma of the kidney. *J Natl Cancer Inst* 1974;53:1619-34.

502. Hu J, Ugnat AM, Canadian Cancer Registries Epidemiology Research Group. Active and passive smoking and risk of renal cell carcinoma in Canada. *Eur J Cancer* 2005;41:770-8.

503. Boeing H, Schlehofer B, Wahrendorf J. Diet, obesity and risk for renal cell carcinoma: results from a case control-study in Germany. *Z Ernahrungswiss* 1997;36:3-11.

504. Wolk A, Gridley G, Niwa S, et al. International renal cell cancer study. VII. Role of diet. *Int J Cancer* 1996;65:67-73.

505. Chow WH, Gridley G, Mclaughlin JK, et al. Protein intake and risk of renal cell cancer. *J Natl Cancer Inst* 1994;86:1131-9.

506. Mclaughlin JK, Gao YT, Gao RN, et al. Risk factors for renal-cell cancer in Shanghai, China. *Int J Cancer* 1992;52:562-5.

507. Yu MC, Mack TM, Hanisch R, et al. Cigarette smoking, obesity, diuretic use, and coffee consumption as risk factors for renal cell carcinoma. *J Natl Cancer Inst* 1986;77:351-6.

508. Benhamou S, Lenfant MH, Ory-Paoletti C, et al. Risk factors for renal-cell carcinoma in a French case-control study. *Int J Cancer* 1993;55:32-6.

509. Brownson RC. A case-control study of renal cell carcinoma in relation to occupation, smoking, and alcohol consumption. *Arch Environ Health* 1988;43:238-41.

510. Mahabir S, Leitzmann MF, Virtanen MJ, et al. Prospective study of alcohol drinking and renal cell cancer risk in a cohort of Finnish male smokers. *Cancer Epidemiol Biomarkers Prev* 2005;14:170-5.

511. Prineas RJ, Folsom AR, Zhang ZM, et al. Nutrition and other risk factors for renal cell carcinoma in postmenopausal women. *Epidemiology* 1997;8:31-6.

512. Nicodemus KK, Sweeney C, Folsom AR. Evaluation of dietary, medical and lifestyle risk factors for incident kidney cancer in postmenopausal women. *Int J Cancer* 2004;108:115-21.

513. Hirvonen T, Virtamo J, Korhonen P, et al. Flavonol and flavone intake and the risk of cancer in male smokers (Finland). *Cancer Causes Control* 2001;12:789-96.

514. Mattioli S, Truffelli D, Baldasseroni A, et al. Occupational risk factors for renal cell cancer: a case - control study in northern Italy. *J Occup Environ Med* 2002;44:1028-36.

515. Lindblad P, Wolk A, Bergstrom R, et al. Diet and risk of renal cell cancer: a population-based case-control study. *Cancer Epidemiol Biomarkers Prev* 1997;6:215-23.

516. Talamini R, Baron AE, Barra S, et al. A case-control study of risk factor for renal cell cancer in northern Italy. *Cancer Causes Control* 1990;1:125-31.

517. Lee JE, Giovannucci E, Smith-Warner SA, et al. Total fluid intake and use of individual beverages and risk of renal cell cancer in two large cohorts. *Cancer Epidemiol Biomarkers Prev* 2006;15:1204-11.

Chapter 4.9

1. United States Environmental Protection Agency. 2004. *Pesticides Industry Sales and Usage: 2000 and 2001 Market Estimates.* http://www.epa.gov/oppbead1/pestsales/01pestsales/market_estimates2001.pdf.

2. International Agency for Research on Cancer. 1987. *Androgenic (Anabolic) Steroids.* In: IARC Monogr Eval Carcinog Risks Hum no S7.

3. Rietjens IM, Boersma MG, van der Woude H, et al. Flavonoids and alkenylbenzenes: mechanisms of mutagenic action and carcinogenic risk. *Mutat Res* 2005;574:124-38.

4. Jukes D. *Food additives in the European Union.* http://www.foodlaw.rdg.ac.uk/additive.htm. 2006.

5. From the Centers for Disease Control. Public Health Service report on fluoride benefits and risks. *JAMA* 1991;266:1061-2, 6-7.

6. National Research Council. *Fluoride in Drinking Water. A Scientific Review of EPA's Standards.* Washington, DC:

National Academy Press, 2006.

7. Bassin EB, Wypij D, Davis RB, et al. Age-specific fluoride exposure in drinking water and osteosarcoma (United States). *Cancer Causes Control* 2006;17:421-8.

8. Douglass CW, Joshipura K. Caution needed in fluoride and osteosarcoma study. *Cancer Causes Control* 2006;17:481-2.

9. Centres for Disease Control and Prevention. *CDC Statement on water fluoridation and osteosarcoma.* http://www.cdc.gov/fluoridation/safety/osteosarcoma.htm. 2007.

10. Food and Agriculture Organization of the United Nations, World Health Organization. *Summary of evaluations performed by the Joint FAO/WHO Expert Committee on Food Additives.* http://jecfa.ilsi.org/. 2006.

Chapter 4.10

1. WHO. 2002. *Diet, nutrition and the prevention of chronic diseases: report of a joint WHO/FAO expert consultation.* In: WHO Technical Report Series no 916. http://www.who.int/entity/dietphysicalactivity/publications/trs916/download/en/index.html.

2. Calder PC. n-3 polyunsaturated fatty acids, inflammation, and inflammatory diseases. *The American journal of clinical nutrition* 2006;83:1505S-19S.

3. Bentley TG, Willett WC, Weinstein MC, et al. Population-level changes in folate intake by age, gender, and race/ethnicity after folic acid fortification. *Am J Public Health* 2006;96:2040-7.

4. Levine N, Moon TE, Cartmel B, et al. Trial of retinol and isotretinoin in skin cancer prevention: a randomised, double-blind, controlled trial. Southwest Skin Cancer Prevention Study Group. *Cancer Epidemiol Biomarkers Prev* 1997;6:957-61.

5. Moon TE, Levine N, Cartmel B, et al. Effect of retinol in preventing squamous cell skin cancer in moderate-risk subjects: a randomised, double-blind, controlled trial. Southwest Skin Cancer Prevention Study Group. *Cancer Epidemiol Biomarkers Prev* 1997;6:949-56.

6. Levine N, Meyskens FL. Topical vitamin-A-acid therapy for cutaneous metastatic melanoma. *Lancet* 1980;2:224-6.

7. Le Marchand L, Saltzman BS, Hankin JH, et al. Sun exposure, diet, and melanoma in Hawaii Caucasians. *Am J Epidemiol* 2006;164:232-45.

8. Goodman GE, Thornquist, M. D., Balmes, J., Cullen, M. R., Meyskens, F. L. Jr, Omenn, G. S., Valanis, B., and Williams, J. H. Jr. The Beta-Carotene and Retinol Efficacy Trial: incidence of lung cancer and cardiovascular disease mortality during 6-year follow-up after stopping beta-carotene and retinol supplements. *J Natl Cancer Inst* 2004;96:1743-50.

9. Omenn GS, Goodman GE, Thornquist MD, et al. Effects of a combination of beta carotene and vitamin A on lung cancer

and cardiovascular disease. *N Engl J Med* 1996;334:1150-5.

10. Omenn GS, Goodman GE, Thornquist MD, et al. Risk factors for lung cancer and for intervention effects in CARET, the Beta-Carotene and Retinol Efficacy Trial. *J Natl Cancer Inst* 1996;88:1550-9.

11. Musk AW, de Klerk NH, Ambrosini GL, et al. Vitamin A and cancer prevention I: observations in workers previously exposed to asbestos at Wittenoom, Western Australia. *Int J Cancer* 1998;75:355-61.

12. Paganini-Hill A, Chao A, Ross RK, et al. Vitamin A, beta-carotene, and the risk of cancer: a prospective study. *J Natl Cancer Inst* 1987;79:443-8.

13. Shibata A, Paganini Hill A, Ross RK, et al. Intake of vegetables, fruits, beta-carotene, vitamin C and vitamin supplements and cancer incidence among the elderly: a prospective study. *Br J Cancer* 1992;66:673-9.

14. Samet JM, Skipper BJ, Humble CG, et al. Lung cancer risk and vitamin A consumption in New Mexico. *Am Rev Respir Dis* 1985;131:198-202.

15. Wu AH, Yu MC, Thomas DC, et al. Personal and family history of lung disease as risk factors for adenocarcinoma of the lung. *Cancer Res* 1988;48:7279-84.

16. Virtamo J, Pietinen P, Huttunen JK, et al. Incidence of cancer and mortality following alpha-tocopherol and beta-carotene supplementation: a postintervention follow-up. *JAMA* 2003;290:476-85.

17. Albanes D, Heinonen OP, Taylor PR, et al. Alpha-Tocopherol and beta-carotene supplements and lung cancer incidence in the alpha-tocopherol, beta-carotene cancer prevention study: effects of baseline characteristics and study compliance. *J Natl Cancer Inst* 1996;88:1560-70.

18. Cook NR, Le IM, Manson JE, et al. Effects of beta-carotene supplementation on cancer incidence by baseline characteristics in the Physicians' Health Study (United States). *Cancer Causes Control* 2000;11:617-26.

19. Lee IM, Cook NR, Manson JE, et al. Beta-carotene supplementation and incidence of cancer and cardiovascular disease: the Women's Health Study. *JNCI Cancer Spectrum* 1999;91:2102-6.

20. de Klerk NH, Musk AW, Ambrosini GL, et al. Vitamin A and cancer prevention II: comparison of the effects of retinol and beta-carotene. *Int J Cancer* 1998;75:362-7.

21. Michaud DS, Feskanich D, Rimm EB, et al. Intake of specific carotenoids and risk of lung cancer in 2 prospective US cohorts. *Am J Clin Nutr* 2000;72:990-7.

22. Woodson K, Stewart C, Barrett M, et al. Effect of vitamin intervention on the relationship between GSTM1, smoking, and lung cancer risk among male smokers. *Cancer Epidemiol Biomarkers Prev* 1999;8:965-70.

23. Ratnasinghe DL, Yao SX, Forman M, et al.

Gene-environment interactions between the codon 194 polymorphism of XRCC1 and antioxidants influence lung cancer risk. *Anticancer Res* 2003;23:627-32.

24. Liu C, Russell RM, Wang XD. Low dose beta-carotene supplementation of ferrets attenuates smoke-induced lung phosphorylation of JNK, p38 MAPK, and p53 proteins. *The Journal of nutrition* 2004;134:2705-10.

25. Goodman GE, Schaffer S, Omenn GS, et al. The association between lung and prostate cancer risk, and serum micronutrients: results and lessons learned from beta-carotene and retinol efficacy trial. *Cancer Epidemiol Biomarkers Prev* 2003;12:518-26.

26. Heinonen OP, Albanes D, Virtamo J, et al. Prostate cancer and supplementation with alpha-tocopherol and beta-carotene: incidence and mortality in a controlled trial.[see comment]. *J Natl Cancer Inst* 1998;90:440-6.

27. Wu K, Erdman Jr JW, Schwartz SJ, et al. Plasma and Dietary Carotenoids, and the Risk of Prostate Cancer: A Nested Case-Control Study. *Cancer Epidemiol Biomarkers Prev* 2004;. 13:260-9.

28. Cook NR, Stampfer MJ, Ma J, et al. Beta-carotene supplementation for patients with low baseline levels and decreased risks of total and prostate carcinoma.[see comment]. *Cancer* 1999;86:1783-92.

29. Frieling UM, Schaumberg DA, Kupper TS, et al. A randomised, 12-year primary-prevention trial of beta carotene supplementation for nonmelanoma skin cancer in the physician's health study.[see comment]. *Archives of Dermatology* 2000;136:179-84.

30. Hennekens CH, Buring JE, Manson JE, et al. Lack of effect of long-term supplementation with beta carotene on the incidence of malignant neoplasms and cardiovascular disease. *N Engl J Med* 1996;334:1145-9.

31. Green A, Williams G, Neale R, et al. Daily sunscreen application and betacarotene supplementation in prevention of basal-cell and squamous-cell carcinomas of the skin: a randomised controlled trial. *Lancet* 1999;354:723-9.

32. Greenberg, E.R., Baron, et al. A clinical trial of beta carotene to prevent basal-cell and squamous-cell cancers of the skin. The Skin Cancer Prevention Study Group [published erratum appears in N Engl J Med 1991 Oct 31;325(18):1324] [see comments]. *N Engl J Med* 1990;323:789-95.

33. McNaughton SA, Marks GC, Gaffney P, et al. Antioxidants and basal cell carcinoma of the skin: a nested case-control study. *Cancer Causes Control* 2005;16:609-18.

34. Willis MS, Wians FH. The role of nutrition in preventing prostate cancer: a review of the proposed mechanism of action of various dietary substances. *Clinica chimica acta; international journal of clinical chemistry* 2003;330:57-83.

35. Fleshner N, Fair WR, Huryk R, et al. Vitamin E inhibits the high-fat diet promoted

growth of established human prostate LNCaP tumors in nude mice. *The Journal of urology* 1999;161:1651-4.

36. Bostick RM, Potter JD, Sellers TA, et al. Relation of calcium, vitamin D, and dairy food intake to incidence of colon cancer among older women. The Iowa Women's Health Study. *Am J Epidemiol* 1993;137:1302-17.

37. Kampman E, Goldbohm RA, van den Brandt PA, et al. Fermented dairy products, calcium, and colorectal cancer in The Netherlands Cohort Study. *Cancer Res* 1994;54:3186-90.

38. Zheng W, Anderson KE, Kushi LH, et al. A prospective cohort study of intake of calcium, vitamin D, and other micronutrients in relation to incidence of rectal cancer among postmenopausal women. *Cancer Epidemiol Biomarkers Prev* 1998;7:221-5.

39. Wu K, Willett WC, Fuchs CS, et al. Calcium intake and risk of colon cancer in women and men. *J Natl Cancer Inst* 2002;94:437-46.

40. McCullough ML, Robertson AS, Rodriguez C, et al. Calcium, vitamin D, dairy products, and risk of colorectal cancer in the Cancer Prevention Study II Nutrition Cohort (United States). *Cancer Causes Control* 2003;14:1-12.

41. Feskanich D, Ma J, Fuchs CS, et al. Plasma vitamin D metabolites and risk of colorectal cancer in women . *Cancer Epidemiology Biomarkers and Prevention* 2004;13:1502-8.

42. Lin J, Zhang SM, Cook NR, et al. Intakes of calcium and vitamin D and risk of colorectal cancer in women. *Am J Epidemiol* 2005;161:755-64.

43. Flood A, Peters U, Chatterjee N, et al. Calcium from diet and supplements is associated with reduced risk of colorectal cancer in a prospective cohort of women. *Cancer Epidemiol Biomarkers Prev* 2005;14:126-32.

44. Baron JA, Beach M, Mandel JS, et al. Calcium supplements for the prevention of colorectal adenomas. Calcium Polyp Prevention Study Group.[comment]. *N Engl J Med* 1999;340:101-7.

45. Grau MV, Baron JA, Sandler RS, et al. Vitamin D, calcium supplementation, and colorectal adenomas: results of a randomised trial.[see comment]. *J Natl Cancer Inst* 2003;95:1765-71.

46. Baron JA, Beach M, Mandel JS, et al. Calcium supplements and colorectal adenomas. Polyp Prevention Study Group. *Ann N Y Acad Sci* 1999;889:138-45.

47. Wallace K, Baron JA, Cole BF, et al. Effect of calcium supplementation on the risk of large bowel polyps.[see comment]. *J Natl Cancer Inst* 2004;96:921-5.

48. Bonithon-Kopp C, Kronborg O, Giacosa A, et al. Calcium and fibre supplementation in prevention of colorectal adenoma recurrence: A randomised intervention trial. *Lancet* 2000;356:1300-6.

49. Hofstad B, Almendingen K, Vatn M, et al. Growth and recurrence of colorectal polyps: a double-blind 3-year intervention with calcium and antioxidants. *Digestion* 1998;59:148-56.

50. Hartman TJ, Albert PS, Snyder K, et al. The association of calcium and vitamin D with risk of colorectal adenomas. *J Nutr* 2005;135:252-9.

51. Hyman J, Baron JA, Dain BJ, et al. Dietary and supplemental calcium and the recurrence of colorectal adenomas. *Cancer Epidemiol Biomarkers Prev* 1998;7:291-5.

52. Martinez ME, Marshall JR, Sampliner R, et al. Calcium, vitamin D, and risk of adenoma recurrence (United States). *Cancer Causes Control* 2002;13:213-20.

53. Platz EA, Hankinson SE, Hollis BW, et al. Plasma 1,25-dihydroxy- and 25-hydroxyvitamin D and adenomatous polyps of the distal colorectum. *Cancer Epidemiol Biomarkers Prev* 2000;9:1059-65.

54. Cho E, Smith-Warner SA, Spiegelman D, et al. Dairy foods, calcium, and colorectal cancer: a pooled analysis of 10 cohort studies. *J Natl Cancer Inst* 2004;96:1015-22.

55. Lamprecht SA, Lipkin M. Cellular mechanisms of calcium and vitamin D in the inhibition of colorectal carcinogenesis. *Ann N Y Acad Sci* 2001;952:73-87.

56. Clark LC, Dalkin B, Krongrad A, et al. Decreased incidence of prostate cancer with selenium supplementation: results of a double-blind cancer prevention trial. *Br J Urol* 1998;81:730-4.

57. Duffield-Lillico AJ, Dalkin BL, Reid ME, et al. Selenium supplementation, baseline plasma selenium status and incidence of prostate cancer: an analysis of the complete treatment period of the Nutritional Prevention of Cancer Trial. *BJU Int* 2003;91:608-12.

58. Platz EA, Leitzmann MF, Hollis BW, et al. Plasma 1,25-dihydroxy- and 25-hydroxyvitamin D and subsequent risk of prostate cancer. *Cancer Causes Control* 2004;15:255-65.

59. Reid ME, Duffield-Lillico AJ, Garland L, et al. Selenium supplementation and lung cancer incidence: an update of the nutritional prevention of cancer trial. *Cancer Epidemiol Biomarkers Prev* 2002;11:1285-91.

60. Combs GF, Jr., Clark LC, Turnbull BW. Reduction of cancer mortality and incidence by selenium supplementation. *Med Klin* 1997;92 Suppl 3:42-5.

61. Clark LC, Combs GF, Jr., Turnbull BW, et al. Effects of selenium supplementation for cancer prevention in patients with carcinoma of the skin. A randomised controlled trial. Nutritional Prevention of Cancer Study Group. *JAMA* 1996;276:1957-63.

62. Duffield-Lillico AJ, Reid ME, Turnbull BW, et al. Baseline characteristics and the effect of selenium supplementation on cancer incidence in a randomised clinical trial: a summary report of the Nutritional Prevention of Cancer Trial. *Cancer Epidemiol Biomarkers Prev* 2002;11:630-9.

63. Bostick RM, Potter JD, McKenzie DR, et al. Reduced risk of colon cancer with high intake of vitamin E: the Iowa Women's Health Study. *Cancer Res* 1993;53:4230-7.

64. Ganther HE. Selenium metabolism, selenoproteins and mechanisms of cancer prevention: complexities with thioredoxin reductase. *Carcinogenesis* 1999;20:1657-66.

65. Combs GF, Jr. Status of selenium in prostate cancer prevention. *Br J Cancer* 2004;91:195-9.

Chapter 4.11

1. Cannon G. The rise and fall of dietetics and of nutrition science, 4000 BCE-2000 CE. *Public Health Nutr* 2005;8:701-5.

2. Food and Agriculture Organization of the United Nations. 2004. *Globalization of Food Systems in Developing Countries: Impact on Food Security and Nutrition.* In: FAO Food Nutr Pap no 83.

3. World Health Organization. *Globalization, Diets and Noncommunicable Diseases.* Geneva: WHO, 2002.

4. Nestle M. The Mediterranean (diets and disease prevention). In: Kiple KF, Ornelas-Kiple CK, editors. *The Cambridge World History of Food and Nutrition.* Cambridge: Cambridge University Press, 2000.

5. Prentice AM, Jebb SA. Fast foods, energy density and obesity: a possible mechanistic link. *Obes Rev* 2003;4:187-94.

6. Huijbregts P, Feskens E, Rasanen L, et al. Dietary pattern and 20 year mortality in elderly men in Finland, Italy, and The Netherlands: longitudinal cohort study. *BMJ* 1997;315:13-7.

7. Lagiou P, Trichopoulos D, Sandin S, et al. Mediterranean dietary pattern and mortality among young women: a cohort study in Sweden. *Br J Nutr* 2006;96:384-92.

8. Cottet V, Bonithon-Kopp C, Kronborg O, et al. Dietary patterns and the risk of colorectal adenoma recurrence in a European intervention trial. *Eur J Cancer Prev* 2005;14:21-9.

9. Kim MK, Sasaki S, Sasazuki S, et al. Prospective study of three major dietary patterns and risk of gastric cancer in Japan. *Int J Cancer* 2004;110:435-42.

10. Kim MK, Sasaki S, Otani T, et al. Dietary patterns and subsequent colorectal cancer risk by subsite: a prospective cohort study. *Int J Cancer* 2005;115:790-8.

11. Wu K, Hu FB, Willett WC, et al. Dietary patterns and risk of prostate cancer in U.S. men. *Cancer Epidemiol Biomarkers Prev* 2006;15:167-71.

12. Terry P, Hu FB, Hansen H, et al. Prospective study of major dietary patterns and colorectal cancer risk in women. *Am J Epidemiol* 2001;154:1143-9.

13. Ronco AL, De Stefani E, Boffetta P, et al.

Food patterns and risk of breast cancer: a factor analysis study in Uruguay. *Int J Cancer* 2006;119:1672-8.

14. De Stefani E, Correa P, Boffetta P, et al. Dietary patterns and risk of gastric cancer: a case-control study in Uruguay. *Gastric Cancer* 2004;7:211-20.

15. Bahmanyar S, Ye W. Dietary patterns and risk of squamous-cell carcinoma and adenocarcinoma of the esophagus and adenocarcinoma of the gastric cardia: a population-based case-control study in Sweden. *Nutr Cancer* 2006;54:171-8.

16. Tominaga S, Kuroishi T, Ogawa H, et al. Epidemiologic aspects of biliary tract cancer in Japan. *Natl Cancer Inst Monogr* 1979;25-34.

17. Ishimoto H, Nakamura H, Miyoshi T. Epidemiological study on relationship between breast cancer mortality and dietary factors. *Tokushima J Exp Med* 1994;41:103-14.

18. Rashidkhani B, Akesson A, Lindblad P, et al. Major dietary patterns and risk of renal cell carcinoma in a prospective cohort of Swedish women. *J Nutr* 2005;135:1757-62.

19. Adebamowo CA, Hu FB, Cho E, et al. Dietary patterns and the risk of breast cancer. *Ann Epidemiol* 2005;15:789-95.

20. Michaud DS, Skinner HG, Wu K, et al. Dietary patterns and pancreatic cancer risk in men and women. *J Natl Cancer Inst* 2005;97:518-24.

21. Fung TT, Hu FB, Holmes MD, et al. Dietary patterns and the risk of postmenopausal breast cancer. *Int J Cancer* 2005;116:116-21.

22. Walker M, Aronson KJ, King W, et al. Dietary patterns and risk of prostate cancer in Ontario, Canada. *Int J Cancer* 2005;116:592-8.

23. Palli D, Russo A, Decarli A. Dietary patterns, nutrient intake and gastric cancer in a high-risk area of Italy. *Cancer Causes Control* 2001;12:163-72.

24. Slattery ML, Boucher KM, Caan BJ, et al. Eating patterns and risk of colon cancer. *Am J Epidemiol* 1998;148:4-16.

25. Slattery ML, Edwards SL, Boucher KM, et al. Lifestyle and colon cancer: an assessment of factors associated with risk. *Am J Epidemiol* 1999;150:869-77.

26. Kesse E, Clavel-Chapelon F, Boutron-Ruault MC. Dietary patterns and risk of colorectal tumors: a cohort of French women of the National Education System (E3N). *Am J Epidemiol* 2006;164:1085-93.

27. Sieri S, Krogh V, Pala V, et al. Dietary patterns and risk of breast cancer in the ORDET cohort. *Cancer Epidemiol Biomarkers Prev* 2004;13:567-72.

28. Velie EM, Schairer C, Flood A, et al. Empirically derived dietary patterns and risk of postmenopausal breast cancer in a large prospective cohort study. *Am J Clin Nutr* 2005;82:1308-19.

29. Balder HF, Goldbohm RA, van den Brandt PA. Dietary patterns associated with male lung cancer risk in the Netherlands Cohort Study. *Cancer Epidemiol Biomarkers Prev* 2005;14:483-90.

30. Dixon LB, Balder HF, Virtanen MJ, et al. Dietary patterns associated with colon and rectal cancer: results from the Dietary Patterns and Cancer (DIETSCAN) Project. *Am J Clin Nutr* 2004;80:1003-11.

31. Markaki I, Linos D, Linos A. The influence of dietary patterns on the development of thyroid cancer. *Eur J Cancer* 2003;39:1912-9.

32. Handa K, Kreiger N. Diet patterns and the risk of renal cell carcinoma. *Public Health Nutr* 2002;5:757-67.

33. De Stefani E, Boffetta P, Ronco AL, et al. Dietary patterns and risk of cancer of the oral cavity and pharynx in Uruguay. *Nutr Cancer* 2005;51:132-9.

34. Nkondjock A, Krewski D, Johnson KC, et al. Dietary patterns and risk of pancreatic cancer. *Int J Cancer* 2005;114:817-23.

35. Key TJ, Thorogood M, Appleby PN, et al. Dietary habits and mortality in 11,000 vegetarians and health conscious people: results of a 17 year follow up. *BMJ* 1996;313:775-9.

36. Hirayama T. [A large scale cohort study of dietary habits and cancer mortality]. *Gan No Rinsho* 1986;32:610-22.

37. Jensen OM. Cancer risk among Danish male Seventh-Day Adventists and other temperance society members. *J Natl Cancer Inst* 1983;70:1011-4.

38. Berkel J, de Waard F. Mortality pattern and life expectancy of Seventh-Day Adventists in the Netherlands. *Int J Epidemiol* 1983;12:455-9.

39. Kuratsune M, Ikeda M, Hayashi T. Epidemiologic studies on possible health effects of intake of pyrolyzates of foods, with reference to mortality among Japanese Seventh-Day Adventists. *Environ Health Perspect* 1986;67:143-6.

40. Lemon FR, Walden RT, Woods RW. Cancer of the lung and mouth in Seventh-day Adventists. Preliminary report on a population study. *Cancer* 1964;17:486-97.

41. Phillips RL, Garfinkel L, Kuzma JW, et al. Mortality among California Seventh-Day Adventists for selected cancer sites. *J Natl Cancer Inst* 1980;65:1097-107.

42. Mills PK, Beeson WL, Phillips RL, et al. Cancer incidence among California Seventh-day Adventists, 1976-1982. *Am J Clin Nutr* 1994;59:1136S-42S.

43. Hirayama T. [Primary cancer prevention by life style modification]. 1989;35:163-70.

44. Mills PK, Beeson WL, Abbey DE, et al. Dietary habits and past medical history as related to fatal pancreas cancer risk among Adventists. *Cancer* 1988;61:2578-85.

45. Mills PK, Beeson WL, Phillips RL, et al. Cohort study of diet, lifestyle, and prostate cancer in Adventist men. *Cancer* 1989;64:598-604.

46. Ye EC. [Case-control study of 100 gastric cancer cases]. *Chung Hua Yu Fang I Hsueh Tsa Chih* 1981;15:107-9.

47. Ren TS. [Case-control study of gastric cancer in ten rural counties in China]. *Chung Hua Liu Hsing Ping Hsueh Tsa Chih* 1985;6:29-32.

48. You WC, Blot WJ, Chang YS, et al. Diet and high risk of stomach cancer in Shandong, China. *Cancer Res* 1988;48:3518-23.

49. Tajima K, Tominaga S. Dietary habits and gastro-intestinal cancers: a comparative case-control study of stomach and large intestinal cancers in Nagoya, Japan. *Jpn J Cancer Res* 1985;76:705-16.

50. Graham S, Lilienfe AM, Tidings JE. Dietary and purgation factors in epidemiology of gastric cancer. *Cancer* 1967;20:2224-34.

51. Youm PY, Kim SH. [A case-control study on dietary and other factors related to stomach cancer incidence]. *Korean J Nutr* 1998;31:62-71.

52. Rachtan J. [Clinical control studies of the role of dietary habits in the etiology of stomach cancer]. *Przegl Lek* 1986;43:543-6.

53. Csendes A, Medina E, Gaete MC, et al. [Gastric cancer: an epidemiologic and dietary study in 100 patients and 100 controls]. *Rev Med Chil* 1976;104:761-5.

54. Dalgat DM, Aliev RG, Gireev GI, et al. [Epidemiology of stomach cancer in Dagestan]. *Vopr Onkol* 1974;20:76-82.

55. Demirer T, Icli F, Uzunalimoglu O, et al. Diet and stomach cancer incidence. A case-control study in Turkey. *Cancer* 1990;65:2344-8.

56. Boeing H, Jedrychowski W, Wahrendorf J, et al. Dietary risk factors in intestinal and diffuse types of stomach cancer: a multicenter case-control study in Poland. *Cancer Causes Control* 1991;2:227-33.

57. Cai L. [A case-control study of stomach cancer in Changle, Fujian Province - by the risk state analysis]. *Chung Hua Liu Hsing Ping Hsueh Tsa Chih* 1991;12:15-9.

58. Ren D, Jin J, Wang D, et al. The nutritional factors related to gastric cancer in Tianjin. *Ying Yang Xue Bao* 1992;14:325-8.

59. Ji BT, Chow WH, Yang G, et al. Dietary habits and stomach cancer in Shanghai, China. *Int J Cancer* 1998;76:659-64.

60. Watabe K, Nishi M, Miyake H, et al. Lifestyle and gastric cancer: a case-control study. *Oncol Rep* 1998;5:1191-4.

61. Ye W, Yi Y, Luo R. [A case-control study on diet and gastric cancer]. *Chung Hua Yu Fang I Hsueh Tsa Chih* 1998;32:100-2.

62. Gao CM, Takezaki T, Ding JH, et al. Protective effect of allium vegetables against both esophageal and stomach cancer: a simultaneous case-referent study of a high-epidemic area in Jiangsu Province, China. *Jpn J Cancer Res* 1999;90:614-21.

63. Cai L, Yu SZ, Ye WM, et al. Fish sauce and gastric cancer: an ecological study in Fujian Province, China. *World J Gastroenterol* 2000;6:671-5.

64. Suh S, Koo B, Choi Y, et al. [Lifestyle and eating behaviors of the stomach cancer patients in Daegu and Kyungpook areas in Korea]. *Korean J Nutr* 2002;35:380-93.

65. Fei S, Xiao S. [Diet and gastric cancer: a case-control study in Shanghai urban districts]. *Chin J Gastroenterol*

2003;8:143-7.

66. Tavani A, Pregnolato A, La Vecchia C, et al. Coffee and tea intake and risk of cancers of the colon and rectum: a study of 3,530 cases and 7,057 controls. *Int J Cancer* 1997;73:193-7.

67. Shoff SM, Newcomb PA, Longnecker MP. Frequency of eating and risk of colorectal cancer in women. *Nutr Cancer* 1997;27:22-5.

68. Potter JD, McMichael AJ. Diet and cancer of the colon and rectum: a case-control study. *J Natl Cancer Inst* 1986;76:557-69.

69. de Verdier MG, Longnecker MP. Eating frequency - a neglected risk factor for colon cancer? *Cancer Causes Control* 1992;3:77-81.

70. La Vecchia C, Ferraroni M, Mezzetti M, et al. Attributable risks for colorectal cancer in northern Italy. *Int J Cancer* 1996;66:60-4.

71. La Vecchia C, Gallus S, Talamini R, et al. Interaction between selected environmental factors and familial propensity for colon cancer. *Eur J Cancer Prev* 1999;8:147-50.

72. La Vecchia C, Negri E, Decarli A, et al. A case-control study of diet and colo-rectal cancer in northern Italy. *Int J Cancer* 1988;41:492-8.

73. Fernandez E, La Vecchia C, D'Avanzo B, et al. Risk factors for colorectal cancer in subjects with family history of the disease. *Br J Cancer* 1997;75:1381-4.

74. Franceschi S, Barra S, La Vecchia C, et al. Risk factors for cancer of the tongue and the mouth. A case-control study from northern Italy. *Cancer* 1992;70:2227-33.

75. Favero A, Franceschi S, La Vecchia C, et al. Meal frequency and coffee intake in colon cancer. *Nutr Cancer* 1998;30:182-5.

76. Benito E, Obrador A, Stiggelbout A, et al. A population-based case-control study of colorectal cancer in Majorca. I. Dietary factors. *Int J Cancer* 1990;45:69-76.

77. Calza S, Ferraroni M, La Vecchia C, et al. Low-risk diet for colorectal cancer in Italy. *Eur J Cancer Prev* 2001;10:515-21.

78. Coates AO, Potter JD, Caan BJ, et al. Eating frequency and the risk of colon cancer. *Nutr Cancer* 2002;43:121-6.

79. Fernandez E, La Vecchia C, Talamini R, et al. Joint effects of family history and adult life dietary risk factors on colorectal cancer risk. *Epidemiology* 2002;13:360-3.

80. Fernandez E, Gallus S, La Vecchia C, et al. Family history and environmental risk factors for colon cancer. *Cancer Epidemiol Biomarkers Prev* 2004;13:658-61.

Chapter 5

1. US Department of Health and Human Services. 1996. *Physical Activity and Health. A Report of the Surgeon General.*

2. Food and Agriculture Organization of the United Nations. 2004. *Human Energy Requirements. Report of a Joint FAO/WHO/UNU Expert Consultation.* In: FAO Food and Nutrition Technical Report Series 1.

3. Åstrand P-O, Rodahl K. *Textbook of Work Physiology. Physiological Bases of Exercise.* New York: McGraw-Hill, 1977.

4. World Health Organization. *Handbook on Human Nutritional Requirements.* Geneva: WHO, 1974.

5. Fogel R. *The Escape from Hunger and Premature Death, 1700-2100 Europe, America and the Third World.* Cambridge: University Press, 2004.

6. Pelto G, Pelto P. Small but healthy? An anthropological perspective. *Hum Organ* 1989;48:11-30.

7. Institute of Medicine of the National Academies, Food and Nutrition Board. *Dietary Reference Intakes for Energy, Carbohydrate, Fiber, Fat, Fatty Acids, Cholesterol, Protein, and Amino Acids.* Washington, DC: The National Academies Press, 2005.

8. Hardman AE, Stensel DJ. *Physical Activity and Health.* London and New York: Routledge, 2003.

9. Geissler C, Powers H, editors. *Human Nutrition.* 11 ed. Edinburgh and New York: Elsevier Churchill Livingstone, 2005.

10. Albanes D, Blair A, Taylor PR. Physical activity and risk of cancer in the NHANES I population. *Am J Public Health* 1989;79:744-50.

11. Paffenbarger RS Jr, Hyde RT, Wing AL. Physical activity and incidence of cancer in diverse populations: a preliminary report. *Am J Clin Nutr* 1987;45:312-7.

12. Blair SN, Kohl HW, 3rd, Paffenbarger RS, Jr., et al. Physical fitness and all-cause mortality. A prospective study of healthy men and women. *JAMA* 1989;262:2395-401.

13. Cohen LA, Boylan E, Epstein M, et al. Voluntary exercise and experimental mammary cancer. *Adv Exp Med Biol* 1992;322:41-59.

14. Vainio H, Bianchini F, editors. *Weight Control and Physical Activity, Volume 6.* Lyon: International Agency for Research on Cancer, World Health Organization, 2002.

15. World Health Organization. 2003. *Diet, Nutrition and the Prevention of Chronic Diseases: Report of a Joint WHO/FAO Expert Consultation.* Technical Report Series no 916.

16. Wu AH, Paganini-Hill A, Ross RK, et al. Alcohol, physical activity and other risk factors for colorectal cancer: a prospective study. *Br J Cancer* 1987;55:687-94.

17. Lee IM, Paffenbarger RS, Jr., Hsieh C. Physical activity and risk of developing colorectal cancer among college alumni. *J Natl Cancer Inst* 1991;83:1324-9.

18. Lund Nilsen TI, Vatten LJ. Colorectal cancer associated with BMI, physical activity, diabetes, and blood glucose. *IARC Sci Publ* 2002;156:257-8.

19. Ballard-Barbash R, Schatzkin A, Albanes D, et al. Physical activity and risk of large bowel cancer in the Framingham Study. *Cancer Res* 1990;50:3610-3.

20. Schoen RE, Tangen CM, Kuller LH, et al. Increased blood glucose and insulin, body size, and incident colorectal cancer. *J Natl Cancer Inst* 1999;91:1147-54.

21. Thune I, Lund E. Physical activity and risk of colorectal cancer in men and women. *Br J Cancer* 1996;73:1134-40.

22. Pietinen P, Malila N, Virtanen M, et al. Diet and risk of colorectal cancer in a cohort of Finnish men. *Cancer Causes Control* 1999;10:387-96.

23. Pukkala E, Poskiparta M, Apter D, et al. Life-long physical activity and cancer risk among Finnish female teachers. *Eur J Cancer Prev* 1993;2:369-76.

24. Gapstur SM, Potter JD, Folsom AR. Alcohol consumption and colon and rectal cancer in postmenopausal women. *Int J Epidemiol* 1994;23:50-7.

25. Severson RK, Nomura AM, Grove JS, et al. A prospective analysis of physical activity and cancer. *Am J Epidemiol* 1989;130:522-9.

26. Nilsen TI, Vatten LJ. Prospective study of colorectal cancer risk and physical activity, diabetes, blood glucose and BMI: exploring the hyperinsulinaemia hypothesis. *Br J Cancer* 2001;84:417-22.

27. Colbert LH, Hartman TJ, Malila N, et al. Physical activity in relation to cancer of the colon and rectum in a cohort of male smokers. *Cancer Epidemiol Biomarkers Prev* 2001;10:265-8.

28. Norat T, Bingham S, Ferrari P, et al. Meat, fish, and colorectal cancer risk: the European Prospective Investigation into cancer and nutrition. *J Natl Cancer Inst* 2005;97:906-16.

29. Suadicani P, Hein HO, Gyntelberg F. Height, weight, and risk of colorectal cancer. An 18-year follow-up in a cohort of 5249 men. *Scand J Gastroenterol* 1993;28:285-8.

30. Wei EK, Giovannucci E, Wu K, et al. Comparison of risk factors for colon and rectal cancer. *Int J Cancer* 2004; 108:433-42.

31. Batty GD, Shipley MJ, Marmot M, et al. Physical activity and cause-specific mortality in men: further evidence from the Whitehall study. *Eur J Epidemiol* 2001;17:863-9.

32. Chow WH, Dosemeci M, Zheng W, et al. Physical activity and occupational risk of colon cancer in Shanghai, China. *Int J Epidemiol* 1993;22:23-9.

33. Fraser G, Pearce N. Occupational physical activity and risk of cancer of the colon and rectum in New Zealand males. *Cancer Causes Control* 1993;4:45-50.

34. Gerhardsson M, Floderus B, Norell SE. Physical activity and colon cancer risk. *Int J Epidemiol* 1988;17:743-6.

35. Gerhardsson M, Norell SE, Kiviranta H, et al. Sedentary jobs and colon cancer. *Am J Epidemiol* 1986;123:775-80.

36. Pukkala E, Kaprio J, Koskenvuo M, et al. Cancer incidence among Finnish world class male athletes. *Int J Sports Med* 2000;21:216-20.

37. Bostick RM, Potter JD, Kushi LH, et al. Sugar, meat, and fat intake, and non-dietary risk factors for colon cancer incidence in Iowa women (United States). *Cancer Causes Control* 1994;5:38-52.

38. Chao A, Connell CJ, Jacobs EJ, et al. Amount, type, and timing of recreational physical activity in relation to colon and rectal cancer in older adults: the Cancer Prevention Study II Nutrition Cohort. *Cancer Epidemiol Biomarkers Prev* 2004;13:2187-95.

39. Davey Smith G, Shipley MJ, Batty GD, et al. Physical activity and cause-specific mortality in the Whitehall study. *Public Health* 2000;114:308-15.

40. Ford ES. Body mass index and colon cancer in a national sample of adult US men and women. *Am J Epidemiol* 1999;150:390-8.

41. Giovannucci E, Ascherio A, Rimm EB, et al. Physical activity, obesity, and risk for colon cancer and adenoma in men. *Ann Intern Med* 1995;122:327-34.

42. Glynn SA, Albanes D, Pietinen P, et al. Colorectal cancer and folate status: a nested case-control study among male smokers. *Cancer Epidemiol Biomarkers Prev* 1996;5:487-94.

43. Hsing AW, McLaughlin JK, Chow WH, et al. Risk factors for colorectal cancer in a prospective study among U.S. white men. *Int J Cancer* 1998;77:549-53.

44. Lee IM, Paffenbarger RS, Jr. Physical activity and its relation to cancer risk: a prospective study of college alumni. *Med Sci Sports Exerc* 1994;26:831-7.

45. Malila N, Virtamo J, Virtanen M, et al. Dietary and serum alpha-tocopherol, beta-carotene and retinol, and risk for colorectal cancer in male smokers. *Eur J Clin Nutr* 2002;56:615-21.

46. Martinez ME, Giovannucci E, Spiegelman D, et al. Leisure-time physical activity, body size, and colon cancer in women. Nurses' Health Study Research Group. *J Natl Cancer Inst* 1997;89:948-55.

47. Polednak AP. College athletics, body size, and cancer mortality. *Cancer* 1976;38:382-87.

48. Sanjoaquin MA, Appleby PN, Thorogood M, et al. Nutrition, lifestyle and colorectal cancer incidence: a prospective investigation of 10998 vegetarians and non-vegetarians in the United Kingdom. *Br J Cancer* 2004;90:118-21.

49. Thun MJ, Calle EE, Namboodiri MM, et al. Risk factors for fatal colon cancer in a large prospective study. *J Natl Cancer Inst* 1992;84:1491-500.

50. Tiemersma EW, Kampman E, Bueno de Mesquita HB, et al. Meat consumption, cigarette smoking, and genetic susceptibility in the etiology of colorectal cancer: results from a Dutch prospective study. *Cancer Causes Control* 2002;13:383-93.

51. Wannamethee SG, Shaper AG, Walker M. Physical activity and risk of cancer in middle-aged men. *Br J Cancer* 2001;85:1311-6.

52. Lee DH, Jacobs DR, Folsom AR. A hypothesis: interaction between supplemental iron intake and fermentation affecting the risk of colon cancer. The Iowa Women's Health Study. *Nutr Cancer* 2004;48:1-5.

53. Singh PN, Fraser GE. Dietary risk factors for colon cancer in a low-risk population. *Am J Epidemiol* 1998;148:761-74.

54. Samad AK, Taylor RS, Marshall T, et al. A meta-analysis of the association of physical activity with reduced risk of colorectal cancer. *Colorectal Dis* 2005;7:204-13.

55. Calle EE, Kaaks R. Overweight, obesity and cancer: epidemiological evidence and proposed mechanisms. *Nat Rev Cancer* 2004;4:579-91.

56. Lewin MH, Bailey N, Bandaletova T, et al. Red meat enhances the colonic formation of the DNA adduct O6-carboxymethyl guanine: implications for colorectal cancer risk. *Cancer Res* 2006;66:1859-65.

56A. Chao A, Connell CJ, Jacobs EJ, et al. Amount, type, and timing of recreational physical activity in relation to colon and rectal cancer in older adults: the Cancer Prevention Study II Nutrition Cohort. *Cancer Epidemiol Biomarkers Prev* 2004;13:2187-95.

56B. Friedenreich C, Norat T, Steindorf K, et al. Physical activity and risk of colon and rectal cancers: the European prospective investigation into cancer and nutrition. *Cancer Epidemiol Biomarkers Prev* 2006;15:2398-407.

56C. Schnohr P, Gronbaek M, Petersen L, et al. Physical activity in leisure-time and risk of cancer: 14-year follow-up of 28,000 Danish men and women. *Scand J Public Health* 2005;33:244-9.

56D. Calton BA, Lacey JV, Jr., Schatzkin A, et al. Physical activity and the risk of colon cancer among women: a prospective cohort study (United States). *Int J Cancer* 2006;119:385-91.

56E. Steindorf K, Jedrychowski W, Schmidt M, et al. Case-control study of lifetime occupational and recreational physical activity and risks of colon and rectal cancer. *Eur J Cancer Prev* 2005;14:363-71.

56F. Hou L, Ji BT, Blair A, et al. Commuting physical activity and risk of colon cancer in Shanghai, China. *Am J Epidemiol* 2004;160:860-7.

56G. Zhang Y, Cantor KP, Dosemeci M, et al. Occupational and leisure-time physical activity and risk of colon cancer by subsite. *J Occup Environ Med* 2006;48:236-43.

56H. Huang XE, Hirose K, Wakai K, et al. Comparison of lifestyle risk factors by family history for gastric, breast, lung and colorectal cancer. *Asian Pac J Cancer Prev* 2004;5:419-27.

57. Cerhan JR, Chiu BC-H, Wallace RB, et al. Physical activity, physical function, and the risk of breast cancer in a prospective study among elderly women. *J Gerontol A Biol Sci Med Sci* 1998;53:M351-56.

58. Colditz GA, Feskanich D, Chen WY, et al. Physical activity and risk of breast cancer in premenopausal women. *Br J Cancer* 2003;89:847-51.

59. Dorgan JF, Brown C, Barrett M, et al. Physical activity and risk of breast cancer in the Framingham Heart Study. *Am J Epidemiol* 1994;139:662-9.

60. Hoyer AP, Grandjean P, Jorgensen T, et al. Organochlorine exposure and risk of breast cancer. *Lancet* 1998;352:1816-20.

61. Lee SY, Kim MT, Kim SW, et al. Effect of lifetime lactation on breast cancer risk: a Korean women's cohort study. *Int J Cancer* 2003;105:390-3.

62. Wyrwich KW, Wolinsky FD. Physical activity, disability, and the risk of hospitalization for breast cancer among older women. *J Gerontol A Biol Sci Med Sci* 2000;55:M418-21.

63. Tavani A, Braga C, La Vecchia C, et al. Physical activity and risk of cancers of the colon and rectum: an Italian case-control study. *Br J Cancer* 1999;79:1912-6.

64. Fioretti F, Tavani A, Bosetti C, et al. Risk factors for breast cancer in nulliparous women. *Br J Cancer* 1999;79:1923-8.

65. Friedenreich CM, Courneya KS, Bryant HE. Influence of physical activity in different age and life periods on the risk of breast cancer. *Epidemiology* 2001;12:604-12.

66. Hirose K, Hamajima N, Takezaki T, et al. Physical exercise reduces risk of breast cancer in Japanese women. *Cancer Sci* 2003;94:193-9.

67. John EM, Horn-Ross PL, Koo J. Lifetime physical activity and breast cancer risk in a multiethnic population: the San Francisco Bay area breast cancer study. *Cancer Epidemiol Biomarkers Prev* 2003;12:1143-52.

68. Mezzetti M, La Vecchia C, Decarli A, et al. Population attributable risk for breast cancer: diet, nutrition, and physical exercise. *J Natl Cancer Inst* 1998;90:389-94.

69. Rattanamongkolgul S, Muir K, Armstrong S, et al. Diet, energy intake and breast cancer risk in an Asian country. *IARC Sci Publ* 2002;156:543-5.

70. Wenten M, Gilliland FD, Baumgartner K, et al. Associations of weight, weight change, and body mass with breast cancer risk in Hispanic and non-Hispanic white women. *Ann Epidemiol* 2002;12:435-4.

71. Byrne C, Ursin G, Ziegler RG. A comparison of food habit and food frequency data as predictors of breast cancer in the NHANES I/NHEFS cohort. *J Nutr* 1996;126:2757-64.

72. Thune I, Brenn T, Lund E, et al. Physical activity and the risk of breast cancer. *N Engl J Med* 1997;336:1269-75.

73. Moradi T, Adami H-O, Bergstrom R, et al. Occupational physical activity and risk for breast cancer in a nationwide cohort study in Sweden. *Cancer Causes Control*

1999;10:423-30.

74. Mertens AJ, Sweeney C, Shahar E, et al. Physical activity and breast cancer incidence in middle-aged women: a prospective cohort study. *Breast Cancer Res Treat* 2006;79:209-14.

75. Coogan PF, Newcomb PA, Clapp RW, et al. Physical activity in usual occupation and risk of breast cancer (United States). *Cancer Causes Control* 1997;8:626-31.

76. Ueji M, Ueno E, Osei-Hyiaman D, et al. Physical activity and the risk of breast cancer: a case-control study of Japanese women. *J Epidemiol* 1998;8:116-22.

77. Friedenreich CM, Bryant HE, Courneya KS. Case-control study of lifetime physical activity and breast cancer risk. *Am J Epidemiol* 2001;154:336-47.

78. Dorn J, Vena J, Brasure J, et al. Lifetime physical activity and breast cancer risk in pre- and postmenopausal women. *Med Sci Sports Exerc* 2003;35:278-85.

79. Kruk J, Aboul-Enein HY. Occupational physical activity and the risk of breast cancer. *Cancer Detect Prev* 2003;27:187-92.

80. Steindorf K, Schmidt M, Kropp S, et al. Case-control study of physical activity and breast cancer risk among premenopausal women in Germany. *Am J Epidemiol* 2003;157:121-30.

81. Yang D, Bernstein L, Wu AH. Physical activity and breast cancer risk among Asian-American women in Los Angeles: a case-control study. *Cancer* 2003;97:2565-75.

82. Sesso HD, Paffenbarger RS, Jr., Lee IM. Physical activity and breast cancer risk in the college alumni health study (United States). *Cancer Causes Control* 1998;9:433-9.

83. Moore DB, Folsom AR, Mink PJ, et al. Physical activity and incidence of postmenopausal breast cancer. *Epidemiology* 2000;11:292-6.

84. Breslow RA, Ballard-Barbash R, Munoz K, et al. Long-term recreational physical activity and breast cancer in the National Health and Nutrition Examination Survey I epidemiologic follow-up study. *Cancer Epidemiol Biomarkers Prev* 2001;10:805-8.

85. Dirx MJ, Voorrips LE, Goldbohm RA, et al. Baseline recreational physical activity, history of sports participation, and postmenopausal breast carcinoma risk in the Netherlands Cohort Study. *Cancer* 2001;92:1638-49.

86. Drake DA. A longitudinal study of physical activity and breast cancer prediction. *Cancer Nurs* 2001;24:371-7.

87. Lee IM, Rexrode KM, Cook NR, et al. Physical activity and breast cancer risk: the Women's Health Study (United States). *Cancer Causes Control* 2001;12:137-45.

88. McTiernan A, Kooperberg C, White E, et al. Recreational physical activity and the risk of breast cancer in postmenopausal women: the women's health initiative cohort study. *JAMA* 2003;290:1331-6.

89. Margolis KL, Mucci L, Braaten T, et al.

Physical activity in different periods of life and the risk of breast cancer: the Norwegian-Swedish Women's Lifestyle and Health cohort study. *Cancer Epidemiol Biomarkers Prev* 2005;14:27-32.

90. Patel AV, Calle EE, Bernstein L, et al. Recreational physical activity and risk of postmenopausal breast cancer in a large cohort of US women. *Cancer Causes Control* 2003;14:519-29.

91. Schnohr P, Gronbaek M, Petersen L, et al. Physical activity in leisure-time and risk of cancer: 14-year follow-up of 28,000 Danish men and women. *Scand J Public Health* 2005;33:244-9.

92. Verloop J, Rookus MA, van der Kooy K, et al. Physical activity and breast cancer risk in women aged 20-54 years. *J Natl Cancer Inst* 2000;92:128-35.

93. Matthews CE, Shu XO, Jin F, et al. Lifetime physical activity and breast cancer risk in the Shanghai breast cancer study. *Br J Cancer* 2001;84:994-1001.

94. Moradi T, Nyren O, Zack M, et al. Breast cancer risk and lifetime leisure-time and occupational physical activity (Sweden). *Cancer Causes Control* 2000;11:523-31.

95. Gilliland FD, Li YF, Baumgartner K, et al. Physical activity and breast cancer risk in hispanic and non-hispanic white women. *Am J Epidemiol* 2001;154:442-50.

96. Chen CL, White E, Malone KE, et al. Leisure-time physical activity in relation to breast cancer among young women (Washington, United States). *Cancer Causes Control* 1997;8:77-84.

97. Carpenter CL, Ross RK, Paganini-Hill A, et al. Effect of family history, obesity and exercise on breast cancer risk among postmenopausal women. *Int J Cancer* 2003;106:96-102.

98. Bernstein L, Patel AV, Ursin G, et al. Lifetime recreational exercise activity and breast cancer risk among black women and white women. *J Natl Cancer Inst* 2005;97:1671-9.

98A. Adams SA, Matthews CE, Hebert JR, et al. Association of physical activity with hormone receptor status: the Shanghai Breast Cancer Study. *Cancer Epidemiol Biomarkers Prev* 2006;15:1170-8.

99. Colbert LH, Lacey JV, Jr., Schairer C, et al. Physical activity and risk of endometrial cancer in a prospective cohort study (United States). *Cancer Causes Control* 2003;14:559-67.

100. Silvera SA, Rohan TE, Jain M, et al. Glycaemic index, glycaemic load and risk of endometrial cancer: a prospective cohort study. *Public Health Nutr* 2005;8:912-9.

101. Salazar-Martinez E, Lazcano-Ponce EC, Lira-Lira GG, et al. Case-control study of diabetes, obesity, physical activity and risk of endometrial cancer among Mexican women. *Cancer Causes Control* 2000;11:707-11.

102. Sturgeon SR, Brinton LA, Berman ML, et al. Past and present physical activity and endometrial cancer risk. *Br J Cancer* 1993;68:584-9.

103. Shu XO, Hatch MC, Zheng W, et al. Physical activity and risk of endometrial cancer. *Epidemiology* 1993;4:342-9.

104. Levi F, La Vecchia C, Negri E, et al. Selected physical activities and the risk of endometrial cancer. *Br J Cancer* 1993;67:846-51.

105. Moradi T, Nyren O, Bergstrom R, et al. Risk for endometrial cancer in relation to occupational physical activity: a nationwide cohort study in Sweden. *Int J Cancer* 1998;76:665-70.

106. Weiderpass E, Pukkala E, Vasama-Neuvonen K, et al. Occupational exposures and cancers of the endometrium and cervix uteri in Finland. *Am J Ind Med* 2001;39:572-80.

107. Furberg AS, Thune I. Metabolic abnormalities (hypertension, hyperglycemia and overweight), lifestyle (high energy intake and physical inactivity) and endometrial cancer risk in a Norwegian cohort. *Int J Cancer* 2003;104:669-76.

108. Olson SH, Vena JE, Dorn JP, et al. Exercise, occupational activity, and risk of endometrial cancer. *Ann Epidemiol* 1997;7:46-53.

109. Jain MG, Rohan TE, Howe GR, et al. A cohort study of nutritional factors and endometrial cancer. *Eur J Epidemiol* 2000;16:899-905.

110. Moradi T, Weiderpass E, Signorello LB, et al. Physical activity and postmenopausal endometrial cancer risk (Sweden). *Cancer Causes Control* 2000;11:829-37.

111. Matthews CE, Xu WH, Zheng W, et al. Physical activity and risk of endometrial cancer: a report from the Shanghai endometrial cancer study. *Cancer Epidemiol Biomarkers Prev* 2005;14:779-85.

112. Dosemeci M, Hayes RB, Vetter R, et al. Occupational physical activity, socioeconomic status, and risks of 15 cancer sites in Turkey. *Cancer Causes Control* 1993;4:313-21.

113. Kalandidi A, Tzonou A, Lipworth L, et al. A case-control study of endometrial cancer in relation to reproductive, somatometric, and life-style variables. *Oncology* 1996;53:354-9.

114. Goodman MT, Hankin JH, Wilkens LR, et al. Diet, body size, physical activity, and the risk of endometrial cancer. *Cancer Res* 1997;57:5077-85.

115. Terry P, Baron JA, Weiderpass E, et al. Lifestyle and endometrial cancer risk: a cohort study from the Swedish Twin Registry. *Int J Cancer* 1999;82:38-42.

116. Schouten LJ, Goldbohm RA, van den Brandt PA. Anthropometry, physical activity, and endometrial cancer risk: results from the Netherlands Cohort Study. *J Natl Cancer Inst* 2004;96:1635-8.

117. Folsom AR, Demissie Z, Harnack L. Glycemic index, glycemic load, and incidence of endometrial cancer: the Iowa women's health study. *Nutr Cancer* 2003;46:119-24.

118. Littman AJ, Voigt LF, Beresford SA, et al. Recreational physical activity and

endometrial cancer risk. *Am J Epidemiol* 2001;154:924-33.

119. Hirose K, Tajima K, Hamajima N, et al. Subsite (cervix/endometrium)-specific risk and protective factors in uterus cancer. *Jpn J Cancer Res* 1996;87:1001-9.

120. Trentham-Dietz A, Nichols HB, Hampton JM, et al. Weight change and risk of endometrial cancer. *Int J Epidemiol* 2006;35:151-8.

121. Silvera SA, Rohan TE, Jain M, et al. Glycemic index, glycemic load, and pancreatic cancer risk (Canada). *Cancer Causes Control* 2005;16:431-6.

122. Alfano CM, Klesges RC, Murray DM, et al. Physical activity in relation to all-site and lung cancer incidence and mortality in current and former smokers. *Cancer Epidemiol Biomarkers Prev* 2004;13:2233-41.

123. Lee IM, Sesso HD, Paffenbarger RSJ. Physical activity and risk of lung cancer. *Int J Epidemiol* 1999;28:620-5.

124. Olson JE, Yang P, Schmitz K, et al. Differential association of body mass index and fat distribution with three major histologic types of lung cancer: evidence from a cohort of older women. *Am J Epidemiol* 2002;156:606-15.

125. Steenland K, Nowlin S, Palu S. Cancer incidence in the National Health and Nutrition Survey I. Follow-up data: diabetes, cholesterol, pulse and physical activity. *Cancer Epidemiol Biomarkers Prev* 1995;4:807-11.

126. Thune I, Lund E. The influence of physical activity on lung-cancer risk: a prospective study of 81,516 men and women. *Int J Cancer* 1997;70:57-62.

127. Colbert LH, Hartman TJ, Tangrea JA, et al. Physical activity and lung cancer risk in male smokers. *Int J Cancer* 2002;98:770-3.

128. Bak H, Christensen J, Thomsen BL, et al. Physical activity and risk for lung cancer in a Danish cohort. *Int J Cancer* 2005;116:439-44.

129. Brownson RC, Chang JC, Davis JR, et al. Physical activity on the job and cancer in Missouri. *Am J Public Health* 1991;81:639-42.

130. Farahmand BY, Ahlbom A, Ekblom O, et al. Mortality amongst participants in Vasaloppet: a classical long-distance ski race in Sweden. *J Intern Med* 2003;253:276-83.

131. Knekt P, Raitasalo R, Heliovaara M, et al. Elevated lung cancer risk among persons with depressed mood. *Am J Epidemiol* 1996;144:1096-103.

132. Lee SY, Kim MT, Jee SH, et al. Does hypertension increase mortality risk from lung cancer? A prospective cohort study on smoking, hypertension and lung cancer risk among Korean men. *J Hypertens* 2002;20:617-22.

133. Linseisen J, Wolfram G, Miller AB. Plasma 7beta-hydroxycholesterol as a possible predictor of lung cancer risk. *Cancer Epidemiol Biomarkers Prev* 2002;11:1630-7.

134. Sellers TA, Potter JD, Folsom AR. Association of incident lung cancer with family history of female reproductive cancers: the Iowa Women's Health Study. *Genet Epidemiol* 1991;8:199-208.

135. Huang XE, Hirose K, Wakai K, et al. Comparison of lifestyle risk factors by family history for gastric, breast, lung and colorectal cancer. *Asian Pac J Cancer Prev* 2004;5:419-27.

136. Kubik A, Zatloukal P, Tomasek L, et al. Lung cancer risk among nonsmoking women in relation to diet and physical activity. *Neoplasma* 2004;51:136-43.

137. Yu M, Rao K, Chen Y. [A case-control study of the risk factors of lung cancer in Beijing, Tianjin, Shanghai, Chongqing metropolitan areas]. *Zhonghua Yu Fang Yi Xue Za Zhi* 2000;34:227-31.

138A. Steindorf K, Friedenreich C, Linseisen J, et al. Physical activity and lung cancer risk in the European Prospective Investigation into Cancer and Nutrition Cohort. *Int J Cancer* 2006;119:2389-97.

138. Lam TH, Ho SY, Hedley AJ, et al. Leisure time physical activity and mortality in Hong Kong: case-control study of all adult deaths in 1998. *Ann Epidemiol* 2004;14:391-8.

139. Nilsen TIL, Vatten LJ. A prospective study of lifestyle factors and the risk of pancreatic cancer in Nord-Trondelag, Norway. *Cancer Causes Control* 2000;11:645-52.

140. Lee IM, Sesso HD, Oguma Y, et al. Physical activity, body weight, and pancreatic cancer mortality. *Br J Cancer* 2003;88:679-83.

141. Hanley AJ, Johnson KC, Villeneuve PJ, et al. Physical activity, anthropometric factors and risk of pancreatic cancer: results from the Canadian enhanced cancer surveillance system. *Int J Cancer* 2001;94:140-7.

142. Stolzenberg-Solomon RZ, Pietinen P, Taylor PR, et al. A prospective study of medical conditions, anthropometry, physical activity, and pancreatic cancer in male smokers (Finland). *Cancer Causes Control* 2002;13:417-26.

143. Paffenbarger RS, Jr., Brand RJ, Sholtz RI, et al. Energy expenditure, cigarette smoking, and blood pressure level as related to death from specific diseases. *Am J Epidemiol* 1978;108:12-8.

144. Alguacil J, Kauppinen T, Porta M, et al. Risk of pancreatic cancer and occupational exposures in Spain. PANKRAS II Study Group. *Ann Occup Hyg* 2000;44:391-403.

145. Smith GD, Shipley MJ, Batty GD, et al. Physical activity and cause-specific mortality in the Whitehall study. *Public Health* 2000;114:308-15.

146. Michaud DS, Giovannucci E, Willett WC, et al. Physical activity, obesity, height, and the risk of pancreatic cancer. *JAMA* 2001;286:921-9.

147. Inoue M, Tajima K, Takezaki T, et al. Epidemiology of pancreatic cancer in Japan: a nested case-control study from the Hospital-based Epidemiologic Research Program at Aichi Cancer Center (HERPACC). *Int J Epidemiol* 2003;32:257-62.

148. Patel AV, Rodriguez C, Bernstein L, et al. Obesity, recreational physical activity, and risk of pancreatic cancer in a large U.S. Cohort. *Cancer Epidemiol Biomarkers Prev* 2005;14:459-66.

149. Sinner PJ, Schmitz KH, Anderson KE, et al. Lack of association of physical activity and obesity with incident pancreatic cancer in elderly women. *Cancer Epidemiol Biomarkers Prev* 2005;14:1571-3.

150. Zhang Y, Cantor KP, Lynch CF, et al. Occupation and risk of pancreatic cancer: a population-based case-control study in Iowa. *J Occup Environ Med* 2005;47:392-8.

151. Nkondjock A, Krewski D, Johnson KC, et al. Dietary patterns and risk of pancreatic cancer. *Int J Cancer* 2005;114:817-23.

152. Eberle CA, Bracci PM, Holly EA. Anthropometric factors and pancreatic cancer in a population-based case-control study in the San Francisco Bay area. *Cancer Causes Control* 2005;16:1235-44.

153. Garfinkel L, Stellman SD. Mortality by relative weight and exercise. *Cancer* 1988;62:1844-50.

154. Quadrilatero J, Hoffman-Goetz L. Physical activity and colon cancer. A systematic review of potential mechanisms. *J Sports Med Phys Fitness* 2003;43:121-38.

154A. Berrington de Gonzalez A, Spencer EA, Bueno-de-Mesquita HB, et al. Anthropometry, physical activity, and the risk of pancreatic cancer in the European prospective investigation into cancer and nutrition. *Cancer Epidemiol Biomarkers Prev* 2006;15:879-85.

155. Giovannucci EL, Liu Y, Leitzmann MF, et al. A prospective study of physical activity and incident and fatal prostate cancer. *Arch Intern Med* 2005;165:1005-10.

156. Patel AV, Rodriguez C, Jacobs EJ, et al. Recreational physical activity and risk of prostate cancer in a large cohort of U.S. men. *Cancer Epidemiol Biomarkers Prev* 2005;14:275-9.

Chapter 6

1. Fogel R. *The Escape from Hunger and Premature Death, 1700-2100. Europe, America and the Third World.* Cambridge: Cambridge University Press, 2004.

2. Commission on the Nutrition Challenges of the 21st Century. 2000. *Ending Malnutrition by 2020: An Agenda for Change in the Millennium.* http://www.unsystem.org/scn/Publications/UN_Report.PDF.

3. World Health Organization. 2000. *Obesity: Preventing and Managing the Global Epidemic.* In: Technical Report Series no 894. http://whqlibdoc.who.int/trs/WHO_TRS_894.pdf.

4. Deurenberg P, Weststrate JA, Seidell JC. Body mass index as a measure of body fatness: age- and sex-specific prediction formulas. *Br J Nutr* 1991;65:105-14.

5. World Health Organization. 1995. *Physical Status: The Use and Interpretation of Anthropometry.* In: Technical Report Series no 854. http://whqlibdoc.who.int/trs/WHO_TRS_854.pdf.

6. James WPT, Jackson-Leach R, Ni Mhurchu C, et al. Overweight and obesity (high body mass index). In: Ezzati M, Lopez AD, Rodgers A, et al., editors. *Comparative Quantification of Health Risks. Global and Regional Burden of Disease Attributable to Selected Major Risk Factors.* Geneva: World Health Organization, 2004.

7. World Health Organization/International Association for the Study of Obesity/International Obesity Taskforce. *The Asia-Pacific Perspective: Redefining Obesity and its Treatment.* Melbourne: Health Communications Australia, 2000.

8. James WP, Chunming C, Inoue S. Appropriate Asian body mass indices? *Obesity reviews* 2002;3:139.

9. World Health Organization Expert Consultation. Appropriate body-mass index for Asian populations and its implications for policy and intervention strategies. *Lancet* 2004;363:157-63.

10. Deurenberg-Yap M, Deurenberg P. Is a re-evaluation of WHO body mass index cut-off values needed? The case of Asians in Singapore. *Nutr Rev* 2003;61:S80-7.

11. Swinburn BA, Caterson I, Seidell JC, et al. Diet, nutrition and the prevention of excess weight gain and obesity. *Public Health Nutr* 2004;7:123-46.

12. Sanchez-Castillo CP, Velasquez-Monroy O, Lara-Esqueda A, et al. Diabetes and hypertension increases in a society with abdominal obesity: results of the Mexican National Health Survey 2000. *Public Health Nutr* 2005;8:53-60.

13. Arner P. Regional adiposity in man. *J Endocrinol* 1997;155:191-2.

14. Bigaard J, Tjonneland A, Thomsen BL, et al. Waist circumference, BMI, smoking, and mortality in middle-aged men and women. *Obes Res* 2003;11:895-903.

15. Dagenais GR, Yi Q, Mann JF, et al. Prognostic impact of body weight and abdominal obesity in women and men with cardiovascular disease. *Am Heart J* 2005;149:54-60.

16. Han TS, van Leer EM, Seidell JC, et al. Waist circumference action levels in the identification of cardiovascular risk factors: prevalence study in a random sample. *BMJ (Clin Res Ed)* 1995;311:1401-5.

17. Lean ME, Han TS, Morrison CE. Waist circumference as a measure for indicating need for weight management. *BMJ (Clin Res Ed)* 1995;311:158-61.

18. Misra A, Wasir JS, Vikram NK. Waist circumference criteria for the diagnosis of abdominal obesity are not applicable uniformly to all populations and ethnic groups. *Nutrition* 2005;21:969-76.

19. Lindblad M, Rodriguez LA, Lagergren J. Body mass, tobacco and alcohol and risk of esophageal, gastric cardia, and gastric non-cardia adenocarcinoma among men and women in a nested case-control study. *Cancer Causes Control* 2005,16.285-94.

20. Tretli S, Robsahm TE. Height, weight and cancer of the oesophagus and stomach: a follow-up study in Norway. *Eur J Cancer Prev* 1999;8:115-22.

21. Engeland A, Tretli S, Bjorge T. Height and body mass index in relation to esophageal cancer; 23-year follow-up of two million Norwegian men and women. *Cancer Causes Control* 2004;15:837-43.

22. Blot WJ, Li JY, Taylor PR, et al. Nutrition intervention trials in Linxian, China: supplementation with specific vitamin/mineral combinations, cancer incidence, and disease-specific mortality in the general population.[see comment]. *J Natl Cancer Inst* 1993;85:1483-92.

23. Brown LM, Swanson CA, Gridley G, et al. Adenocarcinoma of the esophagus: role of obesity and diet. *J Natl Cancer Inst* 1995;87:104-9.

24. Chen H, Tucker KL, Graubard BI, et al. Nutrient intakes and adenocarcinoma of the esophagus and distal stomach. *Nutr Cancer* 2002;42:33-40.

25. Chow WH, Blot WJ, Vaughan TL, et al. Body mass index and risk of adenocarcinomas of the esophagus and gastric cardia. *J Natl Cancer Inst* 1998;90:150-5.

26. Kabat GC, Ng SK, Wynder EL. Tobacco, alcohol intake, and diet in relation to adenocarcinoma of the esophagus and gastric cardia. *Cancer Causes Control* 1993;4:123-32.

27. Trivers KF, De Roos AJ, Gammon MD, et al. Demographic and lifestyle predictors of survival in patients with esophageal or gastric cancers. *Clin Gastroenterol Hepatol* 2005;3:225-30.

28. Vaughan TL, Davis S, Kristal A, et al. Obesity, alcohol, and tobacco as risk factors for cancers of the esophagus and gastric cardia: adenocarcinoma versus squamous cell carcinoma. *Cancer Epidemiol Biomarkers Prev* 1995;4:85-92.

29. Wu MM, Kuo TL, Hwang YH, et al. Dose-response relation between arsenic concentration in well water and mortality from cancers and vascular diseases. *Am J Epidemiol* 1989;130:1123-32.

30. Samanic C, Chow WH, Gridley G, et al. Relation of body mass index to cancer risk in 362,552 Swedish men. *Cancer Causes Control* 2006;17:901-9.

31. MacInnis RJ, English DR, Hopper JL, et al. Body size and composition and the risk of gastric and oesophageal adenocarcinoma. *Int J Cancer* 2006;118:2628-31.

32. Ryan AM, Rowley SP, Fitzgerald AP, et al. Adenocarcinoma of the oesophagus and gastric cardia: male preponderance in association with obesity. *Eur J Cancer* 2006;42:1151-8.

33. de Jonge PJ, Steyerberg EW, Kuipers EJ, et al. Risk factors for the development of esophageal adenocarcinoma in Barrett's esophagus. *Am J Gastroenterol* 2006;101:1421-9.

34. Bu X, Ma Y, Der R, et al. Body mass index is associated with Barrett esophagus and cardiac mucosal metaplasia. *Dig Dis Sci* 2006;51:1589-94.

35. Wu M, Zhao JK, Hu XS, et al. Association of smoking, alcohol drinking and dietary factors with esophageal cancer in high- and low-risk areas of Jiangsu Province, China. *World J Gastroenterol* 2006;12:1686-93.

36. Veugelers PJ, Porter GA, Guernsey DL, et al. Obesity and lifestyle risk factors for gastroesophageal reflux disease, Barrett esophagus and esophageal adenocarcinoma. *Dis Esophagus* 2006;19:321-8.

37. Friedman GD, van den Eeden SK. Risk factors for pancreatic cancer: an exploratory study. *Int J Epidemiol* 1993;22:30-7.

38. Shibata A, Mack TM, Paganini-Hill A, et al. A prospective study of pancreatic cancer in the elderly. *Int J Cancer* 1994;58:46-9.

39. Gapstur SM, Gann PH, Lowe W, et al. Abnormal glucose metabolism and pancreatic cancer mortality. *JAMA* 2000;283:2552-8.

40. Michaud DS, Giovannucci E, Willett WC, et al. Physical activity, obesity, height, and the risk of pancreatic cancer. *JAMA* 2001;286:921-9.

41. Stolzenberg-Solomon RZ, Pietinen P, Taylor PR, et al. A prospective study of medical conditions, anthropometry, physical activity, and pancreatic cancer in male smokers (Finland). *Cancer Causes Control* 2002;13:417-26.

42. Calle EE, Rodriguez C, Walker-Thurmond K, et al. Overweight, obesity, and mortality from cancer in a prospectively studied cohort of U.S. adults. *N Engl J Med* 2003;348:1625-38.

43. Lee IM, Sesso HD, Oguma Y, et al. Physical activity, body weight, and pancreatic cancer mortality. *Br J Cancer* 2003;88:679-83.

44. Batty GD, Shipley MJ, Jarrett RJ, et al. Obesity and overweight in relation to organ-specific cancer mortality in London (UK): findings from the original Whitehall study. *Int J Obes* 2005;29:1267-74.

45. Kuriyama S, Tsubono Y, Hozawa A, et al. Obesity and risk of cancer in Japan. *Int J Cancer* 2005;113:148-57.

46. Larsson SC, Permert J, Hakansson N, et al. Overall obesity, abdominal adiposity, diabetes and cigarette smoking in relation to the risk of pancreatic cancer in two Swedish population-based cohorts. *Br J Cancer* 2005;93:1310-5.

47. Navarro Silvera SA, Miller AB, Rohan TE. Hormonal and reproductive factors and pancreatic cancer risk: a prospective cohort study. *Pancreas* 2005;30:369-74.

48. Nothlings U, Wilkens LR, Murphy SP, et al. Meat and fat intake as risk factors for pancreatic cancer: the multiethnic cohort study. *J Natl Cancer Inst* 2005;97:1458-65.

49. Patel AV, Rodriguez C, Bernstein L, et al. Obesity, recreational physical activity, and risk of pancreatic cancer in a large U.S. Cohort. *Cancer Epidemiol Biomarkers Prev* 2005;14:459-66.

50. Rapp K, Schroeder J, Klenk J, et al. Obesity and incidence of cancer: a large cohort study of over 145,000 adults in Austria. *Br J Cancer* 2005;93:1062-7.

51. Sinner PJ, Schmitz KH, Anderson KE, et al. Lack of association of physical activity and obesity with incident pancreatic cancer in elderly women. *Cancer Epidemiol Biomarkers Prev* 2005;14:1571-3.

52. Lukanova A, Bjor O, Kaaks R, et al. Body mass index and cancer: results from the Northern Sweden Health and Disease Cohort. *Int J Cancer* 2006;118:458-66.

53. Nilsen TIL, Vatten LJ. A prospective study of lifestyle factors and the risk of pancreatic cancer in Nord-Trondelag, Norway. *Cancer Causes Control* 2000;11:645-52.

54. Moller H, Mellemgaard A, Lindvig K, et al. Obesity and cancer risk: a Danish record-linkage study. *Eur J Cancer* 1994;30A:344-50.

55. Wolk A, Gridley G, Svensson M, et al. A prospective study of obesity and cancer risk (Sweden). *Cancer Causes Control* 2001;12:13-21.

56. Samanic C, Gridley G, Chow WH, et al. Obesity and cancer risk among white and black United States veterans. *Cancer Causes Control* 2004;15:35-43.

57. Oh SW, Yoon YS, Shin SA. Effects of excess weight on cancer incidences depending on cancer sites and histologic findings among men: Korea National Health Insurance Corporation Study. *J Clin Oncol* 2005;23:4742-54.

58. Robsahm TE, Tretli S. Height, weight and gastrointestinal cancer: a follow-up study in Norway. *Eur J Cancer Prev* 1999;8:105-13.

59. Bueno de Mesquita HB, Moerman CJ, Runia S, et al. Are energy and energy-providing nutrients related to exocrine carcinoma of the pancreas? *Int J Cancer* 1990;46:435-44.

60. Howe GR, Jain M, Miller AB. Dietary factors and risk of pancreatic cancer: results of a Canadian population-based case-control study. *Int J Cancer* 1990;45:604-8.

61. Ghadirian P, Simard A, Baillargeon J, et al. Nutritional factors and pancreatic cancer in the francophone community in Montreal, Canada. *Int J Cancer* 1991;47:1-6.

62. Zatonski W, Przewozniak K, Howe GR, et al. Nutritional factors and pancreatic cancer: a case-control study from south-west Poland. *Int J Cancer* 1991;48:390-4.

63. Ji BT, Hatch MC, Chow WH, et al. Anthropometric and reproductive factors and the risk of pancreatic cancer: a case-control study in Shanghai, China. *Int J Cancer* 1996;66:432-7.

64. Silverman DT, Swanson CA, Gridley G, et al. Dietary and nutritional factors and pancreatic cancer: a case-control study based on direct interviews. *J Natl Cancer Inst* 1998;90:1710-9.

65. Kreiger N, LaCroix J, Sloan M. Hormonal factors and pancreatic cancer in women. *Ann Epidemiol* 2001;11:563-7.

66. Pan SY, Johnson KC, Ugnat AM, et al. Association of obesity and cancer risk in Canada. *Am J Epidemiol* 2004;159:259-68.

67. Eberle CA, Bracci PM, Holly EA. Anthropometric factors and pancreatic cancer in a population-based case-control study in the San Francisco Bay area. *Cancer Causes Control* 2005;16:1235-44.

68. Fryzek JP, Schenk M, Kinnard M, et al. The association of body mass index and pancreatic cancer in residents of southeastern Michigan, 1996-1999. *Am J Epidemiol* 2005;162:222-8.

69. Lin Y, Tamakoshi A, Hayakawa T, et al. Nutritional factors and risk of pancreatic cancer: a population-based case-control study based on direct interview in Japan. *J Gastroenterol* 2005;40:297-301.

70. Pezzilli R, Morselli-Labate AM, Migliori M, et al. Obesity and the risk of pancreatic cancer: an Italian multicenter study. *Pancreas* 2005;31:221-4.

71. Rousseau MC, Parent ME, Siemiatycki J. Comparison of self-reported height and weight by cancer type among men from Montreal, Canada. *Eur J Cancer Prev* 2005;14:431-8.

72. Lyon JL, Slattery ML, Mahoney AW, et al. Dietary intake as a risk factor for cancer of the exocrine pancreas. *Cancer Epidemiol Biomarkers Prev* 1993;2:513-8.

73. Wynder EL, Dieck GS, Hall NE. Case-control study of decaffeinated coffee consumption and pancreatic cancer. *Cancer Res* 1986;46:5360-3.

74. Berrington de Gonzalez A, Spencer EA, Bueno-de-Mesquita HB, et al. Anthropometry, physical activity, and the risk of pancreatic cancer in the European prospective investigation into cancer and nutrition. *Cancer Epidemiol Biomarkers Prev* 2006;15:879-85.

75. Garland C, Shekelle RB, Barrett Connor E, et al. Dietary vitamin D and calcium and risk of colorectal cancer: a 19-year prospective study in men. *Lancet* 1985;1:307-9.

76. Stahelin HB, Rosel F, Buess E, et al. Dietary risk factors for cancer in the Basel Study. *Bibl Nutr Dieta* 1986:144-53.

77. Klatsky AL, Armstrong MA, Friedman GD, et al. The relations of alcoholic beverage use to colon and rectal cancer. *Am J Epidemiol* 1988;128:1007-15.

78. Gerhardsson M, Floderus B, Norell SE. Physical activity and colon cancer risk. *Int J Epidemiol* 1988;17:743-6.

79. Willett WC, Stampfer MJ, Colditz GA, et al. Relation of meat, fat, and fiber intake to the risk of colon cancer in a prospective study among women. *N Engl J Med* 1990;323:1664-72.

80. Chute CG, Willett WC, Colditz GA, et al. A prospective study of body mass, height, and smoking on the risk of colorectal cancer in women. *Cancer Causes Control* 1991;2:117-24.

81. Thun MJ, Calle EE, Namboodiri MM, et al. Risk factors for fatal colon cancer in a large prospective study. *J Natl Cancer Inst* 1992;84:1491-500.

82. Bostick RM, Potter JD, McKenzie DR, et al. Reduced risk of colon cancer with high intake of vitamin E: the Iowa Women's Health Study. *Cancer Res* 1993;53:4230-7.

83. Suadicani P, Hein HO, Gyntelberg F. Height, weight, and risk of colorectal cancer. An 18-year follow-up in a cohort of 5249 men. *Scand J Gastroenterol* 1993;28:285-8.

84. Bostick RM, Potter JD, Kushi LH, et al. Sugar, meat, and fat intake, and non-dietary risk factors for colon cancer incidence in Iowa women (United States). *Cancer Causes Control* 1994;5:38-52.

85. Chyou PH, Nomura AM, Stemmermann GN. A prospective study of colon and rectal cancer among Hawaii Japanese men. *Ann Epidemiol* 1996;6:276-82.

86. Gapstur SM, Potter JD, Folsom AR. Alcohol consumption and colon and rectal cancer in postmenopausal women. *Int J Epidemiol* 1994;23:50-7.

87. Giovannucci E, Ascherio A, Rimm EB, et al. Physical activity, obesity, and risk for colon cancer and adenoma in men. *Ann Intern Med* 1995;122:327-34.

88. Chyou PH, Nomura AM, Stemmermann GN. A prospective study of weight, body mass index and other anthropometric measurements in relation to site-specific cancers. *Int J Cancer* 1994;57:313-7.

89. Glynn SA, Albanes D, Pietinen P, et al. Colorectal cancer and folate status: a nested case-control study among male smokers. *Cancer Epidemiol Biomarkers Prev* 1996;5:487-94.

90. Key TJ, Thorogood M, Appleby PN, et al. Dietary habits and mortality in 11,000 vegetarians and health conscious people: results of a 17 year follow up. *BMJ* 1996;313:775-9.

91. Kato I, Akhmedkhanov A, Koenig K, et al. Prospective study of diet and female colorectal cancer: the New York University Women's Health Study. *Nutr Cancer* 1997;28:276-81.

92. Martinez ME, Giovannucci E, Spiegelman D, et al. Leisure-time physical activity, body size, and colon cancer in women. Nurses' Health Study Research Group. *J Natl Cancer Inst* 1997;89:948-55.

93. Gaard M, Tretli S, Urdal P. Blood lipid and lipoprotein levels and the risk of cancer of the colon and rectum. A prospective study of 62,173 Norwegian men and women. *Scand J Gastroenterol* 1997;32:162-8.

94. Singh PN, Fraser GE. Dietary risk factors for colon cancer in a low-risk population. *Am J Epidemiol* 1998;148:761-74.

95. Ford ES. Body mass index and colon cancer in a national sample of adult US men and women. *Am J Epidemiol* 1999;150:390-8.

96. Pietinen P, Malila N, Virtanen M, et al. Diet and risk of colorectal cancer in a cohort of Finnish men. *Cancer Causes Control* 1999;10:387-96.

97. Schoen RE, Tangen CM, Kuller LH, et al. Increased blood glucose and insulin, body size, and incident colorectal cancer. *J Natl Cancer Inst* 1999;91:1147-54.

98. Kato I, Dnistrian AM, Schwartz M, et al. Serum folate, homocysteine and colorectal cancer risk in women: a nested case-control study. *Br J Cancer* 1999;79:1917-22.

99. Murphy TK, Calle EE, Rodriguez C, et al. Body mass index and colon cancer mortality in a large prospective study. *Am J Epidemiol* 2000;152:847-54.

100. Jarvinen R, Knekt P, Hakulinen T, et al. Prospective study on milk products, calcium and cancers of the colon and rectum. *Eur J Clin Nutr* 2001;55:1000-7.

101. Nilsen TI, Vatten LJ. Prospective study of colorectal cancer risk and physical activity, diabetes, blood glucose and BMI: exploring the hyperinsulinaemia hypothesis. *Br J Cancer* 2001;84:417-22.

102. Colbert LH, Hartman TJ, Malila N, et al. Physical activity in relation to cancer of the colon and rectum in a cohort of male smokers. *Cancer Epidemiol Biomarkers Prev* 2001;10:265-8.

103. Field AE, Coakley EH, Must A, et al. Impact of overweight on the risk of developing common chronic diseases during a 10-year period. *Arch Intern Med* 2001;161:1581-6.

104. Terry P, Giovannucci E, Bergkvist L, et al. Body weight and colorectal cancer risk in a cohort of Swedish women: relation varies by age and cancer site. *Br J Cancer* 2001;85:346-9.

105. Lund Nilsen TI, Vatten LJ. Colorectal cancer associated with BMI, physical activity, diabetes, and blood glucose. *IARC Sci Publ* 2002;156:257-8.

106. Malila N, Virtamo J, Virtanen M, et al. Dietary and serum alpha-tocopherol, beta-carotene and retinol, and risk for colorectal cancer in male smokers. *Eur J Clin Nutr* 2002;56:615-21.

107. Okasha M, McCarron P, McEwen J, et al. Body mass index in young adulthood and cancer mortality: a retrospective cohort study. *J Epidemiol Community Health* 2002;56:780-4.

108. Colangelo LA, Gapstur SM, Gann PH, et al. Colorectal cancer mortality and factors related to the insulin resistance syndrome. *Cancer Epidemiol Biomarkers Prev* 2002;11:385-91.

109. Tiemersma EW, Kampman E, Bueno de Mesquita HB, et al. Meat consumption, cigarette smoking, and genetic susceptibility in the etiology of colorectal cancer: results from a Dutch prospective study. *Cancer Causes Control* 2002;13:383-93.

110. Wu AH, Paganini-Hill A, Ross RK, et al. Alcohol, physical activity and other risk factors for colorectal cancer: a prospective study. *Br J Cancer* 1987;55:687-94.

111. Kmet LM, Cook LS, Weiss NS, et al. Risk factors for colorectal cancer following breast cancer. *Breast Cancer Res Treat* 2003;79:143-7.

112. Saydah SH, Platz EA, Rifai N, et al. Association of markers of insulin and glucose control with subsequent colorectal cancer risk. *Cancer Epidemiol Biomarkers Prev* 2003;12:412-8.

113. Wong HL, Seow A, Arakawa K, et al. Vitamin D receptor start codon polymorphism and colorectal cancer risk: effect modification by dietary calcium and fat in Singapore Chinese. *Carcinogenesis* 2003;24:1091-5.

114. Koh WP, Yuan JM, van den Berg D, et al. Interaction between cyclooxygenase-2 gene polymorphism and dietary n-6 polyunsaturated fatty acids on colon cancer risk: The Singapore Chinese Health Study. *Br J Cancer* 2004;90:1760-4.

115. MacInnis RJ, English DR, Hopper JL, et al. Body size and composition and colon cancer risk in men. *Cancer Epidemiol Biomarkers Prev* 2004;13:553-9.

116. Sanjoaquin MA, Appleby PN, Thorogood M, et al. Nutrition, lifestyle and colorectal cancer incidence: a prospective investigation of 10998 vegetarians and non-vegetarians in the United Kingdom. *Br J Cancer* 2004;90:118-21.

117. Tangrea J, Helzlsouer K, Pietinen P, et al. Serum levels of vitamin D metabolites and the subsequent risk of colon and rectal cancer in Finnish men. *Cancer Causes Control* 1997;8:615-25.

118. Moore LL, Bradlee ML, Singer MR, et al. BMI and waist circumference as predictors of lifetime colon cancer risk in Framingham Study adults. *Int J Obes Relat Metab Disord* 2004;28:559-67.

119. Shimizu N, Nagata C, Shimizu H, et al. Height, weight, and alcohol consumption in relation to the risk of colorectal cancer in Japan: a prospective study. *Br J Cancer* 2003;88:1038-43.

120. Tamakoshi K, Wakai K, Kojima M, et al. A prospective study of body size and colon cancer mortality in Japan: The JACC Study. *Int J Obes Relat Metab Disord* 2004;28:551-8.

121. Terry PD, Miller AB, Rohan TE. Obesity and colorectal cancer risk in women. *Gut* 2002;51:191-4.

122. Tulinius H, Sigfusson N, Sigvaldason H, et al. Risk factors for malignant diseases: a cohort study on a population of 22,946 Icelanders. *Cancer Epidemiol Biomarkers Prev* 1997;6:863-73.

123. van Wayenburg CA, van der Schouw YT, van Noord PA, et al. Age at menopause, body mass index, and the risk of colorectal cancer mortality in the Dutch Diagnostisch Onderzoek Mammacarcinoom (DOM) cohort. *Epidemiology* 2000;11:304-8.

124. Wei EK, Giovannucci E, Wu K, et al. Comparison of risk factors for colon and rectal cancer. *Int J Cancer* 2004;108:433-42.

125. Kreger BE, Anderson KM, Schatzkin A, et al. Serum cholesterol level, body mass index, and the risk of colon cancer. The Framingham Study. *Cancer* 1992;70:1038-43.

126. Le Marchand L, Wilkens LR, Mi MP. Obesity in youth and middle age and risk of colorectal cancer in men. *Cancer Causes Control* 1992;3:349-54.

127. Lee IM, Paffenbarger RS, Jr. Quetelet's index and risk of colon cancer in college alumni. *J Natl Cancer Inst* 1992;84:1326-31.

128. Must A, Jacques PF, Dallal GE, et al. Long-term morbidity and mortality of overweight adolescents. A follow-up of the Harvard Growth Study of 1922 to 1935. *N Engl J Med* 1992;327:1350-5.

129. Nomura A, Heilbrun LK, Stemmermann GN. Body mass index as a predictor of cancer in men. *J Natl Cancer Inst* 1985;74:319-23.

130. Jarvinen R, Knekt P, Hakulinen T, et al. Dietary fat, cholesterol and colorectal cancer in a prospective study. *Br J Cancer* 2001;85:357-61.

131. Meyerhardt JA, Catalano PJ, Haller DG, et al. Influence of body mass index on outcomes and treatment-related toxicity in patients with colon carcinoma. *Cancer* 2003;98:484-95.

132. Hara M, Mori M, Shono N, et al. Body mass index and risk of cancer in men and women. *Tumor Research* 1999;34:29-39.

133. Tartter PI, Slater G, Papatestas AE, et al. Cholesterol, weight, height, Quetelet's index, and colon cancer recurrence. *J Surg Oncol* 1984;27:232-5.

134. Sidney S, Friedman GD, Hiatt RA. Serum cholesterol and large bowel cancer. A case-control study. *Am J Epidemiol* 1986;124:33-8.

135. Bostick RM, Potter JD, Sellers TA, et al. Relation of calcium, vitamin D, and dairy food intake to incidence of colon cancer among older women. The Iowa Women's Health Study. *Am J Epidemiol* 1993;137:1302-17.

136. Feskanich D, Ma J, Fuchs CS, et al. Plasma vitamin D metabolites and risk of colorectal cancer in women. *Cancer*

Epidemiol Biomarkers Prev 2004;13:1502-8.

137. Folsom AR, Kushi LH, Anderson KE, et al. Associations of general and abdominal obesity with multiple health outcomes in older women: the Iowa Women's Health Study. *Arch Intern Med* 2000;160:2117-28.

138. Doria-Rose VP, Hampton JM, Trentham-Dietz A, et al. Body mass index and mortality following colorectal cancer in postmenopausal women. *Am J Epidemiol* 2004;159:S68-S.

139. Lin J, Zhang SM, Cook NR, et al. Body mass index and risk of colorectal cancer in women (United States). *Cancer Causes Control*, 2004:581-9.

140. Otani T, Iwasaki M, Inoue M. Body mass index, body height, and subsequent risk of colorectal cancer in middle-aged and elderly Japanese men and women: Japan public health center-based prospective study. *Cancer Causes Control*, 2005:839-50.

141. Engeland A, Tretli S, Austad G, et al. Height and body mass index in relation to colorectal and gallbladder cancer in two million Norwegian men and women. *Cancer Causes Control* 2005;16:987-96.

142. Pischon T, Lahmann PH, Boeing H, et al. Body Size and Risk of Colon and Rectal cancer in the European Prospective Investigation Into Cancer and Nutrition (EPIC). *J Natl Cancer Inst* 2006;98:920-31.

143. Ahmed RL, Schmitz KH, Anderson KE, et al. The metabolic syndrome and risk of incident colorectal cancer. *Cancer* 2006;107:28-36.

144. Eichholzer M, Bernasconi F, Jordan P, et al. Body mass index and the risk of male cancer mortality of various sites: 17-year follow-up of the Basel cohort study. *Swiss Med Wkly* 2005;135:27-33.

145. Bowers K, Albanes D, Limburg P, et al. A prospective study of anthropometric and clinical measurements associated with insulin resistance syndrome and colorectal cancer in male smokers. *Am J Epidemiol* 2006;164:652-64.

146. Sherman ME, Lacey JV, Buys SS, et al. Ovarian volume: determinants and associations with cancer among postmenopausal women. *Cancer Epidemiol Biomarkers Prev* 2006;15:1550-4.

147. Hou L, Ji BT, Blair A, et al. Body mass index and colon cancer risk in Chinese people: menopause as an effect modifier. *Eur J Cancer* 2006;42:84-90.

148. Chung YW, Han DS, Park YK, et al. Association of obesity, serum glucose and lipids with the risk of advanced colorectal adenoma and cancer: a case-control study in Korea. *Dig Liver Dis* 2006;38:668-72.

149. Tehard B, Lahmann PH, Riboli E, et al. Anthropometry, breast cancer and menopausal status: use of repeated measurements over 10 years of follow-up-results of the French E3N women's cohort study. *Int J Cancer* 2004;111:264-9.

150. Ahlgren M, Melbye M, Wohlfahrt J, et al. Growth patterns and the risk of breast cancer in women. *N Engl J Med* 2004;351:1619-26.

151. Barrett-Connor E, Friedlander NJ. Dietary fat, calories, and the risk of breast cancer in postmenopausal women: a prospective population-based study. *J Am Coll Nutr* 1993;12:390-9.

152. Byrne C, Ursin G, Ziegler RG. A comparison of food habit and food frequency data as predictors of breast cancer in the NHANES I/NHEFS cohort. *J Nutr* 1996;126:2757-64.

153. Chang SC, Leitzmann M, Stolzenberg-Solomon R, et al. Interrelation of energy intake, body size, and physical activity with breast cancer in the PLCO screening trial. *Cancer Epidemiol Biomarkers Prev* 2003;12:1338S.

154. Colditz GA, Rosner BA, Chen WY, et al. Risk factors for breast cancer according to estrogen and progesterone receptor status. *J Natl Cancer Inst* 2004;96:218-28.

155. De Stavola BL, Wang DY, Allen DS, et al. The association of height, weight, menstrual and reproductive events with breast cancer: results from two prospective studies on the island of Guernsey (United Kingdom). *Cancer Causes Control* 1993;4:331-40.

156. den Tonkelaar I, Seidell JC, Collette HJ, et al. A prospective study on obesity and subcutaneous fat patterning in relation to breast cancer in post-menopausal women participating in the DOM project. *Br J Cancer* 1994;69:352-7.

157. den Tonkelaar I, Seidell JC, Collette HJ. Body fat distribution in relation to breast cancer in women participating in the DOM-project. *Breast Cancer Res Treat* 1995;34:55-61.

158. Feigelson HS, Jonas CR, Teras LR, et al. Weight gain, body mass index, hormone replacement therapy, and postmenopausal breast cancer in a large prospective study. *Cancer Epidemiol Biomarkers Prev* 2004;13:220-4.

159. Folsom AR, Kaye SA, Prineas RJ, et al. Increased incidence of carcinoma of the breast associated with abdominal adiposity in postmenopausal women. *Am J Epidemiol* 1990;131:794-803.

160. Fraser GE, Shavlik D. Risk factors, lifetime risk, and age at onset of breast cancer. *Ann Epidemiol* 1997;7:375-82.

161. Gaard M, Tretli S, Urdal P. Risk of breast cancer in relation to blood lipids: a prospective study of 31,209 Norwegian women. *Cancer Causes Control* 1994;5:501-9.

162. Galanis DJ, Kolonel LN, Lee J, et al. Anthropometric predictors of breast cancer incidence and survival in a multi-ethnic cohort of female residents of Hawaii, United States. *Cancer Causes Control* 1998;9:217-24.

163. Gapstur SM, Potter JD, Sellers TA, et al. Increased risk of breast cancer with alcohol consumption in postmenopausal women. *Am J Epidemiol* 1992;136:1221-31.

164. Goodman MT, Cologne JB, Moriwaki H, et al. Risk factors for primary breast cancer in Japan: 8-year follow-up of atomic bomb survivors. *Prev Med* 1997;26:144-53.

165. Graham S, Zielezny M, Marshall J, et al. Diet in the epidemiology of postmenopausal breast cancer in the New York State Cohort. *Am J Epidemiol* 1992;136:1327-37.

166. Hoyer AP, Engholm G. Serum lipids and breast cancer risk: a cohort study of 5,207 Danish women. *Cancer Causes Control* 1992;3:403-8.

167. Huang Z, Hankinson SE, Colditz GA, et al. Dual effects of weight and weight gain on breast cancer risk. *JAMA* 1997;278:1407-11.

168. Jonsson F, Wolk A, Pedersen NL, et al. Obesity and hormone-dependent tumors: Cohort and co-twin control studies based on the Swedish Twin Registry. *Int J Cancer* 2003;106:594-9.

169. Jumaan AO, Holmberg L, Zack M, et al. Beta-carotene intake and risk of postmenopausal breast cancer. *Epidemiology* 1999;10:49-53.

170. Kaaks R, Van Noord PA, Den Tonkelaar I, et al. Breast-cancer incidence in relation to height, weight and body-fat distribution in the Dutch "DOM" cohort. *Int J Cancer* 1998;76:647-51.

171. Key TJ, Sharp GB, Appleby PN, et al. Soya foods and breast cancer risk: a prospective study in Hiroshima and Nagasaki, Japan. *Br J Cancer* 1999;81:1248-56.

172. Kilkkinen A, Virtamo J, Vartiainen E, et al. Serum enterolactone concentration is not associated with breast cancer risk in a nested case-control study. *Int J Cancer* 2004;108:277-80.

173. Knekt P, Jarvinen R, Seppanen R, et al. Intake of dairy products and the risk of breast cancer. *Br J Cancer* 1996;73:687-91.

174. Lahmann PH, Lissner L, Gullberg B, et al. A prospective study of adiposity and postmenopausal breast cancer risk: The Malmo Diet and Cancer Study. *Int J Cancer* 2003;103:246-52.

175. Lahmann PH, Hoffmann K, Allen N, et al. Body size and breast cancer risk: Findings from the European Prospective Investigation into Cancer and Nutrition (EPIC). *Int J Cancer* 2004;111:762-71.

176. Le Marchand L, Kolonel LN, Earle ME, et al. Body size at different periods of life and breast cancer risk. *Am J Epidemiol* 1988;128:137-52.

177. Lee SY, Kim MT, Kim SW, et al. Effect of lifetime lactation on breast cancer risk: a Korean Women's Cohort Study. *Int J Cancer* 2003;105:390-3.

178. Manjer J, Kaaks R, Riboli E, et al. Risk of breast cancer in relation to anthropometry, blood pressure, blood lipids and glucose metabolism: a prospective study within the Malmo preventive project. *Eur J Cancer Prev* 2001;10:33-42.

179. Mills PK, Beeson WL, Phillips RL, et al. Dietary habits and breast cancer incidence among Seventh-day Adventists. *Cancer* 1989;64:582-90.

180. Morimoto LM, White E, Chen Z, et al. Obesity, body size, and risk of postmenopausal breast cancer: The Women's Health Initiative (United States). *Cancer Causes Control* 2002;13:741-51.

181. Overvad K, Wang DY, Olsen J, et al. Selenium in human mammary carcinogenesis: a case-cohort study. *Eur J Cancer* 1991;27:900-2.

182. Patel AV, Calle EE, Bernstein L, et al. Recreational physical activity and risk of postmenopausal breast cancer in a large cohort of US women. *Cancer Causes Control* 2003;14:519-29.

183. Petrelli JM, Calle EE, Rodriguez C, et al. Body mass index, height, and postmenopausal breast cancer mortality in a prospective cohort of US women. *Cancer Causes Control* 2002;13:325-32.

184. Rissanen H, Knekt P, Jarvinen R, et al. Serum fatty acids and breast cancer incidence. *Nutr Cancer* 2003;45:168-75.

185. Saadatian-Elahi M, Toniolo P, Ferrari P, et al. Serum fatty acids and risk of breast cancer in a nested case-control study of the New York University Women's Health Study. *Cancer Epidemiol Biomarkers Prev* 2002;11:1353-60.

186. Schatzkin A, Carter CL, Green SB, et al. Is alcohol consumption related to breast cancer? Results from the Framingham Heart Study. *J Natl Cancer Inst* 1989;81:31-5.

187. Sellers TA, Davis J, Cerhan JR, et al. Interaction of waist/hip ratio and family history on the risk of hormone receptor-defined breast cancer in a prospective study of postmenopausal women. *Am J Epidemiol* 2002;155:225-33.

188. Silvera SA, Jain M, Howe GR, et al. Energy balance and breast cancer risk: a prospective cohort study. *Breast Cancer Res Treat* 2006;97:97-106.

189. Sonnenschein E, Toniolo P, Terry MB, et al. Body fat distribution and obesity in pre- and postmenopausal breast cancer. *Int J Epidemiol* 1999;28:1026-31.

190. Toniolo P, Riboli E, Shore RE, et al. Consumption of meat, animal products, protein, and fat and risk of breast cancer: a prospective cohort study in New York. *Epidemiology* 1994;5:391-7.

191. Tornberg SA, Holm LE, Carstensen JM. Breast cancer risk in relation to serum cholesterol, serum beta-lipoprotein, height, weight, and blood pressure. *Acta Oncol* 1988;27:31-7.

192. Tornberg SA, Carstensen JM. Relationship between Quetelet's index and cancer of breast and female genital tract in 47,000 women followed for 25 years. *Br J Cancer* 1994;69:358-61.

193. van den Brandt PA, Dirx MJ, Ronckers CM, et al. Height, weight, weight change, and postmenopausal breast cancer risk: The Netherlands Cohort Study. *Cancer Causes Control* 1997;8:39-47.

194. Van den Brandt PA, Van't Veer P, Goldbohm RA, et al. A prospective cohort study on dietary fat and the risk of postmenopausal breast cancer. *Cancer Res* 1993;53:75-82.

195. Vatten LJ, Kvinnsland S. Body mass index and risk of breast cancer. A prospective study of 23,826 Norwegian women. *Int J Cancer* 1990;45:440-4.

196. Vatten LJ, Kvinnsland S. Prospective study of height, body mass index and risk of breast cancer. *Acta Oncol* 1992;31:195-200.

197. Vatten LJ, Solvoll K, Loken EB. Coffee consumption and the risk of breast cancer. A prospective study of 14,593 Norwegian women. *Br J Cancer* 1990;62:267-70.

198. Weiderpass E, Braaten T, Magnusson C, et al. A prospective study of body size in different periods of life and risk of premenopausal breast cancer. *Cancer Epidemiol Biomarkers Prev* 2004;13:1121-7.

199. Wirfalt E, Mattisson I, Gullberg B, et al. Postmenopausal breast cancer is associated with high intakes of omega 6 fatty acids (Sweden). *Cancer Causes Control* 2002;13:883-93.

200. Wirfalt E, Vessby B, Mattisson I, et al. No relations between breast cancer risk and fatty acids of erythrocyte membranes in postmenopausal women of the Malmo Diet Cancer cohort (Sweden). *Eur J Clin Nutr* 2004;58:761-70.

201. Wolk A, Bergstrom R, Hunter D, et al. A prospective study of association of monounsaturated fat and other types of fat with risk of breast cancer. *Arch Intern Med* 1998;158:41-5.

202. Wu K, Helzlsouer KJ, Comstock GW, et al. A prospective study on folate, B12, and pyridoxal 5'-phosphate (B6) and breast cancer. *Cancer Epidemiol Biomarkers Prev* 1999;8:209-17.

203. Wu MH, Chou YC, Yu JC, et al. Hormonal and body-size factors in relation to breast cancer risk: a prospective study of 11,889 women in a low-incidence area. *Ann Epidemiol* 2005.

204. Zhang SM, Willett WC, Selhub J, et al. Plasma folate, vitamin B6, vitamin B12, homocysteine, and risk of breast cancer. *J Natl Cancer Inst* 2003;95:373-80.

205. Adami HO, Rimsten A, Stenkvist B, et al. Influence of height, weight and obesity on risk of breast cancer in an unselected Swedish population. *Br J Cancer* 1977;36:787-92.

206. Adams-Campbell LL, Kim KS, Dunston G, et al. The relationship of body mass index to reproductive factors in pre- and postmenopausal African-American women with and without breast cancer. *Obes Res* 1996;4:451-6.

207. Adebamowo CA, Ogundiran TO, Adenipekun AA, et al. Waist-hip ratio and breast cancer risk in urbanized Nigerian women. *Breast Cancer Res* 2003;5:R18-R24.

208. Adebamowo CA, Ogundiran TO, Adenipekun AA, et al. Obesity and height in urban Nigerian women with breast cancer. *Ann Epidemiol* 2003;13:455-61.

209. Agurs-Collins T, Kim KS, Dunston GM, et al. Plasma lipid alterations in African-American women with breast cancer. *J Cancer Res Clin Oncol* 1998;124:186-90.

210. Althuis MD, Brogan DD, Coates RJ, et al. Breast cancers among very young premenopausal women (United States). *Cancer Causes Control* 2003;14:151-60.

211. Atalah E, Urteaga C, Rebolledo A, et al. [Breast cancer risk factors in women in Santiago, Chile.] *Rev Med Chil* 2000;128:137-43.

212. Bagga D, Anders KH, Wang H-J, et al. Long-chain n-3-to-n-6 polyunsaturated fatty acid ratios in breast adipose tissue from women with and without breast cancer. *Nutr Cancer* 2002;42:180-5.

213. Bonilla-Fernandez P, Lopez-Cervantes M, Torres-Sanchez LE, et al. Nutritional factors and breast cancer in Mexico. *Nutr Cancer* 2003;45:148-55.

214. Bouchardy C, Le MG, Hill C. Risk factors for breast cancer according to age at diagnosis in a French case-control study. *J Clin Epidemiol* 1990;43:267-75.

215. Bowlin SJ, Leske MC, Varma A, et al. Breast cancer risk and alcohol consumption: results from a large case-control study. *Int J Epidemiol* 1997;26:915-23.

216. Brinton LA, Potischman NA, Swanson CA, et al. Breastfeeding and breast cancer risk. *Cancer Causes Control* 1995;6:199-208.

217. Brinton LA, Swanson CA. Height and weight at various ages and risk of breast cancer. *Ann Epidemiol* 1992;2:597-609.

218. Bruning PF, Bonfrer JM, Hart AA, et al. Body measurements, estrogen availability and the risk of human breast cancer: a case-control study. *Int J Cancer* 1992;51:14-9.

219. Calderon-Garciduenas AL, Paras-Barrientos FU, Cardenas-Ibarra L, et al. Risk factors of breast cancer in Mexican women. *Salud Publica Mex* 2000;42:26-33.

220. Carpenter CL, Ross RK, Paganini-Hill A, et al. Effect of family history, obesity and exercise on breast cancer risk among postmenopausal women. *Int J Cancer* 2003;106:96-102.

221. Challier B, Perarnau JM, Viel JF. Garlic, onion and cereal fibre as protective factors for breast cancer: a French case-control study. *Eur J Epidemiol* 1998;14:737-47.

222. Chang S, Buzdar AU, Hursting SD. Inflammatory breast cancer and body mass index. *J Clin Oncol* 1998;16:3731-5.

223. Chen CL, White E, Malone KE, et al. Leisure-time physical activity in relation to breast cancer among young women (Washington, United States). *Cancer Causes Control* 1997;8:77-84.

224. Chie WC, Chen CF, Lee WC, et al. Body size and risk of pre- and post-menopausal breast cancer in Taiwan. *Anticancer Res* 1996;16:3129-32.

225. Chie WC, Li CY, Huang CS, et al. Body size as a factor in different ages and breast cancer risk in Taiwan. *Anticancer Res* 1998;18:565-70.

226. Chow LW, Lui KL, Chan JC, et al. Association between body mass index and risk of formation of breast cancer in Chinese women. *Asian J Surg* 2005;28:179-84.

227. Chu SY, Lee NC, Wingo PA, et al. The relationship between body mass and breast cancer among women enrolled in the Cancer and Steroid Hormone Study. *J Clin Epidemiol* 1991;44:1197-206.

228. Coates RJ, Uhler RJ, Hall HI, et al. Risk of breast cancer in young women in relation to body size and weight gain in adolescence and early adulthood. *Br J Cancer* 1999;81:167-74.

229. Cooper JA, Rohan TE, Cant EL, et al. Risk factors for breast cancer by oestrogen receptor status: A population-based case-control study. *Br J Cancer* 1989;59:119-25.

230. Dai Q, Shu XO, Jin F, et al. Consumption of animal foods, cooking methods, and risk of breast cancer. *Cancer Epidemiol Biomarkers Prev* 2002;11:801-8.

231. de Vasconcelos AB, Azevedo e Silva Mendonca G, Sichieri R. Height, weight, weight change and risk of breast cancer in Rio de Janeiro, Brazil. *Sao Paulo Med J* 2001;119:62-6.

232. Do MH, Lee SS, Jung PJ, et al. Intake of dietary fat and vitamin in relation to breast cancer risk in Korean women: a case-control study. *J Korean Med Sci* 2003;18:534-40.

233. Dorn J, Vena J, Brasure J, et al. Lifetime physical activity and breast cancer risk in pre- and postmenopausal women. *Med Sci Sports Exerc* 2003;35:278-85.

234. Drewnowski A, Henderson SA, Hann CS, et al. Genetic taste markers and preferences for vegetables and fruit of female breast care patients. *J Am Diet Assoc* 2000;100:191-7.

235. Eid A, Berry EM. The relationship between dietary fat, adipose tissue composition, and neoplasms of the breast. *Nutr Cancer* 1988;11:173-7.

236. Enger SM, Ross RK, Paganini-Hill A, et al. Body size, physical activity, and breast cancer hormone receptor status: Results from two case-control studies. *Cancer Epidemiol Biomarkers Prev* 2000;9:681-7.

237. Favero A, Parpinel M, Franceschi S. Diet and risk of breast cancer: major findings from an Italian case-control study. *Biomed Pharmacother* 1998;52:109-15.

238. Ferraroni M, Decarli A, Willett WC, et al. Alcohol and breast cancer risk: a case-control study from northern Italy. *Int J Epidemiol* 1991;20:859-64.

239. Fioretti F, Tavani A, Bosetti C, et al. Risk factors for breast cancer in nulliparous women. *Br J Cancer* 1999;79:1923-8.

240. Fowke JH, Chung FL, Jin F, et al. Urinary isothiocyanate levels, brassica, and human breast cancer. *Cancer Res* 2003;63:3980-6.

241. Franceschi S, Favero A, La Vecchia C, et al. Body size indices and breast cancer risk before and after menopause. *Int J Cancer* 1996;67:181-6.

242. Friedenreich CM, Courneya KS, Bryant HE. Case-control study of anthropometric measures and breast cancer risk. *Int J Cancer* 2002;99:445-52.

243. Friedenreich CM, Bryant HE, Courneya KS. Case-control study of lifetime physical activity and breast cancer risk. *Am J Epidemiol* 2001;154:336-47.

244. Furberg H, Newman B, Moorman P, et al. Lactation and breast cancer risk. *Int J Epidemiol* 1999;28:396-402.

245. Gerber M, Cavallo F, Marubini E, et al. Liposoluble vitamins and lipid parameters in breast cancer. A joint study in northern Italy and southern France. *Int J Cancer* 1988;42:489-94.

246. Graham S, Hellmann R, Marshall J, et al. Nutritional epidemiology of postmenopausal breast cancer in western New York. *Am J Epidemiol* 1991;134:552-66.

247. Hall IJ, Newman B, Millikan RC, et al. Body size and breast cancer risk in black women and white women: the Carolina Breast Cancer Study. *Am J Epidemiol* 2000;151:754-64.

248. Hansen S, Cold S, Petersen PH, et al. Estimates of the sources of variation (variance components) of bioelectric impedance and anthropometric measurements in an epidemiological case-control study of breast cancer. *Eur J Clin Nutr* 1997;51:764-70.

249. Harris RE, Namboodiri KK, Wynder EL. Breast cancer risk: effects of estrogen replacement therapy and body mass. *J Natl Cancer Inst* 1992;84:1575-82.

250. Helmrich SP, Shapiro S, Rosenberg L, et al. Risk factors for breast cancer. *Am J Epidemiol* 1983;117:35-45.

251. Henquin N, Trostler N, Horn Y. Nutritional risk factors and breast cancer in Jewish and Arab women. *Cancer Nurs* 1994;17:326-33.

252. Hietanen E, Bartsch H, Bereziat JC, et al. Diet and oxidative stress in breast, colon and prostate cancer patients: a case-control study. *Eur J Clin Nutr* 1994;48:575-86.

253. Hirose K, Tajima K, Hamajima N, et al. A large-scale, hospital-based case-control study of risk factors of breast cancer according to menopausal status. *Jpn J Cancer Res* 1995;86:146-54.

254. Hirose K, Tajima K, Hamajima N, et al. Comparative case-referent study of risk factors among hormone-related female cancers in Japan. *Jpn J Cancer Res* 1999;90:255-61.

255. Hirose K, Tajima K, Hamajima N, et al. Effect of body size on breast-cancer risk among Japanese women. *Int J Cancer* 1999;80:349-55.

256. Hirose K, Tajima K, Hamajima N, et al. Impact of established risk factors for breast cancer in nulligravid Japanese women. *Breast Cancer* 2003;10:45-53.

257. Hirose K, Tajima K, Hamajima N, et al. Association of family history and other risk factors with breast cancer risk among Japanese premenopausal and postmenopausal women. *Cancer Causes Control* 2001;12:349-58.

258. Hirose K, Takezaki T, Hamajima N, et al. Dietary factors protective against breast cancer in Japanese premenopausal and postmenopausal women. *Int J Cancer* 2003;107:276-82.

259. Hislop TG, Coldman AJ, Elwood JM, et al. Childhood and recent eating patterns and risk of breast cancer. *Cancer Detect Prev* 1986;9:47-58.

260. Holmberg L, Ohlander EM, Byers T, et al. Diet and breast cancer risk. Results from a population-based, case-control study in Sweden. *Arch Intern Med* 1994;154:1805-11.

261. Hsieh CC, Trichopoulos D, Katsouyanni K, et al. Age at menarche, age at menopause, height and obesity as risk factors for breast cancer: associations and interactions in an international case-control study. *Int J Cancer* 1990;46:796-800.

262. Hu YH, Nagata C, Shimizu H, et al. Association of body mass index, physical activity, and reproductive histories with breast cancer: a case-control study in Gifu, Japan. *Breast Cancer Res Treat* 1997;43:65-72.

263. Huang CS, Chern HD, Shen CY, et al. Association between N-acetyltransferase 2 (NAT2) genetic polymorphism and development of breast cancer in post-menopausal Chinese women in Taiwan, an area of great increase in breast cancer incidence. *Int J Cancer* 1999;82:175-9.

264. Ibarluzea JM, Fernandez MF, Santa-Marina L, et al. Breast cancer risk and the combined effect of environmental estrogens. *Cancer Causes Control* 2004;15:591-600.

265. Ingram DM, Nottage E, Roberts T. The role of diet in the development of breast cancer: a case-control study of patients with breast cancer, benign epithelial hyperplasia and fibrocystic disease of the breast. *Br J Cancer* 1991;64:187-91.

266. Ingram D, Nottage E, Ng S, et al. Obesity and breast disease. The role of the female sex hormones. *Cancer* 1989;64:1049-53.

267. Joensuu H, Tuominen J, Hinkka S, et al. Risk factors for screen-detected breast cancer. A case-control study. *Acta Oncol* 1992;31:729-32.

268. Kampert JB, Whittemore AS, Paffenbarger RS, Jr. Combined effect of childbearing, menstrual events, and body size on age-specific breast cancer risk. *Am J Epidemiol* 1988;128:962-79.

269. Kato I, Miura S, Kasumi F, et al. A case-control study of breast cancer among Japanese women: with special reference to family history and reproductive and dietary factors. *Breast Cancer Res Treat* 1992;24:51-9.

270. Katsouyanni K, Trichopoulou A, Stuver S, et al. The association of fat and other macronutrients with breast cancer: a case-control study from Greece. *Br J*

Cancer 1994;70:537-41.

271. Kohlmeier L, Simonsen N, van 't Veer P, et al. Adipose tissue trans fatty acids and breast cancer in the European Community Multicenter Study on Antioxidants, Myocardial Infarction, and Breast Cancer. *Cancer Epidemiol Biomarkers Prev* 1997;6:705-10.

272. Kumar NB, Riccardi D, Cantor A, et al. A case-control study evaluating the association of purposeful physical activity, body fat distribution, and steroid hormones on premenopausal breast cancer risk. *Breast J* 2005;11:266-72.

273. Kuru B, Ozaslan C, Ozdemir P, et al. Risk factors for breast cancer in Turkish women with early pregnancies and long-lasting lactation - A case-control study. *Acta Oncol* 2002;41:556-61.

274. Kyogoku S, Hirohata T, Takeshita S, et al. Anthropometric indicators of breast cancer risk in Japanese women in Fukuoka. *Jpn J Cancer Res* 1990;81:731-7.

275. Lam PB, Vacek PM, Geller BM, et al. The association of increased weight, body mass index, and tissue density with the risk of breast carcinoma in Vermont. *Cancer* 2000;89:369-75.

276. Landa MC, Frago N, Tres A. Diet and the risk of breast cancer in Spain. *Eur J Cancer Prev* 1994;3:313-20.

277. Lee SA, Lee KM, Park WY, et al. Obesity and genetic polymorphism of ERCC2 and ERCC4 as modifiers of risk of breast cancer. *Exp Mol Med* 2005;37:86-90.

278. Levi F, Pasche C, Lucchini F, et al. Occupational and leisure time physical activity and the risk of breast cancer. *Eur J Cancer* 1999;35:775-8.

279. Li CI, Malone KE, Porter PL, et al. Reproductive and anthropometric factors in relation to the risk of lobular and ductal breast carcinoma among women 65-79 years of age. *Int J Cancer* 2003;107:647-51.

280. Li CI, Stanford JL, Daling JR. Anthropometric variables in relation to risk of breast cancer in middle-aged women. *Int J Epidemiol* 2000;29:208-13.

281. Lopez-Carrillo L, Blair A, Lopez-Cervantes M, et al. Dichiorodiphenyltrichloroethane serum levels and breast cancer risk: A case-control study from Mexico. *Cancer Res* 1997;57:3728-32.

282. Lopez-Carrillo L, Bravo-Alvarado J, Poblano-Verastegui O, et al. Reproductive determinants of breast cancer in Mexican women. *Ann N Y Acad Sci* 1997;837:537-50.

283. Magnusson C, Baron J, Persson I, et al. Body size in different periods of life and breast cancer risk in post-menopausal women. *Int J Cancer* 1998;76:29-34.

284. Magnusson CM, Roddam AW, Pike MC, et al. Body fatness and physical activity at young ages and the risk of breast cancer in premenopausal women. *Br J Cancer* 2005;93:817-24.

285. Malin A, Matthews CE, Shu XO, et al. Energy balance and breast cancer risk. *Cancer Epidemiol Biomarkers Prev* 2005;14:1496-501.

286. Marubini E, Decarli A, Costa A, et al. The relationship of dietary intake and serum levels of retinol and beta-carotene with breast cancer: Results of a case-control study. *Cancer* 1988;61:173-80.

287. McCann SE, Ip C, Ip MM, et al. Dietary intake of conjugated linoleic acids and risk of premenopausal and postmenopausal breast cancer, Western New York exposures and cancer study (WEB study). *Cancer Epidemiol Biomarkers Prev* 2004;13:1480-4.

288. McCann SE, Muti P, Vito D, et al. Dietary lignan intakes and risk of pre- and postmenopausal breast cancer. *Int J Cancer* 2004;111:440-3.

289. McCredie MRE, Dite GS, Giles GG, et al. Breast cancer in Australian women under the age of 40. *Cancer Causes Control* 1998;9:189-98.

290. McCredie M, Paul C, Skegg DCG, et al. Reproductive factors and breast cancer in New Zealand. *Int J Cancer* 1998;76:182-8.

291. Meeske K, Press M, Patel A, et al. Impact of reproductive factors and lactation on breast carcinoma in situ risk. *Int J Cancer* 2004;110:102-9.

292. Mendonca GAS, Eluf-Neto J, Andrada-Serpa MJ, et al. Organochlorines and breast cancer: A case-control study in Brazil. *Int J Cancer* 1999;83:596-600.

293. Mezzetti M, La Vecchia C, Decarli A, et al. Population attributable risk for breast cancer: Diet, nutrition, and physical exercise. *J Natl Cancer Inst* 1998;90:389-94.

294. Moorman PG, Ricciuti MF, Millikan RC, et al. Vitamin supplement use and breast cancer in a North Carolina population. *Public Health Nutr* 2001;4:821-7.

295. Newcomb PA, Storer BE, Longnecker MP, et al. Lactation and a reduced risk of premenopausal breast cancer. *N Engl J Med* 1993;330:81-7.

296. Newcomb PA, Egan KM, Titus-Ernstoff L, et al. Lactation in relation to postmenopausal breast cancer. *Am J Epidemiol* 1999;150:174-82.

297. Ng EH, Gao F, Ji CY, et al. Risk factors for breast carcinoma in Singaporean Chinese women: The role of central obesity. *Cancer* 1997;80:725-31.

298. Norsa'adah B, Rusli BN, Imran AK, et al. Risk factors of breast cancer in women in Kelantan, Malaysia. *Singapore Med J* 2005;46:698-705.

299. Okobia MN, Bunker CH, Lee LL, et al. Case-control study of risk factors for breast cancer in Nigerian women: a pilot study. *East Afr Med J* 2005;82:14-9.

300. Olaya-Contreras P, Pierre B, Lazcano-Ponce E, et al. [Reproductive risk factors associated with breast cancer in Columbian women.] *Rev Saude Publica* 1999;33:237-45.

301. Olaya-Contreras P, Rodriguez-Villamil J, Posso-Valencia HJ, et al. Organochlorine exposure and breast cancer risk in Colombian women. *Cad Saude Publica* 1998;14:125-32.

302. Park SK, Yoo KY, Lee SJ, et al. Alcohol consumption, glutathione S-transferase M1 and T1 genetic polymorphisms and breast cancer risk. *Pharmacogenetics* 2000;10:301-9.

303. Peacock SL, White E, Daling JR, et al. Relation between obesity and breast cancer in young women. *Am J Epidemiol* 1999;149:339-46.

304. Petrek JA, Peters M, Cirrincione C, et al. Is body fat topography a risk factor for breast cancer? *Ann Intern Med* 1993;118:356-62.

305. Pietinen P, Stumpf K, Mannisto S, et al. Serum enterolactone and risk of breast cancer: A case-control study in Eastern Finland. *Cancer Epidemiol Biomarkers Prev* 2001;10:339-44.

306. Potischman N, McCulloch CE, Byers T, et al. Breast cancer and dietary and plasma concentrations of carotenoids and vitamin A. *Am J Clin Nutr* 1990;52:909-15.

307. Potischman N, Swanson CA, Coates RJ, et al. Dietary relationships with early onset (under age 45) breast cancer in a case-control study in the United States: Influence of chemotherapy treatment. *Cancer Causes Control* 1997;8:713-21.

308. Rattanamongkolgul S, Muir K, Armstrong S, et al. Diet, energy intake and breast cancer risk in an Asian country. *IARC Sci Publ* 2002;156:543-5.

309. Richardson S, Gerber M, Cenee S. The role of fat, animal protein and some vitamin consumption in breast cancer: a case control study in southern France. *Int J Cancer* 1991;48:1-9.

310. Romieu I, Hernandez A, Mauricio, Lazcano P, Eduardo, et al. Breast cancer, lactation history, and serum organochlorines. *Am J Epidemiol* 2000;152:363-70.

311. Rosenberg L, Palmer JR, Miller DR, et al. A case-control study of alcoholic beverage consumption and breast cancer. *Am J Epidemiol* 1990;131:6-14.

312. Sanderson M, Shu XO, Jin F, et al. Weight at birth and adolescence and premenopausal breast cancer risk in a low-risk population. *Br J Cancer* 2002;86:84-8.

313. Sarin R, Tandon RK, Paul S, et al. Diet, body fat and plasma lipids in breast cancer. *Indian J Med Res* 1985;81:493-8.

314. Schapira DV, Kumar NB, Lyman GH, et al. Abdominal obesity and breast cancer risk. *Ann Intern Med* 1990;112:182-6.

315. Shoff SM, Newcomb PA, Trentham DA, et al. Early-life physical activity and postmenopausal breast cancer: Effect of body size and weight change. *Cancer Epidemiology Biomarkers and Prevention* 2000;9:591-5.

316. Shrubsole MJ, Gao YT, Cai Q, et al. MTHFR polymorphisms, dietary folate intake, and breast cancer risk: results from the Shanghai breast cancer study. *Cancer Epidemiol Biomarkers Prev* 2004;13:190-6.

317. Shrubsole MJ, Jin F, Dai Q, et al. Dietary

folate intake and breast cancer risk: results from the Shanghai breast cancer study. *Cancer Res* 2001;61:7136-41.

318. Shu XO, Jin F, Dai Q, et al. Association of body size and fat distribution with risk of breast cancer among chinese women. *Int J Cancer* 2001;94:449-55.

319. Silva ID, Mangtani P, McCormack V, et al. Phyto-oestrogen intake and breast cancer risk in South Asian women in England: findings from a population-based case-control study. *Cancer Causes Control* 2004;15:805-18.

320. Soliman AS, Wang X, DiGiovanni J, et al. Serum organochlorine levels and history of lactation in Egypt. *Environ Res* 2003;92:110-7.

321. Sonnichsen AC, Lindlacher U, Richter WO, et al. Obesity, body fat distribution and the incidence of mammary, cervical, endometrial and ovarian carcinoma. *Dtsch Med Wochenschr* 1990;115:1906-10.

322. Sonnichsen AC, Richter WO, Schwandt P. Body fat distribution and risk for breast cancer. *Ann Intern Med* 1990;112:882.

323. Staszewski J. Breast cancer and body build. *Prev Med* 1977;6:410-5.

324. Swanson CA, Brinton LA, Taylor PR, et al. Body size and breast cancer risk assessed in women participating in the Breast Cancer Detection Demonstration Project. *Am J Epidemiol* 1989;130:1133-41.

325. Swanson CA, Coates RJ, Malone KE, et al. Alcohol consumption and breast cancer risk among women under age 45 years. *Epidemiology* 1997;8:231-7.

326. Swanson CA, Coates RJ, Schoenberg JB, et al. Body size and breast cancer risk among women under age 45 years. *Am J Epidemiol* 1996;143:698-706.

327. Taioli E, Barone J, Wynder EL. A case-control study on breast cancer and body mass. The American Health Foundation - Division of Epidemiology. *Eur J Cancer* 1995;31A:723-8.

328. Taioli E, Wynder EL. Family history, body-fat distribution, and the risk of breast cancer. *N Engl J Med* 1992;327:958-9.

329. Talamini R, La Vecchia C, Decarli A, et al. Social factors, diet and breast cancer in a northern Italian population. *Br J Cancer* 1984;49:723-9.

330. Tavani A, Gallus S, La Vecchia C, et al. Risk factors for breast cancer in women under 40 years. *Eur J Cancer* 1999;35:1361-7.

331. Terry P, Rohan TE, Wolk A, et al. Fish consumption and breast cancer risk. *Nutr Cancer* 2002;44:1-6.

332. Thomas E, Cade J, Vail A. Risk factor analysis of data from assessment clinics in the UK breast screening programme: a case-control study in Portsmouth and Southampton. *J Epidemiol Community Health* 1996;50:144-8.

333. Thorand B, Kohlmeier L, Simonsen N, et al. Intake of fruits, vegetables, folic acid and related nutrients and risk of breast cancer in postmenopausal women. *Public Health Nutr* 1998;1:147-56.

334. Toniolo P, Riboli E, Protta F, et al. Breast cancer and alcohol consumption: a case-control study in northern Italy. *Cancer Res* 1989;49:5203-6.

335. Torres-Sanchez L, Lopez-Carrillo L, Lopez-Cervantes M, et al. Food sources of phytoestrogens and breast cancer risk in Mexican women. *Nutr Cancer* 2000;37:134-9.

336. Toti A, Agugiaro S, Amadori D, et al. Breast cancer risk factors in Italian women: a multicentric case-control study. *Tumori* 1986;72:241-9.

337. Tovar-Guzman V, Hernandez-Giron C, Lazcano-Ponce E, et al. Breast cancer in Mexican women: an epidemiological study with cervical cancer control. *Rev Saude Publica* 2000;34:113-9.

338. Trentham-Dietz A, Newcomb PA, Egan KM, et al. Weight change and risk of postmenopausal breast cancer (United States). *Cancer Causes Control* 2000;11:533-42.

339. Trentham-Dietz A, Newcomb PA, Storer BE, et al. Body size and risk of breast cancer. *Am J Epidemiol* 1997;145:1011-9.

340. Trentham-Dietz A, Newcomb PA, Storer BE, et al. Risk factors for carcinoma in situ of the breast. *Cancer Epidemiology Biomarkers and Prevention* 2000;9:697-703.

341. Tung HT, Tsukuma H, Tanaka H, et al. Risk factors for breast cancer in Japan, with special attention to anthropometric measurements and reproductive history. *Jpn J Clin Oncol* 1999;29:137-46.

342. Ueji M, Ueno E, Osei-Hyiaman D, et al. Physical activity and the risk of breast cancer: a case-control study of Japanese women. *J Epidemiol* 1998;8:116-22.

343. van't Veer P, Dekker JM, Lamers JW, et al. Consumption of fermented milk products and breast cancer: a case-control study in The Netherlands. *Cancer Res* 1989;49:4020-3.

344. Van't Veer P, Kok FJ, Brants HA, et al. Dietary fat and the risk of breast cancer. *Int J Epidemiol* 1990;19:12-8.

345. van't Veer P, Kok FJ, Hermus RJ, et al. Alcohol dose, frequency and age at first exposure in relation to the risk of breast cancer. *Int J Epidemiol* 1989;18:511-7.

346. Verla-Tebit E, Chang-Claude J. Anthropometric factors and the risk of premenopausal breast cancer in Germany. *Eur J Cancer Prev* 2005;14:419-26.

347. Viladiu P, Izquierdo A, de Sanjose S, et al. A breast cancer case-control study in Girona, Spain. Endocrine, familial and lifestyle factors. *Eur J Cancer Prev* 1996;5:329-35.

348. Walker ARP, Walker BF, Funani S, et al. Characteristics of black women with breast cancer in Soweto, South Africa. *Cancer Journal* 1989;2:316-9.

349. Wenten M, Gilliland FD, Baumgartner K, et al. Associations of weight, weight change, and body mass with breast cancer risk in Hispanic and non-Hispanic white women. *Ann Epidemiol* 2002;12:435-4.

350. Yang G, Lu G, Jin F, et al. Population-based, case-control study of blood C-peptide level and breast cancer risk. *Cancer Epidemiol Biomarkers Prev* 2001;10:1207-11.

351. Yim DS, Parkb SK, Yoo KY, et al. Relationship between the Val158Met polymorphism of catechol O-methyl transferase and breast cancer. *Pharmacogenetics* 2001;11:279-86.

352. Yoo K, Tajima K, Park S, et al. Postmenopausal obesity as a breast cancer risk factor according to estrogen and progesterone receptor status (Japan). *Cancer Lett* 2001;167:57-63.

353. Young TB. A case-control study of breast cancer and alcohol consumption habits. *Cancer* 1989;64:552-8.

354. Zaroukian S, Pineault R, Gandini S, et al. Correlation between nutritional biomarkers and breast cancer: a case-control study. *Breast* 2005;14:209-23.

355. Zheng T, Holford TR, Mayne ST, et al. Lactation and breast cancer risk: a case-control study in Connecticut. *Br J Cancer* 2001;84:1472-6.

356. Zheng T, Holford TR, Tessari J, et al. Breast cancer risk associated with congeners of polychlorinated biphenyls. *Am J Epidemiol* 2000;152:50-8.

357. Zhu Z, Parviainen M, Mannisto S, et al. Vitamin E concentration in breast adipose tissue of breast cancer patients (Kuopio, Finland). *Cancer Causes Control* 1996;7:591-5.

358. Zhu ZR, Parviainen M, Mannisto S, et al. Vitamin A concentration in breast adipose tissue of breast cancer patients. *Anticancer Res* 1995;15:1593-6.

359. Zhu K, Caulfield J, Hunter S, et al. Body mass index and breast cancer risk in African American women. *Ann Epidemiol* 2005;15:123-8.

360. Guo WD, Chow WH, Zheng W, et al. Diet, serum markers and breast cancer mortality in China. *Jpn J Cancer Res* 1994;85:572-7.

361. Hakama M, Soini I, Kuosma E, et al. Breast cancer incidence: geographical correlations in Finland. *Int J Epidemiol* 1979;8:33-40.

362. van den Brandt PA, Spiegelman D, Yaun SS, et al. Pooled analysis of prospective cohort studies on height, weight, and breast cancer risk. *Am J Epidemiol* 2000;152:514-27.

363. Michels KB, Giovannucci E, Chan AT, et al. Fruit and vegetable consumption and colorectal adenomas in the Nurses' Health Study. *Cancer Res* 2006;66:3942-53.

364. Garcia-Closas M, Brinton LA, Lissowska J, et al. Established breast cancer risk factors by clinically important tumour characteristics. *Br J Cancer* 2006;95:123-9.

365. Campagnoli C, Abba C, Ambroggio S, et al. Pregnancy, progesterone and progestins in relation to breast cancer risk. *The Journal of Steroid Biochemistry and Molecular Biology* 2005;97:441-50.

366. Hilakivi-Clarke L, Forsen T, Eriksson JG, et al. Tallness and overweight during

childhood have opposing effects on breast cancer risk. *Br J Cancer* 2001;85:1680-4.

367. Pasquali R, Pelusi C, Genghini S, et al. Obesity and reproductive disorders in women. *Hum Reprod Update* 2003;9:359-72.

368. Anderson KE, Anderson E, Mink PJ, et al. Diabetes and endometrial cancer in the Iowa women's health study. *Cancer Epidemiol Biomarkers Prev* 2001;10:611-6.

369. Baanders-van Halewijn EA, Poortman J. A case-control study of endometrial cancer within a cohort. *Maturitas* 1985;7:69-76.

370. Bernstein L, Deapen D, Cerhan JR, et al. Tamoxifen therapy for breast cancer and endometrial cancer risk. *J Natl Cancer Inst* 1999;91:1654-62.

371. de Waard F, de Ridder CM, Baanders-van Halewyn EA, et al. Endometrial cancer in a cohort screened for breast cancer. *Eur J Cancer Prev* 1996;5:99-104.

372. Ewertz M, Machado SG, Boice JD, Jr., et al. Endometrial cancer following treatment for breast cancer: a case-control study in Denmark. *Br J Cancer* 1984;50:687-92.

373. Folsom AR, Demissie Z, Harnack L. Glycemic index, glycemic load, and incidence of endometrial cancer: the Iowa women's health study. *Nutr Cancer* 2003;46:119-24.

374. Folsom AR, Kaye SA, Potter JD, et al. Association of incident carcinoma of the endometrium with body weight and fat distribution in older women: early findings of the Iowa Women's Health Study. *Cancer Res* 1989;49:6828-31.

375. Furberg AS, Thune I. Metabolic abnormalities (hypertension, hyperglycemia and overweight), lifestyle (high energy intake and physical inactivity) and endometrial cancer risk in a Norwegian cohort. *Int J Cancer* 2003;104:669-76.

376. Gapstur SM, Potter JD, Sellers TA, et al. Alcohol consumption and postmenopausal endometrial cancer: results from the Iowa Women's Health Study. *Cancer Causes Control* 1993;4:323-9.

377. Jain MG, Rohan TE, Howe GR, et al. A cohort study of nutritional factors and endometrial cancer. *Eur J Epidemiol* 2000;16:899-905.

378. Lacey JV, Jr., Brinton LA, Lubin JH, et al. Endometrial carcinoma risks among menopausal estrogen plus progestin and unopposed estrogen users in a cohort of postmenopausal women. *Cancer Epidemiol Biomarkers Prev* 2005;14:1724-31.

379. Le Marchand L, Wilkens LR, Mi MP. Early-age body size, adult weight gain and endometrial cancer risk. *Int J Cancer* 1991;48:807-11.

380. Olson JE, Sellers TA, Anderson KE, et al. Does a family history of cancer increase the risk for postmenopausal endometrial carcinoma? A prospective cohort study and a nested case-control family study of older women. *Cancer* 1999;85:2444-9.

381. Pukkala E, Kyyronen P, Sankila R, et al. Tamoxifen and toremifene treatment of breast cancer and risk of subsequent endometrial cancer: a population-based case-control study. *Int J Cancer* 2002;100:337-41.

382. Schouten LJ, Goldbohm RA, van den Brandt PA. Anthropometry, physical activity, and endometrial cancer risk: results from the Netherlands Cohort Study. *J Natl Cancer Inst* 2004;96:1635-8.

383. Silvera SA, Rohan TE, Jain M, et al. Glycaemic index, glycaemic load and risk of endometrial cancer: a prospective cohort study. *Public Health Nutr* 2005;8:912-9.

384. Yamazawa K, Miyazawa Y, Suzuki M, et al. Tamoxifen and the risk of endometrial cancer in Japanese women with breast cancer. *Surg Today* 2006;36:41-6.

385. Zeleniuch-Jacquotte A, Akhmedkhanov A, Kato I, et al. Postmenopausal endogenous oestrogens and risk of endometrial cancer: results of a prospective study. *Br J Cancer* 2001;84:975-81.

386. Augustin LS, Gallus S, Bosetti C, et al. Glycemic index and glycemic load in endometrial cancer. *Int J Cancer* 2003;105:404-7.

387. Augustin LSA, Dal Maso L, Franceschi S, et al. Association between components of the insulin-like growth factor system and endometrial cancer risk. *Oncology* 2004;67:54-9.

388. Austin H, Austin JM, Jr., Partridge EE, et al. Endometrial cancer, obesity, and body fat distribution. *Cancer Res* 1991;51:568-72.

389. Brinton LA, Berman ML, Mortel R, et al. Reproductive, menstrual, and medical risk factors for endometrial cancer: results from a case-control study. *Am J Obstet Gynecol* 1992;167:1317-25.

390. Cusimano R, Dardanoni G, Dardanoni L, et al. Risk factors of female cancers in Ragusa population (Sicily) - 1. Endometrium and cervix uteri cancers. *Eur J Epidemiol* 1989;5:363-71.

391. Elwood JM, Cole P, Rothman KJ, et al. Epidemiology of endometrial cancer. *J Natl Cancer Inst* 1977;59:1055-60.

392. Ewertz M, Schou G, Boice JD, Jr. The joint effect of risk factors on endometrial cancer. *Eur J Cancer Clin Oncol* 1988;24:189-94.

393. Geraci P, Mancuso A, Maggio S, et al. Risk factors of endometrial cancer in Palermo. *Clin Exp Obstet Gynecol* 1988;15:129-33.

394. Goodman MT, Wilkens LR, Hankin JH, et al. Association of soy and fiber consumption with the risk of endometrial cancer. *Am J Epidemiol* 1997;146:294-306.

395. Gruber SB, Thompson WD, Rubin GL, et al. A population-based study of endometrial cancer and familial risk in younger women. *Cancer Epidemiol Biomarkers Prev* 1996;5:411-7.

396. Hirose K, Tajima K, Hamajima N, et al.

Subsite (cervix/endometrium)-specific risk and protective factors in uterus cancer. *Jpn J Cancer Res* 1996;87:1001-9.

397. Horn-Ross PL, John EM, Canchola AJ, et al. Phytoestrogen intake and endometrial cancer risk. *J Natl Cancer Inst* 2003;95:1158-64.

398. Hou Q, Wang QS, Wang JF. [A case control study on risk factors of endometrial carcinoma in Tianjin.] *Zhonghua Fu Chan Ke Za Zhi* 1994;29:30-2, 61.

399. La Vecchia C, Franceschi S, Gallus G, et al. Oestrogens and obesity as risk factors for endometrial cancer in Italy. *Int J Epidemiol* 1982;11:120-6.

400. La Vecchia C, Decarli A, Fasoli M, et al. Nutrition and diet in the etiology of endometrial cancer. *Cancer* 1986;57:1248-53.

401. La Vecchia C, Decarli A, Negri E, et al. Epidemiological aspects of diet and cancer: a summary review of case-control studies from northern Italy. *Oncology* 1988;45:364-70.

402. La Vecchia C, Parazzini F, Negri E, et al. Anthropometric indicators of endometrial cancer risk. *Eur J Cancer* 1991;27:487-90.

403. Levi F, Franceschi S, Negri E, et al. Dietary factors and the risk of endometrial cancer. *Cancer* 1993;71:3575-81.

404. Matthews CE, Xu WH, Zheng W, et al. Physical activity and risk of endometrial cancer: a report from the Shanghai endometrial cancer study. *Cancer Epidemiol Biomarkers Prev* 2005;14:779-85.

405. McCann SE, Freudenheim JL, Marshall JR, et al. Diet in the epidemiology of endometrial cancer in western New York (United States). *Cancer Causes Control* 2000;11:965-74.

406. McElroy JA, Newcomb PA, Trentham-Dietz A, et al. Endometrial cancer incidence in relation to electric blanket use. *Am J Epidemiol* 2002;156:262-7.

407. Newcomb PA, Trentham-Dietz A. Patterns of postmenopausal progestin use with estrogen in relation to endometrial cancer (United States). *Cancer Causes Control* 2003;14:195-201.

408. Newcomer LM, Newcomb PA, Trentham-Dietz A, et al. Hormonal risk factors for endometrial cancer: modification by cigarette smoking (United States). *Cancer Causes Control* 2001;12:829-35.

409. Olson SH, Trevisan M, Marshall JR, et al. Body mass index, weight gain, and risk of endometrial cancer. *Nutr Cancer* 1995;23:141-9.

410. Okamura C, Tsubono Y, Ito K, et al. Lactation and risk of endometrial cancer in Japan: a case-control study. *Tohoku J Exp Med* 2006;208:109-15.

411. Parazzini F, La Vecchia C, D'Avanzo B, et al. Alcohol and endometrial cancer risk: findings from an Italian case-control study. *Nutr Cancer* 1995;23:55-62.

412. Parazzini F, La Vecchia C, Negri E, et al. Smoking and risk of endometrial cancer: results from an Italian case-control study. *Gynecol Oncol* 1995;56:195-9.

413. Potischman N, Hoover RN, Brinton LA, et al. Case-control study of endogenous steroid hormones and endometrial cancer. *J Natl Cancer Inst* 1996;88:1127-35.

414. Salazar-Martinez E, Lazcano-Ponce EC, Lira-Lira GG, et al. Case-control study of diabetes, obesity, physical activity and risk of endometrial cancer among Mexican women. *Cancer Causes Control* 2000;11:707-11.

415. Shoff SM, Newcomb PA. Diabetes, body size, and risk of endometrial cancer. *Am J Epidemiol* 1998;148:234-40.

416. Shu XO, Brinton LA, Zheng W, et al. Relation of obesity and body fat distribution to endometrial cancer in Shanghai, China. *Cancer Res* 1992;52:3865-70.

417. Shu XO, Hatch MC, Zheng W, et al. Physical activity and risk of endometrial cancer. *Epidemiology* 1993;4:342-9.

418. Shu XO, Zheng W, Potischman N, et al. A population-based case-control study of dietary factors and endometrial cancer in Shanghai, People's Republic of China. *Am J Epidemiol* 1993;137:155-65.

419. Swanson CA, Potischman N, Wilbanks GD, et al. Relation of endometrial cancer risk to past and contemporary body size and body fat distribution. *Cancer Epidemiol Biomarkers Prev* 1993;2:321-7.

420. Trentham-Dietz A, Nichols HB, Hampton JM, et al. Weight change and risk of endometrial cancer. *Int J Epidemiol* 2006;35:151-8.

421. Troisi R, Potischman N, Hoover RN, et al. Insulin and endometrial cancer. *Am J Epidemiol* 1997;146:476-82.

422. Weiderpass E, Persson I, Adami HO, et al. Body size in different periods of life, diabetes mellitus, hypertension, and risk of postmenopausal endometrial cancer (Sweden). *Cancer Causes Control* 2000;11:185-92.

423. Tao MH, Xu WH, Zheng W, et al. A case-control study in Shanghai of fruit and vegetable intake and endometrial cancer. *Br J Cancer* 2005;92:2059-64.

424. Xu W, Dai Q, Ruan Z, et al. Obesity at different ages and endometrial cancer risk factors in urban Shanghai, China. *Zhonghua Liu Xing Bing Xue Za Zhi* 2002;23:347-51.

425. Xu WH, Xiang YB, Zheng W, et al. Weight history and risk of endometrial cancer among Chinese women. *Int J Epidemiol* 2006;35:159-66.

426. Zang EA, Wynder EL. The association between body mass index and the relative frequencies of diseases in a sample of hospitalized patients. *Nutr Cancer* 1994;21:247-61.

427. Zhang CY, Wang TG. [A case-control study of endometrial cancer in Beijing.] *Zhonghua Liu Xing Bing Xue Za Zhi* 1989;10:235-7.

428. Benshushan A, Paltiel O, Rojansky N, et al. IUD use and the risk of endometrial cancer. *Eur J Obstet Gynecol Reprod Biol* 2002;105:166-9.

429. Hagen A, Morack G, Grulich D. [Evaluation of epidemiologic risk factors for endometrial carcinoma based on a case-control study.] *Zentralbl Gynakol* 1995;117:368-74.

430. Jain MG, Howe GR, Rohan TE. Nutritional factors and endometrial cancer in Ontario, Canada. *Cancer Control* 2000;7:288-96.

431. Niwa K, Imai A, Hashimoto M, et al. A case-control study of uterine endometrial cancer of pre- and post-menopausal women. *Oncol Rep* 2000;7:89-93.

432. Yamazawa K, Matsui H, Seki K, et al. A case-control study of endometrial cancer after antipsychotics exposure in premenopausal women. *Oncology* 2003;64:116-23.

433. Beard CM, Hartmann LC, Keeney GL, et al. Endometrial cancer in Olmsted County, MN: trends in incidence, risk factors and survival. *Ann Epidemiol* 2000;10:97-105.

434. Iemura A, Douchi T, Yamamoto S, et al. Body fat distribution as a risk factor of endometrial cancer. *J Obstet Gynaecol Res* 2000;26:421-5.

435. Kalandidi A, Tzonou A, Lipworth L, et al. A case-control study of endometrial cancer in relation to reproductive, somatometric, and life-style variables. *Oncology* 1996;53:354-9.

436. Petridou E, Kedikoglou S, Koukoulomatis P, et al. Diet in relation to endometrial cancer risk: a case-control study in Greece. *Nutr Cancer* 2002;44:16-22.

437. Douchi T, Yamamoto S, Nakamura S, et al. Bone mineral density in postmenopausal women with endometrial cancer. *Maturitas* 1999;31:165-70.

438. Gao J, Xiang YB, Xu WH, et al. [Green tea consumption and the risk of endometrial cancer: a population-based case-control study in urban Shanghai.] *Zhonghua Liu Xing Bing Xue Za Zhi* 2005;26:323-7.

439. Hardell L, van Bavel B, Lindstrom G, et al. Adipose tissue concentrations of p,p'-DDE and the risk for endometrial cancer. *Gynecol Oncol* 2004;95:706-11.

440. Inoue M, Okayama A, Fujita M, et al. A case-control study on risk factors for uterine endometrial cancer in Japan. *Jpn J Cancer Res* 1994;85:346-50.

441. Levi F, La Vecchia C, Negri E, et al. Body mass at different ages and subsequent endometrial cancer risk. *Int J Cancer* 1992;50:567-71.

442. Salazar-Martinez E, Lazcano-Ponce E, Sanchez-Zamorano LM, et al. Dietary factors and endometrial cancer risk. Results of a case-control study in Mexico. *Int J Gynecol Cancer* 2005;15:938-45.

443. Salazar-Martinez E, Lazcano-Ponce EC, Gonzalez Lira-Lira G, et al. Reproductive factors of ovarian and endometrial cancer risk in a high fertility population in Mexico. *Cancer Res* 1999;59:3658-62.

444. Soler M, Chatenoud L, Negri E, et al. Hypertension and hormone-related neoplasms in women. *Hypertension* 1999;34:320-5.

445. Swanson CA, Potischman N, Barrett RJ, et al. Endometrial cancer risk in relation to serum lipids and lipoprotein levels. *Cancer Epidemiol Biomarkers Prev* 1994;3:575-81.

446. Lissner L, Kroon UB, Bjorntorp P, et al. Adipose tissue fatty acids and dietary fat sources in relation to endometrial cancer: a retrospective study of cases in remission, and population-based controls. *Acta Obstet Gynecol Scand* 1993;72:481-7.

447. Littman AJ, Beresford SA, White E. The association of dietary fat and plant foods with endometrial cancer (United States). *Cancer Causes Control* 2001;12:691-702.

448. Moradi T, Weiderpass E, Signorello LB, et al. Physical activity and postmenopausal endometrial cancer risk (Sweden). *Cancer Causes Control* 2000;11:829-37.

449. Newcomb PA, Trentham-Dietz A, Storer BE. Alcohol consumption in relation to endometrial cancer risk. *Cancer Epidemiol Biomarkers Prev* 1997;6:775-8.

450. Olson SH, Vena JE, Dorn JP, et al. Exercise, occupational activity, and risk of endometrial cancer. *Ann Epidemiol* 1997;7:46-53.

451. Terry P, Wolk A, Vainio H, et al. Fatty fish consumption lowers the risk of endometrial cancer: a nationwide case-control study in Sweden. *Cancer Epidemiol Biomarkers Prev* 2002;11:143-5.

452. Webster LA, Weiss NS. Alcoholic beverage consumption and the risk of endometrial cancer. Cancer and Steroid Hormone Study Group. *Int J Epidemiol* 1989;18:786-91.

453. Weiderpass E, Adami HO, Baron JA, et al. Organochlorines and endometrial cancer risk. *Cancer Epidemiol Biomarkers Prev* 2000;9:487-93.

454. Weiderpass E, Baron JA. Cigarette smoking, alcohol consumption, and endometrial cancer risk: a population-based study in Sweden. *Cancer Causes Control* 2001;12:239-47.

455. Xu WH, Matthews CE, Xiang YB, et al. Effect of adiposity and fat distribution on endometrial cancer risk in Shanghai women. *Am J Epidemiol* 2005;161:939-47.

456. Blitzer PH, Blitzer EC, Rimm AA. Association between teen-age obesity and cancer in 56,111 women: all cancers and endometrial carcinoma. *Prev Med* 1976;5:20-31.

457. Dahlgren E, Friberg LG, Johansson S, et al. Endometrial carcinoma; ovarian dysfunction - a risk factor in young women. *Eur J Obstet Gynecol Reprod Biol* 1991;41:143-50.

458. Dahlgren E, Johansson S, Oden A, et al. A model for prediction of endometrial cancer. *Acta Obstet Gynecol Scand* 1989;68:507-10.

459. Iatrakis G, Zervoudis S, Saviolakis A, et al. Women younger than 50 years with endometrial cancer. *Eur J Gynaecol Oncol* 2006;27:399-400.

460. Gamble JF, Pearlman ED, Nicolich MJ. A nested case-control study of kidney

cancer among refinery/petrochemical workers. *Environ Health Perspect* 1996;104:642-50.

461. van Dijk BA, Schouten LJ, Kiemeney LA, et al. Relation of height, body mass, energy intake, and physical activity to risk of renal cell carcinoma: results from the Netherlands Cohort Study. *Am J Epidemiol* 2004;160:1159-67.

462. Hiatt RA, Tolan K, Quesenberry CP, Jr. Renal cell carcinoma and thiazide use: a historical, case-control study (California, USA). *Cancer Causes Control* 1994;5:319-25.

463. Washio M, Mori M, Sakauchi F, et al. Risk factors for kidney cancer in a Japanese population: findings from the JACC study. *J Epidemiol* 2005;15:S203-S11.

464. Flaherty KT, Fuchs CS, Colditz GA, et al. A prospective study of body mass index, hypertension, and smoking and the risk of renal cell carcinoma (United States). *Cancer Causes Control* 2005;16:1099-106.

465. Bjorge T, Tretli S, Engeland A. Relation of height and body mass index to renal cell carcinoma in two million Norwegian men and women. *Am J Epidemiol* 2004;160:1168-76.

466. Nicodemus KK, Sweeney C, Folsom AR. Evaluation of dietary, medical and lifestyle risk factors for incident kidney cancer in postmenopausal women. *Int J Cancer* 2004;108:115-21.

467. Bergstrom A, Terry P, Lindblad P, et al. Physical activity and risk of renal cell cancer. *Int J Cancer* 2001;92:155-7.

468. Chow WH, Gridley G, Fraumeni JF, Jr., et al. Obesity, hypertension, and the risk of kidney cancer in men. *N Engl J Med* 2000;343:1305-11.

469. Whittemore AS, Paffenbarger RS, Jr., Anderson K, et al. Early precursors of urogenital cancers in former college men. *J Urol* 1984;132:1256-61.

470. Kurttio P, Pukkala E, Kahelin H, et al. Arsenic concentrations in well water and risk of bladder and kidney cancer in Finland. *Environ Health Perspect* 1999;107:705-10.

471. Hirvonen T, Virtamo J, Korhonen P, et al. Flavonol and flavone intake and the risk of cancer in male smokers (Finland). *Cancer Causes Control* 2001;12:789-96.

472. Prineas RJ, Folsom AR, Zhang ZM, et al. Nutrition and other risk factors for renal cell carcinoma in postmenopausal women. *Epidemiology* 1997;8:31-6.

473. Fraser GE, Phillips RL, Beeson WL. Hypertension, antihypertensive medication and risk of renal carcinoma in California Seventh-Day Adventists. *Int J Epidemiol* 1990;19:832-8.

474. Hu J, Ugnat AM, Canadian Cancer Registries Epidemiology Research Group. Active and passive smoking and risk of renal cell carcinoma in Canada. *Eur J Cancer* 2005;41:770-8.

475. Zhang YW, Cantor KP, Lynch CF, et al. A population-based case-control study of occupation and renal cell carcinoma risk in Iowa. *J Occup Environ Med* 2004;46:235-40.

476. Mattioli S, Truffelli D, Baldasseroni A, et al. Occupational risk factors for renal cell cancer: a case-control study in northern Italy. *J Occup Environ Med* 2002;44:1028-36.

477. Hu J, Mao Y, White K. Renal cell carcinoma and occupational exposure to chemicals in Canada. *Occup Med (Lond)* 2002;52:157-64.

478. Bergstrom A, Lindblad P, Wolk A. Birth weight and risk of renal cell cancer. *Kidney Int* 2001;59:1110-3.

479. Augustsson K, Skog K, Jagerstad M, et al. Dietary heterocyclic amines and cancer of the colon, rectum, bladder, and kidney: a population-based study.[see comment]. *Lancet* 1999;353:703-7.

480. Yuan JM, Castelao JE, Gago-Dominguez M, et al. Hypertension, obesity and their medications in relation to renal cell carcinoma. *Br J Cancer* 1998;77:1508-13.

481. Boeing H, Schlehofer B, Wahrendorf J. Diet, obesity and risk for renal cell carcinoma: results from a case control-study in Germany. *Z Ernahrungswiss* 1997;36:3-11.

482. Chow WH, Mclaughlin JK, Mandel JS, et al. Obesity and risk of renal cell cancer. *Cancer Epidemiol Biomarkers Prev* 1996;5:17-21.

483. Mellemgaard A, Mclaughlin JK, Overvad K, et al. Dietary risk factors for renal cell carcinoma in Denmark. *Eur J Cancer* 1996;32A:673-82.

484. Lindblad P, Wolk A, Bergstrom R, et al. The role of obesity and weight fluctuations in the etiology of renal cell cancer: a population-based case-control study. *Cancer Epidemiol Biomarkers Prev* 1994;3:631-9.

485. Mellemgaard A, Engholm G, Mclaughlin JK, et al. Risk factors for renal-cell carcinoma in Denmark. III. Role of weight, physical activity and reproductive factors. *Int J Cancer* 1994;56:66-71.

486. Kreiger N, Marrett LD, Dodds L, et al. Risk factors for renal cell carcinoma: results of a population-based case-control study. *Cancer Causes Control* 1993;4:101-10.

487. McCredie M, Stewart JH. Risk factors for kidney cancer in New South Wales, Australia. II. Urologic disease, hypertension, obesity, and hormonal factors. *Cancer Causes Control* 1992;3:323-31.

488. Mclaughlin JK, Gao YT, Gao RN, et al. Risk factors for renal-cell carcinoma in Shanghai, China. *Int J Cancer* 1992;52:562-5.

489. Maclure M, Willett W. A case-control study of diet and risk of renal adenocarcinoma. *Epidemiology* 1990;1:430-40.

490. Asal NR, Risser DR, Kadamani S, et al. Risk factors in renal cell carcinoma: I. Methodology, demographics, tobacco, beverage use, and obesity. *Cancer Detect Prev* 1988;11:359-77.

491. Mclaughlin JK, Mandel JS, Blot WJ, et al. A population-based case-control study of renal cell carcinoma. *J Natl Cancer Inst* 1984;72:275-84.

492. De Stefani E, Fierro L, Mendilaharsu M, et al. Meat intake, 'mate' drinking and renal cell cancer in Uruguay: a case-control study. *Br J Cancer* 1998;78:1239-43.

493. Benhamou S, Lenfant MH, Ory-Paoletti C, et al. Risk factors for renal-cell carcinoma in a French case-control study. *Int J Cancer* 1993;55:32-6.

494. Talamini R, Baron AE, Barra S, et al. A case-control study of risk factor for renal cell cancer in northern Italy. *Cancer Causes Control* 1990;1:125-31.

495. Goodman MT, Morgenstern H, Wynder EL. A case-control study of factors affecting the development of renal cell cancer. *Am J Epidemiol* 1986;124:926-41.

496. Mucci LA, Dickman PW, Steineck G, et al. Dietary acrylamide and cancer of the large bowel, kidney, and bladder: absence of an association in a population-based study in Sweden. *Br J Cancer* 2003;88:84-9.

497. Parker AS, Cerhan JR, Lynch CF, et al. Gender, alcohol consumption, and renal cell carcinoma. *Am J Epidemiol* 2002;155:455-62.

498. Pesch B, Haerting J, Rantt U, et al. Occupational risk factors for renal cell carcinoma: agent-specific results from a case-control study in Germany. MURC Study Group. Multicenter urothelial and renal cancer study. *Int J Epidemiol* 2000;29:1014-24.

499. Sweeney C, Farrow DC, Schwartz SM, et al. Glutathione S-transferase M1, T1, and P1 polymorphisms as risk factors for renal cell carcinoma: a case-control study. *Cancer Epidemiol Biomarkers Prev* 2000;9:449-54.

500. Finkle WD, Mclaughlin JK, Rasgon SA, et al. Increased risk of renal cell cancer among women using diuretics in the United States. *Cancer Causes Control* 1993;4:555-8.

501. Yu MC, Mack TM, Hanisch R, et al. Cigarette smoking, obesity, diuretic use, and coffee consumption as risk factors for renal cell carcinoma. *J Natl Cancer Inst* 1986;77:351-6.

502. Muscat JE, Hoffmann D, Wynder EL. The epidemiology of renal cell carcinoma. A second look. *Cancer* 1995;75:2552-7.

503. Jones SC, Saunders HJ, Qi W, et al. Intermittent high glucose enhances cell growth and collagen synthesis in cultured human tubulointerstitial cells. *Diabetologia* 1999;42:1113-9.

504. Takahashi Y, Okimura Y, Mizuno I, et al. Leptin induces tyrosine phosphorylation of cellular proteins including STAT-1 in human renal adenocarcinoma cells, ACHN. *Biochem Biophys Res Commun* 1996;228:859-64.

505. Chiu BC, Gapstur SM, Chow WH, et al. Body mass index, physical activity, and risk of renal cell carcinoma. *Int J Obes (Lond)* 2006;30:940-7.

506. Moerman CJ, Bueno de Mesquita HB, Runia S. Smoking, alcohol consumption and the risk of cancer of the biliary tract; a population-based case-control study in

The Netherlands. *Eur J Cancer Prev* 1994;3:427-36.

507. Zatonski WA, La Vecchia C, Przewozniak K, et al. Risk factors for gallbladder cancer: a Polish case-control study. *Int J Cancer* 1992;51:707-11.

508. Zatonski WA, Lowenfels AB, Boyle P, et al. Epidemiologic aspects of gallbladder cancer: a case-control study of the SEARCH Program of the International Agency for Research on Cancer. *J Natl Cancer Inst* 1997;89:1132-8.

509. Strom BL, Soloway RD, Rios-Dalenz JL, et al. Risk factors for gallbladder cancer. An international collaborative case-control study. *Cancer* 1995;76:1747-56.

510. Endoh K, Nakadaira H, Yamazaki O, et al. [Risk factors for gallbladder cancer in Chilean females.] *Nippon Koshu Eisei Zasshi* 1997;44:113-22.

511. Serra I, Yamamoto M, Calvo A, et al. Association of chili pepper consumption, low socioeconomic status and longstanding gallstones with gallbladder cancer in a Chilean population. *Int J Cancer* 2002;102:407-11.

512. Shukla VK, Adukia TK, Singh SP, et al. Micronutrients, antioxidants, and carcinoma of the gallbladder. *J Surg Oncol* 2003;84:31-5.

513. Liu E, Sakoda LC, Gao YT, et al. Aspirin use and risk of biliary tract cancer: A population-based study in Shanghai, China. *Cancer Epidemiol Biomarkers Prev*, 2005;1315-8.

514. Zhang XH, Gao YT, Rashid A, et al. [Tea consumption and risk of biliary tract cancers and gallstone disease: a population-based case-control study in Shanghai, China.] *Zhonghua Zhong Liu Za Zhi*, 2005:667-71.

515. Chen CY, Lu CL, Chang FY, et al. Risk factors for gallbladder polyps in the Chinese population. *Am J Gastroenterol* 1997;92:2066-8.

516. Jorgensen T, Jensen KH. Polyps in the gallbladder. A prevalence study. *Scand J Gastroenterol* 1990;25:281-6.

517. Segawa K, Arisawa T, Niwa Y, et al. Prevalence of gallbladder polyps among apparently healthy Japanese: ultrasonographic study. *Am J Gastroenterol* 1992;87:630-3.

518. Pihlajamaki J, Gylling H, Miettinen TA, et al. Insulin resistance is associated with increased cholesterol synthesis and decreased cholesterol absorption in normoglycemic men. *J Lipid Res* 2004;45:507-12.

519. Maclure KM, Hayes KC, Colditz GA, et al. Weight, diet, and the risk of symptomatic gallstones in middle-aged women. *N Engl J Med* 1989;321:563-9.

520. Tsai CJ, Leitzmann MF, Willett WC, et al. Prospective study of abdominal adiposity and gallstone disease in US men. *Am J Clin Nutr* 2004;80:38-44.

521. Tsai CJ, Leitzmann MF, Willett WC, et al. Long-term intake of dietary fiber and decreased risk of cholecystectomy in women. *Am J Gastroenterol* 2004;99:1364-70.

522. Attili AF, Capocaccia R, Carulli N, et al. Factors associated with gallstone disease in the MICOL experience. Multicenter Italian Study on Epidemiology of Cholelithiasis. *Hepatology* 1997;26:809-18.

523. Weinsier RL, Wilson LJ, Lee J. Medically safe rate of weight loss for the treatment of obesity: a guideline based on risk of gallstone formation. *Am J Med* 1995;98:115-7.

524. Syngal S, Coakley EH, Willett WC, et al. Long-term weight patterns and risk for cholecystectomy in women. *Ann Intern Med* 1999;130:471-7.

525. Jee SH, Ohrr H, Sull JW, et al. Cigarette smoking, alcohol drinking, hepatitis B, and risk for hepatocellular carcinoma in Korea. *J Natl Cancer Inst* 2004;96:1851-6.

526. Gallus S, Bertuzzi M, Tavani A, et al. Does coffee protect against hepatocellular carcinoma? *Br J Cancer* 2002;87:956-9.

527. Mukaiya M, Nishi M, Miyake H, et al. Chronic liver diseases for the risk of hepatocellular carcinoma: a case-control study in Japan. Etiologic association of alcohol consumption, cigarette smoking and the development of chronic liver diseases. *Hepatogastroenterology* 1998;45:2328-32.

528. N'Kontchou G, Paries J, Htar MT, et al. Risk factors for hepatocellular carcinoma in patients with alcoholic or viral C cirrhosis. *Clin Gastroenterol Hepatol* 2006;4:1062-8.

529. Balder HF, Goldbohm RA, van den Brandt PA. Dietary patterns associated with male lung cancer risk in the Netherlands Cohort Study. *Cancer Epidemiol Biomarkers Prev* 2005;14:483-90.

530. Goodman GE, Schaffer S, Omenn GS, et al. The association between lung and prostate cancer risk, and serum micronutrients: results and lessons learned from beta-carotene and retinol efficacy trial. *Cancer Epidemiol Biomarkers Prev* 2003;12:518-26.

531. Hoffmans MD, Kromhout D, Coulander CD. Body Mass Index at the age of 18 and its effects on 32-year-mortality from coronary heart disease and cancer. A nested case-control study among the entire 1932 Dutch male birth cohort. *J Clin Epidemiol* 1989;42:513-20.

532. Ito Y, Wakai K, Suzuki K, et al. Serum carotenoids and mortality from lung cancer: a case-control study nested in the Japan Collaborative Cohort (JACC) study. *Cancer Science* 2003;94:57-63.

533. Kark JD, Yaari S, Rasooly I, et al. Are lean smokers at increased risk of lung cancer? The Israel Civil Servant Cancer Study. *Arch Intern Med* 1995;155:2409-16.

534. Knekt P, Heliovaara M, Rissanen A, et al. Leanness and lung-cancer risk. *Int J Cancer* 1991;49:208-13.

535. Knekt P, Raitasalo R, Heliovaara M, et al. Elevated lung cancer risk among persons with depressed mood. *Am J Epidemiol* 1996;144:1096-103.

536. Lee J, Kolonel LN. Are body mass indices interchangeable in measuring obesity-disease associations? *Am J Public Health* 1984;74:376-7.

537. Lee SY, Kim MT, Jee SH, et al. Does hypertension increase mortality risk from lung cancer? A prospective cohort study on smoking, hypertension and lung cancer risk among Korean men. *J Hypertens* 2002;20:617-22.

538. Li K, Yao C, Dong L. [Correlationship between body mass index and mortality in the middle-aged and elderly population of Beijing City.] *Zhonghua Yu Fang Yi Xue Za Zhi* 2002;36:34-7.

539. Linseisen J, Wolfram G, Miller AB. Plasma 7beta-hydroxycholesterol as a possible predictor of lung cancer risk. *Cancer Epidemiol Biomarkers Prev* 2002;11:1630-7.

540. Olson JE, Yang P, Schmitz K, et al. Differential association of body mass index and fat distribution with three major histologic types of lung cancer: evidence from a cohort of older women. *Am J Epidemiol* 2002;156:606-15.

541. Ratnasinghe D, Forman MR, Tangrea JA, et al. Serum carotenoids are associated with increased lung cancer risk among alcohol drinkers, but not among non-drinkers in a cohort of tin miners. *Alcohol Alcohol* 2000;35:355-60.

542. Seidell JC, Verschuren WM, van Leer EM, et al. Overweight, underweight, and mortality. A prospective study of 48,287 men and women. *Arch Intern Med* 1996;156:958-63.

543. Tamosiunas A, Reklaitiene R, Jureniene K, et al. [Time trends in mortality from malignant tumors and lung cancer during the period 1971-2000 and the risk of death in the middle-aged Kaunas men.] *Medicina (Kaunas)* 2003;39:596-603.

544. Tsai SP, Donnelly RP, Wendt JK. Obesity and mortality in a prospective study of a middle-aged industrial population. *J Occup Environ Med* 2006;48:22-7.

545. Wannamethee G, Shaper AG. Body weight and mortality in middle aged British men: impact of smoking. *BMJ* 1989;299:1497-502.

546. Alavanja MC, Field RW, Sinha R, et al. Lung cancer risk and red meat consumption among Iowa women. *Lung Cancer* 2001;34:37-46.

547. Alouane LT, Alguemi C, Cherif F, et al. [Serum alpha-tocopherol and apolipoprotein levels in Tunisian lung cancer patients.] *Sem Hop* 1998;74:12-7.

548. Brown DJ, McMillan DC, Milroy R. The correlation between fatigue, physical function, the systemic inflammatory response, and psychological distress in patients with advanced lung cancer. *Cancer Causes Control* 2005;103:377-82.

549. Burgaz S, Torun M, Yardim S, et al. Serum carotenoids and uric acid levels in relation to cancer. *J Clin Pharm Ther* 1996;21:331-6.

550. Chen KX, Xu WL, Jia ZL, et al. [Risk factors of lung cancer in Tianjin.] *Zhonghua Zhong Liu Za Zhi* 2003;25:575-80.

551. De Stefani E, Brennan P, Boffetta P, et al. Diet and adenocarcinoma of the lung: a case-control study in Uruguay. *Lung Cancer* 2002;35:43-51.

552. Fiorenza AM, Branchi A, Sommariva D. Serum lipoprotein profile in patients with cancer. A comparison with non-cancer subjects. *Int J Clin Lab Res* 2000;30:141-5.

553. Goodman MT, Wilkens LR. Relation of body size and the risk of lung cancer. *Nutr Cancer* 1993;20:179-86.

554. Gorlova OY, Zhang Y, Schabath MB, et al. Never smokers and lung cancer risk: a case-control study of epidemiological factors. *Int J Cancer* 2006;118:1798-804.

555. Kanashiki M, Sairenchi T, Saito Y, et al. Body mass index and lung cancer: a case-control study of subjects participating in a mass-screening program. *Chest* 2005;128:1490-6.

556. Kollarova H, Janout V, Cizek L. [Risk factors of lifestyles and lung cancer.] *Hygiena* 2003;48:79-87.

557. Kubik AK, Zatloukal P, Tomasek L, et al. Lung cancer risk among Czech women: a case-control study. *Prev Med* 2002;34:436-44.

558. LeGardeur BY, Lopez A, Johnson WD. A case-control study of serum vitamins A, E, and C in lung cancer patients. *Nutr Cancer* 1990;14:133-40.

559. Mendilaharsu M, De Stefani E, Deneo-Pellegrini H, et al. Phytosterols and risk of lung cancer: a case-control study in Uruguay. *Lung Cancer* 1998;21:37-45.

560. Ozturk O, Isbir T, Yaylim I, et al. GST M1 and CYP1A1 gene polymorphism and daily fruit consumption in Turkish patients with non-small cell lung carcinomas. *In Vivo* 2003;17:625-32.

561. Rauscher GH, Mayne ST, Janerich DT. Relation between body mass index and lung cancer risk in men and women never and former smokers. *Am J Epidemiol* 2000;152:506-13.

562. Scali J, Astre C, Segala C, et al. Relationship of serum cholesterol, dietary and plasma beta-carotene with lung cancer in male smokers. *Eur J Cancer Prev* 1995;4:169-74.

563. Schabath MB, Hernandez LM, Wu X, et al. Dietary phytoestrogens and lung cancer risk. *JAMA* 2005;294:1493-504.

564. Shen H, Wei Q, Pillow PC, et al. Dietary folate intake and lung cancer risk in former smokers: a case-control analysis. *Cancer Epidemiol Biomarkers Prev* 2003;12:980-6.

565. Stam J, Strankinga WF, Fikkert JJ, et al. Vitamins and lung cancer. *Lung* 1990;168 Suppl:1075-81.

566. Stefani ED, Boffetta P, Deneo-Pellegrini H, et al. Dietary antioxidants and lung cancer risk: a case-control study in Uruguay. *Nutr Cancer* 1999;34:100-10.

567. Swanson CA, Brown CC, Sinha R, et al. Dietary fats and lung cancer risk among women: the Missouri Women's Health Study (United States). *Cancer Causes Control* 1997;8:883-93.

568. Torun M, Yardim S, Gonenc A, et al. Serum beta-carotene, vitamin E, vitamin C and malondialdehyde levels in several types of cancer. *J Clin Pharm Ther* 1995;20:259-63.

569. Tsai YY, McGlynn KA, Hu Y, et al. Genetic susceptibility and dietary patterns in lung cancer. *Lung Cancer* 2003;41:269-81.

570. Xiang Y, Gao Y, Zhong L, et al. [A case-control study on relationship between body mass index and lung cancer in non-smoking women.] *Zhonghua Yu Fang Yi Xue Za Zhi* 1999;33:9-12.

571. Yu M, Rao K, Chen Y. [A case-control study of the risk factors of lung cancer in Beijing, Tianjin, Shanghai, Chongqing metropolitan areas.] *Zhonghua Yu Fang Yi Xue Za Zhi* 2000;34:227-31.

572. Zang EA, Wynder EL. Reevaluation of the confounding effect of cigarette smoking on the relationship between alcohol use and lung cancer risk, with larynx cancer used as a positive control. *Prev Med* 2001;32:359-70.

573. Zhou BS, Wang TJ, Guan P, et al. Indoor air pollution and pulmonary adenocarcinoma among females: a case-control study in Shenyang, China. *Oncol Rep* 2000;7:1253-9.

574. Liaw YP, Huang YC, Lo PY, et al. Nutrient intakes in relation to cancer mortality in Taiwan. *Nutr Res* 2003;23:1597-606.

575. Huang Z, Willett WC, Colditz GA, et al. Waist circumference, waist:hip ratio, and risk of breast cancer in the Nurses' Health Study. *Am J Epidemiol* 1999;150:1316-24.

576. Lahmann PH, Key T, Tjoenneland A, et al. Adult weight change and postmenopausal breast cancer risk: Findings from the European Prospective Investigation into Cancer and nutrition (EPIC). *Int J Obes* 2004;28:S4-S.

577. Mattisson I, Wirfalt E, Wallstrom P, et al. High fat and alcohol intakes are risk factors of postmenopausal breast cancer: a prospective study from the Malmo diet and cancer cohort. *Int J Cancer* 2004;110:589-97.

578. Schapira DV, Kumar NB, Lyman GH, et al. Upper-body fat distribution and endometrial cancer risk. *JAMA* 1991;266:1808-11.

579. Goodman MT, Hankin JH, Wilkens LR, et al. Diet, body size, physical activity, and the risk of endometrial cancer. *Cancer Res* 1997;57:5077-85.

580. Elliott EA, Matanoski GM, Rosenshein NB, et al. Body fat patterning in women with endometrial cancer. *Gynecol Oncol* 1990;39:253-8.

581. Barnes-Josiah D, Potter JD, Sellers TA, et al. Early body size and subsequent weight gain as predictors of breast cancer incidence (Iowa, United States). *Cancer Causes Control* 1995;6:112-8.

582. Breslow RA, Ballard-Barbash R, Munoz K, et al. Long-term recreational physical activity and breast cancer in the National Health and Nutrition Examination Survey I epidemiologic follow-up study. *Cancer Epidemiol Biomarkers Prev* 2001;10:805-8.

583. French SA, Folsom AR, Jeffery RW, et al. Weight variability and incident disease in older women: the Iowa Women's Health Study. *Int J Obes Relat Metab Disord* 1997;21:217-23.

584. Lahmann PH, Schulz M, Hoffmann K, et al. Long-term weight change and breast cancer risk: the European prospective investigation into cancer and nutrition (EPIC). *Br J Cancer* 2005;93:582-9.

585. Radimer KL, Ballard-Barbash R, Miller JS, et al. Weight change and the risk of late-onset breast cancer in the original Framingham cohort. *Nutr Cancer* 2004;49:7-13.

586. Harvie M, Howell A, Vierkant RA, et al. Association of gain and loss of weight before and after menopause with risk of postmenopausal breast cancer in the Iowa women's health study. *Cancer Epidemiol Biomarkers Prev* 2005;14:656-61.

587. Jernstrom H, Barrett-Connor E. Obesity, weight change, fasting insulin, proinsulin, C-peptide, and insulin-like growth factor-1 levels in women with and without breast cancer: the Rancho Bernardo Study. *J Womens Health Gend Based Med* 1999;8:1265-72.

588. Radimer K, Siskind V, Bain C, et al. Relation between anthropometric indicators and risk of breast cancer among Australian women. *Am J Epidemiol* 1993;138:77-89.

589. Han D, Muti P, Trevisan M, et al. Effects of lifetime weight gain on breast cancer risk. *Am J Epidemiol* 2004;159:S13-S.

590. Eng SM, Gammon MD, Terry MB, et al. Body size changes in relation to postmenopausal breast cancer among women on Long Island, New York. *Am J Epidemiol* 2005;162:229-37.

591. McElroy JA, Kanarek MS, Trentham-Dietz A, et al. Potential exposure to PCBs, DDT and PBDEs from sport-caught fish consumption in relation to breast cancer risk in Wisconsin. *Environ Health Perspect* 2004;112:156-62.

592. World Cancer Research Fund/American Institute for Cancer Research. *Food, Nutrition and the Prevention of Cancer: a Global Perspective*. Washington, DC: AICR, 1997.

593. World Health Organization. *WHO Child Growth Standards: Length/Height-for-age, Weight-for-age, Weight-for-length, Weight-for-height and Body Mass Index-for age*. Geneva: WHO, 2006.

594. de Onis M, Garza C, Habicht JP. Time for a new growth reference. *Pediatrics* 1997;100:E8.

595. Karlberg J. The infancy-childhood growth spurt. *Acta Paediatr Scand* 1990;367:111-8.

596. Ong KK, Dunger DB. Birth weight, infant growth and insulin resistance. *Eur J Endocrinol* 2004;151 Suppl 3:U131-9.

597. Dabelea D, Hanson RL, Lindsay RS, et al. Intrauterine exposure to diabetes conveys risks for type 2 diabetes and obesity: a study of discordant sibships. *Diabetes* 2000;49:2208-11.

598. Leon DA, Lithell HO, Vagero D, et al. Reduced fetal growth rate and increased risk of death from ischaemic heart disease: cohort study of 15 000 Swedish men and women born 1915-29. *BMJ (Clin Res Ed)* 1998;317:241-5.

599. Lucas A, Fewtrell MS, Cole TJ. Fetal origins of adult disease-the hypothesis revisited. *BMJ* 1999;319:245-9.

600. Ross MG, Desai M. Gestational programming: population survival effects of drought and famine during pregnancy. *Am J Physiol Regul Integr Comp Physiol* 2005;288:R25-33.

601. Cripps RL, Martin-Gronert MS, Ozanne SE. Fetal and perinatal programming of appetite. *Clin Sci (Lond)* 2005;109:1-11.

602. Remacle C, Bieswal F, Reusens B. Programming of obesity and cardiovascular disease. *Int J Obes Relat Metab Disord* 2004;28 Suppl 3:S46-53.

603. Job JC, Quelquejay C. Growth and puberty in a fostered kindred. *Eur J Pediatr* 1994;153:642-5.

604. Gunnell D, Okasha M, Smith GD, et al. Height, leg length, and cancer risk: a systematic review. *Epidemiol Rev* 2001;23:313-42.

605. Wadsworth ME, Hardy RJ, Paul AA, et al. Leg and trunk length at 43 years in relation to childhood health, diet and family circumstances; evidence from the 1946 national birth cohort. *Int J Epidemiol* 2002;31:383-90.

606. Jousilahti P, Tuomilehto J, Vartiainen E, et al. Relation of adult height to cause-specific and total mortality: a prospective follow-up study of 31,199 middle-aged men and women in Finland. *Am J Epidemiol* 2000;151:1112-20.

607. Goldbourt U, Tanne D. Body height is associated with decreased long-term stroke but not coronary heart disease mortality? *Stroke; a Journal of Cerebral Circulation* 2002;33:743-8.

608. McCarron P, Okasha M, McEwen J, et al. Height in young adulthood and risk of death from cardiorespiratory disease: a prospective study of male former students of Glasgow University, Scotland. *Am J Epidemiol* 2002;155:683-7.

609. Dunger DB, Ahmed ML, Ong KK. Effects of obesity on growth and puberty. *Best Pract Res Clin Endocrinol Metab* 2005;19:375-90.

610. Parent AS, Teilmann G, Juul A, et al. The timing of normal puberty and the age limits of sexual precocity: variations around the world, secular trends, and changes after migration. *Endocr Rev* 2003;24:668-93.

611. Wang Y. Is obesity associated with early sexual maturation? A comparison of the association in American boys versus girls. *Pediatrics* 2002;110:903-10.

612. Kulin HE, Bwibo N, Mutie D, et al. The effect of chronic childhood malnutrition on pubertal growth and development. *Am J Clin Nutr* 1982;36:527-36.

613. Hunter DJ, Spiegelman D, Adami HO, et al. Non-dietary factors as risk factors for breast cancer, and as effect modifiers of the association of fat intake and risk of breast cancer. *Cancer Causes Control* 1997;8:49-56.

614. Clavel-Chapelon F, Gerber M. Reproductive factors and breast cancer risk. Do they differ according to age at diagnosis? *Breast Cancer Res Treat* 2002;72:107-15.

615. Clavel-Chapelon F. Differential effects of reproductive factors on the risk of pre- and postmenopausal breast cancer. Results from a large cohort of French women. *Br J Cancer* 2002;86:723-7.

616. de Waard F, Thijssen JH. Hormonal aspects in the causation of human breast cancer: epidemiological hypotheses reviewed, with special reference to nutritional status and first pregnancy. *The Journal of Steroid Biochemistry and Molecular Biology* 2005;97:451-8.

617. Apter D, Reinila M, Vihko R. Some endocrine characteristics of early menarche, a risk factor for breast cancer, are preserved into adulthood. *Int J Cancer* 1989;44:783-7.

618. Stoll BA, Secreto G. New hormone-related markers of high risk to breast cancer. *Ann Oncol* 1992;3:435-8.

619. Kaaks R, Berrino F, Key T, et al. Serum sex steroids in premenopausal women and breast cancer risk within the European Prospective Investigation into Cancer and Nutrition (EPIC). *J Natl Cancer Inst* 2005;97:755-65.

620. Kaaks R, Rinaldi S, Key TJ, et al. Postmenopausal serum androgens, oestrogens and breast cancer risk: the European prospective investigation into cancer and nutrition. *Endocr Relat Cancer* 2005;12:1071-82.

621. Smith GD, Hart C, Upton M, et al. Height and risk of death among men and women: aetiological implications of associations with cardiorespiratory disease and cancer mortality. *J Epidemiol Community Health* 2000;54:97-103.

622. Thune I, Lund E. Physical activity and risk of colorectal cancer in men and women. *Br J Cancer* 1996;73:1134-40.

623. Hebert PR, Ajani U, Cook NR, et al. Adult height and incidence of cancer in male physicians (United States). *Cancer Causes Control* 1997;8:591-7.

624. Giovannucci E, Rimm EB, Liu Y, et al. Height, predictors of C-peptide and cancer risk in men. *Int J Epidemiol* 2004;33:217-25.

625. Albanes D, Taylor PR. International differences in body height and weight and their relationship to cancer incidence. *Nutr Cancer* 1990;14:69-77.

626. Berkey CS, Frazier AL, Gardner JD, et al. Adolescence and breast carcinoma risk. *Cancer* 1999;85:2400-9.

627. Cerhan JR, Grabrick DM, Vierkant RA, et al. Interaction of adolescent anthropometric characteristics and family history on breast cancer risk in a Historical Cohort Study of 426 families (USA). *Cancer Causes Control* 2004;15:1-9.

628. Colditz GA, Rosner B. Cumulative risk of breast cancer to age 70 years according to risk factor status: Data from the Nurses' Health Study. *Am J Epidemiol* 2000;152:950-64.

629. De Stavola BL, dos Santos Silva I, McCormack V, et al. Childhood growth and breast cancer. *Am J Epidemiol* 2004;159:671-82.

630. Drake DA. A longitudinal study of physical activity and breast cancer prediction. *Cancer Nurs* 2001;24:371-7.

631. Freni SC, Eberhardt MS, Turturro A, et al. Anthropometric measures and metabolic rate in association with risk of breast cancer (United States). *Cancer Causes Control* 1996;7:358-65.

632. Hoyer AP, Grandjean P, Jorgensen T, et al. Organochlorine exposure and risk of breast cancer. *Lancet* 1998;352:1816-20.

633. Nilsen TIL, Vatten LJ. Adult height and risk of breast cancer: A possible effect of early nutrition. *Br J Cancer* 2001;85:959-61.

634. Palmer JR, Rao RS, Adams-Campbell LL, et al. Height and breast cancer risk: Results from the Black Women's Health Study (United States). *Cancer Causes Control* 2001;12:343-8.

635. Swanson CA, Jones DY, Schatzkin A, et al. Breast cancer risk assessed by anthropometry in the NHANES I epidemiological follow-up study. *Cancer Res* 1988;48:5363-7.

636. Tryggvadottir L, Tulinius H, Eyfjord JE, et al. Breast cancer risk factors and age at diagnosis: an Icelandic cohort study. *Int J Cancer* 2002;98:604-8.

637. Vatten LJ, Kvinnsland S. Body height and risk of breast cancer. A prospective study of 23,831 Norwegian women. *Br J Cancer* 1990;61:881-5.

638. Adebamowo CA, Adekunle OO. Case-controlled study of the epidemiological risk factors for breast cancer in Nigeria. *Br J Surg* 1999;86:665-8.

639. Amaral T, de Almeida MD, Barros H. Diet and postmenopausal breast cancer in Portugal. *IARC Sci Publ* 2002;156:297-9.

640. Choi NW, Howe GR, Miller AB, et al. An epidemiologic study of breast cancer. *Am J Epidemiol* 1978;107:510-21.

641. Dubin N, Pasternack BS, Strax P. Epidemiology of breast cancer in a screened population. *Cancer Detect Prev* 1984;7:87-102.

642. Kolonel LN, Nomura AM, Lee J, et al. Anthropometric indicators of breast cancer risk in postmenopausal women in Hawaii. *Nutr Cancer* 1986;8:247-56.

643. Magnusson C, Colditz G, Rosner B, et al. Association of family history and other risk factors with breast cancer risk (Sweden). *Cancer Causes Control* 1998;9:259-67.

644. Swerdlow AJ, De Stavola BL, Floredus B, et al. Risk factors for breast cancer at young ages in twins: An international population-based study. *J Natl Cancer Inst* 2002;94:1238-46.

645. Ursin G, Paganini-Hill A, Siemiatycki J, et

al. Early adult body weight, body mass index, and premenopausal bilateral breast cancer: data from a case-control study. *Breast Cancer Res Treat* 1995;33:75-82.

646. Zhang Y, Rosenberg L, Colton T, et al. Adult height and risk of breast cancer among white women in a case-control study. *Am J Epidemiol* 1996;143:1123-8.

647. Ziegler RG, Hoover RN, Nomura AM, et al. Relative weight, weight change, height, and breast cancer risk in Asian-American women. *J Natl Cancer Inst* 1996;88:650-60.

648. Gray GE, Pike MC, Henderson BE. Breast-cancer incidence and mortality rates in different countries in relation to known risk factors and dietary practices. *Br J Cancer* 1979;39:1-7.

649. Baer HJ, Rich-Edwards JW, Colditz GA, et al. Adult height, age at attained height, and incidence of breast cancer in premenopausal women. *Int J Cancer* 2006;119:2231-5.

650. Giovannucci E. Intake of fat, meat and fiber in relation to risk of colon cancer in men. *Cancer Res* 1994;54:2390-7.

651. Ogren M, Hedberg M, Berglund G, et al. Risk of pancreatic carcinoma in smokers enhanced by weight gain. Results from 10-year follow-up of the Malmo preventive Project Cohort Study. *Int J Pancreatol* 1996;20:95-101.

652. Song YM, Smith GD, Sung J. Adult height and cause-specific mortality: a large prospective study of South Korean men. *Am J Epidemiol* 2003;158:479-85.

653. Mack TM, Yu MC, Hanisch R, et al. Pancreas cancer and smoking, beverage consumption, and past medical history. *J Natl Cancer Inst* 1986;76:49-60.

654. Bueno de Mesquita HB, Maisonneuve P, Moerman CJ, et al. Anthropometric and reproductive variables and exocrine carcinoma of the pancreas: a population-based case-control study in The Netherlands. *Int J Cancer* 1992;52:24-9.

655. Kalapothaki V, Tzonou A, Hsieh CC, et al. Tobacco, ethanol, coffee, pancreatitis, diabetes mellitus, and cholelithiasis as risk factors for pancreatic carcinoma. *Cancer Causes Control* 1993;4:375-82.

656. Sarles H, Cros RC, Bidart JM. A multicenter inquiry into the etiology of pancreatic diseases. *Digestion* 1979;19:110-25.

657. La Vecchia C, Negri E, Parazzini F, et al. Height and cancer risk in a network of case-control studies from northern Italy. *Int J Cancer* 1990;45:275-9.

658. Anderson JP, Ross JA, Folsom AR. Anthropometric variables, physical activity, and incidence of ovarian cancer: The Iowa Women's Health Study. *Cancer* 2004;100:1515-21.

659. Engeland A, Tretli S, Bjorge T. Height, body mass index, and ovarian cancer: a follow-up of 1.1 million Norwegian women. *J Natl Cancer Inst* 2003;95:1244-8.

660. Lapidus L, Helgesson O, Merck C, et al. Adipose tissue distribution and female carcinomas. A 12-year follow-up of

participants in the population study of women in Gothenburg, Sweden. *Int J Obes* 1988;12:361-8.

661. Lukanova A, Toniolo P, Lundin E, et al. Body mass index in relation to ovarian cancer: a multi-centre nested case-control study. *Int J Cancer* 2002;99:603-8.

662. Rodriguez C, Calle EE, Fakhrabadi-Shokoohi D, et al. Body mass index, height, and the risk of ovarian cancer mortality in a prospective cohort of postmenopausal women. *Cancer Epidemiol Biomarkers Prev* 2002;11:822-8.

663. Schouten LJ, Goldbohm RA, van den Brandt PA. Height, weight, weight change, and ovarian cancer risk in the Netherlands cohort study on diet and cancer. *Am J Epidemiol* 2003;157:424-33.

664. Cramer DW, Welch WR, Hutchison GB, et al. Dietary animal fat in relation to ovarian cancer risk. *Obstet Gynecol* 1984;63:833-8.

665. Dal Maso L, Franceschi S, Negri E, et al. Body size indices at different ages and epithelial ovarian cancer risk. *Eur J Cancer* 2002;38:1769-74.

666. Kuper H, Cramer DW, Titus-Ernstoff L. Risk of ovarian cancer in the United States in relation to anthropometric measures: does the association depend on menopausal status? *Cancer Causes Control* 2002;13:455-63.

667. Mori M, Nishida T, Sugiyama T, et al. Anthropometric and other risk factors for ovarian cancer in a case-control study. *Jpn J Cancer Res* 1998;89:246-53.

668. Polychronopoulou A, Tzonou A, Hsieh CC, et al. Reproductive variables, tobacco, ethanol, coffee and somatometry as risk factors for ovarian cancer. *Int J Cancer* 1993;55:402-7.

669. Tzonou A, Day NE, Trichopoulos D, et al. The epidemiology of ovarian cancer in Greece: a case-control study. *Eur J Cancer Clin Oncol* 1984;20:1045-52.

670. Zhang M, Xie X, Holman CD. Body weight and body mass index and ovarian cancer risk: a case-control study in China. *Gynecol Oncol* 2005;98:228-34.

671. Barker DJ, Osmond C, Golding J. Height and mortality in the counties of England and Wales. *Ann Hum Biol* 1990;17:1-6.

672. Lacey JV, Jr., Leitzmann M, Brinton LA, et al. Weight, height, and body mass index and risk for ovarian cancer in a cohort study. *Ann Epidemiol* 2006;16:869-76.

673. Peterson NB, Trentham-Dietz A, Newcomb PA, et al. Relation of anthropometric measurements to ovarian cancer risk in a population-based case-control study (United States). *Cancer Causes Control* 2006;17:459-67.

674. Terry P, Baron JA, Weiderpass E, et al. Lifestyle and endometrial cancer risk: a cohort study from the Swedish Twin Registry. *Int J Cancer* 1999;82:38-42.

675. Tretli S, Magnus K. Height and weight in relation to uterine corpus cancer morbidity and mortaliy. A follow-up study of 570,000 women in Norway. *Int J Cancer* 1990;46:165-72.

676. Koumantaki Y, Tzonou A, Koumantakis E, et al. A case-control study of cancer of endometrium in Athens. *Int J Cancer* 1989;43:795-9.

677. Shu XO, Brinton LA, Zheng W, et al. A population-based case-control study of endometrial cancer in Shanghai, China. *Int J Cancer* 1991;49:38-43.

678. De Stavola BL, Hardy R, Kuh D, et al. Birthweight, childhood growth and risk of breast cancer in a British cohort. *Br J Cancer* 2000;83:964-8.

679. Kaijser M, Akre O, Cnattingius S, et al. Preterm birth, birth weight, and subsequent risk of female breast cancer. *Br J Cancer* 2003;89:1664-6.

680. McCormack VA, dos Santos Silva I, Koupil I, et al. Birth characteristics and adult cancer incidence: Swedish cohort of over 11,000 men and women. *Int J Cancer* 2005;115:611-7.

681. Vatten LJ, Nilsen TI, Tretli S, et al. Size at birth and risk of breast cancer: prospective population-based study. *Int J Cancer* 2005;114:461-4.

682. Kaijser M, Lichtenstein P, Granath F, et al. In utero exposures and breast cancer: a study of opposite-sexed twins. *J Natl Cancer Inst* 2001;93:60-2.

683. Mellemkjaer L, Olsen ML, Sorensen HT, et al. Birth weight and risk of early-onset breast cancer (Denmark). *Cancer Causes Control* 2003;14:61-4.

684. Barba M, McCann SE, Nie J, et al. Perinatal exposures and breast cancer risk in the Western New York Exposures and Breast Cancer (WEB) Study. *Cancer Causes Control* 2006;17:395-401.

685. Schack-Nielsen L, Michaelsen KF. Breast feeding and future health. *Curr Opin Clin Nutr Metab Care* 2006;9:289-96.

686. Leung AK, Sauve RS. Breast is best for babies. *J Natl Med Assoc* 2005;97:1010-9.

687. World Health Organization/United Nations Children's Fund. *Global Strategy for Infant and Young Children Feeding.* Geneva: WHO/UNICEF, 2003.

688. World Health Organization. 2001. *Report of the Expert Consultation on the Optimal Duration of Exclusive Breastfeeding.* http://www.who.int/entity/nutrition/topics/optimal_duration_of_exc_bfeeding_report_eng.pdf.

689. World Cancer Research Fund/American Institute for Cancer Research. In press. *Policy and Action for Cancer Prevention. Food, Nutrition and Physical Activity: a Global Perspective.* www.wcrf.org.

690. Wright A, Schanler R. The resurgence of breastfeeding at the end of the second millennium. *The Journal of Nutrition* 2001;131:421S-5S.

691. Yngve A, Sjostrom M. Breastfeeding in countries of the European Union and EFTA: current and proposed recommendations, rationale, prevalence, duration and trends. *Public Health Nutr* 2001;4:631-45.

692. Davies-Adetugbo AA, Ojofeitimi EO. Maternal education, breastfeeding behaviours and lactational

amenorrhoea: studies among two ethnic communities in Ile Ife, Nigeria. *Nutr Health* 1996;11:115-26.

693. Scott JA, Binns CW. Factors associated with the initiation and duration of breastfeeding: a review of the literature. *Breastfeed Rev* 1999;7:5-16.

694. Taylor JS, Risica PM, Geller L, et al. Duration of breastfeeding among first-time mothers in the United States: results of a national survey. *Acta Paediatr* 2006;95:980-4.

695. Dop MC. [Breastfeeding in Africa: will positive trends be challenged by the AIDS epidemic?] *Sante* 2002;12:64-72.

696. Tryggvadottir L, Tulinius H, Eyfjord JE, et al. Breastfeeding and reduced risk of breast cancer in an Icelandic cohort study. *Am J Epidemiol* 2001;154:37-42.

697. Abramson JH. Breastfeeding and breast cancer. A study of cases and matched controls in Jerusalem. *Isr J Med Sci* 1966;2:457-64.

698. Behery A, Kotb. Genetic and environmental risk factors for breast cancer in Alexandria, Egypt. *J Med Res Inst* 2002;23:117-28.

699. Brignone G, Cusimano R, Dardanoni G, et al. A case-control study on breast cancer risk factors in a southern European population. *Int J Epidemiol* 1987;16:356-61.

700. Charlier CJ, Albert AI, Zhang LY, et al. Polychlorinated biphenyls contamination in women with breast cancer. *Clin Chim Acta* 2004;347:177-81.

701. Enger SM, Ross RK, Paganini-Hill A, et al. Breastfeeding experience and breast cancer risk among postmenopausal women. *Cancer Epidemiol Biomarkers Prev* 1998;7:365-9. 37 ref.

702. Freudenheim JL, Marshall JR, Vena JE, et al. Lactation history and breast cancer risk. *Am J Epidemiol* 1997;146:932-8.

703. Gao YT, Shu XO, Dai Q, et al. Association of menstrual and reproductive factors with breast cancer risk: results from the Shanghai Breast Cancer Study. *Int J Cancer* 2000;87:295-300.

704. Haring MH, Rookus MA, van Leeuwen FE. [Does breast feeding protect against breast cancer? An epidemiological study.] *Ned Tijdschr Geneeskd* 1992;136:743-7.

705. Katsouyanni K, Lipworth L, Trichopoulou A, et al. A case-control study of lactation and cancer of the breast. *Br J Cancer* 1996;73:814-8.

706. Kuo HW, Chen SF, Wu CC, et al. Serum and tissue trace elements in patients with breast cancer in Taiwan. *Biol Trace Elem Res* 2002;89:1-11.

707. Romieu I, Hernandez-Avila M, Lazcano E, et al. Breast cancer and lactation history in Mexican women. *Am J Epidemiol* 1996;143:543-52.

708. Rundle A, Tang D, Hibshoosh H, et al. The relationship between genetic damage from polycyclic aromatic hydrocarbons in breast tissue and breast cancer. *Carcinogenesis* 2000;21:1281-9.

709. Stuver SO, Hsieh CC, Bertone E, et al. The association between lactation and breast cancer in an international case-control study: a re-analysis by menopausal status. *Int J Cancer* 1997;71:166-9.

710. Tajima K, Hirose K, Ogawa H, et al. [Hospital epidemiology - a comparative case control study of breast and cervical cancers.] *Gan No Rinsho* 1990;Spec No:351-64.

711. Tashiro H, Nomura Y, Hisamatu K. [A case-control study of risk factors of breast cancer detected by mass screening.] *Gan No Rinsho* 1990;36:2127-30.

712. Tessaro S, Beria JU, Tomasi E, et al. Breastfeeding and breast cancer: a case-control study in Southern Brazil. *Cad Saude Publica* 2003;19:1593-601.

713. Ursin G, Bernstein L, Lord SJ, et al. Reproductive factors and subtypes of breast cancer defined by hormone receptor and histology. *Br J Cancer* 2005;93:364-71.

714. Ursin G, Bernstein L, Wang Y, et al. Reproductive factors and risk of breast carcinoma in a study of white and African-American women. *Cancer* 2004;101:353-62.

715. Wu AH, Ziegler RG, Pike MC, et al. Menstrual and reproductive factors and risk of breast cancer in Asian-Americans. *Br J Cancer* 1996;73:680-6.

716. Yang PS, Yang TL, Liu CL, et al. A case-control study of breast cancer in Taiwan - a low-incidence area. *Br J Cancer* 1997;75:752-6.

717. Yavari P, Mosavizadeh M, Sadrol-Hefazi B, et al. Reproductive characteristics and the risk of breast cancer - a case-control study in Iran. *Asian Pac J Cancer Prev* 2005;6:370-5.

718. Yoo KY, Tajima K, Kuroishi T, et al. Independent protective effect of lactation against breast cancer: a case-control study in Japan. *Am J Epidemiol* 1992;135:726-33.

719. Yu SZ, Lu RF, Xu DD, et al. A case-control study of dietary and nondietary risk factors for breast cancer in Shanghai. *Cancer Res* 1990;50:5017-21.

720. Lubin JH, Burns PE, Blot WJ, et al. Risk factors for breast cancer in women in northern Alberta, Canada, as related to age at diagnosis. *J Natl Cancer Inst* 1982;68:211-7.

721. Kvale GHI. Lactation and cancer risk: is there a relation specific to breast cancer? *J Epidemiol Community Health* 1988;42:30-7.

722. Li W, Ray RM, Lampe JW, et al. Dietary and other risk factors in women having fibrocystic breast conditions with and without concurrent breast cancer: a nested case-control study in Shanghai, China. *Int J Cancer* 2005;115:981-93.

723. London SJ, Colditz GA, Stampfer MJ, et al. Lactation and risk of breast cancer in a cohort of US women. *Am J Epidemiol* 1990;132:17-26.

724. Michels KB, Willett WC, Rosner BA, et al. Prospective assessment of breastfeeding and breast cancer incidence among 89 887 women. *Lancet* 1996;347:431-6.

725. Abou-Daoud KT. Cancer of the breast and breast-feeding. Study of 279 parous women and matched controls. *Cancer* 1971;28:781-4.

726. Becher H, Schmidt S, Chang-Claude J. Reproductive factors and familial predisposition for breast cancer by age 50 years. A case-control-family study for assessing main effects and possible gene-environment interaction. *Int J Epidemiol* 2003;32:38-48.

727. Brandt B, Hermann S, Straif K, et al. Modification of breast cancer risk in young women by a polymorphic sequence in the egfr gene. *Cancer Res* 2004;64:7-12.

728. Byers T, Graham S, Rzepka T, et al. Lactation and breast cancer. Evidence for a negative association in premenopausal women. *Am J Epidemiol* 1985;121:664-74.

729. Chang-Claude J, Eby N, Kiechle M, et al. Breastfeeding and breast cancer risk by age 50 among women in Germany. *Cancer Causes Control* 2000;11:687-95.

730. Chie W, Lee W, Li C, et al. Lactation, lactation suppression hormones and breast cancer: a hospital-based case-control study for parous women in Taiwan. *Oncol Rep* 1997;4:319-26.

731. Coogan PF, Rosenberg L, Shapiro S, et al. Lactation and breast carcinoma risk in a South African population. *Cancer* 1999;86:982-9.

732. Chilvers CED, McPherson K, Peto J, et al. Breast feeding and risk of breast cancer in young women. *BMJ* 1993;307:17-20.

733. Enger SM, Ross RK, Henderson B, et al. Breastfeeding history, pregnancy experience and risk of breast cancer. *Br J Cancer* 1997;76:118-23.

734. Jernstrom H, Lubinski J, Lynch HT, et al. Breast-feeding and the risk of breast cancer in BRCA1 and BRCA2 mutation carriers. *J Natl Cancer Inst* 2004;96:1094-8.

735. Lai FM, Chen P, Ku HC, et al. A case-control study of parity, age at first full-term pregnancy, breast feeding and breast cancer in Taiwanese women. *Proc Natl Sci Counc Repub China B* 1996;20:71-7.

736. Layde PM, Webster LA, Baughman AL, et al. The independent associations of parity, age at first full term pregnancy, and duration of breastfeeding with the risk of breast cancer. *J Clin Epidemiol* 1989;42:963-73.

737. Lee EO, Ahn SH, You C, et al. Determining the main risk factors and high-risk groups of breast cancer using a predictive model for breast cancer risk assessment in South Korea. *Cancer Nurs* 2004;27:400-6.

738. Lucena RA, Allam MF, Costabeber IH, et al. Breast cancer risk factors: PCB congeners. *Eur J Cancer Prev* 2001;10:117-9.

739. Marcus PM, Baird DD, Millikan RC, et al. Adolescent reproductive events and subsequent breast cancer risk. *Am J Public Health* 1999;89:1244-7.

740. Schecter A, Toniolo P, Dai LC, et al. Blood levels of DDT and breast cancer risk among women living in the North of Vietnam. *Arch Environ Contam Toxicol* 1997;33:453-6.

741. Siskind V, Schofield F, Rice D, et al. Breast cancer and breastfeeding: results from an Australian case-control study. *Am J Epidemiol* 1989;130:229-36.

742. Tao SC, Yu MC, Ross RK, et al. Risk factors for breast cancer in Chinese women of Beijing. *Int J Cancer* 1988;42:495-8.

743. Thomas DB, Noonan EA. Breast cancer and prolonged lactation. The WHO Collaborative Study of Neoplasia and Steroid Contraceptives. *Int J Epidemiol* 1993;22:619-26.

744. Wang QS, Ross RK, Yu MC, et al. A case-control study of breast cancer in Tianjin, China. *Cancer Epidemiol Biomarkers Prev* 1992;1:435-9.

745. Wrensch M, Chew T, Farren G, et al. Risk factors for breast cancer in a population with high incidence rates. *Breast Cancer Res* 2003;5:R88-102.

746. Yang CP, Weiss NS, Band PR, et al. History of lactation and breast cancer risk. *Am J Epidemiol* 1993;138:1050-6.

747. Yuan JM, Yu MC, Ross RK, et al. Risk factors for breast cancer in Chinese women in Shanghai. *Cancer Res* 1988;48:1949-53.

748. Zheng T, Duan L, Liu Y, et al. Lactation reduces breast cancer risk in Shandong Province, China. *Am J Epidemiol* 2000;152:1129-35.

749. Collaborative Group on Hormonal Factors in Breast Cancer. Breast cancer and breastfeeding: collaborative reanalysis of individual data from 47 epidemiological studies in 30 countries, including 50302 women with breast cancer and 96973 women without the disease. *Lancet* 2002;360:187-95.

750. Mink PJ, Folsom AR, Sellers TA, et al. Physical activity, waist-to-hip ratio, and other risk factors for ovarian cancer: a follow-up study of older women. *Epidemiology* 1996;7:38-45.

751. Booth M, Beral V, Smith P. Risk factors for ovarian cancer: a case-control study. *Br J Cancer* 1989;60:592-8.

752. Chiaffarino F, Pelucchi C, Negri E, et al. Breastfeeding and the risk of epithelial ovarian cancer in an Italian population. *Gynecol Oncol* 2005;98:304-8.

753. Greggi S, Parazzini F, Paratore MP, et al. Risk factors for ovarian cancer in central Italy. *Gynecol Oncol* 2000;79:50-4.

754. Mori M, Harabuchi I, Miyake H, et al. Reproductive, genetic, and dietary risk factors for ovarian cancer. *Am J Epidemiol* 1988;128:771-7.

755. Purdie D, Green A, Bain C, et al. Reproductive and other factors and risk of epithelial ovarian cancer: an Australian case-control study. Survey of Women's Health Study Group. *Int J Cancer* 1995;62:678-84.

756. Riman T, Dickman PW, Nilsson S, et al. Risk factors for epithelial borderline ovarian tumors: results of a Swedish case-control study. *Gynecol Oncol* 2001;83:575-85.

757. Risch HA, Marrett LD, Jain M, et al. Differences in risk factors for epithelial ovarian cancer by histologic type. Results of a case-control study. *Am J Epidemiol* 1996;144:363-72.

758. Yen ML, Yen BL, Bai CH, et al. Risk factors for ovarian cancer in Taiwan: a case-control study in a low-incidence population. *Gynecol Oncol* 2003;89:318-24.

759. Zhang M, Lee AH, Binns CW. Reproductive and dietary risk factors for epithelial ovarian cancer in China. *Gynecol Oncol* 2004;. 92.

760. Zhang M, Xie X, Lee AH, et al. Prolonged lactation reduces ovarian cancer risk in Chinese women. *Eur J Cancer Prev* 2004;13:499-502.

761. Huusom LD, Frederiksen K, Hogdall EV, et al. Association of reproductive factors, oral contraceptive use and selected lifestyle factors with the risk of ovarian borderline tumors: a Danish case-control study. *Cancer Causes Control* 2006;17:821-9.

Chapter 7

1. World Health Organization. *WHO mortality database.* http://www.who.int/whosis/mort/en/. 2006.

2. International Agency for Research on Cancer. *Globocan 2002.* http://www-dep.iarc.fr/. 2006.

3. Jemal A, Clegg LX, Ward E, et al. Annual report to the nation on the status of cancer, 1975-2001, with a special feature regarding survival. *Cancer* 2004;101:3-27.

4. Kufe D, Pollock R, Weichselbaum R, et al. *Holland Frei Cancer Medicine.* 6 ed. Hamilton, Ontario: BC Decker, 2003.

5. Vikram B. Changing patterns of failure in advanced head and neck cancer. *Arch Otolaryngol* 1984;110:564-5.

6. Cancer Research UK. *UK Cancer statistics.* http://info.cancerresearchuk.org/cancerstats/. 2006.

7. Weaver EM. Association between gastroesophageal reflux and sinusitis, otitis media, and laryngeal malignancy: a systematic review of the evidence. *Am J Med* 2003;115 Suppl 3A:81S-9S.

8. Wilson JA. What is the evidence that gastroesophageal reflux is involved in the etiology of laryngeal cancer? *Curr Opin Otolaryngol Head Neck Surg* 2005;13:97-100.

9. Franceschi S, Levi F, La Vecchia C, et al. Comparison of the effect of smoking and alcohol drinking between oral and pharyngeal cancer. *Int J Cancer* 1999;83:1-4.

10. International Agency for Research on Cancer. *Tobacco smoking and tobacco smoke:* Lyon: International Agency for Research on Cancer, 2004.

11. International Agency for Research on Cancer. 2004. *Betel-quid and areca-nut chewing.* In: IARC Monogr Eval Carcinog Risks Hum no 85. http://monographs.iarc.fr/ENG/Mfonographs/vol85/volume85.pdf.

12. Ha PK, Califano JA. The role of human papillomavirus in oral carcinogenesis. *Crit Rev Oral Biol Med* 2004;15:188-96.

13. International Agency for Research on Cancer. 2005. *Human papillomaviruses.* In: IARC Monogr Eval Carcinog Risks Hum.

14. Syrjanen S. Human papillomavirus (HPV) in head and neck cancer. *J Clin Virol* 2005;32 Suppl 1:S59-66.

15. Maserejian NN, Giovannucci E, Rosner B, et al. Prospective study of fruits and vegetables and risk of oral premalignant lesions in men. *Am J Epidemiol* 2006;164:556-66.

16. Boeing H, Dietrich T, Hoffmann K, et al. Intake of fruits and vegetables and risk of cancer of the upper aero-digestive tract: the prospective EPIC-study. *Cancer Causes Control* 2006;17:957-69.

17. Galeone C, Pelucchi C, Levi F, et al. Onion and garlic use and human cancer. *Am J Clin Nutr* 2006;84:1027-32.

18. Kreimer AR, Randi G, Herrero R, et al. Diet and body mass, and oral and

oropharyngeal squamous cell carcinomas: analysis from the IARC multinational case-control study. *Int J Cancer* 2006;118:2293-7.

19. Goldenberg D. Mate: a risk factor for oral and oropharyngeal cancer. *Oral Oncol* 2002;38:646-9.

20. Goldenberg D, Golz A, Joachims HZ. The beverage mate: a risk factor for cancer of the head and neck. *Head Neck* 2003;25:595-601.

21. Garavello W, Bosetti C, Gallus S, et al. Type of alcoholic beverage and the risk of laryngeal cancer. *Eur J Cancer Prev* 2006;15:69-73.

22. Vlajinac HD, Marinkovic JM, Sipetic SB, et al. Case-control study of oropharyngeal cancer. *Cancer Detect Prev* 2006;30:152-7.

23. Petti S, Scully C. Association between different alcoholic beverages and leukoplakia among non- to moderate-drinking adults: a matched case-control study. *Eur J Cancer* 2006;42:521-7.

24. Vaezi MF, Qadeer MA, Lopez R, et al. Laryngeal cancer and gastroesophageal reflux disease: a case-control study. *Am J Med* 2006;119:768-76.

25. Yu MC, Yuan JM. Epidemiology of nasopharyngeal carcinoma. *Semin Cancer Biol* 2002;12:421-9.

26. Buell P. The effect of migration on the risk of nasopharyngeal cancer among Chinese. *Cancer Res* 1974;34:1189-91.

27. Wei WI, Sham JS. Nasopharyngeal carcinoma. *Lancet* 2005;365:2041-54.

28. Chan AT, Teo PM, Johnson PJ. Nasopharyngeal carcinoma. *Ann Oncol* 2002;13:1007-15.

29. Niedobitek G. Epstein-Barr virus infection in the pathogenesis of nasopharyngeal carcinoma. *Mol Pathol* 2000;53:248-54.

30. International Agency for Research on Cancer. 1994. *Epstein-Barr Virus and Kaposi's Sarcoma Herpesvirus/Human Herpesvirus 8.* In: IARC Monogr Eval Carcinog Risks Hum no 70. http://monographs.iarc.fr/ENG/Monographs/vol70/volume70.pdf.

31. Young LS, Rickinson AB. Epstein-Barr virus: 40 years on. *Nature reviews* 2004;4:757-68.

32. Raab-Traub N, Flynn K. The structure of the termini of the Epstein-Barr virus as a marker of clonal cellular proliferation. *Cell* 1986;47:883-9.

33. International Agency for Research on Cancer. In preparation. *Formaldehyde, 2-Butoxyethanol and 1-tert-Butoxy-2-propanol.* In: IARC Monogr Eval Carcinog Risks Hum no 88. http://monographs.iarc.fr/ENG/Meetings/88-formaldehyde.pdf.

34. Hildesheim A, Dosemeci M, Chan CC, et al. Occupational exposure to wood, formaldehyde, and solvents and risk of nasopharyngeal carcinoma. *Cancer Epidemiol Biomarkers Prev* 2001;10:1145-53.

35. International Agency for Research on Cancer. 2004. *Wood dust and formaldehyde.* In: IARC Monogr Eval

Carcinog Risks Hum no 6.

36. Iwase Y, Takemura Y, Ju-ichi M, et al. Inhibitory effect of Epstein-Barr virus activation by Citrus fruits, a cancer chemopreventor. *Cancer Lett* 1999;139:227-36.

37. Ayan I, Kaytan E, Ayan N. Childhood nasopharyngeal carcinoma: from biology to treatment. *Lancet Oncol* 2003;4:13-21.

38. Shao YM, Poirier S, Ohshima H, et al. Epstein-Barr virus activation in Raji cells by extracts of preserved food from high risk areas for nasopharyngeal carcinoma. *Carcinogenesis* 1988;9:1455-7.

39. Pera M, Manterola C, Vidal O, et al. Epidemiology of esophageal adenocarcinoma. *J Surg Oncol* 2005;92:151-9.

40. Brown LM, Devesa SS. Epidemiologic trends in esophageal and gastric cancer in the United States. *Surg Oncol Clin N Am* 2002;11:235-56.

41. Yang CS. Research on esophageal cancer in China: a review. *Cancer Res* 1980;40:2633-44.

42. Lagergren J, Bergstrom R, Lindgren A, et al. Symptomatic gastroesophageal reflux as a risk factor for esophageal adenocarcinoma. *N Engl J Med* 1999;340:825-31.

43. Cameron AJ. Epidemiology of columnar-lined esophagus and adenocarcinoma. *Gastroenterol Clin North Am* 1997;26:487-94.

44. Cameron AJ, Zinsmeister AR, Ballard DJ, et al. Prevalence of columnar-lined (Barrett's) esophagus. Comparison of population-based clinical and autopsy findings. *Gastroenterology* 1990;99:918-22.

45. Sandler RS, Nyren O, Ekbom A, et al. The risk of esophageal cancer in patients with achalasia. A population-based study. *JAMA* 1995;274:1359-62.

46. Streitz JM, Jr., Ellis FH, Jr., Gibb SP, et al. Achalasia and squamous cell carcinoma of the esophagus: analysis of 241 patients. *Ann Thorac Surg* 1995;59:1604-9.

47. Maillefer RH, Greydanus MP. To B or not to B: is tylosis B truly benign? Two North American genealogies. *Am J Gastroenterol* 1999;94:829-34.

48. Syrjanen KJ. HPV infections and oesophageal cancer. *J Clin Pathol* 2002;55:721-8.

49. Gonzalez CA, Pera G, Agudo A, et al. Fruit and vegetable intake and the risk of stomach and oesophagus adenocarcinoma in the European Prospective Investigation into Cancer and Nutrition (EPIC-EURGAST). *Int J Cancer* 2006;118:2559-66.

50. Yokoyama A, Kato H, Yokoyama T, et al. Esophageal squamous cell carcinoma and aldehyde dehydrogenase-2 genotypes in Japanese females. *Alcohol Clin Exp Res* 2006;30:491-500.

51. Wu M, Zhao JK, Hu XS, et al. Association of smoking, alcohol drinking and dietary factors with esophageal cancer in high-

and low-risk areas of Jiangsu Province, China. *World J Gastroenterol* 2006;12:1686-93.

52. Galeone C, Pelucchi C, Levi F, et al. Folate intake and squamous-cell carcinoma of the oesophagus in Italian and Swiss men. *Ann Oncol* 2006;17:521-5.

53. Veugelers PJ, Porter GA, Guernsey DL, et al. Obesity and lifestyle risk factors for gastroesophageal reflux disease, Barrett esophagus and esophageal adenocarcinoma. *Dis Esophagus* 2006;19:321-8.

54. Gonzalez CA, Jakszyn P, Pera G, et al. Meat intake and risk of stomach and esophageal adenocarcinoma within the European Prospective Investigation Into Cancer and Nutrition (EPIC). *J Natl Cancer Inst* 2006;98:345-54.

55. Goldman R, Shields PG. Food mutagens. *J Nutr* 2003;133 Suppl 3:965S-73S.

56. Ishikawa A, Kuriyama S, Tsubono Y, et al. Smoking, alcohol drinking, green tea consumption and the risk of esophageal cancer in Japanese men. *J Epidemiol* 2006;16:185-92.

57. Wu IC, Lu CY, Kuo FC, et al. Interaction between cigarette, alcohol and betel nut use on esophageal cancer risk in Taiwan. *Eur J Clin Invest* 2006;36:236-41.

58. Samanic C, Chow WH, Gridley G, et al. Relation of body mass index to cancer risk in 362,552 Swedish men. *Cancer Causes Control* 2006;17:901-9.

59. MacInnis RJ, English DR, Hopper JL, et al. Body size and composition and the risk of gastric and oesophageal adenocarcinoma. *Int J Cancer* 2006;118:2628-31.

60. Ryan AM, Rowley SP, Fitzgerald AP, et al. Adenocarcinoma of the oesophagus and gastric cardia: male preponderance in association with obesity. *Eur J Cancer* 2006;42:1151-8.

61. de Jonge PJ, Steyerberg EW, Kuipers EJ, et al. Risk factors for the development of esophageal adenocarcinoma in Barrett's esophagus. *Am J Gastroenterol* 2006;101:1421-9.

62. Bu X, Ma Y, Der R, et al. Body mass index is associated with Barrett esophagus and cardiac mucosal metaplasia. *Dig Dis Sci* 2006;51:1589-94.

63. Proctor RN. Tobacco and the global lung cancer epidemic. *Nature reviews* 2001;1:82-6.

64. Hoffman PC, Mauer AM, Vokes EE. Lung cancer. *Lancet* 2000;355:479-85.

65. Worden FP, Kalemkerian GP. Therapeutic advances in small cell lung cancer. *Expert opinion on investigational drugs* 2000;9:565-79.

66. WHO. The smokers body. http://www.who.int/entity/tobacco/resources/publications/smokersbody_en_fr.pdf. 2006.

67. International Agency for Research on Cancer. 1987. *Overall evaluations of carcinogenicity: An updating of IARC Monographs Volumes 1 to 42.* In: IARC Monogr Eval Carcinog Risks Hum no Supplement 7.

http://monographs.iarc.fr/ENG/Monographs/suppl7/suppl7.pdf.

68. Alexandrov K, Cascorbi I, Rojas M, et al. CYP1A1 and GSTM1 genotypes affect benzo[a]pyrene DNA adducts in smokers' lung: comparison with aromatic/hydrophobic adduct formation. *Carcinogenesis* 2002;23:1969-77.

69. Rylander R, Axelsson G. Lung cancer risks in relation to vegetable and fruit consumption and smoking. *Int J Cancer* 2006;118:739-43.

70. Kang ZC, Tsai SJ, Lee H. Quercetin inhibits benzo[a]pyrene-induced DNA adducts in human Hep G2 cells by altering cytochrome P-450 1A1 gene expression. *Nutrition and cancer* 1999;35:175-9.

71. IARC. 2004. *Some Drinking-water Disinfectants and Contaminants, including Arsenic.* In: IARC Monogr Eval Carcinog Risks Hum no 84. http://monographs.iarc.fr/ENG/Monographs/vol84/volume84.pdf.

72. FAO/WHO. *Summary of Evaluations Performed by the Joint FAO/WHO Expert Committee on Food Additives.* http://jecfa.ilsi.org/. 2006.

73. Liu C, Russell RM, Wang XD. Low dose beta-carotene supplementation of ferrets attenuates smoke-induced lung phosphorylation of JNK, p38 MAPK, and p53 proteins. *J Nutri* 2004;134:2705-10.

74. Goodman GE, Schaffer S, Omenn GS, et al. The association between lung and prostate cancer risk, and serum micronutrients: results and lessons learned from beta-carotene and retinol efficacy trial. *Cancer Epidemiol Biomarkers Prev* 2003;12:518-26.

75. Steindorf K, Friedenreich C, Linseisen J, et al. Physical activity and lung cancer risk in the European Prospective Investigation into Cancer and Nutrition Cohort. *Int J Cancer* 2006;119:2389-97.

76. Lauren PA, Nevalainen TJ. Epidemiology of intestinal and diffuse types of gastric carcinoma. A time-trend study in Finland with comparison between studies from high- and low-risk areas. *Cancer* 1993;71:2926-33.

77. El-Rifai W, Powell SM. Molecular biology of gastric cancer. *Seminars in radiation oncology* 2002;12:128-40.

78. Crew KD, Neugut AI. Epidemiology of gastric cancer. *World journal of gastroenterology* 2006;12:354-62.

79. Coggon D, Barker DJ, Cole RB, et al. Stomach cancer and food storage. *J Natl Cancer Inst* 1989;81:1178-82.

80. La Vecchia C, Negri E, D'Avanzo B, et al. Electric refrigerator use and gastric cancer risk. *Br J Cancer* 1990;62:136-7.

81. Hohenberger P, Gretschel S. Gastric cancer. *Lancet* 2003;362:305-15.

82. Ando T, Goto Y, Maeda O, et al. Causal role of Helicobacter pylori infection in gastric cancer. *World journal of gastroenterology* 2006;12:181-6.

83. Dooley CP, Cohen H, Fitzgibbons PL, et al. Prevalence of Helicobacter pylori infection and histologic gastritis in asymptomatic persons. *The New England journal of medicine* 1989;321:1562-6.

84. Youn HS, Baik SC, Cho YK, et al. Comparison of Helicobacter pylori infection between Fukuoka, Japan and Chinju, Korea. *Helicobacter* 1998;3:9-14.

85. Peterson W, Graham D. H pylori. In: Feldman M, Scharschmidt B, Sleisenger M, editors. *Gastrointestinal and liver disease. Pathophysiology, diagnosis, management.* 6 ed. Philadelphia: WB Saunders, 1998.

86. Correa P, Fontham ET, Bravo JC, et al. Chemoprevention of gastric dysplasia: randomized trial of antioxidant supplements and anti-helicobacter pylori therapy. *J Natl Cancer Inst* 2000;92:1881-8.

87. Leung WK, Lin SR, Ching JY, et al. Factors predicting progression of gastric intestinal metaplasia: results of a randomised trial on Helicobacter pylori eradication. *Gut* 2004;53:1244-9.

88. Ley C, Mohar A, Guarner J, et al. Helicobacter pylori eradication and gastric preneoplastic conditions: a randomized, double-blind, placebo-controlled trial. *Cancer Epidemiol Biomarkers Prev* 2004;13:4-10.

89. Gastric cancer and Helicobacter pylori: a combined analysis of 12 case control studies nested within prospective cohorts. *Gut* 2001;49:347-53.

90. International Agency for Research on Cancer. 1994. *Schistosomes, Liver Flukes and Helicobacter pylori.* In: IARC Monogr Eval Carcinog Risks Hum no 61. http://monographs.iarc.fr/ENG/Monographs/vol61/volume61.pdf.

91. Gallo N, Zambon CF, Navaglia F, et al. Helicobacter pylori infection in children and adults: a single pathogen but a different pathology. *Helicobacter* 2003;8:21-8.

92. Yamaguchi N, Kakizoe T. Synergistic interaction between Helicobacter pylori gastritis and diet in gastric cancer. *The lancet oncology* 2001;2:88-94.

93. La Vecchia C, Negri E, Franceschi S, et al. Family history and the risk of stomach and colorectal cancer. *Cancer* 1992;70:50-5.

94. International Agency for Research on Cancer. 1994. *Some Industrial Chemicals.* In: IARC Monogr Eval Carcinog Risks Hum no 60. http://monographs.iarc.fr/ENG/Monographs/vol60/volume60.pdf.

95. Phukan RK, Narain K, Zomawia E, et al. Dietary habits and stomach cancer in Mizoram, India. *J Gastroenterol* 2006;41:418-24.

96. Campos F, Carrasquilla G, Koriyama C, et al. Risk factors of gastric cancer specific for tumor location and histology in Cali, Colombia. *World J Gastroenterol* 2006;12:5772-9.

97. Fei SJ, Xiao SD. Diet and gastric cancer: a case-control study in Shanghai urban districts. *Chin J Dig Dis* 2006;7:83-8.

98. Larsson SC, Bergkvist L, Wolk A. Processed meat consumption, dietary nitrosamines and stomach cancer risk in a cohort of Swedish women. *Int J Cancer* 2006;119:915-9.

99. Strumylaite L, Zickute J, Dudzevicius J, et al. Salt-preserved foods and risk of gastric cancer. *Medicina (Kaunas)* 2006;42:164-70.

100. Garcia-Falcon MS, Simal-Gandara J. Polycyclic aromatic hydrocarbons in smoke from different woods and their transfer during traditional smoking into chorizo sausages with collagen and tripe casings. *Food additives and contaminants* 2005;22:1-8.

101. Beevers DG, Lip GY, Blann AD. Salt intake and *Helicobacter pylori* infection. *J Hypertens* 2004;22:1475-7.

102. Shikata K, Kiyohara Y, Kubo M, et al. A prospective study of dietary salt intake and gastric cancer incidence in a defined Japanese population: the Hisayama study. *Int J Cancer* 2006;119:196-201.

103. Parkin DM, Whelan SL, Ferlay J, et al., editors. *Cancer Incidence in Five Continents, Volume VIII.* Lyon, France: International Agency for Research on Cancer, 2002.

104. Stewart BW, Kleihues P, editors. *World Cancer Report.* Lyon: International Agency for Research on Cancer, 2003.

105. Zalatnai A. Pancreatic cancer - a continuing challenge in oncology. *Pathology oncology research* 2003;9:252-63.

106. Stolzenberg-Solomon RZ, Graubard BI, Chari S, et al. Insulin, glucose, insulin resistance, and pancreatic cancer in male smokers. *JAMA* 2005;294:2872-8.

107. Li D, Xie K, Wolff R, et al. Pancreatic cancer. *Lancet* 2004;363:1049-57.

108. Larsson SC, Hakansson N, Naslund I, et al. Fruit and vegetable consumption in relation to pancreatic cancer risk: a prospective study. *Cancer Epidemiol Biomarkers Prev* 2006;15:301-5.

109. Larsson SC, Hakansson N, Giovannucci E, et al. Folate intake and pancreatic cancer incidence: a prospective study of Swedish women and men. *J Natl Cancer Inst* 2006;98:407-13.

110. Larsson SC, Hakanson N, Permert J, et al. Meat, fish, poultry and egg consumption in relation to risk of pancreatic cancer: a prospective study. *Int J Cancer* 2006;118:2866-70.

111. Quadrilatero J, Hoffman-Goetz L. Physical activity and colon cancer. A systematic review of potential mechanisms. *J Sports Med Phys Fitness* 2003;43:121-38.

112. Berrington de Gonzalez A, Spencer EA, Bueno-de-Mesquita HB, et al. Anthropometry, physical activity, and the risk of pancreatic cancer in the European prospective investigation into cancer and nutrition. *Cancer Epidemiol Biomarkers Prev* 2006;15:879-85.

113. Lazcano-Ponce EC, Miquel JF, Munoz N, et al. Epidemiology and molecular pathology of gallbladder cancer. *CA Cancer J Clin* 2001;51:349-64.

114. Enzinger PC, Mayer RJ. Gastrointestinal cancer in older patients. *Semin Oncol* 2004;31:206-19.

115. Cottam DR, Mattar SG, Barinas-Mitchell E, et al. The chronic inflammatory hypothesis for the morbidity associated with morbid obesity: implications and effects of weight loss. *Obes Surg* 2004;14:589-600.

116. Diehl AK. Gallstone size and the risk of gallbladder cancer. *JAMA* 1983;250:2323-6.

117. Shaffer EA. Epidemiology and risk factors for gallstone disease: has the paradigm changed in the 21st century? *Curr Gastroenterol Rep* 2005;7:132-40.

118. Misra S, Chaturvedi A, Misra NC, et al. Carcinoma of the gallbladder. *Lancet Oncol* 2003;4:167-76.

119. Wistuba, II, Gazdar AF. Gallbladder cancer: lessons from a rare tumour. *Nat Rev Cancer* 2004;4:695-706.

120. Hu B, Gong B, Zhou DY. Association of anomalous pancreaticobiliary ductal junction with gallbladder carcinoma in Chinese patients: an ERCP study. *Gastrointest Endosc* 2003;57:541-5.

121. Fujii K, Yokozaki H, Yasui W, et al. High frequency of p53 gene mutation in adenocarcinomas of the gallbladder. *Cancer Epidemiol Biomarkers Prev* 1996;5:461-6.

122. Parkin DM, Bray F, Ferlay J, et al. Estimating the world cancer burden: Globocan 2000. *Int J Cancer* 2001;94:153-6.

123. Llovet JM, Burroughs A, Bruix J. Hepatocellular carcinoma. *Lancet* 2003;362:1907-17.

124. Parkin DM, Bray F, Ferlay J, et al. Global cancer statistics, 2002. *CA Cancer J Clin* 2005;55:74-108.

125. Bruix J, Boix L, Sala M, et al. Focus on hepatocellular carcinoma. *Cancer Cell* 2004;5:215-9.

126. Coleman WB. Mechanisms of human hepatocarcinogenesis. *Curr Mol Med* 2003;3:573-88.

127. Buendia MA. Genetics of hepatocellular carcinoma. *Semin Cancer Biol* 2000;10:185-200.

128. Thorgeirsson SS, Grisham JW. Molecular pathogenesis of human hepatocellular carcinoma. *Nat Genet* 2002;31:339-46.

129. Vitaglione P, Morisco F, Caporaso N, et al. Dietary antioxidant compounds and liver health. *Crit Rev Food Sci Nutr* 2004;44:575-86.

130. International Agency for Research on Cancer. 1994. *Hepatitis viruses*. In: IARC Monogr Eval Carcinog Risks Hum no 59.

131. Chang MH, Chen CJ, Lai MS, et al. Universal hepatitis B vaccination in Taiwan and the incidence of hepatocellular carcinoma in children. Taiwan Childhood Hepatoma Study Group. *N Engl J Med* 1997;336:1855-9.

132. Pessione F, Degos F, Marcellin P, et al. Effect of alcohol consumption on serum hepatitis C virus RNA and histological lesions in chronic hepatitis C. *Hepatology* 1998;27:1717-22.

133. International Agency for Research on Cancer. 1999. *Hormonal Contraception and Post-menopausal Hormonal Therapy*. In: IARC Monogr Eval Carcinog Risks Hum no 72. http://monographs.iarc.fr/ENG/Monographs/vol72/volume72.pdf.

134. Talamini R, Polesel J, Montella M, et al. Food groups and risk of hepatocellular carcinoma: A multicenter case-control study in Italy. *Int J Cancer* 2006;119:2916-21.

135. Franceschi S, Montella M, Polesel J, et al. Hepatitis viruses, alcohol, and tobacco in the etiology of hepatocellular carcinoma in Italy. *Cancer Epidemiol Biomarkers Prev* 2006;15:683-9.

136. N'Kontchou G, Paries J, Htar MT, et al. Risk factors for hepatocellular carcinoma in patients with alcoholic or viral C cirrhosis. *Clin Gastroenterol Hepatol* 2006;4:1062-8.

137. Parkin DM, Whelan SL, Ferlay J, et al. *Cancer Incidence in Five Continents, Vol. I to VIII*. Lyon: IARC 2005.

138. Itzkowitz SH, Yio X. Inflammation and cancer IV. Colorectal cancer in inflammatory bowel disease: the role of inflammation. *Am J Physiol Gastrointest Liver Physiol* 2004;287:G7-17.

139. Lynch HT, de la Chapelle A. Hereditary colorectal cancer. *N Engl J Med* 2003;348:919-32.

140. Weitz J, Koch M, Debus J, et al. Colorectal cancer. *Lancet* 2005;365:153-65.

141. Kinzler KW, Vogelstein B. Cancer-susceptibility genes. Gatekeepers and caretakers. *Nature* 1997;386:761, 3.

142. Lynch JP, Hoops TC. The genetic pathogenesis of colorectal cancer. *Hematol Oncol Clin North Am* 2002;16:775-810.

143. Asano TK, McLeod RS. Nonsteroidal anti-inflammatory drugs and aspirin for the prevention of colorectal adenomas and cancer: a systematic review. *Dis Colon Rectum* 2004;47:665-73.

144. Post-menopausal oestrogen therapy. *IARC Monogr Eval Carcinog Risks Hum* 1999;72:399-530

145. Bingham SA, Norat T, Moskal A, et al. Is the association with fiber from foods in colorectal cancer confounded by folate intake? *Cancer Epidemiol Biomarkers Prev* 2005;14:1552-6.

146. MacInnis RJ, English DR, Haydon AM, et al. Body size and composition and risk of rectal cancer (Australia). *Cancer Causes Control* 2006;17:1291-7.

147. Lin J, Zhang SM, Cook NR, et al. Dietary intakes of fruit, vegetables, and fiber, and risk of colorectal cancer in a prospective cohort of women (United States). *Cancer Causes Control* 2005;16:225-33.

148. Shin A, Li H, Shu XO, et al. Dietary intake of calcium, fiber and other micronutrients in relation to colorectal cancer risk: Results from the Shanghai Women's Health Study. *Int J Cancer* 2006;119:2938-42.

149. Otani T, Iwasaki M, Ishihara J, et al. Dietary fiber intake and subsequent risk of colorectal cancer: the Japan Public Health Center-based prospective study. *Int J Cancer* 2006;119:1475-80.

150. Michels KB, Fuchs CS, Giovannucci E, et al. Fiber intake and incidence of colorectal cancer among 76,947 women and 47,279 men. *Cancer Epidemiol Biomarkers Prev* 2005;14:842-9.

151. Bowers K, Albanes D, Limburg P, et al. A prospective study of anthropometric and clinical measurements associated with insulin resistance syndrome and colorectal cancer in male smokers. *Am J Epidemiol* 2006;164:652-64.

152. Wakai K, Hirose K, Matsuo K, et al. Dietary risk factors for colon and rectal cancers: a comparative case-control study. *J Epidemiol* 2006;16:125-35.

153. Sato Y, Tsubono Y, Nakaya N, et al. Fruit and vegetable consumption and risk of colorectal cancer in Japan: The Miyagi Cohort Study. *Public Health Nutr* 2005;8:309-14.

154. Huang XE, Hirose K, Wakai K, et al. Comparison of lifestyle risk factors by family history for gastric, breast, lung and colorectal cancer. *Asian Pac J Cancer Prev* 2004;5:419-27.

155. Tsubono Y, Otani T, Kobayashi M, et al. No association between fruit or vegetable consumption and the risk of colorectal cancer in Japan. *Br J Cancer* 2005;92:1782-4.

156. Turner F, Smith G, Sachse C, et al. Vegetable, fruit and meat consumption and potential risk modifying genes in relation to colorectal cancer. *Int J Cancer* 2004;112:259-64.

157. Juarranz Sanz M, Soriano Llora T, Calle Puron ME, et al. [Influence of the diet on the development of colorectal cancer in a population of Madrid]. *Rev Clin Esp* 2004;204:355-61.

158. Kuriki K, Hamajima N, Chiba H, et al. Increased risk of colorectal cancer due to interactions between meat consumption and the CD36 gene A52C polymorphism among Japanese. *Nutr Cancer* 2005;51:170-7.

159. Jiang Q, Chen K, Ma X, et al. Diets, polymorphisms of methylenetetrahydrofolate reductase, and the susceptibility of colon cancer and rectal cancer. *Cancer Detect Prev* 2005;29:146-54.

160. Zhang SM, Moore SC, Lin J, et al. Folate, vitamin B6, multivitamin supplements, and colorectal cancer risk in women. *Am J Epidemiol* 2006;163:108-15.

161. Brink M, Weijenberg MP, de Goeij AF, et al. Dietary folate intake and k-ras mutations in sporadic colon and rectal cancer in The Netherlands Cohort Study. *Int J Cancer* 2005;114:824-30.

162. Larsson SC, Giovannucci E, Wolk A. A prospective study of dietary folate intake and risk of colorectal cancer: modification by caffeine intake and cigarette smoking. *Cancer Epidemiol Biomarkers Prev* 2005;14:740-3.

163. de Vogel S, van Engeland M, Luchtenborg M, et al. Dietary folate and APC mutations in sporadic colorectal cancer. *J Nutr* 2006;136:3015-21.

164. Otani T, Iwasaki M, Hanaoka T, et al. Folate, vitamin B6, vitamin B12, and vitamin B2 intake, genetic polymorphisms of related enzymes, and risk of colorectal cancer in a hospital-based case-control study in Japan. Nutr Cancer 2005;53:42-50.

165. Larsson SC, Rafter J, Holmberg L, et al. Red meat consumption and risk of cancers of the proximal colon, distal colon and rectum: the Swedish Mammography Cohort. Int J Cancer 2005;113:829-34.

166. Chao A, Thun MJ, Connell CJ, et al. Meat consumption and risk of colorectal cancer. JAMA 2005;293:172-82.

167. Lin J, Zhang SM, Cook NR, et al. Dietary fat and fatty acids and risk of colorectal cancer in women. Am J Epidemiol 2004;160:1011-22.

168. Norat T, Bingham S, Ferrari P, et al. Meat, fish, and colorectal cancer risk: the European Prospective Investigation into cancer and nutrition. J Natl Cancer Inst 2005;97:906-16.

169. English DR, MacInnis RJ, Hodge AM, et al. Red meat, chicken, and fish consumption and risk of colorectal cancer. Cancer Epidemiol Biomarkers Prev 2004;13:1509-14.

170. Chan AT, Tranah GJ, Giovannucci EL, et al. Prospective study of N-acetyltransferase-2 genotypes, meat intake, smoking and risk of colorectal cancer. Int J Cancer 2005;115:648-52.

171. Brink M, Weijenberg MP, de Goeij AF, et al. Meat consumption and K-ras mutations in sporadic colon and rectal cancer in The Netherlands Cohort Study. Br J Cancer 2005;92:1310-20.

172. Sato Y, Nakaya N, Kuriyama S, et al. Meat consumption and risk of colorectal cancer in Japan: the Miyagi Cohort Study. Eur J Cancer Prev 2006;15:211-8.

173. Oba S, Shimizu N, Nagata C, et al. The relationship between the consumption of meat, fat, and coffee and the risk of colon cancer: a prospective study in Japan. Cancer Lett 2006;244:260-7.

174. Butler LM, Duguay Y, Millikan RC, et al. Joint effects between UDP-glucuronosyltransferase 1A7 genotype and dietary carcinogen exposure on risk of colon cancer. Cancer Epidemiol Biomarkers Prev 2005;14:1626-32.

175. Balder HF, Vogel J, Jansen MC, et al. Heme and chlorophyll intake and risk of colorectal cancer in the Netherlands cohort study. Cancer Epidemiol Biomarkers Prev 2006;15:717-25.

176. Rao CV, Hirose Y, Indranie C, et al. Modulation of experimental colon tumorigenesis by types and amounts of dietary fatty acids. Cancer Res 2001;61:1927-33.

177. MacLean CH, Newberry SJ, Mojica WA, et al. Effects of omega-3 fatty acids on cancer risk: a systematic review. JAMA 2006;295:403-15.

178. Siezen CL, Bueno-de-Mesquita HB, Peeters PH, et al. Polymorphisms in the genes involved in the arachidonic acid-pathway, fish consumption and the risk of colorectal cancer. Int J Cancer 2006;119:297-303.

179. Slattery ML, Neuhausen SL, Hoffman M, et al. Dietary calcium, vitamin D, VDR genotypes and colorectal cancer. Int J Cancer 2004;111:750-6.

180. Sesink AL, Termont DS, Kleibeuker JH, et al. Red meat and colon cancer: the cytotoxic and hyperproliferative effects of dietary heme. Cancer Res 1999;59:5704-9.

181. Huang X. Iron overload and its association with cancer risk in humans: evidence for iron as a carcinogenic metal. Mutation research 2003;533:153-71.

182. Chan AT, Ma J, Tranah GJ, et al. Hemochromatosis gene mutations, body iron stores, dietary iron, and risk of colorectal adenoma in women. J Natl Cancer Inst 2005;97:917-26.

183. Cho E, Smith-Warner SA, Spiegelman D, et al. Dairy foods, calcium, and colorectal cancer: a pooled analysis of 10 cohort studies. J Natl Cancer Inst 2004;96:1015-22.

184. Lamprecht SA, Lipkin M. Cellular mechanisms of calcium and vitamin D in the inhibition of colorectal carcinogenesis. Ann N Y Acad Sci 2001;952:73-87.

185. Lin J, Zhang SM, Cook NR, et al. Intakes of calcium and vitamin D and risk of colorectal cancer in women. Am J Epidemiol 2005;161:755-64.

186. Larsson SC, Bergkvist L, Rutegard J, et al. Calcium and dairy food intakes are inversely associated with colorectal cancer risk in the Cohort of Swedish Men. Am J Clin Nutr 2006;83:667-73; quiz 728-9.

187. Larsson SC, Bergkvist L, Wolk A. High-fat dairy food and conjugated linoleic acid intakes in relation to colorectal cancer incidence in the Swedish Mammography Cohort. Am J Clin Nutr 2005;82:894-900.

188. Kesse E, Boutron-Ruault MC, Norat T, et al. Dietary calcium, phosphorus, vitamin D, dairy products and the risk of colorectal adenoma and cancer among French women of the E3N-EPIC prospective study. Int J Cancer 2005;117:137-44.

189. Gallus S, Bravi F, Talamini R, et al. Milk, dairy products and cancer risk (Italy). Cancer Causes Control 2006;17:429-37.

190. Department of Health 1998. Nutritional Aspects of the Development of Cancer. Report of the Working Group on Diet and Cancer of the Committee on Medical Aspects of Food and Nutrition Policy. In: Report on Health and Social Subjects no 48.

191. Cho E, Smith-Warner SA, Ritz J, et al. Alcohol intake and colorectal cancer: a pooled analysis of 8 cohort studies. Annals of internal medicine 2004;140:603-13.

192. Jin MJ, Chen K, Song L, et al. The association of the DNA repair gene XRCC3 Thr241Met polymorphism with susceptibility to colorectal cancer in a Chinese population. Cancer Genet Cytogenet 2005;163:38-43.

193. Wakai K, Kojima M, Tamakoshi K, et al. Alcohol consumption and colorectal cancer risk: findings from the JACC Study. J Epidemiol 2005;15 Suppl 2:S173-9.

194. Chen K, Jiang Q, Ma X, et al. Alcohol drinking and colorectal cancer: a population-based prospective cohort study in China. Eur J Epidemiol 2005;20:149-54.

195. Kim DH, Ahn YO, Lee BH, et al. Methylenetetrahydrofolate reductase polymorphism, alcohol intake, and risks of colon and rectal cancers in Korea. Cancer Lett 2004;216:199-205.

196. Hong YC, Lee KH, Kim WC, et al. Polymorphisms of XRCC1 gene, alcohol consumption and colorectal cancer. Int J Cancer 2005;116:428-32.

197. Diergaarde B, Tiemersma EW, Braam H, et al. Dietary factors and truncating APC mutations in sporadic colorectal adenomas. Int J Cancer 2005;113:126-32.

198. Chao A, Connell CJ, Jacobs EJ, et al. Amount, type, and timing of recreational physical activity in relation to colon and rectal cancer in older adults: the Cancer Prevention Study II Nutrition Cohort. Cancer Epidemiol Biomarkers Prev 2004;13:2187-95.

199. Friedenreich C, Norat T, Steindorf K, et al. Physical activity and risk of colon and rectal cancers: the European prospective investigation into cancer and nutrition. Cancer Epidemiol Biomarkers Prev 2006;15:2398-407.

200. Schnohr P, Gronbaek M, Petersen L, et al. Physical activity in leisure-time and risk of cancer: 14-year follow-up of 28,000 Danish men and women. Scand J Public Health 2005;33:244-9.

201. Calton BA, Lacey JV, Jr., Schatzkin A, et al. Physical activity and the risk of colon cancer among women: a prospective cohort study (United States). Int J Cancer 2006;119:385-91.

202. Steindorf K, Jedrychowski W, Schmidt M, et al. Case-control study of lifetime occupational and recreational physical activity and risks of colon and rectal cancer. Eur J Cancer Prev 2005;14:363-71.

203. Hou L, Ji BT, Blair A, et al. Commuting physical activity and risk of colon cancer in Shanghai, China. Am J Epidemiol 2004;160:860-7.

204. Zhang Y, Cantor KP, Dosemeci M, et al. Occupational and leisure-time physical activity and risk of colon cancer by subsite. J Occup Environ Med 2006;48:236-43.

205. Ahmed RL, Schmitz KH, Anderson KE, et al. The metabolic syndrome and risk of incident colorectal cancer. Cancer 2006;107:28-36.

206. Otani T, Iwasaki M, Inoue M. Body mass index, body height, and subsequent risk of colorectal cancer in middle-aged and elderly Japanese men and women: Japan public health center-based prospective study. Cancer Causes Control

2005;16:839-50.

207. Engeland A, Tretli S, Austad G, et al. Height and body mass index in relation to colorectal and gallbladder cancer in two million Norwegian men and women. *Cancer Causes Control* 2005;16:987-96.

208. Rapp K, Schroeder J, Klenk J, et al. Obesity and incidence of cancer: a large cohort study of over 145,000 adults in Austria. *Br J Cancer* 2005;93:1062-7.

209. Pischon T, Lahmann PH, Boeing H, et al. Body size and risk of colon and rectal cancer in the European Prospective Investigation Into Cancer and Nutrition (EPIC). *J Natl Cancer Inst* 2006;98:920-31.

210. Lin J, Zhang SM, Cook NR, et al. Body mass index and risk of colorectal cancer in women (United States). *Cancer Causes Control* 2004;15:581-9.

211. Eichholzer M, Bernasconi F, Jordan P, et al. Body mass index and the risk of male cancer mortality of various sites: 17-year follow-up of the Basel cohort study. *Swiss Med Wkly* 2005;135:27-33.

212. Kuriyama S, Tsubono Y, Hozawa A, et al. Obesity and risk of cancer in Japan. *Int J Cancer* 2005;113:148-57.

213. Lukanova A, Bjor O, Kaaks R, et al. Body mass index and cancer: results from the Northern Sweden Health and Disease Cohort. *Int J Cancer* 2006;118:458-66.

214. Oh SW, Yoon YS, Shin SA. Effects of excess weight on cancer incidences depending on cancer sites and histologic findings among men: Korea National Health Insurance Corporation Study. *J Clin Oncol* 2005;23:4742-54.

215. Sherman ME, Lacey JV, Buys SS, et al. Ovarian volume: determinants and associations with cancer among postmenopausal women. *Cancer Epidemiol Biomarkers Prev* 2006;15:1550-4.

216. Hou L, Ji BT, Blair A, et al. Body mass index and colon cancer risk in Chinese people: menopause as an effect modifier. *Eur J Cancer* 2006;42:84-90.

217. International Agency for Research on Cancer. Arsenic in drinking water. *IARC Monogr Eval Carcinog Risks Hum* 2004;84.

218. Chung YW, Han DS, Park YK, et al. Association of obesity, serum glucose and lipids with the risk of advanced colorectal adenoma and cancer: a case-control study in Korea. *Dig Liver Dis* 2006;38:668-72.

219. Sainsbury JR, Anderson TJ, Morgan DA. ABC of breast diseases: breast cancer. *BMJ* 2000;321:745-50.

220. McPherson K, Steel CM, Dixon JM. ABC of breast diseases. Breast cancer-epidemiology, risk factors, and genetics. *BMJ* 2000;321:624-8.

221. Ries L, Eisner M, Kosary C, et al., editors. *SEER Cancer Statistics Review, 1975-2002.* Bethesda, MD: National Cancer Institute, 2005.

222. MacMahon B. General Motors Cancer Research Prizewinners Laureates Lectures. Charles S. Mott Prize.

223. Reproduction and cancer of the breast. *Cancer* 1993;71:3185-8.

223. Lippman ME, Dickson RB, Gelmann EP, et al. Growth regulation of human breast carcinoma occurs through regulated growth factor secretion. *J Cell Biochem* 1987;35:1-16.

224. Murray PA, Barrett-Lee P, Travers M, et al. The prognostic significance of transforming growth factors in human breast cancer. *Br J Cancer* 1993;67:1408-12.

225. Anderson DE, Badzioch MD. Familial breast cancer risks. Effects of prostate and other cancers. *Cancer* 1993;72:114-9.

226. Blackwood MA, Weber BL. BRCA1 and BRCA2: from molecular genetics to clinical medicine. *J Clin Oncol* 1998;16:1969-77.

227. Modan B, Chetrit A, Alfandary E, et al. Increased risk of breast cancer after low-dose irradiation. *Lancet* 1989;1:629-31.

228. Hamajima N, Hirose K, Tajima K, et al. Alcohol, tobacco and breast cancer—collaborative reanalysis of individual data from 53 epidemiological studies, including 58,515 women with breast cancer and 95,067 women without the disease. *Br J Cancer* 2002;87:1234-45.

229. Smith-Warner SA, Spiegelman D, Yaun SS, et al. Alcohol and breast cancer in women: a pooled analysis of cohort studies. *JAMA* 1998;279:535-40.

230. Boffetta P, Hashibe M. Alcohol and cancer. *The Lancet Oncology* 2006;7:149-56.

231. Li CI, Daling JR, Malone KE, et al. Relationship between established breast cancer risk factors and risk of seven different histologic types of invasive breast cancer. *Cancer Epidemiol Biomarkers Prev* 2006;15:946-54.

232. Adams SA, Matthews CE, Hebert JR, et al. Association of physical activity with hormone receptor status: the Shanghai Breast Cancer Study. *Cancer Epidemiol Biomarkers Prev* 2006;15:1170-8.

233. Key TJ, Appleby PN, Reeves GK, et al. Body mass index, serum sex hormones, and breast cancer risk in postmenopausal women. *J Natl Cancer Inst* 2003;95:1218-26.

234. van den Brandt PA, Spiegelman D, Yaun SS, et al. Pooled analysis of prospective cohort studies on height, weight, and breast cancer risk. *Am J Epidemiol* 2000;152:514-27.

235. Key T, Appleby P, Barnes I, et al. Endogenous sex hormones and breast cancer in postmenopausal women: reanalysis of nine prospective studies. *J Natl Cancer Inst* 2002;94:606-16.

236. Campagnoli C, Abba C, Ambroggio S, et al. Pregnancy, progesterone and progestins in relation to breast cancer risk. *The Journal of steroid biochemistry and molecular biology* 2005;97:441-50.

237. Hilakivi-Clarke L, Forsen T, Eriksson JG, et al. Tallness and overweight during childhood have opposing effects on breast cancer risk. *Br J Cancer* 2001;85:1680-4.

238. Pasquali R, Pelusi C, Genghini S, et al. Obesity and reproductive disorders in women. *Human reproduction update* 2003;9:359-72.

239. Michels KB, Giovannucci E, Chan AT, et al. Fruit and vegetable consumption and colorectal adenomas in the Nurses' Health Study. *Cancer Res* 2006;66:3942-53.

240. Garcia-Closas M, Brinton LA, Lissowska J, et al. Established breast cancer risk factors by clinically important tumour characteristics. *Br J Cancer* 2006;95:123-9.

241. Baer HJ, Rich-Edwards JW, Colditz GA, et al. Adult height, age at attained height, and incidence of breast cancer in premenopausal women. *Int J Cancer* 2006;119:2231-5.

242. Innes K, Byers T, Schymura M. Birth characteristics and subsequent risk for breast cancer in very young women. *Am J Epidemiol* 2000;152:1121-8.

243. Hilakivi-Clarke L. Mechanisms by which high maternal fat intake during pregnancy increases breast cancer risk in female rodent offspring. *Breast Cancer Res Treat* 1997;46:199-214.

244. Barba M, McCann SE, Nie J, et al. Perinatal exposures and breast cancer risk in the Western New York Exposures and Breast Cancer (WEB) Study. *Cancer Causes Control* 2006;17:395-401.

245. Smith-Warner SA, Spiegelman D, Adami HO, et al. Types of dietary fat and breast cancer: a pooled analysis of cohort studies. *Int J Cancer* 2001;92:767-74.

246. Kaaks R, Berrino F, Key T, et al. Serum sex steroids in premenopausal women and breast cancer risk within the European Prospective Investigation into Cancer and Nutrition (EPIC). *J Natl Cancer Inst* 2005;97:755-65.

247. Wu AH, Pike MC, Stram DO. Meta-analysis: dietary fat intake, serum estrogen levels, and the risk of breast cancer. *J Natl Cancer Inst* 1999;91:529-34.

248. Tamakoshi K, Kondo T, Yatsuya H, et al. Trends in the mortality (1950-1997) and incidence (1975-1993) of malignant ovarian neoplasm among Japanese women: analyses by age, time, and birth cohort. *Gynecol Oncol* 2001;83:64-71.

249. Chaitchik S, Ron IG, Baram A, et al. Population differences in ovarian cancer in Israel. *Gynecol Oncol* 1985;21:155-60.

250. Bell DA. Origins and molecular pathology of ovarian cancer. *Mod Pathol* 2005;18 Suppl 2:S19-32.

251. Jordan SJ, Webb PM, Green AC. Height, age at menarche, and risk of epithelial ovarian cancer. *Cancer Epidemiol Biomarkers Prev* 2005;14:2045-8.

252. Riman T, Nilsson S, Persson IR. Review of epidemiological evidence for reproductive and hormonal factors in relation to the risk of epithelial ovarian malignancies. *Acta obstetricia et gynecologica Scandinavica* 2004;83:783-95.

253. Brekelmans CT. Risk factors and risk reduction of breast and ovarian cancer.

Curr Opin Obstet Gynecol 2003;15:63-8.

254. Koushik A, Hunter DJ, Spiegelman D, et al. Fruits and vegetables and ovarian cancer risk in a pooled analysis of 12 cohort studies. *Cancer Epidemiol Biomarkers Prev* 2005;14:2160-7.

255. Lacey JV, Jr., Leitzmann M, Brinton LA, et al. Weight, height, and body mass index and risk for ovarian cancer in a cohort study. *Ann Epidemiol* 2006;16:869-76.

256. Peterson NB, Trentham-Dietz A, Newcomb PA, et al. Relation of anthropometric measurements to ovarian cancer risk in a population-based case-control study (United States). *Cancer Causes Control* 2006;17:459-67.

257. Huusom LD, Frederiksen K, Hogdall EV, et al. Association of reproductive factors, oral contraceptive use and selected lifestyle factors with the risk of ovarian borderline tumors: a Danish case-control study. *Cancer Causes Control* 2006;17:821-9.

258. Hicks ML, Phillips JL, Parham G, et al. The National Cancer Data Base report on endometrial carcinoma in African-American women. *Cancer* 1998;83:2629-37.

259. Pecorelli S. *23rd FIGO Annual Report on the Results of Treatment in Gynaecological Cancer*: Martin Dunitz, 1998.

260. Amant F, Moerman P, Neven P, et al. Endometrial cancer. *Lancet* 2005;366:491-505.

261. Hardiman P, Pillay OC, Atiomo W. Polycystic ovary syndrome and endometrial carcinoma. *Lancet* 2003;361:1810-2.

262. Lochen ML, Lund E. Childbearing and mortality from cancer of the corpus uteri. *Acta obstetricia et gynecologica Scandinavica* 1997;76:373-7.

263. Xu WH, Dai Q, Xiang YB, et al. Animal food intake and cooking methods in relation to endometrial cancer risk in Shanghai. *Br J Cancer* 2006;95:1586-92.

264. Iatrakis G, Zervoudis S, Saviolakis A, et al. Women younger than 50 years with endometrial cancer. *Eur J Gynaecol Oncol* 2006;27:399-400.

265. Waggoner SE. Cervical cancer. *Lancet* 2003;361:2217-25.

266. Schorge JO, Knowles LM, Lea JS. Adenocarcinoma of the cervix. *Curr Treat Options Oncol* 2004;5:119-27.

267. Holcomb K, Runowicz CD. Cervical cancer screening. *Surg Oncol Clin N Am* 2005;14:777-97.

268. Garcia-Closas R, Castellsague X, Bosch X, et al. The role of diet and nutrition in cervical carcinogenesis: a review of recent evidence. *Int J Cancer* 2005;117:629-37.

269. Melikian AA, Sun P, Prokopczyk B, et al. Identification of benzo[a]pyrene metabolites in cervical mucus and DNA adducts in cervical tissues in humans by gas chromatography-mass spectrometry. *Cancer Lett* 1999;146:127-34.

270. Piyathilake CJ, Henao OL, Macaluso M, et al. Folate is associated with the natural

history of high-risk human papillomaviruses. *Cancer Res* 2004;64:8788-93.

271. Romney SL, Ho GY, Palan PR, et al. Effects of beta-carotene and other factors on outcome of cervical dysplasia and human papillomavirus infection. *Gynecol Oncol* 1997;65:483-92.

272. Piyathilake CJ, Macaluso M, Brill I, et al. Lower red blood cell folate enhances the HPV-16-associated risk of cervical intraepithelial neoplasia. *Nutrition (Burbank, Los Angeles County, Calif* 2007;23:203-10.

273. IARC. *Human Papillomaviruses*: IARC, In preparation.

274. Stanley M. HPV and pathogenesis of cervical cancer. 2006.

275. International Agency for Research on Cancer. 1998. *General conclusions on sex hormones*. In: IARC Monogr Eval Carcinog Risks Hum no 21. http://monographs.iarc.fr/ENG/Monographs/vol21/volume21.pdf

276. Giuliano AR, Papenfuss M, Nour M, et al. Antioxidant nutrients: associations with persistent human papillomavirus infection. *Cancer Epidemiol Biomarkers Prev* 1997;6:917-23.

277. Oliver SE, May MT, Gunnell D. International trends in prostate-cancer mortality in the "PSA ERA". *Int J Cancer* 2001;92:893-8.

278. Gronberg H. Prostate cancer epidemiology. *Lancet* 2003;361:859-64.

279. Frankel S, Smith GD, Donovan J, et al. Screening for prostate cancer. *Lancet* 2003;361:1122-8.

280. Etzioni R, Penson DF, Legler JM, et al. Overdiagnosis due to prostate-specific antigen screening: lessons from U.S. prostate cancer incidence trends. *J Natl Cancer Inst* 2002;94:981-90.

281. Loman N, Bladstrom A, Johannsson O, et al. Cancer incidence in relatives of a population-based set of cases of early-onset breast cancer with a known BRCA1 and BRCA2 mutation status. *Breast Cancer Res* 2003;5:R175-86.

282. Kirchhoff T, Satagopan JM, Kauff ND, et al. Frequency of BRCA1 and BRCA2 mutations in unselected Ashkenazi Jewish patients with colorectal cancer. *J Natl Cancer Inst* 2004;96:68-70.

283. Chan JM, Stampfer MJ, Giovannucci E, et al. Plasma insulin-like growth factor-I and prostate cancer risk: a prospective study. *Science* 1998;279:563-6.

284. Cunha GR, Hayward SW, Wang YZ, et al. Role of the stromal microenvironment in carcinogenesis of the prostate. *Int J Cancer* 2003;107:1-10.

285. Rodriguez C, McCullough ML, Mondul AM, et al. Meat consumption among Black and White men and risk of prostate cancer in the Cancer Prevention Study II Nutrition Cohort. *Cancer Epidemiol Biomarkers Prev* 2006;15:211-6.

286. Wu K, Hu FB, Willett WC, et al. Dietary patterns and risk of prostate cancer in U.S. men. *Cancer Epidemiol Biomarkers*

Prev 2006;15:167-71.

287. Rodriguez C, McCullough ML, Mondul AM, et al. Calcium, dairy products, and risk of prostate cancer in a prospective cohort of United States men. *Cancer Epidemiol Biomarkers Prev* 2003;12:597-603.

288. Lokeshwar BL, Schwartz GG, Selzer MG, et al. Inhibition of prostate cancer metastasis in vivo: a comparison of 1,23-dihydroxyvitamin D (calcitriol) and EB1089. *Cancer Epidemiol Biomarkers Prev* 1999;8:241-8.

289. Morris JK, George LM, Wu T, et al. Insulin-like growth factors and cancer: no role in screening. Evidence from the BUPA study and meta-analysis of prospective epidemiological studies. *Br J Cancer* 2006;95:112-7.

290. Kesse E, Bertrais S, Astorg P, et al. Dairy products, calcium and phosphorus intake, and the risk of prostate cancer: results of the French prospective SU.VI.MAX (Supplementation en Vitamines et Mineraux Antioxydants) study. *Br J Nutr* 2006;95:539-45.

291. Giovannucci E, Liu Y, Stampfer MJ, et al. A prospective study of calcium intake and incident and fatal prostate cancer. *Cancer Epidemiol Biomarkers Prev* 2006;15:203-10.

292. Kirsh VA, Mayne ST, Peters U, et al. A prospective study of lycopene and tomato product intake and risk of prostate cancer. *Cancer Epidemiol Biomarkers Prev* 2006;15:92-8.

293. Stram DO, Hankin JH, Wilkens LR, et al. Prostate cancer incidence and intake of fruits, vegetables and related micronutrients: the multiethnic cohort study (United States). *Cancer Causes Control* 2006;17:1193-207.

294. Goodman M, Bostick RM, Ward KC, et al. Lycopene intake and prostate cancer risk: effect modification by plasma antioxidants and the XRCC1 genotype. *Nutr Cancer* 2006;55:13-20.

295. Kirsh VA, Hayes RB, Mayne ST, et al. Supplemental and dietary vitamin E, beta-carotene, and vitamin C intakes and prostate cancer risk. *J Natl Cancer Inst* 2006;98:245-54.

296. Cohen HT, McGovern FJ. Renal-cell carcinoma. *N Engl J Med* 2005;353:2477-90.

297. Kim WY, Kaelin WG. Role of VHL gene mutation in human cancer. *J Clin Oncol* 2004;22:4991-5004.

298. McLaughlin JK, Blot W, Devesa S. Renal cancer. In: Schottenfeld D, Fraumeni JJ, editors. *Cancer Epidemiology and Prevention*. 2nd ed. New York: Oxford University Press, 1996.

299. International Agency for Research on Cancer. 1987. *Phenacetin and analgesic mixtures containing phenacetin*. In: IARC Monogr Eval Carcinog Risks Hum.

300. MacDougall ML, Welling LW, Wiegmann TB. Renal adenocarcinoma and acquired cystic disease in chronic hemodialysis patients. *Am J Kidney Dis* 1987;9:166-71.

301. Bisceglia M, Galliani CA, Senger C, et al.

Renal cystic diseases: a review. *Adv Anat Pathol* 2006;13:26-56.

302. Lee JE, Giovannucci E, Smith-Warner SA, et al. Total fluid intake and use of individual beverages and risk of renal cell cancer in two large cohorts. *Cancer Epidemiol Biomarkers Prev* 2006;15:1204-11.

303. Takahashi Y, Okimura Y, Mizuno I, et al. Leptin induces tyrosine phosphorylation of cellular proteins including STAT-1 in human renal adenocarcinoma cells, ACHN. *Biochem Biophys Res Commun* 1996;228:859-64.

304. Jones SC, Saunders HJ, Qi W, et al. Intermittent high glucose enhances cell growth and collagen synthesis in cultured human tubulointerstitial cells. *Diabetologia* 1999;42:1113-9.

305. Pischon T, Lahmann PH, Boeing H, et al. Body size and risk of renal cell carcinoma in the European Prospective Investigation into Cancer and Nutrition (EPIC). *Int J Cancer* 2006;118:728-38.

306. Chiu BC, Gapstur SM, Chow WH, et al. Body mass index, physical activity, and risk of renal cell carcinoma. *Int J Obes (Lond)* 2006;30:940-7.

307. Tawfik HN. Carcinoma of the urinary bladder associated with schistosomiasis in Egypt: the possible causal relationship. *Princess Takamatsu Symp* 1987;18:197-209.

308. Droller MJ. Biological considerations in the assessment of urothelial cancer: a retrospective. *Urology* 2005;66:66-75.

309. Garcia-Closas M, Malats N, Silverman D, et al. NAT2 slow acetylation, GSTM1 null genotype, and risk of bladder cancer: results from the Spanish Bladder Cancer Study and meta-analyses. *Lancet* 2005;366:649-59.

310. Brennan P, Bogillot O, Cordier S, et al. Cigarette smoking and bladder cancer in men: a pooled analysis of 11 case-control studies. *Int J Cancer* 2000;86:289-94.

311. Infection with schistosomes (Schistosoma haematobium, Schistosoma mansoni and Schistosoma japonicum). *IARC Monogr Eval Carcinog Risks Hum* 1994;61:45-119.

312. Pisani P, Parkin DM, Munoz N, et al. Cancer and infection: estimates of the attributable fraction in 1990. *Cancer Epidemiol Biomarkers Prev* 1997;6:387-400.

313. IARC. 1987. *2-naphthylamine*. In: IARC Monogr Eval Carcinog Risks Hum no 7.

314. Geller AC, Annas GD. Epidemiology of melanoma and nonmelanoma skin cancer. *Semin Oncol Nurs* 2003;19:2-11.

315. Marks R. Epidemiology of non-melanoma skin cancer and solar keratoses in Australia: a tale of self-immolation in Elysian fields. *Australas J Dermatol* 997;38 Suppl 1:S26-9.

316. Woodhead AD, Setlow RB, Tanaka M. Environmental factors in nonmelanoma and melanoma skin cancer. *Journal Epidemiol/Japan Epidemiological Association* 1999;9:S102-14.

317. Thompson JF, Scolyer RA, Kefford RF. Cutaneous melanoma. *Lancet* 2005;365:687-701.

318. Abdulla FR, Feldman SR, Williford PM, et al. Tanning and skin cancer. *Pediatric dermatology* 2005;22:501-12.

319. Corona R. Epidemiology of nonmelanoma skin cancer: a review. *Annali dell'Istituto superiore di sanita* 1996;32:37-42.

320. Bliss JM, Ford D, Swerdlow AJ, et al. Risk of cutaneous melanoma associated with pigmentation characteristics and freckling: systematic overview of 10 case-control studies. The International Melanoma Analysis Group (IMAGE). *Int J Cancer* 1995;62:367-76.

321. Marrett LD, King WD, Walter SD, et al. Use of host factors to identify people at high risk for cutaneous malignant melanoma. *Cmaj* 1992;147:445-53.

322. Clydesdale GJ, Dandie GW, Muller HK. Ultraviolet light induced injury: immunological and inflammatory effects. *Immunol Cell Biol* 2001;79:547-68.

323. Goldstein AM, Tucker MA. Genetic epidemiology of cutaneous melanoma: a global perspective. *Arch Dermatol* 2001;137:1493-6.

324. International Agency for Research on Cancer. 1992. *Solar and Ultraviolet Radiation*. In: IARC Monogr Eval Carcinog Risks Hum no 55. http://monographs.iarc.fr/ENG/Monographs/vol55/volume55.pdf.

325. Saladi RN, Persaud AN. The causes of skin cancer: a comprehensive review. *Drugs Today (Barc)* 2005;41:37-53.

326. Levine N, Meyskens FL. Topical vitamin-A-acid therapy for cutaneous metastatic melanoma. *Lancet* 1980;2:224-6.

327. Le Marchand L, Saltzman BS, Hankin JH, et al. Sun exposure, diet, and melanoma in Hawaii Caucasians. *Am J Epidemiol* 2006;164:232-45.

328. International Agency for Research on Cancer. 2000. *Ionizing Radiation, Part 1: X- and Gamma (g)-Radiation, and Neutrons*. In: IARC Monogr Eval Carcinog Risks Hum no 75. http://monographs.iarc.fr/ENG/Monographs/vol75/volume75.pdf.

329. Epstein MA. Historical background; Burkitt's lymphoma and Epstein-Barr virus. *IARC Sci Publ* 1985:17-27.

330. Carneiro-Proietti AB, Catalan-Soares BC, Castro-Costa CM, et al. HTLV in the Americas: challenges and perspectives. *Rev Panam Salud Publica* 2006;19:44-53.

331. IARC. 1996. *Human Immunodeficiency Viruses and Human T-Cell Lymphotropic Viruses*. no 67. http://monographs.iarc.fr/ENG/Monographs/vol67/volume67.pdf.

Chapter 8

1. World Health Organization. 2000. *Obesity: Preventing and Managing the Global Epidemic*. In: Technical Report Series no 894. http://whqlibdoc.who.int/trs/WHO_TRS_894.pdf.

2. Cummings JH, Roberfroid MB, Andersson H, et al. A new look at dietary carbohydrate: chemistry, physiology and health. Paris Carbohydrate Group. *Eur J Clin Nutr* 1997;51:417-23.

3. Erlanson-Albertsson C. How palatable food disrupts appetite regulation. *Basic Clin Pharmacol Toxicol* 2005;97:61-73.

4. Prentice AM, Jebb SA. Fast foods, energy density and obesity: a possible mechanistic link. *Obes Rev* 2003;4:187-94.

5. World Cancer Research Fund/American Institute for Cancer Research. *Food, Nutrition and the Prevention of Cancer: a Global Perspective*. Washington, DC: AICR, 1997.

6. World Health Organization. *Obesity and overweight. Fact sheet no 311*. http://www.who.int/mediacentre/factsheets/fs311/en/. 2006.

7. World Cancer Research Fund/American Institute for Cancer Research. *Policy and Action for Cancer Prevention. Food, Nutrition, and Physical Activity: a Global Perspective*, In press.

8. Deurenberg P, Weststrate JA, Seidell JC. Body mass index as a measure of body fatness: age- and sex-specific prediction formulas. *Br J Nutr* 1991;65:105-14.

9. World Health Organization. *BMI classification* http://www.who.int/bmi/index.jsp?introPage=intro_3.html. 2007.

10. Fogel R. *The Escape from Hunger and Premature Death, 1700 - 2100. Europe, America and the Third World*. Cambridge: Cambridge University Press, 2004.

11. Stubbs RJ, Tolkamp BJ. Control of energy balance in relation to energy intake and energy expenditure in animals and man: an ecological perspective. *Br J Nutr* 2006;95:657-76.

12. Dulloo AG, Jacquet J, Seydoux J, et al. The thrifty 'catch-up fat' phenotype: its impact on insulin sensitivity during growth trajectories to obesity and metabolic syndrome. *Int J Obes (Lond)* 2006;30 Suppl 4:S23-35.

13. United Nations Children's Fund (UNICEF). 2006. *The State of the World's Children 2006: Excluded and Invisible*. http://www.unicef.org/publications/files/SOWC_2006_English_Report_rev(1).pdf.

14. Commission on the Nutrition Challenges of the 21st Century. 2000. *Ending Malnutrition by 2020: An Agenda for Change in the Millennium*. http://www.unsystem.org/scn/Publications/UN_Report.PDF.

15. Popkin BM. The nutrition transition in low-income countries: an emerging crisis. *Nutr Rev* 1994;52:285-98.

16. Popkin BM, Conde W, Hou N, et al. Is there

a lag globally in overweight trends for children compared with adults? *Obesity (Silver Spring)* 2006;14:1846-53.

17. Garrow J. *Take Obesity Seriously. A Clinical Manual*. Edinburgh: Churchill Livingstone, 1981.

18. Department of Health (England)/ Medical Research Council. 1976. *Research on Obesity*.

19. Popkin BM. Technology, transport globalization and the nutrition transition. *Food Policy* 2006;31:554-69.

20. Swinburn BA, Caterson I, Seidell JC, et al. Diet, nutrition and the prevention of excess weight gain and obesity. *Public Health Nutr* 2004;7:123-46.

21. Seidell JC. Epidemiology of obesity. *Semin Vasc Med* 2005;5:3-14.

22. Peeters A, Barendregt JJ, Willekens F, et al. Obesity in adulthood and its consequences for life expectancy: a life-table analysis. *Ann Intern Med* 2003;138:24-32.

23. Department of Health (England). 2004. *Choosing Health: Making Healthy Choices Easier*. http://www.dh.gov.uk/assetRoot/04/09/47/55/04094755.pdf.

24. World Health Organization. 2002. *Diet, Nutrition and the Prevention of Chronic Diseases: Report of a Joint WHO/FAO Expert Consultation*. In: Technical Report Series no 916. http://www.who.int/entity/dietphysicalactivity/publications/trs916/download/en/index.html.

25. World Health Organization. *Obesity and overweight. Fact sheet no 311*. http://www.who.int/mediacentre/factsheets/fs311/en/. 2006.

26. Deckelbaum RJ, Williams CL. Childhood obesity: the health issue. *Obes Res* 2001;9 Suppl 4:239S-43S.

27. Cole TJ, Bellizzi MC, Flegal KM, et al. Establishing a standard definition for child overweight and obesity worldwide: international survey. *BMJ* 2000;320:1240-3.

28. Lobstein T, Baur L, Uauy R. Obesity in children and young people: a crisis in public health. *Obes Rev* 2004;5 Suppl 1:4-104.

29. Wang Y, Lobstein T. Worldwide trends in childhood overweight and obesity. *Int J Pediatr Obes* 2006;1:11-25.

30. Guo SS, Roche AF, Chumlea WC, et al. The predictive value of childhood body mass index values for overweight at age 35 y. *Am J Clin Nutr* 1994;59:810-9.

31. Must A, Jacques PF, Dallal GE, et al. Long-term morbidity and mortality of overweight adolescents. A follow-up of the Harvard Growth Study of 1922 to 1935. *N Engl J Med* 1992;327:1350-5.

32. Freedman DS, Dietz WH, Srinivasan SR, et al. The relation of overweight to cardiovascular risk factors among children and adolescents: the Bogalusa Heart Study. *Pediatrics* 1999;103:1175-82.

33. Pinhas-Hamiel O, Dolan LM, Daniels SR, et al. Increased incidence of non-insulin-dependent diabetes mellitus among

adolescents. *J Pediatr* 1996;128:608-15.

34. United Nations. Urban and Rural Areas 2005: UN, 2006.

35. Popkin BM. Urbanization, lifestyle changes and the nutrition transition. *World Dev* 1999;27:1905-16.

36. Jain A. *What works for obesity? A summary of the research behind obesity interventions*. http://www.unitedhealthfoundation.org/obesity.pdf. 2004.

37. Popkin BM. Global nutrition dynamics: the world is shifting rapidly toward a diet linked with noncommunicable diseases. *Am J Clin Nutr* 2006;84:289-98.

38. Popkin BM, Gordon-Larsen P. The nutrition transition: worldwide obesity dynamics and their determinants. *Int J Obes Relat Metab Disord* 2004;28 Suppl 3:S2-9.

39. Mendez MA, Monteiro CA, Popkin BM. Overweight exceeds underweight among women in most developing countries. *Am J Clin Nutr* 2005;81:714-21.

40. Ezzati M, Vander Hoorn S, Lawes CM, et al. Rethinking the "diseases of affluence" paradigm: global patterns of nutritional risks in relation to economic development. *PLoS Med* 2005;2:e133.

41. Monteiro CA, Conde WL, Lu B, et al. Obesity and inequities in health in the developing world. *Int J Obes Relat Metab Disord* 2004;28:1181-6.

42. Blaxter SK. *The Energy Metabolism of Ruminants*. London: Hutchinson Scientific and Technical, 1967.

43. Jebb SA, Prentice AM, Goldberg GR, et al. Changes in macronutrient balance during over- and underfeeding assessed by 12-d continuous whole-body calorimetry. *Am J Clin Nutr* 1996;64:259-66.

44. Brehm BJ, Seeley RJ, Daniels SR, et al. A randomized trial comparing a very low carbohydrate diet and a calorie-restricted low fat diet on body weight and cardiovascular risk factors in healthy women. *J Clin Endocrinol Metab* 2003;88:1617-23.

45. Foster GD, Wyatt HR, Hill JO, et al. A randomized trial of a low-carbohydrate diet for obesity. *N Engl J Med* 2003;348:2082-90.

46. Samaha FF, Iqbal N, Seshadri P, et al. A low-carbohydrate as compared with a low-fat diet in severe obesity. *N Engl J Med* 2003;348:2074-81.

47. Skov AR, Toubro S, Ronn B, et al. Randomized trial on protein vs carbohydrate in ad libitum fat reduced diet for the treatment of obesity. *Int J Obes Relat Metab Disord* 1999;23:528-36.

48. Howarth NC, Saltzman E, Roberts SB. Dietary fiber and weight regulation. *Nutr Rev* 2001;59:129-39.

49. Uauy R, Diaz E. Consequences of food energy excess and positive energy balance. *Public Health Nutr* 2005;8:1077-99.

50. Diaz EO, Prentice AM, Goldberg GR, et al. Metabolic response to experimental overfeeding in lean and overweight healthy volunteers. *Am J Clin Nutr*

1992;56:641-55.

51. Stubbs RJ, Whybrow S. Energy density, diet composition and palatability: influences on overall food energy intake in humans. *Physiol Behav* 2004;81:755-64.

52. Rolls BJ, Roe LS, Meengs JS. Larger portion sizes lead to a sustained increase in energy intake over 2 days. *J Am Diet Assoc* 2006;106:543-9.

53. Flood JE, Roe LS, Rolls BJ. The effect of increased beverage portion size on energy intake at a meal. *J Am Diet Assoc* 2006;106:1984-90; discussion 90-1.

54. Ello-Martin JA, Ledikwe JH, Rolls BJ. The influence of food portion size and energy density on energy intake: implications for weight management. *Am J Clin Nutr* 2005;82:236S-41S.

55. Stock M. Gluttony and thermogenesis revisited. *Int J Obes Relat Metab Disord* 1999 23:1105-17.

56. O'Rahilly S, Farooqi IS. Genetics of obesity. *Philos Trans R Soc Lond B Biol Sci* 2006;361:1095-105.

57. Bouchard C, Tremblay A, Despres JP, et al. The response to long-term overfeeding in identical twins. *N Engl J Med* 1990;322:1477-82.

58. Samaras K, Kelly PJ, Chiano MN, et al. Genetic and environmental influences on total-body and central abdominal fat: the effect of physical activity in female twins. *Ann Intern Med* 1999;130:873-82.

59. Wade J, Milner J, Krondl M. Evidence for a physiological regulation of food selection and nutrient intake in twins. *Am J Clin Nutr* 1981;34:143-7.

60. Bouchard, Chagnon, Perusse. *The Pennington Biomedical Research Centre* http://www.obesite.chaire.ulaval.ca/genemap.html. 2006.

61. Laaksonen DE, Lakka HM, Niskanen LK, et al. Metabolic syndrome and development of diabetes mellitus: application and validation of recently suggested definitions of the metabolic syndrome in a prospective cohort study. *Am J Epidemiol* 2002;156:1070-7.

62. Rexrode KM, Buring JE, Manson JE. Abdominal and total adiposity and risk of coronary heart disease in men. *Int J Obes Relat Metab Disord* 2001;25:1047-56.

63. Rexrode KM, Carey VJ, Hennekens CH, et al. Abdominal adiposity and coronary heart disease in women. *JAMA* 1998;280:1843-8.

64. Yusuf S, Hawken S, Ounpuu S, et al. Obesity and the risk of myocardial infarction in 27,000 participants from 52 countries: a case-control study. *Lancet* 2005;366:1640-9.

65. Dagenais GR, Yi Q, Mann JF, et al. Prognostic impact of body weight and abdominal obesity in women and men with cardiovascular disease. *Am Heart J* 2005;149:54-60.

66. 1996. *The Third National Health and Nutrition Examination Survey, NHANES III (1988-94)*.

67. Hu FB, Willett WC, Li T, et al. Adiposity as compared with physical activity in

predicting mortality among women. *N Engl J Med* 2004;351:2694-703.

68. Lean ME. Pathophysiology of obesity. *Proc Nutr Soc* 2000;59:331-6.

69. Fogelholm M, Kukkonen-Harjula K, Oja P. Eating control and physical activity as determinants of short-term weight maintenance after a very-low-calorie diet among obese women. *Int J Obes Relat Metab Disord* 1999;23:203-10.

70. Ludwig DS, Gortmaker SL. Programming obesity in childhood. *Lancet* 2004;364:226-7.

71. Schmitz KH, Jensen MD, Kugler KC, et al. Strength training for obesity prevention in midlife women. *Int J Obes* 2003;27:326-33.

72. Borg P, Kukkonen-Harjula K, Fogelholm M, et al. Effects of walking or resistance training on weight loss maintenance in obese, middle-aged men: a randomized trial. *Int J Obes* 2002;26:676-83.

73. Fogelholm M, Kukkonen-Harjula K, Nenonen A, et al. Effects of walking training on weight maintenance after a very-low-energy diet in premenopausal obese women: a randomized controlled trial. *Arch Intern Med* 2000;160:2177-84.

74. Wen W, Gao YT, Shu XO, et al. Sociodemographic, behavioral, and reproductive factors associated with weight gain in Chinese women. *Int J Obes* 2003;27:933-40.

75. Alfano CM, Klesges RC, Murray DM, et al. History of sport participation in relation to obesity and related health behaviors in women. *Prev Med* 2002;34:82-9.

76. Heitmann BL, Kaprio J, Harris JR, et al. Are genetic determinants of weight gain modified by leisure-time physical activity? A prospective study of Finnish twins. *Am J Clin Nutr* 1997;66:672-8.

77. Schmitz KH, Jacobs DR, Jr., Leon AS, et al. Physical activity and body weight: associations over ten years in the CARDIA Study. *Int J Obes* 2000;24:1475-87.

78. Koh-Banerjee P, Chu N, Spiegelman D, et al. Prospective study of the association of changes in dietary intake, physical activity, alcohol consumption, and smoking with 9-y gain in waist circumference among 16587 US men. *Am J Clin Nutr* 2003;78:719-27.

79. Hughes VA, Frontera WR, Roubenoff R, et al. Longitudinal changes in body composition in older men and women: Role of body weight change and physical activity. *Am J Clin Nutr* 2002;76:473-81.

80. Di Pietro L, Dziura J, Blair SN. Estimated change in physical activity level (PAL) and prediction of 5-year weight change in men: The Aerobics Center Longitudinal Study. *Int J Obes* 2004;28:1541-7.

81. Wier LT, Ayers GW, Jackson AS, et al. Determining the amount of physical activity needed for long-term weight control. *Int J Obes* 2001;25:613-21.

82. Schoeller DA, Shay K, Kushner RF. How much physical activity is needed to minimize weight gain in previously obese women? *Am J Clin Nutr* 1997;66:551-6.

83. Ma Y, Olendzki B, Chiriboga D, et al. Association between dietary carbohydrates and body weight. *Am J Epidemiol* 2005;161:359-67.

84. Taylor CB, Jatulis DE, Winkleby MA, et al. Effects of life-style on body mass index change. *Epidemiology* 1994;5:599-603.

85. Sundquist J, Johansson SE. The influence of socioeconomic status, ethnicity and lifestyle on body mass index in a longitudinal study. *Int J Epidemiol* 1998;27:57-63.

86. Sternfeld B, Wang H, Quesenberry CP, et al. Physical activity and changes in weight and waist circumference in midlife women: findings from the Study of Women's Health Across the Nation. *Am J Epidemiol* 2004;160:912-22.

87. Sammel MD, Grisson JA, Freeman EW, et al. Weight gain among women in the late reproductive years. *Fam Pract* 2003;20:401-9.

88. Tataranni PA, Harper IT, Snitker S, et al. Body weight gain in free-living Pima Indians: effect of energy intake vs expenditure. *Int J Obes* 2003;27:1578-83.

89. Macdonald HM, New SA, Campbell MK, et al. Longitudinal changes in weight in perimenopausal and early postmenopausal women: effects of dietary energy intake, energy expenditure, dietary calcium intake and hormone replacement therapy. *Int J Obes* 2003;27:669-76.

90. Forster JL, Jeffery RW, Schmid TL, et al. Preventing weight gain in adults: a Pound of Prevention. *Health Psychol* 1988;7:515-25.

91. Jeffery RW, French SA. Preventing weight gain in adults: design, methods and one year results from the Pound of Prevention study. *Int J Obes Relat Metab Disord* 1997;21:457-64.

92. Jeffery RW, French SA. Preventing weight gain in adults: the Pound of Prevention study. *Am J Public Health* 1999;89:747-51.

93. Kuller LH, Simkin-Silverman LR, Wing RR, et al. Women's Healthy Lifestyle Project: a randomized clinical trial: results at 54 months. *Circulation* 2001;103:32-7.

94. Simkin-Silverman L, Wing RR, Hansen DH, et al. Prevention of cardiovascular risk factor elevations in healthy premenopausal women. *Prev Med* 1995;24:509-17.

95. Leermarkers EA, Jakicic JM, Viteri J, et al. Clinic-based vs. home-based interventions for preventing weight gain in men. *Obes Res* 1998;6:346-52.

96. Harrell JS, Johnston LF, Griggs TR, et al. An occupation based physical activity intervention program: improving fitness and decreasing obesity. *AAOHN J* 1996;44:377-84.

97. Proper KI, Hildebrandt VH, Van Der Beek AJ, et al. Effect of individual counseling on physical activity fitness and health: A randomized controlled trial in a workplace setting. *Am J Prev Med* 2003;24:218-26.

98. Burke V, Giangiulio N, Gillam HF, et al. Physical activity and nutrition programs for couples: A randomized controlled trial. *J Clin Epidemiol* 2003;56:421-32.

99. Pritchard JE, Nowson CA, Wark JD. A worksite program for overweight middle-aged men achieves lesser weight loss with exercise than with dietary change. *J Am Diet Assoc* 1997;97:37-42.

100. King AC, Freyhewitt B, Dreon DM, et al. Diet vs exercise in weight maintenance - the effects of minimal intervention strategies on long-term outcomes in men. *Arch Intern Med* 1989;149:2741-6.

101. Lefevre J, Philippaerts R, Delvaux K, et al. Relation between cardiovascular risk factors at adult age, and physical activity during youth and adulthood: The Leuven Longitudinal Study on Lifestyle, Fitness and Health. *Int J Sports Med* 2002;23:S32-8.

102. Sherwood NE, Jeffery RW, French SA, et al. Predictors of weight gain in the Pound of Prevention study. *Int J Obes* 2000;24:395-403.

103. Klesges RC, Isbell TR, Klesges LM. Relationship between dietary restraint, energy intake, physical activity, and body weight: a prospective analysis. *J Abnorm Psychol* 1992;101:668-74.

104. Eck LH, Pascale RW, Klesges RC, et al. Predictors of waist circumference change in healthy young adults. *Int J Obes* 1995;19:765-9.

105. Paeratakul S, Popkin BM, Keyou G, et al. Changes in diet and physical activity affect the body mass index of Chinese adults. *Int J Obes* 1998;22:424-31.

106. Klesges RC, Klesges LM, Haddock CK, et al. A longitudinal analysis of the impact of dietary intake and physical activity on weight change in adults. *Am J Clin Nutr* 1992;55:818-22.

107. He XZ, Baker DW. Changes in weight among a nationally representative cohort of adults aged 51 to 61, 1992 to 2000. *Am J Prev Med* 2004;27:8-15.

108. Hannerz H, Albertsen K, Nielsen ML, et al. Occupational Factors and 5-Year Weight Change among Men in a Danish National Cohort. *Health Psychol* 2004;23:283-8.

109. Parkes KR. Demographic and lifestyle predictors of body mass index among offshore oil industry workers: cross-sectional and longitudinal findings. *Occup Med* 2003;53:213-21.

110. Bell AC, Ge K, Popkin BM. Weight gain and its predictors in Chinese adults. *Int J Obes* 2001;25:1079-86.

111. Bak H, Petersen L, Sorensen TIA. Physical activity in relation to development and maintenance of obesity in men with and without juvenile onset obesity. *Int J Obes* 2004;28:99-104.

112. Williamson DF, Madans J, Anda RF, et al. Recreational physical activity and ten-year weight change in a US national cohort. *Int J Obes Relat Metab Disord* 1993;17:279-86.

113. Haapanen N, Miilunpalo S, Pasanen M, et al. Association between leisure time physical activity and 10-year body mass change among working-aged men and women. *Int J Obes Relat Metab Disord* 1997;21:288-96.

114. Kahn HS, Tatham LM, Rodriguez C, et al. Stable behaviors associated with adults' 10-year change in body mass index and likelihood of gain at the waist. *Am J Public Health* 1997;87:747-54.

115. Nooyens ACJ, Visscher TLS, Schuit AJ, et al. Effects of retirement on lifestyle in relation to changes in weight and waist circumference in Dutch men: a prospective study. *Public Health Nutr* 2005;8:1266-74.

116. Fortier MD, Katzmarzyk PT, Bouchard C. Physical activity, aerobic fitness, and seven-year changes in adiposity in the Canadian population. *Can J Appl Physiol* 2002;27:449-62.

117. Droyvold WB, Holmen J, Kruger O, et al. Leisure time physical activity and change in body mass index: An 11-year follow-up study of 9357 normal weight healthy women 20-49 years old. *Journal of Women's Health (Larchmt)* 2004;13:55-62.

118. Droyvold WB, Holmen J, Midthjell K, et al. BMI change and leisure time physical activity (LTPA): An 11-y follow-up study in apparently healthy men aged 20-69 y with normal weight at baseline. *Int J Obes* 2004;28:410-7.

119. Delvaux K, Lysens R, Philippaerts R, et al. Associations between physical activity, nutritional practices and health-related anthropometry in Flemish males: a 5-year follow-up study. *Int J Obes* 1999;23:1233-41.

120. Petersen L, Schnohr P, Sorensen TIA. Longitudinal study of the long-term relation between physical activity and obesity in adults. *Int J Obes* 2004;28:105-12.

121. Wagner A, Simon C, Ducimetiere P, et al. Leisure-time physical activity and regular walking or cycling to work are associated with adiposity and 5 y weight gain in middle-aged men: The PRIME study. *Int J Obes* 2001;25:940-8.

122. Hu FB, Li TY, Colditz GA, et al. Television watching and other sedentary behaviors in relation to risk of obesity and type 2 diabetes mellitus in women. *JAMA* 2003;289:1785-91.

123. Mosca CL, Marshall JA, Grunwald GK, et al. Insulin resistance as a modifier of the relationship between dietary fat intake and weight gain. *Int J Obes* 2004;28:803-12.

124. Mo-suwan L, Pongprapai S, Junjana C, et al. Effects of a controlled trial of a school-based exercise program on the obesity indexes of preschool children. *Am J Clin Nutr* 1998;68:1006-11.

125. Sallis J. Project SPARK. Effects of physical education on adiposity in children. *Ann N Y Acad Sci* 1993;699:127-36.

126. Flores R. Dance for health: Improving fitness in African American and Hispanic adolescents. *Public Health Rep* 1995;110:189-93.

127. Neumark-Sztainer D, Story M, Hannan PJ, et al. New Moves: a school-based obesity prevention program for adolescent girls. *Prev Med* 2003;37:41-51.

128. Pangrazi R. Impact of promoting lifestyle activity for youth (PLAY) on children's physical activity. *J Sch Health* 2003;73:317-21.

129. Maffeis C, Talamini G, Tato L. Influence of diet, physical activity and parents' obesity on children's adiposity: a four-year longitudinal study. *Int J Obes Relat Metab Disord* 1998;22:758-64.

130. Mo-suwan L, Tongkumchum P, Puetpaiboon A. Determinants of overweight tracking from childhood to adolescence: a 5 y follow-up study of Hat Yai schoolchildren. *Int J Obes* 2000;24:1642-7.

131. Davison KK, Birch LL. Child and parent characteristics as predictors of change in girls' body mass index. *Int J Obes* 2001;25:1834-42.

132. Twisk JW, Kemper HC, van Mechelen W, et al. Which lifestyle parameters discriminate high- from low-risk participants for coronary heart disease risk factors. Longitudinal analysis covering adolescence and young adulthood. *J Cardiovasc Risk* 1997;4:393-400.

133. Twisk JWR, Kemper HCG, Van Mechelen W. The relationship between physical fitness and physical activity during adolescence and cardiovascular disease risk factors at adult age. The Amsterdam Growth and Health Longitudinal Study. *Int J Sports Med* 2002;23:S8-S14.

134. Twisk JWR, Kemper HCG, van Mechelen W, et al. Body fatness: longitudinal relationship of body mass index and the sum of skinfolds with other risk factors for coronary heart disease. *Int J Obes* 1998;22:915-22.

135. van Lenthe FJ, van Mechelen W, Kemper HCG, et al. Behavioral variables and development of a central pattern of body fat from adolescence into adulthood in normal-weight whites: The Amsterdam Growth and Health Study. *Am J Clin Nutr* 1998;67:846-52.

136. Stevens J, Suchindran C, Ring K, et al. Physical activity as a predictor of body composition in American Indian children. *Obes Res* 2004;12:1974-80.

137. Moore LL, Gao D, Bradlee ML, et al. Does early physical activity predict body fat change throughout childhood? *Prev Med* 2003;37:10-7.

138. Moore LL, Nguyen USDT, Rothman KJ, et al. Preschool physical activity level and change in body fatness in young children. The Framingham Children's Study. *Am J Epidemiol* 1995;142:982-8.

139. Figueroa-Colon R, Arani RB, Goran MI, et al. Paternal body fat is a longitudinal predictor of changes in body fat in premenarcheal girls. *Am J Clin Nutr* 2000;71:829-34.

140. Berkowitz RI, Agras WS, Korner AF, et al. Physical activity and adiposity: a longitudinal study from birth to childhood. *J Pediatr* 1985;106:734-8.

141. Tammelin T, Laitinen J, Nayha S. Change in the level of physical activity from adolescence into adulthood and obesity at the age of 31 years. *Int J Obes* 2004;28:775-82.

142. Ku LC, Shapiro LR, Crawford PB, et al. Body composition and physical activity in 8-year-old children. *Am J Clin Nutr* 1981;34:2770-5.

143. Horn OK, Paradis G, Potvin L, et al. Correlates and predictors of adiposity among Mohawk children. *Prev Med* 2001;33:274-81.

144. Burke V, Beilin LJ, Dunbar D. Family lifestyle and parental body mass index as predictors of body mass index in Australian children: A longitudinal study. *Int J Obes* 2001;25:147-57.

145. Berkey CS, Rockett HRH, Gillman MW, et al. One-year changes in activity and in inactivity among 10- to 15-year-old boys and girls: Relationship to change in body mass index. *Pediatrics* 2003;111:836-43.

146. Janz KF, Dawson JD, Mahoney LT. Increases in physical fitness during childhood improve cardiovascular health during adolescence: the Muscatine Study. *Int J Sports Med* 2002;23:Suppl 1 S15-21.

147. O'Loughlin J, Gray-Donald K, Paradis G, et al. One- and two-year predictors of excess weight gain among elementary schoolchildren in multiethnic, low-income, inner-city neighborhoods. *Am J Epidemiol* 2000;152:739-46.

148. Datar A, Sturm R. Physical education in elementary school and body mass index: evidence from the Early Childhood Longitudinal Study. *Am J Public Health* 2004;94:1501-6.

149. Achten J, Jeukendrup AE. Optimizing fat oxidation through exercise and diet. *Nutrition* 2004;20:716-27.

150. Blundell JE, Stubbs RJ, Hughes DA, et al. Cross talk between physical activity and appetite control: does physical activity stimulate appetite? *Proc Nutr Soc* 2003;62:651-61.

151. Reilly JJ, Kelly L, Montgomery C, et al. Physical activity to prevent obesity in young children: cluster randomised controlled trial. *BMJ* 2006;333:1041.

152. Daley AJ, Copeland RJ, Wright NP, et al. Exercise therapy as a treatment for psychopathologic conditions in obese and morbidly obese adolescents: a randomized, controlled trial. *Pediatrics* 2006;118:2126-34.

153. Goldfield GS, Mallory R, Parker T, et al. Effects of open-loop feedback on physical activity and television viewing in overweight and obese children: a randomized, controlled trial. *Pediatrics* 2006;118:e157-66.

154. Meyer AA, Kundt G, Lenschow U, et al. Improvement of early vascular changes and cardiovascular risk factors in obese children after a six-month exercise program. *J Am Coll Cardiol*

2006;48:1865-70.

155. Kim HD, Park JS. [The effect of an exercise program on body composition and physical fitness in obese female college students.] *Taehan Kanho Hakhoe Chi* 2006;36:5-14.

156. Atlantis E, Chow CM, Kirby A, et al. Worksite intervention effects on physical health: a randomized controlled trial. *Health Promot Int* 2006;21:191-200.

157. Fenkci S, Sarsan A, Rota S, et al. Effects of resistance or aerobic exercises on metabolic parameters in obese women who are not on a diet. *Adv Ther* 2006;23:404-13.

158. Racette SB, Weiss EP, Villareal DT, et al. One year of caloric restriction in humans: feasibility and effects on body composition and abdominal adipose tissue. *J Gerontol A Biol Sci Med Sci* 2006;61:943-50.

159. Hays NP, Bathalon GP, Roubenoff R, et al. Eating behavior and weight change in healthy postmenopausal women: results of a 4-year longitudinal study. *J Gerontol A Biol Sci Med Sci* 2006;61:608-15.

160. Yang X, Telama R, Viikari J, et al. Risk of obesity in relation to physical activity tracking from youth to adulthood. *Med Sci Sports Exerc* 2006;38:919-25.

161. Parsons TJ, Manor O, Power C. Physical activity and change in body mass index from adolescence to mid-adulthood in the 1958 British cohort. *Int J Epidemiol* 2006;35:197-204.

162. Williams PT, Thompson PD. Dose-dependent effects of training and detraining on weight in 6406 runners during 7.4 years. *Obesity (Silver Spring)* 2006;14:1975-84.

163. Williams PT, Wood PD. The effects of changing exercise levels on weight and age-related weight gain. *Int J Obes (Lond)* 2006;30:543-51.

164. Dennison BA, Russo TJ, Burdick PA, et al. An Intervention to Reduce Television Viewing by Preschool Children. *Arch Pediatr Adolesc Med* 2004;158:170-6.

165. Ball K, Brown W, Crawford D. Who does not gain weight? Prevalence and predictors of weight maintenance in young women. *Int J Obes* 2002;26:1570-8.

166. Kaur H, Choi WS. Duration of television watching is associated with increased body mass index. *J Pediatr* 2003;143:506-11.

167. Hancox RJ, Milne BJ. Association between child and adolescent television viewing and adult health: a longitudinal birth cohort study. *Lancet* 2004;364:257-62.

168. Jago R, Nicklas T, Yang S, et al. Physical activity and health enhancing dietary behaviors in young adults: Bogalusa Heart Study. *Prev Med* 2005;41:194-202.

169. Kettaneh AJ, Oppert M. Changes in physical activity explain paradoxical relationship between baseline physical activity and adiposity changes in adolescent girls: the FLVS II study. *Int J Obes* 2005;29:586-93.

170. Skinner JD, Bounds W. Longitudinal calcium intake is negatively related to children's body fat indexes. *J Am Diet Assoc* 2003;103:1626-31.

171. Reilly JJ, Armstrong J, Dorosty AR, et al. Early life risk factors for obesity in childhood: cohort study. *BMJ* 2005;330:1357.

172. Elgar FJ, Roberts C, Moore L, et al. Sedentary behaviour, physical activity and weight problems in adolescents in Wales. *Public Health* 2005;119:518-24.

173. Berkey CS, Rockett HR, Field AE, et al. Activity, dietary intake, and weight changes in a longitudinal study of preadolescent and adolescent boys and girls. *Pediatrics* 2000;105:E56.

174. Dietz WH, Gortmaker SL. Do we fatten our children at the television set? Obesity and television viewing in children and adolescents. *Pediatrics* 1985;75:807-12.

175. Robinson TN, Hammer LD. Does television viewing increase obesity and reduce physical activity? *Pediatrics* 1993;91:273-80.

176. Saelens BE, Sallis J. Home environmental influences on children's television watching from early to middle childhood. *J Dev Behav Pediatr* 2002;23:127-32.

177. Bogaert N, Steinbeck KS, Baur LA, et al. Food, activity and family - environmental vs biochemical predictors of weight gain in children. *Eur J Clin Nutr* 2003;57:1242-9.

178. Skinner JD, Bounds W, Carruth BR, et al. Predictors of children's body mass index: A longitudinal study of diet and growth in children aged 2-8y. *Int J Obes* 2004;28:476-82.

179. Karnehed N, Tynelius P, Heitmann BL, et al. Physical activity, diet and gene-environment interactions in relation to body mass index and waist circumference: the Swedish young male twins study. *Public Health Nutr* 2006;9:851-8.

180. Silveira D, Taddei JA, Escrivao MA, et al. Risk factors for overweight among Brazilian adolescents of low-income families: a case-control study. *Public Health Nutr* 2006;9:421-8.

181. Arenz S, Ruckerl R, Koletzko B, et al. Breast-feeding and childhood obesity - a systematic review. *Int J Obes Relat Metab Disord* 2004;28:1247-56.

182. Owen CG, Martin RM, Whincup PH, et al. The effect of breastfeeding on mean body mass index throughout life: a quantitative review of published and unpublished observational evidence. *Am J Clin Nutr* 2005;82:1298-307.

183. Kvaavik E, Tell GS, Klepp KI. Surveys of Norwegian youth indicated that breast feeding reduced subsequent risk of obesity. *J Clin Epidemiol* 2005;58:849-55.

184. Butte NF. The role of breastfeeding in obesity. *Pediatr Clin North Am* 2001;48:189-98.

185. Araujo CL, Victora CG, Hallal PC, et al. Breastfeeding and overweight in childhood: evidence from the Pelotas 1993 birth cohort study. *Int J Obes (Lond)* 2006;30:500-6.

186. Burdette HL, Whitaker RC, Hall WC, et al. Breastfeeding, introduction of complementary foods, and adiposity at 5 y of age. *Am J Clin Nutr* 2006;83:550-8.

187. Ong KK, Emmett PM, Noble S, et al. Dietary energy intake at the age of 4 months predicts postnatal weight gain and childhood body mass index. *Pediatrics* 2006;117:e503-8.

188. Toubro S, Astrup A. Randomised comparison of diets for maintaining obese subjects' weight after major weight loss: ad lib, low fat, high carbohydrate diet v fixed energy intake. *BMJ* 1997;314:29-34.

189. Simkin-Silverman LR, Wing RR, Boraz MA, et al. Maintenance of cardiovascular risk factor changes among middle-aged women in a lifestyle intervention trial. *Women's Health* 1998;4:255-71.

190. Ebbeling CB, Leidig MM, Sinclair KB, et al. A reduced-glycemic load diet in the treatment of adolescent obesity. *Arch Pediatr Adolesc Med* 2003;157:773-9.

191. Stern L, Iqbal N, Seshadri P, et al. The effects of low-carbohydrate versus conventional weight loss diets in severely obese adults: one-year follow-up of a randomized trial. *Ann Intern Med* 2004;140:778-85.

192. Shah M, Baxter JE. Nutrient and food intake in obese women on a low-fat or low-calorie diet. *Am J Health Promot* 1996;10:179-82.

193. Sheppard L, Kristal AR, Kushi LH. Weight-loss in women participating in a randomized trial of low-fat diets. *Am J Clin Nutr* 1991;54:821-8.

194. Jeffery RW, Hellerstedt WL, French SA, et al. A randomized trial of counseling for fat restriction versus calorie restriction in the treatment of obesity. *Int J Obes* 1995;19:132-7.

195. Swinburn BA, Metcalf PA, Ley SJ. Long-term (5-year) effects of a reduced-fat diet intervention in individuals with glucose intolerance. *Diabetes Care* 2001;24:619-24.

196. Harvey-Berino J. Calorie restriction is more effective for obesity treatment than dietary fat restriction. *Ann Behav Med* 1999;21:35-9.

197. Fleming RM. The effect of high-, moderate-, and low-fat diets on weight loss and cardiovascular disease risk factors. *Preventive Cardiology* 2002;5:110-8.

198. Dansinger ML, Gleason JA, Griffith JL, et al. Comparison of the Atkins, Ornish, Weight Watchers, and Zone diets for weight loss and heart disease risk reduction: a randomized trial. *JAMA* 2005;293:43-53.

199. Epstein LH, Gordy CC, Raynor HA, et al. Increasing fruit and vegetable intake and decreasing fat and sugar intake in families at risk for childhood obesity. *Obes Res* 2001;9:171-8.

200. Matvienko O, Lewis DS, Schafer E. A college nutrition science course as an

intervention to prevent weight gain in female college freshmen. *J Nutr Educ* 2001;33:95-101.

201. Bazzano LA, Song Y, Bubes V, et al. Dietary intake of whole and refined grain breakfast cereals and weight gain in men. *Obes Res* 2005;13:1952-60.

202. Halkjaer J, Sorensen TIA, Tjonneland A, et al. Food and drinking patterns as predictors of 6-year BMI-adjusted changes in waist circumference. *Br J Nutr* 2004;92:735-48.

203. Koh-Banerjee P, Franz MV, Sampson L, et al. Changes in whole-grain, bran, and cereal fiber consumption in relation to 8-y weight gain among men. *Am J Clin Nutr* 2004;80:1237-45.

204. Liu S, Willett WC, Manson JE, et al. Relation between changes in intakes of dietary fiber and grain products and changes in weight and development of obesity among middle-aged women. *Am J Clin Nutr* 2003;78:920-7.

205. Ludwig DS, Pereira MA, Kroenke CH, et al. Dietary fiber, weight gain, and cardiovascular disease risk factors in young adults. *JAMA* 1999;282:1539-46.

206. Ishihara T, Takeda Y, Mizutani T, et al. [Relationship between infant lifestyle and adolescent obesity. The Enzan maternal-and-child health longitudinal study.] *Nippon Koshu Eisei Zasshi* 2003;50:106-17.

207. Burton-Freeman B. Dietary fiber and energy regulation. *J Nutr* 2000;130:272S-5S.

208. Field AE, Gillman MW, Rosner B, et al. Association between fruit and vegetable intake and change in body mass index among a large sample of children and adolescents in the United States. *Int J Obes* 2003;27:821-6.

209. Schulz M, Kroke A, Liese AD, et al. Food groups as predictors for short-term weight changes in men and women of the EPIC-Potsdam cohort. *J Nutr* 2002;132:1335-40.

210. He K, Hu FB, Colditz GA, et al. Changes in intake of fruits and vegetables in relation to risk of obesity and weight gain among middle-aged women. *Int J Obes* 2004;28:1569-74.

211. Parker DR, Gonzalez S, Derby CA, et al. Dietary factors in relation to weight change among men and women from two southeastern New England communities. *Int J Obes Relat Metab Disord* 1997;21:103-9.

212. McAuley KA, Smith KJ, Taylor RW, et al. Long-term effects of popular dietary approaches on weight loss and features of insulin resistance. *Int J Obes (Lond)* 2006;30:342-9.

213. Howard BV, Manson JE, Stefanick ML, et al. Low-fat dietary pattern and weight change over 7 years: the Women's Health Initiative Dietary Modification Trial. *JAMA* 2006;295:39-49.

214. Iqbal SI, Helge JW, Heitmann BL. Do energy density and dietary fiber influence subsequent 5-year weight changes in adult men and women?

Obesity (Silver Spring) 2006;14:106-14.

215. Bes-Rastrollo M, Martinez-Gonzalez MA, Sanchez-Villegas A, et al. Association of fiber intake and fruit/vegetable consumption with weight gain in a Mediterranean population. *Nutrition* 2006;22:504-11.

216. Lindstrom J, Peltonen M, Eriksson JG, et al. High-fibre, low-fat diet predicts long-term weight loss and decreased type 2 diabetes risk: the Finnish Diabetes Prevention Study. *Diabetologia* 2006;49:912-20.

217. Nicklas TA, Farris RP, Smoak CG, et al. Dietary factors relate to cardiovascular risk factors in early life. Bogalusa Heart Study. *Arteriosclerosis* 1988;8:193-9.

218. Colditz GA, Willett WC, Stampfer MJ, et al. Patterns of weight change and their relation to diet in a cohort of healthy women. *Am J Clin Nutr* 1990;51:1100-5.

219. Halkjaer J, Tjonneland A, Thomsen BL, et al. Intake of macronutrients as predictors of 5-y changes in waist circumference. *Am J Clin Nutr* 2006;84:789-97.

220. James J, Thomas P, Cavan D, et al. Preventing childhood obesity by reducing consumption of carbonated drinks: cluster randomised controlled trial. *BMJ (Clin Res Ed)* 2004;328:1237.

221. Newby PK, Peterson KE, Berkey CS, et al. Beverage consumption is not associated with changes in weight and body mass index among low-income preschool children in North Dakota. *J Am Diet Assoc* 2004;104:1086-94.

222. Ludwig DS, Peterson KE, Gortmaker SL. Relation between consumption of sugar-sweetened drinks and childhood obesity: a prospective, observational analysis. *Lancet* 2001;357:505-8.

223. Schulze MB, Manson JE, Ludwig DS, et al. Sugar-sweetened beverages, weight gain, and incidence of type 2 diabetes in young and middle-aged women. *JAMA* 2004;292:927-34.

224. Bray GA. The epidemic of obesity and changes in food intake: the Fluoride Hypothesis. *Physiol Behav* 2004;82:115-21.

225. Ebbeling CB, Feldman HA, Osganian SK, et al. Effects of decreasing sugar-sweetened beverage consumption on body weight in adolescents: a randomized, controlled pilot study. *Pediatrics* 2006;117:673-80.

226. Bes-Rastrollo M, Sanchez-Villegas A, Gomez-Gracia E, et al. Predictors of weight gain in a Mediterranean cohort: the Seguimiento Universidad de Navarra Study 1. *Am J Clin Nutr* 2006;83:362-70; quiz 94-5.

227. Thompson OM, Ballew C, Resnicow K, et al. Food purchased away from home as a predictor of change in BMI z-score among girls. *Int J Obes* 2004;28:282-9.

228. Burke V, Beilin LJ, Simmer K, et al. Predictors of body mass index and associations with cardiovascular risk factors in Australian children: A prospective cohort study. *Int J Obes* 2005;29:15-23.

229. French SA, Harnack L, Jeffery RW. Fast food restaurant use among women in the Pound of Prevention study: Dietary, behavioral and demographic correlates. *Int J Obes* 2000;24:1353-9.

230. Pereira MA, Kartashov AI, Ebbeling CB, et al. Fast-food habits, weight gain, and insulin resistance (the CARDIA study): 15-year prospective analysis. *Lancet* 2005;365:36-42.

231. Jeffery RW, French SA. Epidemic obesity in the United States: are fast foods and television viewing contributing? *Am J Public Health* 1998;88:277-80.

232. Isganaitis E, Lustig RH. Fast food, central nervous system insulin resistance, and obesity. *Arterioscler Thromb Vasc Biol* 2005;25:2451-62.

233. Niemeier HM, Raynor HA, Lloyd-Richardson EE, et al. Fast food consumption and breakfast skipping: predictors of weight gain from adolescence to adulthood in a nationally representative sample. *J Adolesc Health* 2006;39:842-9.

234. Robinson TN. Reducing children's television viewing to prevent obesity: a randomized controlled trial. *JAMA* 1999;282:1561-7.

Chapter 9

1. Hewitt M, Greenfield S, Stovall E, editors. *From Cancer Patient to Cancer Survivor: Lost in Transition / Committee on Cancer Survivorship: Improving Care and Quality of Life*. Washington, DC: The National Academies Press, 2006.

2. Micheli A, Mugno E, Krogh V, et al. Cancer prevalence in European registry areas. *Ann Oncol* 2002;13:840-65.

3. Mackay J, Jemal A, Lee NC, et al. *The Cancer Atlas*. Atlanta, Georgia: American Cancer Society, 2006.

4. Doyle C, Kushi LH, Byers T, et al. Nutrition and physical activity during and after cancer treatment: an American Cancer Society guide for informed choices. *CA Cancer J Clin* 2006;56:323-53.

5. Davies AA, Davey Smith G, Harbord R, et al. Nutritional interventions and outcome in patients with cancer or preinvasive lesions: systematic review. *J Natl Cancer Inst* 2006;98:961-73.

6. Sopotsinskaia EB, Balitskii KP, Tarutinov VI, et al. [Experience with the use of a low-calorie diet in breast cancer patients to prevent metastasis]. *Vopr Onkol* 1992;38:592-9.

7. de Waard F, Ramlau R, Mulders Y, et al. A feasibility study on weight reduction in obese postmenopausal breast cancer patients. *Eur J Cancer Prev* 1993;2:233-8.

8. Berglund G, Bolund C, Gustafsson UL, et al. One-year follow-up of the 'Starting Again' group rehabilitation programme for cancer patients. *Eur J Cancer* 1994;30A:1744-51.

9. Isenring EA, Capra S, Bauer JD. Nutrition intervention is beneficial in oncology outpatients receiving radiotherapy to the gastrointestinal or head and neck area. *Br J Cancer* 2004;91:447-52.

10. Ovesen L, Allingstrup L, Hannibal J, et al. Effect of dietary counseling on food intake, body weight, response rate, survival, and quality of life in cancer patients undergoing chemotherapy: a prospective, randomized study. *J Clin Oncol* 1993;11:2043-9.

11. Persson CR, Johansson BB, Sjoden PO, et al. A randomized study of nutritional support in patients with colorectal and gastric cancer. *Nutr Cancer* 2002;42:48-58.

12. Petersson LM, Nordin K, Glimelius B, et al. Differential effects of cancer rehabilitation depending on diagnosis and patients' cognitive coping style. *Psychosom Med* 2002;64:971-80.

13. Ravasco P, Monteiro-Grillo I, Vidal PM, et al. Impact of nutrition on outcome: a prospective randomized controlled trial in patients with head and neck cancer undergoing radiotherapy. *Head Neck* 2005;27:659-68.

14. Macia E, Moran J, Santos J, et al. Nutritional evaluation and dietetic care in cancer patients treated with radiotherapy: prospective study. *Nutrition* 1991;7:205-9.

15. Black HS, Thornby JI, Wolf JE, et al. Evidence that a low-fat diet reduces the occurrence of non-melanoma skin cancer. *Int J Cancer* 1995;62:165-9.

16. Evans WK, Nixon DW, Daly JM, et al. A randomized study of oral nutritional support versus ad lib nutritional intake during chemotherapy for advanced colorectal and non-small-cell lung cancer. *J Clin Oncol* 1987;5:113-24.

17. Chlebowski RT, Blackburn GL, Thomson CA, et al. Dietary fat reduction and breast cancer outcome: interim efficacy results from the Women's Intervention Nutrition Study. *J Natl Cancer Inst* 2006;98:1767-76.

18. Thiebaut AC, Schatzkin A, Ballard-Barbash R, et al. Dietary fat and breast cancer: contributions from a survival trial. *J Natl Cancer Inst* 2006;98:1753-5.

19. Pierce JP, Natarajan L, Caan BJ, et al. Influence of a diet very high in vegetables, fruit, and fiber and low in fat on prognosis following treatment for breast cancer. *JAMA* 2007;298:289-98.

20. Jyothirmayi R, Ramadas K, Varghese C, et al. Efficacy of vitamin A in the prevention of loco-regional recurrence and second primaries in head and neck cancer. *Eur J Cancer B Oral Oncol* 1996;32B:373-6.

21. Kokron O, Alth G, Cerni C, et al. [Results of a comparative therapy study for inoperable lung cancer]. *Onkologie* 1982;5:20-2.

22. Kucera H. [Adjuvanticity of vitamin A in advanced irradiated cervical cancer (author's transl)]. *Wien Klin Wochenschr Suppl* 1980;118:1-20.

23. Meyskens FL Jr, Kopecky KJ, Appelbaum FR, et al. Effects of vitamin A on survival in patients with chronic myelogenous leukemia: a SWOG randomized trial. *Leuk Res* 1995;19:605-12.

24. Meyskens FL Jr, Liu PY, Tuthill RJ, et al. Randomized trial of vitamin A versus observation as adjuvant therapy in high-risk primary malignant melanoma: a Southwest Oncology Group study. *J Clin Oncol* 1994;12:2060-5.

25. Pastorino U, Infante M, Maioli M, et al. Adjuvant treatment of stage I lung cancer with high-dose vitamin A. *J Clin Oncol* 1993;11:1216-22.

26. van Zandwijk N, Dalesio O, Pastorino U, et al. EUROSCAN, a randomized trial of vitamin A and N-acetylcysteine in patients with head and neck cancer or lung cancer. For the European Organization for Research and Treatment of Cancer Head and Neck and Lung Cancer Cooperative Groups. *J Natl Cancer Inst* 2000;92:977-86.

27. Bairati I, Meyer F, Gelinas M, et al. A randomized trial of antioxidant vitamins to prevent second primary cancers in head and neck cancer patients. *J Natl Cancer Inst* 2005;97:481-8.

28. Greenberg ER, Baron JA, Stukel TA, et al. A clinical trial of beta carotene to prevent basal-cell and squamous-cell cancers of the skin. The Skin Cancer Prevention Study Group. *N Engl J Med* 1990;323:789-95.

29. Mayne ST, Cartmel B, Baum M, et al. Randomized trial of supplemental beta-carotene to prevent second head and neck cancer. *Cancer Res* 2001;61:1457-63.

30. Toma S, Bonelli L, Sartoris A, et al. Beta-carotene supplementation in patients radically treated for stage I-II head and neck cancer: results of a randomized trial. *Oncol Rep* 2003;10:1895-901.

31. Creagan ET, Moertel CG, O'Fallon JR, et al. Failure of high-dose vitamin C (ascorbic acid) therapy to benefit patients with advanced cancer. A controlled trial. *N Engl J Med* 1979;301:687-90.

32. Moertel CG, Fleming TR, Creagan ET, et al. High-dose vitamin C versus placebo in the treatment of patients with advanced cancer who have had no prior chemotherapy. A randomized double-blind comparison. *N Engl J Med* 1985;312:137-41.

33. Lamm DL, Riggs DR, Shriver JS, et al. Megadose vitamins in bladder cancer: a double-blind clinical trial. *J Urol* 1994;151:21-6.

34. Pathak AK, Bhutani M, Guleria R, et al. Chemotherapy alone vs. chemotherapy plus high dose multiple antioxidants in patients with advanced non small cell lung cancer. *J Am Coll Nutr* 2005;24:16-21.

35. Clark LC, Combs GF Jr, Turnbull BW, et al. Effects of selenium supplementation for cancer prevention in patients with carcinoma of the skin. A randomized controlled trial. Nutritional Prevention of Cancer Study Group. *JAMA* 1996;276:1957-63.

36. Duffield-Lillico AJ, Dalkin BL, Reid ME, et al. Selenium supplementation, baseline plasma selenium status and incidence of prostate cancer: an analysis of the complete treatment period of the Nutritional Prevention of Cancer Trial. *BJU Int* 2003;91:608-12.

37. Duffield-Lillico AJ, Reid ME, Turnbull BW, et al. Baseline characteristics and the effect of selenium supplementation on cancer incidence in a randomized clinical trial: a summary report of the Nutritional Prevention of Cancer Trial. *Cancer Epidemiol Biomarkers Prev* 2002;11:630-9.

38. Reid ME, Stratton MS, Lillico AJ, et al. A report of high-dose selenium supplementation: response and toxicities. *J Trace Elem Med Biol* 2004;18:69-74.

39. MacGregor CA, Canney PA, Patterson G, et al. A randomised double-blind controlled trial of oral soy supplements versus placebo for treatment of menopausal symptoms in patients with early breast cancer. *Eur J Cancer* 2005;41:708-14.

40. Van Patten CL, Olivotto IA, Chambers GK, et al. Effect of soy phytoestrogens on hot flashes in postmenopausal women with breast cancer: a randomized, controlled clinical trial. *J Clin Oncol*

2002;20:1449-55.

41. van der Merwe CF, Booyens J, Joubert HF, et al. The effect of gamma-linolenic acid, an in vitro cytostatic substance contained in evening primrose oil, on primary liver cancer. A double-blind placebo controlled trial. *Prostaglandins Leukot Essent Fatty Acids* 1990;40:199-202.

42. Jebb SA, Osborne RJ, Maughan TS, et al. 5-fluorouracil and folinic acid-induced mucositis: no effect of oral glutamine supplementation. *Br J Cancer* 1994;70:732-5.

43. Arnold C, Richter MP. The effect of oral nutritional supplements on head and neck cancer. *Int J Radiat Oncol Biol Phys* 1989;16:1595-9.

44. Breitkreutz R, Tesdal K, Jentschura D, et al. Effects of a high-fat diet on body composition in cancer patients receiving chemotherapy: a randomized controlled study. *Wien Klin Wochenschr* 2005;117:685-92.

45. Douglass HO, Milliron S, Nava H, et al. Elemental diet as an adjuvant for patients with locally advanced gastrointestinal cancer receiving radiation therapy: a prospectively randomized study. *J Parenter Enteral Nutr* 1978;2:682-6.

46. Elkort RJ, Baker FL, Vitale JJ, et al. Long-term nutritional support as an adjunct to chemotherapy for breast cancer. *J Parenter Enteral Nutr* 1981;5:385-90.

47. Meng WC, Leung KL, Ho RL, et al. Prospective randomized control study on the effect of branched-chain amino acids in patients with liver resection for hepatocellular carcinoma. *Aust N Z J Surg* 1999;69:811-5.

48. Ovesen L, Allingstrup L. Different quantities of two commercial liquid diets consumed by weight-losing cancer patients. *J Parenter Enteral Nutr* 1992;16:275-8.

49. Poon RT, Yu WC, Fan ST, et al. Long-term oral branched chain amino acids in patients undergoing chemoembolization for hepatocellular carcinoma: a randomized trial. *Aliment Pharmacol Ther* 2004;19:779-88.

50. Ravasco P, Monteiro-Grillo I, Vidal PM, et al. Dietary counseling improves patient outcomes: a prospective, randomized, controlled trial in colorectal cancer patients undergoing radiotherapy. *J Clin Oncol* 2005;23:1431-8.

51. Yu-Chung C, Fukuda T, Hamazoe R, et al. Long-term oral administration of branched chain amino acids after curative resection of hepatocellular carcinoma: a prospective randomized trial. The San-in Group of Liver Surgery. *Br J Surg* 1997;84:1525-31.

52. National Institutes of Health State-of-the-Science Panel. NIHSS conference statement: multivitamin/mineral supplements and chronic disease prevention. *Ann Intern Med* 2006;145:364-71.

53. Greenlee H, White E, Patterson RE, et al. Supplement use among cancer survivors in the Vitamins and Lifestyle (VITAL) study cohort. *J Altern Complement Med* 2004;10:660-6.

54. Rock CL, Newman VA, Neuhouser ML, et al. Antioxidant supplement use in cancer survivors and the general population. *J Nutr* 2004;134:3194S-5S.

55. Jones LW, Demark-Wahnefried W. Diet, exercise, and complementary therapies after primary treatment for cancer. *Lancet Oncol* 2006;7:1017-26.

56. Barton DL, Loprinzi CL, Quella SK, et al. Prospective evaluation of vitamin E for hot flashes in breast cancer survivors. *J Clin Oncol* 1998;16:495-500.

57. Delanian S, Porcher R, Balla-Mekias S, et al. Randomized, placebo-controlled trial of combined pentoxifylline and tocopherol for regression of superficial radiation-induced fibrosis. *J Clin Oncol* 2003;21:2545-50.

58. Gothard L, Cornes P, Earl J, et al. Double-blind placebo-controlled randomised trial of vitamin E and pentoxifylline in patients with chronic arm lymphoedema and fibrosis after surgery and radiotherapy for breast cancer. *Radiother Oncol* 2004;73:133-9.

59. Cunningham BA, Morris G, Cheney CL, et al. Effects of resistive exercise on skeletal muscle in marrow transplant recipients receiving total parenteral nutrition. *JPEN J Parenter Enteral Nutr* 1986;10:558-63.

60. Nieman DC, Cook VD, Henson DA, et al. Moderate exercise training and natural killer cell cytotoxic activity in breast cancer patients. *Int J Sports Med* 1995;16:334-7.

61. Marchese VG, Chiarello LA, Lange BJ. Effects of physical therapy intervention for children with acute lymphoblastic leukemia. *Pediatric Blood Cancer* 2004;42:127-33.

62. Wall LM. Changes in hope and power in lung cancer patients who exercise. *Nurs Sci Q* 2000;13:234-42.

63. Segal RJ, Reid RD, Courneya KS, et al. Resistance exercise in men receiving androgen deprivation therapy for prostate cancer. *J Clin Oncol* 2003;21:1653-9.

64. Berglund G, Bolund C, Gustavsson UL, et al. A randomized study of a rehabilitation program for cancer patients: the 'Starting Again' group. *Psychooncology* 1994;3:109-20.

65. Burnham TR, Wilcox A. Effects of exercise on physiological and psychological variables in cancer survivors. *Med Sci Sports Exerc* 2002;34:1863-7.

66. Dimeo F, Fetscher S, Lange W, et al. Effects of aerobic exercise on the physical performance and incidence of treatment-related complications after high-dose chemotherapy. *Blood* 1997;90:3390-4.

67. Dimeo FC, Thomas F, Raabe-Menssen C, et al. Effect of aerobic exercise and relaxation training on fatigue and physical performance of cancer patients after surgery. A randomised controlled trial. *Support Care Cancer* 2004;12:774-9.

68. Thorsen L, Skovlund E, Stromme SB, et al. Effectiveness of physical activity on cardiorespiratory fitness and health-related quality of life in young and middle-aged cancer patients shortly after chemotherapy. *J Clin Oncol* 2005;23:2378-88.

69. Cella DF, Tulsky DS, Gray G, et al. The Functional Assessment of Cancer Therapy scale: development and validation of the general measure. *J Clin Oncol* 1993;11:570-9.

70. Chlebowski RT, Aiello E, McTiernan A. Weight loss in breast cancer patient management. *J Clin Oncol* 2002;20:1128-43.

71. Courneya KS. Exercise in cancer survivors: an overview of research. *Med Sci Sports Exerc* 2003;35:1846-52.

72. Rock CL, Demark-Wahnefried W. Nutrition and survival after the diagnosis of breast cancer: a review of the evidence. *J Clin Oncol* 2002;20:3302-16.

73. Holmes MD, Chen WY, Feskanich D, et al. Physical activity and survival after breast cancer diagnosis. *JAMA* 2005;293:2479-86.

74. Abrahamson PE, Gammon MD, Lund MJ, et al. Recreational physical activity and survival among young women with breast cancer. *Cancer* 2006;107:1777-85.

Chapter 10

1. Cannon G. *Food and Health: The Experts Agree. An Analysis of One Hundred Authoritative Scientific Reports on Food, Nutrition and Public Health Published Throughout the World in Thirty Years, Between 1961 and 1991*. London: Consumers' Association, 1992.

2. Doll R, Peto R. The causes of cancer: quantitative estimates of avoidable risks of cancer in the United States today. *J Natl Cancer I* 1981;66:1191-308.

3. US Department of Health. 1988. *Surgeon General's Report on Nutrition and Health*.

4. Bengoa J, Torun B, Behar M, et al. Nutritional goals for health in Latin America. *Food Nutr Bull* 1989;11:4-20.

5. Ulbricht T. *Medical Aspects of Dietary Fibre: a Report of the Royal College of Physicians*. Tunbridge Wells: Pitman Medical, 1980.

6. National Research Council Committee on Diet Nutrition and Cancer. *Diet, Nutrition, and Cancer*. Washington, DC: National Academy Press, 1982.

7. National Research Council Committee on Diet and Health. *Diet and Health, Implications for Reducing Chronic Disease Risk*. Washington, DC: National Academy Press, 1989.

8. Food and Agriculture Organization of the United Nations, World Health Organization. 1994. *Fats and Oils in Human Nutrition: Report of a Joint Expert Consultation*. In: FAO Food and Nutrition Papers no 57.

9. Food and Agriculture Organization of the United Nations, World Health Organization. 2002. *Living Well with HIV/AIDS. A Manual on Nutritional Care and Support for People Living With HIV/AIDS*.

10. Dewey K, Lutter C. *Guiding Principles for Complementary Feeding of the Breastfed Child*. Washington DC: Pan American Health Organization, World Health Organization, 2003.

11. United Nations Children's Fund (UNICEF), United Nations University, World Health Organization. *Iron Deficiency Anaemia: Assessment, Prevention and Control*. Geneva: WHO, 2001.

12. World Health Organization. *New Data on the Prevention of Mother-to-child Transmission of HIV and Their Policy Implications: Conclusions and Recommendations. WHO Technical Consultation*. Geneva: WHO, 2001.

13. Regional Office for the Eastern Mediterranean, World Health Organization. *Guidelines for the Control of Iron Deficiency in Countries of the Eastern Mediterranean, Middle East and North Africa*. Geneva: WHO, 1996.

14. World Health Organization, United Nations Children's Fund (UNICEF), International Vitamin A Consultative Group Task Force. *Vitamin A Supplements: a Guide to their Use in the Treatment and Prevention of Vitamin A Deficiency and Xerophthalmia*. Geneva: WHO, 1997.

15. World Cancer Research Fund, American Institute for Cancer Research. *Food, Nutrition and the Prevention of Cancer: a Global Perspective*. Washington, DC: American Institute for Cancer Research, 1997.

16. World Health Organization. 1990. *Prevention in Childhood and Youth of Adult Cardiovascular Disease: Time for Action*. In: Technical Report Series no 792.

17. World Health Organization. *The Management and Prevention of Diarrhoea: Practical Guidelines*. Geneva: WHO, 1993.

18. World Health Organization. 1997. *Obesity: Preventing and Managing the Global Epidemic. Report of a WHO Consultation on Obesity*.

19. World Health Organization. *Management of Severe Malnutrition: a Manual for Physicians and Other Senior Health Workers*. Geneva: WHO, 1999.

20. World Health Organization. WHO consensus statement on the role of nutrition in colorectal cancer. *Eur J Cancer Prev* 1999;8:57-62.

21. World Health Organization. 2002. *Complementary Feeding: Report of the Global Consultation, Summary of Guiding Principles*.

22. World Health Organization. *Diet, Nutrition and the Prevention of Chronic Disease*. Geneva: WHO, 2003.

23. World Health Organization. *Prevention and Management of Osteoporosis*. Geneva: WHO, 2003.

24. American Academy of Pediatrics. National Cholesterol Education Program: report of the expert panel on blood cholesterol levels in children and adolescents. *Pediatrics* 1992;89:525-84.

25. American Academy of Pediatrics. Human milk and breastfeeding and the transmission of HIV in the US. *Pediatrics* 1995;96:977-9.

26. American Academy of Pediatrics. Cholesterol in childhood. *Pediatrics* 1998;101:141-7.

27. American Academy of Pediatrics. Preventing pediatric overweight and obesity. *Pediatrics* 2003;112:424-30.

28. American Academy of Pediatrics. Prevention of rickets and vitamin D deficiency: new guidelines for vitamin D intake. *Pediatrics* 2003;111:908-10.

29. Byers T, Nestle M, McTiernan A, et al. American Cancer Society Guidelines on Nutrition and Physical Activity for cancer prevention: reducing the risk of cancer with healthy food choices and physical activity. *CA Cancer J Clin* 2002;52:92-119.

30. American Diabetes Association. Position statement: nutrition principles and recommendations in diabetes. *Diabetes Care* 2004;27:S36-S46.

31. American Diabetes Association. Position statement: prevention or delay of type 2 diabetes. *Diabetes Care* 2004;27:S47-S54.

32. American Diabetes Association. Management of dyslipidemia in adults with diabetes. *Diabetes Care* 2004;27:S68-S71.

33. American Gastrointestinal Association. AGA technical review on osteoporosis in gastrointestinal diseases. *Gastroenterology* 2003;124:795-841.

34. American Heart Association. Diabetes and cardiovascular disease. *Circulation* 1999;100:1134-46.

35. American Heart Association. Guide to preventive cardiology for women. *Circulation* 1999;99:2480-4.

36. American Heart Association. AHA dietary guidelines: revision 2000. *Circulation* 2000;102:2284-99.

37. American Heart Association. Soy protein and cardiovascular disease. A statement for healthcare professionals from the Nutrition Committee of the AHA. *Circulation* 2000;102:2555-9.

38. American Heart Association. Primary prevention of ischemic stroke: a statement for health care professionals. *Circulation* 2001;103:163-82.

39. American Heart Association. Fish consumption, fish oil, omega-3 fatty acids and cardiovascular disease. *Circulation* 2002;102:2747-57.

40. American Heart Association. AHA guidelines for primary prevention of cardiovascular disease and stroke: 2002 update. *Circulation* 2002;106:388-91.

41. American Heart Association. AHA guidelines for primary prevention of atherosclerotic cardiovascular disease beginning in childhood. *Circulation* 2003;107:1562-6.

42. American Heart Association. Physical activity and exercise recommendations for stroke survivors. *Circulation* 2004;109:2031-41.

43. American Heart Association. Evidence-based guidelines for cardiovascular disease prevention in women. *Circulation* 2004;109:672-93.

44. American Heart Association/American College of Cardiology. AHA/ACC guidelines for preventing heart attack and death in patients with atherosclerotic cardiovascular disease: 2001 update. *Circulation* 2001;104:1577-9.

45. Canadian Diabetes Association. Canadian Diabetes Association 2003 clinical practice guidelines for the prevention and management of diabetes in Canada. *Can J Diabet* 2003;27:S1-S152.

46. Canadian Hypertension Recommendations Working Group. The 2004 Canadian recommendations for the management of hypertension: part III - lifestyle modifications to prevent and control hypertension. *Can J Cardiol* 2004;20:55-9.

47. Canadian Task Force. 2003. *The Role of Vitamin E Supplements in the Prevention of Cardiovascular Disease and Cancer: Systematic Review and Recommendations*. In: CTFPHC Technical Report no 03-6.

48. Cheung AM, Feig DS, Kapral M, et al. Prevention of osteoporosis and osteoporotic fractures in post-menopausal women: recommendation statement from the Canadian Task Force on Preventive Health Care. *Can Med Assoc J* 2004;170:1665-7.

49. Lewis DW, Ismail AI. Periodic health examination, 1995 update: 2. Prevention of dental caries. The Canadian Task Force on the Periodic Health Examination. *Can Med Assoc J* 1995;152:836-46.

50. Centers for Disease Control and Prevention. Recommendations for using fluoride to prevent and control dental caries in the United States. *MMWR Recomm Rep* 2001;50:1-42.

51. Centers for Disease Control and Prevention. Recommendations to prevent and control iron deficiency in the United States. *MMWR Recomm Rep* 1998;47:1-36.

52. National Academy of Sciences, Institute of Medicine, Food and Nutrition Board. 1997. *Dietary Reference Intakes for Calcium, Phosporus, Magnesium, Vitamin D, and Fluoride*.

53. National Academy of Sciences, Institute of Medicine, Food and Nutrition Board. 2002. *Dietary Reference Intakes for Energy, Carbohydrates, Fiber, Fat, Protein and Amino Acids (Macronutrients)*.

54. National Academy of Sciences, Institute of Medicine, Food and Nutrition Board. 2004. *Dietary Reference Intakes for Water, Potassium, Sodium, Chloride and Sulfate*.

55. National High Blood Pressure Education Program Working Group. Report on primary prevention of hypertension. *Arch Intern Med* 1993;153:186-208.

56. Whelton PK, He J, Appel LJ, et al. Primary prevention of hypertension: clinical and public health advisory from the National High Blood Pressure Education Program. *JAMA* 2002;288:1882-8.

57. National Institutes of Health Consensus Development Panel on Physical Activity and Cardiovascular Health. Physical activity and cardiovascular health: NIH consensus statement. *JAMA* 1996;276:241-6.

58. North American Society for Pediatric Gastroenterology Hepatology and Nutrition. Nutrition support for pediatric patients with inflammatory bowel disease: a clinical report of the North American Society for Pediatric Gastroenterology, Hepatology and Nutrition. *J Pediatr Gastroenterol Nutr* 2004;39:15-27.

59. Osteoporosis Society of Canada. 2002 clinical practice guidelines for the diagnosis and management of osteoporosis in Canada. *Can Med Assoc J* 2002;167:S1-S34.

60. Registered Nurses Association of Ontario. *Prevention of Constipation in the Older Adult Population*. Toronto: Nursing Best Practice Guidelines Project, 2002.

61. US Preventative Task Force. Routine vitamin supplementation to prevent cancer and cardiovascular disease: recommendations and rationale. *Ann Intern Med* 2003;139:51-5.

62. US Department of Agriculture, Advisory Committee on the Dietary Guidelines for Americans. *The American National Dietary Guidelines*. Washington DC: USDA, 2000.

63. British Diabetic Association. Dietary recommendations for people with diabetes: an update for the 1990s. *Diabetic Med* 1992;9:189-202.

64. British Hyperlipidaemia Association. Management of hyperlipidaemia: guidelines of the British Hyperlipidaemia Association. *Postgrad Med J* 1993;69:359-69.

65. Arens U, editor. *The Report of the British Nutrition Foundation's Task Force. Oral Health: Diet and Other Factors*. Amsterdam: Elsevier, 1999.

66. Aggett PJ, Haschke F, Heine W, et al. Committee report: childhood diet and prevention of coronary heart disease. ESPGAN Committee on Nutrition. European Society of Pediatric Gastroenterology and Nutrition. *J Pediatr Gastroenterol Nutr* 1994;19:261-9.

67. Boyle P, Autier P, Bartelink H, et al. European Code Against Cancer and scientific justification: third version (2003). *Ann Oncol* 2003;14:973-1005.

68. The European Heart Network. 1999. *Physical Activity and Cardiovascular Disease Prevention in the European Union*.

69. The European Heart Network. 2002. *Food, Nutrition and Cardiovascular Disease Prevention in the European Region: Challenges for the New Millenium*.

70. Rotilio G, Berni Canani R, Barba G, et al. Nutritional recommendations for the prevention of ischemic stroke. *Nutr Metab Cardiovasc Dis* 2004;14:115-20.

71. Scientific Advisory Committee on Nutrition. *Salt and Health*. London: The Stationery Office, 2003.

72. Scientific Advisory Committee on Nutrition. *Advice on Fish Consumption: Benefits and Risks*. London: The Stationery Office, 2004.

73. Scottish Intercollegiate Guidelines Network. 1999. *Lipids and the Primary Prevention of Coronary Heart Disease*. In: SIGN Publication no 40.

74. Scottish Intercollegiate Guidelines Network. 2000. *Preventing Dental Caries in Children at High Caries Risk: Targeted Prevention of Dental Caries in the Permanent Teeth of 6-16 Year Olds Presenting for Dental Care*. In: SIGN Publication no 47.

75. Scottish Intercollegiate Guidelines Network. 2000. *Secondary Prevention of Coronary Heart Disease Following Myocardial Infarction*. In: SIGN Publication no 41.

76. Scottish Intercollegiate Guidelines Network. 2001. *Management of Diabetes*. In: SIGN Publication no 55.

77. Scottish Intercollegiate Guidelines Network. 2001. *Hypertension in Older People*. In: SIGN Publication no 49.

78. Third Joint Task Force of European Societies. European guidelines on cardiovascular disease prevention in clinical practice. *Eur Heart J* 2003;24:1601-10.

79. UK Department of Health. 1994. *Weaning and the Weaning Diet. Report of the Working Group on the Weaning Diet of the Committee on Medical Aspects of Food Policy*. In: Report on Health and Social Subjects no 45.

80. UK Department of Health. 1994. *Nutritional Aspects of Cardiovascular Disease. Report of the Cardiovascular Review Group Committee on Medical Aspects of Food Policy*. In: Report on Health and Social Subjects no 46.

81. UK Department of Health. 1997. *Preventing Coronary Heart Disease: the Role of Antioxidants, Vegetables and Fruit. Report of an Expert Meeting*.

82. UK Department of Health. 1998. *Nutrition and Bone Health with Particular Reference to Calcium and Vitamin D. Report of the Subgroup on Bone Health: Working Group on the Nutritional Status of the Population of the Committee on Medical Aspects of Food and Nutrition Policy*. In: Report on Health and Social Subjects no 49.

83. UK Department of Health. 1998. *Nutritional Aspects of the Development of Cancer. Committee on Medical Aspects of Food Policy: Working Group on Diet and Cancer*. In: Report on Health and Social Subjects no 48.

84. UK Heart Health and Thoracic Dieticians Specialist Group of the British Dietetic Association. Dietetic guidelines: diet in the secondary prevention of cardiovascular disease (first update, June 2003). *J Hum Nutr Diet* 2004;17:337-49.

85. Australian College of Pediatrics. Policy statement: vitamin A supplementation in measles. *J Pediatr Child Health* 1996;32:209-10.

86. Australian College of Pediatrics. Policy statement: soy protein formula. *J Pediatr Child Health* 1998;34:318-9.

87. Dieticians Association of Australia and the Australian College of Paediatrics. Recommendations for dietary intervention in the prevention and treatment of hyperlipidaemia in childhood. *J Paediatr Child Health* 1995;31:79-82.

88. National Health and Medical Research Council (Australia). 1999. *Dietary Guidelines for Older Australians*.

89. National Health and Medical Research Council (Australia). 1999. *Evidence-based Guidelines for Type 2 Diabetes: Primary Prevention, Case Detection and Diagnosis*.

90. National Health and Medical Research Council (Australia). 1999. *Guidelines for the Prevention, Early Detection and Management of Colorectal Cancer*.

91. National Health and Medical Research

Council (Australia). 2003. *Dietary Guidelines for Australian Adults.*

92. National Health and Medical Research Council (Australia). 2003. *Dietary Guidelines for Children and Adolescents in Australia Incorporating the Infant Feeding Guidelines for Health Workers.*

93. National Heart Foundation of Australia. Position statement on dietary fats. *Aust J Nutr Diet* 1999;56:S3-S4.

94. National Heart Foundation of Australia. Position statement on dietary fat and overweight/obesity. *Nutr Diet* 2003;60:174-6.

95. National Heart Foundation of Australia's Nutrition and Metabolism Advisory Committee. *The use of antioxidant supplements in heart disease. Position statement.* http://www.heartfoundation.com.au/downloads/AntioxidantPolicy%20Oct%202002.pdf. 2002.

96. National Heart Foundation of Australia, The Cardiac Society of Australia and New Zealand. Lipid management guidelines - 2001. *Med J Aust* 2001;175:S57-85.

97. National Heart Foundation of Australia, The Cardiac Society of Australia and New Zealand. *Reducing risk in heart disease 2004.* http://www.heartfoundation.com.au/downloads/RRIHD_fullguide_update_010405.pdf. 2004.

98. New Zealand Dietetic Association. Cardiovascular health for New Zealanders: the role of diet. *J N Z Diet Assoc* 2000;54:58-86.

99. Indian Society of Hypertension. Indian Consensus Group: Indian consensus for prevention of hypertension and coronary artery disease. *J Nutr Environ Med* 1996;6:309-18.

100. Singh RB, Mori H, Chen J, et al. Recommendations for the prevention of coronary heart disease in Asians: a scientific statement of the International College of Nutrition. *J Cardiovasc Risk* 1996;3:489-94.

101. South African Medical Association. Diagnosis, management and prevention of the common dyslipidaemias in South Africa. *S Afr Med J* 2000;90:164-74.

102. Kushi LH, Byers T, Doyle C, et al. American Cancer Society Guidelines on Nutrition and Physical Activity for cancer prevention: reducing the risk of cancer with healthy food choices and physical activity. *CA Cancer J Clin* 2006;56:254-81; quiz 313-4.

103. International Agency for Research on Cancer, World Health Organization. 2002. *Weight Control and Physical Activity.* In: IARC Handbooks of Cancer Prevention, Volume 6.

104. National Institute for Health and Clinical Excellence. 2006. *Obesity: The Prevention, Identification, Assessment and Management of Overweight and Obesity in Adults and Children.*

105. US Department of Health and Human Services, US Department of Agriculture. *Dietary Guidelines for Americans 2005.*

6th ed. Washington DC: US Government Printing Office, 2005.

106. National Institutes of Health. 1998. *Clinical Guidelines on the Identification, Evaluation, and Treatment of Overweight and Obesity in Adults.*

106B. World Health Organization. Obesity: preventing and managing the global epidemic. Report of a WHO consultation. Geneva, Switzerland: World Health Organization, 2000.

107. Food and Agriculture Organization of the United Nations, World Health Organization. 1992. *World Declaration and Plan of Action for Nutrition.*

108. United Nations Children's Fund (UNICEF). *Strategy for Improved Nutrition of Children and Women in Developing Countries.* New York: UNICEF, 1990.

109. Scrimshaw NS, Taylor CE, Gordon JE. *Interactions of Nutrition and Infection.* Geneva: World Health Organization, 1967.

110. US Senate Select Committee on Nutrition and Human Needs. *Dietary Goals for the United States.* Washington DC: US Government Printing Office, 1977.

111. World Health Organization. *Diet, Nutrition, and the Prevention of Chronic Diseases.* Geneva: WHO, 1990.

Index

The cancer process

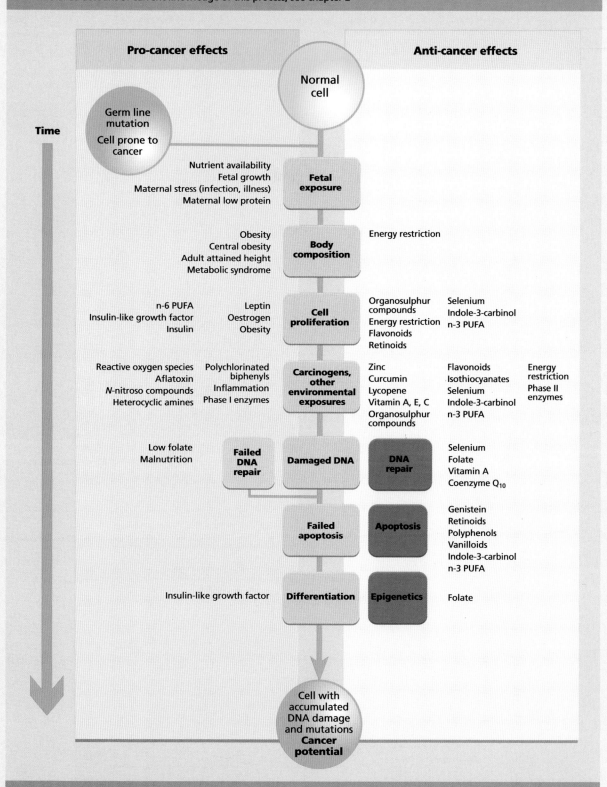

The influences of food, nutrition, obesity, and physical activity on the cancer process
For a detailed account of current knowledge of this process, see chapter 2

Mouth, pharynx, larynx | Nasopharynx | Oesophagus | Lung | Stomach | Pancreas | Gallbladder | Liver

Foods containing dietary fibre
Aflatoxins
Non-starchy vegetables
Allium vegetables
Garlic
Carrots
Chilli
Fruits
Pulses (legumes)
Foods containing folate
Foods containing carotenoids
Foods containing beta-carotene
Foods containing lycopene
Foods containing vitamin C
Foods containing selenium
Foods containing pyridoxine
Foods containing vitamin E
Foods containing quercetin
Red meat
Processed meat
Foods containing iron
Cantonese-style salted fish
Fish
Foods containing vitamin D
Smoked foods
Grilled or barbecued animal foods
Diets high in calcium
Milk and dairy products
Milk
Cheese
Total fat
Foods containing animal fat
Butter
Salt
Salted and salty foods
Foods containing sugars
Energy-dense foods
Low energy-dense foods
Fast foods
Arsenic in drinking water
Maté
High temperature drinks
Coffee
Sugary drinks
Alcoholic drinks
Beta-carotene*
Calcium*
Selenium*
Retinol*
Alpha-tocopherol*
Physical activity
Sedentary living
Television viewing
Body fatness
Abdominal fatness
Adult weight gain
Low body fatness
Adult attained height
Greater birth weight
Lactation
Being breastfed

KEY

Convincing decreased risk | Probable decreased risk | Limited–suggestive decreased risk | Limited–suggestive increased risk | Probable increased risk | Convincing increased risk | Substantial effect on risk unlikely

*The evidence is derived from studies usin
†Judgement for physical activity applies t

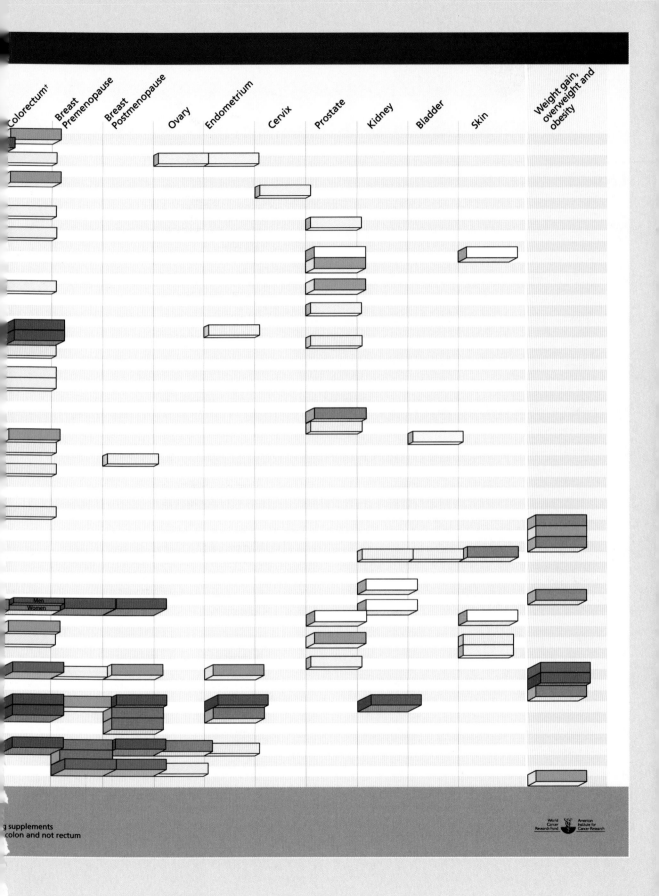

Colorectum† Breast Premenopause Breast Postmenopause Ovary Endometrium Cervix Prostate Kidney Bladder Skin Weight gain, overweight and obesity

Men
Women

World Cancer Research Fund   American Institute for Cancer Research

Recommendations

The Panel's goals and recommendations are the culmination of five years of work. They are based on the best available evidence, which has been identified, collected, analysed, displayed, summarised, and judged systematically, transparently, and independently. The general statements here are headlines of the more detailed recommendations in Chapter 12 of this Report. The recommendations also include public health goals, for populations and therefore principally for health professionals; and personal recommendations, for people, as communities, families, and individuals. Eight general recommendations are followed by two special recommendations. Together they are designed to be integrated and to contribute to healthy dietary patterns, healthy ways of life, and general well-being.

The 10 recommendations, of which the headlines are shown in the panel to the right, derive from the evidence on food, nutrition, and physical activity but not on their wider socioeconomic, cultural, and other determinants. *The Panel is aware* that patterns of diet and physical activity, as well as the risk of diseases such as cancer, are also crucially influenced by social and environmental factors. These broader factors, and recommendations designed as the basis for policies and programmes that can create healthier societies and environments, are the subject of a further report to be published in late 2008.

The Panel concludes that the evidence that high body fatness and also physical inactivity are causes of a number of cancers, including common cancers, is particularly strong. For this reason, the first three recommendations are designed as a basis for policies, programmes, and choices whose purpose is to maintain healthy body weights and to sustain physical activity, throughout life. The remaining five general recommendations are not in any order of priority. After the eight general recommendations, there are two special recommendations, one on breastfeeding and one for cancer survivors, that are targeted at specific groups of people.

These recommendations are concerned with food and nutrition, physical activity, and body fatness. Other factors that modify the risk of cancer outside the remit of this Report include smoking, infectious agents, radiation, industrial chemicals, and medication. *The Panel emphasises* the importance of not smoking and of avoiding exposure to tobacco smoke.

RECOMMENDATIONS

BODY FATNESS
Be as lean as possible within the
normal range of body weight

PHYSICAL ACTIVITY
Be physically active as part of everyday life

FOODS AND DRINKS THAT PROMOTE WEIGHT GAIN
Limit consumption of energy-dense foods
Avoid sugary drinks

PLANT FOODS
Eat mostly foods of plant origin

ANIMAL FOODS
Limit intake of red meat and avoid processed meat

ALCOHOLIC DRINKS
Limit alcoholic drinks

PRESERVATION, PROCESSING, PREPARATION
Limit consumption of salt
Avoid mouldy cereals (grains) or pulses (legumes)

DIETARY SUPPLEMENTS
Aim to meet nutritional needs through diet alone

BREASTFEEDING
Mothers to breastfeed; children to be breastfed

CANCER SURVIVORS
Follow the recommendations for cancer prevention

The Panel's judgements

This matrix displays the Panel's judgements of the strength of the evidence causally relating food, nutrition and physical activity with the risk of cancer of the sites reviewed, and with weight gain, overweight and obesity. It is a synthesis of all the matrices introducing the chapters in Parts 1 and 2 of the Report, and shows judgements of "convincing", "probable", "limited - suggestive", and "substantial effect on risk unlikely", but not "limited – no conclusion".   Usually judgements of convincing and probable generate public health goals and personal recommendations. The recommendations are detailed in full in chapter 12.